C000166133

THE LETTERS OF
T. S. ELIOT
VOLUME 4

By T. S. Eliot

THE COMPLETE POEMS AND PLAYS

verse
COLLECTED POEMS 1909–1962
FOUR QUARTETS
THE WASTE LAND AND OTHER POEMS
THE WASTE LAND:
A Facsimile and Transcript of the Original Drafts
edited by Valerie Eliot
INVENTIONS OF THE MARCH HARE:
POEMS 1909–1917
edited by Christopher Ricks
SELECTED POEMS

plays
MURDER IN THE CATHEDRAL
THE FAMILY REUNION
THE COCKTAIL PARTY
THE CONFIDENTIAL CLERK
THE ELDER STATESMAN

literary criticism
THE SACRED WOOD
SELECTED ESSAYS
THE USE OF POETRY AND THE USE OF CRITICISM
VARIETIES OF METAPHYSICAL POETRY
edited by Ronald Schuchard
TO CRITICIZE THE CRITIC
ON POETRY AND POETS
FOR LANCELOT ANDREWES
SELECTED PROSE OF T. S. ELIOT
edited by Frank Kermode

social criticism
THE IDEA OF A CHRISTIAN SOCIETY
edited by David Edwards
NOTES TOWARDS THE DEFINITION OF CULTURE

letters
THE LETTERS OF T. S. ELIOT
Volume 1: 1898–1922
Revised Edition
edited by Valerie Eliot and Hugh Haughton
THE LETTERS OF T. S. ELIOT
Volume 2: 1923–1925
edited by Valerie Eliot and Hugh Haughton
THE LETTERS OF T. S. ELIOT
Volume 3: 1926–1927
edited by Valerie Eliot and John Haffenden
THE LETTERS OF T. S. ELIOT
Volume 4: 1928–1929
edited by Valerie Eliot and John Haffenden

THE LETTERS OF

T. S. Eliot

EDITED BY

VALERIE ELIOT

AND

JOHN HAFFENDEN

VOLUME 4
1928–1929

faber and faber
LONDON

First published in 2013
by Faber and Faber Limited
74–77 Great Russell Street, London WC1B 3DA

Typeset by Donald Sommerville
Printed in England by T. J. International,
Padstow, Cornwall

A CIP record for this book is available from the British Library

ISBN 978-0-571-29092-5

2 4 6 8 10 9 7 5 3 1

CONTENTS

ILLUSTRATIONS

1   Portrait of T. S. Eliot. Drawing by William Rothenstein, 1928. Plate V from *Twelve Portraits*, London: Faber & Faber Ltd, 1929. © *Estate of William Rothenstein. Collection Faber Archive*

2   Vivien Eliot in the garden of 57 Chester Terrace, with Peter the dog, June 1928. *By permission of the Houghton Library, Harvard University, MS Am. 2560 (185)*

3   Eliot with 'Charlie Chaplin moustache', taken by E. McKnight Kauffer, 1928. *Copyright © Simon Rendall. Collection Valerie Eliot*

4   T. S. Eliot, with pet dog Peter, at 57 Chester Terrace, May 1928. *Collection Valerie Eliot*

5   T. S. Eliot's mother, Charlotte, in Cambridge, 1928. Photograph by Henry Ware Eliot. *Collection Valerie Eliot*

6   Eliot in the garden of 57 Chester Terrace, May 1928. *Collection Valerie Eliot*

7   Leonard and Virginia Woolf on holiday in Cassis, French Riviera, 1928. © *The Granger Collection, New York/Topfoto*

8   T. S. Eliot reading, photographed by Maurice Beck and Helen McGregor, *c.*1928. *Collection Valerie Eliot*

9   I. A. (Ivor Armstrong) and Dorothy Richards on their honeymoon in Nara, Japan, 1927. © *Lorna Caputo. Private Collection*

10   A. L. (Alfred Leslie) Rowse. Photograph by Dorothy Lesty, late 1920s. *Courtesy of Special Collections, University of Exeter*

11   Edward McKnight Kauffer. Vintage bromide print by Howard Coster, 1927. © *National Portrait Gallery, London*

12   Thomas MacGreevy, looking from his rooms at the École Normale Supérieure, *c.*1928. © *Margaret Farrington and Robert Ryan, estate of Thomas MacGreevy*

Every reasonable effort has been made to trace copyright holders. The publishers would be pleased to rectify at the earliest opportunity any omissions or errors brought to their notice.

ACKNOWLEDGEMENTS

For help and advice in many capacities, including copyright permissions, the publishers and editors would like to thank the following individuals and institutions. (Sadly, some of those named below are now deceased, but we wish still to put on record our gratitude to them.) Dr Donald Adamson; The American Jewish Archives, Cincinnati, Ohio; Dr Norma Aubertin-Potter, Librarian in Charge, Codrington Library, All Souls College, Oxford; Joan Bailey; Owen Barfield; Tansy Barton, Special Collections Administrator, Senate House Library, London; H. Baugh; T. O. Beachcroft; Anne Olivier Bell; Bibliothèque Nationale, Paris; Kenneth Blackwell, McMaster University; Michael Harry Blechner, McFarlin Library, University of Tulsa; Mary Boccaccio, McKeldin Library, University of Maryland; Maxwell Bodenheim; John Bodley; William H. Bond; University of Bonn Library; Ann Bowden; British Library; Valerie Brokenshire; Jewel Spears Brooker; Robert Brown, Archivist, Faber & Faber Ltd; Richard Buckle; Penelope Bulloch, Balliol College Library; Professor P. H. Butter; William R. Cagle and Saundra Taylor, Lilly Library; University of California, Los Angeles; Douglas Campbell; Humphrey Carpenter; François Chapon, Bibliothèque Littéraire Jacques Doucet; Mrs Charlton; Dr Joseph Chiari; Alexander P. Clark, Firestone Library, Princeton University; Alan Clodd; Marguerite Cohn; John Constable; Joyce Crick; Arthur Crook; Tony Cuda; Dr Robin Darwall-Smith, Archivist, University College, Oxford; Roy Davids; Dr A. Deiss, General Secretariat, Swiss Medical Institutions; Giles de la Mare; the Literary Trustees of Walter de la Mare; Rodney G. Dennis; Valentine Dobrée; Kenneth W. Duckett, Southern Illinois University at Carbondale; Ellen S. Dunlap, Harry Ransom Humanities Research Center; Peter du Sautoy; Donald D. Eddy, Department of Rare Books, Cornell University Library; Professor Charles W. Eliot; Sarah Ethier, University of Wisconsin-Milwaukee Libraries; Matthew Evans; Sir Richard Faber KCVO; Toby Faber; Elizabeth A. Falsey; Christopher Farley; David Farmer, Harry Ransom Humanities Research Center (and Warren Roberts, Mary Hirth, Mrs Sally Leach, and other members of staff); Anton Felton, Continuum Ltd; Mrs Harry Fine; Mrs Burnham Finney; Henri Fluchère; Fondren Library; Jennifer Formichelli; Donald Gallup;

Special Collections, Isabella Stewart Gardner Museum, Boston, Mass.; K. C. Gay, Lockwood Memorial Library, State University of New York, Buffalo; Herbert Gerwing, University of Victoria; Mrs Ghika; Catherine Gide; Robert Giroux; Estate of Enid Goldsmith; Warwick Gould; Herbert T. Greene; J. C. Hall; Dr Michael Halls; Saskia Hamilton; Sir Rupert Hart-Davis; Professor E. N. Hartley, Institute Archives, MIT; Harvard University Archives; Michael Hastings; The Library, Haverford College; Cathy Henderson, Harry Ransom Humanities Research Center; Nicky Hemingway; Robert Henderson; David Higham Associates Ltd; Roger Highfield; Robert W. Hill, New York Public Library; Michael Hofmann; Michael Holroyd; Judith Hooper; Hornbake Library, University of Maryland; Lélia Howard; Penelope Hughes-Hallett; J. W. Hunt, Royal Military Academy, Sandhurst; Jeremy Hutchinson; Lord Hutchinson; Robin Jackson, The British Academy; Carolyn Jakeman; P. D. James; Dorothy O. Johansen, Reed College, Portland, Oregon; Gregory A. Johnson, Alderman Library, University of Virginia; William Jovanovich; William L. Joyce and Howard C. Rice, Jr., Princeton University; Paul Keegan; Professor John Kelly, St John's College, Oxford; Dr P. Kelly, National Library of Scotland; Mary Kiffer, Assistant Secretary, John Simon Guggenheim Memorial Foundation, New York; Modern Archives Centre, King's College, Cambridge; Monique Kuntz, Bibliothèque Municipale, Vichy; Major N. Aylward Leete; Mrs Dorothy Milburn Léger; Lockwood Memorial Library; Kenneth A. Lohf, Librarian for Rare Books and MSS, Butler Library, Columbia University; London Library; Pat Lowe; Richard Luckett; Richard M. Ludwig, and Howard C. Rice Jr., Princeton University Library; Jim McCue; Mary C. McGreenery, Harvard Alumni Records; Ed Maggs; Professor B. K. Matilal; Francis Mattson, Berg Collection, New York Public Library; R. Russell Maylone, Special Collections Department, Northwestern University Library; Bernard Meehan, Keeper of Manuscripts, Trinity College Dublin; Wim van Mierlo; Mrs Edward S. Mills; University Library, Missouri History Museum; Joe Mitchenson; Kate Mole, Librarian/Archivist, The British Academy; Frank Vigor Morley; Leslie A. Morris, Houghton Library, Harvard University; Lewis Morris; Tim Munby; Mary Middleton Murry; The Bursar, New College, Oxford; Richard Ollard; James M. Osborn; Anne Owen; Martin Page; Stephen Page; Alasdair Paterson, University of Exeter Library; Fondation Saint-John Perse; Lord Quinton; Craig Raine; Graham Wallas and Angela Raspin, London School of Economics; Benedict Read; Real Academia de la Historia; Dr R. T. H. Redpath; Joseph Regenstein Library, University of Chicago; Clare

Reihill; Dorothy Richards; I. A. Richards; Canon Pierre Riches; Helene Ritzerfeld; Alain Rivière; Sir Adam Roberts; Galleria Nazionale d'Arte Moderna, Rome; Rosenbach Museum & Library; Anthony Rota; Carol Z. Rothkopf; Mme Agathe Rouart-Valéry; A. L. Rowse; Lord Russell; Mrs N. Ryan; Professor Alfred W. Satterthwaite; Marcia Satterthwaite; Schiller-Nationalmuseum, Marbach am Neckar; Gerd Schmidt; Susan Schreibman; Rev. Karl Schroeder, SJ.; Ronald Schuchard; Grace Schulman; Timothy and Marian Seldes; Miranda Seymour; Christopher Sheppard, Brotherton Collection, Leeds University Library; Ethel C. Simpson, Trustee, John Gould Fletcher Literary Estate; Samuel A. Sizer, Special Collections, University Libraries, University of Arkansas; Janet Adam Smith; Theodora Eliot Smith; Natasha Spender; Sir Stephen Spender; Tom Staley; Dom Julian Stead; Alix Strachey; James Strachey; Kendon L. Stubbs, University of Virginia Library; Barbara Sturtevant; University of Sussex Library; Lola L. Szladits, Berg Collection, New York Public Library; Allen Tate; Elizabeth Stege Teleky, The Joseph Regenstein Library, University of Chicago; David S. Thatcher, University of Victoria, British Columbia; Alan G. Thomas; Dr Michael J. Tilby; Kathleen Tillotson; Trinity College, Cambridge; Francois Valéry; Judith Robinson-Valéry; The Paul Valéry Collection, Bibliothèque Nationale, Paris; University of Virginia Library; Michael J. Walsh; Jemma Walton; J. Waterlow; Dr George Watson; John Weightman; John Wells, Cambridge University Library; James White, National Gallery of Ireland; Brooke Whiting, Department of Special Collections, University Research Library, University of California, Los Angeles; Widener Library, Harvard University; Helen Willard; David G. Williams; Dr Charlotte Williamson; George Williamson; Patricia C. Willis, Beinecke Rare Book and Manuscript Library, Yale University; Harriet Harvey Wood; Woodson Research Center, Rice University; Dr Daniel H. Woodward, Huntington Library; Yale University Archives; Michael Yeats. For permission to quote from copyright material, we thank Alastair Kershaw (Richard Aldington); The Ezra Pound Literary Property Trust, and James Laughlin (Ezra Pound).

Special thanks go to Tom Chandler for copy-editing; to Donald Sommerville for typesetting; to Iman Javadi for swift and skilful help with translations; to David Wilson for proof-reading; to Mark Bolland for indexing; and to Mrs Valerie Eliot's assistant Debbie Whitfield for her steadfast commitment and long hard work. John Haffenden is most grateful to the Arts and Humanities Research Council for assistance with research expenses, and to the Institute of English Studies, University of London, for hosting the AHRC-funded T. S. Eliot Editorial Research Project.

PREFACE

Volume 4 of the *Letters of T. S. Eliot*, which brings the poet, critic, editor and publisher into his forties, documents a period of professional recuperation, personal strain, and spiritual consolidation.

Following the withdrawal of support by his patron Lady Rothermere, Eliot works hard to cultivate others who might help to secure the future of his influential literary-critical periodical *The Monthly Criterion*. He gradually wins support from ten prominent guarantors: they include his wealthy and well-connected cousin Marguerite Caetani, Princesse de Bassiano; Bruce Richmond, editor of the *Times Literary Supplement*; and the novelist May Sinclair. The magazine goes back to being a quarterly, resuming its original title, *The Criterion*; and in time the young publishing firm of Faber & Gwyer takes over the full financial responsibility. Then in February 1929 Faber & Gwyer becomes Faber & Faber, following the ultimate withdrawal of the Gwyer family interest.

Eliot writes of his career at this time: 'I have a good deal more of general publishing business on my hands than before: advising on manuscripts, discussing with authors and possible authors, and general matters of policy and finance. The business is fairly promising; and the management very harmonious.' He tells his brother: 'It is a young firm, so that success is not certain. When it began as Faber & Gwyer it was very weak and inexperienced, and wasted money; since then it has been reorganised, and is much more promising.' He is paid a salary of £400 a year. 'It is nothing like what a man should be earning at my age, and if the firm flourishes, I shall of course insist on more pay. But I can't do that at the present juncture; so I must supplement my income, just as I did ten years ago, by reviewing, articles, prefaces, lectures, broadcasting talks, and anything that turns up. I begin, I confess, to feel a little tired at my age, of such irregular sources of income. I have begun life three times: at 22, at 28, and again at 40; I hope I shall not have to do so again . . .'

Determined that his work as periodical editor and general publisher should be internationalist above all else, Eliot – an ardent European, committed to cultural cross-fertilization – writes to, and frequently makes personal contact with, a great number of both eminent and emergent writers and thinkers from Great Britain and Europe, as well as from the USA. They include W. H. Auden, Virginia Woolf, H. E. Bates, I. A. Richards, A. L. Rowse, Ernst Robert Curtius, Max Scheler, E. McKnight Kauffer, Allen Tate, Robert Frost, Irving Babbitt, Paul Elmer More, R. P. Blackmur and Lincoln Kirstein (Eliot greatly likes the American magazine *Hound & Horn*, which is explicitly modelled on *The Criterion*). In addition, he seeks to promote the careers of various other writers, such as Louis Zukofsky and Edward Dahlberg (who tells D. H. Lawrence that Eliot has been 'wonderfully gentle' to him in London).

He forges links with foremost reviews including *Europæische Revue* (Berlin), *Nouvelle Revue Française* (Paris), *Revista de Occidente* (Madrid), and *Nuova Antologia* (Milan); claiming of this great enterprise: 'All of these reviews, and others, have endeavoured to keep the intellectual blood of Europe circulating throughout the whole of Europe.'

His own remarkably extensive publications during this period – produced against a background of professional stress (which includes the death from pulmonary tuberculosis, at the untimely age of twenty-eight, of his invaluably astute, devoted secretary Pearl Fassett) and domestic disruption – include the much-loved poems *A Song for Simeon*, illustrated by E. McKnight Kauffer; 'Perch'io non spero' (Part I of *Ash-Wednesday*) and *Animula*; *For Lancelot Andrewes: Essays on Style and Order*; an illuminating introduction to Wilkie Collins's *The Moonstone*; 'A Dialogue on Poetic Drama', for a 1928 edition of John Dryden's *Of Dramatick Poesie: An Essay*; essays including 'The Humanism of Irving Babbitt', 'Second Thoughts on Humanism', and 'Religion without Humanism'; a selection with introduction of Ezra Pound's poems; six talks on 'Seventeenth Century Poetry' for BBC radio; a study of Dante – 'a sort of pamphlet . . . into which I have worked a few notions . . . the idea of the *Vita Nuova* as a manual of sex psychology, and the idea of the difference between philosophy as philosophy and philosophy in poetry'; and an introduction to a translation by Christopher Isherwood (which he considers 'bad') of Baudelaire's *Journaux Intimes*. He finishes too a translation of *Anabase*, by the diplomat Alexis St Leger Leger – writing as St-John Perse – which will prove widely influential.

The heavy roster of his responsibilities extends to caring for his wife, who returns home to London after months in a psychiatric hospital in France. Her behaviour continues to be erratic, sometimes sharply perceptive and caring but at other times fractious and accusatory: 'as you can see, he simply hates the sight of me,' she alleges to one friend. Virginia Woolf gossips: 'Tom is in a great taking with Vivien as mad as a hare.' The evidence of the letters to family and friends in this collection shows that

Eliot persists in looking after his wife with anxious fortitude.

He finds strength in the dogmatic, exacting Christianity he has espoused. 'I . . . feel as if I had crossed a very wide and deep river.' Of his hopes, he writes: 'I do not expect myself to make great progress at present, only to "keep my soul alive" by prayer and regular devotions . . . I feel that nothing could be too ascetic, too violent, for my own needs.'

The principle of editorial selection in this volume, as in the whole series, is straightforward. The letters here printed represent the vast majority that are known to survive: all letters of any importance or significance whatsoever, professional or personal, are to be published. The only letters left out of the printed record are items of little moment or consequence.

For reasons that cannot be exactly determined after all these years, there is only one surviving letter to his brother during the period of this volume, even though he had become accustomed to writing to Henry on a fairly regular basis, at least as often as once a month. Valerie Eliot may well have pinpointed the reason, in her Introduction to volume I of the *Letters*, when she noted that on the deaths of his mother and brother, in 1929 and 1947, Eliot recovered his correspondence with them and burnt a good part of it. All the same, happily for us, there are still some few good letters to his mother – including one notable letter in which he reflects on the deficiencies of his education at Harvard, and others which comment on topics including household arrangements, Vivien's well-being, and the novel challenges of talks broadcasting. However, the dependably newsy but not altogether candid letters to Charlotte Eliot end with her death in September 1929. The compensation is that Eliot comes to write much more openly and expansively to other friends and associates: this is an aspect of his life which gathers pace in the 1930s, and particularly after 1933 as he comes to feel more settled in his career and so delights in exchanging letters with a remarkable range of poets, critics, students, churchmen, historians, philosophers, theorists and thinkers, and also fans.

It is understood too that at about this time he renewed contact with an old friend, Emily Hale; and it is disappointing that his letters to her are yet embargoed. However, it is worth repeating in this connection what Valerie Eliot wrote in Volume I: 'During the course of his correspondence with Emily Hale, between 1932 and 1947 – when Vivien died, after nine years in a mental home – TSE liked to think that his letters to her would be preserved and made public fifty years after they were dead. He was, however, "disagreeably surprised" when she informed him in 1956 that she was giving the letters to Princeton University Library during their lifetime. It seemed to him "that her disposing of the letters in that way at that time threw some light upon the kind of interest which she took, or had come to take, in these letters. The Aspern Papers in reverse."

'On 24 January 1957 the Librarian wrote stating that the letters would remain sealed until fifty years from the death of the survivor [2020]. TSE's reaction was to ask a friend to incinerate Emily Hale's letters to him.'

It is now known that Eliot's letters to Hale span the years from 1930 to 1956, and that the collection adds up to approximately 1,131 letters and related enclosures. These too should be published in time; but in the meantime we must all wait for a few more years to find out the details of their relationship. For the rest, it is a matter of interpretation or speculation; and that is for the biographers and critics, not for his editors.

JOHN HAFFENDEN
2012

BIOGRAPHICAL COMMENTARY
1928–1929

1928 JANUARY – TSE seeks to raise money to keep *The Criterion* in business. The sum of £750 a year is needed to subsidise the magazine. Arnold Bennett, after a personal appeal by TSE and Humbert Wolfe, refuses immediate help. 'I showed little interest,' Bennett recorded in his journal. 'The *New Criterion* is a dull production and always will be.' 13 JANUARY – TSE dines with the businessman F. S. Oliver, who proves to be a generous benefactor: he contributes towards the production of the magazine no less than £250 a year for three years. In time, nine other guarantors (assiduously cultivated) come forward with significant support: TSE's affluent and well-connected cousin Marguerite Caetani, Princesse de Bassiano; Charles Whibley; Bruce Richmond (editor of the *TLS*); May Sinclair, novelist; Alan Lubbock; D. O. Malcolm, diplomat and businessman (Director of the British South Africa Company); J. Hugh Smith; Ethel Sands, American heiress and artist; and Conrad Ormond (director of Doubleday Doran & Co., publishers). 16–23 JANUARY – TSE, in Paris, reports that Vivien 'is not fit' to come home from Malmaison. He loyally defends the right-wing writer Charles Maurras against charges that he is anti-Christian. In 'The *Action Française*, M. Maurras and Mr Ward', *The Monthly Criterion* (March 1928), TSE says he has been 'a reader of the work of M. Maurras for eighteen years', and, far from 'drawing him away from' Christianity – during 1926 Maurras was even condemned by the Pope, with five of his books being placed on the *Index* – Maurras's writings had had the opposite effect on himself. 31 JANUARY – Vivien writes to Ottoline Morrell: 'I am very miserable, & it is all quite *useless*. You must have gathered from Tom what a *horrible* mess all this is. But as you can see, he simply hates the sight of me. And I *don't know what to do*.' FEBRUARY – TSE publishes 'From *Anabase*' (extracted from his translation of *Anabase*, by St-John Perse) in *The Monthly Criterion* 7. By mid-February he is in Paris once more. Vivien returns with

TSE to London in the third week of the month. TSE tells Morrell (20 February), 'It *may* not be a bad thing.' Seven years later, VHE will write in her diary, remembering this moment: 'My dear Tom brought me back with him, but he did not want to. He would have much preferred for me to remain in France ... [T]hey were all *furious* at my leaving ... It was a very bad time & I felt *terribly frightened* at what I had done. So that I was out *of my mind*, & so behaved *badly* to Tom & got very excited. It seemed that everything he said was a *sneer* or an *insult*. When we got to Victoria we were met by Mother & Maurice & their behaviour was *sinister* & *unkind*.' Vivien calls on Morrell and writes to her afterwards, 'I am sorry I talked so much about Tom – of course he is a very old friend of yours – & a great friend & no one likes hearing their old friends spoken against. I am very unhappy, & as you agreed with me – *quite* defenceless. So there it is. If you hear of me being murdered, don't be surprised!' 23 FEBRUARY – TSE attends the Pepys Feast at Magdalene College, Cambridge, as the guest of I. A. Richards. MARCH – TSE makes his first confession, to Father Francis Underhill (whom he calls 'my spiritual director'). He tells William Force Stead: 'I . . . feel as if I had crossed a very wide and deep river.' He takes a vow of celibacy. 1 MARCH – publication of Wilkie Collins's *The Moonstone*, with an Introduction by TSE ('The World's Classics no. 316': 5,000 copies printed); it will be republished in *SE* as 'Wilkie Collins and Dickens'. TSE gives a talk on Tennyson and Whitman at the Poetry Bookshop, London. Mid-month, Vivien suffers from influenza. 25 MARCH – TSE delivers 'Preface' and 'A Dialogue on Poetic Drama' for publication in *Of Dramatick Poesie: An Essay 1668* by John Dryden (London: Frederick Etchells & Hugh Macdonald, 1928). In the Spring of 1928, he publishes 'Perch'io non spero' (with the English text facing a French translation by Jean de Menasce), in *Commerce*: the poem will be Part I of *Ash-Wednesday* (1930). TSE assures Paul Elmer More, who is on a visit to England, that he is a 'strong High Churchman and an enemy to Rome'. 10 APRIL – he tells Force Stead, of his progress in religion: 'I do not expect myself to make great progress at present, only to "keep my soul alive" by prayer and regular devotions . . . I feel that nothing could be too ascetic, too violent, for my own needs.' In mid-month his invaluable secretary Irene Pearl Fassett falls gravely ill with tuberculosis and can no longer go to work: she offers her resignation. Still it is finally decided that the *Criterion* will continue as a quarterly; disingenuously, F&G puts out this statement: 'We are now able to announce that in consequence of reorganisation, and in conformity with the preference of many supporters, The MONTHLY CRITERION will henceforth appear in QUARTERLY form, resuming its original title, THE CRITERION. The next number will be published in June . . . The form will be similar to that of THE CRITERION immediately before its conversion into a Monthly, but the scope will be gradually extended.' MAY – TSE's essay 'The Humanism of Irving Babbitt' is accepted for publication in *The Forum* (New York): he is paid $125 for it. The second edition of *The Sacred Wood* is published. 'A Dialogue on Poetic Drama' is published in an edition of John Dryden's *Of Dramatick Poesie: An Essay*. 2 MAY – TSE visits Cambridge to speak to the Heretics Society: he stays at King's College. The following week, 16 MAY, he visits University College, Oxford, where he dines and talks to the Martlets. Vivien undergoes an operation on her teeth. Throughout the summer, the Eliots' house at 57 Chester Terrace has to be repaired and decorated: but the work is found to have been done so sloppily that in places it has to be done all over again. JUNE – Early in the month, Ottoline Morrell chats with TSE and subsequently gossips to Virginia Woolf; whereupon Woolf conveys the gossip to her sister: 'Tom is in a great taking with Vivien as mad as a hare, but not confined, and they give parties, where she suddenly accuses him of being in love with Ottoline (and me, but this Ott: threw in as a sop) and Tom drinks, and Vivien suddenly says when talk dies down "You're the bloodiest snob I ever knew" – so I have refused to dine there.' In MID-JUNE, TSE is happy to report to Caetani, 'We have been managing . . . very much better this spring, and I am hopeful. Vivien has been running her house well and we have seen a good many people.' 26 JUNE – TSE and VHE go to dinner at the Hutchinsons. TSE later writes to Mary Hutchinson: 'I was . . . extremely nervous as I anticipated that V. would make some statement: I hope it was not too trying for you, but she had had it disturbing her mind for so long that it was perhaps best to get it off.' At the dinner, VHE had managed to break a pearl necklace, which is recovered and returned to her only at the end of September. JULY – TSE goes on a weekend retreat. He publishes 'The Humanism of Irving Babbitt' in *The Forum*. Irving Babbitt and Paul Elmer More visit TSE in London, which he enjoys. TSE later writes of More that in him he found what he called 'an auxiliary to my own progress of thought, which no English theologian could have given me . . . I might almost say that I never met any Christians until after I had made up my mind to become one. It was of the greatest importance, then, to meet the work of a man who had come by somewhat the same route, to the same conclusions, at almost the same time: with a maturity, a weight of scholarship, a discipline of thinking, which I did not, and never shall, possess . . . My first meeting with [More] in London . . . seemed more like the renewal of an old acquaintance than the formation of a new one.' In the final week of the month, the death of Pearl Fassett causes considerable upset to both TSE and Vivien. AUTUMN – Virginia and Leonard Woolf, Mary Hutchinson and E. McKnight Kauffer discuss TSE's poetry at Chester Terrace. Woolf notes her recollections of TSE reciting poems in his 'curious monotonous sing-song'. 17 SEPTEMBER – TSE contributes a 'Preface' to *This American World*, by Edgar Ansel Mowrer: 1,000 copies are printed. He registers his sense of permanent displacement: 'it was not until years of maturity that I perceived that I myself had always been a New Englander in the South West, and a South Westerner in New England.' 24 SEPTEMBER – he publishes *A Song for Simeon* (Ariel Poem no. 16), illustrated by E. McKnight Kauffer: 3,500 copies. 26 SEPTEMBER – his fortieth birthday. 4 OCTOBER – TSE contributes an anonymous 'Preface' (recalling the town of Gloucester where he had spent his summers as a child) to *Fishermen of the Banks*, a collection of short stories by James B. Connolly. 11 OCTOBER – Geoffrey Faber invites TSE to write a pamphlet on Dante for publication in the F&G series 'The Poets on the Poets'. TSE moves to accept, but has to extricate himself gently from his prior commitment to write on Dante for the 'Republic of Letters' series put out by Routledge. It is agreed that he may write the 10,000-word pamphlet for F&G, on the understanding that he will make use of the material in a fuller monograph for Routledge at a later date. In the final week of October, he dines with Robert Frost, who is visiting London. 'Frost I rather like,' says TSE. But Frost's biographer Lawrence Thompson later told of a contrary reaction on the part of Frost: 'What annoyed Frost most was the way in which this native of St. Louis affected an English accent. Long before the evening was over, Frost decided to go on disliking Eliot as a tricky poet – and as a mealy-mouthed snob.' Allen Tate, in a letter to a friend written after a *Criterion* lunch that summer, says: 'Eliot, of course, was due to be the most interesting, but he is a Sphinx'. 9 NOVEMBER – Vivien reports that TSE has taken up dancing again, to the gramophone. TSE sits for a drawing by William Rothenstein which is published in *Twelve Portraits* (1928). 20 NOVEMBER – TSE publishes *For Lancelot Andrewes: Essays on Style and Order* – 1,500 copies are printed – dedicated 'For My Mother'. He declares in the preface: 'The general point of view may be described as classicist in literature, royalist in politics, and anglo-catholic in religion.' He says too that he is working on three books: 'The Outline of Royalism'; 'The Principles of Modern Heresy'; 'The School of Donne' – of which only the second will ever appear, in the form of *After Strange Gods: A Primer of Modern Heresy* (1934). 22 NOVEMBER – Vivien writes to Mary Hutchinson: 'I had a horrible affair at a hair-dresser's last Monday week, & I *very nearly died*. All last week I felt terribly ill, & I had to have 2 interviews with doctors. I have been afraid to go out, as I keep on having queer "turns" & feeling faint.' 23 NOVEMBER – publication of Ezra Pound, *Selected Poems*, edited with an Introduction by TSE – who writes in one advance copy: 'For Vivienne, in memory of many happy days with Ezra & Dorothy Pound. 21. 9. 1928'. DECEMBER – writes an introduction to *The Merry Masque of Our Lady in London Town*, by Charles A. Claye, performed by the Players from St Mary's, Graham Street, at Chelsea Palace Theatre, on 8, 12 and 22 Dec. 1928 (posthumously printed by Stanley Revell: not in Gallup, 1988).

1929   JANUARY – TSE writes 'Second Thoughts on Humanism'. He is in contact with the Americans Richard Blackmur and Lincoln Kirstein, of the periodical *The Hound & Horn* (New York), which he admires, and which is modelled on *The Criterion*. Vivien falls ill with what TSE calls 'the current form' of influenza. TSE refuses evening engagements throughout January. For two months they have two servants – 'a middle aged cook-general and a girl' – and 'old Janes [74] every morning to do the heavy work' – to run their house at 57 Chester Terrace (now Chester Row). TSE meets Allen Tate in London. FEBRUARY – The Eliots begin house-hunting in Bloomsbury: they hope to be able to move into a flat at 51 Gordon Square (Lytton Strachey's former address). TSE takes an interest in the work of the young American Edward Dahlberg, who tells

D. H. Lawrence that TSE had been 'wonderfully gentle' to him in London. 11 FEBRUARY – Ottoline Morrell calls on Vivien Eliot, who becomes fractious when Ottoline does not remember Pearl Fassett (who had just died and for whom Vivien felt considerable affection). When TSE comes into the room in company with Prince Mirsky (whom Morrell did not like), Morrell said she felt annoyed by TSE's references to 'uneducated' writers such as Blake and Lawrence. TSE is offered by Paul Elmer More the opportunity to deliver the Vanuxem Lectures at the University of Virginia; he declines. TSE works on six talks on 'Seventeenth Century Poetry', to be delivered on BBC radio: the series – 'The Tudor Translators', 'The Elizabethan Grub Street', 'The Genesis of Philosophic Prose: Bacon and Hooker', 'The Prose of the Preacher: The Sermons of Donne', 'Elizabethan Travellers' Tales', 'The Tudor Biographers' – will be published in the *Listener* in June and July. TSE has two teeth pulled. Faber & Gwyer becomes Faber & Faber, following the withdrawal of the Gwyer family interest. TSE writes: 'Now that Faber & Gwyer has become Faber and Faber instead, I find that I have a good deal more of general publishing business on my hands than before: advising on manuscripts, discussing with authors and possible authors, and general matters of policy and finance. The business is fairly promising; and the management very harmonious; we have taken on to the Board an American named Frank Morley, who is the representative here also of the Century Company; the others, besides Geoffrey Faber and myself, are Stewart (the general manager) and Richard de la Mare, a son of Walter de la Mare.' He tells his brother: 'I am a director of Faber & Faber: I sold a bond to invest in shares in the new firm. Of course we have no expectations of dividends for the next three or four years; but I want to strengthen my position with them. If the firm goes on and prospers, I shall stay with them; the only danger is of its not succeeding, and having to sell up, and then I do not know what I should or could do. It is a young firm, so that success is not certain. When it began as Faber & Gwyer it was very weak and inexperienced, and wasted money; since then it has been reorganised, and is much more promising.' Formerly he earned £475 per annum: with the reorganisation he volunteers to take a cut to £400 p.a. 'Of course it is nothing like what a man should be earning at my age, and if the firm flourishes, I shall of course insist on more pay. But I can't do that at the present juncture; so I must supplement my income, just as I did ten years ago, by reviewing, articles, prefaces, lectures, broadcasting talks, and anything that turns up. I begin, I confess, to feel a little tired at my age, of such irregular sources of income. I have begun life three times: at 22, at 28, and again at 40; I hope I shall not have to do so again, because I am growing tired.' He launches a series of 'The Poets on the Poets'. APRIL – TSE reports to John Middleton Murry that the problem of moving house was 'worrying to the last pitch of nervous exhaustion, and takes all of our time and attention'. MAY – they decide to move to 68 Clarence Gate Gardens, rather than to share Gordon Square with Lytton Strachey's sister Philippa. TSE's cousins, the Hinkleys – Susan, Eleanor, TSE's niece Theodora Eliot Smith, and Abigail Smith – visit London. The Rothenstein portrait of TSE – which TSE considered 'true' – is put on exhibition in London. TSE is invited by Theodore Spencer to contribute an essay to *A Garland for John Donne, 1631–1931*. A new prize, 'The Five Reviews' Award', is launched by five European reviews – *The Criterion*, *Europäische Revue* (Berlin), *Nouvelle Revue Française* (Paris), *Revista de Occidente* (Madrid), *Nuova Antologia* (Milan) – with the first of five annual awards going to the best short story written in German; subsequently for stories in English, French, Italian and Spanish; and with the winning fiction being printed as nearly simultaneously as possible in all of the five reviews. The first award is to be judged by Max Clauss, editor of the *Europäische Revue*; E. R. Curtius and the novelist Thomas Mann (replacing the late Hugo von Hoffmansthal). TSE hailed this development in his 'Commentary', in the *Criterion*, in January 1930: 'It is not merely a means of bringing to notice new prose writers in five languages . . . We remark upon it still more as visible evidence of a community of interest, and a desire of co-operation, between literary and general reviews of different nations . . . All of these reviews, and others, have endeavoured to keep the intellectual blood of Europe circulating throughout the whole of Europe.' 21 MAY: TSE completes *Dante*: 'a sort of pamphlet . . . into which I have worked a few notions . . . the idea of the *Vita Nuova* as a manual of sex psychology, and the idea of the difference between philosophy as philosophy and philosophy in poetry: the distinction between Belief and Poetic Assent or Acceptance.' TSE tries to find a publisher for Paul Elmer More's manuscript *Pages from an Oxford Diary*. JUNE – the Eliots move from their bijou house on

Chester Terrace to a large ground-floor flat at Clarence Gate Gardens. Vivien Eliot tells a friend: 'it is a most terrible flat. It is quite awful. It is *enormous*. And very *very* expensive. And hideous. And the most terrible uproar of great buildings going up all around it.' TSE publishes in the *Criterion* a review-article entitled 'Mr. Barnes and Mr. Rowse'. He also places 'Second Thoughts on Humanism', in the *New Adelphi* (June/Aug.). JULY – F&F launches the *Criterion Miscellany*. TSE is approached by the Blackamoor Press to write an introduction for a new edition of Baudelaire's *Intimate Journals*, translated by Christopher Isherwood, for a fee of £25. Vivien suffers from pleurisy: the couple plan to go to the seaside for two weeks. TSE begins having driving lessons: presently they buy a Morris Minor – 'a small car, a very small car, a minimal car,' as TSE puts it. He negotiates to bring out a portion of Joyce's work-in-progress *Anna Livia Plurabelle*, as well as Stuart Gilbert's study of James Joyce's *Ulysses*: to a large extent because the book is endorsed by Joyce himself. In consequence, Joyce tells Harriet Weaver: 'T. S. E. most friendly.' AUGUST – TSE works on 'Religion without Humanism', and submits his essay on 13 August: it will be published in *Humanism and America*, edited by his contemporary Norman Foerster, in 1930. He writes of Foerster's brand of humanism that it seemed to him merely 'a bargain sale remnant, shopworn. What I should like to see is the creation of a new type of intellectual, combining the intellectual and the devotional – a new species which cannot be created hurriedly. I don't like either the purely intellectual Christian or the purely emotional Christian – both forms of snobbism. The co-ordination of thought and feeling – without either debauchery or repression – seems to me what is needed. Most critics appear to think that my catholicism is merely an escape or an evasion, certainly a defeat. I acknowledge the difficulty of a positive Christianity nowadays; and I can only say that the dangers pointed out, and my own weaknesses, have been apparent to me long before my critics noticed them. But it [is] rather trying to be supposed to have settled oneself in an easy chair, when one has just begun a long journey afoot.' At long last TSE receives from the poet and diplomat St-John Perse corrections to his long-laboured translation of *Anabase*, to be published by F&F in May 1930. 10 SEPTEMBER – Charlotte Eliot, the poet's mother, dies. 'I fear for Tom, at this time,' writes Vivien. 27 SEPTEMBER – publication of *Dante*, dedicated to Charles Maurras;

the dust-jacket is designed by Rex Whistler. 1 OCTOBER – the Eliots move to 177 Clarence Gate Gardens, Regent's Park, London: 'much smaller than the last, and rather cramped, but cheaper, quieter, and big enough for us,' says TSE. *Animula* (Ariel Poems, No. 23), decorated with wood engravings by Gertrude Hermes, is published on 9 OCTOBER. 'Som de l'escalina' (English text with French translation by Jean de Menasce) appears in *Commerce* (Autumn 1929); it will ultimately be reprinted as Part III of *Ash-Wednesday* (1930). NOVEMBER: TSE receives galley proof of the text and translation of *Anabasis*. He completes his introduction to Baudelaire's *Intimate Journals*. 25 NOVEMBER – his talk 'An Experiment in Criticism' is published in *Tradition and Experiment in Present-Day Literature: Addresses Delivered at the City Literary Institute*. TSE recommends to Oxford University Press the essays of G. Wilson Knight, whose volume will be brought out in July 1930 as *The Wheel of Fire: Essays in Interpretation of Shakespeare's Sombre Tragedies*, with an 'Introduction' by TSE. He suffers from 'a variable though slight influenza' – 'a mild but ineffectual' illness. TSE admires the work of Adrian Stokes, and accepts an essay by him. He considers translating into a version of Jacobean verse one or two of Hofmannsthal's 'Jacobean' verse plays. DECEMBER – TSE lectures at the Children's Theatre, Endell Street, on poetry and philosophy (Whitehead's appreciation of poetry), by way of making a contribution to the repair of the organ at St George's Church, Bloomsbury. He makes suggestions for the improvement of Isherwood's translation of Baudelaire's *Journals* – which he regards as 'bad'. 'Cantique pour Siméon', translated by Jean de Menasce, appears in *Chroniques* 7 (1929). TSE is invited to become a member of the Council of the Shakespeare Association. He supports Louis Zukofsky, Edward Dahlberg, and Walter Lowenfels in their applications to the Guggenheim Memorial Foundation. When invited by John Tucker Murray to give a course of lectures at Harvard, TSE is tempted but declines. His life has been a matter of 'struggling with intermittent ill health punctuated by work and business engagements . . . crowded into the intervals.' W. H. Auden submits *Paid on Both Sides*, which TSE accepts for *The Criterion*. George Williamson publishes *The Talent of T. S. Eliot*.

ABBREVIATIONS AND SOURCES

SA	*Sweeney Agonistes: Fragments of an Aristophanic Melodrama* (London: Faber & Faber, 1932)
SE	*Selected Essays: 1917–1932* (London: Faber & Faber, 1932; 3rd English edn, London and Boston: Faber & Faber, 1951)
SW	*The Sacred Wood: Essays on Poetry and Criticism* (London: Methuen & Co., 1920)
TCC	*To Criticise the Critic* (London: Faber & Faber, 1965; New York: Farrar, Straus & Giroux, 1965)
TUPUC	*The Use of Poetry and the Use of Criticism: Studies in the Relation of Criticism to Poetry in England* (London: Faber & Faber, 1933)
TWL	*The Waste Land* (1922, 1923)
TWL: Facs	*The Waste Land: A Facsimile and Transcript of the Original Drafts*, ed. Valerie Eliot (London: Faber & Faber, 1971; New York: Harcourt, Brace Jovanovich, 1971)
VMP	*The Varieties of Metaphysical Poetry*, ed. Ronald Schuchard (London: Faber & Faber, 1993; New York: Harcourt Brace, 1994)

PERIODICALS AND PUBLISHERS

A.	*The Athenaeum* (see also *N&A*)
C.	*The Criterion*
F&F	Faber & Faber (publishers)
F&G	Faber & Gwyer (publishers)
MC	*The Monthly Criterion*
N.	*The Nation*
N&A	*The Nation & The Athenaeum*
NC	*New Criterion*
NRF	*La Nouvelle Revue Française*
NS	*New Statesman*
TLS	*Times Literary Supplement*

PERSONS

CA	Conrad Aiken
RA	Richard Aldington
RC-S	Richard Cobden-Sanderson
BD	Bonamy Dobrée
CWE	Charlotte Ware Eliot, TSE's mother

EVE	(Esmé) Valerie Eliot
HWE	Henry Ware Eliot (TSE's brother)
TSE	T. S. Eliot
VHE	Vivien (Haigh-Wood) Eliot
GCF	Geoffrey (Cust) Faber
IPF	Irene Pearl Fassett (TSE's secretary)
EMF	E(dward) M(organ) Forster
MHW	Maurice Haigh-Wood
JDH	John Davy Hayward
MH	Mary Hutchinson
AH	Aldous Huxley
JJ	James Joyce
GWK	G. Wilson Knight
DHL	D. H. Lawrence
WL	Wyndham Lewis
FVM	Frank (Vigor) Morley
OM	Ottoline Morrell
JMM	John Middleton Murry
EP	Ezra Pound
HR	Herbert Read
IAR	I. A. Richards
ALR	A. L. Rowse
BLR	Bruce Richmond
BR	Bertrand Russell
ES	Edith Sitwell
WFS	William Force Stead
CW	Charles Whibley
OW	Orlo Williams
LW	Leonard Woolf
VW	Virginia Woolf
WBY	W. B. Yeats

ARCHIVE COLLECTIONS

American Jewish Archives	Jacob Rader Center of the American Jewish Archives, Cincinnati, Ohio
Archives Nationales	Archives Nationales, Paris
Arkansas	Special Collections, University Libraries, University of Arkansas
Beinecke	The Beinecke Rare Book and Manuscript Library, Yale University

Berg	Henry W. and Albert A. Berg Collection of English and American Literature, the New York Public Library
Bodleian	The Bodleian Library, Oxford University
Bonn	Universitäts und Landesbibliothek, Bonn University
BL	British Library, London
Brotherton	The Brotherton Collection, Leeds University Library
Butler	Rare Books and Manuscripts Division, Butler Library, Columbia University, New York
Caetani	Fondazione Camillo Caetani
Cambridge	Cambridge University Library
Cornell	Department of Rare Books, Olin Library, Cornell University
Durham	Special Collections, University Library, Durham University
Exeter	Exeter University Library
Faber	Faber & Faber Archive, London
Guggenheim	Guggenheim Foundation, New York
Harvard	University Archives, Harvard University
Herrick	Herrick Memorial Library, Alfred University, New York
Houghton	The Houghton Library, Harvard University
House of Books	House of Books, New York
Huntington	Huntington Library, California
King's	Modern Archive Centre, King's College, Cambridge
Lilly	Lilly Library, Indiana University, Bloomington
McFarlin	Special Collections and University Archives, McFarlin Library, University of Tulsa
McMaster	Mills Memorial Library, McMaster University, Hamilton, Ontario
Magdalene	Old Library, Magdalene College, Cambridge
Morris	Morris Library, Southern Illinois University at Carbondale
National Library of Scotland	National Library of Scotland, Edinburgh
Northwestern	Special Collections, Northwestern University Library, Evanston, Illinois

CHRONOLOGY OF *THE CRITERION*

The Criterion

Vol. 1. No. 1. 1–103, Oct. 1922; No. 2. 105–201, Jan. 1923;
  No. 3. 203–313, Apr. 1923; No. 4. 315–427, July 1923.

Vol. 2. No. 5. 1–113, Oct. 1923; No. 6. 115–229, Feb. 1924;
  No. 7 231–369, Apr. 1924; No. 8 371–503, July 1924.

Vol. 3. No. 9. 1–159, Oct. 1924; No. 10. 161–340, Jan. 1925;
  No. 11 341–483, Apr. 1925; No. 12. 485–606, July 1925.

The New Criterion

Vol. 4. No. 1. 1–220, Jan. 1926; No. 2. 221–415, Apr. 1926;
  No. 3. 417–626, June 1926; No. 4. 627–814, Oct. 1926.

Vol. 5. No. 1. 1–186, Jan. 1927.

The Monthly Criterion

Vol. 5. No. 2. 187–282, May 1927; No. 3. 283–374, June 1927.

Vol. 6. No. 1. 1–96, July 1927; No. 2. 97–192, Aug. 1927; No. 3.
  193–288, Sept. 1927; No. 4. 289–384, Oct. 1927; No. 5. 385–480,
  Nov. 1927; No. 6. 481–584, Dec. 1927.

Vol. 7. No. 1. 1–96, Jan. 1928; No. 2. 97–192, Feb. 1928;
  No. 3. 193–288, Mar. 1928.

The Criterion

Vol. 7. No. 4. 289–464, June 1928

Vol. 8. No. 30. 1–183, Sept. 1928; No. 31. 185–376, Dec. 1928;
  No. 32. 377–573, Apr. 1929; No. 33. 575–772, July 1929.

Vol. 9. No. 34. 1–178, Oct. 1929; No. 35, 181–380, Jan. 1930;
  No. 36, 381–585, Apr. 1930; No. 37, 587–787, July 1930.

EDITORIAL NOTES

The source of each letter is indicated at the top right. CC indicates a carbon copy. Where no other source is shown it may be assumed that the original or carbon copy is in the Valerie Eliot collection or at the Faber Archive.

del.   deleted

MS   manuscript

n. d.   no date

PC   postcard

sc.   *scilicet*: namely

ts   typescript

<   >   indicates a word or words brought in from another part of the letter.

Place of publication is London, unless otherwise stated.

Some obvious typing or manuscript errors, and slips of grammar and spelling, have been silently corrected.

Dates have been standardised.

Some words and figures which were abbreviated have been expanded.

Punctuation has been occasionally adjusted.

Editorial insertions are indicated by square brackets.

Words both italicised and underlined signify double underlining in the original copy.

Where possible a biographical note accompanies the first letter to or from a correspondent. Where appropriate this brief initial note will also refer the reader to the Biographical Register at the end of the text.

Vivienne Eliot liked her husband and friends to spell her name Vivien; but as there is no consistency it is printed as written.

'Not in Gallup' means that the item in question is not recorded in Donald Gallup, *T. S. Eliot: A Bibliography* (1969).

THE LETTERS
1928–1929

1928

TO *Frank Morley*[1]

CC

2 January 1928[2]   [*The Monthly Criterion*]

Dear Morley,

I find that the sum needed immediately for payments to contributors is £42.3.0. I have spoken to Faber about the matter and he agrees that the best way is for you to send a cheque to him made out to Faber & Gwyer Limited. In this way no entries will appear in *The Criterion* books and the cheques will be sent by Faber & Gwyer as usual.

I also think it is better only to send this amount so that Faber & Gwyer should only have exactly what is needed for immediate disbursement.

I have not had any reply from either Whibley or Richmond.[3] If I do not hear from Whibley by tomorrow morning I shall assume either that he is away or that the post in his part of the country has been very much delayed, and I will send him a wire asking him to wire me at Oliver's[4] address.

Yours,
[T. S. Eliot]

TO *John Gould Fletcher*[5]

CC

2 January 1928[6]   [London]

My dear Fletcher,

I am returning herewith your cheque made out to *The Monthly Criterion* and will ask you whether you will be so kind as to cancel this

---

1–Frank Vigor Morley (1899–1980), writer and editor; director of Faber & Gwyer: see Biographical Register. Though formally employed at this time by the Century Company, and not yet as a Faber lieutenant, his first undertaking with F&F was to look after money matters (inc. payments and subscriptions) for *The Criterion* – a job he tackled with gusto.
2–Misdated 1927.
3–Charles Whibley; Bruce Richmond: see Biographical Register.
4–F. S. Oliver (1864–1934), businessman, author, polemicist: see Biographical Register.
5–John Gould Fletcher (1886–1950), American poet and critic: see Biographical Register.
6–Misdated 1927.

cheque and make out a new one to the order of F. V. Morley. The reason is that for the present we think it much safer that no moneys pass through the *Criterion* account and consequently that no cheques be endorsed on behalf of the *Criterion*. The arrangement is that Morley will collect the money and will then make out a cheque to Faber & Gwyer Limited who will pay contributors, etcetera out of it. In view of the attitude taken up by Lady Rothermere, we think it is best to adopt every precaution.

You might, if you will, send the new cheque to F. V. Morley, c/o The Century Company, 10 Essex Street, w.c.2.

You need not be so punctilious as you are about returning books so quickly. Many thanks, however, for the *Stained Glass*[1] which reached me this morning. I have one or two new French books which may interest you.

I hope you can turn up for lunch on Thursday. We had a very small party last week.

> With very many thanks,
> Yours always,
> [T. S. Eliot]

Cheque enclosed T. S. E.

TO *Richard Aldington*[2]   CC

3 January 1928[3]   [*The New Criterion*]

My dear Richard,

I am writing in haste in connection with a letter just received from Fred Manning[4] who is in Rome. He tells me, under date of December 31st, that Alec Randall[5] has been extremely ill with typhoid and is not likely to live. Apparently he has been unconscious most of the time. He has a specialist named Bastianelli whose name I think I have heard before. When Manning wrote, they did not seem to have entirely given up hope, but all the chances were against him.[6]

1–Herbert Read, *English Stained Glass* (1926).
2–Richard Aldington (1892–1962), poet, critic, translator, biographer, novelist: see Biographical Register.
3–Misdated 1927.
4–Frederic Manning (1882–1935), Australian writer: see Biographical Register.
5–Alec Randall (1892–1977), diplomat and writer: see Biographical Register.
6–Amy Randall had written to Manning (31 Dec. 1927): 'He is in such a very grave condition that it would be ridiculous to have much hope of recovery.' Randall, a Roman Catholic, was Second Secretary to the Holy See. It is said he recovered from the fever only after a holy image was brought to his bedside by special dispensation of the Pope.

I am giving you all this information because Manning says that Mrs Randall sent him a letter which she had written to you and asked him to address it to you. Manning is not sure that it reached you because he addressed it to 'Padhurst'.[1] I hope to see you on Thursday at lunch. I have never met Mrs Randall but when the question is decided one way or the other [I] will certainly write to her.

Yours ever,

[Tom]

TO *Frederic Manning*   cc

3 January 1928[2]   [*The New Criterion*]

Dear Manning,

I have your letter with the enclosure for Mrs Randall to yourself and am horrified to hear this news. I have written to Aldington as you suggested, and will certainly tell Read as soon as he returns to London next week.

I should be very grateful if you would let me know immediately the question of Randall's life is decided.

Yours ever,

[T. S. Eliot]

TO *Godfrey Childe*[3]   cc

9 January 1928   [London]

Dear Childe,

You are by no means a nuisance in sending me your brother's poems,[4] and if there were anything to be done about it I should be very glad indeed. But I know that the series for next year has already been fully arranged by

---

1 – RA's out-of-town address was Malthouse Cottage, Padworth, near Reading.
2 – Misdated 3 January 1927.
3 – Godfrey Childe (b. 1901), author of *Short Head: A Tale* (Cobden-Sanderson, 1927).
4 – Wilfred Childe (1890–1952), poet and critic; a convert to Roman Catholicism in 1914. Editor of *Oxford Poetry* (1916, 1917), he was Lecturer in English Literature at the University of Leeds for thirty years from 1922. His publications include *The Little City* (1911) and *Dream English: a Fantastical Romance* (1917). TSE was to write to the Revd Geoffrey Curtis on 12 Oct. 1945: 'Wilfred Childe I only know very slightly. I remember him as a young poet at the end of the last war, of rather stained-glass aesthetic religious tendencies and I believe that he became a Roman. I have met him on my visits to Leeds and conserve an impression of a rather depressed and disappointed man.'

Richard de la Mare[1] who has the matter in his hands. I will mention it to de la Mare in case the series survives its second year.

And as the prospects of the *Criterion* are at present so vague, I think that it is safest to let you have the poems back. Please tell your brother that I hope he will send me something later on when we know where we are.

Yours sincerely,
[T. S. Eliot]

TO *A. L. Rowse*[2]   TS Exeter

11 January 1928[3]   *The Monthly Criterion*

Dear Rowse,

May we not now drop the Mr? I am very sorry indeed that it is too late to publish your letter in the February *Criterion*. It always surprises people to know how early we have to go to press, and, in fact, the February number is entirely in page. But I should like very much indeed to print your letter and I hope you will not consider it absolutely essential for it to come out in February.[4] As a matter of fact, it is almost impossible to make

---

1–Richard de la Mare (1901–1986) – elder son of the poet Walter de la Mare – joined F&G as production manager in 1925 and became a principal director in 1928; he would rise to become Chairman in 1960, and later President of F&F Ltd. On 2 Oct. 1924 GCF wrote to Mrs M. L. Gwyer: 'He is 24 and appears to be all that a young man ought to be. Very pleasant mannered, intelligent and not afraid of hard work . . . The de la Mares, as I expect you know, have an extraordinarily wide circle of literary friends and acquaintances, and the association of your de la Mare with us may prove a very useful one.' Dick de la Mare became expert in all aspects of book design and production, which he helped to revolutionise, and he commissioned designs and illustrations from artists including Edward Bawden, Rex Whistler, Paul Nash and John Nash; he also introduced to the firm writers including Siegfried Sassoon (a family friend) and David Jones. On 30 May 1941 TSE told ALR, of de la Mare: 'He is the greatest living producer of books and his word is final and your difficulty will be that if you do not crash against his sense of what is beautiful and suitable in production, you may suffer shipwreck on the other rock of his businesss acumen and sense of economy.' TSE was to tell de la Mare directly, on 27 Sept. 1963, 'how happy I have been in this long association with you – since 1925. A long time!' And Peter du Sautoy, a later chairman of Faber & Faber Ltd, said of him: 'He had no use for tricks and quirks that impaired legibility. "For heaven's sake don't show off," was advice he often gave' (*The Bookseller*, 5 Apr. 1986). De la Mare gave the 6th Dent Memorial Lecture, *A Publisher on Book Production*, 1936.
2–A. L. Rowse (1903–1997), historian; Fellow of All Souls College, Oxford: see Biographical Register.
3–Misdated: a note by ALR reads, 'This is evidently a mistake for 1928.'
4–ALR, letter to the Editor, MC 7 (Mar. 1928), 260–3 – a rejoinder to John Gould Fletcher on the subject of Marxism.

any such correspondence quite consecutive except by a method which I regret having overlooked: that is to say, I wish I had sent you a proof copy of Fletcher's letter as soon as it was ready. For this oversight please accept my apologies.

I should like very much to see you again and incidentally to hear your opinions on Massis and Gide. Your invitation is one I should like to accept; but if I can get to Oxford at all during this term, I have tentative engagements at Worcester and University which I should have to fulfil.

With many thanks,
Yours sincerely,
T. S. Eliot

TO *Ramon Fernandez*[1]   CC

11 January 1928[2]   [*The Monthly Criterion*]

My dear Fernandez,

I am glad to hear from you after such a long time.[3] It seems that you have been very busy indeed, and so, in fact, have I. During December the *Criterion* was on the point of being stopped altogether as Lady Rothermere suddenly decided that she wished to withdraw her capital from the enterprise. We now, however, have some hope of replacing this from other sources and meanwhile have brought out a January number and expect to produce a February number. In the circumstances, therefore, I have to be cautious, to explain the somewhat precarious situation to the people whom I desire to contribute to future numbers. I should be very glad indeed to have either the 'George Eliot' or the essay on Comedy; whichever you send will certainly appear in one of the spring numbers if the *Criterion* survives this crisis.

I am relieved to hear that you are satisfied with my translation. I was not satisfied myself and hesitate a good deal over the English equivalents for the abstract words. I thought that I would let you know that I was

---

1–Ramon Fernandez (1894–1944), philosopher, essayist, novelist, was Mexican by birth but educated in France, where he contributed to *NRF*, 1923–43. Works include *Messages* (1926) – which included an essay on 'Le classicisme de T. S. Eliot' – *De la personnalité* (1928), and *L'Homme est-il humain?* (1936). In the 1930s, he was a fierce anti-fascist, but during WW2 he became a collaborationist.

2–Misdated 1927.

3–Fernandez apologised (8 Jan.) for being unable to deliver his essay on George Eliot: he had had too many commitments. He could have finished off his essay on Comedy – 'refutation de Bergson' – if TSE had opted to take that piece first.

very much pleased with your translation of my 'Mallarmé' and apologise for not having done so.[1]

What has happened to the book on Personality which we are all eagerly waiting for in London?

I have to come to Paris occasionally for a few days at a time, and if you are settled again I will telephone to you in the hope that you can come and lunch with me in Paris.

With all best wishes for your wife and your daughter.

Yours ever sincerely
[T. S. Eliot]

TO *Antonio Marichalar*[2]   TS Real Academia de la Historia

11 January 1928   *The Monthly Criterion*

Cher ami,

Merci bien de votre aimable lettre et aussi du numéro de 900 que vous m'avez envoyé pour le jour de l'an. Aujourd'hui Trend[3] est venu déjeuner chez moi et nous avons beaucoup parlé de vous.

Je dois vous dire que l'avenir du *Criterion* est toujours assez précaire. Nous avons lancé le numéro de janvier et nous avons à peu près assuré l'apparition du numéro de février. Au delà de février nous n'y pouvons pas encore voir clair. Tout de même nous espérons obtenir un capital suffisant pour fonder la revue sur des bases plus solides. La crise a été causée par la decision de Lady Rothermere de retirer les fonds qu'elle avait mis à notre disposition.

Donc, si nos projêts viennent à bout, j'aurai grand besoin d'une chronique de vous pour le numéro d'avril. Tous les sujets que vous proposez m'intéressent vivement, mais je tiens surtout à avoir de vous un

1–Fernandez loved TSE's translation of 'A Note on Intelligence and Intuition', C. 6 (Oct. 1927), 332–9, and hoped he had done justice to TSE's essay 'Note sur Mallarmé et Poe', *La Nouvelle Revue Française* 14: 158 (1 Nov. 1926), 524–6.

2–Antonio Marichalar, Marquis of Montesa (1893–1973): Spanish author, critic, biographer and journalist; contributor to the newspaper *El Sol* and the periodical *Revista de Occidente* (on subjects including Claudel, Joyce, Valéry, and Virginia Woolf). His books include *Mentira desnuda*: 'The Naked Lie' (essays on European and American culture, 1933); *Riesgo y ventura del duque de Osuna* (1932): *The Perils and Fortune of the Duke of Orsuna*, trans. H. de Onís; *Julián Romero* (1952).

3–J. B. Trend (1887–1958), journalist, musicologist, literary critic – he wrote the music chronicles for *The Criterion* – was to be Professor of Spanish at Cambridge, 1933–52.

article sur Goya.[1] Je vous donnerai de nos nouvelles dans deux ou trois semaines.

Merci bien de votre sympathie qui m'a beaucoup encouragé, et croyez moi toujours votre dévoué.

T. S. Eliot[2]

TO *Ezra Pound*[3]   TS Beinecke

11 January 1928   Faber & Gwyer Ltd

Dear Ezra,

I can now take up the interrupted correspondence. I have discussed carefully the question of a complete text reproduction of Guido [Cavalcanti] with the business people here and others and they consider that the cost would be prohibitive. It would make the initial outlay about double: that is to say from close on to a thousand pounds; and they don't quite see their way. What they would be very keen to have, however, would be a complete variorum edition and they would like to know what you have to say about that. Also, as my own idea, I should like to enquire if there is any portrait of Guido which could be reproduced to make a frontispiece, or alternatively, for the same purpose, some selected piece of manuscript genuinely in his own handwriting.

Yrs. ever
T.

1 – Marichalar proposed (2 Jan.) to write for *The Criterion* an article on Goya.
2 – *Translation*: Dear Friend, Many thanks for your kind letter, and also for the copy of 900 you sent me as a New Year gift. Trend came to lunch with me today, and we spoke about you a lot.

I have to tell you that the future of the *Criterion* is still uncertain. We have brought out the January issue, and have more or less ensured the appearance of the February number. We cannot yet see what will happen after February. However, we hope to find enough capital to establish the review on a more solid base. The crisis has been caused by Lady Rothermere's decision to withdraw the funds she had put at our disposal.

So, if our plans work out, I shall be in great need of one of your Letters from Spain for the April issue. All the subjects you propose greatly interest me, but I am particularly keen to have an article by you on Goya. I shall let you have further news in two or three weeks' time. Many thanks for your understanding attitude, and believe me your ever faithful. T. S. Eliot
3 – Ezra Pound (1885–1972), American poet and critic: see Biographical Register.

TO *Charles Whibley*[1]   CC

11 January 1928[2]   [London]

My dear Whibley,

It will seem very rude of me not to have written immediately to thank you for your letter and wire and for your letter to Oliver. It is simply that I have been very busy for the last fortnight and also rather under the weather. I am very grateful to you indeed, although I fear that nothing will come of it. I had a very pleasant letter from Oliver and am going to lunch with him on Friday. He says, however, that he does not believe he is in a position to be of much use.[3] I will let you know if anything else turns up.

> In haste,
> Yours ever affectionately,
> [T. S. E.]

TO *W. H. Hindle*[4]   CC

12 January 1928[5]   [*The Monthly Criterion*]

Dear Sir,

Thank you for your letter of the 11th instant.[6] I am returning herewith your cuttings which interested me. I should like to consider the possibility of having regular, or irregular, film notices in *The Criterion* and will certainly keep your name in mind. But at the present moment I am afraid it is out of the question as it is extremely difficult to keep each number

---

1 – Charles Whibley (1859–1930), journalist, author, editor: see Biographical Register.
2 – Misdated 1927.
3 – Oliver wrote on 1 Jan.: 'I'm sorry to say I'm not in a position to finance anything, unless you will take two farms & a variety of other encumbrances off my shoulders.'
4 – Wilfrid Hope Hindle (1903–67), journalist and consultant, was educated at St Edmund Hall, Oxford, and at the Sorbonne. Following a stint as leader-writer for the *Yorkshire Post*, he joined the editorial staff of *The Times*, 1927–33; later he was literary editor of the *Evening Standard*, 1934–6; editor of *The English Review*, Jan.–July 1936; editor of the *Review of Reviews*, 1933–6; and leader-writer of the *Morning Post*, 1936–7. From the late 1930s he worked in the British Embassies in Budapest and Teheran; he was editor of *Britain*, 1943–5; and ultimately he worked as a United Nations Officer, 1947–64, and as a Consultant to the United Nations. His writings include *Portrait of a Newspaper* (1937), *Foreign Correspondent* (1939), and *A Guide to Writing for the United Nations* (1965).
5 – Misdated 1927.
6 – Hindle asked (11 Jan.) if he might undertake to write film chronicles for *MC*.

within our present limitation of ninety-six pages, so that as things are we already have to omit a great deal of matter that we should like to include.

Yours very truly,

[T. S. Eliot]

TO *Herbert Read*[1]

TS Victoria

14 January 1928   *The Monthly Criterion*

Dear Herbert,

I felt pretty sure that you would have to go to bed again. Still, I am sorry that you cannot come on Monday, as I shall probably be going to Paris on Tuesday for the rest of the week. I hope you will be able to come on the following Monday.

Thank you for criticising the Worringer review. I don't think I can conscientiously reject the review without reading the book, which I have wanted to do in any case; and when I have read it I will write to Smith.[2] But it hardly looks as if the review would be printed. I lunched yesterday with Oliver, who is a most delightful person.[3] He said that he would subsidise a March number, if we brought out February; and that he would contribute £100 a year for two or three years.[4] Bennett, whom Humbert and I saw in the afternoon, proved less helpful; and as he would contribute nothing himself and would not touch Beaverbrook[5] for anything, we drew blank.[6]

1 – Herbert Read (1893–1968), poet, critic and administrator: see Biographical Register.

2 – James Smith's review of *Ägyptische Kunst* (1927; *Egyptian Art*, 1928) – by the German art historian Wilhelm Worringer (1881–1965) – did not appear in C.

3 – F. S. Oliver had sent his car to collect TSE for lunch at Kenry House, Kingston Hill, Kingston upon Thames, Surrey, on Fri., 13 Jan.

4 – F. S. Oliver confirmed in a letter to TSE (16 Jan.): '1) That if *for any reason whatsoever* you would like to bring out the March Number of the *Criterion* (whether or not you propose to go on with it after that date) I will pay £100 towards the expenses of that issue. 2) In the event of your succeeding in raising a Guarantee Fund to carry on the paper I will contribute £100 a year to it for two years.'

5 – Max Aitken, 1st Baron Beaverbrook (1879–1964), Canadian-born business tycoon, politician, press baron – 'a magazine king', as TSE once called him – writer and philanthropist; proprietor of the *Evening Standard*, *Daily Express* and *Sunday Express* – he was so wealthy that he never took a salary – knighted in 1911; granted a peerage in 1917. Lampooned by Evelyn Waugh as Lord Copper in *Scoop*; as Lord Monomark in *Put Out More Flags* and *Vile Bodies*. See A. J. P. Taylor, *Beaverbrook* (1972).

6 – Cf. Reginald Pound, *Arnold Bennett* (1952), 326: 'T. S. Eliot and Humbert Wolfe called to discuss the future of the *New Criterion* magazine. "Their real object [said Bennett] was to find out whether I would find capital. I showed little interest. The *New Criterion* is a dull production and always will be."' For his part, Wolfe would recall their encounter in his memoirs and sketches, *Portraits by Inference* (1934): 'the back drawing room of no. 75

The only suggestion they had between them was that Gollancz[1] would probably be willing to take it over; but I could *Not* ask Faber to do that. It is unlucky that Richmond is away, as he had two or three other people in mind whom he was willing to try after Oliver. We will bring out February, but if nothing turns up I propose to stop March, and ask Oliver to relieve some of the February expenses. I tell you all this now (when, being in bed, you shouldn't worry about anything) because I shan't see Morley until week after next, unless he is back on Monday. I never had much hope about it anyway; and I do not feel sure that anybody except Morley takes enough interest to justify the trouble.

My aims have been 'contingent' merely because I did not have the money to run a paper for myself, and because I felt considerable obligation to the people who were running it, and who became less enthusiastic as it cost more and more. I do not blame them for that in the least. I should have preferred to continue to do a quarterly at less cost, than a monthly which would have to pay for itself or sink. As for my aims being indefinite, they are rather so definite that I have deliberately tried to keep them in the background; or rather to make them indefinite enough to be shared with a number of persons; to find the least common denominator for the smallest workable number. I haven't liked to expound my own views except so far as I felt they were shared by others. I should probably feel freer merely as a contributor to other people's journals. But I could only work with Lewis[2] to a very limited extent, as the things he wants (if I have any notion of what he does want) are probably quite different from mine.

ever yours
T. S. E.

[Cadogan Square] with the beautifully bound manuscripts of [Arnold's] novels behind his head. Arnold with his dark tuft, rising like Shagpat's Identical, myself dark and conciliatory, and T. S. Eliot, pale, cold and speaking slowly with his soft persuasive voice like a white kid glove. And I dare say we did want money. Why not? as Arnold himself would have said . . .' (cited in Philip Bagguley, *Harlequin in Whitehall: A Life of Humbert Wolfe, Poet & Civil Servant, 1885–1940* [1997], 266).
1 – Victor Gollancz (1893–1967), publisher and writer, had launched Gollancz Ltd in 1927; later founder of the Left Book Club.
2 – Wyndham Lewis.

TO *Marguerite Caetani*[1]   TS Caetani

14 January 1928   *The Criterion*

Dear Marguerite,

Thank you very much for your note enclosed in one to Vivien. It was very very kind of you to send the flowers, which arrived just at the right moment, and gave a vast deal of pleasure; and the cheque, part of which she spent on toys for the village children.

There is much that would be very difficult to explain without seeing you. It is all very difficult. I should have written before but for *The Criterion* crisis. There is no need to go into details about squabbles, but Lady R[othermere]. was so outspoken in her dislike and disagreement with the review, and her resentments against me, that I was very glad to have her withdraw her money from it. That means, however, that we cannot carry it on unless she is replaced by others; which does not seem likely. But I have had to waste a good deal of time interviewing financiers etc., meanwhile it has been paid for for January, and partly for February, by a small number of contributors; probably we shall have to wind it up in February.

                              ever yours affectionately (in haste)
                              Tom.

TO *Marguerite Caetani*   TS Caetani

16 January 1928   57 Chester Terrace

Dear Marguerite,

Thank you very much for your kind letter. I quite understand your embarrassment. It is very difficult to say whether you could do *anything*, being so far away. I am disturbed to hear that perhaps the Malmaison is not up to date.[2] All the more because I doubt whether Vivien would

---

1–Marguerite Caetani, née Chapin (1880–1963) – Princesse di Bassiano – patron and editor: see Biographical Register.

2–The Sanatorium de la Malmaison, housed in a mansion in Rueil, to the west of Paris, was built in the early 19th century (the Empress Josephine had died there); in 1911 it was transformed into a sanatorium specialising in '*des affections du système nerveux*'. The dramatist Georges Feydeau (1862–1921) died there; and Zelda Fitzgerald was to pass a few days there following a nervous breakdown in Apr. 1930 (Kendall Taylor, *Sometimes Madness Is Wisdom: Zelda and Scott Fitzgerald: A Marriage*, 2002). Since 1965 it has been the headquarters of the Institut Française du Pétrole. See M. de Brunhoff, *Le Sanatorium de la Malmaison* (1913).

accept being moved anywhere else; what she wants is to come home; and for that, alas, she is not fit. I do not know what she has written to you; and I do not want to interfere with her writing as she wishes to anyone; but I cannot help saying that her reports are often anything but exact, though I am quite sure that she believes them. You are quite right in saying that she has confidence in you (though she has every suspicion of all of my immediate family and of our friends). Is there any likelihood of your being in Paris before long? I don't want to drag you into this affair, but on the other hand I have not the slightest desire to keep you out of it! Please believe that you have my confidence also, and that I would willingly tell you anything that I would tell anybody.

I am just leaving for Paris: Cecil Hotel, 30 rue St Didier XVI but hope to return to London on Saturday next. ever affectionately and gratefully,

Tom

TO *William McC. Stewart*[1]   cc

16 January 1928   [*The Monthly Criterion*]

Dear Mr Stewart,

I am just leaving London for five days and am writing in haste.[2] I was very sorry not to see you but have been extremely busy for the last six weeks. I have not had the chance of comparing your translation with the original, but it seems to me indeed excellent. Will you not show Cape your Introduction also, with the possibility of his putting that into the same volume. You are certainly at liberty to tell Cape I thought the Introduction admirable and would myself have accepted it for the *Criterion* but for two reasons. First that it was rather too long for our purposes, and second that it is primarily an Introduction to the work which would be much more suitable prefixed to a translation than in any other form. I don't think I

1 – William McCausland Stewart (1900–89) was born in Dublin and educated at Trinity College, Dublin. Resident Lecteur d'Anglais at the Ecole Normale Supérieure, Paris, 1923–6 (while studying at the Sorbonne), he taught too at the Ecole des Hautes Etudes. He was Lecturer in French, University of Sheffield, 1927–8, and taught at St Andrews and Dundee before becoming Professor of French at Bristol, 1945–68. He was elected Chevalier de la Légion d'Honneur, 1950; Officier des Palmes Académiques, 1950; Commandeur, 1966. His works include translations of Paul Valéry's *Eupalinos, or, The Architect* (Oxford, 1932) and *Dialogues* (Bollingen Series XLV, 1956).

2 – Stewart thanked TSE (6 Jan.) for introducing him to Leonard Woolf, and sent his introduction to Valéry (as TSE had asked). He anticipated meeting Jonathan Cape on 18 Jan. – 'I should be glad however to know your opinion before seeing him.'

can give you any other hints. But if some arrangement could be made by which the other dialogue translated by Madame Bussy could be included to make one volume, I think that would be a good thing.[1]

A translation of *Variété*[2] has, I see, come out in America. I do not know who did it or whether it is any good; and I do not know whether any other publisher has taken that translation for this country. If not, Cape might care to make a corner in Valéry and take everything. I wish I could be more helpful, but I do not know Cape personally.[3]

Yours sincerely
[T. S. Eliot]

P.S. MS sent to Cape today.

TO *Ezra Pound*   TS Beinecke

23 January 1928   Faber & Gwyer

Dear Rabbit,

Yours of the 15th and 18th instants received today on my return from Paris. Re my discourse of reception into the academy. My question marks were intended to be of the rhetorical variety and were introduced primarily in order to give an effect of well balanced, sound critical opinions etcetera instead of mere funeral oration. I don't think they are worth taking up as it would be a long business and I suppose I should be expected to develop the theme touched on so lightly by my steam roller which I agree was not an excessively felicitous metaphor.[4] I am not sure that this sort of

---

1 – Dorothy Strachey (1865–1960), eldest of the Stracheys, was married to the French artist Simon Bussy and lived in France, where she was friendly with Matisse and Gide.
2 – By Paul Valéry.
3 – Jonathan Cape (1879–1960) founded his publishing house in 1921.
4 – TSE, in 'Isolated Superiority' (*The Dial* 84: 1 [Jan. 1928], 4–7) – his review of *Personae: The Collected Poems of Ezra Pound* – saluted EP's 'complete and isolated superiority as a master of verse form . . . A man who devises new rhythms is a man who extends and refines our sensibility; and that is not merely a matter of "technique" . . . I cannot think of any one writing verse, of our generation and the next, whose verse (if any good) has not been improved by the study of Pound's.' Next he considered *The Cantos* 'the most interesting' of all EP's poetry: 'The only criticism which could be made of the Cantos is that Pound's auditory sense is perhaps superior to his visual sense.' Yet he declared too, 'I confess that I am seldom interested in what he is saying, but only in the way he says it. That does not mean that he is saying nothing; for ways of saying nothing are not interesting . . . But Pound's philosophy, I suspect, is just a little antiquated. He began as the last disciple of the Nineties, and was much influenced by Mr Yeats and Mr Ford Madox Ford. He added his own extensive erudition, and proceeded to a curious syncretism which I do not think he has ever set in order. He is, of course, extremely Romantic.' And TSE's final reckoning: 'My own

13

discussion would be good for the public either. However, have it your own way; if you feel unjustly caricatured below the belt, I don't want to stop you from rising in your own defence. The main thing is to salt that two thousand down into good sound bonds or preferred stock.

Re Variorum Edition. You put the matter so clearly that there is nothing more to be said. I will go into the matter of the reproductions again and would be glad if at the same time you could find out Italian prices.[1]

Yours etcetera,

T.

P.S. *Criterion* still in the air. Will let you know later.

———

critical debt to him is as great as my debt in versification. Yet I feel that there is a muddle somewhere. Pound has gone on, and will go on, with vast and restless curiosity in everything that is said and written; it is not that he does not keep up with the times. But I sometimes wonder how he reconciles all his interests: how does he reconcile even Provençal and Italian poetry? He retains some mediaeval mysticism, without belief; this is mixed up with Mr Yeats's spooks (excellent creatures in their native bogs); and involved with Dr Berman's hormones; and a steam-roller of Confucian rationalism (the Religion of a Gentleman, and therefore an Inferior Religion) has flattened over the whole. So we are left with the question (which the unfinished Cantos make more pointed) what does Mr Pound believe?'

EP responded on 18 Jan.: 'Tis indeed a most nobile oration. How seereeyous are the questions? I mean, am I expected to answer 'em; and tell how I reconcile a taste for tennis with a preference for corn-whusky that has been at least ten years in the cask? . . .

'Your infinitely suggestive metaphor of a steam-roller as a gents' religion !!!! with the certainly-by-you-not-comprehended middle term Confucius is a marvel. If I din't love you I wd take it up wiff ghustOO.

'several terms, such as "RRRomantic" need a bit of explaining. But perhaps not in public.

'Do you think I "owe it to myself" to respond publicly to your suggestion that I live in a hopeless and unsorted mental muddle, composed of Uncle Wm. and Mr Ford's cast off luggage? Or shd I keep silent . . .'

1–EP wrote on 15 Jan.: 'A complete variorum Guido [Cavalcanti] would be a pedantic imbecility. There are 81 MSS and 95% of the variations are of *no* interest *whatsoever* . . .

'There is no portrait. There are no scraps of the gent's own handwriting (nor are there of Dante's, whose stuff is much more voluminously preserved) . . . Why the hell should they think I want to spend time on making a complete variorum for nothing? . . .

'Why it shd take 600 pund to reproduce 50 photos, some of 'em only about 3 inches square I dont quite make out.

'Of course you have no means of knowing it, but given the condition of the MSS a "complete variorum", is THE shit, and to a degree almost passing the bounds of the most pre-war-teutonic imbecility . . . [T]he proposed facsimiles were intended to STOP the godbloody idiocy and illegibility of excessive varia, and stupid discussion of same.'

23 January 1928   *The Monthly Criterion*

Dear Rowse,

I have just got back and am very pleased to find your kind letter.[1] It is not yet quite certain whether the *Criterion* will continue or stop, but we should know before very long. I shall be all the more sorry if we cannot go on with it because I had hoped to entice you as a contributor in more ways than merely as a correspondent. If it does go on, I can certainly say that it will be under such auspices as will make it possible for us to widen its scope a little and tackle more seriously the kind of problems in which you are particularly interested. And I want to get more men of about your own age whatever their views.

I am very sorry that it was impossible either to get your letter into the February number or to print it in the form you suggested. The February number was actually with the binders when you wrote. It goes without saying that if there is a March number your letter will appear in it.

If any event please do not fail to let me know whenever you are in London.

> With many thanks,
> Yours very sincerely,
> T. S. Eliot

P.S. I have got your little book on History but have not yet had time to read it.[2]

1–ALR wrote on 18 Jan. 'I am really more sorry for the sake of people like me, if the *Criterion* really is to go. It had the potentiality of being, and was beginning to be a centre for the discussion of ideas which have the greatest importance for us of the youngest generation. On a great many points, it did not represent my views, nor of the various sets of people I have come most in contact with; but we always valued the freshness of its critical outlook, and are self-confident enough to believe that yet more might have been expected from the convergence of its tendencies with ours.'
2–ALR, *On History: A Study of Present Tendencies* (1927).

TO *M. C. D'Arcy*[1]   CC

23 January 1928   [*The Monthly Criterion*]

Dear D'Arcy,

Thank you very much for the review of *Duns Scotus* which is extremely interesting and seems to me very sound.[2] If we bring out a March number it will appear in that; if not, I hope very much that it can be published somewhere else, as I think it ought to be. I could possibly get it published in America if you were willing; but on the other hand you may have some periodical in mind yourself. I shall let you know at once as soon as the future of the *Criterion* is settled.

Sincerely yours,

[T. S. Eliot]

TO *John Middleton Murry*[3]   CC

24 January 1928   [London]

My dear John,

Thank you very much for your kind letter.[4] I cannot yet tell definitely by what time I can get the 'Babbitt' done, and I am afraid there will have to be a little delay, for, as I told you, I shall want to try to place it in America simultaneously, and I do not know what is the best magazine for it there. I should think either the *Forum* or the *Yale Review*.[5]

1 – Martin D'Arcy (1888–1976), Jesuit priest and theologian: see Biographical Register.
2 – See untitled review of C. R. S. Harris, *Duns Scotus*, in MC 8 (Mar. 1928), 266–9. D'Arcy wrote again on 24 Jan.: 'After looking again at the real Scotus I am beginning to fear he was on the wrong track altogether & paved the way for some very wretched systems of philosophy.' IPF responded on 27 Jan.: 'Mr Eliot asks me to thank you for your letter and to say that he believes you to be right about Duns Scotus.'
3 – John Middleton Murry (1889–1957), writer, critic, editor: see Biographical Register.
4 – JMM had written on 21 Jan.: 'I do hope you have succeeded in getting through the difficulties with the *Criterion*. Oddly enough I feel almost as keenly about it as I do about the *Adelphi*.

'Is there any chance of your letting me have what you promised on Irving Babbitt in the near future?

'I would tell you how things are with us here, if only I knew. But, alas, I don't.

'I wish I had you to talk to sometimes. A couple of hours once a week would be very good, for me at any rate. I should like, very much, to understand where you have gone. But I suppose that is impossible. You always said that you did not understand me. It is very strange, for I fancy we are both simple people.

'Well, God bless you, since that has now a meaning for you.

'Ever yours affectionately / John'
5 – TSE, 'The Humanism of Irving Babbitt', *Forum* 80: 1 (July 1928), 37–44.

I wish also that I could give you more definite news of the *Criterion*. The February number will appear and probably the March, but beyond that I have nothing to say as I know nothing.

I wish that I might have more news of yourself. You are often in my thoughts.

Ever yours affectionately,

[T.]

TO *Bonamy Dobrée*[1]   TS Brotherton

24 January 1928   *The Criterion*

Dear Buggamy:

Oh Bwana, your letters would be more satisfactory if they were (1) more frequent (2) more coherent (3) more legible. I am at a loss to reply to all these tumultuous and undecipherable matters. But let us dispose first of

Odds & Ends:

The tune is 11th century, the words were adapted by J. Wesley from the original and literal translation.[2] The tune has also been used for 'Auld Lang Syne', 'Of All the Fish that Swim the Sea' etc. There is no relation between Wuxianity and Islam. I await your report upon the King of Aphghanistan's HAT. Is it true that your University refused the King of Aphghanistan an Honorary Degree because he would wear a grey frock coat, elastic sided boots, and a brown TOP HAT? If so, it reflects great credit upon you, and I suppose that it is only from modesty that you do not allude to the incident, except by the remark that 'you do not like to be associated with a local hatter'.

The male Bolovians were divided into Modernists and Fundamentalists, but the females communicated in both kinds. This supports the assertion of Ovid, in re Tiresias.

Your award re Stoic Shakespeare is appreciated. Many thanks. I ought to let you know that Richmond, and others indeed, have expressed great

1 – Bonamy Dobrée (1891–1974), scholar, editor and critic: see Biographical Register.
2 – TSE had sent greetings by means of a drawing (done by TSE) of 'your old friends' – 'Bolo Rex and Pansy Regina' – and these verses attributed to J. Wesley ('11 century'):
            "'Tis WUX that makes the world go round,
                And sets the balls a-rolling;
            WUX fills with ecstacy our soul,
                Our soul in whole consoling.'

approval of your Kipling, which I thought first rate.[1] Also that I liked the Halifacts,[2] and F. S. Oliver (whose good opinion is worth having, he made a lot of money out of Debenham & Freebodys) wholly approves of it.

The Criterion is still in no man's land. But I am so tired of giving information about that that I asked Herbert to inform you of the situation. We have gloomy meetings at the Grove once a week, and are all getting to the bread & cheese condition.

I was seasick crossing the channel before Epiphany. Herbert went to Yorkshire, and then took to his Bed for ten days. Mr Tandy of the Museum[3] is being sent to the Great Barrier Reef, but whether to gather seaweed, investigate the Thames flood or convert cannibals, he is not certain. It is hoped that he will be devoured by the Banyeg, a fabulous monster inhabiting those Parts. Today I went to a Wedding with the Rev. Force Stead, and we got a bottle of not very good champagne out of it. Father D'Arcy S.J. and Richard Aldington came to lunch with me. Codrington has got down to cheese without bread, and Wheen[4] to bread without cheese. Flint (Frank S.)[5] has gone to Paris for the fiancialles of his brother. He continues to pose as one of the proliatirariat. There is no

1 – 'Rudyard Kipling', MC 6 (Dec. 1927), 499–515.
2 – 'George Savile, Lord Halifax', TLS, no. 1350 (1927), 941–2.
3 – Geoffrey Tandy (1900–69) worked as Assistant Keeper in the Department of Botany at the Natural History Museum, London 1926–47; he also did broadcast readings for the BBC (including TSE's Practical Cats on Christmas Day 1937). During WW2 he served as a commander in the Royal Navy, working at Bletchley Park. He and his wife Doris ('Polly') were to become intimate friends of TSE. FVM would tell W. W. Norton on 1 May 1931, that Tandy was 'a very promising scientist . . . He has the possibilities of a Jennings or even of a Bateson.' Tandy was to write to Martin Ware (who had invited him to talk about TSE to a small literary society) on 20 Nov. 1935: 'I believe that anything I may be able to do to help anybody to a better understanding of Eliot's work will be a good work. Against that I have to set the fact that he is a pretty close personal friend (whatever that locution may mean) and my judgement may be vitiated in consequence. The text of "this side idolatry" may be used against me. However, having asked the man himself if he have any serious objection, I say yes and hope that you will not regret having asked me.' See Miles Geoffrey Thomas Tandy, A Life in Translation: Biography and the Life of Geoffrey Tandy (thesis for the degree of MA in Arts Education and Cultural Studies, Institute of Education, University of Warwick, Sept. 1995).
4 – Arthur Wheen (1897–1971), librarian and translator, grew up in Sydney, Australia, and came to Europe with the Australian Expeditionary Force in WW1 (he received the Military Medal for bravery in action). A Rhodes Scholar at New College, Oxford, 1920–3, he worked for the rest of his career in the Library of the Victoria & Albert Museum, becoming Keeper, 1939–62. He translated novels relating to WW1 and won great praise for his translation of Erich Maria Remarque's All Quiet on the Western Front (1929); and he wrote one novella, Two Masters (1924, 1929). See We talked of other things: The life and letters of Arthur Wheen 1897–1971, ed. Tanya Crothers (Woollahra, NSW, 2011).
5 – Frank Stuart ('F. S.') Flint (1885–1960), English poet and translator, and civil servant: see Biographical Register.

one to pay for the Port but Morley & me, and soon there will be only Morley, and then no one will pay income Tax except Humbert Wolfe and Arnold Bennett. Harrold Monro was carried home speachless from the Aldingtons Reception. My next door neighbour Miss Rivers Thompson[1] continues to play Mendellsohn & Company. Quaxo the Cat is going bald. I am going to help the Flood sufferers by presenting a Young Talking Parot to the pub. in Hammersmith.

[unsigned – incomplete]

TO *The Editor of* The Forum   TS

24 January 1928   *The Monthly Criterion*

Dear Sir,

Thank you for your letter of the 9th instant.[2] I should indeed be happy to contribute to a series which includes the names of More and Babbitt. I have two essays in mind, which I want to write in any event. One is on Julien Benda's last book: that is to say, it would not require any previous knowledge of the book on the part of the reader (*La Trahison des Clercs*) but would discuss the question that he raises: whether the intellectual theorist is ever justified in becoming a political influence. The other is on Irving Babbitt himself, and would put the question of his attitude towards Christianity as shown in his last book (*Democracy & Leadership*).[3] Would either of these fit in? If so, I am sure that we could come to an understanding about the compensation.

The Babbitt article would appear in England, though of course not before you printed it; the other, I have made no English arrangements about, and could give you exclusively, if that is an inducement to you.

Yours sincerely,

T. S. Eliot

I should prefer to do the Benda essay; especially as I half promised the other elsewhere.[4] I have just remembered this.

1–Ruth Rivers Thompson (1865–1937), daughter of Sir Augustus Rivers Thompson, was married to Richard Bosanquet, merchant.
2–H. G. Leach, editor of *Forum* (New York), petitioned TSE: '*The Forum* is planning and publishing a series of critical literary articles. Mr. Paul Elmer More and Professor Irving Babbitt have already contributed papers and we should deem it a special privilege if we might include in our series a literary essay by you on some subject, preferably dealing with the contemporary movement, either in America or England.'
3–'The Humanism of Irving Babbitt', *Forum* 80 (July 1928), 37–44.
4–'The Idealism of Julien Benda', *The Cambridge Review* 49 (6 June 1928), 484–8.

TO *Messrs Methuen & Company*   CC

25 January 1928   [London]

Dear Sirs,

In reply to your letter of the 14th instant, I do not think that I wish to make any revision to the body of the book of *The Sacred Wood* as I am now too far out of touch with it, but I should like to write a short preface.¹ Furthermore, as you propose to reset the book, I should be glad to know whether you could consider issuing it in a slightly different form. I should like a larger page, to make the book uniform in size with my *Collected Poems*, and I think that readers of the book would find a larger type more pleasant to the eye. Finally I should like to enquire whether you consider it necessary to publish the new edition at the same price at which the old one was issued. I should feel better pleased if it could be issued in the form I have suggested, and on a rather better quality of paper; and I think that this could be done at the price of 7/6d.²

I remember that some years ago you remaindered part of the edition.³ Have you any information as to whether these remaindered copies have all been taken up and at what price they were sold to the public?

                          Yours faithfully,
                          [T. S. Eliot]

TO *Marguerite Caetani*   TS Howard

25 January 1928   *The Monthly Criterion*

Dear Marguerite,

Thank you very much for your kind letter. It is good of you to suggest that I again become 'English correspondent' for *Commerce*, but I remember that I never did any work, or rather never accomplished anything, when I was. Anyway, the *Criterion* is hanging on for another month at least, so I haven't time yet to take on anything else. It is all very tiresome. I appreciate your kindness; also in asking me to Menton. But it is a long and rather costly journey for a short stay, and I even feel that I

---

1 – *The Sacred Wood*, 2nd edn (May 1928), contains 'Preface to the 1928 Edition'.
2 – Methuen & Co. replied on 26 Jan. that they would be happy to meet his wishes and asked to see a copy of *Collected Poems*. In the event, they kept the price at 6s. net – 'for we feel that it will have a considerable effect on the sales' (9 Mar.).
3 – Methuen had disposed of 119 copies of *The Sacred Wood* at a reduced rate in 1923, and assumed that they had 'long since passed into the hands of the public.'

see so much of France – I go over regularly every three weeks to Paris for several days – that if I could take a holiday it would have to be somewhere else! but I can't take one at present.

By the way, I have not told Vivien about the *Criterion*. There is no need to yet. Thinking over your suggestions, I don't think that a change of sanatoriums or of doctors would be anything but unsettling for her. She likes Claude[1] very much, and the people about her, and they are kind to her.

With many thanks
ever affectionately,
Tom

I shall be over again about the 11th February.

TO *F. S. Oliver*   CC

25 January 1928   [London]

Dear Oliver,

Thank you very much for your telegram. I shall be delighted to come. I should have liked very much to stay over till Monday; but I shall have certain things to attend to Sunday night and finally a dentist's appointment early Monday morning settles the matter. If it is convenient for you to have the car call for me as before, about 5. or 5.30., that would suit me very well as I usually like to get a full day's work at home on Saturday. If it were more convenient to have the car call later, that would not matter as I should stay in till it came, but if you found it more convenient to send the car earlier, I should be grateful if you would have me rung up at Sloane 3184 to give me warning.

Sincerely yours,
[T. S. Eliot]

1–Henri Claude (1869–1946) was elected to the Académie de Médecine in 1927. He would also look after Zelda Fitzgerald during her brief stay at the Sanatorium de la Malmaison in 1930.

TO *Messrs. Methuen & Company*   cc

27 January 1928   [London]

Dear Sirs,

Thank you for your letter of the 26th instant. I should be very glad if
you could bind the new edition of *The Sacred Wood* as similarly to the
binding of my poems as possible. I am not quite sure, however, whether
the paper label is very satisfactory and should be glad to have your
opinion as to whether in your judgment it would be better to have the
lettering say in gilt.

Yours faithfully,
[T. S. Eliot]

TO *Charles Maurras*[1]   TS Texas

Le 27 janvier 1928   *The Monthly Criterion*

Cher Monsieur et Maître,

Je veux vous expliquer comment j'ai dû arranger la publication de votre
Prologue dans le *Criterion*. Vous aurez depuis longtemps reçu le numéro
de janvier et le chèque pour la première moitié du Prologue. Comme je
vous avais expliqué, je n'avais pas à ma disposition à ce moment-là un
traducteur de la hauteur de vous traduire et j'ai dû m'en charger moi-
même. Je n'avais terminé que la première moitié de la traduction au mois
de décembre quant est survenu une crise de laquelle nous ne sommes pas
encore sortis. Un des fondateurs du *Criterion* a inopinément retiré tous
les fonds qu'il y avait mis. Pendant quelque temps nous ne savions pas s'il
nous serait de faire paraître le numéro de janvier et je n'avais aucun espoir
de faire paraître celui de février. Dans ces circonstances là, et étant tracassé
de mille besognes et inquiétudes, j'ai dû remettre un travail du traduction
que je jugeais, hélas! inutile. Au dernier moment nous avons reçu assez
d'appui pour assurer les numéros de février et de mars; mais à ce moment,
je suis navré de vous le dire, la traduction n'était pas faite et j'ai dû insérer
un autre article au lieu de la suite du votre. Je n'ai pu que mettre en tête
une note pour avertir les lecteurs que la suite de votre article paraîtra
dans le numéro de mars.[2] J'espère adjoindre une autre note de moi sur un

---

1 – Charles Maurras (1868–1952): poet, critic, political philosopher, polemical journalist;
founding editor of *L'Action Française*: see Biographical Register.
2 – 'Prologue to an Essay on Criticism [I]', *MC* 7 (Jan. 1928), 5–15; 'Prologue to an Essay on
Criticism [II]', *MC* 7 (Mar. 1928), 204–18.

petit livre par un certain Leo Ward qui s'appelle *The Condemnation of the Action Française*. C'est un livre sans grand importance, mais puisque c'est le premier livre sur ce sujet qui est parû en Angleterre, je tiens à y répondre.[1]

Donc, je vous offre toutes mes excuses pour le delai, et j'espère que vous me pardonnerez un accident qui fait une partie de la crise que nous traversons.

Recevez, cher Monsieur, l'assurance de ma grande admiration et de ma sympathie cordiale.

T. S. Eliot[2]

TO *Charles Whibley*   CC (photocopy at Houghton)

27 January 1928   [London]

My dear Whibley,

Thank you for your letter. I will send you the Coty book[3] in a few days, as I have not yet finished looking at it myself. As I said, I am told that he is in sympathy with the *Action Française*, but it is thought better not to make this too evident to the public. I find him rather more broad

1 – TSE, 'The *Action Française*, M. Maurras and Mr Ward', MC 7 (Mar. 1928), 195–203.
2 – *Translation*: Dear Sir and Master, I would like to explain how I have had to proceed in the matter of the publication of your Prologue in the *Criterion*. You must have received the January number some time ago, as well as the cheque in payment of the first part of the Prologue. As I explained to you, at the time I had no available translator of the required standard, and so I had to undertake the task myself. I had finished only the first part of the translation by the month of December, when there occurred a crisis from which we have not yet emerged. One of the founders of *The Criterion*, without warning, withdrew all her financial support. For a while, we were uncertain whether it would be possible to bring out the January number, and I had no hope of bringing out the February one. In the circumstances, harassed by a multitude of tasks and worries, I had to postpone the work of translation, which I supposed to be, alas, pointless. At the last moment, we received enough support to ensure the publication of the February and March numbers, but at that point, as I am distressed to have to tell you, the translation was still unfinished, and I had to insert another article in place of the second part of yours. All I could do was to include a note at the beginning to inform our readers that the second part of your article would appear in the March number. I hope to add another note, written by myself, about a little book by a certain Leo Ward, entitled *The Condemnation of the Action Française*. It is not of any great importance, but since it is the first book on the subject to appear in England, I feel I must reply to it.
I therefore offer you all my apologies for the delay, and I hope you will forgive me for an accident which is part of the crisis we are going through.
Allow me to express my great admiration and warm fellow-feeling. T. S. Eliot.
3 – François Coty, *Contre le communisme* (Paris: B. Grasset, 1927).

minded with regard to the position of Great Britain than either Maurras or Bainville is apt to be.[1]

As for the *Criterion*, I do not know whether I told you that I liked <Fredk. Scott> Oliver immensely and that he was sincerely interested and perfectly honest about what he could do. I told him that the young contributors who are interested expected to scrape up enough money for the February number. He volunteered to guarantee the March number and also to contribute a hundred a year for two years. Of course this is nothing like enough for a start, but in the circumstances I think it was very generous of him, and it was obvious that he had given thought to the matter and was anxious to do all he could. Very different from Arnold Bennett, who not only declined to try to interest any of his plutocratic friends, but did not offer the smallest contribution himself. This in spite of the fact that he has always expressed interest in the paper and before there was any question of money being wanted spoke to me about it in the highest terms. Oliver seems enough interested to be willing to give his support toward interesting other people. Meanwhile, as Richmond, who had a few people in mind, is away until next week, we are going to bring the February number out and will prepare a March number as slowly as possible. Oliver thought that Robert Brand[2] might be interested, at least to the same amount as himself. Do you think there is anything in this? I could get Richmond to write to Brand as soon as he returns.

I must explain that the second part of the Maurras essay does not appear in the February number but will be in the March number if that number appears. The reason is that there was no one else to translate Maurras but myself. I therefore only translated the first half for the January number. As I then thought that the February number would not appear, I did not translate the second half in time, but if there is a March number the rest will appear as I have completed the translation. It was not a small task either.

If the March number appears, I intend to put into it a note of my own on Leo Ward's pamphlet which has just appeared, about the *Action Française*.

1–CW had written to TSE (24 Jan.), of Coty: 'A man of brains and character, combined with wealth, may do much with the *Figaro*, & such help is necessary to France just now.'
2–Robert Brand (1878–1963), who took a first in modern history from New College, Oxford, and was elected a Fellow of All Souls, was a civil servant and financier. He worked in colonial administration in South Africa, 1902–9, and then joined the merchant bank Lazard Brothers, as managing director till 1944, and as a director till 1960. During WW1 he worked for the Ministry of Munitions, and in WW2 he was head of the British Food Mission to the USA, 1941–4. A skilful counsellor, he was a director of the Times Publishing Company, 1925–59. In 1946 he accepted a peerage, becoming Baron Brand.

The pamphlet itself is not very good and not very important but it is the first book on the subject to appear in England and therefore I think it ought to be dealt with. I have talked to Leo Ward about the subject and have lunched with him and shall probably have to ask him to lunch with me, but in spite of this exchange of hospitality I consider him a worm. I don't think it will be very difficult to demolish his book.[1] Incidentally, have you seen the book by Marquis de Roux, which is very good?[2] I am afraid that my article, however, may displease Maurras: because I really am compelled to the conclusion that the *Chemin de Paradis*[3] contains a good deal of out of date Hellenism *en toc*, and also I feel that Maurras, at

1 – TSE had lunch with Father Leo Ward at the Wellington Club on 3 Jan. 1928.

Six years later, Father John V. Simcox (St Edmund's College, Ware, Hertfordshire) wrote to TSE out of the blue on the subject of Maurras and the *Action Française*: 'I think that Maurras himself would fully agree with your refusal to associate yourself quite unreservedly with the *A. F.* [*Action Française*] After all, even before his condemnation, he had often warned Catholics against a too unlimited adhesion to his school. Personally, I must own up to a feeling of regret over his condemnation. I can, of course, see that there was plenty of justification for it. But, in my own case, Maurras had only helped me to see much in Catholicism that I had never seen before. He had (through his books) been such a good friend to me that I could not but be sorry when he was condemned.

'My own impression is that many of his Catholic opponents either could not or would not understand him. Certainly that was so with Father Leo Ward in England. I once asked him whether he really believed in his own case against Maurras as set out in his pamphlet on the *A. F.*; but he simply refused to discuss it. He told me that you had replied to his pamphlet and that he was still so sore from your handling of him that he wished never to hear of the *A. F.* again.'

TSE responded to Father Simcox on 14 Feb. 1935: 'I had some conversation with Leo Ward at the time, as well as controversy, and formed the impression that he had taken up the matter with more zeal than knowledge. The book which appeared in England a little later, by Denis Gwynn [*The 'Action Française' Condemnation* (1928)] on the subject, showed a much more intimate acquaintance, although its point of view was one which I could not really accept.'

After reading TSE's article attacking Ward's pamphlet (TSE had sent him a copy), Simcox wrote further: 'I can now understand Father Ward's refusal to discuss the subject of the *A. F.* when I asked him about it. Your reply must have convinced him that he was quite incompetent to deal with the matter. There is, so far as I can see, no reply possible from his side to your criticisms of his incompetence. He may of course have been right in his main view that Maurras deserved condemnation; but, if so, he was right because of luck rather than because of knowledge. Your article proves that up to the hilt.

'My own impression is that he simply "got up" his case against Maurras . . . In any case, in view of the years of blood and sweat that Maurras had put into the exposition of his political views he deserved something better than that type of answer . . . Father Ward should never have been guilty of such a trivial reply to him. However, I imagine that even Léon Daudet himself would agree that your *Criterion* article inflicted chastisement adequate to the offence committed. Poor Father Ward!'

2 – Marquis de Roux, *Charles Maurras et la nationalisme de l'Action française* (1927).

3 – Maurras, *Le Chemin du Paradis: mythes et fabliaux* (1894).

any rate in early life, associated himself so closely with that preposterous philosophy of Comte[1] as to appear a little silly. These points will have to be touched on very lightly.[2]

I was glad to read your very favourable note about Massis' book.[3] Especially as I was myself responsible for the book's appearance in England – it was of course Massis who asked for the Preface from Chesterton – and as it has not gone extremely well it is on my conscience. I don't consider it an extraordinarily good book, but I feel that the questions raised are in themselves so important that the book deserves to be pushed so that people in Britain should at least think about these matters.

Ever yours affectionately,

[T. S. E.]

[Note by Henry Eliot:
'In a letter to me from T. S. E. dated at London June 2, 1939, he remarks:
    "Going through some old files to destroy papers, I picked out a few which might interest you. The correspondence with Whibley is obviously too intimate to be suitable for Eliot House or for anyone to see but yourself." H. W. E. Jr']

---

1 – Auguste Comte (1798–1857), founder of Positivism, insisted upon confining his attention to observable phenomena and deduction, and so disdained metaphysical enquiry and transcendental religion. His writings include *Cours de philosophie positive* (1930–42); *Catéchisme positiviste* (1852), and *Système de politique positive* (4 vols, 1851–4).

2 – CW responded (29 Jan.): 'I was sure that you would like Oliver. There is no one like him, in mind or heart, and he has the rare gift of a practical intelligence. I am glad that he will help, especially as his help will encourage others. I am glad, also, in a fashion, that Arnold Bennett will not. He is dipped in the poison of the worst journalism.

'If it is of any service, & the *Criterion* goes on beyond March, I shall be delighted to subscribe £25 a year to its funds.

'I have read de Roux' book on Maurras & think it very good. There are certain weaknesses in Maurras which should not be forgotten. Like all Frenchmen, he is narrow-minded where other countries are concerned, & often ignorant. He knows practically nothing about England, & very little about America. And he has the Hellenism of one who is not a scholar. As to his admiration for Comte, that beats me altogether. It might be the error of youth, & even then would be unintelligible. I speak of the old humbug with feeling, for when I was an undergraduate I fell in with the Comtists, & have ever since had a horror of their pompous folly . . .

'I don't know if Oliver will be able to influence Brand, whose sympathies never seemed to me to be with any literary enterprise.'

3 – Whibley's note on Henri Massis's *Defence of the West* (1927) has not been found.

TO *The Master, University College, Oxford*   CC

27 January 1928   [London]

Dear Master,

Thank you for your letter.[1] I trust that nothing will occur to interfere with my visit on May 2nd. I should be very happy indeed to stay the night with you and I look forward to meeting you with much pleasure.

Yours very sincerely,

[T. S. Eliot]

TO *Frank Morley*   TS Berg

30 January 1928   *The Monthly Criterion*

Dear Morleigh,

What do you think I have just heard of a pub in the Roman Road Islington way this pub is called the ALBERT Well it Seems this pub has the most remarkable Parret You wouldnt believe the Tales they tell about this Parret How it told the barman Off when he robbed the Till etc. Well I would have rung you up last night the minute I heard but it was Raining but anyway I think we ought to go down to Islington way and see about this Parret.[2]

Well I spent Sunday with Oliver he was very Aimiable & the Long and Short is he would increase his share if the *Criterion* became a Quarlterly (¼ly) as he likes Quarleterley so much Better He would make it £250 per annum for three year anyhow[3] Well if we got 2 others like that we could do it and 4 others would do it handsome & I suppose a Quarterley is better than nothing and personally I perfer it. However £250 a annum

1 – M. E. Sadler had invited TSE to dine with the Martlets at University College, Oxford, on 21 Mar. He wrote again on 26 Jan. to confirm TSE's visit on 2 May. 'We shall dine 7.30, I expect . . . Short coat & black tie. And we hope you will stay the night with us.'

2 – In 1939 TSE was to publish some light verses entitled 'Billy M'Caw: The Remarkable Parrot' (*The Queen's Book of the Red Cross*). Nearly ten years later, he wrote to his friend Jack Isaacs: 'I am pleased that you liked the Parrot . . . I daresay it was composed about the same time as *The Rock*, or a year or so later . . . [T]he episodes in the Life of Bill M'Caw are entirely my own invention. His figure was inspired by a very gifted parrot which used to belong to the licensee of a bar in Islington. The adventures of the real parrot were just as incredible as those of mine!' (29 Dec. 1948). The public house in question, the Prince Albert, Angel, Islington, London, is now the Charles Lamb.

3 – Oliver confirmed his preferential offer in a note to TSE (3 Feb.): 'If you decide to convert the *Criterion* into a quarterly after the issue of the March number, I ~~should~~ shall be willing to guarantee £250 a year for the next 3 years towards its production.'

wont do it or anything so we need more Tomorrow afternoon I go to Tea with Richmond Could you come Too if So ring me up during afternoon Museum 9543 or morning Sloane 3184 and I will arrange with him.

Yours etc.

T. S. Eliot

FROM *Vivien Eliot* TO *Ottoline Morrell*[1]   MS Texas

31 January 1928   4 Place Bergère, Rueil, Seine et Oise

My dearest Ottoline,

I was very very pleased & touched by your sweet letter of Jan. 22nd. It was *wonder*ful of you to find time to write to me at all at such a moment. And the photograph you enclosed is simply *perfect*. I have never seen any photograph of you I like so much, or which does you so much *justice*. Thank you, *thank* you. There is one thing I wish you had done, & that is to sign it. I would send it back to you to sign, but I am afraid I should not get it again. *Should I?*

I have been trying to find a suitable frame for it, but there are not any nice frames to be found in Rueil. But I shall get one.

My mother sent me all the notices of Julian's wedding,[2] & told me about it. So did Tom. And I saw her photograph in *The Daily Mail*. She looked charming, I thought. And her husband looks very nice indeed. I need not say how much I wish I could have seen the wedding. Was Bertie[3] there? Do you see Bertie much now? *Do* write to me again, *please, when you have a moment,* and *do* tell me all you are doing and who you see? Won't you come to Paris, & spend a little time there, & come to see me? How I *should love* it. I am very miserable, & it is all quite *useless.* You must have gathered from Tom what a *horrible* mess

---

1–Lady Ottoline Morrell (1873–1938), hostess and patron of the arts: see Biographical Register.
2–In 1923 OM's daughter Julian had fallen in love with the Russian-born Igor Vinogradoff (1901–87), son of Sir Paul Vinogradoff (1854–1925), Professor of Roman Law at Oxford. But Philip Morrell and OM so disapproved of the engagement – they thought Igor wild and penniless, albeit the brilliant young man had taken a first in Modern History at New College, Oxford – that it was called off. In 1928 Julian married Victor Goodman (1899–1967), later to become Clerk of the Parliaments, but the marriage was dissolved after WW2 – whereupon Julian at long last married her one true love, Igor (with whom she had carried on an affair throughout the war).
3–Bertrand Russell (1872–1970), British philosopher: see Biographical Register.

all this is. But as you can see, he simply hates the sight of me. And I *don't know what to do*. Write to me – I beg.

> Your outcasted friend
> Lovingly
> Vivienne Eliot

TO *Mario Praz*[1] cc

31 January 1928   [London]

My dear Praz,

Thank you very much for your letter of the 27th and for sending your review which I return herewith.[2] It is perhaps unduly flattering to me, but I am grateful for your tactfulness in dissociating me from responsibility in the text. The review is extremely interesting and I am rather envious of it: for it contains a great deal that I ought to have said myself in the Introduction.

It is quite true that the future of the *Criterion* is uncertain. All that I can say at present is that the March number will appear, but after that I have no idea yet what will happen. I hope to see you when you come to London; I am going abroad for a few days at the end of next week, but hope to be back by the 15th or 16th.

> Yours ever,
> [T. S. Eliot]

TO *Bonamy Dobrée* TS Brotherton

[Early February (?) 1928]   [London]

[No salutation]

They have been reduced from 40/- to 30/-. The poems by Cafavy seem to me excellent and unless I hear from you to the contrary I will keep them, as, if the *Criterion* survives, which is doubtful, I shall want them.[3] Many

---

1 – Mario Praz (1896–1982), scholar and critic of English life and literature: see Biographical Register.

2 – Untitled review of *Seneca his Tenne Tragedies* trans. into English, ed. Thomas Newton anno 1591; introduced by TSE: The Tudor Translations, Second Series, ed. Charles Whibley (2 vols, 1927), in *English Studies* (Amsterdam), 10 (1928), 79–87.

3 – C. P. Cavafy, 'Two Poems. For Ammones. If He Did Die', trans. G. Valassopoulo, C. 8 (Sept. 1928), 33–4.

thanks. I brought back from Switzerland several quite new anecdotes of Lady Rothermere, but have already related them in every pub. in London. Is there any innuendo intended in your remark that you are going to lecture about me, and then saying that your lectures are vulgarisation. I do not like being vulgaricised. I am glad you met the excellent Jean de Menasce, (or Ben Menasseh).[1] He is the nicest type of Jew, without the usual thick skin, neither the Hampstead nor the Lancaster Gate nor the Park Lane type at all. You seem however to 'react' somewhat as I do to the Semitic facility and at-easiness with every idea invented by any Gentile. But Jean has what is rare a real tendency towards saintliness, though I doubt if he will ever get there or anywhere else. Up to a point, there is no better companion on earth. But my Christianity is always running up against this question of inferior races: of course a Jew of that sort or of any sort is superior to most Indians or .... passage deleted by Censor) .... [sic][2] but there you are, you couldn't marry into it. But to change the subject it is excellent for Jean to be a Papist, because he is an Egyptian and has no country, so to speak; the Holy See serves the purpose and gives him a sheet anchor. It is also all right for Britons to be Papists when they have been so since before Henry VIII consecutively. But (except as a consequence of political events which I hope will not occur), I should think it unseemly for a naturalised British subject to support any but the church as by Law established. I am meditating a Pamphlet against Leo Ward. I.e. I shall stay in the Est. Church until I am forced out of it, which might happen if it came to an issue on the question of Reservation. I don't quite know what Jean means by saying (as you report it) that my Truth is the Lobster God. I may be very dense, but I don't see how truth and God can be the same thing except by an extension of terms depriving both of meaning. What I tried to do was to say what I believe without bringing in any theological implications; I mean I simply put myself at the point of view of Babbitt which is mine so far as it goes, and tried to say only what I thought an intelligent atheist could agree with. As to your own schism between head and heart, I don't quite follow. I am myself aware of the 'dangers' of 'creating a system'; though I should say that the dangers come not from creating it but from one's way of holding it. Some of these Frenchmen, for instance, risk compromising Christianity by seeming to make it depend upon St. Thomas. The categories are quite different. But I see also great danger in deliberately refraining from a system: that is a kind of *coitus retractatus* (is it *retractatus*? <or

1–Jean de Menasce (1902–73), theologian and orientalist: see Biographical Register.
2–This passage is represented as TSE typed it.

reservatus>) because that merely becomes another kind of system, and a merely negative system. One has to take risks, and trust to one's common sense. You say you can't pay the price; that's what I thought myself & it is a tenable point of view, for the only people who get nowhere are those who get the system without paying for it. The next step is to audit what one has got. It don't send up the price of stock. All Babbitt has to offer positively, I'm afraid, is Babbitt's idea of what is proper, and that is pretty vague. I hate mixing things up and at the same time I find it more & more impossible to isolate any purely 'literary' etc. problem, but am forced to a 'synthesis'. A 'passionate activity' is good until it is self-conscious, i.e. so long as it is a passionate activity TOWARDS something else, but when it comes to the conclusion that its own passionateness is what is admirable then the passion cools into sentiment etc. do I make myself clear I do not. QUESTIONS TO ANSWER: What makes the World go Round? Why did they wear Bowler Hats? Why did their Chariots have square Wheels?

The Mandrake, when discovered, has to be raised with the Mass for the Departed, said backwards (this is very difficult) and then buried at a crossroads, with a hatpin stuck through it. This makes it harmless. When ground to a Powder, and grated over fried onions, it makes a potent aphrodisiac.

> Arnold Bennett was a mistake.[1] No
> one liked it except M. Cattaui.
> Morley is reformed and now al-
> Ways wears a Bowler or Melon.
> Would you do a Clarendon for
> the Times? It is well to remember that   *Typical Mandrake*[2]
> King Bolo's Big Black Bastard Queen
>   Was very seldom sober –
> Between October and July
> And then until October;
> Ah Yes King Bolos Big Black Queen
> Was call'd a Heavy Drinker:
> But still she always kept Afloat
>   And nobody could Sink her.

1 – Arnold Bennett, 'Florentine Journal', MC 6 (Dec. 1927), 484–98; 7 (Jan. 1928), 16–30; 7 (Feb. 1928), 139–53.
2 – TSE had included a photograph (snipped from a magazine) of the Revd Montague Summers, with the printed caption: 'One of the founders of the Phoenix – a society dedicated to revival of old plays. An authority on the Restoration drama.' TSE's handwritten comment, below the caption, was 'Typical Mandrake'.

TO *Sally Cobden-Sanderson*[1]   TS Texas

2 February 1928   *The Monthly Criterion*

Dear Sally,

What I am going to write about is now what about this Parret I mean are you really ready to take delivery of this Parret Because if so it is essential to know clearly what are your wishes in the matter I mean to put it clearly do you want a Male or a Femaile Perret I mean it makdes no Difference in so much As there Is no difference in Plumiage Noise etc. and you get a Cage in either case & a pkt. of birdseed, only This that if later on you wanted to make it a Pair it would make a difference which was which if you grasp my meaning you would want a Proper pair only this time it will only be a single Parret What I think is that as a Parret should be named Pansy but some say Alexander only tastes differ. Hoping to Hear from you on this small point I remain, yours faithfully

T. S. Eliot

TO *F. S. Oliver*   CC

2 February 1928   [London]

Dear Oliver,

It will seem rude of me not to have written at once to thank you for your cheque; but I have been very busy the last two days; and had to dine out the two evenings; I am a bad hand at writing in haste. I say again that it is very generous of you. I do not at the moment quite know what to do with the cheque, but will consult my friend F. V. Morley who has been acting as treasurer of the interim fund. The trouble is that the profits from sales of the January and February numbers will have to be distributed amongst the contributors to that fund, and the profits of the March sales are yours; and it will be some time before we can know what the profits are.

Meanwhile I have had a long talk with Richmond; I have not since discussed this point with anyone interested, but we came round – or he came round, as I was there already – to the conclusion that a quarterly was best. Incidentally, it can be done on much less money; £750 a year would just do it, I believe, and £1000 a year would do it handsomely.

1–Gwladys (Sally) Cobden-Sanderson was the wife of Richard Cobden-Sanderson (1884–1964), printer and publisher: see Biographical Register.

Whibley has promised £25 a year, and I am sure that I could get £25 out of a wealthy relative; so that is a good start. Richmond is going to tackle several people of his acquaintance: and if any names occurred to you, I should be very grateful [*text runs off the page*].

Your support has given us confidence to push on. I suppose that if we got in touch with anyone who seemed friendly, but perhaps did not know the *Criterion* and was not quite certain of the worthiness of the cause, that you would not mind being referred to – especially if it was someone who knew you? Many people, who would from time to time find things in it to interest them, start with the false impression that it is merely an esoteric review devoted [to] the more eccentric manifestations of modern art.

I should have written in any case, to say how much I enjoyed the weekend, and that I should like to come again. It is the most profitable and the only un-fatiguing kind of weekend visit.

With kindest regards to Mrs Oliver,

Yours sincerely,

[T. S. Eliot]

TO *Orlo Williams*[1]   CC

3 February 1928   [London]

Dear Williams,

I am glad that you reminded me about Angioletti.[2] The March number is going to be a very crowded one; partly because we are not yet sure (though hopeful) that the *Criterion* will continue, and therefore there are certain things I must put in. All the space that I have left is two pages of Commentary. I suppose that I ought to mention Thomas Hardy but that can be done very briefly. Would you be willing to write a very short paragraph – less than a page – about Angioletti's prize? This could go into the Commentary. And could you let me have it by Monday, as I ought to get the Commentary ready over the week-end. I shall be very grateful if

---

1 – Orlando (Orlo) Williams (1883–1967), Clerk to the House of Commons, scholar, and critic: see Biographical Register.
2 – Williams wrote: 'Something ought to appear in the March no. about Angioletti's prize and book . . . He would be very hurt otherwise. Shall I write something . . . ? (2 Feb.) The prize had been won by *Il Giorno del Giudizio*: see MC 7 (Mar. 1928), 194.

you can. Thanks also for the tip about Siegfried's article which I have not seen.[1] I will try to get hold of a copy of yesterday's *Times* at once.

Yours ever,

[T. S. Eliot]

TO *The Editor of* The New Statesman   CC

4 February 1928[2]   [London]

Sir,

I did not see Mr Turner's article in your paper to which Mr Desmond MacCarthy replies in a letter in your number of January 21st. But I have seen Mr MacCarthy's letter and have endeavoured to reconstruct the relevant parts of Mr Turner's article from that. As Mr MacCarthy refers twice to the *Criterion*, I hope I may be permitted to comment on his letter.[3]

---

1 – 'What about commenting on André Siegfried's article in today's *Times* . . . ? I think you could write a very good little pendant on England's *intellectual* position vis-à-vis Europe.' Siegfried, in 'A Frenchman On Britain, II: Empire and Continent: Europe's Vital Link' (*The Times*, 2 Feb. 1928, 13), lamented the 'incomplete "Europeanity" of Great Britain' in the postwar world: 'England, Scotland (and Ireland), by their history and millennial traditions, really belong to the truest Europe; and, by their culture, they are at least as European as we ourselves are. On that ground we feel not only an economic but an intellectual solidarity. That is why many of us would prefer (if we were asked to express our wishes) a Great Britain whose attractions should remain not merely Imperial, or extra-European, but Continental as well. She would thus be preserved to us as the vital link without which Europe would be positively and permanently weakened.' TSE commented ('A Commentary', *MC* 7 [Mar. 1928], 194): 'To M. Siegfried it seems that Britain must choose between Europe and an imperial non-European group. To our mind, the peculiar position of Britain is this: that she is on the one hand a part of Europe. But not only a part, she is a mediating part: for Britain is the bridge between Latin culture and Germanic culture in both of which she shares. But Britain is . . . or should be, by virtue of the fact that she is the only member of the European community that has established a genuine empire – that is to say, a world-wide empire . . . – not only European but the connection between Europe and the rest of the world.'
2 – Published under the title 'Frenchified' in *NS*, 4 Feb. 1928, 528–9.
3 – W. J. Turner, in his music column 'A Chamois in the Queen's Hall' (*NS*, 14 Jan. 1928, 433–4), mocked the unwonted influence of Paris upon the arts, such that even Mozart and Schubert were played in an ultra-French fashion. 'Mr Lytton Strachey can find nothing to say about Shakespeare, but writes a heartfelt panegyric on Racine. Mr Desmond MacCarthy admires Shaw because he is the nearest approach to Gallicism that we have ever had in the English theatre . . . Mr T. S. Eliot re-discovered Dryden on finding that he had died a Catholic, and was therefore part of European culture, and Mr Eliot's monthly *Criterion* is a review published in London but written in Paris.'
In a letter published under the title 'Frenchified' (*NS*, 21 Jan. 1928, 460), Desmond MacCarthy protested that while he had 'certainly admired many of Mr Shaw's plays

Mr Turner, it appears, observed that 'our younger poets, writers and artists have all succumbed to influence from Paris,' and the use of the word 'succumb' suggests that Mr Turner considers this influence undesirable. Apparently Mr Turner finds that our younger poets, etc., have consequently exalted the eighteenth century above all others. Mr MacCarthy in his turn finds traces of Parisian influence in London, but not a trace of what he calls 'eighteenth century reasonableness and respect for clarity'; Mr MacCarthy then draws a distinction between 'moral conviction', towards which the *Criterion* appears to have striven, and 'intellectual integrity', which apparently the *Criterion* has overlooked. As Mr MacCarthy does not proceed to define what he means by either moral conviction or intellectual integrity, I am not in a position to argue with him. I would only point out that both Mr Turner (again, judging only from Mr MacCarthy's letter) and Mr MacCarthy himself seem to think this question of Parisian influence much more simple than it is, and especially with regard to the *Criterion*. Again, Mr MacCarthy sees in the *Criterion* the influence of three things which are supposed to be Parisian: Literary Nationalism, Neo-Thomism, and what he calls Rimbauism. I was not myself aware of any influence upon the *Criterion* which could be called Rimbauism, whatever that is. As for Literary Nationalism, I may observe that the *Criterion* has been far more international than any literary review in England, and perhaps more than any literary review published on the Continent. As for Neo-Thomism, I would remark that this is no longer limited to France. As for French influence in general, I should like to point out that the *Criterion* has done its best to introduce into this country important foreign writers irrespective of their nationality.

Yours, etc.
T. S. Eliot

---

immensely', he never thought of them as 'particularly French'; and the other evidence adduced by Turner was either 'absurdly far-fetched' or 'untrue' – with the exception of the case of *The Criterion*: 'yes, there I see the influence of modern Paris – literary nationalism, Neo-Tomism [*sic*], Rimbauism, but, please note, not a trace of eighteenth century reasonableness and respect for clarity; of striving towards moral conviction, but not after intellectual integrity, which in my judgment is inseparable from it.'

TO *F. S. Oliver*

7 February 1928   [London]

Dear Oliver,

Thank you very much indeed for your two letters of the 3rd instant.[1]
I believe that the fact that you have shown your interest in the paper so
substantially is likely to influence others, and that is why I asked whether
you would consent to your name being mentioned.

I asked my secretary to write to you yesterday but I am not sure whether
the letter was clear. What I meant is that in order to be on the safe side
I estimated the cost without allowing for selling a single number. As we
do sell a certain number of copies of the *Criterion*, although not over
one thousand, the receipts less the overhead expenses are obviously the
property of anyone who subsidises the particular number.

I am not disposed to disagree with you about the excessive proportion
of metaphysics in the *Criterion*. But if I am able to run the *Criterion*
on the lines on which I should like to run it I think that you would get
less impression of an excessive amount of philosophy. I am not willing
to say that there would be less metaphysics, but I can say that I think
there would be more of other things which would put the metaphysical
element in better proportion. So far there has been nothing to balance
the metaphysics except what may be called pure literature. What I want
to do is to make a review, and preferably a quarterly review, which
should contain all of these things and also a proper amount of political
philosophy and articles dealing with historical narrative.

Yours ever sincerely,

[T. S. Eliot]

1 – Oliver's first letter of 3 Feb. was in response to TSE's of the 2nd: 'I don't understand what
you mean by the profits of the March sales being mine. I don't anticipate there will be any
profits, and if there are I don't want them. I would much rather you carried them into your
fund for producing future issues.

'Having looked at your copy of the Quarterly, I am clearer than I was before, that I very
much prefer it to the Monthly. I am glad Richmond has come round to the same opinion
. . . I do think, however, (if I may make a criticism from the point of view of a common
reader) that your Quarterly <not so much the monthly> does produce rather too much the
impression of being what is called an esoteric review. I think there is an undue proportion
of metaphysics in it. I don't mean articles which are frankly of this character, but also the
standpoint of reviewers of certain books.'

Oliver's second letter suggested that a quarterly review, running to *c.* 200 pages, had
better be priced at 7/6 rather than 5/-. He harked back too to TSE's visit: 'Our sun is shining
& our daffodils are out. I wish you were here today sitting in a long chair in the verandah:
we have abandoned the winter garden as too hot.'

TSE at thirty-nine

TO *His Mother*[1]   TS Houghton

7 February 1928   *The Monthly Criterion*

My dearest Mother,

A few days ago I sent you an account of Haig's funeral and a poppy which I bought on that occasion.[2] I saw the funeral procession from the beginning. What a wonderful ceremony a British military funeral [is]. I say British, not English, because Haig was Scotch. In foreign affairs, there is no difference between English and Scotch; but at home, they are two different peoples. The funeral started at the Scotch Church,[3] which was flying the Scotch flag at half-mast. I always have to be tactful with Scotch people, because they think my name is *Elliot*, and they say you must be Scotch, why do you spell it *Eliot*. So then I apologise for not being Scotch. Well then there were the Scotch pipers of the Guards, and they started the 'Lament for Flodden',[4] the national Scotch anthem, and there is nothing more dismal and melancholy than the pipers playing that tune. It tears your nerves to pieces. The crowd was very quiet, with its hats off; so you heard only the guardsmen marching to the slow step that is only used for funerals, shuffling, and that horrible Scotch dirge grinding away on the bagpipes. Then came Grenadier Guards, and Coldstream Guards, and shuffle of feet, and all very quiet; and then Belgian troops and French troops; and then Haig's horse, led by his old servant; and the gun carriage with the coffin on it, covered with a Union Jack and lots of red poppies; and then the pallbearers, innumerable fieldmarshalls [field marshals] with hats covered with feathers; old Lord Methuen, the senior Field Marshal and a Boer War veteran, first; and then French, and Foch, and Pétain, and all the English generals; and then the Prince of Wales and his brothers; and then the diplomatic representatives; and everybody you could think of; and church dignitaries; and more Guards and troops all with arms reversed and shuffling in the silence; and then it was Chopin's Dead March, and you could hear it going on blocks and blocks away as everyone was so quiet; and that is how they buried Haig. So he went to the Abbey; and from the Abbey to Euston Station; and thence to Edinburgh; and thence to be buried with his family at Bemersyde in Scotland.[5]

1–Charlotte Champe Stearns Eliot (1843–1929): see Biographical Register.
2–Field Marshal Earl Haig was Commander-in-Chief of the British Expeditionary Force in France and Flanders during WW1.
3–St Columba's Church.
4–'A Lament for Flodden', by Jane Elliot (1727–1805), was included in *The Oxford Book of English Verse: 1250–1900*, ed. Arthur Quiller-Couch (1919).
5–Haig was buried at Dryburgh Abbey.

That was better than Thomas Hardy's funeral. That was a scandal: if Mrs Hardy did not know better, his executor J. M. Barrie should have known better. They put his body in Westminster Abbey, and they buried his heart in Dorchester. Curio hunting I call it. Why not divide him joint from joint, and spot him about the country? I think that if one is buried at all one should decently be buried all in one place.[1]

I was very happy to get your last letter. I sent your cheque to Vivien. I shall go over to Paris and see her again on Sunday. No doubt she will write now and thank you. I was overjoyed to get a letter written so strongly in your own clear hand.

The March *Criterion* will appear, as that delightful person, the author of the biography of Alexander Hamilton, F. S. Oliver, will pay for it. After that, it will more likely be a Quarterly. Bruce Richmond, the Editor of the *Times Literary Supplement*, whom I have often mentioned, is working hard to get guarantors. I myself should prefer a Quarterly to a monthly; I only agreed to the change from quarterly to monthly under protest. A monthly is really more than I can manage, it takes too much of my time; also one can give a Quarterly a certain shape and proportion; and it seems less ephemeral. And I shall have more time for other work.

It is always a great joy to get a letter in your own hand. Everything you say is precious to me; for I feel more closely in sympathy with you than with anyone living.

your very loving and devoted son,
Tom

Mrs Haigh-Wood speaks of you and asks of you often, and with the warmest affection and admiration.

TO *Bruce Richmond*[2]   cc

7 February 1928   [London]

Private and Personal
Dear Richmond,

I spoke to Morley on the telephone this morning and he told me that he had recently seen you and discussed the *Criterion*.

---

1 – TSE made public his view in 'A Commentary': 'We hope sincerely that the manner in which Hardy was interred will not be allowed to establish a precedent for the burial of other great men. We continue to hope that in the future as in the immediate past our great men will be buried in one place instead of being dismembered in a fashion intolerable in any society which is not given over to idolatry of relics and fetishes' (*MC* 7 [Mar. 1928], 193).
2 – Bruce Richmond (1871–1964), editor of the *TLS*: see Biographical Register.

He mentioned to me the question of approaching the Morrells. I have seen them several times lately and have talked to Lady Ottoline about the *Criterion*. I do not think that it is of any use approaching them about it on their own account, because I think that if there was any possibility Lady Ottoline would have volunteered, especially as she is an old friend of mine. She offered, however, to approach two people whom she herself suggested. One being Leo Myers[1] and the other Billy Smith, the son of Lord Hambleden[2] whom she knows quite well. Anyway I think that that is all there is to be done in that direction.

I had tea yesterday with Virginia Woolf[3] and again talked about the *Criterion*. She suggested that we ought to approach Bob Trevelyan. It appears that Bob Trevelyan, who has always been obliged to live on eight hundred a year, has just inherited ten thousand a year from his mother and is very embarrassed as to what to do with it.[4] She thought that he might be glad to relieve his conscience by means of the *Criterion*. Do you know him? If there is no one else who knows him well enough I am willing to ask Virginia to write to him about it herself, but on the other hand if you know him at all or if you are in touch with someone else who knows him well it might be better to approach him in that way. I know him slightly, but very slightly.

I cannot think of anyone else at the moment. On Sunday I came across a man named Lane-Fox-Pitt-Rivers who seems to have no end of money

1 – L. H. Myers (1881–1944): British novelist (who received in 1906 a substantial inheritance from a godfather); author of the trilogy *The Root and the Flower* (winner of the James Tait Black Memorial Prize and the Femina Vie Heureuse Prize, 1935).

2 – William Henry Smith (1903–48) became 3rd Viscount Hambleden on the death of his father, 16 June 1928; he was Governing Director of W. H. Smith & Son, Ltd.

3 – VW was to report of this encounter, to her brother-in-law Clive Bell, on 7 Feb., 'I've been talking for two hours to Tom Eliot about God' (*A Change of Perspective: Letters of Virginia Woolf, III: 1923–1928*, ed. Nigel Nicolson [1977, 1994], 455); and to her sister, on 11 Feb.: 'I have had a most shameful and distressing interview with poor dear Tom Eliot, who may be called dead to us all from this day forward. He has become an Anglo-Catholic, believes in God and immortality, and goes to church. I was really shocked. A corpse would seem to me more credible than he is. I mean, there's something obscene in a living person sitting by the fire and believing in God' (ibid., 457–8). Lord David Cecil would recall for Robert Sencourt on 16 Nov. 1966 a similar encounter at OM's home in London: 'the only thing that sticks in my memory is [Eliot's] modest but formidable defence of his religious beliefs one evening at Gower Street' (Donald Adamson Collection).

4 – R. C. Trevelyan (1872–1951): poet; brother of the historian G. M. Trevelyan (1876–1962). His works include *Poems and Fables* (Hogarth Press, 1925) and *Meleager* (1927). VW was to write to her sister on 11 Feb. 1928: 'Bob Trevelyan had come in for £10,000 a year on his mother's death, and is almost frantic with worry. His miserliness, great as it was when he had £800, has to be vast to cope with £10,000' (*Letters of Virginia Woolf, III*, 457.)

and a certain amount of good intentions,[1] but I did not want to attack him directly myself and in the special circumstances I did not want to ask the man through whom I met him to do so. I merely mention his name in case you may have heard of him and know of someone else who might be willing to tackle him.

I told you when I saw you that I was about to dine with the Malcolms. I am still in ignorance as to why I was invited there. It was a large, extremely formal, dinner party and I had no conversation either with host or hostess.[2] However, although I do not know why I was asked, Malcolm seemed to be fairly clear as to who I was, and I do not believe that I was asked by mistake instead of someone else of the same name.

Yours ever sincerely,

[T. S. E.]

P.S. Oliver says that if he can think of anyone likely to add to the fund he is quite willing to approach such person but that he cannot at the moment think of anyone. He also gives permission to mention his name and support to anyone who is likely to attach any weight to that support.

1–George Henry Lane Fox Pitt-Rivers (1890–1966), anthropologist and landowner, was grandson of the founder of the Pitt Rivers Museum, Oxford; author of *The World Significance of the Russian Revolution* (1920) and *The Clash of Culture and the Contact of Races* (1927). As years went on, he was to become involved with radical, quasi-fascist and racialist groups, and he was interned from 1940 until 1942. In a review of *The Clash of Culture*, Geoffrey Tandy would tactfully remark upon his 'less palatable observations': 'The gravamen of the charge against him is "clerkly treason". The time is still not yet and the anthropologist should stick to his anthropology' (*C.* 7 [June 1928], 440).

2–Dougal Orme Malcolm (1877–1955), a Fellow of All Souls, worked for the Colonial Office before joining in 1913 the board of the British South Africa Company – he was to be Director and President – which enjoyed remarkable profits from Rhodesian mineral rights and railways. See Malcolm, *The British South Africa Company, 1889–1939* (1939). A widower since 1920, Malcolm had married in 1923 Lady Evelyn Farquhar (1877/8–1962), widow of Col. F. Farquhar and daughter of the 5th Earl of Donoughmore. He had been on the losing side in giving support to TSE's candidature for a research fellowship at All Souls in May 1926. A. L. Rowse recalled, in *All Souls in My Time* (1993): 'Sir Dougal Malcolm, Dougie to us, was eminently clubbable . . . and sat long over the port . . . Cousin to half the Scottish aristocracy, he was . . . a gifted linguist as well as Latin versifier . . . Rich and kindly, he invited me to dine at his London house' (85).

TO *Messrs Methuen & Company*

8 February 1928 [London]

Dear Sirs,

Thank you very much for your letter of the 6th instant. I have compared your specimen page with that of the edition of my poems issued by Faber & Gwyer Ltd and it seems to me in respect of type and size of page to be quite satisfactory. The paper on which it is printed is certainly inferior to that on which my poems are printed, but I presume that your specimen, being merely a proof sheet, is not intended to represent the paper on which you would print the book. I am entirely satisfied with the type you have used and I am glad to learn that the volume will run to 192 pages.

Yours very truly,
[T. S. Eliot]

TO *Orlo Williams* CC

8 February 1928 [London]

Dear Williams,

I am very much indebted to you. Without your suggestions I should have had much more difficulty in composing the Commentary. The only subject that imposed itself on me was Thomas Hardy and I wished to say as little as possible about that subject. This I have done. I obtained the *Times* and have written a note on Siegfried's extremely interesting article which, however, really deserves the full treatment of a separate essay. I am also extremely grateful to you for your note on Angioletti. As you will see, I have had to cut it down unscrupulously. This is due to the fact that, not even yet being sure that the March number will not be the last, I have felt bound to include things which otherwise I could decently have postponed until April. Therefore I have only been able to allow two pages for Commentary, and of course I could not give the whole or greater part of that to this subject. I have therefore had to boil Angioletti down to the absolute minimum. But I am very glad to have been able to get it in at all and am very much obliged to you.

I am going away at the end of this week but will try to see you again in about a fortnight.

With many thanks,
Yours ever,
[T. S. Eliot]

TO *Archibald MacLeish*[1]   CC

10 February 1928   [London]

Dear MacLeish,

I owe you an apology for having delayed writing to you for so long.[2] But I have had to be away a good deal and also it took us a long time to make up our minds. We were finally forced to come to the conclusion that we could not undertake at the present time to publish any book of verse which consisted of one long poem. A volume of poetry means, I am sorry to say, a loss to the publishers in any case in this country; and long poems are still more difficult to sell. We had several new volumes already arranged for when yours arrived, otherwise we might have been able to do better.

I am very sorry about this because parts of the poem seem to me very fine and the whole thing is an uncommon achievement.[3] I am not returning the poem until I hear from you. Would you like me to try any other publishers? I should be very glad if you would let me take the matter up on your behalf with the Hogarth Press. They are friends of mine and I think it is a book which would appeal to them.[4]

Yours ever sincerely,
[T. S. Eliot]

1 – Archibald MacLeish (1892–1982), American poet and playwright, studied at Yale and Harvard (where he took a degree in law), and then lived in France for a while in the 1920s. His poem *Conquistador* (1933) won a Pulitzer prize. *Collected Poems, 1917–1952* (1953) won three awards: a second Pulitzer prize, the Bollingen Prize, and the National Book Award. His verse play *J.B.* (1957) won the Pulitzer Prize for Drama and a Tony Award. During WW2, at President Roosevelt's bidding, he was Librarian of Congress, and he served with the United Nations Educational, Scientific and Cultural Organization. He was Boylston Professor of Rhetoric and Oratory at Harvard, 1949–62. TSE wrote on 29 June 1932 to Ferris Greenslet, Houghton Mifflin Co., 'There is no living poet in America who seems to me to have greater technical accomplishment than MacLeish.'
2 – MacLeish had submitted his long poem *The Hamlet of A. MacLeish* on 7 Dec. 1927; it was to be published by Houghton Mifflin in the USA in 1928.
3 – On 30 Dec. 1927 TSE had written this reader's report on MacLeish's work: 'This poem has on the whole disappointed me after MacLeish's earlier work, and a good deal of it seems to me to be a pastiche of Ezra Pound and myself. But partly for this reason I should like to have another opinion before returning it.'
4 – MacLeish was delighted (18 Feb.) by TSE's offer of help.

TO *Ezra Pound* TS Beinecke

10 February 1928   [London]

Rabbit ben Ezzum,

Much pleased to get your nihil obstat or waffenstillstand or whatever you call it.[1] Can't say yet about future of *Criterion* or consequent possible amalgamation of Flint and myself with *Exile*. If *Criterion* stops should be delighted to be of any use to *Exile* but suspect my name might do you more harm than good.

Am waiting to hear your figures for reproductions of Guido MSS. Meanwhile another subject has arizzen, which I take no responsibility for. Our Mr Stewart has received a letter from one Mr Pulitzer or Politzer or Porringer of Curtis and Brown. To my astonishment my colleagues seemed to be interested in the idea of producing a[n] edition of your select poetical works similar to but not necessarily identical with the expurgated edition recently produced by Horatio Liveright. Don't blame me for this idea. I had nothing to do with it. Mr Porringer aforesaid seems to take kindly to the idea of a few notes by myself to explain the more heretical passages and justify your orthodoxy. Well this is all I have to say about it at the moment, except that the labour of scholarship on my part will be so great that I cannot consider putting any price about it. Should be glad to hear from you further. Am willing to fall in with almost any requirements.[2]

Yours respectfully,

T. S. E.

---

1 – EP wrote, of TSE's review of *Personae*: 'No, I didn't think I wuz bein' caricatured below the belt . . . A mos' nobl' roration.' He went on to express his sympathy with TSE: 'If the Crit. is imperiled not by but against your will, do let me know if there is anything I can do to bolster . . . Am ready to come to aid of sinking ferry with anything save the two grand . . . I dont feel that a mouthy letter from me wd save the *Criterion*, or lure the timorous buyer . . . Not knowin' wot the raw'z abaht I dont know whether the giraffe needs more spots, or needs to be demaculated.'

2 – EP, *Selected Poems*, ed. with Introduction by TSE (F&G, 1928). Pollinger, a literary agent with Curtis Brown Ltd, wrote further to EP on 1 Mar.: 'I wrote to Faber & Gwyer asking if Mr Eliot had yet given them the list of poems he has selected for your book. They reply that he has not yet done so, and they will let us have a copy for you, as soon as they can.' EP, who forwarded Pollinger's curt letter to TSE on 3 Mar., typed on the back of it: 'I knew nothing about this unseemly haste. Please don't think I had any hand in attempting to hustle, accelerate, or otherwise impinge. I spose the excellent Pollinger imagines me to be a furious person boiling with impatience.' In 1926 Boni & Liveright had published in New York a collected volume entitled *Personae of Ezra Pound*.

P.S. When things have shaken down a bit shall be able to let you know more about *Criterion* and what anybody can do. Only present requirement is vast sums of money. Cause of crisis: sudden revolt of Harmsworth underworld; consequent inconvenient withdrawal of capital. This of course is all to the good from the point of view of civilisation.

TO *I. A. Richards*[1]   TS Magdalene

10 February 1928   *The Monthly Criterion*

Dear Richards,

I should like very much to come to your dinner on February 23rd, both because it is an honour to be invited on such an occasion and because it is a long time since I have seen you and I want to see you again. I don't mind any sort of quarters, and hope that you will have time for a long talk the next morning.[2]

> Very many thanks,
> Yours sincerely,
> T. S. Eliot

1–I. A. Richards (1893–1979), theorist of literature, education, and communication studies: see Biographical Register.
2–TSE was to go to the Pepys Feast at Magdalene. IAR had written (2 Feb.), 'We could put you up at our temporary home 10 King's Parade if you don't mind rough quarters in an attic . . . I have one or two general questions I badly want to talk out with you.' Dorothy Richards noted in her diary that TSE on arrival 'came up the stairs looking to me very gaunt & grim – as if he had burnt himself out. His queer coloured, strangely piercing eyes in a pale face are the most striking thing about him. He is pale with special wrinkles which run horizontally across his forehead & his nose is delicately Jewish. He doesn't understand all I say nor do we him. His questions are surprising – disconcerting because so simple, sometimes almost inane. We talked of skye scrapers – of Canada & drinking – we took the initiative' (Magdalene). Afterwards, in IAR's college rooms, she 'found Eliot absurdly drunk – not talkative – just fuddled'. At one in the morning they repaired for two more hours of conversation at the Richardses' flat, as Mrs Richards further noted: 'An hour ago Eliot was sleeping: looking exhausted with the effort to keep his eyes open. But true American that he is – as soon as there is at last a general move and any ordinary Englishman would have sighed relief and quickly disappeared to bed – Eliot wakes up, puts on more records and is once more absorbed by the "mechanical toy".' The 'séance' (as Mrs Richards called it) went on until four in the morning, with the consequence that 'Eliot's early breakfast didn't happen'.
    IAR was to recollect, in 'On TSE' (*T. S. Eliot: The Man and His Work*, ed. Allen Tate [1967], 5–6), that 'after my marriage, [TSE] got into the way of coming fairly often to stay with us in Cambridge . . . He used to arrive wearing a little rucksack which protected him,

TO *Marguerite Caetani* TS Caetani

10 February 1928 *The Monthly Criterion*

Dear Marguerite,

Thank you very much for your letter of the 2nd. I am going to Paris on Saturday for several days and if all goes well I shall be there again early in March and shall look forward to meeting you. I don't think I shall have time to make another attempt to see Leger on this occasion but I hope that you will back me up as soon as you are in Paris. Also it would be a great pleasure to see something more of Groethuysen.[1] As for the Seneca, I am afraid that you are throwing away money, and you might have consulted me about it before ordering a two guinea book. I also am wondering when my book is coming out, or which book. Your poem is on my conscience: I regret to say that at present that is the only place where it is to be found. I am so glad you have found such a wonderful tutor. I think, however, that you will have to get an English tutor eventually so as to let Camillo down gently before he is precipitated into the Oxford vortex.

Woolf will be doing extremely well if he can get anything of Hardy's for *Commerce*; as now I believe the only people to deal with are Mrs Hardy and Sir J. Barrie.

I will write again soon more privately,

Yours ever affectionately,
Tom

---

he felt, from molestation by porters. It contained night things and a large new, and to us awe-inspiring, Prayer Book: a thing which in my innocent mind hardly chimed with, say, "The Hippopotamus".

'This, in those days, with "Mr. Eliot's Sunday Morning Service", represented for us what we took to be his position on the Church. I suppose a more experienced reader would have felt the Catholic trend in them. But we were listening to other things. I lent my copy of *Ara Vos Prec* to A. C. Benson, whose comment was: "Watch out! I hear the beat of the capripede hoof!"'

1–Bernard Groethuysen (1880–1946), philosopher, taught at Berlin University from 1906. In 1932, appalled by the rise of Nazism, he moved to France and was naturalised there.

TO *Messrs Methuen & Company*   CC

10 February 1928   [London]

Dear Sirs,

Thank you for your letter of the 9th instant.[1] I shall be glad to inspect the proof of the new setting of *The Sacred Wood*.

Yours faithfully,
[T. S. Eliot]

TO *Harold Kamp*   CC

10 February 1928   [London]

Dear Sir,

I am not quite clear from your letter of the 21st ultimo whether you wish my autograph on the book; but as you seem to wish to have my autograph, here it is.[2]

Yours faithfully,
[T. S. Eliot]

TO *A. S. J. Tessimond*[3]   CC

10 February 1928   [London]

My dear Sir,

I have considered your letter.[4] I have no ready-made reply for such an enquiry but I should suggest that you might come to tea with me here first of all. Would Tuesday week, the 21st, suit you?

Yours very truly,
[T. S. Eliot]

1–Methuen & Co. wrote (9 Feb.): 'We shall use an Antique Laid paper quite equal to the quality of that used for your poems.' Did TSE wish to see proofs of the new setting?

2–Kamp (who wrote from Fresno, California) asked on 21 Jan. for TSE's signature on his copy of the first edn of *The Waste Land*.

3–A. S. J. Tessimond (1902–62), English poet. Works include *Walls of Glass* (1934) and *The Collected Poems of A. S. J. Tessimond*, ed. Hubert Nicholson (1985).

4–Tessimond asked (2 Feb.): 'Is there any way in which someone who has lived in the provinces (till he was 25) and is intensely interested in experimental, progressive literature – who writes fairly bad but fairly wellmeaning poetry – etc., etc. – can meet other people who are similarly interested?' IPF noted on his letter: 'I do not actually remember his stuff; but we returned all his various contributions without hesitation.'

TO *Thomas H. Nesbitt* CC

10 February 1928 [London]

Dear Sir,

I have your letter of the 2nd ultimo and send you my autograph hereunder.[1]

[T. S. Eliot]

TO *Harold Monro*[2] TS Beinecke

17 February 1928 *The Monthly Criterion*

Dear Harold,

I have just got back from Paris and find your letter. Many thanks for sending the reviews. I should be delighted to send Iolo Williams's poetry book except that I do not like to ask publishers for books, or for that matter to ask anyone to write anything to order, until we know definitely where the *Criterion* stands.[3] The March number will of course appear, but that is already in page. After that, all that I can say is that we have about a third of the necessary guarantees and hope to exhaust all the possibilities within the next few weeks.

I am sorry to hear that you have been laid up.[4] As I was longer in Paris than I intended I did not get back in time for yesterday's lunch but will be there next week. I shall look in on you some time on Monday or Tuesday and hope you will be better.

Yours ever,
T. S. E.

1–T. H. Nesbitt, Town Clerk of the City of Sydney, New South Wales, requested TSE's autograph, 'preferably on a slip of headed note paper', for insertion in his 'official and Imperially representative Autograph Book. This Book [is] not a mere collection of names, but a classified historical record of those distinguished in the days march . . .'

2–Harold Monro (1879–1932), poet, editor, publisher, bookseller: see Biographical Register.

3–Monro had asked (15 Feb.) to review I. A. Williams's *Poetry Today*.

4–'I've been laid up over a fortnight with a poisoned leg . . . Do come & see me.'

TO *The Editor of* The New Statesman   CC

18 February 1928[1]   [*The Monthly Criterion*]

Sir,

I read in your issue of today's date a letter about myself signed by 'Alan Ebbutt'. The name is unknown to me. The facts stated by Mr Ebbutt were also unknown to me. I had always been under the illusion that *The Criterion* was published and printed in England; on the cover appear the words 'published by Faber & Gwyer Limited, 24, Russell Square, London'. On the last page appear the words 'made and printed in Great Britain by Trend & Co., Mount Pleasant, Plymouth'. Are London and Plymouth really in France? I had also supposed that the town in which I live, a small fragment of which is visible from my window, was not Paris but London. The date stamps on my passport seem to support my opinion.

I observe that Mr Ebbutt (if that is his name) has the candour to date his letter from Geneva. I persist in dating my correspondence from the place in which I believe myself to be, namely LONDON.

I am, Sir,
Your obliged obedient servant,
[T. S. Eliot][2]

1–This letter appeared in the *NS* (25 Feb. 1928, 622), though without the bracketed words in the second paragraph: 'if that is his name'.

Alan Ebbutt's letter (13 Feb.) was published in *NS*, 18 Feb. 1928, 591: 'I forget whether it was Mr Belloc or Mr Chesterton who wrote a diatribe on the use of the phrase "this country" instead of "England". It has become so universal a practice among politicians and leader-writers that one is forced to tolerate it; but Mr T. S. Eliot, in a letter published in your issue of February 4th, goes really too far.

'Mr Eliot writes as editor of the Paris-published *Criterion*; he lives in Paris; and, in the absence of any contrary indication, he may therefore be assumed to have written from Paris. He writes: "As for the French influence in general, I should like to point out that the *Criterion* has done its best to introduce into this country important foreign writers irrespective of their nationality."

'What does he mean by "this country"? The context suggests England; the geographical facts demand France. It is really time for people from whom we are accustomed to expect good writing to abandon this sloppy habit, and say what they mean. No doubt it was mere oversight on Mr Eliot's part; but such oversights are alarming symptoms.'

2–Ebbutt followed up TSE's letter with a letter (27 Feb.) published in *NS*, 3 Mar. 1928, 656: 'I must confess that the statements I made about Mr Eliot and the *Criterion* were made, in my impetuosity, without verification, on authority which I had always found to be reliable (though the names of my informants, like my own, would be unknown to Mr Eliot). I owe him, and hereby offer him, an unreserved apology for my errors.

'Mr Eliot, I observe, "persists" in dating his correspondence from London. A minor point raised by me, however, was precisely that he did not date his previous letter from anywhere.'

TO *Leonard Woolf*[1]   CC

20 February 1928   *[The Monthly Criterion]*

Dear Leonard,

I have a book of poetry, or rather one long poem, which was sent to me by a young man named Archibald MacLeish. I know something of his work and he seems to me to be decidedly one of the most interesting of the younger American poets. The book does not fit into our list: in particular it is one long poem and therefore not very saleable, and also it is rather too short for a book of our size. Would you care to look at it as I have his permission to send it on? I had in mind partly that it was the sort of book in which Lady Gerald Wellesley might or ought to be interested.[2]

Yours ever,

[Tom]

TO *Mark Wardle*[3]   CC

20 February 1928   [London]

Dear Mark,

I am delighted to hear from you because I was very vexed at not seeing you again. It is true that I was a good deal between here and Paris and therefore all the more busy when in London; nevertheless I have reproached myself for missing any opportunity that there may have been. It was a great pleasure to have you in London and I wish that I might have seen more of you and your wife.

I at least, as I am glad he recognizes, had the "candour" to date mine from the place in which I was and am.'

The editor of the *New Statesman* appended this note to Ebbutt's letter: 'The fact that no address was attached to Mr Eliot's first letter was probably our omission, not his.'

1 – Leonard Woolf (1880–1969), writer and publisher: see Biographical Register.

2 – Dorothy Wellesley, née Ashton (1889–1956), poet and editor – who in 1914 married Lord Gerald Wellesley, afterwards 7th Duke of Wellington (1885–1972) – edited and subsidised the Hogarth Living Poets. She was an intimate of Vita Sackville-West, and her *Genesis* was published by the Hogarth Press (1926). In later years she became a close friend of W. B. Yeats, who introduced *Selections from the Poems of Dorothy Wellesley* (1936). See *Far Have I Travelled* (1952); *Letters on Poetry from W. B. Yeats to Dorothy Wellesley* (1940). LW said (13 Feb. 1928) he would 'like to consider' MacLeish's work.

3 – Mark Wardle, a regular army officer, translated Valéry's *Le Serpent* (intro. by TSE, 1924); his other works include *An Alphabet from the Trenches* (1916) and *Foundations of Soldiering: A New Study of Regimental Soldiering in the British Army* (1936).

I am glad to say that my wife is very much better and has just returned to London.[1]

I am glad to hear that you are such a good sailor as the weather ever since Christmas has been frightful. I had never been seasick in my life but I had to cross from Dieppe to Newhaven on a day on which none of the other lines was running and I had that unpleasant experience for the first time. It has made me very humble about my nautical qualifications and I now fast religiously on such occasions.

If you should hear any more rumours of my having become a Roman Catholic I should be very much obliged if you would deny them. It is not true. It is true that I have become a British subject but there is no logical connection between the two; rather the contrary. As a matter of fact I believe I am rather unpopular with the Roman world and perhaps likely to be more so.

When I do come to Boston, and I hope it may not be very long, I shall certainly look you up, and of course Elizabeth as well.

With kindest regards to Mrs Wentworth.

Yours ever sincerely,
Tom

TO *Ottoline Morrell*

MS Texas

Monday, 20 February [1928]   *The Monthly Criterion*

My dear Ottoline

This is rather in haste. I stayed longer than I had expected, as our plans changed – V. has come back with me. It *may* be not a bad thing. I am keeping any engagements already made, but not making any new ones yet, & I shd like V. to see you first. Could you possibly suggest a day & come to tea with us? Could you drop V. a line. I know she wants to see you, & has spoken of you constantly with affection. Then I should like to see you soon afterwards.

In haste
Ever affectionately
Tom.

Many thanks indeed for the invitation!

---

1 – VHE was to write in her diary on 16 Feb. 1935: 'Seven years ago today that I returned to England from France. My dear Tom brought me back with him, but he did not want to. He would have much preferred for me to remain in France . . . . they were all *furious*

TO *John Cournos*[1]   CC

20 February 1928   [London]

Dear Cournos,

I am sorry to hear that you have been in London and that I missed you.[2] I have not written to you about the *Criterion* because it is still uncertain whether it will continue or not. The March number is certain to appear but beyond that I can say nothing. It is possible that the *Criterion* may revert to its quarterly form. In the circumstances it has been difficult for me to know whether to ask regular contributors for work which possibly may never be published. Fortunately your Report is not due again for several months and I hope to be able to give you definite news within a few weeks.

I am very sorry indeed to hear that after your wife's illness you have been ill yourself. I am afraid that you must have had much anxiety and worry.

> With all best wishes,
> Sincerely yours,
> [T. S. Eliot]

TO *Messrs Methuen & Company*   CC

20 February 1928   [London]

Dear Sirs,

I return to you herewith the correspondence from Curtis Brown Limited re Mr Arundell del Re's projected anthology of English prose for Japanese students. I have no objections myself to Mr del Re's use of extracts providing of course that he makes the proper references for particulars about the book. I think that in an anthology of this sort the Editor ought to say something himself about the books from which he

---

at my leaving . . . It was a very bad time & I felt *terribly frightened* at what I had done. So that I was out *of my mind*, & so behaved *badly* to Tom & got very excited. It seemed that everything he said was a *sneer* or an *insult*. When we got to Victoria we were met by Mother & Maurice & their behaviour was *sinister* & *unkind*. Mabel Read was the maid at 57 Chester Terrace, & W. L. Janes the man. That same evening Nurse E. A. Gordon came to see us – to say that she would come in as Nurse the following day' (Bodleian).

1–John Cournos (1881–1966), American poet, novelist, essayist and translator: see Biographical Register.

2–Cournos asked (15 Feb.) whether he should trouble to write his Russian Chronicle in view of the rumour that C. was closing down. He had 'just come out of the clinique'.

draws his selections. This point might be put to him. And especially I think, as a matter of principle, that some fee, even though nominal, to be divided between author and publisher ought to be charged. If anthologists can get their contents without paying for them there will soon be a great many too many anthologies.

Yours faithfully,
[T. S. Eliot]

TO *Ronald J. Politzer*[1]   CC

20 February 1928   [London]

Dear Mr Politzer,

Thank you for your letter of the 9th. You are very kind. It is difficult to resist such an invitation which makes everything for me. I hope that the few words in question does not mean a comic story. So far as it is humanly possible to predict one's own movements so far ahead, your date is approximately possible, though if you could manage it I should prefer a week or so later as I have to go to Oxford on the 2nd of May.

Yours sincerely
[T. S. Eliot]

TO *Henry Goddard Leach*[2]   CC

21 February 1928   [London]

Dear Mr Leach,

Thank you for your letter of February 8th.[3] As my projected essay on Babbitt seems to fall in so well with your programme I have written to the editor of the other periodical to whom I mentioned it before. I do not

---

1 – President, The Hesperides, Trinity Hall, Cambridge.
2 – Henry Goddard Leach (1880–1970), editor of *Forum*; scholar of Scandinavian civilisation.
3 – Leach 'would be almost willing to sell my soul (if the market on souls were not already glutted) for the privilege of publishing' the paper on Babbitt TSE had proposed: 'It seems to me from what I know of Babbitt that you have singled out the salient point in his philosophy that most needs clearing up. Many of his own students believe that his attitude toward Christianity is equivocal. One of his former students who happens to be a member of my staff assures me that this is not so; that although Babbitt is committed to humanism, he would infinitely prefer the voice of authoritative Christianity to the babble and confusion of thought that comes from the romantic philosophy of self-expression. However this may be, I am glad that you have decided to enter the wedge at this point.'

think there will be any difficulty as this particular article will be more suitable for your paper than for his.

You very kindly suggest that I should follow it up by a paper on Benda. I do not feel that I have at present enough to say about Benda to justify an article of that size, although I am much interested in the subject and have certain things that I do want to say about him. If you cared to have me follow up my essay on Babbitt with something else, I would suggest that I could do something much more suitable on either Monsieur Charles Maurras or Monsieur Jacques Maritain both of whom I know, and in whose work I have been for a long time interested.

I will get to work on the Babbitt as soon as possible, and meanwhile thank you again for your letter.

Yours sincerely,
[T. S. Eliot]

TO *Edmund Wilson*[1]   CC

21 February 1928   [*The Monthly Criterion*]

Dear Mr Wilson,

Referring to my letter of the 7th November last. On thinking matters over I should like to offer you something else more suitable for a weekly periodical than my projected essay on Babbitt. The Babbitt will have to be pretty long and it happens that the *Forum* would like from me an article on this subject to fit in with a series of theirs. I think that what I want to write about Babbitt is more suitable for them than for you, and if you are agreeable I should very much like to write for you what I could do at any time, or as soon as you could use it, i.e. a shorter essay on Julien Benda with particular reference to his new book which has not yet been translated, and also to the translation of *Belphégor* which I believe is soon to appear in America.[2] I hope that this will suit you just as well. May I hear from you? And will you let me know when you want it?

Yours sincerely,
[T. S. Eliot]

1 – Edmund Wilson (1895–1972), American journalist, literary and social critic: see Biographical Register.
2 – 'The Idealism of Julien Benda' – on *The Treason of the Intellectuals* – *The New Republic* 57 (12 Dec. 1928), 105–7.

TO *Allen Tate*[1]   TS Princeton

21 February 1928   *The Monthly Criterion*

Dear Mr Tate,

Thank you for your very kind letter of the 9th instant. You are very much more considerate than many contributors, some of whom seem to expect their work to be published even if there is nothing in which to publish it. I shall not keep your essay any longer than need be: that is to say as soon as I know whether the *Criterion* is to continue or not I will let you know; if it continues I shall want to keep your essay, if not I will send it back at once. I note that you want to revise it before publication. I should be glad if you would drop me a line to say whether your revision is slight enough to be executed in proof or whether I had better send you back the typescript.[2]

Yours very sincerely,
T. S. Eliot

TO *Mario Praz*   CC

21 February 1928   [London]

My dear Praz,

I was extremely sorry to miss you while you were in London. I was only away a week but of course your visits to London are unfortunately even more brief than that. I saw Orlo Williams today who said that he had seen you and that he had told you what there is to tell about the future of the *Criterion*. The March number is certain to appear as one of our friends has generously guaranteed it, but beyond that nothing is certain. As I was not sure that the March number would not be the last, I had to cram into it certain things which might otherwise have been postponed: that is to say had I been certain of the April number I should have included Montale and omitted something else. I can only assure you that if the review continues Montale's poem will be among the first pieces of verse. Personally I have hopes that the *Criterion* will continue, not as a monthly but as a quarterly; the latter form, if less popular, at least suits my editorial mentality, such as it is, better than the monthly form.

1–Allen Tate (1899–1979), American poet, critic and editor: see Biographical Register.
2–Tate had written on 9 Feb.: 'I should be glad, still glad, to have you print my essay at your leisure ... However ... if for any reason, after so long a time, you no longer find it convenient to use the essay – you took it when your journal was still a quarterly – I should have no reason whatever for complaint.'

Many thanks for your remarks about the review of my Seneca in the *Times*. I wrote a letter to the *Times* about it and then cancelled it; for after all there is seldom much point in wrangling with reviewers unless they are actually libellous. What did make me foam at the mouth was exactly that allusion to Lucas.[1] You at least will know that whatever my obligations and whatever my defects of scholarship in the book, I found Lucas's book to be the one book which was wholly useless. I should be interested to know, by the way, what you think of my own review of Lucas's *Webster* in the *Times*.[2]

And now may I ask when will be the next opportunity of seeing you in London?

Yours ever,
[T. S. Eliot]

TO *Jane Heap*[3]   CC

21 February 1928   [London]

I am distressed by your letter of the 15th instant. I have been pallbearer at the funeral of several periodicals and have, like the speaker in Tom Moore's famous poem, become used to the expectation that anything in which I am interested should die. But although I have not had the honour to contribute to *The Little Review* for some years, it is very hard to have such a landmark disappear. In fact it makes me feel that I am approaching old age. I have, I believe, a complete file of *The Little Review* of the days in which Pound was foreign editor and both he and Lewis and I were occasional contributors, and the serial parts of *Ulysses* were eagerly awaited. In those days *The Little Review* was the only periodical in America which would accept my work, and indeed the only periodical there in which I cared to appear.

---

1 – 'Senecan Tragedy' – on *Seneca his Tenne Tragedies* – *TLS*, 9 Feb. 1928, 92: 'Mr Eliot has known how to make use of the work of more heavily equipped investigators; and his own attitude, in appreciation and criticism, is always fresh, sincere, and stimulating. He has made good use in particular of Mr F. L. Lucas's *Seneca and Elizabethan Tragedy*, a volume which, published in 1922, remains the best and most scholarly study of the subject.' Praz exclaimed on 14 Feb.: 'I have just read a silly review of yr *Seneca* in the T.L.S. The reviewer says you are indebted to Lucas, of all Seneca's students! (Of course his Webster is a fine performance but what about his Seneca!)'
2 – 'John Webster', *TLS*, 26 Jan. 1928, 59.
3 – Jane Heap (1883–1964), American publisher, was co-editor (with her lover Margaret Anderson) of *The Little Review* (1916–29). This tribute, written at Heap's request, was published in the final issue of *The Little Review*, 12: 2 (May 1929), 90

If it is certain *The Little Review* is no longer to be controlled by Margaret Anderson and yourself, may I express the hope that it may disappear altogether? *The Little Review* did stand for so much that was important that I should not like to see the same title used for other purposes.

> With all best wishes.
> Sincerely yours,
> [T. S. Eliot]

TO *Oliver Elton*[1]   cc

21 February 1928   [London]

My dear Sir,

I return to you herewith the answers from Father Yealy which you sent me with your letter of the 30th January.[2] I apologise for the delay but I have been abroad.

I find myself somewhat handicapped in replying to your letter. In the first place I had not heard from Mr Tillyard since I sent him my original report and therefore can only draw inferences from your letter to me about your own report. Furthermore I could have wished that Father Yealy had chosen a subject for his dissertation which would have lent itself more readily to an examination of his qualifications. The subject seemed to me too vague, and indeed too trifling, to be suitable for the purpose of a dissertation for the doctorate of philosophy. I was informed that Father Yealy was to be examined only on questions arising out of the subject he had chosen.

Being rather in the dark as to what your opinion was, I find myself at first sight of somewhat different opinion, but probably with the same result. That is to say that I was more impressed by Father Yealy's thesis

---

1–Oliver Elton (1861–1945), English literary scholar, editor and translator, was Professor of English Literature at the University of Liverpool, 1900–25. His works include *A Survey of English Literature*, covering 1730–1880 (6 vols, 1912–28).

2–Fr F. J. Yealy, SJ (1888–1977), an American Jesuit from the St. Stanislaw Seminary, Florissant, Missouri, had submitted a doctoral thesis on 'Emerson and the Romantic Revival' at Christ's College, Cambridge; TSE had undertaken to be an external examiner. Elton had written on 30 Jan.: 'I send you the answers from Father Yealy which I believe Mr Tillyard will have told you to expect from me. They seem to me to improve his position considerably, and I am very willing to concur in any recommendation for the M. Litt. I do not even now, however, feel equal to recommending him for the higher degree, for the reasons given in my report. You will be aware of the drift of my report . . . and Mr Tillyard has explained how you and I unluckily differed. I only wish the system had lent itself to our exchanging ideas directly.'

than I am by his replies to questions. As I have intimated, the subject of the dissertation did not seem to me particularly suitable for exhibiting the applicant's attainments either in breadth or profundity of scholarship, nor did the dissertation itself seem to me to have very great coherence or singleness of point. I confess that I remain very much in the dark as to what Father Yealy has read and whether what he has read was worth reading. I may perhaps be influenced by a prejudice against what I call qualification for academic titles by correspondence; but the upshot of it is that I also feel some hesitation, after your letter, in supporting Father Yealy for the Ph.D. I think, however, that he is certainly qualified for the M. Litt.

As I say, I have heard nothing from Mr Tillyard, but perhaps you will communicate with him and I may hear from you further.[1]

Yours very truly,

[T. S. Eliot]

TO *May Sinclair*[2]   CC

21 February 1928   [London]

Dear Miss Sinclair,

You may be surprised to hear from me after such a long time. It is unlikely that you will have heard of the crisis in the affairs of the *Criterion* which has occupied the whole of my available time – for I have had to be abroad a good deal in connection with private affairs – since the end of November.

To put it briefly, the fact is that Lady Rothermere who had always financed the *Criterion* suddenly decided in November that she was no

---

1 – Tillyard wrote (29 Feb.): 'I had not written as I had understood that Elton was asking you in forwarding the papers to send them on to me. I am sorry that the candidate's absence from England has necessitated the cumbrousness of the written examination and the consequent delays.' He confirmed on 8 Mar. that Fr F. J. Yealy had been unanimously recommended for the M. Litt. Degree.

2 – May Sinclair, pseud. of Mary St. Clair (1863–1946): English novelist; active in the movement for Women's Suffrage, and an early apologist for psychoanalysis; author of *The Three Sisters* (1914), *Mary Olivier: A Life* (1919), and *The Life and Death of Harriet Frean* (1922), of which TSE said that it exhibited 'the soul of man under psychoanalysis' ('London Letter: The Novel', *The Dial* 73 [Sept. 1922], 329–31). TSE reviewed her *A Defence of Idealism: Some Questions & Conclusions* (1917) in *NS* 9 (22 Sept. 1917), while she reviewed *Prufrock and Other Observations* in *Little Review* 4 (Dec. 1917). She was a good friend to TSE, who printed her work in *The Egoist* and her story 'The Victim' in *C.* 1 (Oct. 1922). See further Suzanne Raitt, *May Sinclair: A Modern Victorian* (2000).

longer interested in the paper – in fact she really disliked it – and found that she preferred to use her money in other ways. This left us with the alternative of stopping publication or finding funds from other sources. I was myself resigned to abandoning the venture, but some of my younger friends were anxious that it should be continued and assembled privately the money necessary to pay for the numbers of January and February. The March number has also been assured by one generous guarantor, but beyond that we are quite uncertain.

We no longer hope to accumulate enough support to run the *Criterion* as a monthly but we still hope to be able to continue it in its quarterly form. For this purpose we need a minimum guarantee of about eight hundred pounds a year and a maximum of a thousand a year would be more satisfactory. We have already secured guarantees to about three hundred and twenty five pounds a year. The persons who have concerned themselves with gathering this money have been chiefly Mr Bruce Richmond, Mr Humbert Wolfe and Mr Frank Morley.

I am not writing to you to ask you to contribute yourself, but, at Bruce Richmond's suggestion to ask you whether you can give us any advice about other people whom we might approach. The name of Hugh Walpole was suggested. I have no knowledge myself of Hugh Walpole's means; and I have not seen him for several years; I only know that at one time he took a very keen interest in the *Criterion* and that he was also very kind to me. Do you think that Hugh Walpole would be able and willing to contribute? And can you suggest anyone else?

What we want are guarantees of support for a period of three years if possible, to the extent of sums of £25 a year up. But it is hardly likely that we shall be able to continue the review unless we have two or three more assurances to the extent of £100 a year. If we get enough guarantees we propose to organise the affair in a business way; that is to say we should allocate stock in the existing company, The New Criterion Limited, in proportion to the size of the guarantees. If the *Criterion* ever paid for itself, therefore, the guarantors as shareholders would be entitled to dividends.

I do not know whether you are in London but if so, and if you should be enough interested to have any suggestions to make, I should be very happy to come to see you and incidentally to renew an acquaintance which from my point of view has too long lapsed.

Yours very sincerely,
[T. S. Eliot]

TO *Thomas McGreevy*[1]   TS TCD

21 February 1928   *The Monthly Criterion*

My dear McGreevy,

Your letter of the 10th instant is received. Your impressive card with that formidable word propagation is being pasted into my scrap book. I am more than flattered: my name is printed in full, and correctly. I should like to hear more about the conference and my curiosity and vanity are such that I should like to see a copy of the conference if it exists in writing.

Furthermore your reference to my 'Salutation' gives me extreme pleasure.[2] More particularly as almost nobody else has had the interest, or possibly the courage, to say what he thinks of it. I thought that it had fallen flat. There is only one exception and that is your compatriot *The Dublin Review* which spoke well of it. Anyway I am so used to perceiving that people always think my last work inferior to something I did years ago that I can assure you that it is a great encouragement to have a letter like yours. The only news, official or unofficial, about the *Criterion* is this: that we have gone a certain distance toward obtaining the guarantees; that we are not without hope of continuing, if not as a monthly at least as a quarterly. Personally I should prefer the quarterly.

Let me have news of yourself as well.

Yours ever,
T. S. Eliot

P.S. Your André Gide was well received and still seems to me admirably fair and just.[3]

TO *HM Inspector of Taxes*   CC

21 February 1928   [London]

Dear Sir,

I have to acknowledge receipt of your letter of the 11th instant. With regard to royalties from books stated on my income tax return, these

---

1 – Thomas McGreevy (1893–1967), poet, literary and art critic, and arts administrator: see Biographical Register.
2 – McGreevy sent his 'warmest congratulations on your *Salutation*. It seems to me that it equals and possibly even surpasses the finest passages in *The Waste Land* – certainly the most beautiful thing you have done since.'
3 – See McGreevy's review of works by André Gide, including *Les Faux-monnayeurs* and *Voyage au Congo*, in *MC* 7 (Jan. 1928), 65–9.

do not represent the average gross receipts for three years but the exact receipts for the year under review. Had I given the average for three years, I believe that the sum would have been appreciably smaller, but this figure would have been difficult to arrive at.

Income arising from America. The period of accrual for which this was calculated was the British fiscal year in question apart from the question of American tax which I presume does not concern you. This is a statement of gross income none of which had been subjected to British income tax before receipt.

Fees from Faber and Gwyer. I agree to the amount of tax as proposed by you.

Yours faithfully,
[T. S. Eliot]

то *The Collector of Taxes*   CC

21 February 1928   [London]

Dear Sir,

I have received from you a demand for payment of income tax for the year 1927–28. Number of assessment: 4149, to be payable within ten days.

As I have just settled my income tax for 1925–26 and as I am still in correspondence with your Inspector concerning my tax for 1926–27 which I should have paid long since had we been able to arrive at the correct figure; and furthermore as I have not yet made a return for 1927–28 and as your assessment is therefore incorrect and probably less than the amount due from me, I hope that you will take consideration of these matters and accord a certain delay.

I may say that the delay in settling the arrears has not in my opinion been by any means chiefly my own fault; so far as I am concerned these matters would have been settled long hence [since]. But your office in Covent Garden has been unable to reply to my letters except after very long delay. In the circumstances I should find it a little hard if I were obliged to pay three years tax within a few weeks.

I am, dear Sir,
Yours faithfully
[T. S. Eliot]

TO *Allanah Harper*[1]   CC

21 February 1928   [London]

Dear Sir,

Thank you for your letter of the 25th ultimo.[2] I should be very glad to assist at the debut of your new publication but I am very doubtful, considering my other engagements many of which are long overdue, whether I could make any promise. If it proves possible I will write to you again in the hope of being of use. Your programme is certainly more than interesting. The support of Mr Bonamy Dobrée is quite enough to ensure my good will and my own contribution if I can manage it.

If you want an essay on Virginia Woolf may I suggest two names? Either Mr E. Morgan Forster or Mr Orlo Williams, both of whom know her work very well; and I can think of no one more competent to interpret it.

I hope that we may meet when you are again in London, and with all best wishes, believe me,

Yours sincerely
[T. S. Eliot]

TO *Paul Gilson*[3]   CC

22 February 1928   [London]

Dear Sir,

Thank you for your letter of Monday's date. I have no objection to your publishing in your new review[4] a French translation of my verses entitled

---

1–Allanah Harper (1904–92), socialite and editor. From 1929 to 1931 she was to edit in France an Anglo-French review aptly named *Échanges*, publishing writers including TSE, Auden, Stein, VW, Léon-Paul Fargue, and André Gide. See Harper, 'A Magazine and Some People in Paris', *Partisan Review* (July–Aug. 1942).

2–Harper wrote from Cairo on 25 Jan. to ask TSE to contribute a poem or an article to a review that she was to edit with Roger de Leval (a young Belgian poet), for publication in Apr. or June. She had a poem and an essay by Edith Sitwell; an article on Stravinsky by Sitwell's companion Helen Rootham; a poem by Thomas Driberg; and the promise of an essay by Gide. 'Mr Bonamy Dobrée gave a lecture on your poetry here last month. And said he would be very pleased to let me have a copy of his lecture for the Review. But he would have to write to you first for permission.'

3–Paul Gilson (1865–1942), distinguished Belgian musician and composer (his oeuvre ran to three operas, three ballets, and over 50 orchestral works), writer, editor, teacher of music. Having studied at the Brussels Conservatory, in 1899 he was appointed Professor of Composition there; then in Antwerp. From 1909 to 1930 he was General Inspector of the Belgian Musical Schools; and he was Director of the Revue Musicale Belge, 1925–32.

4–A French literary and philosophical review, called *1928*, was to feature contributions from Max Jacob, Henri Massis, Jacques Maritain, and Virginia Woolf.

'The Journey of the Magi' on three conditions. One that you publish only the French translation and not the English text. Two that the translation should be one seen and approved by myself. Three that you indicate that the original text may be procured from Faber and Gwyer Limited for a shilling.

Your list of contributors is important and interesting and I look forward with great interest to the appearance of the review for which I wish you all success.

Yours very truly,
[T. S. Eliot]

TO *Angel Flores*[1]   TS Flores

22 February 1928   [London]

Dear Mr Flores,

Thank you very much for your letter of the 30th ultimo and for your kind remarks about my poem.[2] I have read your translation, which I return herewith, with great interest and it seems to me that certain parts of the poem read very much better in Spanish than in any other language except English. I regret that my knowledge of Spanish is not adequate for expert criticism. I am particularly anxious to improve my smattering of Spanish as there are many things in that language which I wish to be able to read. But however proficient I might yet become, my knowledge would never be enough to allow me to criticise your translation. So far as I can tell it seems to me admirable and I do not hesitate to authorise its publication.

---

1 – Angel Flores (1900–92) was a Lecturer in Spanish Literature, Rutgers University, New Brunswick, New Jersey, and later Professor of Romance Languages and Comparative Literature at Queen's College, City University of New York; author of *Spanish Literature in English Translation* (1926), and English adviser for Editorial Cervantes of Barcelona.
2 – Flores sent TSE his translation into Spanish of *TWL* – *La Tierra Baldía* – which he had done for two reasons: 'One . . . my deep love for this great poem – great because it is a summation of a fundamental attitude towards the crumbling ideologies of our time, and great also because in its tone of disgust at the status quo of our souls it seems to promise a herculean desire to escape from the blighting atmosphere, made possible by our present metaphysicless world of ideas. Secondly, your poem promises much esthetically. The youth of the Spanish-speaking world is in search of new values, and I believe that *The Wasteland* in its Spanish avatar will be a welcomed gift from the English language.' Federico García Lorca, a friend of Flores, is said to have read the translation while it was in the making in New York; and it exerted an influence upon his *Poeta en Nueva York*.

I have made one or two trifling suggestions and I should be very glad if you could see that the same spacing is observed in the translation as in the original; for I attach great importance to spacing. There is only one other point. On page 13 of your translation you put 'consumiéndome'. Would not simply 'consumiendo' be enough? My original is 'burning', and after all I was merely translating myself quite literally from the Pali original.

I should be indeed honoured if your translation could appear in either the *Revista de Occidente* or *Gaceta Literaria,* but particularly glad if it appeared in the *Revista de Occidente* with the editors of which I have always had the most sympathetic relations.[1]

I am, dear Sir,
Yours very truly,
[T. S. Eliot]

P.S. The title, by the way, is not 'The Wasteland' but 'The Waste Land'. The only exact translation of the title is one which my French translator, Jean de Menasce, discovered, although alas! too late to use in his version – 'La Gaste Lande'.[2] This is absolutely the exact equivalent as it alludes to the same mediaeval fiction.

T. S. E.

TO *F. R. Morrish*   cc

22 February 1928   [London]

Dear Sir,

Thank you for your kind letter of the 13th instant.[3] On thinking over matters, however, as I dislike publicity and in particular dislike having my photograph published, I think I must decline your kind offer.

With many thanks,
Yours faithfully,
[T. S. Eliot]

1–Flores's translation was published by Editorial Cervantes, Barcelona, in 1930.
2–Jean de Menasce's translation, 'La terre mise a nu', had appeared in *Esprit*, 1 (May 1926), 174–94; it was to be reprinted, as 'La terre gaste', in *Philosophies*.
3–TSE had been invited to include a biographical sketch of himself, and a photograph, for entry in *The Illustrated Who's Who*, to be published by Whitehall Publishing Co. Ltd. Morrish, a co-director of the publishing firm, had assured TSE in his letter of 13 Feb. that he would incur no expense from being included.

TO *The Editor of* The Church Times CC

24 February 1928 24 Russell Square, London

L'ACTION FRANÇAISE

Sir,

Being a regular reader of your paper, and being in most matters wholly in sympathy, perhaps I may be permitted once again to protest against your attitude towards *L'Action Française*, as exhibited in your Summary paragraph of last week.[1] I feel the greater obligation, as I believe that I am one of the few defenders of *L'Action Française* in this country who cannot be accused of seizing upon this affair for the purpose of 'No Popery' or Protestant propaganda. I should much have preferred to believe that the operations against *L'Action Française* were amply justified. I consider that I am a Moderate. I do not choose to question either the motives of the Pope or the motives of his counsellors. The matter of influences does not interest me; I am not concerned either with what went before or with what has happened since. I concern myself only with the question, whether the work of Charles Maurras was damnable or praiseworthy.

1 – 'Summary', *The Church Times*, 17 Feb. 1928, 179: 'The controversy between the Vatican and the Paris *L'Action Française* has a real European significance, and it is regrettable that a quite unnecessary and over-heated controversy in England should have obscured the facts. *L'Action Française* is a Royalist and Nationalist newspaper, conducted by M. Charles Maurras and M. Léon Daudet. M. Maurras is a writer of very great distinction, a pagan who does not even pay lip homage to the Church, but who has contrived to attract a considerable section of French Catholics by his violent anti-Republican agitation. M. Daudet is a nominal Catholic, the author of a number of erotic novels, and, incidentally, is obviously a little mad. All that is best in Catholic France and practically the whole hierarchy have deplored and denounced the exploitation of the Faith by these reckless political adventurers. And the Pope's denunciation of *L'Action Française* is quite clearly due, not to any hostility to French Royalism, or, as had been insinuated, to proper French national demands, but to the fear that Catholicism might be associated with the wildest and most pernicious form of Nationalism. The Pope's offence, in the view of M. Maurras, is that he has steadily and courageously backed Locarno. His Holiness, with Cardinal Gasparri, and that very enlightened prelate, Cardinal Ceretti, has played the part of a good European. M. Maurras is preaching the devil's doctrine that a good European must necessarily be the enemy of France.'

The Locarno Treaties (1925) were proposed both to define the borders of France and to conciliate Germany for the punitive terms of the post-war Treaty of Versailles (1919). Led by Austen Chamberlain (GB), Aristide Briand (France), and Gustav Stresemann (Germany), the Locarno Conferences, which involved the participation of seven countries in all – the others being Italy, Belgium, Poland, and Czechoslovakia – agreed to secure once and for all time an inviolable western border for Germany and to establish a western alliance to protect France and Belgium from Germany. The 'Locarno spirit' of goodwill that followed enabled Germany to join the League of Nations in 1926, but anger and dissent in both Germany and France soon wrecked all good intentions.

Your paragraph of last week seems to me, on this ground, unfair. As for M. Daudet, I have met him only once, and then under formal conditions; and I do not defend his methods or what are called his 'erotic' novels, which I have never read. But, if you, Sir, or any other journalist, referred to me as 'obviously a little mad', I should certainly consult my legal advisers about the law of libel. I can only say that on the one occasion on which I have met him, M. Daudet seemed to me as sane as anyone whom I have ever met.

Next, I protest against your wording, 'M. Maurras . . . has *contrived* to attract,' etc., where you might have said simply 'has attracted'. The phrasing suggests an unscrupulous policy. If there is one quality more than another by which M. Maurras is distinguished, it is that of honesty and probity.

Naturally, 'the whole hierarchy' has 'denounced and deplored' the views of the *L'Action Française*; but the hierarchy is bound to obey the decree of the Holy Father. Were I a member of 'the hierarchy', I should probably be silent and obey.

I am not concerned with impugning the Pope's motives, which are probably of the highest. But it is at present you, Sir, who qualify the doctrine of M. Maurras as 'the wildest and most pernicious form of Nationalism'. I am prepared to assert at least that this cannot be the 'wildest' or the 'most pernicious', because I can mention a wilder and more perverse, which is that of the late Maurice Barrès, after whom a small square in the centre of Paris has lately been named. Will you prove to us that the Nationalism of Marshal von Hindenburg or the Nationalism of Mussolini is less 'wild' and 'pernicious' than that of Maurras? In so serious a matter as this, words ought to be used with precision.

Finally, you say that M. Maurras is preaching the 'devil's doctrine', that a 'good European must necessarily be an enemy of France'. Can you produce any statement of M. Maurras to reinforce this affirmation? I am aware that M. Maurras would assert that a 'good European' must be a friend of France; and I should make the same assertion myself. In conclusion, I would mention the fact that the phrase 'good European' was given currency by Nietzsche; that Maurras is accused by his opponents of being a disciple of Nietzsche: so that in any case, people who talk of 'good Europeans' (Mr Lloyd George, who wanted to hang the Kaiser, is a good European?) ought to make acknowledgment of somebody.

T. S. Eliot

TO *Max Clauss*[1]   CC

27 February 1928   [London]

Dear Dr Clauss,

I am not quite sure when you said you were leaving London but I hope
that you will still be here on Thursday as I should like to take you to
lunch to meet some of my colleagues.[2] We have weekly meetings on that
day of a very informal sort; so I am not quite sure who will be there next
Thursday, but I think that Herbert Read will certainly be there.

If you can come, I suggest that I should call for you at your hotel a little
before one o'clock, as the restaurant is rather hard to find. If you cannot
lunch on Thursday, would you care to come to tea here on Wednesday at
half past four?

                             Yours sincerely,
                             [T. S. Eliot]

TO *Max Rychner*[3]   CC

28 February 1928   [London]

Dear Dr Rychner,

You may remember that some time ago you asked me either to write
myself or to suggest someone else who could write an essay for you on
the cultural position in Europe with reference to Curtius's essay on the
relation of France and Germany in the *Europäische Revue*. I should much
have liked to do this myself but unfortunately I have been and am too busy
to consider it for a long time. But one of my colleagues and contributors,
Mr Orlo Williams, whose name you may have seen in the *Criterion*, is
very much interested in this subject and I am sending him the copy of the
Europäische Revue containing Curtius's essay. Would you care to have
an essay by Orlo Williams on this subject? I am sure that he would be
interested, and I think that he would be very glad to do it.[4]

                             Yours sincerely,
                             [T. S. Eliot]

1–Max Clauss (1901–88), German journalist and writer; editor of *Europäische Revue*
(Berlin).
2–Clauss, who had arrived in London on 19 Feb., replied on 28 Feb. from the Regent Palace
Hotel, Piccadilly Circus, that he would be delighted to come to lunch.
3–Max Rychner (1897–1965), writer and critic; editor of *Neue Schweizer Rundschau*.
4–Rychner was sorry (1 Mar.) that TSE felt unable to write the essay; but he would be glad
to have a piece from Orlo Williams as soon as possible.

TO *Mario Praz*   CC

28 February 1928   [London]

My dear Praz,

Thank you very much for your letter. If you are to be in London about the 21st March you are pretty certain to find me here, and I hope very much to hear your lecture if I may.[1]

It is very kind of you to suggest subscribing to the *Criterion* and your subscription would be more than welcome but I suggest that you should wait until we are certain that there will be a *Criterion*. At present it is extremely unlikely that we shall be able to continue it as a monthly, and it is more than likely that we shall continue it as a quarterly.

Your book on Spain[2] has just arrived. I had already heard of it from Williams who liked it very much indeed. If the *Criterion* continues I will try to get J. B. Trend, who knows more about Spain than anyone of my acquaintance, to review it for us.

I have sent a note in the proper direction to ask that a review copy of the *Thomas Browne* should be sent to *English Studies*.[3] But you understand that the complete set of six or seven volumes is to be published only one volume at a time, so if you want a complete set you should arrange with the Editor of *English Studies* to send you the other volumes as they appear.

Your criticism of my review of Lucas surprises me.[4] My review was aimed at the popular reader of the *Supplement* who would be more interested in Lucas's critical opinions than his editorial ability. I thought that I had rendered due tribute in a general way to Lucas's merit as Editor; if I have not done so I am very sorry. The notes are certainly extremely interesting though no doubt a more learned person than myself might discover in

1–Praz was to lecture on Machiavelli at the British Academy, 21 Mar.
2–*Unromantic Spain* (1928) was to be reviewed by Trend in C. 9 (Apr. 1930), 572.
3–Praz wished (27 Feb.) to review the works of Sir Thomas Browne (F&G) in *English Studies* (The Netherlands).
4–'Your review of Lucas's in the *Times* surprised me . . . I found that most of the remarks would have been very appropriate in a long review with plenty of space to dedicate to the evident merits of the work. But you dismiss this latter part and seem to refer the reader to technical reviews for it, and just pick up what is Lucas's feeble side, his indulgence to a kind of pathetic journalese, a defect of which, however, I think he is getting cured. I dislike as much as you do the passages about Pompeii etc.: there the critic as an artist is at his worst. But those passages disappear in the whole, and the whole is full of good points and many original remarks. You thought my review of Lewis unfair: but I am afraid you beat me this time, so far as unfairness is concerned. Note that I was very unfavourably prejudiced against Lucas, because of his rotten Seneca; still I find much to praise in his Webster, both from a scholarly and a literary point of view.'

such a huge mass of information inaccuracies and omissions. What I was really interested in discovering was why Lucas had chosen to edit Webster at all. That is to say, what was the conception of Webster which made him so important to Lucas with reference to Lucas's own temperament? But I am afraid that the choice of subject was due to weakness rather than to strength on the part of Lucas; though having chosen the subject he did his job extremely well. But I do not feel that Lucas has given us anything like a judicial criticism of Webster, and so far no one has done that.

Yours ever,
[T. S. Eliot]

TO *E. McKnight Kauffer*[1] TS Morgan

28 February 1928   Faber & Faber

Dear Ted,

Thank you very much for the photographs. I think they are excellent – especially of Marion and John: the only faults in mine are the Charlie Chaplin moustache (due, I suppose, to the lighting) and my not having bathed my eyes – and the next time you photograph your male guests at 11 p.m. or so you ought [to] give them a rub over first with your electric razor, that is, if you use such a powerful lens. Otherwise, they are a great deal better than Elliott & Fry have done for me. When shall I come and

---

1–E. McKnight Kauffer (1890–1954) – christened Edward Kauffer, he took the middle name McKnight in tribute to Professor Joseph McKnight (University of Utah) who had sponsored him to study in Paris – was an American artist and designer who became renowned in particular for his graphic designs, book illustrations and posters. He lived from 1914 to 1940 in England, gaining fame for his London Underground posters; he also illustrated books and book covers. On his return to New York in 1940, his chief client was American Airlines. His wife Marion Dorn was also a successful creative designer. See Mark Haworth-Booth, *E. McKnight Kauffer: A Designer and His Public* (1979); *The Poster King: E. McKnight Kauffer* (Estorick Collection of Modern Italian Art, 2011). Asked in 1949 to contribute to a 'profile' of Kauffer, TSE promptly wrote out for him these words: 'I almost never succeed in remembering the first occasion of meeting anybody, especially after they have been friends of mine for a long time. I think it was at the end, or shortly after the end of the first World War that I met McKnight Kauffer, who was already, I think, better known and remarked among the younger artists than I was amongst the men of letters. He was in appearance very much the same figure that he is to-day: tall, slender and elegantly dressed, and wearing whatever he wore with a grace that would make the best of the best efforts of the best tailor. (I cannot venture to say much about his appearance, because there is said to be a facial resemblance between Kauffer and myself – at any rate, when I have asked for him at the building in which he lives, several successive porters have taken for granted that I was his brother).'

dine? After the 21st – not on a Wed. or Fri. and not during the period Apr. 2–9. Awaiting the further word from you,

yours ever
Tom

TO *E. M. W. Tillyard*[1]   cc

28 February 1928   [London]

Dear Mr Tillyard,

I did not hear from you again about Father Yealy's dissertation but I have recently had some correspondence with Professor Elton. Professor Elton has shown me his own report and he is under the impression that you are expecting to hear from me.

Professor Elton's criticisms seem to me almost entirely right, and the points which he chooses for attack are exactly the points on which I felt that the applicant was weakest. I must confess that I did not consider the subject a very good one for a dissertation for that degree: I would even say that the subject is trivial. Some of the weakness to which Professor Elton objects seems to me intrinsic in the subject matter. It is true that the thesis lacks unity and that it does not make any point worth making; I was finally influenced in recommending the candidate because I felt that the subject itself was an impossible one. I assumed that the subject had been approved by the University. It is not the sort of subject which makes it necessary for the candidate to exhibit his full scholarship. I dare say that Father Yealy's scholarship, especially in philosophy, exceeds the evidence of it in his dissertation.

There is only one point on which I disagree directly with Professor Elton. I have not the dissertation at my hand and cannot make any direct comparison, so that I can only say that I was much more impressed by the dissertation itself than by the candidate's answers to questions. Professor Elton was more interested by the answers than by the dissertation.

1–E. M. W. Tillyard (1889–1962): Fellow in English of Jesus College, Cambridge, 1926–59; Master, 1945–59. Publications included *The Personal Heresy: A Controversy* (with C. S. Lewis, 1939), *The Elizabethan World Picture: A Study of the Idea of Order in the Age of Shakespeare, Donne and Milton* (1942), *Shakespeare's History Plays* (1944), *Milton* (1946), *Shakespeare's Problem Plays* (1949), and *The Muse Unchained: An Intimate Account of the Revolution in English Studies at Cambridge* (1958).

But in short I am now disposed to concur fully with Professor Elton in his recommendation for the M. Litt. rather than the Ph.D.

Yours sincerely,
[T. S. Eliot]

TO *E. R. Curtius*[1]   CC

28 February 1928   [London]

My dear Curtius,

I must apologise for not having written to you sooner to thank you for your very kind thought in sending me the book of Stefan Georg inscribed by yourself at Christmas time. I shall treasure it because of the inscription, but also I find it a good way of attempting to penetrate what is for me the Georg mystery. I say 'mystery' because I admit that I have always found his poems extremely difficult (a little bit, no doubt, because of the type), but I have a very strong feeling that Georg is a much more important person than Rilke whom I find easier to understand, and I want to confirm this.

I thank you also for sending, or causing to be sent to me, the translation of Ortega's[2] essays with your Preface. I am glad to have [it] because I do not read Spanish fluently and I have already read your Introduction which I find interesting and even exciting.

With very many thanks,
Yours ever sincerely,
[T. S. Eliot]

1–Ernst Robert Curtius (1886–1956), German scholar of philology and Romance literature: see Biographical Register.
2–José Ortega y Gasset (1883–1955), Spanish liberal philosopher and essayist, educated in Spain and Germany, was appointed (1910) Professor of Metaphysics at the Complutense University of Madrid. In 1917 he began contributing to *El Sol*; and in 1923 founded *Revista de Occidente*, which he directed until 1936. For ten years from the outbreak of the Civil War he exiled himself in Argentina and Portugal; but in 1948 he returned to Madrid where he founded the Institute of Humanities. Works include *España invertebrada* (*Invertebrate Spain*, 1921) and *La rebelión de las masas* (*The Revolt of the Masses*, 1930), which TSE called a 'remarkable book' (Leslie Paul, 'A Conversation with T. S. Eliot', *Kenyon Review* 27 [1965], 14).

TO *May Sinclair*   CC

28 February 1928   London

Dear Miss Sinclair,

Thank you very much for your letter.[1] It is slightly embarrassing, however, first because I did not propose to ask you to contribute yourself and second because I have so far only asked for guarantees, except from people who have been asked to contribute for the January, February and March numbers; and therefore I am not quite sure what to do with your cheque until I have seen Mr Frank Morley who is taking charge of the funds.

I shall be very pleased to dine with you on Thursday the 8th and look forward to see you again with much pleasure.

                                   With many thanks,
                                   Yours very sincerely
                                   [T. S. Eliot]

TO *John J. Claffey*   CC

28 February 1928   [London]

Sir,

I apologise for the delay in replying to your letter of the 7th instant as I have been abroad.[2] For your records I beg to inform you that I am married; that my wife's maiden name was Vivienne Haigh Haigh-Wood and that we were married at the Hampstead Registry Office, London, on the 26th June 1915. My wife was British born. We have no children. I last resided in Cambridge Massachusetts. I left the United States in June 1914 but returned for a short visit in 1915 – consequently I left it last about the end of August or the beginning of September 1915. I am sorry that I cannot give you the exact date but hope that this information will be sufficient.

1 – Sinclair (23 Feb.) was 'sorry to hear that Lady Rothermere has dropped the *Criterion*. I send you a cheque for £25 towards expenses. I can't send more, because I have not written a book. I'll give the same each year, as long as my present income continues.

'Will you dine with me on Thursday, the 8th at 7.30? . . . It will be so nice to see you again.'

2 – The American Vice Consul in London had just been made aware that TSE had taken British citizenship, and needed to file a report for the Department of State. TSE answered the requisite questions, and he included a certified statement from the Home Office. The Vice Consul responded (2 Mar.) that he would be filing a report 'to be used in connection with proceedings to cancel your former citizenship record'.

In addition I may say that my family was originally in Saint Louis, Missouri, where I was born and brought up, but that after my father's death my mother removed to Cambridge, Massachusetts, where she still lives.

Yours faithfully,
[T. S. Eliot]

TO *Oliver Elton*   CC

28 February 1928   [London]

Dear Professor Elton,

I have just written to Mr Tillyard to say that having considered your objections I am finally in agreement to recommend Father Yealy for the M. Litt. But not for the Ph.D. I still feel that the choice of subject was unfortunate; that it is not a subject which compels the candidate to display his whole scholarship; and therefore I was inclined to give the candidate the benefit of the doubt. The answers do not seem to me particularly satisfactory. I find no particular fault with them but they seem to me on the one hand lacking in original thought and on the other hand do not bring very much scholarship to bear. But as we are now in agreement these details hardly matter.

I return to you herewith Mr Tillyard's letter to you and the copy of your report with many thanks.

If you are ever in London I hope that you will drop me a line to this address so that we may meet. I visit Oxford from time to time but always as a guest and therefore if you should be in London we could meet at more leisure here.

Yours very truly,
[T. S. Eliot]

28 February 1928   [London]

Dear McSweeney,

I am sending you the copy of *L'Action Française et le Vatican* that I promised you. I found some difficulty in getting it in Paris and had to leave an order which has only just been filled. Please keep it as I have another copy. I have also read *Sous le Terreur* which is the sequel to this but it is not nearly so important and interesting.

I have another letter about the matter in *The Church Times* of last Friday.[1]

I hope to get you to come and lunch with me in a week or so and will write again.

Yours ever,
[T. S. Eliot]

Vivien Eliot TO *Ottoline Morrell*   MS Texas

28 February [?1928]   57 Chester Terrace, S.W.I.

Dearest Ottoline

I enjoyed seeing you very much indeed. It was good of you to come & see me.

I am sorry I talked so much about Tom – of course he is a very old friend of yours – & a great friend & noone likes hearing their old friends spoken against.

I am very unhappy, & as you agreed with me – *quite* defenceless. So there it is. If you hear of me being murdered, don't be surprised!

Are you really coming again next Monday – ? Please do, & please send me a card to say positively. I really do want to see you again.

Yrs ever –
Vivienne Eliot

---

1 – McSweeney (who worked in the Colonial Office) replied on 1 Mar.: 'I read your letter to the *Church Times* – it is, is it not, of a studied moderation? i.e. you have renounced many weapons that you could have used to create effect, though perhaps in the *C.T.* it would not be judicious. The Editor's footnote is, of course, the result of a verbal confusion: if Maurras understood "l'esprit de Locarno" as the editor probably does, he would no doubt be its fervent supporter – insofaras it is a "spirit".'

TO *Ursula Roberts*[1]

29 February 1928   [London]

Dear Madam,

Thank you for your kind invitation to address the Aesthetics Section of the British Psychological Society. I am afraid, however, that it will be impossible for me to find time to prepare a paper to read before your Society during the coming season. Even were I able to do so, I should still be diffident about addressing a learned society of this kind. I am not a psychologist and I am afraid that I know very little about aesthetics. But it is primarily from lack of time that I must decline this honour and only secondly from modesty.

Yours very truly,
[T .S. Eliot]
P.S. I recognise you very well by your pseudonym.[2]

TO *Arnold Bennett*[3]

29 February 1928   [London]

My dear Bennett,

You may remember that when Humbert Wolfe and I came to discuss the *Criterion* with you you suggested that in the circumstances we ought not to pay our contributors. I disagreed with you at the time, and still disagree as a general principle, but it has occurred to us that you might be disposed to back up your own suggestion. We are still hoping to obtain enough capital at least for a quarterly as the amount required for that is much more modest. As for the March number, which is about to appear, that has been guaranteed by Oliver. But we are still embarrassed by the necessity for paying for the February number.

---

1 – Ursula Roberts (1887–1971), author, was married to the Revd William Corbett Roberts, vicar of St George's Church, Bloomsbury, London. She was a member of the Church League for Women's Suffrage (later the League of the Church Militant); hon. treasurer and hon. press secretary of the East Midland Federation of the National Union of Women's Suffrage Societies; a member of the Anglican Group for the Ordination of Women; and a member of the interdenominational Society for the Ministry of Women in the Church. As 'Susan Miles' she published collections of poetry including *Dunch* (1918), *Annotations* (1922), *The Hares, and other verses* (1924), and *Blind Men Crossing a Bridge* (1934); *Lettice Delmer* (novel in verse, 1958; repr. 2002); and a biography of her husband, *Portrait of a Parson* (1955).
2 – On the back of her letter, dated 28 Feb., TSE asked himself: ''?a poetess – author of a slim book of verse entitled "March Hares"? ?daughter of Rev W. C. Roberts?'.
3 – Arnold Bennett (1867–1931), author and journalist: see Biographical Register.

As I think we explained at the time, the January and February numbers were guaranteed chiefly by a number of young men interested in the *Criterion*. These people, of course, have put their hands in their pockets for the January number already. But it will be impossible to pay for the February number without slightly more capital, unless we call upon these same men, some of whom cannot afford such claims at all. I have put up fifteen pounds myself and cannot do more. I remember that you seemed annoyed rather than otherwise at being paid for the 'Florentine Journal'; and indeed the amount that the *Criterion* did pay was so small for such a contribution as to leave it in the category of gifts. Would you be willing to contribute the total amount paid toward the expenses of the February Issue? We should then be doubly in your debt.[1]

Yours very sincerely,
[T. S. Eliot]

TO *Richard Aldington*   TS Texas

29 February 1928   Faber & Gwyer Ltd

My dear Richard,

Please excuse me for not having answered your letter sooner. Very many thanks for your information about Alec Randall.[2] I shall be glad to have any further news that you receive.

When I got your letter I sent a message down to de la Mare asking him to give you the information direct, so I presume that you have heard from him.[3]

I am glad to hear that you are going to have a time in Paris, though I do not suppose it will be a holiday. If there is anyone in Paris of my acquaintance whom you would like to meet, please let me know; but I dare say you know more people there than I do. But I should like very much in any case to give you an introduction to the Princess de Bassiano who is an extremely nice woman. They live in Versailles.

It goes without saying that if there is any translation to be done we shall be delighted to secure your services. I doubt if we have anything in view

---

1–Bennett responded on 1 Mar.: 'But I have spent all that money long since! However, I enclose cheque for the total amount I have received, namely £17. 16. 0., & the cheque received today for £8. 16. 0.'
2–RA had written on 20 Feb., 'I think the poor lad is out of danger . . . I have asked Scott-Moncrieff to send me the latest reports on the situation, and will forward them to you.'
3–'Could you find out from R[ichard] de la Mare if he received the proofs of my 50 Romance Poems . . . and what number of copies F. and G. have decided to take.'

in the way of foreign translations at present, but I have asked Faber to make a note of it. Are you equally open to translating from Italian if the case should arise?

Ever yours,
Tom

TO *Mona Wilson*[1]   CC

1 March 1928   [*The Monthly Criterion*]

Dear Miss Wilson,

I must apologise for not having written to you sooner to explain that since December the *Criterion* has been passing through a crisis from which it has not yet emerged. The crisis was caused by the sudden, unexpected withdrawal of capital by one of the proprietors, and we thought at first that we should be obliged to stop publication immediately. But the January and February numbers, and subsequently the March number, were guaranteed by some generous friends of the *Criterion* and it is now hoped with a certain amount of confidence that the capital will be replaced from other sources and that we shall be able to continue publication. We shall probably be obliged, however, to revert to the old quarterly form, and in this case our next number would not appear until June.

I had hoped to publish your essay before now, but since December I have been faced with the possibility that every number published might be the last, and I have had to change and rechange my editorial plans to try to include as much as possible of the material I had accepted in normal times.

I am hoping that in spite of these unsatisfactory circumstances you will be willing to leave your essay with me. In the event of our stopping publication I would of course have it returned to you at once; but I sincerely hope that this will not be necessary.

With many apologies and all best wishes,

Yours sincerely,
[T. S. Eliot]

1–Mona Wilson (1872–1954) was educated at Newnham College, Cambridge, and became a civil servant (her work took her from the National Insurance Commission to the Ministry of Reconstruction). A close friend of the writer T. Sturge Moore, and a long-time companion to the historian G. M. Young, she published a series of biographical studies on subjects including Sir Philip Sidney and William Blake.

TO *The Editor of* The Church Times

2 March 1928   24 Russell Square, London, W.C.1.

L'ACTION FRANÇAISE

Sir,

Your note following my letter in last week's issue enables me to prevent a possible misunderstanding. I assert merely that Charles Maurras's political philosophy is a reasonable one, and not a gospel of militarism. It is constructed, of course, for France; but it does not require the hegemony of France; it is capable of being applied to other countries, and it is consistent with the peace of Europe.

But I am not concerned to defend the accuracy of all of M. Maurras's information or the wisdom of every one of his views. As for his policy towards Locarno, I could not go into that without expressing my own views, which are of no interest. As for M. Maurras's political judgment in general, I cannot do better than quote the words of Mr Denis Gwynn, who certainly cannot be accused (in his book *The Action Française Condemnation*) of being too favourable in his opinions:– 'There can be few publicists in all Europe who have had their consistent political predictions so literally fulfilled as M. Maurras.'[1]

T. S. Eliot

1–Gwynn replied (*The Church Times*, 9 Mar. 1928, 272–3): 'As Mr Eliot pays me the compliment of quoting my recent book about *L'Action Française* condemnation, as having some authority in his discussion of M. Maurras, may I intervene merely to say that I think he attaches rather too much importance to the sentence which he has quoted? It is obviously true that many of the political prophecies of M. Maurras have been fulfilled. He has constantly preached that democracy meant weak government, while the autocracy of Germany gave the Germans an immense advantage in their rivalry before the war. He showed that the party system in the Republic must paralyse France in time of war, while Germany possessed a single controlling authority. He denounced the tendency of parties before the war to bid against each other for popular support by reducing the period of military service. He proclaimed that the Republic was inherently hostile to the Church, and by its persecution of Catholics was creating internal dissensions while Germany was preparing war. He explained the various weaknesses of the party system, which he regarded as being inevitable in any democratic system; and foretold that international finance must gradually become more powerful than any political party.

'In all these and various other matters it is surely impossible to question Mr Eliot's claim that the political philosophy of Charles Maurras "is a reasonable one". But he is on much more debatable ground when he says that M. Maurras does not aim at, or at least desire, the "hegemony of France", the loss of which he so constantly deplores. As for his claim, that it is "not a gospel of militarism", M. Maurras himself might object to Mr Eliot's statement until a fuller explanation of it was forthcoming. Mr Eliot must have forgotten, among other thoroughly characteristic expressions by M. Maurras, the extremely significant article in which *L'Action Française* newspaper denounced Mgr. Maglione, the Papal Nuncio in Paris, for the few and carefully worded sentences in which he proclaimed, in January, 1927,

TO *Arnold Bennett*   CC

2 March 1928   [*The Monthly Criterion*]

My dear Bennett,

Thank you very much indeed for sending the cheques. I appreciate your kindness. Very many thanks also on behalf of my colleagues. I am sending the cheque to Mr Morley.

                              Sincerely yours,
                              [T. S. Eliot]

TO *Frank Morley*   TS Berg

2 March 1928   *The Monthly Criterion*

Dear Morley,

Bennett coughed up by return of post. He returned two cheques. One is the cheque he had just received from the *Criterion* and not yet cashed, for the February number, amount of eight pounds sixteen shillings, which

---

the gratification of the Holy See at the pacific policy which France's Foreign Minister (M. Briand) has pursued at Locarno.

'Space limitations prevent my quoting the Nuncio's statement here, and I can only refer Mr Eliot to my book for the full text of it, and also of the passionate denunciation which it produced from M. Maurras two days later, after he had given himself a whole day to think over the implications of Mgr. Maglione's speech.

'But one extract from the article in *L'Action Française* must be quoted (the capitals were inserted in the original text): "The dream of peace, as Briand has indicated it, involves in the internal organization of France such a relaxation, such a weakening, such a surrender of the military spirit, the military spirit which IN FRANCE is the true spirit of peace, that those who are unfortunate or miserable enough to follow it would be, in a few years, perhaps in a few months, given over to the spectacle of a new hecatomb. It is not possible to give free rein to such a spirit. We have fought against it in the past; we will fight against it more energetically than ever."

'In face of that quotation, I find it difficult to accept Mr Eliot's statement that the political philosophy of M. Maurras "is consistent with the peace of Europe". And when M. Maurras himself uses capital letters to distinguish the case of France from that of other countries, I am doubtful as to whether he would himself accept generally Mr Eliot's statement that "it is capable of being applied in other countries".

'Even if it were – which would obviously imply a revival of competing armaments among the nations – I wonder, would Mr Eliot regard the prospect with equanimity? Surely it was just this conflict between the pacific policy of the Holy See and the avowedly militarist policy of *L'Action Française* that forced the Pope, in view of converging representations against *L'Action Française*, on various grounds and from various sources, to issue the condemnation a year ago?'

accordingly reduces the amount you have to collect. Please accordingly deduct that amount from the cheque that you send us.

The second cheque herewith – seventeen pounds sixteen shillings. Please cash into your *Criterion* account. It represents payment on the first two instalments of Bennett. Note the signature, E. A. Bennett. Kindly acknowledge receipt.

Yours,
T. S. E.

P.S. What about *The Bookman*?

TO *Orlo Williams*   CC

5 March 1928   [London]

My dear Williams,

Rychner, the Editor of the *Neue Schweizer Rundschau*, knows about you and would be very happy if you would undertake that article, and I send you herewith a circular which seems to be meant for you. I am sure that they would like to have the article as soon as possible.

I say again that I was very sorry to be obliged to cut down your notes on Angioletti practically to nothing.[1] I now perceive that by my so doing the rubric becomes meaningless. What I had in mind was that this number unfortunately, because it was possibly the last number, could not be well arranged and was already very foreign. I had my own note about the French affair, an essay by the Frenchman, then an essay by Quennell about another Frenchman which I had long since promised to print in this number, and finally the story by Linati.[2] So that the casual reader might well say that the *Criterion* deals with nothing but foreign material. I was all the more grateful to you for suggesting that note about Britain. I wish that the note was worthy of the suggestion.

Yours ever,
[T. S. Eliot]

1 – Williams's note, published as the final section of the anonymous 'Commentary' (*MC* 7 [Mar. 1928], 194), reads – under the subtitle 'A New Form of Literary Prize' – 'Public attention in Italy was directed two months ago to a new literary prize, awarded to our contributor, G. B. Angioletti, for his prose book, *Il Giorno del Giudizio*. We offer Mr Angioletti our warmest congratulations.'

2 – The headline contents of *MC* 7 (Mar. 1928) were: TSE, 'The *Action Française*, M. Maurras and Mr Ward'; Charles Maurras, 'Prologue to an Essay on Criticism. II; Peter Quennell, 'Notes on a Reading of Jules Laforgue'; Carlo Linati, 'One of the Claque'.

P.S. Can you tell me anything about two people named Domenico Giordani and Giuseppe Raimondi,[1] both of whom have sent me books inscribed to 'S. T. Elliot'?

TO *Messrs Methuen & Company*   CC

5 March 1928   [London]

Dear Sirs,

I send you herewith my brief preface to the new edition of *The Sacred Wood*. I should be glad if you would let me have proof at your early convenience, and I will not delay the correction.

I have your proof of the text of the new edition. I like the page and the type very much better than the first edition and it seems to me reasonable to sell the book at 7/6d; but of course I leave the price entirely to you. You shall have corrected proof within two days.

Yours faithfully,
[T. S. Eliot]

TO *D. C. J. McSweeney*   CC

5 March 1928   [London]

My dear McSweeney,

Yes, as you say, it is on the cautious side. Do you perhaps not know that your Cardinal Bourne[2] has started a libel action against the XIX century and Dr Longford?[3] Besides I do not really know enough about these other matters and do not want to be bothered with them; I am only playing my own suit.

Let me know a good time before you go to Paris so that I can let you have those letters of introduction.

Yours ever,
[T. S. Eliot]

1 – Williams (6 Mar.): 'Raimondi, who is also the author of the little book entitled *Domenico Giordani*, is one of the Solaria group [Edizioni di Solaria] in Florence.'
2 – Francis Bourne (1861–1935): Roman Catholic Archbishop of Westminster, 1903–35; elevated to the cardinalate, 1911; a traditionalist, he resisted temporising on any doctrine.
3 – See W. W. Longford, 'The Vatican, France and L'Action Française', *The Nineteenth Century and After*, DCIX (Nov. 1927), 611–23; 'The Vatican, France, and L'Action Française', DCXI (Jan. 1928), 1–31; Carrol Romer, 'Apology', DCXVI (June 1928), 721.

I. P. Fassett[1] TO D. C. J. McSweeney

6 March 1928

Dear Sir,

Mr Eliot has asked me to say that he was mistaken in saying that the action was at the instigation of Cardinal Bourne. I enclose a cutting from *The Universe* of March 2nd.[2]

Yours faithfully
[I. P. Fassett]
Secretary

TO I. A. Richards

6 March 1928   [*The Monthly Criterion*]

My dear Richards,

I have asked Ramon Fernandez to send you a copy of his new book on Personality[3] and he tells me that he is doing so. I hope that you will have time to look at it and tell me what you think of it. I am very curious about Fernandez, and I think you are probably the only person in England who is qualified to pass an opinion on him.

I enjoyed my brief visit to Cambridge immensely and I hope that I may come again soon. The next time I shall be better prepared against the

---

1–Irene Pearl Fassett (1900–28), born in Paddington, London, was TSE's invaluable secretary at *The Criterion*.
2–*The Universe* (2 Mar. 1928, 1) reported that the Bishop of Oran (Algiers), Mgr Léon Durand, had issued a writ claiming damages for libel against the Editor and Publisher of *The Nineteenth Century and After* on account of the follow-up to the article by 'a certain Dr W. W. Longford entitled "The Vatican, France and *L'Action Française*"' which was publicly criticised by the Cardinal Archbishop. 'In reply to a letter from Dr Longford asking for substantiation of the criticism, His Eminence wrote that the article "seems largely composed of unfounded statements not corroborated by proof".' The extensive correspondence that ensued was published in the Jan. 1928 issue of the periodical. But as *The Universe* reported too – seemingly not without prejudice – 'The same issue contained a lengthy article by Dr Longford, and at the end of it appeared certain statements highly defamatory to Mgr. Durand.' (Born in 1878, Mgr. Léon Durand studied in Marseilles and at the French Seminary, Rome; and in 1902 took up a place at the Academy of Noble Ecclesiastics. After taking his doctorate in Philosophy, Theology and Canon Law, he was ordained and became successively chaplain at Notre Dame de la Garde at Marseilles, Professor of Dogma and Canon Law at the Grand Seminary, 1913, and military chaplain, 1914. In 1919 he was elevated to the titular See of Hetalonie, thence to the See of Tricomia as auxiliary to the Bishop of Marseilles. He was transferred to Oran in 1920.)
3–Fernandez, *De la Personnalité* (1928).

blandishments of Ogden,[1] and we must insist upon having an opportunity for serious conversation.[2] Alternatively I hope that you and Mrs Richards may decide to settle in London and occasionally visit Cambridge for the benefit of undergraduates.

Yours ever,
[T. S. E.]

TO *Richard Aldington*   CC

6 March 1928   [*The Monthly Criterion*]

My dear Richard,

I am afraid that I am not likely to get over to Paris while you are there. It is unfortunate that we should have just missed each other. But Vivien has just returned to London and so I have no excuse at present for the expense of another visit. It is a great pity that I should not see you there.

I am taking the liberty of giving you three introductions. Use them or not as you like. I like having introductions myself but hate feeling any obligation to present them. You have none.

I will take up the matter of the 'Vie de Bohème' series with Faber and Gwyer but I doubt whether they will look favourably upon it. There does not seem to be much market in this country for French Translations except the market with which you are already in touch. But if anything turns up I will certainly direct it in your way.

With best wishes,
Ever yours affectionately,
[Tom]

1–At the Pepys Feast on 23 Feb., C. K. Ogden (who had been elected a temporary Bye Fellow) sat on one side of TSE.
2–'I knew Eliot pretty well . . . But I always had a difficulty in making him talk about truly serious matters,' said IAR in interview in a later year. 'He preferred not to on the whole . . . He may have had special cronies with whom he could be intimate, but with me he usually dodged it' ('Beginning and Transitions: I. A. Richards Interviewed by Reuben Brower', in *I. A. Richards: Essays in his Honor*, ed. Reuben Brower et al. (1973), 30.

6 March 1928   [*The Monthly Criterion*]

Dear Morley,

Thank you for your letter of the 5th instant. I am sending you herewith for your guidance the *Criterion* estimate. This table shows that the annual expenditure not including any share in overhead or handling expenses, of the quarterly *Criterion*, assuming an edition of one thousand to be printed, would be about £329 x 4 = £1316. The receipts for the year on the average net sale of 550 copies + 200 direct subscriptions (which is about what we always have), total sale 750 copies, would be £137 x 4 = £548. To that would be added whatever could be obtained for advertisements. The net deficit for the year would be, on this estimate, in the neighbourhood of £750.

The actual amount of the sales and subscriptions in 1926 was some £625, and the gross advertisement revenue was over £100. If these figures are maintained, the deficit on the year will be nearer £600 than £750.

If it be supposed that the circulation of the magazine were doubled and the printing order raised to two thousand, the figures would work out as follows:

Expenditure	Receipts	
£351 x 4 = £1404	Sales & Subs £270 x 4 = £1080	
	Advertisements (say)	£124
	Loss on year	£200
£1404		£1404

If the circulation rose to two thousand, and two thousand five hundred were printed:

Expenditure	Receipts	
£362 x 4 = £1448	£360 x 4 =	£1440
Profit £200	Adverts (say)	£208
£1648		£1648

These instances suggest that the paper could be made to pay but in order to reach this point it would be necessary to put in a lot of continuous sales promotion work. So far as Faber and Gwyer are concerned, it would be unremunerative work, at any rate for some time. To be done properly it would I suppose require an expenditure of at least a couple of hundred a year, unless some person were found sufficiently interested in the future of the paper to do this work without remuneration.

As regards the machinery. The paper is owned by *The New Criterion Ltd.* This company has a capital of £1000 ordinary shares, fully paid, the majority of which are held by Faber and Gwyer, and £5000 preference shares 12/- paid, of which Lady Rothermere holds 3500 and Faber and Gwyer 1500. The control belongs to the ordinary shares.

Lady R. could probably be persuaded to part with her shares for a nominal consideration as she has intimated that we can do as we like with the paper so long as she need have nothing more to do with it. Faber and Gwyer accordingly would take over her shares and transfer them to the guarantors in proportion to the amount of their guarantee.[1]

Faber and Gwyer's position is rather difficult. Faber and Gwyer would probably be willing to stand the risk above £750; but if they did that they ought to be allowed the benefit if the expenses are less than £750, especially as they would be making no charge for handling.

Yours sincerely,
[T. S. E.]

TO *Paul Gilson* CC

6 March 1928   [London]

Dear Sir,

I return herewith your translation of 'The Journey of the Magi'. I do not feel competent to criticise it except on a few points:

When I say 'Three trees on the low sky', I mean that three trees are outlined against the sky on the top of a very low hill. I am not sure whether your translation expresses quite that.

Second, you say 'Six mains, près d'une porte ouverte'. What I mean is that the six hands are around a table inside the door and are seen through the door. Your translation seems to me to suggest that the hands were outside of the door.

Third, when I say, a few lines further on in brackets, 'you may say', it is more 'perhaps', or 'pour ainsi dire'. A certain doubt is left.

Finally, as to the last line: in the English text I think it is quite clear to the readers that the speaker of the verses means that he would be glad

---

1–On 8 Sept. 1928 Lady Rothermere – in consideration of the sum of £4. 2s. 6d. – transferred 9,500 Ordinary Shares and 3,500 Preference Shares to Faber & Gwyer.

to die himself. As I read your translation I cannot call it incorrect, but it would seem to me, if I did not know the original, that the speaker would be glad if *somebody else* died. The whole point is that in his state of indecision he would be glad if his own death came to settle it.

I do not know whether it would help the French readers if you informed them that the first five lines which I have enclosed in inverted commas are taken from a sermon on the Nativity preached by Bishop Andrewes before James Ist of England.[1]

Yours very truly,
[T. S. Eliot]

TO *Lincoln Kirstein*[2]

6 March 1928   *The Monthly Criterion*

Dear Mr Kirstein,

Thank you for your thoughtfulness in sending me a copy of Mr Blackmur's essay with your letter of the 11th ultimo.[3] As you say that the essay will appear on the 5th March, that is yesterday, I am not returning to you the essay. I find that I made two or three minor queries on the MS. but as it is impossible for Mr Blackmur to consider them, and as they are so very unimportant, there is no need for me to let you know what they are.

---

1 – Sermon preached before the king on Christmas Day 1622. In 'Lancelot Andrewes' TSE calls the passage one of 'the sentences in which, before extracting all the spiritual meaning of a text, Andrewes forces a concrete presence upon us': 'A cold coming they had of it at this time of the year, just the worst time of the year to take a journey, and specially a long journey in. The ways deep, the weather sharp, the days short, the sun farthest off, *in solstitio brumali*, "the very dead of winter"' (*FLA*, 22–3).

2 – Lincoln Kirstein (1907–96), writer, impresario, connoisseur of art, was born into a wealthy and cultivated Jewish family (his father was chief executive of the Boston department store Filene's). At Harvard he set up, with a contemporary, Varian Fry, the periodical *Hound & Horn: A Harvard Miscellany* – specifically modelling it on *The Criterion* – which ran from 1927 until 1934. Smitten by what he styled 'balletptomaine', he launched in 1933, with his friend M. M. Warburg, the School of American Ballet, and then the American Ballet, which became the resident company of the Metropolitan Opera in New York. In 1946, he founded, with George Balanchine, the Ballet Society, later the New York City Ballet, of which he became General Director, 1946–89. In the 1960s he commissioned and helped to fund the New York State Theater building at the Lincoln Center. He published *Dance: A Short History of Classic Theatrical Dancing* in 1935. See further Martin Duberman, *The Worlds of Lincoln Kirstein* (2007).

3 – Richard Blackmur's article 'T. S. Eliot' appeared in *The Hound & Horn* in two parts: I: 3 (Mar. 1928), 187–213 (poetry); I: 4 (June 1928), 291–319 (criticism).

I find that it is quite impossible for me to bring any critical judgment to bear on any criticism of my own work. The flattery of being discussed at all entirely obscures my judgment. I hope that you will forgive my inability to comment on this most interesting essay.

I hope that you will send me a copy of *The Hound and Horn* in which this appears; indeed I should like to receive it regularly.

With many thanks to Mr Blackmur and yourself,

Believe me,
Yours sincerely,
T. S. Eliot

TO *John Gould Fletcher* TS Arkansas

6 March 1928   Faber & Gwyer Ltd

My dear Fletcher,

Thank you very much for your letter. It is true that I was going to write to you and did not, but I knew that you were leaving London almost at once. It was a great pleasure to me to hear that you liked what you please to call my *lecture* on Whitman and Tennyson: it seemed to me a very poor attempt and I felt that the audience was of my opinion.[1] It was very hastily prepared and was incomplete. It is very difficult to prepare anything for 35 or 40 minutes; it is either too long or too short. I only did it to please Harold and if he was satisfied that is all that is necessary. I am a very poor lecturer. I have had a certain experience and I never improve and I never find it any easier; even this short and badly prepared talk ruined my peace of mind for two or three days beforehand. I will try to take your tip about the mantrams although, as I say, I never speak in public when I can help it; the idea sounds plausible.[2] It reminds me of my own idea for making money: that is, to make gramophone prayer records to be fitted to electrical gramophones to be sold in Thibet. I believe there is plenty of water power in Thibet, so there ought to be no difficulty about the electricity. There should be millions in it.

1–TSE gave a talk on Whitman and Tennyson at the Poetry Bookshop on 1 Mar.
2–Fletcher thought (3 Mar.) TSE's talk 'admirable: far from saying the obvious thing, you said something that was unobvious (I doubt if any of the company had thought of the matter in that light before) and something that really illuminated the whole question of what poetry is, and what poets can do with it.' He offered a remedy for nervousness: 'Learn a mantram, and repeat it to yourself before beginning. It always cools you down. "An old Oxford ox eating oysters" is a good mantram' (*Selected Letters of John Gould Fletcher*, 105).

I don't know on what basis you know yourself to be inferior to me as a critic because you are so careful to write as little criticism as possible.[1] At any rate I have committed myself far more often than you have. I often have very grave doubts about my own merit as a poet, but I console myself with the reminder that I often have doubts about everybody else, and that after all it doesn't matter and that none of us will ever know.

Your invitation is attractive but I find myself too involved to leave London for a couple of weeks at least.[2] In any case let me know as soon as you are back and come to dinner. How delightful to be the only guest in a hotel. I have only had that experience once, but it was a Swiss hotel, and it was Christmas Eve [1925], and I had a large Christmas tree and the complete works of Nietzsche bound in calf all to myself.

Yours ever,
T. S. E.

TO *Archibald MacLeish*   CC

6 March 1928   [London]

Dear MacLeish,

I am sorry that I have had no success with your poem with the Hogarth Press. They seem to be filled up for the next season or two. I am not returning the poem to you until I hear from you because if there is someone else in London you would like to try or like me to try I should be glad to hear from you about it.[3]

There is a possibility of the *Criterion* continuing at least in a quarterly form, and in that case I will let you know so that you may keep it in mind for future contributions.

Yours sincerely,
[T. S. Eliot]

---

1 – Fletcher remarked, 'sometimes I hope that I am not inferior as a poet to you, but always I know myself to be inferior as a critic.'
2 – Fletcher was staying in an otherwise empty hotel in Lyme Regis, Dorset, and urged TSE to come down and spend a little time there.
3 – 'Would you, perhaps, if you have time,' MacLeish asked in an undated reply, 'suggest a publisher & let me write to him to see if he would be willing to look at the thing?'

TO *W. W. Longford*[1]   CC

6 March 1928   [London]

Dear Dr Longford,

   I am very sorry to hear that the Bishop of Oran is making trouble for
you. Please accept my sympathy.[2]

                         Yours very truly,
                         [T. S. Eliot]

TO *Ramon Fernandez*   CC

6 March 1928   [London]

My dear Fernandez,

   I am hoping to see you in England this week but I suppose that you
will be in Paris more or less of the time for the next two months and I am
therefore giving this letter of introduction to you to my great friend and
colleague, Mr Richard Aldington. Mr Aldington, as you probably know,
is a distinguished poet and man of letters and he will be settled for some
time in Paris. I should very much like you to meet him.

                         Yours ever sincerely
                         [T. S. Eliot]

TO *Leonard Woolf*   CC

7 March 1928   [*The Monthly Criterion*]

Dear Leonard,

   I have just received from you for review Sherard Vines's *Movements in
Modern English Poetry and Prose*. I had received a review copy for the
Criterion a couple of days before and have glanced at the book. I am sorry
if I seem cantankerous, but if you don't mind I should very much prefer
not to review this book because he mentions me a good deal in it and it
would be very difficult for me to say anything about it.[3] So I am sending

---

1 – W. W. Longford was vicar of Caversham Rectory, Reading, Berkshire.
2 – Longford replied (7 Mar.): 'To parody an Irish title it is rather a case of Oranmore &
Bourne! I dont think Oran is the responsible person, but I cannot say much at present.'
3 – In the event, *Movements in Modern English Poetry and Prose* was reviewed by HR in
C. 8 (Dec. 1928), 362: 'we need not hesitate to recommend this survey of contemporary
literature as one which is not only up-to-date and impartial, but also full of acute perceptions

the book back to you with apologies. I should be delighted to get anything else you think fit to send me.

I hope to see you soon. Vivien is in London and I should like to bring her to tea with you and Virginia whenever convenient.

Yours ever,
[Tom]

TO *Richard Aldington* TS Texas

8 March 1928   *The Monthly Criterion*

My dear Richard,

Thank [you] for your letter. I wish that you might have been taking your period in London now instead of in Paris. However, that cannot be helped and I hope you will enjoy Paris. I believe that Princess Bassiano is at least an acquaintance of Miss Barney. Incidentally, she is my cousin and an extraordinarily nice woman; and I can recommend you to see her with no doubt whatever. I should like to know Rouveyre.[1]

Even if I had not received your letter of the 7th this morning I should have written to you today. I applaud your pamphlet which you sent me with inscription. It is the best thing that has ever been written about Rémy and certainly the only thing in English. Is it to be a preface to your anthology? I ask because if it is not appearing elsewhere I suggest that it ought to appear in the Hogarth pamphlets; and I believe that I could make them do it. It pleased me extraordinarily.

It is unnecessary to say that if, as I hope, the *Criterion* continues in quarterly form we shall devote a long review to Rémy and yourself; and if possible I will write it myself. You know Gourmont much better than I do and I expect that you will surprise me with innumerable good things that I do not know. After all, I owe a tremendous debt to him. I will certainly

---

and judgments.' HR had urged TSE on 16 Oct.: 'I think that perhaps Sherard Vines's book on all of us, which is so well-intentioned, ought to be mentioned.'

1 – RA had asked on 7 Mar. whether Princess Bassiano was a friend of Natalie Barney's? 'Do you know there is a chance that we may get Rémy [de Gourmont]'s old apartment in the Rue des Saints Peres? Miss Barney and Rouveyre are working on my behalf.' André Rouveyre (1879–1962) was a writer, caricaturist, and graphic artist; friend of Matisse; author of *Le Reclus et le retors, Gourmont et Gide* (Paris, 1927).

try to get Richmond to give it to me, but if I cannot get it from him and if the *Criterion* continues you may count on my doing it in that way.[1]

Ever affectionately,
Tom

TO F. S. Oliver

CC

8 March 1928   [London]

Dear Oliver,

Thank you for your letter of the 3rd which I should have answered sooner, except that I wanted to have the enclosed ready to send you. I think that there is a great deal to be said for your suggestion of the 7/6d price and I am going to chew it over and discuss it with Faber and others.[2] It is obvious that unless we can make an attack on a large public (and it is difficult to do that except with a shilling monthly or at most a half crown quarterly) we should probably do better to squeeze the maximum out of the small public that is really interested. My only question is whether the difference between 5/- and 7/6d will not seriously affect the bookstall sales. I feel that the subscribers who number about two hundred might nearly all be quite willing to pay 7/6d instead of 5/-; but will the people who buy odd numbers at bookstalls or order them from booksellers feel the same way? 7/6d still seems to most people the price of a book and they expect to get a periodical for less. I should like to know how many bookstall sales has the *Quarterly Review*, or any other review that sells for 7/6d.

At the present moment we have with yourself a total of about £400 a year guaranteed, and we need a minimum of £750. I am still hopeful of getting the rest. The enclosures, upon which I should be very grateful for your comments, give some notion of the possibilities. When matters have gone a little farther, I should like very much to come out again and talk things over with you.

With many thanks,
Yours sincerely,
[T. S. Eliot]

1–'I am anxious for you to see this book, for I believe even you, who know Rémy's work so well, will be surprised to see how admirably he comes out in extracts.' He wished TSE would seek to review his sizeable Gourmont anthology for the *TLS*.
2–Oliver wrote: 'if you decide to have a quarterly, let the price be 7/6 (instead of 5/-). This will avoid interfering with the annual subscription to wh. your clients have become accustomed. Nor does 7/6 seem too much for (say) 200–210 pages.'

P.S. Your last paragraph is rather teasing.[1] I wish you would expand it as soon as you can decide what particular sect of obscurantists I ought to attack.

TO *Henri Massis*[2]   CC

9 mars 1928   [*The Monthly Criterion*]

Mon cher ami,

  Merci beaucoup de votre gracieuse lettre. Je vous enverrai d'ici deux jours quelques petits renseignements quoique je le trouve un peu difficile de savoir au juste ce qui conviendra à vos exigences. Vous connaissez peut-être le petit article que Fernandez a consacré à mes ouvrages dans *Messages*.[3] Ces renseignements sont assez exacts puisque c'est moi qui les lui ai fourni. Je vous écrirai lundi.

Toujours votre dévoué
[T. S. E.][4]

TO *Humphrey Whitby*[5]   CC

9 March 1928   [London]

Dear Father Whitby,

  I am so sorry that I was not at home when you called. I am seldom at home in the afternoon, but I am now settled in London again as my wife has returned from abroad; so that I hope I may see you when you have time.

  I had in mind to ask you a question which is nothing to do with anything else. My friend Henri Massis, the Editor of *La Revue Universelle*, asked

1–'You will have to begin thinking about some Provincial Letters; but against what particular sect of obscurantists I can't quite make up my mind.' Oliver was alluding to *Lettres provinciales* (1660), by Blaise Pascal.

2–Henri Massis (1886–1970), right-wing Roman Catholic critic: contributor to *L'Action Française*; co-founder and editor of *La Revue Universelle*: see Biographical Register.

3–'Le classicisme de T. S. Eliot', *Messages: première série* (1926), 216–22 – part 3 of 'Notes sur trois aspects de la pensée moderne' (the other parts were on Freud and Pater).

4–*Translation*: My dear friend, Thank you very much for your gracious letter. I will send you in the next two days some information even though I find it difficult to understand what it is that will meet your requirements. You know perhaps the little article that Fernandez dedicated to my works in *Messages*. This information is quite correct since I myself gave it to him. I will write on Monday. Yours truly as always, [T. S. E.]

5–Vicar of St Mary's Church, Graham Street (now Bourne Street), Sloane Square, London SW1, 1916–46.

me to write for him an article explaining the Prayer Book controversy to the French public. I felt obliged to decline, first from lack of time, second because I did not feel possessed of the technical competence, and finally because I was afraid of fathering my private opinions upon a group of people. Can you suggest the best man to do it? It would have to be someone with ample time to write an article for which the remuneration would be very small. But I think that it [is] worth doing because so far as I know the matter has not been explained in France. The article would have to be simple and elementary of course, as the public in France could not be expected to know the A.B.C. of the matter.

La Revue Universelle is a highly respectable paper of some importance and the circulation, I believe, is over five thousand. It is a fortnightly review.

Yours very sincerely,

[T. S. Eliot]

TO *Leonard Woolf* CC

12 March 1928 [London]

Dear Leonard,

Another suggestion to answer at your leisure: I have just seen a MS verse play by Sturge Moore[1] which seems to me very good of its kind – you know the kind – and certainly worth publishing but which is not at all in our line. I don't suppose the sales would be very large, and it would be in my case too small a book for us to handle. Would you or would the Wellesley[2] be interested? Or is she only concerned with juveniles?

Yours ever,

[Tom]

P.S. Your letter of the 13th just received. Please return MacLeish to me.[3]

1 – A one-act play in rhymed couplets entitled 'Psyche in Hades'.
2 – Dorothy Wellesley.
3 – LW had decided against MacLeish: 'He is intelligent, but he is too much under the influence of Mr T. S. Eliot. I like Mr Eliot from the pure and undefiled source of his own inspiration, and not bottled at second hand with the analysts certificate on the label. I am sorry, but the young must really begin to find some legs of their own to stand on.'

TO *Howard V. O'Brien*[1]   CC

12 March 1928   [London]

Dear Mr O'Brien,

   If I am a myth it is partly your own fault.[2] Why the devil when you
called did you not say exactly who you were. I was, as a matter of fact,
out on both occasions, but if I had know[n] who you were the first time,
I might have been able to arrange a meeting. The failure is partly due to
my confusing you with another gentleman of the same name whom I was
in no hurry to meet. I am very sorry to miss you again this time as I have
heard of you so often from Henry for so many years. Do let me know
at least what are your plans now, when you are likely to be in Paris and
whether there is any chance of your returning to London. If you do return
to London you may count upon my wanting to see you.

                              Sincerely yours,
                              [T. S. Eliot]

Geoffrey Faber[3] TO *A. L. Rowse*   TS Faber

13 March 1928   Faber & Gwyer Ltd

My dear Rowse,

   I meant to have a talk with you about *The Criterion* last weekend; but I
had so much Bursary work to do that it slipped my mind. As I expect you
know the Review has been mainly financed by Lady Rothermere; but at
the end of 1927 she decided to discontinue her support. I can't very well
go into all that in a letter. Enough to say that while she could be legally
compelled to go on, it would be in practice impossible to compel her
to do so. Private announcements were therefore made that *The Monthly
Criterion* would stop with the December number. These caused something
like consternation in the 'inner circle' of letters; and a small contingent
of admirers, including Bruce Richmond, Charles Whibley, Frank Morley,

---

1–Howard Vincent O'Brien (1888–1947), newspaper columnist, critic, and novelist, passed
his entire life in Chicago. A graduate of Yale, he worked for a magazine called *Printers
Ink*, and then founded and edited *Art* magazine. After putting out several novels, in 1928
he became literary editor of the *Chicago Daily News*, where he wrote book reviews and
a regular column called 'Footnotes'. But he became famous for his column 'All Things
Considered', which he launched in 1932 and kept up for the rest of his life.
2–O'Brien had lamented in a letter of 8 March, from Paris, 'I'm afraid you are a myth! This
is my second attack upon you – flanked by my wife – and I find you out both times.'
3–Geoffrey Faber (1889–1961), publisher and poet: see Biographical Register.

Humbert Wolfe and others, provided enough to guarantee the January and February numbers. F. S. Oliver is paying for the March issue. The guarantors have further raised £400 a year for three years – which is rather more than half the amount necessary to maintain *The Criterion* in its old form as a *Quarterly* review for that period.[1]

Faber & Gwyer have spent a good deal of money on the review from first to last, and we are willing to publish and handle it free of charge (so long as there is a deficit), and even to bear some of the deficit ourselves. But we cannot provide the three or four hundred extra a year still required.

It occurred to me that it might be possible to raise something in Oxford, and I wondered if you would be willing or able to help. (Malcolm, by the way, is already one of the guarantors.) There are, I know, few more thankless tasks than the raising of money for such an object as this; and I could not be surprised at your refusing to do it. Nevertheless, knowing that you are an admirer of T. S. E. and of this one gleam of periodical intelligence in the cultural desert of British journalism, I am bold enough to make the suggestion to you. In brief, would you be a collector of guarantees, large or small? The period must be for three years; and the guarantees will almost certainly have to be translated regularly into cash, paid yearly or quarterly in advance.

If you are willing to do this difficult thing, will you communicate with Eliot himself? We (Faber & Gwyer) have nothing to do with the guarantee fund; and I am only writing to you because of our personal relationship.

Yours ever,
Geoffrey C. Faber

1–The guarantors were F. S. Oliver (£250), B. L. Richmond (£25), Charles Whibley (£25), D. O. Malcolm (£10), Marguerite Caetani (£30), Conrad Ormond (£59), Ethel Sands (£10), John Hugh Smith (£25), Alan Lubbock (£25), May Sinclair (£25). (However, on 15 July 1929 Ormond advised FVM that he thought of his contribution as an 'outright payment': 'This has always been my understanding of the position and I am very sorry if in any way I have raised false hopes. Circumstances compel me to stick to my guns, for I should gladly have come into line had my river been flowing with milk and money.')

TO *Charles Whibley*

CC

15 March 1928   [London]

My dear Whibley,

Very many thanks for your kind letter.[1] I am so sorry to hear that you have been ill. As that is the case, I shall not persecute you with a long letter about French politics which I might have written, but will wait to hear from you again in the hope that your news will be better. I am delighted to know that you and Mrs Whibley are going south and hope that you will be able to forget the worries of European politics in the light of southern Italy.

Ever yours affectionately,
[T. S. Eliot]

TO *Richard Cobden-Sanderson*

TS Texas

15 March 1928   *The Monthly Criterion*

Dear Cobden,

I am so sorry about Wednesday. We have had builders in the house redecorating three rooms; at the same time we have had the Practical chimney-sweep; simultaneously we have had the Gas Company to clean the boiler; coincidentally my ex-detective brought in two dozen wallflowers to plant in the garden. Furthermore my wife has been in bed in the one room left us, with influenza. So I hope you will pardon my apparent rudeness.

Will you lunch with me one day next week? Either Tuesday or Friday by preference; or alternatively or preferably both lunch with me on Tuesday *or* Friday and *join us at the Grove on Thursday.*

Please tell Mrs Cobden-Sanderson that I should have written to her but that I have not yet seen any straight Jerboas.

Ever yours,
Thos.

1–CW thanked TSE (8 Mar.) for his introduction to *The Moonstone*; he had been in a nursing home with a 'bad' head, but hoped to set off to Italy 'as soon as I am fit for it'.

TO *William Force Stead*[1]   TS Beinecke

15 March 1928   *The Monthly Criterion*

My dear Stead,

I should have written to you long before, but for domestic preoccupations: my wife is home again, and is ill in bed with influenza, and we have had the gasman and the chimney sweep and the decorators at work painting three rooms, so I have hardly had [any]where to sit down to write. I should have told you that Fr. Underhill[2] asked me to dine with him, and I liked him very much: I have since read a small book on prayer by him,[3] which also I like very much, and I hope to go to see him again soon. Incidentally, I also find I like Whitby more as I know him a little better.

I have also made my first confession, and feel as if I had crossed a very wide and deep river: whether I get much farther or not, I feel very certain that I shall not cross back, and *that* in itself gives one a very extraordinary sense of surrender and gain.[4]

                                ever yours
                                T. S. E.

TO *G. C. Heseltine*[5]   CC

15 March 1928   [London]

Dear Sir,

I hasten to reply to your courteous letter of the 14th instant.[6] The information which you so kindly convey had already reached me but I

1–Willliam Force Stead (1884–1967), poet, critic, diplomat, clergyman: see Biographical Register.
2–Revd Francis Underhill, DD (1878–1943): eminent Anglican priest and author; Warden of Liddon House and priest in charge of Grosvenor Chapel, Mayfair, London, 1925–32; later Dean of Rochester, 1932–7; Bishop of Bath and Wells from 1937. His publications include *The Catholic Faith in Practice* (1918), *Can We Enjoy Religion?* (1926), *Prayer in Modern Life* (1928), and *Christian Life in the Modern World* (1934). He was to become TSE's spiritual counsellor.
3–Either *Prayer in Modern Life* (1928) or *The Life of Prayer in the World* (1923).
4–TSE made his confession on Shrove Tuesday, 20 Feb., before the beginning of Lent.
5–G. C. Heseltine's writings included *William of Wykeham: A Commentary* (1932), *The English Cardinals* (1931), *A Christmas Book: An Anthology for Moderns* (co-ed., 1931).
6–'I have just read with much pleasure your criticism of Mr Leo Ward's pamphlet on the *Action Française*. As a Catholic, I dislike the imputation of dishonesty to Maurras & I dislike Mr Ward's method. My only point in writing to you is to suggest . . . that you should not assume that Catholic writers may not read books on the Index.'

am sorry to say too late for me to modify my article. I am perfectly ready to admit, if the occasion presents, that the Index does not prevent serious Roman Catholic students from reading anything they wish which might be useful to them.[1] I may, however, point out that toward the end of my article I tried to leave open the question of whether Mr Ward had or had not been able to read the texts. I may say privately, and will whenever possible say publicly, that I have not the slightest doubt that Mr Ward has read the texts, because I have received assurances on this point not only from Mr Ward but from others.

I am sorry about *The Journey of the Magi*, especially as I am flattered that you should have cared to include it in your Christmas book. But I consulted my firm with whom I had made a definite contract, and the answer was equally definite.

Yours very truly,
[T. S. Eliot.]

TO *Mario Praz*   CC

16 March 1928   [London]

My dear Praz,

I return to you with compliments your review of Lucas's *Webster* which I wish that I had written myself.[2] I still feel, however, that I intended to pay every compliment to Lucas's scholarship, and if my review suggests any derogation that is a misfortune of phrasing. As a piece of editorship the work seems to me delightful; but as literary criticism the Introduction

---

1–TSE wrote later in the year: 'We should ... draw a distinction between a reasonable censorship and an unreasonable one; and when we say "reasonable", we mean only that it should, right or wrong, be reasoned. The Index of the Roman Church is in this sense reasonable, whether we approve of it or not' ('Commentary', C. 8 [Sept. 1928], 3).

2–Review of F. L. Lucas, *The Complete Works of John Webster*, *English Studies* (Oct. 1928), 146–54. Praz had written on 29 Feb.: 'Now I see what irritated me in your review was the hint that possibly a more learned person might discover omissions and inaccuracies: it implied that you could not well judge this side (after all, the principal one) of the book, but, since your article was unsigned, the reader did not know whether the opinion was given by a professional scholar or by a literary critic. Perhaps the work ought to have been judged only or at least principally by a person who felt sure he could commit himself to a positive statement on that account. That is the trouble of the *T.L.S.* anonymity. I by no means pretend to be a very learned person: but you may feel sure that I did my best to detect flaws in his commentary: I came across only a few: perhaps because Lucas had been helped by Dugdale Sykes ... You will find in my review many hazardous suggestions: I will be very thankful if you will tell me frankly your opinion, which in this case is more authoritative than mine, since you have studied Webster more thoroughly than I have.'

still seems to me lamentable. But you have tackled it from a very different point of view from that from which I wrote for the *Times*. I am sorry if Lucas thinks that I failed to do him justice.

I remain of the opinion that Dugdale Sykes is a much sounder scholar than Lucas.[1]

I am looking forward to hearing your lecture on the 21st March. If you are free for lunch on that day or the day after, please let me know. There is a man here, Isaacs[2] of King's College, who is also an admirer of your work and who hopes to see you.

Yours ever,
[T. S. Eliot]

TO *Richard Aldington*

TS Beinecke

16 March 1928   *The Monthly Criterion*

My dear Richard,

Thank you for your letter of the 10th.[3] Your experience in England with Gourmont is rather like my experience in England with Maurras. The fact is that no one is interested, and if there is to be any interest it must be slowly and painfully fabricated. A paper like the *Nation*[4] is of course no more interested in Gourmont than in Maurras.

Thinking over your letter, perhaps I ought to wait until I have seen your Preface to the Gourmont anthology before I press your Gourmont essay on the Hogarth Press. If I see the Woolfs soon, I am likely to raise the subject of their reprinting your Gourmont essay but I shall refrain from saying that I have consulted you about it. I will merely show them the essay and see what happens.

Candidly, I don't expect that Gourmont, any more than any other serious French writer, will be read with any enthusiasm in England. I have

---

1-H. Dugdale Sykes was author of *Sidelights on Shakespeare* (1919), *Sidelights on Elizabethan Drama* (1924), and other works.

2-Jacob (Jack) Isaacs (1896–1973), Lecturer in English, King's College, London.

3-Many months before, when RA began his anthology, *Rémy de Gourmont: A Modern Man of Letters* (1928), he had offered extracts to LW for *N&A*; but LW had responded that he was not interested in Gourmont. 'I confess, dear Tom, this irritated me intensely.' His Introduction 'is more positively an exposition; my pamphlet was composed in the mistaken belief that there were people in England who knew Gourmont. The experience of delivering it as a lecture at Newcastle and Cambridge undeceived me, and I have written my Introduction on different lines.'

4-*The Nation & Athenaeum*.

been so well disillusioned myself. But if the *Criterion* continues, you may be sure that we will devote a good deal of space to Gourmont when your anthology appears, and indeed I think of making an article about him myself.

I hope that you will see those three people in Paris, and if I can think of any others I will send you letters. I don't suppose you would care to go to see Maurras, but if so I would arrange it. You ought to see Charles du Bos, and if you have no better means of getting at him I should be very happy to send you a letter.

Ever affectionately, and hoping to hear from you frequently from Paris,

Tom

TO *T. Sturge Moore*[1]   Senate House

16 March 1928   [London]

Dear Mr Sturge Moore,

I am very sorry that we have delayed so long in deciding whether *Psyche in Hades* was suitable for us. I am sorry to tell you that the committee has decided that verse plays, no matter by what author, are not suitable for the line which we pursue. Meanwhile I have taken the liberty of mentioning it to my friend Mr Leonard Woolf of the Hogarth Press and he would like very much to see it; especially as it would make the size of book which is more in the line of the Hogarth Press than ours. May I send it to him?

We have some hope that the *Criterion* may continue in quarterly form. It appears impossible to get sufficient guarantees to run it as a monthly, but we have obtained guarantees to the extent of about two thirds of what we need as a quarterly. We could probably continue to run it as a quarterly on a subsidy of £750 a year. When the matter is settled I will let you know so that we may hope to receive contributions from you.

Sincerely yours,

[T. S. Eliot]

1–Thomas Sturge Moore (1870–1944), English poet, playwright, critic, and artist: see Biographical Register.

TO *R. Piccoli*[1]   CC

16 March 1928   [London]

Dear Mr Piccoli,

I must apologise very deeply for not having answered your letter of October 16th. The fact is that almost immediately after your contribution arrived, and ever since, the *Criterion* has been in a state of crisis. Certain support having been suddenly withdrawn, we have been faced with the necessity of seeking fresh support in the form of yearly guarantees from every source possible.[2] It is indeed likely that the *Criterion* may continue as a quarterly, but even that is not yet quite certain. Meanwhile I will hold your MSS. at your disposal, and if the review continues I will let you know, and shall be happy to consider them.

Indeed I remember you very well at Cambridge, and an excursion on the Cam in a punt. If you are ever in England again I hope you will not fail to let me know.

Yours sincerely,
[T. S. Eliot]

TO *Richard Cobden-Sanderson*   TS Texas

19 March 1928   *The Monthly Criterion*

Dear Richard,

I shall with great pleasure expect you here at any time before one o'clock tomorrow morning to lunch with me.

Please tell Sally that Miss Fasset is in communication with the zoo about jerboas.

Yours ever,
Tho[s.]

1–Raffaello Piccoli (1886–1933) was at this time Professor of English Literature at the University of Naples. From 1929 he was to be Professor of Italian at Cambridge University. His publications include *Astrologia Dantesca* (1909), *Benedetto Croce: An Introduction to His Philosophy* (1922), *Italian Humanities: An Inaugural Lecture* (1929), and edited translations of works by Elizabethan dramatists and by Sir Thomas Browne.
2–Piccoli (who had met TSE when punting on the Cam in 1914) had submitted both a translation of an introduction by himself to a new edition of *Hamlet* and a translation of a recent essay by Benedetto Croce on Racine.

TO *Marguerite Caetani*   TS Caetani

19 March 1928   *The Monthly Criterion*

Dear Marguerite,

I regret very much not having written to you before. You may have wondered why you had not heard from me. But since I wrote to you last it was decided that Vivien should come back to London, so we are now in London as usual. I am sorry for this reason, that otherwise I should have been in Paris during this month and should have hoped to see you.

I shall be writing to you more privately before long. This letter is merely to explain my silence and my absence.

After much hesitation I enclose a kind of poem which I have written.[1] If you think it is good enough for *Commerce*, you may use it. If *not*, send it *back*, because I hope to have other poems in the same series which begins with 'Salutation', which you said you liked, within the next few months. So far as *Commerce* is concerned, remember that this poem or the next one which you like well enough to use in *Commerce* is already paid for.[2]

Ever yours affectionately,
Tom

TO *Bruce Richmond*   CC

19 March 1928   [London]

Dear Richmond,

I hate to bother you, especially as you have sent me a number of review books which I am going to review but have not yet been able to review; and more especially as I know how much trouble you have had lately on account of your generous efforts on behalf of the *Criterion*. But this is quite a separate matter and I think you are the person whom I should ask.

I have had in mind for publication a series of cheapish texts of sixteenth century and seventeenth century English theological literature. Faber and Gwyer are favourable and I have only to find the Editor. A name has been suggested: Hutton the Dean of Winchester.[3] I have an impression that

---

1–'Perch' Io non Spero' (part I of *Ash-Wednesday*: 'Because I do not hope to turn again'), *Commerce* 15 (Spring 1928), 5–11. See Schuchard, *Eliot's Dark Angel*, 246–7.
2–Caetani cabled on 29 Mar.: 'Thank you a thousand times splendid poems writing.'
3–William Hutton (1860–1930): Dean of Winchester, 1919–30. A scholar and don, he taught at St John's College, Oxford, 1889–1909 (holding a Fellowship from 1884), and had been University Reader in Indian History, 1913–20; and authored works including *William*

you know him and that he has reviewed for the *Times*. Do you think that he is the best person to edit a series of such cheap texts in seventeenth century theology or not? It is necessary to find someone who has both a general standing among theologians and who has a special knowledge of the seventeenth century. The texts would be intended both for the general public and for such clergymen of scholarly interests who are not able to purchase, and if they purchased would not have time to read, that old library of 'Anglo Catholic Theology'. What I have in mind is a series of selected sermons and essays or books to be sold at about three and sixpence each.

If you would rather say nothing about it I shall not expect to hear from you. If you feel in a position to say whether you think Hutton is the right man with the right scholarship to edit such a series I should be very grateful for a line from you merely to say yes.

Yours ever,
[T. S. E.]

TO *Messrs Methuen & Company* CC

19 March 1928   [London]

Dear Sirs,

In reply to your letter of the 16th instant I am afraid that I cannot accept your point of view and I cannot see that the phrase to which you object is likely to prejudice the sales of Mr Kipling's poetry.[1] No one has

---

Laud (1893), *The English Church from the Accession of Charles I to the Death of Anne (1625–1714)* (1903), *The Age of Revolution: Being an Outline of the History of the Church from 1648 to 1815* (1908), and *Thomas Becket, Archbishop of Canterbury* (1910). Hutton had been suggested by WFS on 8 Feb.: 'He knows the period, and, (what is commercially as important), it is known that he knows the period. He delivered the Bampton Lectures on The English Saints – the first thing of the kind that has been done.

'I gather that Rawlinson thinks that people like Laud, Andrewes & Law would go well because they are known by name even if their writings and sermons are neglected, but he seemed doubtful whether the less known would catch on. The Church of England is strangely neglectful of its past; but if interest could be aroused it would be well worth doing. However, Hutton is the man to consult . . . These people exist to be known and are easy to approach.'

1 – Methuen & Co. – 'the publishers of Mr. Kipling's poetical work' – asked TSE to do them the 'favour' of removing the phrase 'with all its racketing fanfaronade' from this sentence of the preface he had written for the second edition of *The Sacred Wood*: 'If I ask myself, for instance, why I prefer the poetry of Mr. Kipling, with all its racketing fanfaronade, to the poetry of Thomas Hardy, I have to tell myself that it is because the poetry of Kipling seems to me to have a better moral tone.'

a higher admiration for Mr Kipling's work than I have and on the other hand I am fully aware that no word of mine can carry any weight either for or against Mr Kipling's work or can carry any benefit or prejudice to you as his publishers. But as I am anxious to meet you in every way possible I will ask you to omit the whole sentence beginning 'If I ask myself for instance why I prefer the poetry of Mr Kipling' and ending 'better moral tone'. I shall then ask you to omit the phrase in brackets in the next sentence 'to take a comparison on a higher plane'.[1] These omissions ought to be satisfactory to everyone concerned and will, as you say, not impair the sense.

Yours faithfully,
[T. S. Eliot]

TO *Francis Underhill* CC

19 March 1928   [London]

Dear Father Underhill,

Thank you very much. I shall be delighted to come to lunch with you on Monday the 26th at one. I should have been very happy if my wife could come also but she is in bed with a slight attack of influenza and I do not believe that she will be up to going out to lunch within a week. I look forward to seeing you.

Yours very sincerely,
[T. S. E.]

1–In the event, the following sentence was to be kept in the new preface just as TSE had drafted it, albeit there was no longer any other comparison to justify the parenthesis: 'If I ask myself (to take a comparison on a higher plane) why I prefer the poetry of Dante to that of Shakespeare, I should have to say because it seems to me to illustrate a saner attitude towards the mystery of life' (SW, 2nd edn, x).

TO *John Crowe Ransom*[1]   CC

20 March 1928   [London]

Dear Mr Ransom,

Knowing your work so well, I am delighted that the *Criterion* should receive a contribution from you (your letter of the 5th February).[2] It is unfortunately uncertain whether the *Criterion* is to continue, but I hope that you will let me retain your essay a little while and at least show it to some of my colleagues in the hope of our survival. If meanwhile you choose to publish it elsewhere, you have only to let me know.

Sincerely yours,

[T. S. Eliot]

1 – John Crowe Ransom (1888–1974), poet and literary critic, was associated for some while with The Fugitive literary group (with his fellows including Allen Tate and Robert Penn Warren), which espoused the virtues of agrarianism and the conservative south. Educated at Vanderbilt University, Nashville, Tennessee, and at Oxford (where he read classics as a Rhodes Scholar, 1910–13), he taught at Vanderbilt, 1914–37, then at Kenyon College, Ohio, 1937–59, where he set up the Kenyon School of English (an international summer school with visiting faculty including William Empson, Robert Lowell, and Delmore Schwartz) and was editor of *The Kenyon Review*, 1939–59. A reputable poet in his early career – his works included *Chills and Fever* (1924) and *Gentlemen in Bonds* (1927); he was later awarded the Bollingen Prize for Poetry, 1951, and the National Book Award for *Selected Poems* (1963) – he became better known in the 1930s as proponent of the New Criticism. His works include *God without Thunder: An Unorthodox Defense of Orthodoxy* (1930), *The World's Body* (1938), *The New Criticism* (1941). See further *Selected Essays of John Crowe Ransom*, ed. Thomas Daniel Young and John Hindle (1984); *Selected Letters of John Crowe Ransom*, ed. Daniel Young and George Core (1985); Marian Janssen, *The Kenyon Review 1939–1970: A Critical History* (1990); and Thomas Daniel Young, *Gentleman in a Dustcoat* (1976).

In 1946, when the *Sewanee Review* was planning a special issue in honour of Ransom and invited TSE to write on his poetry, TSE owned up to Allen Tate on 1 Nov.: 'I should very much like to help but I am obliged to make the confession that I don't really know Ransom's work well enough to be able to produce such an article. I have a great respect for Ransom as a poet and also as a critic, but I have read very little of his poetry and don't happen to possess any of it' (Princeton).

2 – Ransom sent 'Pictures and Things' – 'a chapter of a book which I have had under way for two or three years now dealing with the general aesthetic problem; in this case with the painter's problem. It takes Leo Stein's recent book, *The A.B.C. of Aesthetics*, as a point of departure but constitutes in no sense a review.'

TO *Johanna Culpin*[1]   CC

20 March 1928   [London]

Dear Aunt Johanna,

It was indeed very nice to hear from you and although I am so long in replying I hope that this letter will reach you at the same address.[2] About that time I went over to Paris and Vivien came back with me to London where she still is. She has been getting on pretty well but the last two weeks has been in bed with influenza, so that apart from my regular work I have not had much time for anything else. I am disappointed that you say nothing about coming back soon to London because I am still looking forward to that dinner at Schmidt's. I did rather imagine what were some of the reasons why you needed to get away from London for a time and I do sympathise with you. I should find it very difficult myself. I am very happy to know that you are able to rest where you are, among congenial society, and I imagine you with plenty of good reading and good music. I envy you being in that beautiful old cathedral town of Ulm, where you have your family. I should like to be able to come and pay you a visit in the spring when the asparagus season begins, and drink some really good Rheinwein with you. It is wonderful to find a spiritual home anywhere, but one finds it, I think, more among simple people than among these complicated sects.

I should love to hear from you again, and I know that Vivien would be very happy to have even a postcard from you. And do give us some hint of when you are likely to come back to London.

Yours ever affectionately,
[Tom]

1 – Johanna Culpin was mother of Karl Culpin, whom TSE had met at Oxford in 1914. Brand Blanshard, another friend, was to recall: 'Culpin was in his final year for a BA in history. He came from a tragically mixed parentage, his father being English, his mother, with whom he lived in England, being German. His own sympathies were British through and through. He wore spectacles for a weakness of sight that kept him for a time out of active service, though he was accepted later, and, like so many other of the best young Oxonians, was killed in France. Culpin was . . . a ready and humorous talker, and a delightful companion' (*T. S. Eliot: Essays from the 'Southern Review'*, ed. James Olney [1988], 31).

2 – Culpin wrote (11 Feb.) from Ulm, Württemberg, that she had found 'a spiritual home' in which to recover, with her 'beloved books', from 'my nervous breakdown and then my separation'. She closed her letter, 'somehow or other, when I meet you, write to you or even think of you I feel Karl so close and near and my heart opens and I always wish in return I could be something to you and Vivien. I hope you have better news of her'; and she signed off with 'much love' from an 'old friend'.

20 March 1928   *The Monthly Criterion*

Dear Stead,

I read your travel diary with great interest and enjoyment. I have no hesitation in saying that it not only seems to me excellent but that it is just the sort of thing which would help to make up a well rounded number of the *Criterion*. I have especially in mind the probability that the *Criterion*, if it survives at all, will almost certainly survive as a quarterly, and I think it will be much easier and much more appropriate to fit in such a thing as an item in a quarterly than in a monthly. For instance, Arnold Bennett's 'Florentine Journal' would have looked much better and been much more in place in a quarterly *Criterion* than in a monthly *Criterion*.

Your essay incidentally seems to me extremely well written.

At the moment I hardly know what to say to you any more than to anyone else. The *Criterion* is extremely unlikely to survive as a monthly and is still likely to survive as a quarterly. But there is so much material on hand which was received on the supposition that the *Criterion* was to continue as a monthly that I cannot consider any new material for more than one or two quarters hence. Now your 'Night on La Verna' seems to me just the sort of thing that ought to go down with a periodical like the *Cornhill*. I do not know the *Cornhill* and therefore cannot do anything in that direction. What I should suggest to you in your own interest is to send a copy of this to the *Cornhill* (which, by the way, pays much better than the *Criterion*) and see what happens. If it is accepted, that is our loss. If you do not publish this thing anywhere else and if the *Criterion* continues, then I can only say that I shall be delighted to use it in the first number possible.

Part of your letter is answered by a letter which I sent you before I received yours.[1] When may I hope to see you again in London?

                Yours ever,
                T. S. E.

1–WFS enquired on 14 Mar. whether TSE had 'found Underhill helpful & sympathetic'.

20 March 1928   *The Monthly Criterion*

My dear McGreevy,

I am sorry to receive your letter of the 16th instant. First, I will write direct to Sturge Moore and ask him what he thinks about it.[1] You will hear from me in due course.

As for Lady Gerald Wellesley, I have seen her once and once is enough.[2] When, however, you have enough poems for a book, please consider Faber and Gwyer Limited as a possibility. I know that Faber and Gwyer cannot entertain the consideration of any books of poems before the 1929 season, but if you cannot get anyone else to do your poems before then, send me the lot and I will see what can be done.

I am not quite clear about your lecture although I have enclosed with yours of the 1st instant what appears to be a synopsis of it. I am not surprised to hear that your admirable note on Gide in the *Criterion* has cut you out of the *N.R.F.*[3] I suggest that you should send me your lecture in the form in which you would print it. If I think it possible, I will try to get the *Revue Universelle,* with which I am on friendly relations, to print it instead. In any case remember that there are many other reviews in Paris besides the *N.R.F.* and believe that I mean all of my suggestions quite seriously.

Ever yours,
T. S. E.

1 – McGreevy lamented that his translation of Valéry's poems, which LW had rejected for the Hogarth Press, was being held at Heinemann. 'I thought wildly that Yeats might ask Sturge Moore to do a prefatory note and that Macmillan's might take it, and have just written but he (Yeats) is so unwell and he mayn't feel like speaking to Sturge Moore.' See TSE's letter to T. Sturge Moore, 28 Mar.

2 – 'Money is an awful business,' wrote McGreevy. 'I made up enough poems for a book and sent it to Leonard Woolf also but Lady Gerald Wellesley wouldn't look at 'em.'

3 – McGreevy's review of four works by Gide, *MC* 7 (Jan. 1928), 65–9. 'The surveillant here thinks I ought to send my lecture to the Nouvelle Revue Française, but I hear Gide is the power there, so tho' I have begun to feel I'd rather like to write it for its own sake I doubt its chances of entry there.' The lecture in question, which McGreevy had sent off to TSE in the form of a single page of TS notes on 1 Mar., discussed the literature of 'the sunset of a civilisation', including work by JJ and TSE. The notes included the following remarks: 'Eliot's preoccupation with idea of rebirth of resurrection more avowed than Joyce's. Shantih Shantih Shantih. Preoccupation with new synthesis. Thomism in early Joyce and late Eliot . . . Eliot's new work less gay than Joyce but imagery more beautiful, more splendid than in his own early work . . . Joyce lyrical, Eliot intellectual, Joyce flighty, Eliot sober, difference between freely thinking Catholic and Thomist Protestant? Both extraordinarily capable of establishing equilibrium between their material and treatment of it, of imposing artistic form on it.'

P.S. I know all about the decades of the rosary but I agree that the casual reader of your poem would need information.[1] I like the poem.

TO *Howard Morris*   TS Lewis Morris

20 March 1928   Faber & Gwyer Ltd

My dear Howard,

Well. Well. Well. I am delighted to hear from you after this long interval.[2] I gather from your letterhead that you have shoved off your partner and are now running the show yourself and am very glad to hear that you have made a success of it. You may not know that I am no longer a banker and am now in the publishing business. I wish I could say that the publishing business had been a healthy one, but the last two years have been very bad for everyone. It is something, however, to say that my firm is still solvent, which is more than all publishers can say.

I am also glad to hear that you have two sons, so far, and hope that you will have many more. I trust that they are to go to Milton and I am sure that they will all supply powerful material for the football team. I was so very sorry not to meet your wife on your first visit to London, and so hope that you will soon be here again.

Being in the business myself, I have never done anything in the book collecting way. Most of the books I own are either presented to me by authors or purchased for professional purposes or obtained by reviewing, and I get rid of them as quickly as I can. You seem to be very much on the spot for first editions which is a subject of which I am entirely ignorant.

---

1 – McGreevy had sent his poem 'St Senan's Well' – 'I make a response to lips I would kiss once / And wonder where tangents finish. / The sunlit circle is small, / The end of a tangent is very far away. // I began my rounds with the sorrowful mysteries / Instead of the joyful, / Ready, therefore, all ready, already / For the without of glory' – along with this note: 'This is about the best of the rhymes you haven't seen. It probably requires a note to say that the decades of the rosary are 15, 5 joyful, 5 sorrowful & 5 glorious in succession.' In the event, Marianne Moore accepted the poem for *Poetry* (Chicago).

2 – Howard Morris (b. 1887), who had been at Milton Academy (est. 1798), Massachusetts, with TSE, wrote to renew contact on 4 Feb. 1928; the two friends had last met at the Carlton Club, London, in the early 1920s. Morris had been stirred to write by seeing TSE mentioned in Forster's *Aspects of the Novel*. He had done very well in the finance business, and now had a wife and two boys: a four-and-a-half-year-old, another aged one-and-a-half. He had 'ease[d] up on work a trifle' and taken up book collecting, and had so far acquired first editions by authors including George Moore, Aldous Huxley, T. F. Powys, Norman Douglas, and H. M. Tomlinson, as well as Cabell and Dreiser. Which authors would TSE recommend?

You might, however, add the name of Wyndham Lewis to your list. Not D. B. Wyndham Lewis but just Wyndham Lewis who is not at all the same person. His first book, *Tarr*, is, I believe, likely to be particularly valuable. It is true that I do now and then talk earnestly to young men of Oxford and Cambridge, but everyone does that.

Dear old George Moore, he is getting a bit weak in the knees now so you'd better pick up everything you can of his because there won't be anything more in a year or two. He is a very nice man and used to be very lecherous, but don't say I said so.

I am glad to hear that you don't have to work so hard now, which I hope will give you a chance to put on a little flesh. If you ever have a panoramic photograph made of yourself, send me a copy to put up on my desk. It will interest you to hear that King Bolo is still going strong, and in fact I had the pleasure of putting the London Bolovian Society on its feet. Mr Frank Morley is President because he is the heaviest weight man here and has a bowler hat; what you call a Derby. Do you remember why the Bolovians wore bowler hats? It was because their monarch wore a silk hat. The Bolovians are still up to their old antics and the Bolovian Society meets once a week for lunch. We lunch until it is time for dinner and then we dine.

Well, no more at present but all best wishes from your comic friend

Tom Eliot

TO *Bonamy Dobrée*   TS Brotherton

20 March 1928   *The Monthly Criterion*

My dear Bomany

By this time you have received *The Moonstone* and I hope that by now you will have digested it and profited by it. I acknowledge receipt of your *Restorationstragoedie*[1] upon which I will report later. I do not understand, however, why you say about it 'this is a mint'.

Re Clarendon, there is no lovely edition of Clarendon to put on your bookshelves and I doubt whether there is likely to be. If you will seriously consider that author, there is no hurry about it but I will do my best to squeeze some standard edition out of the Oxford Press to present you. If the *Criterion* continues, I am positively of the opinion that the author of

1 – BD's *Restoration Tragedy 1660–1720* was to be published in 1929.

the article in the *Times* on George Savile, Marquess of Halifax,[1] should do some equally important work on Edward Hyde, Earl of Clarendon, who, I believe, is a very important and neglected writer, not to be confused with Charles Wood, Viscount Halifax,[2] whom I will deal with myself. <This sentence is rather confused & after lunch.>

I don't know about Ramadan very much but am writing in mid-lent.[3] I am not interested in straight bananas but if you can pick up any straight jerboas I should be very glad if you could bring me a pair.

Yours faithfully,
Tho.

TO *W. T. T. Elliott*   CC

20 March 1928   [London]

Sir,

I must apologise for my delay in replying to your reprint from *The Times* of November 5th 1927. I am much interested in the subject which you discuss and I regret that I did not see the *Times* on that date, otherwise I would have written to you before now.[4] So far as I have been able to discover, there is no connection whatever between the English Eliots (spelt variously Eliot, Aliot, Elyot and Eliott) and the Scotch Elliots. You have probably seen the genealogy of the Eliot family by Walter Graeme Eliot[5]

1 – [BD], 'George Savile, Lord Halifax', *TLS*, no. 1350 (1927), 941–2.
2 – C. L. Wood, 2nd Viscount Halifax (1839–1934): Anglo-Catholic ecumenist: President of the English Church Union, 1868–1919, 1927–34
3 – TSE took a vow of celibacy – possibly for Lent – in Mar. 1928 (Ronald Schuchard, *Eliot's Dark Angel: Intersections of Life and Art* [1999], 157).
4 – W. T. T. Elliott wrote to the editor ('The English Elliots', *The Times*, 5 Nov. 1927, 8): 'Thirty years ago the late Mr George F. S. Elliot published privately a fairly full and very carefully compiled account of the Border Elliots and the family of Minto. Mr Elliot confined the scope of his work to the history of the Elliots of the Scottish Border, and omitted any treatise of English families of the name. Little relating to the latter has ever been printed, but, as the result of many years' research, I have collected extensive material relating to them which is now almost complete so far as families of any importance, and some others, are concerned down to the latter part of the 18th century. Since that date junior branches have been scattered and numerous, and I am anxious to get into touch with members of the family in any parts of the Empire and the United States who possess authentic pedigrees relating to the periods of the 18th and 19th centuries which have hitherto never appeared in print. May I, through your columns, ask any English Elliots who are in possession of such information to write to me? The name is variously spelt Eliot, Elliot, and Elliott.'
5 – Walter Graeme Eliot, *A Sketch of the Eliot Family* (New York: Livingston Middleditch, 1887), traces the history of the family from 1527 to 1887. It may be the book from which TSE derived the name 'Stetson' in *TWL*: Eliot mentions on p. 123 that one of the daughters of Thomas Dawes Eliot married 'Stetson, of New Bedford'.

of which a copy is preserved in the British Museum. Mr Walter Graeme Eliot is my relative.[1] There is every reason to believe that the Eliots of Somerset, Devon, Cornwall and Wiltshire are connected with Eliots who still exist in Normandy; but I have not found any reason for believing that these Eliots are connected with the Elliots or with the Eliotts of Scotland.[2]

I am, I believe, the only representative in England of the Somersetshire branch of the Eliot family, which branch emigrated to America under the Commonwealth.[3]

I should be most interested to hear from you.[4]

Yours faithfully

[T. S. Eliot]

TO *Lady Colefax*[5]   CC

21 March 1928   [London]

Dear Lady Colefax,

I have just realised that I never followed my telegram by a letter. Please forgive me for my apparent rudeness, but I have been very busy and distracted for some days. I was so sorry that I was out of London when your invitation arrived and so could not answer it at once. Since then my wife has been in bed with influenza and my house has been full

1 – Walter Graeme Eliot (b. 1857) was a civil engineer based in New York City, specialising in water and sanitation; a member of the New York State Board of Licensing for Professional Engineers, 1921–30 (Chair, 1925); President of the Technical League of Engineers, 1908–11; founder member of the Society of Municipal Engineers, New York. He was a remote cousin of TSE in line of descent from Andrew Eliot of East Coker.

2 – On 13 May 1954 TSE was to write to Robin Mirrlees (step-nephew of his close friend Hope Mirrlees), who was Rouge Dragon at the College of Arms, London: 'There is certainly no connection between my family and the Elliots or Eliotts, both of whom are Scotch. As for the Elliotts, I remember discussing them with Walter Elliot, and his quoting a Scottish rhyme from which one would gather that Elliotts are any other kind of Eliots who have come down in the world. Why poverty should make people spell their names with more letters remains a mystery.'

3 – Andrew Eliot (1627–1703/4) emigrated from East Coker, Yeovil, Somerset.

4 – W. T. T. Elliott, in 'Elliott Family' – *Notes and Queries*, 157: 8 (24 Aug. 1929), 133 – rehearses the lineage of the Elliotts who are unrelated to the East Coker Eliots.

5 – Lady Colefax, née Sybil Halsey (1874–1950) – 'The Colebox' – salonière and patron of the arts. On 12 Dec. 1917, TSE had participated in a poetry reading (with Edmund Gosse, the Sitwells, and Aldous Huxley) at her house in Onslow Square on behalf of an unknown charity – 'at the house of some rich person for the benefit of something,' as TSE told his mother at the time (*L* I, 240). He had been invited to dine at her subsequent abode, Argyll House in Chelsea, London. In later years, after losing much of her fortune in bad investments, she did well as an interior designer.

of workmen distempering the walls; so that my memory is not what it should be. Please forgive me and accept my expression of regret at being unable to dine with you.

Sincerely yours,
[T. S. Eliot]

TO *Messrs Methuen & Company*   cc

22 March 1928   [London]

Dear Sirs,

Thank you for your letter of the 21st instant.[1] I only desire to have the text as correct as possible. I presume that the edition by Buchler to which you refer is the edition which I have by Buecheler (Berlin. Weidmann. 1904). The text in that edition, page 56, reads as follows:

'ecce autem, ego dum cum ventis litigo, intravit pinacothecam senex canus, exercitati vultus et qui videretur nescio quid magnum promittere, sed cultu non proinde speciosus, ut facile appareret eum ex hac nota litteratum esse, quos odisse divites solent.'

The variant 'literatorum' is given in the gloss.

Perhaps you are referring to another edition? Or a more recent one? I should be glad to know.

Yours faithfully,
[T. S. Eliot]

1–Methuen proposed: 'A further point has arisen in connection with the quotation in Latin which you make from Petronius on the page facing the title page. In this connection we have consulted Buchler's text of Petronius and find that for "et" in the 3rd line he reads "ut" keeping the comma before it, and that for "litteratum" in the 4th line he gives "litteratorum". His edition is not so fully equipped as to make it clear whether these are variant readings of the MS or emendations of his own, but we feel that in both cases they constitute a distinct, if not essential, improvement, and we wonder if you would not prefer to accept them.' TSE won the second point.

TO *E. M. W. Tillyard*   TS King's

22 March 1928   *The Monthly Criterion*

Dear Tillyard,

Thank you very much for your kind letter.[1] It is true that I had often thought of writing a critical book on Elizabethan drama, although the older I get the more ignorant I feel myself to be. If you ever have any suggestions as to what form you would like such a book to take to fill in the gap which you find, your suggestions might be very helpful.[2]

                              With many thanks,
                              Yours sincerely,
                              T. S. Eliot.

TO *W. T. T. Elliott*   CC

22 March 1928   [London]

Dear Sir,

Thank you for your letter of the 21st. I am surprised to hear that Mr Walter Eliot's book cannot be found in the British Museum catalogue. I feel pretty certain that I had the book out and examined it in the British Museum, but that was many years ago. My impression is that it was catalogued under the name of Walter Graeme Eliot.[3] There was a copy in

---

1 – On 21 Mar. Tillyard wrote from Cambridge that he had found TSE's essay on Marlowe's blank verse (*SW*) 'very helpful and suggestive': 'I was having to write a couple of lectures on Marlowe and this essay was the only piece of writing I came across that gave anything more than what a person of average intelligence and taste might find out for himself. In particular your remarks on the *Jew of Malta* were most illuminating and save us from the desperate theory of diverse authorship. I could not help feeling how badly wanted a book was on the Elizabethan drama generally and how much I wished you would write it. You did contemplate it once, did you not?' In fact, TSE had had it in mind at least since 1922 to write a book on 'Elizabethan Drama', and he declared his purpose in the preface to his Clark Lectures in 1926. However, in 1932, when he included 'Four Elizabethan Dramatists (1924)' in *SE*, he made public the fact that he had finally abandoned the intention by adding the subtitle 'A Preface to an Unwritten Book'.

2 – Tillyard replied on 13 Apr., 'I certainly have ideas about the sort of book I feel is wanted though I don't feel at all competent to have them, still less to be airing them to you . . .

'Anyhow what I've long felt (and others have felt too) is that if you could develop and extend what you've already said in the *Sacred Wood* to cover all the more important Elizabethan dramatists you'd be doing us all a very great benefit indeed . . . It's the main lines not the details that matter.

'I had a talk with Richards on the matter. He said he might be seeing you; and if I've been repeating what he said he might be passing on please forgive me.'

3 – TSE's memory was sound: the book is in the British Library at 9919.de.22.

my father's library, but that library was dispersed some years ago and I do not know what became of the book.

I am sorry that I cannot be more helpful. I have no copy of the pedigree. I remember that my family was descended from one Mychel Elyot of Devonshire, and that one of the family married the Heiress of Sigdon in the fourteenth century. The arms of Eliot were quartered with those of Sigdon and were so used by Sir Thomas Elyot of Wiltshire. You could probably get information about the remoter ancestry of this branch of the family from the Earl of St Germans.[1]

Yours faithfully,
[T. S. Eliot]

TO *H. J. C. Grierson*[2]

TS Brotherton

22 March 1928   *The Monthly Criterion*

Dear Professor Grierson,

I have not at all repented of accepting your Milton article; the delay in publication was merely owing to the fact that it was rather difficult to fit in anything of that length, and I had one or two other contributions so long that they had to appear in two or three instalments which I had accepted before yours. But I ought to have written to you before now to explain the present situation of the *Criterion* and give you the option to withdraw your article if you want to publish it elsewhere. Several months

1–Earle Morse Wilbur, in *Thomas Lamb Eliot: 1841–1936* (Portland, Oregon: privately printed, 1937), observed: 'The Eliots are one of the ancient families of England. Their ancestral seat was in Cornwall, and in the fine old Norman parish church of St German's a few miles west of Plymouth, one may to-day see tombstones of nearly forty members of the family; while hard by is Port Eliot, the spacious mansion which, after having once been part of a monastic establishment, has for generations been the family seat' (2). TSE protested in the margin of his copy of the book, 'No! that is the other side of the family.' The Earl of St Germans in Cornwall was created in 1815 for John Eliot, 2nd Baron Eliot. Granville John Eliot (1867–1942) had succeeded as 7th Earl on the death of his first cousin in 1922 . TSE wrote to Robin Mirrlees on 13 May 1954: 'If, as you say, the St. Germans Eliots go back no further than 1500, it seems to me that they and my own family are both quite bogus so far as the arms go, since we both claim them by descent from a certain Walter Eliot who was an M.P. in one of Henry VI's Parliaments. <An earlier Elyot, ancestor of this Walter married the heiress of Sigdon & took a quartering, since abandoned. I am merely giving you some of the mythology of all Eliots.> So if no Eliots have any rights to these arms, I can't quite see the point of my getting Letters Patent. However . . . I shall certainly try to get you to lunch with me again, and you can explain to me why you recommend this course.'
2–H. J. C. Grierson (1866–1960), Regius Professor of Rhetoric and English Literature, University of Edinburgh, 1915–35: see Biographical Register.

ago, Lady Rothermere suddenly withdrew the support which she had given the paper and we have been obliged to look about for other capital. We have gathered promises amounting to about two thirds of the sum needed to run the *Criterion* at least as a quarterly, but we still want two or three hundred pounds more; that is to say in the form of guarantees of so much a year for three years. We have every hope that we shall be able to continue and if so our next number will appear in June; but I cannot make any definite promises.

In the circumstances, therefore, as so much time would still elapse before your 'Milton' appeared in the *Criterion*, if the *Criterion* continues, I think I ought to place the article at your disposal to send to some other periodical. But I want to make it quite clear that I like the essay very much and shall be very disappointed if I see it appear elsewhere.[1]

It is kind of you to invite me to contribute to your series of lectures.[2] I would do so with pleasure and am much honoured by the invitation. The only question is that I do not know at present, and perhaps shall not know for some time to come, whether I shall be in London during August or on holiday. I can only say at the moment that if I were certain to be here I should accept with pleasure, but of course such a reply is, I am sure, too vague to be of any use to you. I hope we may meet again when you are next in London.

Yours very sincerely,
[T. S. Eliot]

TO *H. E. Bates*[3]   cc

23 March 1928   [London]

Dear Sir,

I must apologise for the delay in giving you a decision about your story,

---

1 – 'John Milton', C. 8 (Sept. 1928), 7–26; 8 (Dec. 1928), 240–57.
2 – Grierson invited TSE (18 Mar.) to 'conduct a class in Literary Appreciation for the Board of Education', Oxford, in Aug. Desmond MacCarthy would be giving a class.
3 – H. E. Bates (1905–74), writer. Mentored by Edward Garnett at Jonathan Cape – see Bates's *Edward Garnett: A Personal Portrait* (1950) – he developed into one of the great short-story writers of the century. His many collections include *Day's End* (1928), *The Woman who had Imagination* (1934), *Cut and Come Again* (1935), and – the outcome of his experiences during WW2 as a flight lieutenant in the Royal Air Force – *The Greatest People in the World*, published under the nom de plume 'Flying Officer X' (1942); novels including *The Two Sisters* (1926), *Fair Stood the Wind for France* (1945), *The Jacaranda Tree* (1952), and the nostalgic *The Darling Buds of May* (1958), which was adapted for

'The Fuel Gatherers',[1] but the fact is that owing to the sudden withdrawal of capital by one of the proprietors the *Criterion* has since last December been passing through a grave crisis. It is now hoped with some confidence that the review will continue, but if it does continue it is almost certain to revert to quarterly form; and in that case the next number would appear in June. I am afraid, however, that owing to congestion of material which came into my hands when the *Criterion* was established as a monthly review, it would be impossible to use your story before the autumn. As you say that Cape's are publishing the story in a book in June, it seems as though it would in any case be impossible for it to appear in the *Criterion*. I am very sorry about this confusion and can only hope that if the *Criterion* continues you will soon be able to let me see something else.

Yours faithfully
[T. S. Eliot]

TO *Hugh Macdonald*[2] TS Williamson

25 March 1928 *The Criterion*

Dear Macdonald,

Here is the dialogue, such as it is.[3] You will see that it is preceded by a short preface, but I suggest printing it straight ahead, leaving merely a double spacing between the end of the preface and the beginning of the dialogue.[4] I hope that the dialogue is long enough for your purpose, whatever else it may not be.

––––

television to considerable acclaim in 1991; and other works including *The Modern English Short Story: A Critical Survey* (1950). He was appointed CBE in 1973.

1–TSE had been tipped off about Bates's work by HR on 27 Dec. 1927: 'I think it might be very good.' Bates sent two stories on 1 Jan. 1928 (the other was 'The White Mare', which was used by another periodical). On 22 Mar. Bates wrote again to say that 'The Fuel-Gatherers' was to appear in a volume – *Day's End* (Jonathan Cape, June 1928).

2–Hugh Macdonald (1885–1958), who trained as a solicitor, went into partnership with Frederick Etchells to produce fine editions under the imprint of The Haslewood Books, 1924–31. His own works include *England's Helicon* (1925), *The Phoenix Nest* (1926), *John Dryden: A Bibliography of Early Editions and of Drydenianae* (1939), *On Foot: An Anthology* (1942), *Portraits in Prose* (1946), *Andrew Marvell's Poems* (1952), *Bibliography of Thomas Hobbes* (1952).

3–Macdonald had pressed TSE on 20 Mar. to deliver his Dryden 'Dialogue': they needed at least a month in order to publish in May. 'Can you be influenced by cheques?'

4–'Preface' and 'A Dialogue on Poetic Drama', in *Of Dramatick Poesie: An Essay 1668* by John Dryden (London: Frederick Etchells & Hugh Macdonald, 1928), ix–xxvii.

If any difficult questions arise, do ring me up and come to tea here.

Sincerely yours,

T. S. Eliot

No, cheques make no difference – that is, I do like getting money for what I do, but I hate to do the work after I have had the money and spent it. I am very sorry indeed for the delay, which I believe has been about three years.

I will send you back the Ker in a day or two.

TO *Bruce Richmond*   cc

27 March 1928   [London]

PRIVATE

My dear Richmond,

Please accept my apologies for the delay. I really have not had the courage to write to you until I had sent you officially some review or other. I sent a review of one book last night. I hope that it will do. I have several other books of yours most of which I will deal with, but I cannot conscientiously think that any of them is worth more than half a column.

Many thanks for your valuable information about Hutton.[1] I will wait to hear Murray's opinion.[2] I should think that he would be as competent a person as any to decide on the right man: I am much interested in the idea and if Murray were sufficiently interested, and willing to see me, I should find it much more satisfactory to talk the matter over with him, explain what I have in view, and accept his advice. Perhaps you would convey this message to him?

I tried to ring you up some days ago after seeing Morley. Morley showed me the letter from Hugh Smith[3] and I said that I would ring you up and acknowledge it and thank you for your trouble.

1 – BLR wrote on 20 Mar., in response to TSE's enquiry, that William Hutton 'has reviewed for us for many years; he really knows the period . . . But he is getting old; and he is, I think, getting lazy. He still reviews for us; but it is now rather slapdash . . . I think you ought to be able to get someone better. D. L. Murray would probably know the man.' Murray (1888–1962) worked for the *TLS* from 1920 and became editor, 1937–45, in succession to BLR. From the late 1920s he was a popular historical novelist.

2 – Murray, who took an interest in theological issues – his works include *Reservation: Its Purposes and Methods* (1923) – was to advise TSE on 12 June that he thought Duncan-Jones 'your best man, because (1) he has written on Laud (2) his admirable Hulsean Lectures, *Ordered Liberty*, are built up on a study of Laud, Bramhall, Hooker and the rest.' Failing him, the Dean of Winchester, or Canon Sparrow Simpson, or Canon Ollard.

3 – John Hugh Smith (b. 1881), English banker; close friend of Edith Wharton.

Whenever you have leisure, I should like to see you soon and talk over ways and means. We are still a short distance from having the funds that we need. You have already done so much yourself that I should not dream of asking you to tackle anyone else, but I think that it would be helpful if I could discuss with you what more may be done.

Someone has just suggested to me that Sir Charles C. Wakefield who is a former Lord Mayor might subscribe.[1] I don't know why he should, but if you know anything about him I should be glad of the information. He was, as a matter of fact, a friend of my wife's family – my father-in-law painted his portrait – but I don't consider this sufficient claim upon him in itself.

Yours sincerely,
[T. S. E.]

TO *Sally Cobden Sanderson*   cc

27 March 1928   [London]

Dear Sally,

I enclose herewith, for what it is worth, the introduction from my mother for your brother to Albert Perkins of St Louis, Mo. My mother forgot to put Mr Perkins's address but I have just discovered it in the American *Who's Who*. I believe that the said Perkins is a wealthy and important railway magnate. He was born in 1865. I may mention that I remember him as an old family friend who wanted to marry one of my sisters. He subsequently married one of her friends.[2]

Mr Perkins ought to be the sort of person who would know all of the Society in St Louis for what it is worth.

1–Mark Wardle suggested to TSE (undated) the name of Sir Charles Wakefield, so long as he was 'promised a little publicity . . . He loves subscribing, but loathes anonymity.' Charles Cheers Wakefield (1859–1941) was an oil industrialist: the firm he nurtured, C. C. Wakefield & Co., dealt in lubricating oil and equipment, and by 1912 he was marketing Wakefield Motor Oil. His Castrol range of lubricants, developed by his own scientists, reaped tremendous profits and prestige. The dividends and salary he received between the world wars added up to over £3 million. Married but childless, he became a lavish philanthropist, assisting causes including the Guildhall Library and Art Gallery, the Mental Aftercare Association, the National Children's Home and Orphanage, and the British Museum. He was Mayor of London, 1915–16, received a baronetcy in 1917, and was created Baron Wakefield in 1930, becoming Viscount Wakefield in 1934.
2–Albert T. Perkins, of St Louis Missouri, was co-owner of the Marshall and East Texas Railway Company, chartered in 1908 to acquire the Texas Southern Railway Company; he was associated too with the St Louis Union Trust Company.

In explanation of the letter I may tell you that my mother is eighty six and extremely feeble, so that the letter is not quite so coherent and intelligible as most letters of the sort; but I do think that it is an introduction which might be useful and pleasant.

I hope to see you on Saturday.

Yours ever,
[T. S. E.]

TO *Messrs Methuen & Company*   CC

27 March 1928   [London]

Dear Sirs,

I have your letter of the 26th instant.[1] I agree to your *ut* and trust that you will agree with me that on the other point it is better to stick to the Buecheler edition of 1904.

Yours faithfully,
[T. S. Eliot]

TO *Kenneth Ingram*[2]   CC

27 March 1928   [London]

Sir,

I have undertaken on behalf of my French friend Henri Massis, the Editor of *La Revue Universelle*, to find the suitable person in England to write an article for his review on the Prayer Book crisis in England.

La Revue Universelle is a serious fortnightly review with, I believe, a circulation of considerably over five thousand. I imagine that its public is very largely Catholic, and certainly must represent a considerable part of the more intelligent conservative and reactionary opinion in France. I imagine that, like most French reviews, its fees are almost negligible when

1 – Methuen had returned: 'The edition of Petronius which I looked up was the only one I happened to have, Buecheler's edition of 1882, published in Berlin by Weidmann. That edition has "ut", and I think you will agree that this is better than "et". On the other point I do not think that anyone can feel very strongly. My edition has "literatorum" in the text and "literatum" as a variant. I think we might as well follow your 1904 edition and print the variant (with or without the double T).'
2 – Kenneth Ingram (1882–1965), author, founded and edited *Green Quarterly* (The Society of SS Peter & Paul, Ltd, Westminster House, London) in 1924. His works include *Why I Believe* (1928) and *Has the Church Failed?* (1929).

translated into sterling. The only reason for anyone's writing such an article for a French review is that it would instruct French opinion. There has appeared a certain amount of information in French periodicals lately concerning the affairs of the English Church but a good deal of it has, I believe, been produced either by Frenchmen who cannot understand the affair or by rather ill-informed English correspondents. Being in close relations with *La Revue Universelle*, I am anxious for them to have a statement from the correct point of view.

An article of anything up to four or five thousand words is what the review wants, and it would of course be written in English and translated in Paris.

If you were willing to consider undertaking such a task, I should consider that I had acquitted my undertaking toward my French friends. If you hesitate about it, I should be very pleased to give you any further assistance or information within my power. I am writing to you at the suggestion of Father Child, who has furnished me with your address.

Yours faithfully,
[T. S. Eliot]

TO *T. Sturge Moore*   Senate House

28 March 1928   [London]

Dear Mr Sturge Moore,

I am taking the liberty of writing to you about a young and promising friend of mine, Mr Thomas McGreevy. Tom McGreevy is, as his name suggests, an Irishman. He came to me originally with an introduction from Yeats; he has written some good poems in the Irish manner, one or two of which I have published in the *Criterion*, and he has also done some excellent reviewing for me and I have got him a certain amount of reviewing for the *Times* and the *Nation* where he appears to have given satisfaction. He is now lecturer at the Ecole Normale in Paris, by appointment from Trinity College Dublin.

He has done some translations of Valéry which have been approved by various people and he has been in direct contact with Valéry himself and with Monod[1] about them. He is very anxious to get them published in this country and there is a possibility that Heinemann might undertake publication; but Heinemann want to get a Preface by someone of standing

1 – Julien-Pierre Monod was a cousin of T. Sturge Moore.

in England. McGreevy is very anxious to approach you on the subject of writing a short Preface, so I told him that I would write to you first and see whether you might be influenced to do it. If I hear from you at all favourably I will tell McGreevy to send you the translations to read; you will not of course be engaged in any way until you have read and approved the translations; and it will be enough at that point if you will drop me a line to say whether you consider the translations good enough to be approved by a short Preface by yourself. I know that McGreevy would set great store by a Preface from you, and if you think well enough of his translations to give the support of your name I should feel very happy about it. But I have not yet examined these translations myself and it is a question entirely open whether you will find them good enough to be willing to do this. May I tell McGreevy to send you a copy of his translation?[1]

It was a great pleasure to see you the other day and I hope that I may soon have the benefit of a more private talk with you.

Sincerely yours,
[T. S. Eliot]

TO *D. C. J. McSweeney* CC

28 March 1928 [London]

Dear McSweeney,

I have given away one copy of *La Trahison des Clercs* and have lent another copy, but as soon as I get the latter back I will send it to you.[2]

I do not think that it is worth your spending twelve francs on, but if and whenever you want French books I recommend you to write to my friend Mademoiselle Adrienne Monnier, 7 rue de l'Odéon, Paris (VI), mentioning my name, and she will probably send any books you want promptly and on account.

---

1 – Sturge Moore replied (29 Mar.): 'I shall be very pleased to see Mr McGreevy's translations after Valéry and will do the best I can for him, though I can promise nothing till I have seen them.'

2 – McSweeney wrote on 24 Mar.: 'I wonder if you could lend me a copy of *La Trahison des clercs* which I am still unable to get from booksellers? It occurred to me that Benda wrote the book round an idea which is important and just – one that as an Irishman (& the Irish are a fractious people), I appreciate – but that he disfigured it because he propounded it by means of a machinery (if I may say so) which derived from his prejudices and not from his idea. And this suspicion of mine I should like to test from the book.'

I don't know whether you ever read *Times Literary Supplement*, but there was a review of Benda's book in that periodical which seems to me quite satisfactory.[1] It seems to me satisfactory because I wrote it myself.

Yours ever,

[T. S. E.]

TO *W. T. T. Elliott*   CC

28 March 1928   [London]

Dear Sir,

Thank you for your letter of the 24th instant. I am very sorry to appear so incompetent but I must confess that I do not know Mr Walter Graeme Eliot personally and cannot introduce you to him. Even in America some relatives are so remote that one does not know them personally. But I find from the American *Who's Who* that his address is 1, West 54th Street, New York City, N.Y. In his biography in the American *Who's Who* his genealogy of the Eliot family is dated 1889.

But if you do not succeed in getting into touch with Mr W. G. Eliot, I suggest again that you might get information from the Earl of St Germans, as I know that his predecessor assisted Mr W. G. Eliot in the compilation of the book which I have mentioned.

I am very sorry that I cannot be more helpful. I shall continue to be interested in any discoveries you may make.

Yours faithfully,

[T. S. Eliot]

TO *Thomas McGreevy*   TS TCD

29 March 1928   *The Monthly Criterion*

My dear McGreevy,

I am very glad indeed to hear your good news and hasten to congratulate you. It is more of a compliment to you than if Trinity had merely continued your appointment.[2] All my congratulations and expressions of personal pleasure.

1 – 'Culture and Anarchy', *TLS*, 23 Feb. 1928, 118.
2 – McGreevy wrote (25 Mar.) that, in response to the express request of the Director of the École Normale, the Ministry of Education had agreed to allow him to stay in post in Paris.

Sincerely yours,
T. S. Eliot

I have written to Sturge Moore.

TO *Hugh Macdonald*   TS Williamson

30 March 1928   *The Criterion*

Dear Macdonald,

Thank you very much for your letter of the 28th and Cheque for £20. It is extremely good of you (and a reproach to me) to pay up in 24 hours after waiting 3 years. I am exceedingly pleased to know that the Dialogue seems to you suitable.[1] I hope that the sales will justify your enterprise. I am ready to sign the 55 copies whenever you send them.[2] I suppose I may have 6 copies of the plain edition for myself?

I hope to see you again soon.

Yours sincerely,
T. S. Eliot

I wonder if you couldn't get rid of some copies <sheets> to an American Publisher? I should think that Rudge, or Payson and Clark, or Harcourt Brace might be interested. You could pay me the usual sort of diminished royalty on sale of sheets to America.

TO *Kenneth Ingram*   CC

3 April 1928   [London]

Dear Mr Ingram,

I am very glad to hear that you are able to undertake the article, and am sure that the Editors of *La Revue Universelle* will be highly pleased to know that you are doing it. I quite agree with you that it would be better to wait a few weeks, and have written to Henri Massis to explain.[3] I am

---

1 – Macdonald was 'very glad indeed that you thought of writing in this form instead of that of the usual introduction' (28 Mar.)

2 – Macdonald had asked (27 Feb.) whether TSE would be willing to autograph 45 copies of the edition printed on hand-made paper.

3 – Ingram advised (28 Mar.): 'Within the next month the fate of the Prayer Book will probably be decided one way or the other, and anything which is written now will be a very incomplete account.'

sure that he will agree. I shall look forward with great interest to reading your article myself.[1]

Yours sincerely,
[T. S. Eliot]

TO *Edouard Roditi*[2]   TS UCLA

4 April 1928   *The Monthly Criterion*

Dear Sir,

I have your letter of March 29th.[3] It is, I am sorry to say, quite true that I have translated *Anabase* by St-John Perse.[4] My translation was completed about a year ago, and would have been published immediately but that I have been waiting all this time to hear if Monsieur Leger had any corrections to make. As you may know he is an extraordinarily busy man, and I dare say not very business-like about his private affairs, and I have been unable to get him to give the time to it. But in the normal course of events my translation would certainly have been published a year ago. I am very sorry indeed to hear that you have had all this trouble for nothing. But it is not the first case that I have known of two people translating an author independently and not discovering each other till the last minute.

I have not made any arrangements whatever for translating any other of Monsieur Leger's works, and so far as I am concerned I would not stand

1 – See Ingram, 'L'affaire du Prayer-Book et l'Église Anglicane', *Revue Universelle* 32 (1928), 554–64.

2 – Edouard Roditi (1910–92), poet, critic, biographer, translator, essayist: see Biographical Register.

3 – The 18-year-old Roditi wrote from Paris (29 Mar.) that he had been engaged since Jan. 'in translating Anabase, by St-John Perse, into English, hoping thereby to make my literary début. When, having finished this translation about ten days ago, I entered into communication with the author, I was much surprised and, naturally, disappointed though flattered to hear that you yourself were translating this same poem, and were thus . . . my rival.

'Miss Sylvia Beach, Mlle Adrienne Monnier and Pierre de Lanux all three of whom were kind enough to take a certain interest in my efforts at a translation, have advised me to write to you so as to find out whether you also intended to translate "La Gloire des Rois" by the same author, and which I have also already translated.

'Should you intend this, I would be much obliged if you would kindly inform me, in which case I would immediately relinquish all further competition, if such it can be called, with your superior experience and talent – thus also avoiding a second disappointment of this sort.'

4 – St-John Perse, pen name of Alexis St Leger Leger (1887–1995), poet and diplomat: see Biographical Register.

in your way if you wished to do so yourself. I would suggest however that you might be well advised to communicate with the author first, in order to be sure that the same difficulty does not arise again with some unknown third translator.

I should of course be very much interested to see your translation, though perhaps it would be wiser for me to wait until my own is in type.

With many regrets and all good wishes,

Sincerely yours,

T. S. Eliot

TO *Antonio Marichalar*   TS Real Academia de la Historia

4 April 1928   *The Monthly Criterion*

Mon cher Ami,

Quoique je savais bien d'après vos lettres que votre mère n'avait pas grande chance de vivre longtemps, je suis désolé d'apprendre vos nouvelles.[1] J'ai été pendant l'hiver passé à peut près de la même situation: ma mère, qui habite Boston et qui a quatre-vingt-six ans, est très faible, et on avait à un certain moment désésperé de sa vie. En tout cas elle ne peut guère survivre l'hiver prochain.

Reçevez mon cher ami l'expression de ma sympathie.

Quant au *Criterion*, nous ne sommes pas encore décidés, mais il est probable que désormais il paraîtra triemestriellement à partir du mois de Juin. Je vous donnerai plus tard des renseignements plus précis. Je peux éclaircir le problème de l'article dans *The Times* dont vous parlez.[2] C'est notre ami et collaborateur, F. S. Flint, qui l'a écrit. Si vous voulez bien lui écrire je sais qu'il sera bien reconnaissante. Son adresse est: 11 Buckland Crescent, Swiss Cottage, London N.W.8.

Croyez moi toujours en tout sympathie votre dévoué.

[T. S. Eliot][3]

1 – Marichalar wrote on 27 Mar. that his mother had died on 3 Jan.
2 – Marichalar wanted to know the identity of the author of the review 'Paul Valéry' – on *Hommage des écrivains étrangers à Valéry* – in *TLS*, 22 Mar. 1928, 216.
3 – *Translation*: My dear Friend, Although I knew from your letters that your mother had not much longer to live, I am very sorry to learn your news. Last winter, I found myself almost in the same situation: my mother, who lives in Boston and is eighty-six, is very weak, and at one point her life was despaired of. In any case, she is unlikely to survive next winter.
 Dear friend, please allow me to express my sympathy.
 As regards *The Criterion*, we haven't yet made up our minds, but it will probably be published as a quarterly from June onwards. I will send you more definite information later.

TO *Thomas McGreevy* TS TCD

4 April 1928 *The Monthly Criterion*

Dear McGreevy,

I am just dropping you this line to say that I have spoken to Sturge Moore who of course cannot promise to do the Introduction until he has seen your translation, but who is very willing in principle, and asks me to tell you to send on a copy of the translation to him to read.[1] His address is: 40 Well Walk, Hampstead, N.W.3.

Yours in haste,
T. S. Eliot

TO *Marguerite Caetani* CC

4 April 1928 [London]

Dear Marguerite,

I am very happy to know that you like the poem, and if you intend to use it I will ask you to make one small alteration at once. At the beginning of each of the last two lines please alter the words 'be with' to 'pray for'.[2] One might as well stick to the exact quotation.

I shall be writing to you shortly about another matter, but meanwhile as you have mentioned Leger, and intimate that you may see him, do you think that you could stir him up once more about *Anabase*? Everyone is grumbling about it here, and it would be a great satisfaction if we could get it done. All he was asked to do was to send back the contract form so that we could alter it to suit him in the sense of limiting our copyright to a maximum of 2,000 copies in one edition. I also of course wanted him to send back the copy of the translation which he has in his hands with his comments, as I should not like to publish the translation without having his detailed approval.

I can enlighten you about *The Times* article you mention. It was written by our friend and collaborator, F. S. Flint. If you care to write to him, I know he will appreciate it. His address is 11 Buckland Crescent, Swiss Cottage, London N.W.8.

With warmest regards, [T. S. Eliot]

1 – McGreevy would report to TSE on 23 Apr.: 'I'm afraid Sturge Moore was one of my bad ideas. He wrote a week ago, at great length, returned my translation and had not one good word to say for it. Also he said he wrote to Monod to explain why he couldn't write the introduction, which seemed to me gratuitous.'

2 – 'Pray for us sinners now and at the hour of our death / Pray for us now and at the hour of our death.'

I think Tomlinson is quite good enough and I will try to get hold of him. He is a difficult person to get anything out of, but I saw him a couple of weeks ago, and may be able to speak to him about it.

Yours ever affectionately,
[Tom]

TO *Ezra Pound*　　　　　　　　　　　　　　TS Beinecke

10 April 1928　　　　　　　*The Monthly Criterion*

Dear Eza:

Very Well, if you and D. both prefer notes, will se what can be Done, and let you know. Promise nothing at Preseant.

Question how much to give out in notes e.g. Benett. Nimmim.

Agreed that order is to remain same, and my inculsions to be in form of Appendix, omissions to the Mentioned in Preface.

Note that can get A.L.S. from Flint and Mrs S.

Complete Bilblio. certainly of Poems Only. Should be glad of Pages torn of This Quarter.

What do I know about the deaths dates of Leope de Vega Dates death birth & marriage: if that to go in please furnish Copy Immediately.

Other Notes noted.

What about Criterium dand if I know will let you know when I know.

yrs. etc.
T. S. E.

Yes you Bet any Number of Other deths. WOT the WORD unable to Speak a Word?[1] Infans Natus? Wot about it?

TO *William Force Stead*　　　　　　　　　TS Beinecke

10 April 1928　　　　　　　*The Monthly Criterion*

My dear Stead,

It was very good to have such a good and helpful letter from you at this season. If Easter is a season of hope, it is also a season when one wants to be given hope. First about practical matters, I should have written to you before. I am afraid that the present publication of La Verna settles the matter. I can only say that the five pounds or so that you would eventually

---

1 – 'The word within a word, unable to speak a word' (*Gerontion*, l. 17).

have received from the *Criterion* would have been nothing to what you have received from the American review.[1] When our contributors have a chance of selling the same thing in America, I never want to stand in their way; if simultaneous publication can be arranged, so much the better for us. But I hope that there will be other fragments from the volume in which La Verna will appear, which you may offer to us (if we continue to exist) if and when you do not care to bother to send them to America. With the *Dial*, I can usually arrange; and I could probably get something of yours there if you wished; but there are many other American periodicals which pay better than the *Dial*.

About the rest of your letter, I had rather have an hour of talk with you than an infinity of correspondence. I wholly agree. I do not expect myself to make great progress at present, only to 'keep my soul alive' by prayer and regular devotions. Whether I shall get farther, I do not know. I know that you will, and that you will certainly go far beyond me. I do not know whether my circumstances excuse my going no farther or not. This is a matter which is more for conversation, when and whenever we can meet, than for correspondence.

I like Fr Underhill very much; but I feel that Whitby,[2] when I can see him, is more in my line. I feel that I need the most severe, as Underhill would say, the most Latin, kind of discipline, Ignatian or other. It is a question of compensation. I feel that nothing could be too ascetic, too violent, for my own needs.[3]

1 – WFS had reported on 25 Mar. that the *Virginia Quarterly Review* had accepted his travel piece 'A Night on La Verna', and had paid $95 for it.
2 – Fr Humphrey Whitby, St Mary's Church.
3 – WFS had written on Easter Day: 'Sometime when you have an hour to spare I should like to hear of your experiences with Fr Underhill. I am going to look out for a Spiritual Guide among the Cowley Fathers in Oxford; my life is too chaotic and while ultimately one's progress in the interior life depends upon one's own power of concentration – and of course upon one's will power – I think that actual guidance should come from without, if only to eliminate the danger of self-indulgence, on the one hand, and of morbid over-scrupulousness on the other. Also there is the question of technique, which is as important in the art of "living more abundantly", as in the arts of music and poetry. And technique to some extent can be taught, though the music can only come from within – but the music that is within, is useless, without the technique to bring it forth: and so, that we may have life, and that we may "have it more abundantly", which is the real purpose of Christianity, we must learn the technique by which this life can express itself and emerge into actual living. – Don't you think so?

'I am wondering whether I can hope to make much progress while continuing to suck in the delirious dope of cigarettes – and forgive me if I wonder whether the same is true of you. It would take a terrific and sustained effort of will to give them up permanently, and it would involve a nervous strain amounting to the pains of hell – because that is what hell means: living for the body until the body decays and the soul is left craving what it cannot

When can I see you again?

In confidence,
yours ever,
T. S. E.

TO *René Taupin*[1]   MS Valerie Eliot

12 April 1928   *The Monthly Criterion*

Dear Sir,

Thank you for your letter of March 30th.[2] I am interested to hear of
the work which you are undertaking. I can only give you the following
facts. I came across the work of Jules Laforgue in 1908, and from that
time on for several years was very much under the influence of that poet.
I was already familiar with the work of Baudelaire. I did not think that
my friend Pound became aware of Laforgue until some years later, and
in any case there is no trace of that influence on any of Pound's work.
Of course I cannot say to what causes was due the influence of this type
of French poetry in America; I can only speak for myself. I am rather
doubtful whether there is much direct influence by Laforgue on any of the
poets now writing in America. As for Rimbaud, I did not myself study the
work of Rimbaud seriously until some years later, and I cannot say that
that poet has ever had very much influence on myself. I have indeed been
very much more affected by Tristan Corbière.[3]

---

satisfy. Buddhism gets that far by aiming at a Nirvana in which craving has been killed. But
Christianity not only goes this far, but further – dead, but alive in Christ – Nirvana, and
beyond – where our lives are hid with Christ in God. That is our Resurrection. Buddha and
Christ are parallel up to and including the Transfiguration: from there Christ descended into
the dark night of Calvary, and emerged far ahead of Buddha in the first Easter Morning. It
is a long journey – and I am still faced with a long day's march before I even reach Nirvana
– We must meet and talk.'

1–René Taupin (1905–1981), French translator and critic who moved in the 1920s to the
USA, where he was lecturing in Romance Languages, Columbia University, New York.
A friend of Louis Zukofsky, and correspondent of EP, he was author of *L'Influence du
symbolisme français sur la poésie américaine, de 1910 à 1920* (1929): *The Influence of
French Symbolism on Modern American Poetry* (rev. edn 1981).

2–Taupin asked whether the influence of Laforgue and de Gourmont was brought to
prominence on account of EP, or had TSE discovered Laforgue and Rimbaud for himself?

3–E. J. H. Greene, when undertaking research for his book *T. S. Eliot et la France* (Paris,
1951), remarked to TSE on 13 June 1947, inter alia: 'According to René Taupin you have
said in a letter that you "read Rimbaud much later (i.e. than Laforgue) and (were) hardly
influenced by him . . . ", If my memory does not deceive me, you told me in 1939 that
Rimbaud was "an influence which grew".' TSE responded to Greene on 30 June 1947: 'I do

I reply to your letter with some hesitation, and you will understand that I can only speak for myself and that I am ignorant of the influences on contemporary American poetry, which is a subject in which I am not instructed.[1]

Yours very truly,

T. S. Eliot

TO *William S. Knickerbocker*[2]   CC

12 April 1928   [*The Monthly Criterion*]

Dear Sir,

I am sorry that my allusion to Matthew Arnold at the beginning of *The Sacred Wood* misled you.[3] I was referring only to verbal and unspoken comments and not to anything that I had written; I am afraid that there is nothing in print to which I can point as an expression of my earlier opinion.

I will take note that you want to subscribe to *The Criterion*, and you will hear from us as soon as the reorganisation of the paper is completed. With many thanks.

Yours sincerely

[T. S. Eliot]

---

not know what I said to Taupin as that was so many years ago. My present impression is that I read a good deal of Rimbaud within the same year in which I made the acquaintance of Laforgue. At that time, however, from perhaps 1908 until 1912 I was so much under the influence of Laforgue that Rimbaud could have made only a slighter impression. In subsequent years however I have certainly reread Rimbaud as well as Mallarmé a number of times. Whereas Laforgue is a poet to whom I have felt no need to return . . . Before I went to France in 1910 I was acquainted with Corbière only in the *Van Bever* anthology, but I bought a copy of his poems in Paris during that year. I should say that it was Corbière rather than Rimbaud who succeeded Laforgue in my affections.'

1 – Taupin thanked TSE for this 'prompt and amiable' letter (28 Apr.), noting that TSE's 'useful' remarks had not caused him to change his first ideas but to modify them a little.

2 – William S. Knickerbocker (1892–1972), Professor of English, University of the South, 1926–43, was editor of *The Sewanee Review*, 1926–42. His writings include *Creative Oxford* (1925) and *Victorian Education and the Concept of Culture* (1949).

3 – Knickerbocker asked TSE to point him to the earlier comments on Matthew Arnold to which he had referred in *The Sacred Wood*. (Knickerbocker had published an edition of *Culture and Anarchy* in New York in 1925.)

TO *Conrad Aiken*[1]   CC

12 April 1928   [London]

My dear Conrad,

I receive your letter of the 31st ultimo. I do not know whether I am to congratulate you or to weep over you on account of the various fortunes or misfortunes which you impart to me.[2] To be on the safe side I will say merely that you have all my sympathy. The most cheerful item in your letter is your remark that you may come to London. Come as quickly as possible and we will cheer you up. You are obviously not a fit person to be loose in America. Especially among University circles.

Yours ever affectionately,

[Tom]

1–Conrad Aiken (1889–1973), American poet and critic: see Biographical Register.
2–'As for me,' wrote Aiken on 31 Mar., 'I've been fired for moral turpitude: politely fired: which is to say, "there is no vacancy in the tutorial department next year" . . . It appears that four Graduates called at the Office in University Hall to protest that the author of *Blue Voyage* [his first novel, 1927] was not a fit teacher of the young.' Elsewhere in the letter he stated: 'As for the united Bolovian and Royal Coprophilic Associations, Ltd. I hereby apply for honorary membership. My illegitimate children are in Nashville, Tenn., Birmingham, Ala., and on the shores of Lake Tahoe. They may be seen on application.' (*Selected Letters of Conrad Aiken*, ed. Joseph Killorin [1978], 142–3).
    TSE responded in the same spirit with this undated communication:
        Mr. CONRAD POTTER AIKEN is
            Hereby Notified of
            His Election To the United
        BOLOVIAN COPOPHILIC AND DEIPNOSPOHISTICAL
            Societies
        Which Election to take Effect upon his 1st
        Presentation of himself at
        THE GROVE TAVERN, Beauchamp Place,
        Brompton Road s.w.1. on any THURSDAY
        between the Hours of 1 and 1: 15

            FOR
        The President . . . . .   F. V. Morley
        the Secretary . . . . .   F. S. Flint
        the Cellarman . . . . .   Harold Mungro
        the Treasurer . . . . .   Father Tandy V.O.P.

            The Honaray Vice Presidents:
                Winston Churchill M.P., P.C.
                George Robey P.M.
                Clive Bell W.C.1.

TO *John Crowe Ransom*   CC

12 April 1928   [London]

My dear Mr Ransom,

   Knowing your poetry as I do I am delighted that you should consider offering a contribution to the *Criterion*.[1] I must explain to you that in our present circumstances I think it is better to return it now and ask you to send it back to me later, or whatever you care to submit. You probably do not know that *The Criterion* has been going through a critical period and that we are endeavouring to accumulate sufficient funds to enable us to continue. It is probable that we shall survive, but only in a quarterly instead of a monthly form. But the whole thing is still very much in the air and even if we continue I cannot say definitely when the next number will appear. So as I do not want to retain manuscripts which I am not certain of being able to use I am returning you this very interesting essay. I should like to let you know when the matter is settled and we can then start afresh. With all good wishes I am,

                                        Sincerely yours,
                                        [T. S. Eliot]

TO *Conrad Ormond*[2]   CC

12 April 1928   [London]

Dear Mr Ormond,

   I should like to go further with you into the matter of American sheets of *The Criterion* as I now have the necessary figures. Could you suggest one or two afternoons next week when you would be able to come in and discuss the matter with me and with either Mr Stewart or Mr de la Mare.[3] Wednesday afternoon is impossible up to tea time, but I should be delighted if you would come to tea at 4.30 on Wednesday or any other day. If that time does not suit you I hope you can call one other day, not Wednesday, at some time during the afternoon.

                                        Yours very truly,
                                        [T. S. Eliot]

1–At Allen Tate's suggestion, Ransom had sent 'Pictures and Things', a chapter from a forthcoming book dealing with 'the general aesthetic problem; in this case with the painter's problem'. It did not appear in C.
2–Doubleday Doran & Company, publishers, London.
3–TSE's colleagues C. W. Stewart and Richard de la Mare, directors of F&G.

TO *Marguerite Caetani*   CC

12 April 1928   [London]

Dear Marguerite,

I have your wire today and am sending off tonight a copy of the poem
to Menasce. I hope that he will like it enough to be able to translate it
quickly for you, and I am asking him to send the translation direct to
you.[1] I don't know how quickly that will be as I have not heard from him
for some time and do not know whether he is in Alexandria or Jerusalem.

Ever yours affectionately,

[Tom]

TO *The Editor of* The Nation & Athenaeum[2]

17 April 1928   24 Russell Square, London

Sir,

Mr Edwin Muir, in his interesting review of Mr Sherard Vines's book in
your issue of April 14th, speaks very amiably of what he calls 'the school
of criticism which . . . is represented chiefly by *The Monthly Criterion*'.[3]
For this we should be grateful, but I should like to forestall a possible
misconception. It would be unfortunate if a myth arose to the effect
that 'the *Criterion* school of criticism' consisted of a compact body of
theorists all holding one and the same theory. Someone would eventually
demolish this myth, and the 'group' itself would be held responsible for
its propagation. I see the danger of misunderstanding in the way in which

---

1–Jean de Menasce translated two poems by TSE for Caetani: 'Perch' Io non Spero',
Commerce XV (Spring 1928), 5–11; 'Som de l'escalina', *Commerce* XXI (Autumn 1929),
99–103 – the latter being published as by 'T. S. Elliott'.
2–Published in *N&A* (21 Apr. 1928, 74), under the heading *The Monthly Criterion*.
3–Edwin Muir's review of Sherard Vines, *Movements in English Poetry and Prose* – 'Past
and Present' – declared: 'Mr Vines in his interesting volume is biased, as he was bound to be;
he is in favour of the school of criticism which exalts Reason and is represented chiefly by
The Monthly Criterion. But one cannot help wishing that his bias had been more frank . . .
The truth seems to be that he is a not quite convinced adherent of the theories of Mr Eliot,
Mr Read, and Mr Richards; and that, on the other hand, he has no salient theory of his own.
It is a pity, for if he had had a theory he might have been able to subject the *Criterion* school
of criticism to the test which it most needs at present: a friendly but rigorous examination. So
far Mr Eliot and his collaborators have either received undivided allegiance or encountered
unconditional opposition . . . Mr Eliot and Mr Read have written valuable criticism; but it
is a pity that they have wasted so much time latterly in rendering homage to Reason which
does not serve it in any way' (49).

Mr Muir joins the names of 'Mr Eliot, Mr Read, and Mr Richards'. I have great respect for the theories of the two latter: but it does not follow that I accept all of their theories, or that they accept all of mine or each other's. There are manifest divergences of which everyone is aware; and if we add the names of other *Criterion* contributors, including foreign writers such as Mr Fernandez and Mr Curtius, the scope of divergence will be still more patent. In short *The Criterion* is not a 'school', but a meeting place for writers, some of whom, certainly, have much in common; but what they have in common is not a theory or a dogma.

As for Mr Muir's other criticisms, I should be very glad if he would develop them at more length than is possible within the limits of a review of a book.

Yours, &c.,
T. S. Eliot

TO *I. P. Fassett*   CC

19 April 1928   [London]

Dear Miss Fassett,

I am very sorry to hear your news, but after what I had last heard from your father, it is not wholly unexpected.[1] I have discussed the matter with Mr Stewart. For the present Miss Hawkesley will be able to give me all the time necessary, and it is probable that the office can make some working arrangement after Mr Faber's return. Mr Stewart and I therefore think that it would be a pity to make your resignation definite, and we do not wish at the present time to engage a new secretary, whom it would take several months to train. We have therefore agreed that you shall be paid your salary to the end of this month; and that if everything works out as hoped you may count upon finding the position kept open for you when you are sufficiently recovered.

With all best wishes for a rapid convalescence,

Yours sincerely,
[T. S. Eliot]

1–IPF, who had been diagnosed with tuberculosis, had dictated a letter to TSE on 18 Apr.: 'This is to send you my resignation, with very deep regret, as I shall not be fit for work again for two or three months. When I wrote to you at the beginning, I had no idea that my illness would be so protracted.'

TO *Archibald MacLeish*   CC

19 April 1928   [London]

Dear MacLeish,

I am sorry to have been so slow in replying to your letter.[1] It is rather difficult to suggest a British publisher, but the following names occur to me: Victor Gollancz. Gollancz is a new publisher who was formerly with Benn Bros. He might be keen on new work, and I recommend him especially because Humbert Wolfe is a friend and adviser of his, and Humbert Wolfe has always expressed warm appreciation of your work. If you write to Gollancz you might mention the fact that you understand that Mr Wolfe has expressed approval of some of your poetry. I also suggest Jonathan Cape and Secker, though with rather more diffidence. Unfortunately I do not know any of these people. Martin Secker has published all of Conrad Aiken's work in this country, and might be interested.

If I can think of any better suggestions I will let you know. With all good wishes,

                                   Yours ever,
                                   [T. S. Eliot]

TO *Charles Whibley*   CC

19 April 1928   [London]

My dear Whibley,

Thank you very much for your kind letter.[2] I had already written to your wife to express my regret at finding it very difficult to get away from London at present. I have made an engagement in Oxford and one in Cambridge during May, and even these I shall find rather difficult to fill. I wish that I might see you, as I have much to talk about. I went out to lunch with Morley the day before yesterday. It is now decided that *The Criterion* will continue as a Quarterly, and I am trying to compile a number to appear in June.

Is there any possibility of your running up to London for a few nights within the next month?

                              Ever yours affectionately,
                              [T. S. E.]

1–MacLeish asked in an undated letter if TSE could suggest a publisher for his poem.
2–CW wrote (16 Apr.), 'When my wife wrote to you yesterday, we were a little confused about dates. On April 28th, we are ourselves engaged.' He proposed a meeting on 5 May.

23 April 1928   [London]

My dear Richard,

It happened that I received your letter this morning and that I was
having lunch with Bruce, so I can answer your enquiry at once.[1] The
upshot is that Bruce is completely unconcerned about the matter, supports
you entirely, considers E.'s letter impossible but amusing; and that neither
he nor I can understand why you should be in the least disturbed. I
mentioned that I had read your review and considered it remarkably
favourable towards E. You have NOTHING to worry about.

Go ahead with Benda.[2] As a matter of fact, I turned it down for F.
& G. (confidential), but we are probably taking *Belphégor*. As for [a]
preface, I am flattered, but it is quite impossible for me to do it: I have
reviewed the book in the *T.L.S.*[3] and am writing on it at more length
for the *New Republic*; and in any case I am too much involved with the
Action Française group to be able to sponsor Benda. But why shouldn't
you do it yourself.

I hope you have seen something of Maggie (Bassiano) at Versailles if she
is back from Menton.

I reply'd to your P.C., to 20 rue Jacob: I merely reminded you that
the Anglican translation was PURGE whereas the Papists say SPRINKLE
(with hyssop).[4]

ever aff
[Tom]

1 – EP had sent to the *TLS* a letter supposedly prompted by RA's review of his *Poems*. 'I am
not talking of opinion,' EP reproached the editor Bruce Richmond, 'I am talking about your
penchant for getting ignorami who express their ignorance with a gravity that is an insult to
the literate.' RA implored TSE (22 Apr.) 'to put me right with Bruce if you get the chance.
Could you say to him that I am greatly distressed by the whole occurrence, and do not quite
know how I stand with him? . . . Do what you can for me, dear Tom.'
2 – 'Routledge have bought rights of Benda's *Trahison*,' said RA, 'and ask me to translate.
Have you any objections? I have suggested they ask you to write a brief foreword.'
3 – 'Culture and Anarchy', *TLS*, 23 Feb. 1928, 118.
4 – 'Purge me with hyssop, and I shall be clean: wash me, and I shall be whiter than snow'
(Psalm 51: 7, King James Version). The Douay-Rheims version has 'Sprinkle'.

Monday St George's Day   [London]
[23 April 1928]

Dear Herbert,

I wish I had seen your article in the *Sat. Review*[1] before I wrote the enclosed preface,[2] as you will see the confusion seems to complicate matters. But it can't be helped.

You may have thought that my comments on Hawthorne were just negative: I meant to say that I like the essay very much, and some of the comments were for private discussion rather than for public alterations. So don't take them too seriously. I only felt (1) that introduction of James in that way that is of James as critic of Hawthorne, complicates it undesirably and (2) that there [is] another essay to be written about H. Possibly the other essay is far less critical than yours, and for [the] English public probably less useful; it would merely be from the point of view of someone to whom the N[ewl] E[ngland] granite, lichens, clapboards etc. were in the beginning. Even I, being born on the Mississippi, do not feel sure that I could write about H. as a native.

Some day I want to write an essay about the point of view of an American who wasn't an American, because his America ended in 1829; and who wasn't a Yankee, because he was born in the South and went to school in New England as a small boy with a nigger drawl, but who

1–Herbert Read, 'Hawthorne' – a review-essay on Lloyd Morris, *The Rebellious Puritan: Portrait of Mr Hawthorne* (1928) – *Saturday Review of Literature*, 16 Apr. 1928; repr. in *Collected Essays in Literary Criticism* (1938), 265–79.
2–The opening sentences of this letter are possibly ambiguous: there may or may not be a connection between the first and second paragraphs, so that the phrase 'my comments on Hawthorne' may, and probably does, refer to comments that TSE had made in private conversation with HR, or else the phrase refers back to 'the enclosed preface'. The 'preface' as such probably refers to TSE's preface to Edgar Ansel Mowrer, *This American World* (F&G, 1928), ix–xv. However, it is just possible that TSE was using the term 'preface' loosely, so that it might otherwise refer to his essay 'Le roman anglais contemporain' (*NRF* 28 [1 May 1927], 669–75), which opens (in TSE's original): 'In his little book on Nathaniel Hawthorne, published many years ago, Henry James has the following significant sentences:

> The charm of Hawthorne's slighter pieces of fiction is that they are glimpses of a great field, of the whole deep mystery of man's soul and conscience. They are moral, and their interest is moral; they deal with something more than the mere accidents and conventionalities, the surface occurrences of life. The fine thing in Hawthorne is that he cared for the deeper psychology, and that, in his way, he tried to become familiar with it.

The interest of this passage lies in its double application: it is true of Hawthorne, it is as true or truer of James himself' (669).

wasn't a southerner in the South because his people were northerners in a border state and looked down on all southerners and Virginians, and who so was never anything anywhere and who therefore felt himself to be more a Frenchman than an American and more an Englishman than a Frenchman and yet felt that the U.S.A. up to a hundred years ago was a family extension. It is almost too difficult even for H. J. who for that matter, wasn't an American at all, in that sense.[1]

T.

TO *G. B. Harrison*[2] CC

24 April 1928   [London]

Dear Mr Harrison,

I have just received the following cable:

'Could New Republic reprint Shakespeare Seneca address? Cable our expense.

Edmund Wilson.'

It does not matter to me either way whether the address you printed as a pamphlet is republished in America; but I should like to hear your

1–In his preface to Mowrer's study, TSE says: 'I have a background . . . which is different from that of many Americans. My family were New Englanders, who had been settled – my branch of it – for two generations in the South West . . . The family guarded jealously its connexions with New England; but it was not until years of maturity that I perceived that I myself had always been a New Englander in the South West, and a South Westerner in New England; when I was sent to school in New England I lost my southern accent without ever acquiring the accent of the native Bostonian. In New England I missed the long dark river, the ailanthus trees, the flaming cardinal birds, the high limestone bluffs where we searched for fossil shell-fish; in Missouri I missed the fir trees, the bay and goldenrod, the song-sparrows, the red granite and the blue sea of Massachusetts. I remember a friend of my school-days, whose family had lived in the same house in the same New England seaport for two hundred and fifty years. In some ways his background was as different from mine as that of any European' (xiii–xiv).

2–G. B. Harrison (1894–1991), literary scholar, wrote many studies of Shakespeare and his contemporaries, and would become renowned as general editor of several series of popular editions of Shakespeare. Having been taught at Queens' College, Cambridge, by E. M. W. Tillyard, Mansfield Forbes, and IAR (he was proud to have been Richards's first pupil in English), he was at the time of this letter Assistant Lecturer in English at King's College, London, and Honorary Secretary of the Shakespeare Association.

opinion of it. Of course I understand that if the pamphlet has any sale in America you may not care to give your consent.[1]

Yours sincerely,

[T. S. Eliot]

THE CRITERION

A Quarterly Review

Edited by T. S. Eliot.

ANNOUNCEMENT

April, 1928.

We are now able to announce that in consequence of reorganisation, and in conformity with the preference of many supporters, The MONTHLY CRITERION will henceforth appear in QUARTERLY form, resuming its original title, THE CRITERION.

The next number will be published in June.

The number of pages will be at least double that of the Monthly, and may be further increased. The form will be similar to that of THE CRITERION immediately before its conversion into a Monthly, but the scope will be gradually extended.

The price will be 7s. 6d. for the single number: the subscription price will remain unchanged – 30s. per annum.

Subscribers already listed will receive one Quarterly for each three issues of the Monthly paid for. Those whose subscriptions expire within the next three months will receive the next Quarterly issue.

THE CRITERION, if it is to maintain its quality, can appeal only to a highly intelligent public. It is vital that everyone who desires THE CRITERION to continue should support it by subscription.

If every present subscriber would undertake to obtain at least two new subscriptions, the success of the review would be assured.

We therefore enclose forms for subscription, which may be sent direct to the Publishers, or through a bookseller or newsagent.

Will you try to obtain at least TWO new subscriptions to THE CRITERION?

1–Harrison replied on 30 Apr. that Sir Israel Gollancz had suggested 'that if you wish to allow the NEW REPUBLIC to print your SENECA address [*Shakespeare and the Stoicism of Seneca*, 1927] you should give them the licence to *print* in America only, but not allow them to establish any American copyright'.

FABER & GWYER LTD.,
24, Russell Square,
LONDON W.C.I.

TO *Orlo Williams*   CC

24 April 1928   [London]

Dear Williams,

Many thanks for your letter. I should be glad if you could lunch with me
any day next week so that we can discuss your part in the next number.
Meanwhile I have remembered that I have on hand a review, which I
enclose, of the novels of T. F. Powys. It is a review by a writer some of
whose works have been published by Faber & Gwyer, and who is very
anxious to appear in *The Criterion* and who accordingly suggested the
subject himself. Now I know nothing about T. F. Powys and his work,
and I am sending this review to you to ask you whether you consider that
it can be published in *The Criterion*. If you disagree violently with the
author's opinions I should be glad to know. If not, and if you think the
review printable, I should like to print it. I shall be very grateful if you
will return it as quickly as possible with your confidential opinion.[1] Will
you not also let me know what day next week you would be able to lunch
with me? Wednesday is inconvenient and Thursday is impossible; I think
that all other days are free.

Yours ever,
[T. S. Eliot]

TO *R. Ellsworth Larsson*[2]   CC

26 April 1928   [*The Criterion*]

My dear Larsson,

I am very glad to hear from you at last, and to know that your luck has

---

1–Review by C. Henry Warren of eight novels by T. F. Powys, C. 7 (June 1928), 422–5.
Williams responded on 25 Apr.: 'I don't see why you shouldn't print this review. Personally,
I haven't read the latest work of T. F. Powys because I stopped short at what Mr. Warren
rightly calls his exploitation of the physical, which disgusted me, though I appreciate Powys'
form and power of delineation. But the view here taken is a possible one, though not
perfectly clear to me . . . As a review it seems to me very decent.'
2–Raymond Ellsworth Larsson (b. 1901), poet and journalist, grew up in Wisconsin and
worked in newspapers until journeying in 1926 to Europe, where he visited France (his

changed after so many vicissitudes. I had indeed been worrying about you for some time.

I very much appreciate your interest in the future of *The Criterion*. I have not heard from either Miss Storm Jameson or Miss Spedding, but I have just written to the latter as you suggest.[1] We are going to continue *The Criterion* as a Quarterly, but even for that we still need guarantees amounting to about £250 a year for three years.

I understand that Mr Simon is away from London, but will return, and I will certainly try to see him when he comes. Very many thanks for your hints. I look forward to seeing your new poem. I am afraid that it is possible that there is a poem of yours among the manuscripts here.[2] To tell the truth, during our state of suspense I have hardly bothered to look at manuscripts, not knowing whether I should be able to publish anything. I will let you know as soon as possible whether your manuscript is here or not.

With all good wishes,
[T. S. Eliot]

TO *Mary Spedding*   CC

26 April 1928   [*The Monthly Criterion*]

Dear Madam,

I have just received a letter from Mr Ellsworth Larsson, who has asked me to write to you about *The Criterion*. If the matter is not of interest to you, please ignore this letter; I am merely following out Mr Larsson's request, as he told me that you would like to know what is to happen to this Review.

It is quite true that Lady Rothermere withdrew her support rather suddenly. The Review was of course still very far from being self-supporting, and had only been running as a Monthly for seven months. As a certain number of people seemed to desire strongly that the Review should continue, we have attempted to secure guarantees which range

---

poetry appeared in *transition* in 1927), England, and Belgium. After returning to the USA in 1929, he worked for a while as an advertising manager. He entered the Roman Catholic Church in 1932. In Jan. 1939 TSE wrote to Henry Allen Moe, The Guggenheim Foundation: 'Mr Larsson is . . . rather a minor imitator of myself, on the devotional side.'

1–Larsson had heard from a friend, Mary Spedding, that Storm Jameson 'was interested in trying to save *The Criterion* from oblivion': TSE would do well to write to Jameson.

2–Larsson had enclosed a poem, 'O City, Cities', and asked after another, 'Listen! Listen', submitted earlier.

from £25 up for three years, so that *The Criterion* may have a chance of getting on its feet. We have not been able, within the time at our disposal, to secure enough guarantees to continue in a monthly form, so that we shall revert to the quarterly form, which is less costly. For other reasons also I shall be glad to revert to a form which I myself prefer.

What we actually require in order to carry on *The Criterion* as a Quarterly is a total of £750 guaranteed each year for three years. At the moment we have guarantees of about £500. Although this is inadequate we are intending to continue publication in the hope of making up the balance gradually. A quarterly number will appear in June.

We are also issuing a circular to subscribers, appealing to them to get us more subscribers. If we could triple the subscriptions our position would be very much stronger. I will send you one of these circulars as soon as they are printed.

> I am, Dear Madam,
> Yours faithfully,
> [T. S. Eliot]

TO *John Middleton Murry*   CC

26 April 1928   [London]

My dear John,

Many thanks for your letter. I hope you did not consider my communication too violent.[1] On the other hand I might have made it very much longer by taking up one or two points that occurred to me.

I wish you might be a little more communicative about yourself, as I have been anxious for news of you, and have not had any from any source. Do please write and tell me more about yourself.

As for *The Criterion*. It seems destined to revive in the form of a Quarterly. I can give you more definite news of it later, but I should like to know whether you would consider doing for me a long review based on a certain number of recent Shakespeare books, including the first volumes of two new editions: The Cambridge edition of Quiller-Couch and the folio facsimiles of Dover Wilson.[2]

1–TSE's letter on 'Parliament and the New Prayer Book', *Adelphi*, June 1928.
2–See JMM's review of George Connes, *The Shakespeare Mystery*; Clara Longworth de Chambrun, *Shakespeare: Actor-Poet*; and *The Taming of the Shrew*, ed. Sir Arthur Quiller-Couch; and two volumes in the series of Facsimile Editions of Individual Plays in the Shakespeare First Folio (F&G), ed. J. Dover Wilson, in C. 8: 30 (Sept. 1928), 134–9.

Yours ever affectionately,
[T.]¹

TO *Herbert Read*   CC

26 April 1928   [*The Monthly Criterion*]

Dear Herbert,

Many thanks for your letter. I now enclose two manuscripts which I should have given you had I been able to come to The Grove to-day. If you would prefer me to return either of them myself, let me know and I will do so. I should like to know your opinion, but it doesn't seem to me that Calverton's essay is very interesting for an English public.² Most of it seems to me rather general and vague, and to have no particular merit of style, and his illustrations are mostly from authors whom I at least do not know, but I should like to have your opinion before we decide to return it.

Yours ever,
[T. S. E.]

P.S. As a matter of fact I lunched to-day with Ogden at the Royal Societies.³ I was rather disturbed to see Montague Somers there, and to learn that he is a member. He is certainly one of the most odious persons in existence.⁴

JMM replied promptly (28 Apr.): 'I was very pleased to hear that Vivien is with you again. Please give her my love.

'I shall, of course, be delighted to write something about Shakespeare for the quarterly . . . I am working hard at him (for the nth time) and conclusions are hardening.

'I would have given you more personal particulars; but I am chary. There is no personal situation apart from Violet's condition. That has undoubtedly improved immensely since December, when it was zero. It is supposed to be a miracle – certainly is contrary to all prognosis – that she is now alive. But, alas, there are many degrees between death & life. I *think* she will continue to make progress; but it's very precarious, still.' (JMM's wife, Violet, was suffering from pulmonary tuberculosis.)

1 – Postscript apparently missing: TSE must have mentioned that VHE was back at home.

2 – On 22 Feb., V. F. Calverton, an editor of *The Modern Quarterly* (Baltimore, Maryland), had posted an article (on an American topic) to Herbert Read in the hope that it would be considered for publication in C. HR had forwarded it to TSE.

3 – The Royal Societies Club, St James's Street, London, of which TSE became a temporary member in Apr. 1928.

4 – Montague Summers (1880–1948), scholar of Restoration theatre, occultist and demonologist, graduated in theology from Trinity College, Oxford, and attended Lichfield Theological College, whereafter he was ordained and practised as a deacon. However, in 1909 he migrated to the Roman Catholic Church and thereafter posed and garbed himself as a religious (researchers have found no record of an ordination). A man of great scholarly industry, he published editions of works by writers including Aphra Behn, Congreve, Wycherley, Otway and Dryden; and he was instrumental in setting up the Phoenix Theatre, 1919–25, which was followed by the Renaissance Theatre, 1925–8.

P.P.S. I should like to discuss on Monday with you the question you raise in your letter.

TO *Thomas McGreevy*   TS TCD

26 April 1928   *The Monthly Criterion*

Dear McGreevy,

There is just a remote chance of a job for which I have ventured to mention your name; so I ought to warn you both that I have mentioned you, and that I imagine the chances are rather remote.

Robert Nichols[1] has been enquiring about someone who might take, for a few years, a position at Uppsala, as Assistant in English Literature. Apparently no knowledge of Swedish is expected, but the remuneration is said to be £400 a year with the possibility of making a bit more tutoring. I don't know when the successful candidate will be required, nor do I know for how long you are tied in Paris; but you need only answer this letter if you feel quite certain that the job is one which you do not want.[2]

Yours sincerely
T. S. Eliot

TO *Messrs A. D. Peters*   CC

26 April 1928   [*The Monthly Criterion*]

Dear Sirs,

I have to inform you that *The Criterion* is being reorganised and will be resumed as a Quarterly, the first number to appear in June. You will remember that I reported very favourably on Mr O'Flaherty's story 'The Alien Skull', and that we have retained it for publication if the review continues. Since then you have sent me another story by Mr O'Flaherty called 'The Letter' and I like this story even better than the first. I should

---

1–Robert Nichols (1893–1944), poet and playwright, was educated at Trinity College, Oxford, and served in WWI as a Second Lieutenant in the Royal Field Artillery (though shell shock was to cut short his service): his war poetry, *Invocation* (1915) and *Ardours and Endurances* (1917), brought him renown. He was Professor of English at Tokyo Imperial University, 1921–4, and then worked for a time as adviser to Douglas Fairbanks in Hollywood. His works include *Aurelia* (verse, 1920) and *Guilty Souls* (play, 1922). At the time of this letter, he was living in Winchelsea, E. Sussex. See William and Anne Charlton, *Putting Poetry First: A Life of Robert Nichols, 1893–1944* (2003).

2–McGreevy said (4 May) he was willing to go to Sweden.

like therefore to retain 'The Letter' definitely and send it immediately to press for the June number,[1] and if you so desire, return to you 'The Ancient [*sic*] Skull'. I suggest that 'The Ancient Skull' should be the easier of the two to place, as it is more nearly the normal length of magazine fiction.

Yours faithfully,
[T. S. Eliot]

TO *John Cournos*

28 April 1928   [London]

Dear Cournos,

I apologise for the delay in writing. It is, however, due to the fact first that I got my typewriter ribbon into confusion, which has delayed me for half an hour, but secondarily and primarily to the fact that I hope to get to the Law Stationers' Society, who provide the forms which one uses for Naturalisation. The forms will give you the information you want; and I will send them to you as soon as possible. Meanwhile here is all the information I have.

To get naturalised, you need five sponsors. One of them should swear that he knows everything you say to be true, he should know that you have lived wherever you say you have lived on those dates: six years continuous residence in Britain (short holidays abroad don't count) or if you have been absent then a longer period of residence. The other four are easy to get: for they have simply to say that they *believe* that what you say is true. When you have got these five persons you make a statement of your residences in England. When everything is filled up you send it in to the Home Office. You then keep telephoning the Naturalisation Dept. of the Home Office until they do something about it. What happens first is that a Scotland Yard Inspector visits all of your five and yourself, and asks a few simple questions.

Pending the forms which I will send, my only tips are these: (1) once you know that Scotland Yard is on the job (and they are very slow about it) it is better to be in England than elsewhere (2) before you put in your application, see that your (American) passport has a good time to run, say about nine months or a year. I got into a fix myself, because my American passport was about to expire two months before I could

---

1 – Liam O'Flaherty's story 'The Letter' appeared in C. 7 (June 1928), 346–51.

hope to get naturalised, and I didn't like to be without a passport and thought (rightly) that it might make trouble if I meanwhile took out a new American passport. So I had to pull a few wires to hustle things up. But so far as I can find, all that you can do by wirepulling is to accelerate; so if you arrange matters so that you can wait your time, there is no need to bother.

I can't be of any direct use to you, because it is written that all of the five sponsors must be British born. So you have next to choose your five.

About the *Criterion*: we are finally going to go on – as a Quarterly. I have started sending you our Russian periodicals again. I should like to have a review of them and of any more that come in, in time for the October number. Can you manage that?

Yours cordially,

[T. S. Eliot]

TO *Richard Braithwaite*[1]   CC

30 April 1928   [London]

Dear Mr Braithwaite,

Thank you very much for your kind letter.[2] I should be delighted to accept your invitation, and look forward with much pleasure to meeting you. The only doubt about it is that I have accepted an invitation to dine with another society, which I think is called The Hesperides on the Saturday night.[3] It is very disappointing that I cannot come to your dinner that evening. If you still care to have me on the condition of my being obliged to be absent on Saturday night I shall be delighted; in the circumstances I can hardly hold you to your invitation. Do let me hear from you again.

Yours sincerely,

[T. S. Eliot]

1–R. B. Braithwaite (1900–90), philosopher specialising in the philosophy of science, ethics, and the philosophy of religion, was elected in 1924 to a Fellowship at King's College, Cambridge – where he was, at the time of this exchange, President of the Heretics Society. He was University Lecturer in Moral Sciences, 1928–34; Sidgwick Lecturer, 1934–53; Knightbridge Professor of Moral Philosophy, 1953–67. His writings include *The State of Religious Belief: An Inquiry based on 'The Nation and Athenaeum' Questionnaire* (1927); *Scientific Explanation* (1953); *Theory of Games as a Tool for the Moral Philosopher* (1955); *An Empiricist's View of the Nature of Religious Belief* (1955)

2–Braithwaite wrote on 29 Apr. to invite TSE to dine (along with IAR) on Sat., 12 May: TSE was due to speak to the Heretics on 13 May. (Braithwaite had been introduced to TSE in the rooms of Goldsworthy Lowes Dickinson following one of the Clark lectures.)

3–TSE read at the Hesperides his essay 'The Idealism of Julien Benda'.

TO *Edwin Muir*¹   cc

3 May 1928   [London]

Dear Muir,

Thank you very much for your letter. I was very much interested in your review, and my letter to *The Nation* was written more generally to correct what I felt to be a current notion than to object to anything particular that you said.²

As for McLeod's book.³ I have glanced at it, and it seems to me, as you say, the work of a very young man who may be able to do some serious criticism later on. If you think so, I suppose that a review of two or three hundred words would do very well. But it certainly doesn't deserve more. When I first looked at the book I hoped more from it, but I was disappointed.⁴

If your poem appears in America soon I wish you would let me know.⁵ All my promises of publication have had to be cancelled and altered. *The Criterion* is to be changed again from a Monthly to a Quarterly, with the next number appearing in June. Therefore nothing that I have accepted can appear when I said it would appear. If anything appears in America in the meantime, that is our loss.

If you are ever in town I wish you would let me know and have lunch or tea with me again, and if you notice anything that you would like to review for *The Criterion* I wish you would let me know. Also if your poem appears in America before we can use it in *The Criterion* – and it would now be impossible to use it in the June number – I hope that you will send me something else.

                        Always yours sincerely,
                        [T. S. Eliot]

Enclosed circular explains our position.

1 – Edwin Muir (1887–1959), Scottish poet, novelist, critic; and translator (with his wife Willa) of Franz Kafka: see Biographical Register.
2 – Having been away on holiday, Muir wrote on 2 May – apropos TSE's letter to *N&A* (17 Apr.) criticising his review of *Movements in English Poetry and Prose* – 'It is too late, I am afraid, to admit my carelessness of phraseology in some parts of my review, but perhaps my silence will be sufficient admission of my agreement with what you say.'
3 – Joseph Todd Macleod, *Beauty and the Beast: Essays on Literature* (1927).
4 – Muir had chosen not to write a review of Macleod's volume (even though he had specifically requested it): 'I really can make nothing of it; for the author uses a most extraordinary vocabulary, never defines what he means by it, and is obviously most pleased where he is obscure. I fancy he is a very young man, and I should not be surprised if he should turn out to have some talent later on.' No review was forthcoming.
5 – A poem accepted by TSE for *MC* was to appear shortly in *The Atlantic Monthly*.

TO *Edouard Roditi*   TS UCLA

3 May 1928   *The Monthly Criterion*

Dear Sir,

Thank you for your letter of April 27th.[1] I should be most interested to
see both your translations and your original work whenever you care to
send some to me.

> With all best wishes,
> Yours very truly,
> T. S. Eliot

TO *Leo Ward*[2]   CC

7 May 1928   [*The Monthly Criterion*]

Dear Mr Ward,

Thank you for your letters and your reply. I am sending you the proofs
of your and my previous notes, and will let you have proofs of the last
note in due course. If you wish to omit anything in your own first note,
then I will alter mine accordingly when I receive your corrected proof.[3]

About your last note, there is one point where I think you are a little
obscure. You imply that Maurras denies the legitimacy of representative
institutions. I should first of all question your absolute antithesis between
representative and monarchical institutions, and second point out that
Maurras urges only that the monarchical institutions are the proper ones
for France. He has made it quite clear that different races and nations are
suited to different kinds of government, and that the representative form
of government for instance appears to be that best suited to Switzerland.
The only form of government which he would absolutely repudiate is

---

1–Roditi had written: 'I am very grateful to you for your kind reply [4 Apr.] to my letter
[29 Mar.], and especially for your valuable advice. I was unable to answer more promptly
on account of ill-health; however, I will be delighted to send you a copy of my translation of
Anabase as soon as you should find it convenient.

'Mr Archibald MacLeish, who has read this translation, was, if I may say so, frankly
enthusiastic and has been giving me some very interesting advice concerning both my
translations of St-John Perse and Ungaretti, and my own original poetry, of which I showed
him a few examples.'
2–Author of *The Condemnation of the Action Française*.
3–Leo Ward, '*L'Action Française*: A Reply to Mr Eliot', MC 7 (June 1928), 364–72; 'Reply
by T. S. Eliot', 372; 'A Rejoinder by L. Ward', 376. 'Of course I have not touched the proof
of your Note in which I notice several misprints,' said Ward (16 May).

unlimited democracy, for which I do not think there is anything to be said anyway.

I hope to see you soon and will write again to ask if you can lunch with me one day next week.

Yours sincerely,

[T. S. Eliot]

I thought you were quite correct in your objections to Gwynn. His book in fact makes too much of the political motives.[1]

TO *The Master, University College, Oxford*　　　cc

7 May 1928　　　　　　　　　　[London]

Dear Sir Michael Sadler,[2]

Thank you for your letter of 30th April which I find I have not yet answered. I will drop you a line later on to let you know my train which will probably be late on Wednesday afternoon.[3]

With many thanks,

Yours sincerely

[T. S. Eliot]

P.S. I am rather appalled at your previous suggestion that I should speak to the Society on some literary subject. The fact is that my mind will have been drained rather dry by an afternoon with the Heretics at Cambridge a few days sooner. I will however try to scrape up a few ideas for a very informal talk, but I should also be glad if the Martlets would think of anything that they want to talk about and start a discussion themselves.

---

1 – Denis Gwynn, *The Action Française Condemnation*.
2 – Sir Michael Sadler (1861–1943) was Master of University College, Oxford, 1923–34.
3 – 16 May.

TO *W. H. Auden*[1]   CC

7 May 1928   [London]

Dear Mr Auden,

Thank you for your letter.[2] It is true that I am coming to Oxford on the 16th but I shall only have time to arrive the night before and leave before lunch the next day. Thank you very much for your kind invitation to lunch which I should have been delighted to accept if I had had more time. But I am exceedingly busy, more particularly as I have to spend the previous weekend in Cambridge. I am sorry to say that I have not yet done anything about your poems. Most of my time for the last few months has been taken up with the reorganisation of *The Criterion* into a Quarterly, and I have therefore neglected considering manuscripts. I will try to look at them soon and write to you more fully.

With many thanks, yours very sincerely,

[T. S. Eliot]

In any case remember to come & lunch with me when you come down in June – I shall be here.

TO *G. Rostrevor Hamilton*[3]   TS Bodleian

7 May 1928   *The Monthly Criterion*

Dear Mr Hamilton,

I am writing to you *before* having read your article on Rossetti to explain that however good your article may be there is a very small chance of my being able to use it.[4] As you probably do not know *The Criterion* is now being re-transformed from a Monthly to a Quarterly, and there is therefore no chance of accepting anything for publication before the October number. Meanwhile unluckily I have given a kind of encouragement to a distinguished German author who wants to send an essay on the same subject. Of course it is quite possible that his article may be useless, and that I might be able to use yours, but as I am only just

1 – W. H. Auden (1907–73), poet, playwright, librettist, translator, essayist and editor: see Biographical Register.
2 – Auden had invited TSE (6 May) to lunch in Oxford. 'You have some poems of mine still I believe which I should be most grateful if you would bring with you.'
3 – George Rostrevor Hamilton (1888–1967), poet and critic, studied classics at Oxford and worked as a civil servant: he was knighted in 1951. *The Tell-Tale Article: A Critical Approach to Modern Poetry* (1949) includes a section on the achievement of TSE.
4 – 'Dante Gabriel Rossetti: A Review of His Poetry', *C.* 7 (June 1928), 379–91.

now looking through the manuscripts on hand and have found yours, I am writing at once so that you may not lose any more time if you want to submit it elsewhere for publication. If you would like to do this during the next few months please go ahead. If I do not hear from you I will report in due course.[1]

I hope that I may meet you again, as on the first occasion we began an interesting conversation which we left unfinished.

Yours sincerely,

T. S. Eliot

TO *Robert Nichols* CC

7 May 1928   [London]

Dear Nichols,

I have been meaning to write to you personally but have not yet had time. Meanwhile in case McGreevy is not considered eligible for the job in Uppsala do you think that your friends would consider the great James Joyce[2] himself? I have private information, not direct from Joyce, that he might be ready to accept any such position.[3] I do not make this suggestion in order to supplant McGreevy; for as a matter of fact I think McGreevy would do as well or better on account of his experience. But Joyce would of course be better known, and they might prefer to have him.

Either McGreevy or Joyce could as a matter of fact get strong recommendations from W. B. Yeats, who of course has official connections in Sweden. It is through Yeats that I first knew McGreevy.

Yours in haste,

[T. S. Eliot]

<I believe J. J. knows some Swedish, as of most languages.

P.S. This does *not* mean that I have a *penchant* for Irishmen. It is accidental.>

---

1 – Rudolf Kassner's proposed essay on Rossetti did not appear in C.

2 – James Joyce (1882–1941): Irish novelist, playwright, poet; author of *A Portrait of the Artist as a Young Man* (1916), *Ulysses* (1922), and *Finnegans Wake* (1939). TSE saluted *Ulysses* as 'the most important expression which the present age has produced' ('*Ulysses*, Order and Myth', *Dial* 75: 5 [Nov. 1923]).

3 – McGreevy had reported to TSE on 4 May that JJ (with whom he had worked for four weeks early in the year) had recently written to him: 'Ask Eliot could he recommend a bag of bones like myself if you do not go.' McGreevy added: 'If you think of Joyce don't hesitate to recommend him because of me. I'd be pleased to see him honoured.'

TO *Kenneth Ingram* CC

7 May 1928 [London]

Dear Mr Ingram,

Thank you very much for your essay[1] which seems to me to be admirable for the purpose, and which as it was interesting and informative to me can hardly fail to be interesting and informative to French readers. I am sending it to Monsieur Massis and will ask him to communicate with you direct.

With many thanks,
Yours sincerely,
[T. S. Eliot]

If you have the time, I should like to get you to review some book for the (Quarterly) *Criterion* one day. I was to have met you at Fr. Whitby's once, but was in Paris.

TO *Butler Hallahan* CC

7 May 1928 [London]

Dear Mr Hallahan,

Thank you for your kind letter.[2] I am very sorry that I cannot accept your further hospitality beyond the pleasure of dining with you, as I have accepted an invitation to stay at King's with Mr R. B. Braithewaite [*sic*]. I shall come down rather late on Saturday afternoon. I wonder if someone would be so kind as to call for me at King's in time for the dinner, asking for me care of Mr Braithewaite?

In reply to your other question, I think if you don't mind that I prefer Sherry or even the humble gin and bitters to a cocktail.*

Looking forward to meeting you.

Yours very sincerely,
[T. S. Eliot]

<* You see American standards in cocktails are *very* high!>

1–Kenneth Ingram, 'L'affaire du Prayer-Book et l'Église Anglicane', *Revue Universelle* 32 (1928), 554–64.
2–Looking forward to entertaining TSE at the Hesperides on 12 May, Butler Hallahan of Trinity Hall, Cambridge (secretary of the Society), asked TSE if he could dine with them: 'Do let me know . . . are you still enough of a U. S. A. man to prefer a cocktail to sherry?'

TO *R. B. Braithwaite*   CC

7 May 1928   [London]

Dear Braithwaite,

Thank you for your letter.[1] I will let you know by what train I am coming on Saturday afternoon and will ask for you at the College, or for any instructions you may have left. I certainly hope to return on Saturday night *before* midnight!

I have sent your secretary the post-card. Looking forward to meeting you,

With many thanks
[T. S. Eliot]

TO *James Smith*[2]   CC

7 May 1928   [London]

Dear Smith,

Thank you for the proof and the book which you returned to me.[3] I will write to you later about Worringer.[4] I am to be staying in Cambridge this weekend at King's College with Mr Braithewaite and will hope to see you either at the Heretics or the Hesperides.

Yours sincerely,
[T. S. Eliot]

TO *Edmund Wilson*   TS Beinecke

8 May 1928   *The Monthly Criterion*

Dear Mr Wilson,

In reply to your kind enquiry about my 'Seneca' address I am enclosing a copy of a letter from the secretary to the Shakespeare Association.[5] It appears that if you wish to reprint the paper in *The New Republic* you are

---

1–It had been arranged that TSE would sleep in Braithwaite's rooms on the Sunday: since there was no night porter, TSE had to return from the Hesperides by about 12.15
2–James Smith (1904–72), critic and educator: see Biographical Register.
3–Smith had returned 'Schoell's book on Chapman' on 3 May.
4–Smith's review of Wilhelm Worringer's *Egyptian Art* did not ultimately appear in C.
5–Wilson had cabled on 25 Apr., 'Could New Republic reprint Shakespeare Seneca address cable our expense.' He wrote at length about the same enquiry on 15 May.

at liberty to do so, but that The Shakespeare Association wish to reserve the book-rights. This is how I interpret the enclosed letter.

As I get no royalty in any case, it is a matter of indifference to me, but out of courtesy I should be glad to conform with the desires of The Shakespeare Association.

Yours sincerely,
T. S. Eliot

Benda preparing.

TO *H. G. Leach*   CC

8 May 1928   [London]

Dear Mr Leach,

Thank you very much for your cheque for a hundred and twenty-five dollars. I am glad that you will be able to use my essay, and it would suit me very well if it appeared in July.[1] I am probably in London in June and look forward to meeting you.

Yours sincerely,
[T. S. Eliot]

TO *Alsina Gwyer*   CC Faber

10 May 1928   [Faber & Gwyer Ltd]

Dear Mrs Gwyer,[2]

I had a long talk with Faber this afternoon, with Stewart and De la Mare present for a part of the time. It seems to me that there is every possibility of an agreement, and Faber's modified demands seem to me

1–'The Humanism of Irving Babbitt', *Forum*, 80: 1 (July 1928), 37–44.
2–This letter is an example (others may be inferred from other documents but have not yet been found) of TSE's reluctant and cautious involvement in the altercations over policy and strategy that took place in the period 1925–9 between Geoffrey Faber and Maurice Linford Gwyer (1878–1952) – the latter was to be knighted in 1928 – and his wife Alsina (daughter of the philanthropist Sir Henry Burdett), who were co-proprietors of the company that ran the joint enterprise of the Scientific Press (launched by Sir Henry Burdett, who had died in 1920), the *Nursing Mirror*, and the general publishing house of Faber & Gwyer – of which Faber was chairman. Although the Gwyers were co-owners – Mrs Gwyer understandably felt it her duty to be the trustee of her late father's interests – Maurice Gwyer was a major shareholder but did not serve as a director of the company, and was otherwise fully employed in public service, as Treasury Solicitor. Thus Gwyer's criticisms and interventions soon came to be regarded by Geoffrey Faber as a form of outside interference in his governance of the

business. Faber's concern was to build up and invest in general publishing, whereas Gwyer expected a safer, quicker, and better return on investment. Also, Gwyer went so far at one point as to question why Richard de la Mare and C. W. Stewart (Faber's appointees) were sitting on the Board at all: 'In my view a Board of six is too large; four would be ample.' Yet he favoured the appointment to the Board of someone – namely a chartered accountant – 'with practical experience of Company finance'. Gwyer was averse to risk – 'I could not contemplate without the gravest apprehension,' he told Faber on 6 May 1927, 'the saddling of the Company with a debenture debt of £10,000 merely for the purpose of continuing what is admittedly a speculation . . . The Company has lost all its liquid resources and has nothing to show for them, and it seems to me, though I say it with all respect, nothing but wild-cat finance to hang a further liability of £10,000 round its neck' – whereas Faber was convinced that with reasonable extra investment the publishing business would flourish in the medium term. Faber had faith in his team and the books they were producing; and he wanted 'the balance of power' to be shifted in favour of the personnel who properly ran the business. In the event, the long-lasting and increasingly personalised and rancorous contestation was resolved in 1929 when the Gwyers duly sold their shares, and the *Nursing Mirror* was sold for a profit – and the house of Faber & Faber Ltd was well and truly established.

As early as Apr. 1927, Faber had proposed to Gwyer: 'You chose your language with your usual care; but that you have lost your confidence in me, and in the Board, is something that the choice of words cannot conceal. I am quite clear that the policy I wish to follow is the right one [and] it is clear that no satisfactory solution can be found, except a separation of interests . . . It would be better if either you or I disposed of our interest in the business. I venture, therefore, to ask you if you would be prepared to sell your ordinary shares . . . I make this suggestion – rather than its reverse – for the obvious reason, that the fortunes of the book-publishing depend on me, & that I am far too deeply engaged in the whole business to think of withdrawing, without the most imperative reasons. I feel, also, responsible for & to the staff which I have brought together.'

Both Gwyer and his wife came to place a fair level of trust in TSE for his good sense and moderating manners, and also presumably for the experience he had acquired during his years at Lloyds Bank. Mrs Gwyer also displayed – throughout the protracted period which led up to the parting of the ways – considerable tact and politesse; she evidently knew her husband could be difficult, and sought very often to conciliate Geoffrey Faber too. She wrote for example on 11 Dec. 1927 to express to Faber her sympathy for the fact that, as she put it, he had not enjoyed 'an entirely free hand': 'I fear that the strain will be too great for you. There are also the question of security & happy confidence without which it is (as I know from experience) impossible to give of one's best. You have had criticism but not help from one quarter [her husband], whereas I contribute help where I can, but cannot here bring an informed or useful criticism to bear. It is these two factors which make me anxious, & this is the reason I tried to bring in Mr Eliot – for if he was prepared to be interested & really master the financial side I thought he would bring strength to the Board, for on this subject I ignore the other two directors [de la Mare and Stewart].' In another communication of Dec. 1927, she stated that her husband '(like yourself) feels that it would not be easy for either of you to discuss the situation as it stands today without repercussions from the past disturbing you both. He is willing to discuss the position with Mr Eliot. He says that he has never succeeded in making his views intelligible to you, so perhaps Mr Eliot might be a useful intermediary. I am asking Mr Eliot to have supper with him next Sunday night (I shall be away) – I feel an absolute brute for troubling you at this time & so does he. (*This is true* not tact! He said "I don't want to hurt Faber" – & I know that this was most sincerely said.' On 5 Jan. 1928 she wrote likewise: 'it is a great satisfaction to know that Mr Eliot made things clearer. It is most distressing to me to be at variance with you.' And Geoffrey

possible of acceptance. Particularly as I cannot see any alternative to further negotiation than a General Meeting which could hardly result in anything but a complete revolution. As I told your husband and yourself, I should deprecate a Board Meeting on this matter; if it is on so complete a difference of policy, it would satisfy neither Faber nor yourselves, and could only lead to a General Meeting.[1]

My own opinion is quite simple: the pursuit of Faber's memorandum has to be contingent (1) on the continuance of the present dividend (2) on the ability to reduce the overdraft by £2000 annually (3) of course upon the continuance during that period of the present prosperity of the Mirror.[2] If either (1) or (2) should be jeopardized, or if the Mirror should for any reason undergo an unexpected depression, then that programme must be modified; and it is assumed that if the results for any half year fall short of the prediction, the programme must be revised. With this proviso that the Board is entitled to revise or revoke the programme according to half-yearly progress, Faber's demand for £5000 for three years (subject to the three conditions mentioned) does not seem to be unreasonable. But it seems to me, in any case, that any profits of the Mirror, beyond the usual %100 dividend, not devoted to books, should be placed to reserve during that period.

It is understood, at least as far as I am concerned, that the memorandum is to be reviewed each half year in connexion with the relation of the results to the prediction.

Faber, for his part, always trusted his colleague Eliot to help make things better; he wrote tactfully to Gwyer on 30 May 1928: 'Eliot tells me that he had some talk with you yesterday, & that you were disposed to think that some form of arbitration by a firm of Chartered Accountants would be the best solution. Would it not be a good thing if you & I could discuss this together at an early date – either alone, or with Eliot to help us, whichever you prefer? . . . If you agree – as I am inclined to think – that Eliot's presence would be valuable, would lunch next Wednesday be a convenient date & hour for you?'

1 – GCF's 'Memorandum', written and circulated in Dec. 1927, has not yet been found; but evidently it stated the differences between the factions – that is, Faber himself and Maurice Gwyer – so categorically that if it had been brought to the vote at a General Meeting it would have necessitated the resignation of one of the rivals. TSE's advice was clearly more conciliatory: his stated position took the risk of attempting to go some way to meet Gwyer's demands while always, and fundamentally, supporting Faber's position. Only the day before this letter from TSE to Mrs Gwyer (9 May 1928), Gwyer himself had written to GCF: 'I saw Eliot today (it was merely a coincidence that he happened to be lunching with me the day after our conversation) & he expressed that tho' a discussion at the Board might be very useful a definite vote at the end of it was to be deprecated. There is perhaps a good deal to be said for this & you may like to consider it: but it is, I think, for you to decide. It is of course obvious that a vote will not settle anything, and possibly a full & frank discussion would serve the purpose of clearing the air equally well.'

2 – The Nursing Mirror, the successful journal owned by Faber & Gwyer Ltd.

I remain convinced that the Board ought to be enlarged as I have suggested. While all the members of the present Board seem to me to be individually suitable, I do not feel that the Board as at present constituted is either, on the one hand, sufficiently representative of the shareholders or on the other hand sufficiently representative of publishing experience in general or of general financial experience, to be made responsible for such matters of policy.

I speak with great diffidence, either to you or to Faber, as my position is an anomalous one. I hope you will not consider it impertinent.

By the way, my wife wanted to let you know how grateful she was to you for coming the other afternoon. She had never met the Cobden-Sandersons before, and had not seen Dorothy Pound for two years, so was extremely nervous; and it was a great support to her to have you there.

Yours sincerely,
[T. S. Eliot]

TO *Geoffrey Faber*   MS Faber

Thursday [10 May 1928]   *The Monthly Criterion*

Dear Geoffrey

Enclosed is copy of letter sent to Mrs Gwyer. Its intention is wellmeaning; but it is only fair to let you see it at once. Ring me up in the morning if you have any comments.

Yrs
T. S. E.

TO *Frederic Fassett*[1]   cc

Thursday, 10 May 1928   [London]

Dear Mr Fassett,

I was very busy with a meeting this afternoon or would have rung you up. Tomorrow I shall be very busy with private affairs, and shall not be at my office for more than a few minutes. I am then going away for the weekend, as I have two engagements in Cambridge; so the first afternoon

---

1 – Frederic Fassett (1873–1960), company director, was the father of TSE's secretary, I. P. Fassett, who was seriously ill.

of which I am certain is Tuesday. Could you come in any time on Tuesday afternoon, but preferably for tea (4 o'clock) on Tuesday? I am sorry not to be able to see you sooner.

Also I do hope that you have no bad news for me. I rang up the other afternoon and spoke to a nurse who could not tell me very much. Please believe that we are all anxious for good news, and that we all wish to believe that your daughter can eventually return to her position with Faber & Gwyer.

If the matter should be more urgent, please ring me up in the morning at Sloane 3184.

> With sympathy and all good wishes,
> Yours sincerely,
> [T. S. Eliot]

TO *Maurice Gwyer*   MS Faber

14 May 1928   57 Chester Terrace,
                                     Eaton Square, s.w.1.

My dear Gwyer

I saw Faber today – I have been in Cambridge since Friday – & he showed me a letter he has drafted to you. The letter seemed to me to be unsatisfactory for several reasons, so I dissuaded him from sending it & it struck me that it would be better to have a conversation, if you & he could meet me somewhere.[1]

1–GCF wrote in his draft letter, dated 13 May: 'Since our interview on Tuesday evening I have had several talks with Eliot, Stewart & de la Mare. I repeated your views to them, as nearly as I could in your own words. In what I am going to write, I believe myself to be expressing their opinions equally with my own, though I should not wish to be thought to commit them to my actual words . . . I also felt that, as you had asked Archibald to act for you, I should like to have similar assistance. As Harry Cohen [a solicitor], of Linklater's, is a friend of Archibald's as well as mine (& I believe of yours too?) I went to him. I understand that in his view, as a practical lawyer with a large experience of company work, my general attitude is not an unreasonable one.

'It seems to me that the really important question, which is to some extent at issue between us . . . is this question of "control". I am very anxious to avoid being controversial, but I really do not feel able to accept your contention (if I have rightly understood it) that the Directors have not "the uncontrolled spending of the shareholders' money". Surely the Directors have the right, & indeed the duty, to employ the Company's resources as they think desirable, within the limits of the borrowing powers expressly conferred upon them by the Articles . . . It is not possible to distinguish . . . between ordinary "policy" and "financial policy" . . . It would be impossible to secure efficient and progressive management, if the purse-strings were held, not by the Directors, but by the shareholders . . . [T[he industrial difficulties of 1925 & 1926 & the depression of 1927 – all unforeseen when we began, & falling with maximum severity on a newly-started business – constitute a factor which can't be left out of account . . . You referred last Tuesday to the Board as a "packed Board" – packed, that is, in my interest; and in a recent letter you spoke of "the mere ipse dixit of the Chairman."

'The last part I should cast myself for would be that of autocrat. My whole object from the start has been & still is to build up a business organization which should take its own way, & have its own continuous life. Anyone at Russell Square would tell you, if you asked them about my methods of work, that I *never* impose my own views (except where the decision is obviously for me to take) . . . I have never once attempted to enforce a line of action upon any member of the Board. Even if I were to do so, I should certainly not succeed. Eliot, as you know, could not be any man's creature. That is equally true of Stewart & de la Mare. They owed their appointments to me in the first instance; but neither could I ask for, nor would they dream of recognizing, any obligation arising out of that . . . Of course I should not dispute the fact that my opinion must carry weight with the Board. It would be a disastrous state of affairs if it did not. But that is a very different thing from exercising an improper or excessive influence.

'I feel it due to myself, in this connection, to add that far from delighting in "unfettered personal control", which you say I have exercised, I have been seriously embarrassed by it & have consistently sought to rid myself of it. No single serious decision has ever been taken without the consent either of yourself or of Mrs Gwyer, or of both of you, as well as the formal approval of a Board Meeting. As you know, I urged you more than once to become a director, & when that was impossible I cordially adopted Mrs Gwyer's suggestion that you should be invited to attend Board Meetings & Book Committee meetings . . . In the course of 1926 the need of sharing my load of responsibility became pressing. I persuaded you & Mrs Gwyer to agree to the appointment of the two additional Managing Directors, and initiated the weekly Book Committees. The Memorandum of last December did, it is true, embody my personal views; though I had reason to think that the views of the Directors were not dissimilar . . .

'I am sure you will do me the justice to admit that if your interests are not sufficiently represented on the Board it is no fault of mine. Much as I disliked your proposal to nominate a Chartered Accountant to the Board, I did agree to it. I propose now that we should raise the numbers of the Board to 7, & appoint two additional directors: one to be a nominee of your own, approved of course by myself & the Board; one to be appointed by the existing Board, & to be approved by you. The latter to be, if possible, a man of suitable age & experience to act as understudy to myself . . .

'In the Board, so constituted, the control of policy in the fullest sense of the word permitted by the Articles would have then to rest . . .

'I propose . . . that we should continue to act at Russell Square on the assumption that for the 3 years – 1928 to 1930 – the books will be able to draw on the rest of the business to the extent of £5000 a year . . . [Y]ou said that the balance-sheet for the Books would show a great excess of liabilities over assets; that it would take at least 15 years from the initiation of the books before they could begin to provide money for the business as a whole . . . But I'm quite clear that if in 1934 the books are earning 15% they will be doing well enough to justify themselves . . . The comparison with the private investor is surely quite erroneous. The investor can't afford to wait, a business can; & the loss of interest while the development was being financed, would be made good within a few years . . . The F & G books are not a private enterprise of mine, or the Directors; they are part of the business. Not only were they undertaken because the S[cientific] P[ress] books offered an obvious point of departure, but they & the S. P. books are closely connected . . . So, as it seems to me, the only thing to be done is to enlarge the Board in the way I have suggested, & to agree to differ, and to make the Board be truly & in fact, as well as in theory, the arbiter of the Company's destiny.'

I suggest that you and Faber should lunch with me one day soon. Would either Friday or Monday next be possible for you? The Royal Societies Club has a very bad kitchen, & I have not yet found any good wines there: but it is apt to be empty, & most of the members old and deaf.

Sincerely yours
T. S. Eliot

TO *A. L. Rowse*   TS Exeter

18 May 1928   *The Monthly Criterion*

Dear Rowse,

Thank you very much for your letter, which I ought to have acknowledged sooner. Thank you also for your own generous subscription to the *Criterion*, which I acknowledge hereby. If you come across anyone in Oxford who might be induced to become a subscriber we should be very grateful to you.

I have received Campbell's poem and Massis' book:[1] don't bother about the others, keep them as long as you like. I am very glad that you agree with me about Campbell; I shall try to get him to contribute to the *Criterion*. About Massis, well, I had rather wait for an opportunity to talk to you.

I wish that I could accept your invitation immediately and spend a weekend with you in Oxford. But I have recently had to spend a weekend in Cambridge and a night in Oxford at University,[2] and I do not feel that I could afford the luxury of any more visits during the present term. Perhaps I could come to stay with you during the Michaelmas term, but meanwhile I shall hope to see you in London. When one is very busy it is surprising how much time one loses by these extremely agreeable and sometimes extremely useful visits.

About your other suggestion concerning myself.[3] It is extremely flattering and kind of you. I am not able to consider it seriously at present, because the possibility seems to me so remote. But we can talk of this later.

1–Roy Campbell's 'Tristan da Cunha' 'has the quality of greatness I feel,' wrote ALR (11 May). (In Jan. 1928 TSE had invited ALR to translate Kuhlemann's *Tristan da Cunha*.) Massis's *Jugements* ALR found just as 'frénétique' as Massis had found Gide. 'Perhaps they both are: but then, one's prejudice is in favour of variety of experience.'
2–University College, Oxford.
3–ALR suggested that TSE should stand for election to the Oxford Chair of Poetry.

Meanwhile and more urgent, you have not answered my suggestion that you should write an article for the *Criterion*. I shall not be satisfied with little reviews. Apart from the immediate political questions of the day, is there not some more general problem on which you would like to write?

May I add, as it is a great compliment to yourself, that my friend Fletcher has much admiration for you?

Yours sincerely,
T. S. Eliot

TO *Thomas McGreevy* TS TCD

18 May 1928   *The Monthly Criterion*

My dear McGreevy,

Don't worry in the least about the Uppsala business. If you can't bring yourself to face it I sympathise with you; I merely wanted it to come your way if it suited you. It was no trouble to me, and I have since been asked to recommend one or two others.[1]

I am afraid that your review of Lewis, to which I look forward, will be too late for the June number. I shall hope to print it in the October issue.

I also understand your difficulties about the École Normale. One is always finding oneself between two stools in this way. Probably you are wise to stick to the present situation.

With all good wishes,
Yours ever,
T. S. Eliot

TO *John Gould Fletcher* CC

18 May 1928   [*The Monthly Criterion*]

Dear Fletcher,

Likewise I have been intending to look you up for some weeks past.[2] Things have been very unsettled lately: my wife had to have an operation on her teeth, and after that I had to pay a visit to Cambridge and another

---

1 – McGreevy sent his deepest apologies (undated): he had decided after all not to apply to Uppsala. For one consideration, the École Normale had been dismayed by the idea that he might quit his post by 1 July, a month before the end of the academic year.

2 – Fletcher wrote on 9 May that he had meant 'to look you up for a month'.

to Oxford, and we are only now settling down. Would you be able to come to lunch at Chester Terrace one day, as my wife also would very much like to see you again, and it is so long since we have met that I should like to have a good talk with you about things in general, and about the future of *The Criterion* in particular.

Yours ever,

[T. S. Eliot]

TO *Edmund Wilson*   CC

18 May 1928   [*The Monthly Criterion*]

My dear Wilson,

I am sending you herewith my essay on Benda's last book.[1] If you care to publish it you may use it whenever you like; if not, would you let me know immediately so that I may dispose of it elsewhere?[2]

Yours sincerely,

[T. S. Eliot]

1 – In 'The Idealism of Julien Benda' (*The New Republic*, 12 Dec. 1928), TSE found Benda's thesis 'fallacious' for grouping 'all the intellectuals who may be accused of doing somebody else's business, or of pandering to popular political passions, into one category': writers such as D'Annunzio, Kipling, William James, and H. G. Wells, were varied in 'scope and direction'. Benda's solution was inadequate: 'He holds up to the artist, to the critic, to the philosopher, an ideal of detachment from passions of class, race, nation and party, which . . . looks very admirable. But it implies a complete severance of the speculative from the practical which is itself impossible, and leads, in M. Benda's implications, to an isolation which may be itself a romantic excess . . . The only moral to be drawn, therefore, is that you cannot lay down any hard and fast rule of what interests the *clerc*, the intellectual, should or should not have. All you can have is a standard of intellect, reason and critical ability which is applicable to the whole of a writer's work. If there is a right relation of emotion to thought in practical affairs, so there is in speculation and art too. A good poem, for instance, is not an outburst of pure feeling, but is the result of a more than common power of controlling and manipulating feelings . . .' In a later, unpublished piece, 'On the Place and Function of the Clerisy' (1944), TSE reflected on *La Trahison des clercs* (which he had not read since 1928): 'I did not think it so good as the author's *Belphégor*. My impression remains that Benda was an example of the Cretan Liar, and that he fell into treason while accusing others; but also that he did not distinguish different grades of *clerc*. The higher grades are those, whether philosophers or artists, who are concerned with the word (the discovery of truth or beauty) rather than with the audience, and the lower those who are more concerned with the audience – either to *influence* it or to *entertain* it, or both. (This does not exclude the possibility that a particular lower-grade cleric may be a *greater* man than a particular high-grade one). Benda, as I remember, seemed to expect everybody to be a sort of Spinoza . . .'

2 – Wilson replied on 11 June that he was keen to run TSE's piece as the leading article in their Fall literary supplement.

TO *Mario Praz*   CC

18 May 1928   [London]

My dear Praz,

In reply to your letter of the 9th, I think that your alterations are all to the good.[1] I am submitting your letter with Montale's desires to our Publications Manager; I am not sure that we shall be able to manage this, and in any case Montale must understand that expenses would have to be deducted from his payment.[2] I suggest that we might send him the off-prints of the page proofs, which would only be printed on one side, and that he should have them bound himself; it could probably be done more cheaply in Italy.

I note that the whole payment, such as it is, should be sent to Montale. In most cases it is divided between author and translator; but I will fall in with your wishes.

I have not yet read your lecture.[3] When I have I shall write to you again if I have anything to say; but you know so much more about this subject than I do that I do not suppose I can make any comments that will be useful to you.

Yours ever,
[T. S. Eliot]

TO *Montgomery Belgion*[4]   CC

18 May 1928   [London]

Dear Belgion,

Thanks for your letter. I continue to plan a number of the *Criterion* in which the Whitehead matter will be thrashed out. I shall be delighted to send you the forthcoming book by Whitehead unless Herbert Read would like to have it.[5] He is at present away so I cannot ask him; but he has

---

1 – Praz had returned the proofs of his translation of Eugenio Montale's poem 'Arsenio': C. 7 (June 1928), 342–3.
2 – Montale desired 20 offprints of poem and translation bound up in coloured paper.
3 – Unidentified.
4 – Montgomery ('Monty') Belgion (1892–1973), author: see Biographical Register.
5 – Belgion asked (4 May) to review Alfred North Whitehead's *The Philosophy of Organism* – a review which would aim 'to set going the same discussion now still-born'. Belgion did not in fact review the book in question; but he was later to review Whitehead's *Process and Reality: An Essay on Cosmology*, C. 9 (Apr. 1930), 557–63.

reviewed two of Whitehead's previous books for the *Criterion*,[1] and I feel that he ought to have the first option.

I await with interest your suggestion of another contribution.

I should be very glad if you would let me know by return when you expect your translation of Fernandez' book to appear.[2] I want to write an article about this book, and I intend to offer it to some American periodical. But even if my article appeared before your translation I hope that it would do the translation more good than harm.

Yours sincerely,

[T. S. Eliot]

TO *C. K. Ogden*[3]   Copy of MS

21 May 1928   *The Monthly Criterion*

Dear Ogden,

I heard from Richards last week that you were lying ill at the R. S.[4] I had hoped to see you in Cambridge. I rang up the R. S. a couple of days ago & heard that you were up and about. Are you allright now, if not will come & see you.

Yours ever,

T. S. E.

1 – HR had reviewed *Science in the Modern World*, NC 4 (June 1926), 581–6; and *Religion in the Making*, MC 5 (May 1927), 259–63.

2 – 'There will be no English translation of Fernandez's little book *De la Personnalité*,' wrote Belgion (1 June). The part that had appeared so far was only an introduction to a much longer work (contracted with the *NRF*): all would depend on how Fernandez got on.'

3 – C. K. Ogden (1889–1957), psychologist and linguistician. Educated at Magdalene College, Cambridge, where he co-founded the Heretics Society and founded the weekly *Cambridge Magazine*, he went on in 1922 to translate Ludwig Wittgenstein's *Tractatus Logico-Philosophicus*. In 1927 he set up in London the Orthological Institute to develop and disseminate 'the international auxiliary language' called Basic English (converts to the cause included William Empson, who found Basic English an invaluable teaching resource in Japan and China in the 1930s), and put out supportive texts including *Basic English* (1930). Other publications include *The Foundations of Aesthetics* (with I. A. Richards and James Wood, 1922) and *The Meaning of Meaning* (with Richards, 1923). See further W. Terrence Gordon, *C. K. Ogden: A Bio-bibliographical Study* (1990).

4 – Royal Societies Club, London.

TO *The Master, University College, Oxford*   TS Bodleian

22 May 1928   *The Monthly Criterion*

My dear Master,

Thank you very much for your kind letter of the 18th with the money order for thirty shillings, which I think rather more than covers my expenses.

I should have written to you in any case to tell you how much I enjoyed meeting you, and what a pleasure it was to me to meet your undergraduates. As I hope I said at the time, it was one of the most interesting evenings of that sort that I have ever spent, and I was particularly impressed both by the intelligence and the intelligent interest in one subject which the young men displayed.[1]

I am very much relieved to hear your good news about Shelley.[2] It was certainly extremely distressing; what perhaps is the most painful is to think of the state of mind of the culprit. In France or Germany one would I think always assume that such an act of vandalism had some theoretic motive, as an expression of political or theological opinion. I am afraid that with us no such excuse can be given.

1 – A. T. K. Grant, the undergraduate president of The Martlets Society, had read a paper on 'The Criticism of Poetry' as a basis for the discussion led by TSE on 16 May. Stephen Spender, who was also present at the meeting, would recall: 'Inevitably, the club being half literary, half philosophical, the discussion turned to the problem, "How can we prove that a work of art is beautiful? . . . "

'T ——, an undergraduate who was reading philosophy and who grew tenser and tenser in his cups, and more and more voluble about Santayana, said that he did not believe there could be any absolute aesthetic criterion unless there was God. Eliot bowed his head in that almost praying attitude which I came to know well, and murmured something to the effect of: "That is what I have come to believe."' ('Remembering Eliot', *Sewanee Review* 74, Winter 1974; repr. in Spender, *The Thirties and After* [1978], 238).

2 – The Shelley Memorial, which houses a romantic sculpture of the dead nude poet sculpted by Edward Onslow Ford in a domed room designed by Basil Champneys and erected in 1893, had been vandalised on Ascension Day. E. J. Bowen (1898–1980), chemist, Fellow of the College, worked to remove the ink daubed over the white marble by three student pranksters. Sadler reported on 18 May: 'You will be glad to hear that a scouring with bleaching powder has left Shelley clean. We had an anxious time but the operation was successful. It is a sickening business. We have found the offenders but have not yet clear evidence as to the responsibility for pouring the ink on the marble.' He wrote again on 19 Dec. 1929: 'All has gone well. The worst man is a reformed character . . . And we didn't lose our tempers! Shelley improved by chemical washing, & by my gently removing his copper wreath, which was dripping green on his forehead. Now he is wreathless, & looks less "dramatic".'

With very many thanks, and the happiest memories of my visit, I am,
Yours very sincerely,
[T. S. Eliot]

TO *V. F. Calverton*[1]   CC

22 May 1928   [*The Monthly Criterion*]

Dear Mr Calverton

I hope you will excuse me for writing to you directly about the interesting manuscript of yours[2] which you sent to Herbert Read toward the end of February. I must admit that I kept it a long time before I read it, for the reason that during a long period of uncertainty about the future of *The Criterion* I read no manuscripts at all. My excuse for writing to you direct is that Read is away in France.

I am afraid that this manuscript, interesting as it is, is not quite suitable for our public. The chief difficulty is that some of the instances are much better known in America than here, and I think that you would be able to impress your points on an English public better by an essay aimed at that public. I must say that I have been very much interested in *The Modern Quarterly*, and in your own work, and I hope that you will let me see more of the latter later.

Yours very truly,
[T. S. Eliot]

TO *Leonard Woolf*   CC

22 May 1928   [London]

Dear Leonard,

I am now at last replying to your kind letter of the 9th instant concerning the Hogarth lecture series.[3] As I have explained, when I became a director

---

1–Victor Francis Calverton (1900–40) – originally George Goetz – Marxist literary critic; editor of *The Modern Quarterly*. See Leonard Wilcox, *V. F. Calverton: Radical in the American Grain* (1992). On 6 Oct. 1934 TSE wrote to D. G. Bridson, with reference to *Passing of the Gods*: 'I don't think that a book by Calverton is likely to be worth notice in *The Criterion*. The man can't write English, he doesn't know anything, and I don't believe he has any standing in America among Communists or any other people.'
2–Unidentified.
3–LW again urged TSE to agree to write for the Hogarth Lecture Series a volume on 'Revolutions in Literary Technique', or else 'Mystery as Motive in Literature', or some such

of Faber & Gwyer I made an arrangement which seemed to me perfectly fair, to give them the first refusal of any books that I wished to publish. Such a contract is of course easily modified by friendly arrangement. It is true that they have had my *Collected Poems*, but I feel that I ought to give them one or two more books before I arrange to publish a book elsewhere. Furthermore, I feel that if I do a book for some other publishing firm, then I ought to have some compensation to offer to my own firm. That is why I made the proposal to Virginia; although I must say that my firm would have been more than glad to barter a book by me against one by Virginia.

It appears however that the volume of essays which I have in mind will be ready for publication this autumn,[1] whereas even if Virginia consented to write for us a small book on Scott, which we are extremely anxious to get from her, she could not have it ready for another year at least. I cannot ask my own firm to surrender my little autumn book for the possibility of another book at least a year hence, if not more. What I suggest therefore is this. I will turn over my small book of essays to Faber & Gwyer for publication in the autumn; and they will have my book based on my Clark lectures for the following spring. I shall then feel free to publish a third book elsewhere, and should be very glad to make it one of your series. It would however be much easier for me to arrange this if Virginia would make a contract with us to write a small book on Walter Scott, to be ready within the next two years at most.

If we can agree on these points I will settle on the subject for my book for your series. I have no objection to make to the terms, and it would probably be possible for me to let you have the manuscript within a year from the present date.[2]

Yours ever,
[Tom]

---

topic. Harcourt Brace & Co. would bring out the first ten volumes in the USA, and LW would need the manuscript by the next spring, for publication in Autumn 1929.

1 – *For Lancelot Andrewes* was to be published by F&G on 20 Nov. 1928.

2 – In a letter of 19 Sept. 1928 – responding to a (now lost) letter from TSE – LW notably enthused: 'We would gladly wait for your book on TYPES OF LITERARY CRITICISM until 1930 for the series. I think it a very good idea. It would fit in extremely well with our scheme . . . But do also do the smaller book THE RIVER AND THE SEA at once in your "spare time". It sounds fascinating and we should love to publish it.'

TO *George Williamson*[1]

TS Williamson

22 May 1928   *The Monthly Criterion*

Dear Mr Williamson,

Please accept my apologies for not having written to you before. I have been very much interested by the parts of your book which you have sent me, and so is my friend, Herbert Read, to whom I have shown them, and who as you may know shares our interest in the same subject.[2] I was at first afraid, I admit, that your book would forestall my own; but our methods of treatment are so different that I hope rather that your book and my own will supplement each other. I am sorry that neither of the chapters seem to me quite suitable for *The Criterion*. I think that they are so obviously parts of a book rather than detached essays that it would be a pity to publish them separately, and I may also have been influenced by the fact that you make too many references to my own work. I await the book itself with impatience.

Yours sincerely
T. S. Eliot

TO *Jean de Menasce*

CC

22 May 1928   [London]

Dear Menasce,

I was delighted to get your letter of the 1st May. I have sent your translation on to Madame de Bassiano without any alterations whatever.[3]

1–George Williamson (1898–1968), author and educator, taught at Pomona College, Claremont, California, 1925–7; then in the Department of English, Stanford University, and later at the University of Chicago (1936–68), where he was Professor of English from 1940. Works include *The Talent of T. S. Eliot* (1929), *The Donne Tradition* (1930), and *A Reader's Guide to T. S. Eliot* (1953).
    Williamson wrote on 19 Oct.: 'Although the enclosed essay has been damned by an American magazine as too scholarly, I thought it might interest you, though perhaps not to the extent of printing. It at least makes clear a debt of pleasure that I owe to the author of *The Waste Land*.' Arguing for 'the very close relation between Eliot's aesthetic theory and his practice in *The Waste Land*', the essay was to be made use of as part II of Williamson's study *The Talent of T. S. Eliot* (1929), 20–6.
2–Williamson had submitted on 31 Dec. 1927 sections from *The Donne Tradition in English Poetry*, with acknowledgements to TSE.
3–Jean de Menasce had deprecated (1 May) his version in French of 'The Hollow Men': 'Its directness has become pompous and abstract in translation, its cadence, almost a drumbeat!' His translation of TSE's 'Perch' Io non Spero' – subsequently published as Part I of *Ash-Wednesday* – came out first in *Commerce*, 15 (Spring 1928), 5–11.

I assume of course that your last two lines are the usual French version of the Ave Maria.[1] It seems to me that your version is as near as it is possible to get, and unless I found any quite obvious misunderstanding I should never question any translation of yours.[2] I trust that you know the beautiful Ballata of Guido which suggested the poem to me.[3]

Your remarks about my controversy with Murry interest me very much, and it is hardly necessary to say that your point of view seems to me very much my own.[4] In fact the criticisms that you make deal with the fundamental differences between Catholicism and modern Protestantism. I am not quite sure to what you allude in my manuscript book, but I know that there is a good deal in that book to revise, and that my own ideas have developed rapidly since I put down the text which you have seen. I will only say that from my point of view my views are extremely like your own; although from your point of view I have no doubt that mine is quite untenable. I owe a great deal in my present position to conversation with Lord Halifax, but I am not sure whether such matters will seem to you of any importance.

I am very glad to say that Lady Ottoline is slowly improving. She is now at home although she still has two nurses. We are hoping to be able to see her within a week or two. At any rate she seems now to be out of danger.[5] When I see her I will tell her that you enquired; but I am sure that she

1 – The last two lines are: 'Pray for us sinners now and at the hour of our death / Pray for us now and at the hour of our death.'

2 – Menasce was to write to Valerie Eliot after TSE's death: 'I have a very vivid reminiscence of the process of translating that piece from *Ash Wednesday*: when it came to "teach us to care and not to care, teach us to sit still", I found the only satisfactory version was somewhat too precise and that I might be "cheating". But not knowing what to do I sent my rendering to TSE with a letter asking him whether my Christian interpretation was at all correct and apologizing for it. I had rendered: "enseignez-vous le don et l'abandon, enseignez-vous la Paix". TSE answered the translation was perfectly adequate and that was the way I gathered he had become an Anglican' (10 Jan. 1965).

3 – 'Perch' Io Non Spero' comes from Ballata XI: 'Perch'io non spero di tornar giamai.'

4 – Menasce extolled the *Criterion* controversy with JMM – 'a controversy interesting as documentary evidence as to the average sentimental . . . attitude towards God displayed by those who think of God only in terms of their own needs . . . thus . . . doing away altogether with that bond or free gift we call faith, which is after all the A B C of the spiritual life . . . and a moral life centred towards and emanating from life in God.' Then, switching to French in the middle of his letter, Menasce more directly praised TSE's attitude as it was exemplified in the draft of his book on metaphysical poetry: '*cher ami, n'avez vous pour un instant confondu, dans votre livre encore manuscrit – l'idée du vague avec l'idée de la transcendance ineffable, Trine et Saint Jean de la Croix, le creux humain et la vide divine, le relâchement et le Don, la satisfaction et la Paix.*'

5 – OM had been diagnosed with necrosis of the jaw, and had undergone an operation to remove the diseased portion of bone.

would be pleased if you would write to her yourself, as she has spoken to me about you often.[1]

Yours ever,
[T. S. Eliot]

TO *Richard Braithwaite*   CC

22 May 1928   [London]

Dear Braithwaite,

I have asked my grocers to send you a bottle of their usual whiskey,[2] which is especially useful for medicinal purposes. I hope that you will accept this on account of dilapidations by your sub-tenant![3]

Yours sincerely,
[T. S. Eliot]

TO *I. M. Parsons*[4]   CC

22 May 1928   [London]

Dear Mr Parsons,

Thank you for your letter.[5] I am having my address re-typed and will send you the copy in a few days. I am not very well satisfied with it, but

---

1–'And will you let me know about Lady Ottoline?' asked Menasce in conclusion. 'I was glad to hear from someone in London . . . that she was saved.' OM had at some time presented De Menasce with copy no. 2 of *Ara Vos Prec* (1920).

2–TSE ordered Liqueur Whiskey.

3–It is not known in what way TSE had trashed Braithwaite's rooms in King's College.

4–Ian Parsons (1906–80), who was reading English at Trinity College, Cambridge, was student editor of *The Cambridge Review* (in which he published poetry and criticism by William Empson – who was his contemporary at Winchester and Cambridge – and F. R. Leavis). On graduation he joined Chatto & Windus, initially as a typographer but soon as a junior partner under the chairmanship of Harold Raymond. His successes included Empson's *Seven Types of Ambiguity* (1930) and Leavis's *New Bearings in English Poetry* (1932). In 1954 he became chairman of Chatto & Windus (which had taken over LW's Hogarth Press in 1946); and he was President of the Publishers' Association, 1957–9. Later years saw Chatto & Windus merge with Jonathan Cape, 1969, and with the Bodley Head, 1973: Parsons became joint chairman. His works include *The Progress of Poetry: An Anthology of Verse from Hardy to the Present* (ed., 1936), *Men Who March Away* (an anthology of poetry of the First World War, ed., 1965), and *The Collected Works of Isaac Rosenberg* (1979). He was made a CBE in 1971, and retired in 1975.

5–Parsons asked (18 May) whether he might be able to publish in the May Week number of *The Cambridge Review* the paper that TSE had read at the Hesperides Society Dinner.

if it will be of any use to you, you are welcome to it, as I sympathise with other editors. It will probably be printed in the same or a modified form in America, but I do not think that that will make any difference to either you or the American editor.[1]

If you should be in London at the end of the term, do let me know. I shall probably be here.

Yours sincerely
[T. S. Eliot]

TO *R. Ellsworth Larsson* CC

22 May 1928   *[The Monthly Criterion]*

Dear Larsson,

I am returning your poem[2] because, if I may say so, it doesn't seem to me quite your best, and I should not like you to be represented in *The Criterion* but at your best. I am not quite sure about the rhythms. I wonder how it would seem to you if you had it typed out in regular lines. I do feel that there is a tendency in modern verse to make the eye do duty for the ear. That is to say there is always a danger which I have experienced myself of making typographical arrangement a substitute for rhythm. I don't know whether it could be of any use to you, but I have found myself that it is a great assistance to me to correct my verses by reciting them aloud to myself with the accompaniment of a small drum.

Do let me hear from you again soon, and send me some more manuscript.

With all good wishes,
Yours sincerely,
[T. S. Eliot]

TO *Hugh Macdonald* MS Williamson

29 May 1928   *The Criterion*

Dear Macdonald,

Please forgive me for not writing at once. We have had a great deal to occupy us at home in the last 10 days; furthermore I have been concerned

---

1–'The Idealism of Julien Benda', *The Cambridge Review* 49 (6 June 1928), 485–8.
2–Larsson had submitted a poem entitled 'Listen! Listen!'

with getting the June *Criterion* to press, without my secretary, who is ill, & with no skilled help whatever – You know what it is to have to read quantities of proof for other people who never reply punctually.

This is to say that if it is still possible, my wife & I should be delighted to come to dinner on the 6th June (Wednesday). And if yes, then the more informally, the better it will suit us. I suppose it will be only Mrs Macdonald & yourself, & Etchells?

Please apologise to Mrs Macdonald for my delay.

I want to say also that I & my wife are delighted with the book.[1] You have done me extremely well in every way: I only hope that the book will sell, so that I may look forward to doing Saml. Johnson for you.

Sincerely yours
T. S. Eliot

TO *V. W. W. S. Purcell*[2]   CC

29 May 1928   [London]

Dear Sir,

I am returning to you herewith some essays which you sent to Mr Herbert Read, who has shown them to me. I should not venture to write to you direct, but Mr Read is abroad on a holiday.

I was very much interested by these essays, but we do not find any of them quite suitable for a review of our type. I still hope, however, that anyone who can write so well as you do will have further material to send us.

Yours very truly,
[T. S. Eliot]

1–Dryden, *Of Dramatick Poesie . . .*, with 'A Dialogue on Poetic Drama' by TSE.
2–Victor Purcell (1896–1965), colonial administrator and historian, served in the Green Howards during WW1 (being wounded and taken prisoner in France), and then studied International Law at Trinity College, Cambridge, but left without taking a degree. He served in various capacities in the Malayan Civil Service – primarily in the Chinese Protectorate – which included a stint as Director-General of Information. During WW2 he was senior Chinese expert in the Malayan planning unit, and afterwards worked for the British Military Administration. He was University Lecturer in Far Eastern History at Cambridge, 1949–63. His writings include *The Spirit of Chinese Poetry* (1929), *Chinese Evergreen* (1938) – about a trip across China with I. A. Richards and William Empson in 1937 – *The Chinese in Malaya* (1948), and *The Memoirs of a Malayan Official* (1965). He also published, masked as 'Myra Buttle', a verse satire on TSE, *The Sweeniad* (1957).

TO *The Editor of* The New Adelphi

Published June 1928

Parliament and the New Prayer Book

Sir,

I was so much interested by your admirable editorial notes in the March number of *The New Adelphi* that I hope you will permit me to make a few comments.[1]

I find it a little difficult to reconcile your various statements about the Church of England. First, you say that the House of Commons, in rejecting the new Prayer Book at the beginning of this year, 'voiced the dormant sentiment of the nation.' Being struck by this remark, I read further in the hope of finding out what the dormant sentiment of the nation might be.

1–JMM wrote in 'Notes and Comments' (*The New Adelphi*, 1: 3 [Mar. 1928]) about the recent unexpected rejection by the House of Commons of the proposed New Prayer Book: 'In this matter the House of Commons voiced the dormant sentiment of the nation. Hundreds of thousands of men and women who scarcely ever take part in a Church service are concerned for and attached to the Church of England . . . Englishmen are shy about religion – so shy, indeed, that many of them never go to church at all.' All the same, he went on: 'What happened when the House of Commons rejected the New Prayer Book was that the nation, which is in the last resort the real Church of England, rejected a manifest tendency towards Roman sacerdotalism which the more professional or more specialized Church had found it necessary to yield to . . . [A]ll those changes which seemed to the ordinary man to bring the sacramental doctrine of the Church of England nearer to that of the Roman Church were defeated. The House of Commons did well . . .' Murry argued further: 'It would be easy to . . . show that Anglo-Catholicism can trace a noble, though of late years sadly contaminated, descent from Andrewes, Laud and Hooker; it would be easy to admit that the majority of Anglo-Catholics are a high-minded and devoted body of men. But the fact is that they represent a doctrine totally opposed to that upon which the Established Church of England really rests.' The rejection of the New Prayer Book, Murry proceeded, had thus amounted to a fundamental 'blow' to Anglo-Catholicism. There have even been extreme cases of representative individuals seeking to contest the power of the Commons concerning the doctrines of the Church of England: 'Since the publication by the Bishops of their proposed amendments to the Deposited Book, controversy has been hot and furious. Lord Hugh Cecil has repeatedly enounced the wild theory that Parliament has no right to pronounce upon doctrinal issues in the Church of England. The theory in a vague form is shared by many Anglo-Catholics. Lord Hugh Cecil deserves the credit of stating it clearly, though it is so remote from the reality that it is interesting chiefly as showing what views *can* be held by responsible Anglo-Catholic laymen.' The heart of the matter, Murry concluded, is that what has transpired by way of the vote in the Commons is acute: 'The doctrinal basis of the Church of England has collapsed.' And there is one fundamental sticking point that has become 'the real danger to the Church of England. The fact is simple. Educated men find it daily harder to take orders. And the reason for that is also simple . . . The reason is that educated men do not believe in the Resurrection of Christ . . . The educated man who can believe in the Resurrection will go to Rome, the educated man who cannot will – what will he do? That is the question the Bishops should be trying to answer' (194–9).

I admit that I am not yet clear in my mind what the dormant sentiment of the nation is, unless it be a dormant sentiment for remaining dormant: in which it seems to resemble the dormant sentiment of a dormouse. The nation, apparently is (at least, in hundreds of thousands) attached to the Church of England: it is surely our business to analyze this sentiment of persons who, as you say, 'scarcely ever take part in a Church service'. But I think, Sir, that you alter the case by assuming, as you seem to do, that the new Prayer Book represents a tendency towards 'Roman sacerdotalism'. I have no doubt that to you, and to the hypothetical hundreds of thousands who 'scarcely ever take part in a Church service', because they are so 'shy' – not because they are occupied with more important matters, but solely because of that schoolboy shyness, that precious quality which must be preserved at all costs unless the race is to degenerate – the rejected Prayer Book stands for 'Roman sacerdotalism'. But I find no admission in your admirable notes, that to those who like what you (and no doubt the hundreds of thousands as well) call 'sacerdotalism', the Prayer Book represents a restriction of this 'sacerdotalism'. Accordingly, you speak of the rejection of the Book as a 'blow' to Anglo-Catholicism. Yet you have read the report of the speeches in the Lords, including the speech of Lord Halifax, so you can hardly suppose that the 'Roman sacerdotalists' received the Book with great enthusiasm.

In one or two points of detail I cannot accept your statement of fact. It is interesting, of course, to hear that Lord Hugh Cecil is an Anglo-Catholic, for I did not know that fact.[1] But it is not interesting to hear that, according to the Anglo-Catholic view, Parliament has no right to pronounce upon doctrinal issues. The fact is that, according to the law of the land, Parliament has not only the right but the duty so to pronounce. To some of us, this is a legal absurdity which ought to be altered; but none of us question the legal right and duty of Parliament to pronounce, according to existing law. You refer to Hooker: but you must know as well as I know that the whole social situation was very different in Hooker's day; the relation of Crown to Estates was different; and it is hardly likely that Hooker envisaged the prospect of a Commons in which nonconformists, Jews, Parsees, Atheists and women took part. I doubt even whether Hooker realized that in the House of Lords an Isaacs would be a Marquis, a Smith an Earl, a Samuel a Baron.[2]

1–Lord Hugh Cecil (1869–1956), Conservative MP for Oxford University, 1920–37; Fellow of Hertford College, Oxford, 1891–1936; raised to the peerage as Baron Quickswood, 1941.
2–Rufus Isaacs, first Marquess of Reading (1860–1935): politician and judge. F. E. Smith, first Earl of Birkenhead (1872–1930), barrister and poitician. Marcus Samuel, first Viscount

One other point. You say that the hundreds of thousands, who listen in or ride about in Morris cars on Sunday because they are too British in their 'shyness' to go to Church, the hundreds of thousands who are too shy to take communion, the great broad-shouldered Englishmen who are such sensitive creatures that they cannot make confessions, these great generous, boisterous schoolboys, these persons constitute the Church of England. The Church of England is not a visible Church of communicants, but a wholly invisible Church of shy schoolboys. And yet you admit that there is a real danger to the Church of England. The shy schoolboy attitude does not, in fact, work. They are so shy that they will not take holy orders! It is not that they are not religious: no, there is no one more religious. No, it is that they are 'educated', the hundreds of thousands; and being educated – they *cannot* believe in the Resurrection.

Now I wonder, Sir, whether you suppose that the 'uneducated' believe in the Resurrection, and that the 'educated' do not. My opinion is that it has nothing to do with education or illiteracy in the ordinary sense. I suspect that in England today there are more 'educated' people who believe in the Resurrection than there are 'uneducated' who so believe. But, perhaps, your standards of 'education' are different from mine.

I can only suppose that your view of the Church is exactly the opposite of mine. According to your view, the Church of England consists of those people who never go to church (except, perhaps, to be baptized, married and buried), and who are too honest and too religious to think of becoming clergymen.

Yours, etc.,
T. S. Eliot

Vivien Eliot TO *Ottoline Morrell* MS Texas

1 June 1928   57 Chester Terrace

Dearest Ottoline

Just a wee line to say I am so pleased to hear that you are getting a little better.

It was so good of you to have Tom telephoned to, & to say that you would actually see us, separately, soon. It is wonderful news. I am

---

Samuel (1853–1927), petrol entrepreneur, was raised to the peerage as Baron Bearsted in 1921 and advanced to a viscountcy in 1925; he was succeeded by his son, Walter Samuel, second Viscount Bearsted (1882–1948), art collector and philanthropist.

thankful.[1] Your illness has been too terrible, & what you have suffered is impossible to think of. Aldous & Maria [Huxley] spoke affectionately of you, & with such great sympathy. We liked them better than ever.

> With so much love –
> Affectly
> *Vivienne*

TO *W. Swan Stallybrass*[2]   MS Williamson

1 June 1928   [London]

Dear Mr Stallybrass,

Thank you for your letter of the 31st.[3] I am flattered by your suggestion that you would like to have me write a preface to Aldington's translation of Benda's book. I should have been very glad to do so, but it would be a little awkward for me. My criticisms of the book were rather severe even in *The Times* article which you have seen, and are still more severe in another article which I am publishing in America.[4] And the fact is that I am too much involved with certain people in Paris who are partly the object of Benda's attack to feel that it would be possible for me to introduce his book. Even without this complication it is a little difficult to introduce the book unless one has a more wholehearted approval of it.

This does not mean that I do not admire the book. I think it is well worth translating, and I wish it all success. But for these reasons I should have been delighted to write the introduction.

> Sincerely yours,
> [T. S. Eliot]

1–OM would presently gossip about her interview with TSE, as VW was to relate in a letter to Vanessa Bell on 7 June: 'Tom is in a great taking with Vivien as mad as a hare, but not confined, and they give parties, where she suddenly accuses him of being in love with Ottoline (and me, but this Ott: threw in as a sop) and Tom drinks, and Vivien suddenly says when talk dies down "You're the bloodiest snob I ever knew" – so I have refused to dine there' (*Letters* III, 508).

2–W. S. Stallybrass (1855–1927), Managing Director of George Routledge and Sons Ltd.

3–Stallybrass wrote on 31 May, having seen the review by TSE (anon) of Benda's *La Trahison des Clercs*: 'Culture and Anarchy', *TLS*, 23 Feb. 1928, 118. RA's translation of the book was to be published in Sept.

4–'The Idealism of Julien Benda', *The New Republic*, 12 Dec. 1928.

TO *Hugh Macdonald*   ts Williamson

5 June 1928   57 Chester Terrace

Dear Macdonald,

Can I have six more copies of the Dryden at trade prices with invoice? I refuse to accept them without payment: they are for Gifts to people to whom I owe gifts.

I have put my wife to bed this afternoon, and I am not sure whether she will be fit for me to allow her to come tomorrow, she wishes to come but I may leave her at home. If so, I will ring up tomorrow (I have no number for your private address). And in that case, I shall tell her that I will persuade you and Mrs Macdonald to dine with us here soon. I look forward to seeing you and the Etchells tomorrow.

Sincerely,

T. S. E.

TO *John Gould Fletcher*   cc

11 June 1928   [*The Monthly Criterion*]

My dear Fletcher,

Please let me know as soon as you are back. I should be very happy if you would do that review on contemporary poetry which you suggested for the October number, and shall have several books to send you. Incidentally, I think that Harold Monro's last book of verse[1] is extremely good, and I should like to see you as soon as you get back. Would you lend me that book of Aline Lion's on Fascism which I gave you?[2] I have several other books on the subject, and think of doing something about it myself.

Yours ever,

[T. S. Eliot]

1–Monro, *The Earth for Sale*, published by the Poetry Bookshop on 24 May 1928.
2–Aline Lion, *The Pedigree of Fascism* (1928), was among the books reviewed by TSE in 'The Literature of Fascism', C. 8 (Dec. 1928), 280–90. TSE would later write of Lion, in an undated reference (1936): 'I have known Miss Lion for some years as an occasional contributor to *The Criterion*. She has struck me as a person of philosophic mind, and of wide learning in philosophic subjects, and of literature both French and English. I have always found her essays, both published and unpublished, to be of very serious interest, and to exhibit rigorous and conscientious thinking, and I have no doubt that any lectures she gave would contain matter deserving the attention of the most serious audience.'

TO *Mary Hutchinson*[1]   MS Texas

14 June 1928   Faber & Gwyer Ltd

Dear Mary

Thank you very much for your letter. I should like to lunch with you but it would have to be the week after next as the renewed *Criterion* activity has been responsible for a series of business lunches. And in any case – I think you should come to 57 Chester Terrace, Eaton Square, first: it has been done up, & the garden is not bad. Besides, Vivien also has been pining to see you. Could you, perhaps, come to tea on Tuesday or Friday? We should be very happy.

                                         T. S. E.

Do let us meet soon, anyway.

TO *Mario Praz*   CC

14 June 1928   [*The Monthly Criterion*]

My dear Praz,

I am taking the liberty of asking your opinion so far as you can give one off-hand, on our forthcoming edition of Guido Cavalcanti about which I told you. It is, you may remember, to be published together with the translations by Ezra Pound and Rossetti and with textual criticism. Pound is extremely desirous of including collotype reproductions of the manuscript. He is convinced that these reproductions would add very much to the value of the book from the point of view of Universities and libraries. These reproductions would of course add to the cost, and we do not want to go to that trouble and expense unless it will really make a difference to a monumental edition. What is your opinion so far as you can give one?

The June *Criterion* with Montale's poem will be out in a few days. We will send him two copies as you suggest. I hope to see you again in London before long.

                              Yours ever,
                              [T. S. Eliot]

1–Mary Hutchinson (1889–1977), a half-cousin of Lytton Strachey; prominent hostess, author: see Biographical Register.

TO *Richard Braithwaite*   cc

14 June 1928   [London]

Dear Mr Braithwaite,

I wonder whether I can persuade you to allow me to send you two books which you have probably seen already: *Astronomy & Cosmogony* by J. H. Jeans, and *Beyond the Electron* by Sir J. J. Thomson. I am quite incompetent to hold any opinion about them, but I thought that if you would be willing to look at them and see if a review for *The Criterion*, of any length you like, could be made, I should be very glad indeed. If you thought that nothing could be said about them suitable for a review like *The Criterion*, you would merely let me know and keep the books. Please let me send them.[1]

Yours ever sincerely,
[T. S. Eliot]

TO *Kenneth Pickthorn*[2]   cc

14 June 1928   [London]

My dear Pickthorn,

I wonder if you could give me any suggestions. After a great deal of trouble we have more or less reorganised *The Criterion* as a Quarterly. The June number is about to appear, and I am now turning my attention to the October number. I should like to have more or less regular essays of historical narrative or biography. I assume from what you have told me that you are too busy to do any writing yourself, but can you suggest any other intelligent historian who might be enlisted?

I hope to see you again in London at the end of term, and then you and your wife must certainly come and see us.

Yours ever sincerely,
[T. S. Eliot]

1–HR had advised TSE on 4 June 1927: 'I think R. B. Braithwaite . . . is a possibility for some kinds of books (particularly the dangerous No Man's Land between Philosophy & Science). I don't think he would be much good for the purely scientific book. And perhaps he is rather inhuman. But I do decidedly feel that he would fill an appropriate niche. He is probably very lazy.' Braithwaite (28 June) was not able to accept the invitation: his wife was 'very seriously ill . . . not expected to recover'. She died later in 1928.
2–Kenneth Pickthorn (1892–1975), historian and politician; Fellow of Corpus Christi College, Cambridge: see Biographical Register.

TO *H. W. B. Joseph*[1]   CC

14 June 1928   [London]

Dear Mr Joseph,

You may remember that some time ago you did *The Criterion* the honour of writing a very interesting review of Bertrand Russell.[2] *The Criterion* has again been reorganised in quarterly form, and I am writing to ask whether you would care to review *Realism* by S. K. Hasan with a Foreword by J. A. Smith for us for publication, if possible, in October. If the subject interests you I should be very glad to hear from you, and I very much hope that you may care to do this. I may mention, in case you have not seen the book, that you yourself are discussed; but this would make a review by you all the more interesting.[3]

Yours sincerely,
[T. S. Eliot]

TO *R. S. Wilson*   CC

14 June 1928   [London]

Dear Mr Wilson,

It is very kind of you to write to me.[4] Indeed I remember very well meeting you on a voyage which left me at Marseilles, but which I believe took you on to India. I am nearly always in London, and if you are ever here I hope that you will let me know.

Yours sincerely,
[T. S. Eliot]

1–H. W. B. Joseph (1867–1943): philosopher; Fellow of New College, Oxford, from 1891. His works include *An Introduction to Logic* (1906), *Some Problems in Ethics* (1930), and *Essays in Ancient and Modern Philosophy* (1935). See H. A. Prichard, 'H. W. B. Joseph, 1867–1943', *Mind*, new series 53: 210 (Apr. 1944), 189–91; A. H. Smith, 'Joseph, Horace William Brindley, 1867–1943', *Proceedings of the British Academy*, 31 (1945), 375–98.
2–Joseph on Russell, *The Analysis of Matter*, MC 6 (Dec. 1927), 548.
3–Joseph did not write again for *The Criterion*.
4–Wilson wrote from North Shields that he had just realised the identity of the man he met on board the 'Billy Oxfordshire' in 1925: it was TSE himself, who had been sailing in Nov. 1925 to have a rest at the Savoy Hotel, Alpes Maritimes. 'Had I then known your identity our conversation might have been different and not quite so fatuous!'

TO *A. L. Rowse*

TS Exeter

14 June 1928   *The Monthly Criterion*

My dear Rowse,

I have been meaning to write to you for some time. I have your interesting review of Crump which will appear in the October number;[1] it was just too late for the June number, which is already printed and bound. What you suggest writing is exactly what I wanted from you. I will try to get the books of Hearnshaw and Stalin.[2] Meanwhile please try to find time to meditate such an article for the December *Criterion*.

I should be interested to hear more about the large masses of matter which you say you have on hand.[3]

I still hope that you may come to London. Fletcher in particular is most anxious to meet you.

Yours sincerely,
T. S. Eliot

TO *A. E. James, Messrs James & James*

CC

15 June 1928   [London]

Dear Mr James,

Re Haigh Estate: Dun Laoghaire.

As Maurice has now returned, I have handed him Coall's cheque for £552 odd to collect and distribute between his mother, Vivien and himself. One point however occurs to me. The cheque is for the calendar year 1927. Strictly speaking, should ¼ of the amount which would have accrued to Mr Haigh-Wood personally, not go to capital account for investment by the trustees? But as the amount is so small, and the proceedings so complicated, would it (in that case) not be feasible to arrange privately among the trustees and beneficiaries, so that the whole sum be treated as

---

1–ALR on C. G. Crump, *History and Historical Research*, C. 8 (Sept. 1928), 159–61.

2–ALR suggested (20 May) 'a full-dress article on the present impasse of Socialist theory & its likely solution in relation to academic culture: Hearnshaw's big book *A Survey of Socialism*, plus Stalin's book on *Leninism*, would provide my text if you would care to get them for me.' TSE had reviewed F. J. C. Hearnshaw (ed.), *The Social and Political Ideas of Some Great Thinkers of the Sixteenth and Seventeenth Centuries* (1926) – 'Hooker, Hobbes, and Others', *TLS*, 11 Nov. 1926, 789.

3–ALR wrote, 'I have large masses of more literary matter remaining over from youth and all the years when writing was my only devotion, and I thought never to be able to come to universities.'

income, and divided into three equal parts for Mrs Haigh-Wood, Maurice and Vivien?

With regard to this rearrangement into three equal parts: Maurice showed me your figures for it, and of course I wholly concurred both about principle and method. Is any other formality necessary beyond the acceptance by Maurice and Vivien of the cheques in payment for the shares required to adjust the estate into three equal parts?

Yours sincerely,

[T. S. Eliot]

TO *Messrs Houghton Mifflin Company*   CC

15 June 1928   [London]

Dear Sirs,

I have your two letters of the 4th instant.[1]

As for Mr Hart Crane's poem, I must refer you to him, as *The Criterion* always leaves book and anthology rights to the author.

As for 'Salutation', you are quite welcome to reprint that upon payment of £5:5/- (five guineas) anthology rights to me. I must mention that Messrs Knopf's anthology rights for the poems mentioned[2] extend only to America; so that if there is any question of an English edition of your anthology, you will have to negotiate with me about the rights for Great Britain.

Yours faithfully,

[T. S. Eliot]

1–Houghton Mifflin Company wished to reprint Hart Crane's 'The Bridge' and TSE's 'Salutation', in an anthology of contemporary English and American poetry (ed. by John Drinkwater, Henry Seidel Canby, William Rose Benet), for college and general readers.
2–'Morning at the Window', 'Portrait of a Lady', 'La Figlia Che Piange', and 'Conversation Galante' (all published in the USA by Alfred A. Knopf & Company).

15 June 1928   [Faber & Gwyer Ltd]

Sir,

I have suggested to the members of my Board a series of small books of English Theology.[2] If I can succeed in interesting you in the notion, we hope that you will consider editing this series for us.

What I have had in mind is this. The works of the great English theologians are bulky, expensive, and largely out of print. The 'Library of Anglo-Catholic Theology', even so far as obtainable at all, is too voluminous and too expensive for the intelligent layman, or the parish priest, or the amateur of letters. I have in mind a series of small books to be sold at about 3s.6d., somewhat the size of *The Ancient and Modern Library of Theological Literature*, published some years ago by Griffith, Farran, Okeden & Welsh, of which I have Andrewes's *Sermons on the Incarnation*. I should wish to include select sermons (not selections *from* sermons, like Pearsall Smith's useless Oxford text of Donne), and any important theological works of the same compass. The public in view would be the intelligent layman and the parish priest, and also, to a large extent, the person really interested in English prose style. I thought that we might begin with select sermons of such as Andrewes, Latimer, Taylor,[3] and some of the great XVII century divines, and possibly include such interesting essays as Bramhall's 'Just Vindication'.[4] If the series thrived, we might find place later for a new edition of Hooker etc.

I may say that I read with great admiration and enjoyment your book on Laud, in Sidney Dark's series; but that my own opinion that you are the natural choice for editor of such a series has been fortified by the judgment of others.

---

1 – The Revd Arthur Stuart Duncan-Jones (1879–1955) held various incumbencies (including St Paul's, Knightsbridge, London) before becoming Dean of Chichester Cathedral, 1929–55. His publications include *Archbishop Laud* (1927).

2 – D. L. Murray, whom TSE consulted anent the editing of the series, recommended Duncan-Jones because '(1) he has written on Laud (2) his admirable Hilsean lectures, *Ordered Liberty* [1917], are built up on a study of Laud, Bramhall, Hooker and the rest'.

3 – TSE wrote, in 'The Prose of the Preacher', *Listener*, 3 July 1929, 22–3: 'Donne was by no means either the first or the last of the great English preachers; I believe that his contemporary, Bishop Andrewes, is greater, and Jeremy Taylor certainly must take equal rank. But Donne is undoubtedly the most readable. Hugh Latimer, Bishop of Worcester, was a great preacher and a great prose writer long before Donne' (22).

4 – See TSE's 'Archbishop Bramhall', *Theology* 15 (July 1927), 11–17; repr. as 'John Bramhall' (*SE*).

If the idea interests you, will you let me know? And then you might do me the honour of having lunch or tea with me, and discussing the venture.

I am, Sir,
Your obedient servant,
[T. S. Eliot]

TO *Marguerite Caetani*   TS Caetani

15 June 1928   *The Monthly Criterion*

My dear Marguerite,

I have been meaning to write to you for a long time, though there is one matter about which I did not wish to write until *The Criterion* was at least likely to continue.

We have been managing (this is private I mean personal information, not the *Criterion*) very much better this spring, and I am hopeful. Vivien has been running her house well and we have seen a good many people. We had Mirsky[1] to dinner the other night, just before his departure, and enjoyed him immensely. He seemed to get on very well with Clive Bell, whom I hope you will see soon. Also I am giving an introduction to you to our old friends Aldous and Maria Huxley (Maria is a Belgian, but very agreeable) who are taking a house at Suresnes so that I should like them to come out to see you.[2]

1–Dmitri S. Mirsky (1890–1939), Russian scholar, was the son of Prince P. D. Svyatopolk-Mirsky, army officer and civil servant (on his mother's side he was descended from an illegitimate son of Catherine the Great). Educated at the University of St Petersburg, where he read Oriental languages and classics, he served for several years as an officer in the army, and was wounded during WW1 while fighting on the German front; later he was to serve in the White Army. In 1921, he was appointed lecturer in Russian at the School of Slavonic Studies, London (under Sir Bernard Pares), where his cultivation and command of languages brought him to the attention of a wide literary circle: he became acquainted with, among others, TSE, E. M. Forster, Leonard and Virginia Woolf. He published several books, including *Contemporary Russian Literature* (2 vols, 1926) and *A History of Russian Literature from the Earliest Times to the Death of Dostoevsky, 1881* (1927), and articles on literature, culture and history. In 1931 he joined the Communist Party of Great Britain (see 'Why I became a Marxist', *Daily Worker*, 30 June 1931), and in 1932 returned to Russia where he worked as a Soviet literary critic (and incidentally became acquainted with Edmund Wilson and Malcolm Muggeridge). In 1937 he was arrested in the Stalinist purge, found guilty of 'suspected espionage', and sentenced to eight years of correctional labour: he died in a labour camp in Siberia. See G. S. Smith, *D. S. Mirsky: A Russian-English Life, 1980–1939* (2000).

2–In June the Huxleys had taken no. 3 Rue du Bac, Suresnes, Paris, by the Seine north of the Bois du Boulogne, though in the event they did not occupy it until three months later.

Are you never coming to England? I have my hands full here, publicly and privately, and cannot get even to Paris, to say nothing of Boston.

What I want to put bluntly to you is this. I did not, as I said, wish to bother you about the *Criterion* until something was definite. But now we have collected a certain amount of subsidy: F. S. Oliver has promised a good deal, and various other people, such as Richmond, Whibley, Dugald[1] Malcolm, have made promises. So we have enough guarantee to justify going on, and the first number of the new Quarterly *Criterion* is just ready. But we are still about £250 a year short of what we need (which is about £800 for three years).

You asked me most tactfully to become correspondent for *Commerce* again. What I should like to ask is this. I should like to be of use to *Commerce*, in the way of getting suitable contributions, but I should not like to accept any stipend (which was never earned anyway). Also I would give *Commerce* a poem a year, if it wanted it, for nothing: if you could guarantee £25 a year for *The Criterion*. But now having made the suggestion, I don't want to say anything more about it.[2]

I hear that Jean de Menasce is to be in Paris. I hope he will see you.

yours ever affectionately,
Tom.

TO *Charles Whibley*   CC

15 June 1928   [*The Monthly Criterion*]

My dear Whibley,

Thank you very much for your kind letter. I am distressed to hear that you have had more pain and trouble; I hope that it may soon pass off. It would be delightful if you found a *pied-à-terre* in London, and if that meant that I might hope to see more of you. We were both most pleased by your kind general invitation, and if, towards the end of the summer, it seems practicable for us to attempt such a weekend, I shall certainly venture to propose us.

I shall be writing to you next week about the *Criterion*. The June number is ready. What I want to find (in default of contributors like yourself) is a few young men who are properly educated and can write

1 – *Sc.* Dougal.
2 – Caetani wrote (April 1928): 'I will give you yearly £30–0–0 for the Review & a poem but I think you ought to have Commerce in your care also. I cannot go on with Hogarth. I do not think it is worth while whereas with you it is another story. You think it over.'

history and biography. I have written to ask Pickthorn; I don't suppose you know of any?

> In haste,
> ever affectionately,
> [T. S. Eliot]

I had an extremely intelligent and sympathetic review of my Dryden in the *T.L.S.*,[1] which made up for Squire's bilious grumpiness in the *Observer*.[2]

TO *Edouard Roditi*   TS UCLA

18 June 1928   *The Monthly Criterion*

Dear Mr Roditi,

I have your letter of the 15th instant.[3] I am sorry to say that I have not yet had time to read carefully your translation of *Anabase*, and the others; I have not had time to read anything lately, as I have had to do without my secretary who is ill, and have had to prepare the June *Criterion* by myself. I hope to read your manuscript very soon and will write again.

Meanwhile I am writing to say that it is really not for me to say, one way or the other, anything about the publication of your translation. It would really be impertinent of me to intervene; the real question, as it

---

1–'Of Dramatick Poesie', *TLS*, 14 June 1928, 447.
2–J. C. Squire (1884–1958), editor of the *London Mercury*, 1919–34, and prolific reviewer. 'This is a pleasant, if rather expensive reprint,' decreed Squire ('Dryden and the Drama', the *Observer*, 10 June 1928, 6). 'But Dryden's plays are not good for acting'; and of 'A Dialogue on Poetic Drama': 'Mr Eliot is still further from treating the Dialogue as a branch (though a branch for mere reading) of the Drama. It is perhaps symbolical that he does not even give his characters fanciful Greek names as did Dryden: he calls them, in the desiccated modern manner, A, B, C, D and E . . . These characters of his are all in deadly earnest, and they are all of one type . . . Mr Eliot's remarks about the drama are, as compared with Dryden's, handicapped by the fact that Dryden was a practising dramatist and that Mr Eliot (up to the present) is not. Mr Eliot has very interesting things to say about the present confusion of thought and the absence of agreed beliefs, it may well be that a certain measure of agreement, not at present to be found in any European society, is necessary if the drama is to flourish . . . All students of the drama should read [Dryden] (though, pace Mr Eliot, he never wrote a great play) and they will lose nothing by reading Mr Eliot as well. But why not a few (other than textual) annotations?'
3–Roditi wrote on 15 June to say that Eugène Jolas, editor of *transition*, had offered to publish 'a few portions' of Roditi's translation of *Anabase*, by St-John-Perse. 'However he fears that he might thereby incur your displeasure so that he is unwilling to act without your consent . . . I would therefore be much obliged to you should you (if you have found time to read the copy of my translation which I have sent to you) write me some letters which I might show to Mr Jolas as a proof of your entire consent. After which I should try to come to an agreement, if possible, with Monsieur Leger before the end of July.'

seems to me, is what the author wants done. If I were the author, instead of simply one of the translators, I should expect to be consulted. I am afraid therefore that I must refer you to St Leger Leger, 26 rue de la Tour, *Passy*. You can tell him that I have no point of view whatever and that it is entirely for him to decide what he wishes done. If I said more than this, I should be exceeding my province, but you have all my good wishes. And I will write to you about your translations as soon as I, in a very busy life, can.

> Yours very truly,
> T. S. Eliot

TO *Marguerite Caetani*   CC

18 June 1928   [London]

My dear Marguerite,

   A new situation has arose, as you will see from the enclosed copy of letter. I don't know this bird Roditi, I suppose he is one of These hyphenatedamericans. He wrote to me some time ago about this, and I told him I had done the Authorised translation and was only waiting for Leger's corrections, and tried to steer him onto Robinson Crusoe. Now this comes. It is Leger's or Briand's fault, and is what happens under a Democracy; our english civil servants have Time for Literature, and the job of running the world is done as well or better.

   I am writing to say this is an affair over which I have no Control, but that he should in Courtesy consult Leger first. I thought I ought to warn you; perhaps you may be able to use influence on Roditi (an unpleasant name like Rodent) as well as on Leger. Have you ever heard of Roditi

   [typescript runs off page].

> With love from both,
> In haste,
> [Tom]

Vivienne Eliot TO *Mary Hutchinson* MS Texas

19 June 1928   57 Chester Terrace, s.w.1.

Dear Mary

I am just writing to tell you how happy it made me to see you again, after such a long time. I am so very very glad we are to continue our very *old* friendship.

Thank you for coming to tea today, & for bringing me the heliotropes – which I shall plant in the garden.

I look forward to coming to tea with you next Wednesday – & to seeing yr house & garden.[1]

There are a great many things I want to say to you which I could not today, but I will when I see you again.

> With love, & very happily
> Vivienne Eliot

TO *A. E. James, Messrs James & James* CC

19 June 1928   [London]

Dear Mr James,

Thank you for your letter of the 18th instant. There is one point where I do not quite follow. You say that ¼ of the amount paid by Coall as net rents for 1927 should be treated as capital. But Vivien and Maurice were already in enjoyment of practically ¼ each of the income, and further I should suppose that their Aunt Emily's share should be deducted, so that the amount to be now treated as Capital woud be ¼ of 1/3, i.e. 1/12th of £552.15.3d. that is £46.1.3. Am I correct? In that case the division should be £184. 5.1d. each to Maurice and Vivien, £138.3.10d. to their mother; but however they chose to divide the interest the capital deduction would be only £46.

I note what you say about the Memorandum.

> Yours sincerely,
> [T. S. Eliot]

---

1 – The Hutchinsons had recently moved from River House, on the Upper Mall in Hammersmith (next door to Kelmscott House), to a house on Albert Road, Regent's Park.

TO *Herbert Read*

21 June 1928   [*The Monthly Criterion*]

My dear Herbert,

I have asked Trend to lunch on Monday at the Royal Societies at one. If it isn't too far for you to look in too I wish you would come and have a look at the place. If you take the Piccadilly tube from South Kensington you get out at Dover Street, and it is only a few steps to 63 St James's Street.

Blackwells say that they have no more review copies of Coulton's *Art and the Reformation*, I am still waiting to hear from the Cambridge Press about the other book.

By the way, how would Richards strike you if he could be got hold of as a reviewer for *English Prose Style*?[1]

Yours ever,

[T. S. E.]

TO *Frank Morley*

21 June 1928   *The Monthly Criterion*

My dear Morley,

If you have that various correspondence from Richmond I should be very grateful if you would let me have a list of the *Criterion* guarantors, with amounts and if possible the addresses of the people to whom to write. Some of the people of course are people whom I have dealt with myself, such as May Sinclair and Madame Bassiano. If you still have the actual letters from these people which Richmond passed on to you, I should find them useful, as the terms of my letter to them perhaps should vary from case to case.

1–Four months later, when TSE let HR see a proof of IAR's review (of Herbert Read's *English Prose Style*, C. 8 [Dec. 1928], 315–24) of his book, HR wrote on 31 Oct.: 'I don't think I want to answer it now; perhaps not at all. It is respectful, which is all that matters. Some of his criticisms are very useful; others are a matter of opinion. As for Anglican & Roman, I admit he has scored half a point, but I would maintain that good prose is via media, & that is what my version aims at. The book can, of course, be immensely improved by more time & deliberation: I don't pretend to produce a masterpiece of reasoning in the odd hours most men devote to tiddley-winks & push-penny. The book has come in for much more serious criticism than I ever expected it to; I'm afraid I had in mind a less critical audience. It is a dreadful confession, but the world is too hard on academic saints.

'There is more to be said about Richards' attitude in general, but this sometime in conversation.'

I should like to see you again soon privily, and when you have time I wish you would ring up and suggest a day next week when you could come and have tea with me here, or if you would prefer I could come to you.

Yours ever,
T. S. E.

TO *Nancy Cunard*[1]   cc

21 June 1928   [London]

Dear Nancy,

Thank you for your letter of the 19th.[2] I am delighted to hear of your new venture with a printing press; it is much better than the suggestion I once made to you that you should breed blue Bedlingtons. I await further news of the Press with much interest. I wish that I had anything to offer at the moment, but my very infrequent productions are for the immediate future tied up already with Faber & Gwyer and with the Hogarth Press and with Etchells and Macdonald. But I will keep your press in mind, and hope that I may eventually have something to submit.

I am very glad to hear that you are living in the country. You have found out at last that it is quite impossible to live in Paris; I never stay in that town now for more than a week at a time, if I can help it.

1–Nancy Cunard (1896–1965), writer, journalist, political activist; daughter of Sir Bache Cunard, heir to the Cunard Line shipping business, and of an American heiress named Maud Alice Burke, who flourished as a London hostess under the name of 'Emerald' Lady Cunard (1871–1945). Nancy cultivated lovers and friends including Michael Arlen, Aldous Huxley, and Louis Aragon. In 1920 she moved to Normandy where she ran the Hours Press (successor to Three Mountains Press), 1928–34: her productions included works by Pound and Beckett. Her own works include *Black Man and White Ladyship* (1931); *Negro: An Anthology* (1934); *Authors Take Sides on the Spanish War* (1937) – a pamphlet sponsored by *Left Review* – and *These Were the Hours: Memories of My Hours Press, Réanville and Paris, 1928–1932* (1969). See *Nancy Cunard: Brave Poet, Indomitable Rebel*, ed. Hugh Ford (1968); Anne Chisholm, *Nancy Cunard* (1981); Shari Benstock, *Women of the Left Bank: Paris, 1900–1940* (1986). Lois G. Gordon, *Nancy Cunard: Heiress, Muse, Political Activist* (2007), surmises an affair with TSE.

2–Nancy Cunard wrote on 19 June – from Puits Carrée, 9 Chapelle Réeanville, EURE, Vernon – to say she had taken over printing (on a hand-press) 'the one-time Three Mountains . . . bought from Bird'. Did TSE have anything she might print in 'a small edition of 100 or 150 – about 40–60 pages (or less)'? She wrote again on 19 July to ask if she might put his 'name on prospectus (without time-element) as author of poems . . . No commitment, just name, and then eventually – .' (The Hours Press published sixteen books between 1930 and 1932.)

If I should be coming over to France I would let you know, but I see no immediate prospect.

Yours ever,
[T. S. E.]

TO *H. W. B. Joseph*   CC

21 June 1928   [London]

Dear Mr Joseph,

Thank you very much for your kind letter and especially for your kind remarks about my poem.[1] I quite understand how you feel about the book I suggested; and indeed if I had taken the time to examine the book more carefully I would have anticipated your objection. I hope however to get from you soon either an article or another long review, and if you have any suggestions to make yourself I should accept them with pleasure. I may say that your review of Russell's book was greeted with great applause by all my colleagues.

Yours sincerely,
[T. S. Eliot]

TO *Marguerite Caetani*   CC

25 June 1928   [London]

Dear Marguerite,

Thank you very much for your kind letter and for your generous contribution of thirty pounds toward guaranteeing *The Criterion* on the terms mentioned in my last letter. It is very good of you. I think that either you slightly misunderstood my reference to *Commerce*, or else that I have slightly misunderstood yours. I suggested, as you will find by referring to my letter, that I should again occupy myself with trying to find and suggest to you suitable contributors to *Commerce*. About the Hogarth Press. I did not have in mind replacing your arrangement with them. Of course I do not know at all how your arrangements with them have worked, and if you feel that you would rather close that up and start on a different basis I

1–Joseph (15 June) could not review *Realism*: he had been Dr Hasan's supervisor at New College, Oxford (where the work began as a thesis). He added, 'I wonder if you will think it impertinent of me to say with how much admiration I read your poem on the Magi last Xmas.'

should like to hear more from you, because I should like to do everything that I can in England and America for *Commerce*.[1]

I am committing the impertinence of enclosing a few subscription forms for *The Criterion* in case you should know of anyone in Paris who might like to subscribe. As the circular points out, *The Criterion* as a Quarterly will have to depend chiefly upon subscribers, and every additional subscriber is a cause of rejoicing.

I will wait to hear from you further about *Anabase*. It was a rather embarrassing position, but I did not know what else to do than to refer this person[2] to Leger. In any case I do not think it is right for anyone to publish the translation of any poem without the consent and approval of the author. I can easily imagine how busy Leger must have been and still is during this political crisis.

Yours ever affectionately,
[Tom]

TO *R. G. Collingwood*[3]   CC

25 June 1928   [London]

Dear Mr Collingwood,

I hope you remember that some time ago you honoured *The Criterion* with a very interesting review. The fortunes of *The Criterion* have been doubtful for many months, but the Review has now been reorganised in quarterly form. I should much like to get something else from you. I have two books on hand which I should be glad to send you for examination: if you did not care to review them you need not bother to return them. One is Tennant's *Philosophical Theology* and the other is R. C. Lodge's book on *Plato's Theory of Ethics*. If you care to examine either or both of them, please let me know.[4] In any case I much hope to have more of your writing in *The Criterion*.

Yours very truly,
[T. S. Eliot]

1–Caetani replied (24 Aug.): 'I think for the moment Commerce will simply be on sale at the Hogarth Press and at the bookshop which interest themselves [*sic*] with the review (they aren't many) and then when you and I meet we can discuss the question together.'
2–Edouard Roditi.
3–R. G. Collingwood (1889–1943), philosopher and historian; Fellow of Pembroke College, Oxford: see Biographical Register.
4–Collingwood reviewed Lodge's work in C. 8 (Sept. 1928), 157–9.

TO *Harold Monro*

25 June 1928   *The Monthly Criterion*

Dear Harold,

1. First about those books. I *had* sent Madariaga to Trend, but I have seen him today & he will let me have it back, & I will send it to you. The other book *was* reviewed in the *Monthly C.* months ago, by Quennell. Any others? What about '*English Prosody on Inductive Lines*' by Sir George Young *Bt.* (Cambridge) – something might be done with that.[1]

2. *Also.* You said you wd send me some more of your stories.

3. I shd like to ask *Trend* to our dinner on the 4th July: he is qualified and will be out of town 2 weeks later.

4. I was very sorry I could not come to yr party, but I am getting on in years and late parties are more and more difficult for me.

5. Am sending you a copy of *The Sacred Wood*, 2nd Edition.[2]

Yours ever,
T. S. E.

TO *John Gould Fletcher*

25 June 1928   [*The Monthly Criterion*]

Dear Fletcher,

I am sending you a book entitled *Race and Civilisation* which seems to be in your line.[3] I should be grateful if you would glance at it and let me know whether you think it is worth a review.

I sent you a few days ago two small pamphlets, a Confuscian [*sic*] translation by Ezra Pound and a pamphlet on Jules Gautier.[4] If you are willing to do a couple of short notices of them, or on one of them, I should be very much obliged.

I hope to see you again soon, and in any case at our dinner on the 4th of July.

Yours ever,
[T. S. Eliot]

1–Not reviewed.

2–Published by Methuen & Co., with new 'Preface to the 1928 edition', in May 1928.

3–Fletcher responded on 30 June: 'The book on Race you sent is entirely worthless – a mere rehash of all old theories on the subject refuted by an impenitent Bergsonian sentimentalist. No good. I don't think it's even worth disputing.'

4–Wilmot F. Ellis, *The Art Philosophy of Jules de Gaultier*, was reviewed in *C.* 8 (Sept. 1928), 170–1.

193

TO *I. A. Richards*   CC

25 June 1928   [London]

Dear Richards,

I don't know where you are at the moment but hope that this will reach you quickly. You have a number of books from *The Criterion*, but I am wondering whether you would care to review Herbert Read's *English Prose Style* for us.[1] Read as well as myself would be particularly interested to have your judgment upon it, favourable or unfavourable. Of course I should like to have a review of the book for the September number; but time is short, and if you were too much occupied I should prefer to have a review by you in the December number rather than a review by someone else in September.

If you get this letter, please let me hear from you. If you should be passing through London, do let me know in advance.

                              Yours ever,
                              [T. S. Eliot]

TO *Jean de Menasce*   CC

26 June 1928   [*The Monthly Criterion*]

Dear Jean de Menasce,

I have your letter and should very much like to see you. I think the best thing would be if you would ring me up at home when you arrive, and we will arrange a meeting. My private address is: 57 Chester Terrace, Eaton Square, s.w.1., and my telephone number is Sloane 3184.

                              Yours ever,
                              [T. S. Eliot]

TO *I. A. Richards*   TS Magdalene

28 June 1928   *The Criterion*

Dear Richards,

Thanks for your letter. I am delighted to send you Read's book. You say nothing about dates, so I will repeat that if you find time to deal with it by

---

1–C. 8 (Dec. 1928), 315–24; repr. with headnote in IAR, *Complementarities: Uncollected Essays*, ed. John Paul Russo (1976); I. A. Richards, *Selected Woeks 1919–1938*, ed. John Constable (2001), vol. 9.

July 15th I can get it into the September number, but I know that Read as well as myself would prefer to have you do it for the December number than to have anyone else do it for the September, so if you cannot get it to me by the 15th of July it is understood that you will do something about it for the following number.

The last paragraph of your letter makes me anxious to see you as soon as possible. Do let me know when you are passing through London, and if possible give me a few days notice.[1]

Yours ever
T. S. Eliot

TO *H. E. Bates*[2]   CC

29 June 1928   [London]

Dear Sir,

Thank you for your letter of the 26th, about which we will write to you again as soon as we have had an opportunity of carefully considering the suggestion it contains.[3]

Yours faithfully
Faber & Gwyer Ltd

TO *A. L. Rowse*   TS Exeter

2 July 1928   *The Monthly Criterion*

My dear Rowse,

I have not heard from you since my letter of the 14th June, but if you received this I should be very glad if you could let me know whether you think you can do such an article as we discussed in time for the December *Criterion*.[4] It would fit in very well because we have in view and recently

---

1–IAR (26 June): 'I had hoped to send you my draft of *Practical Criticism* before now. Many thanks for your notes on the poems. I expect you realise that in some instances your opinions clash violently with your other opinions of some months ago. I'll leave the whole thing with you when I go abroad – in about a fortnight's time – and will let you know of my passage through London in good time so that we can have a meeting.'

2–The signature on the letter was misread as 'Butler'.

3–On the recommendation of A. E. Coppard, Bates had submitted two long stories ('fantasies') – 'The Peach Tree' and 'The King who Lived on Air' – which he hoped F&G might like to issue in a limited-edition volume.

4–'The Literature of Communism: Its Origin and Theory', C. 8 (Apr. 1929), 422–6.

discussed a series of investigations of contemporary creeds as a study of contemporary Socialism and Communism. I have thought of dealing myself with the question of Fascism, and have recently worked through four or five books on the subject.[1] The more I read about the more uninteresting it seems; but it might be worthwhile to say even that. What I am trying to do is to find out whether there is any idea in Fascism at all; if not it might be at least worth while to say so. The books on the subject seem to be of two types: Those written by people who wish to prove either how virtuous or how wicked the regime has been; and those who wish to prove that Fascism is the realisation of a magnificent political ideal. The former have a certain scandalous interest, the latter being extremely dull. I only chatter about this in order to give you some notion of the possible series. The question is not to examine particular facts of government, but the importance of certain political ideas.

Yours ever,
T. S. Eliot

TO *John Hayward*[2]

MS King's

2 July 1928　　　　　　　　　　　　　　57 Chester Terrace, Eaton Square

Dear Hayward,

I am afraid tomorrow is not good for Donne – as I have got to have a man from abroad who is here for one day – I am extremely sorry – but would *Friday* next be possible for you, when we could be definitely alone?[3]

With apologies
Yours ever
T. S. E.

Make it *Friday* if you can – if not, *Monday* following?

1–TSE, 'The Literature of Fascism', C. 8 (Dec. 1928), 280–90.
2–John Hayward (1905–65), editor, critic, and anthologist: see Biographical Register.
3–JDH wanted to discuss the edition of John Donne's *Complete Poetry and Selected Prose* that he was preparing for the Nonesuch Press (1929).

TO *Mario Praz*   CC

2 July 1928   [*The Monthly Criterion*]

Dear Praz,

Thank you for your letter of June 28th. I find that two copies of *The Criterion* have already been sent to Montale: one to Florence and another to a country address which we received from you. I will send a third copy to the latter address.

I am glad to hear that we may expect the Vanbrugh.[1]

I hear that you called this morning. I am very sorry to have missed you. I am not very often here in the mornings, but usually in the afternoon, and I had been counting upon seeing you this afternoon. I suppose now that there is no likelihood of seeing you until September.

I look forward with great interest to your Chaucer essay.[2]

                         With best wishes,
                         Yours ever,
                         [T. S. Eliot]

TO *G. K. Chesterton*[3]   MS Dorothy Collins

2 July 1928   *The Monthly Criterion*

Dear Mr Chesterton,

I should like you to know that it was apparently your 'sympathetic reviewer', not I, who made the remark about alliteration; to which it seems he added a more general criticism of mine: so that *such* is not the

---

1 – Praz reviewed *The Complete Works of Sir John Vanbrugh*, ed. Bonamy Dobrée and Geoffrey Webb, C. 8 (Sept. 1928), 153–6.

2 – 'At present I am very busy with a Chaucer essay for the Oxford Press: but you may depend upon my promise for the Vanbrugh [review]'.

3 – G. K. Chesterton (1874–1936), writer, journalist; an Anglican who converted in 1922 to Roman Catholicism; author of novels including *The Napoleon of Notting Hill* (1904) and *The Man who was Thursday* (1908), and shorter fictions including the popular Father Brown stories. His non-fiction includes studies of Browning (1903), Chaucer (1932), and St Thomas Aquinas (1933); and collections of essays including *Heretics* (1905) and *Orthodoxy* (1908). See *The Autobiography of G. K. Chesterton* (1936); Maisie Ward, *Gilbert Keith Chesterton* (1944); Joseph Pearce, *Wisdom and Innocence: A Life of G. K. Chesterton* (1996). TSE was to write of 'G. K. C.', in a memorial note in C. (Oct. 1936), 69: 'It is not for his attainments in pure letters that he should be celebrated here: though it may be said that if he did nothing to develop the sensibility of the language, he did nothing to obstruct it. Nor are his religious convictions precisely our affair. What matters here is his lonely moral battle against his age, his courage, and his bold combination of genuine conservatism, genuine liberalism, and genuine radicalism.'

right connective. Some of your comments seem to be based on a belief that *I* object to alliteration.

And may I add, as a humble versifier, that I *prefer* my verse to be quoted correctly, if at all.[1]

Yours very truly,
T. S. Eliot

TO *James Smith*   CC

2 July 1928   [London]

Dear Smith,

I am frightfully sorry about the Realism book.[2] Not hearing from you I assumed that you were away, and that there would not be time to do anything, so as someone else expressed an interest in it I have sent it to him. Please accept my apologies. Is there any other recent book that you

---

1–In 'An Apology for Buffoons' (*The London Mercury* 18: 104 [June 1928], 162–71), Chesterton – referring to a note by TSE in *N&A*, 27 Dec. 1927 – remarked: 'It is commonly alleged of writers that they resent mild criticisms as infamous personal imputations. Without affectation, I fancy my own case to be rather different and even opposite . . . For instance, a very sympathetic reviewer in this paper said that I used too much alliteration; and quoted Mr. T. S. Eliot as saying that such a style maddened him to the point of unendurance . . .' But alliteration can scarcely be avoided, he went on: 'If an English writer does not avoid it, he is perpetually dragged into it when speaking rapidly or writing a great deal, by the whole trend and current of the English speech . . . Take, for instance, the case of Mr. T. S. Eliot himself. I recently saw a poem of his praised very highly and doubtless very rightly . . . But the passage specially quoted for commendation ran, if I remember right:
    Evening . . . of the smell of steak in passages.'
  (Chesterton was misquoting 'Preludes', 1–2: 'The winter evening settles down / With smell of steaks in passageways.')
  When he came to reprint the article in *The Well and the Shallows* (1935), Chesterton wrote in an 'Introductory Note': 'Since I wrote it, I have come to appreciate much more warmly the admirable work of Mr. T. S. Eliot; and I should like to offer an apology to him for some errors that occurred accidentally in the article itself. It was not he, but another critic, with whom I confused him, who made the particular point against alliteration; and the quotation from him was made from memory; and I have not been able to trace it to reproduce the exact order of words. The inaccuracy, if any, does not affect the argument; but the article which I had already planned to put in the same magazine, called "Apology to T. S. Eliot" would have gone far beyond any such verbal point. It would be adding impudence to injury to dedicate a book to an author merely on the claim of having misquoted him; but I should be proud to dedicate this book to T. S. Eliot, and the return of true logic and a luminous tradition to the world' (vii).
2–Smith had been asked by TSE's secretary (25 June) to review Hasan's *Realism*; on 29 June he sent a postcard to say he was willing to review the book.

would like to have? I very much enjoyed your review of Russell.[1] When is there a possibility of seeing you in London?

Yours sincerely,

[T. S. Eliot]

TO *I. A. Richards*   TS Magdalene

3 July 1928   *The Criterion*

Dear Richards,

Friday is a good day for lunch except that it is possible that John Hayward may be lunching with me as well. But as I may be going away Friday evening till Monday will you come to lunch with me on Friday in any case. If you are in town for a few days we might lunch again on Monday or Tuesday. I am looking forward to your documents.[2] Unless I hear from you to the contrary I will expect you here about one o'clock.

Yours ever,

T. S. Eliot

TO *Bruce Richmond*   CC

5 July 1928   [*The Criterion*]

Dear Richmond,

Thank you very much for your cheque for £25 being your annual endowment of *The Criterion*. It is very generous of you. I shall have to keep the cheque a few days and will then endorse it to Faber and Gwyer.

Thank you for the addresses and suggestions. I will write as you say. When you have had a chance of glancing at the new number I should very much like to have a talk with you.

Are you to be in town in the usual way during August, and if so would you ever be free for one or two more expeditions to the City?

Yours ever,

[T. S. Eliot]

1 – Review of Bertrand Russell, *An Outline of Philosophy*, C. 7 (June 1928), 419–21.
2 – 'Writing on the 2nd of July to arrange a meeting in London when they could discuss the book [*Practical Criticism*], Richards remarked that he would "bring a bundle of strange documents with me", meaning the protocols themselves' (John Constable, 'Introduction', *I. A. Richards and his Critics* [*Selected Works 1919–1938*, vol. 10], xxxi).

P.S. What I call the Bang text of Ford[1] is a large paper-bound book which I have just received from you. I still have two other books on hand which deserve reviewing.

TO *H. J. C. Grierson*

MS National Library of Scotland

5 July 1928   *The Monthly Criterion*

Dear Professor Grierson

I am deeply sorry. I thought that [I] had answered your first letter, but I am rather at sixes and sevens as I have no secretary at present, & so seem to have taken my own will for the deed. I am very sorry to have put you to this trouble and still more sorry that I cannot lecture: there are two reasons – one that I may take a holiday, and two that if I do not, it will be because I have many arrears of work to clear up. I hope you will forgive me, as the invitation was very tempting and I am more sorry than the audience will be.

Is there any chance of seeing you again in London?

Sincerely yours
T. S. Eliot

TO *Alan Lubbock*[2]

CC

6 July 1928   [London]

Dear Sir,[3]

I learned from Mr Bruce Richmond that you had generously offered to contribute £25 a year for three years to the continuance of *The Criterion*.

1 – *John Ford's Dramatic Works Reprinted from the Original Quartos*, ed. Henry de Vocht – the completion and continuation of the *Materialien zur Kunde des älteren englischen Dramas*, founded by Prof. W. Bang – new series, volume I (Louvain, 1927).
2 – Alan Lubbock (1897–1990) was educated at Eton and King's College, Cambridge, and served in the Royal Artillery in WWI. A Fellow of King's College, 1922–8, he subsequently worked for Hampshire County Council, 1932–74 (Chairman, 1955–67). He was a member of the National Park Commission, 1954–61; Royal Commission on Common Land, 1955; and War Works Commission, 1959–64; and he was High Sheriff of Hampshire, 1949, and Deputy Lieutenant of Hampshire, 1951. He was Chairman of the Council of Southampton University, 1957–69 (Pro-Chancellor, 1967–83). Author of *The Character of John Dryden* (Hogarth Press Essays, 1925). He was knighted in 1963.
3 – This letter was sent also to other 'angels' including John Hugh-Smith and Ethel Sands.

We have now reached the point at which it is quite certain that *The Criterion* will be continued, and after consultation with Mr Richmond and other supporters it has been decided that I should write to advise the guarantors. In the present circumstances it would be most convenient for the paper if the guarantors could pay their year's subsidy at this moment. It is understood that the subsidy applies from the June number which has appeared, and that the annual guarantee covers that and the following three quarterly issues.

You will probably prefer not to be bothered with details of the re-organisation at present. This is only to say that probably Messrs Faber & Gwyer will take over Lady Rothermere's shares in The New Criterion Ltd; and if it seems advisable as a matter of business procedure, these shares will be allocated proportionately to the guarantors. It is still a little premature to say anything, but the guarantors will be advised in due course. At my suggestion the guarantors will receive a copy of *The Criterion* as it appears.

We are now on the point of paying the contributors and printers of the June number.

Yours faithfully,
[T. S. Eliot]

TO *G. K. Chesterton*   TS Dorothy Collins

6 July 1928   *The Monthly Criterion*

Dear Mr Chesterton,

Very many thanks for your kind letter.[1] I had no notion of suggesting that your screed in *The Mercury* was hostile; I merely wished to clear myself of an imputation. I have now recovered and re-read my note in

---

1–Chesterton had replied on 5 July to TSE's letter of 2 July: 'I am so very sorry if my nonsense in the Mercury had any general air of hostility, to say nothing of any incidental injustices of which I was quite unaware. I meant it to be quite amiable; like the tremulous badinage of the Oldest Inhabitant in the bar parlour, when he has been guyed by the brighter lads of the village. I cannot imagine that I ever said anything about you or any particular person being a snob; for it was quite out of my thoughts and too serious for the whole affair. I certainly did have the impression, from the way the reviewer put it, that you disapproved of my alliteration; I also added that you would be quite right if you did. I certainly did quote from memory, and even quote from a quotation; I also mentioned that I was doing so casual a thing. Of course, on the strictest principles, all quotations should be verified; and I should certainly have done so, if I had in any way resented anything you said, or been myself writing in a spirit of resentment. If you think a letter to the Mercury clearing up these points would be fairer to everybody, of course I should be delighted to write one.'

The Nation of December 27th and I find, as I believed, that I said nothing about alliteration. As I have rather a weakness for alliteration myself I only felt in a slightly false position. But I certainly do not want you to trouble to write a letter to *The Mercury* about such an insignificant matter. I was also quite aware that you stated that you were quoting from me from memory. The last time that I ventured to quote from memory in print, a correspondent of the paper for which I wrote pointed out that I had made twelve distinct mistakes in well-known passages of Shakespeare.

What I really have in mind however is to use this correspondence as a means of suggesting to you that I should like you to think of *The Criterion* as a medium for making any unpopular statements which might not be suitable either for *The Mercury* or for your own paper. The remuneration is negligible, being only £2 per thousand words. I merely suggest it as a possible vehicle for remarks unsuitable to any more popular paper.

With many thanks,
Yours sincerely,
T. S. Eliot

I *did* however say that you seemed to assume that all of your readers were heretical & ignorant!

TO *Jean de Menasce*   CC

10 July 1928   [*The Criterion*]

Dear Menasce,

I forgot to say last night that *The Criterion* is having an informal dinner on Wednesday July 25th, and if you are still in London I shall be very glad if you will come as my guest.

We enjoyed seeing you very much, and want if possible to arrange a day next week for you to come and lunch or have tea quietly with us when there is no one else.

Yours ever,
[T. S. Eliot]

TO *William Force Stead*   CC

10 July 1928   [*The Monthly Criterion*]

Dear Stead,

I must apologise for not having answered your card sooner, but I have been very busy.[1] I am afraid that this week is no good, as I am going away for a long weekend Retreat and am therefore being very rushed. Would it be possible for you to come up the following week or the week after, and if so would Mrs Stead be coming with you? I should very much like to see you.

Incidentally I have been meaning to write to ask you about those books you have. Do any of them together give you the material for a long review or article?

Yours ever,
[T. S. Eliot]

TO *A. L. Rowse*   TS Exeter

10 July 1928   *The Monthly Criterion*

Dear Rowse,

Thank you very much for your letter of the 7th. Go ahead with your article in your own way, and don't worry about fitting it into anything else. I shall be very glad of any reviews also.[2]

It is very good of you to ask me to stay with you in Oxford, but unfortunately I am going away for three days towards the end of this week, and therefore cannot afford to go away again the following week. I am wondering if you might possibly be in London about the 25th July. There will be a small *Criterion* dinner on that date, and I should be very happy if you would come as my guest.

Yours ever,
T. S. Eliot

P.S. I should like to see anything you write. I have got *The New Statesman*, but have not yet read Connolly's article.[3]

---

1 – WFS wrote on 5 July that he would be in London the following week, and could meet up with TSE 'pretty much as you like'.
2 – Review of C. G. Crump, *History and Historical Research*, C. 8 (Sept. 1928), 159–61.
3 – ALR had recommended Cyril Connolly's review of Wyndham Lewis's *The Childermass*: 'Chang!', *New Statesman* 31 (7 July 1928), 426–7.

TO *Marguerite Caetani*   CC

10 July 1928   [London]

Dear Marguerite,

Thank you for your letter. I am very glad of the news about Leger. But does he realise that I am still waiting chiefly for his comments on the translation, but also for the form of contract which was to be revised? You understand that I would very much dislike publishing my translation without having had his criticisms. About *Commerce*, I shall expect to hear from you later.

I have not bothered to give the Huxleys an introduction to you yet, because they are spending the summer I think at Spezia[1] and will not be back in Paris until the autumn. I will urge them to write to you as soon as I am sure that they are in Paris. Clive Bell also will probably not be in Paris again until September or October. We are thinking of going to Rapallo for a few weeks in December, and may stay in Paris and see you if you are there. Otherwise we shall probably be in London throughout the summer. I do wish you would come here for a short visit.

Affectionately yours,
[T. S. Eliot]

TO *Alan Lubbock*   CC

10 July 1928   [London]

Dear Sir,

Thank you very much for sending your cheque for £25 (Twenty-five pounds) as the first year's contribution to *The Criterion*. If any more formal arrangement is made, you will be notified immediately.

Yours faithfully,
[T. S. Eliot]

1–The Huxleys stayed in Forte dei Marmi, Italy.

TO *D. C. J. McSweeney*   CC

10 July 1928   [London]

Dear McSweeney,

Thank you very much for your letter.[1] I appreciate the trouble you have taken. It deserves very serious consideration, and if you have no objection

---

1–McSweeney wrote on 9 July: 'I have read very carefully the latest number [June 1928] of the *Criterion* and after finding that the views I have formed on it are shared by only too many other people I think that, as an average reader, I should be very negligent if I didn't express them to you. I shall make no apology (at the outset) for their tenor.

'I take it, from the remarks you have made in your editorial, that you intend the *Criterion* to be a review having, above all, a certain magnitude and also a certain tendency not too strictly followed. That means, I assume, that articles appearing in it should be something more than mere aperçus of their subjects and that, furthermore, they should exhibit elements, at least, of a specific attitude towards literature and thought. A further justifiable assumption is, I assume, that some familiarity with the commonplaces of English literature will be presupposed in the regular reader.

'I now venture to examine the articles in the last number . . . from memory. It is necessary to say that I consider the articles as pure cyphers in a general argument.

'I will not saying anything of Dobrée's dialogue except that I thought it admirable. Of Fletcher's article I will say this, however, that, whatever its merits it is no more than a *mise en point* on an aspect of a large and important question. It is extremely dangerous to confine oneself to such articles. The result will be that you run the risk of being thought little more than a disoriented critic without a programme and (may I say it?) afraid of a programme. But if you are afraid of a programme you will get no following. People will begin to look and pass! Cannot the *Criterion*, indeed *must* not the *Criterion*, supply a dogma? There are no dogmas of interest in current English literature except where, perniciously enough, they appear in papers like the *Adelphi*. Therefore, to turn to another paper in the *Criterion*, why be so strictly reserved about the A.F. [Action Française]? I have not allowed my strong favour of the A.F. to influence my criticism of your correspondence with Ward. I just repeat that there is a crying need (forgive my cliché) for something not non-committal about that sort of matter. I shall return to this article from another standpoint.

'Then consider the Rossetti paper. Surely the *Criterion* presupposes all that that had to say as already given? Should its criticisms not begin precisely where that one left off? I ask, but I am really sure that they should. Not dissimilar is the article by Sirdar Iqbal Ali Shah: there is no *method* in it, it is disoriented, it does no more than cite information (very vulnerable when you begin to infer from it) which, again, should be presupposed in an average reader of the *Criterion*.

'I think that the articles that I have just mentioned are most of them open to adverse judgements on the point of merit. There are two, not so vulnerable, which are on other grounds – your correspondence with Ward and Read's note on Behaviourism. As to the former I have said that it is unwise to be so non-committal. But supposing that the non-committal is justified I really don't think that the *Criterion* is the place for that sort of correspondence *tout court*, which would more appropriately find its place in the columns of the A.F. Most readers of the *Criterion* will know nothing of the matter; from the correspondence they will learn nothing helpful to them and at the present stage if you are to mention the A.F. you must give a resumé (impartial if you will) of the background of the matter i.e. the sudden reversion to modernism, Blondelism etc. on the part of the Church

I should like to have one or more copies made of the letter, and to discuss it with some of my colleagues. I should of course, if you wished, have it copied without your name, and keep your name out of it. But I should like to discuss it with a few of the regular contributors, as it is too serious a matter to be overlooked.

Of course there are many things that I might say, mostly about the difficulty of getting the material that I want. But I should prefer to leave that until I have talked to others about the matter, and until I can see you again in London.

With many thanks,
Yours ever,
[T. S. Eliot]

TO *R. E. Gordon George*[1]   CC

10 July 1928   [London]

My dear Gordon George,

I am very glad to hear from you that you are making another of your unexpected visits to England. I am going away for a few days this week, but shall be back early next week and will write to you then. Meanwhile

---

which is of great general interest. This is purely an example, not a recommendation; but I hold the principle to be capital.

'Read's paper on behaviourism is open to this objection: you say in your editorial something to the effect that the articles in the *Criterion* must be, as I have put it, of a certain magnitude. But Read almost confines himself to a definition (debateable moreover) of value which, in view, surely, of what you say, should be expanded, defended, urged . . . What the paper [by Read] does is to satisfy nothing and only to leave a want to know how Read will defend and apply his definition. Is this appropriate to a quarterly?

'I am a little diffident about writing what you may think an attempt to teach you your own business. But I am most anxious that the *Criterion* should be a success and yet I feel that in its present form it won't be. It could really afford to be much more highbrow – it must not fall between two stools. And so long as it is not belligerent, conscious of a defined aim, & above all dogmatic & self-confident it will not be respected and will never create a school – (I do *not* mean a coterie). I repeat that I write as an average reader, and you can't run a review (can you?) without the assent of the reader which, in England, is often gained by a little bullying. I can't say everything that I would because, being accustomed to dictating, I can't write and I hope that, if you can forgive my pretension, you will give me an opportunity of expounding my views sometime, verbally. In any case you can be assured of my utmost anxiety that the *Criterion* should prosper and of all the support I can give it.'
1–Robert Esmonde Gordon George – Robert Sencourt (1890–1969) – critic, historian and biographer: see Biographical Register.

please let me know how long you are to be in England. There is indeed a great deal to talk about.[1]

Yours sincerely
[T. S. Eliot]

TO *St John Hutchinson*[2]   TS Texas

10 July 1928   Faber & Gwyer Ltd

Dear Jack,

I believe that I had some hope of seeing you before you left town. Could you possibly lunch with me on Friday the 20th? I hope you can. I am going away for a few days in the meantime, but after that shall probably be in London through most of July and August.

I enjoyed dining very much the other night, but my pleasure, or rather my capacities were somewhat blunted by having lunched much too well and long with a parson; and I was also extremely nervous as I anticipated that V. would make some statement: I hope it was not too trying for you, but she had had it disturbing her mind for so long that it was perhaps best to get it off. But that is only one of the reasons for my wanting to see you again soon.

yours ever,
T. S. E.

TO *Charles Whibley*   CC

10 July 1928   [London]

My dear Whibley,

Thank you again for your reply.[3] I am glad at least that you are free from pain and find it quite natural that you should be suffering from the effects of the extremely painful operations which you had in London.

---

1 – George wrote on 6 Aug.: 'Lord H[alifax] is not quite happy about your support of the Action Française.'

2 – St John ('Jack') Hutchinson (1884–1942): barrister-at-law; husband of Mary Hutchinson. Educated at Winchester and Magdalen College, Oxford, he was an unsuccessful Liberal parliamentary candidate, but acted as a legal adviser to the Ministry of Reconstruction, 1917; Recorder of Hastings from 1930. TSE was later to refer to him as 'an old and valued friend of mine' (letter to Bishop Bell, 8 Sept. 1948).

3 – 'My head is better & free from pain,' wrote CW, 'but I am suffering from an intolerable feeling of "shock"' (7 July).

I have no doubt that your recovery will be sudden and complete, and you are quite right to try not to do anything at present. But as soon as you do feel better I shall hope to see you in London; more especially as we are having to have certain repairs done to our house, and probably cannot be absent from London until after the middle of August. I am going away for this weekend, but otherwise shall be steadily in London until then.

I ought to tell you that we are now collecting the various guarantees for *The Criterion*. With the exception of Oliver, who has promised £250 a year, most of our guarantees are for about £25 and it was thought more practical to collect these guarantees annually than to ask the guarantors for smaller sums more frequently. You generously offered £25 a year yourself to this cause. Would it be possible for you to supply this sum now? It is understood that each annual guarantee is for a period covered by four quarterly numbers, and therefore begins with the June number, for the expenses of which we now wish to make payment.

When you have time to look over the number I should be very glad to have any comments. What we seem to suffer from particularly is a dearth of intelligent and informed historical and biographical matter; so if you could ever think of any writer of that type whom we ought to have I should be very glad to hear from you about it.

Yours ever affectionately,
[T. S. E.]

TO *Richard Aldington* TS Texas

10 July 1928 *The Monthly Criterion*

My dear Richard,

I am very glad to hear from you, and to receive the copy of Rémy.[1] I like everything about it except the cover. I have just read your introduction with much pleasure. I want to write about the book at length, but it will take time, and I cannot do anything for *The Criterion* before the December number. I wonder whether there is any possibility of getting Richmond to have it reviewed in the *Supplement*, and am writing to him.

1–*Rémy de Gourmont: A Modern Man of Letters* (Seattle: University of Washington Chapbooks, no. 13, 1928). TSE called RA's study 'the best critical introduction to the work of Gourmont that has been written. Mr Aldington places Gourmont very judicially . . . No one is so well qualified as Mr Aldington to expound the ideas and explain the place of this critic and moralist who occupied an important position in the literary world of Paris during the latter part of the last century' (*MC* 7 [June 1928], 458).

Your letter gives me much pleasure.[1] I assume that you are now going to be at Padworth throughout the summer, and it is quite possible that we shall both like to come and spend a week-end with you, but I would give you due warning, and a choice of dates.

Yours ever affectionately,

Tom

TO *D. O. Malcolm*

CC

12 July 1928   [London]

Dear Mr Malcolm,

Richmond informed me in February that you had generously promised help to *The Criterion* fund to guarantee its existence for the next three years.[2] I did not write to you at the time as it was still uncertain whether we should gain enough support to justify continuation. I presume that you have been informed that *The Criterion* is to continue as a Quarterly instead of a Monthly, a form which is much more satisfactory to myself as well as to many readers.

The present situation is this. The sum actually required to continue *The Criterion* as a Quarterly is £750 a year. We have now secured guarantees for £490 a year, so that there is still a considerable deficit. The sum of £750 is the sum required so to speak to replace the capital withdrawn by Lady Rothermere, and at that figure the same proportion of the expenses will still be borne by Faber and Gwyer.

We felt, however, that with nearly £500 a year already guaranteed as a result of the efforts of a few persons, we were justified in continuing indefinitely, while we pursued our efforts to obtain capital from other quarters. During the first year at least we are therefore asking the guarantors to contribute the whole sum of their guarantee.

The majority of the guarantees at present are for £25 a year each. In the case of one or two larger sums we are arranging for half-yearly payments, but with the sums of £25 a year it will, at least for the first year, be very

---

1–'It was good to see you in London,' RA had written (8 July), 'and I felt more deeply than I can say the friendship and sympathy in your look and hand-clasp.'

2–Malcolm told BLR (18 Feb.) he would promise £10 a year for three years; he would subscribe a further £15 a year for three years if it were really needed. However, by July he failed to remember what he had promised and so referred TSE's letter to BLR, who (perhaps cannily) told him 'that he "did promise & vow" £25 a year for 3 years . . . This is my (I hope, correct) recollection of his letter – which I think I sent to you' (BLR to TSE, 15 July).

much more convenient if the guarantors can pay in one sum, and we are collecting the subscriptions in that way.

The question of the eventual arrangement with the guarantors is still in abeyance owing to the fact that the negotiations with Lady Rothermere for liquidating her interest are not yet completed. It may prove desirable at a future date to distribute among the guarantors proportionate quantities of the shares taken over from Lady Rothermere. But meanwhile the June number has appeared and the Review has to be financed, and I am asking the guarantors to be so kind as to pay their subscriptions informally to Faber and Gwyer.

Yours very truly,
[T. S. Eliot]

FROM *TSE's secretary* TO *Gorham B. Munson*[1]   CC

16 July 1928   [London]

Dear Sir,

Mr Eliot asks me to say that he had no objection to your making use mentioned in your letter of that review, but he would have thought you could have found something of his that was better written. He thinks however that the title you suggest is a little misleading, if it is meant to apply to his subject-matter. Mr Eliot would suggest that 'The Critic and the Perception of Values' would be a better title.[2]

Yours faithfully,
Hawksley[3]
[Secretary]

1–Gorham Bert Munson (1896–1969), American journalist and editor, educated at Wesleyan University; close friend of Hart Crane; co-founder in Paris of *Secession*, a magazine of experimental writing, 1922–4; editor of *New Democracy*, the American periodical of the Social Credit movement, 1933–9; teacher of writing at the New School for Social Research, New York, 1927–69; author of works including *Waldo Frank: A Study* (1923); *Destinations* (critical essays, 1928); *The Dilemma of the Liberated* (1930).
2–Munson asked permission (4 July) to include in a textbook TSE's untitled review of HR's *Reason and Romanticism* and Ramon Fernandez's *Messages* – from NC 4 (Oct. 1926) 750–7. He proposed to give TSE's piece the title 'The Critic as a Creator of Values'. See *Style and Form in American Prose* (1929).
3–Successor to I. P. Fassett.

16 July 1928   [London]

Dear Dr Stewart,

    I shall be very glad to consider James Smith's dissertation if you care to send it to me.[1] This address will always reach me as I shall probably not

---

1 – Stewart wrote on 14 July that Smith was sitting again for a Fellowship – 'his last chance'. He had 'shelved' Logic and Wittgenstein and returned to Aristotle and the drama. Earlier on, in an undated letter, Smith had sent TSE, 'for you to read at your convenience, my sketch of a new thesis which bases itself on a criticism of Wittgenstein. It is the sketch which [Bertrand] Russell read, & partially approved. After your remarks on Thursday, I shall not proceed with the sketch as a thesis . . . It is an attempt at the removal of the hampering dichotomy, of "emotional" and "scientific", which has hung over speculation of late years. I become more convinced every day that the method I suggest will effect this, without yielding either to the crude "science" of Richards, or to the repressive "rationalism" of Maritain.' Then, in a letter of 29 July 1928 (presumably misdated?), Smith informed TSE: 'I am labouring at a thesis on Aristotle – do you remember your advice, to concentrate on Aristotle? I cannot, however, promise that the thesis will be finished in the requisite time for the next Fellowship Election at Trinity.'

TSE received 'Character in Drama' by 27 Aug. His undated report reads:

'The fundamental weakness of this thesis is one which I have noticed in previous work by the same author. He is intelligent and is well versed in both philosophy and literature, and keenly interested in both. In this thesis I think he has hold of the right end of the stick, but he cannot be said to make effective use of it when grasped. His great fault is a defect of form – which is not only in expression but in thought; he does not seem to make use of his just philosophic premises to draw any important literary conclusions. In this essay he has built a very firm foundation for a critical structure, but the structure is left for the reader to build.

'The essay as it stands is therefore to be judged rather as a study in the Aristotelian philosophy than as an essay on its nominal subject. So far as I am competent to judge – not having been for many years in immediate contact with the text of Aristotle – it is a careful and trustworthy piece of scholarship. But it will no doubt be submitted to some greater authority on Greek philosophy than I, and upon the opinion of this authority everything depends. But considering the subject of the essay, I feel that the first part could have been much condensed, unless the author had chosen to write a thesis twice as long. One forgets, long before the conclusion, his reason for going so thoroughly into Aristotle's philosophy; we are reminded of it abruptly within a few pages of the end. He could have made his point, which is, I believe, a good one, very much better. He could have contrasted with Aristotle some definite specimens of more modern theory of "personality" in philosophy and psychology, and shown the influence of modern philosophy upon the dramatic criticism of modern times. To make his thesis well formed he should I think have dealt at some length with the influence of Descartes and Locke. As it is, the thesis remains only half a thesis, and the view of Aristotle remains vague simply by not being contrasted with more recent views.

'If it is feasible, I think, that the author ought to be encouraged to *finish* this essay, by an equally full account of the modern views to be contrasted with that of Aristotle, and evidences of their effect upon dramatic criticism. He might then produce a really valuable work. I do not know whether during the writing of this essay he was under any direction, but I should judge not.

'I am prejudiced in the author's favour for the following reasons: I know him personally, and know him to be well read, to have sound principles of scholarship, and to be extremely

be away for any length of time during the summer. I am afraid that it is impossible for me to come to Pontigny, but I hope very much that I may have a chance of seeing you again before very long.[1]

Yours sincerely,

[T. S. Eliot]

Vivien Eliot TO *Mary Hutchinson*   MS Texas

16 July 1928   57 Chester Terrace, S.W.1.

My dear Mary

I was very stupid to accept yr invitation to tea on Wednesday – I was so delighted that you asked me, that I quite forgot that Tom's *neice* is to come & stay with us, & will arrive on Wednesday afternoon. Please forgive me – & could you possibly arrange *another afternoon.*

Will you *& Jack* come to tea on *Sunday*? Please do. *Or Saturday.* I thought it better to write & not telephone. Tom does not *seem* to be anxious to be photographed but I shall <u>ask</u> him to ring you up first thing tomorrow morning.

Yrs. ever

Vivienne Eliot

Please let me know which day you, or you *& Jack* will come to tea.

---

alert to everything of importance in the contemporary world; also I am naturally in favour of any young man who takes Aristotle seriously as a literary critic and who is not unaware of scholasticism. I think that in this dissertation he is on the right lines, though the right lines must so to speak be read partly between the lines. And I think that this dissertation fails chiefly because he did not know how to write it. The decision should lie, in my opinion, with the specialist in Greek philosophy who will report upon it.'

H. F. Stewart wrote to TSE on 29 Sept., 'The Aristotelians are looking at the thesis, & honestly they don't think much of the presentation. He is like a boy with a ball too big for his hands. But I quite think he shd be encouraged to go on with his enquiry even if it does not lead him into a Fellowship.'

1–For the years 1910–14, 1922–39, the philosopher Paul Desjardins (1859–1940) set up at the Abbey of Pontigny (originally a Cistercian monastery founded in 1114), near Auxerre in Burgundy, colloquia he styled 'Decades of Pontigny' (each conference went on for ten days), where leading intellectuals from all over Europe would gather to discuss issues of literature, arts, politics and society. Stewart asked in a postscript, 'Any chance of your coming to Pontigny this year?'

Vivien Eliot TO *Mary Hutchinson*   MS PC Texas

17 July 1928   57 Chester Terrace, Eaton Square

I wonder if you ever *did* get my letter, which I wrote last night. It is very strange if not. It was a nice letter. Is it right that we are to expect you both to tea next *Tuesday*? I do *hope* you will come, & look forward to seeing you *immensely*.

> Yrs ever
> Vivien Eliot

FROM *TSE's secretary* TO *F. V. Morley*   TS Valerie Eliot

20 July 1928   *The Monthly Criterion*

Dear Sir,[1]

Your presence is required at a dinner of *The Criterion* at 7 p.m., on Wednesday next, the 25th, at The Swiss Hotel, Old Compton Street, Soho (Upstairs).

Each member may bring *one* guest at his own expense, but the guest should be a person who either has been, will be, or might be useful in one way or another to *The Criterion*.

> Yours faithfully
> Hawksley
> Secretary.

TO *E. R. Curtius*   MS Bonn

23 July 1928   *The Monthly Criterion*

My dear Curtius,

I am immensely flattered to have your translation of *Perch' Io non Spero*, which I like *very* much.[2] I am delighted to think that you have found these verses worth translation – I have been on the point of writing to you for

---

1 – This letter was sent to: Harold Monro, F. S. Flint, Bonamy Dobrée, J. B. Trend, Richard Aldington, F. V. Morley, Orlo Williams, Humbert Wolfe and Roger Hinks.
2 – Not published.

some time: now that the *Criterion* is to continue – as a quarterly – *Can you let me have an essay soon*: we need you.

Yours ever,
T. S. Eliot

TO *John Cournos*

5 August 1928   Faber & Gwyer Ltd

Dear Cournos,

Many thanks for yours of the 30th July. It is very kind of you. If you can hold up the book till Oct. I should very much like to use the *Bolivar*.[1]

With more time, I should have selected the Amiel-Adams group in toto, but it happens that *Bolivar* is just the thing needed to diversify the contents of the Sept. no. and will fit in admirably.

Will you let me know at once, and I will send it to press.

Yours ever,
[T. S. Eliot]

The whole book will be extremely interesting. With whom is Bolivar compared?[2]

TO *Edouard Roditi*

TS UCLA

9 August 1928   Faber & Gwyer Ltd

Dear Mr Roditi,

I fear that you will have as much trouble in getting M. Leger to write a letter as I have had.[3] You might write to a friend of his (and mine) the Princesse de Bassiano, Villa Romaine. Av. Douglas Haig, Versailles, and ask her what to do, and whether it would be possible to arrange for you to see Leger at his bureau.

---

1 – Cournos had submitted extracts from his forthcoming book, *A Modern Plutarch*: they included essays on Henri-Frédéric Amiel and John Adams, and on Simón Bolívar. His publisher was willing to put off publication until 1 Oct. if it suited his serialisation plans. 'Simon Bolivar – Liberator', C. 7 (Sept. 1928), 88–98.

2 – 'I have compared Bolivar with Lee,' Cournos responded on 7 Aug.

3 – Roditi had written on 28 July: 'Meanwhile I am slowly translating the rest of St-John Perse's poetry: "La Gloire des Rois" and "Les Éloges"; and hope to have finished before the end of the year, unless my first term at Oxford keeps me too busy.'

I have been extremely busy for some weeks past and am sorry that I have not had time to consider your poems thoroughly or write to you about them. I will do so as soon as I can.

You say you are going to Oxford this term, so I dare say you may be in London now and then. Will you come and see me?[1]

Sincerely yours,
T. S. Eliot

TO *E. R. Curtius*

TS Bonn

9 August 1928   Faber & Gwyer Ltd

My dear Curtius,

I am writing a line in haste to let you know of a curious coincidence. About a week after you kindly sent me your translation of "Perch' Io non Spero" I received another translation from Rychner. He asks if I would object to his publishing it in the *N.S.R.* I have just written to inform him of the existence of your translation, which so far as I am concerned has priority, as I received it first. But as you know better than I do, I explained the situation to him and asked him to consult you – so for my part, I should only be pleased if *both* translations appeared. The comparison is very interesting for me, though I am not competent to judge between them.[2]

I have one or two other things, unpublished, which I should like to show you.

And I hope that you will soon come out into the Promised Land and have something to say in the *Criterion*. Soon.

Ever cordially yours
T. S. Eliot

1–TSE and Roditi were to meet for the first time at 24 Russell Square on 9 Oct.
2–Max Rychner's German translation of 'Perch' Io non Spero' (Part I of *Ash-Wednesday*) was to appear in *Neue Schweizer Rundschau* 23 (Dec. 1930), 917–18.

9 August 1928   Faber & Gwyer Ltd

My dear MacGreevy,

I am sorry that I did not answer your letter more promptly.

I do not know what Rodker[1] is doing in the publishing way at present, and indeed have not seen him for some years. I think he can be depended upon to make a good book of it.[2] He did my volume *Ara Vos Prec* some years ago when he first started and called himself the Ovid Press. That was very good, but he has had much more experience and I think has done better work since. My relations with him were quite satisfactory: I think he lost some money on the book, which now sells for two or three times the price.

I think I would accept if I were you, but I would have a proper legal agreement with a stipulation as to the proportion to Author and Translator. I think it would be unsatisfactory to have to do the dividing up yourself, and I don't see why you should make yourself responsible for what is the publishers' business. Of course I don't know quite what the situation is between yourself and Valéry, but it might be best if you had his formal approval as well.

I look forward to seeing you in the *Dublin Review* (which is published in London and edited I believe in Berkshire).[3]

I will let you know later about the *Wild Body*. I agree with your review, but there are considerations.[4]

Will you be in Britain at all this summer?

yours ever
T. S. E.

---

1 – John Rodker (1894–1955): British poet, novelist, publisher, launched in London in 1919 the Ovid Press, publishing TSE's *Ara Vos Prec* (1920), EP's *Hugh Selwyn Mauberley* (1920), and his own *Hymns* (1920), as well as portfolios of drawings by Wyndham Lewis, Henri Gaudier-Brzeska, and Edward Wadsworth. In the 1920s he worked in Paris on the second edition of JJ's *Ulysses* and set up the Casanova Press.

2 – McGreevy wrote (31 July) that, on the advice of RA and JJ, he had offered his Valéry translation to John Rodker, who had offered him a 10% royalty. Rodker published McGreevy's translation, *Introduction to the Method of Leonardo da Vinci*, in an edition of 875 numbered copies (with 50 being signed by Valéry), in 1929.

3 – McGreevy's poem 'The Gift of the Holy Ghost' had been accepted for the Oct. issue of *The Dublin Review*.

4 – 'Do you hate my Wyndham Lewis?' asked McGreevy in his letter. 'I shouldn't like you to, but if you don't care to publish it I shan't feel hurt.'

TO *Ezra Pound*   CC

10 August 1928   [London]

Dear Ezra,

Many thanks for manuscript translation of Schloezer's essay on Stravinsky. It looks all right, and I am much obliged. I will write to Marianne about this and find out what she wants, and whether simultaneous publication could be arranged.[1]

I am now busy on introduction to your poems, which is a nuisance.[2]

Yours etc.,

[T.]

TO *Marianne Moore*[3]   TS Texas

10 August 1928   *The Monthly Criterion*

Dear Miss Moore,

Ezra Pound has sent me a copy of the first part of an essay by Boris de Schloezer on Stravinsky, which he says he has done for you. I have not seen the whole book, but the material looks interesting, and I should like very much to know what part of the book you intend to publish in *The Dial*, and when. As the idea is your own I should not think of asking you to fit it in with simultaneous publication in *The Criterion*, but if you will let me know the publication dates I should be very happy to use some of the material and fit it in with *The Dial*, if possible. Pound says he is not quite sure whether you wanted to use the whole of the book, or whether you would take selections.[4]

1–EP had sent his translation of chapter 1 of Boris de Schloezer's book on Stravinsky. 'Prob. the most serious mus. crit. in Paris,' EP wrote in an undated covering letter. 'Seems to be sort of thing Crit. goes in for. He's one of mainstays of Revue Musicale.' EP had posted the same portion to Marianne Moore at *The Dial*: 'I think it might be too much fuss to try for simultaneous pub. in Dial and Crit. but as I dunno if they mean to print the WHOLE book as serial, or want only this, or will take stray chaps. you might send me yer opinyum.' In the event, the extract from de Schloezer's work did not appear in C.; the book was to be serialised over several months from Oct. 1928 in *The Dial*.

2–EP's *Selected Poems*, ed. TSE, was to be published by F&G on 23 Nov. 1928.

3–Marianne Moore (1887–1972), American poet and critic: see Biographical Register.

4–Moore replied on 23 Aug.,'If Ezra Pound will translate the de Schloezer, we plan to publish the whole book but are suggesting to him that the French version be allowed to precede our version. If you should wish to use some or all of the material, simultaneous publication could no doubt be arranged by you and us.' She added: 'I think I have never told you how deeply we appreciated your giving us not only priority but the sole honour of publishing your critique of Ezra Pound.'

I hope to send you soon the review of Adler's *Dialectic* which you asked for.[1] But I have been extremely busy this summer.

With all good wishes,
Yours sincerely,
T. S. Eliot

TO *Henri Massis*

CC

10 août 1928   [London]

Mon cher ami,

Quelle fâcheuse aventure! J'étais en villégiature pendant le week-end passé, et j'ai trouvé votre lettre en rentrant à mon bureau. Je suppose que vous êtes parti immédiatement pour Paris avec votre fille. J'espère qu'elle va beaucoup mieux, et qu'elle ne garde pas des souvenirs ennuyeux de l'Angleterre. Donnez-moi, s'il vous plaît, de vos nouvelles. C'est d'autant plus embêtant de ne pas avoir pu vous voir puisque j'ai beaucoup à vous dire, et puisqu'il me sera impossible de venir à Paris pendant quelque temps.

D'abord j'avais envie de vous demander de nous donner un autre article. J'ai pensé à une série d'articles sur quelques maîtres de la pensée politique: deux ou trois politiques Anglais et quelque politiques Français. Par exemple je voudrais avoir de quelqu'un un article sur l'œuvre de Fustel de Coulanges. J'ai pensé d'abord à vous, et puis à Painville, à Gaxotte et à Benoist. J'aurais préféré vous causer de ces idées; mais je vous prie mon cher ami d'en réfléchir, et de me dire franchement si vous croyez que je pourrais obtenir la collaboration de ces autres; et dîtes moi d'abord ce que vous préférez vous-même.

Second chapitre. Je cherche maintenant un chroniqueur Français pour me donner une chronique de Paris semblable à nos chroniques de Madrid, de Milan, d'Allemagne, d'Amsterdam et de New York. Nous avions député Kessell; mais Kessell ne m'a fourni qu'une seule chronique. J'ai pensé à Julian Green; qu'en pensez-vous? Il s'agit de trouver quelqu'un de l'esprit libre, et qui s'intéresse à suivre toute la pensée actuelle.

Écrivez-moi bientôt. Croyez-moi toujours votre dévoué,

[T. S. Eliot][2]

---

1 – Not written.

2 – *Translation*: My dear friend, What a misadventure! I was travelling last weekend and I found your letter on my return to my office. I suppose you left immediately for Paris with your daughter. I hope she is much better now and that she does not bear any unpleasant

TO *Nancy Cunard*   CC

10 August 1928   [London]

Dear Nancy,

I have been frightfully busy for the last month, so please excuse me for not having written before. I had to have a note written to you to say that it was quite impossible for me to do anything for your Press at once, as you wished to know before the 28th of July. So far as I can see my verse, if I write any, is tied up for 2 or 3 years to come. I hope to have a small volume next year which is already entangled with Faber & Gwyer, and an American publisher; and the only other thing I am working on, or wish to work on, is a sort of play,[1] which I should like to have produced if possible before publication; so I am afraid that any announcements made in my name would be utterly fallacious, much as I should like to have my name on your list.

If I come across the work of anybody who seems to me worth your notice, I will let you know.

Yours ever,

[T. S. E.]

---

memories of England. Please give me your news. It is all the more a nuisance that I was not able to see you as I had a lot to say and that it will be impossible for me to come to Paris for some time.

First I wanted to ask you to give us another article. I thought of a series of articles on the masters of political thought, two or three English politicians and a few French ones. For example I would like from someone an article on the works of Fustel de Coulanges. I thought of you first and then of Painville, Gaxotte and Benoist. I would have preferred to discuss these ideas with you; but I would ask you to think about it and to tell me frankly if you think you could get these others to contribute; and tell me first of all what you prefer yourself.

Second chapter. I am looking now for a French chronicler to give me a similar chronicle to the ones from Madrid, Milan, Germany, Amsterdam and New York. We had asked Kessel but Kessel has only given me one chronicle. I thought of Julian Green; what do you think? It is about finding a free thinker who is also interested in following current thinking.

Write to me soon. Believe me your loyal friend, [T. S. Eliot]

1 – *Sweeney Agonistes.*

FROM *Frederic Fassett*   TS Valerie Eliot

12 August 1928   32 Pembroke Road, w.8.

Dear Mr Eliot

My wife and I were deeply touched on receiving the beautiful tribute which the contributors to the *Criterion* sent on the occasion of the funeral of our daughter Irene Pearl Fassett.[1]

May I ask that you will accept and convey to those who joined with you in sending the lovely flowers, our great appreciation of the kindly thought underlying this graceful gesture?

To be thus assured of the esteem in which our daughter was held by those with whom her work brought her into contact, has given us no small measure of comfort in our sorrow.

Yours very sincerely
Frederic Fassett

P.S. A formal acknowledgment will be sent to each of those who so kindly united in sending the flowers.

TO *Humbert Wolfe*[2]   CC

13 August 1928   [London]

My dear Humbert,

In reply to yours of the 10th instant you have my permission.[3]

You are not cut off the list, but you are being cut off review books until you give me some satisfaction about that Dialogue between yourself and George Moore, or indeed any dialogue signed by Humbert Wolfe, as

---

1 – Pearl Fassett had died of tubercular peritonitis on 25 July 1928, aged 27. TSE sent to each of the 'inner circle' of his contributors – Richard Aldington, Bonamy Dobrée, F. S. Flint, J. G. Fletcher, Harold Monro, Herbert Read, F. V. Morley, Orlo Williams, and J. B. Trend – this memo: 'On behalf of certain individuals closely associated with *The Criterion*, a wreath was sent for the funeral of Miss I. P. Fassett, which took place at Golders Green Crematorium, today at 12 o'clock.' He wrote in his 'Commentary': 'We regret to announce the death of Miss I. P. Fassett, who had been Secretary of *The Criterion* almost since its beginning. Not only the Editor and the office staff, but also the regular contributors had come to depend upon Miss Fassett's powers of organization and management, and upon her enthusiasm for the review' (*C.* 8 [Sept. 1928], 6).
2 – Humbert Wolfe (1885–1940), poet, satirist, critic, civil servant: see Biographical Register.
3 – Wolfe wanted to reprint his 'English Bards and French Reviewers' (from *NC*, Jan. 1927) in his autumn book, *Dialogues and Monologues*. He asked too: 'Have you cut me off your list or are you going to send me some books presently?'

promised me about a year ago. Can I, or may I not expect a dialogue from you to swell the sales of our December number?[1]

Unless you are departing immediately for Geneva, could we lunch together one day next week?

[T. S. Eliot]

TO *Roy Campbell*[2]   CC

14 August 1928   [*The Criterion*]

Dear Sir,

I have for a long time been interested in your poetry, and should be very happy if you could let me see any unpublished manuscript with a view to publication in *The Criterion*.[3]

Yours very truly,
[T. S. Eliot]

TO *John Gould Fletcher*   CC

14 August 1928   [London]

My dear Fletcher,

Thank you for your letter. It is rather difficult to support my statement with a reasoned argument, but it might be easier in conversation. I do

1 – Wolfe replied on 14 Aug., 'Alas! The George Moore Dialogue will appear in my autumn book "Dialogues and Monologues" . . .'
2 – Roy Campbell (1901–57), South African-born poet, satirist, and translator, arrived in England in 1918 and was presently taken up by the composer William Walton and the Sitwells, and by Wyndham Lewis. He made his name in London with the long poem *Flaming Terrapin* (1924). His later poetry includes *Adamastor* (1930), *The Georgiad* (1931), and *Talking Bronco* (1946). See Peter F. Alexander, *Roy Campbell: A Critical Biography* (1982). In a letter to the publisher Henry Regnery (26 Dec. 1953), TSE was to volunteer this endorsement for the US edition of Campbell's *Poems*: 'I am astonished that no collection of Roy Campbell's poems should have hitherto been published in the United States, since he has been for many years one of the most conspicuous figures in English poetry in my time. His work is unclassifiable: it cannot be defined in terms of any movement. But the best of his work will surely be included in whatever assemblage of the poetical remains of our time, later generations will consider of permanent worth.'
3 – Campbell replied (undated): 'Your interest in my work is gratifying and encouraging . . . At present I am working on a long poem and have disposed of nearly all my unpublished shorter poems (none of which are much good) to the weekly papers . . . But I shall send you the next good poem I write. I have not completed anything good since *Tristan da Cunha* except one poem which I gave [Wyndham] Lewis for *The Enemy*.'

feel, however, that you would be making a great mistake if you thought of settling again in America. Your interests and your point of view are European, indeed much more European than that of most English people, and I have a feeling that the things in which you are interested are such as can be much better discussed here than in America. I could write a very long and no doubt completely unsatisfactory and unconvincing letter, but I will only say now that I think you are more appreciated and valued here than you realise; even if it is by a small number of persons, that doesn't matter; and I think that in the end you will have accomplished much more everywhere if you stay here.

I hope to try and see you soon, and talk about these things.

Yours ever,
[T. S. Eliot]

TO *Alec Randall*   TS McFarlin Library

14 August 1928   *The Monthly Criterion*

My dear Randall,

It is delightful to hear from you after this long time. I had news of your illness from time to time from Richard Aldington, and was indeed very anxious.[1] I had avoided writing to you about *The Criterion* until I knew that you were well enough to deal with such matters. Of course I shall be delighted if you will resume the German periodicals, and deal with them in the same way and at the same length as before. So much has happened here, the disorder of suspense and reconstruction, and also the death of Miss Fassett our secretary, that I am not sure what periodicals you have been receiving direct. Will you let me know what you get and what you want? If you are well supplied I should like to have some notes for the December number, so please let me know.

I understand how you feel about Fletcher's attitude as well as about that of Massis.[2] My own point of view is neither that of Fletcher, nor of

1–Randall said (31 Aug.) he had 'been ill with typhoid fever since last December, and the various complications were so serious that my life was despaired of four times; I am convinced that nothing but prayer finally saved me.'
2–'Fletcher's review of Massis's book stirred me. Not that I disagree with his criticism of Massis's central argument – this kind of Catholic Mediterranean-ism has always seemed to me wrong and dangerous. But to argue from a refutation of Massis's fallacies to a general condemnation of the Papacy seems to me absurd, and even rather offensive (I mean particularly the sneer about the Syllabus). At the moment, however, I don't feel equal to writing a reply to Fletcher, and if I did, I don't know whether you would have room for it.

Massis, nor your own. I think it is probably nearest to Massis, although I see great faults and dangers in his particular argument, and I deprecate the artificial Latinism. The difficulty with *The Criterion* is of course that among the group of intelligent supporters there are not enough points of agreement, hence a certain vagueness in the policy, which I dislike. On the other hand I should dislike equally to force upon the paper views which are shared either by none, or a minority of the important contributors.

I wish you would write your letter in reply to Fletcher. It is not too late to do so, only you would have to bear in mind that most of the readers would have forgotten what Fletcher said, so that you would have to give your letter more the form of an article than if it followed close upon that which it criticises. Fletcher is a very good and honest man. There is a strong strain of Scotch Protestant in him, which somewhat narrows his outlook. Of course I cannot accept your remark about Maurras without great qualifications.

It is very good news indeed to know that your health is so improved, and that we may again hope for your collaboration. Is it possible that you may take a holiday in England?[1]

Yours ever sincerely,
T. S. Eliot

TO *F. S. Oliver*   cc

14 August 1928   [London]

Dear Oliver,

It was very pleasant indeed to hear from you, especially as there was no pressure upon you to write to me on any matter whatever, and your letter gave me great pleasure.[2] I should of course be curious to have your

---

But one thing I feel strongly – more than I did before my illness – that those who do not feel the Papacy to be an instrument of saving souls as well as a political institution can never quite understand those who are convinced of both facts. For Fletcher (and incidentally for Maurras) the Papacy is nothing but a convenient political institution: hence all these words.'

1–Randall wrote again on 26 Nov.: 'It is now too late for any reply to Fletcher in the next number, also . . . for any "German Periodicals" . . . I have been pronounced cured by the specialists, but given severe warnings about going slow, taking a day a week in bed . . . and so on. Outside my office work I am now doing hardly anything, but when the official rush is over, with the new Minister settled down, I hope to be able to do more.'

2–Oliver had written from Jedburgh in Scotland (17 July): 'Your friend Read seems to have produced an exceedingly interesting book. I'm slowly making my way through it.' In addition, he expressed his best wishes for the improving health of VHE (who had visited the Olivers in company with TSE over the summer).

impressions of our last number, but I respect the laziness of others, being naturally very lazy myself, and will postpone enquiries until you have returned to Kenry House.

I am glad to hear that you are reading Read's book, and no doubt he will be still more glad himself. That is another matter on which I hope you will express yourself in speech.

I have nearly completed the September number, and am now looking forward with dread to the preparation of the following number. I am still worried about the difficulty of getting good historical and biographical work. The material offered is large in quantity, but on the whole limited to a very few kinds, and I am asking everywhere for suggestions of names of suitable writers whom I may ask. So if you could think of any I wish you would let me know.

When I saw you last you suggested that you would like to pay your *Criterion* guarantee half-yearly, in the autumn and the spring. If you are not too lazy to write to me again within a few weeks I wish you would let me have two dates which would suit you, so that I can notify Faber.

My wife is very well, but very tired, as most of our summer has been spent in the company of builders and decorators, who have been making necessary repairs to my house, and most of the repairs have had to be made twice over. She joins me in sending kind regards to Mrs Oliver and yourself.

Yours ever sincerely,
[T. S. Eliot]

TO *Norman Foerster*[1]   CC

14 August 1928   [London]

Dear Mr Foerster,

I am very sorry to have missed you in London, and think that it is much more my fault than yours, as I was so very busy that I overlooked your limited dates.[2] I am very sorry not to have seen you while you were in Europe, and hope that you will soon be here again.

I look forward to reading your book, and to reading your note in the *Forum*. I have read Benda's book, and have written a hasty note on it, I think, for *The New Republic*. I do not think it is a very good book.[3]

                        With all good wishes,
                        Yours sincerely
                        [T. S. Eliot]

1–Norman Foerster (1887–1972), educator, critic, humanist – who was a contemporary of TSE at Harvard, though they appeared not to have met there – was teaching at the University of North Carolina, Chapel Hill; he was later Director of the School of Letters, University of Iowa, 1930–44. See Robert Falk and Robert E. Lee, 'In Memoriam: Norman Foerster 1887–1972', *American Literature* 44 (Jan. 1972), 679–80; J. David Hoeveler Jr., *The New Humanism: A Critique of Modern America, 1900–1940* (1977). TSE wrote in 'American Critics', *TLS*, 10 Jan. 1929 – a review of *The Reinterpretation of American Literature*, ed. Foerster – 'Mr Norman Foerster is one of the most brilliant of Mr Babbitt's disciples, and one of those nearest to the master. His recent work, *American Criticism* . . . contains, besides much sound criticism, an authoritative exposition of the "New Humanism".' He would characterise Foerster, in *Thoughts after Lambeth* (1931), as 'the fugleman of Humanism. Mr Foerster, who has the honest simplicity to admit that he has very little acquaintance with Christianity beyond a narrow Protestantism which he repudiates, offers Humanism because it appeals to those "who can find in themselves no vocation for spiritual humility"! without perceiving at all that this is an exact parallel to saying that Companionate Marriage "appeals to those who can find in themselves no vocation for spiritual continence". It is true that to judge from his next paragraph he has at the back of his mind some foggy distinction between "spiritual humility" and "humility" plain, but the distinction, if present, is not developed. One can now be a distinguished professor, and a professional moralist to boot, without understanding the devotional sense of the word *vocation* or the theological sense of the virtue *humility*; a virtue, indeed, not conspicuous among modern men of letters' (*SE* [1932], 359–60).
2–Foerster wrote first on 15 June in the hope of meeting TSE during a visit to England in July. Irving Babbitt had shown him TSE's 'thoughtful article' – 'The Humanism of Irving Babbitt' – in *Forum*, and Foerster had written 'a few remarks by way of reply'. He had asked his publisher to send TSE a copy of his book *American Criticism* (1928).
3–Foerster, who had not been able to meet TSE in London, asked TSE on 1 Aug., 'I imagine you have seen Benda's very interesting new book, *La Trahison des Clercs* . . . ?'

TO *Charles Maurras*   TS Archives Nationales

15 août 1928   London

Cher Maître,

Votre petite brochure, *L'Anglais qui a connu la France*, m'est infiniment précieuse, d'autant plus à cause de l'inscription que vous m'avez fait l'honneur d'y mettre. C'est un souvenir précieux d'une influence et d'une amitié inestimable.

Je voudrais oser vous demander la permission de réimprimer cette brochure dans le *Criterion*, puisque je crois que cette étude pourrait avoir un grand intérêt pour nos lecteurs anglais. Il est possible que je serais forcé de l'abréger un peu.

Dans l'attente de votre réponse favorable, je me soussigne, cher Monsieur et Maître, toujours votre dévoué.[1]

T. S. Eliot[2]

TO *Ethel Sands*[3]   CC

15 August 1928   [London]

Dear Miss Sands,

Thank you very much for your letter of the 12th. May I say how much I appreciate your support toward continuing the life of *The Criterion*. I ought to mention, however, that your cheque does not seem to have been enclosed in your letter.

1–Maurras assented (20 Aug.), though he wanted to review any proposed abridgements; but in the event his pamphlet was not used in *The Criterion*.

2–*Translation*: Dear Master, Your little pamphlet, *L'Anglais qui a connu la France* [The Englishman who has known France] is very precious to me, particularly because of the inscription you have done me the honour of inserting. It is a precious memento of an influence and a priceless friendship.

I would like to dare to ask for your permission to reprint this pamphlet in the *Criterion*, as I think this study could be of great interest to our English readers. It is possible I would have to shorten it a little.

In anticipation of your favourable reply, I am, dear Sir and Master, yours truly as always, [T. S. Eliot]

3–Ethel Sands (1873–1962), American heiress (the family's wealth derived from the manufacture of patent medicines) and artist, spent the best part of her life in France and England, where – along with her lifelong companion, the American painter Anna Hope Hudson – she was a generous hostess and patron to writers and artists including Walter Sickert and Boris Anrep. See Wendy Baron, *Miss Ethel Sands and Her Circle* (1977).

May I hope to see you again this winter when you are back in London?

Sincerely yours,

[T. S. Eliot]

TO *J. B. Orrick*[1]   CC

17 August 1928   [London]

Dear Mr Orrick,

Thank you for your letter of the 14th. I could not say whether Faber &
Gwyer would be likely to accept your book until we have seen it, but the
parts you have shewn me have interested me very much.[2] We should be
very glad if you would let us look at the book.

Yours very truly,

[T. S. Eliot]

TO *Walter Lowenfels*[3]   CC

17 August 1928   [London]

Dear Mr Lowenfels,

Thank you for your letter of the 14th August. I am retaining 'Ode'
and 'Hot for Certainties' and return the other poems herewith.[4] The

---

1–J. B. Orrick published *Matthew Arnold and Goethe* (Publications of the English Goethe
Society, ns 4, 1928), and articles in *The London Mercury* and *Review of English Studies*.
In later years he was to become Chief of the Section of Nongovernmental Organisations
Services of the Department of Public Information of the United Nations.

2–Orrick enquired whether F&G might like to publish a book, *Matthew Arnold as a Critic*,
that he had just completed. TSE had been interested in the sections Orrick had shown him
in 1927 – one on Sainte-Beuve; the other on 'Matthew Arnold and Goethe' – that had been
reviewed in the *TLS*, 15 Mar.

3–Walter Lowenfels (1897–1976): American poet, journalist, author, political activist;
member of the Communist Party; editor of the *Daily Worker* from the late 1930s until
1953. After working for his father (a butter manufacturer), 1914–26, he lived from 1926 to
1934 in Paris, where he came to know expatriates including Ford Madox Ford and Henry
Miller, and where he co-founded in 1930 the Carrefour Press. In 1953 he was to be arrested
by the FBI and charged with conspiracy to overthrow the US government: his conviction in
1954 was overturned for lack of evidence. His works include *Episodes & Epistles* (1925),
Steel, 1937 (1937), and *Where is Vietnam? American Poets Respond: An Anthology of
Contemporary Poems* (co-ed., 1967). See Hugh Ford, *Published in Paris: American and
British Writers, Printers, and Publishers in Paris, 1920–1939* (1975).

4–The poems chosen by TSE were excerpts from 'Finale of Seem', the title poem of a
volume that was to be published in the USA and the UK in 1929. Lowenfels's work had
been submitted to TSE from Paris by George Antheil, who thought the poetry 'extremely
fine' (undated).

earliest possible date at which I could use them now that *The Criterion* is a Quarterly, is December, and I am not quite sure whether I shall have room then, but if you will be so kind as to leave them with me, I shall be grateful to you.

I have passed over 'The Passionate Pilgrim' because I do not know whether *The Enemy* is coming out or not.[1] I seem to remember having made a contribution to it myself about a year ago which has not yet been published.[2]

Yours sincerely,
[T. S. Eliot]

TO *W. Olaf Stapledon*[3]   CC

23 August 1928   [London]

Dear Mr Stapledon,

I have read your essay with great interest, and have also discussed it with one of my colleagues.[4] I think, frankly, that it already marks an advance in expression on the previous essay which you showed me, but I still find your way of writing too vague and general for our purposes, although it is in line with our tendencies. What we need is really something less comprehensive, but more detailed analysis of particular authors and writings. I still think that your tendency is to try to cover too much ground too quickly. I suggest that you should think of this essay as if it were an introduction to a large book, and try to give us instead of the Introduction, one essay on a specific problem or other, with careful citation of texts.[5]

1–Lowenfels wrote: 'Wyndham Lewis wrote me about a year ago that he was using "The Passionate Pilgrim" in *The Enemy*; I dare say that offer has lapsed by now.'
2–TSE, 'A Note on Poetry and Belief', *The Enemy* 1 (Jan. 1927), 15–17.
3–Olaf Stapledon (1886–1950), science fiction writer and philosopher, took a degree in History at Balliol College, Oxford, and then worked for a while in his father's shipping company in Liverpool. But in 1913 he abandoned his father's business in favour of making his living by teaching for the Workers' Educational Association (WEA). After WW1 (he served as a conscientious objector in the Friends' Ambulance Unit), he earned his doctorate at Liverpool University and subsequently essayed poetry and philosophy: *A Modern Theory of Ethics* was to be published in 1929. However, fame and fortune came to him in 1931–44, when he produced a series of celebrated works of science fiction (including *Last Men in London*; *Last and First Men*; *Sirius*) and books of philosophy and cultural criticism. See Richard Crossley, *Olaf Stapledon: Speaking for the Future* (1994).
4–Stapledon had submitted his long essay (on a subject now unknown) on 30 June.
5–Stapledon answered (3 Sept.): 'as I do not feel able or inclined to analyse particular authors and writings, I must evidently give up the idea of contributing to the *Criterion*.'

If you do not see my point, will you let me know at once and I will try to write to you more lucidly. In any case please understand that I want you to keep on writing on these lines, and that is why I wish to take the trouble to make you understand what I mean.

Yours sincerely,
[T. S. Eliot]

TO *Hans Siemsen*[1]   CC

23 August 1928   [London]

Dear Sir,

A friend has recently shown me a copy of your story, 'Die Geschichte meines Bruders'. I think that I had already read and admired this story some time ago in some German Review; in any case I admire the story very much, and should be glad if you would let me have permission to reprint it in *The Criterion*. Our rates are two pounds per thousand words, less the expense of translation. Of course I do not know whether the foreign rights of this story belong to you or to your publishers, and I should be glad to have confirmation.

The Criterion is a literary Quarterly Review, which publishes only original work of the highest quality. I may mention that among German authors it has published work by Hermann Hesse, E. R. Curtius, Max Scheler and Wilhelm Worringer.

I hope that you will consent to our republishing this admirable story.[2]

Yours faithfully,
[T. S. Eliot]

TO *H. E. Bates*   CC

23 August 1928   [London]

My dear Sir,

I have been already interested in your work. The enclosed manuscript[3] was submitted for publication as a small book to our firm, who considered

1–Hans Siemsen (1891–1969), German journalist and writer, was working at this time as a freelance author in Berlin; author of *The Story of My Brother* (1923), *Forbidden Love* (1927), and *Hitler Youth* (1940). See also *Hans Siemsen Reader* (ed. D. Sudhoff, 2003).
2–'The Story of My Brother', trans. Marjorie Gabain, C. 8 (July 1929), 592–615.
3–Details unknown.

that a book of that size was unsuitable for the programme of Faber &
Gwyer. The stories were handed to me as editor of *The Criterion*. I liked
them and, as I say, I have been previously interested in your work; but I
feel that this type of fantasy is not altogether suitable for *The Criterion*.
I should be very grateful, however, if you would let me see more of your
work.

Yours very truly
[T. S. Eliot]

TO *Ruth M. Harrison*[1]   CC

23 August 1928   [London]

Dear Madam,

I am very grateful to you for your letter of the 22nd instant which I
have today discussed with two or three of my colleagues and which we
all found very much to the point.[2] I am not able at the moment to tell
you what will come of it, but merely that your letter fits in with several
criticisms that we have made among ourselves, and that it will not be
without influence on the future form of the paper.

I wish that more of our readers might have as useful suggestions to
make.

With very many thanks,
Yours faithfully,
[T. S. Eliot]

1 – Ruth Harrison was Secretary to the Headmistress of Roedean School.
2 – 'As a very ordinary reader of the *Criterion*, striving a little breathlessly after the truths it
reveals & conceals, may I presume to make a small suggestion?

'The *Criterion* is absolutely the only paper of its kind in England (as far as I know) & it
meets a very urgent need (though one that appears to be still partially unconscious).

'I should like to see its sense of continuity strengthened: I know it exists, but I should like
more stress to be laid on it. In saying this I am thinking of the *Nouvelle Revue Française*,
where the interest which passes on from number to number is that of one point of view
directed to various subjects, as well as being that of various points of view on a given
subject . . .

'If you yourself were able to amplify your Commentary, the step would be taken. If once
a year or so Mr Middleton Murry were to write one of his provocative articles, a section of
the next numbers of the *Criterion* being devoted to articles sorting out his arguments from
half-a-dozen points of view – one would again feel that each quarterly number was not only
complete in itself but a definite forerunner of future numbers.'

TO *Frederic Fassett*

CC

23 August 1928   [London]

Dear Mr Fassett,

Thank you very much for your letter of the 21st. I was very much touched and pleased that you should have thought of sending me the beautiful copy of *The Anglo-Saxon Review* (vol. 1, June 1899). I remember quite well that Pearl showed it to me some time ago, and that I was very much interested to see it. I shall be very happy to keep it with the inscription to her from her grandmother as a memorial.

I hope that you will let me know as soon as Mrs Fassett and yourself are again settled in London, because my wife and I would very much like to call.

With many thanks,
Yours sincerely,
[T. S. Eliot]

TO *Harold Laski*[1]

CC

23 August 1928   [*The Criterion*]

Dear Mr Laski,

I hope you may remember meeting me one day in South Kensington. Ever since I have had in mind to seek for an opportunity of asking you to contribute to *The Criterion*. I should hardly venture to ask anyone like yourself to review for us, but I have another idea which I have hoped might meet with your approval. I feel that Bernard Shaw's big book has been on the whole rather poorly dealt with, and I should like to get a few notes about it from people of a variety of opinion. Would you be willing to give in brief space the gist of your opinions of the book? I want to ask several people of different shades of opinion, and yours is the first name that occurred to me.

1–Harold J. Laski (1893–1950), Professor of Political Science, London School of Economics, 1926–50.

In any case I hope that when you are in London you will come and lunch with me one day.[1]

Yours sincerely,
[T. S. Eliot]

TO *John Gould Fletcher*   MS Arkansas

23 August 1928   [London]

Dear Fletcher

I stupidly forgot your cheque yesterday. What we need is for you to endorse it to Faber & Gwyer Ltd. In that way the books will show that the *Criterion* have paid you, and also that you have contributed the same amount to the *Criterion*.

May I add that Faber also expressed warm appreciation of your generosity.

We enjoyed seeing you very much, & look forward to coming to Sydenham.

Yours ever
T. S. E.

TO *Henri Massis*   CC

27 août 1928[2]   [London]

Mon cher ami,

Merci beaucoup de vos nouvelles. Je suis bien content de savoir que votre fille se retablit, et qu'elle va rentrer en Angleterre. Vous dites qu'elle veut se placer à Londres. Voulez-vous bien me donner quelques précisions, en cas que je puisse vous aider un peu?

Naturellement, si je peux venir passer quelques jours à Paris, je ne manquerai point de vous prévenir d'avance. Je vous remercie vivement de vos démarches chez Gaxotte, et je lui écris. Mais soyez sûr que je veux bien

---

1 – Laski replied on 30 Aug., 'Do not let us "mister" one another. I have too great a regard for your work to venture upon titles before your name. I shall at any time be proud to write for your review. If you will tell me how long a note you would like on Shaw, I will send you one with pleasure; but there must be no question of payment until you can assure me that the *Criterion* is on its feet.' He would contribute to a symposium on Shaw's *The Intelligent Woman's Guide to Socialism*, in C. 8 (Dec. 1928), 191–4.
2 – Misdated 17 août.

recevoir quelque chose de vous, et j'attends avec impatience un morceau de votre manuscrit sur Proust.

Dans l'attente de vos nouvelles, croyez-moi toujours

Votre dévoué

[T. S. Eliot]¹

TO *M. Pierre Gaxotte*²   CC

27 août 1928   [London]

Monsieur,

Notre ami Henri Massis vous aura parlé de la question de votre collaboration au *Criterion*. Massis peut bien vous expliquer le caractère de notre revue, mais je vous envoie un exemplaire sous pli séparé. Pourriez-vous m'envoyer quelque chose avant le 16 septembre, afin de nous donner le temps de la faire traduire? Si vous voulez bien nous accorder un article sur Fustel, je serais très content; sinon, je vous prie de m'indiquer un autre sujet qui vous convient.³

Je vous prie d'agréer l'expression de mon admiration pour votre œuvre sur la Révolution,⁴ œuvre qui sera très utile et importante de ce côté de la Manche. Recevez, monsieur, l'expression de ma haute considération.

[T. S. Eliot]⁵

---

1 – *Translation*: My dear friend, Thank you very much for your news. I am happy to hear that your daughter is getting better and that she will come back to England. You say that she wants a placement in London. Could you give me some more details, just in case I could help a little?

Naturally if I can come for a few days to Paris, I will make sure to let you know in advance. I wish to thank you for your introduction to Gaxotte and I am writing to him. But be assured that I would like to receive something from you and that I look forward with impatience to the extract of your manuscript on Proust.

In anticipation of news from you, I am, Yours truly as always, [T. S. Eliot]

2 – Pierre Gaxotte (1895–1982), French historian and right-wing journalist; author of *La Révolution française* (1928), *Le Siècle de Louis XV* (1933), and other works on the French eighteenth century. He was to be elected to the Académie Française in 1953.

3 – See Gaxotte, 'Fustel de Coulanges' (trans. TSE), C. 8 (Dec. 1928), 258–69.

4 – TSE's secretary requested a copy of *La Révolution française* from Adrienne Monnier in Paris on 27 Aug.

5 – *Translation*: Sir, Our friend Henri Massis will have talked to you about the question of your contribution to the *Criterion*. Massis can easily explain to you the character of our review, but I am sending you a copy under separate cover. Could you send me something by 16 September in order to give us the time to have it translated? If you are willing to give us an article on Fustel, I would be very happy; otherwise, could you suggest another subject that is convenient for you.

TO *Peter Quennell*[1]   CC

27 August 1928   [London]

Dear Quennell,

I wonder if you would care to review for the December *Criterion* the
large work of Lafourcade's on *La Jeunnesse de Swinburne*, together with
our own edition of *Swinburne's Hyperion*. I don't know whether it will
interest you or not, but it is at least a peg on which to hang a long review
of Swinburne himself.[2] If you don't like this subject I wish you would
suggest some other. I should like to see you again soon, and find out how
you are getting on with Corbière.

                                        Yours sincerely,
                                        [T. S. Eliot]

TO *A. L. Rowse*   TS Exeter

27 August 1928   *The Monthly Criterion*

Dear Rowse,

I don't know whether this will reach you or when. The point is: I will
let you off your Communism article until the next (March) number if
(1) I can arrange a symposium on Shaw's *Intelligent Woman's Guide* (2)
and you would contribute to it about 1000 words opinion. Have you
read the book? I thought of asking Laski, Belloc and Fr. D'Arcy among
other representative views.[3] But if you are not agreeable, or if I can't

---

Please accept the expression of my admiration for your work on the Revolution, which
will be very useful and important on this side of the Channel.

Please accept, Sir, the expression of my highest esteem. [T. S. Eliot]

1 – Peter Quennell (1905–93), biographer, essayist, editor. Though rusticated from Balliol
College, Oxford, he became a man of letters (encouraged by figures including Harold
Monro, Edward Marsh, and Edith Sitwell). Works include *Baudelaire and the Symbolists*
(1929); *Four Portraits* (1945); *Alexander Pope: The Education of Genius 1688–1728* (1968);
Samuel Johnson: His Friends and Enemies (1972); and works of autobiography including
The Marble Foot (1976) and *The Wanton Chase* (1980). He edited *The Cornhill Magazine*,
1944–51; co-edited (with Alan Hodge) *History Today*, 1951–79.

2 – Quennell agreed (4 Sept.) to write a review; he was writing a superficial review for the
New Statesman, he said: 'the level of *immediate intelligibility* the editor demands is very
high'. See his review of Georges Lafourcade, *La Jeunnesse de Swinburne*, and *Swinburne's
Hyperion and other Poems*, C. 8 (Dec. 1928), 328–30.

3 – 'Bernard Shaw's *Intelligent Woman's Guide*: Some Opinions' (C. 8 [Dec. 1928], 191–214)
comprised contributions by H. J. Laski, Revd M. C. D'Arcy, ALR, and Kenneth Pickthorn.
In an undated note to TSE, ALR called his own contribution 'an opinion with a vengeance!
Though I read carefully and took heaps of notes I found it impossible to say anything in
review of the book in so short a space: so I said what I thought *about* it.'

work it, I shall try to hold you to your engagement for the December number!

Yours ever sincerely,
T. S. Eliot

TO *Charles Smyth*[1]

CC

27 August 1928   [London]

Dear Smyth,

(May we drop the Mr) When I send the books, or make suggestions, I want your opinion primarily, and your review only if you think the books worth it. In the case of books which you cannot praise, but do not wish to damn, please drop them into the waste-basket or the secondhand bookseller's.[2]

What I had in mind was (1) a full dress review of Belloc's History of England up to date, including his book on James II. If this leaves you cold, would you consider (2) *Great Britain from Adam Smith to the Present Day* by C. R. Fay of Christ's (3) Junius[3] (4) anything that appeals to you in the autumn lists of publishers? I may have some important suggestion for you before long. Incidentally have you read Shaw's *Intelligent Woman's Guide?*[4]

Yours always sincerely,
[T. S. Eliot]

1 – Charles Smyth (1903–87) was an eminent ecclesiastical historian and a fine preacher in the Anglican communion. In 1925 he gained a double first in the History Tripos at Corpus Christi College, Cambridge, winning the Thirlwell Medal and the Gladstone Prize, and was elected to a Fellowship of Corpus (R. A. Butler was elected a Fellow on the same day). He edited the *Cambridge Review* in 1925, and again in 1940–1. He was ordained deacon in 1929, priest in 1930; and in 1946 he was to be appointed rector of St Margaret's, Westminster, and canon of Westminster Abbey. (On 28 Apr. 1952 TSE expressed the view, in a letter to Janet Adam Smith, that Smyth should be 'moved up to where he so eminently belongs, an episcopal see.') Smyth's publications include *Cranmer and the Revolution under Edward VI* (1926); *The Art of Preaching (1747–1939)* (1940); the Birkbeck Lectures, *Simeon and Church Order*, given at Trinity College, Cambridge, 1937–8; and a biography of Archbishop Cyril Garbett (1959).

2 – Smyth had written (25 Aug.) of Christopher Hollis's *The American Heresy* (1927): 'That book is one which has been very well, if not very critically, received by the Press: I cannot praise, but feel no wish to damn it. I think I had better write a short notice of it . . .'

3 – *The Letters of Junius*, ed. C. W. Everett (F&G, 1927).

4 – Smyth replied (29 Aug.) that he was 'inclined to fight shy of Belloc . . . But Fay's book I should like . . . ; also the Junius . . . As to new books, there are two . . . they are both

TO *Max Rychner*   CC

27 August 1928   [London]

My dear Mr Rychner,

Thank you very much for your kind letter of the 23rd August. I should be very glad if you would let me have your Chronicle by the 15th September at the latest. Is this possible?

I am glad you and Curtius have been able to discuss the matter of my poem. Certainly, I should be very happy if your version appeared in your review, and you have entire liberty to reprint the English text if you think best. I leave that to you.

But if I send you the other poems for translation (if you like them well enough to think them worthy of translation) I shall have to ask that the English text is not reprinted; as it will not have appeared in England, and one has to be very careful about copyright especially in America.

I will send you them shortly, and meanwhile hope for an assurance that you will be able to let me have a German Chronicle for the December number.

With all best wishes,
always yours
[T. S. Eliot]

---

important . . . : A History of Medieval Political Theory in the West, vol. V, The Political Theory of the XIIIth Century, by R. W. and N. J. Carlyle . . . ; and Social and Political Ideas of some English Thinkers of the Augustan Age, edited by F. J. Hearnshaw.' As for Shaw's book, he went on: 'I have not yet had an opportunity to read the Intelligent Woman's Guide beyond such gobbets as the newspapers extracted from it. I am glad Shaw slangs the Capital Levy. It looks very much as if the Socialist intelligentsia will have to confine themselves to literary activity for some time to come; the Trades Unionists are becoming very exclusive; and that Ramsay Macdonald should have had to go down to Oswald Mosley's country mansion to defend his possession of it was, I think, a portent. An Illiterate Woman's Guide to Socialism might be more to the point.'

TO *Messrs Clymo & Company*

27 August 1928   [London]

Dear Sirs,

I consider that Mr Lin's delay in paying his account for gas, electricity and telephone and for dilapidations to the furniture of the flat is very much overdue, and in case of illness of long duration it is usual for some other person to be empowered to act as attorney. I should be obliged if you would inform Mr Lin that in default of an early settlement proceedings will be taken.

Amongst the dilapidations, I shall be interested to hear about one curtain missing from two sets of silk curtains, and also about a brass tea canister which is missing.

Yours faithfully
[T. S. Eliot]

TO *Estate Department, W. H. Smith & Sons*

29 August 1928   [London]

Dear Sirs,

In reply to your verbal enquiry of to-day concerning Mr Clement [*sc*. George] Lawrence Smith of New York, I have to inform you that I have known Mr Smith and his family for many years. His father was a distinguished Professor of Harvard University, and his elder brother married one of my sisters.[1] Mr Smith is headmaster of a successful preparatory school for boys in New York, and is also, I believe, connected with a similar establishment in Paris. He is highly respectable and, in my opinion, quite good for any engagements that he would undertake.

Yours faithfully,
[T. S. Eliot]

1–Professor Clement Lawrence Smith (1844–1909) taught Greek and Latin at Harvard University from 1870, becoming Professor in 1883. His son George Lawrence Smith married TSE's sister Charlotte (1874–1926) in Sept. 1903.

TO *John Purves*   CC

30 August 1928   [London]

Dear Sir,

Mr Paterson[1] has shown me your letter of the 17th instant.[2] May I as Editor express my appreciation and gratitude for such criticisms? Incidentally, you will find Grierson's 'Milton' beginning in our next number. Your criticisms fall in with others that I have heard, but I hope and trust that you will continue to find in the *Criterion* the things which you like.

I also appreciate your sending a list of addresses. As a Quarterly, the *Criterion* does not hope to appeal to casual interest, and must depend chiefly upon subscribers.

Yours very truly,
[T. S. Eliot]

1–A. J. B. Paterson (b. 1900) was Sales Manager of Faber & Gwyer, appointed in 1926. GCF had written to Mrs M. L. Gwyer on 15 Jan. 1926: 'I have just taken a very important step in provisionally engaging, as Sales and Circulation Manager, a young Scotchman of 26, who has for the last five years been in the head office of Collins & Sons and Co., Glasgow. His name is Alistair Paterson, and we are giving him the salary which he is getting from Collins, namely £350 a year. I had advertised in two Scotch papers as well as in the Daily Telegraph and The Publishers' Circular for a couple of weeks, and of course I had shoals of replies; amongst which Paterson's was by far the most promising. However, before I saw him I interviewed a good many of the more likely applicants in London. Practically all of them were unsuitable, and so I wired to Paterson to come down and see me, which he did yesterday. I was very favourably impressed. He is clear-headed, his experience with Collins has been very much what we want; he has a particular aptitude for the commercial side of publishing, though he also has a sense of literary values. He is ignorant of the distribution and sales promotion of periodicals, but I have no doubt at all that he will soon master the essentials. He comes to us in a month's time, with a quite remarkable testimonial from the Sales Manager of Collins.'
2–John Purves had written from Edinburgh to Paterson: 'I hope that some of the announcements made under the monthly regime will be fulfilled: e.g. M. Valery Larbaud's promised papers on Landor & Prof Grierson's on Milton.
   'The larger size of the quarterly issue should also, I hope, make for variety; as, indeed, your last number proves. I have heard murmurs that too much space has been taken up by the "Action Française" group; but that was perhaps accidental & temporary. And if the balance can be adjusted and you can give, as before, a wide synopsis of continental literature & thought – literature as well as thought – many, I am sure, will find the review indispensable.'

TO *A. L. Rowse*   TS Exeter

30 August 1928   *The Monthly Criterion*

Dear Rowse,

Many thanks for your letter. That's very good so far, and I am delighted to have you contribute to the symposium, if there is one (I will let you know a little later); but I shall hold you to the Communism sooner or later, as there is no one whose opinions on the subject would interest me more.

What about a note on the Liberal Industrial Report, if it can be done from a non-party point of view?[1]

I am glad you liked my piece[2] about Benda.[3] I am still a little doubtful about making much of the matter in the *Criterion*, for the reason that we are sometimes accused of devoting too much attention to ephemeral French bickerings. We must keep on thinking about it however. The book is slight, and he does not make the best of his thesis.

Yours ever,
T. S. Eliot

TO *Charles Smyth*   CC

30 August 1928   [London]

Dear Smyth,

Many thanks for your letter. I will see that the books you want are obtained and sent to Corpus for you, and I will write to you again about them.

As for Shaw, what I wondered is whether you might be willing to contribute briefly to a small symposium about this book which I hope to assemble? A. L. Rowse of All Souls, whom I should much like to have you meet some day, is contributing, and I hope to get two or three elder people, of divers points of view.

Yours always sincerely,
[T. S. Eliot]

1 – The Liberal Industrial Report is 'a splendid piece of work,' said ALR (undated).
2 – TSE typed 'speech'.
3 – 'Are you writing in the *Criterion* on Julien Benda?' asked ALR. 'I admired very much your article on him in the *Cambridge Magazine* . . . But these Frenchmen make a good deal of pother and smoke out of their disagreements: two enormous controversies in such a short time. La Poésie Pure and now this one. I've just read Benda's *N.R.F.* reply.'

TO *Herbert Cysarz*[1]   CC

30 August 1928   [London]

Sir,

I am writing to ask you whether *The Criterion* might have the honour of publishing an essay by you, as I and several of my colleagues are desirous of having your name in our review.

The Criterion is a Quarterly Review which publishes the work of serious artists and philosophers, and has always been distinguished by its cosmopolitan character. It is the first English periodical to publish new work by Herman Hesse, E. R. Curtius, Hugo von Hoffmansthal [*sic*], Max Scheler and Wilhelm Worringer among German authors; and of Jacques Rivière, Larbaud, Valéry, Cocteau, Proust and Maritain in France. I send you two copies, one of which contains a short article on yourself.[2] The review was for a time published monthly, but is now published four times a year.

Our rates of payment are £10 for 5000 words, and articles should be about that length. When articles have to be translated, we are obliged to deduct from the payment the expenses of translation, which are 15 shillings per 1000 words.

I should be greatly honoured if you would suggest a subject for an essay in *The Criterion*.[3]

> I am, Sir,
> Your obedient servant,
> [T. S. Eliot]

1–Herbert Cysarz (1896–1985), German scholar of literature and philosophy – zealous proponent of the German language and culture, and of the rights of Sudeten Germany – was associate professor at the University of Vienna, 1927–38. In 1928 he was appointed to the Germanistic Chair at the German University of Prague. His writings include *Erfahrung und Idee: Probleme und Lebensformen der deutschen Literatur von Hamann bis Hegel* ('Experience and Ideas: Problems and Ways of Life of German Literature from Hamann to Hegel', 1921) and *Literaturgeschichte als Geisteswissenschaft: Kritik und System* ('Literary History as a Spiritual Science: Criticism and the System', 1926).

2–See A. W. Wheen's review of Cysarz, *Literatur-Geschichte als Geisteswissenschaft*, C. 7 (June 1928), 432–5.

3–No essay was forthcoming.

TO *Alfred Zimmern*[1]   CC

30 August 1928   [London]

Dear Mr Zimmern,

You may not remember that some months ago you kindly wrote to me enclosing a pamphlet of the Institute of Intellectual Relations. At the time, or shortly after, the *Criterion* was in jeopardy, and I could not look very far ahead.

Now we are settled again as a Quarterly, and I should like to return to the subject, and make the Institute a little better known here. Would you yourself be willing to let me have an article about it? I should be delighted if you would; but if you should be too busy, perhaps you will make another suggestion. But I do think that *The Criterion* is the place for something of the sort, and it ought to be by you.

Yours very sincerely,
[T. S. Eliot]

TO *Harold Laski*   CC

6 September 1928   [*The Criterion*]

My dear Laski,

Thank you for your kind letter. I have delayed writing to you until I had heard from a few other of the prospective contributors, so that I might know how much length I could give. There are one or two still missing, but we now have enough to make an interesting and important symposium. Would you be willing to write from a thousand to fifteen hundred words, and could you let us have it by the 20th of September? I need hardly say that I attach particular importance to your own contribution. The next

1–A. E. Zimmern (1879–1957), Fellow and Tutor of New College, Oxford, 1904–9; enthusiast for working-class education (serving as an inspector of the Board of Education, 1912–15), had written in a testimonial, 22 Aug. 1918: 'Mr T. S. Eliot is well-known to me. He has done successful work as a lecturer to working men under the auspices of London University. I have the highest opinion of his character and ability.' (See TSE's letter of thanks, 27 Oct. 1916: *L* I, 172.) In 1920 he was a founder of the Institute of International Affairs (Chatham House); and after teaching as Wilson Professor of International Relations at the University College of Wales, Aberystwyth, and at Cornell University, he became Deputy Director of the League of Nations' Institut International de Coopération Intellectuelle (forerunner of UNESCO). He was the first Montague Burton Professor of International Relations at Oxford, 1930–44; Deputy Director of Chatham House, 1943–5; and in 1945 he became Secretary-General of UNESCO. Publications include *The Greek Commonwealth* (1911), *Europe in Convalescence* (1922), and *The Third British Empire* (1926).

contributor on the same side will be the Rev. M. C. D'Arcy, S.J., and I have still to hear from Belloc. I have also two or three men of less note.

When you are back in London I hope to see you privately, and I also hope that you will drop in on any Thursday for lunch at The Grove, which is in Beauchamp Place, near Brompton Road Station.

With many thanks,
Yours ever,
[T. S. Eliot]

TO *Peter Quennell* CC

6 September 1928   [London]

My dear Quennell,

In reply to the last paragraph of your letter, I hope that you will not write anything about me, however flattering, until I have had an opportunity to talk to you. Your mention of *The Waste Land* rather alarmed me, because I feel that that is now a little out of date, even with respect to my own composition.[1]

Yours in haste,
[T. S. Eliot]

TO *A. E. James, Messrs James & James* CC

10 September 1928   [London]

Dear Mr James,

I enclose a letter received today from the Hampstead Inspector of Taxes, of which I have kept a copy. I am writing saying that I am consulting you. I do not appear to hold a letter from him of 4/7/27, and may have sent it to you. Perhaps it would be simplest if you would kindly reply to him yourself? I do not understand his last question. Surely, any interest received

1–'Mr T. S. Eliot', *Life and Letters* 2: 10 (Mar. 1929), 179–90. Quennell had written on 4 Sept., 'I have been feverishly engaged during the last week upon an article on The Waste Land for Desmond McCarthy's new paper. If you happen to see it – which I trust you won't – please be indulgent.' Quennell later related that he had received a further letter from TSE, now lost: he recalled only 'that, commenting on a critical essay of mine, in which I had suggested that the author of *The Waste Land* was still a Puritan at heart, he had asserted that he was proud of his Puritan ancestry, and that a long line of studious clergymen and judges had firmly fixed his mental pattern' (*The Wanton Chase: An Autobiography from 1939* [1980], 16).

after 25/3/27 is divisible into two parts: that which is capitalised, and therefore I presume not taxable as income, and that which accrues to Mrs Haigh-Wood, and therefore returnable by her as income for 1927/1928?

Yours sincerely,
[T. S. Eliot]

TO *Roy Campbell*   CC

11 September 1928   [London]

Dear Mr Campbell,

Very many thanks for your kind letter. I shall look forward to receiving some manuscript from you as soon as you have anything that you are willing to part with. I hope that we may meet again in London. You may not remember that we met one evening some years ago at Osbert Sitwell's.[1]

Yours sincerely,
[T. S. Eliot]

TO *Bonamy Dobrée*   CC

11 September 1928   [*The Criterion*]

My dear Bonamy,

Thanks for your letter. I am much more sorry than you that it was impossible to make any of those dates, but I wish you would give me a more exact timetable of your movements. When you have settled down as a country squire in Norfolk[2] will you not be back in London on your way to resuming your pedagogics in Egypt? Especially I should like it if you could be here some time in September, as the celebrated Paul More will be in town for a bit, and ought to be worth meeting.

Ever yours,
[T. S. E.]

1–Campbell replied on 7 Feb. 1929, from Martigues, France (where he urged TSE to visit him): 'I remember meeting you very clearly indeed at Osbert Sitwell's but I did not think you would remember me. At that time I was quite certainly the worst writer in England. I had neither properly absorbed what was going on in Europe nor relinquished my feeling of inferiority as a colonial . . . Mentally and socially I am an ordinary Victorian bourgeois and I believe only in the mental and moral standards of my Presbyterian ancestors . . . But I can promise you that I am infinitely more erudite in English poetry than I have ever been able to show in my work.'
2–BD had bought a house in Norfolk.

TO *Paul Elmer More*[1]   CC

11 September 1928   [London]

Dear Mr More,

Thank you very much for your kind letter. I am looking forward keenly to seeing you as soon as you come to London. I will write to your London hotel next Sunday.

I am writing to Ivor Richards and will give him your Cambridge address, and I am sure that he will be very anxious to see you. I am also writing to Spens (the Master of Corpus), and will ask you to accept an introduction to him. But I doubt whether he will be in Cambridge himself until you return there. Richards knows all of the literary, philosophical and psychological people in Cambridge and Spens knows all the theologians. He was a physicist by profession, but you may have read his essay in the volume of *Essays Catholic and Critical*.[2]

May I add a line to say that I am deeply grieved to hear of the death of your wife, of which the Babbitts had not told me. I never knew her myself, but my sister, Ada,[3] had often spoken of her.[4] I am extremely sorry for having written in ignorance, and beg you to accept my expression of sympathy.

                                   Yours very sincerely,
                                   [T. S. Eliot]

TO *I. A. Richards*   CC

11 September 1928   [London]

My dear Richards,

I am awfully sorry not to have been able to see you when you were passing through London, and must apologise for not having written at once. I was at the moment extremely busy with domestic as well as business affairs, and our servant was away on a holiday, otherwise we should have asked you and Mrs Richards to lunch or dinner with us. I hope

1–Paul Elmer More (1864–1937), critic, scholar and writer: see Biographical Register.
2–Spens, who had thought when young of taking Holy Orders, contributed an article on 'The Eucharist' to *Essays Catholic & Critical by Members of the Anglican Communion*, ed. Edward Gordon Selwyn (1926), 425–48.
3–Ada Eliot Sheffield (1869–1943), eldest of the seven Eliot children; author of *The Social Case History*; *Case Study Possibilities*; *Social Insight in Case Situations* (New York, 1937). TSE thought her 'a very exceptional woman': the Mycroft to his Holmes.
4–Henrietta ('Nettie') More had died on 20 Jan. 1928. She had grown up in St Louis.

for my own sake that you will carry out your project of living in London and going up to Cambridge during the week, although I doubt whether anyone but Ogden can survive such a regime. But if you abandon that notion, then I must try to get down to Cambridge some time for a night, so as to talk over the manuscript which you left with me. I will return it as soon as you like. I found it immensely interesting, and particularly want to have a talk to you about it.[1]

Will you please let me know whether you have discovered the copy of Read's book which was sent to you in Cambridge. It should have been waiting at 10 King's Parade. If not, I will get you another immediately, because I particularly want your review of this book for the December number, and we go to press on October 15th.[2]

Lastly, I should be extremely grateful if you would look up Paul Elmer More in Cambridge, and think that you would find him well worth the trouble. I believe that you have already met him in America, so I don't need to tell you much about him. Of course he has gone over almost entirely to theology, but is still, I think, the most interesting critic in America after Babbitt himself. He is staying with his daughter, Mrs Dymond, 10 Hills Avenue. He doesn't seem to have many acquaintances in Cambridge, and I am very anxious that he should meet everyone worth meeting, particularly among the younger men. Could you try to get hold of him?[3]

Yours ever,
[T. S. Eliot]

1 – IAR wrote on 20 Sept. to ask if TSE would send the typescript of *Practical Criticism* to his wife in London. 'Many thanks for Simeon who has just come. Admirable, I think & well got up – but *not* the illustration. I wish I could see how you get lines to look so settled & final, so fixed and finished.' (Houghton) (The illustration to *A Song for Simeon*, to be published on 24 Sept., was by E. McKnight Kauffer. The *TLS* review – 'Ariel Poems', 20 Dec. 1928, 1007 – would concur with IAR's negative view of the illustration: 'Mr McKnight Kauffer's mechanical visions are not a very appropriate comment on the quivering and romantic sensibility of Mr T. S. Eliot.') IAR wrote again, in an undated letter: 'an evening over Practical Criticism would be of immense benefit to me.'

2 – 'Read's book I have found & looked through,' replied IAR. 'You shall have the review before Oct 15. I noticed some things that made me very angry – the last sentence on p 96, for example – and I would like to have cooled off before writing' (undated). See IAR's review of Herbert Read, *English Prose Style*, C. 8 (Dec. 1928), 315–24.

3 – 'I remember Paul Elmer More well & have asked him to come to tea tomorrow. I will make some of the young people meet him' (undated; IAR's letter is given in *Selected Letters*, p. 45, as [June/July 1928], but it appears rather to date from mid-Sept.).

TO *Peter Quennell*   CC

11 September 1928   [London]

Dear Quennell,

I quite understand the difficulty, but have no fears in any case.[1] I am
rather crowded this week, but will drop you a line early next week and
suggest a day to meet.

>   With many thanks,
>   Yours ever sincerely,
>   [T. S. Eliot]

TO *André Mazower*   CC

11 September 1928   [London]

Dear Mazower,

I am glad to hear that there is no difficulty about your getting into
America.[2] We can now pursue our enquiries about Harvard at leisure. I
will write as soon as I can to Professor Lowes[3] as I suggested, and ask him
for any information that he can give. I must say that I do not yet see any
way in which you will be likely to be able to support yourself in America
while studying, but there is plenty of time to find out. I suppose that after
the opening of term I should write to you at Cambridge?

>   Yours sincerely,
>   [T. S. Eliot]

1–Quennell said of the article he was writing for McCarthy: 'the result, though I daresay
silly and *obviously* inadequate, was I think *unobjectionable*. It is q. likely indeed that D. M.
won't use it this month after all, &, in that case, I shall have it back & be able to turn it
inside out. It doesn't deal particularly with *The Waste Land* (I don't know why I said it did)
& is mostly intended as a refutation of that silly creature Edwin Muir in his stupid book,
Transition, & his complaint that your work "*lacks seriousness*".' Muir's 'T. S. Eliot', *Nation*
121 (5 Aug. 1925), was reprinted in *Transition* (New York, 1926), 131–44.
2–TSE had interviewed Mazower on 29 June. By 7 Sept., Mazower ascertained that since
he had been born in Paris he would be entitled to enter the USA on the French quota in the
summer of 1929. He proposed to read for a PhD in English Literature at Harvard; but, since
he had no means – 'I am not in a position to accept an allowance, even if it should be offered
me, from my parents' – he hoped he might either work for his living and fees while studying
or win a scholarship.
3–John Livingston Lowes (1867–1945), American scholar of English literature – author
of the seminal study of Coleridge's sources, *The Road to Xanadu: A Study in the Ways of
the Imagination* (1927) – had taught for some years, 1909–18, at Washington University,
St Louis, where he become known to TSE's family. He later taught at Harvard, 1918–39.

TO *Charles Smyth*   cc

Dear Smyth,

I have your letter of the 7th instant incorrectly dated 7th October, which shows me how extremely conscientious you are. As a matter of fact I was lunching with Pickthorn to-day, and in compliance with your suggestion I asked him to write about Shaw, and he has accepted. I did not tell him that I had written to you first, but I think I will do so. I may say, however, that he immediately remarked that you would do such an essay much better than he would; but nevertheless he seemed interested to do it.

If you are not going to be in the symposium I shall hold you to a long review of 1500 words or so for the December number. You have several books, and if none of them seems to you worthy, I wish you would let me know at once.[1] Also I wish you would try to think of some subject on which you would care to write a long essay for a following number.[2]

I hope to spend a night or two in Cambridge during the term, and shall certainly see you.

Yours very sincerely,
[T. S. Eliot]

P.S. Would you care to have for review also *Canada and World Politics* a Study of the Constitutional and International Relations of the British Empire by P. E. Corbett and H. A. Smith?

TO *Orlo Williams*   cc

11 September 1928   [London]

My dear Williams,

I am writing first to remind you of the Italian Notes which you promised me for the December number. Could you manage to let me have something early in October?

Also, do you think that Norman Douglas is or is not a good subject for a long review? I know nothing of his work at first hand, but I am reminded of it by the receipt of a new novel by him.[3]

---

1 – Smyth reviewed *Social and Political Ideas of some English Thinkers of the Augustan Age*, ed. F. J. C. Hearnshaw, C. 8 (Dec. 1928), 333–7.

2 – 'A Note on Historical Biography and Mr. Strachey', C. 8 (July 1929), 647–60.

3 – OW wrote on 15 Sept. about Norman Douglas (1868–1952), 'his last novel isn't up to much, though his style is nice. He had written one really amusing book *South Wind*, &

I suppose you are in the country now and trust that you will let me know as soon as you are settled again in London.

> Yours ever,
> [T. S. Eliot]

TO *E. R. Curtius*   TS Bonn

11 September 1928   *The Monthly Criterion*

My dear Curtius,

Thank you very much for your kind letter of 2nd September.[1] I should be very glad of course if your translation as well as Rychner's might appear, but that I suppose is not my affair. I will shortly send you one or two unpublished poems, and should be glad to have your opinion. If you should think any of them worthy of translation I should be flattered, and you will have complete liberty with them, except that I cannot allow the English text to appear at present. Everyone to whom I have shown your translation of *The Waste Land* admires it, and it is also agreed that my verse translates better into German than into any other language. That is another reason why I find your translations extremely useful to myself.

Your remarks about English novels interest and amuse me, and I should like to suggest that at some moment of leisure when you have nothing more serious to do, you might write for me some notes expressing your opinion of the modern English novel in general, which we could publish.[2] Your list of names of course has several notable exceptions; chiefly Virginia Woolf and E. M. Forster. If you are not well acquainted with the

---

two admirable books of travel, *Old Calabria* & *Fountains in the Sand*. One *could* write a retrospect of him, but I doubt if it is really worth while.' Douglas would be noticed for the first time in the *Criterion* in Oct. 1930.

1 – Curtius had discussed with Rychner their respective versions of 'Perch' Io non Spero', and had agreed that Rychner should publish his. 'He prefers it to mine. I like mine better. If you wanted to send me something from your unedited poems, I would be very happy. I don't know, of course, whether I am going to translate it or not. One can never tell beforehand. Some sort of inspiration is also required for the practice of translating (poetry).'

2 – 'During the holidays I read a few English novels, chosen at random from the supplies of Tauchnitz [editions] in Swiss bookshops: Wells, Somerset Maugham, Aldous Huxley, M[aurice] Baring, Hugh Walpole, Galsworthy. An odd product, this standardised English novel, of an aesthetic naivety that one cannot compare with continental literary standards. I understand Joyce better now as a reaction against this comfortable way of writing.' Curtius wrote a number of studies of Joyce at the end of the 1920s: 'James Joyce' (*Literatur*, Dec. 1928), 'Technik und Thematik von James Joyce' (*Neue Schweizer Rundschau*, Jan. 1929); and the influential *James Joyce und Sein Ulysses* (Zurich: Verlag der Neuen Schweizer Rundschau, 1929).

work of either of these writers I should like to see that some of their books are sent you. There is also an American writer who is worth notice named Ernest Hemingway.

Apart from your own work, and I have no need to repeat that anything you ever care to send me will be very gratefully received, I wish that you would from time to time suggest new German writers who ought to be represented in *The Criterion*. I was very sorry indeed to hear of the death of Max Scheler whose essay in *The Criterion* I found very interesting, and whose acquaintance I owe to you.[1]

Always your friend,
T. S. Eliot

TO *Glenn Hughes*[2]   TS Texas

12 September 1928   *The Criterion*

Dear Mr Hughes,

I shall be delighted to see you in London as soon as possible.[3] I expect to be in town continuously for some time. In case of an unexpected visit you are more likely to find me here in the morning, at any rate from 10.30 or 11 o'clock, than in the afternoon; but I would suggest that you meet me here for lunch at 12.30 or 1 o'clock on Wednesday the 19th, if that is convenient.

Yours sincerely,
T. S. Eliot

---

1 – Scheler had died on 19 May 1928. TSE wrote in his next 'Commentary': 'When more of Dr Scheler's work is translated into English, his importance will be more apparent. His *Philosophical Anthropology* was still in preparation, and we hope will appear in some form' (*C*. 8 [Sept. 1928], 6).

2 – Glenn A. Hughes (1894–1964), who taught at the University of Washington, was travelling in Europe for nine months on a Guggenheim Fellowship to study the Imagist poets, many of whom he was to interview, for *Imagism and the Imagists: A Study of Modern Poetry* (1931). From 1930 to 1961 he was Head of the Division of Drama at Washington, pioneering 'theatre in the round' at the Penthouse Theatre.

3 – Hughes – who was staying for a while (with wife and child) at Richard Aldington's cottage in Padworth, near Reading (RA had gone away on urgent family business to Italy) – requested to meet TSE in London at some time.

TO *H. E. Bates*   CC

12 September 1928   [London]

Dear Mr Bates,

I shall be glad to use your story 'The Child' but cannot at the moment
tell you in what number of *The Criterion*.[1] I will let you know at the
earliest possible moment, and you will of course receive proof in due
course.

Yours sincerely
[T. S. Eliot]

TO *E. N. da C. Andrade*[2]   CC

12 September 1928   [London]

Sir,

I am venturing to ask whether it would ever be possible for you to
contribute to *The Criterion*, or occasionally to review some important
book at length. *The Criterion* is of course a Quarterly Review of general
interest, and its interest in science is not technical. I am not myself
competent in scientific matters, but am especially influenced in asking you
by the fact that I admire your style of writing. It seems to me that you are
more competent than any other scientific authority of equal standing to
write of scientific matters in a way intelligible to the ordinary intelligent
reader, without ever descending to 'popular science'.

1–C. 8 (Dec. 1928), 215–19. Bates wrote on 24 Aug.: 'Edward Garnett thought it delicious
– and Edward Garnett was wise enough to know that though it was light it wasn't written
hastily. You're probably aware that one doesn't write hastily for Garnett – one writes
remorselessly or not at all.' He was writing another novel, he added. 'You know what this
novel-writing means for one whom the critics *will* call absurdly young – long & wearying
effort with no practical support until afterwards.' Could he do 'a little reviewing' for TSE?
'My only credentials are that I periodically review for *The Nation* & *The Adelphi*.'

   Bates replied to this letter from TSE on 14 Sept.: 'If only for financial considerations, do
print it early if possible. My income from literature is that of a bad farm labourer.' HR, to
whom TSE showed the story, had told TSE on 30 Aug. that he would be 'inclined to publish'
the story: 'Bates deserves encouragement: he is a bit sentimental & a bit provincial, but
might do good things if he will come under our wings. Our costive medicine would do him
good.'

2–E. N. da Costa Andrade (1887–1971): Professor of Physics at the Artillery College,
Woolwich, London, 1920–8. A historian of science, he also wrote poetry. *The Structure of
the Atom* (1923) ran to many editions.

I have often discussed your writing with our mutual friend, Kenneth Pickthorn, who has also shown me some of your poems which I very much liked.

I should very much like to have a long review of Jeans's *Astronomy and Cosmogony* for our readers.[1] I do not know what time you have at disposal, and have no notion whether you will be inclined to contribute to *The Criterion*. I can only say that I should be extremely happy to have you as a contributor.

I am sending you a specimen copy of the Review.[2]

I am, Sir,
Yours very truly,
[T. S. Eliot]

TO *Seán Ó'Faoláin*[3]   CC

12 September 1928   [London]

Dear Mr O'Faolain,

I am writing first to acknowledge the receipt of your story which has just arrived, and which I have not yet read.[4] I am writing also to apologise to you for not having informed you that your article on Words will appear in the September number of *The Criterion*, which will be out in a few days time.[5] Owing to a certain confusion and reorganisation of staff, I was unable to select the material for this number until rather late, and therefore had no time to send you proof of it for correction. I hope

1 – Jeans's work was to be reviewed by Montgomery Belgion only in Apr. 1930.

2 – Andrade replied that he was very busy, since he had just been appointed to the Quain Chair of Physics at University College, London; he might be able to write something after Christmas. He added: 'I am particularly grateful to you for your reference to my poems, as poetry is the one subject that I think ought to be taken seriously' (14 Sept.).

3 – Seán Ó'Faoláin (1900–91): novelist and short-story writer. Brought up in Ireland (where he was born John Francis Whelan), he attended University College, Cork – for a while in the early 1920s he was an ardent nationalist and joined the Irish Volunteers (later the IRA) – and he was a Commonwealth Fellow at Harvard University, 1926–8. Later founder-editor of the Irish periodical *The Bell*, he also served as Director of the Arts Council of Ireland, 1957–9. Following *Midsummer Night Madness and Other Stories* (1932), he produced a wealth of stories: see *Collected Stories of Seán Ó'Faoláin* (1983).

4 – Writing from Boston, Mass., Ó'Faoláin said he had sent his article on Words 'many months ago'. On 28 Aug. he submitted a story based on an incident recorded in the memoirs of Wilfred Scawen Blunt.

5 – 'Style and the Limitations of Speech', C. 8 (Sept. 1928), 67–87.

however that you will not find many errors in the text. A copy of *The Criterion* will, of course, be sent to you next week.

Yours very truly,
[T. S. Eliot]

TO *F. S. Flint*   cc

12 September 1928   [London]

Dear Frank,

As I have not seen you for some time I wish you would drop me a line to let me know whether you have any time at present for *The Criterion*. I don't want to bother you, but I should be glad to have notes on French Periodicals whenever it is possible for you to do any. Also would *Criterion* translations, apart from books, be a nuisance? Also would you, or would you not, care to review Fletcher's new book of poems which is just out, and which I think is the best that he has done?[1]

I want to see you soon. I expect to be at The Grove on Thursday and hope you will come.

Ever yours,
[T. S. Eliot]

TO *Thomas McGreevy*   MS TCD

Thursday 13 September 1928   Faber & Gwyer Ltd

Dear McGreevy,

I am afraid I am rather crowded tomorrow, but shd be glad to see you if you would call here about 12.50 for lunch. Sherard Vines,[2] who is rather

1–In a Faber & Gwyer reader's report (6 Sept. 1927), TSE wrote of Fletcher's proposed collection *The Black Rock*: 'My opinion of his work, which is a high opinion, is not reduced by this MS, but as I was the one who recommended "Branches of Adam" [1927] which has failed so conspicuously, I hesitate to urge this by myself.' He remarked too that this new collection was not 'long, continuous and difficult' like *Branches of Adam*.

Flint responded on 18 Sept.: 'I will do whatever you will, within my powers.

'Your best plan is to give me good notice, and say you want such and such a job done by such and such a date . . .

'Translations, yes: French and German; but give Italian to Orlo [Williams] and Spanish to [J. B.] Trend, and call on me only if they fail or are absent. Other languages – Danish, Swedish, Norwegian, Dutch, Portuguese, if necessary. Russian – not yet!'

Flint reviewed *The Black Rock* (1928) in *C*. 8 (Dec. 1928), 342–6.

2–Sherard Vines (1890–1974), poet and academic, taught at Keio University, Tokyo,

a good poet, is lunching with me, but if you don't mind the presence of a 3rd person, you will be very welcome.

If you turn up at 24 Russell Sq. at 12.50 we shall have a few minutes to discuss your volume.[1]

Yours ever
T. S. E.

TO *The Editor of* The Nation & Athenaeum

Published 15 September 1928   24 Russell Square, London

Sir,

I should like to add a line in support of the admirable protest made by Mr Forster and Mrs Woolf in your last issue against the 'withdrawal from circulation' of *The Well of Loneliness*. I do not like the book, but I agree that it is perfectly decent; and I see no grounds for the suppression. I wish only to suggest that some more organized protest might be made, before the practice of suppression *by these means* – articles in Sunday newspapers – becomes an established custom.[2]

Yours, &c.,
T. S. Eliot

1923–8; and was G. F. Grant Professor of English at University College, Hull, 1929–52. Publications include *The Kaleidoscope* (1921), *The Pyramid* (1926), *Triforium* (1928), and *Tofuku: or Japan in Trousers* (travel, 1931).

1 – McGreevy, who was in London en route to Ireland, wished to meet TSE in order to talk about a book of poetry by himself that was being considered by F&G.

2 – *The Well of Loneliness*, the novel about lesbian love by Radclyffe Hall (1886–1943), had been published in July by Jonathan Cape, who had to withdraw it in Aug. in the face of expressions of outrage in the popular press, especially the *Sunday Express*, and the threat of legal action by the Home Secretary, Sir William Joynson-Hicks (1865–1932). Forster opposed the suppression in principle, and he and VW published a letter, 'The New Censorship', *N&A* 43 (8 Sept. 1928), pointing out that the novel had 'obviously been suppressed because of the theme itself . . . The subject-matter of the book exists as a fact among the many other facts of life. It is recognized by science and recognizable in history. It

17 September 1928   [London]

Dear Forster,

Thank you for your letter. I had not known that any such combined protest had been attempted.[2] What you say rather discourages me; I should be quite ready to support any public protest which did not pretend that the book in question was a good book. I wish that it was; but it seems to me a very poor thing indeed; and I have just said so in the *Criterion*, to make it quite clear that I am not defending *this* book but attacking the censorship.[3] So if the lady objected to your draft, she would certainly not

---

forms, of course, an extremely small fraction of the sum-total of human emotions, it enters personally into very few lives, and is uninteresting or repellent to the majority; nevertheless it exists, and novelists in England have now been forbidden to mention it by Sir W. Joynson-Hicks . . . [W]riters . . . cannot produce great literature until they have free minds. The free mind has access to all the knowledge and speculation of its age, and nothing cramps it like a taboo . . . That is why we feel that Miss Hall's fellow writers ought to protest vigorously against the action of the Home Office, an action which is apparently illegal and is in any case detrimental to the interests of literature. Not only has a wrong been done to a seriously minded book, a blow has been struck at literature generally' (725). The question was brought to court at Bow Street, London (VW and LW attended), where the judge in the case, who refused to permit any defence on the grounds of literary merit, declared the novel obscene and ordered copies to be destroyed.

1–E. M. Forster (1879–1970), novelist and essayist: see Biographical Register.

2–On 25 Feb. 1945 TSE was to recall, in a letter to HR, the efforts made to publish an appeal: 'we based that on the liberty of the press, Miss Hall wanted it based on the greatness of the novel, which was such a dull one that nobody could have read it through except as a preparation for signing a letter about it: and so the letter never appeared.'

3–TSE wrote of Radclyffe Hall's novel ('A Commentary', C. 8 [Sept. 1928], 1–4): 'Its literary merit is not so great as the author hoped it might be. She is passionately sincere; she is obviously a cultivated person with literary standards and ambitions; and has tried to write something which should be both a literary masterpiece and a monument of special pleading for the social status of the sexual invert. She does not succeed either as writer or as pleader, and for the same reason: that she has no sense of humour. The book is not in the least pornographic. But it is long, it is dull, it is solemn, and it is not well written.

'We dislike the book, not because of the subject discussed, but because of its humourlessness, its hysteria, and the philosophy which seems to underlie it. There is the mistaken belief in what is sometimes called "the right to happiness" . . . There is a good deal of romantic slop about Miss Radclyffe Hall's attitude . . . And . . . her subject is neither so important nor so interesting as she thinks . . . If you are a believer in some definite and dogmatic Church, so that your morality is not mere prejudice and habit, but is dependent upon a definite religious faith, then you can consider the book from the point of view of that religion. But if you have not this definite religious background, your only other possible standpoint is that of public order. And most "censorship" of books in Britain and America springs neither from religious dogma nor from a clear conception of public order. Miss Hall's book is certainly no menace to public order . . .

like mine. And my hands are not quite free, because being associated with a publishing house, I could not, I think, say all my opinion of Cape.

[T. S. Eliot]

TO *J. B. Orrick*   CC

17 September 1928   [London]

Dear Mr Orrick,

Our readers and finally our directors have considered carefully the MSS. of your book 'Matthew Arnold as a Critic'. It was unanimously approved as a scholarly and valuable book which ought to be published; but decided that it was not a book suitable for our list at any time in the near future. It was my own opinion, after reading it, that the book should be submitted to one of the University Presses; and if you care to have it, and if you do not already know him, I will gladly give you a line to Mr Gerard Hopkins of the Clarendon Press.

May I also say that I hope that you will have something from time to time to offer *The Criterion*, remembering that our length is 5000 to 6000 words?

I will keep the manuscript until I hear from you.

Sincerely yours,
[T. S. Eliot]

TO *Will Spens*[1]   CC

17 September 1928   [London]

Dear Spens,

Many thanks for your kind letter. I shall be very glad to come for a weekend to Corpus; unfortunately, I am afraid it cannot be very soon. As soon as I can come to Cambridge at all, which will not be for several

---

'The general question of censorship is, we think, a question of expediency rather than principle, when it is not the censorship of a Church . . . [T]he censorship of books is almost beyond human powers to carry out well.'

1–Will Spens (1882–1962), educationist and scientist, was Master of Corpus Christi College, 1927–52. Early in his career he gave a course of lectures on *Belief and Practice* (1915); he wrote on the Eucharist in *Essays Catholic and Critical by Members of the Anglican Communion*, ed. Edward Gordon Selwyn (1926), and on birth control in *Theology* (1931); and he was a member of the commission on Christian doctrine appointed by the Archbishops of Canterbury and York, 1922–38.

weeks, I have engaged myself to stay at Magdalene with Richards, as we have some literary questions to discuss in connexion with his new book. I had already, as a matter of fact, had a general invitation from Pickthorn, whom I lunched with a few days ago, to occupy his room for a weekend during this term, so I was hoping to see you in any case. I should very much like to have a discussion with you on these matters. What you mention is very interesting.

Meanwhile, if I find I cannot get down till rather late in the term, may I give More a line to you?[1] I believe that he is to be in London for a few weeks. I have already mentioned him to Pickthorn.

Sincerely yours,
[T. S. Eliot]

Don't you think that the young men who edit 'Protest' at Oxford need a little curbing now and then?[2]

TO *J. B. Trend*   cc

18 September 1928   [London]

Dear Trend,

Many thanks for your card. I should like the Chronicle by the 15th October if possible, but the 20th is not too late. I want to get the number out as near the 1st December as possible.

Would you care to have any copies of September sent to you for distribution in Spain. And if you could entice or hale in Ortega or any other Spaniard you approve, to contribute something, I should be very grateful; it is a long time since Spain has been represented by any but the faithful Marichalar, to whom give my best regards.

Yours ever,
[T. S. Eliot]

---

1 – 'By all means give [Paul Elmer] More an introduction,' replied Spens (18 Sept.), 'or if you prefer send me his address and I will send him an invitation to a meal.'
2 – The periodical *Protest* was issued by 'Young Catholics', Oxford. 'The "Protest" people seem to me pretty hopeless,' wrote Spens to TSE. 'At present I feel more & more the real strength of the Anglo Catholic position as against Protestant or Roman criticism; on the other hand the hopeless weakness of its presentation & of A-C pokey in general.'

TO *Orlo Williams*

21 September 1928   [London]

Dear Williams,

Many thanks for sending me the Italian Notes before leaving. I have sent them to press and proof should be ready before you return.

If you get this letter in time, would you please ask Trend to let me know whether he can conveniently send a Music Chronicle for December by October 15? I am aiming to get the number out on December 1st if possible.

I remember about Mansfield; I will send you the books as soon as they appear, but I doubt, for the reason above, whether there will be time to get a review done for December.[1] It is not a job you want to be hurried over, in any case.

I hadn't heard anything about the Union Européenne yet.[2] Do let me know as soon as you are back. Best wishes for a successful voyage.

Yours ever,
[T. S. E.]

TO *Ezra Pound*   MS Beinecke

22 September 1928   Faber & Gwyer Ltd

Dear EP

Here is proof of my bloody oration.[3] As it is for you please make any objections you like, only make 'em at once.

Notes: I find to be an impossible impertinence. <I have no business to write such.> Here's a sample and it is rotten stuff, & I want to be *let off*. Reply by return of courier s.v.p.

Yrs
T.

Exclnt copy of XVI Cantos rc^d.[4] I like them better than ever.

1–Williams wanted to write an essay on Katherine Mansfield, including some comment on the *Journal* and the two volumes of her letters that were due out in the autumn.
2–Williams mentioned in his latest notes on Italian periodicals 'this Union Européenne Littéraire which is in the air & wh. proposes to meet in Paris in October. Comment on it really ought to be editorial, so you can cut out all my remarks if you wish. Only I make this point, that it is just like Latin effrontery wholly to ignore what the P.E.N., of purely English origin, had already done to promote European solidarity in literature.'
3–EP's *Selected Poems*, with intro. by TSE, was to be published on 23 Nov.
4–*A Draft of XVI Cantos of Ezra Pound for the Beginning of a Poem of Some Length* (Paris: Three Mountains Press, 1925).

Vivien Eliot TO *Mary Hutchinson*   MS Texas

23 September 1928   57 Chester Terrace, Eaton Square

My dear Mary,

I am writing while you are speaking to T. on the telephone!!

I was quite overjoyed to hear your voice. It *has* been such a long time that you have been away. How I have missed you.

I am just writing to say that it is T.'s birthday on Wed. so will you send him just a picture post card, as a surprise, & for a treat? I want him to have a nice birthday, but he would not have any party, & wd only have the members of <u>my</u> family to dinner, on Tuesday night. So it won't be much. I shd have liked a *large* gathering of old friends, & a great feast. But now I must wait till Christmas.

You have promised to ring up on Friday, so I look forward to that.

It's, as you say, a perfect moment. We walked through the Mall, this evening, & it was glorious – so clear.

Good night
Vivienne Eliot

TO *John Hayward*   TS King's

25 September 1928   Faber & Gwyer Ltd

Dear Hayward,

It is simply that I have had no time for engagements for weeks; all my spare time being filled by American pilgrims who were always here for a very short time and therefore had to [be] fitted in somehow, relatives, relatives of relatives, friends of relatives and friends of relatives' relatives etc. I have wanted to see you. Could you lunch say on Tuesday Oct. 2nd at my asylum[1] at 63 St James's Street?

yours ever,
T. S. Eliot

1–Royal Societies Club.

25 September 1928   [London]

Dear Marguerite,

I have your letter of the 19th and I think it is most kind of you to send all those subscriptions: thank you very much indeed. And on the other hand I am very glad to have those particular persons (such of them as I know) receive the *Criterion*. But a steady increase in the subscription list is what will enable the *Criterion* to survive; we are now aiming at that, and worrying less about bookstall sales; after all, an eventual subscription list of 1000 does not seem arrogantly ambitious.

Please do not judge the Quarterly *Criterion* by the June or September issue. In order to keep it up to its proper level, I have to plan and correspond for nine months ahead; for six months I could do nothing about future contributions, as I did not know whether the *Criterion* was to continue or not; so that the June number had to be put together at the last moment out of what I had, and the September number was not much better.

It is distressing, but not unexpected, to hear that you cannot come to London; and annoying that you will be so little even in Paris. I am however writing to Aldous Huxley, and hope that you will be able to see him during your sojourn in Versailles; as Aldous and Maria are among our best friends.

About *Commerce*: I had, a few weeks ago, written to Roy Campbell to ask him for something for the *Criterion*; he said that he had nothing worthy, but promised to send a thing on which he was working. I will try to get enough to share with *Commerce*. Tomlinson I have been attacking for years, but without result, but I will try again.[1] He is very elusive. So is David Garnett.

I don't like to think of your leaving the Villa Romaine. Will you go practically into Paris?[2]

1–Caetani wrote on 19 Sept., 'I wish you could get a poem from Roy Campbell for "C[ommerce]". I found that poem in the last *Life & Letters* ['The Palm', 1: 4 (Sept. 1928), 287–9] *very fine* and [H. M.] Tomlinson sometime. Tomlinson has been asked by Mrs Woolf but answered that he only had a story about the war which Mrs Woolf presumed I wouldn't want and I don't think I do.'

2–Caetani said that she and her husband were 'looking for a house to replace the Villa Romaine [at Versailles], nearer Paris'.

I hope you have had the *Song for Simeon* which I have sent you. Let me have more news of *Commerce* too.

ever affectionately, and with love from Vivien,

[Tom]

TO *The Editor of* The Times Literary Supplement

Published 27 September 1928   24 Russell Square, London w.c.1

'Questions of Prose'

Sir,

In your interesting leading article of September 13[1] your reviewer makes one point which seems to me of some importance, and which may easily be overlooked. He quotes the well-known passage from North's *Plutarch* (Coriolanus's speech to Aufidius), and follows it with the equally famous version of Shakespeare, which he prints as prose. He observes that the version of Shakespeare is 'a far better piece of prose than the original.'

I make precisely the opposite observation. The prose of North is fine prose, the verse of Shakespeare is great poetry. And printed as prose, the verse of Shakespeare seems to me to be bad prose. As prose, it is difficult to grasp; as prose, it is badly constructed. North's I find much superior – as prose.[2]

What I think your reviewer, like many other people, has overlooked is this: that verse, whatever else it may or may not be, is itself a system of *punctuation*; the usual marks of punctuation themselves are differently employed. If your reviewer were right, the method ought to be reversible;

1 – 'Questions of Prose' – *TLS*, 13 Sept. 1928, 637–8 – a review of Herbert Read, *English Prose Style*; W. Rhys Roberts, *Greek Rhetoric and Literary Criticism*; *A Treasury of English Prose*, compiled by Logan Pearsall Smith; and *Prose of To-day*.

2 – In a later radio talk, 'The Tudor Translators', TSE cited the same passages from North's translation of Plutarch (Temple edn, III, 35) and Shakespeare's *Coriolanus* (IV. v), with this commentary: 'My first feeling about these astonishing parallels is certainly not moral indignation against Shakespeare for robbing so openly; nor do I raise the cry of "lack of originality"; no, I admire the self-confidence of the master, and the consummate skill of the man who would, by altering *so little*, turn a piece of fine prose into a piece of great poetry. But, second, these verses of Shakeseare are a concentrated piece of literary criticism of the style of North. The fact that Shakespeare altered so little, is the best possible testimonial to the beauty of North's prose; and his alterations are a comment on its limitations . . . Every change made by Shakespeare is not merely the change from prose to verse, but an absolute improvement in force, concision, and ease of syntax. The verse of Shakespeare is more mature than the prose of North; but it proves how very fine the prose of North is; and indicates one way in which the prose of the translators contributed to the development of the English language' (*The Listener*, I [12 June 1929], 834).

so that some passages of great prose could be converted into fine verse; and I do not believe he can find an example.

Yours,
T. S. Eliot

TO *Allen Tate*   CC

27 September 1928   [*The Criterion*]

Dear Mr Tate,

I like your essay on Emily Dickinson[1] very much indeed, and want to use it in the *Criterion*. It was too late to use in the December number, which was already arranged, but I should like to publish it in March. I must try to find out who are the English publishers of her poems, for the benefit of English readers of the *Criterion* who do not know her work.

Sincerely yours,
[T. S. Eliot]

TO *Mary Hutchinson*   TS Texas

27 September 1928   57 Chester Terrace, s.w.1.

My dear Mary,

It was a very delightful surprise to get your card yesterday morning, and will be a permanent memory that this peculiar solstitial point on my progress from birth to death was distinguished by your thought & hand. The present arrived punctually by the next post, and was a beautifully printed & bound set of books, the suitable books too, and such as I would choose to receive on such an occasion from such a giver. *Sieti racommendato il mio tesoro!*[2] Thank you very very much, and for the comfortable words with them. I shall treasure the books. When will you appear? You are expected and awaited to ring up tomorrow.

1–Allen Tate had submitted his essay on Emily Dickinson on 3 Aug. 1928.
2–Dante, *Inf.* 15, 119–20: 'Sieti raccommendato il mio Tesoro, / Nel quale io vivo ancor – ' ('But let my Treasure, where I still live on, live in your memory – '). The lines are spoken to Dante by Brunetto Latini, author of *Il Tesore* (*The Treasure*), by way of a fervent behest. TSE quoted the lines in a copy of *Ara Vos Prec* (1919) that he sent to his friend Emily Hale in Sept. 1923 (see Lyndall Gordon, 'Eliot and Women', in *T. S. Eliot: The Modernist in History*, ed. Ronald Bush [1991], 12–13; Schuchard, *Eliot's Dark Angel*, 154); and also in a copy of *The Waste Land* (1923) given to GCF, 27 May 1925. It is not known what books Mary Hutchinson gave him for his fortieth birthday on 26 Sept.

I had a lovely birthday altogether.

> ever affectionately
> Tom

TO *John Maynard Keynes*[1]   TS King's

27 September 1928   Faber & Gwyer Ltd

Dear Keynes,

The directors of Faber & Gwyer would very much like to persuade you to write a book to express your views on Free Trade and Protection, and I have been detailed to endeavour to make the suggestion acceptable. They have in mind of course the prospect of a general election. I have no notion whether you would be willing to write such a book at all, or whether you have the time, or whether you are engaged with other publishers. All I can say is, that if the idea attracted you, then we, having made the proposal, might be said to have some moral claim upon the book! We wanted the expression of a Liberal view of the situation at the present time, which obviously you are the best qualified person to expound. As for the length of the book, it might be hardly more than a pamphlet, or it might be two volumes: that would be for you to decide.[2]

I don't suppose that you are either in London or in Cambridge at the moment, but I hope that the Gordon Square address will soon reach you.

> Sincerely yours,
> T. S. Eliot

1–John Maynard Keynes (1883–1946), influential economist and theorist of money (expert on macroeconomics); pamphleteer; patron of the arts (begetter and financier of the Arts Theatre, Cambridge); government adviser and negotiator; editor of *The Economic Journal*, 1912–45; columnist for the *Nation and Athenaeum* (of which he was chairman from 1923); intimate of the Bloomsbury circle; Trustee of the National Gallery; author of *Indian Currency and Finance* (1913); *A Treatise on Probability* (1921); *The Economic Consequences of the Peace* (1919); *A Treatise on Money* (2 vols, 1930); and *The General Theory of Employment, Interest and Money* (1936). He married in 1925 the ballet dancer Lydia Lopokova (1892–1981). TSE declared in an obituary notice that *The Economic Consequences of the Peace* was 'the only one of his books which I have ever read: I was at that time occupied, in a humble capacity [at Lloyds Bank], with the application of some of the minor financial clauses of that treaty' ('John Maynard Keynes', *The New English Weekly*, 16 May 1946, 47).

2–Keynes regretted (28 Sept.) he could not undertake a book or pamphlet on Free Trade. 'I am struggling to finish a big Treatise on Money which has been turbulently gestating for four years now, and that has the claim on all my time.'

TO *M. C. D'Arcy*

28 September 1928   [London]

My dear D'Arcy,

Very many thanks for your kind letter. I am delighted with your Shaw, which has just the form I should have wished it to have. So far as I can say without having yet read the book myself, I believe myself to be thoroughly in agreement with what you say.[1]

I feel quite certain that Andrewes is now regarded, at least by Anglicans, as among the great Anglicans. I have never read his controversy with Bellarmine – and I don't pretend that he was Bellarmine's equal in ability by any means[2] – and I dare say he was not quite gentlemanly – but some of the Fathers – the only one within my slight knowledge any of whose impolite phrases I remember is Justin Martyr[3] – were occasionally guilty of lapses from decorum weren't they?

But what you say about the essays in general not only gives me great pleasure, coming from such a critic, but revives my courage. When

---

1 – D'Arcy remarked (19 Sept.) of his contribution to the symposium on Bernard Shaw's *The Intelligent Woman's Guide to Socialism* – to be published in C. 8 (Dec. 1928), 195–201 – 'I can never look long at Shaw without beginning to dislike him.' He remarked too, on 27 Sept.: 'I have chosen a religious and Catholic point of view.'

2 – D'Arcy praised 'wholeheartedly' TSE's forthcoming *For Lancelot Andrewes*: 'The criticism seems to me to be so firm, strong & penetrating . . . I liked immensely your criticism of Hobbes and your definition of heresy . . . Of course I agree too with your remarks about humanity and the need of "superhuman Grace", the private self & the higher self and your decisive criticism of Babbitt. I go most of the way with you in your appreciation of Bradley. He is a giant & universal compared with those you mention . . . I liked also your essay on Lancelot Andrewes, but it surprised me. I hesitate to say why . . . because you naturally think I am prejudiced. I assure you I am not; I am only too glad to acknowledge holiness in those not of my communion, and I think there are few things so detestable as blackening opponents' characters in the interests of religion. But I say I am surprised because I had the impression from [John] Lingard's pages on Andrewes, and that he was not one of the great Anglicans. And isn't he exceedingly violent in his controversy with Bellarmine? And until I read the extracts you gave I had the idea that his sermons were elegant and rather too much filled out with Latin.' (Bishop Andrewes had published in 1605 *Tortura Torti* in controversion of Cardinal Bellarmine's *Matthaeus Tortus*, which had attacked James I's book on the oath of allegiance; Bellarmine replied with his angry *Apologia pro responsione sua* (1610), and in the same year Andrewes struck back with *Responsio ad apologiam Card. Bellarmini*.)

3 – St Justin Martyr (*c.*100–*c.*165): the child of a Greek-speaking pagan family in the Roman city of Flavia Neapolis, Samaria, he converted to Christianity in about AD 130, defending the faith in Asia Minor and in Rome, where he was beheaded during the persecution of the Christians under Marcus Aurelius, *c.*165 – so acquiring his posthumous surname. His extant works are two 'Apologies' and *The Dialogue with the Jew Tryphon*.

one writes a book only once in eight or ten years, one becomes often fainthearted.

> With many thanks,
> Yours sincerely,
> [T. S. Eliot]

TO *I. A. Richards*   TS Magdalene

28 September 1928   *The Criterion*

Dear Richards,

I am an incompetent ass when I am left temporarily without any secretary, and I have mislaid the letter in which you gave me Mrs Richards's address to send your MSS. to. Will you please let me have it again and forgive the delay?

I am now venturing to send you herewith for inspection and return a copy of most of a group of poems I have been working on. I am not sure whether their weakness is a question of detail, or whether they are fundamentally wrong. They seem to get feebler towards the end too. No. 2 was published in the *Criterion*, No. 1 in *Commerce*; the rest are unprinted.[1]

I will let you know as soon as I can come to Cambridge; and I will give you a wide choice of dates, as soon as I have the time to leave London at all for a night.

> Yours ever,
> T. S. E.

1–Parts I and II of *Ash-Wednesday*. IAR responded on 1 Oct.: 'I don't think there is *much* wrong with the poems. Perhaps you have been working at them too closely. They are stronger – to a stranger's eye – than you suggest. May I keep them a little to see how they *wear*. The last thirds of some of them are perhaps a little thin and a little evidently deliberate. I certainly don't think there is anything *fundamentally* at fault . . . . Tit for tat, herewith a chapter on Belief belonging to the third part of *Practical Criticism* which is now about finished. The same view, I think, exactly that I tried to maintain in *Science & Poetry* but I hope clearer and not as easily misunderstood. I had your review before me most useful!' (*Selected Letters*, 47.)

29 September 1928   57 Chester Terrace, S.W.1.

My dear Mary

It is nearly 8 o'clock, & I am expecting a masseuse in a short time, so I must rush up & take a bath. But I just wanted to write to you at once, after seeing you this afternoon. It was very sweet of you to ring up, after we had got home, to tell me that you had found, & kept, that little pearl necklace which I broke at yr dinner-party on *June 26th.*

I remember that it broke during dinner, & that afterwards I put it up on *that cupboard,* or *chest,* on the *left* of yr drawing-room.

I thought about it today, while I was dressing to come & see you this afternoon, but when I got to you I forgot to mention it.

It was given to me by Pearl Fassett, the Christmas before last. You will *keep* it for me, won't you? & if you could remember to bring it with you when you come on Wed. *week,* I should be very glad.

I was glad I made the effort to speak to you about Pearl Fassett today. *It was an effort.* But I want you please to promise not to speak about it to anyone else. On the whole people have been very kind to me about it. But one person was not. And her death is the most *terrible loss,* & gap, in my life that you could possibly imagine. In fact it is no use expecting anyone to realise it at all. But it leaves me *frightfully* lonely. She was constantly with me. And there is no-one who can in the least bit take her place. She was Tom's right hand, in the *Criterion,* & I really *do not know* how he gets on without her. Of course he is *so* reserved & peculiar that he never says anything about it, & one cannot get him to speak. That makes one much more lonely. Pearl knew all about you, and we *often* spoke of you together. She was the most perfect *companion* & friend that anyone ever had. I have never known anyone like her.

So now this is to tell you how thankful I am that you have suggested these meetings to read Tom's poems & criticize them. He needs his <u>old</u> friends, Mary, the new ones aren't the same. It doesn't seem to me that they take much interest in his poetry side. There are heaps of people I wd like you to see, & to say what you think of.

I don't know whether you are really lonely over there at Regent's Park, but I thought you seemed so. Perhaps that is because I am so very very lonely over here in *Chester Terrace.*

I never get resigned to the loss of Clarence Gate, & the life we had there. I miss *Ellen,*[1] you remember *Ellen* – & of course *she* can never be

---

1 – Ellen Sollory, née Kellond, had been Vivien's maid until 1926.

replaced. She comes to see us sometimes, but she lives out at Watford, & can't find rooms in town.

The maid I have here is glum & silent, *although* a good-natured girl, & *hard-working*. But she depresses me. The house is too small to have anyone *living in*. And it is horribly lonely & cut-off.

I feel too, that it wld. be nicer & easier for *both* Tom & me if he lived a little nearer to his office. It is a *long way*.

I have one or two plans to better our conditions, but these I must put to you when I see you. I feel Tom needs *ever* so much more in his life, *more* people of the *right* sort, (& less of the *wrong*).

I must stop now. But we expect you *& Jack* to dinner on Wed. week, Oct. 1*oth* at 7 o'clock. You will receive copies of the poems next week. I shall write to Virginia & Leonard myself, & leave Tom to deal with McKnight Kauffer.

Your most affectionate friend
Vivienne H. Eliot

Do you know Sullivan, & would *he do*?

TO *Paul Elmer More* CC

30 September 1928 57 Chester Terrace

My dear (Mr) More,

First let me say that your letter gave me a vast deal of pleasure.[1] When I send you the final volume perhaps you will have time to treat me to

---

1 – TSE had sent More a proof copy of *FLA*. More wrote on 28 Sept. – 'My dear Eliot (if I may address you so *sans façon*)' – that he had read the volume 'with sustained interest and almost complete approval. I see in them no trace of that tendency to sever art and life of which I spoke to you as marring my pleasure in Read's work and of which I thought I saw signs in your own earlier writing. On the contrary you seem to me to have a wholesome view of literature as at once a reflexion and function of life and its efflorescence. I think I stand closer with you than with any other literary critic I know. You may set this down as rather a naïve form of commendation, but you will acknowledge its sincerity. I could make one or two specific detractions from my eulogy, if you care to hear them. I still feel . . . that the truth about Middleton, as of most of the other renaissance dramatists including even Shakespeare in part, is that they were rather interested in the display of individual exhibitions of passion without much thought of the continuity or development of character. But I will admit that you have made a good case for Middleton, and that you may be right and I wrong. Your Bradley is excellent so far as it goes, but I wish that, in revising it for more permanent publication, you had made a little clearer just what the man in himself stands for. It is not safe to assume that your readers have any such understanding of him. So with Crashaw, I wish that something were added more definite about his own qualities apart from comparison with Keats and Shelley. That is to say, your book would be more satisfactory if

the marks of journalism were more perfectly obliterated. I rather regret too the tone of the article on Baudelaire . . . But these blemishes, if such they are, must be accounted very slight in comparison with the clarity and soundness and solidity of the book as a whole. As I told you, your attitude towards Babbitt agrees pretty well with what I myself have come to feel, although I would never say just what you say. The first essays, on Andrewes and Bramhall, rather frightened me. I feared you had forestalled me in making a study of the seventeenth century such as I have long had in mind to attempt. But you have left me my chance.'

On 10 July 1928, when opening his correspondence with TSE – 'My dear Mr Eliot, – I have in past years been so intimately connected with your family in St Louis – one of your brothers I think I once taught – that I dispense with a more formal mode of address' – More praised TSE's article 'The Humanism of Irving Babbitt' (Forum [New York] 80: 1, July 1928, 37–44): 'it has interested me very much because it takes precisely the line of argument that has developed between Babbitt and myself of recent years. The difference that has grown between us – I need not say there has been no rift in our friendship or in our mutual loyalty – is partly strategic. He thinks that the best point of attack is from the positive humanistic side; I feel that there can be no general or wide return to humanism except *through* religion. But more than that: he, though at heart himself deeply religious, is sceptical of any form of revelation and scornful of the Church; I have been brought, slowly and, as Ste.-Beuve would say, *à corps défendant*, to acknowledge that loose talk about religion without a certain amount of dogma and without allegiance to the Church is at the best precarious and ineffective.'

More was to write to his sister on 18 Nov. 1928: 'Eliot himself, in the preface to a new book of essays which he has sent me, comes out clearly on his new platform: classicism, royalism, and Anglo-Catholicism. This is the sort of thing that is going on in England. There is some claptrap mixed up in it, but they mean something serious too – at least there are elements of a wholesome reaction from the maelstrom of follies that has almost engulfed the world. With their classicism they contrive to mix the freest of free verse, with their royalism an ultra democracy, and with their Anglo-Catholicism a good dose of skepticism plus bravado; but they may come to terms with themselves later on' (quoted in A. H. Dakin, *Paul Elmer More* [Princeton, 1960], 266).

To the critic Austin Warren, More wrote on 11 Aug. 1929: 'I remember that last summer after reading his *Andrewes* with its prefatial program of classicism, royalism (the divine right of kings!) and Anglo-Catholicism, I asked him whether, when he returned to verse, he would write the same sort of stuff that he once called poetry, or whether he had seen a new light. His answer was: "I am absolutely unconverted" . . . He is avowedly and, no doubt, sincerely religious; but just what his religion means to him, I do not know' (Dakin, *Paul Elmer More*, 269 n. 1).

TSE would later record (after More's death in 1937): 'It was not until one or two of the volumes of *The Greek Tradition* [5 vols, 1924–31] had appeared, that More began to have any importance for me. It was possibly Irving Babbitt himself, in a conversation in London, in . . .'28, during which I had occasion to indicate the steps I had recently taken [in becoming a Christian], who first made me clearly cognizant of the situation. In the later volumes of *The Greek Tradition*, and in the acquaintance and friendship subsequently formed, I came to find an auxiliary to my own progress of thought, which no English theologian could have given me. The English theologians, born and brought up in surroundings of private belief and public form, and often themselves descended from ecclesiastics, at any rate living mostly in an environment of religious practice, did not seem to me to know enough of the new world of barbarism and infidelity that was forming all about them. The English Church was familiar with the backslider, but it knew nothing of the convert – certainly not of the convert who came such a long journey. I might almost say that I never met any Christians until after

some detailed destructiveness; but I sent you the proofs just in the hope that they might elicit, as a general criticism, the remark that you made, that you detect no trace of the tendency to sever art from life. I am well aware that the essays have not been adequately rewritten: the article on Bradley should have gone into his metaphysic as well; and the two notes on Crashaw and Baudelaire are particularly unsatisfactory and formless. Had I had the time, I would have done much more; but the book was precisely pushed forward quickly in order to prepare my few readers for some change of orientation, and also to correct what seemed to me wrong interpretation of *The Sacred Wood*. It was perhaps an act of impatience, but the other book I am working on will not be ready until next year.

But what pleased me far more than any overt praise could do, is your word about the similarity of my point of view to your own.

I very much hope that you will eventually write the study of the seventeenth century you mention. I do not know of anyone else who could do it; I have not the scholarship myself; my next book will be on Donne and his 'school', but I could never cover the whole field; and my essays on Andrewes and Bramhall are the merest sketches. I once thought of tackling Laud, but that is really beyond me, and still more so is Hooker.

I have spoken to Read, and he will be very glad to dine on next Wednesday the 3rd. But what I want to ask you is that you shall both dine here. My wife also asks you to do so; it is convenient for Read; it is quieter than a restaurant; and there is another man whom I may have in after dinner. We will dine with you in Cambridge or New York or Princeton, or even here if you will stay long enough; but this time you shall come to us again. And I have a gramaphone [*sic*] record which I should like to draw to your notice.[1]

With very many thanks,
Sincerely yours,
[T. S. Eliot]

I had made up my mind to become one. It was of the greatest importance, then, to meet the work of a man who had come by somewhat the same route, to the same conclusions, at almost the same time: with a maturity, a weight of scholarship, a discipline of thinking, which I did not, and never shall, possess ... My first meeting with him in London ... seemed more like the renewal of an old acquaintance than the formation of a new one: More was a St. Louisan, and had known my family' (*Princeton Alumni Magazine* 37 [5 Feb. 1937], 373–4).

1–More dined chez Eliot on 3 Oct. On 11 Oct. More wrote: 'I count as about the best thing that happened to me on this trip your friendship, as I trust you will permit me to call our present relation. One meets so few men with whom one can agree ... With kind regards to Mrs Eliot and gratitude for her hospitality, I am ...'

TO *A. I. Palmer*   CC

1 October 1928   [Faber & Gwyer Ltd]

Dear Mr Palmer,

I must apologise for the delay in replying to your letter of September
25th, and hope that this delay has not caused you great inconvenience.
Your novel passed through the hands of several readers, ending with
myself, and I am afraid that I was very busy at the time, and took too
long over it. It interested us all very much. Many parts of the book are
extremely impressive, and the picture of Turkish life is certainly very vivid.
We hesitated for some time over the book, but finally decided that as our
immediate lists are well filled we ought, though with regret, to decline it.
With very many thanks for letting us see the book.[1]

                                    I am,
                                    Yours sincerely,
                                    [T. S. Eliot]
                                    Director

TO *Ottoline Morrell*   TS Texas

2 October 1928   Faber & Gwyer Ltd.

My dear Ottoline,

It is very pleasant to know that you are back, but I am sorry to gather
that you are still not very well. But no doubt you are much better than
when I saw you last, and steadily improving. You have had a very long
siege of it.[2]

This has been a long tiring summer; we have been here the whole time,
with necessary repairs and decorations in the house almost continuously,
and successions of American visitors, my nieces, and various other friends
and relatives. It has been particularly good to have had Irving Babbitt and
Paul More here in the same summer. Otherwise, it has been very fatiguing.

1–Palmer had submitted 'Zenin' to F&G in Aug. TSE wrote of it in his report for F&G, 13
Aug. 1928: 'This novel "Zenin" by A. I. Palmer has been strongly recommended to me by
my friend J. B. Trend, the music editor of *The Criterion*. Trend tells me that the author of
the book is an eccentric Englishman who lives in Turkey, and has become a Turk, or at least
a Mahomedan; and that this is a novel about native and Turkish life. Trend has read the
book and thinks very highly of it. I should be glad to have either an outside opinion, or the
opinion of another member of the Committee before I read the book myself. Trend himself
seems to think that the author is another T. E. Lawrence.'
2–OM was still recovering from necrosis of the jaw.

The enclosed may interest you, partly because of Jean; it has only appeared in Marguerite Bassiano's review.

I am rather doubtful what to do. I should like to see you soon, but I should not like V. to think that you wished to see me and not her. Suppose you write to us both, at 57 Chester Terrace, and announce your return, but say you are not very well, and can only see people one at a time at present, and would like to see us severally, without specifying any date? V. is much better everyone thinks. I think it would be unwise to have any concealment or discrimination, and so would rather delay a bit, much as I should like to see you.

Always affectionately yours
Tom.

TO *Mario Praz*   CC

3 October 1928   [London]

My dear Praz,

This is just a line to thank you in arrears for your letter of the 22nd. Do let me know something about the Italian Chair when you can, and I should like to put my finger into the matter, although I am afraid my influence is slight.[1]

Yours ever,
[T. S. Eliot]

TO *Ian Parsons*   TS Texas

3 October 1928   *The Monthly Criterion*

Dear Mr Parsons,

I remember you very well indeed at the pleasant meeting of the Hesperides Association, and I am interested to know that you have settled in London with Chatto & Windus.[2] I should be very glad to see you again. Would a day next week, say Tuesday the 9th, suit you for lunch? It happens that I have got to take my typewriter to be repaired at a shop

---

1–Praz had written on 22 Sept.: 'There will be an election to the Italian chair in Cambridge during the autumn term. I will let you know about it later on, but they tell me Mr Bullough is almost sure to be elected.'

2–Parsons had written on 28 Sept. to reintroduce himself: he had met TSE at the Hesperides Society Dinner in Cambridge earlier in the year.

almost next door to Chatto, and I could arrange to come on that day or some other and pick you up for lunch in your neighbourhood.

Yours sincerely,
T. S. Eliot

TO *Glenn Hughes*   TS Texas

3 October 1928   *The Criterion*

Dear Mr Hughes,

Very many thanks for letting me see the astonishing manuscript, which filled me with wonder.[1] I am returning it herewith.

I have nothing on hand at the moment, but it may well be that I shall before long have something of that length for publication in England, and I shall be very happy to submit something for your approval as soon as the occasion appears.[2]

I should be very glad if you would let me see the translation of modern Japanese poetry with a view to publication by Faber & Gwyer, and should they not prove suitable for us I would suggest that I propose them to my friends of the Hogarth Press, as it would be a very suitable book for them.[3] But I hope you will be so kind as to let me see them before sending them to anyone else.

I enjoyed meeting you, and hope that we may see you again, especially if you spend a few weeks in London.[4]

Yours sincerely,
T. S. Eliot

P.S. Could you give me Richard Aldington's present address?

1–Hughes had sent on to TSE (27 Sept.) an amusing manuscript (now unidentifiable) that had been submitted to him as a possible Chapbook: he thought it 'quite amazing'.

2–Hughes asked if TSE had a MS of 4,000 or 5,000 words in length (perhaps published in England but not in the USA) that might make a Chapbook?

3–Hughes and Yozan T. Iwasaki were going to combine into a single volume the two Chapbooks of their translations of modern Japanese poetry; they had proved very popular in the USA, where the first – *Three Women Poets of Modern Japan* – had sold 1,500 copies 'without any display advertising'. Would Faber & Gwyer be interested in such a book?

4–Hughes was to reveal one personal detail of his meeting with TSE, when he noted that EP had 'never achieved the cool detachment of T. S. Eliot, whose eyebrows scarcely lift at even the most moving mention of the United States' (*Imagism & The Imagists*, 249).

TO *M. C. D'Arcy*   cc

3 October 1928   [London]

My dear D'Arcy,

Thank you for your note and for the warning, which I regret to hear, that you will not be much longer in London. We both wish very much to see you again before you leave, and I will drop you another line in a day or two.

Certainly I shall be very glad to meet your friend Thomas Burns. Will you tell him just to drop me a line, and we will arrange to meet.[1]

Yours ever,

[T. S. Eliot]

TO *T. M. Muggeridge*[2]   cc

3 October 1928   [London]

Dear Sir,

I am sorry for the delay in writing to you about your sketches.[3] I do not find either of them quite suitable for *The Criterion*, but they may interest

1–D'Arcy wished (1 Oct.) to introduce to TSE a 'young man Thomas Burns . . . He is a poet friend of mine . . . & is practically in charge of the publishers Sheed & Ward.' Tom Burns (1906–95), whom D'Arcy had taught at Stonyhurst, was with the Catholic publishers Sheed & Ward, 1926–35. From 1935 he worked for Longman Green – where among other undertakings he managed to arrange to finance Graham Greene's mission to enquire into the persecution of the Catholic Church in Mexico: that exploit eventuated in *The Lawless Roads* (1939) and *The Power and the Glory* (1940) – and he became in addition a director of the Tablet Publishing Company, 1935–85. During WW2 he was press attaché to Sir Samuel Hoare, British Ambassador to Spain: his qualifications were that he knew Spain and the Spanish language. He was chairman of Burns & Oates, the premier Catholic publishing house, 1948–67; and he was editor of *The Tablet*, 1967–82.

2–Malcolm Muggeridge (1903–90), journalist and broadcaster, graduated from Selwyn College, Cambridge, and taught in India, 1925–7, then for three years in Cairo. From 1930 he wrote for the *Manchester Guardian*; and from 1932 he lived for a while in Russia; later in Switzerland. Later still, he wrote for the *Calcutta Statesman* and the *Evening Standard* (London). His work for the Intelligence Corps in WW2 earned him the Légion d'honneur and the Croix de Guerre with palm. In 1945 he became a leader writer for the *Daily Telegraph* (he served too as Washington correspondent, 1946–7); and he edited *Punch*, 1952–7. From the 1950s he won fame as a TV presenter. In 1982 he was received into the Roman Catholic Church. Works include a biography of Samuel Butler (1936), *The Thirties* (1940), and autobiographies. See also Richard Ingrams, *Muggeridge: The Biography* (1995), and G. Wolfe, *Malcolm Muggeridge: A Biography* (1995).

3–Prompted by BD, Muggeridge (who had met him while working in Cairo) had submitted two short essays on 3 June. He submitted a further story on 6 Dec. 1928.

me enough to lead me to say that I should be very glad if you could send me more of your work.

Yours faithfully,
[T. S. Eliot]

TO *Huw Menai*¹   CC

3 October 1928   [London]

Dear Mr Menai,

I must apologise for the delay in replying to your two letters, but I have been very busy particularly during the holiday season.² I may say that your poem interested me very much. I mean 'The Passing of Guto'. The shorter poems unfortunately seem to me inferior. I say unfortunately because the long one is much too long for me to use. I should suggest your sending the long poem, and perhaps a number of short poems as well, to The Hogarth Press, 52 Tavistock Square, W.C.1., who often publish very small books of verse, particularly by new poets. You are quite welcome to use my name in writing to The Hogarth Press, and I should very much like to see more of your work.³

Sincerely yours,
[T. S. Eliot]

1–Huw Owen Williams (1886–1961) – 'Huw Menai' – went to work at the age of 16 in the pits at Gilfach Goch, Glamorgan; he published poems in local newspapers including *Merthyr Express* and *Western Mail*; his first book was *Through the Upcast Shaft* (1920).
2–Menai had submitted some poems on 9 July. He wrote again on 15 Sept.: 'After reading some of your profound literary criticism I congratulate myself that in many of my poems, and I have written a few hundred of them, I have stumbled in my amateurish & uneducated way into much of the form & content which you extol.' He never forgot 'the prosaic basis of it all, that I am a citizen not of the world or the universe, but of a pair of boots and those, very often, leaky ones.' He had written 500 poems over nine years; and *The Nation*, *The Spectator* and *Cornhill Magazine* had accepted work by him in 1928.
3–VW had written to LW on 25 Sept. 1928: 'On Vita [Sackville-West]'s advice she [Dorothy Wellesley] is going to publish the Welsh Miner' (*Letters* III, 535). *The Passing of Guto and Other Poems* was published in Mar. 1929 in the Hogarth Living Poets series.

TO *Richard Church*[1]   CC

3 October 1928   [London]

Dear Church,

I was sorry not to find you at the Grove last week, and hope that it does not mean that you are ill. I am writing to ask whether you have enough material for a longish review on Goldsmith. I sent you one book, but was under the impression that one or two more were coming out.[2] Have you seen any announcements? I am sorry for the delay about your story, but I am returning it now, as after a good deal of thought I don't think it is quite suitable for us, and I should not be able to use it for some long time in any case. Do let me hear from you.

With all good wishes,
Yours ever,
[T. S. Eliot]

TO *H. V. Fitzroy Somerset*[3]   CC

3 October 1928   [London]

Dear Somerset,

I am very sorry indeed that I cannot use your interesting note on the Salzburg Festival, but I am afraid that it is just the sort of thing that I cannot use. You see, we have a regular music chronicler (J. B. Trend) who has written quarterly notes on music especially covering foreign musical festivals like this, and as he is in the position of an associate he must have a free hand, and I leave everything of that sort to him. This does not mean at all that *The Criterion* is not open to articles on music by other people. It only means that such accounts of contemporary activities must be covered by one regular chronicle.

I don't know much about *The Saturday Review*, but I should certainly try Squire. I haven't seen *The London Mercury* for a long time and do not know whether it would be in the same position concerning musical notes as myself, but it is certainly worth trying.

1–Richard Church (1893–1972), poet, critic, novelist, journalist, worked as a civil servant before becoming in 1933 a full-time writer and journalist. His first book of verse, *Mood without Measure*, was published by TSE in 1928.
2–Richard Church, 'Oliver Goldsmith', C. 8 (Apr. 1929), 437–44.
3–H. Vere Somerset (1898–1965), Fellow of Worcester College, Oxford.

I should be delighted if you would suggest some other subject for an essay. I hope very much that we may meet again before very long, either in Oxford or in London.

Yours sincerely,
[T. S. Eliot]

P.S. I am just trying to write a review of the English translation of *Les Trois Réformateurs*, but it is difficult to write about the works of people one knows.[1]

TO *N. C. Wilson*   CC

3 October 1928   [London]

Dear Mr Wilson,

Very many thanks for your kind letter of appreciation.[2] I should have been very happy to sign your copy of my poems, but unfortunately I have to refuse all invitations, however flattering, to sign this particular volume, except of course the few copies which I gave myself to friends. The reason is that a limited edition, now exhausted, was published which I signed, and I do not feel that it would be quite fair to the people who bought that edition to sign other copies. I hope that you will understand my position. I am always ready to sign copies of any books of mine when there is no limited signed edition.

I shall hope to see you in London. I have always wanted to visit Scotland, but have never had the opportunity

Yours sincerely,
[T. S. Eliot]

---

1 – [TSE], 'Three Reformers' – on Jacques Maritain, *Three Reformers: Luther, Descartes, Rousseau – TLS*, 8 Nov. 1928, 818.
2 – N. C. Wilson of Lockerbie had asked TSE to sign his copy of *Poems 1909–1925*.

TO *W. Edward Crankshaw* [1]

cc

3 October 1928   [London]

Dear Sir,

I have your letter of the 25th of September and regret that I have not replied immediately.[2] It is, as you appear to be quite aware, difficult to say anything to a writer whose work one does not know, except that I should be very glad to read anything you care to send. I would only suggest that if you want to send notes from Vienna you should look carefully at *The Criterion* to be sure that they did not conflict or overlap with our German Chronicle or any other regular features. If you have any specimens of your writing on hand I should be very glad to look at them now. If not, by all means send me something from Vienna, and I will at least give it my full attention.

Yours faithfully,
[T. S. Eliot]

TO *Charles Norman* [3]

cc

3 October 1928   [London]

Dear Mr Norman,

Please forgive my delay in replying to your letter of the 6th September. I remember your poem quite well. I am quite willing that you should use

---

1–Edward Crankshaw (1909–1984): writer, translator, and commentator on Soviet affairs. Soon after leaving Bishop's Stortford College, he went off to live in Vienna, teaching English at the Berlitz School, learning the German language, and becoming absorbed by Austrian and German culture. On the outbreak of WW2 he was contacted by the British secret services and sent to work at the Military Mission in Moscow (where he also quickly learned Russian). He later worked as a journalist for the *Observer*, 1947–68, writing authoritative commentaries on the USSR. His many publications include *Vienna: A Culture in Decline* (1938), *Gestapo* (1956), *Russia without Stalin* (1958), *The Fall of the House of Habsburg* (1963), *Maria Theresa* (1969), *The Shadow of the Winter Palace* (1976), and *Bismarck* (1981). In addition, he translated into English five plays by Ernst Toller (who had become a close friend while in Austria): *Nie Wieder Friede* he translated as *No More Peace! A Thoughtful Comedy*, with lyrics adapted by W. H. Auden (1937). In 1964 the Austrian government awarded him the Ehrenkreuz für Wissenschaft und Kunst; and he won both the Heinemann Award, 1977, and the Whitbread Prize, 1981.
2–Crankshaw, who said he was going 'to get first hand knowledge of the Continental Theatre', offered 'Reports of the Artistic state of affairs in Vienna'.
3–Charles Norman (1904–96), Russian-born poet and biographer (his parents emigrated to the USA in 1910), made a name for himself as poet and journalist. After WW2 he taught for a time at New York University and went on to become better known for his biographies

my name, and will also write a letter.[1] Will you tell me what form the letter ought to take and to whom I should address it, and at the same time send me a few of your poems to have at hand when I write it. With many thanks for what you say of my own work.

Yours sincerely,
[T. S. Eliot]

TO *Ezra Pound*

TS Beinecke

6 October 1928   Faber & Gwyer Ltd.

Dear E:

Your 2 letters and corrected proof received with thanks. I have incorporated practically All your suggestions, and am also obliged for correction of several slips & slops of my own.

Was not unaware of element of satire in S.P.[2] or for that matter in *Mauberley*. Didn't think it profitable to call attention of Publikum to that; if they can't see it for emselves its no use telling em, and wd only mix em up. Have now added note to say *Quia Pauper Amavi* can be obtained from Faber & Gwyer.

Eddition shd now appear Nov. 9th.[3]

---

of Samuel Johnson (1951), E. E. Cummings (1958), Ezra Pound (1960), and Christopher Marlowe (1971). His poetic output includes *The Far Harbor: A Sea Narrative* (1924) and *Poems* (1929).

1 – Norman wrote from New York to ask if TSE would sponsor him for a Guggenheim Fellowship in Creative Writing. TSE might remember writing to him about his poem 'Dead Men Under Buildings' on 30 July 1926 (see *L* 3). Recently, his poem 'Ode' had appeared in *The Dial*, June 1928 (Marianne Moore had told him that he was 'an authentic poet', he said); and 'Saint in Modern Dress' in *The Bookman* in July.

2 – *Homage to Sextus Propertius*.

3 – TSE's edition of EP's *Selected Poems* would appear on 23 Nov. When TSE was asked in a later year whether his introduction to the volume was designed to be a counterblast to the criticisms that Wyndham Lewis had levelled at EP, he responded: 'My recollection is that my introduction to Pound's *Selected Poems* was in no way inspired by a desire to counterbalance the criticism by Wyndham Lewis. I certainly read *Time and Western Man* when it appeared but I do not believe that I had Lewis's comments on Pound consciously in mind when I wrote the introduction. Indeed, it seemed to me at the time that Lewis's brilliant criticism, if, as so often, somewhat exaggerated for the sake of effective phrases, was on the whole justified and I think it gave me a good deal of pleasure. Besides, I was aware that criticism from Wyndham Lewis, even as strong as this, would not be likely to disturb Pound. They had, of course, worked together in the past and the fact that Lewis, like Pound himself, was to a considerable degree an *écrivain maudit*, would have effectively prevented the criticism from arousing in Pound the rancour which criticism from some different sources would have provoked.

Have had discussiums about Guido reps. with DelaMare and others; upshot seems to be that we can only afford them if we can get enough American support. DelaMare was to figger out how much support needed. This sort of thing is primarily his job & he is supposed to be authority on prices of production of books. Pussume you shall hear from him pressently; I will stir him up on Monday.

herzlichem Gruss.[1] V. adds love to both.

T.

I should have liked to take advantage of your benefolent proposal about the Dial, but there aint time. Will send a copy of the book for review: a few persons in America might like to posses a copy of the book, even if they have the Liveright text, merely as curiosity of literature.

TO *Mary Hutchinson* TS Texas

8 October 1928   57 Chester Terrace, s.w.1.

Dear Mary,

Vivien has been in bed all day with that cold she had yesterday, which became more feverish; and I don't think she will be up tomorrow. We don't want to postpone the small party on Wednesday, as it is not always easy once postponed to get just the right people together again quickly. So I want to suggest that we should have the dinner party for you and Jack as soon as possible, and that on this Wednesday you should all come at 9 after dinner. Perhaps Vivien will be in bed, but then she won't give anybody her cold; and if she was not about to see to the dinner herself, it would not be a very good one. So will you please, Mary, ring me up in the morning early to say if that is convenient.

We enjoyed your visit very much. And Valéry's essay is excellent; I am not sure that he is not romanticising Poe a bit; and the statement that

---

¹'Pound did not really resent criticism of this sort from people whom he considered to be in the same boat as himself. He might have been violently offended by the same sort of criticism from somebody amongst the successful and established critics. But Lewis was a kind of outlaw in addition to being also a kind of metic – he was born in Nova Scotia of American parentage – and I am quite sure that Pound felt no resentment. My introduction, in fact, was inspired simply by a general sense of the neglect of Pound's poetry, a neglect which seemed to me largely due to irrelevant causes, that is, the extent to which Pound's personality both in society and as expressed in some of his critical outbursts, irritated the literary powers of the day' (letter to H. W. Häusermann, 5 Dec. 1946).

1 – *herzliche Grüße*: with best wishes.

Poe is completely ignored in America is quite wrong.[1] The book is very nice; and Baudelaire and Dante are the two poets of whom I cannot have enough copies about, as I want them at any moment.

affectionately

Tom

P.S. I think it would be more fun if we put it off altogether for a few days, and you all came to dinner together. Will you say which nights you and Jack are free, of Saturday, Monday, Tuesday and Wednesday next, and I will find which nights the Woolfs are free and fix it by telephone.

TO *Caresse Crosby*[2]   CC

8 October 1928   [London]

Dear Mrs Crosby,

Thank you for your letter of the 2nd.[3] I am sorry that I can do nothing about *Anabase* for the following reasons. My translation was completed two years ago, and it was then arranged that a limited edition should be published by my firm, Faber & Gwyer, who should have world rights for my translation in that (first) edition. My translation was sent to the author, as was also a contract form. We have been waiting for two years only for him to sign the contract and make any suggestions about my translation, which I did not wish to publish until he had approved it.

So I cannot, obviously, consider publishing it anywhere else; as but for M. Leger's delay – owing no doubt to pressure of official business – it

1 – Paul Valéry, 'On Poe's *Eureka*' (preface to 1923 edition of Baudelaire's translation of Poe's cosmogonic poem): *Œuvres* I, ed. Jean Hytier (Gallimard, 1957, 1960), 854–62; *Collected Works of Paul Valéry*, ed. Jackson Mathews (Princeton, 1956–75), 8, 161–76. See further TSE, 'From Poe to Valéry' (1948), in *To Criticize the Critic* (1965), 27–42.

2 – Caresse Crosby (1892–1970), née Jacob (her parents were wealthy New Yorkers), married in 1922 the poet Harry Crosby, with whom she set up in Paris an imprint called Editions Narcisse, which presently became the Black Sun Press: they published writers including James Joyce, D. H. Lawrence, Hart Crane, and Ezra Pound. Following Harry Crosby's suicide in 1929, she continued to run and to expand the Black Sun Press – publishing notable works including Hart Crane's *The Bridge* (1930) and editions of her late husband's writings – before returning to the USA in the mid-1930s. In later years she took initiatives in various fields: she opened the Crosby Gallery of Modern Art, Washington, DC; she launched a quarterly journal, *Portfolio: An Intercontinental Review*; and she became active in the international peace movement, co-founding and supporting both Citizens of the World and Women Against War. Her writings include *Graven Images* (1926); *Poems for Harry Crosby* (1931); *The Passionate Years* (memoir, 1953).

3 – Crosby asked to produce a 'very limited edition de luxe' of TSE's translation of *Anabase* with a foreword by TSE; or else any other poem by TSE – '(100 copies only)'.

would have been published two years ago by us. Indeed I have long given up hope that it can ever be published by anybody!

I am glad to hear that you may be in London early next year, and shall look forward to meeting you.

Sincerely yours,
[T. S. Eliot]

Vivien Eliot TO Mary Hutchinson   MS Texas

Wednesday 8 October 1928   57 Chester Terrace, S. W. 1.

My dear Mary

Thank you very much for telephoning this morning. And I am really *awfully sorry indeed* that you *did catch my cold* on Sunday. You *knew* I *was* afraid, & I told you I had a fever. You remember how you came over hot – & felt queer. What a disaster. And I caught it from an elderly gent: called Paul Elmer More who dined here last Wed. And we have heard from Sullivan, who was also here that night, that he is also infected. So it may turn into another Plague of London. Conveyed by the Americans to spite England. Tom looks pulling [puling] tonight, & I believe is about to be ill. So he will send for 2 gentlemen for tea. He has *not* written to Virginia, & I have *NOT* had time, so do, for *all* our sakes, I beg – ring her up & say it is Monday night at 8.30.

Yrs. ever
Vivienne

Let me hear *how you are.*

FROM Geoffrey Faber   TS Valerie Eliot

11 October 1928   Faber & Gwyer Ltd.

My dear Tom,

I was asked at the Book Committee yesterday to find out if you would be willing to do an essay for The Poets on the Poets Series. The position here is that Walter de la Mare is writing on Thomas Hardy, and Chesterton on Chaucer; but both these two essays will not be ready for publication till the autumn. For the spring there is only as yet arranged for Blunden's essay on Coleridge. Do you think you could or would do one for us for spring publication? I suggested Dante as a possible subject and everybody agreed that if you would do this it would be a first-rate essay to start the series with. I rather fancy that you originally said something about doing an essay on more than one man. We feel that that would be rather unsatisfactory from our point of view. The terms that we are giving to de la Mare and Chesterton are an advance of £25 on a 10% royalty for an essay of 12,000 words.[1]

Another matter. We are doing Rothenstein's next collection of portraits. The list is a very interesting one, but is two short of the full number. He has asked us to suggest two additions; and we wonder if you would consent to be drawn by Rothenstein for the purpose? I don't really know whether I ought to mention this to you, as Rothenstein himself has not yet had our suggestions![2]

One other small matter. F. L. Lucas has written to Curtis Brown to say that he is too busy to tackle Sir Walter Raleigh and the Atheists, and suggests John Hayward for the purpose who has edited The Nonesuch *Rochester* and the forthcoming Nonesuch *Donne*. Can you tell me anything about Hayward?

The porringer is a most beautiful thing, and has caused great delight.

Yours ever,
Geoffrey Faber

TO *F. L. Lucas*[3]   CC

20 October 1928   [London]

Dear Lucas,

Some weeks ago the suggestion was made to us that you should be asked to write a book on Raleigh and the Atheists. I with the others approved of

---

1 – TSE, *Dante* (1929).
2 – William Rothenstein's *Twelve Portraits* (F&F, 1928) includes a drawing of TSE.
3 – F. L. ('Peter') Lucas (1894–1967), poet, novelist, playwright, scholar; Fellow and Librarian of King's College, Cambridge. Author of *Seneca and Elizabethan Tragedy* (1922) and *Euripides and his Influence* (1924), he was extensively praised for his edition *Complete Works of John Webster* (4 vols, 1927) – TSE considered him 'the perfect annotator'. Lucas published an unfavourable review of *The Waste Land* in the NS (3 Nov. 1923); and he attacked TSE in *The Decline and Fall of the Romantic Ideal* (1936). VW characterised Lucas, on 3 Mar. 1925, as 'a bony rosy little austere priest; so whole, & sane, & simple throughout one can't help respecting him, though when it comes to books we disagree.' As E. M. W. Tillyard would report, Lucas was to become 'openly hostile' to TSE (*The Muse Unchained: An Intimate Account of the Revolution in English Studies at Cambridge* [1958], 98); and T. E. B. Howarth gossiped that matters were to become so rancorous that Lucas 'would not even allow Eliot's work to be bought for the [King's College] library' (*Cambridge Between Two Wars* [1978], 166).

this, and we were very sorry to learn that you cannot consider it. But it is owing to your suggestion that John Hayward should be asked that I am writing to you; and I should be very grateful for your advice.

I was doubtful at the time whether there was enough material for such a book; but I knew that you would know; and I knew that a book by you would justify itself. Of course I know and like Hayward, and should like to have a book of some kind from him. But when it is [a] question of an author who is still unknown, the subject of the book needs more careful thought. If there is really enough important or interesting or new material for a book on this subject, I am sure Hayward would do it well; but as his name would not carry it, I should like to know whether you consider that there is enough fresh material to make such a book? The subject would be interesting, if there is enough to be found out: but it was always my impression that the information was scanty and vague. I wish you would let me know what you think of the subject, independently of Hayward or anyone else as possible author.

I hope you will not find this enquiry a nuisance: it is the result of your own suggestion.[1]

Yours sincerely,
[T. S. Eliot]

TO *Paul Elmer More* CC

21 October 1928 [London]

My dear More,

I was very happy to get your essay (your letter of the 18th), and have read it twice.[2] The only thing I am not sure about is the length (speaking as Editor); but if you will allow me, I shall have it set up in galley, then measure the length; and if it should prove to be much too long you can

---

1–Lucas replied (21 Oct.): 'My impression is that a very interesting essay might certainly be written on the subject, but that to commission a *book* on it would be rather a gamble, until one knew more of the sort of information available: and to know that it would be necessary to do some preliminary research, unless possibly someone like Greg could tell you offhand. It would no doubt be possible, if information ran short about the Raleigh affair, to fill up the book with a wider study of atheism at the time, in general. But that might of course prove, on the other hand, too formidable.'

2–More, 'An Absolute and An Authoritative Church', C. 8 (July 1929), 616–34 – an abbreviated version of a chapter written for *The Greek Tradition*. More claimed of the subject of the essay, in his covering letter (18 Oct.): 'The question itself seems to me of vital, perhaps the most vital, importance for religion today.'

then consider whether it is possible to abbreviate it – though I doubt the possibility. I think that I am (with of course far less knowledge of the subject) on nearly all points in close agreement; though I am perhaps less worried about magic. Of course there are innumerable political dangers as well, resulting from any acceptance of an absolute church in the modern world, but it is certainly better not to touch upon these. I doubt sometimes whether the idea of authority which is not absolute can ever be driven into the human skull – but for me that doubt is near to despair.

No, I did not write about Cleopatra: it may have been my friend Bonamy Dobrée, but I have not yet read the leader so cannot be sure.[1]

May I have your essay set up? I have to add, that I very much admire it.

Sincerely yours
[T. S. Eliot]

TO *G. K. Chesterton*

TS Dorothy Collins

21 October 1928   *The Monthly Criterion*

Dear Mr Chesterton,

Very many thanks for your kind and unexpected letter.[2] I did not want to bother you with a small matter, it is merely that I did not like to be judged by anyone of your importance at second hand – and as I said, my letter was a pretext. I know very well that the letters which I want to answer myself – that is, to type myself, as I never use a pen – are the ones which remain unanswered. But I hope that you are now quite restored to health.

What you say about my note in the *Forum* gives me great pleasure, especially as I am reprinting it in a small book next month (*Lancelot Andrewes*). It also disconcerts me, for this reason: I have wanted to start in the *Criterion* some discussion of the question of Humanism and Religion, to which I had hoped to induce you to contribute; and possibly you may feel that your article in the *Forum*, to which I look forward,

1 – More asked whether TSE had written 'Cleopatra and "That criticall warr"', *TLS*, 11 Oct. 1928, 717–18. It was in fact written by BD (as TSE suspected).
2 – Chesterton, who had been overworking, had been ordered by his doctor to take a month's holiday; his correspondence had been badly neglected and he apologised elaborately to TSE. 'I should like to add that I would certainly write for your paper if you still desire it.' He praised TSE's article on Babbitt in the *Forum* – 'which I have just had occasion to read: as they asked me to contribute to the discussion.'

covers all that you want to say. What I wished to do is not quite the same as the *Forum's* inquest: I want to generalise the question beyond the work of Babbitt, into the question of the possibility of any Humanism as a substitute for organised religion. There are other contemporary documents besides Babbitt's writings: the work of Benda, and Fernandez, and perhaps Scheler, and particularly a book on *American Criticism* by Norman Foerster, which states the general humanistic position, and which I can let you have. Perhaps you would be willing to adapt your *Forum* essay for this purpose? It would be for the March (Quarterly) number, so there would be considerable time.[1]

But I must add that our rates are necessarily very low: £2 per 1000 words; and I have never varied from the principle of paying all contributors at exactly the same rate.

With many thanks,
Yours sincerely,
T. S. Eliot[2]

TO *A. M. MacIver*[3]   CC

22 October 1928   [London]

Dear Mr MacIver,

I hope you will forgive my delay in answering your kind letter, which is chiefly due to something like influenza which attacked my wife and myself.[4] I remember what I said, but am afraid that I still have no right to accept even such a flattering invitation as that of the Jowett Society for any time so near as 'next term' which is now already the present term.

---

1 – Chesterton, 'Is Humanism a Religion?' C. 8 (Apr. 1929), 382–93.
2 – Chesterton responded on 22 Oct.: 'I certainly should be very pleased to write for you on the general subject you mention; as I only said a small part of what there is to say in my Forum article. Indeed I merely took a text or two from the other Forum articles; in this case, if you would kindly send me any book like "American Criticism", I have no doubt I can find some text in that. It does not matter anyway about the payment; and I think you are perfectly right to pay everybody equally.'
3 – Arthur Milne MacIver (1905–72) was reading Philosophy at New College, Oxford; he subsequently taught at Edinburgh, Leeds and Birmingham before joining the faculty at University College, Southampton, where he became Professor of Philosophy, 1960–70. He was President of the Mind Association, 1958; President of the Aristotelian Society, 1961–2.
4 – MacIver (President of the Jowett Society) wrote on 2 Oct. that since Father D'Arcy had recently addressed them on 'Modern Thomism', 'it might profit us to hear something of other sides of Neo-Scholasticism ... The Jowett is a philosophical society and consists entirely of undergraduates, with the exception of one or two Research students.'

I have many engagements to fulfil, so that I shall be unable to read or speak in public before the summer, except on one occasion in March.

I should be very happy to meet the Jowett Society when I can conscientiously do so, but incidentally I am afraid that Neo-Scholasticism is not quite my subject. It is a study which I have done what I can to encourage, but in which I am by no means an authority, and I certainly could provide no worthy parallel to Father D'Arcy. But perhaps a more modest subject could be agreed upon later?

I see that you asked me to reply before the 12th; and I hope you will accept my sincere apologies. I add that I am rather frightened of the Jowett Society.

Sincerely yours,
[T. S. Eliot]

TO *W. Swan Stallybrass*   CC

23 October 1928   [London]

Dear Mr Stallybrass,

You may remember that some time ago I made a contract with you to write a 'Dante' for the Republic of Letters. The circumstances were that we were having amicable negotiations to avoid the possibility of conflict between that series and a series which I was to edit for Faber & Gwyer; and in view of certain limitations which you and Dr Rose were prepared to make, I agreed to do a book for your series. Our series was subsequently abandoned, so that the Republic of Letters is quite free to deal with any of the authors who would otherwise have been excluded – but this has nothing to do with my undertaking with you. I happened to suggest that what I should like to do would be a book on Dante, although I doubted my competence; Dr Rose took up this suggestion, though I warned him that it would be such a difficult subject for me that I could hardly hope to do a book even within five years. The contract was consequently made without any time limit whatever.

I am now writing because Faber & Gwyer have asked me to write a pamphlet of about 10,000 to 12,000 words on Dante. If I did so, it would be during 1929. As it is still quite impossible for me to do a book on the subject, of the solidity required for the Republic series, for a number of years, I do not think that there would be any conflict; if it was successful it might even increase the demand for the larger work. Nevertheless, I felt that such a performance might be technically a breach of my contract with you; I am therefore writing to ask your opinion of the matter. If you consider that it would be to your disadvantage for me to write this essay, I will of course choose a different subject, if I write a pamphlet for Faber & Gwyer.

Sincerely yours,

[T. S. Eliot]

TO *Leonard Woolf*   TS Sussex

24 October 1928   57 Chester Terrace, s.w.1.

Dear Leonard,

This week has been rather unexpectedly filled up for me, so far as lunchtime goes, particularly by the appearance of Robert Frost.[1]

Would Thursday or Friday of next week be convenient for you to lunch with me?

I congratulate the Hogarth Press in having done Robinson Jeffers's book;[2] it is the best verse out of America for a long time. Flint has reviewed it very enthusiastically for the Dec. *Criterion*.

May I send the Hogarth two things which F. & G. have balked at? One is Tom MacGreevy's collected poems,[3] which I should earnestly recommend to the mercy of Lady Gerald; the other is some translations of

---

1–Robert Frost, who was visiting London, was invited by Harold Monro to read at the Poetry Bookshop. TSE would be there, HM assured him; but in the event TSE had to send his apologies. Monro took Frost out to dinner with TSE the next day. Lawrence Thompson relates: 'The two Americans entered into conversation easily by comparing notes on how their host had and had not assisted them more than a decade earlier . . . [But] there was something strained about the entire evening. What annoyed Frost most was the way in which this native of St. Louis affected an English accent. Long before the evening was over, Frost decided to go on disliking Eliot as a tricky poet – and as a mealy-mouthed snob' (*Robert Frost: The Years of Triumph 1915–1938* [1970], 337–8). (Thompson cites in evidence only a letter that Frost wrote to him on 24 Jan. 1943.) TSE never flagged in his respect: in June 1957 he would propose the toast to Frost at a Books Across The Sea Dinner hosted by the English-Speaking Union of the Commonwealth.

2–*Roan Stallion, Tamar, and Other Poems*.

3–On 3 Oct. 1928 TSE had reported to the F&G Book Committee on MacGreevy's proposed volume of poetry entitled 'Submarine and Aerial': 'Thomas McGreevy is a young Irishman who has a lectureship in Paris and who was introduced to me several years ago by W. B. Yeats. He has done some very good reviewing for *The Criterion*, and subsequently has reviewed also for *The Nation* and *The Times*. One poem in this small volume appeared in *The Criterion*, and there is another which I should have liked to use had it not appeared elsewhere. The stuff is very Irish, not very even, but I think some of it is good and promising. I should like, however, to have an intelligent opinion on the poems as a book. If they are no use to us, I shall urge the Hogarth Press to do the book in their new series.'

modern Japanese poetry, put on me by Glenn Hughes of the University of Washington: for the latter I take no responsibility at all.[1]

Yours ever

T. S. E.

Can you also tell me what one should say to Rubinstein, Nash & Co. who quote your name among others, in writing about the *Well of Loneliness*? I am quite willing to give my support, if the people are all right.[2]

TO *G. K. Chesterton* TS Dorothy Collins

24 October 1928 Faber & Gwyer Ltd

Dear Mr Chesterton,

Your kind letter gave me great pleasure. I made bold to send you Foerster's book at once: it is the last chapter that is relevant. I saw Babbitt when he was in London a few weeks ago, and I understand from him that he considered Foerster's formulation a fair statement of his own views also.

I will send you the proof of a preliminary note on this affair by Herbert Read which will appear in the December *Criterion*, which is now in the press. If it were possible for you to write something for the March number

---

1–LW replied (25 Oct.), 'I am glad you think well of Jeffers: he is I feel an interesting poet at the least. Lady Gerald has already talked to MacGreevey and I rather doubt it being much use trying her again. I will certainly consider the other book, though I do not feel that it sounds very likely.'

2–Rubinstein Nash & Co., Solicitors, had written to TSE on 23 Oct.: 'We are concerned for the Pegasus Press in connection with the seizure of copies of Miss Radclyffe Hall's novel *The Well of Loneliness.*

'In view of the probable course of events, we are anxious to be prepared with a body of responsible and authoritative opinion to rebut the opinions expressed in the matter by the Home Secretary and by Mr James Douglas in *The Sunday Express.*

'We might mention that we have already secured promises of support from a large number of distinguished ladies and gentlemen including Miss May Sinclair, Mr E. M. Forster, Miss Sheila Kaye-Smith, Miss Virginia Woolf, Miss Rose Macaulay, Mr Leonard Woolf, Dame Mary Scharlieb, Dr Stella Churchill, Mr Ashley Dukes and others.

'We venture to believe that you will be taking a sympathetic interest in the matter, and we shall be much obliged if you will inform us whether we may count upon your support on the lines indicated, should the occasion arise . . .

'*P.S.* In case you should not have read Miss Radclyffe Hall's book, we shall be happy to lend you a copy for that purpose.'

LW replied to the question in TSE's postscript: 'I think one ought to give evidence in the case [of *The Well of Loneliness*] if possible, though I dont like the people. But the book is perfectly decent and it is monstrous to suppress it.' He had published his judgement in 'The World of Books', *N&A*, 4 Aug. 1928, 593.

(the review is a quarterly) I should be very grateful indeed. I should like to get, in time, several views, English and foreign.

I will also send you the December *Criterion* itself as soon as it is ready.

With many thanks,
Sincerely yours,
T. S. Eliot

TO *William Rothenstein*[1]   TS Houghton

25 October 1928   57 Chester Terrace, Eaton Square

Dear Mr Rothenstein,

If you care to make a drawing of me, nothing would give me more pleasure.[2] I would suggest a day, but you do not say where. Do you prefer your own studio, or my office at Russell Square, or my house? I should be glad to know also how long a sitting you like; so that I can arrange both time and place to suit you, and without interruption. If you can give me this information, I will suggest a day or two in the near future, at your convenience.[3]

Yours sincerely
T. S. Eliot

3 o'cl. suits me as well as any other time –
– But if you chose my house, I should try to include my Cat in the picture.

---

1 – Sir William Rothenstein (1872–1945), artist and administrator: see Biographical Register.
2 – Rothenstein wrote (undated), 'I have long had the habit of making drawings of my contemporaries. It has been suggested that I shd make one of yrself. Indeed, nothing wd please me more.'
3 – Rothenstein replied (29 Oct.), 'Will you suggest an afternoon next week, at about 3 o'clock. I will keep it free. . . . . My studio is here [at the Royal College of Art].'

TO *Messrs George Routledge & Sons*   CC

25 October 1928   [London]

Dear Sirs,
Your ref. GRF: for attention of Mr [Cecil A.] Franklin.
    I thank you for your kind letter of the 24th instant.[1] It is understood that the pamphlet on Dante in question will be published during 1929, and that I am at liberty to use the material therein towards my volume on Dante for the Republic of Letters.

Sincerely yours,
[T. S. Eliot]

TO *Paul Elmer More*   CC

25 October 1928   [Faber & Gwyer Ltd]

Dear More,
    Very many thanks for the review of Scott, which I am delighted to have, and have sent off immediately to the printers.[2] You will get the proof, and probably the other proof,[3] in Cambridge.
    As for payment, I cannot avoid that.[4] No one ever gets more than the usual rates; but no one so far has succeeded in avoiding receiving payment at those rates.
    Apparently our printers still charge according to the final copy, not for everything sent to them. In this case, however, I am sanguine and believe that they will not be cheated.[5]

Yours very sincerely,
[T. S. Eliot]

---

1 – Replying for Stallybrass to TSE's letter (23 Oct.), Franklin made it known: 'We have no objection to your writing for Faber & Gwyer a pamphlet of 10,000 to 12,000 words on Dante, on condition that, when the bigger book is printed, you are at liberty to use the material in the pamphlet, or as much of it as you require for the bigger book.'
2 – Unsigned review of S. Herbert Scott, *The Eastern Churches and the Papacy*, C. 8 (Dec. 1928), 353–8.
3 – The 'other proof' refers to More's essay 'An Absolute and an Authoritative Church'.
4 – More had told TSE (24 Oct.) not to pay him for the review.
5 – More (22 Oct.) admired 'the generosity of your publisher or the cheapness of composition in England, which enables you to set in type an article the utilization of which is doubtful.'

TO *John Gould Fletcher*   MS Arkansas

26 October 1928   57 Chester Terrace, s.w.1.

My dear Fletcher

I was sorry you could not come on Thursday: it was rather pleasant, as it is when Flint comes, and as it often is not when he is absent. Frost I rather like.

I am sorry about Jeffers: you could have dealt with him wisely; but as this is his first appearance here, there is no harm in a Puff.[1] I admire him; but fear the development of an American Claudel.[2] Too many words.[3]

Would you care to tackle my edition of Ezra, soon to appear? Or Wingfield Stratton's huge *History of British Civilisation*? I want the Maritain–Gill essay.

My wife and I would be very happy to come to supper on Sunday week, as you suggest. Perhaps, before then, you will give us directions.[4]

I ought to have typed this: I become more and more illegible.[5]

Yours ever,
T. S. E.

TO *Paul Elmer More*   cc

28 October 1928   [London]

My dear More,

Please forgive my apparent negligence. *The Demon of the Absolute* arrived several days ago; I postponed writing to acknowledge it until I had

---

1 – Fletcher argued (n.d.): 'Benét's book – as an American phenomenon – is as interesting as Jeffers', and Flint will probably be carried away by one of his momentary enthusiasms into writing nonsense about Jeffers. I thought the two books formed an interesting and very instructive contrast, and as I have spent a good part of my life studying my country from the vantage-ground of Europe, I believe I could do a more balanced survey of both books than Flint.'
2 – Paul Claudel (1868–1955), poet and playwright, served in the French diplomatic corps, 1893–1936. A devout Catholic, he wrote several verse plays including *L'Otage* (1911), *L'Annonce faite à Marie* (1912), and *Le Soulier de Satin* (1925–8).
3 – TSE's phrase glances at the reproach by the Emperor Joseph II to Mozart, apropos *The Marriage of Figaro*: 'Too many notes.' In a later year, when E. J. H. Greene questioned TSE by letter about Claudel (21 Nov. 1947), TSE responded on 28 Nov. 1947: 'If there is any influence of Claudel it is unconscious and probably dates from 1910–11. I have read very little of his work since then and always with far less attention than it deserves.'
4 – Fletcher was living at Holme Lea, Crystal Palace Park Road, Sydenham.
5 – This sentence, and the sign-off, are typed.

read it through, and in haste forgot to mention the receipt in my last letter. I am very sorry that you and your daughter should have this unnecessary trouble; but if the other copy arrives, I can make good use of it.[1] So far I have only read the title essay and the second, which I had read before in the *Forum*. I think there is nothing in the first to which I can give anything but applause; and I had particular pleasure from the paper on Whitehead. Of the second, I can only say that you seem a little kinder to a few people like Cabell[2] than I should be: of Cabell I could only say that it seems to me one of the most uninteresting forms of humbug that any public has ever swallowed. But one of the worst results of censorship is to propagate a belief that every author 'censored' must be an artist.

Perhaps I shall have some more intelligent comments to make later. And thank you very much for the book: it has given me great satisfaction.

Sincerely yours,
[T. S. Eliot]

TO *Amabel Williams Ellis*[3]   CC

28 October 1928[4]   [London]

Dear Madam,

I have your letter of the 27th instant.[5] I have a meeting on that afternoon (Thursday November 1st) but if possible I shall be glad to come. All the more so because I am anxious to know, before giving support, what form the movement will take. I am as anxious as anyone that this affair should not be repeated, and that the censorship movement should be checked;

---

1 – Anxious that a copy of his book sent from Princeton had not reached TSE, More had asked his daughter to send another copy to him from Cambridge, England.
2 – James Branch Cabell (1879–1958), American writer; author of *Jurgen: A Comedy of Justice* (1910).
3 – Mary Annabel (Amabel) Williams-Ellis (1894–1984), author and journalist – daughter of Joe St Loe Strachey, owner and editor of the *Spectator* – had married the architect Sir Clough Williams-Ellis in 1915. See her memoirs, *All Stracheys are Cousins* (1983).
4 – Misdated 28 August 1928.
5 – Williams-Ellis invited TSE to a tea party at her husband's studio, 22b Ebury Street, on 1 Nov. to discuss the upcoming case of Radclyffe Hall's *The Well of Loneliness*; others who had agreed to be there included LW and VW, Vita Sackville-West, Bernard Shaw, Rose Macaulay, and the lawyer Rubinstein: it is not known whether TSE went along. See VW, *Diary* III, 204. In due course, when the chief magistrate, Sir Chartres Biron, ruled against the novel, an appeal was fixed for Friday, 14 Dec., at the London Sessions at Newington Butts. TSE agreed to make himself available for the defence, but in the event he was not called upon.

but if what is needed is enthusiasts for this book, I am not one of them. But I am prepared to do what I can for the general principle.

Yours very truly,

[T. S. Eliot]

TO *The Modern Library*

TS Butler

29 October 1928   [London]

Dear Sirs,

I thank you for your kind letter of August 31st.[1] I should have replied sooner, but that I was extremely busy; and I could not in any case have provided the introduction before the 1st of this month. I should have been glad to do so had you been able to give me a few months longer; but this autumn was exceptionally full of engagements for me.

Yours faithfully,

T. S. Eliot

I am afraid that complications of American copyrights with several publishers prevent any consideration of an edition of my poems in America for several years, but I thank you for the suggestion.

T. S. E.

TO *L. J. Potts*[2]

cc

29 October 1928   [London]

Dear Mr Potts,

Thank you very much for your kind letter of the 22nd.[3] Had I the leisure I should be delighted to accept your invitation, by which I feel highly

---

1 – Bennett A. Cerf, President of the Modern Library, New York, had written on 31 Aug. – having read TSE's review of *The Golden Ass*, in the *Dial* – to ask whether TSE would be interested in writing a short introduction, for a fee of $50, for a reprint of the *Golden Ass* to be published in the Modern Library series later in the year.

2 – L. J. Potts (1897–1960): Fellow of Queens' College, Cambridge. His pupils included the novelist T. H. White (author of the Arthurian sequence *The Once and Future King*), who called Potts 'the great literary influence in my life': see *Letters to a Friend: The Correspondence between T. H. White and L. J. Potts*, ed. François Gallix (1982). Potts was author of *Comedy* (1948); *Aristotle on the Art of Fiction* (a translation of Aristotle's *Poetics*, 1953); and a translation of Strindberg's *Tales* (1930).

3 – Potts had invited TSE to a College Feast on 3 Dec. He had earlier consulted TSE about the text of Donne (presumably 'A Nocturnal upon St Lucy's Day', l. 7), for on 6 Oct. he wrote: 'Thank you for troubling about my question. I didn't want the passage emending, but

flattered. But it is difficult for me to get out of London for the present, and I have in fact promised to make a particular visit in Cambridge on the first occasion when I can go. So I am afraid I must decline your invitation with very many regrets. I hope that we may meet again in London in any case.

Yours sincerely
[T. S. Eliot]

TO G. Wilson Knight[1]

CC

29 October 1928   [London]

Dear Sir,

I must apologise for the delay in answering your letter of September 4th; but a temporary illness held up my work. I have since re-read your essay[2] very carefully, and although it is an interesting study, I do not feel that *The Criterion* is quite the place for an essay of such restricted scope, which might well find a place in a technical journal. I should however be very glad if you would let me see anything of less restricted scope.

With apologies for the delay,
Yours faithfully,
[T. S. Eliot]

---

thought perhaps there might be some literary or scientific allusion of which I was ignorant. It still seems slightly strange that Donne should have written "feet" when he meant "foot" – but the difficulty is probably met by your belief that Donne's thought here, as elsewhere, outstripped his syntax.'

1–G. Wilson Knight (1897–1985) served in WW1 and took a degree in English at St Edmund Hall, Oxford, in 1923. In the 1920s he held a variety of teaching posts before being appointed Professor of English at Toronto University, where he worked until 1940; thereafter he taught at Leeds University, ultimately as Professor, until 1962. Publications include *The Wheel of Fire* (1930) – for which TSE wrote the introduction, having recommended the work to OUP – *The Imperial Theme* (1931), and *Principles of Shakespearian Production* (1936). TSE would later write of him, in a reference addressed to the Universities Bureau of the British Empire, 31 May 1937: 'I have known Mr Wilson Knight in connexion with his essays on Shakespeare's plays, which have attained a considerable reputation. My opinion of these essays is sufficiently indicated by my having committed myself in writing the introduction to the first of the volumes, which was published by the Oxford University Press (*The Wheel of Fire*). Although I think Mr Wilson Knight sometimes presses a point too far, I have a very high opinion of his Shakespeare scholarship.' On 29 Oct. 1956, TSE was to write to Helen Gardner, of Wilson Knight: 'I found his first book about Shakespeare's imagery very stimulating indeed – in fact, I wrote a preface to it, but by the time the third volume came out, I began to feel that it was enough to submit a few of Shakespeare's plays to such analysis, but I did not want to read any more.' Wilson Knight was to situate himself in relation to TSE in 'My Romantic Tendencies', *Studies in Romanticism* 9: 1 (Winter 1967), 556–7.

2–Wilson Knight had submitted in July 1928 an essay on Shakespeare's *Macbeth* and Kyd's *The Spanish Tragedy*; he asked after it on 4 Sept.

29 October 1928   [London]

Dear Jack,

Yes, I have more than anyone else to regret that I could not arrange to come to Ann Arbor this year.² But under present conditions, with the *Criterion* to run singlehanded, it would be impossible for me to spend so much time lecturing in one place in America; as to any visit I made, a month must be added for a visit to my family in Boston.

I am afraid that it will be a long time, owing to existing agreements with divers publishers, before I can arrange a collected edition of poems in America.³ A new edition of *The Sacred Wood* has been done by Methuen, but I don't know whether they have made any arrangements for America. I have lost interest in that book. A new prose book of mine is to be done by Doubleday Doran, I believe.

You kindly say that you are 'listing below' names of persons who might be interested in *The Criterion* – but they are *not* given! Perhaps you will supply the defect?

Smith has disappeared mysteriously. I supposed him to be at Princeton, and am giving him an introduction to P. E. More on that supposition, but Charles Smyth told me the other day that Smith is teaching at Repton!⁴

What about W. Pater? And tell Little⁵ that I *shall* be writing to him.

                           Yours sincerely,

                           [T. S. Eliot]

1–Peter Monro Jack (1896–1944), born in Scotland, graduated from Aberdeen University before becoming a doctoral research student at Trinity Hall, Cambridge, where E. M. W. Tillyard was to supervise his thesis on the 'Aesthetic teaching of Walter Pater' – and where TSE was retained as his adviser (see *L* 3). He edited *The Gownsman*, and in 1926–7 was 'Skipper' (Literary Editor) of *The Granta*. In the late 1920s he taught at Michigan University before moving in 1930 to New York, where he became a lecturer and freelance writer. He was a regular reviewer for the *New York Times Book Review*.

2–TSE, in a letter now lost, had told Jack that he would have liked the chance to visit Ann Arbor for a year, but that his personal circumstances made it an unlikely prospect.

3–'I am worried about the American editions of your books,' wrote Jack on 13 Oct., 'especially the collected poems . . . I have been driven to send to England for bundles of copies. I wish some arrangement might be made.'

4–'A letter from James Smith rather dismally asks for a welcome to America,' wrote Jack. 'I tried to get him here; still, Princeton is better, and we are nearer each other than before.' Smith had told TSE on 29 July: 'I am to spend next year as a Visiting Fellow at Princeton. I do not know whether you will approve of this: I remember some strong expressions which dropped from you on the subject of emigration.' Charles Smyth confirmed on 9 Nov.: 'By the way, you were right about James Smith. The Repton appointment fell through, & he has gone out to Princeton as a Jane Eliza Procter Fellow.'

5–Clarence C. Little (1881–1971), American scientist; Harvard contemporary of TSE: see note on p. 655.

TO *Maurice Haigh-Wood*[1]   CC

29 October 1928   [London]

Dear Maurice,

In reply to your letter of the 23rd instant, concerning allotment of Buenos Ayres Gt. Southern Rwy. Preference Shares to the Trustees of Charles H. Haigh-Wood, considering the fact that the Trustees have been allotted only four shares, I do not consider that it is worth while for the Estate to keep these shares, and I trust that the other Trustees will concur with me in deciding to sell these new shares. If you and your mother agree, please instruct the brokers to sell the shares; the proceeds to be credited to the Trustees account at the bank, for re-investment.

Sincerely yours,
[Tom]

TO *Herbert Read*   CC

29 October 1928   [*The Criterion*]

Dear Herbert,

Thanks for your letter of the 28th.[2] I am of opinion that as I have the Siemsen story, and the Powys story, I should write to the agents to say that I cannot use the Williamson unless they are willing to wait a sixmonth. Also, I should like to use the Dobrée yarn; I may get a second opinion; but I don't want to discourage her, and as you say, it could do no harm.

If you think well of Clark, go ahead and tell him to write it; we could certainly use it if not really too bad, and it won't conflict with anything else.[3]

---

1 – MHW was working at this time for the British Italian Banking Corporation, London.

2 – TSE had sent a number of items to HR for his opinion: they included a story by Valentine Dobrée, another by Henry Williamson. HR responded on 28 Oct.: 'I don't know what to say about Mrs Dobrée's short story. I would personally rather read it than Williamson's story, which seems good of its kind (village idiot school – but not quite so bizarre as Powys). I think she will probably feel rather crushed if you turn it down, but that is not a proper consideration. I don't think it would do any harm & I still think it has got decided merits. It is too laboured, but it is fairly vivid. On the balance I should say "yes", but you could probably easily convince me that "no" was the proper answer.

'Williamson is rather amusing, but has it any specific interest for the *Criterion*? Mrs D does at least attempt something more than amusement.'

3 – HR wrote of the budding art historian Kenneth Clark: 'I have met him once or twice . . . & I think he is going to be a useful man. His recent book on *The Gothic Revival* is distinctly good. His suggestion seems an interesting one, & if you approve I will ask him to go ahead.'

I sent you a copy of More's last book. If you feel inclined, use it, if not, don't; it is a spare copy, and was not sent primarily for review. Also a book on Havelock Ellis: merely on the assumption that he interests you.

yours ever
[T. S. E.]

TO *Conrad Aiken*   CC

29 October 1928   [London]

Dear Conrad,

Thanks for your letter of the 5th. I had been wondering for months what had become of you. In your last letter, which was written a very long time ago, you mentioned your affairs and spoke of a visit to Spain which would bring you eventually to London. I judge that you changed your mind and decided to endure Cambridge for a little longer. I hope that your notion of returning to London in mid-winter is less illusory than the last.

About your inclusions of the poems mentioned in your Modern Library Anthology.[1] That unfortunately is nothing to do with me. Knopf has, I am sorry to say, full anthology rights, and can do as he pleases. He also pockets the cash, and turns over something to me. So you need not worry about me at all.

The anthology rights for *The Waste Land* are in my own hands, as I was wiser by the time that I made a contract with Liveright, but it would infringe Liveright's rights if I let anybody print the whole of *The Waste Land* in an anthology, as he printed it as a book by itself. Furthermore the reason why I insisted on keeping the anthology rights was that I did not want anybody to read the poem in bits, and I shall always insist on its being published as a whole, if at all.

(In an earlier letter – 30 Aug. 1928 – HR had said he considered Clark 'rather promising. He is Berenson's secretary, & is doing a book on the Gothic Revival. We had better wait & see what it is like. But he is well read & speaks very intelligently: he was expected to take a First in History at Oxford, but didn't. He may be rather a duplicate of Roger Hinks, & no better. But he is worth watching.')

1–Aiken was preparing for the Modern Library an anthology of American verse, 1671–1927, and wanted to include 'Prufrock', 'Gerontion', 'Sweeney among the Nightingales', 'Whispers', and 'perhaps La Figlia'. 'Also, I unhappily suppose there wouldn't be a ghost of a chance of getting the Waste Land for this – even if it were very handsomely paid for?' He asked too: 'Do you think Faber & Gwyer might be interested in this here anthology? . . . I think it will be better than any previous collection of American verse.'

You might suggest to The Modern Library, if they have the British rights, that they should let Faber & Gwyer see a copy of the anthology. But if the rights are in your own hands, please send us a copy yourself. I cannot say that we are keen on anthologies, for which the market in England seems to be exhausted; but if yours is on a new plan we should at any rate like to have a chance of getting it.

Ever yours affectionately,

[Tom]

TO *Glenn Hughes*   TS Texas

30 October 1928   *The Monthly Criterion*

Dear Hughes,

Faber & Gwyer have decided against taking up the Japanese poetry. We do not publish a great deal of verse, and small books are not much in our line. So I have taken the liberty of sending them on to Leonard Woolf for the Hogarth Press. I have given him your address, and you may hear from him.

Let me know when you are in London again.

With many thanks,

Sincerely yours,

T. S. Eliot

TO *Leonard Woolf*   CC

30 October 1928   [London]

Dear Leonard,

Here are the two small books of Japanese verse. I am writing to Mr Glenn Hughes, whose address is Malthouse Cottage, Padworth, Nr. Reading, to say that I have taken the liberty of sending them on to you. I doubt however if either you or Lady Gerald will think it worth while.

I shall expect you here about one o'clock on Friday.

Yours ever,

[Tom]

to *I. A. Richards*   TS Magdalene

30 October 1928   Faber & Gwyer Ltd

My dear Richards,

I have just read in proof your review of Read (which I trust will reach you by this post).[1] I am sending him a copy. Some of your criticisms (I might say censures) strike me very forcibly; and in commenting for instance on Read's paraphrase of that passage on the English Church I think you score very heavily.[2] Anyway, it is what I want: it will be good for Read, as it is the only really serious criticism his book has had; and it will be good for the *Criterion*, which is popularly considered to be the organ of a 'clique'. So I am pleased editorially, and excited personally.

I am coming to see you as soon as I can: but I should like also to arrange a meeting between you and Read in London.

Many thanks. Yours ever,
T. S. E

to *Marguerite Caetani*   TS Caetani

30 October 1928   *The Criterion*

Dear Marguerite,

Thank you very much for your letter. It is very generous of you to take out some more subscriptions as you have already done so much for *The Criterion*, and I appreciate it very keenly. I am very glad to hear that there is some prospect of *Anabase* turning up. I hope that you will remind him that we also want back the form of agreement which was sent out to

---

1–Review of Herbert Read's *English Prose Style*, C. 8 (Dec. 1928), 315–24.
2–IAR notes that 'the use of metaphor to convey our feeling about what we are speaking of is . . . important. On page 29, Mr Read re-writes a flowery passage on the Oxford Movement and in doing so gives us one of the few examples of imperfect sensibility to language that this book – no slight test – contains. In his translation of this passage into direct language a very important part of its meaning is certainly lost – the whole expression of the author's feeling towards the Oxford Movement, the Anglican Church and the Church of Rome. *The Anglican sands* is certainly not equivalent to *the looser elements of the Anglican Church*. The first gives the feelings of a Romanist, the second those of an Anglican. Similarly *failed to uncover any rock-bottom underlying them* (the Anglican sands) is not equivalent to *failed to reach any fundamental body of opinion*. No more is *the Rock of Peter* equivalent to *The Church of Rome*. Mr Read was nodding when he made this paraphrase; the original presents one set of sympathies, the paraphrase another. I suspect in part a prejudice against elaborate metaphors in prose as the explanation, but also the influence of ideas about "meaning" which are altogether too simple' (318–19).

him. You will remember that he wanted one alteration in the agreement: the reversion of the copyright of the French text after printing a certain number of copies, and we agreed to this and asked to have the agreement back for alteration. I dare say he has lost it by now, but I should like to know, and if so we must prepare a new one. I suspected that Briand and Berthelot had put all the work on him in connection with this unfortunate document, and I am sorry for him.

It is pleasant to hear that you are likely to keep the Villa Romaine, as it is such a lovely place.

I am asking the Sales Manager to send you a catalogue, and to enter you as a subscriber for the edition of Sir Thomas Browne. The Webster is published by Chatto & Windus. I am asking Jones & Evans to send you a copy. It is a very fine edition indeed. I reviewed it in *The Times*.

I am sending Aldous Huxley an introduction to you, and hope that you will be able to see him and his wife before you leave Paris.

Yours ever affectionately,
Tom.

TO *Aldous Huxley*[1] CC

30 October 1928   [London]

Dear Aldous,

I am sorry to have to write care of the Athenaeum, but I have mislaid your address. I suppose I could get it from Mary, but it is quicker really to do it this way. I find that the Bassianos are in Versailles until the 15th of November. I have written to her and should be very glad if you would drop her a line as she would very much like to meet you and Maria. Her address is: Villa Romaine, Avenue Douglas Haig, Versailles.

I heard from Mary that you were likely to be in London for a few days very soon. I hope that is true.

Yours ever,
[T. S. E.]

---

1 – Aldous Huxley (1894–1963), novelist, poet, and essayist: see Biographical Register.

TO *Conrad Ormond* CC

30 October 1928   [London]

Dear Ormond,

Very many thanks for your cheque which is indeed welcome, and which I have endorsed to the firm. Perhaps I have not adequately expressed my appreciation of your generous support, and the appreciation of those most interested in the success of *The Criterion*.

I enjoyed our lunch the other day, and hope we may meet again soon.[1]

Sincerely yours,

[T. S. Eliot]

TO *A. S. Duncan-Jones* CC

31 October 1928   [London]

Dear Mr Duncan-Jones,

You will remember our meeting in the spring to discuss the possibility of an inexpensive theological library, chiefly of the English seventeenth century. You were then about to leave for a holiday abroad. I hope you have not forgotten that you promised to take the matter up with me again in the autumn. If you are now in London I should be very happy if we might discuss the matter.

Yours sincerely,

[T. S. Eliot]

1–Ormond (Doubleday Doran & Company, London) had entertained TSE to lunch at the Eiffel Tower Restaurant.

TO *Gerard Hopkins*[1]   CC

31 October 1928   [London]

Dear Mr Hopkins,

I hope that you will remember that we have seen each other from time to time at those dreary meetings of The Phoenix Society. I am glad to say that I am writing about something quite different.

A young man who I do not know personally, but with whom I have had a little correspondence, has submitted to us a book on Matthew Arnold. His name is J. B. Orrick; I think he has been an occasional contributor to *The New Adelphi*, and possibly other publications. I first saw a section of this book which he submitted for *The Criterion*, and it would have been sufficiently interesting for me to use but was much too long. He then sent the complete book. It seemed to me a scholarly and interesting work, but we did not feel that it was the type of book for publishers like ourselves. I told him that I would write to you and ask whether the manuscript might be considered by the Clarendon Press; if this is only a nuisance, please forgive me for troubling you.

Yours sincerely,
[T. S. Eliot]

TO *Norman Dakers*[2]   CC

31 October 1928   [London]

Dear Mr Dakers,

I am replying to your letter of the 17th, enclosing 'Billy Goldsworthy's Cow' by Henry Williamson. I have a great respect for Mr Williamson's work, and although I do not think this is one of his best, I should be glad to publish it. On the other hand it will be quite impossible for me to use it before next June, and as that is so far ahead, I think you might prefer to send it elsewhere meanwhile. So I hold it at your disposal.

---

1 – Gerard Hopkins (1892–1961): publisher, and translator from the French. A nephew of Gerard Manley Hopkins – whose poetry, letters and diaries he would put into print – he was educated at Balliol College, Oxford (where he was president of the OUDS), and went on to win the Military Cross during WW1. In 1919 he joined Oxford University Press, serving as publicity manager and later editorial adviser. He became well known for his prodigious feats of translation: his output included vols. 7–27 of Jules Romain's *Men of Good Will* (a work he had loved since his schooldays); biographies by André Maurois; and Proust's *Jean Santeuil*, as well as other biographies, memoirs, broadcasts and plays. He was made a Chevalier de la Légion d'Honneur, 1951.
2 – The Andrew H. Dakers Literary Agency.

I shall always be interested to see any other work by Mr Williamson.

Yours sincerely,

[T. S. Eliot]

TO *Mario Praz*   cc

31 October 1928   [London]

My dear Praz,

Thank you for your letter of the 26th.[1] No, I did not write the leader in *The Times* on Brémond's book,[2] but it seemed to me very interesting, so I am flattered that you should think I wrote it. However, I have the book, I mean the English edition, and will send it to you. If you would care to write about it in the March number I should be very happy. But I leave that to you.[3]

I find your dialogue extremely interesting.[4] I will write to you again when I have re-read it, but meanwhile should like to know when the English edition of your book is to appear, because I should like to ask you whether I might publish it in *The Criterion* say for March, if I find it possible.

Yours ever,

[T. S. Eliot]

1 – Praz had written: 'I have just seen in the T.L.S. the leader on Brémond's book on *Prayer and Poetry*. I suppose you have written it. In that case could you lend me both Brémond's book and its translation? . . . My pleasure in reading it has been a trifle spoilt by the fact that I had just finished writing a new chapter, on Mysticism, for the English edition of my book on Spain.' He asked too, 'Could you go through my Dialogue one of these days, and then send it back with your remarks? . . . what I want from you is an opinion on the contents.' Praz's book was published as *Unromantic Spain* (1929), with one section, 'Mysticism or Advocatus Diaboli', appearing in C. 8 (Apr. 1929), 460–79.

2 – 'Pure Poetry' – on *La Poésie Pure*, by Henri Brémond and Robert de Souza; *Prière et Poésie*; *Prayer and Poetry*, trans. Algar Thorold – TLS 1,395 (25 Oct. 1928), 765–6. The review was written by John Middleton Murry.

3 – Praz reviewed Henri Brémond, *Prayer and Poetry: A Contribution to Poetical Theory*, in C. 8 (July 1929), 740–5.

4 – 'La Censura. Dialogo tra Roma e Londra', *L'Italiano*, year 4 (1929), 5–6.

TO *Edmund Wilson*   cc

31 October 1928   [London]

Dear Mr Wilson,

A most unfortunate thing has happened. I have your letter about Léonie
Adams.[1] I suppose that it was posted by her in London, and no doubt
she merely put her address on the envelope, as there was no enclosure;
but unfortunately having left my affairs in some disorder for a few days,
the envelope had disappeared by the time that I took up your letter. I
should be very sorry for her to think that I have deliberately avoided, or
even neglected, making her acquaintance. It is possible that some friend of
mine in London may happen to know her whereabouts, and if so I shall
certainly try to meet her. With many regrets and apologies,

                              Yours very sincerely,
                              [T. S. Eliot]

TO *I. A. Richards*   cc

31 October 1928   [London]

My dear Richards,

I am now down to grappling as best I can in a letter with your chapter
VIII.[2] I think that so far as you go in this chapter I am in agreement. It is

---

1 – Wilson had written on 18 Sept. to invite TSE to 'look up' the poet Léonie Adams during
her visit to London: 'she is so shy that in the ordinary course of things she would never meet
anybody but herself . . . but I feel that she is a really distinguished person who deserves more
consideration than she is likely to get on her own initiative.'
2 – IAR explores in the chapter (VIII) that he gave TSE to read – it would become ch. VII,
'Doctrine in Poetry', of *Practical Criticism: A Study of Literary Judgment* (1929) – the
question of belief and disbelief (intellectual or emotional) in poetry, and the question of
sincerity. 'For it would seem evident that poetry which has been built upon firm and definite
beliefs about the world, *The Divine Comedy* . . . or Donne's *Divine Poems* . . . must appear
differently to readers who do and readers who do not hold similar beliefs. Yet in fact most
readers, and nearly all good readers, are very little disturbed by even a direct opposition
between their own beliefs, and the beliefs of the poet. Lucretius and Virgil, Euripides and
Aeschylus, we currently assume, are equally accessible, given the necessary scholarship, to a
Roman Catholic, to a Buddhist and to a confirmed sceptic . . . But the same problem arises
with nearly all poetry; with mythology very evidently; with such supernatural machinery as
appears in *The Rime of the Ancient Mariner* . . . but equally, though less obtrusively, with
every passage which seems to make a statement, or depend upon an assumption that a reader
may dissent from . . . But as the assumptions grow more plausible, and as the consequences
for our view of the world grow important, the matter seems less simple. Until, in the end,
with Donne's Sonnet ['At the round earth's imagined corners'] . . . it becomes very difficult
not to think that actual belief in the doctrine that appears in the poems is required for its full

certainly right to include Virgil (who to my mind belongs with Tennyson and Whitman and beats them both hollow at laureate verse). I am not sure that there is not a sharper division to be made between poetic fictions (*Ancient Mariner*) and poetic beliefs (Dante or Donne). One difficulty of course is that civilisation has proceeded more in some respects than others: i.e. that emotions which persist can only be represented or evoked by the pretence of beliefs which we no longer hold. The consequences might be alarming: that the earlier man was better shaped, so to speak, mentally, than we are, and that we have at present no 'beliefs' to correspond to some of our feelings. This leads to a quagmire from which it is more your business than mine to deliver us! Your problem is, I fancy, to find out whether we can exercise the complete scale of feeling (assuming that that is valuable, as I think we both do assume) on the present meagre instrument of belief. The range of human feeling has been restricted by the restriction of belief; feelings which find no outlet in belief are dangerous, instance the wild passions which distort the rationalism of a B. Russell. I experiment in believing; you will experiment in other ways.

To continue. What seems to me to follow inexorably from this chapter of yours is a division into two quite distinct (I think) questions: that of belief in the mind of the poet and belief in the mind of the reader. It is certain that if the poet has done his work properly belief is not required of the reader – though a certain knowledge and understanding may be required – as the curious answers to your quotation of Donne's sonnet testifies. An incidental query is how far this knowledge is required for enjoyment of the poem, and how far merely to neutralise or disinfect the ideas of the reader – as some of your pupils went astray, I believe, not so much by failing to understand Donne's theology as by interposing some confused modern theology of their own. But the question of how much 'belief' was necessary to Dante, or to Donne (the latter an extremely

---

and perfect imaginative realization.' However, since 'all [the] importance' of a poetic thought rests in its 'effect . . . upon our feelings and attitudes', IAR posits a difference between intellectual belief and emotional belief. And happily the 'desirability or undesirability of an emotional belief has nothing to do with its intellectual status', for 'the question of belief or disbelief, in the intellectual sense, never arises when we are reading well'. The quality 'we most insistently require in poetry', and that 'we most need as critics', is 'sincerity', he argues. Sincerity he defines as that which helps us towards 'self-completion'; which effects 'a tendency towards increased order'. Yet how do we establish 'standards for sincerity'? he queries. 'When our response to a poem after our best efforts remains uncertain, when we are unsure whether the feelings it excites come from a deep source in our experience . . . we may perhaps help ourselves by considering it in a frame of feelings whose sincerity is beyond our questioning . . . It might be said . . . that the value of poetry lies in the difficult exercise in sincerity it can impose upon its readers even more than upon the poet.'

difficult case of 'belief') seems to me quite separate from the question of the 'belief' or suspension of belief required of the reader.

It seems to me that the psychological basis of Gray's owl,[1] and of the last canto of the *Paradiso*, are different. Really, I should say that the type of *Annahme*[2] involved in moping owls etc. is conspicuously absent from Dante. Dante is apt at the explicatory simile (as distinct from the obfuscatory simile) but rather shy of the metaphorical.

There is a further question – which I hand over to you – that of the relation of the 'belief' of the poet to the 'belief' of the philosopher, theologian or scientist. How far can you say that Lucretius' 'motive' was to propagate Epicureanism, or Dante's Thomism? or that they merely made use of the philosophies which happened to excite feeling? or can you speak of a 'motive' at all?

Yours ever,
[T. S. E.]

TO *Ottoline Morrell*   MS Texas

1 November 1928   *The Criterion*

My dear Ottoline,

It would have been difficult for me this afternoon in any case, & I feel it will be better if V. sees you *first*. I hope you understand.[3]

Affectionately
T.

1 – Thomas Gray, *Elegy Written in A Country Church-Yard* (1751): 'The mopeing owl does to the moon complain / Of such, as wand'ring near her secret bow'r, / Molest her ancient solitary reign' (10–12) – verses on which IAR wittily remarked: 'Even so honest a man as Gray attributes very disreputable motives to his Owl' (*Practical Criticism*, 279).

2 – TSE had defined *Annahme*, in 1926, as 'something entertained but not precisely believed' (*VMP*, 88). He had assumed the term from Alexis Meinong's study in object-theory, *Über Annahmen* (1900, 1910), of which he had made use in his Harvard doctoral dissertation: 'The *Annahme*, as I understand it, is such a floating idea. If reality is all of a piece, as the epistemologist believes, then the imaginary must be cut off and floating "like Mahomed's coffin" between earth and sky' (*KEPB*, 126).

3 – 'Ottoline was hurt, however, and accused Tom of "Neglect"' (Carole Seymour-Jones, *Painted Shadow: A Life of Vivienne Eliot* [2001], 460).

TO *John Simon Guggenheim Memorial Foundation*

TS Guggenheim

2 November 1928   24 Russell Square w.c. 1.

My name is not F. S. Eliot but T. S. Eliot.[1] I know Mr Norman only by correspondence. A year or two ago, I imagine long before he thought of applying for a Fellowship, he sent me some poems. I did not consider them suitable for the *Criterion*, but was much interested: I thought I found in them intellect and poetic ability, and wrote to the author about them. Their chief defect was immaturity; but they were good enough to make me remember them and wish to keep in touch with the author. I believe that with maturity, experience and study, Mr Norman may take a high rank among poets of his generation. I may add that a great many young poets send me their verses, and that Mr Norman is one of a very small number, in either England or America, whose work I have thought good enough to follow up.

I have read Mr Norman's synopsis of his projected work.[2] If he is granted a fellowship, and spends at least a part of his year in London, I shall certainly look forward to meeting him, and discussing his work with him, and introducing him to other poets and critics from whose society he might profit.

Having made clear that my knowledge of Mr Charles Norman is derived entirely from correspondence and from reading some of his verse, I have nevertheless no hesitation in recommending him for a fellowship. I look forward to his future development, both as poet and as critic, with great interest; and from what I know of him, I believe that his appointment would be wholly in accordance with the intentions of this Foundation.

T. S. Eliot
Editor of *The Criterion*; Director of Faber & Gwyer Publishers

1 – On the 'Report Form' supplied to TSE his name had been given as 'F. S. Eliot'.
2 – Norman's synopsis does not survive; but he wrote in a letter (16 Oct. 1928) to Henry Allen Moe, Secretary of the Guggenheim Foundation, that he was 'revising my novel, and attempting what is at best a precarious living by freelance work for the magazines. I have now heard from the last of my three sponsors, Mr T. S. Eliot, and within a day I will send you the papers you requested, such as my essay on pure poetry, and my project for the Fellowship year, as well as the letters from Edwin Arlington Robinson, Prof. Hyder E. Rollins, and T. S. Eliot, a few of my best poems, and a list of my accomplishments.'

TO *William Rothenstein*

5 November 1928   57 Chester Terrace, s.w.1.

Dear Mr Rothenstein,

I am very sorry to disturb an appointment, & particularly with anyone so busy as yourself, when you have given me the honour of an appointment – but I find I simply can't manage tomorrow at all. I am very disappointed; & it may be merely an impertinence to say that I could arrange _any_ day _next_ week to suit you unless, as is likely, you may have changed your mind.

With many apologies – but yet hoping that I may sit to you.

Yours sincerely

T. S. Eliot

TO *T. H. White*[1]

cc

6 November 1928   [London]

Dear Mr White,

I must apologise for my delay in writing to you about the manuscript you sent me.[2] As so often happens, especially when one is busy, I deal most quickly with the manuscripts in which I am not interested, and often put aside and delay those about which I want to write at length. I have found your book very interesting, and am inclined to agree with you in your preferences. That is a greater compliment than if I said I liked them all.

One of the reasons why I had not felt pressed to write to you the detailed letter which I should like to have written was that I knew that it was impossible to use any of these in *The Criterion* before March, and as your book will appear in February I must wait until you can send me something new. May I say that I hope that you will soon have other things to send me, and that I shall look forward to the appearance of your book with much interest.

1 – T. H. White (1906–64) was reading English at Queens' College, Cambridge, where he had become a friend of Ian Parsons. His works include the bestselling Arthurian trilogy *The Once and Future King* (1958) – adapted as the popular musical *Camelot* (1959).
2 – White had submitted on 26 Sept. a copy of his volume *Loved Helen and Other Poems* (forthcoming from Chatto & Windus in Spring 1929), in the hope that TSE might like to use one or more of his poems in the *Criterion*. He said of his poems that he liked in particular 'Induction to Propter Hoc', 'The Diving Bell', 'The Deaf Mutes', and 'Interim'. He asked also if TSE might please give a further paper to the Erasmus Society.

It is kind of you to ask me to appear again before the Erasmus Society. I am afraid that it is quite impossible this term, and probably also during the next term, as I have already made several appointments in Cambridge which I shall have to postpone from this term to the next; but I feel very pleased and flattered to be asked to meet the society again, and I should very much like to do so.

And will you send me any verse that you have written too recently for inclusion in your volume. With apologies for the delay.

Yours sincerely,
[T. S. Eliot]

TO *Ian Parsons*   TS Reading

6 November 1928   *The Criterion*

Dear Mr Parsons,

I am sorry to have given you and White all this trouble. It would have been impossible for me to have used any of his verse before the book is published, but I am very glad that Chatto & Windus are going to publish it. I had put the manuscript aside because it interested me, and I was waiting for a period of leisure to consider it more thoroughly. I have now sent it back to him.

I have it in mind that I should like to see you, and hope to write or ring you up one day next week.

Yours sincerely,
T. S. Eliot

TO *H. E. Bates*   CC

7 November 1928   [London]

Dear Mr Bates,

In reply to your letter of the 31st October, which I have only received yesterday, I should certainly be interested in a story by you, even of the length you mention, although that is longer than most of the stories we publish.[1] The chief difficulty however about a story of that length if I want to publish it is that it may have to wait for a number in which there

---

1 – Bates was offering a story of 7,000–8,000 words. In answer to this letter, he said (9 Nov.) he would try elsewhere.

happens to be ample room. In any case you will understand that *The Criterion* since becoming a Quarterly publishes such a small proportion of fiction that we cannot repeat the same author more than once in a year. It is therefore unlikely that I should be able to use this story, however good, until next October or June at the earliest. I therefore feel that you ought to dispose of it elsewhere in the meantime, and am sure that you could do so. But if not, I need hardly say that I should be very happy to have you send me the manuscript.

Yours sincerely
[T. S. Eliot]

TO *Mario Praz*   CC

7 November 1928   [*The Criterion*]

My dear Praz,

Thank you for your letter of the 4th November. I suspect that the author of the article in which you were interested was Middleton Murry, but I am not sure.[1]

Yes, I should like to use your 'Mysticism' very much. But I am not sure yet whether I should be able to squeeze it into the March number, and in any case I do not want to delay your book. But if [you] would be so kind as to find out from your publisher exactly when he expects the book to appear, it would be useful to me, and then I would let you know as soon as possible whether I could get the essay in. I hope that I can. It would not matter to *The Criterion* if the book appeared very soon after the publication of our March number.[2] I am sorry that the Brémond book has been sent off, so that it went to the University instead of to your private address. I hope, however, that you have now received it.

Yours ever,
[T. S. Eliot]

---

1 – TSE was correct in thinking that the anonymous *TLS* review of Brémond was by JMM.
2 – 'Mysticism or Advocatus Diaboli', a conversation piece inspired by Jean Baruzi's *St Jean de la Croix et le Problème de l'Expérience Mystique* (Paris, 1924–6) – an extract from Praz's forthcoming book *Unromantic Spain* (Knopf) – C. 8 (Apr. 1929), 460–79.

TO *Harriet Shaw Weaver*[1]   CC

9 November 1928   Faber & Gwyer Ltd

Dear Miss Weaver,

I have your letter of the 8th instant, and am glad to hear your interesting news. I was just making up my short notices for page, and I enclose copy of the note on Miss Marsden's book which I am adding at the end, and which is all that I can say from the information you give.[2] If you could provide the price of the book, and the future address of the Egoist Press, it would be useful.

You do not say whether the revival of the Press will bring you to London. I hope so, as my wife and I would very much like to see you; it is a long time since we have met.

I should also like to know whether the Egoist Press has any further intentions of publication. I believe that there is still work for it to do, besides this book, and should like to help it in every way possible. And it occurs to me that it might like to recover the volumes which it entrusted to *The Criterion*, and subsequently by devolution to Faber & Gwyer. Of course I have not mentioned the matter yet to my directors, and shall not do so until I hear from you in more detail.

With all good wishes,
Yours sincerely,
[T. S. Eliot]

1–Harriet Shaw Weaver (1876–1961), editor and publisher: see Biographical Register.
2–TSE wrote in C. (Dec. 1928), of Dora Marsden's work: 'among the readers of *The Criterion*, we trust, are many of those who used to read *The Egoist*, and we are sure that they will be glad to hear of the revival of the Egoist Press, and the publication of a book by Miss Marsden, which will be followed by three other volumes' (367). He chose to omit the detail Weaver supplied: 'The title of this first volume is *The Definition of the Godhead: Based on a Trinitarian Conception of the Structure of the Universe*. Miss Marsden has three further volumes almost ready, the titles of which are: *The Mystery of Time*; *The Immemorial Cross*; *The Constitution of Mind and Knowledge*. All the volumes form a single work the underlying idea of which is that the mysterious-seeming dogmas which make up the dogma of Christian theology are, actually, the foundational positions of the science of the first principles of physics: a science which was elaborated by man at a time so remote as to be lost to history. The net result is to take the findings of the comparative study of religions and present these as Christian dogma interpreted as findings of the science of the first principles conceived organically. It amounts to an intellectual rehabilitation of Christian theology without the loss of one single dogma. It ought to mean a most profound theological, philosophical and scientific change.'

9 November 1928   [London]

My dear More,

You will forgive me, I hope, for my delay in replying to your interesting, and I feel, flattering letter.[1] I quite agree that there is a place for such a book; but I am equally certain that it is not within my capacities to write it. I am old enough to have a modest opinion of what I can do, and how long it will take me to do it. I have three prose books in mind that I want to write, and two more that I have promised to write; if I succeed in writing all these I shall have written enough prose; and I want to devote the remainder of my energies to experiments in verse. So what you suggest is too much for an autumnal talent like mine!

Have you yet seen Pickthorn or Spens?

I have sent you proof of the Scott review. I have just received proof of the Essay:[2] it is appallingly long for *The Criterion*; but I want a morning to go through it carefully and see whether I can make any suggestions for abbreviating, or dividing, for our use. It is so much in line with the views which I wish expressed in *The Criterion*, that I will go to almost any lengths to print it.

And we hope that you will be in London again, if only for a day.

Sincerely yours,

[T. S. Eliot]

---

1 – More urged TSE (30 Aug.) to write a religious – specifically Anglo-Catholic – novel: 'we have a considerable number of novels in English written from the Roman Catholic point of view, but since *John Inglesant* [by J. H. Shorthouse (1881)] almost nothing that is Anglo-Catholic. I do not of course mean fiction like Trollope's that deals with the Church and with priests as a formal part of society, but stories which turn upon the inner life frankly and upon theological questions . . . There is material from the Anglo-Catholic side, both historical and modern, for wise and deeply emotional writing – and the field is practically virgin. Now to the point, why are not you the man to do what I suggest? I really believe you could . . . [F]or a modern treatment of the theme there is needed an Englishman, or one who knows England. The questions at issue are scarcely felt in America, and there is something banal in the form religious disputes take over there . . . I do wish you would ponder what I have said. A really good novel such as I have in mind would be more efficacious than a cartload of homilies and treatises.'

2 – 'An Absolute and An Authoritative Church'.

Vivien Eliot TO *Mary Hutchinson*   MS Texas

Friday 9 November 1928   57 Chester Terrace, S.W.1.

My dear Mary,

   Do let us hear from you. No news! Are the Huxleys about? Tom
sends his love. He has taken up dancing again, & is quite enjoying it
(gramophone). We think another small gathering is *needed*. (Yes *please*)
Are you going to the party at Miss S¹ next week? I shan't, as I have no
dress – am ugly & have rough hands.

                                        Yr friend
                                        Vivienne H Eliot

TO *R. B. Braithwaite*   CC

9 November 1928   [London]

Dear Braithwaite,

   After our last communication I did not like to bother you, and during
the vacation I had no opportunity of getting news of you. It was not
so very long ago that I learned on enquiry that you had lost your wife.
Please accept my expression of deep sympathy, and do not consider it an
impertinence.

   I should like to have news of you. Also I wonder whether I can yet
tempt you to write for the *Criterion*. I have two books, for instance,
which I ordered with you in mind, and which I should be loth to send
elsewhere if you would take them: Jeans's astronomical work² which is
completely unintelligible to me, and Eddington's recent book,³ which
looks important, and comparatively popular.

                                        Sincerely yours,
                                        [T. S. Eliot]

1 – Probably a party at Ethel Sands's London apartment.
2 – *Astronomy and Cosmogony* (1928).
3 – *The Nature of the Physical World* (1928).

TO *Jean Paulhan*[1]   CC

10 November 1928   [London]

Cher monsieur et ami,

Merci de votre aimable lettre.[2] J'ai honte de ne pas pouvoir vous donner une chronique à temps, pour le numéro de décembre; mais j'espère pouvoir la préparer d'ici quelques jours, et vous écrirai en même temps plus à la longue.

Toujours votre dévoué,
[T. S. Eliot][3]

TO *William Rothenstein*   MS Houghton

11 November 1928   57 Chester Terrace, s.w.1.

Dear Mr Rothenstein

I ought not to have made the appointment with you for tomorrow morning, for I have realised that I already had business to fill both morning and afternoon. *Thursday*, the other morning we mentioned, is quite free, and of course I will come then; but if you would like another morning this week either Tuesday or Friday is possible. So if either suits you please let me know, and I will come on Thursday at 10.30 in any case.

With many apologies for wasting your time.

Sincerely yours
T. S. Eliot

---

1 – Jean Paulhan (1884–1968), editor of *Nouvelle Revue Française* (in succession to Jacques Rivière), 1925–40, 1946–68. He was active in the French Resistance during WW2. His works include *Entretiens sur des fait-divers* (1930); *Les Fleurs de Tarbes, ou, La Terreur dans les lettres* (1936); *On Poetry and Politics*, ed. Jennifer Bajorek *et al.* (2010). See Michael Syrotinski, *Defying Gravity: Jean Paulhan's Interventions in Twentieth-Century French Intellectual History* (1998); Martyn Cornick, *Intellectuals in History: The 'Nouvelle Revue Française' under Jean Paulhan, 1925–1940* (1995); Anna-Louis Milne, *The Extreme In-Between: Jean Paulhan's Place in the Twentieth Century* (2006); William Marx, 'Two Modernisms: T. S. Eliot and *La Nouvelle Revue Française*', in *The International Reception of T. S. Eliot*, ed. Elisabeth Däumer and Shyamal Bagchee (2007), 25–33.

2 – Paulhan had written on 2 Oct. 1928, eager for a chronicle from TSE.

3 – *Translation*: Dear Sir and Friend, Thank you for your kind letter. I am ashamed at being unable to provide you with a chronicle in time for the December issue; but I am hoping to be able to get it ready a few days hence, and at the same time will write to you at greater length.

Always your devoted, [T. S. Eliot]

TO *Glenn Hughes*

TS Texas

12 November 1928   *The Criterion*

Dear Hughes,

Thank you very much for sending me your book and the manuscript which I shall put forward immediately to be read, and will also look at myself as soon as I have time.[1] I shall be interested in your book on the theatre, though I doubt whether there is anything like the possibility of sale for such a work here as in America; for the public which is interested in the problems of the theatre is very small. I will let you know about these books as soon as I can.

> Yours sincerely,
> T. S. Eliot

TO *John Gould Fletcher*

CC

12 November 1928   [*The Criterion*]

Dear Fletcher,

I have read your essay on Gill[2] and like it very much, and it seems to me high time that such an article should be published, especially as Gill's theories do not seem yet to have had the notoriety they apparently deserve. There is no question about my wanting to publish this essay; I only wonder whether it will fit into the March number. There will be some theological matter in that number. I do not yet know how much, but the point is that I don't want any one number of *The Criterion* to be too much taken up with such subjects. I have a very long essay on the Roman Church at the present time by Paul Elmer More. It is much too long to publish, and I am writing to him to ask whether he can shorten it for our purposes. If it can neither be shortened nor divided, then I shall have to cast it out, and should probably use yours in March. If not, I should have to hold yours over till June. But if that is too long to wait, let me know

---

1–Glenn Hughes submitted on 10 Nov. (i) a MS of three modern Japanese plays in translation, with an introduction; (ii) a book by himself, *The Story of the Theatre*, which had been published in New York, and which he hoped F&G might bring out in the UK.
2–Eric Gill (1882–1940), artist, type designer, sculptor, draughtsman, wood-engraver, essayist, social critic; convert to Catholicism, 1913; member of the third order of St Dominic, the lay order of the Dominicans, 1919–24; neo-Thomist; socialist; practitioner of the ideal craft community; devotee of a 'holy tradition of workmanship'. His publications include *Art-Nonsense* (1929); *Art and a Changing Civilisation* (1934); *Work and Leisure* (1935); *The Necessity of Belief* (1936); and *Autobiography* (1940).

and you shall have it back; but I hope to be able to tell you in a few days whether I can get it into March or not.[1]

Yours ever,
[T. S. Eliot]

TO *Paul Elmer More*   CC

12 November 1928   [*The Criterion*]

My dear More,

I don't quite know what to do about your essay on the Absolute Church, and am sending it back to you with a proof copy to ask you to tackle it yourself. Of course, 9,000 words is much too long, and the essay is now much longer than I estimated it. Would it be possible for you, and if possible would you be willing, to cut it down for our purposes to about 6,000 words; or alternatively could you divide it at any point into two parts? I had rather do the latter than not use it, but if you dislike both alternatives I shall have no choice but to surrender it.

Yours sincerely,
[T. S. Eliot]

TO *Charles Smyth*   CC

12 November 1928   [London]

Dear Smyth,

Your letter of the 9th crossed mine.[2] I like your idea very much, and it seems to me that there is an opportunity for a very lively essay, and I agree

---

1–Fletcher (13 Nov.): 'I am afraid I could not agree to postponing my article till the June number, though I quite appreciate your desire to have the contents of each number as varied as possible. If More is able to cut his essay, I shall of course withdraw my article; if not, you may keep it for the March number.' His essay on Gill did not appear.

2–Smyth wrote: 'I have been trying to think of something that would be satisfactory to you for a full-dress article. Would you care to have one on Historical Biography, or How Not To Do It? There are one or two things that do need saying very badly at present, and that need saying to the general non-professional-historian public in all its varying degrees of exaltation, including (high up the scale, of course) the *Criterion* public; at least, I think so. These reviews of Guedalla's latest masterpiece, e.g. the one in last Sunday's Observer, are progressively reducing it to a condition of blood-expectorating incoherence. I want to make an entirely unpedantic attack on the Historiomastix cult – Guedalla, Maurois, Ludwig, and Americans like Rupert Hughes and Woodward. It could be made quite amusing. I don't know whether it is sufficiently your line, catholic as your principles of selection appear to

with you that it is very much needed. I am trying to get the Mary Ann
Disraeli book for you, and hope you will go ahead.

Yours very sincerely,
[T. S. Eliot]

P.S. I have just brought out a small book of essays but my Clark Lectures
will not be out until next year.

TO *William Rothenstein*   MS Houghton

14 November 1928   57 Chester *Terrace*, s.w.1.

My dear Rothenstein,

I have just had your note, which went to Chester *Street*. Certainly, I will
come as soon after 2.30 as possible.

It is very kind of you to ask me to supper on Friday. I wish I might come,
but am sorry that I am already engaged. I hope it may be another time.

Sincerely yours
T. S. Eliot

TO *Henri Massis*   cc

16 novembre 1928   [London]

Mon cher ami,

J'ai été convié à collaborer à une revue qui m'est inconnue, qui s'appelle
La Gazette des Nations.

Pourrez-vous m'en donner des renseignements?

Je vais vous envoyer sous peu un petit volume de mes articles que j'ai
recueillis.

———

be. But the present situation is really an impasse, so far as reviewing goes: the professional
historians in their own professional journals go on saying that these amateur historical
biographies by journalists are not worth reading, while the journalists in papers that
reach "the wider public" go on patting each other's backs and saying that the professional
historical biographies by "pedants" (people like KWMP and me, to look no further) are
unreadable. Neither is wholly true. If you approve, I should like to take Dizzy and Mrs D.
for my battleground: that offers the best chance to sock Guedalla & Maurois in the eye, as
I do happen to know the field tolerably well. It would be ideal if Benn would send James
Sykes' Mary Anne Disraeli . . . I have read the book cursorily, but closely enough to see that
it would furnish the ideal text. Sykes is a journalist who has made an honest & on the whole
extremely successful effort to be an historian, for which he deserves more praise than he has
yet received . . .

'Is it true that you are publishing your Clark Lectures?'

Et puis-je attendre un grand article de vous pour le *Criterion* trimestriel de 1929?

Mes meilleurs vœux pour vous at pour Madame Massis. Et j'espère que votre fille va bien et qu'elle est rentrée en Angleterre?

Toujours votre
[T. S. Eliot]

Donnez-moi, je vous en prie, de vos nouvelles.[1]

TO *H. V. Routh*[2]   CC

16 November 1928   [London]

Dear Mr Routh,

I should [be] very glad in principle, to accept your kind invitation to participate in a course of lectures at Bedford College, if convenient dates can be arranged, and for the emolument mentioned.[3] Wednesday afternoon is not very convenient for me, nor is always Thursday, but other days at 3 o'clock are quite convenient. I should like also, before accepting definitely, to have a more precise idea of what is wanted. I do not even know on what subject I can be supposed to be an authority. Who else is lecturing, and on what subjects?

Yours sincerely,
[T. S. Eliot]

---

1 – *Translation*: My dear friend, I have been invited to contribute to a review which is unknown to me, called *La Gazette des Nations*. Could you send me some information about it? I am going to send you shortly a small volume of essays of mine that I've gathered together. And can I expect a big article from you for the *Criterion* quarterly in 1929? My best wishes to you and to Mrs Massis. And I hope that your daughter is well and has returned to England?

Always your [T. S. Eliot].

Do please send me your news.

2 – H. V. Routh (1878–1951): University Reader in English, London University, 1919–37; first Byron Professor of English Literature and Institutions, University of Athens, 1937; founder and director of first Institute of English Studies in Greece, 1938–9. His works include *Money, Morals and Manners* (1935) and *Towards the Twentieth Century* (1937).

3 – Routh, who was at this time Acting Head of the Department of English Literature, Bedford College for Women, University of London, invited TSE on 7 Nov. to 'join in a course of lectures which is to be given . . . by specialists who are recognised as authorities on their subject . . . Wednesday at 3 p.m., as far as I know at present, is the most convenient for us.' (The college offered a cab fare of £8 for each lecture.)

TO *George Rostrevor Hamilton*

16 November 1928   [57 Chester Terrace, s.w.1.]

Dear Mr Hamilton,

I have your letter of yesterday. I should be quite ready to write a short preface to your book, especially if you think that it would help to stimulate interest in Aiken's work.[1] I have only one objection. If Aiken was a stranger to me, it would not arise. But he is a very old friend of mine, so I think he ought to be consulted first. I think the suggestion to him would come better from you than from me – even if you do not know him personally. Would you object to writing to him yourself, and enquiring his views? You could say perhaps that you feel sure that I should like to do it. If so, I will get my secretary to send you his address – I have not got it at home.

Yours sincerely
[T. S. Eliot]

TO *Lincoln Kirstein*

16 November 1928   *The Criterion*

Dear Mr Kirstein,

Thank you for your letter of the 25th October.[2] I should like very much to write for *The Hound and Horn*, and your terms seem to make it possible. I feel more than diffidence, however, in dealing with the subject you propose. Much as I admire James, and much as I have learned from him, I am not yet ready to write about him again; and as for the subject of expatriation, I think I may have something to say about that in twenty-five years time: I do not want to speak of it until I can do so from the retrospective tranquillity of old age. And in any case, having a busy life, I find I can only accomplish anything by fitting in the subjects I write

---

1–Hamilton asked TSE (15 Nov.) to write a preface to a booklet, *Conrad Aiken: A Poet of Genius*. 'The title of my booklet does not imply *wholesale* panegyric, but I do think he has genius . . . [T]he mainspring of the book is the desire to honour Aiken . . .' Aiken wrote to Robert Linscott on 7 Dec.: 'Here's a Bergsonian poet and critic hight George Rostrevor Hamilton who wants to do a book on Haiken, with a preface (mind you) by T. S. Eliot. Now by god this is too much' (*Selected Letters of Conrad Aiken*, 149).
2–Kirstein hoped to commission from TSE an essay of between 7,000 and 8,000 words, for a payment of $150; he suggested 'as a possible subject the expatriation of Henry James and its effect on his work – did this expatriation lead to success or failure, and were the implications of the success or failure ethical or artistic?'

about to some scheme of my own. At the moment, I am more interested in the New Humanism, and Babbitt and his disciples (vide a note of mine in the July *Forum*).[1] So I will write for you, but I want to give you the opportunity of suggesting any other subject that you like.

With all best wishes for *The Hound and Horn*,

Yours sincerely,

T. S. Eliot

TO *The Editor of* The Forum[2]

16 November 1928   24 Russell Square, London

Sir,

I have read with interest Mr Granville Hicks's article in your December number, and believe that I am in the main in agreement with him.[3] There are one or two excellent points made by him which I think would bear a little heavier stress.

In any discussion of the frankness and realism, as it is called on the one hand, or the 'filthiness', as it is called on the other, of contemporary

1 – Kirstein responded (6 Dec.): 'As Mr Babbitt is contributing a series of articles on humanism to ensuing numbers of The Hound & Horn, it would be extremely pertinent to have you write on "the New Humanism, and Babbitt and his disciples," as you suggest.'

2 – Published in *Forum* 81 (Feb. 1929), xlvi–xlvii, under the heading 'Contemporary Literature: Is modern realism frankness or filth?'

3 – Granville Hicks, in 'The Gutter – and Then What?' (*Forum* 80: 6 [Dec. 1928], 801–10), argued that the modern age was 'an age of indecency . . . an age of negation': 'it is hard to think of a time when authors have been so preoccupied with unpleasantness for its own sake'; and this produces the consequence that 'the distinguishing characteristic of modern literature . . . is its devotion to whatever is stark, brutal, disgusting . . . The demise of the theory of progress, the skepticism about democracy, the decadence of liberalism – all these are evidence of the extent to which the old articles of faith are being questioned . . .' What has occurred is that 'the rise of science has changed the views of most people and destroyed the religious faith of many, and that the new psychology, combined with the disillusioning events of the last decade or two, has modified our optimism regarding mankind.' The bored sophistication of a work such as Huxley's *Antic Hay* shows just such 'a reflection of what might be called the modern mind . . . Bereft of faith in God and faith in man, self-conscious and cynical with regard to his own pretensions, unable to justify the conviction that the work he is trying to do is somehow significant, the literary artist is in no mood to place high value on ideals and aspirations.' Notwithstanding, Hicks claimed, we still seek faith in life itself: a writer like Eugene O'Neill extends 'the courageous venturing of his own spirit' in order 'to say that life is good'. And albeit the traditional system expressed in the *Divine Comedy* has 'broken to bits', and is not to be revived, still we must needs look for a new tradition: 'that tradition must begin by reaffirming faith in life, by reaffirming it in such a way that the minds and imaginations of men can face without fear the worst negations of science and history.'

literature, I think that the whole point is lost if the discussion is restricted to the question of propriety and decency. So far as my own work goes, I happen not to have a taste for such methods as those of Mr Joyce or Mr Lawrence, but I consider that merely a question of method, so that it is hardly more than a trifling accident that Joyce and Lawrence are censored and I am not. A certain number of books (not by Joyce or Lawrence) are produced which I deplore; but it is in the greater good that they should be allowed to circulate and sink by their own weight. A recent case in London gives this observation its point. But where I cordially support Mr Hicks is in his alliance of the problem of decency in writing to a more general and more important problem. He remarks:

> The demise of the theory of progress, the skepticism about democracy, the decadence of liberalism – all these are evidence of the extent to which the old articles of faith are being questioned, even as were the articles they superseded. [803]

This is the real point. The people whose work Mr Hicks discusses are fighting – even when, like Mr Huxley, they are doing so unconsciously and in spite of themselves – the battle which Arnold, in *Culture and Anarchy*, tells us that Newman was fighting against nineteenth century liberalism. I shall not expect the Roman hierarchy of Massachusetts, which, like the rest of Ireland, north and south, seems to be thoroughly Puritanised, to be able to understand this statement. But to my mind the phenomena that Mr Hicks discusses are evidence of a transition, a revolt against the paganism of progress of the nineteenth century, toward a rediscovery of orthodox Christianity. Even 'Freudianism', crude and half-baked as it is, is a blundering step toward the Catholic conception of the human soul. The religious faith which Mr Hicks suggests has been destroyed by 'science' was a faith much better destroyed. Perhaps the most interesting example, from the point of view from which we are looking at the matter, is the spectacle of the grandson of Thomas Huxley discovering that human nature is fundamentally corrupt. This seems to me a very healthy sign. Mr Huxley is on the way toward orthodoxy.

Certainly, a healthy movement like this will carry along a great deal of rubbish with it, like the negligible work of Mr Cabell;[1] but oblivion will soon take care of that. And to paraphrase Mr Hicks's words, one who thinks is only now justified in any surrender to church or to state, as the

---

1 – Hicks remarks, 'The victory of *Jurgen* has so emboldened [James Branch] Cabell that we have the spectacle of our preeminent romanticist employing his allusive, archaic style to describe organs and functions of which most of the realists still fight shy' (801).

terminus of a voyage directed by 'the courageous venturing of one's own spirit'.

T. S. Eliot

TO *The Editor of* Time & Tide[1] CC

17 November 1928   [London]

Sir,

I have read with great interest Mr Bernard Shaw's article on the Irish Censorship in your issue of November 16th.[2] After this article and that of Mr W. B. Yeats in *The Spectator*, it seems that there is little more to be said.[3] Yet I am tempted to write, both because it is a rare pleasure for me to find myself in almost complete agreement with anyone so eminent as Mr Shaw, and because I feel that this is a subject upon which every man who writes or thinks (or both) ought to speak his mind.

It pleases me to find that opinions which I have expressed elsewhere coincide with those of Mr Shaw. It is important to recognise that this outburst of Puritanism in Southern Ireland will injure the Catholic Church in the opinion of Englishmen. It may not be important, but it is interesting

---

1–Published as 'Censorship', *Time and Tide*, 23 Nov. 1928, 1131, this letter was written at the request of the novelist Winifred Holtby, Director of the periodical.

2–'Bernard Shaw Fulminates against the Irish Censorship' (*Time and Tide*, 16 Nov. 1928, 1099–1100) scorned the Irish Censorship Bill for its 'specific and avowed objects': 'to prevent our learning the truth about the various methods of Birth Control (some of them in urgent need of criticism) now in irresistible use, and to hide from us the natural penalties of prostitution until we have irrevocably incurred them, often quite innocently at second hand'. The 'Irish moral panic' promoted by the Catholic Church will be ruinous to Eire, he argued: 'if, having broken England's grip of her, she slops back into the Atlantic as a little grass patch in which a few million moral cowards are not allowed to call their souls their own, by a handful of morbid Catholics, mad with heresy-phobia, unnaturally combining with a handful of Calvinists mad with sexphobia (both being in a small and intensely disliked minority of their own co-religionists) then the world will let "these Irish" go their own way into insignificance without the smallest concern.'

3–See TSE's 'Commentary', C. 8 (Dec. 1928), 185–7: 'In the *Spectator* of September 29th last, Mr W. B. Yeats published an admirable essay on the proposed Irish censorship. In his words, the "Free State" Government has drafted "a bill which it hates, which must be expounded and defended by Ministers full of contempt for their own words" . . . The question in Ireland is not whether the Church, or its lay zealots, is right, but whether the views of Churchmen can be imposed upon those who avow no allegiance to the Church . . . It is not in the interest of the Roman Church in England that its Irish Branch should abuse its power . . . The tyranny of religion is bad; if religion should prosper, it should not prosper by such means. But the tyranny of "morality", with some wholly vague religious backing, or wholly divorced from any exact religion, is still worse.'

to me personally, to find myself agreed with Mr Shaw, and Mr Yeats, against the powers of Ulster, and of Dublin, and against the author of a book entitled *The Prayer Book Crisis*.[1]

Yours, etc.,

[T. S. Eliot]

TO *Charles Davies*

17 November 1928 [London]

Dear Mr Davies,

Your letter gives me much pleasure. It is always a compliment to have any reader interested enough to write about any question.[2]

I seem to have expressed myself rather badly. I do not wish to distinguish quite so sharply between promise and performance. Any promise worth talking about in print is partly a performance – though of course a final 'performance', such as 'Samson Agonistes', need not 'promise' anything further. I certainly think, and thought that I had made clear, that Keats and Shelley would probably have become poets on a much larger scale than Crashaw. I don't wish to press the beam in favour of 'Romantics', or to put forward Crashaw as a 'classical' poet merely because I have more sympathy for the things in which he believed than for the various things in which Keats and Shelley believed. The difference between major and minor is not the same as that between classic and romantic. Wordsworth is uncontestably a much greater poet than Crashaw, though I prefer Crashaw. I referred expressly to 'The Triumph of Life' because it approaches Dante more nearly than any other English poem. I do not say

1–William Joynson-Hicks, Viscount Brentford, *The Prayer Book Crisis* (1928).
2–Charles Davies wrote (16 Nov.) from the University College of North Wales, Bangor, to question one point in FLA: 'In the essay on Crashaw you speak of him as a poet of full and mature performance and state that Shelley and Keats showed promise only. I do not infer from this that you mean that Shelley and Keats's promise was better than Crashaw's performance . . . Such inferences would weight the scale in favour of "the Romantics" in a most uncritical way . . . I conclude then that whereas you view the accomplishment of Keats and Shelley with a dubious look (there is a hint of something like disparagement) you at the same time envisage the possibilities of their fulfillment (had they lived to see it) with every expectation of its proving to be proportionately vast and moving. But if it were proportionate to the promise of the actual poems how could it be so great seeing that their actual performance is faulty? I am not concerned to defend Shelley and Keats. I am inclined to accept your view of them as it is implied in this essay, but I don't quite understand what your standard or term of reference is in this matter as it stands between the "perfection" of Crashaw and the promise of the Romantics.'

that the promise of Keats or Shelley would necessarily have been fulfilled. They might have proceeded to write only rubbish. Nevertheless the frame of 'Hyperion' or 'The Triumph of Life' is much bigger than any Crashaw could have filled.

One other point. The observation on which you compliment me, about Baudelaire, is original in English; but perhaps it would never have occurred to me unless I had read the admirable essay of my friend Du Bos.[1]

If you are in communication with Zimmern, you might remind him that I wrote to him in Paris some weeks ago, and have had no answer.[2]

With many thanks,
Yours very truly,
[T. S. Eliot]

TO *A. L. Rowse*   TS Exeter

17 November 1928   *The Criterion*

Dear Rowse,

Thank you for your card. That's satisfactory about Eden; but when I send you a book you must remember that I not only leave the length of the review to your judgment, but also whether it is worth reviewing *at all*.[3] About the other thing; make it as long as you can: for I told you that I wanted an article and not a review. So if you can write an article about Communism, you needn't bother about more than a reference to the books (with publisher & price). In the December *Criterion* you will see a very superficial article by me called 'The Literature of Fascism'; what I want is something of at least the same length by you to succeed (not eclipse) mine, on The Literature of Communism, though you need not call it that.[4]

About the Professorship of Poetry, may I say that Faber has already talked to me about it. I merely don't want you to waste time. The point is

---

1–Davies wrote, 'When you write of Baudelaire "to him the notion of Original Sin came spontaneously, and the need for prayer", it puts him in a new light and helps me to know him in terms of my experience as I have not done before, at least to the same extent.'

2–Alfred Zimmern had introduced Davies, while in Geneva, to *The Waste Land*.

3–ALR wrote: 'I have received [Frederic] Eden's *State of the Poor* [1928] and will write a short review of it the moment term ends.' But he had 'got hung up over' other books he had been minded to review, including '[F. C. J.] Hearnshaw's *Socialism*, which is however a silly book.' See his untitled review of *A Survey of Socialism, Analytical, Historical and Critical*, C. 9 (Oct. 1929), 150–5.

4–'The Literature of Communism: Its Origin and Theory', C. 8 (Apr. 1929), 422–36.

that it is an appointment only for a period, so would leave me at the end looking for another job; also that I should have to take an M.A., and I have no time for such kickshaws unless they were pressed into my hand; and I am too disreputable a figure anyhow; and in short I don't want my friends to take that trouble for nothing, as it would be.[1]

Yours ever,
T. S. Eliot

TO *Paul Elmer More*   CC

18 November 1928   [*The Criterion*]

My dear More,

Thank you for your letter of the 15th.[2] And for all the trouble you have taken for me; much more than the value to you of having the essay in an obscure periodical would justify. On thinking it over, I believe that for our readers the essay will be more effective in one number, even in its deplorably mutilated form, than in two. I want it to be read; and many people, when they see that a particularly serious article which demands some exertion is to be continued, pass on to something which is complete.

1–ALR responded ('Monday'): 'It's more about the Professorship I want to write, though not to bother. I kept Faber in touch with the proceedings, instead of worrying you. But the upshot of the affair is very hopeful: so please, for our sake, don't think fatalistically about it. There's a body of people here who would regard it as the greatest good fortune if we could get you here: and the prospect for next time is greatly advanced.

'You see it was a *statutory* qualification, which could not be changed in time, that the Professor should be an M.A. This not only ruled out you but several others, notably Oliver Elton and (I believe) Humbert Wolfe.

'But the effect so far has certainly been to extend the notion of your candidature; and there is every prospect for the next election (in five years) that the statute will be changed and the Chair thrown open without qualification.

'I did find out in the course of such efforts as I was able to make that there were one or two really weighty people who were inclined to back you for next time: notably our Warden and Professor Gordon. [G. S. Gordon (1881–1942) was Merton Professor of English Literature, Oxford University; later President of Magdalen College; Vice-Chancellor, 1938–42.] Also by that time, there'll have been a considerable propaganda among the younger dons. It really is nothing to do with disreputability that counts so much: as the average don's pure ignorance of contemporary literature.

'It's true, of course, that from your point of view your coming to the Professorship is not so important, as it is from ours that you should be elected. But though it's at most only a ten year job at an inadequate stipend, it might be the very best road for a full Professorship if you should want one.'

2–More had chosen to cut 'An Absolute and an Authoritative Church', not to divide it into two parts (option B) as TSE had otherwise proposed: see C. 8 (July 1929), 616–34.

Even the *Criterion* public is largely made up of wellmeaning intellectual weaklings!

So I return you your B, as you ask, with many thanks. Can we still hope to see you again in London (if not in Cambridge) before you leave?

Yours always sincerely,

[T. S. Eliot]

TO *Mario Praz*   cc

18 November 1928   [London]

My dear Praz,

Thank you for your letter of the 15th, with the review of Brémond, which I shall use in the March number.[1] I should question, myself, whether there is in any Christian (orthodox) mysticism any identification with the ONE comparable with that in oriental mysticism, and the passage which you quote from S. John of the Cross seems to me very remote from the Upanishads.[2] I speak subject to correction from your greater knowledge of Christian mysticism. But I think that my most positive view on mysticism would be, that no tenable defence of mysticism can be made which is not a defence of the human reason as well. There are so many mysticisms, one at least for every religion, that any 'mystical experience' is not in itself testimony of any religion.

I have just finished the December *Criterion*, and shall be starting the March this week, so I shall be able to tell you whether I can fit your essay in, within a few days.

I am not *sure* that Murry wrote that leader. But I still think it was his. You must remember that the Murry of the *Supplement* is not the same as the Murry of the *Adelphi* – I mean that he sometimes more than changes his style according to the periodical in which he is writing.

I hope to see you on your way to Italy.

Yours ever,

[T. S. Eliot]

1 – Praz's review of Henri Brémond's *Prayer and Poetry: A Contribution to Poetical Theory* ultimately appeared in C. 8 (July 1929), 740–5.
2 – Praz was to respond (19 Nov.): 'The passage about the identification of the mystic with the One occurs apropos of Plotinus: there is no mention of the Upanishads in Brémond.' The passage in question was cut from the printed text, at Praz's suggestion.

TO *John Rodker*   CC

19 November 1928   [*The Criterion*]

Dear Rodker,

I am glad to have a copy of Ezra Pound's new cantos for review (which
are indeed beautifully done) especially as I am having reviewed his selected
poems in the March number, and should like to have these reviewed
with them. I should be glad if you could let me have particulars of price,
number of copies available etc., or whether all sold out, for this purpose.[1]

> Sincerely yours,
> [T. S. Eliot]

TO *I. A. Richards*   MS Magdalene

[Postmark 20 November 1928]   57 Chester Terrace, s.w.1.

Let me know at once whether you can come to dinner here on Saturday
& whether Mrs Richards can come too.

Re 8th – not certain – wd be pleasant, but, had I not better come one
night when we shd have more opportunity to talk?

> Yrs ever,
> T. S. E.

Did you get a foolish letter from me about yr chapter?

TO *I. A. Richards*   MS Magdalene

20 November 1928   57 Chester Terrace, s.w.1.

Dear Richards,

It transpires that our recently reorganised cooking staff is not efficient,
and until it can be reorganised again we are debarred from asking people
to dinner. We are disappointed at being unable to offer the semblance of
hospitality; but would you be able to come in after dinner and have coffee
and port instead? If we can ask you to dine out with us I will send you a
wire, but my wife has not been very well lately and dining out is apt to
tire her.

1–John Gould Fletcher reviewed *A Draft of XVI Cantos for the Beginning of a Poem of
Some Length* (Paris: Three Mountains Press, 1925), and *A Draft of Cantos XVII to XXVII
of Ezra Pound* (John Rodker, 1928), in C. 8 (Apr. 1929), 514–24.

I hope to see you on Saturday, anyway.

Yours ever,
T. S. Eliot

TO *William Rothenstein*   TS Houghton

20 November 1928   57 Chester Terrace, S.W.I.

My dear Rothenstein,

I am very sorry about today and hope it did not inconvenience you, though I fear it must have done. The truth is that I find the afternoon rather difficult at present, and today proved impossible. Would it be possible for you to give me a morning instead at your convenience? I expect to be in London continuously, so it can be as far ahead as you like (Wednesday is never a very good day, and Thursday not always). Please forgive me.

Yours sincerely,
T. S. Eliot

TO *Mary Hutchinson*   TS Texas

20 November 1928   57 Chester Terrace, S.W.I.

My dear Mary,

I ought to have written to you two days ago to say that I had not asked Ethel Sands or anyone else for this Thursday because I remembered that we have agreed to have 2 bores on that day: only tonight the bores have telephoned to say they will come on Thursday week instead, but that is no help. But I dare say as you have a serious dinner party in the evening you will be glad; but I hope I did not prevent you from accepting some pleasant invitation. We shall be at home, I think; unfortunately the commissariat is rather demoralised at present. But please do ring up or see Vivien when you can. It is difficult for her to get about to see people, and she is a bit unsteady since that accident which I touched upon (and which you need not mention to her).[1] I wish we might meet more often.

Affectionately,
Tom

1–See letter from VHE to Mary Hutchinson, 22 Nov. 1928, below.

TO *Humbert Wolfe*   TS Berg

20 November 1928   *The Criterion*

My dear Humbert,

> Are you a –
> live and a –
> bout, and
> if
> so, why
> should we not
> have lunch
> , one day
> before too
> long?
> ?
> Yours e-
> ver
>
> ,
>   T. S. Eliot

TO *William Force Stead*   CC

22 November 1928   [London]

Dear Stead,

   Your invitation would be very tempting indeed if I were free; but I am afraid that for me to run down for a night needs rather longer notice, and so I must very reluctantly decline. I should very much have liked to hear Rawlinson and hope that you will remember me to him.[1]

   As for our never meeting. Why do you never come to London?

   By the way, I have written to Richmond to ask him to send me that review if he isn't using it.[2] I gather that he has been very busy for the last fortnight, but am hoping to see him next week, and will mention the matter again.

---

1 – WFS invited TSE (undated) to visit Worcester College to hear Rawlinson speak on the subject 'Preparation for Communion'.
2 – WFS told TSE on 24 Oct. that he had written for the *TLS* as long ago as Jan. a review of Flowers's *Psychology of Religion*, and that evidently BLR was not inclined to use it. Nor did it appear in *C*.

Please come to London if you can, and give me a day or two notice.

Ever yours,

[T. S. Eliot]

TO *John Hayward*

MS King's

22 November 1928   57 Chester Terrace, s.w.1.

My dear Hayward,

I have realised today with chagrin & discomfiture that we had already made a lunch engagement for Friday – in fact I only realised it when it came to postponing it because of another more urgent engagement at 2.30 in another part of town.

Could you manage *Wednesday* or next week instead? I am very sorry. If not Wednesday, *Thursday*?

I am starting to revamp my Donne lectures & shall want to show you some.

I hope *either* Wed. or Thurs. is possible. Please forgive me.

Yours ever

T. S. Eliot

TO *G. K. Chesterton*

TS Dorothy Collins

22 November 1928   *The Criterion*

Dear Mr Chesterton,

I don't want to be a nuisance, but you did hold out to me hope that you might write a paper on Humanism, perhaps rather fuller than your article in the *Forum*, which I have not seen, for *The Criterion*. I am just starting to make up the March number. Is there any hope that I might have such an essay from you in time for that number, that is by the end of the year? If that is not convenient. I would gladly wait to have it for the June number; but it would be a great help to me to know. And I should be immensely grateful if I could have it for March.[1]

---

1 – 'Is Humanism a Religion?' C. 8 (Apr. 1929), 382–93.

I enclose proof of a note by Mr Herbert Read which will appear in the December number.[1] Mr Read's views and mine are not necessarily identical.[2]

Yours sincerely,
T. S. Eliot

Vivien Eliot TO *Mary Hutchinson*   MS Texas

Thursday 22 November 1928   57 Chester Terrace, s.w.1.

My dear Mary

It was very nice of you to telephone to me this morning. *Of course* I should have rung you up before this, but I have really been very very unwell. I had a horrible affair at a hair-dresser's last Monday week, & I *very nearly died*. All last week I felt terribly ill, & I had to have 2 interviews with doctors. I have been afraid to go out, as I keep on having queer 'turns' & feeling faint.

However, I am really better today, although I wonder I am 'still alive'. It is delightful for you to be going to stay with Lytton Strachey, & I must say I envy you.

If no *more* disasters happen, I will ring you up, as I said, on Monday about 6.30.

I don't think I shall undertake much Christmas shopping.

Ever yours
V. H. Eliot

Enjoy yr weekend, & tell me *all about it.*

1–HR, 'Humanism and the Absolute', C. 8 (Dec. 1928), 270–6.
2–HR recalled, in 'T. S. E. – a Memoir' (1965), one morning when he was staying with the Eliots in Belgravia (presumably in 1927): 'I lay still and saw first a hand and then an arm reach round the door and lift from a hook the bowler hat that was hanging there. It was a little before seven o'clock and Mr. Eliot was on his way to an early communion service. It was the first intimation I had had of his conversion to the Christian faith' (14).

23 November 1928   *The Criterion*

Dear Mr Tate,

Thank you very much for your revised version of your essay on Emily Dickinson.[1] I am just completing the December number of *The Criterion*, and in a few days I shall be making up the body of the March number. I hope to be able to let you know very soon whether I can use this essay in the March number, or not. I expect to be able to do so, but I am not sure, and if I could not do so would very much want to have it for the June number, as it interests me extremely.

If you are to be in London between the 10th and 15th of December, will you not let me know, and give me a more direct address? I was very sorry not to see you again privately while you were in London before, and should like to have a talk with you.[2]

Yours sincerely,
T. S. Eliot

---

1 – Tate sent his revised version on 20 Nov. 'Emily Dickinson' did not appear in C. – it had appeared in *Outlook* 149 (15 Aug. 1928), 621–3, and was reprinted with revisions as 'New England Culture and Emily Dickinson', *Symposium* 3 (Apr. 1932). The revised version was included, as 'Emily Dickinson', in *Reactionary Essays on Poetry and Ideas* (1936), 3–25. He next contributed 'The Fallacy of Humanism', C. 8 (July 1929), 661–81.

2 – In Oct. 1928 FVM had taken Tate to a *Criterion* lunch with TSE and HR. Tate wrote: 'Herbert Read is the best mind in England ... Eliot, of course, was due to be the most interesting, but he is a Sphinx' (*Literary Correspondence of Donald Davidson and Allen Tate* [1974], 218; cited in James King, *The Last Modern: A Life of Herbert Read* [1990], 88). Years later, in 'Homage to T. S. Eliot' (1966), Tate put a rather more indulgent gloss on his memory of the occasion, recalling 'the perfect simplicity of manners that was Tom Eliot's. There were times when he was silent: I remember a luncheon at a London club, at which Bonamy Dobrée and Herbert Read were also present, when he was *withdrawn*; but he was not withdrawn from us; he was withdrawn into himself. This ... I take to be a form of civility' (*Sewanee Review*, Winter 1966; repr. in *T. S. Eliot: The Man and His Work*, ed. Dobrée [1966]; *Memories & Essays old and new 1926–1974* [1976], 88).

TO *Maria Cristina Chambers*[1]   CC

23 November 1928   [London]

Dear Miss Chambers,

I am writing to thank you for your kind letter of 30th October.[2] Your appreciation is not only very encouraging, but you have done exactly what we should wish all readers to do, in giving me addresses of persons who might be interested. We have written to both of the persons whose names and addresses you gave.

I shall look forward to seeing your new story, as I so much enjoyed 'John of God'.[3]

> With very many thanks,
> Yours sincerely,
> [T. S. Eliot]

TO *Messrs Alfred A. Knopf*   CC

23 November 1928   [London]

Dear Sirs,

I have to acknowledge your cheque with statement of sales of my poems from January to June 1928, the payment being thirty-eight dollars twenty cents. While thanking you for this cheque I beg to call your attention to the fact that my address is not, and never has been, 18 Crawford Street. It is only owing to the odd coincidence that someone named Elliott lives there, and that this person took the trouble to look me up, that your letter reached me. I should be obliged if in future you would address all correspondence to me as above, 24 Russell Square. As a matter of fact your previous remittances had been reaching me here.

> Yours faithfully,
> [T. S. Eliot]

1–Maria Cristina Mena (1893–1965), Mexican-born writer of short stories and children's books. Educated at an English boarding school (where she became fluent in Spanish, English, French and Italian), she was sent in 1907 to live in New York. In 1916 she married the playwright and journalist Henry Kellet Chambers. She contributed stories to *The Century Magazine* and *American Magazine*, but published nothing between 1916 and 1942. See *The Collected Stories of Maria Cristina Mena*, ed. Amy Doherty (1997).

2–Chambers said she had sent a new story to her agent, A. D. Peters: 'A story I really wrote for the *Criterion*.' She added names of possible subscribers. (She had earlier submitted a story called 'Marriage by a Miracle', which was rejected on 1 Jan. 1928.)

3–'John of God, the Water Carrier', *MC* 6 (Oct. 1927), 312–31.

TO *John L. Donaghy*[1]   CC

23 November 1928   [London]

Dear Mr Donaghy,

I am, as you request, returning your manuscript poems and the volume which you lent me, and have great pleasure in keeping the two other volumes which you say I may keep; though I regret the absence of your signature in them.[2] I will only say at the moment that your poems interest me very much. Curiously enough the one which you say needs revision entitled 'The Pit' interested me particularly. I should be very happy if you would let me see any poems which you might care to submit for publication in *The Criterion*.

I am very sorry that our meeting was so brief, and hope that you will warn me before you pass through London on your way to California.

Yours sincerely,
[T. S. Eliot]

TO *The Bureau of Authors*   CC

23 November 1928   [London]

Dear Sirs,

I have your letter of the 20th concerning an article by André Maurois entitled 'The Past and Future of Love'.[3] I have of course a great respect for Monsieur Maurois' work, but I must say that the title of this article does not suggest that it is particularly suitable for *The Criterion*. Nevertheless I should be very glad to examine it and give you my decision at the earliest possible moment. I must make clear however that I cannot use, except for very special reasons, any contribution by a French author which has already been published either in America, or in any European country.

Yours faithfully,
[T. S. Eliot]

1–John Lyle Donaghy (1902–49), Irish poet and teacher, was educated at Larne Grammar School, County Antrim, and Trinity College, Dublin. His works include *Into the Light, and Other Poems* (Dublin: The Cuala Press, 1934).

2–Donaghy asked TSE to return his *At Dawn over Aherlow* (Dublin, 1926), since the copy in question belonged to his sister; he wanted TSE to keep *Ad Perennis Vitae Fontem* (Dublin, 1928), and *Primordia Caeca* (Dublin, 1927). Of the work in the last-named volume, he said, '"Pit" . . . is the poem among them which most needs drastic revision.' TSE accepted 'The Pit' for C. 9 (Oct. 1929), 89–95.

3–'The Past and Future of Love' had already appeared in *Harpers Monthly*, June 1928.

TO *H. J. Laski*   CC

23 November 1928   [London]

My dear Laski,

I am writing to ask if you would be so good as to tell me what you think
about a book which I am given to understand you are acquainted with.
The enquiry is of course with a view to translation, and the question of
the possible public in England. It is a book on Machiavelli by someone
named Janni. I should be extremely grateful for your opinion about the
book, and especially for your opinion of the possible sale for such a book
in this country.[1]

When am I going to see you again? You might, for instance, have turned
up at lunch yesterday.[2]

> Yours ever sincerely,
> [T. S. Eliot]

TO *Seán Ó'Faoláin*   CC

23 November 1928   [London]

Dear Mr O'Faolain,

You wrote to me to ask me to destroy the enclosed story, which I cannot
consider doing, so I venture to return it to you. I agree with you that it
needs re-writing, but I hope that you will let me see this or some other
contribution before very long.[3]

1–Laski replied (25 Nov.): '[Ettore] Janni's *Machiavelli* is an admirable combination of
biography and historical critique – much the best book on its subject since [Pasquale] Villari
[*Machiavelli e i suoi tempi*, 1878] fifty years ago. The standpoint is that of the Acton–Burd
edition of the Prince [*Il Principe*, ed. L. Arthur Burd; introd. by Lord Acton (1891)]. I think
it would have a general interest, and it would be of real academic value.'
2–'I have a real consciousness of sin about Thursday. But this term I have lectures on that
day from 12–1 and a seminar at 2.30 – ruinous to decent adventures. Are you in town on
Sunday nights? Could you come to supper here on Dec 9th? It would be a delight to us.'
3–Ó'Faoláin wrote on 28 Oct.: 'I will save you the trouble of returning my story of the
Great Irish Famine – please destroy it . . . When rewritten somewhat it may suit a journal
with more space than the *Criterion* and perhaps a less serious reason for existence.'

I will send you a copy of the December *Criterion*, as in my commentary I am referring to your interesting article in *The Irish Statesman* on the Boston Censorship.[1]

Yours sincerely,

[T. S. Eliot]

TO *John Gould Fletcher*   CC

23 November 1928   [London]

Dear Fletcher,

I have just heard from Paul Elmer More, who has reduced his article in such a way as to make it possible for publication in one number of *The Criterion*. On looking over that article in relation to other articles already accepted for that number, I think it would be better, for the reasons which I gave you, not to include yours in the same number. At the same time I am very regretful to lose it, as it is just the thing which ought to appear in *The Criterion*, and as I feel that it is time that we devoted some attention to the theories of Eric Gill. However, I think you had better go ahead with it elsewhere, and if by any chance it could not be published anywhere else much before June, be quite certain that I should like to have it for that issue.

I have had an advance copy of Pound's poems sent to you, and I think I also wrote to ask whether, if you took this on, you would also consider dealing with the new lot of cantos which John Rodker has published, and which I would send you. I should be glad if you would let me know. I shall be writing to you before very long, as we still hope to get you and your wife to come to dinner.

Yours ever,

[T. S. Eliot]

1–Having read Ó'Faoláin's article 'Censorship in America' (*The Irish Statesman*, 6 Oct. 1928), TSE wrote in his 'Commentary' that he was saddened to learn that Boston, which was no longer the Puritan city it once was, had the most severe standards of censorship in the USA: it was a sorry irony that books would sometimes sell well in other parts of the country precisely because they had been censored in Boston. 'Censorship has made impossible a critical estimate of Joyce's *Ulysses* for at least a generation; by setting up a false relationship between art and morals it has obstructed the efforts of all those who recognize the true relationship between art and morals' (*C*. 8 [Dec. 1928], 187–8).

TO *John Gould Fletcher*

PC partly torn [? late November 1928]   57 Chester Terrace, S.W.1.

Dear Fletcher,

I quite understand how you feel. I certainly should *not* be offended by anything you said in criticism of my introduction, so long as I have the credit of sincerity.[1] I daresay I do not see E.[P.] impartially, as I [am tre]mendously in his debt. *There is no hurry* – keep the book for a time, while I think whether there is anyone to whom the job wd be more congenial.

Yr,
T. S. E.

TO *H. S. Bennett*[2]

CC

25 November 1928   [London]

My dear Sir,

Thank you for your letter of the 20th.[3] I shall be very much interested to know if I am wrong. J. G. Robertson was of course a scribal slip which

---

1 – Introduction to *Ezra Pound: Selected Poems*.
2 – H. S. Bennett (1889–1972): Fellow of Emmanuel College, Cambridge. His publications include *The Pastons and their England* (1922), *England from Chaucer to Caxton* (1928), and *English Books and Readers 1475–1557* (1952).
3 – Bennett wrote, 'I notice in your new edition of *The Sacred Wood* that you reprint your article on "The Blank Verse of Christopher Marlowe", & I therefore venture to write to you about it for two reasons. First because I am now editing *The Jew of Malta* for Methuen in an edition [*The Jew of Malta and The Massacre at Paris*, 1931] similar to the Arden Shakespeare, & secondly because I find many of my colleagues & pupils accept the interpretation you give of the play from 83ff (old edn). I am therefore most anxious to be sure that I am not mis-reading your meaning before I write my own Introductn.
'As I understand your view it is that from *Tamburlaine* onwards "there was the powerful presence of [Spenser] immediately precedent" (p. ??81) & again on p 82/3 "M gets into blank verse the melody of Spenser, etc." The examples you quote, including the passage discovered by "J. G. Robertson", are both from the *Faery Queene*. I find it difficult to be sure if this is what you have in mind because I think the second part of *Tamburlaine* cannot be later than 29 March 1588, whereas the F. Q. was not even entered ar Stationer's Hall till 1 Dec. 1589. Does not this make any argument from the F. Q. difficult, or am I wrong in thinking that it is mainly that poem you have in mind?
'My main concern, however, is with your view that *The Jew* has been misunderstood; & that, I take it, is bound up with your statement that the movement of the verse is "towards this intense & serious great poetry which . . . attains its effects by something not unlike caricature". To support this view you make use of *Dido*, & certainly give me the impression that you believe it to be a late play. No doubt you are aware of the many problems of that play, & that many writers think it to consist in its present state of work by Marlowe &

336   TSE at forty

I really ought to have corrected. The reference is to Robertson's small *Elizabethan Literature* p. 78.

Instantly after the issue of the first three cantos, Marlowe in the printed Tamburlaine chants over again etc.

I shall write to Robertson and ask him what he now thinks. I certainly thought that the first three cantos circulated before *Tamburlaine*. How would you yourself explain the coincidence?

As to *Dido*, I must look into that too! Some at least of the versification still strikes me as late Marlowe.

I do not think, however, that either of these points would induce me to revise my opinion of the *Jew*. I was careful not to call it 'Caricature' straight out, and I qualified my suggestion of farce: I mean that by using these terms cautiously one gets nearer to the play than by treating it merely as huffe-snuffe tragedy. My impression was only confirmed when I saw the Phoenix performance of the *Jew*. And I feel a quality in it which differentiates it in this way from the common run of Elizabethan blood and thunder.

I may be writing again to you about the two important points you raise. If you are right, it is a pity that I had not discovered them sooner.

Yours very truly,

[T. S. Eliot]

TO *John Simon Guggenheim Memorial Foundation*

TS Guggenheim

26 November 1928   Faber & Gwyer Ltd

Confidential Report on Candidate for Fellowship
Name of Candidate: Mr Sean O'Faolain

I had never heard of Mr O'Faolain until he sent me an essay on language which interested me and which I published in the *CRITERION* of last September.[1] This is itself a recommendation, as it is only rarely that such

---

Nashe. There is also the important consideration of its date: if we cannot agree it is the earliest play of M, as some scholars aver, can we fairly make use of it for the purposes of supporting a view which would seem to imply that *Dido* shows "progress" & represents the direction in which M's verse might have moved it? And this with no indication to the reader of the doubtful nature of the material?

'And if this position is untenable, as I frankly admit the dates make it seem to me, do you still feel safe in regarding *The Jew* as caricature? Is it really out of line with many other pieces of Elizabethan love of tempestuousness & lack of sensitiveness generally?'

1 – 'Style and the Limitations of Speech', C. 8 (Sept. 1928), 67–87.

an unsolicited contribution by a person unknown to me is acceptable. Since then I have had some correspondence with him, and have seen one or two things of his which interested me, particularly in *The Irish Statesman* and *The Hound and Horn*.[1]

From what I know of Mr O'Faolain, however, which is as I have stated above, I should consider him a highly suitable candidate. His programme of work is for what should be an interesting and valuable study, well up to the standards of the Foundation; and I believe that Mr O'Faolain is probably particularly well qualified to carry it out. I am sufficiently convinced of this to be ready to give him a personal letter of recommendation to Mr Yeats, whom he could see either in Dublin or in Rapallo. I hope that he may be granted a Fellowship, as I believe that the work he would produce in fulfillment would well justify it. I think he might do well to spend some time at the British Museum as well as in Dublin or Rapallo, and meet the specialists there, such as Mr Robin Flower.[2]

I am quite ready to stand as one of Mr O'Faolain's sponsors.[3]

TO *Marianne Moore*   TS Beinecke

7 November 1928[4]   *The Criterion*

Dear Miss Moore,

I have just heard from Ezra Pound enclosing a letter of the 24th October which you wrote to him. I do not want you to delay any part of the Schloezer essay on our account.[5] I was as a matter of fact on the point

1–Ó'Faoláin wrote to TSE on 14 Nov. 1928: 'I am aware that you know very little about me personally beyond reading my work as printed by you, and two stories submitted at intervals: you may have read my "Fugue" in the Hound and Horn . . . I certainly did not name you because I expected you to praise me, (though, to be honest, I scarcely thought you would dispraise me.) My proposed study is: (A) The examination for interpretation of the symbolism in the later Yeats – drawn, as you know, mostly from magic, Rosicrucianism, theosophy and what not of the same type. This examination must be undertaken some time: without it Yeats is almost as unintelligible at times as uninterpreted Blake. Of the value of such a study there can be little question. My plan is to follow John Livingstone Lowes' method – more humbly than he about poetry I hope – by steeping myself in what Yeats read, and in what Yeats wrote . . . . The (B) section of my project I scarcely expect you to be interested in – i.e. the finishing of a book of short stories.'
2–Robin Flower (1881–1946), English poet; scholar of Anglo-Saxon and Celtic literature; Deputy Keeper of Manuscripts at the British Museum from 1929.
3–Ó'Faoláin's application was not successful.
4–This letter was mistakenly printed in *L* 2, 269, under date of 7 Nov. 1923.
5–Boris de Schloezer (1881–1969): émigré Russian literary and music critic, translator and philosopher; author of studies of Scriabin, Stravinsky and Bach. EP's translation from the French of Schloezer's *Igor Stravinsky* was serialised in the *Dial*, starting in 85: 4 (Oct. 1928).

of writing to you to ask you to let me know immediately what point you would have reached in your issue of next March. I could not possibly use any of the book before that issue. But if there is part of it which you would ordinarily be publishing in that issue I wish you would let me know what part it is, as I should like to consider using it simultaneously. I will communicate with Pound on hearing from you.

Yours sincerely,
T. S. Eliot

TO *J. S. Barnes*[1]   CC

29 November 1928   [London]

Dear Barnes,

I am writing to you in a great rush. Mary[2] sent me your essay day before yesterday, and I have hardly had a quiet moment to sit down and read it. She said that I must let you know today. I like it very much on a very cursory reading. What I should like to do would be to have it in my hands for a couple of weeks and submit it to someone who knows much more about aesthetics, and about Maritain's theory of art, than I do. If you can let me see it at that much leisure I should like very much to consider it for the *Criterion*.[3] From my point of view, there is no great hurry, as I should not have room for it before June at the earliest; but as Mary put it to me, I feel obliged reluctantly to return the MS. at once herewith, and merely hope that you can let me have it back.

1–J. S. Barnes (1890–1955), son of Sir Hugh Barnes. Brought up in Florence by his grandparents, Sir John and Lady Strachey, he went on to Eton College and King's College, Cambridge. During WW1 he held commissions in the Guards and the Royal Flying Corps. Enamoured by the country of his childhood, he came in time to forge a friendship with Mussolini; and as a Roman Catholic he sought to credit the notion that Fascism and Catholicism were compatible. TSE was to write to HWE on 7 Jan. 1937: 'There is a man whom I have known for some years named Jim Barnes, otherwise Major James Strachey Barnes. I don't know him intimately. It is rather that he is the brother of a Mrs. [St John] Hutchinson who is an old friend of mine . . . Jim is rather a queer bird. He is a cousin of the Stracheys and I think his father is a head of the Anglo-Persian Oil Company or something of the sort. He is very correct, having been to Eton, Cambridge, in the Blues and ended the War in the Air Force. He is a violent Italophile, a pal of Mussolini, and wrote a couple of books about Fascism in its early stages. He is also some kind of honorary valet to the Pope, being a R. C. convert.'
2–Mary Hutchinson, Barnes's sister.
3–Barnes's essay on Maritain and aesthetic theory was not printed; his next contribution was 'Fascism', C. 8 (Apr. 1929), 445–59.

Incidentally, I send you herewith proof of a superficial article of my own.[1] Perhaps you will want to reply to it in the following (March) *Criterion*? In great haste – I should like to see if you are to be in London at any time.

Yours sincerely,

[T. S. Eliot]

TO *E. McKnight Kauffer*   MS Morgan

Tuesday [? late November 1928]   57 Chester Terrace, s.w.1.

Dear Kauffer

I am sorry to hear you are laid up, & disappointed not to see you today. Will you drop me a line as soon as you are about & we will arrange a lunch next week.

Thank you for your kind remarks about Andrewes. You seem to be the first person to look inside the book! Certainly I will send you a copy of the poems, but I have not done anything to improve them yet.

With best wishes to both,

Yours ever

T. S. Eliot

My wife has not been very well the last few days either.

---

1 – TSE, in 'The Literature of Fascism' (C. 8 [Dec. 1928], 280–90), argued that Barnes's study *The Universal Aspects of Fascism* was 'anxious to persuade us that the political philosophy of fascism is a modern development of the philosophy of the Catholic Church, and especially of Aquinas . . . I am in accord with the desirability of the "independent moral authority", but I cannot see why any fascist should necessarily recognize the need for it, unless a fascist also has to be a Christian, which is not demonstrated . . . In spite of Mr Barnes's able apology, I remain (as an outsider) unconvinced of the essential harmony between fascism and Roman Catholicism.'

Barnes replied to this letter from TSE on 30 Nov.: 'As for your article on fascism, I do not think it is at all superficial, because it raises questions of great interest . . . I . . . have been working in an Institute [Centre International d'Études sur le Fascisme, Lausanne] whose aim is to examine Fascism in an entirely objective & scientific spirit; and this, if it has not modified my belief in Fascism as a good thing with universal lessons for us all, has taught me to make many distinctions which before escaped me and to see things in a much better perspective. All the questions you raise need answers & explanations – and I think I can throw a lot of light on them. So I accept your offer with pleasure & gratitude.'

TO *William Rothenstein*   MS Houghton

2 December 1928   57 Chester Terrace, S.W.1.

My dear Rothenstein,

I have remembered a tentative agreement for lunch on Tuesday at 12.30 in the neighbourhood of Bloomsbury. If this holds good, it prevents my coming to you at 12 on that day. May I ring up on Tuesday if I find I can come, but don't bother to keep it open. I could *certainly* come on Thursday at that time, were you free.[1]

Yours sincerely
T. S. Eliot

TO *A. W. G. Randall*   CC

2 December 1928   [London]

My dear Randall,

I am delighted to hear from you, and to know that beyond the natural limitations after such a severe illness, your complete restoration to health is assured. It is very good of you to offer to take up the reviews again, and of course I shall be very happy when you can. We have had no German notes or reviews since your illness. The December number is complete. If you could let me have some notes for the March number, I should be very grateful; but at the same time I will arrange to be able to do without them for that number, so that you need not feel pressed. For that number they ought to be in by the end of January. Don't bother to write meanwhile; but if your notes turn up they will be very welcome, also as a sign that you are much improved in health.[2]

Ever yours,
[T. S. Eliot]

1–Rothenstein wrote on 14 Dec.: 'My dear Eliot – thanks indeed for the beautiful poem [*A Song for Simeon*]: the dark night of the soul. Which is the significant moment of a man's life, his moment of hope, or of ecstasy or sorrow, his youth, his manhood or the autumn of his age? To an artist it doesn't finally matter – through his work he will be all these moments, though they will be linked together & form a pattern, & he will be called hopeful or hopeless. I liked the gravity of the writing: you must forgive me for having read so little of yr. work.'
2–Randall replied (27 Dec.) that he would be able to submit his review of German periodicals by the end of Jan. 1929.

3 December 1928   [London]

Dear Rabbitt,

I am Happy to say as I have received yours of the 29th ultimo and ave Pleasure. to Reply[1] Now what about This monnograph by W. B. Yeats is there anny posibilty that it might be posble for Faber & Gwyer to publish It. I shd like to Hear from you on This point Well now about the Prose book the points is two If the Poems goes Off well. Has there seems some reason to Believe then I shd Propose next. a Selected Prose book But Has you say I am ignorant I shd suggest You select first and then I select and then you select If you See my meaning But as for Daniel Book that will Depend not on Selected poems but Of course on success of Cavalcanti I understand Has you say that daylight as finally been Seen between DelaMare & you, so Hopes matters will go forward. About my writing introductions the only introductions I have written voluntarily as been. for you & jno. Dryden. I also wrote a preface at request of Faber 7gwyer for a book about american Civilisattion[2] also was paid 15 1bs. for Wilke Collins If I did preface for yr prose shd not want roylties. damn it everybody is sposed to ave some spare time You see. how it is we shall know by jan. or feb. how the Selected poems is & then I will proppose Selected Prose uniform 7/6. thanks for kindness to tom Mcgreevey.

Am annimatverting in dec. number on Irish censorship[3] if. that is what you Mean I dont know about ungarrians but welcome information am trying to attack censorship in all forms[4] fix up Guido as soon as possible and I shall approach selected prose next so now no more I will close

always yours very truly
[T.]

1–EP: 'You will be glad to hear that Mr Yeats, unable to do the comment on Guido, now announces a small brochure on your old frien Ezzry!!!

'//// So you wont be alone. ////

'What I am getting at is this. I hear circumventiously that you write introds. fer A., B., C, etc. . . .

'Was your rash outbreak about wanting to edit my prose, polite hot air, or wd you prefer it to doing Wilkie Collins etc.

'On a basis of 25% of royalties up to 5000 copies. I.E. 25% of whatever royalties were accorded the edited author??'

2–Preface to Edgar Ansel Mowrer, *This American World* (1928), ix–xv.

3–'Commentary', C. (Dec. 1928), 185–7

4–EP (29 Nov.): 'As editor, I suggest that you cast a few words of Ridicule, on the Oirish and Hungarians for copying our god damnd idiotic article 211 . . . I shd think the Crit. was sufficiently well entrenched to stroike a blowgh for freedom and lightenment nown again . . . This is NOT politics, but the affair of ever writer and ever intellexshul.'

3 December 1928   [London]

My dear Robertson,

I am enclosing a copy of a letter which I have recently received from a Don at Cambridge.[2] It may interest you, as my instances were taken from you, and my affirmation that Marlowe was influenced by Spenser was supported from p. 78 of your Home U. Lib. *Elizabethan Literature*. I should very much like to know what you think about this. I have written to the man to ask him how he explains the parallel if he denies that Marlowe knew the 3 books of the *F.Q.*; he surely must either reverse the derivation or else point to a close common source. I am not myself greatly impressed by Stationers' Hall at that time, but I am no scholar, and I should very much like to have your opinion.

About *Dido*, he may have caught me out; but if there are not verses in that play which are late Marlowe then I should like to know what they are.

Of course neither point in the least affects my main contention, as he somewhat pedantically seems to think they should. And I am not impressed by the intelligence of a man who after actually quoting my carefully worded phrase 'something *not unlike* caricature' then proceeds in the next breath to assume that I said it *is* caricature, a totally different statement, and one which I should not have dreamt of making.

May I use this occasion as a pretext for getting into touch with you again after a long silence? And I will remind you that the *Criterion*, after tempests and vicissitudes, is now on an even keel for several years to come; that it is no longer under the Harmsworth regime but under the protection of a group of people who do not wish to control it in any way; and that it would welcome something by yourself as of yore. And I should like at your convenience to have another chop and whisky with you at Gatti's or elsewhere.

                    Sincerely yours,
                    [T. S. Eliot]

1–J. M. Robertson (1856–1933), author, journalist, politician: see Biographical Register.
2–H. S. Bennett's letter of 20 Nov.

4 December 1928

My dear Eliot

The Marlowe problems raised by your correspondent are rather elusive. In *The Sacred Wood* you explained that you used 'farce' in a special sense, far removed from the modern one, and the argument about 'caricature' should take note of it. As to Spenser's influence on Marlowe, again, B[ennett] is not heedful of the possibilities.

Note that whereas Spenser is echoed in the printed 2 *Tamburlaine*, there is internal reason to surmise that the lines were added *for* the printed version, and were not in the first stage copy. On that view, M. may have had S's printed text before him; though it is pretty certain that even long poems were often current in MS. before printing, in those days.

But the date of 1590 still leaves two-and-a-half years for Marlowe to be influenced by Spenser. Now, I have never been able to believe that *Dido* was Marlowe's first play. The chief reason for that view is the very small percentage of double-endings. I admit that that fact takes some explaining on any other view. But it is a kind of fact usually ignored by the academics who in this case lean to the early date. And they are not good guides, inasmuch as they almost unanimously put the translations of D. I of Lucan as a work of M's university days.

That it *cannot* be, inasmuch as it has the very *highest* percentage of double-endings in all Marlowe – barring *Richard III*.

Now, my notion as to *Dido* is that here, in a *classic* tragedy, M. would intelligibly eschew double-endings, even if we did not know from *Nashe's* practice that *he* disliked the d. e. form. I used to wonder whether Nashe deliberately cancelled double-endings in *Dido* when he edited it. (There are a few left.)

But here are the broad facts. Marlowe only gradually took to double-endings. He gets to his highest only in *Richard III* (which I say he wrote) and in the Lucan translation. Some of the scenes in which he gets pretty high in *Ed II* are pretty clearly late insertions; & those in *Titus* belong to 1593. Then, supposing *Dido* to have been written in or soon after 1590, there is plenty of room for Spenser's influence there – *if you can trace it*. And I agree with you that the diction in *Dido* is certainly not that of the beginner. That is why I can't count it his first play.

It is not easy to settle such a point by internal evidence, but you may note in *Dido* various tags which seem to belong later than 1586 –

e.g. 'brazen doors' (I, i) (a Kyd–Peele–Greene phrase)

'buckled with' – also Greene

'map of weather-beaten woe' – the 'map' figure is in Greene & Lodge

'lawnds' is in *Orlando Furioso*;

'fatal instrument' recalls Peele;

and I used to think it was Spenser who set the fashion of 'gloomy' – found also in Greene.

Of course when we come to special Marlowe phrases – as 'And he'll make me immortal with a kiss' (iv) and 'Nor sent a thousand ships unto the walls' (v), we can't argue confidently that these *preceded* the phrases in *Faustus* or that they are later echoes. But inasmuch as they are *weaker applications* I have always counted them *later*.

Mind you, I don't feel that M's visible *joy* in S's music when he first heard it means that he would go on modifying his verse in response. How far could he? Drama is one thing and stanza-music another. Remember that Jonson *disliked* Spenser; & Shakespeare doesn't seem to have taken to him. His outstanding adorers are Greene and Peele.

If Marlowe were *enduringly* fascinated, ought you not to find Spenser in *Hero and Leander*? Well, do you? You will find 'thirling car' (which I think is from Spenser) in Sestiad I (near 'gloomy'), but the verse is hardly Spenserian, is it? and I don't seem to recall Spenserian phrasing [*sentence terminates here*].

I'll leave it at that: you can work out your own salvation.

I am very glad to learn that the *Criterion* is now on velvet for a term of years; and much obliged to you for the invitation to chip in again, and to have a hob-nob with you again. Both I hope to do soon. But for two years I have been chained to a big task – a 'History of Free Thought in the Nineteenth Century', which may sound ill to you in your present incarnation! It is to come out in fortnightly parts, beginning in January. If you think you could give it a word of notice, it shall be sent.

Anyway, I am just putting finishing touches to the later chapters, and shall be absorbed with proofs & index yet awhile.

Then I shall return to the haunted house of literary analysis, belike! Herbert Read has been provoking me lately; and the other man, Rylands,[1] seems to have no ears for non-Shakespeare matter in the Folio.

Yours sincerely

J. M. Robertson

---

1 – George Rylands (1902–99), Fellow of King's College, Cambridge, since 1927.

5 December 1928   [London]

My dear Grierson,

I wonder if I may bother you with a question on a small point of Elizabethan scholarship? I have had a letter from Bennett of Cambridge who is editing *The Jew of Malta* in a school series. He questions two assumptions that I make in my short essay on Marlowe's versification in *The Sacred Wood*. First he does not believe that Marlowe's *Tamburlaine* would have been influenced by Spenser – on the grounds that *Tamburlaine* was entered at Stationers Hall earlier than *The Faery Queen*. I feel however that the parallel which I quoted, following J. M. Robertson, is so close as to need some explanation. I am not myself greatly impressed by the Stationers Hall dates of that period, though I confess that they do create a presumption, and that any argument which ignores them ought to have more support than mine. But it seems to me more than likely that the first few books of *The Faery Queen* may have been in private circulation for some time previous, especially among Walter Raleigh's group, which Marlowe frequented.

The other point is rather more serious. It is that I have treated *Dido* as a late play, whereas the bulk of opinion is against me. I do agree that I overemphasised the lateness of *Dido*, but I cannot believe that it is anything like an early play in its present form. Some of the verses which I should myself attribute to Marlowe rather than to Nash seem to me manifestly mature Marlowe. But I should very much like to know your views on these two points. If you are very busy at the moment however, pray ignore this letter.

Is there any possibility of ever seeing you in London again?

Yours sincerely,

[T. S. Eliot]

FROM *H. J. C. Grierson*   TS Faber

6 December 1928

Dear Eliot,

I hope you will excuse my typing if it is not perfect. My secretary only types for me at College. But no one can read my handwriting. I am much interested in the questions you raise which have made me look up several things. I do not carry dates about with me easily. I do not remember what book of Robertson you are quoting from. I do not give all the weight you do to Robertson though I respect his work and have corresponded with him. But it was, I think, [Charles] Crawford in his *Collectanea* (1906) that first drew my attention to the borrowings of Marlowe from Spenser; and they are too numerous and pointed to be ignored. Besides the one you refer to I might quote one more:

> He lowdly brayd with beastly yelling sownd,
> That all the fieldes rebellowed againe:
> As great a noyse, as when in Cymbrian plaine
> An heard of bulles, whom kindly rage doth sting,
> Do for the milky mothers want complaine,
> And fill the fieldes with troublous bellowing,
>
> F. Q. I. viii. xi.

> I'll make ye roar, that earth may echo forth
> The far-resounding torments ye sustain;
> As when an heard of lusty Cimbrian buuls
> Run mourning round about the females' miss,
> And stung with fury of their following,
> Fill all the air with troublous bellowing.
>
> 2 Tamb. iv. p 63 Dyce

But Crawford gives several and you probably know his book. He was a surface-man on the Great Western Railway. Now as to the dates. This difficulty was pointed out, but Crawford says that though the F. Q. was not published till 1590 the same year as Tamburlaine 'a portion of the poem was in circulation as early as 1588, some lines of Book II. being accurately cited by Abraham Fraunce that year, in his *Arcadian Rhetoric* and he cites a note by [Alexander] Dyce. Moreover it was Raleigh who brought over Spenser in 1589 and as we know Marlowe was one of Ralegh's freethinking circle. If Spenser read the poem aloud to Ralegh may he not have done the same to *his* friends? Even if *Tamburlaine* was acted so early as 1587 that is not to exclude the possibility that it was revised before printing.

As to *Dido*, I fear I have not given close study to that play but I reread it in going over Miss [Una] Ellis-Fermor's book [*Christopher Marlowe*, 1927]. Chambers declares frankly that 'the play has affinities both to early and to late work and cannot be dated.' This seems to be your opinion and Chambers is a great authority.

I have been reading your essays on Andrew[e]s and others with interest. I feel a little with your reviewer in the T. L. S. but not altogether. I am probably to lecture at Bedford College in March or April on 'Humanism and the Churches in the Seventeenth Century', a lecture I gave in America. It will be necessary to define 'humanism' a little more closely for the word is being rather loosely used. My old teacher Professor Minto used to say you never knew what a man meant by a word till you knew what he was opposing it to, the contra-positive he had in his mind. When Pope talks of 'Nature' he does not quite mean what Wordsworth does. Roughly Pope is contrasting nature with the fantastic, Wordsworth with the conventional. So Babbit by Humanism means something which is opposed to the Naturalism of Rousseau and those whom he influenced; but in the seventeenth century the opposite of humanism is rather fanaticism. A humanistic Christianity is what Erasmus wished to see namely 'the philosophy of Christ', In my view humanism is very much Aristotle's doctrine of the mean, allows that there is good in many things which an intransigeant Christianity would rule out, as drama, poetry, the arts, &c. if you give them their right place and measure. So that the Anglican *via media* was essentially a humanistic ideal. Andrew[e] s and Hooker and Herbert and the Cambridge Platonists are admirable expressions of that spirit and temper; but the English Church today seems to have abandoned the *via media* for the extremes of Evangelicalism and Joynson Hicks on the one side and Anglo-Catholicism on the other. I was in Exeter Cathedral this year and when I picked up some of the books laid out for contemplative Christians to read in the Church I felt there was something wrong with a movement that could recommend people to contemplate such tripe. I do not write as a Scottish Presbyterian for I was brought up in the Scottish Episcopalian Church which is in open communion with the Church of England and very sympathetic with the Oxford Movement. The word Romantic too is still very vague. To me nothing could seem more romantic than to be a 'royalist' to-day. Royalism implies that God has given us a king whom we must obey but in the past he seems so often to have made a bad selection that various excuses had to be made from time to time to get rid of him, just as the difficulty about divorce was got over at times by calling it 'nullity'. After all St Paul did not commit Christians to Kings but simply to the 'powers that be', an excellently pragmatic decision. But I must not launch into statements that might easily be misunderstood. I have not studied the later developments of Anglo-Catholicism from within.

I think of being in London round about Christmas and if I am will try to find out if you are in town. I have my American lectures to bring up to Chatto and Windus. I must thank you for the fee you gave me for Milton.

Sincerely yours
H. J. C. Grierson.
P.S. It is a great pleasure to hear from you occasionally. I see your 'Seventeenth Century Poetry' is still going on.

TO *Edouard Roditi*   TS UCLA

5 December 1928   *The Criterion*

Dear Mr Roditi,

   I must apologise for the delay in answering you letter of the 23rd. I am returning your poems as you request,[1] and have made a few marginal comments on the first few pages which will give you some idea of the line of criticism which I should take. Perhaps when you come up to London you will look in and see me here.

                                   Yours sincerely
                                   T. S. Eliot

TO *Vita Sackville-West*[2]   CC

6 December 1928   [London]

Dear Mrs Nicolson,

   Thank you very much for sending me Roy Campbell's poem.[3] It is not, perhaps, one of his best; but it is definitely his own and undoubtedly good enough for me. It happens, however, that I might be able to place

---

1–Roditi wrote from Balliol College, Oxford, asking TSE to return the poems he had left at F&G in Oct.; his father had offered to meet some of the cost of publishing a selection.
2–Vita Sackville-West (1892–1962), only child of the 3rd Baron Sackville; writer, poet, and landscape gardener (famous for her development of the gardens at her house near Knole and at Sissinghurst Castle, Kent), wrote novels including *The Edwardians* (1930) and *All Passion Spent* (1932), and works of poetry, non-fiction and biography. Sustaining an unorthodox relationship with her husband, the diplomat and writer Harold Nicolson (1886–1968) – both being essentially homosexual – she had love affairs with Violet Trefusis (1894–1972), daughter of Mrs Alice Keppel (mistress of Edward VII) – her relationship with Trefusis earned the tribute of Virginia Woolf's fantasy-fiction *Orlando* (1928) – with the poet Dorothy Wellesley, and with others, as well as a close relationship with Woolf herself, 1925–8. See Nigel Nicolson, *Portrait of a Marriage* (1973); Victoria Glendinning, *The Life of Vita Sackville-West* (1983); Suzanne Raitt, *Vita and Virginia: The Work and Friendship of V. Sackville-West and Virginia Woolf* (1993); *The Letters of Vita Sackville-West to Virginia Woolf*, ed. L. De Salvo and M. A. Leaska (1984).
3–Sackville-West wrote on 3 Dec.: 'I am sending you Roy Campbell's poem ["The Gum Trees"] as I promised.'

it more to his financial advantage: I have only this morning a letter from Princess Bassiano asking me to get her a poem by Campbell for *Commerce*. If this is published in *Commerce* (that is to say the text with a translation by someone quite competent, like Larbaud or Leger) he will get pounds more for it than from the *Criterion;* and as she has asked me for a poem, I should like to offer her this. Should I ask Campbell first, or go ahead?[1]

I have ordered the *Radio Times*, and await it with great interest. You may be quite sure that there will be no offence, in any case![2] I cannot understand how anyone can be offended by criticism; the only thing that ever upsets me (and I think that is quite normal) is not being mentioned at all. In other words I prize criticism frankly by quantity rather than by praise.

I enjoyed meeting you very much, and hope that we may meet again.

With many thanks,
Yours sincerely
[T. S. Eliot]

1–See Campbell, 'Poèmes' – 'The Gum Trees' and 'The Palm', trans. Georges Limbour – *Commerce* XVIII (Hiver 1928), 67–85.

2–'I was so glad to meet you at last, and I sincerely hope that none of my remarks have given you offence, if you have read them in the Radio Times!' Sackville-West's article 'The Formidable Mr Eliot' (*Radio Times*, 30 Nov. 1928, 589, 628), was rude enough: 'Mr Eliot . . . is not a popular poet; he is too difficult, and too selfish, to achieve general popularity . . . Nevertheless, I do not think I shall exaggerate if I say that Mr Eliot has had more immediate influence than any other living poet on the younger generation of his fellow poets . . . [F]or my own part, much as I admire Mr Eliot as a poet, I think that his influence as an intellect has had many disastrous consequences . . . (He is, I may add incidentally, as well as being a poet, a fine and fastidious critic.) But it is perhaps on account of . . . his American birth that his culture has gone slightly to his head. English literature, with all its implications, was not his by birthright, as it is ours; he acquired it, so to speak, and the draught proved a little too heady for him . . . Being a man of severe intelligence, endowed with a highly susceptible sense of literature, he must have found himself almost forced into adopting an attitude of his own, where another and less coldly intellectual man would have been content with mere intoxication and surrender. The result is manifest in his poetry: it is a strange compound of indebtedness and independence . . . He is, in short, an intellectual poet . . . Mr Eliot within his own limitations is undoubtedly a genuine poet . . . I mean that he has a genuine poetic attitude towards life, and has evolved a means of expression exactly suited to his purpose.'

10 December 1928   Faber & Gwyer Ltd.

Dear Grierson,

Very many thanks for your letter of the 6th, and for taking so much pains to answer my questions. Your reply is entirely satisfactory for me.

I wish that I might see you to answer your letter, as you let loose several formidable genii who will not easily go back into their bottles. Minto was right. But I am quite sure that Babbitt is not only putting up humanism against Rousseau etc. where of course I follow him all the way, but definitely offering a substitute for religion. Perhaps the finest example of a word which means anything and everything according to the opposition in the mind of its user, is 'Romanticism'; and perhaps the only legitimate way to use it, except when talking about its historical use in a particular generation, is to define it clearly without pretending that your meaning is that of any other person or any other time.

Of course the lamentable extremes of the English Church to-day do push each other further each in its own direction; and I quite admit that there is plenty of unpleasant Sainte-Sulpicerie in Anglo-Catholicism, often a disposition to feel that whatever is Roman is right, an exaggeration of ritualism (outside of the Mass) – and of course there is the Immaculate Conception, which I cannot swallow, and which is not accepted by the Greeks. I think that P. E. More is doing good service by his insistence upon the Greek tradition, in the seventeenth century English church, as against the excessively legal Latin tradition. As for Royalism, I must leave that until I have got my Donne book off, which I hope will be early in the spring. Which reminds me to remind you of your promise to read and criticise a few chapters of it in manuscript, when they are ready.

I do hope that you will be in town about Christmas time. As just at Christmas I may be absent from my office for several days on end, it would be safer to write to me at 57, Chester Terrace, Eaton Square S.W.1. (in the telephone book).

> With very cordial thanks,
> Sincerely yours,
> T. S. Eliot

[P.S.] this also is my own amateur typing.

TO *Hugh Macdonald*   TS Williamson

10 December 1928   [London]

Dear Macdonald,

Many thanks for your two letters, and apologies for not having previously answered the first.[1] It would be more satisfactory to see you about this matter, but I am still very busy and it is likely that I shall have no time till after Christmas, but as soon as I can I will ring you up and ask you to come and lunch with me.

I will say, however, that I do not consider that you are under any obligation to compensate me even in part for the *Bookman* offer. If you had made a formal contract (and I conjure you in your own protection to do that with all authors in future!) you would presumably have been guarded against that sort of thing. Our original informal arrangement, by your letter, which I must look up, was £20 down in advance of a certain royalty, I forget what rate; and I wish to stick to that. Also I entirely agree that it would be damaging for you to have the essay reprinted so soon.

Of course I will accept the £14 you kindly send, but I hope that when you have time you will work out an exact royalty statement for me. I like to have them, and possibly I am now overpaid to date.

                                         Yours ever,
                                         T. S. Eliot

TO *H. S. Bennett*   CC

10 December 1928   London]

Dear Mr Bennett,

I have been in correspondence with Robertson and with Grierson, and it may interest you if I summarise their conclusions.

---

1 – *American Bookman* wished to reprint TSE's 'A Dialogue on Dramatic Poetry'. Macdonald responded first on 3 Dec., 'I would . . . prefer that it should not be re-printed except in a book of your collected essays. We will of course not allow you to suffer any pecuniary loss . . . We didn't make any definite arrangement with you & it might be as well to get the matter settled.' He wrote again on 9 Dec.: 'Etchells & I are of course anxious not to stand in the way of your making as much as you can out of the *Dialogue* but we feel that its reappearance in an American magazine less than six months after its first publication might do us some harm . . . As a compromise, do you consider £40 fair payment for the *Dialogue* on condition that we retain the copyright but only till the end of next May – a year from publication? I have been into the figures again & I find that to compensate you for the loss of payment by the *Bookman* would tax us too heavily.'

1. They both think it more probable that Marlowe saw a draft or drafts of the first three books of the *Faery Queen* before publication. Grierson refers me to Crawford's *Collectanea*, a book which you probably know, and adds himself that the borrowings of Marlowe from Spenser are 'too numerous and pointed to be ignored'. He mentions as one other example *F.Q.* I.viii.xi versus 2 *Tamb.* iv.1. p 63 (Dyce).

2. Robertson says merely about *Dido* that he does not believe it to be so early as is supposed. Grierson hazards no opinion but quotes Chambers as saying that 'the play has affinities both to early and to late work and cannot be dated'. – I agree with you however to this extent, that I should not have used *Dido* at all, in view of the doubts about it, as it is not essential to my argument.

I should be very glad to hear from you further about these matters.

Yours very truly,
[T. S. Eliot]

TO *Gerard Hopkins* CC

11 December 1928 [London]

Dear Mr Hopkins,

Thank you for your letter of the 4th.[1] It is kind of you to write to explain why you could not accept Mr Orrick's work, and I am really in agreement with your criticisms. It was not a personal matter, as Mr Orrick is not a personal friend of mine, and I merely felt that I ought to do anything I could to get his manuscript published.

With many thanks,
Yours sincerely,
[T. S. Eliot]

1–Hopkins wrote (4 Dec.) that Orrick's submission 'Matthew Arnold as a Critic' 'reads a little too much like that abomination of desolations the university thesis, and we all feel that Mr. Orrick has laboured a little heavily and a little at length to produce his mouse which, however interesting, remains a mouse.'

11 December 1928   57 Chester Terrace, s.w.1.

Dear Aunt Susie,

I have been a very long time in answering your kind letter but I am writing now in the hope that this may reach you about Christmas time, as a Christmas greeting. Your enjoyment of my poem[2] gave me great pleasure; it is always a pleasure and a surprise to hear from anyone that they like my work, but always particularly so when the expression comes from one of my family.

We were very sorry to miss Barbara altogether this summer. I do not think it was our fault: you have heard no doubt that she wrote suddenly to say that she was in London for a few days, and omitted to say at what hotel she was staying! We were very busy this summer, with repairs and decorations to the house here, as well as everything else, and so were unable to accept her invitation to visit them at Falmouth. I should have liked very much to see her and to meet Roger Wolcott.

There had been rumours that you and Eleanor[3] would return to England during the past summer; I hope that it is merely a postponement, and that you will be coming next year: if possible, in May or June, rather than in the middle of the summer, when nothing is going on.

I hear from Marion[4] that Mother is very active and alert, so I hope you will all be having a happy Christmas together.

Vivien joins me in good wishes for Christmas for you and Eleanor.

Affectionately your nephew,
Tom

TO *John Gould Fletcher*   CC

11 December 1928   [*The Criterion*]

Dear Fletcher,

Many thanks for your review of Pound.[5] I have only read it through once, but I see no reason whatever why we should not publish it, and I shall send it to press directly. Very many thanks.

1–Susan Heywood Hinkley, née Stearns (1860–1948): TSE's maternal aunt.
2–*A Song for Simeon*.
3–Eleanor Holmes Hinkley (1891–1971), TSE's cousin.
4–Marion Cushing Eliot (1877–1964), fourth child of Henry Ware and Charlotte Champe Eliot; TSE's favourite sister, she had visited him with their mother in 1921.
5–Fletcher's review appeared in C. 8 (Apr. 1929), 513–24.

When I see you again I have an interesting letter to show you from Mr J. C. Banerjea, who writes from Rosy Bower, Patna, India, and who says that he is an ex-professor of English at Patna College. He points out a great number of specimens of bad English in the September *Criterion*, and I think that some of them occur in your own writing.[1]

Drop me a line to let me know whether you expect to be in London over Christmas.

Yours ever,
[T. S. Eliot]

TO *Marguerite Caetani*

CC

11 December 1928   [London]

Dear Marguerite,

You asked me some time ago and reminded me in your last letter, that you wanted to get a poem by Roy Campbell. It is difficult to get anything out of him as he is diffident and distrustful of his own work. I have however secured the enclosed poem[2] from Vita Sackville West who says that I may use it for either *The Criterion* or *Commerce*. I could use it for *The Criterion*, but I have actually a great deal more material of all kinds than I could use in the next six months, so you are quite welcome to it if you like it. I am not sure that it is Campbell quite at his very best, but it is an interesting poem, and certainly could not have been written by anyone else. Could you let me know as soon as possible whether you care to use it or not.

In haste,
Yours ever affectionately,
[Tom]

TO *Bonamy Dobrée*

TS Brotherton

11 December 1928   *The Criterion*

Dear Bonamy,

I have been so busy for the last two months that I have no time to write to you any letters on the philosophical subjects which interest you

---

1 – Banerjea gave twelve examples of poor English usage in the Oct. number of C.
2 – 'The Gum Trees'.

so keenly. This hasty note is merely to say that I have sent you Lytton Strachey's *Elizabeth & Essex* and hope that you will see fit to review it for the March number.[1] Say anything you like about it; I may say that had I been reviewing it under my own name I should probably have been more severe than I was in last week's *Literary Supplement*.[2]

Will you please give my regards to Mrs Dobrée and tell her that I have her second draft of her story.[3] I am not quite sure however that I shall be able to use it until June; the fact is that owing to absence of mind I have involved myself with a story by D. H. Lawrence for the March number which turns out to be much longer than I thought it was when I accepted it.[4] So that I may not have room for another story until June.

Yours in haste,
T. S. E.

TO *Max Clauss*

TS Brotherton

11 December 1928   [London]

Cher Docteur,

Merci bien pour votre aimable lettre du 23 passé; je vous prie de me pardoner le delai, parce que j'ai été tres affairé ces derniers jours.

Les nouvelles que vous recevez, que je 'viens de fonder un journal littéraire', sont un peu fausses. Ce qui est vrai, c'est que nous avons réussi à rétablir le vieux *Criterion* comme revue trimestrielle avec l'appui de nouveaux amis. Est-ce que vous ne recevez le *Criterion* regulièrement? Le numéro de décembre paraîtra en peu de jours.

J'ai honte de ma défaillance, en ne vous signalant pas un article pour votre numéro de janvier; mais j'aurais du vous demander quelques renseignements. Exigez-vous des inédits? Autrement, je pourrais m'arranger avec vous pour vous passer des articles qui paraîtraient *simultanément* dans le *Criterion*. Quand vous recevez notre numéro de décembre, indiquez-moi si vous y trouvez un article, essai ou conte que vous *auriez* voulu publier en même temps: pour l'avenir, je pourrais vous envoyer des épreuves d'avance des choses que je pense pourraient vous plaire.

J'ai à vous remercier de votre gracieuse invitation. J'ai grande envie de voir Berlin, puisque jusqu'ici je ne connais que l'Allemagne méridionale.

1–BD's review appeared in C. 8 (Apr. 1929), 524–9.
2–'Elizabeth and Essex', *TLS*, 6 Dec. 1928, 959.
3–'Nearer God'.
4–DHL, 'Mother and Daughter', C. 8 (Apr. 1929), 394–419.

Il me ferait le plus grand plaisir de visiter cette ville comme votre invité, et d'y faire la connaissance de vos amis littéraires. A ce moment, je n'ai pas la chance de quitter Londres; mais le cas échéant, je ne manquerai pas de vous rappeler votre gentille invitation.

Et comptez toujours sur un bon acceuil quand vous venez à Londres. Votre bien dévoué, pour le Weinachtsfest, mit herzlichem Gruss –

[T. S. Eliot][1]

TO *Märit Scheler*[2]   TS Brotherton

17 December 1928   [London]

Dear Madam,

You may remember having had some correspondence with me on the occasion of *The Criterion* having the honour to be the first English periodical to publish some of your late regretted husband's work. I am now writing, first, though belated, to express to you my sympathy and that of all my colleagues in England, for the loss of one whom we considered among the very most important living Europeans. I am having sent to you a copy of the latest *Criterion*, in which you will find both a review of his most recent book, by Mr Herbert Read, and a fuller notice by Dr Max Rychner in Zurich.

I am however writing also, not as Editor of *The Criterion*, but as a Director of this firm of publishers who publish *The Criterion*, to

1 – *Translation*: Dear Doctor, Thank you for your kind letter of 23 November; please forgive me for the delay as I have been very busy these last few days.

The news that you receive, that 'I have just founded a literary review', is a little false. What is true is we have managed to re-establish the old *Criterion* as a quarterly review with the support of new friends. Don't you receive the *Criterion* regularly? The December issue will be published in a few days.

I am ashamed by my failure to point out an article for your January issue, but I should have asked you some information. Are you demanding unpublished material? Otherwise I could arrange to forward you articles, which would be published *simultaneously* in the *Criterion*. When you receive our December issue, please tell me if you find an article, essay or story that you would have liked to publish at the same time: in future I could send you the proofs (drafts) of the things I think you would like.

I must thank you for your gracious invitation. I really would like to see Berlin, as until now I have only known southern Germany. It would give me great pleasure to visit this city as your guest and to meet your literary friends. At this time I do not have the opportunity to leave London, but if I do, I will not forget to remind you of your kind invitation.

And you can always count on a warm welcome when you come to London. Yours truly, with hearty Christmas greetings – [T. S. Eliot]

2 – Märit Furtwängler, who became Max Scheler's second wife in 1912, was a sister of the conductor Wilhelm Furtwängler.

enquire whether the *Philosophische Anthropologie* is being prepared for publication; and if so, whether the firm of Faber & Gwyer, which I represent, may have the honour of considering it with a view to producing an *English translation*.

Receive, Dear Madam, the assurance of my highest respects.

Yours very truly,
[T. S. Eliot]

TO *Charles Mauron*[1]   TS Brotherton

17 décembre 1928   [London]

Cher Monsieur Mauron,

Toutes mes excuses.[2] La lettre que vous avez recue était une simple affaire de routine, envoyée à tous les contribuables. D'aucune importance de chercher le coupable. En somme, je serai heureux de publier ou la moitié ou votre article entier; donc nous en sommes quitte; vous recevrez le *Criterion* regulièrement (étant du très petit public qui l'apprécie); nous publions quelque chose de vous aussitôt que possible, et vous remettons le solde.

Et je vous remercie d'un article du plus grand intérêt.

Recevez, cher monsieur, l'assurance de mes sentiments très sympathiques.

[T. S. Eliot][3]

1–Charles Mauron (1899–1966) trained as a chemist but suffered from increasingly impaired eyesight. Author of *The Nature of Beauty in Art and Literature*, trans. Roger Fry (Hogarth, 1927), he translated into French VW's *To the Lighthouse* and *Orlando*, and collaborated with Fry on translations from Mallarmé. His later works include *Aesthetics and Psychology* (1935) and *Des métaphores obsédantes au mythe personnel* (1962).

2–Mauron wrote on 19 Nov. that he had received a request to renew his subscription to the *Criterion*. But the truth is, he confessed, that he had never actually paid for a subscription: one of his friends, English or French, must have paid it on his behalf – possibly the Princess de Bassiano. Since he admired the *Criterion* but considered the cost of a subscription too 'onerous', he offered an article in exchange for a subscription.

3–*Translation*: Dear Mr Mauron, All my apologies. The letter you have received was just a formality, sent to all contributors. Of no importance to find the culprit. In short, I would be happy to publish the half or the whole of your article: so we are quits; you will receive the *Criterion* regularly (being part of the small number who appreciate it); we will publish something of yours as soon as possible and send you the balance.

And I wish to thank you for your most interesting article. Yours sincerely, [T. S. Eliot]

17 December 1928   [*The Criterion*]

Dear Sir,

Your letter gives me much pleasure. Your name of course is well known to me, and needs no introduction even from our friend Fr D'Arcy, or our common friendship for Maritain. I am more than gratified by your kind gift of *Prayer and Intelligence*. I had given my copy to Mrs Irving Babbitt, and was going to procure another. I might as well admit that it was I who reviewed the book,[2] as well as *Three Reformers,* in the *Times Literary Supplement.*[3]

Whenever you may be in London, I hope that you will let me know, and if possible lunch with me.

May I take the opportunity of saying how much I always enjoy *The Dublin Review*. It has, I flatter myself, more in common with *The Criterion* than any review in England.

Sincerely yours,

[T. S. Eliot]

1 – Algar Thorold (1866–1936), diplomat, author, journalist: son of Bishop Anthony Wilson Thorold of Winchester, was editor of *The Dublin Review*, 1926–34. Publications include *Dialogue of St Catherine of Siena* and *Catholic Mysticism*. TSE wrote in a memorial note in C. (Oct. 1936, 68) that Thorold 'had been a frequent contributor since very early in our history: his knowledge especially of modern French philosophy and theology was invaluable. Having written very few books – his [*Six*] *Masters of Disillusion* has been out of print for many years – he was not known to a very wide public, and another generation will not be aware that *The Dublin Review*, under his editorship, was one of the most distinguished periodicals of its time. Being half-French by birth [his mother was Emily Labouchère], and at the same time thoroughly English, with the culture of the past and the curiosity of the present, he held a position as a man of letters such that we could say of him, that he was the sort of man whom we could ill afford to lose.' On 24 Nov. 1954, when Dom Michael Hanbury, OSB (St Michael's Abbey, Farnborough), asked TSE to recall Thorold for the *Dublin Review*, TSE said (1 Dec.) he was 'a valued contributor . . . but I liked him very much indeed as a man . . . I certainly remember the man himself not only with regard and respect, but affection.'

2 – 'The Life of Prayer'– on J. and R. Maritain, *Prayer and Intelligence*, trans. Algar Thorold – *TLS*, 21 June 1928, 460: 'It is not a book for those who approach religion solely through their emotional nature: it is rather for those who approach it intellectually, and is itself a corrective to the authors' intellectualism . . . [T]he book is important for the study of Maritain also. Perhaps one of the most incontestable virtues of this philosopher is his reminder that the development of the mind and the development of the emotions should proceed together . . . It is, for some, easier to believe in God than to love Him.' (not in Gallup.)

3 – 'Three Reformers' – on *Three Reformers: Luther, Descartes, Rousseau,* by Jacques Maritain – *TLS* 1,397, 8 Nov. 1928, 818.

TO *Godfrey Childe*   Photocopy of TS

17 December 1928   *The Criterion*

My dear Childe,

I have been thinking of you often. I should like to see you again soon. I am afraid however, that with the responsibilities, the business interruptions, and the pagan ceremonies which turn Christmas into a hideous farce, I cannot make any engagements till after the festival is behind us. I suppose you will be going to Yorkshire. Please give my regards to your brother. Will you let me fetch you for lunch one day soon after the new year.

All best wishes,
sincerely,
T. S. Eliot

TO *Mary Hutchinson*   TS Texas

27 December 1928   57 Chester Terrace, s.w.1.

My dear Mary,[1]

I was very happy & proud to receive the handkerchief – it is a very lovely one, & will serve my best occasions; but especially I was pleased to be remembered by you in such a way.

I hope I may see you soon to thank you.

Always affectionately
Tom.

Vivien Eliot TO *Mary Hutchinson*   TS Texas

27 December 1928   57 Chester Terrace, s.w.1.

My dear Mary

I was just writing to thank you for those 3 lovely handkerchiefs, when you telephoned. But I shall go on writing just the same.

The handkerchiefs are really very fine, & I am very delighted with them. It was very good of you, I think, to bother. And also to choose something so nice for me. It was very jolly to see you & Jack on Christmas Day.

1–This letter came with a card inscribed 'Mary from Tom Xmas 1928', and this message: 'Best wishes for Christmas and the General Election from T. S. Eliot'.

We shall be very pleased *indeed* if you will come in & see us after dinner tomorrow, as you suggested. It will be very nice indeed. So please do come, & we will expect you at about 8.30 – may we?

With love, & many many good wishes for the New Year, to you & to Jack & to yr children.

Yrs. ever
Vivienne Eliot

TO *Ottoline Morrell* MS Texas

27 December 1928   57 Chester Terrace, S.W.1.

My dear Ottoline,

I was very happy to find that you had remembered 'my diary', as I now call it, having had four in succession from you. I have come to depend on it. It was a particular pleasure that you should not only have remembered that, but added – & marked – Pusey's Prayers, which I did not know at all. I shall treasure them always.

You need not have returned the Andrewes – but it is a nasty little edition. I think there is a better edition, which I will try to find for you. They are almost indispensable.

I hope you will come and see us again soon. I was very glad to see you looking so well.

Ever affectionately
Tom.

TO *Bonamy Dobrée* CC

28 December 1928   [London]

Dear Bonamy

In reply to yours of the 5th instant I do indeed think that you might have written before, but so on the other hand might I.[1]

About business first. If those books you mention are worth short notes and if the short notes are not too much trouble, please dash them off;[2] but if they are not worth it, or if you have something better to do, such

---

1 – 'I do think I might have written before, don't you?' wrote BD (5 Dec.).
2 – BD asked about 'the Ibsen lady? . . . And the Life of Colley with a survey of the Restoration stage?'

as swearing at your gardener in Arabic,[1] please forget them altogether. I should however like you to take the *Elizabeth & Essex* seriously. Although I do not think it a good book, it seems to me worth taking as a symptom of popular taste. Please let me hear from you when you have looked at it.

I have no particularly interesting or cheerful information to give you about life in London; and I imagine that you are looking forward more keenly to Norfolk than to London. But we all look forward to your return in the early Spring, and your company has been missed at two or three small dinners.

Yours ever,
[T. S. E.]

P.S. I have the Ibsen in cold storage, and will see what I can do about having it copied.[2]

TO *Homer L. Pound*[3]

TS Beinecke

28 December 1928 *The Criterion*

Dear Mr Pound,

Your letter of the 10th gave me a great deal of pleasure.[4] I understand from Ezra that he liked my introduction, and if you like it also that is all the approval I need. I will certainly send you any reviews that may be interesting. *The Times* has not yet reviewed the book, but it is probably all the better that it should be reviewed after Christmas than before.

I agree with you that a real collection is wanted. Ezra's own collection does not fulfil the need. I do not believe that it is any use for a poet to suppress any poem that he has once published. Someone is sure to want it, and it is annoying not to be able to have the whole of Ezra's work together.

1–BD had written in his letter, 'at the end of the last paragraph, I was called away to argue about manure for my lawn, and talking Arabic and gestures is very forgettifying.'
2–BD had asked TSE to send him a copy of his essay on Ibsen 'as soon as possible'.
3–Homer Loomis Pound (1856–1942) was at the time of EP's birth a Federal land official in the Midwestern town of Hailey, Idaho; but the family moved to the suburb of Wyncote, Philadelphia, when Homer was appointed to the US Mint there.
4–'The new book *Selected Poems* has just arrived. Am very much pleased especially with your introduction. I would appreciate it very much if you see any reviews of the book you would send me copies. Maybe the Times will review it. Of course if I had anything to do with the collection there would have been more of Ezra's poems in it. There never has been a real collection of all his poems. Am glad that you and Ezra manage to keep together, and hope you will continue.'

It is a long time since I have seen Ezra, but we communicate frequently. We saw Dorothy several times this summer, and learned from her that there was some prospect that you and Mrs Pound might transplant yourselves very soon to Rapallo. I hope that this is so as it encourages me to believe that we may meet.

With very many thanks, and all good wishes for the New Year,

Sincerely yours,

T. S. Eliot

TO *Ralph Grote*

CC

28 December 1928   [London]

Dear Mr Grote,

I am now answering your letter of the 11th November.[1] I found your letter and your essay extremely interesting. Your essay I like very much, and I hope that I have profited from it. At the same time I am afraid that it is quite impossible for me to publish in *The Criterion* any paper that is so much concerned with a discussion of my own work. I regret this as I have found the essay very illuminating to my own advantage. I hope for my own sake that it will be published somewhere else.

I will assure you of my interest in your work, and I hope that you may send me something which I shall not be obliged to decline for the reason above.

With all good wishes,

Yours sincerely,

[T. S. Eliot]

1 – Grote, an American, submitted 'an essay about one of the numerous phases of aesthetics that you have written on. It is largely a critical essay, and not a laudatory one.' A friend of his, who had written on 'some of the more abstract and personal beliefs' in TSE's poetry, had received a letter from TSE 'assuring him of a difference in opinion'. Since the friend had criticised TSE's poetry, it had been agreed between the two of them that Grote – 'being . . . the prosier person' – would 'deal with [TSE's] prosier opinions'. He hoped TSE would print 'The Critic in the Sacred Wood' in C., even though he knew 'that as editor and because of a strange Custom of Self-Modesty ordained more or less by the ruling classes of England you might or would be reluctant to publish anything which contains your name and your theories. On the other hand, I thought that since it is not laudatory, and possibly dyslogistic, it might receive the unusual encouragement of being published.' Grote informed Marianne Moore, when he subsequently submitted his essay to *The Dial*, that he 'valued' this letter from TSE, and thought it might be 'a breach of honour' for him to show it to her (explained in letter from Moore to TSE, 6 Apr. 1929).

TO *Kenneth Ingram*   CC

28 December 1928   [London]

Dear Mr Ingram,

I must apologise for having left your letter of the 18th until after
Christmas. I was very busy during the last week. I feel very much honoured
that the Association should wish me to speak, but apart from my general
feeling about public meetings I am rather sceptical about my own utility.[1]
If there is time I wish you would drop me another line to make the subject
a little clearer. I am not quite sure what you mean by Literature in this
context. Will you be so patient as to enlighten me a little more fully.

I went to a similar meeting about a year ago. I say similar because I
am not quite sure that it was the same thing. The speakers certainly took
considerably more than ten minutes each, and it was in fact a long oration
by Russell Thorndike[2] that drove me from the room before the end. I did
not feel very much enlightened by that meeting, but perhaps this will be
different.

I shall write to you again in about a week to ask you to come and lunch
with me.

With all good wishes for the New Year.

                                        Yours sincerely,
                                        [T. S. Eliot]

TO *John Gould Fletcher*   TS Arkansas

[December 1928]   *The Criterion*

              The Fifth Epiphany Dinner of the
              CRITERION will have [*sc*. take] place
              on Wednesday the 2nd January
              evening 6.45 for 7 o'clock
              at the SCHWEIZERHOF
              53, Old Compton Street, W.C.1 (Sohoo)

1–Ingram: 'The Literature Association of the Anglo-Catholic Congress [Catholic Literature
Association, Westminster] have asked me to write to you to see whether you would be
willing to speak at their Annual Meeting on Wednesday, January 30th in the Church House
at 5 pm. Evoe Knox is going to speak, and Dr Waggett will be in the Chair. It is a very largely
attended meeting. The speeches are not more than 10 minutes, so that it is not a very big
undertaking. The object of the meeting is to emphasize the value of literature in any religious
movement.'
2–Russell Thorndike (1885–1972), actor and writer; brother of the more famous Sybil.

Your presence is requested
reply to
Harold Monro Esqre., 38,
Great Russell St. w.c.1. quickly.

J. G. Fletcher Esq.

TO *Herbert Read, F. S. Flint, J. G. Fletcher, J. B. Trend, Harold Monro, Richard Church, Roger Hinks, Conrad Aiken, F. V. Morley*   cc

28 December 1928   [*The Criterion*]

It has unfortunately been found necessary to alter the date of the *CRITERION* New Year's Dinner by one week, to Wednesday Evening, January the 9th.

You are asked to take note of this alteration, and particularly to notify Mr Harold Monro, at the Poetry Bookshop, 38, Great Russell Street, w.c.1. whether you will be able to be present. Several persons failed to reply to the last invitation, and it is essential that Mr Monro should know the number, before arranging with the Swiss Hotel.[1]

Secretary.

TO *John Gould Fletcher*   TS Arkansas

30 December 1928   57 Chester Terrace, s.w.1.

My dear Fletcher

Your kind invitation for Thursday would have brought us but unfortunately god damn it we have a New Years Dinner with my in laws put off from Jan. 1st to Jan. 2nd and then to Jan 3rd. so we shall have to be in Hampstead instead of with you. Our best wishes both for a happy New Year and a happy Birthday. It is as a matter of fact our turn to try to get you here, and we shall try to do so as soon as possible. Meanwhile I

1–Conrad Aiken wrote to Robert Linscott on 7 Dec. 1928: 'I attended the *Criterion* Christmas dinner, and got tight as a tick ... Tom is a lost man. He's unsure of himself, more dependent than he used to be, wary, and now faced with a growing opposition and a shrinking fellowship, so I read the situation, anyway. They are all of them on the defensive, I think, a little bit wary and frightened, a little shrunk in size, feeling the frost' (*Selected Letters of Conrad Aiken*, 149).

am free for lunch any day next week and hope also that you will turn up at the Epiphany dinner on the 9th at the Schweizerhof. With very many regrets from both and most cordial birthday wishes yours ever

T. S. E.

TO *Ada Leverson*[1]

TS Berg

30 December 1928   57 Chester Terrace, s.w.1.

Dear Mrs Leverson,

Very many thanks for your letter of Christmas Day, which we both enjoyed and appreciated.[2] I do not think that I ever properly answered your much earlier letter; but it is hardly necessary to say that *of course* I did not mind your reference to me! I have several times been questioned about my relationship to the great novelist, and sometimes (by foreigners) have been (accidentally or maliciously) confused with that Mrs Cross.[3]

Please remember that we expect to be still at this address (though it is not quite so charming as it sounds) when you return to London in April, and shall expect you to announce your arrival, so that we may really see you this next time. *The Criterion*, which was for a time a Monthly, is now reorganised more solidly as a Quarterly again, and everyone says that it is much better in that its true form than it was as disguised as a Monthly Magazine. The December number has just appeared.

I look forward to seeing in print the whole of 'Before the Fall of the Curtain' and also 'Reading from Left to Right!' which sounds delightful.

1–Ada Leverson, née Beddington (1862–1933): notable salonière (her friends included Beardsley and Beerbohm); novelist and contributor to the *Yellow Book* and *Punch*. She was an intimate friend of Oscar Wilde, who called her 'The Sphinx' and saluted her as 'the wittiest woman in the world', and she was loyal to him in his trials. TSE's friend Sydney Schiff was her brother-in-law. See Violet Wyndham, *The Sphinx and her Circle: A Biographical Sketch of Ada Leverson 1862–1933* (1963); Julie Speedie, *Wonderful Sphinx: The Biography of Ada Leverson* (1993).
2–Leverson had written from Florence to acknowledge a Christmas card from the Eliots: inter alia, she said, she hoped presently to be finishing off a sketch entitled *Before the Fall of the Curtain* as well as a humorous play *Reading from Left to Right*.
3–In a letter of 5 Oct. she had enclosed a short sketch, 'Husbands of Interesting Women', taken from a projected longer work entitled *Memorable Moments*, including this passage:
   'The late Captain Patrick Campbell . . .
   'I have been interrupted by a misinformed gink who rang me up to ask me to put in my list the brilliant American poet and critic, T. S. Eliot, thinking him to be the husband of the late George Eliot! And so obstinate about it!'

With all best wishes for the New Year from Vivienne and myself, and both looking forward to seeing you in April, when we trust you will be again at the Hotel Washington, I am,

yours ever sincerely,
T. S. Eliot

TO *Ramon Fernandez*   TS Dominique Fernandez

31 December 1928   *The Criterion*

My dear Fernandez,

I was very glad to hear from you, after having despaired of ever getting into touch with you again. I think you will probably find Freeman Wills Crofts more to your taste than Austin Freeman.[1] Did I give you *The Cask*, which I think might be particularly suitable for translation? I am told that his latest, *The Mystery of Starvel Farm*, is the best, but have not read it. I also hear that Pamela Wentworth[2] is a good writer, but do not know any of her works.

I am looking forward to the January *N.R.F.*, with the paper you mention. But in any case I should very much like to have a part of your essay on Humanism for publication in the JUNE *Criterion*.[3] It would fall in very well: I am sending you the December issue, which contains a short essay by Herbert Read on Humanism,[4] and in the March number the same subject will be taken up by G. K. Chesterton.[5] So if you would follow, I should be delighted; and I shall ask Norman Foerster to do the same. Will you let me know about this as soon as you can.

---

1 – Fernandez, who had got in touch on 11 Dec., commented: 'I must say that I have read other [Dr] Thorndyke marvels [by R. Austin Freeman] which I find better perhaps than *Angelina*, though I find very good parts in that book. I think Freeman's formula is a very interesting one.'

2 – Patricia [*sic*] Wentworth (1878–1936), British crime fiction writer.

3 – Fernandez had completed a paper on the classical spirit, for the *NRF* in Jan., and he was writing an essay on Humanism – 'in a very different sense from Schiller's'.

4 – 'Humanism and the Absolute', C. 8 (Dec. 1928), 270–6. HR wrote of his contribution in a letter to TSE of 12 Oct.: 'I have purposely given it rather an aggressive title, to provoke discussion. I think we are now getting down to bedrock – & that some interesting revelations may be provoked. Perhaps, if you publish it, you can invite one or two people to define their positions on the subject.' (He remarked further: 'I hope the next number is shaping well. I feel in a way that it will be a critical number. We have had time to recover from our "Umschwung" & to show our mettle. I grow more & more skeptical of the wisdom of conceding anything to the demand for fiction at any price.')

5 – G. K. Chesterton, 'Is Humanism a Religion?', C. 8 (Apr. 1929), 382–93.

Very well, we will get on with your Personality, if, as you say, the sequel is not soon forthcoming.[1] I shall be tempted to deal with you myself, if I am not too pressed by tedious duties.

Have you any prospects of visiting England again during the winter or spring? If so, let me know in good time, as we should like to see you here; and meanwhile my wife joins me in sending the best wishes for the New Year to yourself and Madame Fernandez.

Yours ever sincerely,
T. S. Eliot

Yes, the 'counterpart' of your Classical Spirit would be very welcome to the *Criterion*.

TO *E. E. Phare*[2]   CC

31 December 1928   [London]

Dear Madam,

Thank you for your kind letter of the 27th instant. I am much flattered by being invited to address the Newnham College Arts Society during the next term, and much wish that I could do so. But I have unfortunately and inadvertently agreed to speak on several occasions in London during that term, and am obliged to forgo any further imprudences of this kind. I very much regret it for my own sake, and hope that I may be given the same opportunity at some later time.

Yours very sincerely,
[T. S. Eliot]

1–Fernandez said he would not be working on 'Personality' again 'for a long time'.
2–Elsie Phare (1908–2003) read English at Newnham College, Cambridge, where she was taught by IAR, F. R. Leavis, and Enid Welsford; she took a starred First with Special Distinction in both parts of the Tripos. As President of the Newnham College Arts Society, she invited VW (whom she found 'haughty') to give the talk that would become *A Room of One's Own* (1929). She went on to teach at Southampton University, 1931–4; at Birmingham University, 1936–75. She published *The Poetry of Gerard Manley Hopins: A Survey and Commentary* (1933); articles on subjects including T. S. Eliot (1946); a British Academy Warton Lecture, 'A Great Master of Words: some aspects of Marvell's poems of praise and blame' (1976); and the third edition (with Pierre Legouis) of H. M. Margoliouth's *The Poems and Letters of Andrew Marvell* (2 vols, 1971). In 1933 she married Austin Duncan-Jones (1908–67), who was to become Professor of Philosophy at Birmingham. TSE wrote to Frank Morley on 20 Aug. 1945: 'Miss Phare is a Cambridge product who used to send contributions to the *Criterion* in the old days and I think did a little reviewing. She subsequently married a son of Duncan Jones, the Dean of Chichester.'

TO *J. S. Barnes*

CC is at top right

CC

31 December 1928   [London]

Dear Jim Barnes,

Very many thanks for your interesting essay in reply to my questions.[1] I have sent it to the printers to set up for the next (March) number of the *Criterion*, so that you will have a proof to correct before publication.

Your other essay[2] is still in the hands of one or two friends who know more about the subject than I do, but I hope to write to you about it very soon.

I enjoyed seeing you again, though for so few moments, and certainly hope that we shall be able to meet at more leisure and privacy on your next visit.

With best wishes for the New Year

Yours ever sincerely
[T. S. Eliot]

TO *A. L. Rowse*

TS Exeter

31 December 1928   Faber & Gwyer

Dear Rowse,

Faber has shown me an essay on the Pitcairn Islanders which amused me very much. I understand that your object in sending it was to get it published as a book, but that if you could not get it published as a book – and I doubt if any publisher would undertake anything so small – you would try the reviews. I should like to use it in the *Criterion*, if there is no great hurry. On the other hand, if you really prefer to get it done separately, I would gladly urge it on the Woolfs for a Hogarth Pamphlet.

Shall I try the latter first, and if not will you consider the *Criterion*? I am a little diffident, because it is a type of article that the more respectable reviews might snap at, because it is 'informative'.[3]

1–J. S Barnes, 'Fascism', C. 8 (Apr. 1929), 445–59. 'I believe that Fascism will become not only the means of reconciling the claims of Church and State in Italy, but provide the impetus necessary to enable the Church to assimilate modern culture.'
2–On Maritain's theory of art.
3–ALR replied on 9 Feb. 1929 that the Pitcairn essay was by a friend, W. K. Hancock, who wrote on Australia for the *New Statesman*; he hoped TSE would find out whether the Woolfs might make a booklet out of it. See 'Politics in Pitcairn', *Nineteenth Century and After* 109 (1931), 575–87; *Politics in Pitcairn and Other Essays* (1947). W. K. (later Sir Keith) Hancock was to become Australia's foremost historian; author of *Ricasoli and the Risorgimento in*

Incidentally, you spoke vaguely of getting at a certain piece of work that I suggested to you for the *Criterion*, during the vacation. I don't want to hustle you, but I should like to know whether it will be ready soon, or whether I should arrange to have room for it in the June, instead of the March number?[1]

With best wishes for the New Year,
Yours ever,
T. S. Eliot

TO *Ezra Pound*

TS Beinecke

31 December 1928
this last day of the
Old Year Goddam.

57 Chester Terrace, S.W.1.

Dear Rabbit,

No I Hope you Wont see the Book, whatever Unc. Wm. says about It. Anyway, you wouldnt like it, but it may satisfy You to Know that in Bloombsbury it is regarded like our youngest daughters Bastard: it is not Spoken Of, like the Bargee's daughter, Our Embly, she's in the fambly way but were keeping of it Quiet. Anyway, I had thought of trying the influence of the Bassiano famly on Richard but they are in the South of Cannes so no use at present, I have heard from him and have received his carrol,[2] the worst piece he has ever done and you know what that means he's ready for the looney bin Klotz Hennessey a la Sante etc yrs. more in sorrow than what you may think it there aint many sane people here or anywheres yrs etc.

T.

Tuscany (F&G, 1926) and *Australia* (1930); accounts of British mobilisation on the home front during WW2; a Survey of British Commonwealth Affairs; and a biography of the South African statesman Jan Smuts. He was a founder of the Australian National University. See Jim Davidson, *A Three-Cornered Life: The Historian W. K. Hancock* (UNSW Press, 2010).

1 – 'The Literature of Communism: its Origin and Theory', *C.* 8 (Apr. 1929), 422–36.

2 – Aldington, *Hark the Herald* (Paris: Hours Press, 1928).

TO *John Hayward*   TS King's

Thursday [? January 1929]   57 Chester Terrace, s.w.1.

Dear Hayward.

But if you will address letters to me at *15*, Chester Terrace, then of course they do not reach me so quickly. I think your explanation is as good as one could wish. I always go on instinct in such matters: that is to say, if I have read a thing many times without being troubled by it or realising that there is anything to explain, then I conclude that if there really is anything to explain it is not worth explaining.

As you said you had a copy of the Ariel I didn't press another on you, but here it is, and I am pleased that you should want it.

Yours ever
T. S. E.

TO *Alan M. Boase*[1]   CC

4 January 1929   [London]

Dear Sir,

I have your interesting letter of the 1st instant about the film censorship. I shall be very glad to know whether you will permit me to print this as correspondence in *The Criterion*.[2] Possibly, as Censor of *The Criterion*,

1 – Alan Boase (1902–82): Lecturer in French at the University of Sheffield at the time of this letter; subsequently Professor of French at Southampton, 1936–7; and Marshall Professor of French at Glasgow, 1937–65; an officer of the Légion d'Honneur; and winner of the Grand Prix du Rayonnement Française. Author of *Fortunes of Montaigne* (1935), and an authority on the work of Montaigne's contemporary Jean de Sponde, he also contributed to *The Criterion*, *Scrutiny*, the *Mercure de France*, and the *Revue des Sciences Humaines*. See too *The French Renaissance and Its Heritage: Essays presented to Alan M. Boase by colleagues, pupils and friends*, ed. D. R. Haggis et al. (1968).
2 – TSE had written in his 'Commentary' (C. 8 [Sept. 1928], 4): 'The general question of censorship is, we think, a question of expediency rather than principle, when it is not the censorship of a Church. The censorship of the theatre, so far as we know, seems to work pretty well; the censorship of films might be better indeed if it were more severe.'

I might question the desirability of referring to an anonymous and unknown censor as 'feeble-witted' (I am afraid that none of them is, for pathological purposes). But if you will permit your letter to be printed, you shall have proof of it.

I am afraid that, not being very much interested in the cinema, I expressed myself badly. I am quite ready to admit that probably the good films are suppressed (censorship has always much more to do with politics, moral prejudice and fear, than with religion); but I should have been glad if several I have seen, and others I have heard about, had been suppressed too. I particularly object to one called *The King of Kings*[1] (which I understand O'Connor[2] would have suppressed, but was overridden by the L.C.C.[3]) and one on the Madonna.[4] The Russian films in question I should have liked to see. What I should have said, perhaps, is that the film

Boase challenged him ('Correspondence', C. 8 [Apr. 1929], 501–3): 'one may agree that there is too much vulgarity and suggestiveness which deserves the film-censor's blue pencil and which now escapes, but heaven forfend that you should encourage Mr O'Connor's staff in their activities, until their personnel has been greatly changed, or, at least, until they have been 're-educated'. The more intelligent film-going public would probably be shortly robbed of what little good foreign stuff they can at present see, if you stimulated these gentlemen's "moral sense".' Boase instanced three films which had been crassly censored in the UK – G. W. Pabst's *Die Geheimnisse einer Seele* and *Jeanne Ney*, and Galeen's *Alraune*, in addition to other 'films of value, Russian and others' – and argued: 'so far as censorship is made use of on "moral grounds", it is the question of children which makes it difficult to deal with the cinema. In Switzerland the sensible arrangement prevails that children under the age of fourteen are not admitted except with their parents or except when special performances are given. Failing this, it is very necessary to obtain a more broad-minded treatment for 'A' Certificate Films (Adult Exhibition) and to create a new class for films of artistic or social interest which cannot pay in the ordinary commercial cinema house. These should be dealt with by a board of censors with some qualifications for appreciating the work they are required to see.'

1 – *King of Kings*, produced and directed by Cecil B. DeMille (1928).
2 – Thomas Power O'Connor (1848–1929), journalist and politician. Educated at Queen's College, Galway, O'Connor combined careers in journalism – writing for newspapers including the *Daily Telegraph*, the *New York Herald*, and the *Pall Mall Gazette*, and even starting some of his own (including in 1902 the popular *T.P.'s Weekly*) – and in politics, being elected in 1880 a Parnellite, home-rule-urging MP; and he was president of the Irish National League of Great Britain, 1883–1918. In 1917 he was appointed the first president of the British Board of Film Censors; and in 1924 he was made a member of the Privy Council. His works include *The Parnell Movement* (1886) and *Memoirs of an Old Parliamentarian* (2 vols, 1929) – for several years he was 'Father of the House'. See further L. W. Brady, *T. P. O'Connor and the Liverpool Irish* (1983), and J. C. Robertson, *The British Board of Film Censors: Film Censorship in Britain, 1896–1950* (1985).
3 – London County Council.
4 – Possibly *Madonna of Avenue A* (1929), dir. Michael Curtiz; starring Dolores Costello.

censorship shows that censorship always prohibits the wrong things, and lets by the things which ought to be prohibited. Anyway, I am sure that the stricter the literary censorship, the greater will be the sale of really salacious books.[1]

Yours faithfully,
[T. S. Eliot]

TO *Leonard Woolf*

TS Berg

5 January 1929   *The Criterion*

Dear Leonard,

I have received through A. L. Rowse of All Souls a very interesting and amusing essay on the history of the Pitcairn Islanders by one Hancock, whom I do not know, but who I understand writes about Australia in the *New Statesman*. I offered to use it in the *Criterion*, but Hancock wants to publish it as a booklet, which is how we got it. It is much too small for us to deal with but might be just about a good Hogarth Pamphlet length. So I told Rowse that I would offer it to you, as I could not see any other way of publishing it by itself; and if you don't like it or think it suitable then I will use it in the *Criterion*. It is quite light, but I imagine accurate; and is a sort of study of religious fanaticism and utopias.

Please let me know whether you would care to see it or not.

I should like to get you to lunch with me again when convenient. And to know whether you have had the opportunity of speaking to Adrian Stephen about that matter. There is one question of etiquette, in that connexion, which I should like to put to you.[2]

yours ever,
T. S. E.

---

1 – TSE wrote further about film censorship in his 'Commentary' (C. 9 [Apr. 1930], 384), where he proposed that Bernard Shaw 'ought to agree that an intelligent censorship would be a good thing. And this is precisely the question which has never been thoroughly discussed: whether an intelligent censorship is possible; and, if not, whether the effects of a stupid censorship are worse than those of no censorship at all.' See also David Trotter, 'T. S. Eliot and Cinema', *Modernism/Modernity* (Apr. 2006), 237–65.

2 – Adrian Stephen (1883–1948), brother of VW and Vanessa Bell; author and psychoanalyst: trained by Ernest Jones and James Glover, he practised from the 1920s. TSE's reference to 'that matter' presumably refers to the possibility of referring VHE to Stephen.

I am very dissatisfied with my review of the Goethe: I wanted to point the book (which I like) to the public which Dickinson seems to aim at, but it looks feeble.[1]

TO *Darsie R. Gillie*[2]   CC

6 January 1929   [London]

Dear Gillie,

We should have been hard pressed to produce the Pilsudski Memoirs[3] this spring even if we had it in hand, so we are reconciled to autumn publication. But I am afraid that August would be much too late. You see, the spring season begins in March, and the autumn season by the middle

1 – 'Introduction to Goethe' – a review of F. Melian Stawell and G. Lowes Dickinson, *Goethe and Faust: An Interpretation*, and *Goethe's Faust*, trans. by Anna Swanwick – *N&A* 44 (12 Jan. 1929), 527. LW said he found TSE's review 'admirable' (8 Jan. 1929).
2 – Darsie R. Gillie (1903–72) was Berlin correspondent of *The Morning Post*; later in the 1930s he reported from Warsaw, and as Paris correspondent of the *Manchester Guardian*. During WW2 he was to work for the BBC as French News Editor; and in 1944 he returned to the *Guardian*; ultimately, he would be the BBC's representative in Paris.
3 – Jósef Pilsudski (1867–1935), Polish nationalist, born in Lithuania, educated at Kharkov University, joined in 1892 the Polish Socialist Party and built up a private revolutionary army of 10,000 men, then the Polish Legions, which during WW1 fought against Russia alongside the Austro-Hungarians and Germans. Having secured Poland's independence (after 123 years of ever-varying partitions), Pilsudski became Chief of State, 1919–22, representing Poland at the Versailles Treaty, and Commander of the Polish Forces in the Polish-Soviet War. In 1923 he gave up his leadership of the army, but three years later he staged a coup and became the virtual dictator of the Second Republic of Poland, 1926–35. F&F advertised Pilsudski's memoirs (published as *The Memories of a Polish Revolutionary and Soldier*, 1931) in 1930: 'These memoirs of the great Field Marshal, one of the most powerful and remarkable figures of post-war Europe, have an interest beyond that of most memoirs of notable people. They have not been written since the Marshal has become famous; they are the events of his full and adventurous life put down as they occurred, some of them long before his name was known. The Marshal has been a revolutionary, a warrior, and a governor of a great people. Here is his analysis of various periods in his career, written not for notoriety, but for the interest of discovering what, in a man of action, have proved the mainsprings of action. Such memoirs, covering his career from the beginning, have a unique directness and documentary value; they have also the dramatic quality which belongs to great events as they are seen 'from the inside'.
'Thus the *Memoirs of Marshal Pilsudski* is not one of those books which are published only because they bear a world-famous name. It is the more thrilling because it is not a mere "looking backwards" over past adventures, or a mere narrative of political intrigue. It is an important document in the history of the liberation of Poland; and yielding insight into the mind of their leader, it yields insight also into the character of the Polish people.
'The memoirs have been translated and carefully knit together by Mr D R Gillie, Foreign Correspondent of the *Morning Post*.'

of September. So I am returning your contract with the latest possible date for our autumn season, viz. May 31st 1930. I do hope that you can see your way to finishing it by then, so that it shall not be held up for another year. Can you initial opposite the place where we have inserted that date and return to me?

Do let me know as soon as you can. Meanwhile I hope that you enjoy Berlin, and that your work, though arduous, is not unpleasant.

Yours ever cordially,
[T. S. Eliot]
Director.

TO *A. L. Rowse*   TS Exeter

9 January 1929   [London]

Dear Rowse,

I am replying to your letter merely on one point to say that I should particularly like to have your article for the March number.[1] The date January 25th would suit me very well but I am afraid I cannot give much longer. I look forward to reading it but would much more like to have a talk with you. Some day I hope to get you and Smyth in the ring together.[2] I am rather puzzled by what you say about Lancelot Andrewes as there is so little matter in the book which could be called political.[3]

Best wishes for the New Year,
Yours always sincerely,
T. S. Eliot

---

1 – 'The Literature of Communism: Its Origin and Theory', C. 8 (Apr. 1929), 422–36.
2 – 'What nonsense,' said ALR (9 Feb.) of Charles H. Smyth's review of *Social and Political Ideas of the English Thinkers of the Augustan Age*, ed. F. J. C. Hearnshaw, in C. 8: 31 (Dec. 1928), 333–7.
3 – ALR had remarked, 'Shall I say, what is the truth, that I was greatly disquietened by the political essays of *For Lancelot Andrewes*: or is this merely an impertinence?'

TO *Vita Sackville-West*   CC

9 January 1929   [London]

Dear Mrs Nicolson,

I cannot remember whether I wrote to report to you that Madame de Bassiano will be very glad to publish Campbell's poems.[1] Anyway at the risk of repeating myself I will say that she would like to be put in touch with Campbell. I wonder whether you would mind writing to her and explaining what has happened and perhaps you would prefer to suggest that he wrote to her direct.

Her present address is –

    Villa Caldena,
    La Californie,
    Cannes.

I hope that we may meet again this year.
With all best wishes and many thanks,

                     Yours sincerely,
                     [T. S. Eliot]

TO *John Cournos*   CC

9 January 1929   [London]

Dear Cournos,

I was very glad to hear from you and to know that you are better and look forward to your return to London.

I am sending you back the Russian stories almost without having read them although they look very interesting especially the second and third.[2] The fact is that I have so much fiction on hand which has been definitely accepted and which I must take in rotation that I could not publish any of these before the autumn. It is due wisely or unwisely to my having accepted a story from Lawrence which turns out to be even longer than I

1–Sackville-West had already answered on 5 Dec. that she was sure Roy Campbell 'would be delighted if you were to send his poem to *Commerce*'.
2–Cournos was bringing out a collection of translations: *Tales out of Soviet Russia* (Dent). He explained (31 Dec. 1928): "The Tale About Ak and Humanity", a piece of pure satire, written at the time of the Red Terror, undoubtedly personifies Lenin in the character of Ak. "A White Night" is a little take-off on romanticism ... "The Affair in Basseynaya Street" is an amusing tale which shows the effort of a pre-revolutionary writer to become revolutionary. It states something of Russia's attitude to the West.'

thought so that I shall not be able to publish any other story in the March number.[1]

This throws forward till June two other stories which were accepted for March.

All good wishes for the New Year for yourself and your family,

Yours ever

[T. S. Eliot]

I wrote this before you rang me.

TO *David Higham*[2]

CC

9 January 1929   [Faber & Gwyer Ltd]

Dear Mr Higham,

Thank you very much for your letter of the 3rd inst.[3] The situation is rather a peculiar one and I want to make it quite clear. I have never put any of my work in your hands or in those of any other bureau, not merely for the reason that I am so unproductive but chiefly because as a director of this firm I naturally give them the option of everything I write, and so far the option has always been exercised. Furthermore my arrangement is to leave arrangements for American publication in the hands of this firm, that is to say with Mr Stewart,[4] as my agents.

The present situation is of course rather different as it is a question of American publication of a limited edition of which Faber and Gwyer should of course have the English Agency, but it is complicated by the fact that I have been in indirect communication with the Crosby Gaige people about this matter for some months.[5] I had discussed it with Richard de

---

1–D. H. Lawrence, 'Mother and Daughter', C. 8 (Apr. 1929), 394–419.

2–David Higham, Curtis Brown literary agency. TSE was to write, in a letter to Joseph Chiari, 7 Feb. 1953 (when Higham was with Pearn, Pollinger, and Higham): 'David Higham is a very active and pushing agent.'

3–Higham wrote (3 Jan.) to say that 'Crosby Gaige's publishing organisation, now known as The Peregrine Press and under the control of James Wells ... has been discussing possibilities for future volumes with us and your name naturally came up.' Curtis Brown could represent TSE in negotiating a limited edition prior to publication.

4–Charles W. Stewart, Managing Director of F&G.

5–Crosby Gaige (1882–1949) – born Roscoe Conkling Gaige – theatrical agent and producer, had made a fortune of some $5m by producing Broadway hits (initially with the Elizabeth Marbury agency, then with Edgar and Arch Selwyn, and finally by himself) by the likes of George S. Kaufman and Channing Pollock. At the suggestion of his friend Bennett A. Cerf (founder of Random House), he set up a publishing house to produce fine editions: his productions included titles by Siegfried Sassoon, Richard Aldington, Humbert Wolfe,

la Mare and with Humbert Wolfe both of whom have talked about it to one or another of the American principals. Only the day before I got your letter Mr Wolfe had written to me to say that he had been discussing the matter with Mr Wells[1] and that he was asking Mr Wells to make an appointment to see me. I am therefore waiting to hear from Mr Wells so that you will understand that I do not feel that I am in a position to take advantage of your kind offer as things stand.

I should be very happy to meet you and possibly you may be calling soon one day when I am here.

> With many thanks,
> Sincerely yours,
> [T. S. Eliot]

TO *Ramon Fernandez*   CC

9 January 1929   [*The Monthly Criterion*]

My dear Fernandez,

Thank you for your second letter of the 5th. If you can let me have your essay ready by Easter it ought to be in time for our June number.[2]

I will ask Miss Stewart to let me see Schlumberger's story although I have a good deal of material on hand which I have definitely accepted.[3]

As for your comment on my footnote it is perhaps a feeble reply but a true one to say that I had altered this note considerably in my proof but owing to the illness of the head printer none of my final alterations to that article appeared, but I am pleased that you like the essay on the whole.[4]

Joseph Conrad, Virginia Woolf, and W. B. Yeats (*The Winding Stair* was the last such title, put out before the Wall Street Crash of 29 Oct. 1929 did away with his reserves). His own writings included *New York World's Fair Cook Book: The American Kitchen* (1939), *The Standard Cocktail Guide* (1944), and *Macaroni Manual* (1947). See also Gaige's ghost-written memoirs, *Footlights and Highlights* (1946?).

1–James R. Wells, who worked with Gaige, ran the Bowling Green Press until May 1929. GCF wrote to H. M. Cohen on 6 Jan. 1930: 'Mr James R. Wells is the head of the Fountain Press of New York. This firm is a sort of "middleman": it arranges for expensive editions and for their publication through certain American firms.'

2–Fernandez's essay on Humanism.

3–Jean Stewart had translated a story called 'L'enfant qui s'accuse' by the novelist, dramatist and poet, and co-founder of the *Nouvelle Revue Française*, Jean Schlumberger (1877–1968), whose writings include *L'Inquiète Paternité* (1911), *Un homme heureux* (1921), *Saint-Saturnin* (1931), *Plaisirs à Corneille* (1937) and *Éveils* (1950). Schlumberger, who corrected the translation, wondered whether it was suitable for C.

4–TSE remarked in 'The Literature of Fascism' (C. 8, Dec. 1928), 'M. Maurras and his friends have often displayed a lamentable and even grotesque ignorance of foreign affairs' –

Is there any likelihood of your lecturing in England this year?

Yours always sincerely,
[T. S. Eliot]

TO *I. A. Richards*

CC

9 January 1929   [London]

My dear Richards,

It is all very well and I shall preserve your post card[1] as a document in the case but it does not seem to me to improve Freud's position in the least. My main point is after all that he is dealing with a subject to which his own knowledge is irrelevant. If he has dealt with the same subject more fully and clearly elsewhere then I should like to know where to find it. But his chief difficulties in this book[2] do not seem to me psychological errors at all but logical and epistemological.

It is a minor point and a merely forensic one that he should not have written such a book, which touched another of those subjects, likely to be read by a great number of people who have not mastered his other works.

I should like to come to Cambridge but all that I can say at present is that when I can I will make bold to press myself on you and Mrs Richards before applying elsewhere.

With all best wishes to you both for the New Year.

Yours ever,
[T. S. E.]

TO *Leonard Woolf*

CC

10 January 1929   [*The Criterion*]

Dear Leonard,

Thank you for your letter of the 8th. I am sending you herewith Hancock's essay and hope that you will like it, but if it is no use to you

---

and added this footnote: 'An ignorance which, however, is not by any means limited to this political party, but is, it seems, characteristically French. The French are an insolent people, and inclined often to repudiate their best friends' (289). Fernandez commented: 'I do not think that what you say about the Action Française's knowledge of foreign affairs can apply to the French in general. We have here wonderful "informateurs" and this deficiency of Maurras, Daudet and even Bainville reacts on the whole theory.'

1–Not found.

2–Sigmund Freud, *The Future of an Illusion* (London, 1927).

will you return it to me here. If you think you could use it will you let me know and I will write to Rowse and ask him to get Hancock to write to you.

I am afraid that it is unlikely that I shall be able to lunch before the 16th.[1] In that case I may write to you to ask you your opinion on one point. If I do not see you before the 16th I will write again on the 25th and ask you to lunch [with] me as soon as possible after that.

Yours ever,

[Tom]

TO *Bruce Richmond*   CC

10 January 1929   [London]

Dear Richmond,

I believe that I wrote to you some time ago but am writing again about this point. I understand that you have a long review of a book or books on the *Psychology of Religion* by W. F. Stead. Stead told me that you had it for a long time and I offered to use it in the *Criterion* if you would be glad to get rid of it. I don't want to bother you but if you can find his review and don't want to use it yourselves I should be very glad to have it.[2]

I hope that the review I sent you the other day will satisfy Boas.[3]

Yours ever,

[T. S. E.]

TO *J. B. Trend*   CC

10 January 1929   [London]

Dear Trend,

I am very sorry you could not come to dinner last night, but I understood from Monro that you have not been well. I hope that you will not leave England again, or even go to the country without giving me a chance of seeing you. I should like very much to know [how] you are and what are your plans for the immediate future.

---

1 – The Woolfs were going to Berlin, 16–25 Jan.
2 – Not found.
3 – 'Turbervile's Ovid' – *The Heroycall Epistles of Ovid, Translated into English Verse by George Turbervile*, ed. with introd. and glossary by Frederick Boas – *TLS*, 17 Jan. 1929, 40.

I am counting upon a Music Chronicle from you for March, but should like to be reassured.[1] I do not suppose that you would care or have time to do any notes on Spanish periodicals. There is very little to be sure. Hardly more than the *Gaceta Literaria* which comes on. I don't know whether to send these to you or not. With all good wishes for the New Year.

Yours ever,
[T. S. Eliot]

TO *Roger Hinks*[2]   CC

10 January 1929   [London]

Dear Hinks,

Thank you very much for your post card which is most satisfactory. I am writing to ask you whether you think that Kenneth Clarke's [*sic*] book on the Celtic Revival is worth either a long or short review. Please let me know as soon as you can whether you want to do anything with this book or with any other books as separate reviews so that I may have the space for them.[3]

I was sorry that you could not come to the dinner last night but hope that we may arrange another within a month or so.

Yours ever
[T. S. Eliot]

---

1 – Trend, 'Music Chronicle', C. 8 (Apr. 1929), 480–6.

2 – Roger Hinks (1903–63) – son of Arthur Hinks (Secretary of the Royal Astronomical Society and Gresham Lecturer in Astronomy) – was educated at Trinity College, Cambridge, and at the British School in Rome. From 1926 to 1939 he was Assistant Keeper in the Department of Greek and Roman Antiquities, British Museum, from which he resigned in consequence of a scandal caused by his arrangements for deep-cleaning the Elgin Marbles. He later worked at the Warburg Institute, at the British Legation in Stockholm, and for the British Council (Rome, The Netherlands, Greece, Paris). His writings include *Carolingian Art* (1935), *Myth and Allegory in Ancient Art* (1939), and *Caravaggio: His Life – His Legend – His Works* (1953). See also 'Roger Hinks', *Burlington Magazine* 105: 4738 (Sept. 1964), 423–34; and *The Gymnasium of the Mind: The Journals of Roger Hinks, 1933–1963*, ed. John Goldsmith (1984).

3 – Hinks, untitled review of Kenneth Clark, *The Gothic Revival*, C. 8 (Apr. 1929), 529–32.

TO *Hugh Fraser Stewart*   CC

Dear Dr Stewart,

I hope you will not think it impertinent or intrusive of me to write to you on the following matter. Mario Praz, of Liverpool University, tells me that he is applying for the Italian Professorship at Cambridge, and I understand that you are one of a committee which has to do with the selection. Praz has asked me if he might use my name. I do not know who else is to be considered, and therefore my commendation has not absolute significance. But I should be very glad if he were appointed. I met him first through reviewing his book (*Secentismo e Marinismo in Inghilterra*) for *The Times*;[1] I was also so impressed by it that I wrote to him, without knowing who he was; but I have been more and more impressed since then, by his immense scholarship and his command over his own scholarship. And last year I heard him deliver, in fluent English, an admirable, even masterly lecture on Machiavelli to the British Academy.[2] I am sure that Grierson would speak warmly of him, as he has discussed him with myself; and among my own acquaintance I should put him second only to Grierson in knowledge of seventeenth century English poetry. I do not know him at all intimately, but he has very agreeable manners.

The other point on which I had to write is that Fernandez has just let me know that your daughter has translated a story of Schlumberger which Fernandez much admires. I have never met your daughter – I think she was in Paris when I was in Cambridge – but I should be very grateful if you would tell her that unless she has other ends in view, and unless the story is too long for my purposes, I should very much like to see it for *The Criterion*. I have forgotten which story it is, but it is one that I have not read.[3]

With all best wishes for the New Year to Mrs Stewart and yourself,

Sincerely yours,

[T. S. Eliot]

---

1 – 'An Italian Critic on Donne and Crashaw', *TLS*, 17 Dec. 1925, 878.
2 – *Machiavelli and the Elizabethans* (Annual Italian Lecture of the British Academy, 21 Mar. 1928), *Proceedings of the British Academy*, vol. 13 (Humphrey Milford, 1928).
3 – Jean Schlumberger, 'L'enfant qui s'accuse', trans. Jean Stewart: not published in *C*.

TO *O. Reeman Clarke*   CC

11 January 1929   [London]

Dear Sir,

I have your letter of the 3rd inst.[1] I am afraid it is impossible for me to send books for review for the *Criterion* by anyone whose work I do not already know. I have found it necessary to make this an invariable rule. I should however be very glad to see any specimens of your work, either published or unpublished that you care to submit.

With regard to your second request I am naturally honoured and flattered at being asked to become a patron of a new periodical. I do not feel however that such patronage is of the slightest value unless the patrons whose names are published know and approve in advance what they are patronising. I should wish to give every encouragement to your review but I should much prefer to see a copy of it before I give my name as I feel that I should like my sponsorship to have some meaning. So that I hope you will kindly send me the first copy of the periodical.

Yours very truly,

[T. S. Eliot]

TO *Walter Lowenfels*   CC

11 January 1929   [London]

Dear Mr Lowenfels,

I have been thinking over your letter of the 7th December and the manuscript of your poem.[2] It seems to me that the most likely publisher for your work is the Hogarth Press, the proprietors of which are friends of mine, that is Leonard and Virginia Woolf. If you will drop me a line to say that you concur I will write to the Woolfs about your work and ask them to consider your book.

Sincerely yours,

[T. S. Eliot]

---

1 – Clarke wanted to review Osbert Sitwell's *The People's Album of London Statues*. In addition, he asked TSE to become one of the patrons of a new periodical he was editing, *The Critic*, which was 'published chiefly for a literary and classical society in Liverpool'.
2 – 'Finale of Seem.'

11 January 1929   *[The Criterion]*

My dear Herbert,

I am bothering you again with a few manuscripts that I think are worth looking at. One is a short play by a boy named Auden whom I have seen and talked to several times.[1] I think he has some merit and he really wants seriously to do something with some form of verse play. You will see I think places where he breaks down completely and becomes stupidly imitative but I should like to know whether you see any promise in it. The second is the essay on Shelley by Douglas Garman[2] which also seems to me to have some force. It might be as well to annex the better members of the old Calendar Group. I don't know

1 – W. H. Auden had submitted his play 'Paid on Both Sides' from Berlin on 30 Dec. 1928 – 'I feel it wants revising at several points, but I want to leave it alone for a bit, and should like you to see it now', he wrote – and then a corrected version on 4 Apr. 1929. 'Paid on Both Sides' was to appear in *C.* 9 (Jan. 1930), 268–90.

Auden would say, in a radio broadcast following TSE's death in 1965, that TSE 'once stated that in literature he was a classicist. This seems misleading, because whatever he may have intended by the term, it inevitably suggests a poet whose work can be viewed as a logical and inevitable step in the historical development of English poetry. To me, on the contrary, he seems one of the most idiosyncratic of poets, both in his subject matter and in his technique . . . His influence as a critic upon taste is much clearer . . . In Eliot the critic, as in Eliot the man, there's a lot, to be sure, of a conscientious church-warden. But there was also a twelve-year-old boy, who liked to surprise over-solemn wigs by offering them explosive cigars, or cushions which fart when sat upon . . . Another quite definite influence he's had upon younger poets was concerned with manners and conduct. None of us, I think, imitated him exactly by taking to a bowler hat and a tight-rolled umbrella, but he certainly taught us it was unbecoming to dress or behave in public like the romantic conception of a poet. More importantly, he taught us that a poet's conduct is subject to exactly the same moral judgments as that of a person in any other walk of life. He cannot claim special privileges . . . So long as one was in Eliot's presence, one felt it was impossible to say or do anything base.'

2 – Douglas Garman (1903–69), editor and journalist, read English at Cambridge and went to work, with Edgell Rickword (a fellow socialist), for Wishart & Company, the publishing house set up by his friend Ernest Wishart. Garman became assistant editor of their quarterly literary review, *The Calendar of Modern Letters*, 1925–7 (contributors included E. M. Forster, Robert Graves, AH, and DHL). See Bernard Bergonzi, 'The Calendar of Modern Letters', *The Yearbook of English Studies* 16: *Literary Periodicals Special Number* (1986), 150–63. From Mar. 1933 Garman was a director of Wishart & Company (he also became the lover of Peggy Guggenheim, and was briefly married to her). In 1934, with Wishart and Rickword, he joined the Communist Party; and in 1935 the publishing house, now Lawrence and Wishart, became the official press of the Communist Party of Great Britain (CPGB); it also published the anthology *New Writing*, and *Negro*, an anthology of black culture edited by Nancy Cunard. During WW2 Garman was education officer for the CPGB. For all the ins and outs of the Garmans and their world, see Cressida Connolly, *The Rare and the Beautiful: The Lives of the Garmans* (2004).

Garman myself or anything about him except the somewhat jaundiced opinion of Wyndham.

The third are some poems by a boy whom I think I mentioned to you named Roditi. Roditi is a young undergraduate who on first appearance is a sort of second rate Menasce. He is a French Jew of Spanish extraction who speaks the most fluent English and is now at Balliol; or rather he started at Balliol and is now in a sort of consumptive home in Switzerland.[1] Do you think that he is worth encouraging?

I hope to see you privately for lunch next week if you can manage it so don't bother to post this stuff back.

Yours ever,

[T. S. E.]

---

1 – Roditi (who was in fact American) had written to TSE on 18 Dec. 1928: 'When I returned to Paris, my parents and doctor found that I was in a very bad state of health; so that I was immediately exiled to a nursing-home in Switzerland where I must now stay for at least two months . . .

'Of course this is most annoying both for my studies and for all my other occupations; but bad lungs make bad scholars, and (my doctor tells me) bad poets – which last statement seems perhaps less true.

'I am enclosing a few short poems, which really form one longer poem, being different aspects of the same idea. As you said, when you were kind enough to read them, there are considerably less adjectives.

'If they interest you at all, I have several others which I could send in a few weeks – in fact I have a whole book of some 60 pages ready; which, although the poems are not all of the same nature, shows a certain development towards a different idea, which would form my second "plaquette". I would very much like to see them published, for different reasons: to convince my parents, to be able to judge them from a less personal point of view, and to see whether they are of any use to others than myself and my friends. Do you know whether they would be of interest to any particular English or American publisher? I somehow feel that they would not command as vast a public as Miss Millay; but I do not think that that can discourage me.

'While out here I will finish my translations of St-J. Perse, and try to translate a few poems of [Léon-Paul] Fargue.

'I am scarcely allowed to work at all so do not expect to achieve much.

'I hope that when I see you again, I shall be as large and as healthy and as muscular as a "professional" mountaineer.

'It would certainly make life much easier for me, if I recovered; but the life I have to lead here is so dull that I often loose [sic] hope.'

He was still at the sanatorium, Val-Mont, Glion, Lac Leman, in Mar. 1930.

TO *John Macmurray*[1]   CC

15 January 1929   [London]

Dear Mr Macmurray,

I am writing to ask you whether you would be willing to consider reviewing Professor Eddington's latest book for the next number of the *Criterion* which will appear in March. As you probably do not know the *Criterion* as well as I know your work I am sending you a copy of the September and December number. We have, from time to time, merely technical philosophical reviews and do not expect reviewers to write down to any level, though of course our public is the ordinary cultivated public which cannot be expected to be versed in higher mathematics. We should be very honoured if you would do this and I hope that you will consent.[2]

                              Yours very truly,
                              [T. S. Eliot]

TO *David Higham*   CC

15 January 1929   [London]

Dear Mr Higham,

I must apologise for my delay in answering your letter of the 11th.[3] I should be delighted to lunch with you but I afraid that to-morrow is now too short notice. Would you care to suggest a day next week, Wednesday is as good for me as any day.

                              With many thanks,
                              Yours sincerely,
                              [T. S. Eliot]

1–John Macmurray (1891–1976), moral philosopher, educated at Glasgow and Balliol College, Oxford, was Grote Professor of the Philosophy of Mind and Logic at University College, London, 1928–44; Professor of Moral Philosophy at Edinburgh University, 1944–58. His works include *Freedom in the Modern World* (1932); *The Self as Agent* (1957); *Persons in Relation* (1961). See J. E. Costello, *John Macmurray: A Biography* (2002); *John Macmurray: Critical Perspectives*, ed. D. Fergusson and N. Dower (2002).
2–See Macmurray, untitled review of E. S. Eddington, *The Nature of the Physical World*, C. 8 (July 1929), 706–9.
3–'Of course we understand your very natural attitude and acquiesce in it with goodwill. Our object was not in the least to butt in, but only to be helpful.'

TO *Sherard Vines*   CC

16 January 1929   [London]

Dear Vines,

I hear that you called at this office the other day but you left no message and no address, which was unkind of you so that I have no means of getting hold of you if you are in London. If this letter is forwarded to you and if you have not left London I hope you will let me know.

What I am writing to ask is whether you would ever do any writing <reviewing> for the *Criterion*. All that I have in my mind for the moment is two books published in the Hogarth Lecture Series. One by Grierson on Modern Poetry and the other by Herbert Read on Phases of English Poetry.[1] If this subject does not attract you I hope you will suggest something else.

With all best wishes,
Yours sincerely,
[T. S. Eliot]

TO *Charles Smyth*   CC

16 January 1929   [London]

Dear Smyth,

Thank you for your letter. I will accordingly use for the March number one of the reviews which I have in mind. I think that it would suit me quite as well to have your essay for the June number, which I trust will give you plenty of time.[2] I say I think it will, because I am depending on certain other material which has been promised me; at any rate I would rather that you finished your essay at your leisure.

Yours ever,
[T. S. Eliot]

---

1 – *Phases of English Poetry*, Hogarth Lectures on Literature, First Series, no. 7 (1928). No review was forthcoming.

2 – Smyth had written (undated): 'I have no review for the March number. I have an article in hand, which I promised you – an attack on Lytton Strachey, Maurois, & Guedalla in particular, for which I propose to use as my text Mary Anne Disraeli by James Sykes . . . Do you want that for March? On the whole, I personally should prefer to take my time over it: but I could perfectly easily polish it off in a fortnight, if you would like it.' 'A Note on Historical Biography and Mr Strachey', C. 8 (July 1929), 647–60.

TO *Humphrey Whitby*[1]   CC

[16 January] 1929[2]   [London]

Dear Father Whitby,

I must apologise for my delay in answering your kind letter, but as your suggestion was preliminary to a definite date I was really waiting to see how things would be. At present it is still rather difficult for several reasons to make evening engagements but I could find lunch or tea possible. If the evening becomes possible I will let you know but it always means a special arrangement as we cannot have any servant living in, in so small a house.

Even if you could not arrange with Mr Claye[3] I should like to come and see you whenever you have the leisure. It is very kind of you to take so much trouble.

Sincerely yours,
[T. S. Eliot]

TO *Francis Underhill*   CC

16 January 1929   [London]

Dear Father Underhill,

I was very happy to hear from you again and it is very kind of you to ask me to dinner.[4] It has been on my mind for a long time that I should like to see you again. Unfortunately evening engagements are rather difficult for me at present and I wonder whether you would have the patience to suggest, at your convenience, some day for lunch or even tea. I hope that it will be possible as I should like very much to see you.

With very many thanks,
Yours sincerely,
[T. S. Eliot]

P.S. My private address is 57 Chester Terrace, Eaton Square, s.w.1.

1–Fr Humphrey Whitby was vicar of St Mary's, Graham Street (now Bourne Street), Sloane Square, London s.w.1, 1916–46.
2–Misdated 28 Feb. 1929.
3–Charles A. Claye was author of a masque, *The Merry Masque of Our Lady in London Town*, performed by the Players from St Mary's at Chelsea Palace Theatre, on 8, 12 and 22 Dec. 1928. (TSE's introduction to the piece was posthumously printed by Stanley Revell as 'Not in Gallup', 1988.)
4–Underhill wrote to TSE on 13 Jan. from Liddon House, South Audley Street, London.

TO *John Hayward*   TS King's

16 January 1929   57 Chester Terrace, S.W.1.

My dear Hayward,

Your Donne has arrived – a book which does credit to the Press – it is very cheap at eight and six – and to the Editor (though this statement is so far made largely on faith, for I have had only a few minutes examination) – and more than my due to me, in the Preface. I should of course like a limited edition too – but if that is inconvenient, don't bother, but in that event you must sign this copy for me. I don't think the *Criterion* need have another copy – as I shall want to write a note on it myself – how long and when is a question of time, but the later the longer.[1] I shall try to get you to lunch in a week or so, and hope you are well. I liked Clutton-Brock,[2] and should like to see him again. May I count upon a review and a note from you, for the March number?[3]

Yours ever,
T. S. Eliot

Incidentally, the book will be very convenient for my own work!

TO *Desmond MacCarthy*[4]   CC

22 January 1929   [Faber & Gwyer Ltd]

Dear MacCarthy,

Mrs Nicolson recently gave me an unpublished poem[5] by Roy Campbell, which I passed on to the Princess Bassiano to use in *Commerce* – not that I did not like it, but because *Commerce* can pay better than *The Criterion*.

---

1 – JDH's edition of John Donne, *Complete Poetry and Selected Prose*, and Herbert J. C. Grierson's shorter edition of *The Poems of John Donne*, were ultimately to be reviewed by T. O. Beachcroft in C. 9 (July 1930), 747–50.
2 – Alan Clutton-Brock (1904–76), JDH's contemporary at King's College, Cambridge (where he took a first in English in 1926), would write for *The Times* and *TLS* from 1930, and was to become Art Critic of *The Times*, 1945–55 and Slade Professor of Fine Art at Cambridge, 1955–8. His publications include *Italian Painting* (1930), *Introduction to French Painting* (1932), and *Cézanne* – 2 vols, co-authored with Adrian Stokes – published 1947–55 in the Faber Library under the general editorship of R. H. Wilenski.
3 – JDH, untitled review of *The Poetical and Dramatic Works of Sir Charles Sedley*, ed. V. De Sola Pinto, C. 8 (Apr. 1929), 540–3.
4 – Desmond MacCarthy (1877–1952), literary and drama critic, was closely associated with the Bloomsbury Group. Literary editor of the *New Statesman* 1920–7; editor of *Life and Letters,* 1928–33; and from 1928 principal literary reviewer of the *Sunday Times*.
5 – 'The Gum Trees'.

I now hear urgently from Madame de Bassiano that she would like to publish also in *Commerce* a poem of Campbell's which appeared in *Life and Letters*.[1] It would be the English text with a French translation on the opposite page.

I am not in touch with Campbell; I heard from him some months ago from the South, but have no trustworthy address; and Madame de Bassiano seems to be in rather a hurry. I wrote to Vita Nicolson, but unluckily she had left Surrey for the North, and now, I hear, is back in Berlin.[2] So I am now appealing to you, to ask, first, whether *Life and Letters* would have any objection to this republication; and second, whether you can give me the present address of Campbell to send to Madame de Bassiano. I should be very grateful.

Yours sincerely,
[T. S. Eliot]

TO *Caresse Crosby* TS]

23 January 1929   57 Chester Terrace, s.w.1.

Dear Mrs Crosby,

I am so deeply sorry, because this is, I think, the second time that I have missed you here.[3] I can only hope that you and your husband will soon be in London again. It is merely the current influenza which has brought down my household, not very severe, but I am told very infectious. I hope at least that this will catch you before you sail, if that is the word. Do let me hear more about your Press, though I am so unproductive that I doubt whether I can be of any use personally. And if I come to Paris I shall hope to see you there.

With many regrets,
Sincerely yours,
T. S. Eliot

1–Campbell, 'The Palm', *Life and Letters* 1:4 (Sept. 1928), 287–9.
2–Harold Nicolson was British Ambassador to Berlin.
3–Crosby, who was staying briefly at Claridge's Hotel, had hoped to see TSE.

TO *H. J. C. Grierson*　　　　TS National Library of Scotland

23 January 1929　　　　　*The Criterion*

Dear Grierson

Many thanks for your letter of the 20th.[1] I shall be delighted if you will review the Donne (which I read first as 'Circe') for the (June) *Criterion*. If I had thought that you would care to do it I would have sent to you at once. I had half promised to do it myself: John Hayward is a young friend of mine, in whom I take a good deal of interest; he consulted me from time to time about some of his cruces and variants; so I should prefer not to deal with him myself; but I hope you will be able to be lenient with him – but in any case he ought to feel honoured by being reviewed by the greatest living authority on the subject!

Review copy follows.[2]

I hope that we may meet again whenever chance or duty brings you to London. For your last remark, the only hope for a periodical like the *Criterion* is gradually to reach the people who might like it. There are, I am sure, enough in the world to support it, but they are scattered – one in Bolivia, two or three in China, and so on – and they are not people to be reached by 'circularisation'.

And when you are in London, and have time, I may say that the *Criterion* group will want you as guest of honour at one of their fortnightly dinners.

Sincerely yours,
T. S. Eliot

TO *Alan M. Boase*　　　　　　　　　　　　　　　　CC

24 January 1929　　　　　[London]

Dear Mr Boase

Thank you for your letter of the 18th. I am glad that you will allow your letter to be published; the whole question of film censorship seems to me more difficult than that of any of the other censorships, difficult as they are (for instance, I found myself in a difficult position about the *Well of Loneliness* book, because I considered it a dull, badly written and inartistic book, and even a pernicious one, though not at all for the reasons for which it was suppressed) and airing it can do no harm.

1 – Not found.
2 – See note to TSE's letter to JDH, 16 Jan. 1929 above.

I should be most interested to see your essay on French 'metaphysical' poets.[1] Do send it. I realise how awkward it is, in such an essay, to strike the balance between quotation, exposition, and criticism. But I know there is a good deal to be done in that field.

Yours very truly,
[T. S. Eliot]

TO *A. L. Rowse* TS Exeter

24 January 1929   [London]

Dear Rowse,

The end of the month will still do for your essay, as I am counting upon it and looking forward to it. Can you assure it by then?

I do wish that I had had the suggestion of David Cecil before. I have met him, some years ago, and had kept him in mind as a possible writer, but his name never occurred to me in connexion with Strachey's book, though he should have been an obvious choice.[2] It is too late now, as that is all arranged; but will you tell him that I should be very glad if he would suggest something else – or you might be able to suggest for him something suitable for him to do?

Ever cordially,
T. S. Eliot

TO *John Macmurray* CC

24 January 1929   [London]

Dear Mr Macmurray,

Thank you for your kind letter.[3] Your objection, that you have already reviewed Eddington's book for the *British Weekly*, is not an objection to me; it is not an objection at all unless you yourself dislike reviewing

---

1 – 'Then Came Malherbe', C. 10 (Jan. 1928), 287–306.

2 – 'My friend David Cecil was very anxious to review Strachey's book . . . ,' wrote ALR in an undated note ('Friday'); 'he knows an awful lot about the period and writes very well . . . he'd write a superb article on the subject.' Lord David Cecil (1902–86), younger son of the 4th Marquess of Salisbury, was a Fellow of Wadham College, Oxford, 1924–30; Fellow of New College, Oxford, 1939–69 (being Goldsmiths' Chair from 1949); author of a life of William Cowper, *The Stricken Deer* (1929). He did not write any reviews for C.

3 – Macmurray said (15 Jan.) he would like to review *The Nature of the Physical World*, but he had just done a 'longish review' of the book for *The British Weekly*.

the same book for two papers. I don't suppose the *British Weekly* would mind; our publics hardly ever overlap! and you would have a chance to say all the things you wanted to say, but might have said in *Mind*. So I hope you will reply and say that you will do it; and whether you want our review copy sent to you.

If you ever see Canon Streeter, I wish you would give him my kindest regards.

Very sincerely yours,
[T. S. Eliot]

TO *J. M. Robertson* CC

24 January 1929   [London]

My dear Robertson,

I shall be very happy to publish your jeremiads on scansion, if they can wait until the June number. I thought for a moment of squeezing them in under the guise of a review of the trifling book to which you refer; but decided that they would be lost or overlooked in that form. So may I have them for June or not?[1]

May I say that I am heartily in agreement with you? And also may I ask for chapter and verse for my statement that Shakespeare was no thinker, but that Dante was?[2] I think I can produce some other text to show that I deny that title to *both*. I am an ignorant man, but perhaps I am no more ignorant of anything than of the things that I have myself put into print. Is it to be counted a virtue or a defect, that I find my own words quite unreadable?

Ever yours,
[T. S. Eliot]

---

1 – Robertson, 'The Scansion of Shakespeare', C. 8 (July 1929), 635–41.

2 – Robertson wrote on 9 Jan.: 'You will . . . find yourself tranquilly defied on p. 5; but I don't know that that need disturb you.' See 'The Scansion of Shakespeare': 'When my friend the editor proclaims that Shakespeare had no philosophy, but that Dante had, in respect of his recital of a dogma which stultifies his life – or which his life stultifies – I am willing to waive discussion. That situation can take care of itself' (p. 636).

25 January 1929   24 Pembroke Gardens, W. 8.

My dear Eliot

Certainly hold over the article till June. I am comforted to have you with me against the rotters. And I'll allow any man merit for finding his own work (*pro. tem.*) unreadable. *Selbst-Kritik* is the beginning of wisdom. But now as to Dante & Shakespeare.

You did say (*Sh. & the Stoicism of Seneca*, p. 14):– 'In truth, neither Shakespeare nor Dante did *any real thinking* – that was not their job' – which I confess I didn't take to mean anything. But you go on:– 'When Dante says: *la sua voluntate* (etc.) it is great poetry, *& there is a great philosophy behind it*. When Sh. says 'As flies to wanton boys' (etc.) it is *equally* great poetry, though the philosophy behind it *is not great*.'

Answer. You quote from S. a *dramatic* utterance, & say it is *his*. Yet the philosophy behind *that* is a far more real thing than Dante's vacuous dogma, which has behind it no philosophy at all, but a countersense. The alleged philosophy maintains at the same time that <u>all</u> *that happens* is 'his will'. Then our peace & our dispeace are alike 'in it'.

What S. makes Kent say is not his 'philosophy': it is Kent's *pessimism* – *dramatically* fit. But when in *Winter's Tale* S. makes a character say:

> 'Nature is made better by no mean,
> But nature makes that mean' (etc.)

he is putting his own philosophy into the speaker's mouth, and it *is* true philosophy, out-diving alike Bacon and Dante: the true philosophy which obliterates *la sua voluntate e nostra pace*.

And when S. makes Prospero say with all his soul:

> And like the baseless fabric of this vision . . .
> We are such stuff
> As dreams are made on, and our little life
> Is rounded with a sleep,

he is outdiving them all again, thinking more profoundly than they ever thought, *and* putting it into great poetry which (the context admits) comes of a fervour of feeling & thought that carries him *beyond* dramatic fitness.

I admit you give Dante away, after crediting him with assimilating a 'great' philosophy. But you can't give away the dramatist, save when, by noting *dramatic* unfitness, you confess the dominion of his *philosophy*.

Q. E. D. But I ought to insert an explanatory phrase – or alter the phrase – in my paper.

Yours ever
J. M. Robertson

TO *R. P. Blackmur*[1]   CC

25 January 1929   [London]

Dear Mr Blackmur,

Thank you for your letter of the 14th instant.[2] I have not the previous letter (Mr Kirstein's) by me, but I think that you wanted the essay early in April. You shall have it then (if you need it sooner let me know); I think I will call it 'Second Thoughts on Humanism'.[3] As for the length, I think 4000 will be nearer the mark than 6000; I am a short winded writer; and the length of the longer essays in either of my books is an accurate gauge.

As for simultaneous publication in general, of the *Criterion* and the *Hound and Horn*, I shall be very glad to give you the opportunity of using anything that strikes me as suitable for you. The *Criterion* only asks of its contributors first serial rights in English; if they choose to publish things subsequently in America or in foreign languages, that is for them to arrange. So when I indicate anything to you, and you like it, will you please then write to the author and make your terms with him. For my part, I should be glad to see a certain amount of simultaneity, though an excess might be damaging to both reviews. The *Criterion* does not discriminate, but pays all its contributors at the same low rate of £2 per 1000 words; but if you vary, you would offer to each man on his actual market price.

1–R. P. Blackmur (1904–65): American literary critic who achieved a high reputation without a university degree. He was managing editor from 1928 to 1930 of the literary periodical *Hound and Horn* – which specifically emulated *The Criterion* – and in 1935 published his first, influential book, *The Double Agent: Essays in Craft and Elucidation*. On the recommendation of Allen Tate he taught from 1940 at Princeton, where he ran the Creative Arts Program. He was a Hodder Fellow; a member of the American Academy of Arts and Sciences; Vice-President of the National Institute of Arts and Letters; Fellow in American Letters at the Library of Congress; and Pitt Professor of American History and Institutions at Cambridge University. He was to publish three volumes of poetry.
2–Blackmur asked TSE to supply an exact title, probable length, and earliest date for the delivery of TSE's promised article on Babbitt and Humanism: they hoped to be able to announce it in the spring issue. He asked also after the possibilities of sharing articles.
3–'Second Thoughts on Humanism', *Hound and Horn* 2: 4 (July/Sept. 1929), 339–50; reprinted from *New Adelphi* 2: 4 (June/Aug. 1929), 304–10.

I shall have more concrete suggestions to make later. Meanwhile I take the opportunity of saying that the *Hound and Horn* interests me more at present than any other American periodical, so I take a great interest in its success. It is in the same class as the *Criterion*, the *N.R.F.*, the *Neue Schweizer Rundschau* and the *Revista de Occidente*. Your programme is exciting. Of course my opinion may not have much weight, as I was interested first by your very flattering and acute articles about myself, but I shall be just as keenly interested in the future!

Sincerely yours,
[T. S. Eliot]

TO *S. Walker*[1]   CC

25 January 1929   [London]

Dear Mr Walker,

I beg to acknowledge receipt of your letter of the 24th instant, and to confirm our arrangement that Mr Chesterton's essay which will appear in the March *Criterion* (i.e. the number which will probably appear between the 15th and the 31st March and which will probably be dated 'April') should be released for publication in America for any date after the 1st March.[2]

Yours sincerely,
[T. S. Eliot]
Editor.

TO *Desmond MacCarthy*   CC

25 January 1929   [Faber & Gwyer Ltd]

Dear MacCarthy,

Thank you for your letter of the 24th giving Campbell's address, and saying that you have no objection to the republication of his poem. As for the emolument, I ought to have explained that that was assured: *Commerce* pays very well indeed, according to English, not French standards.[3]

---

1 – A. P. Watt & Son literary agency.
2 – G. K. Chesterton, 'Is Humanism a Religion?', C. 8 (Apr. 1929), 382–93.
3 – MacCarthy urged TSE, 'we must try and secure for [Campbell] the *extra* payment.'

I shall be very glad to follow your suggestion of sending verse on to you (and should be glad if you would reciprocate).[1] There is so much, I find, that is really good enough to publish, though so little that is really first rate, that there is often little to choose between much of what one does use and much of what one does not.

Sincerely yours,
[T. S. Eliot]

TO *J. M. Robertson* CC

28 January 1929   [London]

My dear Robertson,

Your reply clears matters up a little; it reduces, that is, the margin between fact and opinion. You really exonerate me from the charge of saying that Dante was 'thinker'. But I *should* have said 'neither Shakespeare nor Dante did any *philosophical* thinking'; the phrase 'real thinking', I admit, means nothing: because no one really has any notion of what thinking is, except in rough contrast to 'not using one's mind'.

Answer to your answer: I am attacking people who take Shakespeare's dramatic utterances as personal utterances, and therefore it is not quite fair to attack me in return on another ground.

On the other hand, if you attribute one sentence to the figure Kent, rather than to Shakespeare, are you justified in assigning another to Shakespeare rather than to Prospero?

I disagree on one point of fact. Without going into the question of Predestination (which I suggest is a particularly Scottish obsession) I should interpret 'la sua voluntade e sua [*sic*] pace' not in a Calvinistic sense. It seems to me to mean that the happiness of man resides in *conforming* his will to the divine will, which is not at all the same thing as saying that 'all that happens is His will'.[2] But I think that theology might profit by the

---

1 – 'By the bye, if some poem comes to your notice which [you] think well of, and yet, for some reason or other, cannot publish in *The Criterion*, I should always be very grateful if you would ask the author to send it on to *Life and Letters*.'

2 – Cf. TSE's *Dante*, 46: 'Dante is informed by Piccarda ([*Paradiso*] Canto III) in words which even those who know no Dante know:

> *In la sua voluntade e nostra pace.*
> *His will is our peace.*

It is the mystery of the inequality, and of the indifference of that inequality, in blessedness, of the blessed. It is all the same, and yet each degree differs.'

Russell–Whitehead Theory of Types,[1] which is a more formal statement of Bradley's Degrees of Truth.[2]

I can't pretend to give the Dramatist away. But then he never gives himself away.

Yours ever,
[T. S. Eliot]

TO *I. A. Richards*   CC

28 January 1929   [London]

My dear Richards,

I must apologise for not having already answered your enquiry about your MSS., indeed I thought I had done so. I have now looked in all the probable, and some of the impossible places; but I had and have a strong impression that I handed it back to you on the evening you spent with us, and when, you remember, we had a brief discussion: may you not have left it in Dulwich?[3]

I am very sorry that you have been tempted by the orient again; though I dare say that a year or so at Cambridge continuously is enough to make one homesick for Pekin.[4] I suppose you can find mountains which have never been scaled in northern China. My brother in law's father is president of a Missionary College, and invented the first Chinese typewriter, with a circular keyboard on a pivot.[5] But I wish you were not going: my interest in Cambridge is reduced.

1–Alfred North Whitehead and Bertrand Russell, in *Principia Mathematica* (3 vols, Cambridge, 1910–13), sought to demonstrate that mathematics was all a matter of logicism. Vol. I follows 'Preliminary Explanations of Ideas and Notations' with 'The Theory of Logical Types'. TSE acquired his copy of vol. I in July 1914.

2–F. H. Bradley argues, in *Appearance and Reality: A Metaphysical Essay* (1893), that there are degrees of truth in the world of appearance; only the Absolute is absolutely true.

3–IAR asked (n.d.), 'if you can easily send me that scrap of MSS back (the part of a chapter on belief) – if you have sent it to me back in the past sometime and I have mislaid it – which may well be – could you tell me.' He replied to this letter from TSE: 'Sorry to have bothered you over that odd bit of MSS. I've probably left it at Dulwich as you suggest. In any case there is no difficulty for me in having a version typed for the printer.'

4–'It is lucky we didn't take a house or a flat in London as I now have had a tempting invitation to Pekin – to go and be a Professor there at Tsing Hua [University] for a year. So we shall be leaving in June returning in Oct. 1930 – when you will probably be deciding that you have had enough of Chester Terrace, and we – if we bring home a staff of Chinese servants – will be able to take it over!'

5–Alfred Dwight Sheffield (1871–1961) – who married TSE's sister Ada in 1905 – was born in China, where his father, the Revd D. Z. Sheffield (d. 1913), missionary and president

We must certainly get into this belief matter within the next five months: preferably in Cambridge, but if not, in London. But I hope you don't overrate my philosophical and gegenstandological talents: I am only a smatterer. The only value of my collaboration would be, if we could plot it out so as to work from different approaches, and so hope to get some sort of triangulation by it. When I have got the weary Donne book done I should like to tackle it seriously, even if it [. . .] But what I should like to discuss first, is some sort of scheme for me to work on, complementing but not duplicating your own lines.[1]

By the way, I should like to get something more out of you for the *Criterion* before you go. I had been meaning to write and ask whether you would tackle Fernandez' book on Personality, at least as thoroughly as you did Read. I had held it up, understanding that two more volumes were to appear; but I have had a recent letter from him, saying that it will be a long time before he can do more, and that he would be very glad to have an English criticism of it. I think he is worth your trouble, if you have the time: I admit that his prose is very undigestible.[2]

(You are welcome to Chester Terrace, unless someone else snaps at it first: but it is a long way from Liverpool Street, and not very near to Euston.[)]

With best regards to Mrs Richards,
Yours ever,
[T. S. E.]

Do you know anyone in Cambridge who can review mathematical physical books intelligently for the general public?[3]

---

of Tungchow College, invented in 1899 a typewriter capable of printing 4,000 Chinese characters.

1–IAR wrote: 'It seems to me if we are ever going to discuss problems of belief we ought to begin before many more months have passed. I should be sorry to postpone it altogether until the nineteen-thirties.' He replied to TSE's response above (n.d.): 'I shall probably be sending you a sheaf of notes on Belief as a first step to our dividing the subject in discussion later. I am rather anxious to get the main heads of the subject arranged on paper in some form before breaking off with it for my Peking year. I hope it won't mean reading any German, if so I'm completely out of it – but I don't think it should be necessary. There seems to me to be more than enough to say that hasn't been properly reflected upon without' (*Selected Letters*, 49).

2–'I'd like to write something on Fernandez – I'll have another shot at reading him again soon.' (*ibid.*) In the event, Fernandez's book was not reviewed in C.

3–'I'm seeing some of the younger physicists & logicians tonight & will perhaps be able to hear of somebody worth printing. I've been reading Eddington lately with a renewed sense that Physics is reaching a point where its *methods* can be understood. I think they are the methods of *all* denotative explanation, *psychological* as well as physical, only carried further and if so the general consequences as to the inherent limitations of descriptions

TO *Marguerite Caetani*   CC

29 January 1929   [London]

Dear Marguerite,

I must explain to you what happened. After I had your letter saying
that you would like to use also Campbell's poem in *Life and Letters*, I
wrote again to Mrs Nicolson,[1] asking her for Campbell's address in order
to write to him.[2] But it appears that she had left for the North, and I only
recently traced her back to Berlin, where her husband is in the Embassy.
So when I got your wire I wrote to Desmond MacCarthy, who replied
saying that *Life and Letters* would not object to republication, providing
that Campbell himself got paid for it; and it is MacCarthy who gave me
the address I wired to you (Poste Restante, Martigues, Bouches du Rhone)
for Campbell. I trust that you understood that you were to write to him
there yourself; and I am writing to him by this to explain what happened.
I hope that it will all be arranged in time for your next number. I don't
know your translator; but I know that all translations in *Commerce* are
good.

> Always affectionately,
> [Tom]

TO *Orlo Williams*   CC

29 January 1929   [London]

Dear Williams,

This is just to tell you that I like your story very much. The only
question is one of time: usually I wonder where the next printable piece
of fiction is to come from; but at present I have a waiting list of stories
from Powys, Mrs Dobrée, Hans Siemsen, Schlumberger, and one or two
others, all of which have been accepted and ought to [be] printed more
or less in rotation. I don't think I could conscientiously use yours before
the end of the year. So may I keep it, and if you do want to publish it

---

are important. But they don't, as far as I can see, lie at all in the directions Eddington and
[J. W. N.] Sullivan for example, seem to think. It's significant that the physicists should be
trying to hand over the fundamental problems to the psychologists just at the time when
most psychologists are wanting to hand them over to the neurologists!' (*Ibid.*)

1–Mrs Harold Nicolson: Vita Sackville-West.

2–Caetani had asked (7 Jan. 1929) whether TSE thought 'it would a good idea to publish
at the same time as the poem of Roy Campbell you sent me, the poem he gave to Life &
Letters a few months ago[?]'

earlier elsewhere, will you just send Miss Townsend[1] a card, and ask her to return it?[2]

Would lunch one day next week be possible for you? We have not met for a long time.

Yours ever,
[T. S. Eliot]

TO *Richard Church*   CC

Tuesday 29 January 1929   [London]

Dear Church,

Many thanks for your note of the 27th, enclosing short notice. There is no hurry at all about the book on Darley, particularly if the book is a good one. Do a long note on it for the June No.[3] I will send for the Collins for you; and if you think it might make the excuse for a short essay on Collins like your Goldsmith, you will let me know.[4] By all means do a short notice of Strong, who I believe deserves encouragement.[5] I was sorry not to see you at the Grove last Thursday, and hope that you can be there on Thursday week.

Yours ever,
[T. S. Eliot]

TO *John Macmurray*   CC

30 January 1929   [London]

Dear Mr Macmurray,

Thank you very much for your letter [29 Jan.]. As for the length, I should say from 1000 to 1500 words, as it is an important review: as for time, that is now for you to choose. I had really wanted it for the March number; but that number is now nearly all in press; so that I could not

---

1 – TSE's secretary.
2 – Williams, 'An Idyll', C. 9 (July 1930), 689–709.
3 – Church, untitled review of Claude Collier Abbott, *The Life and Letters of George Darley, Poet and Critic*, C. 8 (July 1929), 727–32.
4 – 'Oliver Goldsmith', C. 8 (Apr. 1929), 437–44. Untitled review of H. W. Garrod's *Collins*, and *The Poems of William Collins*, ed. Edmund Blunden, C. 9 (Oct. 1929), 119–22.
5 – 'Shall I do a short notice on L. A. G. Strong, whose little book is full of good work, likely to be overlooked nowadays.' Untitled review of *At Glenan Cross: A Sequence*, C. 8 (Apr. 1929), 562–3.

give you more than a week from Friday next. But if you cannot do it at all by then, or if conscience or desire tells you that you ought to have more time, then do it at your leisure for the June number. The *Criterion* can often afford to be late, and wants its reviewers to be able to write articles under their own conditions and without pressure. At the same time, if (knowing the book so well as you do) you could find time to give me the review for March, I should be very grateful. But I leave it entirely to you; only I should like to know which.

> With many thanks,
> Yours sincerely,
> [T. S. Eliot]

to *M. C. D'Arcy*   cc

31 January 1929   [London]

My dear D'Arcy,

I owe you many apologies for not having answered your kind invitation immediately and also for not having answered your previous letter.[1] I have been very busy lately and my wife is just recovering from the current form of influenza. I should be delighted to go as your guest to some meeting of the L.S.S.R., which must be an extremely interesting affair, even without von Huegel.[2] But I am afraid that I cannot venture to make evening engagements for the immediate present. I am very disappointed and do hope that you will ask me on some other occasion, and not having seen you during the vacation it would have been an additional pleasure. I trust however that we shall meet in any case during the Easter holidays.

One of your young friends has written to me and I am hoping to see him soon.

> Yours very sincerely,
> [T. S. Eliot]

1–D'Arcy sent a postcard (postmarked 19 Jan.) to invite TSE to come as his guest to a meeting of the London Society for the Study of Religion (LSSR), on Fri., 25 Jan.
2–D'Arcy (24 Jan.): 'The L.S.S.R. is rather an interesting society ([Baron Friedrich] Von Hügel used to be the main force in it).'

TO *Herbert Read*   CC

31 January 1929   [*The Criterion*]

Dear Herbert,

I am very sorry to bother you with this stuff but I should be most grateful if you would look at the enclosed four contributions and see if you think any of them are any good. I am rather distrustful of my judgement on Muggeridge's work.[1] As you know he is a protégé of Bonamy's. Kay Boyle you have probably seen in some of the American periodicals, some of it I know is bad stuff but I don't feel quite sure of the rest. Let me have them back when we meet again. I doubt whether the other book you want will come in time but will have it forwarded to you at once.

                                   Yours ever,
                                   [T. S. E.]

TO *H. J. C. Grierson*   CC

1 February 1929   [London]

Dear Grierson,

Thank you for your letter of the 26th.[2] I quite see how you feel about it, although it would have been more interesting to have had a review from you than from anyone else. It is certainly annoying about the Oxford Press and very foolish of them. I should think it would be to the interest of the Press to publish themselves cheaper editions of the texts of that whole series. I also agree with you about the Nonesuch Press.

I look forward to seeing you again in March.

                                   Sincerely yours,
                                   [T. S. Eliot]

1–It is not known what article Malcolm Muggeridge submitted.
2–Grierson had decided not to review Hayward's *Donne*. 'I should have nothing harsh to say of Hayward's work for he has done it very well, though I do not agree with all his amendments. But I was a little sore with the Nonesuch Press for cutting in with a cheap text before I had the opportunity of using mine in that way . . . But it does not matter. My edition in the Oxford Poets will be out soon.'

TO *Desmond MacCarthy*   CC

1 February 1929   [London]

Dear MacCarthy,

Many thanks for your letter of the 31st. First about W. J. Lawrence, I am afraid that I cannot deal with any more of his work at present.[1] He is rather a prolific writer and I have recently accepted from him a sequel to an article which we published some time ago.[2]

I shall be going through our own collection of verse manuscripts in a few days.

I look forward with keen interest to what you will say about my book in the *Sunday Times* and I am delighted to hear that you are reviewing it yourself. I shall probably write to you about it.[3]

Yours sincerely,
[T. S. Eliot]

TO *I. A. Richards*   CC

1 February 1929   [London]

My dear Richards,

I am writing to you now about a matter quite unconnected with any previous correspondence. It is about the case of a young American Jew

---

1–'I think we might occasionally be of service to writers in general by sending each other MSS,' said MacCarthy. 'For instance, [W. J.] Lawrence (the Shakespeare scholar) has sent me a good essay on the Dedication of Early English Plays and the facts which may be deduced from their rarity. I should like to print this, but it strikes me as a little too specialised in interest to suit the make up of Life and Letters at the present time.' W. J. Lawrence (1862–1940) was a theatre and textual historian; author of *The Elizabethan Playhouse and Other Studies* (1912).

2–Lawrence, 'The Pirates of *Hamlet*', C. 8 (July 1929), 642–6, was a sequel to 'The Mystery of the *Hamlet* First Quarto', MC (May 1927), repr. in *Shakespeare's Workshop* (Oxford, 1928).

3–'I have written about *For Lancelot Andrewes* in the Sunday Times this week . . . While writing [the review] I was a little anxious about what you would think of it yourself. I have disputed two points with you – your analysis of Machiavelli and your admiration for Andrewes' prose. I had a great deal more to say, and I am not sure whether I have not left out several things which even in that short space ought to have been said, but I hope I have conveyed to the reader my respect for your book as a whole.

'If by any chance you should have time, or thought it worth while to communicate to me what you thought of my arguments I should be very pleased, but do not do this unless it comes quite natural to you to do so.' See 'The World of Books: Anglo-Catholic Criticism', *Sunday Times*, 3 Feb. 1929, 10; and TSE's letter to MacCarthy, 6 Feb. below.

named Dahlberg who has come to me for advice.[1] I understand that he

1–Edward Dahlberg (1900–77), novelist and essayist, was born in Boston to a single mother, and spent most of his teenage years in the Jewish Orphan Asylum in Cleveland. He went on to the University of California at Berkeley and to Columbia University. In the late 1920s he lived in Paris and in London, where his autobiographical novel *Bottom Dogs* was published with an introduction by D. H. Lawrence. After visiting Germany in 1933, he was for a while a member of the Communist Party, and in later years made his living as a writer and college teacher. Later works include *Those Who Perish* (1934), *Do These Bones Live* (essays, 1941), *Because I Was Flesh* (autobiography, 1964), *Alms for Oblivion* (essays and reminiscences, 1964), *The Confessions of Edward Dahlberg* (1971).

On 7 Jan. 1929 F. S. Flint had written to TSE: 'The author of the enclosed poems is the Edward Dahlberg whom you have met at the Grove.

'I know very little about Dahlberg, except that he has written a novel, which I have read, and which D. H. Lawrence thinks so highly of that he has offered to recommend it to Curtis Brown and to the Viking Press. It is a novel of street and orphanage life in the United States and of the subsequent adventures of the victims, written, but without ostentation, in the dialect of the American streets. I think it shows a great deal of talent.

'Dahlberg is a graduate of Columbia University (I have seen his diploma); and he came to London with the idea of taking the London M.A. Unfortunately for him, his source of money in America went wrong almost as soon as he arrived here, and, although he says he will have about £2 a week on which to live, he hasn't the money to pay his matriculation and other fees. Even if he could save this out of his very meagre income (an income that is by no means certain), he cannot afford the time, because he has to get back to the United States as quickly as possible in order to help keep his mother.

'He wanted to take a part-time job; but apparently this is forbidden by the Ministry of Labour regulations. I sent him off this afternoon to the American Relief Society, to see whether they could do anything for him. Meanwhile, can I ask you to look at these poems, and, if you think well enough of them to accept them for the *Criterion*, would it be possible to pay Dahlberg in advance for them? I would recommend this, if it is possible, only if you think the poems are worth it. I'm afraid Dahlberg may find himself being repatriated at the expense of his government.'

Dahlberg was to write, in a later (undated) letter to HR: 'When I was in London, and a friend of the late F. S. Flint, a true linguist and the real founder of the Imagist movement in poetry, whom Pound scarcely mentions, he asked me whether I should like to come to a pub where Eliot, you [HR], Flint, and the deceased, gallant [T. M.] Ragg, came to lunch. Flint said to me: "Tom does not like Jews." However, Eliot was gracious and kind and did all that he could to be of use to me. I blame Eliot for nothing but the books that he has written' (Edward Dahlberg and Herbert Read, *Truth Is More Sacred: A Critical Exchange on Modern Literature* [London: Routledge & Kegan Paul, 1961], 173).

In a later work, *The Confessions of Edward Dahlberg* (1971), he wrote: 'Frank Flint asked if I would like to lunch with T. S. Eliot, T. M. Ragg, an enchanting Irishman, Frank Morley, and Herbert Read . . . Flint informed me that Eliot did not care for Jews . . .

'To my amazement the literary figures who gathered weekly at the Chelsea pub showed me unusual respect . . . As was my wont, I desired to admire Eliot. I did not care for that dull tractate on Lancelot Andrewes, but I did wish to please though I sought no advantage of him . . .

'At one of the luncheons Eliot engaged Frank Flint in a discourse on Matthew Arnold and Walt Whitman . . . Eliot turned to me abruptly and asked, "Which one do you think is more important, Matthew Arnold or Walt Whitman?" I hadn't the slightest idea, but I had caught his drift and he got no sluggish reply. "Without ambiguity, I would elect Matthew Arnold." . . .

'Eliot was delighted . . .' (222–3).

took a B.A. degree at Columbia University. He wants to teach English in some American College or University but came over to London with the idea of taking an M.A. or Ph.D. at London University, as [the] degree would be very useful in getting a job at home. Since arriving he has been disappointed in two respects.

In the first place his supplies of money from home are not going to be what he expected.

In the second place he wanted to work especially at aesthetics having done a good deal of work in philosophy as well as literature, and does not find anyone at London University of much use to him. He appears therefore to be hungry, both physically and mentally. His problem is rather difficult as he must try to earn a little while he is studying and at the same time he wants to study somewhere there is a teacher who can help him. At present I believe, he has about £2 a week from America and he tells me that he has got a job of indefinite duration as a reader for Putnam at £1 a week. Putnams have also taken a novel of his which I am told D. H. Lawrence thinks highly of. I have seen some of his work which has merit but is rather tediously in the manner of the American Mont Parnasse school.

I told him I would ask you first whether he could get any sort of degree at Cambridge, second whether in your absence there will be any able man doing your sort of work in Literature and Psychology, and third what he could live on in Cambridge. Personally I don't see much hope for him. He could live more cheaply abroad and take a degree at a foreign university but it is doubtful if he could earn any money there. I should imagine it would cost him very much more to live in Cambridge than in London and I don't see how he could pick up any money there either. I simply wanted to find out anything I could for him before advising him to get back to America as quickly as possible.

You needn't bother to write a long letter about this but I should be extremely grateful if you could give me a few lines of opinion before next Tuesday when he is coming to see me again.[1]

[Yours ever,

T. S. E.]

1–IAR responded (n.d.: c. Feb. 1929): 'Comparing the costs for the neediest people I have known recently I make out that about £200 is the least per year that anybody can scrape through with here. Of course by going to no lectures and seeing few people a little could be knocked off. £220 is the minimum contemplated by County Council Scholarship Awards – this for men who are receiving ordinary amounts of tuition etc and membership of some College. A man taking an M.Litt might do things perhaps thirty pounds cheaper – but unless

1 February 1929   *The Monthly Criterion,*
Candlemass Eve   24 Russell Square

Dear Bonamy,

Yours of the 13th ult. received. Also received damn you a well dressed young black named Annam (?) who has deposited portions of an essay on Kant's categorical imperative and who drops in now and then to ask whether I have read it. I think Lloyd ought to prevent you from exporting such things. I understand how you feel about Strachey and perhaps I ought not to have imposed it on you. Gone to press, but I felt you were holding yourself in rather.[1] I lean more and more to the opinion that it is a shoddy piece of humbug. The time however is not quite ripe for showing him up: meanwhile perhaps Lewis will do it, if he does anything.

I am glad you can speak so favourably of Andrewes, beyond my hopes. Your criticism is useful, because it makes me see I have probably given a wrong impression of my attitude towards Babbitt.[2] My point is:

---

he has some great & evident gain to expect from being here – he shouldn't be advised to do it. There isn't anyone doing any real psychology as well as literature here except me. There is Leavis (Dr F. R. Leavis) who is I believe a good supervisor on literary and general critical matters but I shouldn't say he was worth coming here under difficulties for. Nor on the whole are the Research Degrees (M. Litt., Ph.D.s) much good to anyone. We are doing our best in English to abolish them – in most cases they just waste a man's time and their window-dressing value – for good men – is less than is often supposed. I might recommend a medievalist to work for one but not a man who is interested in general critical questions' (*Selected Letters*, 48–9).

1 – 'As to Strachey, I was relieved to get your letter saying that you did not think *E & E* [*Elizabeth and Essex*] a very good book, as I had already roughed out an unfavourable review, & thought that my view might have been due to splenetic afterChristmasheit [*sic*] . . . I am interested in your remark that had you been writing a signed notice in the *Times* you would have been more severe. That is, of course, the right attitude, and I personally like signing attacks. But as far as I am concerned as regards Strachey, I feel that there are things I could say anonymously, which would sound impertinent (I mean cheeky) as coming from a junior and inferior would-be biographer – e.g. 'His style is affected.' I wish I had thought of saying what you say in *Lancelot Andrewes*, namely that he really belongs to the Shaw generation.' TSE had reviewed Lytton Strachey's *Elizabeth and Essex* in the *TLS*, 6 Dec. 1928, 959; BD reviewed it in *C.* 8 (Apr. 1929), 524–9.

2 – Of *FLA*, 'I like it very much indeed, the first and last essays more than anything you have written. My trouble is, that though I wish I could agree, I can't. I see the necessity for God intellectually. The senses can never be satisfied, as Herbert remarks, and nor can the mind: God is the only permanent satisfaction . . . Valentine says the Babbitt essay is just the thing for people in my position. Quite – but then I am in the position of a Babbitt (more or less) who sees the validity of your criticism. You say throughout, I take it, that ethics are no good without God – but cannot one love order without loving God? On the whole I do love order – and I find it in humanism. But since I agree with you about humanism, I am in the

I don't object in the least to the position of Babbitt for Babbitts. It is a perfectly possible position for an individual. I only say: this is not a doctrine which can help the world in general. The individual can certainly love order without loving God. The people cannot. And when I say the people, don't think that I mean the inhabitants of any slum or suburb or Belgravian square; I mean any number that can be addressed in print. I should say of humanism as many say of mysticism: it is unutterable and uncommunicable. It is for each humanist alone. It is not only silly, but damnable, to say that Christianity is necessary for the people, until one feels that it is necessary for oneself. I'm not attacking humanism: I should be more hostile to a catholicism without humanism; I only mean to say that humanism is an ingredient, indeed a necessary one, in any proper catholicism; and I wanted to point out the danger of Babbitt's leading some of his followers to a kind of catholicism which I should dislike as much as he does.[1]

I am sorry that your dancing has been ill-fated, but that is perhaps a proper punishment for imitating a barbarous race such as the Russians.[2]

Yes, I agree that leisure seems to diminish.[3] I have saved the Cleopatra, which I knew to be by you[4] (though a true Bolovian would have drawn the interesting parallel) but have not yet read it – speaking of leisure. I expect to like it, because someone asked me whether I wrote it. I was talking of you to D. Higham of Curtis Brown, who has a very high opinion of your commercial future.

Sure, I will suggest a successor. To begin with, what of Sherard Vines, who has served his time in Tokyo, and is now at Hull? He ought to be able to stand anything.

Ever yours,
Tom

---

disgusting, silly, and patronizing position of people who say that Christianity is necessary for other people but not for them or rather I would be if I could bear to go to church as an example to the lower classes.'

1 – In a letter to HR (9 Apr. 1929), BD was to lament that the *Criterion* seemed to be becoming a 'Religio-Political organ': 'It seems to me to have lost its freedom . . . we are asked to condemn the Revolution because it was not Anglo-Catholic! I am beginning to feel a little uncomfortable in that galley' (Victoria; cited in King, *The Last Modern*, 89).

2 – BD had hurt his knee while trying out a Russian dance at a party – 'a thing by no means becoming the dignity of a middle-aged man and a Professor'.

3 – 'Life is altogether too busy and too nervous here. I was looking at one of my own books the other day. I did *not* say "My God, what a genius I had when I wrote that book!" but "Lord, what a lot of leisure I must have had when I wrote that book!"'

4 – BD wondered whether TSE would 'approve' his essay 'Cleopatra and "That criticall warr"', *TLS*, 11 Oct. 1928, 717–18.

P.S. A good toothpaste is Phillips Dental Magnesia, made by the proprietors of the Milk. I shall have a sample sent to you.

TO *Jean Stewart*[1]   CC

1 February 1929   [London]

Dear Miss Stewart,

Thank you for your letter of the 20th, enclosing your translation of Schlumberger's story, 'L'enfant qui s'accuse'. I liked it very much. I had not seen the story before: I suppose it appeared in the *N.R.F.*?

I should like to use it. That is for me merely a question of time; for I have four or five stories already accepted, which I must use more or less in order; and the *Criterion* cannot use a great deal of fiction. Would you like to send it elsewhere? If so, you shall have it back; but I should like to keep it until you want it.

It is difficult to know what to suggest for translation. Publishers are not, as a rule, keen about translations of French novels, because most of them appeal only to those who read them in French. If you are not averse to heavy work, I wonder whether some of Etienne Gilson's works on mediaeval philosophy might be possible? There is also Fernandez' book on Personality. I liked your translation, although I have not read the original: if you have any authors in mind, whom you do not know personally, I should be glad to help.

[*Incomplete: text runs off the page of the carbon copy*]

TO *Franklin Gary*   Princeton C0896/cc

1 February 1929   [London]

Dear Mr Gary,

It is true that Father D'Arcy has spoken to me of you and your friend more than once.[2] I should be very glad to see you both. You write from Oxford and do not say when you are likely to be in London. It makes very little difference to me as I am here almost all the time, but week ends are not very convenient. Will you give me some idea of your movements?

1–Daughter of TSE's Cambridge friend H. F. Stewart.
2–Franklin Gary (a student at Balliol College, Oxford) wrote (24 Jan.) to seek an audience for himself and his friend James Burnham.

Your name is not a common one. Have you by any chance relatives in Baltimore?[1]

Sincerely yours,
T. S. Eliot

TO *Huw Menai*   CC

1 February 1929   [London]

Dear Mr Menai,

I must apologise for not having written to you before. It was a long time before I was able to read any of your poems with attention; and while I was thinking them over, Mrs Harold Nicolson told me that the Hogarth Press were likely to bring out a volume.[2] I expect to see Mr Leonard Woolf early next week, and shall enquire whether the poems from which Lady Dorothy Wellesley selected, include all of those you sent me. If not, she ought to see them before the book is made up. After that, I hope that I may arrange to publish something of yours – with your permission – in the *Criterion*.

Sincerely yours,
[T. S. Eliot]

TO *His Mother*   TS Houghton

3 February 1929   57 Chester Terrace, s.w.1.

My dearest Mother,

I was very glad to get your sweet letter. Your enclosures about Clarence Little interested me very much; it was the first that I had heard about his resignation; and I know nothing more than what the cutting says.[3] I should think it very likely that he might become president of Harvard in time; but I should hardly expect Lowell to resign for many years. Lowell has accomplished a great deal, I believe, in his term of office; and the position was a difficult one for the immediate successor of Charles Eliot.[4]

---

1 – Gary was not related to the Gary family of Baltimore.
2 – *The Passing of Guto and Other Poems* (1929).
3 – Clarence C. Little (1888–1971), a Harvard contemporary of TSE, was President of the University of Michigan from 1925 – resigning in 1929 (as TSE's letter says); see note on p. 655, below.
4 – Abbott Lawrence Lowell (1856–1943), a brother of the poet Amy Lowell, succeeded

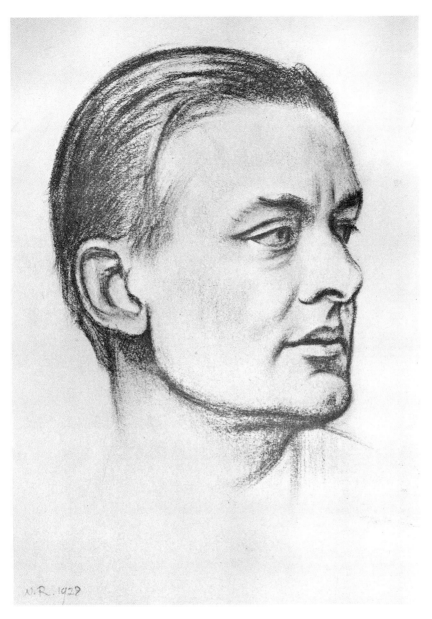

Portrait of T. S. Eliot. Drawing by William Rothenstein, 1928.

Vivien Eliot in the garden of 57 Chester Terrace,
with Peter the dog, June 1928.

Eliot with 'Charlie Chaplin
moustache', taken by
E. McKnight Kauffer, 1928.

Eliot in Chester Terrace garden
with Peter the dog.

T. S. Eliot's mother, Charlotte, in Cambridge, 1928,
taken by Henry Ware Eliot.

Eliot in the garden of
57 Chester Terrace, May 1928.

Leonard and Virginia Woolf
on holiday in Cassis,
French Riviera, 1928.

T. S. Eliot reading,
photographed by
Maurice Beck and
Helen McGregor,
*c.*1928.

I. A. and Dorothy
Richards on their
honeymoon in Nara,
Japan, 1927.

A. L. Rowse, *c.*1928.

Edward McKnight Kauffer, 1927.

Thomas MacGreevy, looking from
his rooms at the École Normale
Supérieure, *c.*1928.

Frontispiece drawing by
E. McKnight Kauffer for
A Song for Simeon,
Faber & Gwyer, 1928.

Alexis St Leger Leger (pen-name, St-John Perse), *c*.1930.

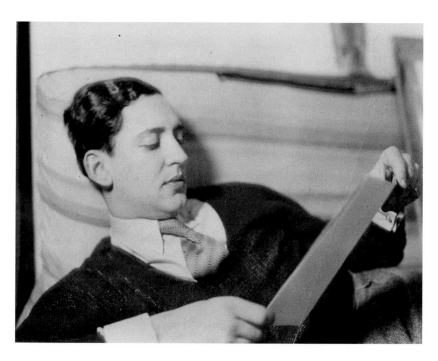

Edouard Roditi, Berlin, 1931.

Mario Praz, 1934.

For Lancelot Andrewes: Essays on Style and Order, Faber & Gwyer, 1928. Jacket design by Edward Bawden.

Marguerite Chapin Caetani, *c.*1930.

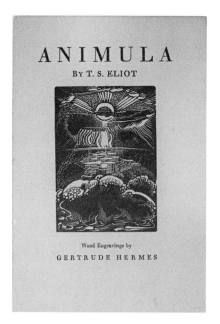

Front cover of *Animula*,
Faber & Faber Ltd, 1929. Wood-
engraving by Gertrude Hermes.

Frontispiece wood-engraving
by Gertrude Hermes
for *Animula*, 1929.

Front cover of *Dante*,
Faber & Faber, 1929.
Jacket design by Rex Whistler.

The next president will have an easier time. I was reading yesterday Lowell's Report to the Overseers. I think I shall hardly be able to find my way about Cambridge, so much seems to have been built and altered and demolished since I was there. I believe that things are much better than they were in my time. I had a talk with Babbitt about it when he was here. I was one of the victims of the 'elective system'. I have always regretted that as an undergraduate I did not stick to Latin and Greek, and some mathematics, and leave alone all the things I dabbled in year after year. As I said to Babbitt, the old system by which a student merely chose his courses in any combination according to caprice, really did the most harm to the most active minds. I was so interested in many things that I did nothing thoroughly, and was always thinking about new subjects that I wanted to study, instead of following out any one. Enough money was spent on my education to have made me a great scholar. Yet I suppose that everyone regrets the imperfections of his own education – I have no one to blame but myself and partly President Eliot.[1] I am sure that I should have made a very poor professor of Philosophy, because, after my first enthusiasm, I found modern philosophy to be nothing more than a logomachy, believed in by its professors, chiefly because they had to make their living out of it. (I might have made a teacher of Latin and Greek, if I had pursued my studies properly). But on the other hand, I learnt all that I know about writing prose from studying the works of F. H. Bradley, and from the criticism I had from H. H. Joachim while at Oxford;[2] and

---

Charles William Eliot as President of Harvard University: he held office 1909–33. Among his mixed achievements, he did away with C. W. Eliot's educational model of 'electives' and established the perdurable system of majoring in a particular discipline.

1 – Charles W. Eliot, who was President of Harvard, 1869–1909, did away with a prescribed classical curriculum in favour of 'electives'. See Samuel Eliot Morison, *Three Centuries of Harvard, 1636–1936* (Cambridge, Mass., 1936); Hugh Hawkins, *Between Harvard and America: The Educational Leadership of Charles W. Eliot* (New York: Oxford University Press, 1972). Gail McDonald remarks, in *Learning to be Modern: Pound, Eliot, and the American University* (Oxford, 1993), that TSE 'was able to select whatever attracted him . . . As a student, T. S. Eliot was the model Charles W. Eliot had in mind in establishing the elective system: one to whom self-discipline would come naturally in the pursuit of an intellectual goal. Given the range of choice, Eliot's selection of courses was conservative, a continuation of the classical and humanistic studies in which he had excelled at the Smith and Milton Academies. Seven of the eighteen undergraduate courses he chose were in Greek and Latin. The remainder were largely in modern languages (German, French, and – through study of Dante – Italian), English and comparative literature, and philosophy. He worked efficiently, finishing the requirements for his BA degree in three years and those for his MA in the fourth' (28).

2 – Harold H. Joachim (1868–1938): Fellow and Tutor in Philosophy at Merton College, Oxford, 1897–1919; British Idealist philosopher and follower of F. H. Bradley; author of *The Nature of Truth* (1906), an influential account of the 'coherence theory' of truth. TSE

my study of philosophy has been of great advantage to me in directions in which I never expected it to be. So one never knows what to regret and what to be glad of!

I wish indeed that I could write a book that would have the sale of Lytton Strachey's. But if one has begun by building up a reputation of one kind, it is usually better to build further on that, in the long run, than to try to reach a new public. My books really do very well, of their kind, though they do not bring in much money. My Poems have sold about 3000 copies, which is very good for poetry; my recent little book of essays has sold about 1200 copies so far in this country, and is to be published separately in America by Doubleday Doran & Co. My single poem, 'The Journey of the Magi', has sold about 2500, and the 'Song for Simeon' so far about 1500. What is agreeable is that all these things go on selling regularly, a few each week. You see, a book like Lytton Strachey's is bought by many people because they think it is the last word in intellectual writing; and as it is really very easy to read they think it proves that they are very intellectual themselves. But I think that my book on Donne, the revision of my Cambridge lectures, will have a larger sale than any of my prose books; because it will be bigger, and will be a continuous book instead of a collection of previously printed essays.

---

recalled buying *The Nature of Truth* at Harvard, and taking it with him in 1914 to Oxford, where Joachim was his tutor. According to Brand Blanshard, it was said that 'if you started any sentence in the *Nichomachean Ethics* of Aristotle, Joachim could complete it for you, of course in Greek' ('Eliot at Oxford', *T. S. Eliot: Essays from the Southern Review*, ed. James Olney, 1988). TSE wrote an obituary letter in *The Times* (4 Aug. 1938), and paid tribute to Joachim in the introduction to *Knowledge and Experience in the Philosophy of F. H. Bradley*, 1964). In a late letter, he said 'he taught me more about how to write good prose than any other teacher I have ever had' as well as revealing 'the importance of punctuation in the interpretation of a text such as that of the *Posterior Analytics*' (24 June 1963: Merton College). Aurelia Hodgson, partner of the poet Ralph Hodgson, took notes from talks with TSE during Jan.–July 1932; her jottings include this anecdote: 'Once he was reading aloud a paper of his, to his tutor. Joachim sat in silence, smoking. Presently he removed his pipe and only commented: "Why do you use metaphors?" The inflection dropped in the middle of the question – as Eliot imitated it – most effectively. The lesson did not need repeating.' (EVE) TSE's notes on Joachim's lectures on Aristotle's *Nichomachean Ethics*, 1914–15, are at Houghton (MS AM1691.14 (17). On 6 July 1915 Joachim penned this testimonial: 'Mr. T. S. Eliot spent last year (Oct. 1914–June 1915) in working at Philosophy at Merton College, Oxford. During that time, he was my pupil, & brought me Essays (partly on modern Logic & Metaphysics, but mainly on the philosophy of Plato & Aristotle) every week. I was greatly impressed with his ability & enthusiasm for the subject, & also with his conscientiousness & patient endeavour to master the details in every piece of work. From what I have seen of him & of his work, I am quite sure that he would make a most successful teacher: & that he would deserve & win the affection, as well as the respect, of his pupils' (copy with EVE).

I have been looking about at houses and flats lately, as we really intend to move into something more easily run than this house, and in a part of town nearer more of our friends. I enclose, to amuse you, some sketches I made of the plan of a house in St. Johns Wood (that is half way between Clarence Gate Gardens and Mrs Haigh-Wood's). It was very attractive, and had a very large studio attached; but the neighbourhood was rather dreary, and also, though rather a bargain, the house would have been difficult and expensive to run. In London, the older sort of houses are expensive to run, because they were built when servants were easily to be had at low wages; and newer houses, where there are any, are expensive to get. But like other cities, London is becoming more and more overrun with flats. Many new blocks of flats are being built, but they are luxurious and very expensive; and apparently are taken by people who had had big houses, and find the cost of maintaining a staff of servants now too much for them. So for people like ourselves it is as difficult to find a moderate priced and easily run small house or large flat as ever. But we could manage with one less room than we have; because all of the rooms in this house are so tiny that it is very difficult and uncomfortable to have more than two or three guests at a time. We are going to see what is called an 'upper part', that is the upper part of a house the ground floor of which is a shop.

I must stop now. Vivienne has been very busy lately, and is very tired; she has had to get two new servants – in a little house like this, one servant can't get through the work, and two seem to crowd the place out! – and train them, and we don't know yet whether they will be satisfactory. But she is very good at handling servants; only she worries if everything is not kept absolutely clean and tidy.

> With very much love from both,
> your devoted son,
> Tom

TO *Leonard Woolf* TS Sussex

5 February 1929 *The Monthly Criterion*

Dear Leonard,

I was particularly disappointed not to be able to lunch with you to-day. I should fake an excuse to anyone else; but you know already that I am never quite sure of being able to keep any engagement. This occasion has to do with a panic about a servant.

I wonder if Wednesday or Thursday of next week would be possible for you, as I am fairly certain of those two days? I hate to be such a nuisance.

I wanted to ask you whether before trying to see Hart[1] I ought first as a matter of form to put the matter to V.'s doctor. She does see him from time to time; he has followed our affairs for years. I had rather be quite open with him about it. I don't know whether it would be professional for him to do so, but if he would communicate what he knows himself, and the clinical notes he had from France, it might be very useful, too.

That is the only personal point I had to bring up when I saw you. I am handicapped here too, as several of the staff are away with flu: but may I send you another MSS. volume of verse, by one Walter Lowenfels. I doubt whether it would do for you, but I promised him to try.

I hope Virginia is better. Your maid was not reassuring when I rang up yesterday.

Yours ever,
Tom

I don't suppose you know of any flats to let about Bloomsbury, do you? We are really going to move if we can find anything tolerable, and I should much prefer to be in Bloomsbury if possible.

TO *Leonard Woolf* TS Reading

5 February 1929 57 Chester Terrace, S.W.I.

Dear Leonard,

There is one matter I forgot to mention to you. I have had for several months, to my shame, an enormous batch of manuscript by a Bard, named Hew [*sic*] Menai. I had praised some other work of his and so he sent me,

---

1–Dr Bernard Hart, MD, FRCP (1879–1966), Fellow of University College, London; Consulting Physician in Psychological Medicine, University College Hospital; Consulting Physician in Psychiatry, National Hospital, Queen Square; author of *The Psychology of Insanity* (1912) and *Psychopathology: Its Development and Its Place in Medicine* (1927).

apparently, everything. He has been very patient, but now he says you are preparing a volume of his things, and making the choice. Shall I send you over what I have, as he thinks that I may have things that you have not seen?

I have told him that after the choice is made for the book I will try to choose something for the *Criterion*; but as I don't know when the book appears, or when I can use anything of his myself, I do not know whether I shall use material from the book or from outside it.

Yours ever,
Tom

TO *A. L. Morton*[1]   CC

5 February 1929   [London]

My dear Morton,

Thank you very much for your review of the book by Mathiez. Your review is by no means too long, but on reading it I feel that the book itself hardly deserves so much notice. I have, therefore, kicked myself for not making another suggestion to you. Have you the patience to read another book on the French Revolution which has not been translated, I mean a book, not very long, by Pierre Gaxotte who contributed to the last *Criterion*. I have only dipped into this book; but I am certain that it is very lively and provocative and would make it possible to build up your review into something much more interesting. It is a bit late to get the present review into the March Number anyway. Would you have the patience to review Gaxotte's book with it if I sent you the book, and make a review about double the length for the June Number? If you prefer not to do so let me know candidly.[2]

I am also sending you another book on the History of the Devil, which I know nothing about, but which may possibly appeal to your anthropological interests.[3]

1–A. L. Morton (1903–87) was to become a leading Marxist historian; educated at Cambridge, he worked in the 1930s for the *Daily Worker*. *A People's History of England* (1938) is a modern classic. Later works include *The English Utopia* (1952), *The Everlasting Gospel: A Study in the Sources of William Blake* (1958), *The World of the Ranters: Religious Radicalism in the English Revolution* (1970). See also *Rebels & Their Causes: Essays in Honour of A. L. Morton*, ed. Maurice Cornforth (1978), and *History and the Imagination: Selected Writings of A. L. Morton*, ed. Margot Heinemann (1990).

2–Untitled review of Albert Mathiez's *The French Revolution* (trans. by C. A. Phillips), and Pierre Gaxotte's *La Révolution Française*, C. 8 (July 1929), 717–20.

3–Untitled notice of R. Lowe Thompson, *The History of the Devil*, C. 8 (July 1929), 764.

Yours very sincerely,
[T. S. Eliot]

P.S. I note your proper address.

TO *Allen Tate*   TS Princeton

6 February 1929   Faber & Gwyer Ltd,
                                         24 Russell Square

Dear Mr Tate,

I am glad to hear from you because I have been waiting to write and explain that I find it impossible to get your essay in the March number. But that if you will be so kind I shall definitely be able to put it in the June number. In the ordinary way I should be sending you proof sometime in March. But if there is any risk of your leaving Paris before this I should be grateful for another address.

I was very much disappointed in not seeing more of you in London, such a meeting as we had is extremely unsatisfactory and I had hoped to have a private talk with you. Do be persuaded to return to London, if only for a few days before you go back to America.[1]

By the way I have not said that your essay in its present form is *admirable* for our purposes.[2]

Yours sincerely,
T. S. Eliot

TO *Hugh Macdonald*   TS Charlotte Williamson

6 February 1929   Faber & Gwyer Ltd,
                                         24 Russell Square

Dear Macdonald,

I find that as a result of several distractions I have been extremely remiss in not even having acknowledged your and Mrs Macdonald's kind invitation of the 31st.[3] I do hope that you will forgive me. I could not have come on that date in any case. But it sometimes happens to

1–Tate had journeyed from Oxford to Paris by way of Southampton (17 Jan.).
2–Tate, 'The Fallacy of Humanism', C. 8 (July 1929), 661–81.
3–Macdonald (16 Jan. 1929): 'I don't know if you ever go to parties. If you feel inclined, do come on the 31st . . . We do not appear to have made any formal agreement about royalties on the *Dryden* – you asked me to look up the correspondence – so I am leaving this and other matters till I see you.'

me that I think I have written to decline an invitation when I have not done so.

I still want to see you as soon as I can and when I am a bit freer I will ring you up at the Law Courts and ask you to lunch with me. I have also that first edition which I should prefer to return to you by hand.

With apologies to Mrs Macdonald and best wishes.

Yours very sincerely,
T. S. Eliot

Even this was delayed – the typists are dropping like flies, with flu.

TO *Desmond MacCarthy*

CC

6 February 1929   [London]

My dear MacCarthy,

I am very much obliged to you for your review in *The Sunday Times*, which I feared might be much less favourable.[1] I can honestly say that it

1 – 'Anglo-Catholic Criticism', *The Sunday Times*, 3 Feb. 1929, 10. MacCarthy opens by praising TSE's verse as 'the best expression . . . of contemporary tendencies and sensibilities'; *The Waste Land* was 'neither histrionic, nor the product of pure aesthetic theory'. However, TSE has moved on from the direction and concerns of *The Sacred Wood* (1920) – 'a collection [which] dealt with separate points in aesthetics and literary history': 'He has been busy orientating himself. The visible sign of the completion of this process is that he has been received into the Anglo-Catholic Church; and these essays *For Lancelot Andrewes* are separate rays of criticism issuing from his new central position . . .

With respect to TSE's revisionary construction of Machiavelli's *The Prince*, MacCarthy notes: 'Mr Eliot is anxious to prove that Machiavelli was not a cynic, and that the historic conception of him as a purveyor of "tips of tyrants" is silly and false. From his new point of view, what appears sympathetic and therefore important in Machiavelli is that his theory of government takes for granted the utter vileness of human nature when untouched by "Grace". Machiavelli seems a sound moralist to Mr Eliot because he thinks of him as one who grasped the dogma of original sin; a sound statesman because he valued order, whatever the means used to establish it, above liberty.'

But MacCarthy argues further: 'What has really shocked mankind down the ages in Machiavelli is not his cynicism, though they may have called it that, but something more devastating (Mr Eliot is right, the professed cynic who writes to cause pain is negligible in comparison), namely, his *unconscious* cynicism; though to call this "purity of heart" is to fail precisely in that quality of candour which is Machiavelli's own rare and redeeming characteristic . . . What shocked mankind was that Machiavelli, having taken firm hold of the fact that the ethics of government are not those of private life, should show such complete indifference to the discord; that he should hold up as an example to all rulers, Caesar Borgia's policy in Romagna, of first appointing a particularly cruel lieutenant to murder and inspire terror, and then, in order to dissociate himself from the odium, having that man murdered in his turn and his slashed body exposed in the market-place; that he should say, "There is, then, no more potent, nor more valid, nor healthier remedy than to murder the sons of Brutus" – before those young men have moved a finger against authority;

417

is the most helpful review that I have received; and I admit that you show me that I have made some exaggerated statements about Machiavelli. Your criticism of my Machiavelli essay seems to me very sound. On the other hand I stand by my guns for Andrewes. When you quote one of my

---

that he should couple such words as "honourable frauds", "generous cruelties", "glorious crimes", and proceed to show how completely he means what he says by giving glaring examples of model treachery and cruelty. It is true that this unconscious cynicism served to expose a problem which has not yet been solved – the relation between political and private morality; it is true, too, that contemporary conditions excused Machiavelli's interpretation of the art of government in terms of the art of ruthless war . . .

'We seem to touch the bottom of Machiavelli in his admiration for a saying of Capponi's that those men are are most admirable "who loved their country better than the safety of their souls", a maxim which still may prove the ruin of civilization. It is, by the by, a thoroughly pagan one; and I am surprised that from his new point of view Mr Eliot should consider Machiavelli a sound moralist.'

MacCarthy praises TSE's interpretation of Baudelaire as greatly superior to the nineteenth-century view of him as 'a diabolist and decadent'. But MacCarthy then finds that TSE overpraises a passage from *Mon cœur mis à nu*, which MacCarthy regards as 'only touching'. He goes on: 'The same exaggeration shows in [Eliot's] praise of the prose of Bishop Andrewes. "Andrewes," he says, "is the first great preacher of the English Catholic Church", and he contrasts Donne with him to Donne's disadvantage. His praise of Andrewes's sermons sent me to them; I did not find it justified. They struck me as crabbed and jerky. My experience, however, is not good evidence . . . I appeal rather to the witness of Alexander Whyte, D.D., who has edited Andrewes's "Devotions", and finds his sermons unreadable; and to Coleridge, who, while adoring and annotating divines of all sorts, had no praise for Andrewes's sermons. Read this passage which Mr Eliot quotes, presumably as one of the best, and ask yourself is it very fine? –

> "I know not how, but when we hear of saving or mention of a Saviour, presently our mind is carried to the saving of our skin, of our temporal state, of our bodily life, and farther saving we think not of. But there is another life not to be forgotten, and greater the dangers, and the destruction more to be feared than of this here, and it would be well sometimes if we were remembered of it. Besides our skin and flesh a soul we have, and it is our better part by far, that also hath need of a Saviour; that hath her destruction out of which, that hath her destroyer from which she would be saved, and these would be thought on. Indeed, our chief thought and care would be for that; how to escape the wrath, how to be saved from the destruction to come, whither our sins will certainly bring us. Sin it is will destroy us all."

Apart from the gravity which is common to all seventeenth century prose; apart from the possibility of interpreting, in the light of the preacher's saintly character, its hitching, inhibited movement as signs of an admirable integrity, is this prose really very fine? Is it not extravagant to rate it above above that of Hooker, Taylor, and Donne? Surely the importance of Andrewes as an Anglican divine has obscured Mr Eliot's vision of a literary man.

'We are dealing with a book of criticism by a critic who has recently discovered that the value of literature does not depend on aesthetic values alone.

'Sometimes his new point of view leads him to exaggerate merits because they are connected with others to which he is now sensitive; sometimes it intensifies his penetration. In the case of Middleton his head for moral values has led him to one of the most subtle and just pieces of aesthetic criticism I have read for a long time. His analysis of where precisely in Middleton's play *The Changeling*, the tragedy lies, is masterly, and by implication an exposure of the fundamental triviality of much Elizabethan drama – indeed, most of it is childish, reckless, rickety stuff.'

quotations as evidence that Andrewes' prose is not first rate I can only throw up my hands. I am afraid that I remain unrepentant on this point and still prefer the style of Andrewes to that of Donne. And by the way, have I explicitly rated Andrewes above Hooker and Taylor?

There is no reason why you should have difficulty, I suppose, but I think you tend to exaggerate the contrast between my present point of view and my point of view in 1920. Certainly some of the papers dealing with the theory of criticism in my 1920 book show an excessive influence of Gourmont, but I did not think that my practice at that time with dealing with particular writers differs very widely from my practice now.

I was surprised to see you praise so highly my essay on Middleton. Richmond liked it but I had rather regretted including it. Perhaps I was over conscious of the problems about Middleton which I had avoided. The Essay, I am afraid, has very little scholarly value because I purposely avoided all the questions of attribution and collaboration which complicate Middleton's work.

There is one other point which will no doubt seem much more important to me than to you. When you say that I have been received into the Anglo Catholic Church I should like to know whether you are speaking ironically. If not, I should like to write to *The Sunday Times* to point out that there is no Anglo Catholic Church for anybody to be received into.

With very many thanks,

Yours ever,

[T. S. Eliot]

TO *E. F. Lydall*   CC

6 February 1929   [London]

Dear Mr Lydall,

Many thanks for your kind letter.[1] I always enjoy coming up to Cambridge to talk to undergraduates and the name of the Nashe Society endears it to me, as I have a particular affection for that vituperative writer. But do not think that I share his quarrelsome nature: I do not enjoy making havoc of college intellectuals and am always most tempted when there is some risk of their making havoc of me. But I am afraid that

---

1–Lydall invited TSE (30 Jan.) to talk to the Nashe Society at St John's College. 'I'm sure you would enjoy making havoc of a bunch of college intellectuals, and they would be all thrilled appreciation at having such an august operation performed upon them.'

health, and various importunate business both public and private warn me not to make any definite engagements of such a sort for several terms. Perhaps you will be so good as to pass me on to your successors and if some months hence I find the leisure which I cannot foresee, I shall be delighted to meet your Society.

With many thanks,
Yours sincerely
[T. S. Eliot]

TO *Elsie Elizabeth Phare*   CC

6 February 1929   [London]

Dear Miss Phare,

I am very honoured by your renewing your invitation.[1] I am afraid that I should be ill advised to make any engagements at Cambridge or Oxford for another two terms. I wish I could do so but I am gradually coming to learn my limitations.

With many thanks and best wishes for your Society.

Yours sincerely,
[T. S. Eliot]

TO *Max Rychner*   CC

6 February 1929   [London]

Dear Dr Rychner,

Thank you for your letter of the 4th inst. I hope to see Mr Williams in a few days and will speak to him again about the essays; but it might be as well for you to write to him yourself. His address is:–

> Orlo Williams, Esq.,
> 16, Aubrey Walk,
> Kensington, London, W.8.

I have pleasure in sending you a copy of my last book and shall be interested in your criticism of it. Please believe that I shall be very happy to co-operate with you and your admirable Review in any way possible. I hope also that you may be persuaded at some time to visit London.

1–Phare (26 Jan.) renewed her invitation to TSE to address the Newnham College Arts Society.

I should like to have you meet some of our colleagues.

Yours sincerely,

[T. S. Eliot]

TO *Freda Kirchwey*[1]   CC

7 February 1929   [London]

Dear Madam,

Thank you so much for your letter of the 7th January.[2] I am flattered that you would like to have me contribute to your series of Poetry Quartos. I should be very glad to do so but I am afraid that my present engagements put it out of the question for a long time. It is not quite certain but I am at present negotiating for a small number of new poems to be published in America. I have therefore nothing in hand to offer; but if I happen to write something which might be suitable for such a series I will write to you again.

Yours very truly,

[T. S. Eliot]

TO *M. C. D'Arcy*   CC

7 February 1929   [London]

My dear D'Arcy,

Thank you for your kind letter, it is a pleasure to look forward to coming with you to some future meeting of the L.S.S.R.

Your invitation is very tempting and flattering and I should very much like to meet the new Poetry Society of which you speak so highly.[3] But

1 – Freda Kirchwey (1893–1976), radical journalist and magazine editor. Educated at Barnard College, she was feminist and socialist, and campaigned in the 1930s against Fascism (while also advocating conciliation with the Bolshevik USSR). In 1918 she went to work for *The Nation*, becoming Managing Editor in 1922, Editor in 1933. See further Sara Alpern, *Freda Kirchwey: A Woman of 'The Nation'* (Cambridge, Mass., 1987).

2 – 'Random House is planning to publish a series of twelve Poetry Quartos, each containing one new poem by an American poet. The quartos will be distinctive and well made . . . I am writing to ask if you have a poem you would like to contribute to this series. The only stipulation is that it shall be new and between 40 and 125 lines in length. I have been authorized to offer you $50.'

3 – D'Arcy reported (5 Feb.) that the new Poetry Society consisted of 'almost all the young poets & aesthetes & remarkable people "up" at present . . . a rather unique membership for a University Society.'

in my present circumstances it is very difficult for me to take the time to come down to Oxford or Cambridge even under such pleasant auspices, and I do not dare to say yes at least for this term. I should like to meet that Society if I had time to come to either University at all, but for the present I can see but little prospect of it.

Looking forward to seeing you at Eastertide.

Yours very sincerely,

[T. S. Eliot]

TO *René Hague*[1]   CC

7 February 1929   [London]

Dear Mr Hague,

Please forgive me for not having answered your letter sooner. But I thought it futile to do so until I could suggest a time for meeting. Mr Gordon George spoke to me about you when I saw him last and I think mentioned you as a friend of Maritain.

I should like very much to see you. The best time for me at present is the morning about 11.30. Would Thurs. or Friday next suit you? If so please write or ring my Secretary here and leave word.

Yours sincerely,

[T. S. Eliot]

TO *Gilbert Seldes*[2]   TS Timothy and Marian Seldes

7 February 1929   *The Monthly Criterion*

My dear Seldes,

I am very glad to hear from you. It seems a very long time since we have had any communication. Certainly, I do indeed want you to continue your American Chronicle. You are aware no doubt that *The Criterion* has reverted to its original and more satisfactory quarterly form, so that

1–René Hague (1905–81), printer and scholar. Born in London of Irish parents, he was schooled at the Benedictine foundation of Ampleforth College in Yorkshire. In 1924–5 he met the craftsman Eric Gill (he would marry Gill's daughter Joan), as well as the artist and writer David Jones; and with Gill he founded the Pigotts Press, which they ran until 1956. Hague's works include *A Commentary on 'The Anathemata' of David Jones* (1977); and *Dai Greatcoat: A Self-Portrait of David Jones in His Letters* (edited, 1980). See further Barbara Wall, *René Hague – A Personal Memoir* (Aylesford Press, 1989).
2–Gilbert Seldes (1893–1970), journalist and critic: see Biographical Register.

I now have six foreign Chronicles to fit into four Numbers, and until we can afford to increase the size of the paper, I can have only one Chronicle a year from each Capital. That, I am aware, increases the difficulty for the chronicler. On the other hand you can choose the time of year that suits you best, as I can well re-arrange the continental people. Will you just let me know when it would suit your convenience and the events of the year to let me have another Chronicle. The subject you suggest seems to me a very good one.[1]

I imagine that Ervine made rather a fool of himself in America because the so called dramatic reports which he has sent to *The Observer* have been dreadful stuff. But I never thought very much of Ervine any way.[2]

I certainly have not seen your book, *The Stammering Century*, I do not know how I overlooked it, but I do not at the moment remember it having been offered to Faber & Gwyer at all. The only books of yours that I have seen in recent years have been those which you have published pseudonymously. I should be very grateful if you would send me a copy.[3]

With all good wishes,
Yours sincerely,
T. S. Eliot

1 – Seldes remarked (19 Jan.) that of the 'two or three signal things' that occurred in the USA last year, he would 'be inclined to speculate more on the weakness of the literature of protest (the Menckenian school) and its derivates in fiction and playwriting: the weakness that all of them rebel against the facts of American existence (roughly, too many motor cars) and all of them accept the underlying philosophy (better to call it a philosophy flatly than to add "or the lack of it").'

2 – The 'most ghastly' event of the year, said Seldes, 'was the appearance of St John Irvine.' St John Ervine – *nom de plume* of John Greer Irvine (1883–1971) – was born into working-class poverty in Belfast but moved to London while still a young man. His first full-length play, *Mixed Marriage* (1911), was produced by W. B. Yeats's Abbey Theatre, Dublin – of which Ervine became (for less than a year) the domineering manager. His successful tragedy *John Ferguson* (1915) was also written for the Abbey. A diehard Unionist, opposed to Irish Home Rule, he enlisted during WW1 in the British Army and was so gravely wounded in action that he had to have a leg amputated. His other plays included *Jane Clegg* (1913), performed at the Gaiety Theatre, Manchester, starring Sybil Thorndike; *The First Mrs Fraser* (1929); and *Boyd's Shop* (1936); his novels include *The Foolish Lovers* (1920) and *The Wayward Man* (1927). In addition, he wrote works of reminiscence and literary biography. *George Bernard Shaw* (1956) won the James Tait Black Memorial Prize. In the 1920s he worked as drama critic for the *Morning Post* and *The Observer*; and in 1929 he was the guest drama critic for the *New York World* – a role in which he aroused resentment for his withering comments on the New York theatre.

3 – Seldes assumed that TSE had read *The Stammering Century* when it was offered to F&G (it had not been published in the UK); if not, he would send a copy.

TO *John Crow*[1]   CC

7 February 1929   [London]

Dear Crow,

Here is the letter I promised you.[2] If it seems to you in any way unsatisfactory I will give you another one.

I will try to think of something else as well.

Yours sincerely,
[T. S. Eliot]

TO *Leonard Woolf*   CC

7 February 1929   [Faber & Gwyer Ltd]

Dear Leonard,

This is to introduce to you Mr John Crow who has been down from Worcester College, Oxford for about a year.

Mr Crow has always wanted to do literary journalism but at Oxford took his degree in physiology, as he had intended to take a medical degree later and make a living out of medicine. Since leaving Oxford he has been at Guy's Hospital but has now decided to abandon medicine if he can get any start in writing.

I have advised him to try to find some sort of secretaryship to keep him going for a time until he is able to explore the chances of London and make up his mind what to do. But meanwhile I hope that he can get a little reviewing as well as other journalistic work. He is especially interested in literature, but he also is an authority on boxing and on the music hall stage and would like to review any books connected with those subjects. He is also well read in detective fiction. I should be very much obliged if you would see him and give him your advice, and perhaps keep him in

---

1–Derwent May describes John Crow as 'a brilliant if eccentric lecturer in English at King's College, London . . . Crow had once written a newspaper boxing column called "From the Crow's Nest"' (*Critical Times: The History of The Times Literary Supplement* [2001], 365).
2–John Crow hoped (24 Jan.) TSE might remember that they had met in 1928 at Worcester College, Oxford, when TSE read *TWL*. 'Might I come and see you some time, if you can give me some advice how best to embark on a "literary life"?' William Force Stead told TSE on 19 Jan. that his friend Crow was 'anxious to get a start in the journalistic or publishing world. He was Editor of the Isis & did his work well: he's an able & humorous fellow . . . He is willing to take a post of any kind from office boy upwards.'

mind for any possible books. He has one or two other literary schemes which I have advised him to talk to you about,

Yours ever.

[Tom]

TO *Edward Dahlberg*[1]   CC

7 February 1929   [London]

Dear Mr Dahlberg,

I have your letter of the 5th.[2] I have not yet had time to read the poems but I am replying at once. I hope you are getting on nicely and unless I hear from you to the contrary, will expect to see you next Tuesday morning about 11.30 a.m. Meanwhile I have heard from Cambridge and must say that the report is not very encouraging. An M.Litt. degree takes two years and a P.H.D. [Ph.D.] three years or two if the candidate is specially qualified. He says that there is no one in Cambridge specially worth working under and he advises against Cambridge except for someone working on an historical subject preferably a medieval subject. He even says that anyone specially interested in technical and general problems, or anyone who wants to rate himself should be warned away from Cambridge. The minimum cost of living in Cambridge seems to be about £200 a year including the vacations.

I am afraid that is a pretty clear indication that you would be wasting your time there. The only man I know who is any good in Oxford is Collingwood. You have already spoken of him. If you say the word I will

1 – Edward Dahlberg (1900–77), novelist: see TSE's letter to I. A. Richards, 1 Feb. above.
    Later in life, in letters to Herbert Read, Dahlberg disparaged TSE's poetry and his purposes: 'You think I am wrong about Eliot. There is too much of the well-fed votary of Helicon in him, and real seers are waifs' (15 Nov. 1951); 'I regard T. S. Eliot's poems as evil' (19 Jan. 1952); 'You know I have a niggard regard for Eliot's poems, but I believe his conception of originality is discerning' (13 Jan. 1954); 'Eliot is a wild son of Ham, and he will not last . . . The evil he is is in the rabble titles of his volumes, *Murder in the Cathedral* and *The Cocktail Party*, which are a claim for cash' (1 Mar. 1955): from *Epitaphs of Our Times: The Letters of Edward Dahlberg* (1967), 62, 69, 75, 94. Later still, in *The Confessions of Edward Dahlberg* (1971), he said of TSE: 'I know of no better description of him than the following I've culled from the *Memoirs* of Saint-Simon: "He was a humble down-looking man, whose physiognomy promised nothing"' (223).
2 – Dahlberg wrote from Sydenham: 'I'm very sorry I was unable to come to the city to see you . . . London fogs and slopy [*sic*] rains have about taken everything out of me. I am sending along some poems I've done since I've been in London . . . It's been very kind of you to bother about me, and your seeing me has made London more liveable.'

write to Collingwood also, but if I do that I suggest that you should give me some outline of the work you want to do for his guidance. We will talk these things over on Tuesday.

Yours sincerely,
[T. S. Eliot]

TO *Mario Praz*   TS Galleria Nazionale d'Arte Moderna, Rome

7 February 1929   *The Monthly Criterion*

My dear Praz,

No I had not seen the news in yesterday's *Times* and I am deeply grieved.[1]

Dr Stewart had written rather encouragingly although he warned me that there was a large field of competitors.[2] I am keenly disappointed. I met Piccoli once in 1915 when he was in Cambridge before.[3] I have no doubt that his previous association with Cambridge made all the difference, though I had not thought of him as a serious competitor. We must still hope, however, to get you out of Liverpool.

I should not have supposed that Q knew anything about Machiavelli.[4]

With many regrets,
Yours ever,
T. S. Eliot

TO *Philippa Strachey*[5]   TS Fawcett Library

8 February 1929   57 Chester Terrace, S.W.1.

Dear Miss Strachey,

I do not know whether you will remember our having met. I hope so, as I feel that I am taking rather a liberty in any case. My wife and I

1–Praz wrote (undated): 'As you have probably seen from yesterday's *Times*, I failed to get the Cambridge post. [Raffaello] Piccoli, of course, is quite a good man . . .'
2–Stewart (14 Feb.) thought Praz 'evidently a serious candidate, & I assure you that his claims will have the consideration wh: they deserve. There is likely to be a strong field.'
3–Piccoli had taught Italian at Cambridge, 1913–16.
4–'I am told that Q. [Sir Arthur Quiller-Couch, who had served on the appointment committee] attacked the substance of my essay on Machiavelli, at the meeting. I wonder what he may have said. It is a criticism to which I will never be able to reply.'
5–Philippa Strachey (1872–1968) – 'Pippa' – one of the many siblings of Lytton Strachey, was prominent in the movement for women's rights. As Secretary of the London National

are looking for another habitation, and preferably in Bloomsbury; and Mary Hutchinson, to whom we were talking about it, suggested that 51, Gordon Square might be available. I spoke to Leonard Woolf this morning: he thought it possible that you might not wish to keep the whole of the house, and urged me to write to you at once.

Of course we do not want a whole house of that size to ourselves, only a couple of floors; but we thought of taking either (1) a house, and letting off part, as the Woolfs do; or (2) taking part of a house as sub-tenants. We would not consider taking a maisonette over people of whom we knew nothing – which makes half of London impossible.

If you consider either disposing of your house altogether, or sub-letting a part of it, I should be extremely grateful if you would let me know at once, and give me an 'option' – but if you have no such intention, I hope you will forgive this impertinence.

Yours sincerely,
T. S. Eliot

I am writing in this way, because I have other things in view which I must decide about – so I hope you can let me hear something about it.

TO *Frances Gregg Wilkinson*[1]   CC

9 February 1929   [London]

Dear Madam,

I must apologise for the delay in considering your interesting story.[2] I have been badly handicapped for some months by a succession of

---

Society for Women's Suffrage she organised in 1907 the first mass feminist demonstration of the National Union of Women's Suffrage Societies, and during WW1 she organised the Women's Service (finding jobs for women and training them for skilled work). She was secretary of the London Society for Women's Service, 1918–51.

1–Frances Gregg (1884–1941), American writer, was brought up in Philadelphia. Friend of EP and intimate of H.D. (Gregg wrote in her diary: 'Two girls in love with each other, and each in love with the same man. Hilda, Ezra, Frances'), she married in 1912 the writer Louis Wilkinson ('Louis Marlow') after breaking with H.D. (and she divorced Wilkinson in 1923). She had contributed poems to the periodicals *The Egoist* and *Others*. See Gregg, *The Mystic Leeway*, ed. Ben Jones (1995), which includes an account of Gregg by her son Oliver Wilkinson; *The Letters of John Cowper Powys to Frances Gregg*, vol. 1, ed. Oliver Marlow Wilkinson (1994); and Richard Perceval Graves, *The Brothers Powys* (1983). Her career is well rehearsed by Helen Carr in *The Verse Revolutionaries: Ezra Pound, H.D. and The Imagists* (2009).

2–Gregg had submitted 'Child and a Goat' on 16 Oct. 1928. 'Mr de la Mare has been good enough to praise it. He said among other things that it 'was clear as a mirror in a garden'. He suggested certain slight alterations which I have made. If you should care to use it for

secretaries, and at times have had to be without; so that in doing a good deal of my own secretarial work I have had to neglect the reading of manuscripts. Your story is at present in the hands of one of my colleagues; but I have asked him to return it immediately, and will give you a decision.

With renewed apologies and regrets,

Yours faithfully,
[T. S. Eliot]
Editor.

Vivien Eliot TO *Ottoline Morrell*   MS Texas

Monday 11 February 1929   57 Chester Terrace, s.w.1.

Dearest Ottoline,

This evening I began a long letter to you, but I have stopped in the middle.

I shall send you the letter later on – very soon.

But at the moment, all I shall say is that I was very happy to see you this afternoon.[1] That I was sorry Mirsky was here – but I was afraid you wld. be too bored if there was no one else.

That I do not want to feel that you & Tom are not the good friends that you used to be, & that so far as I am concerned I should be only too glad for him to have yr intimate friendship.

The Criterion, I would rather like to put – 'to Mr Walter de la Mare' just below the title. But if that would not be in a good taste it should not be done.' On 7 Feb. 1929 she wrote again to ask for a word about her story.

1–Carole Seymour-Jones writes, on the basis of a journal entry by OM (14 Feb. 1929; Goodman Papers): 'When Ottoline eventually called on Vivienne on 11 February 1929, the atmosphere was strained. Although at first Vivienne seemed more normal and "sane" to Ottoline, she became fractious and upset when Ottoline did not remember Pearl Fassett, Tom's secretary, who had died recently. Barely had Ottoline calmed her hostess down when Tom entered with Prince Mirsky, a White Russian writer whom Ottoline disliked intensely; her sympathies began to shift towards Vivienne and against Tom, whose contempt for other "uneducated" writers, such as Lawrence and Blake, annoyed her, as did Eliot's secret holding of Ottoline's hand, which she found patronising. Tom considered himself as infallible as the Pope, decided Ottoline' (*Painted Shadow*, 460).

As extrapolated from OM's diary by Miranda Seymour: 'I went to see Vivienne Eliot (why has she taken to calling herself Vivienne, I wonder: she used to be Vivian). I always go there trembling & fearing a scene . . . Then Tom & Prince Mirsky came in & sat at the other end of the room. Mirsky . . . is a dreadful man – and a fraud – very clumsy & insensitive – a brute. I turned my back on him & talked to VE. TSE said he thought DHL had an "incomplete intellect" and that he couldn't be bothered with Blake's long poems.'

I understand better now that I know you had not known that Miss
Fassett is dead.

With my love
Yrs. affectionately
Vivienne H. Eliot

TO *Alfred E. James, Messrs James & James* [1]   CC

11 February 1929   (London)

Dear Mr James,
Re Irish Estate.

Mrs Haigh-Wood has shown me your letter of the 7th to Maurice.
I have taken copies of it for myself, for Vivienne, and one which I am
sending to Maurice.

Pending any consultation between the Executors, and the Proprietors
(Maurice and Vivienne), one or two points occur to me. It struck me
that we ought to have particulars of the 'improvements and decorative
work' before assenting to Mr Duffy's proposal.[2] Unfortunately, I have
no papers of the Estate before me, and remember nothing of the terms of
his tenancy, whether he is responsible for repairs or not, or whether he
has been in arrears or not. But improvements and decorative work are
not necessarily improvements or decorative from the landlord's point of
view. As for Spencer Hill, I should think that it ought to be renewed if the
'necessary repairs' are reasonable.[3]

I gather that there is no urgency about either of these matters; but I
hope that meanwhile Mr Coall will provide more information about both.

Yours sincerely,
[T. S. Eliot]

1 – Solicitors.
2 – James had advised Maurice Haigh-Wood on 7 Feb. 'that the tenant [of 10 Eglinton Park],
Mr Duffy, is desirous of making improvements and doing decorative and other work at an
estimated cost of £200 but before he undertakes this he asks for a 21 years lease. His present
term of 7 years will expire on 18th May 1931 His rent is £111 per annum but the landlord
pays the rates.'
3 – 'The Freeholders offer to renew this lease at a rent of £30 on condition that necessary
repairs are carried out. I have asked Mr Coall what he estimates these repairs will cost.'

11 February 1929   *The Criterion*

Dear Mr Tate,

(We might drop the mister?) Many thanks for your very interesting letter of the 9th.[1] I do hope you will produce that essay, and let me have the version of which you speak. I am trying to work up Humanism in the *Criterion*: you may have seen Read's note in December; Chesterton is writing about Foerster's book in March;[2] Fernandez has promised a note about *his Humanism* for June; and I have asked Foerster to reply to Chesterton. I also have an essay by More (more theological) for June. So yours would come in very well; probably best in September, for when I should want it in June.

I agree with most of what you say. It is possible that Babbitt is a bigger man, in his kind, than More. I am not sure, however, that you don't underestimate the positive side of More's religious views. I saw a good deal of him this summer, and although I had read *Christ the Word*,[3] I found him a good deal nearer to Catholic orthodoxy than I had supposed. I also read several unpublished writings. He has been slow, but I should be surprised if he died unsacramented.

At the same time, what you say does apply very closely to his published work. Many of his literary judgments are moralistic – that is, based upon nothing. What interests me about him is not his accomplishment, but his striving. He is often, as you say, as unbalanced as the aesthete. The great vice of the modern moralist, in my phrase, is that he expects morality itself to be moral: a logical error, which haunts the humanist as well as the humanitarian. One is not in a position to take a moralist point of view unless one can take a super-moralist point of view. It is the believer in

---

1–'Perhaps you will remember that I speak of [Henry] James as a "post-Emersonian" in whom religion had contracted into an ideal of personal honour. In much the same way (with differences that could be defined) Professors Babbitt and More have tried to erect a doctrine of Humanism on the same plane, and I think an historical discussion of these men would make their positions much clearer than it is at present; it would show, I think, what their limitations are and thereby isolate all the more sharply their value . . .

'I am writing an essay for an American journal [*The Bookman*], and if you feel any interest in these ideas I should like to re-write it later and send it to you . . .

'More's doctrine is historically sounder, I believe, than Babbitt's, but Babbitt can no longer deceive himself, and he is superior to More; he is more intelligent. The point I wish to make is that More is our real starting-point if we are religious; but we must reject his method.'

2–'Is Humanism a Religion?', C. 8 (Apr. 1929), 382–93.

3–Paul Elmer More, *The Greek Tradition, from the Death of Socrates to the Council of Chalcedon*, vol. 4: *Christ the Word* (Princeton, 1927).

dogma, not the Nietzschean, who is beyond good and evil.

But all I started out to say was: by all means write it and let me have it. It is just what the *Criterion* wants.

– But are you sure that Babbitt doesn't deceive himself in his own fashion?

Yours ever sincerely,
T. S. Eliot

I look forward to seeing you in London in the summer.

TO *Paul Elmer More*   TS Princeton

Shrove Tuesday [12 Feb.] 1929   Faber & Gwyer Ltd

My dear More,

I now owe you several letters, and must try to pack several unrelated matters into one. First of all, let me thank you for your kind letter suggesting the lectureship at Princeton.[1] Had I the time at present to contemplate such an extended visit to America, I should jump at it. But as things are at present, I cannot look forward to a visit of any length; when next I come, it will probably be because my mother's health is failing, and then I shall spend all the time at my disposal with her in Cambridge. But I thank you for the kind thought. No doubt by the time I am ready to lecture in America, I shall be despised as an old fogey – that time is not far off.

Second, about your essay. I hope you will not mind if I put this into the June instead of the March number. It is a question of conflict of material. I have a paper on Humanism by Chesterton, from the Chesterton point of view, which I must use in March because I could not stand in the way of his selling it in America too.[2] I felt very strongly that it would confuse the reader, and blur the effect of both, if I printed you with him; as I knew that you had only let me have the essay as a personal favour, and had not intended it for serial publication, I have done accordingly.

Third, about the MSS.[3] It moved me deeply, partly, I dare say, because

1 – More had suggested (19 Dec. 1928) that TSE might like to give the Venuxem Lectures at Princeton: 'it is possible that a word from me would turn the committee to-you-wards.' (He had himself once delivered the Venuxem lectures, which turned into *Platonism*.)
2 – More said (21 Feb.) he had no objection to a postponement to suit TSE's convenience.
3 – During his visit to Oxford in 1928, More had written *Pages from an Oxford Diary*,

431

I know the author, and feel myself to be closely in sympathy in this writing as in others. But I should think it a great pity if the book were not published. Now, will you allow me, first, to put it to Faber & Gwyer, keeping your identity even from the directors of the firm? I am doubtful whether they will accept it under such conditions: if I refuse the author's name, and refuse the sale of American rights, the book is of a type which would make its way but slowly, and would hardly in those circumstances be a moneymaker; and I should hesitate to associate my own name as introducer (for what that is worth) for fear of giving a clue to the author. But I should like to try it on them. Also, I should like to take it to Kenneth Ingram, who runs the Society of SS. Peter & Paul, an Anglo-Catholic press, which might have the public to absorb such a book without any author's name on it.[1] F. & G. would take any book by P. E. More, but that is a different matter.[2]

Have you seen a review of *The Demon of the Absolute* which I was privileged to write for the *Times Literary Supplement*?[3]

I have been reading lately with great enjoyment Huegel's *Letters to his Niece*.[4] There is much one can skip, but much that is precious. I was impressed by one remark – a thing that has often occurred to me, but does not seem to worry many: that there seem to be certain persons for whom religion is wholly unnecessary. I do not think of people like Babbitt, or even Bertie Russell, in whom the religious instinct is very strong, even if diverted into other channels – but of persons of whom I have met a few, in whom it is simply absent. They may be very good, or very happy; they simply seem to miss nothing, to be unconscious of any void – the void that I find in the middle of all human happiness and all human relations, and which there is only one thing to fill. I am one whom this sense of void

---

which he rather hoped to publish anonymously; he submitted the MS to TSE on 28 Dec.

1 – Ingram edited *The Green Quarterly* on behalf of the Society of SS. Peter & Paul Ltd.

2 – More responded to this paragraph on 21 Feb.: 'You are entirely at liberty to give my name to Faber & Gwyer . . . My reason for offering the MS in England is that the Oxford scene would make the book look queer in the hands of an American publisher . . . If the thing really succeeds (i.e. among those who count), I should not care very much whether or not my name became gradually associated with it . . . On the other hand, I should be sensitive about my connexion with the book if it appears, to the intelligent, flat or mawkish or indiscreet . . . I should be glad to have you approach Kenneth Ingram, and even reveal my name to him, if F. & G. prove intractable.'

Pages from an Oxford Diary was published in 1937: see the review 'An Anglican Platonist: The Conversion of Paul Elmer More', *TLS*, 30 Oct. 1937, 792.

3 – TSE, 'Mr P. E. More's Essays', *TLS*, 21 Feb. 1929, 136.

4 – In C. 8 (Apr. 1929), TSE noted that *Letters from Baron Friedrich von Hügel to a Niece*, ed. Gwendolen Greene, was a 'book of great value' (568).

tends to drive towards asceticism or sensuality, and only Christianity helps to reconcile me to life, which is otherwise disgusting. But the people I have in mind – the good ones are much more puzzling than the bad – have an easy and innocent acceptance of life that I simply cannot understand. It is more bewildering than the 'Problem of Evil'.[1]

Yours ever sincerely,
T. S. Eliot

TO *Philippa Strachey*   TS Fawcett Library

13 February 1929   57 Chester Terrace, s.w.1.

Dear Miss Strachey,

Thank you very much for your letter. The possibility you suggest is what would suit us best: it is much more attractive to have you remain in the house, and take two storeys as your tenants, than to take a whole house and have to let off part to strangers.

We do not really want to move until the autumn, so that there would be no hurry for you. The only possibility is that we might have to decide upon something else in the meantime, before you have decided whether you want to let off your two top floors. There is also the question of cost; I should not like to pay more than £200 a year as a maximum; on the other hand we might come to some arrangement about the alterations.

All this is tentative: but if I was forced to decide on something else within the fortnight (I hope that will not happen) I would let you know at once; and on the other hand I shall be very grateful if you will let me know as soon as you have made your own plans.

Sincerely yours,
T. S. Eliot

TO *Kay Boyle*[2]   cc

13 February 1929   [London]

Dear Mr Boyle,

I must apologise for the delay in acknowledging your MSS. This has

---

1 – More replied (21 Feb.) that von Hügel was 'a great man and a great thinker. But in the end, though I go with him very far, I draw back from the *intensity* of his religion'.
2 – Kay Boyle (1902–92), American author whose early novels, including *Plagued by the Nightingale* (1931) and *Year Before Last* (1932), were to be published by F&F. See Robert

been so long that I am no longer sure that this address will reach you: if it does I hope you will let me hear from you at once.

I should like very much to use your MS entitled 'Three Little Men'. The others do not seem to me quite so suitable for the *Criterion*.

I am not quite certain of the date on which I can use 'Three Little Men'. Unfortunately I had already three or four accepted pieces of fiction on hand; I wish that I had had your MS. six months earlier. I should be very much obliged if you would leave it with me until you want it and if you would let me know if you publish it elsewhere in the meantime; otherwise I think I could probably use it towards the end of the year.[1]

I had already read other interesting things of yours in *Transition*.

If I do not hear from you I will write to you c/o *Transition* being uncertain of your address. I am keeping all of the MSS. until I hear.

Yours very sincerely,
[T. S. Eliot]
Editor.

TO *Ottoline Morrell*

TS Texas

13 February 1929   57 Chester Terrace, S.W.1.

My dear Ottoline,

Vivienne has mentioned to me what you have said and written to her about my having 'dropped' you, and your not understanding it. There is no reason for either: it is all quite simple and temporary; and it seems to me that it is time to explain. Neither of us want to lose you, you may be sure. I am sorry that I had Mirsky the other day, as it merely wasted time. It now seems to me however better that we should both see you again by ourselves, before Vivienne comes to tea with you. I should like to suggest that instead of her coming to you on Tuesday, you should come and dine here with us alone the first evening next week that you have free. Please do this. It is most important to me, and to Vivienne, that we should have no misunderstandings; and in the present circumstances there is no necessity for it whatever. There is nothing solemn or worrying about it – but I can best make it clear in talk between V. and you and myself.

Please say what night or nights you could come.

McAlmon and Kay Boyle, *Being Geniuses Together, 1920–1930* (1970), and Jean Mellen, *Kay Boyle: Author of Herself* (New York, 1994).
1 – 'Three Little Men', C. 12 (Oct. 1932), 17–23.

Always affectionately
Tom.

FROM *Geoffrey Faber* TO *Frank Morley*   TS Butler

15 February, 1929   [London]

My dear Morley,

You will have been expecting to hear from me before now; but the law's delays are endless, and I have had nothing definite to tell you.

It is now, however, almost certain that we are going to sell the Nursing Mirror. The principle has been agreed, and there is a prospective buyer whose name I am for the moment under promise not to reveal. All depends on the price, and it looks as if that would be satisfactory.

I would rather wait until things are definitely fixed up, before writing to you. But things may move very fast during the next two or three weeks, and I want to know to what extent I may count on you, in your absence, if things go the way they look like going.

It may be necessary to form a new company, almost immediately, to take over the other assets of Faber & Gwyer Ltd., including both the F. & G. and the S. P. books. The bulk of the money I shall, if the Mirror is sold, be able to find out of my own pocket. The new company would take over these premises.

I want the Board to consist of myself as chairman, you, de la Mare, Stewart, Eliot. I shall not require any return on my capital until the company can comfortably afford to make it; but I shall need a salary of (say) £1200. I propose a salary of £600 each to you, de la Mare, and Stewart, and some interest in profits of a nature to be determined later – whether through shares or through commission.

Your own particular functions would be to advise on MSS., to ingeminate policy, and (most important of all!) to bring grist to the mill. I don't mean that you would be limited to these functions; only that they are what we specially want you for.

One of the most important points we have to settle, and may have to settle quickly, is the name of the new company. There are four principal suggestions in the field.

  1. Geoffrey Faber Ltd.,
  2. Faber & Co., Ltd.,

435

3. Faber & Faber Ltd.,
4. Faber & Morley Ltd.

Of these I prefer the last, and so does Stewart; and I want to know if you would agree to it, supposing it commends itself to the others. It sounds well, and has a real basis in your accession to the firm. Stewart's name is not of value; de la Mare's is impossible.

As regards capital; I should expect every director to put up something – if it were only £500, and I should be very glad if you found it possible, in one way or another, to put up more than this. I don't say it is essential; but I do think it is very desirable, whether now or later.

I can't speak definitely of the amount of capital required – it depends on the value put on the assets we take over. But I have good reason for hoping that we may get these very cheaply. I should say that the authorised capital would not be less than £30,000 nor more than £40,000; and that the capital issued for cash would not be less than £20,000 nor more than £30,000. I should probably provide about £15,000 myself.

Now could you on receiving this letter cable to me your answers to the following questions?

ONE. Will you join the company, if it is formed, as a director on the terms stated?

TWO. Will you permit your name to form part of the title if we want to use it?

THREE. Can you see your way to putting up any money within (say) the first year?

FOUR. If so, how much (in pounds not dollars!)?

FIVE. If not, could you probably do so later on?

SIX. If later on, how much?

SEVEN. When could you be back in England, if the Company is formed?

To save expense, don't in your cable quote the numbers of the questions but give the answers in order; e. g.

Yes Yes No Blank Yes 2500 March 7
    or

Yes Yes Yes 2500 Blank Blank March 7[1]

1–FVM told Cecilia Sempel on 3 June 1948 that GCF 'invited me to join forces with him in the reorganization of Faber & Gwyer, which had not been successful, into a new firm, Faber & Faber. In 1929 the suggestion was, if I could put in capital, to call the firm Faber & Morley, which is an amusing memory! But I had no capital, and came in as an ordinary director . . . The business was not departmentalised, but roughly the division was that de la

I write in some haste, and can't go in to more detail. 'Flu has been raging here. I've had it twice, and all my family! I hope you're having a good time, and enchanting your audiences.

Yours ever,
Geoffrey Faber

TO *Marguerite Caetani*   CC

18 February 1929   [London]

Dear Marguerite,

I ought to have answered your question sooner, but have been having trouble of various kinds, a plague of influenza among the typists and secretaries of the company which has given me a good deal of routine work to attend to myself, and finally I have had some poisoning from my teeth, and am just recovering from an extraction. It is difficult to say what you ought to pay Campbell; as *Commerce* does not seem to have any settled rates; I should think ten guineas would be about right for the two poems, as one of them has been published already.[1] I had a friendly letter from him finally expressing his pleasure at having the poems printed and translated in *Commerce*.

Vivienne is pretty well over her influenza, but is very tired and run down again at present from the fatigue and worry of nursing me. We both send love, and will write at more leisure.

Affectionately,
[Tom]

TO *Ezra Pound*   TS Beinecke

18 February 1929   Faber & Gwyer Ltd,
                                     24 Russell Square

Cher E:

Received your letter of the 14th instant[2] with very many thanks for

---

Mare looked after production, Stewart after advertising, and in the main Eliot and I were responsible for editorial work . . . But as I say, the divisions were not rigid; we all worked as a team, with Faber as a very excellent chairman' (Berg: Morley/Eliot Papers, Box 95).
1 – 'Please send me just a line telling me how much I ought to give him respectively for the two poems?' asked Caetani on 8 Feb.
2 – Not found.

your remarks and cheque, which is however not due to me at all; I have already been paid cash by Faber & Gwyer for my small attempt (10 gui.) and so am not in the least entittled [*sic*] to any more, so please receive the cheque check [*sic*] back as I am not entittled to it and please this closes the matter so far as I have engaged in it all further royalties go to the author. Re Propertius (*Quia Pauper*) I am afraid I have overlooked looking into the matter due to the scourge of influennza in this office it has been difficult lately to get information on any subject; but I will have a statement of the copies on hand sent to you and the 6 copies you want. The arrangement was wholly informal as Miss Weaver merely handed over the stock of *Egoist* to us except what the authors wanted to take over themselves (e.g. *Tarr*[1]) and she said she had never had any formal aggrement [*sic*] with the authors; so we decided simply to pay to authors proceeds of sales less a sum to be estimated for overhead charges, storage and brilliant salesmanship. So you see disposal of stock is a matter for private arrangement with the individual author.

Hoping that the wolves, Vatican etc. plumbling etc. are not troublesome in Rappalo, yrs. with love from both

T.

TO *Allan Chapman*   CC

18 February 1929   [London]

Dear Sir,

I thank you for your letter of the 15th instant, and for inviting me to criticise *Cambridge Poetry 1929*.[2] I quite agree with you that it is desirable to have the book reviewed by someone outside of Cambridge, and wish indeed that I could do it myself. But I am at the moment very much behindhand in my work, owing to the illness of some of the staff here, and finally to a slight illness of my own; and as you need the copy so soon I am afraid that I must decline: though the task would be a very interesting one. If you have no one else in mind I might suggest Mr Herbert Read (Victoria & Albert Museum) or Mr Sherard Vines (The University, Hull).

With many thanks for the compliment, and many regrets,

1–Wyndham Lewis's *Tarr* (London: Egoist Press, 1918) was hailed by TSE in *The Egoist* 5: 8 (Sept. 1918), 106; and 'Contemporanea', *Egoist* 5: 6 (June/July 1918), 84.
2–Allan Chapman, editor of *The Cambridge Review*, invited TSE (15 Feb.) to review *Cambridge Poetry 1929* (Hogarth Press), which was due for publication on 1 March.

I am,

Yours sincerely

[T. S. Eliot]

TO *Paul Elmer More*

19 February 1929   [Faber & Gwyer Ltd]

My dear More,

I am writing again, in haste, on receipt of your kind letter of the 6th, lest you think that my previous letter was a reply; it was posted several days before I received yours.[1] My letter was, I felt, inadequate thanks for your thought of me in connexion with the Vanuxem letters [*sc.* lectures]; but it would have been ungracious in reply to yours. I am very sorry to have been even the unconscious cause of a pickle in the University, and I hope your kindness and zeal on my behalf has not been the cause of any further vexation to you. But, grateful as I am, I am afraid that my decision (in advance of the University decision) is unchanged; I blame myself for not having written to you sooner, and thus saved you the trouble of forwarding my interests. I cannot go fully into the reasons; but I assure you that they are compulsive [*sic*].

Apart from my gratitude, nothing would have pleased me more than to pay a visit under such auspices to Princeton, and make the acquaintance of some of the faculty and undergraduates.

And thank you most cordially for your private hospitality.

Ever gratefully yours,

[T. S. Eliot]

TO *H. P. Collins* TS Private Collection

19 February 1929   *The Criterion*

Dear Mr Collins,

Thank you for your letter. I shall be delighted if you can contribute again in any way to the *Criterion*. We have never yet met, after several years; I hope that you will soon be well enough to meet me in London.[2]

1–A letter is missing from this exchange: Princeton has an envelope from TSE to More postmarked 13 Feb. 1929 but lacking the letter.
2–Collins wrote (7 Feb.) that he had 'been hopelessly incapacitated by illness for many months'. He asked whether he might review a novel, *We are the Dead*, by Ann Reid.

I am not as a rule very keen on reviewing new novels one by one, even in short notes. *The Criterion* aims to be really a 'review'; and we attach more importance to reviewing, from time to time, the total work of a novelist with several notable books to his name, than to noticing individual new novels. But is there no other book, worth a long review, that you would care to deal with for the June number?

The 'Joubert' is to receive a long notice, but my reviewer was unable to finish it in time for March, so it will appear in June.[1]

I do hope that your health will improve, in spite of this destructive weather.

Yours sincerely
T. S. Eliot

TO *Leonard Woolf*   CC

20 February 1929   [Faber & Gwyer Ltd]

Dear Leonard,

This is to introduce to you Mr Edward Dahlberg of New York. Mr Dahlberg came to London primarily to continue studies in philosophy and aesthetics begun at Columbia; with a view to taking a higher degree; but he has found, I am afraid, that there is no one good enough here in his line to make it worth his while. At present he is reading for Putnam's, who are bringing out a novel of his which I am told D. H. Lawrence recommended very strongly.[2]

1–'I wonder if you received a copy of my Joubert which I contributed to Aldington's Broadway series.' Joseph Joubert, *Pensées and Letters*, trans. with Introduction by H. P. Collins, was to be reviewed by Peter Quennell in C. 8 (July 1929), 715–17.
2–*Bottom Dogs*.

I have seen some poems of his which I like, and I should like him to have the opportunity of showing them to you. I shall be grateful if you can see him.[1]

Yours,
[Tom]

TO *Max Rychner*   CC

21 February 1929   [London]

Dear Dr Rychner,

I thank you for your letter of the 14th instant, and have pleasure in authorising you to publish the German translation of my essay on Machiavelli, in the *Neue Schweizer Rundschau*.[2]

I have arranged for a review copy of *Lancelot Andrews* to be sent to your Review.

With all best wishes,
Yours cordially,
[T. S. Eliot]

1–Dahlberg reported to TSE (27 Feb.) on his meeting with LW: 'He looked over my MS of poems and sent it back with great courteous dispatch. He doesn't take to them, simply not interested in the kind of things I see or how I see them . . . I just write straight ahead, too unconscious, he believes. Anyway, we talked for an hour about what he called the modern fake . . . I wanted to go for Mr Woolf, but only made halfhearted gestures, as I had been introduced thru your kindness, and as he had turned down my MS . . . I respect Mr Woolf's reactions to my poems, although I find his syllogisms a bit flaccid.' (In a letter to TSE of 20 Apr., Dahlberg would reconsider his initial negative reaction to LW: 'I have changed my mind about Leonard Woolfe [*sic*]. I think he was right in not taking my poems. At the time I thought, perhaps, I was working out some kind of direction for myself; but the poems, like everything else I have done so far, are so wanting in unity.')

On 13 Mar., Dahlberg left London for Paris. He wrote to TSE (who sent him some money during his first weeks in France) on 12 Mar.: 'You have been beautifully kind to me, and I'm glad I came to London, because I met you.' And on 20 Mar.: 'Last saturday nite I saw D. H. Lawrence for a couple of hours. We spoke of you, your work, and I told him how wonderfully gentle you had been with me during my stay in London.'

2–'Niccolò Machiavelli', trans. Erich Alport, *Neue Schweizer Rundschau* 22: 8 (Aug. 1929), 597–606.

TO *Messrs Talbot Coall & Son*   cc

21 February 1929   (London)

Dear Sirs,

Re Haigh-Wood Estate –

With regard to the proposed renewal of the lease of Spencer Hill from the freeholders I have to inform you that the assent of the Trustees and of the Proprietors has been delayed owing to the absence of Mr Maurice Haigh-Wood on business in Italy. I hope to hear from him on this matter within a few days; I wrote to him some days ago, and am now telegraphing. I understand from your letter of the 18th instant to Messrs. James & James that the nominal time limit of the end of this month can be extended indefinitely; but it is as well that you should know the cause of the delay.

10 Eglinton Park –

Referring to your letter of the 18th ultimo, to Messrs. James & James, I gather that Mr Duffy has declined to consider purchasing this house, and that he has applied for a new lease instead. I understand that he is preparing a list and estimate of the improvements which he desires to carry out, which you will forward to Messrs. James & James in due course.[1]

I am, dear Sir,
Yours faithfully,
[T. S. Eliot]

TO *Messrs. James & James*   cc

21 February 1929   [London]

Dear Mr James,
RE Irish Estate.

On the 11th instant I send Maurice a copy of your letter to him of the 7th, but have had no answer. I am wiring to him tonight, as he has been moving about in Italy and the letter may have missed him.

1–Talbot Coall & Son (Estate Agents, Receivers, Auctioneers & Valuers) replied on 25 Feb. that Mr Duffy had 'not made what we consider an adequate offer. Apparently the highest amount he is prepared to give is £800, and this is not full value for the house . . . [H]e had had preliminary estimates of the work which amount to from £170 to £200.'

I have your letter of the 19th and note that Mr Duffy will submit a list of the work he proposes having done.[1]

Your letter and the enclosure make the situation about Eglinton Park clearer; I should have been surprised if the option expired at the end of this month. I will send copies of these to Maurice as soon as he replies to my wire; and when we hear from him about it, the executors and the beneficiaries can write to you formally. Meanwhile I am dropping a line to Coall to explain the delay.

Meanwhile Maurice forwarded me a letter which he had from you before he left and which he had not had time to answer. Am I to understand that Mr Duffy will not consider purchase, and had made the application for a new lease as a counter-proposal?

Yours sincerely,
[T. S. Eliot]

TO *Ants Oras*[2]   CC

21 February 1929   [London]

Dear Sir,

Thank you for your letter.[3] I am quite willing that you should publish translations of some of my poems into Esthonian in your literary monthly. You mentioned 'The Hollow Men', 'Portrait Of A Lady', and 'Preludes'. I authorise you to publish translations of these. If you wish to translate any others I shall be glad if you will write to me again, as I never like to authorise translations unless I know exactly what is to be translated.

It is understood that this present agreement applies to publications in your literary periodical only.

---

1 – At 9/10 Eglinton Park.
2 – Ants Oras, who had taken a B.Litt. in English Literature at Oxford, was Assistant Lecturer in English Literature (later Professor), University of Tartu, Estonia; Secretary of the Estonian P.E.N. Club; and author of *The Critical Ideas of T. S. Eliot* (Tartu, 1932).
3 – Oras asked permission to translate into Estonian, for the leading Estonian literary monthly *Looming*, 'specimens' of TSE's poetry. He had already translated verse from English, Finnish, German, and Russian. 'I am quite aware that any attempt to translate your verse is a daring enterprise but I hope some of its style and spirit can be retained in Estonian without deviating very much from the wording of the original poems. Our language has attained to a considerable degree of flexibility and precision.' The translations appeared in the issue of May 1929, 562–8.

I wish you all success with your Monthly, and am very sorry that I shall be unable to appreciate your translations.

Yours very truly,
[T. S. Eliot]

TO *Peter Quennell* CC

22 February 1929   [London]

Dear Quennell,

I have read your essay on Corbière with great interest and enjoyment.[1] I find it a little difficult to criticise apart from the rest of the book of which it will be part; which makes me all the more anxious to see as much more of the book as is ready. My point is that I do not quite make out what the plan of the book is to be. None of these poets is really well known in England, even Baudelaire; but Corbière is probably the most obscure of all. Even for a very select public, an essay on Corbière must contain a good deal of simple expository matter, and more quotation; and I doubt whether there are a dozen people in England who know his verse well – as your essay requires them to know it. You may say, of course, that in what you have sent me Corbière himself is merely the text for a general statement. I agree, and I find the statement a very interesting one; but you don't get it across to people who don't know Corbière, because they will think it is necessary to know Corbière to understand it.

Do you think you could send me any more parts? I am a little doubtful whether this part by itself is not above the heads even of *The Criterion* public. The first thing is to make out a case for Corbière as a [*typing runs off the page*] your whole book is pioneer work. There has been no sound criticism of any of these points for the present generation, except of Baudelaire; and about him there is too much.

I should like to see you in a week or two and talk it over.

Yours ever,
[T. S. Eliot]

1 – Quennell submitted his essay with an undated letter: 'I am afraid it is rather long and I don't know how much sense it makes out of its context: the original essay is as long again and longer.' He hoped also to send TSE 'the *Baudelaire* you so kindly said you would look at in a few days time'. TSE reviewed *Baudelaire and the Symbolists* in C. 9 (Jan. 1930), 357–9.

TO *S. L. Gould*   CC

22 February 1929   [London]

Dear Madam,
   In reply to your enquiry of the 2nd instant,[1] addressed to Faber &
Gwyer, I have pleasure in giving you hereunder the dates of the essays in
For Lancelot Andrewes which were published in England:

Lancelot Andrewes	*Times Literary Supplement*	Sep. 23, 1926
John Bramhall	*Theology*	July 1927
Machiavelli	*Times Literary Supplement*	June 16, 1927
F. H. Bradley	*Times Literary Supplement*	Dec. 29, 1927
Thomas Middleton	*Times Literary Supplement*	June 30, 1927

   The *T.L.S.* is weekly, *Theology* monthly; both are published in London.
                              Yours faithfully,
                              [T. S. Eliot]

TO *Allen Tate*   TS Princeton

22 February 1929   *The Criterion*

Dear Tate,
   Thank you for your interesting letter of the 15th.[2] I am sending you
a copy of the Chesterton proof; but as I think I said, you will not find it
anything except what you expect of Chesterton. It always is: but Chesterton
may serve as a megophone [*sic*] to call attention to the problem.[3] I do not
know whether you have seen the *Forum*.

---

1 – S. L. Gould (Book Editorial Department, Doubleday Doran & Company) said that *FLA*
was to be published on 8 Apr.: she therefore asked for a full listing of the essays published
in periodicals, so as to complete the copyright records.
2 – 'I should like to see what Chesterton says of Foerster, upon whom the discussion of
the non-religious part of Humanism is based. Foerster lacks the canniness of the master
Babbitt; he is eager and explicit; and his exposition of the Humanistic programme lies open
to fundamental attack . . . For example, how can a method for the refutation of naturalism
be based on naturalism (he says science)? . . .
   'It is all a desperate muddle, and Babbitt shares it in all its aspects. For this reason, he
does, as you say, deceive himself. But I do think that if Babbitt were religious, as More is,
he would see that religion is not "what you do with your solitude" – which is what More's
religion, at least until recently, comes down to . . . It seems to me that Hulme's identification
of humanism and naturalism will stand.'
3 – Chesterton, 'Is Humanism a Religion?', C. 8 (Apr. 1929), 382–93.

445

I am inclined to agree that Foerster, and even Babbitt, in fact the humanists in general, do suffer from lack of philosophical training. It is this philosophising against a literary, and academic-literary at that, background, which makes them talk as if there was a philosophy explicit in Homer or Virgil or Sophocles. As for science (which to me means only mathematics and mathematical physics) one should know just enough, I think, to avoid getting mixed up with it. Hulme has influenced me enormously.

I wonder what American periodical you mean: besides the *Forum*, the *Hound and Horn* is interested, and I am going to write an article for them to clear up some of the apparent misunderstandings of my note on Babbitt in the *Forum*. I look forward to seeing you again in London.

yours very sincerely,
T. S. Eliot

TO *Roy Campbell*   CC

22 February 1929   [London]

Dear Mr Campbell,

Thank you very much indeed for your letter, which gave me much pleasure.

I do not agree with you about 'The Gum Trees'; I see the effect of the Cantique des Collones;[1] but everything I have seen of yours is quite your own. I am very glad it will appear in *Commerce*; and I am very glad to hear that you will send me something soon that you like better.[2]

I agree with you in not enjoying contemporary poetry;[3] and find no relief in French, German or Italian either. But I doubt whether a poet can judge his contemporaries except within very narrow limits of a technical kind. I doubt whether one should read contemporary verse at all! If a man is trying to do something like what one is trying oneself, it bothers one; if

1 – 'Cantique des colonnes', by Paul Valéry.
2 – Campbell wrote on 7 Feb. that he had 'some better work in preparation' to send to TSE for C.; as for 'The Gum Trees', it was 'a poem about which I am very doubtful indeed – an early poem which I have overhauled about ten times to suit different things. It was originally the mere result of the excitement I got out of reading Les Colonnes. For me it has completely lost its identity . . . The metre, also, is one which I should leave alone. You are about the only modern writer that can use it without a sing-song effect.'
3 – '[F]rom your critical essays it appears that you read the same poets as I do . . . I don't very often feel anything for a contemporary, but I have been forced by my own literary conscience to study everything you have written since I was sixteen years old . . .'

he is not, it bores one; and it seems to me bad for one to read any poetry except that out of which one gets a peculiar delight. There seems to be a great amount of quite competent verse turned out today; but most of it could have been written by any one of half a dozen people.

It is very kind of you to ask me to visit you in Martigues; and I should like immensely both to visit Martigues, which I have never seen, and to visit you, who threaten to become invisible for a long time. But I see no prospect of getting away from London long enough, within the next six months; apart from having no assistant with *The Criterion*, I have engagements dotted about all that period, of greater or less remuneration. I am sad to think that you may not be in London again for several years – people who have left it for a long time seldom want to return here to live; but I had hoped that business of some sort might bring you here. I hope however that we can keep in touch by correspondence.

Please send me a poem for *The Criterion* as soon as you can,[1] and believe me, with most cordial thanks for your kind invitation,

Yours very sincerely,

[T. S. Eliot]

TO *H. P. Collins* CC

23 February 1929   [London]

Dear Mr Collins,

Thank you for your letter of the 21st. I am interested that you should have noticed the review of P. E. More's book, because I wrote the review myself.[2] I have been deliberating whether to have the book reviewed in *The Criterion* or not. If you saw the December *Criterion* you will have noticed a short article on Humanism by Herbert Read. This essay is actually the setting of a problem, which is to be dealt with by others: it is to be followed in March by an article by G. K. Chesterton, and I am expecting contributions by such writers as Norman Foerster, Ramon Fernandez, and Allen Tate. (I have already written on the subject in *The Forum*, a paper which I reprinted in my last small book, and am probably writing again in the June *Adelphi*). Now, I should be very glad to have you participate, and your point of view would be most interesting. But I think

---

1 – No poem by Campbell appeared in *C*.

2 – Collins had noticed in the *TLS* that day the anonymous review of Paul Elmer More's book of essays, *The Demon of the Absolute*, which he thought would make a good basis for an essay-review in the *Criterion*. Failing that, he would like to write on Galsworthy.

a review of one of More's books separately would be merely a dispersal of interest. May I ask whether you are familiar both with the work of Babbitt and of More, and with the differences of attitude of these two men? The texts of the debate are Foerster's book on American Criticism, Babbitt's last two books, and More's *Greek Tradition* and his new book.

I will send you a copy of *The Demon of the Absolute* in any case; and you can write again when you have looked at it?

And I will keep your other suggestions in mind and perhaps make others. I am just completing work on the March number, which is in press; and have hardly begun to think of the reviews for the June number.

Sincerely yours,
[T. S. Eliot]

TO *Charles A. Siepmann*[1]   TS BBC

24 February 1929   *The Criterion*

Dear Mr Siepmann,

I enclose a tentative synopsis of a fairly popular sort. I have had to leave several blanks in the bibliography for books that I shall have to look up at the library. I should glad to hear from you about this <outline> before arranging for a test.[2]

Yours sincerely,
T. S. Eliot

---

1 – Charles Arthur Siepmann (1899–1985), radio producer and educator, was awarded the Military Cross in WW1. He joined the BBC in 1927, and was Director of Talks, 1932–5; of Regional Relations, 1935–6; of Programme Planning, 1936–9. He was University Lecturer, Harvard, 1939–42; worked for the Office of War Information, 1942–5; and was Professor of Education, New York University, 1946–67. His publications include *Radio's Second Chance* (1946), *Radio, Television and Society* (1950), and *TV and Our School Crisis* (1959). See further Richard J. Meyer, 'Charles A. Siepmann and Educational Broadcasting', *Educational Technology Research and Development* 12: 4 (Winter 1964), 413–30. TSE told HWE on 9 Mar. 1937: 'In spite of [Siepmann's] name he is in all appearance a perfectly English person, and was educated at Rugby and Oxford. I think his father or grandfather was German. Siepmann is an extremely serious, not to say solemn, young man, of about 36, who has been in the British Broadcasting Corporation longer than anyone I have ever heard of except Sir John Reith himself . . . [H]is political sympathies are rather liberal and left. He is a very nice fellow, although somewhat humourless.'
2 – Siepmann answered (25 Feb.), 'I am very much attracted by your outline scheme and have no material alterations to suggest . . . You will, of course, remember that a standard of simplicity is essential in such talks.'

Syllabus for a course of six talks on Seventeenth Century Poetry: by T. S. Eliot

I. General characteristics of the period of James I and Charles I. Sixteenth century a period of consolidation, marked by foreign wars and alliances; seventeenth century a period of internal dissensions, which have their political and their religious aspect. The 17th century more sophisticated, more cosmopolitan and more highly civilised. Prose literature develops rapidly. In drama, tragedy declines, whilst comedy becomes more refined and brilliant. Lyrical poetry, that is, poetry to be sung with musical accompaniment, tends to disappear; the lyric to be recited or read is highly developed, and becomes elaborate in meaning and often fantastic in expression. Influence of the Counter-Reformation: bitterness of the struggle for different kinds of political organization and antagonistic kinds of religious belief and church organization. The poet was often an ecclesiastic and a courtier, or was actively engaged in the political conflicts which overshadow everything. Papist, Puritan and Anglican. Shorthouse's novel *John Inglesant* is still an excellent introduction to the atmosphere of Jacobean and Caroline England. Feiling's *England under the Tudors and Stewarts* [sic] (Home University Library) gives a brief statement of the historical facts. Grierson's *Metaphysical Poetry of the XVII Century* is an admirable anthology of the poets to be discussed, with a capital introduction. The spirit of Baroque Art in England.

II. DONNE: Donne the representative poet of his age, although he represents also the transition from Elizabethan to Stewart period in literature. What is meant by calling Donne a *metaphysical* poet. His use of philosophical and theological learning in poetry. His development of lyrical verse. His great popularity at the present time, after long neglect. In what ways he is overrated or misunderstood. His verse inventions, and his development of the Verse Satire. (In the Muses' Library (2s. each) his Satires and Epistles are published in one volume and the lyrical verse in another. The standard text is that of Grierson (Oxford, 2 vols) and Grierson's Introduction should be read.) His use of the *conceit* in poetry, and his influence. Dr Johnson's opinion of Donne.

III. THE DEVOTIONAL POETS: George Herbert, Richard Crashaw, Vaughan and Traherne. Donne's religious verse is eloquent, but in these four men English religious verse finds its highest development. Contrast between Herbert the Anglican and Crashaw the Roman Catholic. We must however consider rather the common religious ground of these men than their sectarian differences from a modern point of view. Contrast between religious verse of the XVII Century and that of the XII and

XIII Centuries. Influence of Spanish mystics. Relation of Vaughan and Traherne to Wordsworth and the poetry of nature. Walton's *Life of Mr George Herbert* should be read, in the volume of Walton's *Lives* (World's Classics 2s).

IV. PURITAN POLITICIANS, AND COURTIERS. Andrew Marvell and John Milton are an interesting subject of comparison, both active in political life and Parliament-men. Contrast of Marvell's verse with Milton's early work, especially *L'Allegro*, *Il Penseroso*, and *Comus*. (Milton's major works will not be discussed). Puritanism produced no great 'devotional' verse except Milton's *Hymn to the Nativity*. On the other hand we have the 'courtly' light poets, such as Carew, Lovelace and Suckling.

V. MINOR 'METAPHYSICALS': We get much evidence of the 'fantastic' in poetry in Donne, Crashaw and Marvell, and in the poetry of Bishop King, who is as near to Marvell as to anyone. But we cannot understand the spirit of the age unless we are willing to examine at least two of the lesser, but more grotesque poets: Cleveland and Benlowes – and to read these poets we must turn to Mr Saintsbury's *Caroline Poets*. Samuel Johnson's essay on Donne, in his *Lives of the Poets*, is an essential document in the history of opinion, and is a criticism of Cleveland as well. What there is to be said for Cleveland and Benlowes. (As these poets are less familiar, the listener may depend upon the extracts to be read during the course of the talk).

VI. ABRAHAM COWLEY: Who, again, is given a good deal of attention by Johnson in his *Lives of the Poets* – and Johnson's critical opinions are always interesting and always to be respected – is particularly interesting because he represents the transition between the intense, if often wildly absurd, poetry of the first part of the XVII Century, and the 'Augustan Age' of Dryden and Pope. Cowley is an important historical document: he shows us how the change in sensibility between the England of Charles I, Wentworth and Laud,[1] and the England of Charles II and

---

1 – William Laud (1573–1645), Archbishop of Canterbury from 1633; leader of the High Anglican party. In 'Lancelot Andrewes', TSE said that the bishop's prayers 'illustrate the devotion to private prayer . . . and to public ritual which Andrewes bequeathed to William Laud' (*FLA*, 18). Laud was a passionate advocate for the powers and rights of the established Church in harmony with the monarchy. He was opposed to Puritanism and nonconformism, insisting that ecclesiastical uniformity was the necessary correlative of order in the state. His conviction as to the catholicity of the Church of England led to suspicions of popery. TSE said of Richard Hooker, in *VMP*, 164: 'it is no wonder that before he joined the Church of Rome he found the church of Archbishop Laud the most sympathetic, of Laud who took his stand for the liturgy and "the beauty of holiness" . . .'.

William and Mary and Anne, could have come about. His feeling is with the later generation, his habit of thought and expression with the earlier. Cowley's influence upon Dryden.

BIBLIOGRAPHY

Several books, the most useful for our purpose being Grierson's anthology of Metaphysical Poetry, have already been mentioned. I should like to add the small book on Marvell by Vita Sackville-West (Faber & Faber, 3s. 6d.); and for those who can read Italian the best book, besides the works of Professor Grierson mentioned, is *Marinismo e Secentismo in Inghilterra* by Mario Praz (La Voce, Florence) which gives some notion also of the continental currents of the times. Among the works which contribute to the background of the period are such books as the *Exercises* of St Ignatius Loyola, the writings of St John of the Cross, the *Private Prayers* of Lancelot Andrewes, and Hooker's *Ecclesiastical Polity*. Duncan-Jones's short biography of Archbishop Laud is a useful book. But for purely literary criticism, Dr Johnson and Professor Grierson are best. The latter has recently brought out *Cross Currents in English Literature of the XVII Century* (Chatto, 15s.)

V. THE MINOR 'METAPHYSICALS' TO COWLEY: Cleveland and Benlowes as examples of the more fantastic minor poets. What there is to be said for them, how they can be read, and how they help us to understand the major poetry of the period. (These two poets are hardly accessible except in Saintsbury's *Caroline Poets*, but extracts will be given in this talk). The curious place of Abraham Cowley: his verse is related to that of Donne before him and to that of Dryden after him. He is the link between early seventeenth century poetry and the poetry of the Augustan Age.

VI. DRYDEN: The last great poet of the XVII Century. Development of the heroic couplet with Denham and Waller, of Satire with Oldham, and of heroic drama with Davenant. Reaction against the early XVII Century. In what the greatness of Dryden consists. His criticism of the earlier age as expressed in his Essays (Everyman's Library). Comparison of the first half and the second half of the XVII Century in their theory and practice of poetry.

TO *R. P. Blackmur*   CC

25 February 1929   [London]

Dear Mr Blackmur,

Your letter and the welcome offprint from the *Hound & Horn* arrived this morning. I am glad to hear that my suggestion is welcome to you. What I have to say will be a kind of sequel to my *Forum* essay, trying to sweep up on the way some misconceptions.[1]

You are right about Fernandez' uncertainty.[2] He has promised me a contribution in time for the June number – not the essay on George Eliot, which was promised a year ago and never written – but an essay on Humanism again, or on the Fernandez brand of Humanism. Would that make too much Humanism for one number? *If* it comes in time, I could write to Fernandez immediately for his consent, and send you a copy. I shall be writing to him tomorrow; having just got the March number made up for the printer I am starting to round up the June contributors.

Some time I hope to discuss your article fully with you – I have never yet found time.[3] But meanwhile I should be extremely interested to know how you react to Andrewes. It is more an apologia than a programme of reform: it is an interim statement, to avoid misunderstanding. But any such statement creates more misunderstanding than it dispels.[4]

1–Blackmur (13 Feb.) liked the title 'Second Thoughts on Humanism': 'I suppose and hope that your "Second Thoughts" will have some relation to your Forum article on Babbitt. I know from personal conversation that a great many people have been struck with the notion of humanism as a *substitute* for religion – myself especially.' TSE, 'Second Thoughts on Humanism', *Hound and Horn* 2: 4 (July/Sept. 1929), 339–50.

2–'The other day in conversation with Mr Montgomery Belgion I learned that Ramon Fernandez was in a very long process of giving you some sort of essay – perhaps on George Eliot – I am not sure now. If you think it would be possible to arrange such an essay with M. Fernandez, this is precisely the sort of thing that we would like to be able to publish simultaneously with the *Criterion* . . . I understand that M. Fernandez is a very slow writer and cannot be depended upon so far as time is concerned.'

3–'T. S. Eliot': Parts I and II, *Hound and Horn* I (Mar. 1928), 187–213; (June) 291–319. 'I am sending you a copy of the reprint of my article on yourself. Believe me, that I am rather ashamed of many paragraphs, both as to style and content, and I am in fact, rather sorry that the thing was reprinted at all. But I hope some time to go over it carefully making corrections, modifications; expanding it generally so as to include the mood, which I think I share, exposed in "Lancelot Andrewes", and the program announced in its preface. I should be enormously grateful if you would be willing to make particular comment on what I have written, either as to point of fact, or "interpretation".'

4–See also Max Stewart, 'The "*Gout pour la Vie Spirituelle*"; T. S. Eliot's Anglican profession and his view of Bishop Lancelot Andrewes', *The Yeats Eliot Review* 9: 2 (Winter 1988), 54–63.

I shall do my best to let you have my paper by the middle of March. By the way, Middleton Murry wants to use it here in his June or July *Adelphi*: I suppose there is no objection? But (although I believe *The Adelphi* pays little or nothing) in that case I should like to be paid by you at your ordinary rates only. I don't want to bleed a goose which lays such excellent eggs.[1]

Yours sincerely,
[T. S. Eliot]

Vivien Eliot TO *Ottoline Morrell*   MS [Texas]

Monday le 25 February 1929   57 Chester Terrace, s.w.1.

Dearest Ottoline

I am dreadfully annoyed with myself, but I have another attack of influenza. Or rather, the *same* attack, for I am sure I never quite got over it. I have felt *terribly* ill since last Friday week, when Tom went to have 2 teeth out. He had a very bad swollen face for some days before that, and was *very queer*. It upset me a *good deal*, one way & *another*, & I have felt very tired ever since. I was in bed all Friday, & most of Saturday. And now today I have a fever & pains all over me. It is very trying, the cold weather. And various other small calamities have happened.

I got a card from you several days too late, as it was addressed to 27 Chester Terrace. I thought it very nice of you to invite me to tea with you – last time you were here. I never said anything against you, except on that *one* occasion under what I consider to have been the *most extreme* provocation, & if I was ever worth knowing, I am worth knowing now. I think you were quite honest with me a year ago – but I don't see what I could have done.[2]

Yours affectionately
V. H. Eliot

1 – The standard rate was 'three dollars and a half a page for prose'. Blackmur later said (20 Mar.) they had no objection to TSE's article coming out also in the *Adelphi* – 'but we do have an insuperable objection to changing, in any way, our arrangement with you about the rate at which you will be paid. Naturally, if in the future you will be willing to let us have things at our ordinary rates, we could hardly be anything but very pleased.' TSE, 'Second Thoughts on Humanism', *New Adelphi* 2: 4 (June/Aug. 1929), 304–10.
2 – OM had apparently advised VHE at some point in 1928 to separate from TSE.

TO *Constance Eastwood* CC

28 February 1929   [London]

Dear Miss Eastwood,

I thank you for your letter of the 25th, and should be highly honoured by serving on the Parish Council.[1] But I am extremely doubtful whether it is possible for me, with my other engagements and obligations, conscientiously to accept a position which I might not be able to fill adequately – in addition to the fact that I have no experience – and if there is any other suitable person, I feel that that person would be more suitable than I.

> With many thanks,
> I am,
> Yours very truly,
> [T. S. Eliot]

TO *Humphrey Whitby* CC

28 February 1929   [London]

Dear Father Whitby,

It is good of you to write to me, and I have been wishing to see you for a long time. For reasons which are partly known to you, it is difficult for me to make engagements; and the only day which I can more or less count upon for tea, is Wednesday of any week. Next Wednesday I have already had to engage; and I [am] afraid Wednesday is not very convenient for you in any case. But if a future Wednesday is possible, it would be a great pleasure to me.

> With many thanks and best wishes,
> Sincerely yours,
> [T. S. Eliot]

1–TSE's neighbour Constance Eastwood (31 Chester Terrace, s.w.1) invited TSE to serve on the Parish Council of St Mary's, Graham Street, London.

TO *Francis Underhill*   CC

28 February 1929   [London]

Dear Father Underhill,
    Very many thanks for your patience. I shall be very happy to lunch with
you on Wednesday, the 27th March at 1, as you suggest.[1]
                                Yours very sincerely,
                                [T. S. Eliot]

TO *Francis Underhill*   CC

28 February 1929   [London]

Dear Father Underhill,
    I have your letter of the 25th about the Liddon centenary.[2] I shall be
very happy to do everything I can to help. I have been thinking about it,
and wish you could let me have further suggestions of any ways in which
you think I might be useful. *The Criterion*, of course, must allow always
about twenty-five years to elapse before any of its ideas can reach the
general public; and it is hopeless as an 'advertising medium'. I *might* be
able to help influence *The Times* (Dawson) to take some interest: they
ought to publish an article on Liddon when the time comes. The weekly
reviews are of very little use, I think. This is an immediate reply, and I
shall continue to think about it; but any suggestions from you would be
useful.
                                Sincerely yours,
                                [T. S. Eliot]

1–Fr Underhill invited TSE to dine at Liddon House, 24 South Audley Street.
2–Underhill asked for advice on launching a 'press campaign' in aid of the centenary of
Dr Henry Liddon: Liddon House and St Edmund Hall were preparing jointly to mark the
centenary. A memorial meeting was to be held in Christ Church Hall. H. P. Liddon (1829–
90), traditionalist theologian (he was devoted to Pusey and Keble) and charismatic and
immensely popular preacher, was born on 20 Aug. 1829. A friend of Lewis Carroll at Christ
Church, Oxford (from where he graduated in 1850), Liddon was made in 1864 prebendary
of Salisbury Cathedral. In 1870 he was appointed at one and the same time Canon of St
Paul's Cathedral, London, and Professor of the Exegesis of the Holy Scripture, Oxford; and
in 1886 he was made Chancellor of St Paul's. He published several series of lectures, essays,
and addresses; and *Some Elements of Religion* (1870).

TO *Maurice Haigh-Wood*   CC

4 March 1929   [London]

Dear Maurice,

I enclose copy of letter and attached list re 10, Eglinton Park which I have from Coall. James observes

> 'I think that the terms offered by the tenant for a new lease are not unreasonable but at the same time I myself should prefer to sell the house for £800 which amount invested would probably bring in an annual return equal to that under the lease. For estate duty the property was valued at £593 only in 1927'.

I do not quite agree. The house property in Ireland was rather under-valued in 1927; and I do not see how £800 is going to bring in £57 a year. But I should have to ask a broker what can be bought to yield that.

You may not have time to answer this before you return, but it is just as well that you should be acquainted with the situation before you come.

                                          Yours ever, aff.,
                                          [Tom]

TO *Mario Praz*   CC

4 March 1929   [*The Criterion*]

My dear Praz,

I must apologise for not having answered your letter. My secretary has been expected back to work every day, after an illness, and thus work has been postponed from day to day in the expectation of her returning to do it.

I should like very much to have the Chaucer MSS. to show my people.[1] At the same time, I am afraid that it will be too technical and advanced for us to market successfully; and it undoubtedly ought to have been taken by the University Press. But I should like to see it: it might be expanded, if you were willing, into a book for the general public, without losing any of its scholarly quality.

1–Praz had written from Liverpool ('this abomination of desolation') a long, scholarly, reference-heavy essay on 'Foreign Influence on Chaucer' for a collection *A Companion to Chaucer* which the Clarendon Press had asked him to recast in shorter, more accessible form. He asked TSE on 10 Feb. if F&G might publish his piece as a pamphlet. (He told TSE on 5 Apr. that ultimately he had agreed to the changes desired by Clarendon Press.)

So far as I know, I shall be at my office during the morning of Tuesday the 12th; and if you cared to look in I should be delighted to see you.[1]

Where should the March *Criterion* (published the 15th) be sent to you (with the Advocatus Diaboli)?[2]

Yours ever,
[T. S. Eliot]

TO *Denys Winstanley*[3]   CC

4 March 1929   [London]

Dear Winstanley,

It is very pleasant to hear from you again.[4] As for Babbitt, you could I believe find no one better; but I should be very much surprised if it were possible for him to accept. I saw him this summer; he had just spent a 'sabbatical' (or is it 'sabbatacal'?) year in Paris, where he has more than once lectured as exchange professor at the Sorbonne; so I doubt whether he will be free again from Harvard for some years to come. Of course you understand that I could not say positively without asking him – but I should consider it extremely unlikely.

I think I mentioned Herbert Read to you several years ago. I think without question that he is a lecturer you ought to have sooner or later; and of course he has much more published work, and a bigger reputation, than he had then. I should say that whether you considered him now or a couple of years hence would depend upon what other good candidates there are in the field. There is a very good German – E. R. Curtius – but I am not quite sure that he could lecture in English; and I don't suppose you want more foreigners at present. But I am speaking strongly in favour of Read, when I say that if you don't have [*typing runs off the page*] him sooner or later.

The name of Babbitt suggests to my mind that of Paul Elmer More, his friend, and, I think, a man of equal importance: but he is not so well

1 – Praz would be passing through London, on his way to Italy. (In the event, he did not find TSE at his office that day.)

2 – Praz, 'Mysticism or Advocatus Diaboli', C. 8 (Apr. 1929), 460–79.

3 – Denys Winstanley (1877–1947), historian, was a Fellow of Trinity College, Cambridge; Senior Tutor, 1925–31; Vice-Master from 1935.

4 – Winstanley wrote on 3 Mar. to say that the College Council was considering the possibility of inviting Prof. Irving Babbitt to become Clark Lecturer for the year 1929–30. Did TSE think Babbitt might accept? 'Herbert Read is also being considered, and I should value your opinion of him.'

known here, though he has friends and relatives in Cambridge. Ivor Richards knows him.

Thank you very much for your invitation. I should be delighted to come down some night as your guest; and if I find it possible during the summer, I shall propose myself.

Yours very sincerely,
[T. S. Eliot]

TO *F. E. Hutchinson*[1]　　　　　　　　　　　　　　　　　CC

4 March 1929　　　　　　　　　　　　[London]

My dear Sir,

I must apologise for not having replied immediately to your kind and flattering letter of the 21st ultimo; but I have been turning you[r] invitation over in my mind.[2] It would have given me great pleasure to accept, and I was very much tempted; but after summing up carefully my engagements for the next four months I am brought to the conclusion that it is more than I have any right to attempt. The period to be treated presents, of course, such a temptation as may never occur again; yet I feel that I have no business to undertake what I am not sure of being able to carry out to my satisfaction.

With many thanks and very many regards,

I am, Sir,
Yours very truly,
[T. S. Eliot]

1–The Revd F. E. Hutchinson (1871–1947) was Secretary to the Delegacy for Extra-Mural Studies, University of Oxford, 1920–34; and Chaplain (1928) and Fellow (1934) of All Souls. An authority on Caroline poetry, he was author of *Richard Crashaw* (1928), *The Works of George Herbert* (ed., 1941), *Henry Vaughan: A Life and Interpretation* (1947), *Milton and the English Mind* (1946), and *Cranmer and the English* (1951).
2–Hutchinson invited TSE to contribute a set of three lectures – perhaps on Lancelot Andrewes, John Donne, and Marvell or Vaughan? he suggested – to the Oxford Summer Meeting in Aug.: the theme of the school was to be 'England and English Literature in the Seventeenth Century'. The fee was five guineas per lecture, plus travelling expenses.

TO *C. A. Siepmann*   TS BBC

4 March 1929   Faber & Gwyer Ltd

Dear Mr Siepmann,

Will you kindly suggest some day when it would be convenient for me to have a voice test, say between 11 and 12:30 in the morning? I could manage any day this week except Thursday (and tomorrow, Tuesday), and I think any day the following week.[1]

Yours sincerely,
T. S. Eliot

TO *Allen Tate*   Princeton/CC

5 March 1929   Faber & Gwyer Ltd

Dear Tate,

Very many thanks for your letter of the 28th and the essay which I have read with the deepest interest. It reached me before I had finished my (briefer) paper for the *Hound & Horn;* I avoided saying some things that you had said better than I could have done, but you may find some overlapping nevertheless.[2] I should have liked to use your paper in the next (i.e. the June) number; but in that number I am publishing an essay by More,[3] and it seemed to me unsuitable to launch More at the same time as a criticism of him, onto a public to which he is almost unknown. So I am using your Emily Dickinson in June, and this essay probably in the following number. Meanwhile I will send you a proof of More's essay, though I dare say it will not modify your judgment. I am not yet quite sure whether your interpretation of More is fair or not; but I am sure that you are perfectly just to Babbitt and Foerster. I think yours is a brilliant article.[4]

Yours sincerely,
T. S. Eliot

1 – Siepmann replied (5 Mar.) with the suggestion of Wed., 6 Mar. at 12 o'clock.
2 – 'I think we are in accord on the main points of the humanism–religion issue . . . Reading it over for the last time, I am astonished to see that it is possible people will suppose that I am unsympathetic to the humanists, particularly to More. I admire More extremely.'
3 – Paul Elmer More, 'An Absolute and Authoritative Church', C. 8 (July 1929), 616–34.
4 – Tate responded to this letter (n.d.), 'I am delighted that you like my essay. If it overlaps with yours for the Hound and Horn, the reason is easy to find: I have followed your writings with great care for more than ten years. But I think there is some remote difference from you. I would call myself a Realist by way of Cartesian rationalism, this doctrine being influenced in its contemporary application by the works of Hulme. My criticism of Babbitt and Foerster is substantially yours, in your essay on Babbitt.

TO *H. P. Collins*   CC

5 March 1929   [London]

Dear Mr Collins,

Thank you for your letter of the 4th instant. I am very glad to know that you are already so deep in the Humanism subject. I like your suggestion very much; the only question is of date. I have already one interesting paper on the subject by Allen Tate, which I should have printed in June, except for the inconvenience that I have an essay by P. E. More himself, already postponed, which I must use in that number; and it did not seem to me suitable to print an article largely criticising More in the same number. That throws More forward till September; and I must also allow for the possibility of Norman Foerster's wanting to publish a reply to Read and Chesterton. But I think I could print yours in December, in any case. I hope that will suit you? I shall be most interested to learn your point of view. I am printing another article of my own on the subject in America (and possibly also in the *Adelphi*) in June.

I am very sorry to hear that you are still suffering from this intolerable winter, and hope that things will be better soon.

Sincerely yours,

[T. S. Eliot]

'I shall be very much pleased if More's article permits me to alter my interpretation of him . . .'

He wrote further after reading More's article (15 Mar.): 'The whole trouble with More, it seems to me, is rooted in his unphilosophical grasp of his terms. No serious Catholic, and no mind familiar with the philosophical vocabularies, would technically apply the word "absolute" to the Roman claim of infallible interpretation or to the Protestant claim of an infallible text. We all know that ultimately these claims are political fictions useful to the masses who must take hold of religion on the lowest plane. More's dilemma is false, and he is betrayed into it because he is unconsciously imbued with the assumptions of eighteenth century rationalism. He is sound in so far as he is uncomfortable about the conclusions of this sort of rationalism, but at present there is no evidence that he will ever be more than uncomfortable. The validity of Catholicism doesn't depend on More's idea of the truth or falsity of the Virgin Birth and the related dogmas, for his idea of them is fundamentally Voltaire's. Before you can talk about the truth of the Virgin Birth you have first to discover a universe in which it can occur; without such a universe, it is neither true nor false; it simply doesn't exist. It really doesn't exist for More because his implicit idea of the absolute is mechanism. The question of the absolute is the question of the nature of truth, and it seems to me that More has never taken the matter back that far. In this essay, again, More relies on common sense, which appears to him to be simple and pure; it is invariably corrupt.

'More is fundamentally sound – if he could only get the right terms. Out of his compromise he may get personal satisfaction, but he will have to forgo authority. I wish I could believe it were otherwise.'

TO *Alsina Gwyer*

5 March 1929   [London]

Dear Lady Gwyer,

I return herewith the copies of your letters to Faber and his letter to you,[1] which I received this morning and showed to Stewart and De la Mare.

I knew nothing of this matter until Friday morning, after your telephone conversation with Mr Faber. I think that his first action was hasty and unmatured, and that the question might have been submitted to the board first, although I understand that it was quite within his powers to deal with it without such consultation. The three months period seemed and seems to me the fair one. But it appears that there was a wide misunderstanding between you and Mr Faber on the telephone. I am quite sure that Mr Faber and the Board will be very glad to approve the three months salary and record their recognition of your brother's services.[2]

1–Lady Gwyer told GCF on 1 Mar. 1929: 'I wish to make my position absolutely clear.

'When I asked you what notice my brother would need your reply was:– "I shall not treat your brother as a housemaid." This however you have now done – He has received one month's notice after four years' work. Such treatment is inexcusable & is directly contrary to the practice of the Firm which has hitherto had an unbroken record of fairness towards those in its employ. As a director I refuse to be a party to any such arrangement, & unless your letter to him has beeen withdrawn previously I shall bring the matter up at the next Board Meeting. I shall also ask the directors to pass a formal vote of thanks to him for his services with an expression of regret that they will not be required after March 31st. I shall also ask that he be voted 3 months' salary in lieu of longer notice.

'Since 1916 I have never known anyone receive less courtesy than this, & whilst I am a member of the Board I shall see that the old tradition is preserved.

'You evidently have other views but the time for putting these into practice will come later. / Yours faithfully / A. H. Gwyer.'

Geoffrey Faber responded on 2 Mar.: 'I am more than sorry to get your letter. Really I have not deserved that you should write to me in such terms. I thought you meant to make yourself responsible for your brother's interests after March. I must have altogether misunderstood you – no doubt very stupidly. In writing to your brother I made no reference to any private arrangement which might have been the subject of discussion between you & him.

'The proposal which your letter makes is identical with the suggestion I made to Eliot and [C. W.] Stewart, after you telephoned on Friday, & – with their consent – I asked Archibald [an accountant] to communicate to you. This, he tells me, he has done.'

Lady Gwyer came back at him on 4 Mar.: 'You are entirely mistaken in thinking that I had any question of money in my mind. I was & am indignant that anyone who has been connected with the Company for over 20 years should have his services summarily dispensed with by the Chairman without any reference to the Board & without a single word of appreciation of his work. That Osbert is my brother is quite irrelevant; I should have felt just as strongly in the case of anyone else. / Yours faithfully / A. H. Gwyer.'

2–Osbert Burdett (1885–1936), Lady Gwyer's brother; author. Works include *The Idea of Coventry Patmore* (1921), *Critical Essays* (1925), *William Blake* (1926), *W. E. Gladstone* (1928), *The Brownings* (1928), *The Two Carlyles* (1930), *Memory and Imagination* (1935).

I am very sorry indeed to learn that you have a chill. This winter has been very unkind to your health. But I hope that you will be well enough to come to the meeting on Thursday without running any risk.

Yours very sincerely,

[T. S. Eliot]

TO *John Middleton Murry*

MS Valerie Eliot

5 March 1929   57 Chester Terrace, s.w.1.

Dear John,

I am afraid that Thursday is not much good; I have a sudden Board meeting on that day at 3, and it is likely to go on for a long time; I don't expect to be able to get home until 5.30 or so. And we have to go out to dinner in the evening. I knew that already, and it would not have interfered by itself, but with the meeting it makes a great rush.

Could you come here to lunch or tea on the day you leave, before you return to Yateley? And could I come to see you before you leave the home?

Or, if you prefer, come on Thursday – Vivien will be at home for tea & all the afternoon & w^d be very glad to see you, but *won't expect* you unless she hears.

Aff.

Tom

Please let me have your London address in any case.

TO *G. K. Chesterton*

MS Dorothy Collins

8 March 1929   57 Chester Terrace, s.w.1.

Dear Mr Chesterton

I much enjoyed your article in *The Forum*, and am writing to express my grateful appreciation of your mention of myself.[1]

GCF had reflected in his diary (18 Nov. 1924) upon Burdett, whom he 'liked very well', that he seemed 'rather unpractical, full of ideas, some valuable others not.' It is not known in what capacity Burdett had worked directly for the publishing business, but presumably he had been closely involved from the early days of the Scientific Press.

1–G. K. Chesterton, 'The Skeptic as a Critic', *The Forum* 81: 2 (Feb. 1929), 65–9. Chesterton complimented 'the admirably sane, subtle, and penetrating article by Mr T. S. Eliot ['The Humanism of Irving Babbitt', *The Forum*, July 1928]; especially that vital sentence in it in which he tells Professor Irving Babbitt (who admits the need of enthusiasm) that we cannot have an enthusiasm for having an enthusiasm' (65–6). Later in his piece, Chesterton

I am having sent to you my recent essays. The book is not important, but if you glance at it, you may get some indication of my position.

Yours very sincerely,

T. S. Eliot

The Criterion should be ready about the 15th.

TO *His Mother*   TS Houghton

10 March 1929   57 Chester Terrace, S.W.1.

Dearest Mother,

The cold spell of weather, which you were worrying about, seems to have passed for good; we have had nearly a week now of moderate and more or less sunny weather. Yesterday was so warm that we had tea in the garden. Perhaps it was rash, so early in the year, but it was very tempting. With so tiny a house, it makes a great difference when the weather is warm enough to use the garden; it seems to give us much more space. Various bulbs are poking their way up, but everything is very late; and the wallflowers which we put in in the autumn are all dead from the frosts. I enclose the first snowdrop of the season; others are budding; the crocus and the other things will not even bud for several weeks.

The house is running very well now. You remember that for several weeks we had two servants, a middle-aged cook-general and a girl; but apart from the expense, which was great, two seemed to be too many, especially with old Janes[1] every morning to do the heavy work, and they were simply tumbling over each other. Now we have got rid of the cook, and have kept the girl, who cooks quite nicely, and is a very efficient

---

declares: 'The Catholic philosophy is mentioned in terms of respect, and even a sort of hope, both by Professor Babbitt ['The Critic and American Life', *Forum*, Feb. 1928] and Mr T. S. Eliot. I do not misunderstand their courtesies, or seek to lure them a step further than they desire to go. But, as a matter of fact, by a series of faultlessly logical steps, Mr Eliot led Professor Babbitt so near to the very gates of the Catholic Church that in the end I felt quite nervous, so to speak, for fear they should both take another unintentional step and fall into it by accident' (69).

1 – W. L. Janes (1854–1939): ex-policeman who worked as handyman for the Eliots. Having been superannuated from the police force early in the century, he worked for a period (until about 1921) as a plain-clothes detective in the General Post Office. TSE reminisced to Mary Trevelyan on 2 Apr. 1951: 'If I ever write my reminiscences, which I shan't, Janes would have a great part in them' ('The Pope of Russell Square', courtesy of the late Humphrey Carpenter). On 12 Dec. 1955 TSE wrote to Adam Roberts: 'I . . . knew a retired police officer, who at one period had to snoop in plain clothes in the General Post Office in Newgate Street – he caught several culprits, he said' (Adam Roberts). Janes would also tell TSE stories of Benjamin Disraeli.

servant, and everything runs very smoothly. Vivien does a good deal of housework herself, under this arrangement; but she prefers that to having too many people about.

My secretary who was ill has not yet returned, so I have been very busy with the *Criterion*, as you may imagine. Nevertheless, I think we have managed to get it out on time, more punctually than the last time; it should be out by the 15th of March (I call it the April number); and I think it is quite an interesting number too. Meanwhile I have written my article on Humanism for the *Hound and Horn*, which will appear in June; and yesterday I finished writing a lecture on Contemporary Literary Criticism which I have promised to deliver at some Working Men's College just before Easter. And I went on Friday to the British Broadcasting Company's offices to have a 'voice test' for my talks which I am to deliver in June. I was taken into a little room, which seemed to be hermetically sealed, and was called a studio, and sat down at a desk and read a few paragraphs aloud in an ordinary voice. There was a little metal box hanging down over the desk, which is the microphone or receiver; and there is a red lamp on the desk which is supposed to go out when one's voice is inaudible. The official who was testing me sat at the other end of the room with a 'headphone' over his ears. The test seemed to be satisfactory. The great difficulty is in timing one's speech: it must be nineteen minutes exactly. It is strange to think that anyone with a *very* powerful wireless set could hear me talking, I suppose, in Boston.

I have not very much news this time. I am anxious to hear from you that the Spring has begun in Cambridge; because your winter is so long and hard, especially for you in a frame house that cannot be properly heated. I look forward so eagerly to your letters, and for news of all the family.

Vivienne sends her love with mine.

Always your devoted son,
Tom.

TO *Bonamy Dobrée*

TS Brotherton Library

11 March 1929 *The Criterion*

Dear Bongamy,

Yours of the 28th ult. received and I trust that you have by now received several Samples of Dentifrices which I have ordered to be sent to you. I have found them very satisfactory[;] having just had Some teeth out and several others condemned I speak with authority.

Re Annamm there is still time for the Strappado, the bastinado, and the bagnio. I will be more careful.

Re Printed Lectures: quoting the 1st Duke of Wellington, I say

'print and be damned'.[1]

Do I mind being libelled? No.

> Yours till June
>
> Tom

Would striplings be considered for Egypt? Young fellows? Can provide scores of Ox. and Cam. youths, if required.

TO *Bruce Richmond*   CC

13 March 1929   [London]

Dear Richmond,

Thank you for your letter of the 12th.[2] The book on the Elizabethan novel would suit me capitally – I have even promised to give a BBC 'talk' of nineteen minutes on the Elizabethan novel – also, I could review with it a reprint of a Greene novel which I had from you some time ago. Perhaps you would prefer to have this review before the Heywood, as the latter is an American University book, and therefore not urgent?

I had thought that you were not really very keen on the Ford, and so had dropped it. But if you do want it, I should like very much to tackle him for some time in May.[3]

I should very much like to see you – but I am afraid that Monday and Tuesday are impossible.[4] With your permission, I will try to get you on the telephone next week, to arrange a day?

I have some rather good news about Read, but perhaps that ought to keep until he has accepted the offer – something I wanted him to have three years ago.

1 – 'Publish and be damned,' said Wellington when threatened with exposure in the memoirs of the courtesan Harriet Wilson in 1824. See Frances Wilson, *The Courtesan's Revenge: The Life of Harriet Wilson, the Woman Who Blackmailed the King* (2003).
2 – BLR asked whether TSE would like to review *The History of the English Novel: The Elizabethan Age and After* – on Sidney, Nashe, Deloney, Dekker, etc. – by Ernest Baker.
3 – 'How is Ford getting on?', asked BLR. 'I should like to have him in May.' BLR responded to this letter on 14 Mar., 'By all means go for the books first. I am not counting on Ford: I shall be glad of it some day – but don't worry over it.' See TSE's review-essay 'John Ford' – based on *Materials for the Study of the Old English Drama (Materialen zur Kunde des älteren englischen Dramas)*, series II, vol. 1, ed. H. de Vocht (Louvain, 1927) – *TLS*, 5 May 1932, 501–2.
4 – BLR had invited TSE to lunch the following week.

By the way, Hachette have recently produced a book called *Le mouvement humaniste aux Etats-Unis* by Professor Louis Mercier, which I think is worth a note: about Babbitt, More and Brownell. Not, please, by me: I have entered the arena of Humanist fighting, and therefore should prefer not to deal with it anonymously any more.

And finally, I have promised my old friend, Miss Harriet Weaver ('The Egoist Press') to do anything I can to get reviewed a book by her friend Dora Marsden which she is publishing, called *The Definition of the Godhead*. It is a tremendous work, demonstrating Christian dogma, a book before which the stoutest will quail; but if you have someone who could look at it, there may, I think, be something there.

Yours ever,
[T. S. E.]

TO *I. A. Richards*

MS Magdalene

19 March 1929   57, Chester Terrace S.W.1.

Dear Richards,

Many thanks. I shall be very glad to come on May 18, but if that is *too late* for you please say so: for it will do as well if we can meet in London.

I am sorry that I am booked for lunch on Thurs. next. I wish I was not. *But* we should be very glad if you & Mrs Richards could come to tea here on that day (4.30?) My wife hopes you can both come. Will you let us know?

Other questions when we meet. Do come to tea on Thursday.

Will you be in London during April?

Yours ever
T. S. E.

TO *The Editor of* The New Statesman[1]

19 March 1929   24 Russell Square, W.C.1

Sir,

Like Mr Edward Garnett, whose letter in your issue of March 16th I read with much interest, I was disturbed by the attitude which you adopted towards the *Sleeveless Errand* case; and I am not reassured by your reply

---

1–Published, under the headline '*Sleeveless Errand*', NS, 23 Mar. 1929, 757.

to Mr Garnett.[1] I have not read the book, but your comments upon it seem to me contradictory. You say, what no one denies, that 'the police must retain the power to prohibit the general publication of prurient and pornographic pictures or writings which have no artistic value'. How this remark applies to Miss James's book is not clear; for you say later that two-thirds of the book, 'contain a very moving and admirably related tale to which no possible objection could be taken', and you 'deny confidently that the book could possibly do any harm to anyone'. If the magistrate had thought as you do, that the book could do no harm, how could he have applied the statute under which it was condemned? If the book could do no harm, then surely all defence or palliation of its suppression falls to the ground.

Furthermore, your counsel is that 'pending the happy day when police supervision is altogether abolished, we think it the business of authors to avoid writing in such a way as positively to invite police interference'. Moses might thus have replied to the Lord: 'Pending the happy day when Pharaoh will see the reasonableness of abolishing all restrictions on the freedom of movement of the children of Israel, I think it the business of my people to avoid acting in such a way as positively to invite the despatch of six hundred chariots'. If authors act with such sweet reasonableness,

---

1 – The editor of the *NS* accepted the case (9 Mar. 1929) that a novel by Norah J. James, *Sleeveless Errand* (published in Paris and the USA), had been suppressed and confiscated (when printed by Eric Partridge for proposed distribution in the UK) for valid reasons. 'It is perfectly obvious that in any circumstances the police must retain the power to prohibit the general circulation of prurient and pornographic pictures or writings which have no artistic value . . . It is an outrage that the manuscripts, decent or indecent, of a writer of the calibre of Mr D. H. Lawrence should be seized in the post, but that is another matter altogether.' Edward Garnett, the publisher's reader, denied in a letter to the editor (16 Mar. 1929, 727–8) that there were 'prurient or pornographic pictures' in James's novel; he held that it was 'spiritually pure, of perfectly sound morality, and one calculated to do public good . . . [I]t is absurd to expect the usual standards of polite conversation in a book which is holding up a mirror to the life of a neurotic "set" of the Café Royal . . . While I agree with you, sir, that it is an outrage that the manuscripts, decent or indecent, of Mr D. H. Lawrence should have been seized in the post . . . I regard it as far more serious that a flood of obloquy should be poured officially on the work of a young, talented authoress who has no means of defence and no remedy against its arbitrary suppression.' Replying to Garnett in the same issue, the editor maintained that the novel contained 'passage after passage which must be described as "obscene" . . . where a greater artist would have produced the same effect without verbal obscenity': 'but after all a line must be drawn somewhere . . . and we do not see how the most broadminded of magistrates could be expected to draw the line below this book and thus give it his official *imprimatur*. That the book could possibly do any harm to anyone we most confidently deny, but pending the happy day when police supervision is altogether abolished, we think it is the business of authors to avoid writing in such a way as positively to invite police interference.'

the happy day is still less likely to arrive, and the bondage will endure for ever. I congratulate you upon your composition of liberalism and prudence.

I am far from believing that all pieces of fiction written by enthusiastic and earnest young women are 'works of art'. This obscure phrase merely confuses the issue, though doubtless the belief that a suppressed book is a work of art wins it many supporters. And the question is not what 'the most broadminded of magistrates' should do when the book is arraigned before him: the point is that it should not be brought before him; the fault is not with Pilate. There is a commonsense knowledge by inspection of pornographic literature of the underworld sort, which is adequate. There is another type of pornographic literature, of which I have seen specimens, and which is always written in such a way as to avoid the possibility of police action. Miss James's book, I am sure from your own testimony, is not pornographic.[1]

Yours, etc.,
T. S. Eliot

TO *I. A. Richards*

MS Magdalene

21 March 1929   57, Chester Terrace S.W.I.

Dear Richards

Mrs Richards will have told you of my mistake, but *next* Thursday will really suit me much better (4.30).

And I also find that May 18 is Whitsun, which won't do. May I hope that May 25, the following week end, will suit you just as well? I do hope so. I am very sorry for my carelessness. And in any case I count on your being available for a time in London.

I am having to do to order a small book on Dante, which I want to ask you about.

'Centifrugal' & 'centripetal' are very crude. Former merely humanists like Babbitt & Fernandez who extract a philosophy & morals out of

1 – The editor replied to TSE's letter, on the same page: 'There is no contradiction in what we have said . . . [D]oes Mr Eliot propose that all supervision should be lifted and that books like *Ulysses* should be freely printed in England as elsewhere, or is he merely talking through his hat about a book which he confesses he has not read? There is no middle course that we can see. Until Mr Eliot, and those who think with him, will come out simply and openly and boldly for the free printing of everything that anybody chooses to write, we do not see that they have any case at all against particular suppressions.'

literature: their bases need to be examined. The opposite is the examination of the terminology of criticism: your work continued.

Yrs.

T. S. E.

TO *A. L. Rowse*   TS Exeter

21 March 1929   [London]

Dear Rowse,

I am returning Mr Crowther's MSS. to you as I received it from you; although it is interesting it seems to me a little thin for our purposes.[1] I have not been able to induce the Hogarth Press to take the essay on the Pitcairn Islanders as a pamphlet. I should be very glad to use it in the *Criterion* but doubt whether that would be possible before the September number. So that if the author would like to try it elsewhere in the mean time please let me know and I will return it.

I shall write to you at greater length later.

Yours, in haste,

T. S. Eliot

TO *Philippa Strachey*   TS Fawcett Library

25 March 1929   57, Chester Terrace S.W.1.

Dear Miss Strachey,

You will remember that you wrote to me on the 14th February, in a way which I took hopefully. I don't want to importune you about your plans; but I have at the moment two possibilities, which I must decide upon almost immediately. Can you let me know whether you have decided to keep your house, and if so whether you have come to any conclusion about letting the top two storeys?

1–Rowse had submitted to TSE (undated) 'a MSS of a friend of mine who is scientific correspondent of the Manchester Guardian. He is a clever man & has many things worth saying: however he writes unprofessionally, and in case the article won't do, I shall be grateful if you would return it either to him or to me: the former preferably.' J. G. Crowther (1899–1984), science journalist, was a professional populariser who contributed from 1928 a well-regarded science column to the *Manchester Guardian*. Other writings include *The Social Relations of Science* (1941) and *Science in Modern Society* (1967).

As I do not know whether you are at home or not, and as time presses me, I shall take the liberty of telephoning tomorrow morning, hoping that you will excuse my haste.

And if you *do* want to let those upper storeys, I should like very much to look at them, at your convenience.

Yours sincerely
T. S. Eliot

TO *Messrs James & James* CC

27 March 1929   [London]

Dear Sirs,

I enclose herewith cheque for £350:12:6 signed by Mrs R. E. Haigh-Wood and myself as Executors of the Charles H. Haigh-Wood Estate, in settlement of your charges for the legal work in winding up the Estate, and with apologies for the delay.

Yours faithfully,
[T. S. Eliot]

TO *Andrew Corry*[1] Copy of TS

2 April 1929   *The Criterion*, 24 Russell Square

Dear Mr Corry,

I hope you will forgive my delay in replying to your kind letter. I knew that it was extremely unlikely that I should be able to come down to Oxford to your dinner on the 8th June; but it was so pleasant to be invited to Merton, to the dinner of a society of which I was once a member, that I dallied as long as I could before declining. It is so uncertain whether I shall be free on that date, whether I shall be able to leave London or if able to leave London whether I shall not have to go somewhere else instead, that I feel I must decline. At the same time I should like to convey to the Bodley Club my pleasure at being invited, and my aspiration towards an invitation for another year.

---

1 – Andrew Corry (1904–81), a graduate of Harvard (Geology and Liberal Arts), was a Rhodes Scholar at Merton College, 1927–9. He would work for the US Foreign Service, as Ambassador to Sierra Leone, 1964–7; Ceylon and the Maldive Islands, 1967–70.

It would be a pleasure to me to meet a man who is of both Harvard and Merton – a combination I have not met with before – and I hope that when you are in London you will let me know, and that we can arrange a meeting.

Again with many thanks,
Yours sincerely,
T. S. Eliot

TO *Roger Hinks* CC

2 April 1929   [*The Criterion*]

Dear Hinks,

I have ordered the Ananias book for you. I had had it in mind that you might care to say something about modern British sculpture, re the two books sent you (one on Eric Gill[1] and one more general) but be that as you wish. It seemed to me to be time that Gill was sized up (or down). But when you have looked over the lot, and considered what is timely, and what interests you, please let me know what you propose to do in chronicle and in long or short reviews, so that I may know how much to allow for, in making up the number.[2]

Yes, we ought to meet again before long. I suggest tomorrow week, tentatively (Wednesday)?

Yours ever,
[T. S. Eliot]

1 – Joseph Thorp, *Eric Gill: With a Critical Monograph by Charles Marriott* (1929).
2 – Hinks replied on 3 Apr. that he had already reviewed Stanley Casson's *Some Modern Sculptors* (1928) in the *Observer*, and he had looked at the Gill: 'I hardly think I could excogitate a chronicle out of such meagre material. But I could do you a review – I think both ought to be publicly sat upon.'

TO *Charles Williams*[1]   CC

2 April 1929   [Faber & Faber Ltd]

Dear Mr Williams,

Many thanks for letting me see the MSS. enclosed – call it essay or chat as you will.[2] As I said, I have no opinion, but am always delighted to read anything about myself, whether flattering or denunciatory does not matter. I have no objection to being called a Mahommedan – these kinks will straighten themselves out in time. My only protest is that which I make to anyone who mentions me – that no account is taken of what I have written since my book of verse: especially the two fragments of *Sweeney Agonistes* (published in *The Criterion*), and less importantly my two Christmas 'Ariel' poems at a shilling apiece. But perhaps they are *not* so good (relatively) as I think they are!

Looking forward to seeing you again,

Sincerely yours,

[T. S. Eliot]

1 – Charles Williams (1886–1945), novelist and writer on theology, worked as a reader for Oxford University Press. After removing in 1939 from London to Oxford (where he lectured and tutored), he became a member, with C. S. Lewis and J. R. R. Tolkien, of the 'Inklings'. TSE greatly admired Williams's 'spiritual shockers', the later novels including *War in Heaven* (1930), *The Greater Trumps* (1932) and *All Hallows' Eve* (1945). See further *Letters of C. S. Lewis*, ed. W. H. Lewis; rev. edn by Walter Hooper (1991)

TSE was to recall, in his Introduction to *All Hallows' Eve* (1948): 'It was in the late 'twenties, I think, that I first met Charles Williams; and it was through the friend who first called my attention to his work that the introduction was effected. A woman with a notable flair for literary talent, who liked to bring together the authors whose work interested her, and who was in a position to do so, made me read Williams's first two novels, *War in Heaven* and *The Place of the Lion*, and at the same time, or a little later, invited me to tea to meet him. I remember a man in spectacles, who appeared to combine a frail physique with exceptional vitality, whose features could be described as "homely" – meaning by that word a face which is immediately attractive and subsequently remembered without one's being able to explain either the attraction or the persistence of the impression. He appeared completely at ease in surroundings with which he was not yet familiar, and which had intimidated many; and at the same time was modest and unassuming to the point of humility: that unconscious humility, one discovered later, was in him a natural quality, one he possessed to a degree which made one, in time, feel very humble oneself in his presence. He talked easily and volubly, yet never imposed his talk; for he appeared always to be at the same time preoccupied with the subject of conversation, and interested in and aware of, the personalities of those to whom he was talking. One retained the impression that he was pleased and grateful for the opportunity of meeting the company, and yet that it was he who had conferred a favour – more than a favour, a kind of benediction, by coming.'

2 – 'Herewith the essay – the chat rather,' wrote Williams (28 Mar.). 'I don't expect you to have an opinion, but Milton (let us say) might have been annoyed if the experience of his poetry had led a reader to suppose him a Mohommedan. And you might have sympathized with Milton.' See 'T. S. Eliot', in *Poetry at Present* (Oxford, 1930), 163–74; repr. in *Selected Modern Critical Essays*, ed. H. S. Milford (Oxford, 1932), 278–87.

TO *A. Den Doolaard*[1]   CC

2 April 1929   [London]

Dear Mr Den Doolard,

It is some time since we have had a Dutch Chronicle – we were then
still a 'monthly', but are now, as you know, a quarterly again, to my great
relief – and I should very much like to have one from you for our next
number, which should appear in June (I trust you have already received
a copy of the April number which has just appeared). I should like very
much to hear from you, especially if you can say that you will let me have
a chronicle by the 25th of April, or about then? The last was admirable
for us, and I have only to ask you to do the same thing for the time that
has elapsed since, in Dutch letters.

With all best wishes, and hoping to hear from you,[2]

Yours always sincerely,

[T. S. Eliot]

TO *Thomas Henderson*[3]   CC

2 April 1929   [London]

Dear Sir,

I beg to express my gratification at the kind invitation of the Association
to speak during the next winter. I am, first, honoured and flattered by the
invitation to address your society; secondly, having never visited Scotland,
and having always wished to do so, I have been greatly tempted to avail
myself of this opportunity to see the country and visit some of the most
interesting towns under such auspices. But unfortunately, it is very difficult

---

1 – A. Den Doolaard (1901–94), pen name of the Dutch poet, novelist, traveller, journalist,
and campaigner Cornelis Johannes George (Bob) Spoelstra, who undertook from the 1920s
several extensive journeys through France and the Balkans and other places. After issuing
early warnings against Fascism in Europe, during WW2 he made his way to London and
became a radio broadcaster for the Free Dutch. For a while after the war he lived in the USA
and in Portugal, but then returned to his homeland where he became famous for his writings,
including documentaries and travelogues. He is honoured with an official memorial in the
Macedonian city of Ohrid.
2 – Den Doolaard was away from home, working on a novel, and would be unable to meet
the date TSE indicated; he would be able to submit a chronicle by June or July (17 Apr.).
3 – Thomas Henderson (Interim Secretary, The Scottish Association for the Speaking of
Verse, Edinburgh) invited TSE on 28 Mar. to speak on a subject of his own choice at two or
more of their branches – Edinbugh, Glasgow, Greenock, Perth, Inverness – during the course
of the coming winter. They would pay an honorarium in addition to expenses.

for me to make any engagements for next winter, which I am not certain of being able to keep; so I have decided that for the next year I ought not to accept.

May I say that I hope that the invitation may be repeated another year. And if the expenses of such a tour were paid, I should consider the pleasure and interest sufficient, without any further honorarium. If the Society should esteem me worthy of a second invitation, I should be glad to know whether the lecturer is required to deliver five different lectures in the five towns mentioned, or one lecture to be repeated?

With many thanks, and many regards,

I am,
Yours very sincerely,
[T. S. Eliot]

TO *Geoffrey Faber*

MS Valerie Eliot

3 April 1929   *The Criterion*

Dear Geoffrey

As you gave no one any opportunity – this is a line to wish you Godspeed & to say that I hope you will both have a most happy (& deserved) holiday.[1] I envy you, but it is a pleasant envy to think of anyone doing what one would like to do, if one feels that they will enjoy it as one would oneself. Somehow, when you go away, I think of all the things I wanted to say, to talk about; and somehow have not – & think – if he does not return, they will never be said. That is silly, of course: it merely means that I look forward to your return.

Yours ever,
Tom.

1 – The Fabers were going on a Mediterranean cruise aboard the *Stella d'Italia*, visiting the Dalmatian coast, Delphi, Athens, Eleusis, and Constantinople.

TO *Glenn Hughes*   TS Texas

4 April 1929   *The Criterion*

Dear Hughes,

Thank you for your letter of the 2nd. I am sending you a copy of the *Criterion* separately.[1] But I am sorry to hear that you are not likely to return to England as I see no prospect of visiting Paris this Spring. But if I do I shall not fail to let you know. It is true that I wrote that small book about Ezra Pound and there is no reason for concealing the authorship, you are quite free to mention it.[2]

With best wishes to yourself and Mrs Hughes,

Sincerely yours,

T. S. Eliot

TO *H. P. Collins*   CC

4 April 1929   [London]

Dear Mr Collins,

Thank you for your letter of the 26th March which I ought to have answered sooner. I agree with you that Chesterton's article does not get the matter much further forward.[3]

Thank you for answering the Sherlock Holmes riddle.[4] I am sure that your answer is the correct one. I only maintain that Clay's remark applies

---

1–Hughes asked from France to be sent a copy of the Apr. issue of the *Criterion* with John Gould Fletcher's review of EP's *Selected Poems* introduced by TSE: 'I need Fletcher's review of Pound's poems, and I am too hard up to buy a copy at Brentano's.'

2–Hughes had spent three days at Rapallo with EP, who mentioned 'that the monograph entitled *Ezra Pound: His Metric and Poetry* was written by you. Do you want this fact kept secret, or could it be mentioned in my chapter on Pound? Entirely as you wish.' Accordingly, Hughes identified TSE as author of that 'authoritative monograph' on EP in a parenthesis of his *Imagism & The Imagists: A Study of Modern Poetry* (1931), 235. See too Ronald Schuchard, *Eliot's Dark Angel: Intersections of Life and Art* (1999), 199, 251.

3–Collins wrote, 'I think Chesterton ['Is Humanism a Religion?', C. 8 (Apr. 1929), 382–93] has merely side-tracked the issue. Foerster's book has merits and also great incidental faults, and I do not think his position has the firm standpoint of Babbitt's or the implicit weight of More's.'

4–TSE remarked, in his review of *The Complete Sherlock Holmes Short Stories* and of Anna Katherine Green's *The Leavenworth Case* (C. 8 [Apr. 1929], 552–6), apropos Conan Doyle: 'It is, of course, the dramatic ability, rather than the pure detective ability, that does it. But it is a dramatic ability applied with great cunning and concentration; it is not spilt about. The content of the story may be poor; but the form is nearly always perfect. We are so well worked up by the dramatic preparation that we accept the conclusion – even when, as in

grammatically to the actual situation rather than to the previous crimes which he had committed.

Sincerely yours,
[T. S. Eliot]

TO *The Manager, Lloyds Bank* CC

4 April 1929   [London]

Dear Sir,

I believe that you hold in safe custody for me [a] share certificate for £10 Preference share in Faber & Gwyer Ltd. I should be very much obliged if you would kindly forward this certificate on my behalf to Mr K. A. Layton-Bennett, of Layton-Bennett Chiene & Tait, 3 London Wall Buildings, E.C.2., as it has to be surrendered for a new certificate.[1]

Yours faithfully,
[T. S. Eliot]

TO *The District Bank* CC

6 April 1929   [London]

Dear Sirs

Securities Department.

I am anxious to trace a Share Certificate for £10 Preference Share of Faber & Gwyer Ltd which was issued to me at some date in 1925 and which must be handed to the Liquidator of the firm in connexion with a reorganisation of the business.[2] I should be obliged if you would let

---

The Red-Headed League, it is perfectly obvious from the beginning. (By the way, was bank robbery subject to capital punishment at that epoch? or else why should John Clay, when caught, have exclaimed "I'll swing for it"? . . .).'

'May I answer your Sherlock Holmes riddle in the new *Criterion*?' wrote Collins. 'Clay was "wanted" for murder as well as for bank-robbery. The Scotland Yard man definitely says so. Hence, I suppose, the aristocratic gesture of losing his own chance of escape for his confrère, though the latter was not liable perhaps to "swing".'

See also TSE's letter to A. P. Rossiter, 8 July 1929, below.

1 – The Assistant Manager responded (10 Apr.) that they had forwarded to Layton-Bennett the 7% Preference Share which they held in safe custody on TSE's account. Layton-Bennett, Chiene & Tait wished to forward to TSE a cheque for £10 representing his share of a return to contributories.

2 – K. A. Layton-Bennett, Liquidator, gave notice on 8 Apr. 1929, 'pursuant to Section 188 of the Companies (Consolidation) Act 1908 that a Meeting of the Creditors of [Faber &

me know at your earliest convenience whether I deposited this with you, either separately or in conjunction with the securities which you hold for Mrs Eliot.

Apologising for troubling you,
I am,
Yours faithfully,
[T. S. Eliot]

TO *F. J. Sheed*[1]   CC

7 April 1929   [London]

Dear Mr Sheed,

I hope that you remember meeting me one day at the 'Grove' in South Kensington.

Gwyer Limited] will be held at 3, London Wall Buildings, London, E.C.2., on Monday the twenty-second day of April 1929, at 12 noon for the purposes provided for in the said Section.' Faber & Gwyer Ltd was thereafter to be reconstituted as Faber & Faber Ltd.

On 11 Mar., GCF explained to his uncle G. Brace Colt that *The Nursing Mirror* and Burdett's Hospital's and Charities were to be taken over by a 'very big newspaper corporation' and would become a new company, Nursing Mirror Ltd. 'The proceeds of these two sales will be such that every ordinary share holder will ultimately receive for each £10 share held by him around £180 . . .

'I have arranged to form a new Company with the title of Faber & Faber Ltd., to carry on the book publishing business; and I intend, after paying off the balance of my loan from the Arthur Faber Trust Estate, to put £20,000 into this new Company.'

He told an unknown correspondent on 18 Mar.: 'The Chairman of Faber & Faber Ltd will be Mr Geoffrey Faber . . . Mr C. W. Stewart and Mr Richard de la Mare will be principal directors. Mr Frank Morley, the London representative of the Century Co. of New York, is also joining the Board as a Principal Director. Mr T. S. Eliot, the editor of the *Criterion*, will also be a director. Mr A. J. B. Paterson will continue to be Sales Manager . . . The change-over will take effect from March 31st next . . . and except for the alteration of name the change will be imperceptible.'

He told A. J. B. Paterson on 22 Mar.: 'Mr T. S. Eliot will be an ordinary Director.'

1–Frank Sheed (1897–1981), publisher and author, was an Australian-born convert to Catholicism. He married in 1926 Maisie Ward (daughter of English Catholic gentry). Educated at Sydney University, he was on a year-long trip to London in 1920–1 when he became an ardent participant in the Catholic Evidence Guild and went on to set up in 1926 the publishing house of Sheed & Ward, specialising in theology and apologetics. The opening in 1933 of the New York office of Sheed & Ward enabled the firm to become for many years the most influential Catholic publisher in the English-speaking world. Author of *Nullity of Marriage* (1932), *Catholic Evidence Training Outlines* (with Maisie Ward, 1925), *Map of Life* (1933), *Communism and Man* (1938), *Theology and Sanity* (1946), *The Church and I* (1974). See Wilfrid Sheed, *Frank and Maisie* (1985)

A lady whom I have known slightly for many years, Miss Arabella Yorke, is anxious to find work translating from the French.[1] My firm does not do very much in that way, and I had nothing to offer her at present. I advised her first to get in touch with American publishers, who publish many translations from French; and then I thought of you. It occurred to me that you might be considering translating other books of the school of Maritain.

If you do, I wish to recommend her. She is thoroughly competent and conscientious. Furthermore, she is going to live in Paris, and could see about translation rights from that end. I shall give her introductions to several writers there, such as Julien Green, Georges Bernanos etc. and could also introduce her to Plon;[2] as it struck me that there might be books in the *Rosseau d'Or* well worth translation, and possibly some in your line.

If you think there is any possibility, I should be very glad; and should then suggest sending her to see you. If not, please accept my apologies for troubling you.[3]

Sincerely yours,
[T. S. Eliot]

1–Dorothy ('Arabella') Yorke (1891–1971), American translator and illustrator, had an affair with John Cournos (see his *Autobiography*, 1935), but on arrival in London in 1917 became mistress to Richard Aldington, who left her in 1928. When H.D. portrayed Yorke as 'Bella Carter', and Cournos as 'Ivan', in her autobiographical fiction *Bid Me to Live* (1960), Yorke groused to Cournos (29 Sept. 1960) that H.D. showed her up as 'an illiterate bunny-brained whore'. See also *Richard Aldington & H.D.: Their Lives in Letters 1918–61*, ed. Caroline Zilboorg (Manchester, 2003). TSE had come to know Yorke through RA.

2–Publisher.

3–Sheed replied (11 Apr.) that they did not at the moment have any work for Miss Yorke. 'I should take this opportunity of thanking you for the review of *Three Reformers* in the Times Lit. Supp. I have been told that you were the author, and the effect of the article on the sale of the book was very remarkable.' 'Three Reformers' – on *Three Reformers: Luther, Descartes, Rousseau*, by Jacques Maritain – *TLS*, 8 Nov. 1928, 818.

On 2 May Yorke was to thank TSE for his help with locating publishers who might commission translations: Stallybrass (George Routledge) was negotiating for the rights to a book that she might be asked to translate. She wrote again on 12 May gratefully to inform TSE that Stallybrass had indeed asked her to translate the book, and to say she had got a job with an American bookseller and publisher in Paris. See Emile Dermenghem, *The Life of Mahomet*, trans. Arabella York (George Routledge, 1930).

TO *John Middleton Murry*

TS Valerie Eliot

8 April 1929   57 Chester Terrace, s.w.1.

Dear John,

We had been counting upon seeing you on Wednesday next; I am not sure whether it would have suited you; but I fear now that we must postpone it for some time. In fact, we are not seeing anybody at present; we are neither of us well, and Vivien is very worn out; and we are in the middle of negotiations for getting rid of this house and taking a flat instead. Which is very worrying to the last pitch of nervous exhaustion, and takes all of our time and attention. We are not really in a state for intelligent conversation or companionability. When we get through this period, if we do – I hope it will be settled and that we may be moved in a few weeks – we want to renew our contacts and I will write to you at once. I hope that meanwhile things are better with you, at least so far as to let you work regularly for a few hours a day, for I think that is absolutely essential for mental health. Let me hear how you are.

affectionately,

Tom

TO *Messrs A. P. Watt & Son*

cc

8 April 1929   [London]

Dear Sir,

I am returning you with many regrets the short article by Mr G. K. Chesterton entitled 'A Note on Classice [*sic*] at College', which you sent me on the 3rd instant.

I shall always be very glad to have good material by Mr Chesterton but you will understand that a quarterly like the *Criterion* has to be careful to space its authors out and not give to readers too much of the same authors in consecutive numbers. We have a longer essay by Mr Chesterton in the number which has just appeared and therefore could not accept any more of his work, unless it was a continuation of the same discussion in which he engaged in the article which we have published, for at least six months. I therefore think it best to return it to you now and hope that you will have something more from him before the end of the year.

Yours sincerely,

[T. S. Eliot]

TO *The Manager, District Bank*   CC

9 April 1929   [London]

Your Reference S. Bn/H
Dear Sir,
    I thank you for your letter of the 8th inst.[1] and shall be greatly obliged
if you will forward the share certificate of the £10 Preference Share in
Faber & Gwyer Ltd., to Mr K. A. Layton-Bennett,[2] of Layton-Bennett
Chiene & Tait, 3 London Wall Buildings, E.C.2., the Liquidator of Faber
& Gwyer Ltd.[3]

                        Thanking you for your trouble,
                        Yours faithfully,
                        [T. S. Eliot]

TO *James Burnham*[4]   CC

9 April 1929   [London]

Dear Mr Burnham,
    I have your letter of the 31st, and shall look forward to seeing you and
Mr Gary at lunch on Wednesday, April 24th.
                        Sincerely yours,
                        [T. S. Eliot]

1 – The District Bank confirmed, 'we hold in safe custody on your account Certificate relating
to one Faber & Gwyer Limited 75% Preference Share of £10, fully paid.'
2 – Kenneth Arthur Layton-Bennett, Chartered Accountant.
3 – Faber & Gwyer Ltd was formally liquidated on 6 June 1929.
4 – James Burnham (1905–87), American political theorist, was educated at Princeton
University, where he came top of the roll, before attending Balliol College, Oxford (where
he was taught by J. R. R. Tolkien and TSE's friend Fr. Martin D'Arcy, SJ). From 1929 he
taught philosophy at New York University, where he co-authored, with Philip Wheelwright,
Introduction to Philosophical Analysis (1932). In the 1930s he became a radical activist,
specifically a Trotskyite, and was instrumental in the development of the Socialist
Workers Party. In 1940, disillusioned with Marxist theory and praxis, he quit the SWP
(see 'Burnham's Letter of Resignation', *The Fourth International* 5: 4 [Aug. 1940], 106–7)
and turned himself into a political conservative, an anti-communist and a liberal. During
WW2 he headed the 'Political and Psychological Warfare' division of the Office of Policy
Coordination; and later he co-founded, with William F. Buckley, the magazine *National
Review* – thus he has been dubbed by some opponents 'the first neocon'. In 1983 President
Ronald Reagan conferred upon him the Presidential Medal of Freedom. His influential
writings include *The Struggle for The World* (1947); *The Coming Defeat of Communism*
(1949); *The Managerial Revolution: What is Happening in the World* (1941); *Suicide of the
West: An Essay on the Meaning and Destiny of Liberalism* (1964).

TO *Hamish Miles*[1]

CC

10 April 1929 [London]

Dear Miles,

I am sorry to hear that you have had such a bad time of it. Please don't bother to do anything about Huxley now. If you find the book worth it we will use the review in March, so don't try to do any work now, but get well and come back to London as soon as you can.

Yours ever,
[T. S. Eliot]

TO *J. S. Barnes*

CC

10 April 1929 [London]

Dear Jim Barnes,

I have been meaning to write to you for some time and I owe you a good many apologies about your essay.[2] It is all the more inexcusable because I shall find it impossible to use it for six or nine months and I should have warned you at once in case you wanted to send it elsewhere. Your essay on Fascism has been very successful and has received a good deal of praise.[3] I am indulging myself to the extent of writing a shorter essay myself for the next number dealing with you and A. L. Rowse[4] together and I hope to provoke replies from both of you although of course discussion on the subject will have to get shorter and shorter.[5] For this reason I shall have to allow a considerable interim before introducing you on another subject. I shall probably send you a proof of my notes before publication.

I am sorry to have seen nothing of Mary for some time but I believe that she has been very busy with Jack in the Isle of Wight preparing for the General Election.[6]

Yours ever sincerely,
[T. S. Eliot]

1 – Hamish Miles (1894–1937), writer; translator of George Sand and André Maurois.
2 – Barnes had asked on 21 Jan. after his article entitled 'The Nature of Art and the Function of Art Criticism', which would ultimately appear in C. 10 (Apr. 1931), 462–79.
3 – Barnes, 'Fascism', C. 8 (Apr. 1929), 445–59.
4 – ALR, 'The Literature of Communism: Its Origin and Theory', C. 8 (Apr. 1929), 422–36.
5 – TSE, 'Mr. Barnes and Mr. Rowse', C. 8 (July 1929), 682–91.
6 – Barnes replied (13 Apr.): 'Mary [Hutchinson] appears to have all her time just now occupied in being pleasant to Jack's electorate. It must be rather trying for her, as she cares not a wit for politics. But no doubt her sense of humour must help her.'

TO *John Gould Fletcher*   PC MS Arkansas

15 April 1929   57 Chester Terrace, S.W.1.

Dear Fletcher,

I have been too busy lately with private affairs – trying to move etc. – to look up anybody – but I have been anxious to know *how* & *where* you are. Do let me hear from you if you get this.

                                                    Yours ever,
                                                    T. S. E.

TO *Herbert Agar*[1]   CC

18 April 1929   [London]

Dear Mr Agar,

I have your letter of the 16th and it is quite true that I have been reading *The Garment of Praise*. Even if I had not I should always be very happy to meet any friend of Paul More.[2]

For the next few days my times are very broken up by private business so that I hardly dare to suggest appointments. You do not say how long you will be here, as you do not, I hope for some considerable time [*sic*]. I expect to be freer towards the end of next week; but if by any chance you should be leaving London before then I hope you will let me know so that we can fit in some sort of meeting.

                                                    Yours sincerely,
                                                    [T. S. Eliot]

1–Herbert Agar (1897–1980), journalist and author; editor of the *Louisville Courier-Journal*. His writings include *The People's Choice: From Washington to Harding – A Study in Democracy* (1933; winner of the Pulitzer Prize for History); *Who Owns America? A New Declaration of Independence* (co-ed. with Allen Tate, 1936); and *The Price of Union: The Influence of the American Temper on the Course of History* (1950).
2–More had given Agar an introduction to TSE which he had hesitated to use. 'However, since I believe that you have been, or will be, reading *The Garment of Praise*, I have decided to send you the card, in case you are sufficiently interested in the book to feel that a meeting would be pleasant.'

TO *Norman Foerster*   CC

22 April 1929   [London]

Dear Mr Foerster,

I was very glad to get your letter of the 9th instant. I hope that your first paragraph means that you will soon have something for the *Criterion*. The paper which you read with chuckles will appear here in the June *Adelphi*,[1] so that by that time you will be well known here: and I am very keen to have something from you for the *September Criterion*. But I suggest, in fairness to yourself and for the interest of our readers, merely that you hold it up until I send you proof of Tate's essay, which I hope to have in a few days.[2]

I shall be delighted to contribute to your symposium. I like the scheme, and think you are quite right to keep French & Germans out of it; the wider you go, the more varieties of Humanism you will find, and we ought to keep the issue to Babbitt's brand. The only possible Englishman to include is Herbert Read. I only suggest that, because, if you could give the book a more comprehensive title – and Humanism *ought* to be as keen an issue here as in America – I should be very glad to urge the firm (Faber & Faber) of which I am a director to take sheets from Doran. We are doing *Belphégor* with Babbitt's preface,[3] and I should be keen to get them to do your book.

I will think over subjects. What suggests itself to me at once is 'Humanism *in* Religion', but would have to be sure that I was not crossing More's territory. I mean that it would amuse me to show the other face of my own theory – insist upon the danger of *religion without* humanism; having already written about humanism without religion. I am in fear of

1 – TSE, 'Second Thoughts on Humanism', *New Adelphi* 2: 4 (June/Aug. 1929), 304–10.
2 – Allen Tate, 'The Fallacy of Humanism', *C.* 8 (July 1929), 661–81. Foerster's ultimate contribution to the debate was 'Humanism and Religion', *C.* 9 (Oct. 1929), 23–32.
3 – TSE wrote in his reader's report, 30 Jan. 1929: 'This preface [by Babbitt] is rather shorter and less informative than I had hoped but I still think that the book is worth doing. No doubt the question will be discussed by this Committee.' It is likely that TSE wrote the copy for F&F's Autumn catalogue: 'M. Julien Benda, mathematician, musician, successful novelist, Commander of the Order of the Legion of Honour, is attached to no party or clique; his independent criticism, especially *Belphégor* and *La Trahison des Clercs*, has made a great stir in Paris and throughout France. Of these two books, *Belphégor* is of the wider, and less purely Parisian, interest. It is a drastic and severe examination of the attitude of modern France – and by implication of all modern society – towards art and philosophy. The study was begun in 1914, but was interrupted by the War. It appeared first in 1918, and has become one of the classical documents of contemporary reaction against the tendencies of the later nineteenth century.'

the power of religious hierarchy, whether Roman or Protestant, which is not truly civilised. It might be called roughly the Erasmic theory. I shall write to More to find out what ground he is taking, and I should like to know whether this would do if there is no overlapping. 'Humanism and Culture' strikes a little vaguely on me, but I will think it over.[1]

I shall be very busy till the middle of July, but I believe I could get my paper done in a fortnight after that. What length?

Yours cordially,
[T. S. Eliot]

TO *Franklin Gary*

TS Princeton

24 April (1929)

Faber & Faber Ltd,
24 Russell Square

Dear Mr Gary,

I had been expecting you & Mr Burnham to lunch today. Unfortunately, my wife is laid up so that she cannot deal with certain domestic complications – & I must default. I have no address to write to you, & so have the shame of letting you come in vain.

I shall be tied up now for about 3 weeks, but could you not both come up to Town one day after that during term? & have lunch with me. I was looking forward to discussing your Review with you.

With deep apologies, & hoping to see you in a few weeks. Do write & let me know.

Sincerely yours
T. S. Eliot

1–TSE, 'Religion without Humanism', in *Humanism and America: Essays on the Outlook of Modern Civilisation*, ed. Norman Foerster (New York, 1930), 105–12. On 2 June 1934 TSE was to tell Walter Tomlin (then a student at Brasenose College, Oxford): 'I remember now that the article was written for a special purpose. I had no desire to associate myself with that group of "humanists" at all: it was only out of courtesy and regard for my old master Irving Babbitt that I took part. I considered it only as a volume in honour of Babbitt; and I took the only possible line that I could at the moment, in his support. To reprint now what is in any case a rather feeble piece of writing, would give it a stamp of my own endorsement which I don't want it to have' (TS Lady Marshall).

TSE at forty

TO *Huw Menai*

29 April 1929   [London]

Dear Mr Menai,

I have owed you a letter of appreciation and apology for a long time. You will probably have realised that when I communicated with the Hogarth Press, on hearing from you, I heard that the selection of poems had already been made. I must say that I think the selection a very good one. When I read your poems in the Hogarth book, I liked them more than ever. There was not one poem which bored me – that may seem an odd commendation, but I think the first thing about a poem is that it should hold one's attention. I liked your book of poems as much as any I had read within the year; and I was very sorry to surrender the copy to *The Criterion* reviewer.[1]

Meanwhile I retain the rest, and hope to choose one or two and ask your permission to publish.[2]

Yours very truly,
[T. S. Eliot]

TO *James Burnham*

29 April 1929   [London]

Dear Mr Burnham,

Thank you for your letter of the 27th. You need not have worried so much as to send a cable, for I am quite content to have my name appear.[3] The only question with me in this connexion is one of time. I do not think I can give you anything before the end of this year.

I will think over your suggestion of Hulme. He ought to be dealt with, certainly, but I wonder whether Herbert Read is not more suitable than I for giving an exposition.[4] He has studied all of Hulme's views more

---

1 – Sherard Vines reviewed *The Passing of Guto and Other Poems* by Huw Menai, together with seven volumes of poetry by other hands, in C. 8 (July 1929), 709–15.

2 – No poetry by Menai appeared in C.

3 – Burnham apologised for the fact that he had printed the name of TSE on a notice advertising the new New York-based magazine *The Symposium: A Quarterly Journal for Philosophical Discussion*, when TSE had not yet actually agreed to be a contributor.

4 – Burnham asked (27 Apr.) whether TSE might perhaps write on T. E. Hulme. 'For such an article we should be able to pay about seventy-five dollars (the financial question, I imagine always a delicate one for an enterprise which does not aim at becoming a commercial success, is one of the many I should be grateful for your advice on).' Herbert Read had edited Hulme's posthumous collection *Speculations* (1928).

carefully than I have, as I have merely leapt off from those of his notes which dealt with subjects in which I was interested. But I will think this over; and if I don't feel competent to deal with Hulme, will suggest some other subject, and let you know.

My only suggestion about payment is: pay everybody a flat rate and make no exceptions; just figure out how much you can afford on each number, and give level rates. Then write as much as you can yourselves, and take no payment for it.

I shall write to suggest a day for lunch as soon as I can.
[Letter incomplete.]

TO *Hugh Macdonald*   TS Charlotte Williamson

29 April 1929   *The Criterion*

Dear Macdonald,

I was glad to hear from you again. I should like to see you soon, but doubt whether it will be possible for several weeks; I will write as soon as I can. I quite agree with you that if the Clarendon Press are going to do Johnson's verse complete it would be better to print the two long poems only.[1] But even so, won't the Oxford Johnson cut in pretty heavily? I mean that if you would like to consider doing any other 17th or 18th [century] poet *instead*, I would be ready to consider it too. I don't know whether Shenstone is worth it, but perhaps you will think of somebody else. But if you still want to go ahead with Johnson, I am quite ready to do so.[2]

With best wishes to Mrs Macdonald,

Sincerely yours,
T. S. Eliot

1 – Macdonald wrote on 17 Apr., 'You will see that we have announced your book as LONDON etc. I thought this best as I have heard that the Clarendon Press is shortly bringing out a complete edition of the [Samuel Johnson] poems. In this case we should either have to ask the Press to allow us to use their text or employ a scholar to produce another, which would probably have less authority and anyway would be superfluous.'
2 – See TSE's 'Introduction', in Samuel Johnson, *London: A Poem and The Vanity of Human Wishes* (London: Frederick Etchells and Hugh Macdonald, 1930).

TO *Harold Monro*   Photocopy of TS

29 April 1929   Faber & Faber Ltd

Dear Harold,

It is quite true that you sent me a long poem by Desmond Harmsworth: rococo but quite striking.[1] I had thought it even too long for one of the long poems of which we spoke; but should like to reconsider it. I had thought of sending it on to the Hogarth Press for the Wellesley Collection, which could be brighter than it is. But I have another notion – not particularly concerning this poem, it is true, – which I have talked over with Morley, and may want to discuss with you; as, if it proved worth going into, it would want your collaboration. I'll speak of that again soon.

No, it would not have made any difference; as a matter of fact I was thinking of a Reading all the time; but if you prefer a Lecture, in the autumn, I will do one then.[2] But I can't do anything more until August at soonest; and it is a question whether I can fulfil all my contracts before then. And this business of moving is the devil; more details and complexities than I remembered. In fact I was going to write anyhow, to say that I am postponing my supper party until the summer after moving: we simply can't manage it at present. I am very sorry for this: but I hope you will be in London part of the time this summer. I will try to get the same people together, and perhaps Bonamy. Meanwhile I will look in one morning soon.

Yours ever,
Tom

TO *Mario Praz*   CC

30 April 1929   [Faber & Faber]

My dear Praz,

Thank you for your letter of the 29th. I hope that you received a copy of the *Criterion* which was sent to Liverpool. I must explain that cheques in payment have merely been delayed by the fact that the firm of Faber & Gwyer has now become Faber & Faber and all our accounts had to be

---

1 – Monro wrote on 26 Apr. to ask after TSE's thoughts on 'a longish poem by a certain Harmsworth of Paris' that he had forwarded.
2 – Monro had asked TSE to give a talk at the Poetry Bookshop in May; now, he said, 'I believe if I'd asked you merely to read, & not to lecture . . . [you] might have managed it.'

submitted as a formality to the Liquidator of the former firm. In future matters will go on as before except for the change of name.

If I can think of any books worth your reviewing for *La Stampa* I will mention them.[1] I don't think that Hemingway has published anything recently but I believe that he has something on the way and perhaps it might be as well to wait for his next book. Have you thought of dealing with David Garnett who has just brought out a new book with Chatto & Windus called *No Love*. I have not read it but have seen several very favourable reviews and think that he is a good enough writer for your purpose. I heard from Williams[2] about *Pegaso* and have written to Ojetti in consequence and have had the April number sent to him.[3]

I have been waiting for your return to thank you for the very interesting and flattering review which you wrote of my book.[4] I do not feel competent to criticise my own critics but can only say that it gave me a great deal of satisfaction. If the book is as good as you say it is I am quite happy about it, and I think that your reservations on my judgement of Machiavelli are wholly justified. No one else has made these points.

With all best wishes,

Yours ever,

[T. S. Eliot]

1–Praz, who had engaged himself to write articles on modern English and American literature for *La Stampa*, hoped TSE might help with suggestions. He would probably write first on Hemingway. 'Has he published anything after *Men Without Women*?'

2–Orlo Williams.

3–Praz had reviewed Siegfried Sassoon's *Memoirs of a Fox Hunting Man* for *Pegaso*. The editor Ojetti (Praz reported to TSE on 29 Apr.) wished to exchange *Pegaso* with C.

4–Praz reviewed FLA in *La Cultura* (Mar. 1929), 177–80. He had written to TSE on 22 Dec. 1928: 'Of your essays. I have read Machiavelli & Crashaw at once. Let me first compliment you for the excellence you have achieved in your prose style: so simple and so forcible, endowed as it is with a quiet power of persuasion. You are almost as spare as Swift in the use of figurative language: a very rare feat for a poet. As for Machiavelli I think you pay too little attention to the change of views that intervened between the *Prince* & the *Discourses*. But what you say for inst. on p. 52 'The impersonality and innocence of Machiavelli is so rare' etc. strikes me as a very acute and new remark. Though, of course, the statement (pp. 59–60) that 'Machiavelli would distort and omit nothing' is disproved by the *Stoni fiorentine*. It is a commonplace to say that M. made facts fit to his ideas, whereas Guicciardini sticked [*sic*] to the bare facts.'

He went on: 'As for Crashaw I thank you for yr generous mention of my book. I see that your query about Shelley (p. 123) has provoked a rejoinder in the T.L.S. I must confess that I am rather surprised at what you are saying there. Of course Shelley's metaphors are far from felicitous: an arrow suggests a bow, not a sphere, and "lamp" for "light", there, is muddling. But the parallel between the voice of the bird growing fainter and fainter in the sky, and the light of the moon "becoming paler and paler" in the morning sky, holds good, after all. And is it true that "Crashaw does not need *such* notes"? What about the passage in the hymn in the holy nativity quoted on p. 236 of my book? "She sings thy Tesses asleepe . . . "'

TO *Susan Hinkley*   TS Houghton

1 May [1929]   57 Chester Terrace, S.W.1.

Dear Aunt Susie,

I am very sorry that you cannot come too on Sunday, and so is Vivienne.
This however is merely to convey a message from Mrs Haigh-Wood. She
says: could you pay your combined visit to her and to your friends in
Hampstead, on either Saturday *or* Monday next? If you can settle on one
or the other day she will be at home all the afternoon. Will you let her
know?

The address is

> Mrs Haigh-Wood
> 3 Compayne Gardens
> N.W.6.

She hopes you can come on one of these two days. No. 2 or 13 Bus to
Finchley Road MET. Station.

I do hope to see you again before you leave. It has been so brief.

                              Your affectionate nephew
                              Tom.

TO *Philippa Strachey*   TS Fawcett Library

2 May 1929   57 Chester Terrace, S.W.1.

Dear Miss Strachey,

I ought to have written to you before, as the matter has been settled
for several days, to let you know that we have finally decided upon and
taken a mansion flat near Baker Street.[1] The deciding reason was that a
purchaser appeared for my house (which was rather important for me)
who wanted to get into it as soon as possible; but still more the question
of stairs. One chief reason for giving up the house is that my wife is
practically crippled at present from going up and down the steep stairs;
and although your flat would have been ideal in every other way, I felt
that it was wiser to take something all on one floor.

I wish that we could have shared your house, which delighted me;[2] and
I regret also that I shall have no excuse now for coming to see you. I do

1 – 68 Clarence Gate Gardens.
2 – 51 Gordon Square.

489

hope that you have been able to make satisfactory arrangements with the estate, and that you will stay in your house.

Yours sincerely,

T. S. Eliot

TO *Virginia Woolf*[1]

MS Berg

2 May 1929

57 Chester Terrace, s.w.1.

My dear Virginia,

Not having heard from you, I don't know whether Sunday was possible for you or not: and must now write to say that we must postpone again – circumstances are too much for us, & indeed I doubt whether we ought to ask anyone to see us till we have moved. It is very depressing; please let me be in letter & telephone communication at least, during this exile. On Sunday we must be saying farewell to my relatives, & then plunge into another week of surveyors, valuers and solicitors.[2]

I am sorry for Rothenstein, but will not press you further. He was extremely anxious to have you as a sitter.[3]

1 – Virginia Woolf (1882–1941), novelist, essayist, and critic: see Biographical Register.
2 – See VW, *Diary* III: 'Poor Tom – a true poet, I think; what they will call in a hundred years a man of genius: & this is his life. I stand for half an hour listening while he says that Vivien cant walk. Her legs have gone. But whats the matter? No one knows. And so she lies in bed – cant put a shoe on. And they have difficulties, humiliations, with servants. And after endless quibbling about visiting – which he cant do these 8 weeks, owing to moving house & 15 first cousins come to England, suddenly he appears overcome, moved, tragic, unhappy, broken down, because I offer to come to tea on Thursday. Oh but we dont dare ask our friends, he said. We have been deserted. Nobody has been to see us for weeks. Would you really come – all this way? To see us? Yes I said. But what a vision of misery, imagined, but real too. Vivien with her foot on a stool, in bed all day; Tom hurrying back lest she abuse him: this is our man of genius. – This is what I gathered yesterday morning on the telephone' (223).
   VW wrote to Clive Bell on 2 May 1929: 'What amuses me, when I hear it in Tom's voice on the telephone, mayn't amuse you. Indeed it should not; it is tragic and sordid in the extreme. "Vivien's legs" – "*Legs*, did you say?" Yes, both legs, but especially the left. "But what's the matter with it?" "She cant get a slipper on this week. Last week she was just able to come downstairs. So of course we have had to give up the Strachey's flat." "My God, Tom, have you seen a doctor?" "We have already had ten doctors." "And what do they say?"(here we settled it for an hour or two, I on the edge of a broken chair too) – Well the long and short of it all is that Vivien is now recumbent for ever; swollen, horizontal – for one can't get any footrest that suits her; 15 cousins from America call daily; what in short is the pleasure to be had from life if you've married Vivien and have only father Darcy [D'Arcy] to fall back on?' (*A Reflection of the Other Person: The Letters of Virginia Woolf, IV: 1929–1931*, ed. Nigel Nicolson [1978], 49–50).
3 – William Rothenstein's *Twelve Portraits*, published by F&G in the autumn of 1928, included a romantic drawing of TSE.

By the way, I sent the Hogarth Press some poems by a Walter Lowenfels. I don't think I let you or Leonard know that I hear from him that they have been accepted by Heinemann, through the offices of Humbert Wolfe.[1]

I wrote to Hew Menai to tell him how much I liked his book, but he does not seem to consider my words adequate. But he is very angry with Humbert: not without reason, but poets can be very trying.[2]

Ever aff.

Tom.

TO *Susan Hinkley* TS Houghton

Monday [6 May 1929]   57 Chester Terrace, s.w.1.

Dear Aunt Susie,

Eleanor suggested that you might all be able to look in on us tomorrow evening to say goodbye. Even if you could only come for 5 minutes, *do* come if you can. We should be full of regret if you had to leave without seeing us once more.

I will ring up after breakfast to make sure.

Your affectionate nephew

Tom.

1 – Lowenfels, *Finale of Seem* (London: William Heinemann, 1929).

2 – Huw Menai replied on 30 Apr. to TSE's letter of 29 Apr.: 'I thank you for your comments on my little book [*The Passing of Guto and other poems*, 1929], although they are somewhat cold and negative. But I daresay you are quite just, in giving it no more and no less than it deserves . . . You are much kinder to my little venture than is Mr Humbert Wolfe – that dilletantic darling of the Do-Nothings! I enclose herewith the beginnings of a letter I once thought of sending to him but thought better of it, feeling that I was seeking to justify myself a little too much.' His letter to Wolfe (26 Mar.) opened: 'A friend has just shown me a cutting from the *Saturday Review* where you comment very severely on my little book of verse . . . Your criticism, or want of criticism, your sweeping & gratuitous statement, seems calculated to discourage me from ever again trying my hand at the writing of verse. But I happen to be middle-aged, and I feel that you are not a very old man yourself, despite the airs of patronage & infallibility which you assume. So your "review" will not altogether crush me as it is obviously intended to do.'

TO *Ursula Roberts*   CC

8 May 1929   [London]

Dear Mrs Roberts,

I shall be very glad to help towards the Renovation Fund at St George's.[1]
It is rather early for me to be able to say definitely that I can speak on one
Wednesday evening in October; but so far as I can see at present, I shall be
very glad to do so. I dislike more than anything reading my own poems;
but even if I did not have the leisure to prepare a lecture, I might perhaps
do a sort of combined reading with critical comment on the work of some
better poet, such as I have done before at Mr Monro's Poetry Bookshop.

I might suggest asking Mr Monro to help in this way himself.

I hope also that I may be able to make another contribution towards
the Fund.

Yours very truly,
[T. S. Eliot]

TO *Herbert Read*   CC

8 May 1929   [Faber & Faber Ltd]

Dear Herbert,

T. O. Beachcroft sent me this essay on Traherne which I think is rather
interesting. He would like you to look at it too but I should like to have
it back at your leisure with your opinion as you probably know Traherne
better than I do.[2]

Yours ever,
[T. S. E.]

1 – Ursula Roberts made her request on 6 May.
2 – HR gave his opinion on 15 May: 'I think this essay of Beachcroft's is quite good, though
somewhat amateurish in style. It doesn't say all there is to say about Traherne, but so far as
it goes it is carefully observed. I should certainly print it.' See T. O. Beachcroft, 'Traherne,
and the Doctrine of Felicity', C. 9 (Jan. 1930), 291–307.

TO *G. K. Chesterton*   TS Dorothy Collins

8 May 1929   57 Chester Terrace, S.W.1.

Dear Mr Chesterton,

I should like extremely to come to see you one day. I do not expect to have the leisure, or the brainpower, before July; but if you are to be at home during any part of the summer after that I should like to arrange to spend a weekend with my friend and colleague Herbert Read at Seer Green, and with your permission bring him with me to call on a Saturday or Sunday afternoon.

May I mention that I have much sympathy with your political and social views, as well as (with the obvious reservations) your religious views?[1] And that your study of Dickens was always a delight to me.[2]

I am publishing in the June *Adelphi* my own criticisms of Mr Foerster, and will send you a copy.

Sincerely yours,
T. S. Eliot[3]

---

1 – In a whimsical postscript to an account of his career to date, written for the Twenty-fifth Anniversary Report of the Harvard College Class of 1910, TSE wrote: 'I believe I am an Honorary Vice-President of the Distributist League of Glasgow, but I am not sure.'
2 – *Charles Dickens: A Critical Study* (1906).
3 – Chesterton replied on 13 May: 'Thank you so very much for your letter, which . . . came to me with a double reproach, because I have long been trying to write to you anything like an adequate appreciation of the most penetrating and significant little book of essays [*For Lancelot Andrewes*] that you kindly sent to me . . .

'As it is, there is no time to write all I should like to write about the book; which contains two or three things at least which I think are of quite pivotal importance. There is one sentence down in the corner of one page, on which I should like to write a whole book; but it is much better as it stands. "The spirit killeth and the letter giveth life." If we could get people to read that riddle (as it would be to them) we should have saved the modern world. As it is, don't be surprised if I someday write an even longer and even more rambling article in the [*London*] *Mercury* called "Apology to T. S. Eliot" entirely upon that text.

'I do hope you will come down and see me as you suggest, or that we may meet somewhere or other . . . I should be delighted to fall in with anything you suggest.'

TO *Sir William Rothenstein*

8 May 1929   57 Chester Terrace, s.w.1.

My dear Rothenstein,

Thank you very much for your letter and card of invitation.[1] I shall do my best to come: partly for the vanity of seeing my own mug in a distinguished exhibition; and because it is a likeness which I consider true and Monro considers flattering; and partly from pleasant memories of my sittings.

Sincerely,

T. S. Eliot

I have broached the matter of a drawing to Virginia Woolf; but she is a very shy bird and says that she loathes it and has refused all offers for ten years, which I believe; but I have not given up all hope.

TO *I. A. Richards*

CC

9 May 1929   [Faber & Faber Ltd]

Dear Richards,

I am sorry about the Fernandez, but half expected it. The *Criterion* can survive, because there is plenty of review material; and I had rather wait until you can do the subject, than assign it to some one else; and as you have not been able to deal with it till now, I doubt whether you could in time for the following number; so please leave it until it becomes convenient.[2]

I am still hoping for the 25th, but have become endlessly involved in business over the sale of my house and the purchase of a flat, and we shall be moving early in June; but I will write later to let you know just how long I can stay. If it does not shorten our time for conversation, I should be very glad to meet the people you mention.[3]

1–Rothenstein wrote on 7 May: 'I am showing the drawing for wh. you so patiently sat, with some others, this week.' Frederic Manning wrote to TSE on 9 May: 'I have just seen a drawing of you, at Rothenstein's private view, and perhaps the averted eyes seemed to reproach me.' See Rothenstein's *Twelve Portraits* (F&F, 1929).

2–IAR wrote (8 May), 'I shall have to break my word. I've had a whole week wiped out with a touch of something which affects me like flue [*sic*] – a specially poisonous kind of cold & now am unable to get Fernandez even properly read by the date I promised. Shall I try to get him done for your next number – or will you hand him over to someone more dependable. It won't be easy for me – what with moving off from here by June 15.' No review of Fernandez by IAR was forthcoming.

3–'The weekend of Sunday 26th we are expecting you [in Cambridge]. Will you when you

494   TSE at forty

Very many thanks,
yours ever,
[T. S. Eliot]

TO *K. Pickthorn*   CC

9 May 1929   [London]

Dear Pickthorn,

Thank you for your letter.[1] I am writing at once in haste to say that if the Namier (I believe he is a Jew) is too much against the grain, will you please dismiss him with a short snort or note?[2] I think I have quite enough material to make up the next number, and I hate to have any one write a long review about a book which isn't worth it. I am very sorry however to hear of both inconveniences and tragedies. I hope not so serious as the latter word? I know about the former, as I am in the midst of selling my house and buying a flat at the same time. For the same reason I doubt whether I can, as I had hoped, visit you or Corpus this term. I had promised definitely to come stay with Richards to discuss certain critical problems we have been brewing over; and as he is leaving for China, I feel that if I can come to Cambridge once I must keep my promise to him. And I doubt whether I can come even once, as we are moving on the 25th June. However, it is still a possibility. With best wishes from my wife and myself (and I hope your troubles will soon be at an end.)

Yours ever sincerely,
[T. S. Eliot]

----

can give us an indication of how long you can stay, when you can come & when you must depart. Make it as long as you can. We won't have any parties except one tea at which a few English School people whose mental balance might be improved thereby might appear. Leavis, Bennett, Tillyard perhaps. But say if you would rather not.'

1 – Pickthorn wrote from Corpus Christi College, Cambridge, 8 May: 'I am ashamed about Namier [L. B. Namier, *Structure of Politics at the Accession of G. III*], but honestly I have been interrupted by almost every sort of inconvenience & tragedy, & loathe the sight or thought of the book now. However, I will do it in the next few days or burst.'

2 – Pickthorn had agreed on 17 Jan. to review Namier's book – 'But I am not really competent to review it . . .' An intervening letter from TSE dated 9 Mar. (to which Pickthorn alludes in a letter of 12 Mar.) is missing. Pickthorn's letter of 12 Mar. includes these remarks: 'I think rather less well of the book [by Namier] than apparently anyone else, but I am sick of being denigratory, and I think that I should be likely to drift into denigration if I had to write very much.' No review of the Namier book was forthcoming. S. E. Morison reviewed L. B. Namier's *England in the Age of the American Revolution* in C. 10 (July 1931), 760–1.

TO *Samuel Eliot Morison*[1]   CC

9 May 1929   [London]

Dear Mr Morison,

Thank you for your note.[2] If all goes well, can you call for me at the Royal Societies Club, 63 St James's St., at one o'clock next Thursday? If not, I shall write to this address, or you will write to me at 57, Chester Terrace, s.w.1.

Looking forward to meeting you,

Sincerely yours,
[T. S. Eliot]

TO *Nigel Sutton*[3]   CC

13 May 1929   [London]

Dear Sutton,

I am writing to you so suddenly, unexpectedly, and on a matter for which you will be quite unprepared, that I ought to remind you first that you lunched with me when in London, and that I at least remember the occasion with much pleasure (I have just seen a cousin of mine, a Professor Morison, who met you also through Gordon George, and spoke of you appreciatively).

1–Samuel Eliot Morison (1887–1976), American historian, was for thirty years from 1925 Professor of History at Harvard. He was a cousin of TSE. In 1922 he became the first Harmsworth Professor of American History at Oxford. His numerous publications include *The Maritime History of Massachusetts* (1921), *The Oxford History of the United States* (1927), *The Growth of the American Republic* (1930), the history of Harvard University (5 vols, 1930–6), the history of the American navy in WW2 – *History of American Naval Operations* (15 vols.) – which is rated by many historians his finest achievement – the *Oxford History of the American People* (1965), and *The European Discovery of America* (1972). A Fellow of the Society of Antiquaries and of the American Philosophical Association, he served too as President of the American Historical Association; and his awards included the Bancroft Prize (twice), the Pulitzer Prize (twice), the Alfred Thayer Mahan Award of the Navy League, the Gold Medal for History, National Institute of Arts and Letters, and the President's Medal for Freedom.

2–Morison wrote from Christ Church, Oxford, on 9 May to say he would be passing through London on Thurs., 16 May, en route to Cambridge.

3–Nigel Sutton was head of the Paris Branch of Kalamazoo Ltd, an Australian-based company (founded by Oliver Morland, English head of the printing firm of Morland and Impey Ltd, with Charles E. Howie) which marketed adding, accounting, addressing, and punch-card machines. The Kalamazoo loose-leaf ledger, or binder, was world-famous.

The present matter is this. I have a Parisian friend named Henri Massis.[1] He is editor of *La Revue Universelle* (with Bainville), is pretty well known in French literary circles, but I don't know whether you have ever met him. He is really one of the A.F.[2] group of Catholics. He has a daughter (whom I have never seen) of about 20. She started to be a religieuse, taught French for two years in a nunnery in Kent, fell ill, returned to Paris, and now apparently has had to abandon the religious life; because her father writes to me to ask if I know of any English or American firms in Paris who might employ a bi-lingual dactylographe.[3] So I am writing to you, as head of the Kalamazoo, merely on the chance: if [you] see any possibility, and can grant an interview to the girl, good; if not, you need not even bother to answer this letter.

I have been lunching to-day with a relative, Professor Samuel Eliot Morison, a friend of Gordon George: as he as well as I is indebted to Gordon George for our acquaintance with you, we talked of you.

Hoping to see you again whenever I may be in Paris, or you in London.

Yours sincerely,
[T. S. Eliot]

TO *Thomas McGreevy*   MS Trinity College Dublin

Postcard 15 May 1929   57 Chester Terrace s.w.1.

My dear McGreevy,

I am very sorry.[4] Of course this is a feminist age and one must put up with that. But London isn't so bad, and I shall be glad if you are here for a spell. Meanwhile I'll think about you and write more fully, and consider about Rodker or some other.

1–Henri Massis (1886–1970), right-wing Roman Catholic critic; contributor to *L'Action Française*; co-founder and editor of *La Revue Universelle*: see Biographical Register.
2–*Action Française*.
3–Stenographer.
4–McGreevy reported on 11 Apr. that he was 'being sacked' from his post at the Ecole Normale, Paris. 'Miss Burt has been telling people this good while that I was not "assez universitaire" which is perhaps true and that I was "too literary" for her needs. It is true that my classes dwindled in size also but then the students are mostly young women whose concern is to pass examinations, and in whom I had no interest. The few who showed any live interest I have kept, men and women.' He said he wanted to go and live in Italy for a while, and to learn Italian better, but 'could put up with London for a few months'. He hoped TSE could place his book with Faber & Gwyer or with John Rodker.

Be of good heart. Best wishes from my wife and myself.

Yours ever,

T. S. E.

TO *Orlo Williams*   cc

16 May 1929   [London]

My dear Williams,

Many thanks for your letter. I have turned down the Evola,[1] on the strength of your ignorance of him: I did not think much of it, but if you had said that he was famous in Italy I should probably have asked you to read it for us. But I have a prejudice against Douglas Ainslie's[2] translations – is that justifiable? He seems to me a mad bad translator.[3]

About Garnett – there is no hurry, for what I contemplated was a long review for September. I don't want you to do it unless [you] really think Garnett worth it: yet I think it is time that *The Criterion* pronounced upon Garnett. If you incline to do it, I will ask Chatto to send you *The Sailor's Return* and any others you want. It seems to me that David Garnett is at least a modern document, like Hemingway. So let me know in due course.

If not Garnett, have you any one else in mind worth a long review for September? And please let me know when it would suit you best to let us have more Italian notes. I am up to the eyes in moving: if I may see you after the 1st July please let me know.

[T. S. Eliot]

1 – Julius Evola – Baron Giulio Evola (1898–1974) – reactionary Italian philosopher and esotericist; author of *Heathen Imperialism* (1928), *Introduction to Magic: Rituals and Practical Techniques for the Magus* (1929), *Three Aspects of the Jewish Problem* (1936).
2 – Douglas Ainslie (1865–1948): Scottish poet, translator, and critic; friend and associate of Oscar Wilde, Aubrey Beardsley, and Walter Pater; and translator of Benedetto Croce.
3 – Williams replied on 17 May: 'You are quite right about Douglas Ainslie: it is a tragedy he nobbled Croce. Evola, I see from the bibliography of Schneider's *The Making of the Fascist State*, writes on the theory of fascism from a Nietzschean point of view.'

TO *H. C. Crofton*[1]   CC

16 May 1929   [London]

My dear Crofton,

It's good to see your handwriting,[2] but I don't want you to feel obliged
to acknowledge *all* the fiction I send: I have one or two more on hand on
which I have almost pronounced my pontifical judgement, and which will
reach you soon after Pentecost; don't bother to write then. But I found
Gaboriau[3] better than I had remembered him to be. I am now reading the
works of a Swedish writer of Kriminal-Romane, named Heller,[4] beginning
with the words (in Gothic letters) 'ALL RIGHT CABBY' supposed to be
pronounced as 'Victoria-Station'.[5]

I had really been about to write to ask you about the following matter.
I have a friend named Henri Massis, an eminent Parisian publicist, editor
of *La Revue Universelle*, etc. He has a daughter (whom I have never seen)
aged about 20. She apparently started to be a religieuse, taught French for
two years in a nunnery in Kent, acquired a mastery of the English tongue,
fell ill, returned to her home, and apparently has abandoned the religious
life. Massis has written to me to ask do I know any English or American
firm in Paris which could employ a dactylographe who is bi-lingual. I take
it that the girl can do shorthand typing in both languages. I have written
to a man named Nigel Sutton, who sells Kalamazoo Loose Leaf Ledgers
in Paris; but I bethought me also of Lloyds Bank (rue des Capucines).
Without putting you to much trouble, is there anybody there whom you
know, to whom I could write, using your name, to ask for an interview
for the girl? I should only say that I know viz. that I don't know her, but
know her parents, and know that her father is highly respectable (red
ribbon) and well known in Paris etc. But if it means much machinery just
drop me a line and say you can't be troubled.

At the moment I am thoroughly empickled with preparing the lectures
(which will be delivered from 2 LO at 7:25, when you ought to be in your
bath before dinner) and a small book on Dante to be delivered by June

---

1 – H. C. Crofton worked in the Colonial and Foreign Department at Lloyds Bank, where
he had been a good friend.
2 – Crofton wrote on 15 May to acknowledge a detective novel that TSE had sent him.
3 – Émile Gaboriau (1832–73), French novelist and journalist; pioneer of modern crime
fiction; author of *Monsieur Lecoq* (2 vols, 1868); and *La vie infernale* (2 vols, 1870).
4 – Frank Heller – nom de plume of Gunnar Serner (1886–1947) – whose novels about the
detective-thief Philip Collin include *The Perilous Transactions of Mr Collin* (1924), *The
London Adventures of Mr Collin* (1924), *The Strange Adventures of Mr Collin* (1926).
5 – 'Victoria Station, sir! . . . All right, cabby!' (*Herr Collins sällsamma äventyr*).

30, and with selling my house and buying a flat and moving on June 25th. If you are to waste any of your time in the City during *August*, I should love to refresh myself with you: at that time of year I am apt to be making pilgrimages to the City Churches and Alehouses with B. L. Richmond, and we might join.

Yours ever,

[T. S. Eliot]

There is another book coming to you shortly called *Nemesis at Taynham Parva*.[1] It is full of Evil Argentines. I hope Aylward[2] is well (and married?). My conscience smites me that I have not been in touch with him lately. Please give my regards to the Head of the Staff Department, when you see him next.

TO *Theodore Spencer*[3]   TS Harvard

20 May 1929   *The Criterion*

Dear Sir,

I am honoured by your letter of the 7th instant, and should be very glad to contribute to your symposium, understanding that contributions must be in hand before April 1st 1930.[4] The only possible objection is that I have in preparation, not very far advanced, a book on Donne and the metaphysical poets, which may appear, I dare say, in the spring or autumn of 1930, unless something else turns up, as has already happened, which I must put my hand to first. This is only a partial difficulty on my part,

1–J. J. Coddington, *Nemesis at Raynham Parva* (London: Gollancz, 1929).
2–James de Vine Aylward was also a colleague and friend at Lloyds Bank.
3–Theodore Spencer (1902–48), writer, poet, and critic, taught at Harvard, 1927–49; as Boylston Professor of Rhetoric and Oratory from 1946. Co-editor of *A Garland for John Donne 1631–1931* (Cambridge, Mass., 1931), for which TSE wrote 'Donne in Our Time'; author of *Shakespeare and the Nature of Man* (Lowell Lectures on Shakespeare, 1951). The Master of Eliot House, Cambridge, Mass., writing to TSE on 24 Apr. 1950, spoke of 'Ted's grace and wisdom'.
4–Anticipating the 300th anniversary of the death of John Donne (31 Mar. 1931), Spencer announced that he was planning a 'tercentennial volume' to commemorate the occasion: a collection of 9 or 10 essays, under the title *A Garland for John Donne*, with contributions from the most eminent scholars of Donne including Sir Herbert Grierson, Evelyn Simpson, Miss Ramsay, and Mario Praz. Would TSE please be willing, he asked, to write for the collection a critical appreciation of Donne's poetry? – 'but I of course do not want to limit you too closely, and I should welcome most warmly any suggestion you might care to make.' The volume would be published by Harvard University Press; and each essay, which should not exceed *c*.5,000 words, would have to be received at the latest by 1 Apr. 1930; a fee of $100 would be paid for each essay.

meaning that it is more difficult to write an essay when you are writing a book on the same subject; but it might be a more serious difficulty from your point of view. Perhaps you will let me know what you think?[1]

Yours very truly,

[T. S. Eliot]

TO *Max Clauss*   CC

20 mai 1929   [London]

Cher ami,

Merci de votre gracieuse lettre du 13 courant. Nous acceptons votre proposition avec un vif plaisir.[2]

Je conviens, de la part de Faber & Faber Ltd., propriétaires du *Criterion*, de contribuer RM 50 au prix littéraire. Mais en outre, je veux stipuler ceci: selon notre règle invariable, nous payons £2 les 1000 mots. Si le manuscrit auquel est décerné le prix est en excès de 1500 mots (c'est-à-dire, si nos honoraires ordinaires dépasseraient RM 50) nous voulons payer la solde direct à l'auteur, si vous nous accordez la permission.

Et vous me permettrez de m'ajouter un autre member du groupe *Criterion*, en jugeant des dix manuscrits?

---

1 – Spencer ventured (1 June), 'I should think that if your book will be delayed until after the symposium appears, the matter could very easily be settled.' Since he planned to be in London from c.25 June, they could meet up and 'discuss the matter more satisfactorily'.

2 – A new award, 'The Five Reviews' Award', was to be conferred by *The Criterion*, *Europäische Revue* (which Clauss edited from Berlin), *Nouvelle Revue Française* (Paris), *Revista de Occidente* (Madrid), and *Nuova Antologia* (Milan), in each of five successive years: first for the best short story in German, then for stories in English, French, Italian, and Spanish; with the winner being printed in the five reviews. The first award was to be judged by Max Clauss, E. R. Curtius, and the novelist Thomas Mann (replacing the late Hugo von Hofmannsthal). TSE would hail this development in his 'Commentary', C. 9 (Jan. 1930), 181–2: 'It is not merely a means of bringing to notice new prose writers in five languages . . . We remark upon it still more as visible evidence of a community of interest, and a desire of co-operation, between literary and general reviews of different nations . . . All of these reviews, and others, have endeavoured to keep the intellectual blood of Europe circulating throughout the whole of Europe . . . It is of vital importance that the best thought and feeling of each country of high civilization should be contributed to the others while it is still fresh. Only so can there be any direction towards that higher community which existed in some ways throughout the middle ages, which persisted into the eighteenth century, and which was only dissolved finally after the Napoleonic wars. And without such intellectual community and co-operation of different organs in one body all peace pacts, world congresses, disarmament discussions, and reform leagues appear merely to be concerned with the body and not with the soul.'

Je vous remercie affectueusement de votre aimable et si flattante invitation. Je vous en écrirai bientôt quand j'aurai réfléchi là-dessus.

Toujours votre dévoué

[T. S. Eliot]¹

TO *Shane Leslie*²   CC

20 May 1929   [London]

Dear Mr Leslie,

Thank you for your letter of the 10th, which I seem to have been very slow in answering.³ Had I already done anything with Maurras's little

1 – *Translation*: Dear friend, Thank you for your kind letter of the 13th inst. We accept your proposal with great pleasure.

I agree, on behalf of Faber & Faber Ltd., owners of *The Criterion*, to contribute 50 RM [Reichmarks] to the literary prize. But I also want to stipulate the following: according to our fixed rule, we pay £2 for every 1000 words. If the manuscript that is awarded the prize exceeds 1500 words (that is, if our ordinary fees are in excess of 50 RM) we want to pay the balance directly to the author, if you grant us permission.

And will you allow me to add another member of *The Criterion* as a judge of the ten manuscripts?

Thank you very much for your kind and flattering invitation. I will write to you as soon as I've had the chance to think about it. Yours faithfully, [T. S. Eliot]

2 – Sir Shane Leslie (1885–1971), diplomat and author. Born into the Anglo-Irish Protestant Ascendancy – he was first cousin on his mother's side to Winston Churchill – he read classics at King's College, Cambridge, where he became a Roman Catholic for life as well as an Irish Nationalist (though christened John Randolph, he thereafter styled himself 'Shane'– the Irish form of his name). He also resigned the Irish estates entailed upon him and was for several years actively committed to Irish nationalist affairs (he stood for Parliament as a Nationalist in the 1910 election, unsuccessfully). In 1907 he went to Russia and visited Lev Tolstoy, and for a while he studied Scholastic Philosophy at Louvain University. He edited the *Dublin Review*, 1916–26, and published many works including *The End of a Chapter* (1916); *Henry Edward Manning: His Life and Labours* (1921); *Mark Sykes: His Life and Letters* (1923); *The Skull of Swift* (1928); *Studies in Sublime Failure* (1932); *American Wonderland* (1936); *The Film of Memory* (1938); and *Long Shadows* (1966). He succeeded as third baronet on the death of his father in 1944.

3 – Leslie wrote: 'In Paris recently I had a long talk with Ch: Maurras about your proposed translation of his bouquin on J. E. C. Bodley (*L'Anglais qui a connu la France*). I am engaged in writing Bodley's life and I am anxious to quote a chapterful in translation from Maurras' delightful work. If you have not proceeded with the translation since Sept Maurras is willing that I should produce it in whole. Otherwise I would quote from your translation if it appears before the Autumn with your permission . . . I know what you have written of Maurras in the *Criterion* I think. I wrote 2 articles on him in the *Outlook* but otherwise he seems singularly ignored on this side.'

J. E. C. Bodley (1853–1925) – a descendant of Sir Thomas Bodley, founder of the Bodleian Library, Oxford – was an English civil servant; secretary to Sir Charles Dilke; friend of Cardinal Manning. His writings include *France* (2 vols, 1898), *L'Anglomanie et les traditions*

book, I should be very willing to have you make use of the translation; but many other more pressing things have intervened; and it will be a long time before I should do it. And as a matter of fact, there are other parts of his work which I am now more anxious to translate. So if you will go ahead and translate the whole, do so by all means.

I should be very happy to meet you and to discuss Maurras, who as you suggest, is only known here, except to half a dozen people, as more than an obscure political agitator. He is suspect to Liberals on the one hand and to Papists and High Churchmen on the other; and I did not have much success in trying to fight his battle in *The Church Times*. At present I have no time to see anyone – but after July I hope to have more time to renew old acquaintances and form new ones.

Yours very truly,
[T. S. Eliot]

TO *Gerard Hopkins* CC

20 May 1929   [London]

Dear Mr Hopkins,

I have glanced at *Shakespeare der Mensch*, which strikes me – without any prejudice, as I never heard of it before – as an interesting book.[1] But it reaches me at an awkward moment, when I have a thousand things to do, and am preparing to move; so I think it really ought to go to someone who could give it the attention it deserves.

The best man I can think of is A. W. Wheen of the Victoria and Albert Museum, who is a remarkable German scholar and a student of Shakespeare, and a widely read man. He has often reported on German works to other firms; possibly you know him already.

Françaises (1899), and *L'Age mécanique et le déclin de l'idéalisme en France* (1913). See Shane Leslie, *Memoir of John Edward Courtenay Bodley* (1930).

1 – Hopkins asked TSE on 14 May to write a short report on *Shakespeare der Mensch*, by Helene Richter: 'It has been proposed that we [Oxford University Press] should translate the work, and I notice that a review in the special German number of the Times Literary Supplement spoke of it with praise. I do hope you will forgive my troubling you, but a combination of German scholarship and Shakespearian judgment is not so common that I can afford to ignore the most distinguished possessor of these two gifts.'

I will hold the book until Wednesday, and will then return it to you, unless you write at once and ask me to send it direct to someone else.

With very many regrets and apologies,

Yours sincerely,
[T. S. Eliot]

TO *Edith Sitwell*[1]   CC

21 May 1929   [London]

Dear Edith,

I should be very much pleased if you were able and willing to review a new collection of Charlotte Mew's poems which Harold Monro has just published. It might be made rather a full review dealing with her work as a whole. I do not remember when *The Farmer's Bride* appeared but it was long before the *Criterion* was founded, so we have never discussed her. I do hope you can do this as I should not need it until mid-summer, that is to say in time for the September issue.[2]

Vivien and I often speak of you and we should so like to see you again. She has had so much trouble with her leg and foot during the last few months that she has hardly been out at all and has seen very few people. The trouble seems to have been greatly aggravated by the steep stairs of our house and so we are moving into a flat at the end of the June quarter.[3] Until then we are of course in a frightful muddle. I suppose that you will be away during the summer but we should like to see you as soon as we can after we have got settled

[*Incomplete, the typing runs off the page.*][4]

1–Edith Sitwell (1887–1964), poet, biographer, anthologist, and novelist: see Biographical Register.
2–ES would submit her review – C. 9 (Oct. 1929), 130–4 – with an undated letter: 'I have tried not to roll on her, because she is dead, and because I respect some of her work, but I do think that a lot of it is simply "Alice where art thou" played on the harmonium.'
3–On 6 Sept. VHE wrote to Mary Hutchinson, of the flat at 68 Clarence Gate Gardens: 'I left it to Tom to choose it. Very stupid & unfair of me. Well my dear it is a most terrible flat. It is quite awful. It is *enormous*. And very *very* expensive. And hideous.'
4–Judging from ES's undated reply to this letter, TSE went on to say that he and Vivien were going for a while to the seaside.

TO *C. A. Siepmann*

21 May 1929   57 Chester Terrace, s.w.1.

Dear Mr Siepmann,

Concerning my B.B.C. talks to begin June 11th, I am writing to make three requests, viz.:

I have written out my first lecture, which I think times pretty closely to your 19 minutes. I should like to have a test of it soon; but should like first to send the MSS to be read by you or someone else, so that you can tell me whether it is what you want, or whether too high- or alternatively too low-brow. I am not sure whether I have struck the right 'note'.

2. May I have another copy of the pamphlet, as I have mislaid my copy of my own prospectus, and am not certain of the order in which my talks were advertised.

3. The third point is rather serious for me. My first talk is fixed for June 11th, the second for June 18th, the third for June 25th etc. It happens, as I could not have anticipated, that I am moving from this house into a flat on June 25th (quarter day): I cannot get possession of my flat earlier, and I must give possession to the purchaser of my house on the following day (June 26th). It will be a *most* inconvenient day for me to lecture on: so if it is humanly possible to change my talk for June 25th to some other day – later in the same week, or at the end of the course – I should be extremely grateful. If impossible, I shall of course fulfil my engagement: but only at much cost and by superhuman efforts.[1]

Yours sincerely,
T. S. Eliot

TO *I. A. Richards*

TS Magdalene

21 May 1929   57 Chester Terrace, s.w.1.

My dear Richards,[2]

I ought to have written to you over Whitsun, but was still dreaming that my engagement with you was a fortnight hence. So I am writing at inexcusably short notice – I now find it at the last moment quite impossible to get away for my weekend with you on the 25th, to which I

---

1 – Siepmann offered (22 May) to comment on TSE's text 'from the point of view of this rather elusory broadcast technique'. But he could not change the dates for recording.
2 – This letter is quoted, in part, in John Constable's 'Introduction' to *I. A. Richards and his Critics* (2001), xxxiii–xxxiv.

had looked forward keenly. I am moving on June quarter day, but am still in daily negotiation with my solicitors who are in daily communication with the solicitors of the Purchasers (of the address above) and with the solicitors of the Vendors (of my new address); and what with this, and the consequent arrears into which everything else has fallen, and the fact that I have got to write at high speed some B.B.C. talks at the beginning of June, and also that my wife, in a crippled condition, is occupied daily in sorting and packing and cataloguing here, I don't feel justified in leaving town, even to visit you. I shall be very sorry to miss a meeting with Tillyard and the others; but the main thing really is that I should see you once or twice before you leave for China: to get some notion of a line which you purpose to work on, and of another for me to work on. How long can you be in London, and when, before you sail? If we could have one or two mornings, or afternoons, it would be useful to me.

I have just finished a sort of pamphlet on Dante into which I have worked a few notions discussed with you: the idea of the *Vita Nuova* as a manual of sex psychology, and the idea of the difference between philosophy as philosophy and philosophy in poetry: the distinction between Belief and Poetic Assent or Acceptance. (Of course the further difference, which I believe can be established, between philosophic theological and scientific belief, does not enter here. And the really exciting point, whether Russell's analysis of the proposition is not as antiquated as Bradley's, does not enter either.) I have merely got down a vague literary adumbration of a few questions I want worked out more thoroughly; so when I send you the proof, please think of it as rough notes incorporated in a popular pamphlet. The only other effect is that having put these remarks in connexion with Dante will alter the form of my Donne, and I think improve it. The only point which I hope I have made, in the little Dante book, is this: that for

[*page missing*]

TO *Kenneth Ingram*   CC

22 May 1929   [London]

Dear Mr Ingram,

I have been meaning to write to you for a long time but have kept postponing it until I could suggest a day for us to lunch together. I have however been extremely busy with both personal and impersonal matters and my affairs are further complicated by arrangements for moving in

June. Paradoxical as it may seem I believe and hope we shall have more opportunities for meeting after I have made this change.

I am now writing to you about a matter which I had hoped to mention to you in conversation. I have a manuscript of a friend of mine which I asked him to submit to my own firm.[1] It is unsuitable for us for two reasons. First we do not like dealing with such short books as this, it is only 88 typed pages, and second because it is not the type of book which we could market, especially as the author desires to remain strictly anonymous.

The book is written by a distinguished elderly scholar and man of letters whose name, however, is very much better known in America than here. He calls it *Pages from an Oxford Diary* and [it] is the record of his philosophical and religious meditations during a prolonged stay in Oxford. He has concealed himself further under a suggestion that the writer is actually an Oxford Don, which he is not. The book would have of course much greater interest to anyone who knew the other work of the author who has written a considerable amount of theological as well as literary work. But if one explained his position in a general way I think it would still be of great interest because it shows a gradual development of a learned and highly cultivated man of an older generation than ours from a sceptical to a Catholic position.

I offered the author to write a preface for the book and he said that he would be very glad for me to do so; partly I think because he thought that it might still further protect his identity by leading people to believe that I was myself the author.[2] If your Society considered the book a signed preface by me might not be desired; but I think that I ought to write a short anonymous preface to explain wherein lies the interest and importance of the whole book.

If you are interested I will have the MSS. sent to you; and if you did care to publish it I would of course put you into communication with the author himself.[3]

Yours sincerely

[T. S. Eliot]

---

1 – Paul Elmer More, 'Pages from an Oxford Diary'.

2 – More had written to TSE on 21 Feb., 'I had no thought of asking you to make yourself responsible for the publication by writing an introduction, but should be flattered if you felt moved to do so. Probably the first result would be to bring the authorship on your own head because of the religious views. That would amuse me vastly.'

3 – Ingram responded (27 May) that he would be glad to read the manuscript, and that a preface by TSE 'would greatly increase the value of the book'.

TO *Erich Alport*[1]

TS Richard Buckle

23 May 1929   57 Chester Terrace, s.w.1.

Dear Mr Alport,

Thank you very much for your note, but I am disappointed to learn that your only free time is Friday afternoon, as that afternoon is filled up for me elsewhere.[2] I had hoped that you might be in London and free for lunch today or tomorrow. I am glad however that we have had an opportunity of meeting though only for a few minutes.

I have not got your address in Hamburg, but if Faber has it you need not bother to let me know.

I trust that we may now keep in touch with each other: I am looking forward with much interest and satisfaction to reading your translation of Machiavelli. I have just finished a little book on Dante which should appear in the autumn: should it receive the approval of Curtius, I think it is as likely to be suitable for German readers as for English. I will send it to you.

I do not know whether you have completed your arrangements with Faber about German books for translation; but I cordially endorsed his views on that subject.[3]

Looking forward to our next meeting either in England or Germany,

I am, yours very sincerely,
T. S. Eliot

TO *Henri Massis*

CC

24 Mai 1929   [London]

Mon cher ami,

J'ai déjà receuilli quelques nouvelles. Suivant un liaison établi par des amis de Lloyds Bank Londres, je peux proposer à votre fille d'écrire à Monsieur L. A. Perkins, 12 rue du Faubourg St. Honoré, un administrateur de Lloyds Bank *Paris* qui m'est personellement inconnu; il est averti de la situation de votre fille.

1–Dr Erich Alport was author of *Nation und Reich in der politischen Willenbildung des britischen Weltreiches* (Berlin, 1933).
2–Alport asked (19 May) to meet TSE at teatime on Fri. 24 May.
3–GCF was to write to Alport on 28 June 1929 of 'the arrangement we made, on your last visit to England, by which we are to have the benefit of your advice on contemporary German books suitable for translation into English'.

Elle aura bientôt aussi une lettre de M. Nigel Sutton, duquel je vous ai parlé; il est en vacances, mais il lui écrira en deux ou trois jours lors de son retour à Paris.[1]

Votre tout dévoué,
[T. S. Eliot][2]

TO *S. Dudley* CC

24 May 1929   [London]

Dear Dudley,

I am extremely grateful to you for your kindness; I really had not expected to call upon anyone to take so much trouble for me on account of my friend's daughter.[3] Please accept my most cordial thanks.

I have read your enclosure with much interest.[4] I hesitate to criticise a tour de force which is far beyond my own capacity; and I hesitate also to say that Macaulay *never* began a paragraph with a preposition, though I think it unlikely that he ever ended a sentence with one. I remember once being taken down by Henry Bell[5] for saying 'under the circumstances', and the following week I came across the same phrase in the first paragraph

---

1 – Massis thanked TSE (undated) for his kind help. However, the situation was not now so urgent, since his daughter had been employed for the last two months as a secretary '*dans les bureaux de Dupont de Remours, la grande affaire américaine*'.

2 – *Translation:* My dear friend, I have already received several pieces of news. In accordance with an arrangement made by friends at Lloyds Bank, London, I am going to suggest that your daughter writes to Mr Perkins, 12 rue du Faubourg St Honoré, an administrator at Lloyds Bank *Paris* who is not known to me personally; he has been advised about your daughter's situation.

She will very soon get a letter from Mr Nigel Sutton, of whom I have spoken to you; he is on holiday, but he will write to her within two or three days of his return to Paris. Yours ever, [T. S. Eliot]

3 – Crofton had mentioned to S. Dudley (a colleague at Lloyds) TSE's concern for Henri Massis's daughter. Dudley wrote to TSE on 17 May, 'As I happen to know the present Assistant General Manager at Lloyds & National Provincial Bank Limited, Paris, I have written to ask him to use what I believe is known as "his good offices" on her behalf.' He wrote again on 22 May that his friend L. A. Perkins, 12, Rue du Faubourg St Honoré, would be glad to consider an application from Mlle Massis: 'He also says that if she is bilingual and an accurate typist there is little doubt that he can find her a position without much delay.'

4 – Dudley – 'being very unlearned' – asked TSE about a cutting that he enclosed, in imitation of Macaulay, with a paragraph opening 'Of their little daughter . . .'; he commented, 'I think it would be a good thing . . . if I could tell the writer that Macaulay would not have started a paragraph with preposition – perhaps he might have, that's what I don't know.'

5 – Henry Bell (d. 1935) was a Director of Lloyds Bank Ltd.

of something by Cardinal Newman.[1] However, I didn't rush up to Bell's room to point that out to him.

Thanks you again for your kindness,

Sincerely yours,
[T. S. Eliot]

TO *Gerard Hopkins*

CC

24 May 1929   [London]

Dear Mr Hopkins,

Since writing to you I have heard that A. W. Wheen is seriously ill and has just been taken to St Thomas's Hospital, so that my suggestion is now useless. I will try to think of someone else, though it is hardly likely to be anyone as good as he would have been. I will post the book to you on Monday, and if I can find a few minutes to dip into it again meanwhile, I will. I am very sorry indeed about Wheen.

Yours sincerely,
[T. S. Eliot]

1 – From the Preface (2 May 1865) to the 2nd edn of *Apologia Pro Vita Sua: Being a History of His Religious Opinions* (1864), by John Henry Cardinal Newman (1801–90), after being attacked in *Macmillan's Magazine* (Jan. 1864) by the Revd Charles Kingsley (Professor of Modern History at Cambridge, chaplain to the Queen). Kingsley wrote, 'Truth for its own sake, had never been a virtue with the Roman clergy. Father Newman informs us that it need not, and on the whole ought not to be; that cunning is the weapon which Heaven has given to the Saints wherewith to withstand the brute male force of the wicked world which marries and is given in marriage. Whether his notion be doctrinally correct or not, it is at least historically so.' Newman opened the second paragraph of his Preface: 'It is now more than twenty years that a vague impression to my disadvantage has rested on the popular mind, as if my conduct towards the Anglican Church, while I was a member of it, was inconsistent with Christian simplicity and uprightness. An impression of this kind was almost unavoidable *under the circumstances* [editorial italics] of the case, when a man, who had written strongly against a cause, and has collected a party round him by virtue of such writings, gradually faltered in his opposition to it, unsaid his words, threw his own friends into perplexity and their proceedings into confusion, and ended by passing over to the side of those whom he had so vigorously denounced' (*Apologia Pro Vita Sua*, ed. Martin J. Svaglic [Oxford, 1967], 1).

TO *Nigel Sutton*   cc

24 May 1929   [London]

Dear Sutton,

   Thank you very much for your letter; and I shall be very grateful if
you will write to Mlle. Massis, or to her father, at 157, Boulevard St.
Germain.[1] As I said, I have never seen the girl, and know nothing directly
of her capacities; but anyway I should be glad to have you meet Henri
Massis, who is intelligent and agreeable.

   I saw Professor Morison (whom I had never met before) a few days ago
and liked him.[2] He spoke most cordially and enthusiastically of you.

   I certainly hope to see you again in Paris, but also in London. During
May and June I am very rushed indeed, but should [you] be in London
during July or August I hope you will let me know.

With very many thanks,
Yours sincerely,
[T. S. Eliot]

TO *H. C. Crofton*   cc

24 May 1929   [London]

My dear Crofton,

   I think it most awfully kind of you and Dudley to take so much trouble
about such a matter, and I am writing to Dudley to thank him. The young
lady ought to recognise herself very much in your debt.[3]

   I am sending on two more tales, with some misgivings: the Connington
story has something to do with White Slave traffic; the other has what
might be taken as an offensive caricature of a deceased statesman; they
are to read and throw away, rather than for your shelves.[4] I don't suppose
most people would see anything objectionable about them, but I feel that
such themes are not appropriate to detective fiction!

1–Sutton had undertaken on 19 May to contact Mlle Massis.
2–Sutton wrote: 'Professor Morison and his wife came to see me when they were in Paris.
We liked them so much . . . Gordon George stayed with me for a few days . . .'
3–Crofton wrote on 17 May that their 'mutual friend' S. Dudley was writing to the Asst.
General Manager of Lloyds in Paris, on behalf of 'the unknown religieuse manquée'
(daughter of Henri Massis) about whom TSE had consulted him.
4–They shared a passion for detective fiction, and TSE often sent him new titles – so often
indeed that Crofton could speak of TSE's 'Detective Story shelf at Middle Farm'.

I am very glad to hear that you will be in town in August, and look forward to a lunch then.

With most grateful thanks,
Yours ever,
[T. S. Eliot]

TO *J. B. Trend*   cc

27 May 1929   [London]

My dear Trend,

If you are now in London or in England, I wonder if you would be willing to read for us the manuscript of a book by Antonio Pastor. It deals with a subject on which you are something of an authority, i.e. with the intellectual influence of the Moors in Spain.[1] It strikes me as extremely interesting but I am completely bewildered by it. What we have is merely the first section of rather a long book but I think it should be enough to judge from. We should of course not ask you to do it without paying our usual reader's fee. I hope that you can as I do not know anyone else whose judgement I should trust. Would you let me have a line from you in any case. I am still looking forward to lunching with you and Dent.[2]

Yours ever
[T. S. Eliot]

TO *M. C. D'Arcy*   cc

27 May 1929   [London]

My dear D'Arcy,

I wonder if you would be so kind as to look at another book for *The Criterion* and at least tell me what you think of it, even if you do not have time to write about it. It is called *The Definition of the Godhead* by Dora Marsden. A book with such a portentous title, also written by a woman of whom you have probably never heard might well frighten you off. I believe however that there is just a possibility that there may be something

---

1–Pedro Antonio de Alarcón (1833–91), *Moors and Christians*.
2–Trend said (29 May) he would be happy to look at the MS. 'Dent has been very difficult to get hold of this term.' Trend submitted his reader's report on 15 June, along with this brief comment in a letter of the same date: 'I hope the report is not too severe. There is certainly a book there, and a very interesting one; but he hasn't quite got it out.'

in it, and I am particularly anxious to find out as I am quite sure that it will be completely ignored by every other review. I will admit that pressure has been brought to bear upon me by a friend of the author, to whom I am indebted, to do something about it; so my conscience makes it necessary for me to find out at least whether it is a good book or not.[1]

I hope that I may see something of you this summer. We shall be moving into a flat on the 25th of June, so it will be very difficult for me to make any engagements until we have settled down a little at the beginning of July. But I trust that you will be in London at least part of the time during July and August.

Yours always sincerely,
[T. S. Eliot]

TO *Edwin Osgood Grover*

CC

27 May 1929   [London]

Dear Sir,

I have your letter of the 9th instant and note your request.[2] For the right to use any of my poems in an anthology in America you should apply to A. A. Knopf and not to me. But please observe that Messrs Knopf's rights do not cover Great Britain or the Colonies except Canada so that for British rights you would have to apply to me; and before granting these rights I should have to know a good deal more about the book.

Yours very truly,
[T. S. Eliot]

---

1 – D'Arcy said (29 May) he would like to see Marsden's book: 'she is tackling a difficult proposition, but who knows?'

2 – Edwin Osgood Grover (1870–1965), publisher and educator – Professor of Books, Rollins College, Winter Park, Florida, 1926–47 – requested permission (9 May) to include 'The Hippopotamus' in an anthology entitled *The Animal Lover's Knapsack* to be published by Thomas Y. Crowell & Co., New York. 'P. S. You may have one or two other animal poems that might be suitable for my "Animal Lover's Knapsack".'

TO *R. E. Gordon George*   CC

27 May 1929   [London]

My dear Gordon George,

I am very glad to hear from you and should be delighted if you would
review Du Bos's two books for the September number.¹ I will let you
know a little later on what date we should have the copy. I have just been
looking through his *Journal* with great interest, and managed to squeeze
a short notice into the June *Criterion* in commendation of it² and should
be all the more glad to have a long review of him later on.

I am very much obliged to you for bringing me into touch with Morison
who I liked very much indeed and hope to see again.

With all best wishes from my wife and myself.

                                        Yours ever,
                                        [T. S. Eliot]

TO *Mario Praz*   CC

28 May 1929   [Faber & Faber]

My dear Praz,

Thank you for your letter of the 27th. I am having the volume of
Randolph's *Poems* sent to you and you will I hope let me know how long
a note you consider it to be worth.³

I have heard from Mr Theodore Spencer of Harvard, whom I do not
know, and have written accepting provisionally but informing him that I
hope to bring out a volume of my own about Donne in 1930 but suppose
that this will make no difference to him. I see no reason why he should

---

1–George asked if he might review the new books on Byron and Gide [*Le dialogue avec
André Gide* (1929)] by Charles du Bos. 'I have been doing his Journal for [Bruce] Richmond
. . . The Byron and Gide are barred from the Supplement because Richmond will not face
the question of the sexual irregularities and vices involved, which Du Bos thinks essential
to his discussion . . . I do not ask for more freedom than I have taken in Michelangelo and
Maupassant' (21 May).
2–TSE, untitled review of Charles du Bos, *Extraits d'un Journal: 1908–1928*, in C. 8 (July
1929), 762 (not in Gallup): 'Charles du Bos is a writer whose name is known to everyone
who knows contemporary French literature, though he writes but little. This is a journal of
a man of culture and taste and insight, who knows well several literatures, including English,
and who in two volumes entitled *Approximations* has written some of the best pieces of
contemporary criticism. It is, in fact, a book of some importance.'
3–Praz reviewed *The Poems of Thomas Randolph*, ed. G. Thorn-Drury, in C. 9 (Oct. 1929),
164–6.

not be able to get a good lot of contributors. But I am writing to Grierson and will ask him whether he is accepting.[1]

In haste,
Yours ever
[T. S. Eliot]

TO *H. J. C. Grierson*

TS National Library of Scotland

28 May 1929

Faber & Faber Ltd,
24 Russell Square

Dear Grierson,

It has occurred to me that there is room for a new critical biography of Burns, and naturally yours was the first name that came to mind as the possible author. I have spoken to one or two of my other Directors about it and they agree with me that it would be a very good thing indeed if we could induce you to undertake the book. I dare say that other publishers have thought of this subject before and have approached you about it. But I should very much like to know how the suggestion strikes you and if there is any chance whatever of your undertaking the book I will bring the matter up immediately before my Board so that they may make you definite proposals. Personally I should be more than delighted to have a book by you on this, or indeed any other subject.[2]

Another matter of minor importance. I have had a letter from a Mr Theodore Spencer of Harvard asking me to contribute to a memorial volume of essays on Donne. He has also asked Praz who is writing to you about it and has written to me as well. I have practically accepted myself and therefore I very much hope that you will be in the same company.[3]

With all best wishes,
Yours very sincerely,
T. S. Eliot

1–Praz responded to this information on 16 June: 'I also have been asked again to write a study of Donne (in book form) for 1930. All things considered, I do not think I'll do it. I begin to think there is too much fuss made about Donne, and what was a quasi-discovery a few years ago threatens to become too much of an open door in the near time to come.'
2–Grierson replied (1 June) that he would have liked to 'try his hand' at a biography of Burns, but he was 'absolutely tied up with the work I have undertaken for Constable of collecting and editing the letters of Sir Walter Scott . . . It would be interesting to try one's hand at a Life free from prejudice national or otherwise, but I fear it is not for me.'
3–'They want me to write on Donne and Later English Poetry . . .' said Grierson (1 June), 'but I fear it is rather beyond me even if I had the time . . . [M]y view is probably a little old-fashioned . . . I have not yet written to Spencer and shall think it over.'

TO C. A. *Siepmann*   TS BBC Caversham

3 June 1929   *The Criterion*

Dear Mr Siepmann,

Thank you very much for your letter, which I found very helpful.[1]
I enclose a revised version (which I understand you want at once for *The
Listener*) and hope that it is about the right length;[2] but I am to have
an audition with Mr Rendall[3] on Wednesday at 2: 30, and if it is found
too long or too short I shall have time to adjust it. After I have delivered
one talk it should be easy for me to gauge the manuscript of those which
follow.

                                        Yours very truly,
                                        T. S. Eliot

TO *Harold Monro*   TS Texas

4 June 1929   Faber & Faber Ltd

Dear Harold,

I have been meditating your letter of the 29th.[4]

You are more than welcome to *The Hollow Men*, *Whispers of
Immortality*, and any other of my published verse except *The Journey
of the Magi* and *The Waste Land*. As for the first, had I had a volume of
verse ready this year I should probably have included it; but as things are,
and as it still sells a little, my co-directors would rather I did not allow it
[to] appear in any anthology. Of course I am legally quite free; but you

---

1 – Siepmann (27 May) liked TSE's talk 'in the main very much indeed'. He had three 'minor
points': (i) since the talk was 800 words too short, it allowed 'room for what I think your
manuscript rather lacks at present, namely a number of pertinent illustrations of the felicity
of style of these Elizabethan translators'; (ii) TSE had 'exerted an almost excessive self-
control. A personal note . . . does not come amiss in a broadcast talk'; (iii) TSE's opening
paragraph was 'a little formal. It is important to win the confidence and interest of your
listeners early . . . The opening at present is, perhaps, a little academic.'
2 – R. S. Lambert, editor of *The Listener*, wrote on 3 June to say that *The Listener* would
be printing the text of TSE's broadcast talks on Tudor Prose; however, they would require
an abbreviated version of the talks, running to a length of about 1800 words. The first of
TSE's talks, 'The Tudor Translators', would appear in *The Listener*, 12 June 1929, 833–4.
3 – R. A. Rendall, Director of Programmes, Adult Education Section, BBC, wrote of TSE's
talk (8 June): 'You will notice I have made two very slight modifications, crossing out
reference to Boot's, Mudie's and the Times, as such things are forbidden fruit to us.'
4 – Monro asked permission to include in an anthology three poems – 'The Hollow Men',
'Whispers of Immortality', *Journey of the Magi* – 'and just one short extract from *The Waste
Land* from page 84 of the *Poems* and consisting only of lines 400 to 409.'

will understand how I feel being so closely associated with the publishers of the poem.

And about the *Waste Land* selection, I really don't feel that I could bear to let one bit be published by itself, even for your anthology. I hope you won't be very disappointed.

I suppose the *Fragment of an Agon* (which I rather like) is too long, and unsuitable. Would you care to consider either the 'Salutation' which was published only in the *Criterion*, or a better poem called 'Perch' Io non Spero', which was published only in Paris? You are welcome to either of these, which have not appeared in any volume or anthology, and which I intended to keep back for a sequence I am preparing.

ever yours,

Tom

TO *Pierre Loving*[1]

5 June 1929   [London]

Dear Mr Loving,

Thank you for your letter of the 2nd June. I am interested to hear that *This Quarter* is to be revived with your help, and your list of contributors makes it sound very much more interesting than the original review.[2] I should be very glad to contribute when I can but I am afraid that I have too much to do to be able to write anything for you for your July number. I should be very glad if you would let me see the number when it appears so that I may have a clearer idea of what you want.

Yours sincerely,

[T. S. Eliot]

1–Pierre Loving (1893–1950), journalist, author, translator, actor, wrote for *The Nation*, worked for the *New York Herald*, and was a correspondent for the International News Service. His works include *The Gardener of Evil* (a novel about Baudelaire, 1931), and translations of works by Pierre Louÿs, Friedrich Hölderlin and Arthur Schnitzler.

2–Loving wrote (? 2 June) that he had become editorial adviser of *This Quarter*, which was to be published henceforth by the American publisher E. W. Titus (1870–1952), with the first number due to appear in July: contributors were to include D. H. Lawrence, Aldous Huxley, Julien Green, Liam O'Flaherty, Herbert Read, and Sherwood Anderson. See Hugh Ford, *Published in Paris: American and British Writers, Printers, and Publishers in Paris, 1920–1939* (1975), 137 ff.

TO *Allen Tate* Princeton

7 June 1929 *The Criterion*

Dear Tate,

I am extremely sorry to find that something has gone wrong. Some months ago I wrote to you to say that I wanted to use the Humanism Essay in this June number after all; having no reply I went ahead.[1] In due course galley proof was sent to you and we discovered at the last moment that you had not returned it corrected, so that we had to do the best we could in the office. The June number will be out within the week with your essay on Humanism in it. I only pray that you will not find a great number of mistakes in it or much that you would like to revise.

Have you had any other trouble with correspondence at this address. Because so far as we can trace both letter and proof were addressed correctly. I am very sorry about this and hope that the change is not inconvenient for you. As I am using the Humanism in June I could not use the Emily Dickinson until December; so that if you want to publish it elsewhere please let me know and I will return it to you with some galley proofs which you may find useful.[2]

With many regrets,
Yours sincerely,
T. S. Eliot

TO *H. J. Massingham*[3] CC

11 June 1929 [London]

Dear Massingham,

I have your essay on Spengler, which I have very much enjoyed reading. The June issue will be out in a few days and in any case I should not have had room for it in that number, but I should like very much to use it in September.[4]

1–Tate, 'The Fallacy of Humanism', C. 8 (July 1929), 661–81. Tate wrote on 4 June to say that he had been expecting the proofs of his essay on Emily Dickinson.
2–Tate published a brief essay on Emily Dickinson in *Outlook* 149 (Aug. 1928), 621–3, and ultimately revised it for inclusion in his *Reactionary Essays on Poetry and Ideas* (1936), 3–25; and *On the Limits of Poetry: Selected Essays, 1928–1948* (1948), 197–213.
3–Harold John Massingham (1888–1952), writer and journalist devoted to rural traditions and crafts: his works included *Downland Man* (1926), *Wold without End* (1932), *Country Relics* (1939), and *Remembrance: An Autobiography* (1941).
4–Allen & Unwin published in 1926 a translation of *Der Untergang des Abendlandes:*

I bought a wireless set only in time to hear your last two talks on birds which interested me very much indeed. I am afraid that you will not find my own worth listening to as I am completely inexperienced in this sort of public speaking. You seem yourself to handle that medium with the greatest ease.[1]

Yours sincerely,

[T. S. Eliot]

TO *Ruth Wainewright*   CC

12 June 1929   [London]

Dear Madam,

I am honoured by your invitation to address the Sussex Poetry Society during next autumn or winter; and I think that the fees that you offer are wholly adequate;[2] but I am afraid that I must decline with regrets this and any further invitations for public speaking for the next year as I shall be extremely busy with other work from which I cannot afford even such a pleasant distraction.

With very many thanks and regrets,

I am,

Yours sincerely,

[T. S. Eliot]

TO *W. J. Lawrence*[3]   CC

12 June 1929   [London]

Dear Mr Lawrence,

I am now writing to you personally about your paper on the Elizabethan private playhouse. I shall be very glad indeed to use [it] if you will give me the time you promise. I might possibly be able to print it in December although it is more likely to be next March. If meanwhile however you

---

Umrisse einer Morphologie der Weltgeschichte (2 vols, 1918–22), by the philosopher Oswald Spengler (1890–1936) – which had sold 90,000 copies in Germany – under the title *The Decline of the West*. In the event, Massingham's essay did not appear in C.

1 – Massingham replied (20 June): 'On the contrary, I am enjoying your Tudor Prose talks immensely. I was also happy to read E. M. Forster's paper on your poems the other day.'

2 – Wainewright (10 June) offered £3. 3. 0d. plus expenses.

3 – W. J. Lawrence (1862–1940), theatre and textual historian; author of *The Elizabethan Playhouse and Other Studies* (2 vols, 1912–13).

want to place it somewhere else you have only to let me know and it shall be returned to you.[1]

Yours sincerely,
[T. S. Eliot]

TO *Messrs. William Jackson*   CC

12 June 1929   [London]

Dear Sirs,

I have your letter of the 31st of May and have to inform you that your client is mistaken.[2] The only mention that has ever been made of the three books you list was in connection with the explicit statement that the[y] are only in preparation. I hope to have the volume of Donne ready written in a year's time.

Yours faithfully,
[T. S. Eliot]

TO *A. L. Rowse*   TS Exeter

14 June 1929   [London]

Dear Rowse,

I am very glad to hear from you and I quite understand as I knew that you were very busy during the election.[3] By all means let us have a review of Pollard's Wolsey as you say it is a really important book. There is

---

1–Lawrence had written on 18 Apr. that he 'should be content to await your convenience in the matter of its appearance . . . say twelve months from date.' He reaffirmed on 13 June that he was prepared to leave his essay with TSE until Dec., or even Mar. 1930. See 'The Elizabethan Private Playhouse', C. 9 (Apr. 1930), 420–9.

2–William Jackson (Books) Ltd of London (Export Booksellers) wrote on 31 May to enquire on behalf of a 'Client' who had placed an order with them for three books by TSE: *The School of Donne*, *The Outline of Royalism*, and *The Principles of Modern Heresy* – all of which had been projected by TSE in his 'Preface' to *FLA* (1928).

3–The General Election, on 30 May, returned a second Labour administration under Ramsay MacDonald. Labour won 287 seats; Conservatives, 261; Liberals, 59; others, 8. (The preceding Conservative Government had run from Oct. 1924. TSE wrote in his 'Commentary' (C. 8 [July 1929], 579): 'The Conservative Party has a great opportunity, in the fact that within the memory of no living man under sixty, has it acknowledged any contact with intelligence . . . It has, what no other political party at present enjoys, a complete mental vacuum: a vacancy . . . Will it, during its holiday, be inclined to take any notice of the fancies of men who like to think, and do not want to hold office of any sort?

---

no hurry about [it] because the July number is already with the binders and should be out in a few days. But the sooner you can let me have it the better and it will go into the September number.[1] The other review I should like also; I could never swear that I should be able to publish two reviews by the same reviewer in the same number but if you think these two books well worth doing I should be glad to have the review and could use it in the following issue.[2]

I enclose a page proof of my note on Barnes and yourself, you will probably think it very silly and amateurish and if you care to show me up I will reserve three or four pages for you in the September number for that purpose.[3]

Yours sincerely,
T. S. Eliot

TO *J. B. Trend* CC

14 June 1929   [Faber & Faber Ltd]

My dear Trend,

I am writing now to put to you a suggestion which was made at a recent Directors' Meeting. We should be very glad to know if you might possibly be interested and if you could possibly find the time to write a book on

---

We are ready to place a bet on the negative.') ALR wrote to TSE (undated): 'I am afraid I have been very remiss about the promised reviews, what with electioneering and tutorials and term.' He meant to write a review of Pollard's *Wolsey* 'in the next two days'.
1–Untitled review of A. F. Pollard, *Wolsey*, *C.* 9 (Jan. 1930), 353–6.
2–ALR reviewed G. D. H. Cole, *The Next Ten Years in British Social and Economic Policy*; Egon Wertheimer, *Portrait of the Labour Party*; F. J. C. Hearnshaw, *A Survey of Socialism*, in *C.* 9 (Oct. 1929), 150–5.
3–'Mr. Barnes and Mr. Rowse', *C.* 8 (July 1929), 682–91. ALR wrote against this paragraph of TSE's letter: 'What a gent!' He replied ('Friday'): 'That was very kind of you to send me the article. I was delighted with it; for, if I may say so, it seemed to me to go to the root of the matter much more than the original on Fascism. And it certainly opens up the essential point about the relation of a system of values to a "materialist" interpretation of history. On that and one or two subsidiary points I have something I am anxious to say; so I shall be glad if you will allow me three or four pages in the Sept number.

'I must confess – perhaps I have done so already – that I was disappointed with my own contribution on Communism. It got out of hand, became long and at the same time was incomplete . . . What I should really like would be someday to complete it with a second article on the Political Aims of Communism; for I scarcely got up to that point in the other. And that is where I most of all disagree with Communism.

'I'm very far from being a Communist you know, but am an ordinary orthodox member of the Labour Party. Only I don't agree with their view of history and think there's a great deal of value in the Marxist approach to politics and economics.'

modern music. What we have in mind is a book rather for the general listener than for the amateur with technical knowledge of music; or rather a book which would cross both frontiers and interest both people with technical knowledge and intelligent people with none. I am sure that there is no one except perhaps Dent who is so closely in touch as yourself with everything that is going on in music in all the musical countries of Europe.

We published a year or two ago a book by Wilenski, called *The Modern Movement in Art*.[1] What we had in mind is something that would perform the same service for the lover of music that that book attempted to perform for people interested in painting. But of course you would not be bound to any programme such as a definite series of books would impose and as it is impossible to treat modern movements in different arts in the same way.

I have put this very tentatively and vaguely rather hoping to stimulate you to make some suggestions yourself, and not at all with the aim of asking you to carry out any previously determined programme. I wish you would let me know what you think of the idea and then I would go into the matter with you more thoroughly.

One more small matter. I am taking the liberty of enclosing some translations of Gongora sent me by a Cambridge undergraduate.[2] He does not give chapter and verse of the original text but I should be grateful if you could let me have a line in returning them to say how they strike you. Any translation of Gongora I am quite unable to decipher.

Yours ever,

[T. S. Eliot]

1 – R. H. Wilenski, *The Modern Movement in Art* (F&G, 1927).
2 – TSE was to publish Edward Meryon Wilson's translation of lines from *Las Soledades* (1614), by Luis de Góngora y Argote (1561–1627), in C. 9 (July 1930), 604–5.

TO *Karl Anton Rohan*[1]   cc

15 June 1929   [London]

Dear Prince de Rohan,

I must apologise for my delay in answering your letter.[2] It will be a great pleasure to see you. I only regret that your visit coincides with a period of extreme stress for me, that is, I shall be in the midst of moving from one private address to another. Nevertheless, I hope to see something of you, and certainly hope that you may meet some of my friends.

Yours very truly,
[T. S. Eliot]

TO *K. Wilson*   cc

17 June 1929   [London]

Dear Madam,

I must apologise for having kept the enclosed essay[3] so long but I put it aside as I found it interesting. I am afraid after all that it is not quite suitable for *The Criterion* and I think that it should appear rather in one of the older quarterly reviews. I should always be glad to see more of your work.

Yours faithfully,
[T. S. Eliot]
Editor

---

1 – Prince Karl Anton Rohan (1898–1975), Austrian landowner and political writer, resided at Castle Albrechtsberg; proprietor of the *Europäische Revue*, 1925–36. His publications include *Umbruch der Zeit 1923–30* (Berlin, 1930), *Schicksalsstunde Europas* (Graz, 1937), and *Heimat Europa: Erinnerungen und Erfahrungen* (Düsseldorf, 1954).
2 – Rohan announced in his letter to TSE (14 May) that he would be staying in London from about 23 to 30 June, and proceeded to say: 'I take therefore the liberty to ask you if I shall have the pleasure of meeting you in London at that time. I should also be very grateful if you would be so kind to introduce me to some of your friends at this occasion.'
3 – 'Psychology in Shakespeare's Tragedies'.

TO *Mary Hutchinson*   TS Texas

23 June 1929   98 Clarence Gate Gardens,
                                      Regents Park

Dear Mary,
   I am rushing off this line to thank you for the wonderful flowers, as
Vivien is up to her eyes in work getting things straight, and nearly at the
end of her strength. It was very sweet of you, and the inscription could
not have been more charming. And we do hope and expect to see you
before the flowers fade. This has turned out much more frightful than was
anticipated; this is a huge barrack and we don't know how we shall ever
run it. You must come soon to see it and tell us what you think.
                                      Ever affectionately,
                                      Tom

TO *Theodore Spencer*   MS Harvard

25 June 1929   98 Clarence Gate Gardens, N.W. 1

Dear Mr Spencer,[1]
   I am doubtful of being able to be at my office tomorrow morning at
11:30 – so if you can, I suggest that you come there about 3:30 and stop
for a cup of tea. I hope you can.
                                      Sincerely yours
                                      T. S. Eliot

TO *J. M. Robertson*   CC

28 June 1929   [London]

My dear Robertson,
   The Criterion is always open for the cause of justice and to your name.[2]
I only ask three questions:

1–Spencer was visiting London from 25 June.
2–Robertson protested on 20 June that his friend John Dover Wilson had 'made a perfectly
priceless mess' of his British Academy Shakespeare lecture, having sought to convict
Robertson of a 'slip' but succeeding only in 'giving the lie to his own explicit critical
doctrines'. Could TSE please 'insert' a response by Robertson in the 'autumn number'?
See Robertson's essay-review 'Shakespearean Idolatry', C. 9 (Jan. 1930), 246–67. J. Dover
Wilson replied with a lengthy open letter to Robertson published under the title 'Idolatry
and Scepticism in Shakespearian Studies', C. 9 (July 1930), 631–41.

How long will your paper be?

How soon can it be ready?

If the paper is short, would you object to my getting Dover Wilson to write a short reply (or apology?) in the same issue, with a rejoinder by you with the final word (He could go at it again in the following number if he must). My editorial sense leads me to hope for a controversy?

Some day *The Criterion* might invite opinions on whether the British Academy is justifying its right to exist.

Yours in haste,

[T. S. Eliot]

TO *A. L. Rowse* TS Exeter

28 June 1929 [London]

Dear Rowse,

Thank you very much for your letter of last week.[1] It is a satisfaction to know that my article passed your approval; I felt that I had ventured on something beyond my competence.

I am also glad to know how you feel about your own; because I had meant to write and suggest that you should follow it up with something which should express your personal views. I found it very profitable reading; but it did lose in vigour from the fact (or as it struck me) that you were merely asking for a fair hearing for something which is maligned but which you cannot support wholly. I liked the tone, but it will be much more interesting to have your own beliefs. So may we say December for your next essay?[2] My secretary will remind you of your notes for September.

There are other things I want to write about, including your poem which I have; but this must do for the moment, as I have many arrears.

With many thanks,

Yours ever,

T. S. Eliot

1 – Not found.

2 – ALR, 'Marxism: A Reply' (in reply to TSE), C. 9 (Oct. 1929), 84–8.

TO *J. S. Barnes*   CC

29 June 1929   [London]

My dear Barnes,

I was away from the office when your letter arrived, as I was moving from a house to a flat; so I had to deal with your letter over the telephone.[1] I am terribly sorry if my remark gives rise to any misunderstanding, and will do everything possible to rectify it in the following issue. I think it will be best if you yourself explain to the readers exactly what the position of the Institute is; and I will put in a note of my own. I supposed that you were a Director of the Institute because you believed in the international importance and value of fascism: and certainly not the other way about.

My secretary will let you know when we should have your rejoinder. With many regrets and all best wishes,[2]

yours sincerely,
[T. S. Eliot]

TO *Kenneth Ingram*   CC

29 June 1929   [London]

Dear Mr Ingram,

I am very much in your debt for the trouble you have taken over my friend's manuscript.[3] I think too that the objections to it are perfectly

---

1–Barnes wrote on 19 June to TSE's secretary Evelyn Townsend (who had sent him the proofs of TSE's article 'Mr Barnes and Mr Rowse'): 'In the first paragraph of Mr Eliot's article he speaks of me as a convinced supporter of Fascism, coupling with this remark that I am a director of the International Centre of Fascist Studies. This might easily be interpreted as implying that I was a convinced supporter of Fascism because I am a director of this Institute; and since the latter has no opinion either for nor [*sic*] against Fascism, and again since there is an erroneous impression abroad that we are a propagandist body, we consider it very important that any expression of opinion by myself in favour of Fascism should not give the impression that such opinions represent those of this Institute. If therefore it is not too late, I should be much obliged if you would delete from the article all reference to the Institute.'
2–Barnes replied on 2 July 1929: 'That is quite all right. It was my chief who made the bother. He is fussed because, since I am known to be a fascist, it is all the more difficult to get over the general opinion in England that my institute is a propagandist body.'
3–Of *Pages from an Oxford Diary* (submitted anonymously by Paul Elmer More), Ingram wrote (20 June): 'Our view is that, although it is interesting and well-written, it is the kind of book which would have a very limited public. It certainly does not read like the work of an Oxford don: any intelligent reader would penetrate that disguise, and there are sentences which from a strictly orthodox point of view are a little doubtful . . .'

valid. If the author would consent to publish it over his own name, they would be less cogent, and the history of a certain development would have more point; so I am afraid it ought to wait till then. And I confess that I had no desire to have the book fathered unto myself.

I hope that we may meet again, and shall write to you when I see an opportunity.

Sincerely yours,
[T. S. Eliot]

TO *Louis Untermeyer*[1]   CC

29 June 1929   [London]

Dear Untermeyer,

I am very glad to hear from you again, and hope that things are indeed well for you.[2] As for the Anthology, you are very welcome to use the *Hollow Men*. About the *Magi*, the situation is this: the shilling leaflet is still selling a little, and after talking it over with the directors of this firm I decided to refuse to allow Harold Monro to use it in an anthology of his; so I don't see how I can allow anyone else to use it yet. I think in another year.

The other poems you mention you are welcome to so far as I am concerned, but you would write to Knopf about them as well.

When shall we have another baked potato and cabbage?[3]

Yours ever sincerely,
[T. S. Eliot]

---

1 – Louis Untermeyer (1885–1977): poet, editor, translator, parodist, and anthologist; co-founder and contributing editor of *Seven Arts* magazine; Poet Laureate Consultant to the Library of Congress, 1961–3; author of *Collected Parodies* (1926), *Long Feud: Selected Poems* (1962), and *From Another World* (autobiography, 1939).

2 – Untermeyer asked on 8 June if he might add to the number of TSE's poems printed in a revised edition of *Modern American Poetry: A Critical Anthology* (1921; 4th rev. edn, 1930); he wanted to use 'Prufrock', 'Sweeney among the Nightingales', 'Gerontion', 'The Hollow Men', and 'Journey of the Magi'.

3 – Untermeyer replied on 12 July, 'Save a sprout & one-half kidney for me. Expect me next January at 1.15 p.m. in front of the Elgin marbles.'

TO *Harold Monro* TS Texas

29 June 1929   Faber & Faber Ltd,
                                24 Russell Square

Dear Harold,

I apologise for the delay in answering your letter of the 17th; but you know, I believe, that I was away moving to my new address. Meanwhile I understand that you arranged prices with Stewart. I can't give American rights on 'Whispers', 'Preludes', and 'Rhapsody',[1] as that is not yet out of Knopf's hands; but I dare say it is not to be published over here.

As soon as we are a bit settled I hope to see you.

Yours ever,
T. S. E.

TO *Desmond Harmsworth*[2] TS Valerie Eliot

29 June 1929   [London]

Dear Mr Harmsworth,

I have your letter of June 18, and reproach myself for my unfulfilled intentions.[3] Mr Leonard Woolf has been abroad, but I will find out whether he has returned, and will certainly send him your poem with

---

1 – 'Whispers of Immortality', 'Preludes I', and 'Rhapsody on a Windy Night'.
2 – Desmond Harmsworth (1903–90). Publisher, poet, and artist; son of the politician Cecil Harmsworth and nephew of the press barons Alfred Harmsworth, Lord Northcliffe, and Harold Harmsworth, Lord Rothermere – the latter the estranged husband of TSE's erstwhile patron Lilian, Lady Rothermere. Educated at Eton and Christ Church, Oxford, Harmsworth made a start in the family business but kicked against the press by going off to art school, the Académie Julian in Paris. In the 1930s he published literary editions at his private press, the eponymous Desmond Harmsworth Ltd: his most famous production, undertaken in collaboration with the Obelisk Press, Paris, was a limited edition of JJ's *Pomes Penyeach* (1932), illustrated by Joyce's daughter Lucia. Desmond Harmsworth succeeded to the title of 2nd Baron Harmsworth on the death of his father in 1948.
3 – Harmsworth wrote 'about a certain poem of mine ["Birth of Aphrodite"] which got to you in rather a roundabout way, having first been sent by me to Harold Monro. Some weeks ago I was in London and went to see Monro who read me some words of yours about the poem, among which were 'rococo but interesting' (or 'interesting but rococo'). Besides this I think you mentioned its being a possible addition to the Hogarth Press series of longish poems . . . If you are familiar with Leonard Woolf (or whoever it is at the Hogarth Press), will you do me the kindness of showing him the poem sometime?' See TSE's letter to Monro, 29 Apr. 1929 above.

my recommendation to publish it. It was, of course, of quite impossible length for the *Criterion* at present; but it interested me very much indeed.[1]

Yours sincerely,

T. S. Eliot

TO *Arthur Calder Marshall*[2]

CC

29 June 1929   [London]

Dear Mr Marshall,

Thank you for your kind invitation of June 27th, to address the Oxford Poetry Society. Father D'Arcy had already spoken to me about

---

1 – Harmsworth responded on 2 July: 'Your help comes as a great blessing as I have been getting rather desperate about finding a publisher, and I feel one's development is difficult without the encouragement of print and of other people's opinions.' Nearly thirty years later, Harmsworth showed 'Birth of Aphrodite' to John Hayward, who dismissed it in a letter of 23 Aug. 1957: 'It may be that you have been sustained all this time by Eliot's good opinion – an opinion which I would find completely baffling if I didn't know from experience how much easier it is (if one can't publish something oneself) to push a MS back to the author with a word of praise & a recommendation to try it on old so & so (!) than to face the disagreeable task of telling him that it's no good. This, alas, is my task. Your poem seems to me to be merely a literary exercise in the rhetorical mode on a highly romantic theme, but written in an outworn poetical convention and diction, which lapses at times into Tennysonian pastiche ... I wish that I could be constructive rather than de-structive – but, alas, I cannot find merit enough in any part of the poem to justify my suggesting how it might be revised & made fit for publication.' A little later, when Harmsworth challenged JDH's unsparing judgement with TSE's supposed approval, JDH replied (24 Oct. 1957): 'I must assure you that I had no intention (as I have no right) to impute to Eliot a lack of integrity. Having known his views on poetry throughout a close association of more than thirty years and bearing in mind the kind of poetry – his own and that of other poets – he was publishing a quarter of a century ago, I was at a loss to understand how he could have "thought well" (the phrase you used) of your poem. His actual comment – "it interested me very much indeed" – which you quote, seems to me a perfectly fair and honest way of tempering his rejection of your poem. "Interest" does not necessarily imply approval; and he may well have been interested very much indeed in a poem so very different from the kind of poetry with which he (as a poet and as a publisher of poetry) has always been associated. Otherwise, why did he pass it on to the Hogarth Press instead of recommending his own firm to publish it? I am sure you must be aware that publishers and editors without (as you put it) betraying their critical standards do try to word their refusals in such a way as to mitigate as much as possible the blow they must so often deliver to the writer's hopes. This is all I meant to suggest that Eliot was trying to do and I much regret that I caused you to be "astounded and amazed" by suggesting otherwise.'

2 – Arthur Calder-Marshall (1908–92), writer, studied at Hertford College, Oxford, and then taught for three years (1931–3) as a schoolmaster at Denstone College, before becoming a full-time writer. His works include novels – *About Levy* (1933), *Dead Centre* (1935), *The Scarlet Boy* (1961) – film scripts and documentaries (including in 1946 the screenplay for the award-winning Paul Rotha documentary *The World is Rich*); biographies including *No*

---

the Society, and aroused my interest in it. I should very much like to address it, especially as your other speakers have been chosen with so much discrimination;[1] but I foresee that I shall have a great deal of work to do during the winter; and these interruptions, delightful as they are, require a little leisure if one is to do them justice. So I hope that you will accept my expression of keen regret, and perhaps I may hope to be invited again at a later time.

With my repeated regret, and my best wishes for the future of such a promising Society.

Yours sincerely,
[T. S. Eliot]

TO *J. B. Trend* CC

29 June 1929 [London]

My dear Trend,

Very many thanks for your extremely useful report and letter of the 15th. I was away from the office when they came (I have been moving to 98, Clarence Gate Gardens, N.W.1) but they were both opened and appreciated. I am very sorry indeed that you cannot do a book for us now, but perhaps we may publish something by you at a later date.[2]

Again most gratefully,
[T. S. Eliot]

Earthly Command, a life of Vice-Admiral Alexander Riall Woods, DSO (1957); and various non-fiction works including *Wish You Were Here: The Art of Donald McGill* (1966) and *Prepare to Shed Them Now: The Ballads of George R. Sims* (1968); and a widely admired autobiography, *The Magic of My Youth* (1951).

1 – 'We hope also to have Wyndham Lewis, Herbert Read, Mrs Woolf and Dr Mansfield Forbes among our guests of next term.' (In 1930 Calder-Marshall invited to Oxford the occultist Aleister Crowley, whose talk on Gilles de Rais was banned by the authorities.)

2 – 'I am not really very anxious to launch out into a book on modern music (even for you!) Yet I can't think of anyone else – Dent being so deeply involved, as to be out of the question – and if I wasn't deeply involved myself, in two Spanish books, I might think about it.'

TO *Charles Du Bos*[1]   TS Texas

29 June 1929   Faber & Faber Ltd

My dear Du Bos,

You have been extremely kind to send me your three books, with such gracious inscriptions, and I am delighted to have them.[2] I wish first to read the *Journal*, of which I had read a fragment, and look forward to it with the greatest interest. I have been exceedingly busy of late, and only had time to insert a short line of commendation into the July *Criterion*;[3] but Gordon George is writing an extended review of you and the other books for the October number.

I wish that we might meet again; I have been too busy to come to Paris; do you never come to London?

Perhaps it is useless to remind you that I have been waiting for a good many years now for a contribution from you for the *Criterion*.

With very grateful thanks and all best wishes,

Sincerely yours,
T. S. Eliot

TO *Hugh Macdonald*   TS Dr Charlotte Williamson

29 June 1929   Faber & Faber Ltd

Dear Macdonald,

Thank you for your letter.[4] I cannot quite see my way until August or September, as I have already many arrears to make up; but I promise to give you a date then for the Johnson preface.

I still hope to see you before the holidays.

Yours sincerely,
T. S. Eliot

1 – Charles du Bos (1882–1939), French critic of French and English literature (his mother was English, and he studied for a year at Oxford), contributed one review to C., in 1935. He wrote essays on Shakespeare, Shelley, Byron, Flaubert, Goethe, Mérimée, and Mauriac, and was admired for his posthumously published journals (6 vols, 1946–55).
2 – Charles du Bos had sent *Extraits d'un Journal 1908–1928* (Editions de la Pléiade, 1928) – 'For T.S. Eliot, this intellectual and spiritual pilgrimage, – as a token of deep sympathy Charles du Bos Versailles, Sunday April 21st 1929' – and two other volumes.
3 – See footnote to TSE's letter to R. E. Gordon George, 27 May 1929 above, which quotes in full TSE's 'line of commendation' of du Bos.
4 – Macdonald wrote on 21 June: 'The Oxford edition of [Samuel Johnson's verse] will be such a different book that I don't think it will get in the way of ours at all. We only propose *London* and *The Vanity of Human Wishes*.'

TO *Mario Praz*   CC

29 June 1929   [London]

My dear Praz,

I am answering your letter of the 25th.[1] I will see about the Browne on
Monday, and look forward to reading your article.

I will have Miss Whittingham-Jones's papers returned to you. She does
not yet know how to write English, but her ideas seem to me very good;
and at least, she is thinking about the right things. Will you give me her
address (and tell me how old she is – so that I may know whether she is
too old to learn[)] – and I think I can find some books to send to her for
review.

If you can, let me know in advance when you will be in London, so that
we may at least meet for a moment.

I can't think of any more authors for the *Stampa* at the moment. Have
you written anything about Wyndham Lewis? Pound's *Cavalcanti* should
be out in the autumn.

Do you know a man in New York named Angel Flores? I can get you
his address; he has started an American-Spanish review there, and no
doubt would like to review your book.[2]

> Yours in haste,
> [T. S. Eliot]

TO *J. M. Robertson*   CC

1 July 1929   [London]

My dear Robertson,

Your letter gave me a shock of disappointment, because my September
number is already largely made up, and what with things already in press
and things I have promised to include, I hardly think that I shall have room
for an essay of that length. I agree that such an essay should be answered
in the following number. Would you consider your paper appearing in

---

1 – Praz, who was writing an article on Sir Thomas Browne, had acquired a defective copy
('see p. 49') of vol. IV of Browne's *Works* (F&F). 'You would oblige me very much if you
could get the publisher to send me in its place a perfect copy, as soon as possible . . .' By the
same post, he sent some papers by Barbara Whittingham-Jones, a 22-year-old Cambridge
law graduate who was 'very interested in politics' and who wanted to write reviews for *C.*
'on subjects of her competence'. She was later to become well regarded as a journalist.
2 – Praz's *Unromantic Spain* was to be published on 26 Sept.: he hoped TSE might make
suggestions 'as to whom copies should be sent'.

December with Dover Wilson to follow in March, and you again a year hence? That seems a long way off, but this controversy evidently needs a deal of space to lash its tail in.[1]

Quite independently of this, I wish you would make any suggestions that occur to you for my documenting myself for an Inquest upon the Academy. I suppose I had better get their 'proceedings' (if that is what they call them) out of the London Library, and study them myself before trying to engage any valiant spirits in the investigation. It seems to open up a long vista of hostile faces. I wish you would give me hints.

We are delighted to have your renewal of subscription, which I have passed on to the proper department, which should acknowledge it.

Yours ever,
[T. S. Eliot]

TO *M. C. D'Arcy*   CC

1 July 1929   [London]

My dear D'Arcy,

Thank you very much for your letter of June 14th, and also for your invitation.[2] I have not only been very much preoccupied by moving, but Tuesdays at present are impossible for me, because of giving some short talks on the wireless, a set of six, which will end by the middle of July. Perhaps I may look forward to attending a meeting with you in the autumn.

I am very glad if you liked my short paper on humanism. I think that I have now said all that I have to say on that subject. Your point about

---

1 – Robertson had replied on 29 June to TSE's polite enquiries (28 June) about his proposed attack on John Dover Wilson: 'The paper is *ready now*. It consists of about 7000 words – a little less perhaps.

'On reflection, I fear this may be too long . . . At the best, it is too long for Dover Wilson to answer in the same number. But I may tell you that I wrote him specifying the main challenges, and saying that I would carefully weigh, before publishing, any defence he should make. I got only a vacuous answer, embodying simply the propositions that Chambers had been his colleague, and Pollard (who backed Chambers 'anyhow') his Revered preceptor . . .

'You may well get up a question as to whether the B.A. [British Academy] shows its right to exist. I find my unworthy self promoted to the glittering eminence of "Aunt Sally" or target for B.A. lecturers on Shakespeare at a loss for original ideas on that large subject . . .

'It would be a real pleasure to open a ball in the *Criterion*. A separate pamphlet would find a much smaller audience. But I fear I may trespass on your space.'

2 – D'Arcy hoped that TSE might be his guest at an upcoming meeting of the London Society for the Study of Religion.

the Jesuits and humanism is very interesting; but I should say also that the Jesuits arrived too late, inevitably, to do much more than point a moral for posterity. I mean that 'humanism', in its various forms, seems to me one of those forms of heresy which I feel had to come, and had to work themselves out to the end. Humanism is perhaps merely a more than usually protean and slippery form.[1]

I should like to know whether you can review either or both of those two books for September; and I wish you would drop me a line to say what you think of them and whether either is worth the trouble. Then, I will give you a date for the copy.

Yours ever sincerely,

[T. S. Eliot]

TO *Bonamy Dobrée*

TS Brotherton

4 July 1929   Faber & Faber Ltd

My dear Prior Bongamy,[2]

I have no red strip on my ribbon, and therefore pass over your incivility to a poor wretch who has just been moving (note new address 98, Clarence Gate Gardens, Regents Park N.W.1.) and say: I will lunch with you on Wednesday 10th, or you will lunch with me, or you will lunch with me on Tuesday and I will lunch with you on Wednesday: on the latter day I have an evening fixture, and as for the former, Sir, you seem unaware of how low I have fallen since we last met: I am delivering Tonic Talks on the Wireless from 2LO on Tuesday evenings, which are supposed to foment the cause of Adult Edjjication; I believe I am billed to talk about Sir Thos. Urquhart on that date. Now I want some reply to the above, in passing on to state that the Comedy book was a Present for the Prior of Limberham's Library, and was not intended for review. Will you be said. Nothing really has turned up worthy of your name, and Smyth has said all the things about Strachey you wanted to say;[3] and 'Achigar' is featured

1–D'Arcy thanked TSE for his article on humanism in the *New Adelphi*: 'there is so much in it that you have said so much better than I could have said it, but it is what I should have liked to have said. I am particularly interested as a Jesuit in Humanism because it is true to say, I think, that the Jesuits came at a moment when Christian civilization & Humanism were being abstracted from each other & they determined to prevent it. I sometimes think their efforts were – and were perhaps bound to be – somewhat artificial.'

2–BD was living at Mendham Priory, Harleston, Norfolk.

3–Charles Smyth, 'A Note on Historical Biography and Mr Strachey', *C.* 8 (July 1929), 647–60. Smyth had written on 14 Apr., 'I have said exactly what I feel about Lytton Strachey, and as strongly as I feel it. Possibly libellous, though obviously true (I think).'

for December,[1] a piece of fiction by a writer of the same name being due for Sept. Why don't you stay over and come to the Grove for lunch on the Thursday, after I have seen you privvily first? The Grove is now spruced up by the presence of Montgomery Belgion (a cousin of the Hares, of course), various American editors, publishers and humanists, and Mr Tandy and Mr Codrington are in good shape and really qualifying for scratch bores the former on Northern Australia and the latter on skiing. On Thursday the 11th I expect there an editor of the N.Y. Bookman, and have told him that he should publish some of your work and that he might see you there.

Well so will Close, looking forward to seeing you on Tuesday Wednesday and Thursday of next week.

> I am, *en t'embrassant sur les 2 joues*
> TSE

<Typed this myself>[2]

TO *J. M. Robertson*   CC

8 July 1929   [*The Criterion*]

My dear Robertson,

Thank you for your letter of the 2nd, checking my enthusiasm about the British Academy.[3] As for the manuscript, your writing is so clear that it is not necessary to have it typed; but I do not like being in possession of unique copies any longer than is necessary so I should be glad if you would let me have it early in September.

> Yours ever,
> [T. S. Eliot]

'I regret that Dobrée's review of Eliz. & Essex in the current number is so favourable. But I don't think that really matters.'

1–BD, 'Achigar, translated from the Basque', C. 9 (Apr. 1930), 476–81.
2–Added by hand.
3–Robertson had cautioned TSE on 2 July: 'As to a general attack on the B. A. [British Academy] I am doubtful. In its legitimate field, I believe, its own papers – i.e. the papers by its members, of which I have heard one or two – seem scholarly and sound, if dull.

'But these Shakespeare lectures (and some other annuals) are delivered on "foundations", & represent merely a popular side show for the Academy.'

TO *John Livingston Lowes*   TS Houghton

8 July 1929   *The Criterion,* 24 Russell Square

Dear Sir,

I have heard from several people recently that you were in London, and having just learnt your address from Mr Lincoln Kirstein, I am taking the liberty of writing to you. I believe that you know my mother, as she has often mentioned you very appreciatively and I think first knew you when you were at Washington University.

May I venture to ask you to let me know whether you would do me the honour of lunching with me one day next week.[1]

Yours very truly,

T. S. Eliot

TO *Leonard Woolf*   CC

8 July 1929   [*The Criterion*]

Dear Leonard,

I heard some little time ago that you were abroad and since then we have been so busy with moving that I have had no time for a great many things. If you and Virginia are in London I should very much like to see you soon. Also may I send you a long poem by a young man named Desmond Harmsworth. It would I think be about the right length for a small volume in the Hogarth Living Poets.[2]

Yours ever,

[Tom]

TO *Allen Tate*   TS Princeton

8 July 1929   *The Criterion*

Dear Tate,

I am glad to hear from you in London but I am much disappointed to know that you will be here for such a short time.[3] I expect to be lunching at the Grove on Thursday. Would you be able to look in here some time

1–JLL responded (10 July) that he would be delighted to meet TSE for lunch.
2–LW's secretary acknowledged receipt on 9 July.
3–Tate was visiting London for a week from 7 July; but in the event he had to leave early for Paris, where his wife had been taken ill. He did not meet TSE during his visit.

before lunch so that we might have a talk and you could join us for lunch if you are free.

Yours sincerely,
T. S. Eliot

This was dictated yesterday. Glad to hear you will come.

TO *Montgomery Belgion*

cc

8 July 1929   [London]

Dear Belgion,

That is exact. I will come to the Savile Club at 1:15 on Wednesday week the 17th July.

Meanwhile I will have the MSS. returned to you for emendations. But my hopes of using it in September have fallen very low this morning; one of the people I invited to 'reply' has written at slightly, and the other at very much greater length, than I intimated. And as they are replying to *myself*, I am not in a strong position to cut them down!

Yours ever,
[T. S. E.]

TO *Seán Ó'Faoláin*

cc

8 July 1929   [London]

Dear Mr O'Faolain,

I was sorry not to see you when you were in London but hope you will be here again before very long. Do let me know as soon as you return.[1] I should like to talk to you about The Silver Branch which I found extremely interesting.[2] I have kept it because although I feel it is really too

---

1 – They were able to meet for lunch in London in mid-Aug.

2 – Ó'Faoláin had submitted on 3 Feb. 1929 a long essay – 'the fruit of many years study of Irish (vernacular) literature' – called 'The Silver Branch: a study of early Irish lyric poetry'. He explained further: 'since Arnold's essay on Celtic Literature nothing has been written from the literary man's point of view about the old Irish literature. It has been in the hands of the scholars and the patriots: the first know so much (and so little) about it that they can make no generalization – the latter have a dream, and no information whatever. In the whole of the controversy about the Irish censorship Bill and the coinage you see that weird dream at work – the belief of the patriot in the essential perfectitude of all Irish traditions: there is a great deal of the same dream in the modern Irish education.' Ó'Faoláin's essay was intended to form the introduction to his work-in-progress: a parallel-text edition of Gaelic lyric poetry written between *c.*700 and 1400.

long for the *Criterion* I have been hoping to find some other way in which it could be published. I should be very glad if you could leave it with me until we meet.

Yours sincerely,
[T. S. Eliot]

TO *H. J. C. Grierson* CC

8 July 1929   [London]

Dear Mr Grierson,

(I had thought that we were on slightly more informal terms). Your letter has made me pore over my timetable:[1] I wish for two reasons that you were to be here next week: first that I am engaged for lunch on Wednesday and Thursday of this week, but second that Read is out of town the whole of this week.

I should much like to have even a short talk with you, and I should be very happy if you cared to come in here for a cup of tea at about 4:15 on Wednesday?

Your suggestion about Read is very interesting.[2] Of course I shall not mention it to anyone; and not to him without your permission. At any other time when you and he are both in London I can easily arrange a meeting.

Sincerely yours,
[T. S. Eliot]

1–Grierson (7 July) invited TSE to dine with him at the Junior Athenaeum Club, 112 Piccadilly, on the following Weds. or Thurs.
2–Grierson wished to meet Herbert Read, whose work had always interested him: 'one or two of us here have thought of him as a possible successor to Professor Baldwin Bruce in the Chair of Fine Art. Of course this is quite among ourselves. The Professor has not said anything of retiring but he was appointed in 1880 which is a fairly long time ago.'

TO *Alan Lubbock*   CC

8 July 1929   [London]

Dear Mr Lubbock,[1]

   It has occurred to me that you as one of the Guarantors of the *Criterion*
might be interested in the *Criterion Miscellany* of which I have pleasure in
sending you herewith the first two issues.[2]

   The *Miscellany* is not a periodical, it will consist of various short
volumes, published from time to time in a form similar to these.[3]

                                   Yours sincerely,
                                   [T. S. Eliot]

TO *M. C. D'Arcy*   CC

8 July 1929   [London]

My dear D'Arcy,

   Thank you for your letter of the 2nd.[4] I remember your speaking about
the Poetry Society some time ago and I have recently heard from its
Secretary. I have had to tell him that I know I shall be extremely busy this
winter and that I do not feel justified in pledging myself so to speak. But
that I should very much like to meet the Society and perhaps might do so
in a subsequent term.

1–This letter was sent to all the guarantors: Marguerite Caetani, D. O. Malcolm, F. S.
Oliver, Conrad Ormond, Ethel Sands, J. Hugh Smith, May Sinclair, and Charles Whibley.
2–GCF wrote to Michael Joseph, 4 Apr. 1930: 'In connection with the *Criterion* . . . we
publish a certain number of books, which explore the less obvious but deeply important
intellectual and spiritual currents of the present time. We have also been successful in reviving,
through the *Criterion Miscellany*, an art which seemed dead – the art of pamphleteering. I
mention this particularly because it marks, most definitely, the character of the policy we
would wish to be known as ours – a policy of new ideas, yet tenacious of good traditions.'
3–GCF wrote to the literary agent David Higham on 25 June 1929: 'The *Criterion
Miscellany* is an experiment, which looks as if it might go very well. But the proof of the
pudding is in the eating – we shall know more in a few weeks. The idea is, of course, to
get at a wide public with cheap books or booklets, from a shilling to (at most) five bob. It's
essential that nothing commonplace should go in to the series, and that it should "feel the
pulse" of the public. At the same time it isn't intended to be "rarefied".' In a letter to Philip
Graves (11 Feb. 1930), GCF said of the *Criterion Miscellany* that 'we want to reserve [it] on
the whole for things of some moral significance'. To Lord Chelmsford (whom GCF hoped
would write about India) on 13 Feb. 1930: 'Generally speaking, what we want in these
Miscellany pamphlets is the vigorous presentation of a definite point of view on a topic
of moral or political importance and relevance. Tepidity or frigidity would be fatal; there
should be some warmth of conviction.'
4–D'Arcy invited TSE to address the Oxford Poetry Society.

I look forward to your review of MacDougall and hope to be able to write before long and suggest a meeting.

Yours ever,

[T. S. Eliot]

TO *Selwyn Williams*   CC

8 July 1929   [London]

Dear Williams,

I am sorry that I was not here when you rang up. As you will know I spoke to Mrs Williams on the telephone afterwards and I am very glad to enclose an introduction to Dr Cyriax.[1] I have not seen him for some years but I think he will probably remember me. I had some treatment from him a year or so before I met you.

I apologise for the delay but hope that this correspondence may renew our acquaintance.

With best wishes,

Yours sincerely,

[T. S. Eliot]

TO *A. P. Rossiter*[2]   CC

8 July 1929   [London]

Dear Sir,

Thank you very much for your letter in the matter of Sherlock Holmes.[3] I agree that I was guilty of an over-statement, even of a mis-statement, and

---

1 – Dr Edgar Ferdinand Cyriax (1874–1955): Swedish-born medical doctor, specialising in physiotherapy, Swedish medical gymnastics, and manipulative treatment. He was the son-in-law of Jonas Henrik Kellgren, a notable figure in the promotion throughout late nineteenth-century Europe of Swedish remedial gymnastics and massage. Based in London, Cyriax lectured in physiology at the Central Institute for Swedish Gymnastics. (His son was Dr James H. Cyriax [1904–85], who coined the term orthopaedic medicine.)

2 – Arthur Percival Rossiter, Shakespearian scholar, was later to be Fellow in English Literature, Jesus College, Cambridge. His publications include *The Gold Insect . . . Being the 'Gold Bug' put into Basic English* (1932), *Statement and Suggestion: The Basic English system as an instrument for reading verse* (1935), *The Growth of Science: An Outline History, in Basic English* (1939), *English Drama from Early Times to the Elizabethans* (1958), *Angels with Horns, and other Shakespeare Lectures* (1961).

3 – Rossiter argued ('June 1929') – with reference to TSE's review of *The Complete Sherlock Holmes Short Stories* and Anna Katherine Green's *The Leavenworth Case*, in *C.* 8 (Apr.

I accept most of your criticisms. As for John Clay it has been pointed out to me that Clay was also 'wanted' on a charge of murder.[1] This seems to me an error of judgement on the author's part as it seems unlikely that a criminal who could easily be recognised and was wanted for so serious an offence could still be operating in London.

Yours truly,
[T. S. Eliot]

TO *C. Henry Warren*[2]

CC

8 July 1929   [London]

Dear Mr Warren,
    I tried to telephone to you today without success. I did not realise until I got your letter that you were the Mr Warren whom I already knew.

1929), 552–56 – 'it seems to me that you are mistaken in saying that Sherlock Holmes "does not seem to be descended from either [Wilkie Collins's] Sergeant Cuff or [Poe's] Dupin" . . . I believe both the Holmes brothers to be children of the Chevalier Dupin, and that a collation of Poe and the Sherlock Holmes stories supports this.

'I should trace Mycroft to the Dupin of [*The Murder of*] *Marie Roget*, Sherlock to the more active mood of the *Rue Morgue* and the *Purloined Letter*, and contend that this combination is proof positive of the Chevalier's paternity of your alleged Melchisadeks.

'I agree that Holmes is a formula; but is it not true that the same plot-formula – the dramatic summoning of the person whose confession elucidates the whole problem – is common to the Rue Morgue and a fair number of the Holmes stories? . . . If Holmes is a formula, he is an intellectual formula: and in both the *Dancing Man* and *The Cardboard Box* he uses Dupin's trick of following his chronicler's train of thought; more than once he echoes his progenitor's comments on the simplicity of the outré, in Chap. VII of *A Study in Scarlet*, almost word for word; and the faculty of Sherlock for sudden taciturnity immediately before a triumphant denouement is as hereditary as his habit of hiding himself in a pensive cloud of smoke . . . There is no need to point Holmes' debt of a body to Dr Bell, but though his methods of storing tobacco and taking revolver practice are endearing, they do not constitute character. These are adroit additions to the formula . . . Finally, when John Clay said "I'll swing for it!", need one conclude that hyperbole is eschewed by gentlemen-burglars? Suppose he had said he would pay the piper . . .'

1 – See letter to H. P. Collins, 4 Apr. 1929 above.

2 – C. Henry Warren (1895–1966), author, broadcaster, reviewer, worked as an English teacher; as a lecturer for the National Portrait Gallery, 1927; and for the BBC, 1929–33. On 13 July 1927 GCF had written this testimonial to Maurice Marston, Organising Secretary, National Book Council: 'Warren has contributed a good deal to the *Spectator* and other papers, both prose and verse; and he has published (with us) two books – *Cobbler, Cobbler*, a collection of short stories, and *Wild Goose Chase*, an account of his experiences in Canada. He writes extremely well, is young (I believe), and more than ordinarily attractive. If you could make any use of him, I think you would not regret it.'

I have thought over your suggestion, and must say that I am afraid it is one with which I can do nothing: it is not a subject on which I am qualified, or, to tell the truth, one in which I am interested. But I could not say that there are no 'possibilities' in it for someone else.[1]

I am very sorry that it cannot be fitted in to my inelastic mind; but thank you very much for the proposal.

Yours sincerely,
[T. S. Eliot]

TO *Paul Elmer More*   CC

8 July 1929   [London]

My dear More,

Your letter arrives before my writing one which is now overdue. My results are so far nil. (1) 'Marketing' an anonymous work[2] is a special business. (2) The brevity of the work makes it a special problem. (3) I believe that Faber and Faber would have published it if it could have been signed. But as it is, it is both because of its shortness and because of its subject matter a type of book that they are not prepared to handle. (4) The Society of SS. Peter & Paul came within an inch of it, and there again, I think might have done so had it not been anonymous. But they felt that with an anonymous work they undertake more responsibility for its orthodoxy; and being religious publishers, could not swallow the responsibility for certain remarks (which in my opinion are essential to express the exact point of view) such as the suggestion that the writer had no desire to communicate – an apology for High Mass which rather embarrassed them.

I must say that I gave no hint of the author's identity to either group of people. And that I think the importance of the book would be immensely increased if the identity of the author could be revealed. Of course, that is your affair; but I do feel that in the 'line up' of which you speak, and which I agree must come, the most important lining must be made by your own footsteps.

1–Warren (5 July) was seeking to publish in *The Radio Times* an article in a series called 'English Eloquence': 'there might be an article in the trend of eloquence in modern America. How far, for instance, are the racy coinages of the modern American compatible with what we have come to understand by the term "eloquence" . . . [O]ur aim must be rather to please than to educate!' Could TSE manage 1,200 words by 12 July?
2–*Pages from an Oxford Diary.*

In some haste, and awaiting the opportunity for a longer letter (by the way, as you are evidently not coming this summer, I must look forward to 1930).

Yours always sincerely,
[T. S. Eliot]

TO *Edgar Cyriax*   cc

9 July 1929   [London]

Dear Dr Cyriax,

I hope that you will not have to rack your brains to remember my identity. I am taking the liberty of writing this letter to introduce to you Mr Selwyn Williams. I met Mr Williams several years ago when he gave me some very remarkable massage; he is extremely interested in that work and I think has made some interesting discoveries in the course of his practice. He would very much like to meet you as he knows a great deal about your work and has read your book. I should be very glad if you could see him.

Yours very sincerely,
[T. S. Eliot]

TO *H. C. Crofton*   cc

9 July 1929   [London]

My dear Crofton,

You and Dudley will think me a confounded nuisance especially as the French girl[1] I bothered you about some time ago turned out to have found another job mean while. But I hope on this next matter you will put yourselves to less trouble.

A young man who has just taken his degree at Cambridge has come to ask me how he can get a job in a bank in Paris. I must say first that he has no claim on me whatever except that he has been the pupil of a friend of mine at Corpus Christi Cambridge[2] and the fact that he has written some very bad verse. All the young men who write bad poetry seem to have a

1–Henri Massis's daughter.
2–Presumably André Mazower had been referred to TSE by Kenneth Pickthorn, his friend at Corpus Christi College.

certain claim on me. This boy is named André Mazower. His nationality is rather uncertain. His father is a Russian refugee who has, I think, some small business in the Midlands. The boy says that he knows no Russian. His French is a little rusty but ought to be very good with some practice as he tells me that French is his native language. He speaks English quite perfectly. He took his degree in Economics and English.

He says that he wants to go over to Paris in a week or two and look for a job there. Rather than give him an introduction to someone in Paris, is there any one in London connected with the Paris Auxilliary who interviews candidates? If there is I should like at least to give this boy a chance to see him.

It is very unsatisfactory to keep imposing upon you in this way and never to see you. I have been very busy lately as we have just moved from our house into a flat. But I should like to know what part of the summer you expect to be in the City and try to get you to come to lunch with me again.

Yours ever,
[T. S. Eliot]

TO *D. S. Mirsky* CC

11 July 1929   [London]

Dear Mirsky,

I am very sorry to have delayed so long in answering your kind letter, but it arrived as I was in the midst of moving and when the moving was completed my wife was taken ill so I have had to be negligent.[1] I would be very glad to discuss this interesting suggestion with your friend Poutermann [*sc.* Pouterman], and hope that he may be coming to London.[2]

I do not know whether this letter will reach you but I hope to see you in the autumn when you return.

Yours sincerely,
[T. S. Eliot]

1–Mirsky wrote (20 June) that J. E. Pouterman, the French publisher, had begun an English publishing house, the Blackamoor Press, and was to issue an English translation of Baudelaire's *Journals*: might TSE be interested in writing an introduction to it?
2–Mirsky replied (20 July) that Pouterman would be in London from the morrow.

11 July 1929   [London]

Dear Mr Lowes,

   Thank you very much for your letter. I am not quite so free at the
moment as I had hoped to be because my wife has been taken ill and
the first time I am sure of is today week, Thursday the 18th for lunch.[1]
Could you possibly lunch with me at one o'clock on that day at the Royal
Society's Club, 63 St. James's Street. I hope you can but if not do let
me know and I will try to make another time as I am very anxious to
meet you.

                             Yours very sincerely,
                             [T. S. Eliot]

P.S. I see from your letter that you are working in the Museum, so perhaps
it would be more convenient for you to call for me here at 24 Russell
Square.

TO *F. S. Flint*   CC

12 July 1929   [London]

Dear Frank,

   I have conscientiously visited the Grove for the last fortnight, but
without seeing you. Will you let me have a line to say where you are
and if there is any possibility of our meeting in the future; and if you are
in London and have any time to spare for *The Criterion* do you think
you could let us have some notices on French Periodicals in time for the
September number?[2]

                             Yours ever,
                             [T. S. Eliot]

---

1 – Lowes replied (12 July): 'I'm grieved to hear of Mrs. Eliot's illness, and I beg you to let
me know if, when the time comes, you'd rather not have me then.'
2 – Flint replied on 23 Oct. – to a further (now lost) letter from TSE – 'I was ashamed to tell
you that I can't possibly do the French periodicals for the December number. I am up to my
eyes in work I cannot do. By the end of the year, I shall be clear, and I intend to take on no
more beastly translations.'

TO *Frank McEachran*[1]   CC

12 July 1929   [London]

Dear McEachran,

I have your letter of the 7th.[2] It is true that the Humanism of Babbitt is rather local to America but I do not by any means think that it has no value elsewhere. I have been publishing in the *Criterion* a succession of papers by various authors dealing with the subject of Humanism and have written about it myself elsewhere; and this should be sufficient evidence that I consider it of importance.

Many years ago I was myself a pupil of Babbitt and although I have now taken issue with him I still feel under a very great debt to him. I consider him one of the most important minds of our time. In other words I agree with you and not with your supervisor.

I still have an essay of yours about which I hope to write to you before very long.[3]

> Yours very sincerely,
> [T. S. Eliot]

1–Frank McEachran (1900–75), schoolmaster, classicist, and author, was to become a friend of TSE and contributor to C. In the 1920s he taught at Gresham's School, Holt, Norfolk (where W. H. Auden was a pupil); subsequently at Shrewsbury School (where Richard Ingrams, editor of *Private Eye*, was a student). Alan Bennett has acknowledged that the eccentric, charismastic schoolmaster Hector, in *The History Boys* (2004), is based on McEachran (Dave Calhoun, 'Alan Bennett: interview', *Time Out*, 2 Oct. 2006). On TSE's recommendation, F&F brought out McEachran's first books, *The Civilised Man* (1930) and *The Destiny of Europe* (1932). His other publications include a study of J. G. Herder (1939), based on his Oxford B.Litt. thesis, and an influential anthology, *Spells* (1955). See further John Bridgen, 'Sometime Schoolmasters All: Frank McEachran and T. S. Eliot . . . and a few others', *Journal of the T. S. Eliot Society (UK) 2010*, 21–40.

2–McEachran wrote: 'Lately I have been busy preparing a thesis on the "Humanitäts" of Herder and as Humanität is the subject I naturally looked into the "humanism" of Irving Babbitt, and incorporated a good deal of it into the work.

'My supervisor objects that the humanism of Babbitt is an American hypothesis of no value whatsoever here. I don't think Babbitt is always right and a good many people disagree with him as far as he touches on religion but I thought his books, especially the one on Rousseau to be full of sound stuff and his summing up of "humanitas" a good one. Would you mind letting me know what your opinion is on Babbitt on the humanistic side – *if you could spare a few lines?*'

3–McEachran, 'Tragedy and History', C. 9 (July 1929), 661–70.

13 July 1929   *The Criterion*

Dearest Mother,

We have now been installed at 98 Clarence Gate Gardens for a fortnight, and very tiring it has been. We got through the actual move pretty easily; but of course in moving the real work begins afterwards: carpets to be fitted, curtains to be made etc. The flat is too big, and nothing that we have seems big enough; after the little house. There is a new carpet to be bought; there are curtains to be made for most of the windows; I had to put up all new curtain rods; and various things proved necessary that we did not have. The flat is certainly very light and very airy, especially compared to the house, and is much higher and drier: we feel a great difference in the air. In that way it is much healthier. But it is a great change. I will enclose a rough plan of the flat, so that you may imagine it; and when it is a little better in order we will take some photographs. Baker Street has changed a good deal; and some huge tall apartment houses are going up, so the clanging of steel goes on all day.

We have not yet got used to it enough to know whether we like it or not; and at present Vivien is in bed with a slight attack of pleurisy, and being nursed. She has a good doctor and a good nurse; and our small maid Eva does her best, though not extremely efficient. Janes still helps us, of course he is half an hour away by tube now; so he only comes three times a week; but we are always glad to see him. He polishes the brass and cleans the balconies and keeps my study tidy and takes the dogs for walks; and the cat is very happy here. Yesterday was Janes's seventyfifth birthday, so we gave him a silver topped walking stick engraved with his name and the date; I looked out of the window and saw him exhibiting it proudly to the porter as he left.

I think Vivien's illness is largely due to getting very overtired and then chilled, and she needs a good rest. The doctor wants us to take a two weeks holiday as soon as she can get out.

We have not yet been able to see Theodora.[1] We did not know when she was coming, and had not heard from her at all until she telephoned. Abigail Smith[2] too has been here but we have not seen her yet, and hardly anyone has seen this flat yet.

I met a very pleasant young man a few days ago named Lincoln Kirstein, from Cambridge, an editor of the *Hound and Horn*, who said that he

---

1 – Theodora Eliot Smith: TSE's niece; daughter of Charlotte (Mrs George Lawrence Smith).
2 – TSE's cousin.

knew you, because he sometimes helped serving in the Dunster House Bookshop; so I told him that if he was ever there again when you came in, he should introduce himself and tell you of meeting me.[1] There are a great many Americans here now. I have just learned that Professor Lowes is here, and have written to ask him to lunch with me on Thursday. I very much want to meet him. I hope to see Samuel Eliot Morison again too; I enjoyed him very much; I found that a friend of mine had staid with him in Cambridge.

The July *Criterion* will have reached you before this letter. Fortunately I had it nearly ready before the move began. I think it is a fairly good number; and the subscriptions are increasing, so I am not discouraged about it. I am now busy with the October number; particularly as the July number was for various reasons, mostly the printers' fault, nearly two weeks late: I meant it to be out on the 15th of June.

My *Dante* has arrived in proof, and I am correcting it slowly; it will be out in the autumn. Now that Faber & Gwyer has become Faber and Faber instead, I find that I have a good deal more of general publishing business on my hands than before: advising on manuscripts, discussing with authors and possible authors, and general matters of policy and finance. The business is fairly promising; and the management very harmonious; we have taken on to the Board an American named Frank Morley, who is the representative here also of the Century Company; the others, besides Geoffrey Faber and myself, are Stewart (the general manager) and Richard de la Mare, a son of Walter de la Mare. Of course interviews take a good deal of time – both for books and for *Criterion* contributors – and we have committee meetings every Wednesday and Thursday afternoon.

On Tuesday I shall be giving the last of my 'broadcast talks', which I have been sending to you week by week as printed in *The Listener*. On the whole, it has been pleasant, and I should be very glad to get more work of the same kind; at the same time, and particularly at the present time, it has been a considerable strain, and I shall not be sorry when this series is over. My only regret in doing this sort of work is that the material is of little or no use to me afterwards. When I have got the *Dante*, and one or two articles which I have promised, off my hands, I must start in the autumn on a small book on the theory of government: that sounds very ambitious for me, but it is less pretentious than it sounds.

1 – TSE had given Kirstein lunch in a Kensington pub.

I must stop now. I am anxious to know how you endure the heat, and whether you can get away at all this summer, and how Aunt Nellie is; do tell me more about her health. Will Henry be with you at any time this summer?

With very much love,
Your devoted son,
Tom

P.S. The doctor has just been & says Vivien is much better, & can get up tomorrow.

TO *John Freeman*[1] CC

16 July 1929   [London]

Dear Mr Freeman,

Thank you for your letter, I am flattered to think that you should have cared to read my very superficial remarks in *The Listener*.[2] I think that the only difficulty between us is my use of the word 'professional' which differs from yours. I do not mean by a professional writer merely a man who writes for his living. I mean just as much a man for whom writing is an art and for whom it is his real vocation. I should in this sense consider you and myself to be professional poets, although we neither of us make a living by it. My distinction was entirely between such people and others like Sea Captains who are obliged to keep records of their voyages or of

1–John Freeman (1880–23 Sept. 1929), poet and businessman, worked for his entire career for the Liverpool Victoria Friendly Society, London (a national health insurance company), starting in his teenage years as a junior clerk and rising to become Secretary and Director in 1927. An autodidact, he taught himself classical Greek and English poetry, and became closely associated with the Georgian poets. His writings ran to ten volumes of poetry including *Stone Trees* (1916) and *Collected Poems* (1928); *Prince Absalom* (play, 1925); criticism including *Portrait of George Moore* (1922) and *Herman Melville* (1926); and reviews for periodicals including the *New Statesman* and *London Mercury*. See *John Freeman's Letters*, ed. G. Freeman and J. C. Squire (1936).
2–Freeman asked (undated): 'Ought you to have said in *The Listener* that [Charles] Doughty's *A.D.* [*Travels in Arabia Deserta*] is 'the work of a very highly sophisticated professional writer'? The words are true enough of Arnold Bennett, Shaw & half-a-dozen others, whether they are writing well or ill; but how can Doughty be reckoned professional, even if he be reckoned . . . sophisticated? He must have chosen the wrong profession, for no man ever took such pain to succeed as Doughty took to fail in it. He – this professional writer – wrote one book in prose, which began to be valued when it couldn't be bought, & several poems which haven't yet begun to win a value except among secret worshippers. In prose and in verse he was an experimenter, an amateur, writing almost exclusively for the only audience he found – himself.'

let us say medical men or scientists who are obliged to write accounts of experiments or interesting cases for technical journals.

It is possible that the meaning which the word has to you is the meaning which it has to most people and if I have an opportunity I will try to make clear what the word means to me.[1]

With very many thanks,
Yours sincerely,
[T. S. Eliot]

TO *H. C. Crofton*   CC

16 July 1929   [London]

My dear Crofton,

Very many thanks for your kind letter and the trouble you have taken. I am writing to the young man to ask him to write and ask Mr Henderson[2] for an appointment.

We may be going away next week for about a fortnight as my wife is just recovering from pleurisy and the doctor has advised a visit to the sea-side. When we get back I will ring you up and try to arrange a lunch.

Yours very gratefully,
[T. S. Eliot]

TO *André Mazower*[3]   CC

16 July 1929   [London]

Dear Mazower,

I have just heard to-day from my friend in the city to whom I promised to write about you. And he has enclosed a letter to him from one of the general managers of the Paris Bank of which I send you a copy. I suggest that you should write to Mr Henderson at Gracechurch Street and ask him when you could hope to see him.

---

1 – Freeman replied to this letter ('Friday'): 'Your interpretation of "professional" is right, & if I hadn't been stupid I should not have asked my question. But I was shaking off the scurf of an influenza & couldn't read intelligently . . .'

2 – C. R. Henderson (Deputy General Manager, and Secretary, Lloyds & National Provincial Foreign Bank Ltd) had told Crofton (12 July) he would see André Mazower and give him an introduction to Paris: his problem would be to get a work permit.

3 – See TSE's letter to H. C. Crofton, 9 July 1929, above.

If you will let me know before you leave for Paris I will give you a line to the man in Paris of whom I spoke.[1]

Yours sincerely,
for T. S. Eliot

As Mr Eliot has had to leave the office early he has asked me to sign this for him as he wants it to [go] this afternoon.

TO *Nigel Sutton*   CC

17 July 1929   [London]

My dear Sutton,

I should be very grateful if you could spare a few minutes to talk to the bearer of this letter Mr André Mazower. He has just taken his degree at Cambridge in English and Economics and is anxious to get into some English bank or business in Paris for a few years. I dare say that there is no sort of opening in your own business but I am sure it would be helpful to him if he could talk to you.

With all best wishes.
Yours very sincerely,
[T. S. Eliot]

TO *R. E. Gordon George*   CC

17 July 1929   [London]

Dear Gordon George,

I am delighted to hear that you are in England again and should like to know how long you are to be here because I am afraid that there is no chance of our meeting until after the bank holiday. My wife is just recovering from a slight attack of pleurisy and I am hurrying to take her away to the sea-side for about a fortnight. Therefore I am in rather a rush in every way as we want to get off before the end of the week if possible. If I find any chance of seeing you I will ring and leave a message. If not please let me know where you will be a fortnight hence. I should be very sorry, and so would my wife, if you left England without seeing us.

[T. S. Eliot]

---

1 – Mazower had in fact written to TSE from Paris to say he had found a job as an office boy in the offices of the White Star Line.

P.S. I should be glad to have your review of Du Bos etc. as soon as possible to send immediately to the printers.[1]

TO *Ethel Sands*   CC

17 July 1929   [London]

Dear Miss Sands,

Thank you very much for your letter of the 13th and your cheque which I have passed in to the proper hands. I am sorry that you added 2/- for the little books. I will not fail to let you know of any future books in this collection which might interest you.

With all best wishes,
Yours sincerely,
[T. S. Eliot]

TO *James Burnham*   CC

17 July 1929   [London]

Dear Burnham,

I have your letter of the 10th and am very sorry indeed that I shall miss you, on this occasion. My wife is just recovering from a slight illness and the doctor has ordered her to the seaside for a short time so we shall probably be leaving before the end of the week. You and I seem to have very poor luck in arranging meetings. I hope that your letter does not mean that you are leaving England permanently.[2] Please let me know your plans and whether and when you will be returning.

With many regrets,
Yours ever,
[T. S. Eliot]

1 – Robert Sencourt, untitled review of Charles du Bos, *Byron et le besoin de la fatalité* and *Le dialogue avec André Gide*, and E. C. Mayne, *Life of Lady Byron*, C. 9 (Oct. 1929), 122–7.
2 – Burnham had graduated from Balliol College, Oxford.

TO *David Higham*

17 July 1929   [London]

Dear Higham,

I wonder if you would be so kind as to advise me on the following points.

I have just given a set of broadcast talks entitled 'Six Types of Tudor Prose'. They have been printed in *The Listener* in the six issues beginning with June 12th. I had not thought to make any further use of them as they are very short – the published version is about 1800 words for each talk. But I have a letter from The Holliday Bookshop of New York suggesting that they would like to use them for publication.[1] The Holliday perhaps imagines that there is much more material than there is but even if there is not enough for their purpose their letter has suggested to me that possibly some American periodical might care to use them.

If you think Curtis Brown could do anything for me I will get copies of *The Listener* and send them to you. In that case of course The Holliday Bookshop ought to have the first look at the stuff.

I am going away for a short holiday but I hope that you can come and lunch with me as soon as we are both in town.

Sincerely yours,
[T. S. Eliot]

TO *Douglas St-Leger Gordon*[2]

19 July 1929   [*The Criterion*]

Dear Sir,

I have read with interest your essay on The Sporting Instinct and regret that it is not quite the type of Natural History article which is suitable for *The Criterion*. It would be indeed more suitable for most other periodicals and there must be several magazines which would be very happy to publish it.

If we accepted articles on subjects of Natural History they would be such as deal with the more theoretic and philosophic aspects of the science or with the importance of new discoveries and inventions.

1–Terence B. Holliday (The Holliday Bookshop, 49 East 49th Street, New York) applied to TSE on 5 July.
2–Douglas St-Leger Gordon was to become a noted writer on Devon and its wildlife; his books include *Under Dartmoor Hills* (1954) and *Portrait of Devon* (1963).

I should of course always be glad to see more of your work.

Yours very truly,
[T. S. Eliot]
Editor

TO *His Mother*

TS Houghton

28 July 1929   98 Clarence Gate Gardens, London

Dearest Mother,

July is nearly over, and we have been in this flat for over a month. Vivien has got over her attack of pleurisy, but we have not yet been able to get away. And naturally, all the work of getting settled here has interrupted our ordinary life. I am not sure that we shall get really settled here; for after living in a house for several years a flat seems very strange and foreign, and we are not now at home in this neighbourhood.

I have just finished correcting the proofs of my small book on *Dante*, a considerable labour, involving numerous alterations and added footnotes. And a good deal of time has been taken up lately for the firm, by books by people whom I know – reading them, discussing them, coming to terms etc. I have had to read, in rapid succession, a philosophical work, a detective story, and the memoirs of Marshal Pilsudski, the dictator of Poland. All these things take time.

Now that my wireless talks are over, I miss them. I hope you received all six from me, as printed in *The Listener*. I have just had a very nice letter from the head of that department of the Broadcasting Company expressing appreciation and a hope that I will give another series later. I should like to do that; once you get used to talking in that way, without seeing any audience, it becomes very easy; and there is a pleasure in thinking that the people who listen really are listening, and not like so many people at a lecture who come merely to find out what you look like.

Now I am going to have lessons in driving a motor car. It is one of the things one ought to know how to do, nowadays, and it is a way of getting fresh air and resting the mind. I hope that afterwards Vivien will learn too. This flat gives her a great deal to do and to oversee, and she needs to get out of doors more.

We hope to see Theodora when she returns from Cambridge, and Abigail Smith when she returns from Sweden. I had Professor Lowes to lunch with me a few days ago, and liked him very much. He spoke most appreciatively of you. He said that Mrs Lowes had seen you and Marion more recently than he had, and I hope we may meet Mrs Lowes later in the summer, when they return to London from Oxford. He told me (this is *confidential* and not to be repeated to anyone) that he and some others were desirous that I should be nominated at some time for the Charles Eliot Norton Professorship, but I gathered that this was unlikely to happen for several years in any case. So I shall be coming just to see you long before I am asked (if at all) to come as a professor. From another source (*not* from Lowes) I learned that the only opposition to me so far had come, not from anyone in the English Department – but from Lawrence Lowell! I thought that perhaps President Lowell disliked the name of Eliot.

I am still anxious for news of how you are passing the summer, and whether Henry is coming on to see you during the summer. I have owed him a letter for a very long time, and I really must try to write to him this week.

The weather in London has been very dry and extremely hot; and I have been wearing, what I always keep for very warm weather, the two pairs of white pyjamas you made me. Do you remember them? I do not wear them a great deal, because I want to keep them to wear for a long long time; and even when they are too worn out to wear I shall still keep them!

With very much love from Vivien and me,

your devoted son,
Tom.

TO *James Joyce* CC

30 July 1929   [Faber & Faber Ltd]

My dear Joyce,

I am sorry that I have not had an opportunity of answering your letter before.[1] *A.L.P.* has arrived from Paris and I have read it with real enjoyment. Personally I should very much like to carry out the project I suggested to you but I shall have to wait a week or so until I can even take the matter up as two out of the five Directors are away on holiday. I shall expect to write to you further about this in a fortnight.[2]

---

1 – JJ wrote from the Imperial Hotel, Torquay, 2 July: 'I hope you got A.L.P. [*Anna Livia Plurabelle*] from Paris' (*Letters of James Joyce* III, ed. Richard Ellmann [1966], 510).
2 – JJ had written to Harriet Weaver on 16 July: 'T. S. E. most friendly. He wants his firm to publish S.G.'s book [Stuart Gilbert's *James Joyce's 'Ulysses': A Study*] and to bring out an English paperback edition of A.L.P.'

I hope that you and your family are enjoying Torquay, and my wife and I look forward to seeing you and Mrs Joyce in September.

Sincerely yours,

[T. S. Eliot]

TO *M. C. D'Arcy*   CC

30 July 1929   [London]

My dear D'Arcy,

Very many thanks for the admirable review of McDougall.[1] I have read your reply to More with great interest and enjoyment. I can see no objection whatever to publishing it and would be glad to do so but its form suggests to me that it would be more suitable in the correspondence column than anywhere else. Would you have any objection to my presenting it as a letter to the Editor?

I am not sure that I was wise to put in *The Criterion* an article dealing with such a contentious subject as Mr More's, but having done so, it seems to me quite right to print any reply to it.[2]

Yours very sincerely,

[T. S. Eliot]

TO *Stuart Gilbert*[3]   CC

30 July 1929   [Faber & Faber]

Dear Mr Gilbert,

I have just received your MS and shall be extremely interested in

1–Untitled review of William McDougall, *Modern Materialism and Emergent Evolution*, C. 9 (Oct. 1929), 127–30.

2–D'Arcy sent on 23 July 'a short article on Paul Elmer More's in the last number of the *Criterion*. But I want you to have no hesitation in returning it, if it does not suit, or again if you think it is ungenerous or would do more harm than good. I hate bickering without a purpose – in this case I think something ought to be said but without making bad blood.' See 'Correspondence', C. 9 (Oct. 1929), 117–18; and a concluding exchange of correspondence between Elmer More and D'Arcy in C. 9 (Apr. 1930), 508.

3–Stuart Gilbert (1883–1969), English literary scholar and translator, was educated at Hertford College, Oxford (taking a first-class degree in Classics), and worked for some years in the Indian Civil Service and then, following military service, as a judge on the Court of Assizes in Burma. It was only after his retirement in 1925 that he undertook work on Joyce, having admired *Ulysses* while in Burma. After befriending Joyce and others in his Paris circle (including Sylvia Beach, Auguste Morel and Valery Larbaud), he wrote *James Joyce's*

reading it.[1] I think that what you have sent should be enough to enable me to decide, but I am afraid that the decision may have to be delayed until your return to Paris. Two Directors are away and I shall want one other Director to read the MS. as well as myself. But I will do my best to get you a quick decision.

> With many thanks,
> Yours very truly,
> [T. S. Eliot]

TO *J. E. Pouterman*   CC

30 July 1929   [London]

Dear Sir,

In reply to your letter of the 26th instant.[2] It is quite true that I told Prince Mirsky that the subject interested me. I did not know how soon you intended to bring out the book and if it is to be during the present

---

'*Ulysses': A Study* (F&F, 1930). He helped JJ with the French translation of *Ulysses*; and in 1957 he edited *Letters of James Joyce* (counselled by TSE). In addition, he translated works by Saint-Exupéry, Roger Martin du Gard, Paul Valéry, André Malraux, Jean Cocteau, Albert Camus, Jean-Paul Sartre and Georges Simenon.

TSE was to write in a letter of recommendation to the British Council, 14 Jan. 1945: 'I have known Mr. Stuart Gilbert for a good many years – ever since he wrote what remains the final work of its kind about my friend James Joyce – a book which was successfully published by my firm. I have known him and Mrs. Gilbert [SG's French-born wife was Moune, née Marie Douin] in Paris as well as in London. He lived there until the fall of France; and is, I know, more at home there, and among French people, than anywhere else. He is a man of culture and charm, who mixed with literary circles in Paris; and is I am sure peculiarly well qualified to forward the work of the British Council in France.

'Mr. Gilbert's academic attainments and qualifications speak for themselves. Besides his original work, he has also done considerable translating from the French.'

1 – Gilbert had submitted on 26 July 'a portion of my *James Joyce's 'Ulysses': A Study*': 'Mr Joyce tells me that you were kind enough to offer to examine my work with a view to possible publication by Messrs Faber & Faber.

'The typescript submitted consists of:–

> a synopsis
> a specimen section of the introduction
> my commentaries on five of the eighteen episodes of *Ulysses*.

'I also enclose a copy of the current *Fortnightly* containing an article by me, illustrating the general lines on which I am treating *Ulysses* in my book. Mr Joyce tells me that you have seen my article on *Ulysse* in the *Nouvelle Revue Française* . . .'

2 – Pouterman (The Blackamore Press) asked: 'I understand from my friend, Prince Mirsky, that you are prepared to consider writing an introduction for an English edition of Baudelaire's "Mon Coeur mis à nu, etc." which we intend to bring out in the course of this autumn.'

autumn there hardly seems time for me to write an introduction which would involve a great deal of work. As I am interested in the subject however I should be glad if you would let me know by what time you would want such an introduction and what terms you would offer for it.

Yours faithfully,
[T. S. Eliot]

TO *James Burnham*   CC

30 July 1929   [London]

Dear Mr Burnham,

Thank you for your letter of the 21st of July.[1] I am very sorry to have missed you especially as there appears no possibility of foreseeing when we can meet again and our first meeting was far too hurried. I think that the third number would suit me very well. I should like to know however whether as the title and the purposes of your review suggest you have any special subject in mind. Otherwise I might be inclined to offer an essay on The Place of Belief in the Appreciation of Poetry, a subject hitherto hardly dealt with except by I. A. Richards in his recent book *Practical Criticism* which you ought to look at.[2]

With all best wishes,
Yours ever,
[T. S. Eliot]

1 – Burnham asked TSE to contribute to *The Symposium*, giving possible dates. Paul Elmer More was scheduled to contribute a piece on TSE's criticism.
2 – Burnham – whose magazine *The Symposium: A Critical Review*; otherwise, *The Symposium: A Quarterly Journal for Philosophical Discussion*, went through birthing bothers, with the consequence that the first issue would appear in Jan. 1930 – responded to this letter by TSE only on 28 Dec. 1929: 'I hope you still wish to write the article "On the

TO *J. L. Donaghy*

30 July 1929   [London]

Dear Mr Donaghy,

I must apologise for having left your letter[1] unanswered for so long. I hope you will not think I have been very rude. I like 'The Fort' very much and should have accepted it already but that it may be a long time before I have room to include so long a poem. I wonder if you will let me keep it and merely inform me in case you publish it elsewhere and also will you have the patience to send me when you can a few more poems and shorter ones.[2]

Hoping to see you again in London.[3]

Yours sincerely,
[T. S. Eliot]

TO *Nigel Sutton*

cc

30 July 1929   [London]

My dear Sutton,

I very much appreciate your kindness and the trouble you have taken over young Mazower.[4] I will certainly advise any more youths who come to me, to secure their license to work before they leave London.

———
Place of Belief in the Appreciation of Poetry". Reading I. A. Richards's chapter has convinced me more than ever that the subject has not yet been adequately treated. He puts the issues clearly enough, and shows their importance; but his solution is discouraging. If we had your article by the end of February, it could be published in the second issue.'

1–Letter of 10 June 1929.

2–'The Fort', C. 9 (Oct. 1929), 89–95. HR, whom TSE asked for an opinion on the poems Donaghy had submitted, and some by other poets, gave his advice on 21 July: 'I have read through them & feel that Donaghy's poem is the only one that matters. If on reading it again you feel the same, it might be worth while asking him to shorten it, or to send in a shorter one.'

3–Donaghy came to London with his wife and child in mid-Nov. 1929.

4–Sutton wrote on 25 July that he had talked with Mazower ('he will probably not have a great deal of difficulty in finding a beginner's job, and indeed he tells me he has already two nibbles') and said he should use a friend in Paris with some 'pull' to secure him a work permit – 'a point on which the French authorities are as intractable as the English'. Mazower thanked TSE on 24 July: 'I think that I should be able to get something at Lloyds almost as soon as I can get the "avis favorable" permitting me to work or failing that Mr Sutton has promised to help me, and says that there should be little difficulty in finding work – the difficulty lies in obtaining the permit from the Ministry of Labour.'

It is very good news to know that you are returning to London in the autumn and I very much hope that after that we may meet much more frequently.

Yours very sincerely,
[T. S. Eliot]

TO *Archibald MacLeish*[1]   CC

2 August 1929   [London]

Dear MacLeish,

I am sorry for the long delay about your poem. I hesitated over it a good deal. Candidly it does not seem to me one of your very best and I should not like to publish anything by you which seems not quite your best work. This is really a compliment although it may not appear so.

Have you settled permanently in Massachusetts or is there any prospect of your returning to Paris now and then? If not I shall regret all the more that I missed seeing you while you were there.

With all best wishes,
Sincerely yours,
[T. S. Eliot]

TO *Darsie R. Gillie*   CC

2 August 1929   [London]

My dear Gillie,

I had hoped to be able to get in to see you today, but business interruptions occurred, and I found I had not time.[2] I trust that the operation was wholly successful, and that you are now perfectly comfortable. If you linger in London over the weekend I hope you will let me know.

The Chairman and myself have both read your manuscript with great interest; we should like to publish the book; and we think that the material supplied is enough to justify pursuing the matter at once. What I have to

---

1–See *Letters of Archibald MacLeish 1907–1982*, ed. R. H. Winnick (Boston, 1983).
2–Gillie had submitted by post on 24 July a translation of 'about a third . . . or a little less' of the memoirs of Marshal Pilsudski. 'I would propose to write a short introduction (geographical and historical), short dry links between the fragments, and explanatory notes.' He went on: 'I shall be up in town on Saturday morning and will ring you up . . . Unfortunately I am going into a nursing home on Sunday in order to have part of my nose removed on Monday . . . I shall be . . . quite competent to consider business propositions if any by Thursday . . .' He added in a postscript: 'I hope that Mrs Eliot has quite recovered.'

propose is briefly this: a royalty of 10% on the first 2000 copies sold; then 15% up to 5000; 17½% to 10,000; and 20% thereafter. We should want to have the American rights; if we got an American publisher to set up the book in New York we should offer 50–50 shares on profits with the author; if the American publisher took sheets we should offer a straight 15% royalty. And to you, as the translator, we should offer £50 outright together with one half of any fee paid by an American publisher for the translation right.

In putting forward this offer we have had to keep two things in mind. First that a translation is more expensive to produce (and the expense considerably precedes the return) than an English book, because the translator must be adequately paid, and on delivery of the final manuscript. Second, that this book is rather more speculative than the name of its author would lead one to suppose. Personally, both myself and Mr Faber felt that this type of memoir is more interesting than the conventional type of political memoir. The view of the workings of the mind of an introspective man of action, Pilsudski's account of his own feelings during his campaigns and battles, is even better than you led me to expect: it is almost unique. But the ordinary public expects something else from the memoirs of a statesman; it expects spicy or acrimonious 'revelations' about diplomacy and diplomats of whom it has read in the newspapers. Mind you, I do not say definitely that this book will fail to sell as well as the conventional circulating library type of political memoir; it *may*, if it catches on, and reaches the right reviewers, sell much better; on the other hand it may fall flat. We take our chance on that, because it is a good book that ought to be published. But it is not going to sell in thousands merely on the name of Marshal Pilsudski; we have got to work hard to get it to the attention of the right people. These are the reasons why I think that the offer made above is reasonable.

I am not quite sure how far you are authorised to go; but if this offer is not accepted I should like to be assured of continuing the negotiations before the book goes elsewhere. Personally, I have great faith in the book: but I know that I am taking a risk.

Two other points arise. Mr Faber and I both think that it is essential that the gaps in the Marshal's life should be filled in, as you yourself suggested, by a running commentary of simple biography. I take it that you intended to provide this in any case.[1] The other point is that we have

---

1 – See Gillie's 'Translator's Note', ix: 'Those of Marshal Pilsudski's writings collected in this book include nearly everything he has written about his personal experiences prior to 1923, except the book *Rok 1920* (The Year 1920), which describes the most critical moments of his campaign against the Red Army.

no wish to delay about it; if we can arrange to publish it we should like to do so as soon as possible; and we should like to know how soon you think you could place the complete manuscript, with your own matter, in our hands. We should be ready to make a contract with the Marshal and with you as translator, immediately; though probably with a clause to the effect that the remaining two thirds of the book should be up to requirements. But I may say that we have noted your remark that what you have presented is probably the best; so that our requirements for the remainder would be quite modest.

Please drop me a line to my private address (98, Clarence Gate Gardens, N.W.1) to acknowledge this; and to tell me when you are leaving London and when you will be back. I take it you are returning to the same address at Bath? If you should be in London over next week, I should be delighted if you could lunch with me on Thursday.

And finally, if you come across any Polish books worth translating, we should recognise (substantially as well as politely) any suggestions that we accepted.

Yours always sincerely,
[T. S. Eliot]

We do want some photographs – but you could select them at leisure in Warsaw.

Dear Sirs,

With reference to the agreement, dated February, 14th, 1930, which has been made between your firm and myself for an English edition of my work, 'Memoirs of Marshal Pilsudski', translated with a biographical commentary by Mr Darsie Gillie, I hereby authorise you to pay Mr Darsie Gillie twenty five per cent. of any sums that may become due to me under the agreement, the balance of such sums to be paid by me.

Yours truly,
Messrs. Faber & Faber Ltd.

'It should be noted that the book before the reader was not conceived as a whole. It contains the major parts of two whole books, one written in 1903 (*Bibula*) and one in 1917 (*Moje Pierwsze Boje*) as well as many articles, fragments of speeches, a letter and orders to troops serving under him. These were produced over a period of twenty-six years (1903–29) on quite different occasions, in very varied circumstances, and without any thought as to their mutual relation. Such unity as they possess is due to the stamp of the author's character and to the consequence of his political purpose.

'The general plan of the book has been approved by Marshal Pilsudski.'

Gillie supplied a series of linking notes A–F.

то *E. J. Dent*[1]

[London]

Dear Dent,

I am writing to you about a matter which I put to Trend a couple of months ago. He was quite sure that it was impossible for him and was extremely discouraging about you. I am aware that it is more than unlikely [*sic*] that you will even consider it. Still you will understand that when publishers have a notion for a book they want written they naturally tackle the greatest authorities first even if there is very little prospect of getting them to write the book. So I hope you will forgive me for this letter.

We have in mind that a book should be written on Modern Music: as I said to Trend 'a book rather for the general listener than for the amateur with technical knowledge of music. Or rather a book which would cross both frontiers and interest both people with technical knowledge and intelligent people with none.' It should give some idea of the tendencies, both general and technical of modern music in the musical countries and should give some guidance, let us say, to the person whose knowledge of music ends with Wagner or with Strauss and who would like to find his way about in what is actually being done.

I put this rather crudely and it may seem to you an unworthy task; but it is obvious that if such a book is worth doing at all there are very few people in England capable of doing it. We have examined a German book which Trend recommended but it is not quite what we want.

Any way I do hope that you will think of this and let me hear from you. If you couldn't do it yourself is there anyone whom you could recommend? Incidentally I should very much like to know your opinion of Boris de Schloezer's essay on Stravinsky.

Sincerely yours,

[T. S. Eliot]

1–Edward Joseph Dent (1876–1957), British writer on music; educated at King's College, Cambridge, he was Professor of Music at Cambridge, 1926–41. He wrote a number of notable studies of musicians including Scarlatti, Busoni, Handel, and Mozart; he also translated several libretti for Sadler's Wells Opera (of which he was a governor).

TO *Algar Thorold*   CC

2 August 1929   [London]

Dear Mr Thorold,
   I shall be very happy to lunch with you on Wednesday the 7th of August
and look forward with much pleasure to meeting you at last.
                                        Yours very sincerely,
                                        [T. S. Eliot]

TO *Jacob Bronowski*[1]   CC

2 August 1929   [London]

Dear Sir,
   I am much interested by those poems which you sent me some time ago,
but on the whole I do not think that they are quite right.[2] I hope you will
send me some more of your work.
                                        Yours very truly,
                                        [T. S. Eliot]

---

1 – Jacob Bronowski (1908–74) – Polish-born scientist, humanist, writer, and broadcaster,
whose family came to the UK in 1920 – was at this time reading mathematics at Jesus
College, Cambridge. After gaining his doctorate in 1933, he taught at the University College
of Hull, 1934–42; and during WW2 he became scientific deputy to the British joint chiefs
of staff mission to Japan (where he wrote a report on the effects of the atomic bombs on
Hiroshima and Nagasaki). For thirteen years from 1950 he was Director of the Coal Research
Establishment of the National Coal Board, working on the development of smokeless fuel;
and 1964 he became Senior Fellow at the Salk Institute for Biological Studies in San Diego,
California. His varied publications include *The Poet's Defence* (1939), a critical study of
William Blake (1944), and *Science and Human Values* (1956). In his later years he won
acclaim for his thirteen-part TV series *The Ascent of Man* (1973).
2 – Bronowski submitted from Cambridge, on 17 Dec. (1928), two poems: 'Betrayal'
and 'October Casuistry'. (In 1929 he published a poem, *For Wilhelmina, Queen of the
Netherlands* (Cambridge: W. Heffer & Sons: 'Songs for Sixpence' no. 6), which was notably
derivative from *The Waste Land*.)

TO *Sherwood Trask*   CC

2 August 1929   [London]

Dear Mr Trask,

I am sorry that none of these poems seems to fit in very well with *The Criterion*, but I liked the one which we published[1] so much that I hope you will continue to let me see your work as it becomes ready for publication.

Yours sincerely,

[T. S. Eliot]

TO *Hart Crane*[2]   CC

2 August 1929   [London]

Dear Mr Hart Crane,

I must apologise for the delay in writing a letter which should have been written a year ago. I return this small poem[3] with the message that I don't like it as much as a great deal of your work. But I do hope you have by now some more and longer pieces which you might send to me.

Yours sincerely,

[T. S. Eliot]

TO *Seán Ó'Faoláin*   CC

2 August 1929   [London]

Dear Mr O'Faolain,

I am sorry for the delay about your poem especially if it has interfered in any way with your arrangements for the *Hound and Horn*. I am now returning it with apologies as I am afraid I could not use it for a considerable time.

I am still hanging on to your essay on Irish poets which I liked so much and hope that you will let me keep it for a remote possibility which I have in view, but of course on the understanding that you are

1 – 'A Footnote of History', C. 5 (Jan. 1927), 43–4.
2 – Hart Crane (1899–1932), American poet; author of *White Buildings* (1926) and *The Bridge* (1930). See Hart Crane: *Complete Poems and Selected Letters*, ed. Langdon Hammer (1997); Lee Oser, *T. S. Eliot and American Poetry* (1998).
3 – Title unknown.

at liberty to publish it anywhere you like if you will let me know of the publication.

With all best wishes,
Sincerely yours,
[T. S. Eliot]

TO *Allen Tate*   CC

2 August 1929   [London]

My dear Tate,

I cannot yet make up my mind about your 'Thoughts for a Friend', but I wish you would let me keep it a little longer and let me know if you publish it elsewhere, and if you have other things you could send me.

I was extremely sorry that you had to leave London on the day when we were to have lunched together and still more sorry to learn the reason.[1] I do hope that your wife is quite recovered and should be glad of a line to know how you are getting on and what your plans may be.

Yours ever,
[T. S. Eliot]

TO *Paul Elmer More*   TS Princeton

3 August 1929   Faber & Faber Ltd

My dear More,

Your letter of the 21st July gave me much pleasure, and contrary to my habits, I am answering it at once.[2]

---

1 – Tate had left London on Thurs., 11 July, because his wife was ill in Paris.
2 – 'I should never have sent the MS of the Oxford Journal to you had I supposed you would give yourself so much trouble over it. Now I have two proposals to make, which I trust will relieve you of difficulty.

'The MS might simply be turned over to some agency, if you think such a move advisable.

'It has occurred to me also that matters might be smoothed over if I offered to pay for publication . . . Then there is the question of anonymity. As I have already said, I have no objection to letting the publisher know my name, but that is a different matter from letting my name appear on the title page. I could not present myself to the world as an Oxford don. The case would be different of course if the authorship were guessed, because then the role of donship would appear as a disguise, which indeed it is. And there are personal reasons for anonymity. I should shrink from deliberately giving such a document to the world ("to the world" is a pleasant phrase) under my name. The subject matter is altogether too intimate . . . But an unacknowledged attribution after all is a different sort of thing from a spontaneous self-revelation – if you understand my scruples.

You need feel no embarrassment about the matter of your MSS. I have had the pleasure of reading it, and the pleasure of trying to get it published. I am doubtful of the possibility of an agency being able to place an 'anonymous' book, unless it were a popular novel, or a sensational work of some sort. And in general, I have been against our publishing books 'on commission', or at the author's expense, except in the case of expensive works of scholarship which ought to be done, but obviously can only be done at a loss. In general, if a publisher thinks a book worth publishing, I think he ought to take the risk himself. But of course I will discuss that possibility with my directors.

I should like anyway to be allowed to keep the typescript for some time, if you will leave it with me, because I have some hope that we might be able to fit it in, later on, with a kind of series or library of small paper bound volumes that we have in view.

I quite agree with your views about the anonymity. And you may be sure that any time I have given or shall give to the problem of this book is purely a satisfaction to me.

I have been struggling to write an essay for Foerster, but find it is a blind alley.[1] I feel that I have said all that I have to say about Humanism in those two articles, and that the further work to be done is a long slow one. I find in Foerster and other disciples of Babbitt a kind of impatience to get quick results, overnight programmes and immediate dogmas. Foerster thinks that he and his fellows are the saving remnant, but they seem to me a bargain sale remnant, shopworn. What I should like to see is the creation of a new type of intellectual, combining the intellectual and the devotional – a new species which cannot be created hurriedly. I don't like either the purely intellectual Christian or the purely emotional Christian – both forms of snobbism. The co-ordination of thought and feeling – without either debauchery or repression – seems to me what is needed. Most critics appear to think that my catholicism is merely an escape or an evasion, certainly a defeat. I acknowledge the difficulty of a positive Christianity nowadays; and I can only say that the dangers pointed out, and my own weaknesses, have been apparent to me long before my critics noticed them. But it [is] rather trying to be supposed to have settled oneself in an easy chair, when one has just begun a long journey afoot.

'I am laying on you a burden of decision . . . But . . . I do not wish the business to cause you any annoyance or to take any appreciable amount of your time. The simplest solution of the affair would be to send the MS back to me without further bother.'

1 – TSE, 'Religion without Humanism', in *Humanism and America: Essays on the Outlook of Modern Civilisation*, ed. Norman Foerster (New York, 1930), 105–12.

I am not intoxicated by the idea of 'leading' anybody, at present, and I want no converts. It's all right to be a leader after you are dead, but dangerous while you are alive.[1] And people only want a few catch words to ease their minds with.

We must look forward to seeing you in 1931 then; for if I am in Boston meanwhile I shall not have time for a pilgrimage to Princeton. With all best wishes from my wife and myself.

Sincerely yours,
T. S. Eliot

TO *Ramon Fernandez*   CC

9 August 1929   [London]

My dear Fernandez,

Being in same condition in which you say you are I naturally reply in this language.

I ought to have written to you before to thank you for Molière which I look forward to reading. It was very kind of you to send it to me.

Do by all means send me your essay on Humanism as quickly as you can. I should like to have it very much indeed and would if possible try to print it in December.[2]

Richards is now in China but I am writing to his publishers to ask them to send you his book. I am sure that Richards would have sent it himself had he been here. I hope that there is a chance of your coming to England this autumn or winter. Meanwhile my wife joins me in sending kindest regards.

Yours very sincerely,
[T. S. Eliot]

1–More had written on 21 July: 'You would be interested to hear how the soi-disant humanistic movement is sweeping over the country. Really, I am amazed . . . And the religious aspect of the question is coming more and more to the front. The younger men are dividing themselves into camps of those who adhere to Babbitt's rather supercilious attitude towards religion, and of those who feel that the purely secular programme is too negative to accomplish anything very valuable or even to correct the disintegrating influences of modern life. These latter would like, most of them I believe, to look to you as their leader, but at present are a little worried to know just where you stand. They want something more positive than your two excellent articles on Babbitt and Foerster.'

2–Fernandez, 'A Humanist Theory of Value', trans. by TSE, C. 9 (Jan. 1930), 228–45. JMM replied to Fernandez in 'The Detachment of Naturalism', C. 9 (July 1930), 642–60.

TO *Marguerite Caetani*   CC

Dear Marguerite,

Thank you very much for your two letters and for the cheque. I did not at first understand what the cheque was for but have transferred it to *The Criterion*. Thank you very much indeed for your continued support.

I do not want to publish the poem separately in English. It is one of a short sequence which I may publish together in a limited edition. But if you use the poem in the December number of *Commerce* that will give me time enough.[1] Menasce's address is 8 rue de Grace, but I do not know where he is at present. If you cannot get an answer from him quickly by all means give the poem to any one else whom you think competent.

I will write to Aldous Huxley in September, and tell him when you are to be in Paris as I am sure he would very much like to meet you.[2]

I am very glad to get Leger's contract and his revision of my translation.[3] I am doubtful however whether it will be possible to have the book ready for publication before the early spring. I shall have to go through Leger's notes very carefully and type out another text and send it to him with explanations wherever I maintain my own version. I am quite aware that from his point of view some of my departures from the exact translation must seem unjustified, but they are often determined by exigencies of rhythm and association which he could hardly be expected to follow. I see however that there are many places where I can fall in with his recommendations.

1–T. S. Elliott [*sic*], 'Som de l'escalina', trans. Jean de Menasce, *Commerce* 21 (Autumn 1929), 99–103.
2–'I would like awfully to meet Aldous Huxley or any friend of yours,' remarked Caetani on 23 July. She was to report on 8 Dec.: 'The Huxleys were very disappointed because I hadn't played croquet with you as a child! I wish I had!'
3–Caetani wrote on 6 Aug.: 'I managed to persuade Leger [St-John Perse] to give me the long-awaited document promising to write in his place . . . I promised to do my best to explain to you that he has delayed so long always wishing to write you at length himself – He wants you to feel how high he places you as a poet and that all his notes and suggestions are simply to explain more clearly his vision and in no way to impose or even ask *any* changes in your text that you do not feel yourself.'

I was very sorry indeed about Hofmannsthal, it is a great loss.[1]

I am writing now rather hurriedly and hope to write again soon but wished to acknowledge your letters and enclosures and reply to your questions at once.

Yours ever affectionately,

[Tom]

TO *Edouard Roditi* TS UCLA

10 August 1929

Faber & Faber Ltd,
24 Russell Square

Dear Mr Roditi,

Although I have been so dilatory, do not think that you and your work have been wholly out of my mind. I think that the book you sent me (I mean the MSS.) is a real advance on your previous work.[2] You are still full of undigested imagery and feeling from Leger, and some from myself, but I think this will work itself out; and the right way is to refuse to worry about it, and never try deliberately to rid oneself of an influence – by so

1 – 'What a tragedy the death of Hofmannsthal!'

TSE was to write in his 'Commentary', C. 9 (Oct. 1929), 5–6: 'Of your charity pray for the soul of Hugo von Hofmannsthal. We mention him in particular because he supported and contributed to the *Criterion*. Hofmannsthal, who is not long dead, was a fine poet and a fine prose writer. He was, during his lifetime, the leading man of letters in Vienna. Not only by his own work, but by his patronage, his influence, and the periodicals which he affected, one of the great European men of letters. Most English readers know him only as the author of the librettos of Strauss's operas, especially *Elektra*. Those who know German recognise the poet and prose writer. Hofmannsthal was a man of European culture. In some of his verse plays, such as *Sobeidens Hochzeit*, he showed himself to be saturated in Elizabethan and Jacobean drama, which he knew intimately; in some of his later work, he showed an equal intimacy with Spanish drama, with Lope and Calderon. Yet his work was never pastiche. He is one of the writers in German whose work appears as fine after the War as it did before, and whose tendency and influence may be described as "classical". And he was a man of great charm and great culture.'

2 – Roditi had sent ('Friday June 20th') a manuscript he entitled 'Emperor of Midnight'. In a separate, undated letter, he had remarked: 'I have just finished my first book, after three months in correcting, changing, criticizing etc. It includes all my poems from 1926 to 1929, that is to say "Oracles" and a lot of vaguely mystical and romantic things which I wrote before this winter. Its title is Emperor of Midnight, and it is of about 60 pages . . .

'Robert Graves has asked me to send it to him as it might interest his Seizin Press. But I am in no hurry to finish it, as the more time I spend over it, the more mature the poems will be.

'I hope these 60 pages of rather effusive poetry will not disgust you too much. I often wonder how I ever wrote some of these poems; but although I would not write such things now, I do not disapprove of them. They seem to me to have been necessary – so far as I am concerned.'

doing one only falls into some worse pitfall. I think it is good enough to be published; so long as you take no notice of what anyone says about it, but do your own criticism, and ignore both praise and censure. But to criticise oneself is terribly painful.[1]

So let me hear from you sometimes and I hope you will soon be able to get back to Oxford.

Sincerely yours,
T. S. Eliot

TO *Bonamy Dobrée*   TS Brotherton

10 August 1929   Faber & Faber Ltd

Dear Father Superior,

Forgive this tardy note of thanks for your inscribed volume, for which some American collector will pay a huge price a hundred years hence.[2] Yes I do like the book, and I think it succeeds. I have just read the Forster, which I like very much, and which goes extremely well with the Kipling. I am not so sure about the Lawrence, but must go over that again. But the more one examines these essays the more coherent they appear, and that I think is as it should be with a book of essays.

We are still stewing in the horrors of modern London. I wonder whether I should find the country any more tolerable. Is there any chance of your coming to tahn between now and the Septennial Saturnalia?

Ever yours,
T.

1 – Roditi was to recall in 1988: 'The annotations that Eliot had made in the margins of these poems were all so useful that I took them into account in revising my own text, but I refrained for many years from publishing *Oracles*, probably because I soon felt that they were already in a way outdated. Forty-five years later, I nevertheless decided to include this revised version of them at long last, in 1974, in *Emperor of Midnight*, published by Black Sparrow Press' ('Corresponding with Eliot', 37).

2 – *The Lamp and the Lute* (1929) included a critical study of the early TSE.

TO *Conrad Aiken*   CC

10 August 1929   [London]

Dear Conrad,

Many thanks. You may be right.[1] Anyway, I am glad to add your acute comments to a file (very select) which I shall draw upon when I write my Apologia. Most of these criticisms I had already anticipated, or made myself. Thrice is he armed who knows what a humbug he is. My progress, if I ever make any, will be in purging myself of a large number of impure motives.

Only, *do* I suggest that 'reason is Bankrupt'???

No, these are not dull subjects: Theology, Bridge, and Detective Fiction are not dull.

No hope of jobs here, no hope at all; am near bankrupt (not being reason) myself.[2] But will look round and hope to make suggestions soon. It's time you returned for a spell – and time I came over there for a spell.

Yours affect.

[Tom]

TO *E. M. Forster*   TS King's

10 August 1929   Faber & Faber Ltd

My dear Forster,

I am not sure whether I wrote to thank you for your essay in *Life and Letters* or not.[3] If I did, please forgive the repetition.

On account of the flattery implied by being written about by you, my opinion is anything but reliable, but I liked the article very much. You are right about the 'horror'; and may be interested to know that the first quotation I chose for the *Waste Land*, before I hit on the more suitable

---

1–On 29 July Aiken sent TSE an offprint of his review of FLA: 'A thin and vinegarish hostility towards the modern world is breathed from these pages. Seeking certainties, or at least a hope of certainties, Mr Eliot sounds a quavering recall, and attempts to lead us back to classicism in literature, to royalism in politics, and to the Anglo-Catholic church in religion. Humanism he condemns as merely a "sporadic" ancillary of religion, a kind of parasite, unable to exist fruitfully in its own right. Reason is bankrupt . . . It is hard to describe this as anything but a complete abdication of intelligence . . . A note of withered dogmatism sounds repeatedly in these pages' ('In Retreat', *Dial* 86 [July 1929], 628–30).

2–Aiken had petitioned: 'I'm keen to find a job. Have you got anything at Gwyer's?'

3–'T. S. Eliot and his Difficulties', *Life & Letters* 2: 12 (May 1929), 417–25 (repr. in *Abinger Harvest*).

one from Trimalchio, was a sentence from the end of *Heart of Darkness*, which you may remember, ending with Kurtz's words 'the horror . . . the horror'. I only think that you exaggerate the importance of the War in this context. The War crippled me as it did everyone else; but me chiefly because it was something I was neither honestly in nor honestly out of, but the *Waste Land* might have been just the same without the War.

I am not sorry that you detect the element of bluff in much of the prose. The relation to James may however be pressed too far, because I do think that I succeed in distinguishing the City of God from London in the Season; but the bluff is there right enough, and I believe that I was the first person to detect it. As for the 'impersonality' doctrine, it has its personal motives of course, and is neither more true nor more false than the opposite doctrine; but I believe that it may have been of some value in its time.

I wish that we might meet occasionally.[1]

Yours sincerely,

T. S. Eliot

TO *Raymond Ellsworth Larsson* CC

10 August 1929 [London]

My dear Larsson,

I am very glad to hear from you and know that your book is to be published in September.[2] I shall look forward to reading it with great interest because of what I have seen of your work; but I am afraid I cannot provide any comments for your publishers to see. I have been asked to do this before but have consistently refused on principle so I do not see how

---

1 – Forster replied (from a ship in the Red Sea), 9 Sept.: 'Your letter gave me very great pleasure; thank you so much for it. As to the war, I put that part wrong in my article. I did see that the Waste Land would have been written anyhow. On the other hand, but for the war, I shouldn't myself have had any preparation for the poem. The article ought to have contained a sentence to the above effect. As it stands, it's misleading. – I'll think over what you say about the "impersonality" doctrine. I want, when your next book or books come out to go through your work very carefully again. – The poems, of course, I keep on reading on and off for "pleasure" as I call it; the sort of thing I love comes to me out of their words again and again, and out of different words as re-read.'

2 – Larsson (27 July): 'Payson and Clarke, who are publishing a book of my things in September under the title *O City, Cities!* have asked me if I thought you would be so kind as to make some statement concerning my work, to be used in advertising . . . Presently, you will receive proofs of the book for Faber and Gwyer, whom I should like to have publish it in England, if you like them.'

I can make an exception. But I hope that you are writing more poetry and that you will soon have some to send me for *The Criterion*.[1]

> With all best wishes,
> Yours very sincerely,
> [T. S. Eliot]

TO *S. George West*[2]   CC

10 August 1929   [London]

Dear Sir,

I must apologise for my delay in answering your letter of the 16th July. I consider it an honour to be asked to address your society; and I have been much tempted to accept. But I have declined all invitations to deliver lectures during the next three terms, being unsure of my time and leisure, and whether at any given date I shall be in England or not; and so I feel that once more I must refuse, on this occasion with particular regret. I hope that I may have another opportunity offered me, and add my sincere good wishes for the success of your season.

> Yours very truly,
> [T. S. Eliot]

TO *J. E. Pouterman*   CC

10 August 1929   [London]

Dear Sir,

Thank you for your letter of the 2nd of August.[3] It might be possible for me to let you have an essay by the time you wish. Before I promise definitely and before I suggest any terms I should be glad if you would let me know about what length you would wish such an introduction to be.

> Yours very truly,
> [T. S. Eliot]

---

1 – Larsson sent the proofs of his book on 22 Aug. 1929.
2 – Hon. Secretary, King's College Literary Society, London.
3 – 'For the time being the date of publication of Baudelaire's Journals has not yet been definitely fixed, and I am quite willing to delay publication so as to give you ample time to write the introduction. If you could let me have it by the end of November ot the beginning of December, I would publish the book in February 1930.' He asked TSE to suggest suitable terms: 'For your guidance I would only mention that I intend to limit the edition to 1000

TO *The Holliday Bookshop, New York*   CC

10 August 1929   [London]

Dear Sirs,

I thank you for your letter enquiring about my Broadcast Talks on Tudor Prose.

It had not occurred to me that those superficial chats could be reprinted; but I am ordering the copies of *The Listener* in which they appeared (6 talks of about 1800 words each, abbreviated from the form in which they were delivered), and if you then care to proceed any further, you may take the matter up with Curtis Brown Ltd. (London). But I dare say you will drop the matter when you read the talks.

Yours very truly,

[T. S. Eliot]

TO *Jean de Menasce*   CC

10 August 1929   [London]

My dear Menasce,

I am writing suddenly and in haste about two things.

I have recently [sent] Madame de Bassiano a new poem for *Commerce*, with a word that if you would care to translate it, I had rather you did [it] than anybody. So you may hear from her.

And I have just heard from a publisher whom I do not know, named Fourcade (22 rue de Condé) suggesting a small book of my poems translated. Of course there are not enough already translated for the book; but if you cared to translate enough more yourself I should be glad to have it published in France on the most modest terms so far as I am concerned, but you should get something out of it. Perhaps you will let me know what you think. You may have better means than I for finding out about Fourcade. And you may be far too busy with other work. I should like news of you, anyway.

Yours affectionately,

[T. S. Eliot]

---

numbered copies on de luxe paper, of which 500 for sale in England at one guinea, and 500, destined for America, to be disposed of through some agency at a wholesale price of about 8 shillings.'

TO *Ruth Harrison*

10 August 1929   [London]

Dear Madam,

I hope that you will pardon my incivility in not answering your letter for three months.[1] I can only say, in partial extenuation, that had there been any opportunity whatever, I should not have let this time elapse.

Your qualifications are so obvious – I do not mean merely your degrees and distinctions, or the position you have just left, but what impressed me more, a very acute letter of criticism that you wrote to me over a year ago – that I very much regretted having no excuse for offering an interview. I very much need someone like yourself. But at present, and probably for several years to come, *The Criterion* is partly dependent for its existence upon the generosity of the guarantors; and until the review is quite self supporting, its editor is not justified in employing anyone to do anything that he can do himself. Even then, the position of secretary will ha [*typing runs off the page*] a remunerative one.

I am writing this tardy note of appreciation merely to let you know that it was a pleasure to me to think that such a position would have attracted you.

Yours very truly,
[T. S. Eliot]

TO *Herbert Read*

TS Victoria

12 August 1929   *The Criterion*, 24 Russell Square

Dear Herbert,

I was very sorry to miss the weekend with you; it was stupid of me not to have taken account of the fact that our maid's holiday had been postponed so that she would be absent over that weekend.[2] It is good of you to renew the invitation, and when I can see my way, I shall suggest myself again, or if possible let you know in advance two or three weekends to choose from.

---

1 – Ruth M. Harrison, who was Secretary to the Headmistress, Roedean School, wrote on 10 May to ask whether TSE needed a secretary; she desired 'a non-resident post where time for reading would more often be possible than it is in a girls' boarding school.'
2 – HR had invited TSE on 20 July to spend the following weekend with him and his wife at Broom House, Seer Green, Beaconsfield.

There were two or three minor things about which I should have liked to talk to you. The most important was about your reason for wanting to get out the war-pamphlet quickly.[1] I think (1) there is no doubt that the book ought to be published sooner or later, and (2) I cordially support your reason for wanting to print it; I am only uncertain whether this book can be counted upon to perform that function. That is to say, insofar as you mean it as a reminder to the public rather than to yourself. To the general public, I fear it may give a superficial impression of scraps sewn together, and will have little weight against the impressive scholarship and bulk of the Clark Lectures. (And don't follow my cunctative example; get your lectures ready for the book immediately after you deliver them, or delay will undermine conviction). I don't see how you can escape for the next year or two, the reputation of being a profound but slightly academic critic; and I don't see that it matters, so long as you can get started privately on the other line.

Incidentally, I should like to know how you feel about Professorships in general: as Grierson has mentioned to me in confidence but with permission to repeat to you, that he and some others had been considering putting your name forward for a Professorship of Fine Art at Edinburgh. Unless the agitation dies out, I think he will want to talk to you about it the next time he comes to town. It is in my experience rather exasperating to have professorships dangled in front of you (sometimes with large salaries attached); and it is very difficult to know how one really feels about it until it is a definite offer. And I can't see why anyone should accept a professorship unless he very much needed the money.

A very small point. It seems to me that the *Criterion* ought sooner or later to express some opinion about Joyce's latest style. There are now two small books of it (*Anna Livia Plurabelle* and *Shem and Shaun*) and a book of essays about it, and a big number of *Transition*. What do you think about it? It's too important a matter, if done at all, to entrust to a man like Williams.[2]

I thought of giving Bonamy's book to Belgion to review. Fletcher has got Richards. How does the matter of the American periodicals stand?

---

1 – See catalogue blurb, Spring 1930, for *In Retreat*: 'The narrative, by an infantry officer and writer of assured position, of the retreat of the British Fifth Army from St Quentin in March, 1918, *In Retreat* was written in 1919, and originally issued in the *Hogarth Essays* in 1925. Though championed by a few, it remained a noble fragment overlooked by many, and *The Times Literary Supplement* of November 29, 1929, mentioned it as "that neglected little masterpiece". It is now available for the first time at a shilling.'
2 – Orlo Williams.

Shall I write to Bonamy about it? I think it would be a very satisfactory arrangement; I can't think of anyone else who would do it and could be trusted.

I believe that the Humanism affair, in its present form, is played out – I am printing a dull essay by Foerster in September, Fernandez has promised a contribution for December, which might possibly add something new, and possibly might not. On the other hand I feel that the controversy has merely scratched the surface of something much more important, and that some preliminary mapping out of the territory might be done. Belgion I think might be of some use; Curtius I feel is perhaps getting a little old to go any farther than sound but rather vague generalities. I should like to find one or two younger Germans of the weight of Scheler.[1]

I hope to see you on Thursday anyhow. Will you find out whether the dugout will be reopened by then? Without the room and the gramophone, we should certainly be better off anywhere else.

ever yours
T. S. E.

TO *Muriel Kent*[2]   CC

13 August 1929   [London]

Dear Madam,
    I very much regret that I cannot use the enclosed study of *Tagore* which I found very interesting but which does not quite fit in to the programme of *The Criterion* at the present moment.[3]
    I should be glad again to see more of your work.

Yours faithfully
[T. S. Eliot]
Editor.

1–Max Scheler (1874–1928), German philosopher specialising in ethics, value theory, phenomenology, philosophical anthropology; Professor of Philosophy and Sociology at Cologne, 1919–28; a notable influence on Karol Wojtyla, the future Pope John Paul II, who wrote his *Habilitation* (1954) on Christian ethics in the light of Scheler. His works, including *Nation und Weltanschauung*, are gathered in *Gesammelte Werke* (Bern, 1963).

2–See *A Diary of St Helena: The Journal of Lady Malcolm, 1816, 1817*, ed. Sir Arthur Wilson, with introd. by Muriel Kent (1929).

3–Kent submitted on 5 July an essay on Rabindranath Tagore and some earlier Indian mystics. She had earlier tried TSE with essays including one on 'A Danish Pilgrim's Progress' – based on the English edition of the Autobiography of Jörgensen (vol. 1).

TO *G. Wilson Knight*   CC

13 August 1929   [London]

Dear Sir,

I shall be glad to see you if you care to call on Friday next the 16th, at about 12 o'clock. Thursday would be more convenient for me, but I think that Friday is quite possible and shall look forward to seeing you.[1]

Yours very truly,

[T. S. Eliot]

TO *Adrian Stokes*[2]   CC

13 August 1929   [London]

Dear Sir,

I am glad to hear from you and to have your address. It is true that Pound gave me for publication the essay you mention.[3] I found it extremely interesting and told Pound that it was very much too long for *The Criterion*. I then heard from him that I might cut it at my discretion to a suitable length. Had I known that you were in England I should certainly have sent the manuscript back to you so that you might make your own cuts; more especially as I found it extremely difficult; and you may consider my abbreviations to be quite irrational. The manuscript

---

1 – Wilson Knight had been plying TSE with essays for some months. Pieces submitted for consideration had included studies of *Timon of Athens* and the technique of *Hamlet*. TSE admired Knight's approach but had not yet accepted an essay for publication in *C*.

2 – Adrian Stokes (1902–72), British art critic, author, and poet. Independently wealthy (having inherited a fortune from his stockbroker father), Stokes studied at Magdalen College, Oxford, and embarked on travels in India, China, and the USA, ultimately in Italy (where in 1926 he met EP). A bisexual who suffered from depression, in 1929 he underwent a course of psychotherapy with the Freudian psychoanalyst Melanie Klein, with the consequence that Freudianism became a key strand in his critical writings. His first publications were *The Thread of Ariadne* (1925) and *Sunrise in the West: A Modern Interpretation of Past and Present* (1926) – published by Kegan Paul, Trench, Trubner. Then F&F put out his influential studies, *The Quattro Cento: A Different Conception of the Italian Renaissance* (1932) and *The Stones of Rimini* (1934), and many later writings. His other works include studies of Cézanne (1947), Raphael (1956), and Monet (1958); *Michelangelo: A Study in the Nature of Art* (1955); and *Reflections on the Nude* ((1967). See further *The Critical Writings of Adrian Stokes*, ed. Lawrence Gowing (3 vols, 1978); *With All the Views: The Collected Poems of Adrian Stokes*, ed. Peter Robinson (1981); and Richard Read, *Art and Its Discontents: The Early Life of Adrian Stokes* (2003).

3 – 'The Sculptor Agostino di Duccio. Extracted from the third of four essays on the Tempio Maletestino at Rimini. Part of a work in progress about the Italian Renaissance', *C*. 9 (Oct. 1929), 44–60.

went to the printer some time ago and I am expecting galley proofs at any moment which I shall have forwarded to you immediately to the address from which you write.

Yours faithfully,
[T. S. Eliot]

TO *Norman Foerster*

CC

13 August 1929   [London]

Dear Mr Foerster,

Here is my proposed contribution to your volume, which has been produced under considerable difficulties. I am aware that (1) it may be too late (2) it may be too short (3) it may be unsuitable. If any or all of these causes have force, please send it back to me, because I can revise it and print it elsewhere. I also believe that it is anything but a model of English prose, as it appears to me to be a jumble of themes which ought to be analysed into a book or perhaps several books.

But let me know as soon as you can.[1] Meanwhile your own essay is appearing in the October *Criterion*, about the third week of September, and you will get a copy at once.

Sincerely yours,
[T. S. Eliot]

TO *F. S. Oliver*

CC

13 August 1929   [London]

Dear Oliver,

I have just realised that with the crowd of business and worry which I had during the month of May, and my wife being ill directly after we moved, I do not appear ever to have answered your letter of the 3rd May or attended to the subscription for Mrs Wallace. I hope you will forgive this delinquency and I have just arranged for the March and July numbers to be sent to her.[2]

1–'Religion without Humanism'. Foerster responded on 23 Aug. that he had read TSE's essay 'with intense interest'.

2–Oliver had written on 3 May, 'I am glad to hear that you have settled your move, and I hope the fatigue and bother won't be too much for your wife and yourself.' He went on: 'Your last remark, that you think it would be a good thing to reduce the price to 5/- is *not*

I take it for granted that you are now in Scotland so am sending this letter to Edgerston. I should like very much to have news of you and hope that you are now in very good health.

About the reduction of the price which you mention in that letter. This point is by no means settled and is in any case for consideration a year or two hence and not at the present time. If and when the question of the reduction in price is raised seriously I shall of course consult you about it before any change is made.

With many apologies and all best wishes from my wife and myself to you and Mrs Oliver.

I am,
Yours sincerely,
[T. S. Eliot]

P.S. Our present address is 98 Clarence Gate Gardens, N.W.1.

TO *E. J. Dent* CC

16 August 1929   [London]

Dear Dent,

Thank you for your letter of the 7th of August which gave me pleasure and a great deal of exasperation.[1] We are very anxious that this book should be written and we are equally convinced that there is no one to do it except yourself and Trend. And as Trend refers to you and you refer to Trend we get no farther. But I feel quite hopeless about Trend as he is always so busy with one thing and another and editorial labours of love

---

my opinion. I don't think you will get any more readers at the lower price; but then not being a publisher, I haven't got any right to think at all on this subject.' He asked if TSE would please send a copy of the *Criterion* to his sister-in-law, Mrs William Wallace.

1–In reply to TSE's desire to commission from him a book on modern music, Dent had replied from a hotel on an Italian mountain: 'It is a book wh. in some ways wd interest me very much: but I could not afford to write a book of that sort unless it was a really super-first-class piece of work – otherwise it wd be mere journalism . . . and I want to keep clear of that now. I can visualize the sort of book you want . . . but it wd require a far more detailed knowledge of modern music than I possess or have time to acquire.'

After recommending (with reservations) Edwin Evans and M. D. Calvocoressi as 'the sort of people who cd write a *fairly* good book for you', he went on: 'At present I am wrestling with the life of Busoni and have retired to these mountains to be undisturbed. I shall get about half the book finished here: must go again to Berlin for more materials, and may with luck be able to write the rest in the course of the next six months.

'After that I may have to devote myself to translating Busoni's letters & miscellaneous writings – I hate translating books, but this is rather a matter of *pietas* . . . I dread writing your book for you . . .'

and other works for which he gets no recognition and which I think he is very foolish to do, that I have no hope of his doing anything else. We are therefore so anxious that you should take it on that we should be willing to wait for a long time if you will consider an approximate date. So will you please think it over once more and if there is any possibility of your tackling it after your Busoni work is done I could make a definite offer on behalf of my board of Directors.

At least please do not give a definite refusal now but if you cannot say yes wait until you return to England and let us make this question the excuse for lunch or dinner.

Yours sincerely,
[T. S. Eliot]

TO *Charles Maurras*   CC

16 août 1929   [London]

Cher monsieur et maître,

J'espère que vous m'accorderez une grande faveur en acceptant la dédicace d'un petit livre (pas plus grand que le votre) que j'ai sous presse, sur *Dante*. Si vous me donnez ce plaisir, je veux ajouter la citation suivante:

'La sensibilité, sauvée d'elle-même et conduite dans l'ordre, est devenue un principe de perfection.'[1]

1–TSE cited this sentence in his dedication to Maurras in the 1st edn of *Dante* (1929), without identifying his source in *Le conseil de Dante* (1928): ch. 2 ('Béatrice'), 54.

  Geoffrey Hill has deplored TSE's dedication and epigraph, writing in 2001: 'As an instance of Eliot's aestheticized – and aestheticizing – politics, consider the epigraph to his *Dante*, a sentence taken from *Le Conseil de Dante*, a (then) recently published book by Charles Maurras, the founder of *Action Française* to whom Eliot's monograph is dedicated: "La sensibilité, sauvée d'elle-meme et conduite dans l'ordre, est devenue un principe de perfection" (Sensibility, redeemed from itself and reduced to order, became a basis of perfection). These words assist our understanding of Eliot's *Ash-Wednesday*, but they do nothing to strengthen our grasp of the *Comedy*' ('Between Politics and Eternity', in *The Poets' Dante*, ed. Peter S. Hawkins and Rachel Jacoff [2001], 329). Christopher Ricks, in his Panizzi Lectures 2002, contested Hill's challenge: 'But when Eliot reprinted his *Dante*, in the only form in which he kept it in print, as section IV of his *Selected Essays*, he dropped the dedication and the epigraph. This is not to say that he thereby disclaimed (or, slightly different, could disclaim) the original commitment, but it might be judged to entail some modification of the charge against him, that in aestheticizing politics he does nothing to strengthen our grasp of Dante. (A charge that is in any case left as say-so [by Hill] and so does nothing to strengthen our grasp of exactly what is at issue.)' (*Decisions and Revisions in T. S. Eliot* [2003], 30.)

J'ai toujours eu le désir de vous dédier un volume, et j'ai choisi mon *Dante* pour deux raisons: mon admiration pour votre *Conseil de Dante*; et je juge mieux de choisir une oeuvre purement *littéraire*. Puisque je ne parle pas de politique, vous n'y trouverez rien de compromettant!

J'espère que vous ne me refuserez pas la permission de témoigner mon [*sc.* ma] gratitude et mon admiration.

Veuillez agréer, cher monsieur et maître, l'expression de mes sentiments dévoués.[1]

[T. S. Eliot][2]

TO *Christopher Dawson*[3]

TS Mrs Rivers Scott? [CC]

16 August 1929

Faber & Faber Ltd,
24 Russell Square

Dear Sir,[4]

I have recently read some of your work and have had it in my mind some little time to write to you to express my interest. But [I] have only been brought to the point at this moment by having had some conversation about you yesterday with Mr Algar Thorold and Father Burdett.[5] I wish

---

1 – Maurras replied on 18 Aug. that he was honoured and moved to be TSE's dedicatee.

2 – *Translation:* Dear Sir and Master, I hope you will grant me a great favour in accepting the dedication of a small book on Dante (no bigger than yours) that I have in press. If you give me this pleasure, I want to add the following quotation:

'Sensibility, saved from itself and brought into order, has become a principle of perfection.'

I have always had the desire to dedicate a book to you, and I have chosen my Dante for two reasons: my admiration for your Conseil de Dante; and I consider it best to choose a purely literary work. As I do not talk about politics, you won't find anything compromising in it!

I hope you will not refuse me permission to show my gratitude and admiration.

I am, dear Sir and Master, yours sincerely, [T. S. Eliot]

3 – Christopher Dawson (1889–1970), historian. See Christina Scott – daughter of Dawson – *An Historian and His World: A Life of Christopher Dawson 1889–1970* (1984); Bradley H. Birzer, *Sanctifying the World: The Augustinian Life and Mind of Christopher Dawson* (2007); James R. Lothian, *The Making and Unmaking of the English Catholic Intellectual Community, 1910–1950* (University of Notre Dame Press, 2009). See too Dawson, 'Mr T. S. Eliot and the Meaning of Culture', *The Month* NS 1: 3 (Mar. 1949), 151–7.

4 – This letter was quoted in full in Scott, *An Historian and His World*, 90–1.

5 – Thorold told Dawson on 15 Aug. 1929: 'I lunched yesterday with T. S. Eliot. He said such gratifying things about *The Dublin [Review]* that I felt quite embarrassed. I naturally think he is an extraordinarily intelligent man; you may find a further ground for his judgement (as I do also) in the fact that he is a great admirer of your work, particularly of *Progress and Religion* [1929]. He timidly asked if I should consider it an unfriendly act were he to ask you to write for the *Criterion* and remembering that in Spinoza's words: "it arises from no

merely to express my conviction that the *Criterion* ought to publish some essay by you and I should be very grateful if you would write to me and make some suggestion.

Also I should very much like to meet you at some time when you are in London.[1]

Yours very truly,
T. S. Eliot

TO *Stuart Gilbert*   CC

16 August 1929   [*The Criterion*]

Dear Sir,

We have been very favourably impressed with the parts which you have shown us of your book on Joyce's *Ulysses* and although we do not believe that it is likely to make money in view of the small number of people in England who have had an opportunity of reading Joyce's work, we yet feel that we should like to publish it. We propose a straight 10% royalty for the English-speaking book rights and on these terms would publish the book within about a year. We should be obliged to allow ourselves a certain liberty in choosing the moment of publication as the book would be one of a kind of series to be associated with the name of the *Criterion*. I do not mean the Criterion Miscellany of which you may have heard, but a number of full size books which we are building up around the periodical. Our proposal is made on the basis of the parts of the book which we have seen and we should of course have to see the complete work before we made a definite agreement. We have also been much influenced by the fact that Joyce approves of your interpretations and we should want to be sure of this same approval for the rest of the book.[2] But I do hope you will

---

accident, but from the nature itself of reason, that the highest good of man is common to all," I encouraged him to do so. I hope you won't make me jealous! I really thought Eliot particularly nice, though looking ill' (Scott, *An Historian and His World*, 90).

1–Scott has noted: 'This was the beginning of a long acquaintance – although the two men had so many intellectual interests in common, a certain lack of communication between them prevented a close friendship' (*ibid.*, 93).

2–This fact was conceded publicly by Gilbert not in the 1st edn of *James Joyce's Ulysses: A Study* (F&F, 1930) but in 'Preface to the 1952 edition', 10: 'it should be mentioned that in the course of writing this Study I read it out to Joyce, chapter by chapter, and that, though he allowed me the greatest latitude in the presentation of the facts and indeed encouraged me to treat the subject on whatever lines were most congenial to me, it contains nothing . . . to which he did not give his full approbation; indeed there are several passages which I directly owe to him' (Peregrine Books, 1963).

give me and my firm the pleasure of publishing what I feel to be a really valuable book.

Yours very truly
[T. S. Eliot]

TO *Ramon Fernandez*   CC

17 August 1929   [London]

My dear Fernandez,

Thank you very much for your essay on humanism, which I have read this morning with great interest and pleasure; and which was all the more welcome because I never expect you to fulfil your promises in the way of contributions to *The Criterion*! I shall translate it, or have it translated, for the December number. It is exciting, in that it gives new life to a debate which between Chesterton and myself on one side, and Babbitt and Foerster on the other, had come to an end. I think that it should be even more disturbing to the American Humanists, who are woefully unphilosophical, than it is to myself; though I shall have to sharpen my own wits to reply to it.

I hope that Routledge the publisher has sent you the copy of Richards's book which I asked them to send you. If not, let me know. And you must also tackle Murry's new book, which I shall ask to have sent to you, and which will be called simply 'God'.[1]

Yours always sincerely,
[T. S. Eliot]

1–In the event, TSE himself reviewed *God: being an Introduction to the Science of Metabiology* in C. 9 (Jan. 1930), 333–6.

TO *His Mother*   TS Houghton

17 August 1929   98 Clarence Gate Gardens, N.W.1

Dearest Mother,

I have not very much news since I wrote to you last. London is very quiet just now, with most people away, and very few visitors. Lawrence Smith rang up unexpectedly last night, and said he and his wife were here for just two days; we are going to ask them to tea tomorrow, but I wish people would give more notice, as it is not always easy to see them in the next day or two. I understand that Theodora is coming back from Cambridge, and we have asked her to spend a few days with us, but have not heard from her.

I suppose that Marion has been to Uncle Chris's and come back by now; and I am very glad if you have had Henry with you for a short time. We have had very warm weather most of the time. I have just finished correcting the proofs of my *Dante* book, which is just 70 pages long; so I ought to have a copy to send you in about a month.[1] And I have written an essay for a collection to be published as a book in New York, edited by Norman Foerster, I believe in the late autumn. I have been too busy to get developed the last photographs that we took of Chester Terrace; but I hope to get that done and sent to you by the end of this week.

Vivien sends much love, and we are always talking of you. Mrs Haigh-Wood and Maurice are well.

I will write again during the week.

Your devoted son,
Tom.

TO *F. McEachran*   CC

19 August 1929   [London]

Dear Mr McEachran,

I am sorry to have kept your essay on Tragedy so long without giving you a reply. I find it very interesting and should like, if I may, to keep it for publication, but I do not believe that I shall be able to get it into the December number and shall be more likely to use it in March. If,

---

1–On 28 Aug. 1929 TSE inscribed a copy of *Dante* for VHE, 'For Vivienne with love from her devoted husband'.

meanwhile, you have an opportunity of placing it elsewhere do not hesitate to let me know and I will surrender it, although with reluctance.[1]

Yours sincerely,

[T. S. Eliot]

TO *J. E. Pouterman*

cc

19 August 1929   [London]

Dear Sir,

I thank you for your letter of the 14th instant.[2] A length of 4000–5000 words would suit me very well and for an essay of that length I should want £25.0.0. on the delivery of the manuscript which I would let you have by the first of December and at an earlier date if possible. Will you let me know what you think of this proposal and if you are in accord I should be obliged if you could let me have copies of the French text and all the matter which you intend to include in your volume as I do not think I have any of it at present in my library.

Yours very truly,

[T. S. Eliot]

1 – 'Tragedy and History', C. 9 (July 30), 661–70, See too McEachran's 'The Roots of Tragedy', *The Bookman* 71: 2 (Apr.–May 1930), 129–37.
2 – Pouterman left it to TSE to decide the length of the introduction, but suggested 4,000–5,000 words.

TO *Stephen Spender*[1]   TS Northwestern

19 August 1929   *The Criterion*, 24 Russell Square

Dear Mr Spender,

I must apologise to you upon receiving your letter of the 14th August.[2] I was under the impression that I had already replied, but it just happened that two or three similar invitations came at the same time and had to be answered very hurriedly. I am extremely sorry for keeping you in suspense.

I am sorry that I have to decline any invitation to speak this year however attractive and on the other hand next year is too far ahead for me to be able to fix arrangements with confidence. I should very much like to meet your society and it would be a pleasure to have something to read that would interest them and I hope for a future opportunity.

With very many thanks and regrets,

Yours sincerely,

T. S. Eliot

1–Stephen Spender (1909–95), poet and critic, won a rapid reputation with his first collection *Poems* (F&F, 1933), following an appearance in Michael Roberts's anthology *New Signatures* (1931). Spender cultivated friendships with some of the foremost younger writers of the period, including W. H. Auden, Christopher Isherwood, John Lehmann, and J. R. Ackerley. For a brief while in the 1930s he joined the Communist party and went to Spain to serve the Republican cause. With Cyril Connolly he set up the magazine *Horizon* in 1940. In the post-war years he was to be a visiting professor at a number of American universities, and he made international trips on behalf of the British Society for Cultural Freedom, the Congress for Cultural Freedom, and PEN. He served too as poetry consultant to the Library of Congress, 1965–6. For fourteen years from 1953 he was co-editor of the magazine *Encounter*, which – as it was ultimately proven – was from the start the beneficiary of funding from the CIA (just as many writers including William Empson had long suspected). Spender's other works include *The Destructive Element* (1935), *Vienna* (1934), *Forward from Liberalism* (1937), *The Still Centre* (1939), *World within World* (autobiography, 1951), *The Creative Element* (1953), *Collected Poems* (1955), *The Struggle of the Modern* (1963), *Love-Hate Relations* (1974), *The Thirties and After* (1978), *Journals, 1939–83* (1985), *New Selected Journals 1939–1995*, ed. Laura Feigel and Jane Sutherland with Natasha Spender (2012), and the novels *The Backward Glance* (1940) and *The Temple* (1989). He was instrumental in setting up *Index on Censorship* in 1971, and worked for five years (1970–5) as Professor of English at University College, London. He was awarded the CBE (1962), elected a Companion of Literature by the Royal Society of Literature (1977), and knighted in 1983.

2–Spender wrote from Bad Homburg to enquire whether TSE might be available to address the Oxford University English Club (of which Spender was Hon. Sec.) in the autumn.

TO *Erich Alport*   CC

21 August 1929   *The Criterion*

Dear Mr Alport,

Thank you for your letter of the 12th of August.[1] I think that Curtius's suggestion is a very interesting one and I have read his essay with much pleasure.[2] Before replying definitely I think that I ought to write to Rychner as a matter of courtesy as he might want to devote his next Chronicle to the same subject and I will write to you again as soon as I have Rychner's reply.[3]

I had also thought, before I got your letter that Hofmannsthal's essay in question, of which he sent me a copy two years ago might possibly do for translation in *The Criterion* and I am asking one or two friends to look at it with that view. If they agree with me I shall want to find out where I should apply for the right to translate.[4]

With many thanks for your letter,

Yours sincerely
[T. S. Eliot]

TO *Algar Thorold*   CC

21 August 1929   [London]

My dear Thorold,

Thank you very much for your card. I will see if I can get the English translation of Lassky [*sic*] from the London Library.[5] And I should be

1–E. R. Curtius had asked Alport to suggest to TSE that his article on Hofmannsthal, in the Aug. issue of *Neue Schweizer Rundschau*, might be suitable for English readers.
2–Curtius published 'Hofmannsthal's deutsche Sendung' ('Hofmannsthal's German Mission'), *Neue Schweizer Rundschau* (Aug. 1929). See also Curtius, 'Hofmannsthal und die Romanität' ('Hofmannsthal and the Romance World'), *Die Neue Rundschau* (Nov. 1929). Both pieces are included in *Essays on European Literature* (*Kritische Essays zur europäischen Literatur*), trans. Michael Kowal (Princeton, 1973), 129–41.
3–Rychner's next 'German Chronicle' (C. 9 [July 1930], 710–17) was indeed devoted to Hofmannsthal.
4–No essay by Hofmannsthal appeared in C.
5–Nikolay Lossky (1870–1965), Russian philosopher. A proponent of Russian idealism, of spiritual and religious regeneration, he styled his philosophy 'intuitive-personalism'. After studying in Germany, he taught philosophy at the University of St Petersburg, but his criticisms of the Russian Revolution and his reversion to the Russian Orthodox Church caused him to be exiled in 1922. He became a professor at the Russian University of Prague; and, from 1947 to 1961, he taught Christian theology at Saint Vladimir's Orthodox Seminary in New York City. His last years were spent in France. His extensive writings include *Value*

very glad to borrow the French one from you at your convenience. But I should have very little time to read it at the moment and I should like to look forward to another lunch with you before very long when perhaps you could let me look at it.

I should like very much to come down to see you in the country but also I hope that we may lunch again one Wednesday before very long.

With many thanks,
Yours sincerely
[T. S. Eliot]

TO *James Burnham* CC

21 August 1929   [London]

Dear Mr Burnham,

Thank you for your letter of the 14th August.[1] I have thought over your suggestion and should like to be allowed to defer my decision a little while longer. I am not quite sure that I have anything to say at present about the idea of Progress, and if nothing occurs to me I shall probably ask you to accept my original suggestion. But you will hear from me again in a month or two.

With best wishes,
Yours sincerely,
[T. S. Eliot]

---

and Existence (1935) and *Sensuous, Intellectual and Mystical Intuition* (1941). The work that TSE mentions in this letter was *The World as an Organic Whole* (1917), translated from the Russian [1917] by Natalie A. Duddington (1928). Thorold was to review Henri Bergson's *Les Deux Sources de la morale et de la religion* and Lossky's *Freedom of Will* in C. 12 (1932), 124–31. Later, Thorold would translate *The Mystical Theology of the Eastern Church* (1957), by Lossky's son Vladimir Lossky.
1–'We are . . . grouping three or four articles in each issue [of *Symposium*] under a general heading. For the third issue, this will be "The Idea of Progress". Benda is definitely writing for it, probably Maritain, and perhaps Lindsay, the Master of Balliol. If you care to contribute to this "symposium", I should think it would work out nicely.' But TSE's suggestion, 'The Place of Belief in Poetry' would 'be quite as suitable – particularly since you mention it in connection with *Practical Criticism*, which we are reviewing at some length in an earlier issue; and since Richards is writing for the second issue'.

TO *Henry S. Canby*[1]   CC

22 August 1929   [London]

Dear Mr Canby,

Thank you for your letter of the 6th of August.[2] I was very sorry that you were snatched away from England just before our meeting but I am glad to hear that your wife's health is improving and hope that you may come again next year and bring her with you.

I should be very glad to let you have an article such as you asked for and will write again as soon as I can make one or two suggestions.

> With all best wishes,
> Yours sincerely
> [T. S. Eliot]

TO *William Force Stead*   TS Beinecke

22 August 1929   *The Criterion*

My dear Stead,

I am very glad to hear from you after this long interval although you say very little about yourself.[3] I had indeed been meaning to write for some time and ask how and where you were. I shall probably be in London pretty continuously for some time so do try to come up some day and meet me. I should very much like to have a talk with you and it is a long

---

1–Henry S. Canby (1878–1961): critic and editor. Having taught for over 20 years at Yale University, where he was the first professor to offer courses in American literature, and where he was assistant editor of the *Yale Review*, 1911–20, he was founder-editor of the Literary Review of the *New York Evening Post*, 1920–4, and co-founded and was the first editor of the *Saturday Review of Literature*, 1924–36. In 1926 he became Chair of the newly founded Book-of-the-Month Club. His publications include *Classic Americans: A Study of Eminent American Writers from Irving to Whitman* (1931), *Thoreau: A Biography* (1939), *Walt Whitman, an American: A Study in Biography* (1943), *American Memoir* (1947), and *Turn West, Turn East: Mark Twain and Henry James* (1951); and he was co-editor of the *Literary History of the United States* (1948).

2–Canby had been visiting London, but had had to rush home when his wife was taken 'critically' ill: happily, she had been recovering. He hoped TSE would write an article for *The Saturday Review* 'in or on criticism running from 3500 to 4000 words, and if it were philosophical in character and had a reference to the underlying spirit, as you see it, of modern literature either here [in the USA], or in England, or both, I should be the more particularly interested.' Payment for the American serial rights would be $100.

3–Stead sent (14 Aug.) a review by his colleague Vere Somerset: 'I do chiefly to oblige him, but also because – although obviously too long for your purposes – it contains some bright flashes. I wonder if you could select the best bits and make a short review of it?'

time since our last meeting. I am returning to you Somerset's review. I don't quite know what I should say to him about it, but of course it is quite impossible for *The Criterion*. For one thing there would be no particular point in our giving so much attention to Murray's novel and for another thing the way in which Somerset has mentioned myself would make his review impossible for *The Criterion*. There are, as you say, good flashes in it. Perhaps you could have a word with Somerset and give him some idea of what is suitable for *The Criterion* and what is not. He is an interesting man and ought to have something to say.[1]

I am afraid a visit to you is impossible at the moment, much as I should enjoy it. So (with many thanks) will you not try to run up to London one day?

Ever yours,
T. S. Eliot

TO *James Joyce*   TS Buffalo

22 August 1929   Faber & Faber Ltd

Dear Joyce,

I am enclosing an agreement for you about *Anna Livia Plurabelle*. Not being sure that I have your present Paris address I have left it to you to fill in. If this is all right will you complete it and let me have it back. I also enclose a specimen page in a type which would allow the whole thing to

1 – Stead responded to this letter on 25 Aug., apropos his colleague Somerset: 'I have bored you with another of Somerset's effusions – his diffusive effusions . . . [He] asked me and I could not refuse . . . I thought you might be able to select a few of his flashes and make a short and amusing notice of it. He bubbles with brilliance – the bubbles are all right, but their substance is soap and water – not wine. When I try to explain to him that he needs concentration, he cries excitedly – "Shut up! – don't be a damn fool!" etc. He is like some wild character in Headlong Hall or Nightmare Abbey. His talk *pours* out in a torrent but he never starts a sentence on one subject without flying off in the midst of it to something else and in the midst of that to something else. He reads five books at once – a serious work on history, some humorous short stories, a play, some memoirs, a book of poems – keeping them around him, before him, behind him, & under him – snatching at them by turns, and running to his piano to improvise a melody – suddenly as the melody develops, crying in anguish – "Good God! I've got these hellish examination papers to correct." He stops, looks mortified by his profanity, crosses himself devoutly to wipe out the stain of swearing, flops into a chair, and exclaims – "O Gosh, I feel all gugger! Oxford doesn't agree with me."

'After an evening in his room I feel quite *mentally* sea-sick – all shaken up by the tossing of his impetuous waves.

'But he has ability: he is brilliant and charming – would that I could save him from himself.'

be printed in 32 pages. 32 pages is a convenient form and would certainly allow us to publish the book at a shilling. We quite agree with you on the question of price and are anxious to keep it down to a shilling if possible but I do not know whether you will think this page too closely crowded. I shall get the opinion of the other directors on that point anyway but if you have any doubt yourself about this page I should suggest that you look in on Monday about noon and we will talk it over with de la Mare who is the Manager responsible for the printing.[1]

Yours ever,

T. S. Eliot

TO *H. J. C. Grierson*

TS National Library of Scotland

23 August 1929   *The Criterion*

Dear Grierson,

Many thanks for your kind letter of the 5th which I should have answered before.[2] I very much appreciate your hospitality and should enjoy a visit to you immensely; also I have never visited Edinburgh and live in hope of doing so. Although my wife is very much better I am afraid it will be impossible for me to leave London this summer and only hope that we may be able to take a holiday in the autumn. But thank you very much indeed; I hope I may be able to visit Edinburgh at some future time.

I have mentioned that matter to Herbert Read, putting it confidentially and making it clear that the suggestion came from you and perhaps a few of your colleagues privately and had nothing of the character of an official feeler.[3] I think he has lectured a little now and then and of course you know that he will be giving the Clark lectures at Cambridge this winter. That I think will be more experience than he has ever had before.

My Donne book has been postponed and during the past year I have been able to do but very little work upon it.[4] One thing after another has

1–TSE had lunch with JJ and Harold Monro on 28 Aug. (Dominic Hibberd, *Harold Monro: Poet of the New Age* (2001), 249).

2–'I wish you could find your way to Edinburgh some day & pay us a visit. As most of my family are now out in the world we have plenty of room, & if ever you wished a short holiday we shd be delighted to have you & Mrs Eliot also if she cared to come so far.'

3–'You are free to say to Mr Herbert Read what I said to you [about the possible Chair of Art at Edinburgh] so long as you let him know that it was just the thought of some of us individually. Does Mr Read lecture? It would be interesting if we could have a lecture from him in Edinburgh.'

4–'I wonder . . . when your "Metaphysical Poets" is to appear.'

come in the way and I don't suppose that I shall be able to settle to it again until the winter.

I hope that I shall have better fortune on your next visit to London.

Yours sincerely,
T. S. Eliot

TO *Max Rychner*   CC

23 August 1929   [London]

Dear Mr Rychner,

I understand from Mr Erich Alport that Curtius who is at present away from home has suggested that his essay on Hofmenstal [*sic*] might be published in *The Criterion*. I am reading the essay with great interest and with this in view. But before I make up my mind about it I should like to know whether you will wish to say much about *Hofmenstal* yourself when you give us another Chronicle. I think that your next Chronicle is due for March but we should be very glad to have one in December if you cared to send it. In that case would you wish to devote all of it to *Hofmenstal* or are there other matters which you would want to discuss as well?

One small point on which I think readers would like to be informed is the present vogue of war novels and war reminiscences in Germany. It has reached this country but we must admit that most of the best recent books of this kind here are translations from the German and we should like to know what the present attitude towards such books is in Germany.

With all best wishes,
Yours sincerely,
[T. S. Eliot]

TO *Orlo Williams*   CC

27 August 1929   [London]

Dear Williams,

I suppose I may take it as certain that you are [at] Newdigate,[1] or at any rate out of town, but I am sending this letter to Aubrey Walk.

1 – Williams lived at 'Simon's', Newdigate, Surrey.

(1) If you are in town, or if you come up to town, could we lunch on Wednesday or Thursday of next week? (2) Are you the author of the review of Toffanin in *The T.L.S.*?[1] and whether so or not, can you give me your private and confidential opinion as to whether he is worth translating for an English publisher? It so happens that he is authorised by Toffanin to translate his works (of which I had not then heard), and that two days after, another man wrote to say that he would like to write an article about Toffanin (Christopher Dawson the latter, one of the Rossetti family the former).[2] So I gather that Toffanin is rather a big gun, and his book (Che cosa . . .) looks interesting after 20 minutes given to it. So I should be grateful for anything you have to say about the man.

Please answer both questions.

Yours ever,
[T. S. Eliot]

TO *Christopher Dawson* CC

27 August 1929   [London]

Dear Mr Dawson,

I was afraid that my letter had not reached you, and am glad to get your reply of the 21st.[3] An article upon Berdaieff[4] and Toffanin would suit me exactly. I read Berdaieff's book in the Roseau d'Or collection, and enjoyed it; I have seen nothing else of his (I suppose that book was translated from German, and that you have read other works of his in German?) Toffanin I had never heard of a week ago; but three people mentioned him to me at once, and then the *Times* reviewed him; which seems a good omen. So please go ahead with it. 5000 to 6000 words is right, and we pay everyone the same, viz. £2 per 1000. I should like the essay for the March number,

---

1–The article on Giuseppe Toffanin (1891–1980), literary critic and scholar of humanism (Professor at the University of Naples from 1928) was in fact by Professor Foligno: 'The Renaissance' – on *Il Cinquecento* (Milan) and *Che cosa fu l'umanesimo: Il risorgimento dell'antichita classica nella coscienza degli italiani fra i tempi di Dante e la riforma* (Florence) – *TLS*, 22 Aug. 1929, 651. Toffanin's other publications include *La fine dell'umanesimo* (1920), *Che cosa fu l'umanesimo* (1929), *Storia dell'umanesimo* (3 vols, 1942–50), and *La fine del Logos: l'Umanesimo europeo* (1946).

2–Geoffrey W. Rossetti, Gonville & Caius College, had lent his copy of *Che cosa fu l'umanesimo* (Torino, 1920, 1929) to TSE.

3–Dawson had written from Yorkshire: 'Would you care for an article on the meaning of the Renaissance, dealing with Berdaieff & Toffanin's views?'

4–Nikolai Berdiayev (1874–1948), Russian philosopher and anti-authoritarian writer.

but should like to know the *title* soon, so as to advertise it with other contributions in December.[1] And please let us meet if, as you promise, you come to London in the autumn.

Yours very truly,
[T. S. Eliot]

TO *Stuart Gilbert*   cc

29 August 1929   [*The Criterion*]

Dear Sir,

Thank you for your letter of the 28th. I am very happy to know that you accept our offer. I am sure that Joyce also will be highly pleased to know that we are publishing your book, as we have arranged to produce an English edition of *Anna Livia Plurabelle*.[2]

We shall have an Agreement prepared and sent to you early next week, and will then write more fully. Meanwhile there is of course no objection to your mentioning the fact that we are to publish your book.[3]

Yours very truly,
[T. S. Eliot]
Director.

P.S. If you should be in England at any time I hope you will let me know, and if possible lunch with me.

TO *Viscount Brentford*[4]   cc

29 August 1929   [London]

Sir,

Having been very much interested by your article on the 'censorship' of books in *The Nineteenth Century* for August, I am taking the liberty

---

1 – 'The End of An Age', C. 9 (Apr. 1930), 386–401.
2 – 'As regards the English edition I had hopes that, if it were brought to public notice that my book contains so many quotations as to constitute practically an abridged version of *Ulysses*, the inaccessibility of the original in England would be actually a point in favour of my study . . . Mr Joyce himself will, I think, speak for the authenticity of my interpretation.'
3 – Gilbert was publishing 'The Aeolus Episode of Ulysses' in the next *Transition*, and wished to know whether he could mention that the book was to be brought out by F&F.
4 – William Joynson-Hicks (1865–1932), solicitor and Conservative politician. As Stanley Baldwin's Home Secretary, 1924–9, 'Jix' (as he became widely known) earned a reputation as a reactionary on account of his personal commitment in the banning of Radclyffe Hall's

of making a suggestion to you about it.[1] My firm is trying to fill what
we consider a real need in British publishing, by producing in more or
less uniform style, in paper binding and at low prices – preferably not
more than a shilling – essays and pamphlets by persons and on matters
of general interest which ought to be accessible to a wide public. The
suggestion I have to make occurred to me, on reading your article, because
we have just arranged to publish in this way an essay on Imperialism by
Mr H. G. Wells, which will be the expansion of a paper which he has
recently published in a periodical.[2]

If you would consider expanding your statement in *The Nineteenth
Century* into an essay of between 5000 and 15,000 words (the minimum
say 20 typewritten pages), it would be a document of the first importance,
which we should be proud to see in our *Miscellany*. I am sending to you
separately a copy of Mr H. M. Tomlinson's essay on *Cote d'Or*,[3] in the

---

The Well of Loneliness – though he would redeem himself in part with his strong support for
the Equal Franchise Act (1928); and he was passionately in favour of penal reform. He was
created Viscount Brentford in 1929. GCF wrote to H.W. Yoxall on 19 Oct. 1928: 'There is
one good point about "Jix" at any rate, and that is the handle which he gives to people who,
like myself, thoroughly dislike him.'

1–TSE was to write in his 'Commentary' (C. 9 [Oct. 1929], 1–3) that Lord Brentford's
article 'Censorship of Books', 'confirms the opinion that we have always held; that the late
Sir William Joynson-Hicks is a very honest, conscientious, public-spirited and bewildered
man . . . [His] defence of his action in the case of *The Well of Loneliness* is conducted against
those opponents whom it is easiest to attack; those who believe that the book is a "work
of art" . . . It is not a question of "art" but of public liberties. We should like to point out
to Lord Brentford that we did not consider *The Well of Loneliness* to be a work of art, but
merely a dull, badly written, hysterical book with an unpleasant strain of religiosity; and
that judging it thus we still insisted that it should have been allowed to circulate . . . He
admits that there *are* "pornographic productions" which even a Home Secretary can detect
without prompting! . . . But there are apparently other productions, in the case of which the
Home Secretary cannot move because he does not trust his own opinion, but only moves
because he takes the opinion of the penny press, or of any busybody who chooses to protest
. . . We fear that Lord Brentford, like many other people, has ceased to be a human being –
that is to say, has ceased to think independently – because he has been a Statesman . . . When
Lord Brentford . . . convinces us that he really knows what the words mean when he talks
glibly of books "debauching the young", or "corrupting", we may be inclined to give him
the attention that we would give to any serious undergraduate. Has he really spent much
time considering *how* the young are debauched, or *how* human souls are corrupted, and
how much *books* have to do with it? Has he, in his busy life, ever had time to think deeply
about the relation of art and morals, and morals and religion? Some men have found these
problems so difficult that they have had no time for anything else.'

2–Wells, *Imperialism and the Open Conspiracy* (1929); Criterion Miscellany no. 3.

3–GCF wrote to Dr E. F. Jacob (Christ Chuch, Oxford) on 4 July: 'Very many thanks for
your appreciative letter. Tomlinson shall be flattered by it. I am very interested in what you
say. Don't you think that any job needs to be hitched on to some sort of staff? I have always
supposed that the minute scientific researcher must be kept going by the idea that his work

proposed series, to show the general appearance; though the paper cover and other details are designed differently for each title.

I am putting this suggestion as briefly as possible, in order not to waste your time; but if it commends itself to you we should be very happy to arrange publication at the earliest possible moment.[1]

We have also been in correspondence with Lord Lloyd about a possible contribution from him.

I am, Sir,
Your obedient servant,
[T. S. Eliot]
Director.

TO *David Higham* CC

31 August 1929   [London]

Dear Higham,

Thank you for your letter of the 17th.[2] As the notion was put into my head by the Holliday Bookshop, I wrote to them to say that I would send them the copies of *The Listener*, and that if they then thought fit to pursue the matter, would they please communicate with you. But unfortunately I have not got round to sending the copies – I hope I shall have the energy next week. If the Holliday Bookshop declines, I will have copies typed and sent to you; though if they don't want the stuff I am not sanguine about its prospects.[3]

Yours sincerely,
[T. S. Eliot]

---

may fit in to something big and beneficent. For some people I suppose truth, with a capital T, is all the star their wagon needs. But truth very soon becomes merely learning, and it isn't a great distance from learning to pedantry. I am glad to think that there is one professor of History, at any rate, who won't go along that road.'

1 – See Viscount Brentford, *Do We Need a Censor?* (Criterion Miscellany, 1929).

2 – Higham wrote (17 Aug.) to suggest they follow up the *Listener* business.

3 – Higham replied on 5 Sept., 'If the Holliday Bookshop can't make any proposal, I think it possible that we might be able to interest someone else. I'd like to try, anyway.'

31 August 1929   *The Criterion*

Dear Mr Roditi,

Thank you very much for your letter of the 27th and your suggestions.[1] You are entirely right on the points you mentioned. What has happened is that Leger has now sent me back my first draft of the poem, with a great many corrections and suggestions, including those which you noticed yourself. So I have rewritten my translation with his alterations in front of me. For this reason I do not think I should accept your kind offer; for I have all I need to ensure approximate accuracy; and I do not want to go

---

1 – 'Dear Mr Eliot, It is now my turn to write an "impertinent letter". When I returned to Paris I read Anabase, my own translation and the fragment of yours which has already appeared in the *Criterion*. Of course I prefer yours – mine is very immature (I was only 16 when I began it); but I cannot help feeling that in one or two passages I am perhaps nearer to the original meaning of Leger.

'Thus "nous vaut ce ciel incorruptible" which you translate by "is more to us than this incorruptible sky" and I: "begets for us . . ."

'I believe that "nous vaut" here means: "grâce à cette terre sans amande *nous avons* ce ciel incorruptible" – which is a perfectly classical French use of the verb valoir.

'Again for "que savons nous du songe, notre aînesse" you have "what know we of the primogeniture of dreams?" and I: ". . . of dreams, our elder sisters".

'This last passage reminds me of the same theme in Eloges – that at dawn man is like a child beginning a new life; and of Eugenio d'Ors' theory of dreams and the sub-history. In other words that this passage translated into unpoetical French means: quand nous nous réveillons purs à l'aube nous ne nous souvenons plus de nos rêves, qui appartiennent à la sub-histoire, et sont notre passé inconscient – which also makes the comma after songe, very important.

'My own translation is useless to me – If you should care to refer to it or use it in any way – that is, if really I am not mistaken and my own interpretations are in certain cases more correct though not so well worded, I would be only too glad to find that my Anabase has been useful to you. As you understand, my own translation is, and cannot help being, very immature. At the moment I have not the time to rewrite it. In another two or three years, when I may find enough time, the inclination will be gone; so that my translation has but one hope of ever being useful to anyone outside of myself; that is that you should use it if you find it in any way profitable.

'I hope you will not find this letter impertinent. I can be impertinent to you, not you to me; it is a question of experience, critical and otherwise –

'I will be in London on Sept 18 19 20 – when I hope very sincerely to see you again and for a little longer, as if I manage to thaw my timidity, I have a lot to say to you.

'Yours very sincerely, Edouard Roditi'.

In an earlier letter ('Friday June 20th'), Roditi remarked: 'I have read your translation of Anabasis and am really most enthusiastic. I scarcely expected that such an accurate and poetic (according to English standards) translation would be possible. But when we meet again I will speak of the different details which I have noted as particularly interesting to me.'

On 16 June 1930 TSE would inscribe a copy of *Anabasis* to Roditi (UCLA).

further and pilfer from another translator. And perhaps in the end your translation will supersede mine.

I hope you will try to find me at my office when you return to London in September.

> With many thanks,
> Yours sincerely,
> T. S. Eliot

TO *Richard de La Mare*   MS Faber: internal memorandum

[?September 1929]

O my God! I forgot there would be 400 of 'em.[1] I am taking the lot home. If I get through an appreciable number by tomorrow or Friday I will ring up & get you to send a boy for them.

> T. S. E.

TO *Roy Campbell*   CC

2 September 1929   [London]

Dear Mr Campbell,

Thank you for your letter. I am ashamed to say, especially after talking to Mrs Campbell, that I have been forced to defer your two poems to the early spring. So if you want to publish them in the *Statesman*, do so; if you don't publish them meanwhile, I shall use them; if you do publish them meanwhile, then be sure to send me something else *before the end of the year*.[2]

I don't know anything about bullfighting but it does not seem kind to the bulls or to your public. But I have a terror of bulls and even of cows, and was brought up to be amiable to animals, so I am prejudiced. I hope you will recover quickly.[3] Who eats the bulls that are killed in this way? I am interested in the theories of the origin of the practice.

---

1 – Presumably entries to the 'Five Reviews' short story competition.
2 – Campbell reported (undated letter, late Aug.) that he had been hurt in a bullfight and needed some money urgently; and if TSE was not going to publish the last two poems – 'not much good' – that he had sent, he would like to submit them to the *New Statesman*. No poem by Campbell appeared in *C*.
3 – 'I managed to take the cockade off the bull which was 1200 frs but the judges were hostile and disqualified me for falling. So I had a lot of trouble for nothing and got my ribs hurt at the same time and my foot a bit crushed.'

Do send me something soon. Do you ever care to do any reviewing?

Yours cordially,

[T. S. Eliot]

TO *Alexis St Leger Leger*   TS Fondation Saint-John Perse

2 septembre 1929   *The Criterion*

Cher ami,

Since your revision of my translation makes evident that you know English much more intimately than I know French, and indeed puts me to shame, I shall write to you henceforward in this language.[1] I was

---

1–St-John Perse (24 Aug.) apologised for having been slow to return TSE's translation of *Anabase*, and went on to express his admiration for TSE's own recent poems, *The Hollow Men* (1925) and *Journey of the Magi* (1927): 'Plus que mon silence au sujet de votre admirable traduction, je me reproche d'avoir pu vous taire la joie que m'ont causée vos dernières poèmes, si pleins de choses exceptionnelles et vraiment authentiques, sous l'armure invisible de l'ellipse et le dédain de toute complaisance. (Ah! que j'aime, cher Ami, votre dégoût de plaire!) ... Une lettre de notre excellente amie, la Princesse Caetani, me fait part de vos intentions au sujet de la revision de votre manuscrit. Je veux que vous sachiez de moi-même que vous n'avez pas à me renvoyer votre traduction révisée, non même à vous astreindre en rien à mes indications. Je vous devais, avant tout, de vous faire exactement, et en faisant abstraction de tout souci littéraire, ce que j'avais voulu dire. Ceci fait, et sous réserve de quelques contre-sens à éviter, vous demeurez entièrement libre d'en prendre tout à votre aise avec les nécessités de transposition que comporte forcément toute traduction vivante – véritable récréation des qu'il s'agit d'y sauvegarder les mystères essentiels de l'incantation, c'est à dire la fois ceux de la suggestion verbale et de la suggestion intellectuelle. Je vous demande même instamment, quels que puissent être vos scrupules envers moi, de ne jamais perdre de vue cette obligation de liberté que je vous fais sincèrement. Quand on s'honore comme je le fais d'être traduit par un poète comme vous, c'est bien le moins qu'on veuille bénéficier de toute sa spontanéité' (Faber Archive; published in full in *Lettres atlantiques*, 37–9).

Translation: I blame myself – rather than for the silence on the subject of your admirable translation – for having been able to remain silent on the pleasure which your last poems have given me, so full of exceptional and really authentic things, under the invisible armour of the ellipsis and the disdain of all complacency. (Ah, how I love, dear friend, your aversion to pleasing!) ... A letter from our very kind friend Princess Caetani informs me of your intentions with regard to the revision of your manuscript. I want you to know it from me that you don't have to send me your revised translation, or to follow my instructions in any way. It was my duty, above all, to show you exactly what I had wanted to say by leaving aside any literary concern. With that done, and subject to some mistranslations to avoid, you remain entirely free to take liberties with the necessities of rearrangement which any living translation inevitably demands – a genuine reconstruction as soon as it becomes a matter of safeguarding in it the essential mysteries of incantation, that is to say, both those of verbal suggestion and of intellectual suggestion. I urge you, whatever your scruples towards me may be, never to lose sight of this obligation to freedom which I genuinely place upon you. When one is honoured as I am to be translated by a poet like yourself, one wants at the very least to benefit from all his spontaneity.

most happy to receive through Madame de Bassiano, your Agreement and the revision which I had awaited with so much impatience. I marvel first at the pains that you have taken, and more at the accuracy of your emendations. You will find that I have used *most* of your suggestions. Where I have not, it has been usually for some reason of rhythm, or for *compensation*: that is to say, trying to supply by a richness of association of the word in English in one place, a richness of the word in French in another place which could not there be conveyed. After all, a translation must be made globalement, by loading in one place to compensate for an impoverishment in another place!

I shall send you shortly a copy of my revision. If you have any alterations to make in that, and if you can let me have them by the end of this year, I shall use them and shall be glad of them. But if you have not time – and I imagine that you are now busier than ever, I dare say that you are at this moment in Geneva with Briand – then the copy you will receive will be printed in the spring.

It is clearly understood, is it not, that the rights of the text belong to you and not to Gallimard, and that *for this edition* we are to publish the French text opposite my paraphrase. Otherwise our book would lose much of its interest. And that on publication, my firm is to pay you £50.[1]

I have only one thing to say which *needs* your answer. As it was Madame de Bassiano who first brought me to study and admire your poem, and as she has acted from time to time as intermediary and intercessor, I should like, if you agree, to dedicate the *translation* to her as from *the author and the translator*.[2] But I cannot do this without your approval in writing.

As for the many charming things you say, I can only reply that I must wait until I can see you again before responding adequately. I hope that may be soon. And I must say that it has been a great pleasure to me to know and to translate your poem, which has indeed, in at least one or two places which I could point out, affected my own subsequent work.

Yours ever sincerely,
T. S. Eliot

1 – St-John Perse, who translated this letter by TSE for the 'Pléiade' edition (p. 1143), omitted the pre-penultimate paragraph: 'It is clearly understood . . . pay you £50'.
2 – When Colin Watson sought in a later year to update *The Times*'s obituary of St-John Perse, TSE responded to his enquiry on 2 Nov. 1960: 'I made his acquaintance first through the Duchess of Sermoneta, who was then Princess de Bassiano and who was in the 20s living at Versailles publishing a literary magazine called *Commerce*. The Duchess is still living . . . I never knew Monsieur Leger intimately, though after the war I frequently visited the United States and when in Washington always called to see him.'

TO *Viscount Brentford*

2 September 1929   [Faber & Faber Ltd.]

Dear Sir,

Thank you for your letter of the 30th.[1] I wrote to you from my private address, where I did not have a copy of Mr Tomlinson's essay; but have had my secretary send you one today. But, as I said, it can give you an idea only of the size, the kind of print and paper, and the price.

I know myself how difficult it is to expand anything once written, or to turn one kind of article into another. But I put 15,000 words only as the maximum possible for the type of publication we have in view; an essay of 5000 words would suit us very well. As for your suggestion to make your statement more inclusive, comprehending all forms of censorship, I welcome it most cordially; we are sure that it would add greatly to the public interest.

We have given a good deal of thought to the question of remuneration to authors for pamphlets in the *Miscellany*. We wish to keep the prices very low – with rare exceptions the price should be a shilling; and on a venture of this sort the margin of profit to the publisher is very small. Such a pamphlet has only paid the publisher his costs when about 3000 copies have been sold. We have therefore been obliged to offer all authors the same royalty – viz. ten per cent. If any issue sold less than 3000 copies, it would be a loss to us, though still, of course, of some profit to the author. And from the point at which it begins to pay the profits to author and publisher are about equal.

I ought to add, of course, that of such an essay as I have suggested to you, particularly if developed in the way that you have indicated, we should confidently expect a very large sale indeed. It should reach a large public which never reads anything in periodical form; and should make much more impression upon its readers than anything that they read in the daily press.

I have however two suggestions to make concerning remuneration. One is that we could, if you wish, engage to pay upon publication, the royalties

---

1–After thanking TSE for his letter, Lord Brentford went on: 'But you have not, as a matter of fact, sent me under separate cover the copy of Mr Tomlinson's essay [as TSE had stated in his letter of 29 Aug.].

'It is always a little difficult to expand an article, particularly as this one is only just over 2,000 words . . . I wonder whether you would care for me to make it on censorship generally, and to include pictures, films and theatres, in which case, however, it would take me a little longer, for, although I was in very close touch with the Lord Chamberlain in my late office, he, and not I, was the Censor.'

on the copies which had been 'subscribed' up to that date, instead of including them in the total royalties on sales at the end of the half-year. The other suggestion is, that as we treat merely for the right to include the essay in our series, I am sure that a publisher could easily be found for it in America. It would add appreciably to the monetary return, and if you cared to have us arrange the American publication for you, I am sure that we could be helpful.

I am,
Yours very truly,
[T. S. Eliot]
Director

TO *E. Geoffrey Curtis*   CC

2 September 1929   [London]

Dear Father Curtis,

It would be discourteous of me not to answer your kind letter as quickly as possible, though I have not yet had time to consider your poems carefully. So I shall hope to write to you again in a week or two.

Meanwhile I write to say that I have not made any engagement to visit Oxford during the autumn or winter, but should I do so I hope that it will be one that will enable me to make your acquaintance. I am too busy to undertake addressing undergraduate societies nowadays, but I might possibly invite myself for a weekend with Stead at Worcester. But as all this is vague, could we not arrange definitely for a meeting in London? Please let me know when it would be convenient for you to lunch with me.

Of course I did not know that it was you who had appealed to the Archbishop, and I do not even know what he said; I only heard casually some days later that [the sheet is torn] which prompted your act. Your approval is really disconcerting for it seems incongruous that anyone who has proceeded such a short distance in their spiritual life should have anything to offer to such as yourself.[1]

---

1 – E. Geoffrey Curtis, Vice-Principal of Dorchester Missionary College, Burcote, Abingdon – who was to 'join or rather demand admission to the Society of St John the Evangelist' the following May – wrote on St Augustine's Day (28 Aug.): 'I need hardly tell you how much I loved *For Lancelot Andrewes*. I was responsible for the Archbishop of York's onslaught on the Times Litt. Sup's review. I sent him the review with an insistent appeal to act. Perhaps you heard how he did so in his S.C.M. broadcast speech?'

The anonymous review in question (written by Alan Clutton-Brock) – 'Mr Eliot's New Essays', *TLS* (6 Dec. 1928), 953 – observed: 'It is now some years since it was first suggested by an acute critic that Mr Eliot would find it possible to reconcile his principles with his practice only "by an act of violence, by joining the Catholic Church". A drawing near to Anglo-Catholicism is the step his new book announces ... More and more one finds Mr Eliot expressing controversial sentiments which he makes little or no effort to support ... In the essay on Bradley ... [he] denies the ability of the individual to stand alone; destroy communion with God, he asserts, and the most enlightened humanism can yield only disappointment. All these issues are brought to a head in the final essay, which is in purpose a questioning of Mr Babbitt's philosophy of secular humanism from the viewpoint of one accepting a religion of revelation and dogma. Can such humanism, he asks, ever provide an alternative to Christianity – save perhaps temporarily and on a basis of Christian culture? Is not the humanist, suppressing the divine, "left with a human element which may quickly descend again to the animal"? Has humanism ever achieved more than a sporadic accompaniment to a continuous Christianity? Can it, in short, be more than parasitical, secondary to religion? ... The characteristic modern refusal to receive anything upon an authority exterior and anterior to the individual he rejects decisively ... The essay in its parts and as a whole leads "to the conclusion that the humanistic point of view is auxiliary to and dependent upon the religious point of view. For us, religion is of course Christianity; and Christianity implies, I think, the conception of the Church."

'Here, certainly, is nothing new, but from the author of *The Waste Land* it is at first sight astonishing, to say the least. We ourselves can only conceive of Mr Eliot's "act of violence" as consequent upon a dynamic fusion of the need for an object of belief with the desire – the increasing desire – for a universal and continuous rather than a living tradition. He has discovered at once a respite and a continuity. But it is our view that by accepting a higher spiritual authority based not upon the deepest personal experience (for that we must still turn to the poems), but upon the anterior and exterior authority of revealed religion, he has abdicated from his high position. Specifically he rejects modernism for medievalism. But most of us, like Mr Babbitt, have gone too far to draw back. It is to the country beyond the Waste Land that we are compelled to look, and many will consider it the emptier that they are not likely to find Mr Eliot there. Recently he recorded his conviction that Dante's poetry represents a saner attitude towards "the mystery of life" than Shakespeare's. Not a saner, we would say, but simply a different attitude, and to the majority, the great majority, to-day no longer a vital one.'

Dr William Temple, in his greatly lauded address, 'The Dedication of the Mind' – given at the Quadrennial Conference of the Student Christian Movement in Liverpool, 2–7 Jan. 1929 – remarked: 'One branch of art is so widely influential as to call for special mention. Literature is in these days a factor of incalculable importance. We have reached a stage where the pundits of literature regard the acceptance of any specific revelation as a confession of weakness. The review of Mr T. S. Eliot's last volume of essays in *The Times Literary Supplement* is a symptom, perhaps a portent. The reviewer holds that a gulf is now fixed between Mr Eliot and himself because Mr Eliot accepts the Christian revelation. To base himself on that instead of on "the deepest personal experience" is held to be an abdication. Now that argues a definite deification of pride or self-centredness. Whether or not a revelation has been given is open to dispute; but if it has in fact been given, how can it be the mark of inferior genius to accept it? It cannot be wrong to be right! Why should not a man's acceptance of, and response to, a Divine self-revelation in a Person be as deep a personal experience as his response to the Divine Self-Revelation in Nature or in History generally?

I have just re-read your letter and find that you have included an invitation to stay at the College. I should enjoy that very much: I at present 'owe' weekend visits to several hospitable friends, but perhaps when I have worked these off I may be allowed to remind you?

With many thanks,

Yours very truly,

[T. S. Eliot]

TO *Erich Alport*

2 September 1929   [*The Criterion*]

Dear Mr Alport,

Thank you for your letter of the 30th. Since writing to you I have heard from Rychner that he intended to write about Hofmannsthal in his Chronicle in the December *Criterion*, so I think that it would be difficult

---

For all experience is a response to something. And the aesthetic quality of a literary work does not depend on the extent to which the artist received his material from without, for there is and can be none which he does not so receive; it depends on the extent to which in receiving it he has really made it his own. Our great need is writers of artistic gifts who will seek to make their own the Christian revelation, and then set it before us recreated by the vividness of their experience. But that very vividness of experience is a snare, for it ministers to self-importance and to an unwillingness to accept the spiritual discipline of seeking to appropriate what at first may seem remote. Hence, as I suppose, springs the attitude of mind which takes it for granted that an artist has abdicated his lofty claim because he has found truth where saints and sages also found it before him' (*The Purpose of God in the Life of the World* [London: Student Christian Movement, 1929], 199–200).

See TSE's letter to William Temple, Archbishop of York, 3 Oct. 1929, below.

TSE was to remark in *Thoughts After Lambeth* (1931), 10–11: 'One of the most deadening influences upon the Church in the past, ever since the eighteenth century, was its acceptance, by the upper, upper middle and aspiring classes, as a political necessity and as a requirement of respectability. There are signs that the situation to-day is quite different. When, for instance, I brought out a small book of essays, several years ago, called *For Lancelot Andrewes*, the anonymous reviewer in the *Times Literary Supplement* made it the occasion for what I can only describe as a flattering obituary notice. In words of great seriousness and manifest sincerity, he pointed out that I had suddenly arrested my progress – whither he had supposed me to be moving, I do not know – and that to his distress I was unmistakably making off in the wrong direction. Somehow I had failed, and had admitted my failure; if not a lost leader, at least a lost sheep; what is more, I was a kind of traitor; and of those who were to find their way to the promised land beyond the waste one might drop a tear at my absence from the roll-call of the new saints. I suppose that the curiosity of this point of view will be apparent only to a few people. But its appearance in what is not only the best but the most respected and most respectable of our literary periodicals, came home to me as a hopeful sign of the times. For it meant that the orthodox faith of England is at last relieved from its burden of respectability.' TSE told his brother on 28 Apr. 1936 that he had 'no grievance' against Alan Clutton-Brock.

to use Curtius's essay.[1] Particularly as Rychner mentions it and says he will quote from it. You understand that I like our regular chroniclers always to have as free a hand as possible.

If you are writing to Curtius, I wish you would reinforce my request, which I am writing to him, that he should let the *Criterion* have something else from him for the March number. We have had nothing from him for a long time.

Do you know Hofmannsthal's work at all well? On second thoughts, the essay I mentioned, remarkable and beautifully written as it is, does not seem to me quite the best thing for an audience which knows his work none too well; especially as it was an address of primarily local application. I should welcome suggestions.

With many thanks,
Yours sincerely,
[T. S. Eliot]

TO *P. Mansell Jones*[2] CC

2 September 1929 [London]

Dear Mr Jones,

I apologise for my delay, and am hurrying to get off to you these letters to Benda, Maurras and Maritain.[3] Let me know if you get them, and of

1 – 'To the Memory of Hofmannsthal', *Essays on European Literature* (*Kritische Essays zur europäischen Literatur*), trans. Michael Kowal (Princeton, 1973), 129–41.

2 – P. Mansell Jones (1889–1968), educated at University College, Cardiff, and Balliol College, Oxford, was teaching at the University College of South Wales and Monmouthshire, Cardiff; he was later Professor of Modern French Literature, University of Manchester, 1951–6. His works include *Tradition and Barbarism* (F&F, 1930), *French Introspectives* (1937), *Background of Modern French Poetry* (1951), *Baudelaire* (1951), and the *Oxford Book of French Verse* (ed., 1957).

Geoffrey Faber had written to Jones on 21 June 1929: 'Mr Eliot and I have both read the manuscript of your book on Tradition and Barbarism. We think it could form an admirable introduction to the conflict of critical opinion in France, and we should certainly like to publish it. But we would rather not do so this year. It is our intention to issue from time to time books by authors or on topics connected with the *Criterion*; and your book would be one of these . . . At present it seems as if the spring of 1930 would be the best moment to choose . . .

'I should be inclined to suggest myself that the final essay on "French Romanticism: A Tradition of Descent", should not be included. It doesn't appear to me to be quite in the same vein as the rest of the book . . . The other two essays "Romantic Degeneration" and "A Critic of Contemporary France" fit on to the earlier part of the book more closely. It is possible that Mr Eliot, who is at present away, may have different views on this point.'

3 – Jones had written on 24 Aug. to remind TSE that he had promised to provide introductions for him in Paris, which he was due to visit for two weeks from 3 Sept.

any other people you want to meet. Shall I see you on your return?

Yours sincerely,

[T. S. Eliot]

TO *Julien Benda*[1]   CC

2 September 1929   [London]

Monsieur,

Je me donne la permission de vous présenter, par cette lettre, Professor P. M. Jones de l'université de South Wales. Il a en train un livre que nous publierons ici, sur les mouvements intellectuels en France, dans lequel il parle beaucoup de vous; et vous me feriez une faveur personnelle en lui accordant quelques minutes.[2]

Je m'aperçois que votre bel article (quoique contestable!) dans l'*N.R.F.* paraît aussi dans *The Realist*. Quand me donnerez-vous quelque chose pour le *Criterion* – n'oubliez pas que nous avons Belphégor sous presse.

Recevez, cher monsieur, l'assurance de mes sentiments cordiaux.

[T. S. Eliot][3]

TO *Jacques Maritain*[4]   CC

2 September 1929   [London]

Cher Monsieur,

Je donne cette lettre à Monsieur P. M. Jones, professeur à l'université de South Wales, actuellement à Paris. Monsieur Jones s'intéresse aux

1–Julien Benda (1867–1956), journalist, philosopher: see Biographical Register
2–Benda agreed on 10 Sept. – 'bien volontiers' – to be interviewed by Jones.
3–*Translation*: Sir, I take the permission to introduce to you, through this letter, Professor P. M. Jones of the University of South Wales. He is working on a book which we will publish here, on the intellectual movements in France, in which he talks much about you; and you would do me a personal favour in granting him a few minutes.

I notice that your fine article (albeit disputable!) in the *NRF* is printed also in *The Realist*. When will you give me something for the *Criterion* – don't forget that we have Belphégor in preparation.

Please believe me, dear Sir, yours faithfully, [T. S. Eliot]
4–Jacques Maritain (1882–1973), philosopher and littérateur. At first a disciple of Bergson, he revoked that allegiance (*L'Evolutionnisme de M. Bergson*, 1911; *La Philosophie bergsonienne*, 1914), and became a Roman Catholic and foremost exponent of Neo-Thomism. For a while in the 1920s he was associated with *Action Française*, but the connection ended in 1926. His works include *Art et scholastique* (1920); *Saint Thomas*

mouvements intellectuels en France, sur lesquels il a en train un livre que nous allons éditer; et je lui souhait le Bonheur de vous faire la connaissance.

J'ai beaucoup causé de vous dernièrement chez M. Algar Thorold.

Recevez, cher monsieur, l'assurance de mon amitié et de ma sympathie fidèles.

[T. S. Eliot][1]

to *Charles Maurras* CC

2 September 1929 [London]

Cher monsieur et maître,

Cette lettre vous sera rendue par Monsieur P. M. Jones, de l'université de North Wales; et j'espère vivement que vous pourrez le recevoir. Il est en train de préparer un livre sur la situation actuelle sur l'intelligence en France, dans laquelle il s'occupe beaucoup de votre pensée; et il peut parler avec plus d'autorité si vous lui accordez quelques minutes. Je m'y intéresse parce que nous éditerons le volume.

Je ne puis pas vous exprimer le plaisir que m'a donné votre gracieuse lettre.

Toujours en sympathie et admiration
[T. S. Eliot][2]

---

d'Aquin apôtre des temps modernes (1923); *Réflexions sur l'intelligence* (1924); *Trois Réformateurs* (1925); *Frontière de la poésie* (1926); *Primauté du spirituel* (1927).

1 – *Translation*: Dear Sir, I give this letter to Mr P. M. Jones, Professor at the University of South Wales, who is currently in Paris. Mr Jones is interested in the intellectual movements in France, on which he is preparing a book that we are going to publish, and I wish him the good fortune of meeting you.

I have talked a lot about you recently at Mr Algar Thorold's.

Please believe me, dear Sir, yours faithfully, [T. S. Eliot]

2 – *Translation*: Dear Sir and Master, This letter will be handed to you by Mr P. M. Jones of the University of North [correctly South] Wales; I hope very much that you'll be able to see him. He is in the process of preparing a book on the current state of intelligence in France, in which he deals much with your thought; and he can talk with more authority if you grant him a few minutes. I am interested in it because we are going to publish the volume.

I cannot tell you the pleasure that your kind letter has given me.

With sympathy and admiration, [T. S. Eliot]

TO *J. M. Robertson*   CC

3 September 1929   [*The Criterion*]

My dear Robertson,

If you are in town and if your invective against Dover Wilson is ready
I should be very glad to have it so that it could be set up at once.

Yours ever sincerely,
[T. S. Eliot]

TO *W. H. Auden*   CC

3 September 1929   [*The Criterion*]

Dear Auden,

I shall be very glad to see you.[1] Could you possibly call for me here for
lunch about one o'clock on Thursday next?

Yours sincerely,
[T. S. Eliot]

TO *Bonamy Dobrée*   TS Brotherton

3 September 1929   *The Criterion*

My dear Bonamy,

This letter is on one subject only and is purely a matter of business.
For some time past Herbert has been anxious to get rid of the American
periodicals for notice at the end of *The Criterion*. He has only gone on
with it because there did not seem to be anyone else about who could deal
with them properly, but I should like to relieve him of the burden for he
has certainly been overworked in other ways for a long time past. He and
I thought that if you would care to take them on you could do them better
than anyone else. You will be aware that a lively sense of humour is one of
the most important qualifications for such a task. Please understand that
you can deal with them in any way that seems to you good, even the most
capricious and irresponsible: read what you like, ignore what you like
and say what you like. If you will accept it will be a great relief to both
Herbert and myself, and living in the country as you do you will be able
to dispose of the periodicals in the form of bonfires.

1–Auden invited TSE (2 Sept.) to have 'lunch or dinner' with him 'any day this week'.

Yours in haste,
Tom

P.S. We are bringing out *Belphégor* on the 15th and are sending you a copy. That is to say I should be glad if you would mention the book to anybody, and it occurred to me that you might possibly care to apply for it to *The Nation* or some other paper.

TO *Theodore Spencer*   TS Harvard

4 September 1929   *The Criterion*

Dear Mr Spencer,

I am very sorry that you are sailing so soon and all the more sorry that I have seen nothing of you this summer.[1] I am afraid that both Monday and Tuesday are bad days, but could you not lunch with me (and John Hayward whom you know) on Wednesday? If you are leaving before then, do try to come in to this office about noon on Monday or Tuesday and see me once more.

Yours always sincerely,
T. S. Eliot

TO *T. O. Beachcroft*   CC

4 September 1929   [London]

Dear Beachcroft,

I am writing to say that I have been forced to postpone 'Traherne' until December. It turned out to be much longer than I expected, and at the same time another contribution which I was obliged to publish in the October number was much longer than I had expected it to be. So I hope you will not mind the delay, for which I am sorry.[2]

Will you not turn up at the Grove again before long? I shall probably be there myself this Thursday.

Yours ever,
[T. S. Eliot]

1 – Spencer, who was visiting London (though soon to depart), had written on 2 Sept.
2 – 'Traherne, and the Doctrine of Felicity', C. 9 (Jan. 1930), 291–307.

TO *Charles Mauron*[1]   CC

4 septembre 1929   [London]

Cher monsieur,

Je vous écris pour vous faire mes excuses. Seulement parce que j'ai tenu
à traduire moi-même votre article, et parce que j'ai été très affairé ces
derniers mois, la traduction n'est pas encore faite, et ne sera prête que
pour le numéro de décembre. Je vous prie d'accepter mes expressions de
regret et d'amitié. Je préparerai la traduction aussitôt que possible.

[T. S. Eliot][2]

TO *Felix Morrow*[3]   CC

4 September 1929   [London]

Dear Mr Morrow,

I like very much the essay[4] which you sent me with your letter of the
15th August, and have only two serious objections, as editor. One is that I
want henceforth to keep out of *The Criterion* references to myself; and the
other is that I think I have already unloaded on the British public about
all the stuff about Babbitt–More that it will stand from one periodical.

1–Charles Mauron (1899–1966), French critic and translator, trained as a chemist but
suffered from impaired eyesight. Author of *The Nature of Beauty in Art and Literature*,
trans. Roger Fry (1927), he translated into French VW's *To the Lighthouse* and *Orlando*,
and collaborated with Fry on translations from Mallarmé. Later works include *Aesthetics
and Psychology* (1935) and *Des métaphores obsédantes au mythe personnel* (1962).
2–*Translation*: Dear Sir, I am writing to give you my apologies. The translation has not
been done yet, and will only be ready for the December issue, only because I wanted to
translate your article myself, and because I have been very busy these past few months.
Please accept my expressions of regret and friendship. I will prepare the translation as soon
as possible. [T. S. Eliot]
3–Felix Morrow (1906–88) – born Felix Mayrowitz – was brought up in an Orthodox
Jewish family in New York City and worked from the age of 16 for the *Brooklyn Daily
Times* and the *Brooklyn Daily Eagle*. After graduating from New York University, he went
on to Graduate School at Columbia University, studying religion in association with the
Philosophy Department. It was at the time of this exchange (when he was working for
The Menorah Journal in Brooklyn) that he changed his surname. In 1931 he joined the
Communist Party, going on to write for *The New Masses* and *The Daily Worker*; he was to
become a prominent figure in the Trotskyist movement, joining the Communist League of
America in 1933; and he edited *The Militant*, the newspaper of the Socialist Workers Party.
After WW2, when he grew alienated from Communism, he worked as head of the Causeway
Books publishing house. See also Alan W. Wald, 'The Menorah Group Moves Left', *Jewish
Social Studies* 38: 3 /4 (Summer/Fall 1976), 289–320.
4–Morrow's essay was about Paul Elmer More.

I quite agree with you that only the surface has been scratched and that the debate must now be generalised; but so far as the *Criterion* is concerned, I want to see that done without reference by name to Babbitt or More or Foerster or Chesterton or myself. I am not returning your essay herewith, because, if I get your permission, I should like to try to get Middleton Murry to publish it in *The Adelphi*. Will you let me know, and perhaps send me something else?[1]

Yours sincerely,
[T. S. Eliot]

Vivien Eliot TO *Mary Hutchinson* MS Texas

Friday, 6 September 1929 98 Clarence Gate Gardens, Regent's Park, N.W.1
Paddington 6930

Dear Mary,

How it pleased me to get a letter from you. And such a letter, & from such a place. Fishbourne, of all places, for I like it best of all. Better than Bosham, or Itchenor or Birdham or even Wittering. I think it is a *very* peculiarly wonderful place. And you did *not* give me the impression that it is completely spoiled.

It quite upset Tom & me to think of you there, & we immediately want to know if you have *taken* this house you are in, or have you only got it temporarily? And we want just as badly to know if you intend to make it a place to go backwards & forwards to again? And *is* there a small vacant workman's cottage?!! *Is there*? This is serious. I am *sorry* about Mrs Fricky. You know how you always said she was a clever woman, & a success. And she was pretty. And of course the other one is congratulating herself now! I think it is very very sad.

Well, here are we. We are in a bad state. We have never been away at all. The summer has seemed like 2 *long hot* summers, never ending. You last saw us at 57 Chester Terrace. And I believe we were congratulating ourselves on moving to a flat. Did I tell you I had never seen the flat? I left it to Tom to choose it. Very stupid & unfair of me. Well my dear it is a most terrible flat. It is quite awful. It is *enormous*. And very *very* expensive. And hideous. And the most terrible uproar of great buildings going up all around it. Hammer hammer hammer. Cranes – drills. etc.

---

1 – Morrow was pleased (18 Sept.) to accept TSE's offer to pass his essay on to JMM. He wrote again on 27 Jan. 1930 to ask whether JMM had expressed any interest in it.

So after nearly 3 months pining we are going to move again if we can *only* get it off our hands.

When are you coming back. Please let me know directly, & then come & see for yourself. We have discovered a really exquisite little house, & if all goes well, we shall take it.

Meanwhile Tom has learned (again) to drive a car. He has done a lot of work, & finished those poems that he read to you – at last. They have gone to America. And also we have had his niece staying with us. I will tell you all about that, & her, when I see you.

I have rather dreaded Barbara,[1] but you must tell her not to be unkind to me, & that you & I must go on being friends. Will you? Now please write soon. Tom sends love.

Yrs.
Vivienne

I *love* your notepaper.

TO *The Manager, District Bank* CC

10 September 1929 98 Clarence Gate Gardens,
Regent's Park N.W.1

Dear Sir,
Securities: Estate of C.H. Haigh-Wood Decd.

I enclose herewith form of Armstrong-Whitworth reorganisation, signed by myself and Mrs R. E. Haigh Wood as Executors and Trustees, and request that you will kindly do the needful with the £300 6½% 2nd Mtge. Deb. Stock which you hold to our account.

Mr M. H. Haigh-Wood, the other Trustee, is at present abroad on holiday, but as I observe that the signature of one holder is sufficient in the case of joint holdings, I take it that his signature is unnecessary.

Kindly acknowledge receipt.

Thanking you for your trouble,
Yours faithfully,
[T. S. Eliot]

1–Barbara Hutchinson (b. 1911), only daughter of Mary and St John Hutchinson.

Vivien Eliot TO *Mary Hutchinson*   MS Texas

Tuesday, 10 September 1929   98 Clarence Gate Gardens, Regent's
                                  Park, N.W.1

Dear Mary,

I wrote, & *answered* your letter last Friday – 6th. Did you get my letter?
I want you to write to me, please.

I told you most of the news.

But now I am just writing to tell you that Tom has had a cable this
afternoon, to say that his Mother is dead. Will you write to him. And
Jack too.

I fear for Tom, at this time.[1]

> With love,
> Vivienne

TO *John Hayward*   MS King's

Wednesday [11 September 1929]   Faber & Faber Ltd

My dear Hayward

If it would interest you – James Joyce is coming in to see me tomorrow
morning, & I might persuade him to lunch with us. I owe *you* a lunch or
two already, which I will return, I trust, every week or two.

But ring up Russell Sq. in the morning to say – otherwise I come alone.
If yes, you lunch with me alone, next week perhaps.

I was sorry not to lunch with you & Spencer, who is a nice fellow – but
Whibley is a very great friend, & I see him seldom now, & I felt I must
lunch with him today.

> Yours ever,
> T. S. Eliot

1–Seymour Jones writes: 'In her later diary [Vivien] remembered it as an agonising time for
Tom, who had not had a chance to see [his mother] Charlotte again since abandoning both
his Unitarian faith and his American nationality' (*Painted Shadow*, 463; citing VHE's diary,
Oct. 1934: Bodleian).

TO *Mary Hutchinson*   MS Texas

15 September 1929   98 Clarence Gate Gardens, N.W.1

My dear Mary,

Your letter touched & pleased me very much. You are a person who can always be depended upon, and your friendship is something that both Vivien and I are very proud of.

It is good to know that you will be in town again tomorrow. We should like to see you. This has been a very difficult summer here and we are tired out.

With much love & gratitude, & please give my love to Jack.

Tom.

TO *Stuart Gilbert*   CC

18 September 1929   [London]

Dear Mr Gilbert,

Thank you very much for your letter of the 9th;[1] for several reasons I have been rather dilatory about correspondence lately, and I apologise for not having sent you your contract sooner. As I am writing this at home, and cannot find a big envelope, I will send the contract on to you tomorrow. Don't bother about a stamp; we can do that when you return it.

About the time of publication – I put it some time ahead, to be on the safe side, but we really should like to be able to publish in the Spring: the idea being to bring out a shilling edition of *Anna Livia Plurabelle* (which I am backing heavily) a few weeks afterwards. Therefore I hope that you can let us have your complete text *in January*, and that you will have the opportunity to go through it with Joyce first. Personally, I am convinced that it will be a good book; but it will be an advantage to us to say that it has all been approved by Joyce.[2]

1–Gilbert, who had yet to write studies of three of the eighteen episodes of *Ulysses*, and to revise other parts, hoped he might be in a position to deliver the full TS in Jan. 1930.
2–See the F&F Catalogue announcement, Spring 1930, presumably written by TSE: 'The situation of James Joyce's masterpiece *Ulysses* is unique in literary history. Of all modern novels it is undoubtedly the most famous and the most influential; most competent judges also consider it the greatest. Yet it is not permitted to enter this country; and even those who are able to read it are not always able to understand it.

'Mr Gilbert's book serves a double purpose. He quotes copiously from *Ulysses*, and his quotations are knit together by a lucid exposition of the whole novel. It is therefore not merely the only substitute for the masterpiece itself, which is available to English readers; it is also the only guide and commentary to it.

One other point: we have only stipulated for the English-speaking rights. But Joyce suggested that very likely his German publishers would like to translate your book, and possibly it might be wanted in other languages too. If you care to leave the matter to us, we should be very glad to act as your literary agents, on an ordinary commission basis, for translation rights; but perhaps you would prefer to deal with foreign publishers yourself. But I should be glad to hear from you on this point.

And if you ever visit your native country, remember that there are other persons, as well as myself, who will be eager to meet you and drink a glass of port with you. May I not even urge you to pay a visit to England? London is very large, and there are some very intelligent people in it.

Sincerely yours,

[T. S. Eliot]

TO *R. B. Braithwaite*   CC

18 September 1929   [London]

Dear Braithwaite,

I am answering your letter of the 10th addressed to Frank Morley. He doesn't know you, and I do – if you remember a weekend on which I drank all your whisky on Saturday night, and astonished you by going to Communion the next morning. Your reply to the 'tempting suggestion' (sic) does not seem to me final.[1] What you call 'entirely negative' is exactly what we had in mind: and I don't see how such an enquiry could be any more than negative. In fact, its whole point is that it *should* be negative. What Morley and I had in mind was just a critical examination of the new *religious physics* of W. and E. The tendency seems to be towards believing

---

'*Ulysses* is enormously long; it embodies an immense erudition, and employs a profound and difficult method of allegorical symbolism. Even therefore if the original were published in England, Mr Gilbert's exposition would be valuable. As things are, it is invaluable.

'The present volume has been written under Mr Joyce's own supervision, and may therefore be regarded as an authoritative interpretation.'

1 – Braithwaite wrote: 'Thank you very much for your letter of the 30th August suggesting that I should write a booklet for the *Criterion Miscellany* on *Sentimental Physics*. It is a tempting suggestion; but I think that I must decline. What I should have to say would be entirely negative (critical of such writers as Whitehead & Eddington) and I don't feel it important enough to popularise a purely negative position to be prepared to write the booklet you suggest . . . It was very kind of Herbert Read to think of me . . .'

that physics is religion and that religion is physical, and the essay we had in mind could be only sceptical and destructive.

So perhaps will you reconsider? I feel myself that sometimes, and certainly here, it *is* important to broadcast a 'purely negative position'. For the actual tendencies seem to [*typing runs off the page*].

Another point. I have been wanting to get you into the *Criterion* for a long time. Would you consider writing for us (I would send you the books) a review of Jeans, telling us exactly what Jeans is worth (compared to Whitehead and Eddington) to the general public? I cannot think of anyone whom I should prefer to do this, and I should be very happy if you would consent.[1]

Yours sincerely,
[T. S. Eliot]

TO *Harold Monro*   CC

18 September 1929   [London]

My dear Harold,

I had forgotten that I had promised to give a reading of my poems, but if I did, I will do it.[2] But I had rather, if you will, arrange it for early next spring. For one thing I shall then be able to release a little new stuff; and for the other, my mother died a week ago, and I am not very eager to appear in public during the rest of this year. I want to be of any use I can, but could you put me into your spring programme instead of this autumn? And I shall want then to discuss the selections with you.

Ever yours,
[T. S. E.]

1–Braithwaite did not write for C.
2–Monro reminded TSE (13 Sept.) that he had agreed to give a reading at the Bookshop: 'I am diffident about writing. I have gathered more or less that you don't dislike reading them aloud and so I endeavour to ride rough shod over my own diffidence.'

TO *J. Ralph Pinker*[1]   cc

18 September 1929   [London]

Dear Mr Pinker,

I must apologise for the delay in answering your letter of the 11th instant.[2] I quite understood from Mr Joyce that all payments should be made to you, and I asked him to let us have his written authority to that effect. I forgot to remind him of this when I saw him last, and I think he has now returned to Paris. I should be very much obliged if you would write to ask him to send me such a letter of authority.

I see that this forthcoming publication has already been spoken of in *T.P.'s Weekly.*

Yours sincerely,
[T. S. Eliot]

TO *A. H. Cooke*   cc

18 September 1929   [London]

Dear Sir,

I have your letter of the 14th instant.[3] Forgive me for saying (1) I don't have anything to do with publishers who will publish poetry if you pay for it: WAIT till you can get some other publisher to publish at his own risk. (2) One can *write* poetry worth publishing at the age of nineteen, but one mustn't expect to get it published. At nineteen, I wrote some verse worth publishing, but I did not get anyone to publish it until I was twenty-eight.

---

1 – (James) Ralph Pinker (1900–59) was a partner, with his brother Eric (b. 1892) in James B. Pinker & Sons, Literary, Dramatic and Film Agents – founded by their father James Brand Pinker (1863–1922) – representing authors including John Galsworthy, H. G. Wells, Henry James, Jack London, Arnold Bennett, Joseph Conrad, and James Joyce.
2 – 'I have received a copy of your agreement with Mr James Joyce for a portion of his *Anna Livia Plurabelle*. I am not quite sure whether Mr Joyce made it clear that he wished you to account for this book to me, but if you like I will ask him to write you a note . . .'
3 – 'I am endeavouring to have published a volume of poems, of which I am the author, and a Publisher has offered to deal with them for £26. Since I earn a mere clerical wage, being nearly nineteen, this initial expense is quite beyond me, and I am wondering if you would be sufficiently interested in my work to help me . . . May I send you a few of my poems? – I am confident that you will not consider them unworthy of your aid.'

Go on with your present job, and better it if you can. Don't publish anything. And send me some of your poems.

Yours faithfully
[T. S. Eliot]

TO *Stuart Gilbert*   CC

3 October 1929   [*The Criterion*]

Dear Mr Gilbert,

I have given very careful thought to your letter of the 25th September, and have discussed it with my fellow directors, whom I find to be in agreement with me about the matter.[1] We should like to meet you in every way possible, because we should like to be associated with, and have some honour for, the publication of such a book. I must say however, frankly, that I do not see any possibility of our offering better terms. We do not expect, even on these terms, to make money out of your book; we rather expect to lose; and we counted merely on the American edition partially to recoup our losses.

If we gave the same royalty on the American sheets as we give on the English sale, we should profit nothing, and should be actually at a loss on account of the office expenses and trouble involved. The terms we offer are those usual – both in the case of [*line missing*] when publishers ask for English-speaking rights.

It may be impertinent, but I cannot help saying that the terms we offer you, for American publication, are the terms which I have always accepted myself, as an author.

If you feel that you could get better terms elsewhere, we should not wish to stand in your way in the least. Possibly the Incorporated Society of Authors (which one ought to join) could advise you about it. But we should very much regret the loss of your book. And I should regret it personally, because of my friendship and admiration for Joyce, and because, at my suggestion, we are publishing *Anna Livia Plurabelle* in the spring; and because we had hoped, and Joyce had desired, that your book might appear shortly before.

1–Gilbert wished to negotiate better terms than those offered by F&F, including a 10% royalty to himself on American sheets. 'I should have preferred to reserve the American rights, but recognize, of course, the position of Messrs Faber & Faber in the matter.'

I hope you will let me know quickly exactly what you think. And in any case I must remind you of your promise to visit London in the spring so that we may have a lunch or dinner together.[1]

Yours sincerely,
[T. S. Eliot]
Director.

TO *C. A. Siepmann*   TS BBC Caversham

3 October 1929   *The Criterion*

Dear Mr Siepmann,

I am sorry that I have delayed answering your letter,[2] but I have been occupied in moving again. And I have had no time for lunching. I wonder if one day, say Thursday, of next week, would be possible for you? I should be very glad to lunch with you, and hope that we can find a day for it.

Meanwhile it would help me to know whether what you have in mind – or what my hint suggested to you – is talks on some poets and poetry of the past – an historical set, or talks on modern or contemporary poetry. The latter would be much more difficult to do for your audience – if one is not to be cheap on the one hand or too technical on the other. I should really prefer the former: especially if it might be Elizabethan or seventeenth century. But that is one important point to discuss.

Hoping to see you next week,

Yours sincerely,
T. S. Eliot

1–Gilbert meant to visit London when he finished his book: 'till then I observe a self-denying ordinance; seventeen years' experience of writing "judgments" tends to "cramp one's style" and I find myself too often writing of Mr Bloom as if he were one of my Burmese murderers! Hence the need for thorough revision of much that I have written.'
2–Siepmann (BBC, Savoy Hill, London) wrote on 25 Sept. in the hope of discussing with TSE the idea of a 'project of a series on Poetry if you were ready to undertake this'.

TO *John Middleton Murry*   TS Northwestern

3 October 1929   *The Criterion*

My dear John,

I rather stupidly did not acknowledge your letter and proof, because I was moving, and because I took it that you would be away. Since then I have been very busy; my mother has died; we have moved again, and are now at 177, Clarence Gate Gardens N.W.1.[1]

I suppose that you are back now. Your book I have read twice, and must write about: it is, I think, much more important than the *Life of Jesus*, and will take all my strength to answer. Of course I believe you to be wrong (as far as the word 'wrong' has meaning); but I think you have made a good job of it, and you have given me something much more difficult to demolish than any constructions of Babbitt or Russell. So you have done what you meant to do. Anyway, the book does clarify the issues: and that will be the chief point of anything I say about it.[2]

Ever affectionately,
Tom

TO *Marguerite Caetani*   CC

3 October 1929   [London]

Dear Marguerite,

Very many thanks for your kind and sympathetic letter. But had I thought that my intervention would be of any use with Coward, I should

1–The Eliots had moved house on 1 Oct. 1929.
2–JMM had sent a proof copy of his *God: being an Introduction to the Science of Metabiology* on 11 Aug.: 'Though it's a rather queer affair, it's the only thing I've managed to say which I care about very much. You can damn it to hell, of course – I don't mind what you do, so long as you meet it fairly – because, as you know, rather more blood & sweat than I care to think about are decocted into it.' TSE reviewed it in *C.* 9 (Jan. 1930), 333–6: 'From my point of view, the book has . . . a very important merit: though Mr Murry seems to me in the end to offer only a variation of biological naturalism, yet he has seen far more clearly than others the real issue; the choice that one must make, the fact that you must either take the whole of revealed religion or none of it.' JMM responded to this letter from TSE on 6 Oct.: 'I am glad that you think I have "made a good job" of it. To me it is important, as making something which I *feel* to be a final liberation, or disintoxication. But whether it is important to anybody else, I don't know; and probably it doesn't matter except to the animal J.M.M. who has his living to earn.'

gladly have done anything possible; it merely seemed to me pointless to try to introduce to each other two people neither of whom I knew.[1]

It seems quite certain, as far as I can see, that *Anabase* will appear in the spring. The poem I sent you of my own is one of a set of six (including 'Perch' Io non Spero' from *Commerce*) which is to be brought out in a limited edition by Faber & Faber and the Fountain Press of New York; but I think it extremely unlikely that the book will be printed before the new year, so it should not affect *Commerce*.

I am discussing with Menasce the possibility of a small book of selected poems in translation to appear in Paris; and I should prefer all the translations to be by him; so I am sure he will do this one.[2]

I will make enquiries about *Wolf Solent*.[3] I saw Aldous Huxley a few days ago and he will probably write or telephone to you. His address is 3 rue du Bac, *Suresnes*. We like his wife very much too.

I have not forgotten the Sterne of Kassner, but of course if I came across anything else by him equally good I might use that instead.[4] But Rychner is doing Hofmannsthal for December, and I have had to turn down one essay on Hofmannsthal already by Curtius for that reason.

I am glad to hear that the Roman villa is getting forward, though I shall be sorry to think of [you] settling still farther away than Paris. But we shall expect you in London in the spring. How is Camillo getting on preparing for Oxford with his tutor?

We are nearly settled in our new flat – much smaller than the last, and rather cramped, but cheaper, quieter, and big enough for us.

Vivienne sends love.

Yours ever affectionately,
[Tom]

1 – Caetani had written ('Tuesday'): 'I am so very sorry to hear of the death of your mother and I wish I had known of it and not written that stupid letter about indifferent things at such a time. Let us say no more of Noel Coward! I quite understand and if I had reflected for half a minute I might have known.'
2 – 'Som de l'escalina', trans. Jean de Menasce, *Commerce*, 21 (Autumn 1929), 99–103.
3 – 'The next time you write please tell me what you think of *Wolf Solent* [the novel by John Cowper Powys (1872–1963)] and if he would be for *Commerce*.'
4 – 'Are you ever going to bring out the Sterne of Kassner? You wouldn't like a fine article he has written on Hofmannsthal . . . [?]'

TO *F. J. Yealy*   CC

3 October 1929   [London]

Dear Father Yealy,

Although I am at the moment buried in arrears of correspondence, I must write to you immediately to say how warmly I appreciate your kind note of sympathy.[1] It is all the more welcome in coming from Missouri – where I was born – and where my mother and father are buried, in Bellefontaine Cemetery at St Louis.

I do not feel that we are strangers, because we nearly met, and because (I do not think it need be a secret) I had the pleasure of reading your interesting dissertation on Emerson for Trinity College. Therefore I look forward with interest to reading your next printed work.

                                        With grateful thanks, I am,
                                        Yours sincerely,
                                        [T. S. Eliot]

TO *The Archbishop of York*[2]   CC

3 October 1929   [London]

My dear Archbishop,

I must apologise for some delay in answering your kind and gracious letter of the 28th, as I have been moving house.[3] It would give me the greatest of pleasure to meet you. You are very kind to suggest my coming to Bishopsthorpe, but I shall be very busy in London for the next month or so, and therefore look forward to meeting you first, as you suggest, when you are here in November.

---

1 – Yealy wrote from St Stanislaus Seminary, Florrisant, Missouri, on 12 Sept. to commiserate with TSE on the death of his mother – 'and, although I can claim no more personal acquaintance with you than could come from exchanging three or four letters with you when I was at Cambridge a few years ago, I feel that this should not keep me from offering you my sincere and respectful sympathy in your bereavement.'

2 – William Temple (1881–1944) – son of Frederick Temple (1821–1902), Archbishop of Canterbury – taught Classics at Oxford University; was ordained in 1908; served as Headmaster of Repton School, Derbyshire, 1910–14; and was Bishop of Manchester until translated in 1929 to the Archbishopric of York. After thirteen years at York, in 1942 he became Archbishop of Canterbury. His writings include *Christus Veritas* (1924), *Nature, Man and God* (1934), *Readings in St John's Gospel* (1939, 1940), and *Christianity and Social Order* (1942). In the 1920s he won authority as a leader of the movement for international ecumenism – 'this world-wide Christian fellowship,' as he proclaimed it.

3 – Dr Temple – 'with apologies for obtruding myself on you' – wished to meet TSE.

I must take the opportunity of thanking you for your generous defense of my small book.[1] Unfortunately I did not hear or see it, else I should have written at the time to thank you. The attitude of the *Times* reviewer is typical of a large number of literary people.[2]

I shall remember that you are to be in London during the second or third week of November, and earnestly hope that I may hear from you then and come to see you.

[T. S. Eliot]

TO *Mario Praz* TS Galleria Nationale d'Arte Moderna, Rome

5 October 1929 Faber & Faber Ltd

Dear Praz,

I am sorry that I could not write in time to catch you in Florence. I shall be at my office on Tuesday and Wednesday mornings, and shall be very glad if you can call. We will discuss the Scholartis, and also, if you please, your Donne & Crashaw.[3]

Yours ever,
T. S. Eliot

TO *Sacheverell Sitwell*[4] CC

5 October 1929 [*The Criterion*]

Dear Sachie,

I am sending you a copy of my essay on Dante (with my respects) and a copy of Vita Nicolson's *Marvell* in a series of essays called 'The Poets

---

1 – *The Student Movement* 31: 5 (Feb. 1929), 99, reported: 'His address on the last morning of the conference probably did more than any other address that was delivered to help the younger members as to how to make their own some of the spiritual experience of the gathering.'

2 – See TSE's letter to the Revd E. Geoffrey Curtis, 2 Sept. 1929, above.

3 – Praz wrote on 22 Sept. that he had prepared an anthology of Italian sonnets, with an introduction, for publication by Scholartis Press; but he no longer trusted the management (Partridge) and expected the outfit to fail; he wondered if F&F might be interested in publishing the volume. TSE had thought to include an adapted version of Praz's *Secentismo e Marinismo in Inghilterra* in the series 'The Poets on the Poets'.

4 – Sacheverell Sitwell (1897–1988): writer, poet and art critic; the youngest of the Sitwell trio. TSE thought him the 'most important and difficult poet' in the anthology *Wheels* (1918). Reviewing *The People's Palace*, he praised its 'distinguished aridity', and said he 'attributed more' to Sacheverell Sitwell than to any poet of his generation (*Egoist* 5: 6, June/

on the Poets' which we have started, and which is my own invention.[1] The chief motive is to induce you, if possible, to contribute an essay to the series yourself: the subject we had in mind for you is Shelley; but it is part of the programme that the poets writing should choose their own subjects; so if there is another poet on whom you would prefer to write I should like you to say so. But I am sure that a great many people would be keenly interested to read you on Shelley.

You will see from the back of the wrappers that the term 'poet' is a wide one; but I venture to think that the two essays I am sending would not disgrace you as company.

[May] the *Criterion* publish some section of *The Gothick North* before it all is published in book form? Do answer this too.[2]

We have had a very trying summer, as we have had to move twice, but I believe are now settled for some time at 177, Clarence Gate Gardens. Will you be in London at all this winter? We hope to see you, and to meet your wife at last.

Yours ever,
[Tom]

TO *Charles Williams* CC

5 October 1929   [*The Criterion*]

Dear Mr Williams,

Very many thanks for your letter of the 26th ultimo. Of course I have no objection to the American *Bookman* reprinting my address:[3] as it is a reprint, I should charge only ten guineas. Will you let them know, or should I? But if you have any intention of publishing the whole volume

---

July 1918). But it was as an idiosyncratic writer of books about travel, art, and literature, including *Southern Baroque Art* (1924), that Sitwell came to be best known.

1 – Vita Sackville-West wrote to TSE on 13 June 1929, 'I am delighted to hear that you are godfathering Marvell.'

On 1 Nov. 1929 GCF wrote to Gilbert Murray to invite him to contribute an essay on Homer to 'The Poets on the Poets': 'Eliot's essay indicates the type of approach which best suits the object of the series – that is to say, not a resumé of scholarship, so much as a mode of appreciation. *Dante* has stimulated me to have another go at the Comedy. Mightn't *Homer* do the same?' And on 7 Nov.: 'In spite of what you say, we would very much rather you wrote about Homer than about Aeschylus, for the purely commercial reason that the former would "draw" much better than the latter.'

2 – No extract from Sitwell's book appeared in *C*.

3 – 'Experiment in Criticism', *The Bookman* 90: 3 (Nov. 1929), 225–33.

in America, I don't want to interfere with its success by having my part appear separately.

I am very glad to hear that you have a book of verse coming out, particularly as I much enjoyed your Shakespeare.[1] I imagine that your 'controller' as you style him thought your poem more frivolous than it appears to me.[2] But it seems to me rather a poem to be printed with others, than by itself to represent the author; and as I am choked with verse for the next nine months, I must return it to you. But I shall look forward [*typing runs off the page*] this was (unjustly) rejected.

> [Sincerely yours
> T. S. Eliot]

TO *Charles Du Bos*   MS Texas

5 October 1929   *The Criterion*

My dear Du Bos,

I am sending you the current *Criterion*, with a review of you by Gordon George.[3]

At the same time we have had to consider the question of publishing a translation of your *Byron*,[4] which your agents have brought us. We hesitated a good deal, because it is a book (and your name) which we should like to have on our list. But unfortunately the Byron market has had a good many books in the last few years, and still more unfortunately Maurois is producing a Byron in the spring, in English. I see no reason to believe that his *Byron* will be any more important than his Shelley but Maurois has a great vogue here among the semi-literate, and we felt that the appearance of his book would limit your audience here to people who like to think – and one always loses money by publishing books which concern only those readers who like to think.[5]

---

1 – *A Myth of Shakespeare* (play in verse, 1928).
2 – Williams explained that he was publishing a volume of poems with a private press, but one of the poems had been set aside by 'the controller'; the *London Mercury* had also rejected the poem, though CW thought it '*not* a bad poem'. Might it be suitable for C.?
3 – Robert Sencourt, untitled review of Charles du Bos, *Byron et Le Dialogue avec André Gide*, and E. C. Mayne, *Life of Lady Byron*, C. 9 (Oct. 1929), 122–7.
4 – *Byron et le Besoin de la Fatalité*. In Aug. 1937 TSE donated his copy of Du Bos's *Byron* to the Eliot House Library at Harvard University; now in Houghton.
5 – GCF wrote separately to Messrs Curtis Brown, literary agents, on 3 Oct.: 'We have no doubt whatever of the excellence of the book; but we feel that it is a book for a somewhat limited public mostly well able to read it in French. In spite of the comparative success of

I am writing to say however that we should very much like [to] have you as an author with Faber & Faber. And that if you do ever write that book on Walter Pater, I feel no doubt that we should jump at it.

I have not yet read your Gide;[1] but may I say how very much I have enjoyed the Extraits d'un Journal?

With all best wishes – and the strong appeal to you to visit London, where many people will be anxious to see you,

I am,

Yours very sincerely,

T. S. Eliot

TO *Max Clauss*   CC

5 octobre 1929   [London]

Cher monsieur et confrère,

Je vous remercie vivement de votre lettre du 30 pp. [sc, 30 Sept.], qui m'expose très clairement la situation. Naturellement, j'apporte mon appui à la décision unanime des trois membres allemands – MM. Mann, Curtius et vous-même – et je mettrai le manuscrit immédiatement dans les mains d'un traducteur qualifié.

Si, par hasard, la décision n'est pas ratifié par un autre membre étranger, de sorte que le prix ne peux pas être décerné, je vous prie de me télégraphier, afin que je puisse arrêter la publication, qui devrait être pour le fin de décembre.

En outre, je trouve le conte très émouvant et d'un intérêt sérieux. Je propose comme titre ou *The Centurion* ou *A Prussian Centurion*.[2]

J'ai reçu une lettre de Simon & Schuster, maison d'éditions à New York, qui voudraient bien publier dans un volume réunis les cinq contes – allemand, anglais, français, italien, espagnol. Je vais leur répondre que le sujet ne peut pas encore être mis en discussion, vu que les cinq prix ne seront décernés que dans l'espace de cinq ans. Mais je n'ai aucun doute, si nous réussissons à aboutir, que nous pouvons bien arranger la publication simultanée du volume dans les cinq pays.

---

the recent life of Lady Byron we do not think that the interest of Byron at the present day is sufficiently strong to justify us in taking the risk of publishing Monsieur du Bos's book . . . Moreover we believe a study of Byron by [André] Maurois is shortly to appear; and this will probably monopolise all the available interest.'

1 – *Le Dialogue avec André Gide* (1929).

2 – Ernest Wiechert, 'The Centurion', trans. Marjorie Gabain, C. 9 (Jan. 1930), 185–200.

Je ne crois pas que je puisse me présenter à Paris pour votre réunion; mais, le cas échéant, je vous désignerai un remplaçant.

Recevez, cher monsieur, l'expression de mes sentiments cordiaux et fraternels.

[T. S. Eliot][1]

TO *Ursula Roberts*   cc

5 October 1929   [London]

Dear Mrs Roberts,

Thank you for your letter of the 1st instant. It is true that I rather rashly and zealously offered to speak during the autumn for the St George's Renovation Fund.[2] I don't wish to go back on my promise; but in order to make it easier for me, I should be grateful if you would give me some notion (1) of the kind of subject suitable and (2) of the kind of audience you expect. (1) really depends on (2). Will it be parishioners, or people interested in literature, or interested in something; or will it be prosperous snobs whose half-guineas we are to extract for a good purpose? Perhaps it would help me if I knew who are the other speakers, and what they are to talk about. You see, it is rather important to me to be able to prepare something that I could use later in some other way.

I will make suggestions for a chairman, if ne- [*typing runs off the page*] November would I think suit me as well as any day.

Yours sincerely,
[T. S. Eliot]

---

1 – *Translation*: Dear Sir and Colleague, Thank you very much for your letter of the 30th, which explains the situation very clearly. Of course I support the unanimous decision of the German members – Messrs Mann, Curtius and yourself – and I will put the manuscript immediately in the hands of a qualified translator.

If, by any chance, the decision is not ratified by another foreign member, so that the prize cannot be awarded, I ask you to send me a telegram, so that I can stop the publication, which should be at the end of December.

Moreover, I find the story very moving and of serious interest. I propose either 'The Centurion' or 'A Prussian Centurion' as a title.

I received a letter from Simon & Schuster, publishers in New York, who would like to collect the five stories in one volume – German, English, French, Italian, Spanish. I am going to reply that the subject cannot be discussed yet, in view of the fact that the five prizes will be awarded in the space of five years. But, if we manage to succeed, I have no doubt that we can arrange the simultaneous publication of the volume in the five countries.

I do not think that I will be able to go to Paris for your meeting, but, if need be, I will appoint a replacement. Please believe me, dear Sir, yours faithfully, [T. S. Eliot]

2 – TSE was to speak at the Children's Theatre, Endell Street, London.

TO *Geoffrey Rossetti*   TS Mary Rossetti Rutterford

5 October 1929   *The Criterion*

Dear Mr Rossetti,

Toffanin has been much in my mind, but I have been so busy, both with public and private business, that I have not got very far with him yet. I appreciate your forbearance and patience. I should like a couple of weeks longer to read and discuss: although I feel that if the Oxford Press will do the book, and probably others of his works, we ought not to stand in the way. If I come to [the] opinion that it is an Oxford Press book, I shall do everything I can to forward Foligno's design.[1]

I hope that you are feeling very well,[2] and hope to see you during the year, either, or both, in Cambridge and London.

> Yours sincerely
> T. S. Eliot
> Director

TO *Jean de Menasce*   CC

5 October 1929   [London]

My dear Menasce,

I have been delayed in answering your letter, as I have been occupied with moving.[3] I must say that with no doubt I much prefer to have such a book of selected poems appear in the series of Fumet than with publishers whom I do not know, so I shall decline the other proposal.

What I should like, if possible, would be a selection made by you and myself, and all of the translations to be by you, instead of using the few other translations – Adrienne Monnier's Prufrock, Germain's Preludes, and Leger's Hollow Men, which have already been made.[4] Would you be

---

1–Rossetti told TSE on 14 Sept. that Professor Foligno had been in touch with Oxford University Press and seemed to think that they would publish a translation of Toffanin.
2–Rossetti had regretted in his letter: 'I very much regret that when I called on you I was in a somewhat overstrung state of nerves, and hope my behaviour was not extraordinary.'
3–Menasce pressed TSE on 16 Sept. to contribute a selection of his poems to a series of 'short works of literary excellence' to be edited by his friend Stanislas Fumet.
4–'La chanson d'amour de J. Alfred Prufrock', trans. Sylvia Beach and Adrienne Monnier, *Le Navire d'Argent* I (1 June 1925), 23–9; 'Préludes' (a translation by André Germain of 'Préludes' and 'Morning at the Window'), *Écrits Nouveaux* 9 (Apr. 1922), 32–3; 'Poème' (a translation by St-John Perse of a poem later published as Part I of 'The Hollow Men': English text and French 'adaptation' on facing pages), *Commerce* 3 (Winter 1924/25), 9–11.

prepared to do this? If so, let us begin making a list. I should rather like to include several of my later poems – the Magi,[1] the Simeon,[2] possibly Animula,[3] which I shall send you shortly, and the set of six which includes Perch' Io non Spero and the one which Madame de Bassiano will have sent you (I have just given her your new address). This set will appear in English for the first time early next year.[4]

Let me know. And I should like to hear more about your own activities and plans, and what you are writing and studying. Is it true that you are contemplating entering an order?

Yours ever sincerely,
[T. S. Eliot]

TO *Erich Alport*   TS Richard Buckle

5 October 1929   *The Criterion*

Dear Dr Alport,

Thank you for your two letters which I have not yet answered. About Hofmannsthal I shall have to think: I have long had the idea myself of trying to translate one of his Jacobean plays into more or less Jacobean English;[5] but I don't know when I could get that done. Meanwhile Rychner is writing about him for December.[6]

About Scheler, I hope to retain that option until December 1st. I am getting hold of copies of those two essays from a friend in England and will write to you again about them. I am personally very keen on publishing Scheler. Am I to understand that Mrs Scheler has in mind to sell the rights of all her husband's works together to one English publisher? I believe there is just a possibility of popularising (to some extent) Scheler in England; perhaps not to the extent of Spengler and Keyserling, because Scheler is (to my mind) so much more important a writer.[7]

You will hear from me again about it in a week or two. Faber is back, and I believe he has written to you.

Yours very sincerely,
T. S. Eliot

1 – *Journey of the Magi* (1927).
2 – *A Song for Simeon* (1928).
3 – *Animula* (1929)
4 – *Ash-Wednesday* (1930).
5 – TSE had in mind Hofmannsthal's *Sobeidens Hochzeit* and *Die Damme am Fenster*.
6 – Rychner, 'German Chronicle' (C. 9 [July 1930], 710–17).
7 – No essay by Scheler appeared in C.

TO *John Hayward*   MS King's

7 October 1929   177 Clarence Gate Gardens, N.W.1

My dear Hayward

This is to try to tell you how much pleasure your letter gave me.[1] It is the first opinion I have had. I cannot take it as indicative of what the world will think – you know me too well to be at all representative of that – but at all events, what you say seems to indicate that the book has been to you what I hoped it might be to persons like yourself. I put a good deal of blood, if little scholarship, into it.

We have been very busy moving, & my mother has just died. But I hope to get you to lunch soon.

Yours ever gratefully,
T. S. Eliot

TO *Walter de la Mare*[2]   TS De la Mare Estate

11 October 1929   *The Criterion*

Dear de la Mare,

I think that you are a little wrong, because I know that it was not only the other day, but several times during the last three years, that I have sent messages to you through Dick, to try to get a story or a poem from you for the *Criterion*.[3] However, I am delighted to have this one at last. I like it very much; even if I did not I should have accepted it – so in saying that I like it I am merely throwing in my personal opinion after the editorial acceptance. But may I keep it to publish in *March*?[4] The reason is that I have got involved with four reviews (French, German, Italian and Spanish) in a prize contest, and the winning (German) story has to be

---

1 – Not found: presumably a fan letter about *Dante* (published 27 Sept. 1929).
2 – Walter de la Mare (1873–1956), prolific poet, novelist, short story writer, anthologist, spent his early career in the Statistics Department of the Anglo-American Oil Company, 1890–1908, before being freed to become a freelance writer by a £200 royal bounty negotiated by Henry Newbolt. He wrote numerous popular works: poetry including *The Listeners* (1912), *Peacock Pie* (1913), and *The Traveller* (1946); novels including *Henry Brocken* (1904), *The Return* (1910), and *Memoirs of a Midget* (1921); and anthologies including *Come Hither* (1923). He was awarded the OM (1953); appointed CH (1948). See Theresa Whistler, *Imagination of the Heart: The Life of Walter de la Mare* (1993).
3 – Walter de la Mare wrote on 3 Oct.: 'Dick [his son, TSE's colleague] told me the other day that you had very kindly said you would like to have a short story for the *Criterion*.'
4 – Walter de la Mare, 'The Picnic', C. 9 (Apr. 1930), 430–49.

published simultaneously in December: so that I have no room till March.

About my poem.[1] Personally, I should be honoured by your including it, and I see no difficulty, but I think I ought to consult the other directors first. The reason is that it is one of a set of six to be produced shortly as a volume: 24 pages at about eighteen pence a page, limited. I think it would do me good and no harm nevertheless if you quoted it (in full): and as the two books are both in the same firm it ought to be simple enough, but I will speak to Faber and the others about it on Monday.

I rather hope that you may like one or two other of the poems better than that one; you will have a copy when it is printed.

I shall have to keep Mr Woodhouse's poem by me for a week or so:[2] I have the greatest difficulty in making up my mind about contemporary verse: it is always more conventional, or more radical, than my own; and I spend much time trying to divest myself of my prejudices in both directions. I dare say you know the feeling. I have an impression that Woodhouse needs to throw overboard a whole dictionary of other people's words, before he can say it in a simple way, but I will write to you again about him in a week or two.

> With very grateful thanks,
> Yours sincerely,
> T. S. Eliot

TO *Stuart Gilbert*   CC

14 October 1929   [*The Criterion*]

Dear Mr Gilbert,

Thank you for your letter of the 10th.[3] I am returning your contract tomorrow. I write now first to say that there is no objection, quite the

---

1 – De la Mare wrote: 'I have just finished a hotch-potch of a book on "Islands etc." (mainly Defoe) . . . It consists of an expanded lecture and what would be called notes, and I am very anxious to include your poem that appeared in *Commerce*, "Because I do not hope to turn again." It would be in reference to this sentence: "But an endless sleep, unstirred, unillumined by any phantom of dream, is unimaginable, since, even in the conceiving of it, the self within hovers over the envied ashes – envied, because the spirit may be compelled to endure a weariness beyond the body's power to allay."' The poem was 'Perch' Io non Spero', *Ash-Wednesday*. See *Desert Islands* (1930), 71, 272.
2 – De la Mare had enclosed poems by a young man named Charles Woodhouse, who was living on 'parish relief' and had walked all the way from Epping to call on him.
3 – Gilbert had returned the signed contract. He was pleased to report that the *Revue de France* and *Neue Rundschau* were asking for extracts from the forthcoming monograph.

contrary, to parts of your book appearing in continental reviews (with reference to us as publishers); and it may increase the demand for translations.

But what I wish to say particularly is that we are very anxious to have the typescript by the end of this year. The reason is that we do not want to bring out *Anna Livia Plurabelle later* than the middle of May; and we want to bring out your book *at least* a fortnight earlier. Joyce also was very anxious that your book should appear first: you see there are many people in England who have read the *Portrait*, and your book must take the place for most of them of the text of *Ulysses* which they have not seen, and provide a very useful stepping stone between the *Portrait* and *A.L.P.* Now if you cannot let us have the *complete* text before the end of January, could you not begin giving us the text, section by section, at once? so that most of the book would be set up, proof-read by you, and ready for paging. This would be a great help; and furthermore I do hope you will try to finish the book altogether as long as possible before the time you said. Will you please give me some idea at once of what you think possible? You will understand that I should not hustle you in this way except for the real importance of getting your book out before the Joyce. I discussed this point fully with Joyce when he was here, as he will tell you.

I look forward to your visit in the spring, and also shall be very glad if I can be of any use to you then in connexion with questions of translation rights. And there also the Society of Authors is very desirable.

One final point. It would very much accelerate our negotiations with American publishers, particularly with a view to pushing the publication (rather than 'taking sheets') of the book over there, if you could send us your final typescript in *duplicate*, so that we could send one copy to America, or show it to American publishers' branches here. If you are having it copied fair, could you have three copies made instead of two – one for our printers, one for the Americans and one for your-[self]

[*typing has run off the page*]

TO *John Gould Fletcher*   TS Arkansas

14 October 1929   [London]

Dear Fletcher,

Many thanks for your letter. I think your idea is a very interesting one. As the series was my own idea, so it was also my idea that the essays should do what you have gathered that they are meant to do. But of course I don't suppose that every writer will take this line; they must be left to see the point, if they can, for themselves.[1]

Shelley has not been assigned, but has been offered. But in any case I think it is better to continue to have each essay ostensibly about one poet only; for we must depend, for the sale, partly on people who don't know much about a poet but would like to know what a contemporary thinks about him. I think the 'Blake' is a good idea. I should like to talk it over with you when we can next meet; there is time, as it could hardly be published before next autumn, and I think we ought to wait a few months to see how the first two go (especially as we are committed to two for the spring) before making any more contracts. I think the series ought to do very well, but you never know what will happen to a book or a series.

I have been very busy at home lately but want to see you as soon as possible.

Yours ever
T. S. Eliot

TO *Max Clauss*   CC

14 October 1929   [London]

Cher ami et confrère,

Je sais que vous êtes à ce moment très affairé, mais j'ose néanmoins vous écrire sur un projet que j'ai eu dans la tête depuis quelque temps.

1–Fletcher wrote on 11 Oct. 'Your new project, The Poets by the Poets, interests me extremely and I would like to discuss with you an idea that has come to me in regard to it. On reading your *Dante*, it seemed to me that your idea was to decide the range and value of a particular poet's mind and individual achievement, as it appeared to a poet born under different conditions, in another age, and possibly with very different problems to face . . . You discussed Dante from the background of your personal experience of his mind . . . I should like to see other poets treated in the same way . . . The poet that interests me in this particular instance is William Blake. It seems to me that no one has said exactly what he intended, and why he failed in the major part of his work, which is the *Prophetic Books*. I regard these as an attempt to build up a philosophic myth on the basis of the French Revolution. The Apocalypse of St John is an example of the same sort of thing. As the author of the Apocalypse used the material of the background, the fall of Jerusalem, the destruction of the Temple, the dispersal of the Jews, as a sort of frame of reference to describe the struggle of the Messiah and the Roman Empire, so Blake (with less skill) used the background of the French Revolution to describe the struggle of instinct and reason in mankind. This idea does not seem to have been brought out by any of Blake's numerous commentators, and it has important corollaries – notably in the practice of Shelley (who I understand has already been assigned in this series), who took a Greek myth as the basis for his own attempt at the same thing.' (This letter is printed, with minor variants, in *Selected Letters of John Gould Fletcher*, 114–16.)

En lisant les journaux, l'idée m'est venue que le temps est mûr pour un exposé, simple mais savant, au public anglais, des idées générales et des combinaisons pratiques, de la jeune Allemagne nationaliste et royaliste.[1] La jeune Allemagne, est-elle, ou non, monarchiste et nationaliste? Quelle signification ont les plusieurs sociétés militantes (Stahlhelm etc.)? à quoi tend la jeune Allemagne, en fait d'organisation politique intérieure, et en fait de sympathie ou d'antipathie internationale? L'Allemagne, a-t-elle, ou non, survécu le Drang nach Osten? les idées monarchistes, sont-elles vraiment royalistes ou purement nationalistes? Se-rapprochent-elles des idées de 'restauration' en France ou chez nous?

[typing runs off the page]

petit livre ou même une brochure. C'est votre livre 'Das politische Frankreich', aussi bien que nos liaisons personelles, qui m'a tenté de vous aborder sur ce sujet. Le livre que nous envisageons serait explicatoire et définitoire, plutôt que théorique; toutefois, vous auriez pleinement la liberté d'y exposer vos propres vues.

Sans plus dire à ce moment, seriez-vous disposé, préalablament, à écrire vous-même un tel volume – un petit livre – pour le public anglais? Nous nous intéressons beaucoup, actuellement, à la politique allemande et nous n'en savons rien; nous n'avons que les mensonges itérés des journaux.

Toujours votre dévoué
[T. S. Eliot][2]

---

1 – GCF wrote to Erich Alport on 15 Oct. 1929: 'Max Clauss. This is an excellent suggestion. Eliot knows Clauss more or less and is writing to him direct. Or so he has promised to do; but it sometimes takes him a little time to fulfil such promises. Let me know [when] you get an answer to your letter.'

2 – *Translation*: Dear friend and colleague, I know that you are very busy at present, but I venture to write to you all the same about a project that I've had in my mind for some time. Reading the newspapers, I've had the idea that the time is ripe for a simple but learned account for the English public of the general ideas and practical combinations of the new nationalist and royalist Germany. Is the new Germany monarchist and nationalist, or not? What significance do the several militant societies (Stahlhelm, etc.) have? What are the tendencies of the new Germany, as to the internal political organisation and international sympathies and antipathies? Has Germany survived the "Drang nach Osten" or not? Are the monarchist ideas really royalist or purely nationalistic? Are they similar to the ideas of "restoration" in France or here? [. . .] small book or even a pamphlet. It's your book *Das politische Frankreich*, as well as our personal contacts, which has tempted me to approach you on this subject. The book that we envisage would be explicatory and definitory, rather than theoretical; however, you would have complete freedom of expressing your own views.

Without saying any more now, would you be willing to write such a volume yourself – a small book – for the English public? We currently take a great interest in German politics, and we know nothing about it; we only have the lies repeated by newspapers. Yours faithfully, [T. S. Eliot]

TO *Clifton P. Fadiman*[1]   cc

14 October 1929   [London]

Dear Mr Fadiman,

Thank you for your letter of the 19th ultimo and your interesting suggestion about the prize stories.[2] I have communicated your suggestion to Dr Max Clauss, of the *Europaeische Revue*, Berlin, from whom the scheme originates. But I think I can say, without waiting to hear from him, that we shall keep your proposal in mind, but that it is premature to make any arrangements. It must be five years before all the prizes are awarded, the notion being to award one each year, and to take the five countries in rotation – Germany, England, France, Italy and Spain. And you will understand that when the time comes for book publication – which is a very good idea, all of the authors as well as the editors must be consulted.

I shall look forward with much pleasure to reading Mr Dahlberg's novel.[3]

With many thanks for your suggestion.

[T. S. Eliot]

TO *E. R. Curtius*   cc

15 October 1929   [*The Criterion*]

My dear Curtius,

Dr Alport has conveyed to me the suggestion, which I believe was his own idea, of combining your essays on Proust, Gide, Joyce and myself[4] for translation and book publication by Faber & Faber. I think the idea

---

1 – Clifton Fadiman (1904–99), American author, radio and TV presenter, and pundit. Educated at Columbia University, he worked for ten years for Simon & Schuster, ending as chief editor; he was then editor of the Book Review section of *The New Yorker*, 1933–43. From the late 1930s he compered various radio and TV chat shows and quizzes.

2 – Fadiman (Simon & Schuster) asked to be able to publish either the single winner of the prize-winning 'novelletes', or a collection if they were to be shorter pieces. 'I should think that with a sponsorship such as yours some remarkable work might develop.'

3 – Dahlberg, *Bottom Dogs* (published in England by Putnam).

4 – Curtius wrote on Marcel Proust in his *Französischen Geist im Neuen Europa* (Stuttgart, 1925); on Gide in *Die literarischen Wegbereiter des neuen Frankreich* (1919); on James Joyce in *James Joyce und sein Ulysses* (Zürich, 1929; repr. in *Schriften der Neuen Schweizer Rundschau*). See *Essays in European Literature* (*Kritische Essays zur Europäischen Literatur* [Bern, 1950]), trans. Michael Kowal (Princeton, 1973), 327–54. For 'T. S. Eliot I' (1927), see also *Kritische Essays zur Europäischen Literatur*, 298–315.

is a valuable one, but before pursuing it further I should like to take up with you once more a suggestion which I made to you some years ago, and which I still think a better one. That is, of course, that you should write two or three more studies of English authors, and bring out a book, simultaneously in Germany and with us, parallel to the *Wegbereiter,* (but of course up to date). There are several good reasons. No one is more qualified than yourself to interpret modern English literature to modern Germany. And England, like every other country, needs foreign criticism of her own work. And from a publishing point of view, such a book would have a far better sale here than a composite book on French and English authors. (Proust has the disadvantage of having been a great deal written about, Gide the disadvantage of being very little known.) For you also, it would have the advantage of being a new book which could be published in Germany and in France also.[1]

It would be an impertinence to suggest the names of writers about whom I should be excited to see your critical opinions, but I should be very glad if I could help you towards obtaining books that you might need. At the moment I merely put the general suggestion – but very strongly – as I want to see the book written, and I can assure you that we should want to publish it. But if for any reason you must decline the suggestion absolutely, I shall take up again Alport's suggestion.

Yours ever cordially,
[T. S. Eliot]

TO *John Middleton Murry* TS Northwestern

15 October 1929 *The Criterion*

My dear John,

There is one matter I forgot to mention when I wrote to you last. I have received unsolicited a good many essays on Humanism, some good, most bad. There is far more than I can use in the *Criterion*: by the end of this year the discussion will have occupied quite as much space as I can afford to give it: but one or two are quite good, and deserve to be published

1–GCF wrote to Alport on 15 Oct. 1929, apropos Curtius: 'Some time ago [TSE] proposed to Curtius that he should write a series of studies on *English* writers parallel to his studies of French writers. I think that such a book would really be very much better than the one you suggest. Don't you agree? The essays on Joyce and Eliot could be taken as a basis for the book which might include another four essays. Eliot is also writing to Curtius to revive his old suggestion, stimulated by yours.'

somewhere. And of course, the subject would be taken more seriously by people if it were now and then discussed in more than *one* review.[1]

Yours in haste,
Tom.

TO *J. S. Barnes* CC

15 October 1929   [London]

Dear Jim Barnes,

I am trying to answer your letter of the 7th as best I can.[2]

First – after congratulating you on your approaching marriage – about the publishing business. (I can understand your feeling that you have been

1 – JMM replied (16 Oct.), 'By all means send one or two or three of the essays on to me; and I will certainly do my best to publish at least one of them.'

2 – Barnes was eager to change the course of his career, he wrote: he wanted to enlarge his 'horizons and activities'. In addition, he had 'very good reasons to hope that next year I should find myself a married man! And this means definitely that I must seek work more remunerative than my present work.' He desired to get away from the 'big soulless business machine,' he added, as well as to be able to write more. 'Publishing & the best kind of journalism appeal to me. Is there in your opinion any opening in this direction, such as would enable me to earn enough to keep myself and a wife in London, without being wretchedly hampered by financial difficulties? Say £1000 p.a. & upwards?

'I would be prepared to invest up to £2000 in a publishing business, provided I was satisfied that it represented a really secure investment. Apart from this, I have qualifications which would be valuable to a publisher – a really first rate knowledge of Italian & French, considerable business experience, and a host of friends & acquaintances in the literary, artistic & political worlds of several countries (to which I shall be able soon to add America . . .' Were there any suitable openings at F&F? Failing Faber, could TSE recommend any other publishers? 'So do tell me all you can about it like a father.'

GCF, to whom TSE showed Barnes's letter before replying to him, responded with this handwritten note: 'What can one say?! Of course Faber & Faber has no room for anyone of B's standing & financial requirements. His only chance would be to be taken on by one of the really big firms. Benn may have a job of the kind – I don't know. £2000 is no good. The successful firms don't want it: the others couldn't pay his salary. I daresay B. might be useful; but I don't know what his connection wld. be worth, & £1000 a year is a lot to pay for undefined usefulness. As you know there aren't many such jobs in existence, & the pressure is such that they fill up almost before they become vacant. In fact it's seldom if ever that there is such a thing as a "vacancy" in publishing. I always feel, too, that it's a mistake for anyone with high falutin ideas to become a professional publisher, & that business is better taken unmixed with things that give you pleasure in themselves. I know I find it harder & harder to judge or read a book for its own sake. But that's a question for the individual. Looking at it practically I fear you will have to return a discouraging answer. Unless B. could get a job as a part-time reader & gradually work himself in somewhere, I don't see where he is going to get a foothold. Wldn't he stand more chance in journalism? This is all very useless to you, & one has said it all scores & scores of times: but I can't think of anything either fresh or helpful.'

long enough in Lausanne, and that you have done all you have to do in your present work, interesting as it must have been). At the same time, I shrink from encouraging you to go into publishing, in preference to other kinds of business. It is less profitable than most, but is no less business. It is notorious that everybody counsels everyone else not to take up his own business – my father did that with his sons[1] – but I am sure nevertheless that illusions do cling tenaciously about publishing. There is a perpetual struggle between one's ideals and the necessity of hitting the market; most of the books one publishes are intellectually and morally worthless; you are interested in poetry and you have to sit up planning the 'lay-out' of a book on cricket, or the memoirs of some eminent nincompoop; and insensibly it becomes harder to read any book for profit or enjoyment, or to judge any book except commercially. You have to work just as hard, and just as commercially, as in any other business; and this business somehow has an odious connexion with your intellectual interests which befouls them.

I put this strongly. Even to be an editor is bad enough, for the constant stream of mean books in smart covers which pours into the office and out again to reviewers is enough to kill any zest one had in reading. One loses the desire to read, and if it were not for financial pressure, would lose the capacity to write. Perhaps I have.

But now for practical advice. Faber & Faber is a young firm, and is staffed in every way – not perhaps up to its needs – but up to what a young firm is justified in carrying. I wish we could have you, as I am sure it would be very valuable to us in the long run. As for other firms, the difficulty is that £1000 is a big salary in publishing; only a large firm could afford it for any but the most experienced heads; the firms which would be glad of an investment of £2000 can't afford £1000 salary; and the firms which can afford it, don't need £2000.

I think it would be more satisfactory if you could come over to London; we could talk about these things; and if you could get any *piston* with people like Macmillan, or Murray, or Methuen (I was going to add Blackwood, but you don't want to live in Edinburgh) that is the type of firm to go for. Constable might be added, and Doubleday-Doran, the American proprietors of Heinemanns. But with any of these the investment would be quite secondary; though if you got the job, it would be worth while. I should say roughly, that no investment less than £10,000 would pull a job at £1000.

---

1 – TSE's father, Henry Ware Eliot (1843–1919), was President and Treasurer of the Hydraulic-Press Brick Company, St Louis, Missouri.

As for journalism, I should think you ought to tackle the *Times* and the *Morning Post*. I know some of the *Times* people, I don't think that I know anyone on the *Post*, but no doubt you would have means of getting at them. The great thing always is to know or pretend to know, something that nobody else knows; and what with Albania, and Mussolini and the Vatican, I should think that you were as well prepared as anyone.

About your essay on aesthetics: I don't see how I can use it before June, or March at the very earliest. In a quarterly, one has to be very careful about spacing contributors – it doesn't of course matter so much in reviews – so that no one contributor shall have a leading article more than twice in a year, and never in consecutive numbers: in fact there are not many instances of people appearing more than once in a year, and these are mostly on controversial topics which have to be dealt with at once. But if you would like to try other reviews meanwhile, I shall be ready to help. For instance, I know Thorold, the editor of the *Dublin Review* (the next best quarterly to the *Criterion*) and he might be able to use it sooner on my recommendation. If you like, I will try him.[1]

I think that your visit to America will be an asset to you in getting a job here: but if you have any time in London before you go there it would be worth while seeing a few people.

I seem to have talked like rather a heavy father of the Vincent Crummles brand:[2] but say what you like, and I will do what I can.

Ever yours,
[T. S. Eliot]

TO *Viscount Brentford*   CC

16 October 1929   [London]

Dear Sir,

I have to thank you for your letter of the 11th instant, enclosing the typescript of *Do We Need a Censor?* I have read it with great interest and satisfaction, and on behalf of my Board, am sending you a form of Contract herewith, as we should like to send the essay to press immediately so as to publish it during November.

---

1 – Barnes was to publish in *The Dublin Review* (185: 371 [Oct. 1929], 264–81) an essay on 'Fascism and the International Centre of Fascist Studies'.
2 – Crummles is the actor-manager who takes on Nicholas in Dickens's *Nicholas Nickleby*.

I must offer a note of explanation. As I had no reply to my second letter to you, I regretfully formed the conclusion that you had either decided to defer the matter, or ceased to entertain the suggestion. Since then we have arranged, at my instance, to publish another pamphlet on the *Censorship*, by Mr D. H. Lawrence. Not only from our point of view, but from that of the public, I am sure that the simultaneous publication of the two pamphlets would have an excellent effect. And personally, because I should deprecate any hasty alteration of the present law or abandonment of its application, I am sure that it will be beneficial to show the public that this is not a simple question of two points of view, but of a good many points of view, all of which must be weighed before even the private citizen can make up his mind. Mr Lawrence's view, for instance, is not diametrically opposed to your own; he rather leads one to believe that he would be strongly in favour of censorship, if it were in his own hands, and would apply it forcibly.[1] And his point of view is widely divergent from that of the 'World League for Sexual Reform', particularly as expressed in the statement of that Society from which you quote.

I have thought it only fair to let you know that we are publishing such a pamphlet – not antecedent, but at the same time as your own. But, as I have said, I am sure that not only for us as publishers but for the public, the coincidence is most useful; for the two essays do more to cast light on the difficulties of a subject which has usually been made to appear too simple, than everything else that I have read.[2]

1–D. H. Lawrence's *Pornography and Obscenity* (Criterion Miscellany, 1929) was written in Aug.–Sept. 1929. DHL wrote on 19 Dec. 1929 to the German physican and playwright Max Mohr, 'That *Obscenity* pamphlet . . . has made the old ones hate me still more in England, but it has sold very well, and had a pretty good effect, I think' (quoted by Harry T. Moore, 'D. H. Lawrence and the "Censor-Morons"', in Lawrence, *Sex, Literature and Censorship*, ed. Harry T. Moore [London, 1955], 34).

Dr William Temple, Archbishop of York, wrote to TSE on 21 Nov.: 'I was left wondering what Lawrence was aiming at with his essay: if only to express his own conviction & mood, no doubt he succeeded; but if to persuade any one who did not agree with him beforehand, it struck me as ill-conceived. No one is converted by having his nose rubbed in what his opponent regards as the mess he has made of his job. Most "grey ones" who read it will be fixed by it in greyness for evermore.'

2–Brentford graciously and properly replied on 17 Oct. that he had, 'of course, no objection to anyone else publishing a pamphlet on whatever lines he may see fit'.

Five years later, GCF was to write to the Secretary of State for Home Affairs, on 7 Sept. 1934: 'I have just been informed by one of our customers, Sequana Limited, of 16 Buckingham Palace Road, s.w.1., that their premises have recently been visited by the police, and a number of publications seized and removed. Among these publications was a pamphlet entitled Pornography and Obscenity published by my firm. This pamphlet was first published in 1929, in a series called the *Criterion Miscellany*, simultaneously with a pamphlet in the same series entitled Do We Need A Censor?, by the then Home Secretary,

I hope that you will be able to let us have the signed agreement at once, so that we may push the pamphlet forward for publication in November. And at your leisure, you will perhaps answer a question raised in my previous letter, and let me know whether you would care to have us take up the matter of American publication for you.

I am,
Yours faithfully,
[T. S. Eliot]
Director

Vivienne Eliot TO *Mary Hutchinson*   MS Texas

17 October 1929   177 Clarence Gate Gardens,
                                Regent's Park

My dear Mary,

I must thank you again for bringing me those wonderful flowers. I am trying to remember the name. Was it Reanthus? They are beautiful against these black & gold curtains. You spoil me, & you always have. So many presents – & you have been such a wonderful friend to us all these years. You do not know how much we both treasure yr. friendship.

But what thick *walls* of reserve grow up between people, & how much one longs to break them down. When I can drive the Morris Minor I shall feel free-er. But I have my own views about driving, & Tom has his. They are not identical. But Tom says he will drive me over to your house as soon as he has the car, & that will be in about a week. After dinner – or in the afternoon. Don't keep *next Wednesday*.

Yours with
Much love
V. H. Eliot

---

the late Viscount Brentford. The two pamphlets represented opposite points of view upon a question of no little public importance.

'It is not, however, upon this fact that we base our protest against the seizure of this particular pamphlet by the police, so much as upon more general grounds. It appears to us so astonishing as to be almost incredible that the police should conceive it proper to seize a copy of a publication, bearing the imprint of a reputable firm of English publishers, upon the premises of one of that firm's customers, without any previous or subsequent communication with the publishers themselves.'

17 October 1929   [London]

Dear Rowse,

Your letter, and the enclosed review, gave me a great deal of pleasure.[1] It is more satisfactory to have you like this essay than to have you like the Andrewes, because it is nearer to the sort of thing that I am qualified to do. And I am glad that you like the poem, though I have rather a low opinion of it myself. I have always abstained from having my own work reviewed in the *Criterion*, and I don't think I should depart from it; certainly not unless the critic found every flaw in the texture – and you have been very lenient. So I return your review with pleasure and regret.

I quite agree with you about Value.[2] It is the subject to which all others lead, and which one always has to tackle, usually amateurishly, if one tries to follow any subject out to the end. The people who write about it are very dull, very long-winded, and very unconvincing. It would certainly be a subject worth taking up in the *Criterion*. I question symposia, because they narrow the interest of one issue to a very select few readers; but a sort of continuing discussion, running for a year or more, seems to me both feasible and desirable. The contributors ought, I think, to be people who have had to try to think it out for themselves and have come upon it from quite different starting points: art, literature, economics etc. Would you take a hand?

I want your article on Communism for the *March* number, so there is plenty of time still.[3] Your Wolsey for this next number.[4]

1–ALR had written (undated): 'I read your study of Dante with such fascination, that I was impelled to write this little commentary. Is it any good for the *Criterion*? If not, or if you have already sent out the book to be reviewed, perhaps you'd let me have it again, for the *Oxford Magazine* would, I know, like to have it . . . May I say that I think the *Dante* is a book of great beauty, and with no reservations such as spoiled my appreciation of the political essays in *Lancelot Andrewes*.'

2–'I feel that all these discussions of ours verge on the complex of subjects connected with *Value*, and it's a subject I do not yet know my way about, nor does anybody else seem to. One wants a guide: or time to think one's way alone. Have you ever thought of a Criterion symposium on the subject of what one means by Value in experience: "the values of life", Value in Aesthetics etc.'

3–'Do you expect my article – a final one – on the Theory & Practice of Communism for the next number? If so I'll do my best: but I'm never happy about doing the subject justice short of a good deal more reading and criticism.' See 'The Thoery and Practice of Communism', C. 9 (Apr. 1930), 451–69.

4–Untitled review of A. F. Pollard's *Wolsey*, C. 9 (Jan. 1930), 353–6.

I must tell you again how much pleasure your commendations have given me. I wish that we might meet sometimes.

Yours ever,
T. S. Eliot[1]

TO *J. B. Trend*

cc

18 October 1929   [177 Clarence Gate Gardens]

Dear Trend,

I have been in a great state of mental confusion of late, because I have been moving, and having to divide my thoughts between the *Criterion*, Shoolbreds,[2] the telephone Service etc. I am just collecting my wits, and have a strong recollection of a suggestion that you and I and Dent should lunch together. I am sure that there is something about it in the files, but I am writing at home: so may we start afresh?

Are you now in London? Are you reading Valdes[3] for us? Will you give me a Chronicle by the 10th November? And also can you review (even if, and perhaps preferably, very briefly) Praz's translated book *Unromantic Spain*? (He is very anxious that you should do it).[4] And can we still arrange that lunch with Dent?

Yours ever,
[T. S. Eliot]

TO *Peter Quennell*

cc

18 October 1929   [London]

Dear Quennell,

Thank you very much for sending me your book, which I have just read. Although it is very well produced – except that I hate the binding ends of illustrations turning up unexpectedly – I think the arrangement does it less than justice. That is, the book is really (as I found) a whole, instead of a collection of incoherent essays like Symons's; but the form suggests

---

1 – ALR jotted on this letter, 'What a pity I held off as usual – as always.'
2 – Shoolbred's Removals and Warehousing, Tottenham Court Road, London.
3 – Presumably Trend was writing a Faber Reader's Report on a (now unknown) work by Menéndez Valdes.
4 – Praz was to tell TSE on 22 Oct. that Trend's (anonymous) review in the *TLS* 'did me much pleasure'. Trend's untitled review of *Unromantic Spain*: C. 9 (Apr. 1930), 572–3.

separate self-contained essays. So I was dissatisfied when I finished the Baudelaire, though it is full of good things, because there is so much more to be said about him. When I got to the end I revised my opinion, because the unity asserts itself more and more. I hope if I can find the time to review it myself for the next number, and if I said more now I should have to repeat myself. But it is a good job.[1]

But I cannot believe that Valéry is more than a pygmy to Mallarmé.

I am satisfied with myself for having suggested [*typing runs off the page*]

[T. S. Eliot]

TO *Viscount Brentford*   CC

18 October 1929   [London]

Dear Sir,

I thank you for your letter of the 17th instant, enclosing signed Form of Agreement concerning your pamphlet 'Do We Need a Censor', and enclose herewith the counterpart thereof. I should be very much obliged if you would acknowledge receipt.

1–TSE's review of *Baudelaire and the Symbolists: Five Essays* (C. 9 [Jan 1930], 357–9) opens: 'Mr Quennell has done for his generation what Arthur Symons did many years ago with his *Symbolist Movement in Literature* [1908]. I am not disposed to disparage Mr Symons's book . . . I myself owe Mr Symons a great debt: but for having read his book, I should not, in the year 1908, have heard of Laforgue or Rimbaud; I should probably not have begun to read Verlaine; and but for reading Verlaine, I should not have heard of Corbière. So the Symons book is one of those which have affected the course of my life.' Of Quennell's 'five chapters in one whole essay', TSE remarks in particular: 'the essay on Baudelaire is an admirable study, and except for the studies of Laforgue and Mallarmé, really the best in the book. It is the first of a sequence of studies in the post-mortem of Romanticism, and in the insurgence of something which can hardly be called classicism, but which may decently be called Counter-Romanticism . . . [But] it will not do to label Baudelaire; he is not merely, or in my opinion even primarily, the artist . . . I should place him with men who are important first because they are human prototypes of new experience, and only second because they are poets.' Quennell notes that Baudelaire 'enjoyed *a sense of his own age*', an observation TSE finds 'certainly true . . . And a "sense of one's age" implies some sense of other ages; so that Baudelaire's sense of Racine is integral with his sense of his own age.' TSE remarks further: 'When we get to Laforgue, we find a poet who seems to express more clearly even than Baudelaire the difficulties of his own age; he speaks to us, or spoke to my generation, more intimately than Baudelaire seemed to do.' TSE warmly concludes that Quennell's volume 'is a good book on what is the most important part of the history of the poetry of the nineteenth century. I look back to the dead year 1908; and I observe with satisfaction that it is now taken for granted that the current of French poetry which sprang from Baudelaire is one which has, in these twenty-one years, affected all English poetry that matters. Mr Symons's book is one milestone, and Mr Quennell's will be another.'

The manuscript has gone to press today, and we hope to publish the pamphlet well before the end of November.

With regard to the *Saturday Evening Post*, I shall be glad to consult a fellow-director who is better acquainted with American periodicals than I am, and will write to you again in a few days.[1] I have also in mind *The Ladies Home Journal*, which published Mr Strachey's *Elizabeth and Essex*, and which is rather more than its name suggests, as a medium.

I may say again that I and my Board are very much honoured and pleased by having the opportunity of publishing this pamphlet.

I am,
Yours very truly,
[T. S. Eliot]
Director

TO *Harold Monro*   CC

18 October 1929   [London]

Dear Harold,

Do you remember that you promised me a review of Richard's poems for the December number? I have been counting upon it, and so would like to know whether you could promise it to me by the 10th November? Make it as long as you like.[2]

How are you? I hope to see you again soon.

Yours ever,
[T. S. E.]

TO *Orlo Williams*   CC

18 October 1929   [London]

Dear Williams,

I apologise for not having written before, but I have recently been moving again, which has decidedly mutilated my editorial duties for a time. Now we are beginning to get settled, and the normal routine of life resumed, I hope to see you soon.

---

1 – Brentford replied on 21 Oct., 'I leave the matter of America in your hands, but do not approach the "Saturday Evening Post" without communicating with me.' (He had a prior relationship with the *Saturday Evening Post*, which was printing some articles by him.)

2 – Monro, untitled review of Richard Aldington, *Collected Poems*, C. 9 (Apr. 1930), 518–22.

I am sorry that the Huxley book of essays had already gone out, to Hamish Miles, before you wrote, else you would have had it.[1] A great mass of stuff has come in, but nothing else that struck me you would care for. I was on the point of posting off to you the first four volumes of Virginia's Woolf's collected works, when I thought that having written about her once, you might not want to write about her again. There is of course one new small book (*A Room of One's Own*) which is a long essay. Please let me know how you feel about this.[2]

Barnes is of course a romantic and not a realpolitiker; and I have been [*typing runs off the page*] of him or for that matter of myself in the role of Interlocutor!

Yours ever,
[T. S. Eliot]

TO *Walter de la Mare*   CC

18 October 1929   [Faber & Faber Ltd]

Dear de la Mare,

This is merely to tell you that the other directors see no more objection than I do to your reprinting the whole of 'Perch' Io non Spero' in *Islands*. I should be glad if you would omit that title, and if possible print it without any title, because I am reprinting the poem later without that title, merely as no. 1 of a sequence of six which I have called provisionally 'Six Poems', but think of calling *Ash Wednesday Music* (but I should like very much to have your frank opinion of that title, about which I feel doubtful).[3] There is no need to give any reference at all.

1–*Do What You Will* (1929); reviewed by Hamish Miles in C. 9 (Jan. 1930), 343–5.
2–OW reviewed the *Uniform Edition of the Works of Virginia Woolf* (*The Voyage Out, Jacob's Room, Mrs Dalloway, The Common Reader, To the Lighthouse*), together with *A Room of One's Own*, in C. 9 (Apr. 1930), 509–12; paying particular attention to the last: 'It may seem rash for a man, in face of Mrs Woolf's scorn for men's lordly propensity to settle women's case, to say that she settles it unexceptionally; yet I am bold enough to assert that she does so, within the limits of her argument. Feminism – nobody can deny – is justified as a protest against an age-old masculinism, yet it defeats its own object by perpetuating the dissidence . . . Mrs Woolf, for all the effective play she makes with the paradox of man's behaviour to woman, and for all the passion of her plea that woman's horizon must be complete unrestricted, sees beyond the dissidence . . . In two acute pages she amplifies the opinion that masculine models in literature – from verse-forms to sentences – were, and are, inappropriate to the motions of a woman's mind. In the future, the book, the poem, the sentence will be adapted to the body; there will be a feminine as well as a masculine tradition in a complete and legitimate sense.'
3–De la Mare responded (21 Oct.): 'In itself I like the title "Ash Wednesday Music". There

The people who don't like the poem would not like the book and the people who do like it would like the book; and also, I consider it a great honour to be printed by you in this way.

[*Incomplete: typing runs off the page.*]

TO *John Middleton Murry*   CC

18 October 1929   [London]

Dear John,

I have taken the liberty of sending you a book by Fausset, dealing with Babbitt etc., in the hope that if you find it good enough (or bad enough) you might be willing to review it before Nov. 12th, for the next *Criterion*. But if it does not appear worth it please drop me a card.[1] The Shakespeare books are sent you rather with the thought that you might accumulate some such, with the notion of later writing a review or article on recent Shakespeare editions – the ordinary reader is rather bewildered by them, and not helped by the battle raging between Robertson, Chalmers, Wilson and Q.

I would have sent you a couple of Humanism essays today, but have mislaid one of them, which I hope to find.

Affectionately,
[Tom]

TO *Christopher Dawson*   CC

18 October 1929   [London]

Dear Mr Dawson,

Some little time ago I sent you a copy of Vossler's *Mediaeval Culture*. Probably I ought to have written first to ask whether you could review it for us. But still I hope you can. The book has had a good deal of notice, mostly rather perfunctory, and on glancing at it I am not satisfied with any of its reviews. Would you please let me know whether you would review it for me (1000 words or so) for the December number? or if that is

---

is a covert poetic nuance between Ash and music. My only hesitation is its ironical tinge. It might have this to some minds; it may indeed be partly your intention. But judging from this one poem it seems to me to be not exactly right. I hesitate to blunder on like this because as a title it is pregnant and arresting.'

1 – JMM reviewed Hugh l'Anson Fausset, *The Proving of Psyche*, in C. 9 (Jan. 1930), 349–53.

pressing you too hard, for the following number. But I should very much like to have it for December, and I think a review of the book by you would be of the greatest interest.[1]

Yours very truly,
[T. S. Eliot]

TO *Henry Eliot*   TS Houghton

19 October 1929   Faber & Faber Ltd

My dear Henry,

I have your two letters, one of the 22nd, and one just received, in front of me. I have also letters from Marion, Margaret and Ada (the last the most satisfactory of the three) which I have not yet answered. Thank you very much for giving me such an exact account,[2] which I should never have had from anyone else. I feel a great craving to see you, and wish you could come to England again. Margaret in her letter suggested that I or I and Vivien should come and stay with them at Concord Avenue before they leave it: but of course that is the last thing on earth I should do: it will be years before I feel up to coming back to America, and I would not stay at Concord Avenue. Whenever I do come I shall want to go directly to St. Louis; certainly now, as I get older, I find myself turning more on St. Louis, and with more pleasure and less pain, than on Cambridge. And oddly enough, the thought of St. Louis is more soothing and less painful to me than the thought of East Gloucester.

I am very thankful, though I have a perfectly irrational (not theological) dislike of cremation, that mother is with father in Bellefontaine.[3] It is partly due, of course, to the feeling I have mentioned above – I not only want them together, but want them in St Louis.

By the way, mother said that when she died – I have the letter in which she said it – that she would leave all the books that I have published, and all the magazine articles I wrote, and any I sent her which mentioned me, to *you*. I do not suppose that she left any instructions, or mentioned it to anyone else; but I wish you to have them, and I shall say this to Marion and Margaret also. As for myself, there are certain books in the library which mother meant me to have, and in which for that reason she put my

1–Review of Carl Vossler, *Medieval Culture: An Introduction to Dante and His Times*, C. 9 (July 1930), 718–22.
2–An account of their mother's death, and the funeral.
3–Bellefontaine Cemetery, St Louis, Missouri.

bookplate. I think there is an Audubon, the works of Addington Symons, and possibly Addison's *Spectator* and a few others. I should like to have them, solely because she meant them for me – for I have too many books, and shall have to clear out some to make room for them.

About mother's poems. I should very much like them to be published. I have a few, but not many. It would be a great pleasure to me to write an introduction or preface for the book, and perhaps if I did so a publisher, or a publisher of limited editions particularly, might be ready to bear part or all of the cost of production. It would be a delicate and possibly invidious task, as whatever I wrote would have to have the approval of all members of the immediate family before it appeared, but I should be glad to do it. Some of them, indeed all of them in some degree, are good poems. I remember when I wrote a poem at Smith Academy, when I was 16, I learned to my surprise that she had had copies typed and distributed (I only heard that from Aunt Rose) and then mother said to me that it was a better poem than any she had written. It wasn't; but even then I had some perception of what such a statement meant.

She wrote to me once, that when she died all my letters to her should be destroyed. I wish that they might be; I do not want to read them again, and I do not want anyone outside of the family ever to have access to them.

One talks and writes and fusses for a long time around a subject, before facing it directly; and so I write about these minor matters.

Your second letter is more informative about yourself than the first, or than the letter you wrote me just before mother's last illness, but still leaves much to be desired. Please think that I want as full information from you about your affairs as possible. I gather that you have ceased active participation in your business. If you go in with any publisher in New York, they would automatically get the U.S.A. rights of all my own writings: but as I know exactly what their sales are, I have no illusions about the financial advantages of that. But they would also get everything desirable from Faber & Faber that I could steer their way. If you have any firm or firms in mind, I should like to hear about it: because we do a good deal of business with New York.

If you don't do that, I agree that a country life (say in southern New England, not too far from either Boston or New York) is the best.

About my own business. As you know, I am a director of Faber & Faber: I sold a bond to invest in shares in the new firm. Of course we have no expectations of dividends for the next three or four years; but I want to strengthen my position with them. If the firm goes on and prospers, I shall stay with them; the only danger is of its not succeeding, and having to sell up, and then I do not know what I should or could do. It is a young firm, so that success is not certain. When it began as Faber & Gwyer it was very weak and inexperienced, and wasted money; since then it has been reorganised, and is much more promising. The directorate and staff work very well; and I got into the firm a very able American named Morley, a brother of Christopher Morley,[1] to supply a business sense which I felt was wanting; who shares my room with me, and whom, fortunately, I find sympathetic.[2] He was a Rhodes Scholar from Baltimore, and was and is still the London representative of the Century Company. While congenial to everybody, he supplies an element of push and initiative, as well as of caution, which was very much needed in this rather close correct Oxford atmosphere of Faber & Faber. Some people are both conventional and impetuous: Geoffrey Faber is that, but personally one of the kindest and most agreeable of men. For a long time my own works were the best sellers of the firm, which gave a very dismal forecast; but latterly that is not the case, and the list, and prospects and prestige of the firm are improving rapidly.

If you engaged in the publishing business in any way in New York, I wonder whether it would be possible for you to do for us in New York something like what Morley does for the Century Company in London: that is to say, try to sell our books (in sheets or setting-up rights) to American publishers, and to send our way any really good American books that might be saleable in England. Of course I have not suggested this to anyone else at this point. But the Anglo-American market is quite active at present.

At present I draw only £400 a year from the firm, which includes my work in running the *Criterion* and my work as director; and in the rearrangement of the firm, I find myself more and more concerned with the publishing side. I first came in primarily as editor, with a salary of £475 p.a. to cover both jobs; when the business was reorganised I offered the reduction. Of course it is nothing like what a man should be earning at my age, and if the firm flourishes, I shall of course insist on more pay. But I can't do that at the present juncture; so I must supplement my income, just as I did ten years ago, by reviewing, articles, prefaces, lectures, broadcasting talks, and anything that turns up. I begin, I confess, to feel a

1–Christopher Morley (1890–1957), novelist, essayist; columnist on *The New York Evening Post*.
2–FVM always acknowledged that he owed his position at F&F to TSE.

little tired at my age, of such irregular sources of income. I have begun life three times: at 22, at 28, and again at 40; I hope I shall not have to do so again, because I am growing tired.

It is a great relief to me to be able to ramble on in this way about my affairs to you, and I wish you would do the same. There is much more than can go into one letter, so consider this an instalment.

Ever your most affectionate brother,
Tom

P.S. I shall be sending you, as soon as I can get round to it, a small book called *Dante* and my 'Ariel Poem'[1] for this autumn. The former I believe will be rather successful. It is very strange now not to send the first copy of such things to mother. I had been looking forward to her seeing both, and had written her about them, and the other things I had in view.

Since I started this letter Vivien has just had a letter from you telling a little more about your plans. I am sure that your health will be much better out of the Chicago climate, and am happy to think of you moving east. I will write again soon.

TO *The Secretary, The English Association*   cc

21 October 1929   [London]

Dear Sir,

I thank you for your letter of the 16th instant, enclosing copy of your previous letter the original of which had not reached me.[2] I am greatly honoured by the invitation to address the Association, but regret that it would be quite impossible to do so during 1929. I have several tasks to accomplish by or about the 1st of December, so that I should have no time to prepare anything worthy, and December is a busy and distracted month at best. I can only thank you for the invitation, and hope that it may be repeated at some later time.

Yours very truly,
[T. S. Eliot]

1–*Animula*, published on 9 Oct. 1929.
2–A. V. Houghton invited TSE (28 Sept. 1929) to address the English Association in the Great Central Hall, Westminster, at the end of Nov. or the first week in Dec.

23 October 1929   [London]

Dear Sachie,

Many thanks for your letter of the 17th.[1] We are delighted to think that you will write an essay on Shelley for my series; for I could not think of any contemporary poet whose views on that subject would be so interesting as yours. You intimate that you need time: I enclose a contract stipulating for delivery of the MSS. of round about 12,000 words (the length of the two I sent you) by May 31st next. That is so we could publish next autumn; and I hope earnestly that it gives you enough time. Otherwise it would have to be for the spring of 1931; but I shall be disappointed if we cannot bring it out in the autumn of 1930.

My notion for the series was, that each writer should write primarily about his own experience of the poet discussed. We don't want a Benn's sixpenny handbook; remember that the interest resides [in] the fact that *that* particular contemporary poet is writing about that particular dead one. In writing my small *Dante* I did not bother to do any reading or re-reading, but just wrote ahead. But I do not want you to think that any particular method is imposed; if so, the series would lose its point altogether.

We should love to see you again, though it is painful to think that eight years have passed. Vivien and I are investing presently in a small car, a very small car, a minimal car; and as soon as one or both of us can learn to drive properly, if ever, we intend to expand our visiting radius considerably. On the other hand, is there no hope of seeing you in London this winter?

                                   Yours ever,
                                   [Tom]

1–Sacheverell Sitwell replied from Weston Hall, Towcester, Northamptonshire: 'I should be delighted to do the little book you suggest, as long as there is plenty of time.' He went on: 'I have given up all hope of ever seeing you, or Vivien, again. It is eight years since I set eyes on you, and more than that since I saw Vivien . . . I suppose it is no use trying to get you and Vivien, or either one of you, down here for a night or two.'

TO *Howard Morris*[1]   TS Morgan

24 October 1929   Faber & Faber Ltd

My dear Fat,

It's good to hear from you like this, and I will see first of all that the
Criterion is sent to you with invoice. Yes, it still exists, in spite of various
vicissitudes; and the Pope, Ramsay Mac,[2] and Herb Hoover[3] are said to
tear it open with trembling fingers once every three months. We will see
how it strikes you. I have a pretty good crew of sturdy Bolovians writing
reviews for it.

I am not quite clear from your account of yourself whether you are
going to succeed Pierpont Morgan or land in jail; but as most of our
contemporaries seem to come to a bad end I expect you will too. Poor
old Duke: I am sorry about him, but he was headed as straight in that
direction as anyone I ever knew; but for my stout Anglo-Saxon constitution
I suppose I should be in a box too. Krumpacker too: well, well, but you
look blooming, and I expect the kids will weigh in to the Primo Carnera
class eventually. Your photo, by the way, looks a lot more like my memory
of your father than the frail and elfin H. Morris jr. that I remember. I'll
send you one of me, and you can draw your own conclusions. However, it
wd seem that you get more & more respectable as you get older; whereas
Tompo becomes more & more dissolute and shady.

I knew about Pete Little having separated himself from Mitchigan
[*sic*] – a disagreement with the board of governors, I gathered, about the
correct use of quinine pessaries – but did not know that he had got rid of
K. as well.[4] Well well, as they say,

1 – Howard Morris (b. 1887), who had been with TSE at Milton Academy and Harvard, had
written to renew contact on 4 Feb. 1928; they had last met at the Carlton Club, London, in
the early 1920s. He had been inspired to write by seeing TSE mentioned in E. M. Forster's
Aspects of the Novel. Morris had done well in the finance business, and had a wife and
two boys. He had 'ease[d] up on work a trifle' and taken up book collecting, and had
acquired first editions by George Moore, Aldous Huxley, T. F. Powys, Norman Douglas,
H. M. Tomlinson, Cabell and Dreiser. Which authors would TSE recommend?
2 – Ramsay MacDonald (1866–1937), leader of the National Government from 1929.
3 – Herbert Hoover (1874–1964), Republican; 31st President of the United States, 1929–33.
4 – Clarence C. Little (1888–1971) – known to his Harvard friends as 'Pete' – scion of an
upper-class Boston family; science researcher specialising in mammalian genetics and cancer;
President of the University of Maine, 1922–5, then President of the University of Michigan,
1925–9 – he quit the post not on account of quinine pessaries, as TSE jokes, but because his
progressive plans were not welcome; founding director of the Roscoe B. Jackson Memorial
Laboratory at Bar Harbor; managing director of the American Society for the Control of
Cancer (later the American Cancer Society); twice President of the American Society for
Cancer Research, President of the American Eugenics Society; and, most controversially,

Now bugger my ear the Boatswain said,
Now WHERE can all my rum go?
My reason leads me to suspect
That Bastard, Chris Columbo . . .

In the Vatican Library (where I worked for a month) I only found one
genuine stanza; the rest of the MSS. being *hopelessly corrupt.* As follows:

The Boatswain was a man of mark
Well known as Worthless Walter.
He found the Chaplain fast asleep
Perusing of the psalter.
He took him swiftly by the pants
And buggered him on the alter;
And the Mate said, (with a knowing look),
'I've seen that done in Malta'.

Yours ever fraternally
T.

TO *Hoffman Nickerson*[1]   CC

24 October 1929   [Faber & Faber]

Dear Hoffman,
    I was glad to get your letter of the 30th September.[2] I am sorry that you
did not get hold of the *Andrewes* in time, as I should have enjoyed your
opinion, but I hope there will be later opportunities. Meanwhile I look
forward to seeing your own book, and if you can come to England during
this winter or spring, you will find me, if anywhere, at the address above.
                        With many thanks,
                        Yours ever,
                        [T. S. Eliot]

Scientific Director of the Scientific Advisory Board of the Tobacco Industry Research
Committee (later the Council for Tobacco Research), 1954–69. In 1911 he had married
Katherine Day Andrews, daughter of a Boston architect, but they were divorced in 1929.
1–Hoffman Nickerson (1888–1965), journalist and historian.
2–Nickerson had attempted to undertake to review *For Lancelot Andrewes*, for either
Commonweal or the *New York Herald Tribune*, but he was too late in both cases. For
himself, he was expecting Doubleday Doran to publish his new book *The American Rich*.

TO *Humbert Wolfe*   CC

24 October 1929   [London]

Dear Humbert,

Referring to yours of the 12th instant HW/HW/ I quite agree with your opinion of the article you mention in the current *Criterion*. My effort is always to get from authors something a little better than their usual, and I note that here I have succeeded (see also the *Nottingham Guardian*).[1]

Mario Praz writes to ask me to ask you for the address of Lafourcade, who he says is a friend of yours.[2] If that is so, could one of your secretary's secretaries give me the address? I understand that Praz wishes to send L. a book.

About books, it would be helpful if you would make suggestions yourself. Please do. And let me know and when you are more or less in London.

Yours ever,
[T. S. E.]

TO *Darsie R. Gillie*   CC

24 October 1929   [London]

My dear Gillie,

I now send you your own contract with us, and also the contract for Pilsudski to sign. I believe that Stachieviez[3] does not figure in the contracts at all? I shall have to leave it to you to obtain Pilsudski's signature and see that we get it: the counterpart of these contracts will of course be sent to you and to him as soon as we have these back.

You will observe that if we can make with America the terms that we hope to make, there will be a further cash payment to you.

1 – Wolfe thanked TSE for the latest number of the *Criterion*; joking: 'I thought the article on Satire by Humbert Wolfe was rather above his normal level. That being so, I commend to your attention a book by the same author, *Notes on English Verse Satire* [1929]. If this is not noticed in *The Criterion* my opinion of that paper will sensibly appreciate.'
2 – Praz asked TSE on 22 Oct. if he could 'kindly get from Humbert Wolfe the address of Georges [de] Lafourcade, the author of La jeunesse de Swinburne [1928]?'
3 – Brigadier General Julian Stachiewicz (1890–1934), Polish military officer, historian and writer, was the director since 1923 of the Biuro Historyczne Wojskowe (Military Bureau of History) in Warsaw. Gillie described Stachiewicz, in his 'Translator's Preface', as 'the administrator of the Marshal's literary interests and joint editor of the complete edition of his writings, now in process of publication by the "Instytut Najnowszej Historji Polskiej"' (Pilsudski, *The Memories of a Polish Revolutionary and Soldier* [1931], ix).

I have discussed with my Board the question of the division of royalties between you and Pilsudski. I suggest (you understand quite informally, and only in the way of giving you my personal advice) that you could ask for a maximum of 25% of Pilsudski's royalties, and that you might accept a minimum of 15% of his royalties. But remember that this arrangement is only for the English-speaking rights, and that you will have to make terms for other translation rights as well. I mean, the 25% is based on the fact that you have made the translation; so if you get 25% you could hardly expect quite so much from him for say German rights; but on the other hand, if you have to take less than 25% for the edition, commentary *and* English translation, then you might even it up on the other foreign translations. But for the English-speaking rights alone, considering that you have conceived the idea, collected and edited the material, and provided commentary, map and photographs as well, I think you have a good case for a full 25%. Possibly you can do better.

I hope these suggestions will help you to make a satisfactory arrangement. Please let me know that you receive this letter, and I shall expect a certain delay before Pilsudski's contract is signed: but we should like to put the whole thing through as quickly as possible.

Yours ever sincerely,
[T. S. Eliot]

TO *Ursula Millett* CC

24 October 1929 [London]

Dear Madam,

I thank you for your letter of the 11th instant.[1] I have a profound dislike of all contemporary anthologies; but if yours is going to happen anyway, and as I cannot prevent you from using my poems in America, I do not see why you should not use them here; providing, of course, that your English publisher pays me a suitable fee. My consent, therefore, depends only on what your English publisher is willing to pay; and I am not unreasonable.

1–Ursula Millett, Houghton Mifflin Company, asked on 11 Oct. about the British rights to poems that TSE had agreed might be included in a forthcoming anthology, *Twentieth Century Poetry*, edited by John Drinkwater, H. S. Canby, and W. R. Benet.

And speaking next as a publisher, may I suggest that the anthology might first be offered to this firm, of which I am a director?

Yours very truly,

[T. S. Eliot]

TO *Bernard Causton*[1]   CC

24 October 1929   [London]

Dear Sir,

I must apologise for the delay in replying to your letters and returning your story.[2] It always happens that the contributions which are obviously useless are dealt with first. Yours I found very interesting, kept aside for further consideration, and mislaid.

I should have written to say that I did not find the story suitable for the *Criterion*, but that it impressed me, and I should from time to time very much like to see more of your work.

Yours faithfully,

[T. S. Eliot]

TO *P. M. Jones*   CC

24 October 1929   [London]

Dear Mr Jones,

I was very sorry indeed to miss you in London, but I hope that you may perhaps be here again the next holidays. I am very glad indeed that you were able to see those people in Paris, although you missed Maurras.[3] It would certainly be an impertinence on my part to ask to see your manuscript; if you will have it typed, I will see it then or in proof; and if

1 – Bernard Causton, journalist, was at this time UK representative of Houghton Mifflin, Boston. (He aso wrote for the *Daily Herald*.)
2 – 'Flight from Shame'.
3 – Jones wrote on 17 Oct.: 'Most of what I picked up in France, thanks to the interviews you so kindly secured for me, is now recorded in an Epilogue which I have been putting together since my return. It makes about a dozen pages of foolscap manuscript, & I am wondering whether you would care to glance at it before it is sent to be typed.' He wrote earlier (17 Sept.), 'I have had a quite exhilarating talk with Maritain & he has put me in touch with Du Bos. Unfortunately I do not seem to be able to find contact with any of the Maurras group . . .'

you wish my opinion you are welcome to it; but I have no desire to censor what you write.

I look forward with much pleasure to your book.[1]

Yours sincerely,
[T. S. Eliot]

TO *Viscount Brentford* CC

24 October 1929   [London]

Dear Sir,

Thank you for your letter of the 21st instant. I have consulted my Board, and we consider the *Saturday Evening Post* is as suitable a periodical as any. I learn that *The Ladies Home Journal* is under the same proprietorship, so that in writing to the *Post*, the essay could be proposed alternatively for the other paper. The next best periodical is, we think, *The Forum*.

I know the management of *The Forum* personally,[2] but not that of the other two papers. If you are already in communication with the *Saturday Evening Post*, perhaps you would prefer to write to them yourself. But if you would like us to do so for you, will you please let me know, and I will take it up at once.

I am,
Yours very truly,
[T. S. Eliot]
Director

TO *John Hayward* TS King's

29 October 1929   *The Criterion*

Dear Hayward,

I think Raleigh is well worth 1000 words,[3] and I hope you can let us have it by November 10th.

1–*Tradition and Barbarism* (F&F, 1930).
2–TSE had met Henry Goddard Leach, editor of *The Forum*, in London in 1927.
3–JDH had suggested (19 Oct.) that Ralegh's *Poems* were worth a review of 900–1000 words. 'Can you afford so much space?' He reviewed *The Poems of Sir Walter Ralegh*, ed. A. M. C. Latham, in C. 9 (July 1930), 753–5.

I shall be very glad if you will do Bonamy's *Restoration Tragedy*, and the other book with it: will you drop me a card of reminder when it comes out.[1]

I wonder if the *T.L.S.* has given you Quennell's book on Baudelaire & the Symbolists. He has an often irritating style, but he says some good things.

Very many thanks for your letter. I hope to see you before long.

Ever yours,
T. S. Eliot

TO *William Empson*[2]   CC

29 October 1929   [*The Criterion*]

Dear Mr Empson,

I have just heard from I. A. Richards that there is a possibility of your coming to London and doing literary work. I hope that this is so; and I wonder whether you would care to do any reviewing for *The Criterion*. Perhaps you will let me know when you come up to town and let us arrange a meeting here at some time.

Yours sincerely,
[T. S. Eliot]

TO *I. A. Richards*   CC

29 October 1929   [London]

Dear Richards,

I am very glad to hear from you. I have written to Empson and asked him to come and see me if and when he comes to London, and of course said nothing about Cambridge. Your recommendation is enough, and

---

1 – JDH (19 Oct.): 'I have not done a note on Bateson's XVIII cent: Comedy. Could I combine it with Bonamy's book on Restoration Tragedy (coming shortly, as they say); both books belong to the same series.' For unknown reasons, BD's *Restoration Tragedy 1660–1720* (1929) was not to be noticed in C.

2 – William Empson (1906–84), poet and critic; author of *Seven Types of Ambiguity* (1930), *Some Versions of Pastoral* (1935), *The Structure of Complex Words* (1951), and *Milton's God* (1961). TSE would later take pains at F&F to publish *The Gathering Storm* (poems, 1940), and to raise interest in Empson's work in the USA in the late 1940s. See further *Complete Poems*, ed. John Haffenden (2001).

when I have printed something of his I will try to get him in anywhere I can.[1]

I don't know who wrote the *T.L.S.* review of *Practical Criticism*.[2] The *Criterion* review by Fletcher was rather rushed; but I thought it best to get someone to write at once to say that it is a good book, and then get others to attack its theory later in articles at leisure.[3] That will be done. I am sending you my small Dante essay, in which you will find traces of conversations. Of course it is an elementary, almost one-syllable essay; but I want you to read the note to Chapter II. I have also revised for publication in the spring those poems which you criticised, and think that I have much improved them; and that the improvements just make all the difference between sincerity and sham.

I am glad that you have not forgotten Fernandez: he has an essay in the December *Criterion* which is worth your noticing.[4] But in your idyllic surroundings have you time to do other things as well.[5] A book

---

1 – IAR wrote from Tsing Hua University, Peiping (n.d.): 'I've just heard today from the best man I've ever had at Cambridge, William Empson <His address Yokefleet Hall Howden Yorkshire> <Oh yes! President of the Heretics when you read your paper to them! Not much good on a platform> that Magdalene after giving him a Bye Fellowship largely under pressure from me have taken it away on the ground of some indiscretion with a feminine direction. I don't know any details but am most indignant.

'He talks of coming up to London & working at the things he is interested in. This covers a good deal of 16th & 17th Century poetry and all sorts of things besides. I think he is a quite exceptionally good poet. *Cambridge Poetry 1929* will allow you to judge of this. He is a very ready hand with a pen and can produce new & valuable ideas about books within a very short time of first handling them. So he could be made great use of in reviewing. I'd always weigh his opinion as carefully as anyone's. I've told him that I would write to you in case you could help him to any criticism. I think he has a *small* private income. Don't mention to him that I have told you of his disaster.' (*Selected Letters*, 52–3.)

2 – 'The *Times* review of *Practical Criticism* was very friendly – I can't imagine who wrote it. Have I to thank you for suggesting someone?' (*ibid.*, 53).

3 – Fletcher called Richards's *Practical Criticism: A Study of Literary Judgment* (C. 9 [Oct. 1929], 162–4) 'a book which seems to me to be by far the best Mr. Richards has written, and one that generally makes for clearness of ideas, and improvement of judgment'. However, his caveats included criticism of IAR's proposal to 'separate emotional from intellectual assent . . . [I]t seems highly doubtful whether they can be so separated in the case of an art which so obviously fuses feeling and thinking as poetry.'

4 – Fernandez, 'A Humanist Theory of Value', trans TSE, C. 9 (Jan. 1930), 228–45.

5 – 'Here at the moment life is Paradisal. We live in a Llama Temple, turned by an ex Prime Minister of China into a Summer palace of his own. "The Temple of True Consciousness" – all flowers and cassia shrubs and aged pines and incense burners and halls and altars – marble steps and red lacquer pavilions, and we live in one of these with grinning attendants with whom we converse at present in gesture language . . . Classes are merely fun and not too many of them. Such charming students . . . I have not forgotten that I'm to write on Ramon Fernandez soon for you. Do send me, when you can, some poems, both those you have published in odd places and any you are going to publish. I have some lines of the

or two turns up from time to time which I should like to send you to review at your leisure. I am sending you also a book we are publishing (at my instance) by one Montgomery Belgion, which I think is worth your looking at,[1] and I may send you another book on *Instinct and Intuition* for your opinion.[2]

Will you return to England next summer, if ever?

With best wishes to both from my wife and myself,

Yours ever,

[T. S. E.]

Why, when you write to me, is the letter addressed care of some Ladies College in Osaka? 'There must he some reason for it, but I wonder what is that reason?' You left England, I believe, in time to escape The Two Black Crows in Hades, which is pitiful.[3] I saw Ogden a little while ago, looking very unhealthy and bursting with energy.

TO *Stuart Gilbert*   CC

29 October 1929   [*The Criterion*]

Dear Mr Gilbert,

I enclose herewith your counterpart to the agreement about your book on *Ulysses*. I should be grateful for your acknowledgement of receipt.

I think it is possible that we may be able to do business in America with the first half of the book in our hands;[4] but at the same time I earnestly

---

leopards poem [Part II of *Ash-Wednesday*] in my head from time to time – the feeling of them rather than the words & only the ghost of their movement.'
1–Montgomery Belgion, *Our Present Philosophy of Life: according to Bernard Shaw, André Gide, Freud, Bertrand Russell* (1929). GCF wrote to FVM on 24 July 1929: 'Eliot has reported favourably on Belgion's book *Our Present Philosophy of Life*. I have glanced at it, and think we certainly ought to publish it this autumn . . . I enclose a copy of Eliot's report.' On 25 Oct. GCF was to send a copy of the book to the editor of the *Daily Mail*: 'The reason I send this copy . . . is that the book contains a vigorous attack on the views of Bernard Shaw, and it occurs to me that, in view of the public's interest in Mr Shaw and his opinions, you may find a news value in this attack.'
2–George Binney Dibblee, *Instinct and Intuition: A Study in Mental Duality* (1929).
3 – 'Two Black Crows' – aka 'Moran and Mack' – George Moran (1881–1949) and Charles Mack (1888–1934) – was a successful blackface comedy act, appearing both on the radio and in movies; 'Two Black Crows in Hades' parts I and II was released in 1929.
4–Gilbert had written on 20 Oct.: 'I am accelerating work on the book as much as possible and will send at least the first half at the end of November . . . May I suggest that the proof sheets of the first half could be shown to possible American buyers?'

hope that you will still be able to let me have the complete manuscript well before the end of January.

Looking forward to meeting you here in the spring,

I am,
Yours sincerely
[T. S. Eliot]
Director.

TO *Christopher Dawson*   CC

29 October 1929   [London]

Dear Mr Dawson,

I am sorry you cannot deal with the Dante book at once, but the article is more important, and I should not like anything to interfere with my having that in good time for the March number. So take the Dante at leisure.

As for the title of your article, I should like, if you can, to have one that did not contain the word 'humanism'. It has appeared on several *Criterion* covers, including the next; the subject remains important, but I am afraid that people will become tired of the word.[1]

I hope very much that I may see you when you are in London. Please let me know as soon as you can, when and where you will be here.

Yours sincerely,
[T. S. Eliot]

1–Dawson wrote (22 Oct.): 'With regard to the title of the article, I would suggest "The Passing of Humanism", unless you think that will be confusing to your readers, who may take the word in an exclusively Babbittian sense. Personally I use neo-humanism to describe Babbitt's doctrine & keep the older & wider sense for humanism. As for Berdiaiev, I think *Der Sinn der Geschichte* is very much his best book, but so far as the Renaissance is concerned, he says very little in it which is not repeated in *Un Nouveau Moyen Age*.' In response to TSE's letter above, Dawson ventured on 31 Oct.: 'I am renaming my article The End of an Age, but I am afraid there is no getting away from the subject of humanism . . . Still I hope that I am covering rather different ground to the other articles you are publishing.' See 'The End of an Age', C. 9 (Apr. 1930), 386–401.

29 October 1929   *The Criterion*

Dear John,

Your criticism is harsh, but I see no reason why it should not appear in *The Criterion*.[1] I could not speak so sharply myself about a master whom I admire and to whom my personal debt is very great indeed, but that is no reason why you should not do so. The only thing is that humanism is going to be hydra-headed, as you will see from Fernandez' article in the next *Criterion*, and that there is much more to be done than just to sit on Babbitt. But actually I am wholly in agreement with you.

About the list of subscribers: I have no objection myself, but the directors seem to think that we ought to go slow on exchange circularising. We have tried it out with the *Hound & Horn*; it does not seem to have had much effect; but what we are afraid of is pestering subscribers with circulars from other reviews. In our case particularly, I imagine that most of the subscribers of each know already about the other – at least, they do if they *read* the periodical to which they subscribe. Why not make that arrangement with some foreign, preferably American periodical?

I wish myself that omnibus subscriptions, at reduced rates, were possible in this country as in America: we could then give alternative collections, including a variety of American and continental reviews: but that system seems to be looked upon askance.

Will you keep that Shakespeare essay in mind, if and when the proper number of editions accumulate?

Ever affectionately,

Tom

---

1 – JMM wrote by pc (24 Oct.), 'There is probably something good in Hugh l'Anson Fausset's book: but I can't say definitely till I have read it.' He added that he wanted to exchange lists of contributors – 'for propaganda purposes'. He wrote again, with his review ('Sunday'): 'Here is something on Fausset & Babbitt: of whom – the latter – I am now completely tired. I have reached the final conclusion that he is, in the worst sense, academic: so, I have felt myself at liberty to punch his head – with charity. If it doesn't suit your book, don't worry, but just return it: because it suits mine. But, as a matter of fact, it suits yours just as well – really. And it's high time you stopped being polite to our common enemies.' See JMM's review of Fausset, *The Proving of Psyche*, C. 9 (Jan. 1930), 349–53.

TO *Joseph Gordon Macleod*[1]   CC

29 October 1929   [London]

Dear Mr Macleod,

I am sorry to find that I have left your letter so long unanswered.[2] I remember your play very well; and shall be very glad indeed to see your poem; though I must say that publication of long poems is rather out of the way of Faber & Faber. But I might be able to suggest some other destination.

Yours sincerely,
[T. S. Eliot]

TO *G. Wilson Knight*   CC

29 October 1929   [London]

Dear Mr Knight,

I must apologise for the delay in answering your letters.[3] Your essays have not left my office, and I propose to discuss them at a committee

---

1–Joseph Todd Gordon Macleod (1903–84), poet, playwright, actor, theatre director, historian, and BBC newsreader, was educated at Balliol College, Oxford (where he was friends with Graham Greene), and in 1927 joined the experimental Cambridge Festival Theatre, of which he became director, 1933–6 (his productions included Ibsen's *The Seagull* and Ezra Pound's Noh plays, as well as five of his own plays). In 1938 he joined the BBC as announcer and newsreader, retiring to Florence in 1955: it was during the BBC period that the poetry he produced under the pseudonym 'Adam Drinan' became sought-after by editors in Britain and the USA; and he was admired by writers including Basil Bunting and Edwin Muir. His first book of poems, *The Ecliptic* (1930), was published by TSE at F&F. His plays included *Overture to Cambridge* (1933) and *A Woman Turned to Stone* (1934). See also James Fountain, 'To a group of nurses: The newsreading and documentary poems of Joseph Macleod', *TLS*, 12 Feb. 2010, 14–15.

2–Macleod had mentioned (25 Sept.) a poem written in the early part of this year: 'It is long, about 1500 lines. Chatto & Windus had no use for it . . .' (He had earlier submitted, in 1927, what he called 'a telescopic play'.)

3–GWK had submitted a selection of his essays on Shakespeare in the hope that F&F would publish a volume including pieces on *Macbeth*, *King Lear*, and *Timon of Athens*. There was also an essay on *Hamlet* which, as he had noted on 3 Oct., 'you kindly promised to use'. In a letter of 5 Oct. he enunciated what his work 'stands for': 'a translation into a suitable logic of the imaginative nature of the poet's vision . . . [T]he kind of work I have been doing has not as yet been ever systematically attempted, as far as I know. That is why I insist often that it is "interpretation" rather than "criticism". The fact that poetic drama has a plot-skeleton apparently analogous to actual human affairs has led commentators to abstract that rigid scaffolding for analysis: this is unjust . . . [O]ne must receive the unique work – if it be admittedly a masterpiece – as it stands, & then proceed to indicate its nature, finding whatever logic best suits its peculiar quality . . . the coherence of poetic vision.' OUP had made an approach to him, but he preferred to try F&F in the first instance. He wrote to TSE

---

tomorrow afternoon. It is possible that the other directors will consider that they are not the type of book by which our firm can do the best; but if so I shall venture to offer some suggestion as to where to take them. So you will be hearing from me again very soon.

Yours sincerely,
[T. S. Eliot]

TO *J. S. Barnes* CC

29 October 1929   [London]

Dear Jim,

In reply to your[s] of the 24th, I enclose, in the form in which I used to draw up such things when in the City, what little I have picked up about Marks, of whom I myself had never heard till you mentioned him.[1] I think that the capital is very small for a new venture. But perhaps I shall learn more about it before you come to London.

Your casual mention of Burns & Oates[2] made me think of Sheed & Ward. You probably know the people: Sheed is a brother-in-law of Leo Ward, the grandson of Wilfred Ward, and there is also Tom Burns in my firm. They are nice people; go-ahead and more popular than Burns & Oates, and considered quite promising. It seems to me the right place. If you don't know them, I could introduce you. Of course, I say this without knowing anything about the firm from the inside.

Yours ever,
[T. S. Eliot]

---

again on 16 Oct., 'I would prefer that the three essays I sent (Macbeth, Timon, Lear) did not go out of your office for the present . . . I am rather anxious that they should not be widely seen before I fix their publication . . .'

1 – Barnes reported his interest in Mr Marks – 'the late Managing Director of Benn's and also of Fisher Unwin': 'He intends to set up on his own, has collected part of the capital (from £10–15,000) and invites me to join him as a Director & working partner – investing £2,000 more.' He was eager to know what TSE knew of Marks's career and reputation in publishing circles, and whether it would be a good for him to join in Marks's enterprise.

2 – Barnes had mentioned in a letter of 17 Oct.: 'In certain circumstances I may have the offer of a job (to be on the Board into the bargain) of Burns, Oates & Washburn, but this depends on a lot of things which have not yet materialized.'

TO *R. B. Braithwaite*   CC

29 October 1929   [London]

Dear Mr Braithwaite,

Thank you very much for your letter of the 20th instant, and for sending me the offprint of your *Mind* article on Eddington, which I have read and enjoyed, though much of it is beyond my depth.[1] I am more than sorry that you are unwilling to do that essay on Sentimental Physics, and am still unconvinced by your reasons. But perhaps some other notion will turn up which will find you more enthusiastic.

Unfortunately, not hearing from you I had given up hope of your writing on Jeans, and gave it to someone else. Had I known sooner I should gladly have kept it over a quarter for you. But here again, I shall return with other suggestions, and hope even that you may make one yourself.[2]

                                    With all best wishes,
                                    Yours sincerely,
                                    [T. S. Eliot]

TO *John Copley*[3]   CC

29 October 1929   [London]

Dear Sir,

Your letter of the 22nd ultimo and your essay on Umano have now been read by myself and two other Directors.[4] The opinions you quote have

---

1 – 'Professor Eddington's Gifford Lectures' – a review of A. S. Eddington, *The Nature of the Physical World* (1928) – *Mind: A Quarterly Review of Psychology and Philosophy* 38: 152 (Oct. 1929), 409–35. Braithwaite wrote to TSE: 'It seems to me that I must have a definite "concern" (to use the Quaker word) in order to propagate my purely negative opinions about Eddington's & Whitehead's "religions". And though I am pretty confident that I am right in thinking that physics has no bearing upon religion and that Eddington & Whitehead's physically-based systems of metaphysics are untenable, yet I don't think that these heresies are so pernicious that I (who have nothing to put in their place) wish to uproot them.'
2 – Braithwaite did not contribute to C.
3 – John Copley (1875–1950), lithographer, studied at the Manchester School of Art and the Royal Academy School, London, and spent two years in Italy. He took up lithography in 1907, and won the chief award and medal at the first International Exhibition of Lithographs at the Art Institute of Chicago, 1930. Examples of his work are in galleries throughout the world.
4 – Copley had submitted a pamphlet about Umano (d. 1927), with the assurance that Umano's friends would subsidise its publication; he said that the proposal was endorsed by Madame Lévi and her sister Rosina Filippi, and Bernard Shaw warmly supported it.

led us to give it very serious consideration. I confess that none of us had ever heard of 'Umano' before.

We are of the opinion that the publication of an introductory pamphlet like yours should, in justice to both author and publisher, be an integral part of a general scheme for launching his works in translation. It ought to be in the hands of the same firm of publishers, and should, I think, appear at the same time as the first of the books, so that it might be put into the hands of reviewers. We should therefore not consider the pamphlet separately; but would consider it in connexion with one or more of Umano's books, if some proposal were laid before us.

Yours faithfully,
[T. S. Eliot][1]

TO *Henry Goddard Leach*   cc

29 October 1929   [London]

Dear Mr Leach,

I am writing to you personally because I have some hope that you may remember meeting me – on, I am sorry to say, only one occasion – when you were in London a couple of years ago. In any case, you may remember me as a contributor to *The Forum*; so I take the liberty of writing to you about another possible contributor.

I have induced the late Home Secretary, Lord Brentford (better known as Sir William Joynson-Hicks) to expand a few pages he wrote for *The Nineteenth Century* into a full essay of some 5000 words, which we are going to publish in England as a pamphlet. It occurred to me that, as we did not require American rights of this, an essay on this subject by such an authority ought to be very desirable to some American periodical, as it is by no means of local interest. As he tells me he does not know you, or anyone connected with the *Forum*, – and I suggested to him that the *Forum* would be the most suitable vehicle, I am writing to you to give you the first refusal of this essay called 'Do We Need a Censor?'.

If you think you would like to have it could you send me a short cable of acceptance quoting terms? Of course your acceptance would be subject to your approval of the manuscript on receipt.

---

1 – Copley responded (30 Oct.), 'I am very glad that there is a possibility of your being interested in his work. I feel sure that he had sane, clear, unsentimental things to say about peace & that principles that must underlie its assumption, that are of value today.' He offered to put TSE in touch with Madame Lévi, Umano's greatest friend in England, who could speak 'authoritatively' about his work.

Yours very truly,
[T. S. Eliot]
You will understand that we have no financial interest in the matter, and
that payment should be made direct to Lord Brentford.

TO *E. G. Selwyn*[1]   CC

30 October 1929   [London]

Dear Dr Selwyn,

Thank you very much for your letter.[2] It is true that Mr Montgomery
Belgion's book was sent you at my suggestion. (I have seen a good deal
of the author lately, and he is a member of a club under that name, and I
have no reason to suppose that he has any other). It would give me great
pleasure to review it, but there are objections: I am a director of the firm
which published it; the book was first submitted to me, and was published
on my strong recommendation; so I incline to the view that it would be
unsuitable for me to recommend in a review a book which I have myself
been responsible for publishing. But, if you are at a loss for a reviewer,
I could mention several friends of mine who are equally competent to
review it, without my embarrassment. The fact that I have got the book
published is enough to show that I think it a book well worthy of the
space you are disposed to give [to it.] [*typing runs off the page*]

Incidentally, I hope that you will read the book yourself. It attacks
several superstitions which I am sure you must detest as strongly as I do:
it is negative in the right way – by leaving a vacuum which I believe can
only be filled in one way.

I have had you on my conscience for some time. You, or rather your
secretary, sent me for review, at a moment when I thought I was freer

1 – The Revd Edward Gordon Selwyn (1885–1959), editor of *Theology: A Monthly Journal
of Historic Christianity*, 1920–33. Educated at Eton and King's College, Cambridge
(Newcastle Scholar; Porson Scholar and Prizeman; Waddington Scholar; Browne's
Medallist; 2nd Chancellor's Medallist), he was Rector of Redhill, Havant, 1919–30; and
Provost in Convocation, 1921–31. He was ultimately to be Dean of Winchester, 1931–58.
His publications include *The Teaching of Christ*; *The Approach to Christianity*; *Thoughts on
Worship and Prayer*; *The First Epistle of St Peter* and *Essays Catholic & Critical by Members
of the Anglican Communion* (ed., 1926).
2 – Selwyn wrote (28 Oct.) that he had been sent by F&F, 'at your suggestion, what looks like
an exceedingly interesting book by one Montgomery Belgion – a *nom-de-plume*, perhaps? –
called *Our Present Philosophy of Life*.' He hoped TSE would review it for *Theology*. 'I am
sure that the book should be discussed by someone who is primarily a man of letters, & at
the same time has a philosophy of life strong enough to take the place of the modern one
discredited in this book.'

than I was, Gore's *Jesus*[1] and an American book on the same subject. I have been meaning to write to apologise for the defect of my review, and to ask you if I might make amends by incorporating it into a brief article from a layman's point of view, and the point of view of a man of letters, on 'Lives of Jesus' in general – comprehending Murry and Ludwig[2] and Gore's Everyman Renan[3] as well. Of course I am not very friendly to such attempts, but some useful distinctions between types might be drawn.

I am hoping that at some time you will be in London with enough leisure to see me.

Sincerely yours
[T. S. Eliot]

TO *Miss Powell*   cc

2 November 1929   [London]

Dear Madam,

It is unfortunate that I was unable to speak to you on the telephone yesterday. I wished to ask you whether Lord Brentford would consider it necessary to revise the proofs of the pamphlet entitled 'Do We Need a Censor?'. It is most important that we should be able to produce the pamphlet by November 14th. We did everything possible, on receipt of the script, to press forward the printing, but only received proofs yesterday; and it is necessary, if we are to keep to our timetable, to be able to return these proofs to the printer on Monday.

I should be very grateful if you would put the matter to Lord Brentford on Monday morning if possible. We have had the proof read very carefully, and have found only one or two slight errors; so we trust that no further revision is required. I should be very glad if you would kindly telephone me on Monday morning at this number; or early Monday afternoon at Paddington 6930.

Yours faithfully,
[T. S. Eliot]
Director

1 – Charles Gore, *Jesus of Nazareth* (1929). Gore (1853–1932) was a theologian and Anglican Bishop (Worcester, Birmingham, Oxford). His other publications include *The New Theology and the Old Religion* (1908) and *The Holy Spirit and the Church* (1924).
2 – Emil Ludwig, *Der Menschensohn: Geschichte eines Propheten* (Berlin, 1928): *The Son of Man*, trans. by Eden and Cedar Paul (London, 1928).
3 – Ernest Renan, *The Life of Jesus*, with introduction by Charles Gore (London, 1927).

TO *G. Wilson Knight*   CC

4 November 1929   [London]

Dear Mr Wilson Knight,

We have considered the essays which you sent me with a view to the publication of a large book of your essays on various plays of Shakespeare. After mature consideration we feel that it would not be quite the type of book with which we are equipped to deal and that there are other publishers who would probably produce it with greater advantage to yourself. And I should myself strongly advise your submitting it to the Oxford University Press and if I could be of any help to you in that connection I should be very glad.

Meanwhile I hold the essays until I hear whether they should be returned to you or sent to some other destination on your behalf.[1]

Yours sincerely,
[T. S. Eliot]

TO *Richard Strachey*[2]   CC

4 November 1929   [London]

My dear Strachey,

I am at last able to report on your book as two other directors have now been able to read it.[3] I have told you more or less how it strikes me and the fact that I wanted to keep it for consideration by the firm is a further indication of my opinion. The feeling of the other directors

---

1 – Wilson Knight said (7 Nov.) he was happy for TSE to send his work on to OUP.
2 – Richard Strachey (1902–76), elder son of Lytton Strachey's brother Ralph, spent his early years in India (where his father was an engineer for the East India Railway). 'Dick' Strachey became best known for his writings for children, the 'Little Reuben' and 'Moonshine' series. See also *A Strachey Child* (1979) and *A Strachey Boy* (1980).
3 – Philippa Strachey had written to TSE on 13 Sept. 1929: 'I am venturing to ask your permission to introduce a young nephew of mine – Richard Strachey – to your benevolence. He has literary aspirations & a profound admiration of your work & has written a novel. None of this sounds very original – but he does take the art of writing very seriously & he wants to be allowed to pay you a visit & ask your advice about his book.' On 2 Oct. Richard Strachey himself made 'tender inquiries after' his own book. 'I am ready to admit that the second chapter is somewhat ingenuous, but I rather wanted S and P to be stage ingénues, in other words youth personified, sublimated, absolutely unreal but quite possibly imaginable. As they move through the book their characters (never really very different) merge into one – this is "symbolized" (shall I say symbolized?) in the act of copulation, and becomes evident in the shipwreck.'

however was that we were not probably the best firm to deal with it. For a book like this it is a question of a limited public all of whom must be reached. I daresay you have already thought of the Hogarth Press but I will add that I should very much like them to see it. Chatto & Windus are another possible firm.[1] So I am not returning the book until I hear from you and if you want me to send it to either of these firms or to any other with a personal note from myself I should be glad to do so.

I enjoyed meeting you very much and hope you will let me know when you are in London again.

Yours sincerely,
[T. S. Eliot]

TO *Viscount Brentford*   cc

11 November 1929   [London]

Dear Sir,

I have received a cable from the editor of *The Forum* of New York offering two hundred dollars for the first American serial rights of *Do We Need a Censor?*

I shall be glad to know whether this offer is acceptable to you. If so, I will send a copy of the pamphlet to the *Forum* and ask them to communicate thereafter direct with yourself. The offer is of course contingent upon their approval of the essay, but I think it is very unlikely that they will have any hesitation.

Yours faithfully,
[T. S. Eliot]

TO *Alexis St Leger Leger*   ts Fondation Saint-John Perse

15 November 1929   Faber & Faber Ltd

My dear Leger,

I am now sending you herewith the galley proof of the text and the translation of *Anabase*.

I know how busy you are, so you need not feel obliged to answer this letter. I merely wished to give you the opportunity of reading the proof,

---

1–Chatto & Windus acknowledged receipt of *These Characters are Imaginary* by Richard Strachey on 16 Nov. 1929. It was to be published by Victor Gollancz in 1931.

detecting any errors in the French text, and making any further criticisms that occur to you of my translation.

You will observe that I have accepted the great majority of your revisions, that in a few places I have compromised, and only in a few have stuck to my first version. I think I could justify most of these; but if you still find any gross alterations of the sense I hope you will let me know quickly.

My Directors were desirous of having a small edition signed by author (and translator); but I told them that it would be asking far too much of anyone so occupied as yourself to sign and return to us a number of sheets within a short time. Even were you not so busy, I know myself the trouble of signing sheets in another country, the trouble with customs offices, post offices etc. It was agreed therefore that you should not be asked to do this, but that I should sign a certain number of copies myself, as the existence of some 'signed' copies would stimulate the sale.

I should very much like to hear from you, and also about the dedication to Madame de Bassiano, which of course I cannot include without your assent. We wish to bring the book out early in the spring, and the production of an elaborate edition is not an undertaking that can be hurried. So I should be very grateful, if you have any alterations to make, or any suggestions, that you would send me a brief line *at once*, so that I shall wait for a longer letter. But if I do not hear from you at all within four or five days, I will take it as your permission to proceed.[1]

> With most cordial good wishes,
> Yours always sincerely,
> T. S. Eliot

1 – Marguerite de Bassiano replied for Leger on 8 Dec.: 'Leger will write to you as soon as he possibly can and I hope you will surely meet when he is in London for the Naval Conference.

'In the meantime he has asked me to thank you de tout coeur for the great trouble you have taken with the translation which he finds most beautiful. He is very touched that you should have taken account of so many of his observations! I thank you with all my heart also. You have really been an angel.

'Is it intentional that you omit two phrases [on] page 2 where I have marked and "his raiment" at the bottom of page 25?

'Leger tells me you want to dedicate the translation to me but it would be unadvisable for reasons which I can tell you better when I see you. Dedicate me one day something really yours!'

TO *M. C. D'Arcy*   CC

18 November 1929   [London]

My dear D'Arcy,

The Directors of my firm have been discussing the possibility of a new popular book on Roman Catholicism, and I have been asked to consult you about it. The notion is not mine; and I confess that I was not very sanguine about it, largely on the ground that Ronald Knox had already done it.[1] Of course, I agree (with them) that Knox's book is not a very good one; it is self-consciously smart, and if a man begins as an Oxford wit he hardly ever gets over it. Still, Knox was trying to do much the same thing: to explain the position of the Church to the ordinary Englishman who is not a theologian and probably not closely associated with any church.

If a new book were to be written at all, it ought, we think, if possible, to be written by a layman, and preferably by a layman who was not a convert, but born into the Church. Anyway, I should like to know whether you think there is anything to be done, after Knox's book; and if so whether you can think of anyone suitable.

I do hope that we may be able to meet during the Christmas holidays.

Yours always sincerely,

[T. S. Eliot]

TO *E. T. Scott*[2]   CC

18 November 1929   [London]

Dear Sir,

I have your letter of the 11th November addressed to me at 27, Chester Terrace (which was never my address) and which had reached me only after considerable delay.[3]

1–Ronald Knox, *The Belief of Catholics* (1927). Knox (1888–1957), theologian, priest, writer of crime fiction (a founding member of the Detection Club), became an Anglican priest in 1912. A High Anglican, in 1917 he converted to Catholicism, being ordained as a Catholic priest in 1918; he taught at St Edmund's College, Ware, Herts, 1919–26, and served as an Oxford chaplain, 1926–39. Other works include *Apologia* (1917), *A Spiritual Aeneid* (1918), *Caliban in Grub Street* (1930), and *Heaven and Charing Cross* (1935).
2–E. T. Scott (1883–1932), younger son of C. P. Scott (editor-owner of *The Manchester Guardian*) worked for the *Guardian* from 1913 and was appointed editor in July 1929.
3–Scott asked if TSE would care 'to write us a letter for publication explaining your views on this question' – i.e. censorship.

I cordially approve your enquiry into the censorship question, and look forward to reading your inquest. But you will I trust understand that it is impossible for me to contribute to the discussion, however much I should like to do so. I am a Director of the firm which publishes these two pamphlets, and they were published at my own suggestion, so that it would be improper for me to take any part in advertising them. I return them with my thanks, so that you may send them in the same way to some other critic.

Yours very truly,
[T. S. Eliot]

TO *James Maxton*[1]   CC

18 November 1929   [London]

Dear Sir,

I am sending you under separate cover copies of three pamphlets recently issued by my firm, under the serial title of *The Criterion Miscellany*, by Mr H. G. Wells, Lord Brentford and Mr D. H. Lawrence, each dealing with some matter of current interest.

It is our design to use the notion of this series to enable men and women in public life to put before the public their ideas on any subject with which they are especially engaged, in a cheap pamphlet which shall be at the same time more permanent, and more conspicuous, than periodical publication. The series has no tendency; it aims only at the rapid circulation of ideas in pamphlet form by persons of importance or of authority on their subjects and views.

With the approval of my Board, I am writing to ask you whether you would care to consider writing such a pamphlet, of from 5,000 to 10,000 words, stating, let us say, your own views of the programme which a Labour government ought to carry out.

As we aim to keep the price of such pamphlets very low, we expect to profit only where there is a very large sale; and therefore we offer to all contributors the same scale of payment, viz., 10% royalty.

We should be very happy if the scheme commended itself to you.

Yours faithfully,
[T. S. Eliot]
Director.

1–James Maxton (1885–1946), Scottish socialist politician; MP for Bridgeton, 1922–46, and in time leader of the Independent Labour Party; advocate of Home Rule for Scotland.

TO *Erich Alport*   CC

18 November 1929   Faber & Faber Ltd

Dear Dr Alport,

I am writing to you again at last about Scheler. I have thought over
carefully the three smaller books – 'Wesen und Form', 'Die Stellung des
Menschen' and 'Mensch und Geschichte', and discussed the matter with
one or two friends. My opinion now is, that it would be a pity to bring out
any small book first. The two pamphlets are part of the *Anthropologie*
anyway, I understand; and Wesen und Form is a distinctly technical work:
if it came out now, it would have very little sale, and the fact that it had
appeared and made only a limited success would injure the later work.
We feel not only that the *Anthropologie* is a book of much wider interest
(so far as one can predict at this point), but that its success would help
the Wesen u. Form; whereas if the latter appeared first, it would injure the
Anthropologie. To introduce an author like Scheler to the English public,
I am sure that the Anthropologie would be the best book.

We should be very grateful if you would put the case for us to the
publishers, and if possible get them to let us have the first option on the
Anthropologie. Have you any news as to when it will appear in German?

Yours always sincerely,

[T. S. Eliot]

TO *Allanah Harper*   CC

18 November 1929   [London]

Dear Madame,

I have your letter of the 8th instant as well as your telegram received today. I have no objection at all to your making a French translation of my
preface to *Le Serpent*, providing, as I said, you give the date of its original
appearance. I should not like it to be thought a new piece of writing.[1]

As for *The Hollow Men*, that is another matter.[2] I am sorry that you
should have much work for nothing, but on the other hand I must protest
against your sending me a translation without previously consulting me,
saying nothing about remuneration, and taking it for granted that I agree

---

1–Harper's telegram requesting the use of TSE's preface has not survived.
2–Harper (8 Nov.) had submitted for TSE's approval what she considered her 'feeble'
translation of 'The Hollow Men': she was proposing to publish it in the first number of
Échanges: revue trimestrielle de littérature Anglaise et Française, due out in Dec. 1929.

to the publication. The question of payment does not actually interest me, but I do not wish at present to have any such translations into French appear. The first part of this poem has already been translated by St Leger Leger and I am at present [*word illegible: typescript runs off the page*] with a friend a volume of selected poems in French translation. You will I hope understand that in the circumstances I do not wish any other unauthorised translations to appear, and that I should regard them as an infringement of copyright.

With many regrets and all best wishes,

Yours very truly,
[T. S. Eliot]

TO *Darsie R. Gillie*   cc

18 November 1929   [London]

Dear Gillie,

Thank you for your letter of the 29th ultimo. You need not worry about our repudiating the contracts if the MSS. is not ready by the 31st December, and if you can let us have it (and I hope the maps and photographs) by the 31st January next we shall be quite satisfied.

So I hope you can let us have the contracts soon, and if you prefer to alter the dates to 31st January please do so. Of course we should be glad to have the MSS. earlier if possible, as every week counts before the spring season, and the earlier books are out the better.

I am not sure whether I sent you the letter for Du Bos or not; if not, here is another one.[1]

Yours always sincerely,
[T. S. Eliot]

1–Gillie had asked for a letter of introduction to Charles du Bos on behalf of a friend, a translator from English into French.

TO *Charles Du Bos*   cc

18 November 1929   [London]

My dear Du Bos,

    This is to introduce to you my friend Mr Darsie Gillie, the Berlin
Correspondent of the *Morning Post*, who wishes himself to introduce
to you a person very highly qualified for translation from English into
French. I am sorry that Mr Gillie cannot at present call upon you; but he
will enclose this note with a letter explaining what he has in mind.
    I have just sent you my small book on Dante, as a partial return for the
volumes you sent me.

                                    Yours very sincerely,
                                    [T. S. Eliot]

TO *Messrs. Chatto & Windus*   TS Reading

18 November 1929   Faber & Faber Ltd

Dear Sirs,

    I have sent to you a manuscript of a novel by Mr Richard Strachey, and
have your acknowledgement. Mr Strachey brought the book to me for
my opinion, and I considered it very carefully. It is immature and uneven,
but seemed to me to have promise. I felt that it was not the type of novel
which my firm was best qualified to handle, and that you would be more
likely to reach the suitable public for it, so Mr Strachey agreed to my
suggestion that I should forward it to you.
    I shall be grateful if you can have it considered carefully; as I am sure
that he deserves that. Will you please let me know your decision direct.[1]

                                    Yours faithfully
                                    T. S. Eliot

1–On 15 Nov. 1930 TSE was to write, in his Faber reader's report on a novel entitled
'Mysognyny over the weekend' (author unknown): 'This book seems to me but the shadow
of laughter like a sigh, or vice versa if you prefer. I doubt if there is much money to be made
by publishing an imitation of the earlier mode of Aldous Huxley. After all, *Crome Yellow*
was a coherent book; and its characters, being copied from life to the best of the author's
ability, were at least simulacra of human beings. But to combine supposedly real and modern
young people – with what names – Denis! – the quintessence of vulgarity – with wholly
preposterous figures talking the best Pavonian they can muster – seems to me to fall on
one's nose between two stools. I think that this sort of harlotry-playing might well be left to
the very, very young publishers. Even young Richard Strachey's book was better than this.'

18 November 1929   [London]

Dear Herbert,

Very many thanks for your letter and the hints. I will come to see the eikons, if possible on a day when we can lunch together.[1] But the Yorkshire lady does not want a matrimonial agency at the moment, but a home; so remember that if you come across any dogless homes.[2]

Now the two volumes of Gundolf's Shakespeare have come from the publisher.[3] You remember that we talked about this. I think we ought to get it read and reported on by some competent authority, and we thought you might advise as to who is a competent authority for this book. I suspected that it is not at all in the line of the regular Shakespeare scholar e.g. Dover Wilson. Am I right? Would it be better to send it to some more philosophical critic, and if so, can you propose anyone? I don't remember whether you have read the book or not, but at least you know where to classify it.[4]

I am not sure about that line; the point had not struck me.[5] I don't think the poem is really first rate, but I do think that it just does escape insincerity, somehow.

I believe that a slow-motion picture of Fernandez' acrobatics would show that he is standing on his own head – there is, I feel, a distinct sleight of hand with his values, but the glibness of the speech deceives the eye. It would have infuriated Hulme, I am sure. But as you say, it is already too wiredrawn for periodical uses, and ought to be handled elsewhere.[6]

1–Read enclosed a card, in a letter of 16 Nov., to remind TSE of an Exhibition at the Victoria & Albert Museum. 'It is really important. There has probably never been so much good art in England before. You must try & come, & if you can take the opportunity of lunching with me at the same time, so much the better.'

2–HR had written on 16 Nov.: 'I haven't found a home for the young lady from Yorkshire, but I suggest that she might join the Club of which I enclose a membership form. Notice the ithyphallic seal. The club has about a quarter of a million members (as bad as the R. A. C.) so she won't be lonely.' The lady and the club are not known.

3–*Shakespeare: sein Wesen und Werk* (Georg Bondi).

4–HR replied (19 Nov.): 'I have not read the Gundolf, but I know the kind of book it is.' He suggested Collingwood or Dover Wilson.

5–'About your poem [*Ash-Wednesday* III], I can only say that I like it very much. The only detail that worries me is the clash of the false & true rhymes of "banister", "stairs" & "despair" at the top of p. 6. I'm not sure, too, that I like "twisted" and "banister" in the same line, but I can see that it might be defended. That is positively the only detail that holds me up at all. The poem as a whole moves splendidly & gives me great pleasure.'

6–'The review of [JMM's book] GOD [by TSE in C. 9 (Jan. 1930), 333–6] is surely all right,' wrote HR (16. Nov.). 'It is so much all right that it might have been written equally

Ever yours,
[T. S. E.]

TO *C. A. Siepmann*   TS BBC Caversham

20 November 1929   Faber & Faber Ltd

Dear Mr Siepmann,

I enclose tentative syllabus for my six talks. You will observe that I give alternatives for V and VI, the second being rather the more popular and comprehensive – a whole half hour on Cleveland and Benlowes is probably too stiff; and the inclusion of Dryden might be more pleasing. Besides, if I give one evening to Dryden no one can say that I am merely rehashing old Cambridge lectures. (They will be very different in any case, and in some respects my opinions have altered since four years ago).

But let me know which you prefer, or if you suggest altering the syllabus in any other way I shall be quite amenable.

I think the second date – from March 8th, would suit me best: January 25th gives me very little time for preparation.

Yours sincerely,
T. S. Eliot

TO *Walter de la Mare*   CC

20 November 1929   [London]

Dear De la Mare,

I did get your first letter, and apologise for not answering at once.[1] I have been considering whether there is any justification for my writing

---

well by a Christian or an atheist – which seems to point to impartiality. Fernandez I found quite interesting, but as you say, people will have had enough of that subject, & in any case it is now getting down to subtleties outside the province of a periodical. Someday, if the subject becomes more urgent, there might be room for a symposium in book form, but the time is not ripe for that yet.'

1 – De la Mare wrote on 4 Nov. on behalf of the Royal Society of Literature to invite TSE to contribute a paper of *c*.5,000–10,000 words to a collection on the 1880s to be published by Cambridge University Press. The paper would be read before the RSL, and a fee of ten guineas would be paid; all other rights were to remain with the author. 'Would you please consider contributing a Paper on *Aesthetic*?' he requested. In a covering note of the same date, he added, '"The Eighteen-Eighties" is, of course, only a very loose title, but roughly Walter Pater and Vernon Lee can be included under it.' Having received no reply after a couple of weeks, de la Mare enquired again on 19 Nov.

on this subject at all, though I appreciate highly the compliment of being invited. My only qualification for writing about the 80s is that I was, by a fair margin, born in that decade; I am not an authority on Aesthetics, or on Walter Pater, and I am remarkably ignorant of the work of Vernon Lee. I mean, I could write about Pater, but there seems no obvious reason why I should be the man chosen for that task; and I have no all round knowledge of the aesthetic of the period. I used to know Symonds's work pretty well, but that is long ago. I should be very happy to be in your volume; but I don't see how I could justify my presence on that subject! Perhaps the name of someone better qualified will occur to you.

> With many thanks,
> Yours sincerely,
> [T. S. Eliot]

TO *J. E. Pouterman*   CC

28 November 1929   [London]

Dear Sir,

Referring to your letter of the 22nd August last, I have to inform you that my Introduction to the translation of Baudelaire's *Journeaux Intimes* is now ready; and I shall be glad to know what address – whether London or Paris – I should send it.[1]

I give my formal acceptance of your offer of £25 (twenty-five pounds sterling) for this introduction; but I should be glad to hear from you in your reply to this letter that you agree to my using my introduction in a collection of my essays, or separately in periodical form, as soon as your limited edition of the translation of *Journaux Intimes* is sold out, or after two years from its publication, whichever date is the nearer. You will see, I am sure, that this is reasonable; for it would not be worth my while to write introductions of this length unless I could make further use of them after a reasonable time.

> Awaiting your early reply,
> Yours faithfully,
> [T. S. Eliot]

1 – Charles Baudelaire, *Intimate Journals*, translated by Christopher Isherwood; Introduction by TSE (London: The Blackamore Press; New York: Random House, 1930).

TO *David Higham*

28 November 1929   [London]

Dear Higham,

I enclose herewith the essay 'Poetry and Philosophy' which I mentioned to you on the telephone; and I should be glad if you could place it advantageously for me with some American periodical. I may mention that it was written for delivery to a small audience for the benefit fund of St George's Bloomsbury – that I have no intention of publishing it in this country – and that therefore any American review that took it would be having practically the first rights. Incidentally, I should like to get proof for alterations and improvements.

I will confirm what I said to you on the telephone about Guy Chapman's offer.[1] It is certainly tempting, but I had already considered (for my own firm) and dismissed the possibility of publishing the two 'Fragments' by themselves. I have not yet given up the hope of finishing the play of 'Sweeney Agonistes'; if I do, it means considerably revising these fragments; and if I finish the play, I have, as I said, definite notions about the form of publication. I think that you will be able to put my reasons to Chapmans in such a way that they will not suppose that I object to them; for indeed I am pleased and flattered by the offer.

I have been suffering from an intermittent influenza for three weeks, and am all behindhand with everything; when I can catch up I shall suggest a return lunch with me.

Yours sincerely,
[T. S. Eliot]

TO *Richard Cobden-Sanderson*

29 November 1929   [London]

Dear Richard,

I was pleased to see in your new catalogue that you are still advertising my mother's *Savonarola*; and I shd be grateful if you wd let me know how many copies you still have on your hands; and if you would let me have six copies with invoice at trade rates. Now that my mother is dead, my

---

1–Higham had advised TSE on 2 Nov. that Guy Chapman wished to publish the two *Sweeney* fragments (C. Oct. 1926, Jan. 1927) in his King's Printers series for Eyre & Spottiswoode. 'The idea is a limited edition in folio – a really fine book in the style of Pope's folios', with a fee based on a 15% royalty of the published price of about 10/6d.

brother and I want to bring out in America some sort of limited edition of her poems, including this one; primarily of course for members of the family. I confess I have forgotten on what terms you retained the copies you have; but if they are a burden to you, we should be very willing to relieve you of them. This is an opportunity for telling you how much I appreciated your kindness and the trouble you took over the book at the time.

Congratulations on the Forget-me-not: I think that most other publishers wish that they had thought of it first. It deserves a great success.

[*Incomplete: typing runs off the page.*]

TO *Gerard Hopkins*   CC

30 November 1929   [London]

Dear Mr Hopkins,

As I once took the liberty of sending you on some manuscript, may I do so again? There are a few of a series of essays on Shakespeare by a man named G. Wilson Knight, a master at Dean Close School, Cheltenham. Another essay I have accepted for the *Criterion*; one has been published in the *Dublin Review*; and as you will see from his schedule enclosed, others have been published or are accepted for publication elsewhere. I told him I thought the book was not in our line, and that a University Press would be the best place. I do think they are worth considering. I understand that he has a chance of going to the University of Calcutta as Professor of English.[1]

There is one point. If you think the MSS. worth sending to a reader, I believe that Murry does not like this man's Shakespeare work, and would probably be against it.[2]

Yours sincerely,
[T. S. Eliot]

1 – Wilson Knight advised TSE on 26 Nov.: 'It seems that I have a fairly good chance of getting a post as Professor of English at Presidency College, Calcutta (University of Calcutta). I interviewed a board yesterday – Sir Israel Gollancz & two India Civil Service officials – & they are forwarding my papers to India. I gathered that my chances were good.'
2 – Wilson Knight had petitioned TSE on 7 Nov.: 'As Mr Middleton Murry is, I believe, at work on a very big Shakespeare treatise for the Oxford Press, it seems more than likely that they will officially refer my essays to him. He is, moreover, at present hostile towards my work.' Hopkins assented on 2 Dec. On 11 Dec. OUP was to acknowledge receipt of the 'specimen chapters of Shakespeare's Plays' (TSE's secretary had posted them on 9 Dec.).

30 November 1929   [London]

Dear Mr Bates,

I have discussed your suggestion of the 22nd with the other directors, and we should be very glad if you would send in your MSS.[1] For the Miscellany we do want a first rate piece of fiction from time to time; but I cannot say in advance at what date we should be able to publish it; our idea being to sprinkle the fiction in with the more topical pamphlets in a small proportion. But I believe that there is more than a chance of our being able to use something of yours, so please send the MSS. as soon as you can.

Sincerely yours,
[T. S. Eliot]

TO *Stuart Gilbert*   Mrs Stuart Gilbert

30 November 1929   [London]

Dear Mr Gilbert,

I must apologise for not having answered your last letter; a variable though slight influenza has thrown all my correspondence into disorder. I thought over very carefully your suggestion about printing one section of the book in the *Criterion*.[2] If it were merely a section of a book to be completed at some indefinite date, I should have been very glad to do so. But the book, we hope, will be out within a measurable time of the publication of the April *Criterion* – the first number in which I could use it. I felt, on the one hand, that the use of one section in that way would do little or nothing to help the book; and on the other hand I have to guard against the possibility of people thinking that we merely use the *Criterion* as an advertising medium for our own books – or alternatively, that we make up the *Criterion* by the facile method of putting in bits of future books. I hope you will see my point: that the *Criterion* and the publishing business cannot afford to appear *too* closely associated.

But anyway, I am quite sure that the book will make its way; and in any case we shall be happy to have published it.

1 – Bates offered (22 Nov.) to 'furnish a story of the right length . . . which is not included' in his forthcoming volume.
2 – Gilbert had written on 3 Nov.: 'May I ask if you would care to consider publishing one of the chapters in the *Criterion*? There are two, either of which might, perhaps, be suitable – the *Proteus* and *Scylla* episodes . . . I could write a page of introduction . . .'

Looking forward to seeing you in the spring,

> Yours sincerely,
> T. S. Eliot
> Director,
> Faber & Faber Ltd.

TO *R. Piccoli*   cc

30 November 1929   [London]

Dear Mr Piccoli,

I am very sorry indeed that at the time when you said you were to be in London[1] I was more or less laid up with a variable sort of influenza; and whenever I have been about again since I have had so much to do that I have only been able to keep up with current matters. I hope that when you are in London next I may have another opportunity of seeing you, though the week end is never a good time for me. It is very disappointing to me that our meeting is so long postponed.

> Sincerely yours,
> [T. S. Eliot]

TO *Adrian Stokes*   cc

30 November 1929   [London]

Dear Sir,

I must apologise for the delay in answering your letter, but I have been intermittently ill for several weeks, and have a vast accumulation of correspondence.

I think your suggestion a very interesting one, and shall be very glad if you will carry it out.[2] In view of certain other essays already accepted or

---

1–Piccoli (Magdalene College, Cambidge) wrote on 9 Nov. to say that he would be in London 'Friday next in the afternoon, and Saturday . . .'

2–Stokes proposed (undated) he write an essay on Giorgione's 'Tempesta' picture, which was to feature in the upcoming Italian exhibition in London. 'I have a good deal to *say* about that picture as it is the pivot of the book I am now writing, but I should confine myself to elucidating the subject of the picture which has always been a mystery. Recent remarks by a young Italian . . . go to show that the picture was commissioned to illustrate a definite kind of neo-Aristotelianism, and I would content myself with writing up his views and putting them into relation with Renaissance painting, particularly Piero della Francesca.' See Stokes, 'Painting, Giorgione and Barbaro', C. 9 (Apr. 1930), 482–500.

commissioned for the March number, I should not like to commit myself to more than 4000 words. Can you do it in that space?

I enjoyed immensely the essay which we published. I have never been to Rimini, I am sorry to say – I nearly got there once by just not taking the wrong train from Ravenna. I wish I had: but no one had ever told me then – it was many years ago – that Rimini was worth seeing.

Yours sincerely,
[T. S. Eliot]

TO *John Cournos*   CC

30 November 1929   [London]

Dear Cournos,

I must apologise for not having answered your letter of the 22nd October sooner, but I have not been very well myself.[1] I am dreadfully sorry to hear that you are still in such wretched luck; and I hope that things are better already. Unless one of you is having treatment – and I know there are first rate doctors in Lausanne – I doubt whether Lausanne is a healthy place about this time of year – it is apt to be very foggy. But when one is ill, November and December are difficult months anywhere in Europe. Let me know again how you are.

So far as I know, there is not yet any Russian delegation in London; when I hear of there being one I will write for those periodicals. The other one in Paris we will try to get.[2] I shd like a chronicle for the March number, and will write to you again.

Meanwhile, let me know again how you and your family are and what you intend to do.

Yours ever cordially,
[T. S. Eliot]

1 – Cournos told how, 'as usual, that filthy wretch Fate has been dogging my footsteps with her usual tricks. My wife has not fully recovered from her ordeal of the last two years; apart from this, my son, while in Paris, had to be rushed to the American Hospital for an emergency appendicitis operation and nearly died. However, it all ended well, except for my poor purse; and now for the boy's convalescence we've come up here, and I expect to remain here for some time.'
2 – Cournos hoped TSE might contact a Russian representative in London to help him secure the periodicals needed for his chronicle; however, the best émigré periodical, *Sovremenniya Zapiski* (also called *Les Annales Contemporaines*) was published in Paris.

TO *Osbert Burdett*   CC

30 November 1929   [*The Criterion*]

My dear Burdett,

Thank you very much for your note on the Blake book; it arrived too late for the December number; but Blake is never out of season, so I shall put him into March.[1]

There has been no intention to insult:[2] if there has been that effect, then I must have offended a couple of dozen other people within the last month. I have been laid up off and on for several weeks, at a time when I had several commissions to work off to date, and the December issue to prepare; so my unanswered correspondence has mounted every day; and most of my unanswered invitations were for dates that have long passed. I should like it very much if you could lunch with me in a fortnight or so.

With many apologies,
Yours sincerely,
[T. S. Eliot]

TO *W. A. Collins*[3]   CC

30 November 1929   [London]

Dear Mr Collins,

I must apologise for the delay in answering your letter of the 29th October, but for the past several weeks I have been in poor health myself, and have been obliged to neglect much correspondence. I was very sorry to hear of your son's continued illness, and sincerely hope that his stay in the nursing home has helped him.[4] I should be very glad to have further news of his condition from time to time. It is a great pity that his literary work has been so hampered for a long time past.

Yours very truly,
[T. S. Eliot]

---

1 – Burdett sent (20 Nov.) 'a short notice of the facsimile of *Urizen*'.
2 – Burdett was offended that TSE had failed to respond to two invitations. 'Such negative insults even an enemy scarcely earns . . .' Burdett's piece on the Blake facsimile did not appear, but he would review Mona Wilson's *The Life of William Blake* in C. 11 (July 1932), 714.
3 – W. A. Collins (1873–1945) was Chairman of the publishers of William Collins, Sons & Co., Glasgow and London, and Collins, Bros & Co., Australia and New Zealand.
4 – H. P. Collins had been unwell for some months.

TO *Bruce Richmond*   CC

30 November 1929   [London]

Dear Richmond,

I suppose the enclosure, which I have not yet received, was a letter complaining that *The Game of Chesse* has not been reviewed.[1] I will do it during the week. I have had an intermittent influenza for a fortnight, and various jobs accumulated and had to be worked off; but I am now a little freer. I am afraid that Dec. 12 is much too soon for me to do anything serious with Ford; I can only apologise.[2]

You are, I must say, extremely patient and long suffering of my delinquencies. I will help to heap coals on my own head by suggesting myself for lunch on Wednesday – let me know if it is at all inconvenient. I ought to ask you to lunch with me, and would prefer it, except that I am tempted by the thought that perhaps your Wensleydale is in good condition.

With many thanks,
Yours sincerely,
[T. S. E.]

TO *Sacheverell Sitwell*   CC

30 November 1929   [London]

Dear Sachie,

Some time ago I wrote in reply to your encouraging letter, and sent you a contract for a *Shelley* dated for receipt of MSS. the 31st May 1930. I have not heard from you. I am writing again to remind you of it, and to say that if that date is too early we will, though reluctantly, put it a sixmonth later – but I do hope that that does not press you too hard, and that we can publish the book next autumn.

---

1 – BLR added in a postscript to a letter of 26 Nov. that he meant to enclose a letter from the editor of Thomas Middleton's *A Game at Chess*. 'I can't find it: but I will.'
2 – 'I am still hoping for the leader on Ford; and . . . it would come in particularly handy for the Supplement of December 12; but I dare say you can hardly finish it off in time?' In due time TSE made up for his remissness with 'John Ford' – a lead review of *Materials for the Study of the Old English Drama, New Series, First Volume: John Ford's Dramatic Works*, vol. II, ed. H. de Vocht – *TLS*, 5 May 1932, 501–2; repr. in *SE*.

I do hope we shall have an opportunity at least of seeing you once in London this winter.

Yours ever,
[T. S. E.]

TO *James Joyce*   cc

30 November 1929   [Faber & Faber Ltd]

My dear Joyce,

(I am sorry I have mislaid your number rue de Grenelle). The Chairman (of Faber & Faber) suggested to me the other day that he thought that there was a remote possibility now that if *Ulysses* were published in England, it might be allowed to circulate. Of course we should have to make discreet enquiries about this; the point at the moment is that if it can be done we should like to do it. But we should like to know first whether you would have any objection, or whether it would conflict with your present arrangements for its publication. I don't see that it could; because copies cannot be imported into this country; but I should like to hear from you first before we look into the possibility further.

Yours always cordially,
[T. S. Eliot]

TO *Herbert Read*   TS Victoria

Friday [early December 1929]   177 Clarence Gate Gardens, N.W.1

Dear Herbert,

Yes, I think any other considerations about Bridges become merely a question of literary politics.[1] I want to know whether you think we should do him in the March *Criterion*, or leave him in silence – either behaviour will be misconstrued, but if the former, who is there to do it, as you can't speak again, and I don't want to?[2]

1–HR wrote on 28 Nov.: 'Thanks for the card of encouragement about Bridges. No reverberations so far, though Dickey [Richard] Church gives me up as a bad job. I agree about the matter: but is it really worth while? Even Murry's God is more in the picture.'
2–HR responded on 4 Dec. to TSE's comments in this letter: 'As for Bridges, Fletcher, in conversation, seemed fairly sound. But he might go off into the deep end about the "matter". All things lead to Manichaeism with him.' Robert Bridges's *The Testament of Beauty* was to be reviewed by John Gould Fletcher in *C*. 9 (Apr. 1930), 533–5. Despite his disinclination, TSE would in due time pay gracious if ultimately canny tribute to the late

I am glad you like *Anabase*.[1] I think it is a big thing myself – as important as *Anna Livia Plurabelle* – but there *is* considerable loss in the translation – which I have tried to compensate as far as possible by drawing on the greater resources of our language – but what Leger has done with French is prodigious.

I feel emboldened to try my hand at translating one or two of Hoffmansthal's [*sic*] Jacobean verse plays back into Jacobean. <e.g. *Sobeidens Hochzeit* and *Die Damme am Fenster*.>[2] Do you think it is possible and worth while? I don't think it is worth while troubling to translate verse into English unless it is going to enrich English somehow; but I do feel that Leger has something to offer in that way.[3]

The interesting point is that Leger wanted to avoid the (French) Bible, and whenever he spotted the Bible in my translation he wanted me to alter it.

Dr Robert Bridges in his 'Commentary', C. 9 (July 1930), 587–8: 'The journalistic flutter of curiosity over his successor owes its interest largely to the fact that Bridges, in his very different way, raised the Laureateship to a dignity which it had not had since the most triumphant days of Tennyson . . . And it is no disparagement of any possible successor, but merely a recognition of the late Laureate's particular gifts and even limitations, to say that there is no one living who can occupy that office with so much grace as its late tenant . . . There could be no reason for Bridges' nomination except that he was a poet. When he became Laureate he not only increased the eminence of the post, but at the same time raised and maintained the estimation of poetry as a dignified occupation even in the modern world . . . [I]t is certain that his "experimentation" has served a valuable purpose. It has helped to accustom readers of verse to a more liberal conception of verse technique, and to the notion that the development of technique is a serious and unceasing subject of study among verse writers; it has helped to protect other versifiers of less prestige, against the charge of being merely "rebels" or "freaks"; or as a writer in *The Morning Post* some years ago nicely named them, "literary bolsheviks" . . . [E]ven those poets who feel that they owe nothing to him directly, and who cannot join the chorus of praise over *The Testament of Beauty*, have reason to bless his memory.'

1 – HR wrote of *Anabase* (28 Nov.): 'It is excellent. It seems to me there is no loss in the translation: you have slightly transposed the "key", perhaps, but kept it all in that key, which goes better in English. The French, that is to say, lacks the English Bible, & to that extent is the poorer. It was well worth doing, & should have some influence.'

2 – *Die Hochzeit der Sobeide* and *Die Frau im Fenster*, by Hugo von Hofmannsthal (1874–1929).

3 – HR responded on 4 Dec.: 'I haven't read the two Hoffmansthal plays you mention & don't quite know what to say about the project. Some of his poetry is extraordinarily good & its qualities would pass over into English. I don't think you would be wasting your time & I don't think we ought to despise translation. One can put practically everything one has into it, God willing. With Anabase before me, I feel inclined to urge you to go ahead with Hoffmansthal, but I really ought to look up the actual plays you have in mind. The only point I hesitate about is the Jacobean touch: it suggests fumed oak. I mean, that other things being equal, I would rather have a contemporary accent.'

I am cutting pages of Gundolf. The colds are being submitted to linctusses and pills. I did mine no good by lecturing at the Children's Theatre in Endell Street on Whitehead's appreciation of poetry for the benefit of the repair of the organ in St. George's Bloomsbury.[1] I want to show you the paper. Miss Professor Stebbing[2] of Bedford College said she agreed with me. But a furious young man said was I unaware that the mechanistic explanation of life was the only one accepted by medical students? Christianity, said he, is merely a particular and insignificant form of vitalism, and vitalism is absurd.

Yours ever,

T

TO *Ottoline Morrell* CC

2 December 1929   [London]

My dear Ottoline,

Certainly *The Greville Papers* come within the scope of the *Criterion*; I have two or three reviewers who I think are competent and will be very glad to get it. I am having my secretary write to the publishers for it; but I have not had much from them before; and they are not among the firms who send me books without being asked; so it would assure their compliance if Philip cared to let them know that we should have a review copy.[3]

Yours ever affectionately,

[Tom]

TO *Muriel Kent* CC

2 December 1929   [London]

Dear Madam,

I am very sorry to have given you so much trouble. I have now read your essay on Spring Rice with much interest. But I cannot feel that his literary activity was enough to justify giving him so much space in the

---

1–TSE talked at St George's Church about poetry and philosophy, including the idea that poetry provides an aesthetic sanction for thought.
2–L. Susan Stebbing.
3–G. Kitson Clark reviewed *Leaves from the Greville Diary*, a new and abridged edn with introd. and notes by OM's husband Philip Morrell, in C. 9 (July 1930), 739–42.

Criterion. Your essays have always interested me and I still hope to find one that might be suitable. Of the three that you mention I should be very glad to see the study of Clough.[1]

Yours sincerely,
[T. S. Eliot]

TO *Orlo Williams*   cc

2 December 1929   [London]

Dear Williams,

Many thanks for your cordial note.[2] Certainly we ought not to let the month pass without meeting. Would Wednesday or Thursday of *next* week be possible for you? I suppose you are going to Surrey for Christmas, but I hope you can manage it. I believe I am lunching with Richmond on this Wednesday, and perhaps I shall see you there.

I was going to write to you anyway; but have had a sort of mild ineffectual FLU for several weeks, so that my correspondence has got completely out of hand. (I am all right now). I am not sure even whether I answered your kind suggestion about the Mussolini book; I ought to have written to say that we considered it carefully, but did not think it a book for us. But thank you very much for the suggestion.

I have just had sent you Hemingway's and also Julian Green's latest books. These are for storage until you think fit to discharge your wrath or blessings upon the respective authors. I think we agreed some time ago that Hemingway should wait; but I have glanced at this book and (speaking personally and not editorially) I feel it is high time that this literature of barbarism was put in its place. Hemingway is at his best when he deals with barbarism in its proper place – i.e. Chicago gunmen at home etc. – but when he lets his barbarians loose in Europe he ought to be arraigned for it. If they were pure barbarians I should not dislike them so much; but Hemingway seems to deny that human beings have any obligation to think, or to feel any but the most elementary emotions, or to express themselves in anything but stuttering repetitions of inanities.

---

1 – Kent had submitted 'The Poems of a Patriot' on 30 Oct. 1929. She said she was working too on Arthur H. Clough; on the poems of Charlotte Mew; and on the Curé d'Ars. See Muriel Kent, 'A Balliol Scholar', *C.* 9 (July 1930), 675–88.
2 – Williams wrote on 1 Dec., 'This is the beginning of the month of Xmas, and we cannot let that ancient festival go by without meeting to exchange seasonable wishes. It is long since we met. Can you not come to lunch one day?'

I don't know whether there might be any interest in doing Green with him, as a contrast on Americanism (it is curious that Hemingway's parents were English, whereas Green is a Franco-American of considerable American descent and tradition). But I believe that Green is a writer worth estimating, sooner or later; and as he is an American writing in French, he might just as well be estimated as an 'English' writer (seeing that he has been so fully translated) as a French writer. I think he is influenced by both Poe and Hawthorne.[1]

Let me know about next week.

Yours ever,
[T. S. E.]

TO *Ashley Sampson*   CC

3 December 1929   [London]

Dear Sir,[2]

I must apologise for having kept your two stories such a long time. I think that the one about the schoolmaster is extremely good.[3] But after much hesitation [I] have decided that it is not quite suitable for *The Criterion*. Yet I hope that you will send me more of your work.

I believe that we were to have met a long time ago and hope that you will make another attempt to find me. I shall probably be very busy until after Christmas, but I should be glad if you cared to suggest a morning after that at your convenience, when you could call and have a talk with me.[4]

Yours very truly,
[T. S. Eliot]

1–OW reviewed Ernest Hemingway, *A Farewell to Arms*, and Julian Green, *The Dark Journey*, together in C. 9 (July 1930), 724–31.

2–Sampson, a schoolteacher from London, had submitted in Apr. 1929 a short story entitled 'The Golden Cage'; he asked after it by letter on 10 Nov. 1929.

3–'The School Master'. On 11 Jan. 1930 Sampson was to report that a story had been accepted by *The Dial*, and that it had also been selected by Edward O'Brien for the next edition of *Best Short Stories*.

4–Sampson wrote two book reviews for C. in a later year.

TO *The Blackamore Press*   CC

6 December 1929   [London]

Dear Sirs,

I am returning herewith the transcript of the translation of the *Journaux Intimes* of Baudelaire. You will observe that at the request of Mr Isherwood and of Mr Pouterman I have made a number of suggestions on the text.[1] Some of these deserve careful attention as they refer to errors in typing. e.g. In one place 'ligne' is translated 'time' instead of 'line'.

In accordance with a letter from Mr Pouterman dated 5th December, I am sending my introduction by the next post.

I should be obliged if you would kindly acknowledge receipt of both of Mr Isherwood's translation and of my introduction.[2]

Faithfully yours,
[T. S. Eliot]

TO *Huw Menai*   CC

6 December 1929   [London]

Dear Mr Menai,

I am very sorry for the delay over choosing your poems for *The Criterion*. I am still anxious to use something of yours early next year but have got confused as I have not the copy of the Hogarth Press book by me, and am not quite sure which poems, among those I am returning to you, have already appeared in that volume. I should be very much obliged if you would now pick out for me some of the poems which you like best among those which did not appear in that volume, and send them to me again to choose from. Therefore I am returning to you the whole of your

---

1–Harold Solomon (The Blackamore Press) had written to TSE on 29 Nov.: 'Mr Isherwood, who translated Baudelaire's Diaries, tells us that you expressed the desire to peruse a typewritten copy of this translation, which we enclose herewith.' (The typescript was posted to TSE in the first week of Dec.) Pouterman wrote on 5 Dec.: 'I understand from Mr Isherwood that you expressed the desire to peruse the text of his translation, and have instructed our London office to send you a copy of the typescript, which I hope has safely reached you. Any suggestions which you may have to make in connection with this translation will be greatly appreciated.' TSE, in signing over his copy of the volume at a later date to Valerie Eliot, wrote on it that it was 'a bad translation' (TSE's Library).

2–Solomon acknowledged receipt of TSE's introduction on 9 Dec. – 'and also your revision of Mr Isherwood's typescript'. In addition, he enclosed the agreed fee of £25.

manuscript and cuttings as well as your book. I hope you can let me have such a selection before the end of the year.[1]

> Yours sincerely,
> [T. S. Eliot]

TO *Erich Alport*

TS Richard Buckle

7 December 1929   Faber & Faber Ltd

My dear Alport,

(as we correspond so frequently may we not drop the Mr and the Dr?) thank you for your reports on Scheler and Gundolf. I remain of the same opinion about Scheler: that he ought to be introduced into England by his biggest work, and that we, if anyone, are the people to do it; but I cannot recommend my firm to publish any smaller works of Scheler, merely on the chance of getting his masterpiece. From every point of view, I believe that the biggest book should appear first; and I hope you may be able to convince Frau Scheler, who seems difficult.

About Gundolf, I can only say at the moment that we are keenly interested, and are making enquiries here. I shall be much disappointed if we don't do it.

I wrote to Curtius about a book of essays, but have not yet heard. Nor have I any news yet from Clauss.

> Yours sincerely,
> T. S. Eliot

TO *Giansiro Ferrata*[2]

CC

9 December 1929   [London]

My dear Sir,

I thank you for your cordial letter of the 6th instant, which I appreciate.[3] My knowledge of Italian is not intimate enough for me to be able to give

---

1 – Menai had written on 9 Nov. to ask after the date of the poems and book he had sent TSE 'about a year ago'. No poems by Menai appeared in *C*.

2 – Giansiro Ferrata (1907–86), critic, scholar, editor of the new literary review *Solaria* (Florence); later a director of the publishing house of Mondadori. See Stefania Salustri, *Giansiro Ferrata and years of 'Solaria': Moral Sentiment in Europe and a Distinguished Republic of Letters* (Florence, 1994).

3 – The editors (Ferrata and Alberto Carocci) of *Solaria* requested permission to print 'A Song for Simeon', in a translation by Eugenio Montale.

an authoritative opinion; but the translation seems to me both graceful and admirably faithful. And in any case, the name of Signore Montale, some of whose poetry I admire highly, is both a guarantee of care and a distinction to any poem which he cares to translate; so that I have no hesitation in authorising your use of this poem in your review. May I ask you to send a copy of the number in which the poem appears to me, and also a copy to Mr Orlo Williams and a copy to Mr Mario Praz?

Yours very sincerely,
[T. S. Eliot]

TO *G. B. Harrison* CC

9 December 1929 [London]

Dear Mr Harrison,

Excuse my apparent neglect in not answering your letter of the 19th ultimo; but I was not well for some time, and my correspondence fell into confusion.[1] It is hardly necessary to say that I am greatly honoured by the compliment paid me by the Shakespeare Association. I feel that I ought, as a matter of conscience, ask first how often the Council meets, what the duties of its members are, before accepting. I should be very happy to be a member, but I should like to be sure whether I shall be able to fulfil the obligations.[2]

With many thanks,
Yours sincerely,
[T. S. Eliot]

1–Harrison (Hon. Sec. King's College, London) invited TSE to become a member of the Council of the Shakespeare Association.

2–Harrison replied on 16 Dec.: 'The Shakespeare Association is not likely to take very much of your time, as the Council normally meets about twice a year and the duty therefore of a member is to attend (if he can) its meetings, which are held prior to one of the lectures.

'I am very glad that you will be able to join us.'

TO *Ezra Pound*   TS Beinecke

9 December 1929   *The Criterion*

Dear Ezra,

(1) about Zukovsky[1] [*sic*]. I agree he is a man of parts, and I shall
have more pleasure in recommending him to Guggenheim than anyone
yet[2] – by the way, I don't think anyone I have sponsored has got in yet.
His verse is highly intelligent and honourably Jewish. The Adams[3] is an
excellent piece of work, & good in the right way, i.e. gives me still better
hopes for his verse. But what the hell can I do with it in London. It's much
too long for the *Criterion,* wouldn't bear mutilation; I would press it as
a pamphlet but hell it implies some knowledge of Adams in the reader.
Adams ought of course to be introduced to the British publikum; nobody
here but Fletcher has ever heard of him; but this book is simply no good
to put over Adams onto a public one hundredth of one per cent of which
may have heard from its grandfather that there was once an American
ambassador named Adams. If Zuk. wd consider that public and write a
simple article introducing Adams that would be my form. But this I fear I
must return with regrets.

(2) The Canto seems to me allright, I take it to be a transitional or
connecting canto summing up or telescoping themes either in retrospect
or anticipation; but not TOO difficult. No loss of vitality observable.

(3) I have recently produced one or two small articles which shall
reach you in due course. The poems only good in moments, but I think
my translation of ANABASE can stand the racket. The Dante will also

1–Louis Zukofsky (1904–78), American poet, son of Lithuanian Jewish parents, grew up
speaking Yiddish and was educated at Columbia University (being taught by Mark van
Doren and John Dewey). In 1927 he sent to EP 'Poem Beginning "The"' – a parody of
TWL – which EP put out in his review *The Exile,* no. 3 (Spring 1928), 7–27. Zukofsky
worked for the Works Projects Administration, 1934–42, and in the English Department of
the Polytechnic Institute of Brooklyn, 1947–66. A leader of the 'Objectivist' group of poets
(associates included William Carlos Williams), his writings include *'A'* (published in full
in 1978), *Prepositions: The Collected Critical Essays of Louis Zukofsky* (1967), *All: The
Collected Short Poems, 1923–1964* (1971), and *Autobiography* (1970). See *Selected Letters
of Ezra Pound and Louis Zukofsky,* ed. Barry Ahearn (1987); and Mark Scroggins, *The
Poem of a Life: A Biography of Louis Zukofsky* (2007).
2–Zukofsky wrote to EP, 8 Sept. 1929: 'One from T. S. Eliot would add the proper academic
weight, but since so far I have only corresponded with his sec'y I don't know what to do
about it' (Beinecke: Ezra Pound Addition YCAL 53, series I, Box 24, 362).
3–'Henry Adams: A Criticism in Autobiography' Parts I, II, III, in *Hound and Horn,* May,
July, Oct., 1930; repr. in *Prepositions: The Collected Critical Essays of Louis Zukofsky,*
80–124.

reach you, but that is merely a small autobiographical fragment, not a contribution to scholarship for my Ph.D.

                    The peace of God etc.
                    T.

TO *John Simon Guggenheim Memorial Foundation*
TS copy Guggenheim Foundation

[9 December 1929]¹   [London]

I do not know Mr Lowenfels except by correspondence and I know him only as a writer of verse. I published some of his verse in *The Criterion* which means that I thought highly of it.² He then sent me the MSS. of a book of verse. I was trying to get this published when I learned from Mr Wolfe that Heinemanns decided to do it.

From this it will be evident that I have a high opinion of Mr Lowenfels' ability and I do not hesitate to recommend him, believing him to be fully qualified for one of your Fellowships.

TO *Henry Allen Moe, John Simon Guggenheim Memorial Foundation*
TS Guggenheim Foundation

9 December 1929   177 Clarence Gate Gardens, N.W.1.

Dear Mr Moe,

I have just heard that Mr Louis Zukovsky is applying for a Guggenheim fellowship, and that he may be referring to me, so I am writing, if possible to save you the bother of writing to me. I do not know Mr Zukovsky personally. But he strikes me as one of about half a dozen American younger poets whom I could recommend – one of them, Tate, has of

---

1 – Henry Allen Moe asked for a reference in a letter of 21 Nov. 1929, enclosing Lowenfels's application 'for a fellowship for creative work as a writer': 'For about the last year and a half I have been working on a book entitled REALITY PRIME and I am submitting myself as a candidate for the purpose of continuing and completing the work, which . . . attempts a restatement of the idea of poetic creation and might be described, briefly, as a philosophy of poetry in terms of modern science. This work requires research into modern scientific thought in the fields of philosophy, physics, psychology, phyiology, and allied subjects.' A handwritten note at the head of the typed copy of TSE's reference reads '1930 application', but TSE actually posted it on 9 Dec. 1929.

2 – TSE was misremembering – he had not yet published any verse by Lowenfels – or else he was mistaking Lowenfels for Louis Zukofsky, two of whose poems he had published in C. 8 (Apr. 1929), 420–1. Lowenfels's application was not successful.

course had a fellowship already. I have published a couple of Zukovsky's poems in *The Criterion*.

I have just sent you your form of enquiry about Lowenfels. If it were a question of picking one man or the other I should hesitate. On the one hand I have seen more of Lowenfels' verse, and think him a little more developed as a poet. On the other hand I have seen none of his prose, and have seen a very acute and scholarly essay by Zukovsky on Henry Adams. So I am not comparing, you understand; and I don't know what other candidates there are simultaneously; but I do sincerely consider both Lowenfels and Zukovsky distinguished and worthy, judging from their work that I have seen they should both do credit to the Foundation in later years.[1]

Yours sincerely,
T. S. Eliot

TO *C. A. Siepmann*   TS BBC

9 December 1929   Faber & Faber Ltd

Dear Mr Siepmann,

I return herewith the proofs;[2] not having called at my office on Saturday, I did not find them till this morning. I call attention to two points: one, the correct title of the book of Grierson's mentioned in talk 1; and the other is that the dates are given, I believe, as for the original Saturdays, instead of for one Thursday (March 6th?) and the following five weeks on the Friday.[3] I have also added the cheap edition of Donne, which appeared only a few days ago.

Yours sincerely,
T. S. Eliot

1 – Zukofsky's application was not successful.
2 – Siepmann wrote on 6 Dec.: 'I enclose herewith proof slips of the summaries of your broadcast talks together with the short biographical note for our forthcoming Talks and Lectures Programme ... I should therefore be obliged if you would be good enough to make any necessary corrections in the attached and return them to me as soon as possible.' The biographical note – for the 'Who's Who' section of the Talks Programme for the spring session – read: 'T. S. ELIOT is a Director of Faber & Faber and Editor of the *New Criterion*. It will be remembered that he gave a successful series in the summer session on Tudor Prose. This time he will give six talks on 17th-Century Poetry.'
3 – TSE's talks had been scheduled for Saturdays, but they were brought forward when Arnold Toynbee found that he could not broadcast his talks on 'The New Map of Europe' on Fridays in the spring. 'I have not forgotten how your face dropped,' wrote Siepmann on 29 Nov., 'when I suggested that your six talks should interfere with your weekends.'

TO *Judith Wogan*[1]

9 December 1929   [London]

Dear Miss Wogan,

I have of course heard of you in connexion with the Arts League of Service. I am interested to hear of your new venture, and am much pleased that you find my dialogue on the drama sympathetic to your aims.[2]

I should like however to understand a little more clearly what you would like to do with my 'Hollow Men'. Is it a reading, in the ordinary sense; or is there to be some scenic background or dramatic or mimetic action in your readings? And when you speak of repertory, how much use would you want to make of the poem?

I confess that I find the idea of public readings of my verse has never appealed to me. It would be ungracious of me to refuse permission for any special reading; but the suggestion of repertory, and the possibility of further interpretation, does I think also justify me in asking for more information.

My objection to a 'repertory' for a poem (not for plays, where of course I approve) is that it may introduce poems to people who are unprepared for them, and also that it stamps a writer (as an-[*bottom edge of page has been torn off*] and perhaps not one by which he cares to be so judged.

With all best wishes,
Sincerely yours,
[T. S. Eliot]

TO *Christopher Dawson*

10 December 1929   [London]

My dear Mr Dawson,

I am sending you separately copies of several pamphlets in the *Criterion Miscellany*. As you will see, the purpose of the Miscellany is to revive the art of pamphleteering, and to publish cheaply and rapidly serious essays on subjects of contemporary importance.

My Board have asked me to ask you to consider whether you would be willing to write a pamphlet for this series, covering somewhat the same

---

1–Judith Wogan, a former Hon. Organizing Secretary of the Arts League of Service, was based at the Grafton Theatre (a former cinema), Tottenham Court Road, London.
2–Wogan, who was starting up a small experimental theatre, wrote on 5 Dec. to ask if she could include 'The Hollow Men' in the repertory of 'an unusual variety programme'.

ground as Bertrand Russell's recent book, *Marriage and Morals*, from the point of view of a Roman Catholic layman. I feel myself that there is a need for the Catholic laymen to speak on these matters about which so many opposite extremists are speaking; for on such points the views of a layman would, I feel, carry more weight with the ordinary public than any official or even semi-official ecclesiastical pronouncement. The views of a practising Catholic layman about marriage reform, birth control, the relations of the sexes in general in the modern world, would I am sure attract much interest and compel much respect; and so much is being said on the opposite side that I should myself be very glad to have such a statement. Not [*the foot of carbon page has been torn off*] both laymen and clerics say about you, I am sure that you could do this admirably. We should want a pamphlet of anywhere from five to ten thousand words; and I hope that you would consider it worth your while to write it quite soon; but I will not go into details until I hear from you. I shall be very grateful if you will let me have some reply at once; merely to say whether you are (as I fervently hope) disposed to pursue our suggestion a little further.[1]

Yours very sincerely,
[T. S. Eliot]

TO *C. C. Martindale*   CC

10 December 1929   [London]

Dear Sir,

There is no reason why I should be writing to you, rather than any other member of my Board of Directors, except that I can present myself as a friend of Father D'Arcy.

I am sending you separately two pamphlets which my firm has recently produced, by Lord Brentford and Mr D. H. Lawrence, on the subject of Censorship. We have thought that it would be very useful to the public which has had the interest to read these two pamphlets – and that is, we find a large public – if a third point of view might be presented: that of the Roman Church. I am quite sure that the ordinary Englishman (not Roman Catholic) who is interested in this subject at all, would like to know first, what is the attitude of a Roman churchman towards the *civil* censorship, and what is the relation, from the Roman point of view, of such censorship to that of the Index. Is the Church censorship sufficient, or should it be

1 – See Christopher Dawson, *Christianity and Sex* (*Criterion Miscellany*, 1930).

supplemented by civil censorship, or have the two quite distinct purposes, and no relation whatever? Incidentally, there is I am sure, among non-Roman Englishmen, ignorance at best, and misapprehension more often, of the purpose, of the functioning, of the limitations and qualifications, of the Vatican Index. Even in popular expositions of Catholicism for the benefit of non-believers, very little is said about this: and among non-Romans, the notions of what a Roman Catholic is forbidden to read, and when, and why, are much worse than vague.

I should be very grateful if you would let me have your opinion as to whether there is a place for such a statement, and secondly I should be more than happy if you would consent to write for us such a statement yourself. If I can first obtain your approval and your consent in principle, I will immediately give you precise terms. Meanwhile I can say that we find that our scheme of a series of pamphlets on current problems does seem to justify itself, and I am sure reaches a large number of people who are immune to articles in serious reviews (which they never buy) and equally to full length books.[1]

> I am, Dear Sir,
> Your obedient servant,
> [T. S. Eliot]
> Director

TO *C. K. Scott Moncrieff*   CC

12 December 1929   [London]

Dear Scott Moncrieff,

I have your letter of the 2nd. You need not have troubled to ask for my permission to reprint the fragment of 'Albertine', for the *Criterion* asks only for first serial rights.[2] Of course I should appreciate it if you could find room for a statement that that part did appear originally in *The Criterion*.

---

1 – Martindale replied ('Thursd night'): 'I hope I can manage something, for the very simple reason that I am earning every halfpenny I can in order to build a Cath. institute in Poplar, E14, a horrible district . . . So, suppose we decide we had better not say anything about the Index, tho' I now would rather like to do so, if you have any other subject that you think I might be competent to treat of, do let me know. This is a vulgar reason or excuse: the reason is not at all vulgar . . . I wish we had had time to talk about those bargees and lightermen . . .'
2 – C. K. Scott Moncrieff's translation of Proust's 'The Death of Albertine' had appeared in C. 2 (July 1924), 376–94.

The history of the manuscript is very curious, and is rather exasperating for you.[1]

I will have your subscription renewed, and also have the pamphlets that you want sent to you.[2] I wish that everyone who cares at all about the existence of *The Criterion* would do the same – people don't realise that it is subscriptions, and only subscriptions, which will ever make it quite self-supporting. At any rate the subscription list does improve; and I appreciate the thoughtfulness of everyone like yourself.

I envy you in your semi-Retreat; but I hope that no physical illness has contributed to making it desirable.[3] If I can be of any further use in sending out books to you, I shall be very glad. Is there ever any hope of seeing you in London again?

Yours ever sincerely,

[T. S. Eliot]

By the way, I ought to thank you for a letter you wrote a long time ago to *The New Statesman* in my interest. The whole question about the Skylark was really beside the point; for the real question is: are not all or most of Shelley's comparisons in that poem irrelevancies? Surely Dante would have shuddered at such a far fetched simile to express 'keenness'. I maintain that the ode is a bad poem and won't stand analysis. And nobody stopped to think whether poor Crashaw is a great poet or not. And I do prefer Crashaw to Shelley, for myself![4]

But the difference of opinion between Sturge Moore and Housman did of course amuse me hugely.

1 – 'A curious point has arisen in this connexion. In several passages my Criterion version does not conform to the French text afterwards published by Gallimard; and in two of these it is quite plain to me that the typescript from which I translated for you was right and that the Gallimard text is wrong. But how did it come to be falsified?'
2 – Scott Moncrieff asked for the *Criterion Miscellany* pamphlets by DHL and Joynson-Hicks (Brentford).
3 – Scott Moncrieff, who was suffering from gastric ulcers, was being cared for by the Little Company of Mary, Calvary Hospital, Rome. 'I am anticipating a long spell of reduced life with these Blue Sisters, with little capacity for work and much drowsy opportunity for mild reading.'
4 – The last three sentences of this paragraph were first printed in *C. K. Scott Moncrieff: Memories and Letters*, ed. J. M. Scott Moncrieff and L. W. Lunn (1931), 194.

TO *The Blackamore Press*

12 December 1929 [London]

Dear Sirs,

I have your letter of the 9th instant, enclosing your cheque for £25 in payment for my introduction to Baudelaire's *Journaux Intimes*, for which I thank you.

I will remind you again that I am anxious to have galley proof of my introduction to correct and alter.

Yours faithfully,
[T. S. Eliot]

TO *Marguerite Caetani*

12 December 1929 [London]

Dear Marguerite,

Thank you very much for your kind letter of the 8th, and thank Leger also for his expressions of appreciation and good will. I very much hope that he will have time to see me when he comes to London; but when he came the last time, with Briand and Doumergue, there was no possibility of getting at him.

The book will now appear in February or March. There is just a faint possibility that there may be some royalties on it – I mean a little more money for Leger – if the book is taken up in America. That we are not sure of yet.[1]

I am very much disappointed that you refuse the dedication.[2] I cannot conceive what these obscure reasons may be, which cannot even be entrusted to paper! But you may be sure I shall demand an explanation when I see you. But you must have something else.

I am glad that *Commerce* will be out in December, because I am bringing out a limited edition of a set of six poems, including that one and the one previously published in *Commerce*, also in February or March, under the title of *Ash Wednesday*.

---

1 – *Anabasis* would appear on 22 May 1930. The first American edition, revised and corrected by TSE, was published by Harcourt, Brace and Company only on 3 Mar. 1938.
2 – 'Leger tells me that you want to dedicate the translation to me but it would be inadvisable for reasons which I can tell you better when I see you. Dedicate me one day something really yours!'

We look forward to revisiting Rome under your auspices; we both like Rome very much, and when you are settled there we shall have a very strong reason for returning. We also welcome very warmly your first faint intimation of the possibility of your coming to London.[1] You must come in the spring. By then we hope to be in a house again. We moved twice last summer, spending all of our time, strength and money in that *folle volo*, and are worse off in both contentment, health and wealth than before we started. We are in a flat; and apparently we had to come into a flat in order to find out that we can only live in a house!

Ever affectionately.
[Tom]

TO *Robert Gathorne-Hardy*[2]   cc

12 December 1929   [London]

Dear Mr Gathorne-Hardy,

You have been on my mind for a long time. I am ashamed about your poems;[3] but in *The Criterion* the worst are served first: the people whose manuscripts are worthless get them back often almost by return of post; when I cannot make up my mind the contributor often waits for years, or until he has forgotten where his manuscript is. I should like to see you and talk to you about your poetry at some time; and meanwhile I should very much like to see anything you have done in the interim; and I will return what I have.

About Dante: it seems to me less difficult to explain how a poet borrows *and improves*, than to explain how he borrows and makes something different, just as good, or rather with no relative valuation possible.

---

1 – Caetani wrote: 'We are leaving here about the 28th I think probably to spend January somewhere on the riviera until we can live in our villa in Rome which should be about February 1st. Next year you *must* come both of you and stay with us. We will be back for Easter as usual and if you don't come here I am going to see you in London.'

2 – The Hon. Robert Gathorne-Hardy (1902–73), author, bibliographer; publications include *Village Symphony and Other Poems* (1931); *Garden Flowers* (1948); editor of *Ottoline: Memoirs of Lady Ottoline Morrell* (1963) and *Ottoline at Garsington* (1974).

3 – Gathorne-Hardy asked (n.d.) after the poems he posted 'about six months ago'. 'If you still have them anywhere, I should be very grateful if you could return them . . . but it does not matter if they have been lost.' (Harold Monro told TSE on 22 Nov. 1928: 'He has been in fact one of my truly difficult cases, which is a reason why (if he doesn't mind) I want to pass him on to you! It seems to me that there is a mind keenly at work, but I hear it battering, more often than not, at a thick wall. I am interested in his last MSS. which perhaps he may send you, but I find myself unable to formulate a written opinion.')

'Veteris vestigia flammae' is the same, and yet utterly different from the segni etc. – partly the difference between veteris and antica: the context does it for both Dante and Virgil, and they both emerge triumphant from the borrowing.[1] The moral seems to be that one test of a man's originality is the success of his borrowing; for to borrow a phrase and make a right use of it in a context utterly different from the original, is as original as

[*Last part of letter missing.*]

TO *Mario Praz*   TS Galleria Nazionale d'Arte Moderna, Roma

13 December 1929   Faber & Faber Ltd

My dear Praz,

I should be very grateful if you could tell me whether you know anything of an Italian political-philosopher named 'Umano' (I forget what his real name was, but that is his pseudonym) who produced an enormous book in 1922. And in any case would you be willing to look at a résumé of the book (in Italian) which is said to have been made by the author, and letting me have your opinion? I find both the style and the matter too hard for me.

I have been approached with a view to publication of an English translation, and I have never heard of Umano.[2]

I have seen Miss Whittingham-Jones, and have hope that she will do some good work.[3]

1 – Gathorne-Hardy wrote in his letter: 'I enjoyed your essay on Dante very much – I had approached him through the same gate as you – the Temple Classics. There's one problem which I think might have a fruitful explanation if one could find it – how Dante has literally translated passages of Virgil (and I suppose other people) and yet made them entirely original – 'veteris vestigia flammae' the ancient flame is one case, and the passages about the cranes flying south and crying is out of a battle scene in the Aeneid, yet it seems one of Dante's most characteristic similes. I believe if one could explain how a poet borrows and improves on his model one could explain the merit of all poetry – but perhaps one couldn't . . .' He was referring, in the first case, to *Purgatorio* XXX, 48 – '*Conosco I segni dell' antica fiamma*': 'I recognise the tokens of the ancient flame' – which Dante had taken from Virgil's '*Agnosco veteris vestigia flammae*' (*Aeneid* IV, 23). TSE quoted in his *Dante* 18 lines from *Purg.* XXX ending with verse 48, but without mentioning Dante's 'borrowing', with the comment: 'We cannot understand fully Canto XXX of the *Purgatorio* until we know the *Vita Nuova*, which in my opinion should be read after *The Divine Comedy*. But at least we can begin to understand how skillfully Dante expresses the recrudescence of an ancient passion in a new emotion, in a new situation, which comprehends, enlarges, and gives a meaning to it.'
2 – Praz replied on 25 Dec.: 'From what I gather from competent friends, I should not think "Umano" worth a translation. The work does not rank at all with philosophers here . . . I have not heard of it until you wrote me . . .'
3 – Barbara Whittingham-Jones was to write three reviews for C. in 1929–30.

I shall be writing to you soon about the Crashaw: we must come to a decision as to what ought to be done.[1]

I am sorry that I did not get Lafourcade's address from Wolfe until after you wrote again.

And finally – do you know anything about a novel by one Nievo – '*Memorie d'un ottogenario*' or something like that?

Yours ever,

T. S. Eliot

I await anxiously your opinion of my *Dante* – I gave you a copy, did I not?

TO *A. C. Bradley*[2]   cc

13 December 1929   [London]

Dear Sir,

I am writing on behalf of my firm to ask whether you would be so kind as to give us your opinion of the *Shakespeare* of Friedrich Gundolf (Bondi-Verlag, Berlin), and to let us know whether you consider it an important enough book to merit translation into English.[3]

If you are not acquainted with the book we should be glad to send you the German text. We should not venture to appeal to you on the matter except that this is a very special case, in which no ordinary reader's report would be adequate. We must therefore appeal to the highest authority that we can get. It is a large book, and with the cost of translation added, would be very expensive to produce. We should hardly expect it to be remunerative; we should publish it for the prestige of the firm and from a sense of public spirit. The reader's fee, in such a case, is very far from representing the value of an opinion such as yours; so we are really asking you to give an opinion for some of the same reasons that impel us to publish the book. We have had very high recommendations from

---

1–Praz had thought (10 Nov.) that his *Secentismo e Marinismo in Inghilterra* – the parts on Donne and Crashaw – would have to be reduced by two-thirds to fit the schema of 'The Poets on the Poets'. 'I wonder if anybody else but myself would be able to do that abridged version. It practically means that I ought to do the translation as well.'

2–A. C. Bradley (1851–1935) – one of his numerous siblings was the philosopher F. H. Bradley, whom TSE studied with passion – English literary scholar; Regius Professor of English Literature, University of Glasgow, from 1889; Oxford Professor of Poetry, 1901–6; author of *Shakespearean Tragedy* (1904) and *Oxford Lectures on Poetry* (1909).

3–HR had written on 4 Dec., 'I see A. C. Bradley is not dead but I suppose he is too old & secluded to be bothered with Gundolf. But he might already have read him & might express an opinion.'

Germany; the book is said to be one of the first importance; but we could not contemplate undertaking it unless we had a favourable opinion from someone like yourself.

– I might even say simply 'from yourself': for it is a work of philosophy as well as scholarship; a purely technical point of view would be insufficient; so that if you cannot help us I shall be very much at a loss whom to ask.

I am, Dear Sir,

Yours faithfully,

[T. S. Eliot]

Director.

TO *George Bernard Shaw*[1]

CC

13 December 1929   [London]

Dear Sir,

I am taking the liberty of writing to you about the work of the Italian political philosopher 'Umano'. His work has been proposed to me for translation and publication by my firm. The work, and even the name, is unfamiliar to me; but I am given to understand that you have a high opinion of it, and that you are even prepared to give financial support to its publication in this country.

I should be very grateful if you could let me have your opinion of the work of Umano, and if you could let me know whether it is true that you are desirous of seeing it published in England; and whether you would also assist such a production with a preface by yourself.

I ought to add that on hurried examination I hardly consider that I could advise my firm to engage on such an expensive venture, for an author still unknown in England, unless it had substantial support from other sources.

Yours faithfully,

[T. S. Eliot]

Director

---

1 – George Bernard Shaw (1856–1950), playwright and pamphleteer, socialist and Fabian, philanderer and pro-feminist, and pacifist; author of several successful plays including *Man and Superman* (1902), *John Bull's Other Island* (1904), *Major Barbara* (1905), *Heartbreak House* (1919), *Back to Methuselah* (1921), *Saint Joan* (1923); and other books including *The Intelligent Woman's Guide to Socialism* (1928). TSE was no enthusiast: he deplored Shaw's plays and opposed his politics.

TO *Richard Cobden-Sanderson*   CC

14 December 1929   [London]

Dear Richard,

Thank you very much for your letter, for sending me the two copies of
my mother's book, and for the cheque. I do not quite know what to do
with the cheque, which comes as a surprise, but I think the best thing is to
collect it myself and account for it to the estate. I won't bother you for a
full statement unless the executors should demand it, pro forma.

All best wishes for your Christmas,

Ever yours,
[T. S. Eliot]

TO *H. E. Bates*   CC

14 December 1929   [London]

Dear Mr Bates,

Replying to your letter of the 2nd instant, we have thought over your
suggestion, but have decided that we should much prefer to have *one* story
of the right length, than two of half-length.[1] For such small pamphlets a
collection of two stories does not seem suitable. Possibly later on we may
publish in the Miscellany rather larger paper bound books; and in that
event we should probably welcome small collections of from four to six
stories by the same author. So keep that in mind; but meanwhile we shall
be very glad if you will send on the story on which you are working, as
soon as it is ready. A good length is 32 *printed* pages: if you have not seen
Tomlinson's essay or Blake's story in [the] series I will send you copies.[2]

Yours sincerely,
[T. S. Eliot]
Director, Faber & Faber Ltd.

1–Bates regretted that 'the story I intended for you seems forced and wrong in some way,
and I shall spend the remaining weeks until Christmas reshaping it. As soon as it is read I
shall send it to you.

'I wish you would let me know, fairly soon, what length you require. And again, if two
stories would be just as acceptable as one, provided the right length were obtained.'
2–Bates submitted his story on 1 Jan. 1930. 'Charlotte Esmond' would be published in
C. 10 (Oct. 1930), 55–74.

to *A. L. Morton*

14 December 1929   [London]

Dear Morton,

I have your letter of the 1st.[1] I shall be glad to do what I can. It would be useful if you could send me some brief biographical account of yourself – schools and college etc. what literary work you have done, and what sort of books you want to review, and on what subjects you are specially competent. Make as much as you can of the latter.

Yours sincerely
[T. S. Eliot]

to *John W. Nance*

14 December 1929   [London]

Dear Sir,

I have your letter of the 12th instant;[2] but I am afraid I cannot give permission for you to use any excerpts of my writings, beyond what may fall within the ordinary legal definition of legitimate unauthorised quotation, unless you can let me know exactly what you wish to use.

Yours faithfully,
[T. S. Eliot]

1–Morton, who had been setting up a bookshop, wanted some reviewing 'or other work of that kind'.

2–'I am writing a study of technique in modern poetry. And I should like to include considerable extracts therein from your various publications.

'The book will be privately printed, in an edition of not more than 250 copies; but will probably be circulated for sale amongst certain specific dealers.'

TO *F. S. Oliver*   CC

14 December 1929   [*The Criterion*]

Dear Oliver,

I was very glad to hear from you.[1] First of all thanks for your opinion, which I am glad coincides with mine.[2] Richmond thought rather differently, so I feared I might have been over-scrupulous.

I had not known quite what a bad time you had been having.[3] It must have been a great tax upon your nervous strength, and no doubt you – or anyone else – will have to take the greatest care of yourself for a long time. And the tedium of having to nurse one's strength is almost intolerable.

Having heard, however, that you had been very ill, I was puzzled to think how you could have written a book which, from the brief announcement I saw, did not appear to be the one upon which I knew you had been working. But I think that after one has been engaged for a certain time upon a particular piece of work, it is well to publish what is done. I shall look forward to reading it. I think it ought to be reviewed in *The Criterion*. The reviewing becomes more and more of an editorial problem, as our scope widens. I want the reviewers to work with all possible time and leisure, and therefore send out any important book as soon as it comes in, [*line missing*] has been, that when the next number has to be composed, I have more reviews on my hands – and of books well worth our reviewing – than I can squeeze in. The more so, because I like as far as possible to allow trusted reviewers to use their own discretion about length. But I do want, as you will notice, to give more space to reviewing historical and political books.

With all best wishes for your Christmas,

Sincerely yours,

[T. S. Eliot]

1–Oliver had written on 6 Sept., 'I've been very much handicapped since March last – 6 dreary months – & during that period have been more in bed than out of it. My complaints fortunately are neither painful nor debilitating but I am a bad hand at letter writing except when I can sit at a table.'

2–Oliver wrote on 10 Dec.: 'I presume you appeal to me, not as a highbrow, but as a medium or middle class brow. My opinion (wh. I give without reasons, for I am at present too weak for argument) is that in a magazine both lines wd be better omitted.'

3–Oliver said (10 Dec.) he had undergone four operations in nine months, 'so that I have literally been unable since Oct 1 to do a stroke of work . . . I have been ill since early in Feby last, & have not had a decent weeks interval in all that time . . . [M]y body is tired & flagging . . . My book to which you refer is not I fear in your line. It is written for the middling classes by a member of their own order. I think you had better leave it alone . . .'

TO *The Editor of* The Ladies' Home Journal cc

15 December 1929   [London]

Dear Sir,

On behalf of Viscount Brentford I send you herewith a copy of a pamphlet by him which we are bringing out today entitled *Do We Need A Censor?*

Lord Brentford (better known as Sir William Joynson-Hicks, the late Home Secretary) has written this pamphlet for us to publish in this form. We are concerned only with the British rights, in this form, and it struck me that the essay would be very desirable for an American periodical. It is an important statement by an authority on a question of the day which is I think as active in the U.S.A. as here.

Should you wish to publish this essay in periodical form, I should be glad if you would send me a short cable stating terms and probable date of publication. You will understand that my part in the matter is purely informal and that future negotiations should be with Lord Brentford himself.[1]

Yours faithfully,
[T. S. Eliot]

TO *Bonamy Dobrée* TS Brotherton

15 December 1929   Faber & Faber Ltd

Dear Bonamy,

You will think me a graceless Dog, but I am all behind with correspondence. I must thank you for the inscribed copy, and for dedicating to me so excellent a book.[2] I do think it is quite first rate, and at least as good as your *Restoration Comedy*. The review copy has been taken by Hayward, who wrote for it long before it was out; I hope he will make a good job of it; I know he is enthusiastic. Many congratulations, and again my grateful appreciation of the honour.

---

1 – After reading the pamphlet – 'with interest' – Chesla C. Sherlock, Managing Editor, replied that she would 'file this pamphlet in our file of data for future reference' (4 Dec.).
2 – *Restoration Tragedy 1660–1720* (1929) is dedicated 'To T. S. Eliot'. Dobrée sent a copy on 20 Nov., inscribing it 'T. S. E. his private copy from B.D.' BD wrote in his covering note: 'I hope you won't find it dull reading, and of course you needn't.'

I hear you are now in London. For about how long?[1] For we should like to have a small *Criterion* dinner soon after Christmas, and it must be, of course, on a Wednesday.

Yours ever,
Tom

to *E. McKnight Kauffer* ts Morgan

15 December 1929   Faber & Faber Ltd

My dear Kauffer,

I ought to have written before to thank you for the *Robinson Crusoe*, with the inscription which I shall prize.[2] I like the illustrations immensely, and some of them have a quality which reminds me of Chirico, and which remind me that it is my duty to finish the play, so that the world may have the benefit of your scenery for it.[3]

Incidentally, I have dipped into the book itself, for the first time since childhood. What a good tale it is!

I enjoyed our lunch, and hope to see you again soon after Christmas.[4]

Again with many thanks,
Sincerely yours,
T. S. Eliot

to *The Master, University College, Oxford* cc

16 December 1929   [London]

My dear Master,

Your letter is a great compliment, and rather an embarrassing one. I should feel greatly honoured by having some manuscript of mine preserved in the Bodleian. My early poems, and the manuscript (largely

---

1 – BD had already told TSE, on 20 Nov.: 'I propose to be in London for two months or so from December 9th.' His wife, he had mentioned, was presently to deliver a baby.

2 – Daniel Defoe, *The Life and Strange Surprising Adventures of Robinson Crusoe of York, Mariner*, with Illustrations by E. McKnight Kauffer (London: Etchells and MacDonald: The Haselwood Books, 1929).

3 – *Sweeney Agonistes*, for which Kauffer would design both the set and the book.

4 – On 10 Oct. 1929 Kauffer had asked if he might do 'a special edition' of *TWL*. 'I would like to do it – not illustrated for that would be impossible – but perhaps annotated – perhaps suggestions arising from some of its sources. Something could be done without in the least affecting the reader too graphically.' The idea was not taken up.

typescript) of *The Waste Land*, are or were in the John Quinn collection in New York: Quinn had them from me – one he bought and the other I gave him – and I have no later manuscripts of any interest. I work mostly on the typewriter from rough notes, which I usually destroy. And my prose writings are typed direct with very few corrections, and those of no importance.

What I could do, if it were considered to have any value whatever, would be to write out the final version of some set of poems in longhand; of course that would be merely a fair copy in my own hand. If you cared to have that, I should suggest giving you a small set of poems which is to appear in the late winter, called *Ash Wednesday*.

With many thanks for the compliment.

Yours very sincerely,
[T. S. Eliot]

TO *Christopher Dawson*   CC

16 December 1929   [London]

Dear Mr Dawson,

Thank you for your letter of the 13th. We do not feel that the (relative) ignorance of the modern literature on the subject to which you confess need be an objection. What is important is your competence from the point of view of your own Church; to explain the principles, as you suggest, with some historical view of their continuous tradition. I should be very glad to see your article in 'Order'.

We should like to have the essay, of from 5000 to 10,000 words, as soon as possible; but certainly by the middle of January. Is that possible for you? Our terms for these pamphlets are the same for all our authors: 10% royalty. We have of course, in publishing work in this form and at this price, to sell a good many to make any profit ourselves. But so far we have done pretty well; and it is certain that articles in this form reach a great many people who do not read articles in periodicals.

I should be very glad to lend you the Russell book, which is a useful compendium of the 'modern' views.

I do hope you will be able to find the time to do this. I am having the copies of the *Miscellany* sent: they will show you merely the general form of publication.

Yours very sincerely,
[T. S. Eliot]

TO *Max Clauss*

18 December 1929   [London]

My dear Clauss,

I must apologise for my delay in answering your letter, and thereby putting you to the trouble and expense of telegraphing.[1]

1–'HAVE YOU RECEIVED MY LETTER YOURS SINCERELY CLAUSS EUROPREVUE.' (17 Dec.) Clauss telegraphed too (date unknown): 'PLEASE WRITE GENERAL AGREEING OR NO WITH NOVEL PRIZE KINDEST GREETINGS.' On 5 Dec. he had written a letter in French in reply to TSE's invitation to him to write a *Criterion Miscellany* pamphlet on Young Germany of which TSE prepared – for the benefit of the Faber Board – a 'summary'; this version is in fact more of a literal translation than a digest: 'It would be difficult to write solely an account of the theories and views of German nationalism, first because none of them are very clear, and secondly because German nationalism only exists as a function of the republican realities . . . We are only at the end of our first decade of republicanism with an undigested revolution in our stomach and the inheritance of the Empire on our back.

'Would you allow me to change the subject slightly and to write for you a brief portrait of political Germany of to-day with commentaries for the benefit of the English or French reader? I assure you I would set to work with all my force at once. I do not wish and am unable to give you a piece of learned sociology. But perhaps just a few very simple opinions of political psychology . . .

'What I should like to explain in the 60 or 80 pages which you offer me would be something as follows:

Currents and Cross currents of German Politics			
INTRODUCTION Western Europe & Ourselves	10 printed pages		
1. The Situation of the Republic	20	"	pages
2. The parties of opposition	20	"	pages
3. Our New Physiognomy	10	"	pages [. . .]

'The first part, the position of a republic, should expose the new social strata and the regime established after the collapse of the empire in November 1918. As for historical ideas I should confine myself to referring only to what is absolutely necessary in order to understand the actual state of people and affairs, which is the whole subject of my essay. In this way I hope to give a definition of certain new phenomena which are very important for our politics: For example the Social democratic Prussia of Braun, the Empire from Ebert to Hindenburg, the inflation and the economic recovery from the point of view of the national psychology and the political consequences only, the policy of Stresemann at the meeting point or at the cross roads of old and new Germany.

'The second part, "The parties of Opposition" would give the other side of the medal and would be concerned with disturbing factors left over from the old Germany. Communism, the margin of the social democratic republic, nationalism in revolt against the policy of carrying out the peace treaty, and both meeting in National socialism and in the person of Hugenberg who is a worthy successor of Ludendorf and Stinnes, and like them a representative of a certain organizing tendency which takes no account of simple human values and therefore fails completely.

'In the third place, "The Political Geography of the Empire" – localism and the different horizons of the Germans of the Rhineland and those of the East.

'The third part "Our New Physiognomy", will take the place of a conclusion as far as possible. Without touching on chimerical ideas I shall try to deduce certain fundamental and positive lines of our first republican decade and to show the foreigner our aspirations of

716   TSE at forty-one

We discussed very thoroughly at several meetings your very careful and excellent outline. I must explain first that when I first wrote to you I was, as are many people in England, [aware] that there was in post-war Germany a well developed Reactionary, Counter-Revolutionary, or even what we might call High Tory tendency; clear cut, with a positive *ideology* and theory. Possibly the wish engendered the thought; for I should myself like to see an *international* philosophy of politics developed, which should provide the modern world with an alternative to Marxism. When I say 'international' I mean of course a community and sympathy between intellectuals, not a matter of congresses, committees and leagues. Perhaps we can [find an] occasion for a meeting of representative groups of intellectuals of the great European nations, of men interested in political philosophy, who would attempt a synthesis between the best elements in political counter-revolution with the best elements in international amity and understanding.

That is a suggestion thrown out to you for the future. As for the present, and speaking merely in the role of publisher. We feel positively that the outline you have given is much more suitable for a book of from 50,000 to 80,000 words, than for a short pamphlet. We are sure that you would need more space than we had in mind, and that the *book* would be for a smaller and superior public than that which we must attract with a pamphlet. Therefore we should like now to hold the matter over, until we can see a propitious moment for asking you to do a book. We have in view another series, of *Criterion* books – that is to say, of books dealing with intellectual questions of the day in which *The Criterion* is interested, a collection of an international character; and into this series a book by you on the intellectual tendencies of Germany would certainly fit. Meanwhile, we think that we should abandon the pamphlet, and wait a little. I may add that we could probably offer better terms for a book than we can for any pamphlet.

Now about the Prize. I have succeeded in printing 'The Centurion' in the January *Criterion*, of which you will shortly receive a copy. I like the story, but I do not know how it will succeed. I have also commented on it editorially.[1] As for next year, I await your suggestions; and shall be glad to

---

today and tomorrow. This with the purpose of forestalling anxiety, of exciting curiosity, & of giving assurances for European confidence in Germany . . .

'Dr Clauss then says that if we accept this programme he can promise us the German text by the 15th of January. He awaits our suggestions and terms.'

1 – 'A Commentary', C. 9 (Jan. 1930), 181–2.

know how you advertised the competition in Germany, and any help you can give me by telling me how you arranged the selection.

Incidentally, do you not think that there might be some advantage in having a sixth review – to represent America? For future prizewinners, to have their story published in an American periodical would considerably increase the financial reward, and would open to every winner the possibility of an American public. It would be a little unfair to Wiechert.[1] But the American periodical that I have in mind is *The Hound and Horn*, which in its aims is really very close to the present five reviews. I think I could induce *The Hound and Horn* to take Wiechert's story, and pay him at their usual rates, if I could invite that review into the group, and add a sixth prize to the five in view. I should like to hear from you as soon as possible on this point.

The Hound and Horn is a very commendable quarterly, the best in America. It is very much on our lines. They are publishing an essay of Fernandez in their next number; and I have hope of getting them to publish people like Curtius, Scheler, Worringer. It would help to link them up if I could engage them in this story prize, and I believe that they would be more than willing. They have just absorbed a new periodical to which I had promised support, and are really alone in the field in the new world.

One other suggestion. When it comes to Spain, I think that Spanish America ought to be included. It is not important enough by itself. But perhaps when the time comes we might suggest it to Ortega?

When can you come to London again? I should like to try to see whether a few lectures were possible, if you would indicate that it would be possible for you to come to give them? And you know that you have now many acquaintances here who would welcome you in an informal way.

Yours ever sincerely,

[T. S. Eliot]

I have been very rushed for time, and I know that you read English readily – and if I had waited to dictate this letter in French, or work it for myself in German, it would have been still more delayed.

---

1 – Ernest Wiechert, 'The Centurion', trans. Marjorie Gabain, C. 9 (Jan. 1930), 185–200.

TO *John Simon Guggenheim Memorial Foundation*

TS Guggenheim Foundation

19 December 1929   [London]

[Reference for Edward Dahlberg]

I met Mr Dahlberg last year when he came to England with the idea of studying aesthetics and taking an English degree. I made enquiries for him, and found, as I expected, that apart from I. A. Richards, who was just going to China, there was no teacher in England who could give him what he wanted. He had succeeded in getting a novel accepted by a publisher here, and was doing certain regular work as a reader for that firm. As he had very small funds, this was necessary for him. I advised him to go to a German university, but as he had no such means of earning any money in Germany he could not do that, and returned to New York.[1]

I have no knowledge of Mr Dahlberg's attainments in philosophy and aesthetics; but I have no doubt there are others to vouch for that. I have not seen his novel.[2] I have seen a number of poems and prose poems, which struck me as having promise; he set down his impressions and feelings sincerely and simply. He struck me as genuinely devoted to literature, and from several conversations with him I got an impression of good sense: he seemed to be sensitive and to know what to avoid in the way of bad writing and in the way of American society abroad; and to be really appreciative of what was good.

I do not consider his actual performance nearly as good as that of two other candidates whom I have just recommended. But I imagine that he wishes to work in aesthetics and the philosophy of literary expression; in this field, from what little I have seen, he would be a pupil whom I could personally recommend to such people as Messrs. Richards and Ogden. I think he deserves the chance, and he certainly needs the financial help to get it. I should not consider him at all unworthy of the fellowship, and his

---

1 – Dahlberg was to recall, in *The Confessions of Edward Dahlberg* (1971), 225: '[F. S.] Flint had advised me to return to the United States. I considered going to Oxford, but Eliot said this would be too sterile for a novelist.'

2 – Dahlerg had written to TSE (in response to an unfound letter from TSE) from New York on 17 Oct. 1929: 'Thanks a great deal for your kind letter . . . Since I left London, nothing much has happened to me. Simon & Schuster are publishing "Bottom Dogs" sometime in February, but that gives me little pleasure, as I don't believe in the novel, I mean my novel. I have been ashamed of it, its structural and anecdotal faults, and even its story value has been somewhat tampered with in the process of expurgation: for Putnam's in London have done some bad literary doctoring. I didn't mind having them castrate certain chapters, but I wasn't expecting them to castrate them.'

aims would be fully within the intention of the founder. I am sure that a fellowship would *not* be in this case merely the possibility of a pleasant holiday, but a real and unique opportunity to get the education he wants.

P.S. On re-reading Mr Dahlberg's outline of what he wants to do. I think he would benefit greatly by a few months in London, where he has already met some of the people worth knowing; and I should always be glad to give him advice and help in reading etc.; I think also that he would do well to spend a semester at a German university. Freed from financial anxiety for a period, he ought to be able to pursue some systematic studies *at the same time* as working on his novel. It must be remembered that I have seen no part of any of his novels.

T. S. Eliot.
Editor <i>The Criterion</i>,
Director Faber & Faber Ltd.

TO *Christopher Dawson* CC

19 December 1929   [London]

Dear Mr Dawson,

I think the end of January will do quite well, and I will have a contract sent to you made out for that date. I will send you the Russell book, and may have a few other suggestions to make later, of books to read.

We are very glad to have arranged to have an essay from you.

With all best wishes,
Yours sincerely,
[T. S. Eliot]
Director.

TO *E. Gordon Selwyn* CC

19 December 1929   [London]

Dear Dr Selwyn,

I owe you many apologies for my delay in replying to two letters, but I have been overwhelmed with other work under difficulties.[1] As for Mr

---

1–Selwyn had written on 8 Nov., apropos Belgion's book *Our Present Philosophy of Life* (F&F, 1929): 'I will gladly avail myself of your offer to suggest the names of some of your friends who would do it. Only I much hope the review – or article-review – might be done by someone of your own definite standpoint. The book seems to me to give an

Belgion's book, I suggest that Mr Hamish Miles, 4, Pilgrims Way, N.W.3. would review it very well. I believe that he has already reviewed it for *The New Statesman*, but that might not be an insuperable difficulty. He has written often in *The Criterion*; he is a very intelligent R.C.

Failing him, I might recommend Mr William Thorpe, Victoria and Albert Museum, South Kensington, S.W.7., [who] would do it very well.

I must apologise also for the failure to send you my promised article on Lives of Jesus. I suppose that it is now too late to be considered for a future number?

I am very sorry that I missed you when you called at Russell Square. Will you not, when you next come to London, give me a little warning and the opportunity of asking you to lunch with me?

Yours very sincerely,

[T. S. Eliot]

TO *William E. Spaulding*   CC

19 December 1929   [London]

Dear Mr Spalding,[1]

I find that by some oversight I failed to answer your letter of November 12. I hope you will excuse this belated acknowledgement.[2]

I brought the matter up and we discussed it fully; but we felt that especially in view of the appearance of Mr Harold Monro's *Twentieth Century Poetry*, it would be impossible to market another anthology at the present time. I hope personally that other publishers may have a different opinion.

As for any verse of my own, of course any publisher who undertakes your anthology in England will communicate with me about that.

Trusting that we may soon be able to publish some other book of yours, I remain,

Yours faithfully,

[T. S. Eliot]

Director.

---

admirable opening to the pen of someone who not only agrees with the author's view as to the incredibility of "our present philosophy", but will go on to claim that the Christian philosophy does fill the place.'

1 – TSE's letter misspelt the name.

2 – Spaulding (Houghton Mifflin Company, Boston, Mass.) had responded to TSE's suggestion that F&F might wish to distribute in the UK market the Houghton Mifflin anthology *Twentieth Century Poetry*.

TO *Gerard Hopkins*

19 December 1929   [London]

Dear Mr Hopkins,

It is very difficult to fix any appointment before Christmas![1] Will you be disposed towards business on the day after boxing day, or if not, the following Monday?[2] We will pray that Mr Knight does not arrive till after that.

I am afraid I probably cannot add much to your knowledge, but I am at your disposal.

Yours sincerely,
[T. S. Eliot]

TO *John W. Nance*

19 December 1929   [London]

Dear Sir,

I have your letter of the 16th instant.[3] I do not see that any harm could be done by your publishing the whole of *The Hollow Men*. In fact, as the poem is one poem it is more to my interest to have you publish the whole than a part. So go ahead and print *The Hollow Men* entire; but, please, indicate somewhere that it is contained in a volume of poems published by Faber & Faber Ltd. at seven and six.

I know nothing of your work, but if there is any question of finding a publisher, remember that I am a member of a firm of publishers, and

---

1–Hopkins wrote on 17 Dec.: 'I don't want to bother you unduly, but it would help me considerably in making up my mind about Mr G. Wilson Knight if I could have a few words with you. Mr Knight is coming to London early in the New Year, and if I could steal half an hour of your time either this week, or, say, on Monday of next week, I should be extremely grateful.'

2–TSE and Hopkins met on the Monday, and Hopkins consequently wrote on 22 Jan. 1930: 'It is really good of you to say that you will do an introduction for Wilson Knight's book. Would you think 15 guineas for 2,500 words a ludicrous underpayment?' Wilson Knight wrote to TSE on 20 Jan.: 'Mr Hopkins has told me that The Oxford University Press can take my book. I am writing to thank you for your great kindness in helping me.'

3–'Apropos of the proposed infringement of your copyright, I have a horrid desire, which must, on other grounds, be most firmly suppressed, to include the whole of your collected poems as an Appendix to my study . . . But I would like your permission, if you would be so kind . . . to use the whole of "The Hollow Men" in my book . . . In any case, the book will probably never be exposed for sale at all, but will be privately printed . . .'

I should be most interested if you cared to send me the manuscript at this address.

But I must record my disgust with the foul word *modernist*. It is, unhappily, necessary in theology; but it could easily be avoided in poetry. It implies a desire to be 'modern'; and no poet should care whether his work is 'modern' or not.[1]

Yours faithfully,
[T. S. Eliot]

TO *Arthur Calder Marshall*   CC

19 December 1929   [London]

Dear Mr Marshall,

I know that you have my promise to address the Poetry Society, and I hope to keep it;[2] but I am afraid that next term again will be impossible for me. I have a book to write, and have also a difficult set of wireless talks to give; and with my ordinary engagements I shall find it very hard to get through my work at best.

I owe you many apologies for deluding you with false expectations; please believe that I am anxious to fulfil my undertaking as soon as it is literally possible.

Yours very sincerely,
[T. S. Eliot]

1 – 'I'm sorry about that word "modernist",' replied Nance (20 Dec.); 'but I don't see how I can alter it. The word I want is "Futurist". But the artists have played such harry with that word that one simply cannot use it. You see I want to draw a distinction between the modern poets – Humbert Wolfe and the rest of them; and the new poets – Pound and the later Graves and yourself . . . In the word "modernist" I am trying to describe the sort of poet who writes intellectual poetry – poetry of which the meaning is of the most fundamental importance – in a rhythmic syllabic form. Cras ingens haruspex – that is what you are. But I daren't call you haruspices.'
2 – Calder Marshall had written from *The Oxford Outlook* on 13 Dec. 1929. TSE had promised some three months earlier to come and talk to the Poetry Society.

TO *Ana M. Berry*[1]   cc

19 December 1929   [London]

Dear Miss Berry,

I was very glad to hear from you, and must apologise for the delay in answering your letter of the 30th October.[2] I should always be glad to do anything I could to support the League, and if I could have seen my way to accepting your kind invitation, I should have written sooner. But I have been, and shall be very busy for the next six months, and do not see how I can possibly make any more lecture engagements. When I can, I look forward to the pleasure of seeing you again; and meanwhile send you my very best wishes for your work with the League.

Yours very sincerely,
[T. S. Eliot]

TO *Walter de la Mare*   cc

19 December 1929   [London]

My dear De la Mare,

I am deep in confusion, because while still humming and hawing and meaning to write to you to say that I still felt that the subject was out of my range, I have received a letter from the Secretary asking me to fix a date![3] I still feel that the original subject you suggested is too much for me; and that I cannot – especially with my commitments to other work, do anything at all suitable for an historical survey of this kind. I am in fact in a panic. 'Aesthetics' is quite beyond me, and if I tackled Pater, I should feel on very uncertain ground about his art criticism.

I am sorry to hear that Dick is ill. I hope it is not at all serious.

Yours sincerely,
[T. S. Eliot]

1–Ana M. Berry was Hon. Organising Secretary, The Arts League of Service, 1919–31. Born in South America of English and Chilean parentage, she came to Europe to study art, and had joined the Arts League of Service from the beginning (in the first year TSE gave a talk on poetry at the Conference Hall, Westminster). In 1931 she was obliged to return to S. America, and she died there in 1947. Her works include *Art for Children* (Special Winter Number of *The Studio*, 1929), and the posthumous *Understanding Art*, ed. Judith Wogan and Bride Scratton in collaboration with Eleanor M. Elder (1952).
2–Berry hoped TSE might be able to contribute a lecture to their winter series, perhaps on poetic drama: maybe on 8 Jan.
3–F. L. Rudston Brown, secretary of the RSL, wrote on 16 Dec. to determine a date.

TO *H. M. Simpson*[1]

19 December 1929   [London]

Dear Madam,

I thank you for your kind letter of the 1st December, and wish that I could accept your invitation. But I have so much to do that I have been compelled for some time to forgo all lecture engagements for an indefinite time. I should be very happy if at a future time I were able to address such an audience as yours.

I must thank you also for expressing approval of my talk.

Yours sincerely,
[T. S. Eliot]

TO *A. E. Taylor*[2]

19 December 1929   [London]

Dear Sir,

I am writing on behalf of my firm to ask whether you would be willing to give us the great benefit of your opinion of a recent work by Professor Kurt Singer, entitled *Platon der Grunder*.

In a case like this a publisher is always in a difficulty. Such a book would be expensive to translate and produce, and we cannot afford to make the venture unless we can have absolutely the most authoritative opinion. On the other hand the reader's fee can never represent the value of an opinion like yours, or the value of your time. As we should publish the book primarily for our prestige and as a work of importance and public value we can only ask for your opinion with the knowledge that it is asking a considerable kindness.[3]

Yours faithfully,
[T. S. Eliot]
Director.

---

1 – H. M. Simpson was Lecturer in English, Avery Hill Training College, a training college for elementary teachers.

2 – Alfred Edward Taylor (1869–1945), Professor of Moral Philosophy in the University of Edinburgh, 1924–41; President of the Aristotelian Society, 1928–9. Publications include *St Thomas Aquinas as a Philosopher* (1924); *Plato, the Man and his Work* (1927).

3 – Taylor agreed (24 Dec.) to give his opinion, but not before Jan. 1930.

TO *Robert Shafer*[1]

19 December 1929   [London]

Dear Mr Shafer,

I must apologise for not having written to you long ago.[2] You are quite right to publish your article in *The Bookman*. I read it with great interest and appreciation, and should very much like to have used it, not only in fairness as a reply to Tate, but for its intrinsic value. But as an editor, I have attempted something very unfamiliar even to the *Criterion* public in England, in pressing Humanism so forcibly on its attention; and I felt that it was wiser to drop the subject for a time, rather than risk spoiling the impression already made by overdoing what seems to many people (quite wrongly) a purely American controversy. I am publishing one more Humanist study, but that is by Fernandez, and is definitely generalised.

I took the liberty of showing your essay to Middleton Murry, who also thought highly of it; but rejected it on the natural ground that it presumed knowledge of another article which had appeared in another review, and was therefore unsuitable for *The Adelphi*.

I am therefore very glad to know that it will appear elsewhere; and can only add that I should very much like to publish something by you, and that I apologise again for the delay.

Yours very truly,

[T. S. Eliot]

1 – Robert Shafer (1899–1956), Professor of English at the University of Cincinnati, 1927–55; author of *Progress and Science* (1922); *Christianity and Naturalism* (1926); *Humanism and America* (co-ed., 1930); *Paul Elmer More and American Criticism* (1935).

2 – Shafer submitted on 27 Aug. 1929 'Retort upon Tate' – a reply to Allen Tate's essay 'The Fallacy of Humanism' (*C.* July 1929). 'I think (if I may say so without being suspected of trying to push my own wares) that a serious responsibility was incurred by the publication of Mr Tate's essay. I don't see how, whatever one's sympathies, one can escape the conclusion that Messrs. More and Babbitt were gravely wronged. And at least your readers should have the opportunity of hearing something from the other side. That "something", however, cannot be said – save as a mere empty counter-assertion – without direct examination of Mr Tate's lucubrations.' He wrote again on 29 Nov., 'Mr Seward Collins, editor of *The Bookman* (New York) heard that I had written a reply to Mr Tate's "Fallacy of Humanism" and that Mr Tate's article was to be published in the U.S.A. in the Winter Number of *The Hound and Horn*. He asked to see my essay, and now desires to print it in the January issue of *The Bookman*, and to this I have consented.'

TO *E. R. Curtius*   TS University of Bonn

19 December 1929   *The Criterion*

My dear Curtius,

Your letter of the 5th December gives me some encouragement. The list of authors you give is admirable; I would only suggest that Robert Graves is not yet important or representative enough. Lawrence, Forster and Huxley are all quite right; and I should certainly like to see you include Virginia Woolf, and Wyndham Lewis, and possibly Lytton Strachey.

It would be difficult to obtain all the books of all of these authors. Perhaps you would care to let me know later what books you have read, and I could suggest any others that seem to me essential; and would try to get them for you from the publishers.

I have failed to thank you [for] a number of gifts from you; but nevertheless have read them all with great enjoyment. Your essay on Hofmannsthal gave me much pleasure; and I was very sorry afterwards that I did not use it for the December *Criterion*, because Rychner has not written his note on Hofmannsthal in time after all. I felt that as our regular chronicler, he ought to have the opportunity of writing on so important a subject.

I wish you would let me know at some time which, if any of Hofmannsthal's plays seem to you suitable for translation into English. It would interest me to try my hand at it, if I could get permission.

Yours ever cordially, and again with many thanks,

T. S. Eliot

P.S. I am very anxious indeed to persuade you to write this book of essays on English authors, and so are my co-directors.

TO *Edwin Berry Burgum*[1]

CC

21 December 1929   [London]

My dear Mr Burgum,

I must apologise for my delay in answering your letter of the 7th ultimo.[2] I have no objection in principle, except that I do not think a writer ought to give his work away; and I should be glad to know what fee you are prepared to offer for using this essay.

Yours very truly,
[T. S. Eliot]

TO *Walter de la Mare*

CC

26 December 1929   [London]

My dear De la Mare,

The imminence of Christmas prevented me from answering your letter of the 22nd at once. I will not discomfit you now – if, that is, I may be allowed to do what I feel competent to do.[3] I have a great deal of other work to do in the next three months, including a set of lectures; and if I write for you it must be on some subject which I can do without much reading, either fresh or refreshment of memory. Would the relation of

---

1 – Edwin Berry Burgum (1894–1979) was Associate Professor of English at New York University, 1924–53. From 1936 to 1938 he was to be President of the College Teachers Union of New York City, contributing to and editing the Marxist quarterly *Science and Society*, and he was therefore possibly affiliated to the Communist Party. In 1952, during the McCarthy witchhunt, he was subpoenaed to answer questions in the Senate about his putative links to the Communist Party, but throughout the ensuing hearings he staunchly invoked both the First and the Fifth Amendments, refusing to confirm or deny his alleged Marxist beliefs. In 1953 he was at first suspended and then dismissed from his New York University post, and he was never reinstated despite concerted campaigns by lawyers, teachers and unions. After his wife committed suicide in 1957, he took up a new career as a lay analyst and psychotherapist (his wife had been a psychotherapist). His writings include *The Literary Career of Edward Bulwer, Lord Lytton* (1926), *Ulysses and the Impasse of Individualism* (1941), and *The Novel and the World's Dilemma* (1947).
2 – 'I am editing for Prentice-Hall, Inc. a collection of essays on esthetics and literary criticism, to be called The New Criticism. I hope to include essays or selections by Santayana, Croce, Maritain, Valery, Fernandez, Richards, Bosanquet, Buermeyer, and so on. I am anxious to be permitted to include among them your Tradition and the Individual Talent . . . May I have your permission to use this essay?' See *The New Criticism* (1930).
3 – De la Mare was now 'in a panic too . . . I shall be dreadfully sorry if you withdraw, & that quite apart from the question of time which is getting rather short. There is no need to keep to aesthetics: just Pater's literary criticism & his work in general, if that would appeal to you . . . There is no need whatever to keep closely to any precise subjects . . .'

Pater to Arnold, with a retrospect at Newman, do? The mutations of the religious sensibility, in that descent, are interesting, and not, I think, without a bearing on literary criticism. *Literature and Dogma* is the *mittelpunkt* of course: my view being that Arnold in surrendering dogma, gave a deplorable bias to literature.[1]

Our previous correspondence is at the office, but as I remember nothing was said about other rights. May I ask (1) whether the contributors get any further benefit from the book than the ten guineas, and (2) whether there are any limitations on simultaneous publication in America and subsequent publication in a volume of my own? I find it essential to sell as much as possible of my work at the best possible price in America as well as here, because I am a slow and fitful writer.

> With all best wishes,
> Sincerely yours,
> [T. S. Eliot]

TO *Mary Hutchinson*   TS Texas

26 December 1929   177 Clarence Gate Gardens, N.W.1

My dear Mary,

I am very much pleased with your bowl of cherry wood curiously carv'd, which shall stand on my desk. I always admire your ability to choose such charming presents as you do – but what also gives a value different from that of others, is the fact that you deliver them yourself: particularly this year, when your Christmas Eve visit delighted us extremely.

And now I hope that before long we shall be coming to see you.

> Yours always affectionately,
> Tom

1–De la Mare responded on 30 Dec., 'the subject you suggest and the way of treating it could not be better; and I don't think the fact that the view you express about Arnold is rather out of my range in the least precludes my saying this.'

TO *St John Hutchinson*   TS Texas

26 December 1929   177 Clarence Gate Gardens, N.W.1

Dear Jack,

How very kind of you to send me a Christmas present. Your thurible will look well on my mantel, where it will hold tobacco; though its age seems to demand that I should take to using snuff instead.

I wish that the present might soon be followed by yourself. I imagine you have been very busy this last year; but your old friends would always be grateful for the refreshment of your company.

I can now drive the car well enough to drive to Albert Road; and I hope that if I pluck up the spirit to drive us there one day, you will be there to greet us, and then to turn the car round so that I can drive back.

Ever affectionately,
Tom

TO *Marion and Ted Kauffer*   MS Morgan

26 December 1929   177 Clarence Gate Gardens, N.W.1

Dear Marion & Ted Kauffer,

Your beautiful hyacinths arrived, to our surprise and pleasure, on Christmas Eve, and added immensely to the pleasure, or alternatively relieved the burden, of our Christmas in this dismal flat. You are extremely generous people, and we both appreciated the gift to the full.

We have had a very trying time these last months, and have not been very well, and dislike our present abode so much that we have had no heart to ask people here. But hope to find a dwelling early in the New Year to which we shall want to invite our friends.

And we thank you again for the hyacinths & the thought behind them.

Yours ever sincerely
T. S. Eliot

TO *William Empson*   cc

26 December 1929   [*The Criterion*]

Dear Mr Empson,

I did get your letter eventually, though as you see the address is 24 and not 25; and you have been on my mind for some time.[1] If you are to be in London only on Friday the 3rd January, I think I could see you then at this address, say at 12 o'clock; or if that is inconvenient let us make another appointment at the end of the month when you say you will be in town for a longer period.

                        Yours sincerely,
                        [T. S. Eliot]

TO *Ottoline Morrell*   TS Texas

26 December 1929   177 Clarence Gate Gardens, N.W.1

My dear Ottoline,

I was very much pleased to have the beautiful diary from you again this Christmas. What I like particularly is the continuity of it, and the sense of permanent friendship. I keep all the diaries you have given me, and it is many years now since I have ever been without one in my pocket; and a Christmas without a diary from you would be a sad one.

I do hope that we shall see you very soon. We both enjoyed extremely the last time you came to tea.

                        Yours ever affectionately
                        Tom

Vivienne Eliot TO *Mary Hutchinson*   MS Texas

26 December 1929   177 Clarence Gate Gardens, N.W.1

My dear Mary,

I want to thank you for coming in to see us on Christmas Eve. It was *good* of you. And I must thank you again for the *delightful* presents. When I opened my parcels – I was *enchanted* with my necklace! It really is too lovely for me.

1–Empson thanked TSE (21 Dec.) for inviting him to an interview: he had written twice to no. 25 Russell Square, and had even called at that address – only to be disappointed.

I would like to have telephoned to you today, but am writing instead.

We managed to get to our Christmas dinner in the Morris Minor, & Tom drove it very very well. A perfect master of it. And again today we had a nice short drive.

I do want you to come & have tea with me, as you *said* you would, as soon as you can. And I now suggest next *Tuesday* afternoon, at 4 o'clock. I do hope you can, & will. If you cannot will you suggest another day?

With love, and again thanking you very very much my dear,

Yours
Vivienne H Eliot

TO *Edwin Muir*   CC

26 December 1929   [*The Criterion*]

My dear Muir,

I should be very glad indeed to see your essay on Kafka.[1] I know the name, but that is all; but if he is as important as Rilke I am very glad that you have translated one of his books. It would be best, I think, if your article appeared after the book is in circulation here; and I could not use it till June anyway; but do let me see it as soon as it is ready.

With best wishes for the New Year to Mrs Muir and yourself,

Yours sincerely
[T. S. Eliot]

TO *Louis Zukofsky*   TS Texas

28 December 1929   *The Criterion*

Dear Mr Zukovsky [*sic*],

I will let you know about your new poems as soon as I can.[2] But you will understand that I cannot get in poems by one author more than once

1–Muir offered (20 Dec. 1929) an article on Franz Kafka. 'Probably you know something of him, although he is almost unknown, I think, in England. My wife and I have translated one of his novels [*Das Schloss/The Castle*] recently, which is to appear in the spring. He is, I really think, the most considerable writer that Austria or Germany has produced, with the possible exception of Rilke, during this century. And he is immensely interesting . . . I have been more excited by his novels than by anything I have read for a long time.'
2–Zukofsky had submitted in June 1929 'the first two movements of a poem entitled "A"'; on 23 Oct. he wrote to ask for a decision, and then again on 10 Dec. He added to the last letter, 'Would you be interested in an essay dealing with Ezra Pound's Cantos?'

a year, as we only have room for four poems, or four sets of poems in a year.

Meanwhile I have read a very interesting essay on Henry Adams, which Pound showed me. It was unfortunately, much too long for *The Criterion*. Also, it does imply that its reader has some elementary knowledge of who Adams was and what he stood for; and his works, except perhaps the *Autobiography,* are practically unknown here. I should very much like to get, if I could, a more elementary essay on Adams to introduce him to the English public.

I should very much like to *see* your essay on Pound's *Cantos*, and I think I might be able to publish it: the chief doubt being that their circulation has been of necessity of price and form very small; so that I hope your paper contains numerous quotations to make it more intelligible to anyone who has never seen the *Cantos* themselves.[1]

I have taken the liberty of writing about your work, at Pound's suggestion, to the Guggenheim Foundation.

Yours sincerely,
T. S. Eliot
Editor

TO *Stephen Spender*

TS Northwestern

28 December 1929   *The Criterion*

Dear Mr Spender,

I find to my discomfiture, in clearing up great arrears of correspondence, that you asked me to reply to your letter before the 21st. So I suppose that this letter must follow you to Switzerland, and I apologise for the inconvenience I am causing you.[2]

I had indeed hoped that I might be able to address the English Club and the Poetry Club this next term. But an excess of engagements of one kind and another, contracted under the human necessity of making a living, makes it impossible for me to make any appointments to visit

---

1 – 'The Cantos of Ezra Pound (one section of a long essay)', C. 10 (Apr. 1931); repr. in *Prepositions: The Collected Critical Essays of Louis Zukofsky* (1967), 61–77.
2 – Spender had asked, on two or three occasions, whether TSE might be able to talk in the spring term to a combined meeting of the Oxford University English Club and the Poetry Club (Spender was the only member of the university who was an officer in both clubs). He wrote again on 9 Dec., 'if you could possibly let me know of your decision before December 21st I would be very grateful as I am going to Switzerland then . . .'

Oxford or Cambridge; and indeed I have had to break one to which I had bound myself. So I can only express the hope that this will be merely a postponement; and add my sincere expression of disappointment.

Yours very sincerely,
T. S. Eliot

TO *Herbert Read*   TS Victoria

28 December 1929   *The Criterion*

Dear Herbert,

Many thanks for your counsel. I am sorry that the Museum has been sweating you; and had we known that you were there we would have asked you over for a lunch of cold turkey.[1] Though both exhausted by Christmas and myself very hoarse from smoking a kind of cigar that was given me.

I have decided to decline the Arts League request.[2] It is Ana Berry's show, you know; and I mistrust their taste and the theatrical talent at their disposal; and as you suggest, they are all women. Of course Craig[3] or Reinhart[4] would be different; and with producers so distinguished as they the author's responsibility would be nil. As I am I believe a member of the Council of the A. L. of S. people might think the Punchandjudy was under my direction. There are about 300 members of the Council.

I think your tip about a *Criterion chapelle* is a good one. That is just where an editor needs the advice of a few persons like yourself. I want to keep off theology for a bit; and I want to discuss with you as soon as

1–HR wrote on 26 Dec. that he was being required to work till 9 p.m. that day.

2–Judith Wogan of the Grafton Theatre had requested permission from TSE on 5 Dec. to stage a version of 'The Hollow Men'. HR advised TSE on 26 Dec.: 'I feel generally that one should let one's work take the natural course of vulgarization . . . But one should guard as far as possible against misrepresentation . . . Gordon Craig or Reinhardt or Diaghlieff (can't spell him) is one question, but what looks like a bitchy set of busybodies, is another. So I should say: if these people are good enough, yes; if not, no.'

3–Edward Gordon Craig (1872–1966), son of Ellen Terry; actor, director, designer, and theorist of theatre. He directed a celebrated production of *Hamlet* at the Moscow Art Theatre in 1911, and his influential writings include *On the Art of the Theatre* (1911).

4–Max Reinhardt (1873–1943), Austrian-born theatre and film director, managed the Deutsches Theater, Berlin, 1905–30, and in 1920 founded (with Richard Strauss and Hugo von Hofmannsthal) the Salzburg Festival. Following the *Anschluss* in 1938 he migrated to the USA, where he was naturalised in 1940. In addition to several notable productions on Broadway, he made films including *Das Mirakel* (1912) and *A Midsummer Night's Dream*, starring James Cagney, Mickey Rooney, Olivia de Havilland (1935). In Vienna he set up the Max Reinhardt Seminar; in Hollywood the Reinhardt School of the Theatre.

possible some other topic[s], such as those suggested in my December commentary. Do you think that some views of the younger generation (meaning ourselves) on such common subjects as Disarmament, International Relations, etc. would be palatable? (Observe that while we are very nearly the older generation in literature, we can still figure as juveniles in politics).

About Scheler:[1] could you send me the book, or if you are lunching at the Grove on Jan 2nd. I will go there.

About the *Listener*.[2] It seems to me no more degrading to write for the *Listener* than for any other periodical for which one writes for money. *Times* Leaders are good, because you can always realise on them in a book. But what use is a *Nation* review? You can't use it again: and you can speak your mind better in the *Criterion*. I am doing another set of broadcast talks in the spring, and am thankful to have them to do. I should certainly take on the *Listener*, if I were you. One only has to acquire a certain thin fluency; and on the other hand, for one's conscience, it is often easier to speak your mind in a more lowbrow paper than in the hidebound *Nation* or *Times*. And anything is better for you than wasting energy on *Times* and *Nation* column reviews.

I shall have to consult Morley on Monday about Wheen's dream.[3] We may have to visit Madame Sosostris to clear it up.

I think we ought to tackle Lippman's *Preface to Morals*. I have been talking to your neighbour Thorold about it. Have you read it, and would you review it yourself? There was a good review in *The Realist* by one Catlin. Who is he?[4]

> With New Year Wishes,
> Yours,
> Tom

---

1 – Worringer had sent HR a volume of Scheler's essays, just published, running to about 150 pp. It 'would be a good introductory volume' for F&F to produce, HR considered.

2 – HR had taken on the job of writing a weekly column on art for *The Listener*. 'I fell to the temptation – my resolve being to substitute this for bread-&-butter reviewing of books in the *Nation* & elsewhere . . . Do you think I have done right?'

3 – 'Wheen . . . dreamt . . . that you and Morley were playing chess in his house at a table suspended over a bottomless pit. What does this portend?'

4 – George Catlin (1896–1979) reviewed Lippman's book in *The Realist* (Dec. 1929). A Professor of Political Science, author of numerous books on political philosophy – including *Thomas Hobbes* (1922) – and later on Anglo-American relations, Catlin was a friend and associate of Harold Laski, Ramsay MacDonald, Herbert Morrison and Nehru; and husband of Vera Brittain (author of *Testament of Youth*). See John Catlin, *Family Quartet: Vera Brittain and her family* (1987). HR wrote to TSE on 3 Jan. 1930, 'Avoid Catlin: he is a dreadful windbag. Morley had lunch with him recently & will concur.'

TO *John Cournos*   CC

28 December 1929   [London]

Dear Cournos,

I am very sorry that your letter arrived only just before Christmas; I
snatched it up with many others on my last visit to the office, and did not
read them till I got home; and there has been no opportunity of getting
a copy of the *Dante* until next Monday the 30th.[1] I regret that I could
not get it off in time for Mrs Cournos's Christmas; but it shall be sent on
Monday. I shall be interested to know whether you both like it.

I send all my sympathy to you. I do not know anyone who has been so
afflicted as you during the past few years. I am particularly sorry that you
cannot tell me that the danger is over. I hope that you keep a little health
yourself under the fearful strain.

You shall have a copy of the December *Criterion*: perhaps it has already
reached you. I should like a Russian Chronicle for March; the Russian
Chronicle is I think one of the most appreciated by the readers. But I will
not bother you further about it at the moment.

Please tell your wife that I hope to see her well and strong in London in
the spring, and accept my sympathy yourself.

                                        Yours ever,
                                        [T. S. Eliot]

P.S. I will also send a copy of my Christmas verses – though they are
rather depressing ones![2]

TO *A. A. Jacobs*   CC

28 December 1929   [London]

Dear Sir,

In reply to your letter of the 12th ultimo, asking for permission to use
a certain four of my poems in a new Anthology, I should be glad to know

---

1–Cournos had written, in reply to a (now lost) letter from TSE, to say that his wife Helen
had just undergone 'another major operation'. 'So far she has survived the ordeal, though
she is by no means out of danger.' Just before the operation she had 'expressed a desire to
read' TSE's *Dante*. Cournos therefore enclosed a postal order for a copy, which he hoped
TSE would inscribe '*to her!*' He hoped it might arrive in time for Christmas.
2–Cournos liked *Animula* 'very much' (as he would write to TSE on 14 Jan. 1930). 'As for
Helen, she says "it's the most disillusioning thing I've ever read!"'

what fee you offer for their use; and whether the volume is to be published in England as well as America.[1]

Yours faithfully,
[T. S. Eliot]

TO *Huw Menai* CC

28 December 1929   [London]

Dear Mr. Menai,

In reply to your letter of the 20th instant, by all means let me see the new volume as soon as it is ready. We publish very little verse, but I liked your first book so much that I should like to have the opportunity of considering and recommending the new one.

Yours sincerely,
[T. S. Eliot]

TO *G. C. Bosset*[2] CC

28 December 1929   [London]

Dear Sir,

I thank you for your kind letter expressing appreciation of my talk at the Children's Theatre.[3] Such expressions are always very welcome.

I meant merely that as poetry on the one hand makes ideas *sensible*, so on the other hand the idea is necessary to the poetry; the meaning

---

1 – 'Your permission is requested for the inclusion of "A Cooking Egg", "The Hippopotamus", "Whispers of Immortality" and "Mr. Eliot's Sunday Morning Service" in *Circumference*, which is an anthology of varieties of metaphysical verse, 1456–1928, edited by Genevieve Taggard, in a signed and numbered edition limited to 1050 copies which we have undertaken to print and make at our expense to sell at cost plus royalty and 10 per cent which is allowed for distribution, by Covici-Friede.'

2 – Georgette C. Bosset, author and translator. Her works include *Fenimore Cooper et le roman d'aventure en France vers 1830* (1928) – a thesis at the Université de Lausanne.

3 – Bosset wrote from London on 2 Dec. that she had 'very much enjoyed' TSE's lecture on poetry and philosophy at Endell Street. 'It gave me great joy of a very rare quality, & provided food for thought for several days . . . I found your idea that poetry provides an aesthetic sanction for thought as valuable as it is beautiful.

'I did not quite understand so clearly, however, the first part of your statement – that it also gives an intellectual sanction for feeling – I wondered whether the word "intellectual" simply referred to the verbal and rhythmical interpretation of the poet's feeling, or whether the function of poetry entails something more rigorously intellectual than that. If so, I am unable to discover it.'

is essential to justify the emotion or sensation. This is very simple, and perhaps commonplace.

> With many thanks,
> Yours very truly,
> [T. S. Eliot]

то *Hugh Sykes Davies*[1] CC

28 December 1929   [London]

Dear Mr. Davies,

Very many thanks for your kind invitation to address The Heretics next term. It is all the more a compliment as I have already addressed that body, and they must know what a poor speaker I am. I wish that I could help; but I have already undertaken probably more work than I can get through in the next three or four months; and I am afraid any visit to Cambridge or Oxford during that time is impossible. Why, by the way, do you not try to get Wyndham Lewis to address you? I cannot think of anyone better, in the present lamentable conditions of which you complain.[2]

1–Hugh Sykes Davies (1909–84), author and critic. Educated at St John's College, Cambridge – where he edited, with William Empson, the magazine *Experiment*, and where he took the Jebb Studentship and the Le Bas Prize, 1931 – he became a University Lecturer and Fellow of St John's. In the 1930s he was a Communist and Surrealist, and co-created the London Surrealist Exhibition, 1936. His novels include *Full Fathom Five* (1956) and *The Papers of Andrew Melmoth* (1960); his poems, though some were published, were not collected in his lifetime. His other writings include *Wordsworth and The Worth of Words* (posthumous, 1986). TSE would write of him on 13 Mar. 1936, when he was applying for a post at the University of Liverpool: 'I have known him pretty well for some years, and I regard his qualifications as exceptional. He has the advantage, not too common in these days, of a sound classical foundation, and I remember an essay of his on the earliest Latin versification which impressed me very much. For the study of criticism he has, I believe, much curious and out-of-the-way learning in Renaissance criticism and philosophy, both in Latin and in Italian, and I regard this as of great importance. He has very wide curiosity and acquaintance with a variety of subjects, as well as a solid knowledge of those which he professes. He is, I believe, something of an authority on the philosophy of Vico, but of this I am not qualified to speak. He has a brilliant mind, and I think also has the temperament which makes it possible for a teacher to acquire the friendship of his pupils. I have great pleasure in supporting his application.' See also George Watson, 'Remembering Prufrock: Hugh Sykes Davies 1909–1984', *The Sewanee Review* 109: 4 (Fall 2001), 573–80.
2–Sykes Davies wrote from St John's College (undated): 'The Lucas-faction in King's have become very vocal in the absence of Richards, and their figurehead of a Lytton is prowling round the courts very significantly. It would be very good of you to come and administer a rap on their knuckles.'

With many regrets and all best wishes,

Yours sincerely,

[T. S. Eliot]

Vivienne Eliot TO *Mary Hutchinson*   MS Texas

29 December 1929   177 Clarence Gate Gardens, N.W.1

My dear Mary,

I am very sorry but I must postpone our meeting on next Tuesday. I shall have much more to do than I anticipated for the next week or 2, & I know I ought not to make any engagements.

So can we put off our meeting for a week? And telephone on tomorrow week (Monday week *evening*) to decide it? If you have not telephoned by *8.30* p.m. on next Monday week, I will ring you up myself.

With love

Yrs. as ever

V. H. Eliot

TO *Judith Wogan*   CC

30 December 1929   [London]

Dear Miss Wogan,

I have thought over your letter of the 17th very carefully, hence my delay in replying; for which I apologise.[1]

I have come regretfully to the conclusion that, however much I appreciate the compliment, and with the most sincere good wishes for the start of the Grafton Theatre, I had rather not have 'The Hollow Men' staged at the present time.

Various considerations have influenced me, with all of which I need not bother you. I have no objection in principle to the dramatic presentation of poems, nor even to such presentation **to** poems by living writers. But there is not yet among my poems any which I care to have marked out in this way, or by which I should care to be represented. And particularly

---

1 – 'Your poetry makes me live emotions keenly, besides being very visual to me . . . This is how I would like to do the poem on a stage.

'Three dimly lit figures grouped against a cyclorama background, making occasional slight concerted swaying movements and possibly altering their positions now and then.

'I should like queer unreal figures with a hint of the scarecrow about them; perhaps rather Picasso-esque figures. I would like the poem spoken by an unseen person.'

with the 'Hollow Men', I feel that it might be misleading; though, if it were done, your ideas of doing it seem to me along the right lines. But it is

[*text missing at foot of the page*]

by a greater mass of later work before I allow it the honour of such notoriety. Perhaps after I have had another edition of *Poems*, considerably enlarged, would be a better time.

Had I ever written a complete *play*, that would be a different matter; for a play stands by itself, without such insidious implications.

I fear that I must fail to make my attitude clear. But believe me, had I thought such production suitable at the present time for this poem, I should not have hesitated.

> With many regrets,
> Yours sincerely
> [T. S. Eliot]

TO *Bonamy Dobrée*   TS Brotherton

30 December 1929   *The Criterion*

Dear Bonamy,

Neuerscheinungen: ACHIGAR von Gutfreund von Obrae: eine knappe, tuchtige, witzige, durchsichtige, prufende Darstellung des Baskischen Seelenwesens: im Monat Maerz.

As for your HOGMANY HILARITIES:[1] I very much regret that it is impossible for me to be present; BUT if on the 8th or the 15th there could be arranged an EPIPHANY EFFERVESCENCE or even a pre-CANDLEMAS CONVIVIALITY I should use my best endeavours to join you. In other words, I couldnt come on the 1st; I would arrange the 8th or the 15th; but Morley can come on the 1st or the 15th but not the 8th. I dont want to disturb matters, & please dont rearrange on my account. But if necessary telephone me here or at <Home> Padd 6930 or Gerard

---

1 – BD had written on 18 Dec.: 'You will hear, no doubt, that a Criterion Festival is being arranged for Jan. 1st . . . Perhaps, however, you will want to avoid me out of shame at not printing *Achigar*. In return I will point out the nasty attack made on you at the Italian Front.
    Signor Mussolini
    Disliked the name Sweeney.
    Anyone bearing it, he said,
    Would get a thump on the head.
'That's all the trouble you get for taking fascisms seriously. "Where are your black shirts?" 'Sir – they are at the wash."'
    BD's 'Achigar, translated from the Basque', was to appear in C. 9 (Apr. 1930), 476–81.

1234 or Sloane 3434 or Museum 4000 or elsewhere.

Yours confusedly,

T. S. E.

I hope all goes well with your family up to date?

OPEN WIRELESS VAUDEVILLE

Epiphany Programme

<u>'Vigorous Frank' Morley</u>
The Telephone Comedian

in a New Sketch entitled

'Good Lad!! God Bless You!!!'

<u>Flint & Codrington</u>
Codrington & Flint

Polyglot Punsters

<u>Humbert Wolfe</u>

Our Hebrew Friend

The Revd. J. G. Fletcher

The Red-hot Revivalist Returns to the Roost
with a Roaring Rhapsody
'Are you Saved?'

<u>Read & Thorpe</u>

The Yodelling Youngsters
in 'Yorkshire Pudding'.

<u>A. W. Wheen</u>

With his Mile-a-Minute Monalogue

<u>T. S. Eliot</u>

The Bellowing Baritone
With Bolovian Ballads
'The Blue Baboon'

<u>Harold Monro</u>

The Sentimental Scotsman
Burns & Bagpipes: A Poetry Reading

SUPPLEMENTARY TOASTS

Pius XI.	Proposer: Mr J. G. Fletcher
Zaghlul Pasha.	Proposer: Major Dobrée, J.P.
The Aga Khan.	Proposer: Humbert Wolfe, C.B.
The Bishop of Birmingham.	Proposer: T. S. Eliot
Mr F. L. Lucas.	Proposer: Mr Herbert Read.

TO *John Middleton Murry*   TS Northwestern

30 December 1929   *The Criterion*

Dear John,

I am very grieved to learn that your corrected proof was not used. The office has only just opened properly today after Christmas, and I found myself very busy; but I shall make enquiries tomorrow. Meanwhile I offer my apologies, and will certainly print the errata in March.[1]

Yes, I will certainly print an article by you on Value. I will try to work out tomorrow what space I have left in the March number and if there is not enough for your needs would you care to send a short preliminary letter and send the article for the following number? but you need not answer this till you hear from me again.[2]

Exactly I want to get the discussion removed from the local and sectarian atmosphere of American Humanism into a more philosophic field, wherefore I welcomed Fernandez. And the less you have to use the word 'humanism' or refer to the Americans the better.

I have got to study Fernandez more closely: to translate an essay is not necessarily to master it as a whole.

I think I understand F.'s terminology much better than I understand yours; but it is most illuminating to know that you find his position so close to yours. Fernandez is most useful I think in clarifying the issues. I am surely not satisfied with my review of you: in fact all that I have been able to say so far is that I cannot understand. But on the other hand I find that the more fully I accept my own views – I mean, the more confidently I accept the dogmas of the Church – the more puzzling and mysterious they become.

1–See 'Errata', C. 9 (Apr. 1930), 564: 'We regret that Mr Middleton Murry's corrected proof of his review of Mr Faussett's [*sc.* Fausset] book, in the last number [Hugh l'Anson Fausset's *The Proving of Psyche*, C. 9 (Jan. 1930), 349–53], was apparently lost in the post. We print hereunder with apologies, a list of Mr Murry's corrections.'
2–JMM, 'The Detachment of Naturalism', C. 9 (July 1930), 642–60.

Some time ago you wrote suggesting a small group for the study of religion. Although (by the way) Huegel's society[1] persists – it may have become a desiccated Aristotelian Society by this time – I think your notion a very good one.[2] The chief questions in my mind are practical ones of my participation. Whether I could take any active part or not I do not know. The membership ought to be small and very carefully chosen. Wyndham Lewis – *if possible* – should be enticed. Anyway, I should like to hear more about it.

Why do you conclude that I understand Fernandez? I am not at all sure.

Belgion's book is good so far as it goes, and I think worth a notice in *The Adelphi*. Have you had a copy?

With all wishes from both of us for the New Year.

Ever affectionately,

Tom

I think you are very tolerant of my review of you.

TO *John Livingstone Lowes*   TS Houghton

30 December 1929   *The Criterion*, 24 Russell Square

Dear Professor Lowes,

I have just learned that you are to fill a Professorship at Oxford next year, and I write to express my pleasure in the event. I dare say my information was very belated: I saw it with a photograph of you in the Harvard illustrated paper. I hope that I shall see more of you on this visit.

A little time ago I received a cable, signed with a name unknown to me 'Tucker Murray', asking if I could give a course of lectures at Harvard this next term.[3] I cabled my regrets, and would have written; but I had expected the cable to be followed by a letter, which never came. It was short notice, as an absence of that length of time would mean very careful preparations in my work here; and furthermore, I did not feel inclined to

---

1 – The London Society for the Study of Religion.

2 – JMM had suggested on 6 Nov.: 'It struck me this morning that it would be a good thing if you & I were to found some sort of informal club meeting say once a month for the discussion of religion, philosophy & psychology. It should be small, & the conditions of membership rather stringent – something like the small society that formed itself round von Hügel. I may be wrong, but it seems to me just the moment for such a thing . . . It is important, I think, that the founding shd be done (if done at all) by you & me together – in our polar capacity.'

3 – John Tucker Murray (b. 1877), taught at Harvard since 1919 and was Professor of English, 1929–39; author of *English Dramatic Companies: 1588–1642* (2 vols, 1910).

visit Cambridge so soon after my mother's death. I hope that I may have an opportunity in some future year.

With all best wishes for the New Year,

Yours sincerely,

T. S. Eliot

TO *Paul Elmer More*   TS Princeton

30 December 1929   *The Criterion*

My dear More,

I have been shamefully dilatory in answering your letter of October 23rd; I can only say that I have many letters still longer unanswered, and am working through them in the Christmas holidays.

As for Tate, I did warn him about *Christ the Word*[1] when I first read his article.[2] I cannot remember whether he subsequently read the book and decided that it did not affect his judgments, or whether, as I fear, he merely decided that it would not affect them if he did read it. In any case, it is I who owe the apology, because I should not have left it at that, but have seen that his essay was sound and complete in the light of that book. I am afraid that sometimes one editor is apt to get a little tired of amending and improving his contributions, and become a bit slack.

Tate is worth watching; he is still in growing pains, and his style is heavy and uncouth; but I think that he is as likely to do well as any of his generation.

I think in any case, that a new article on you is due when the final volume of *The Greek Tradition* appears – an article which should, by the way, be written out of earshot of all the clamour that is now going on over the word Humanism. I am not satisfied with Foerster's book, of

1 – Paul Elmer More, *The Greek Tradition, from the death of Socrates to the Council of Chalcedon*, vol. 4: *Christ the Word* (Princeton, 1927).
2 – 'It was good journalism to print Allen Tate's article ['The Fallacy of Humanism', C. 8 (July 1929), 661–81] in the same issue with my own ['An Absolute and Authoritative Church', 616–34]. As for the paper itself, though heavy and confused in expression, it does contain an idea in the offing that ought to be uttered. But really that note of Tate's on page 675 ['My argument may be doing Mr More an injustice, for I have not been able to find and read his *Christ the Word*'] is extraordinary. *Christ the Word* is on the market and perfectly easy to find. The apparent truth is that Tate had never heard of the book until, presumably, he saw it mentioned in proof of my article (note on page 616). Now that book deals precisely with the issue he raises, and, as a dead editor to a living one, I would suggest that you might have asked him to inform himself on the subject he was discussing before he discussed his views.'

which I have just seen proofs, and least of all with my own contribution.[1] I should have been better advised to keep out of it. The multitude of voices only gives an effect of confusion. I dread something as sterile as the 'New Realism' of seventeen years ago; and I fear the betrayal of Babbitt by his disciples – instead of developing the philosophy, they are apt merely to reiterate with less vitality.

About D'Arcy, I did not know what to do.[2] I could hardly refuse to publish the letter; but I felt that *The Criterion* was an unsuitable place for such a controversy, and so I confess I did not *ask* you to rejoin: but on a point of misquotation you should certainly have been heard. The best I can do now is to call it to the notice of D'Arcy, whom I have not seen for many months, and ask for his explanation, if he has any. This I should have done already: but it will still be done, and some statement printed.

From my point of view, D'Arcy's letter hardly matters. Your essay had the very great value for me of stating what can be taken as the *Criterion* position on the question. Had I tried to say the same things myself, I not only should have said them far less well, but a paper under my name would have given too distinct a theological cast to the *Criterion* itself.

I hope you will read Fernandez' French version of Humanism in the December number. It is an able piece of reasoning, not, I think, without sophistry. And Murry tells me that he finds Fernandez' position to be very close to his own.

I look forward eagerly to your next statement in *Humanism*: I think it will soon be both needed and expected. If and when I can put down anything myself I will send it to you before trying to publish.

---

1 – 'Religion without Humanism', in *Humanism and America: Essays on the Outlook of Modern Civilisation*, ed. Norman Foerster (New York: Farrar & Rinehart, 1930), 105–12.
2 – 'I am a little annoyed over Father D'Arcy's letter in the current issue of the *Criterion*. Some reply from his hand I rather expected . . . Naturally I did not look for friendly treatment from such a critic, but I did expect common honesty. Now observe. I wrote as follows (page 629): "The dogma of *original sin*, . . . corresponds with an indisputable trait of human nature . . . But the dogma of *original guilt* is a pure fabrication of occidental theology." Father D'Arcy accuses me of charging at windmills, and to prove his point quotes me thus: "The dogma of *original sin* is a pure fabrication etc." I am not exactly surprised at this Jesuitical treachery . . . But I am surprised that you, as editor, did not check the error. If Father D'Arcy does not know the difference between "original sin" and "original" guilt, and distrusts my definitions, he may consult any theologican of the Orthodox Church. I hint at ignorance, because otherwise I do not see how he can be exonerated of culpable carelessness or calculated dishonesty.' The letter from M. C. D'Arcy SJ appeared in C. 9 (Oct. 1929), 117–18; Paul Elmer More and Father D'Arcy would further contest one crucial point in an exchange of letters in C. 9 (Apr. 1930), 508.

With very best wishes from my wife and myself for the New Year.

Yours very sincerely,

T. S. Eliot

P.S. I find I have not sent you my small essay on Dante, as I meant to do. I am sending a copy; please take it merely as what my preface claims for it: it is purely a work of popularisation.

TO *Ramon Fernandez* CC

31 December 1929   [London]

My dear Fernandez,

I am very grieved not to have seen you during your brief visit to England. It is a great loss to me, as we so seldom have the opportunity of talking; and you are one of the small number of people with whom I find talk, or I ought to say listening, profitable. But I was at that time struggling with intermittent ill health punctuated by work and business engagements that had to be crowded into the intervals: I kept postponing writing until it was too late. I hope you will be in England for a longer time again during the winter or spring?

I hope you will not be dissatisfied with my translation of your essay. I find that the labour of translation does not always result in complete understanding – one's eye is too close to details to take in the whole: but the essay seemed to me very valuable; and I shall read it now several times in order to find out how to disagree with it.[1] By the way, Middleton Murry says that your position (especially as expressed in this essay) is very close to his own; and he is puzzled because I seem to be able to appreciate your theory but cannot understand his. It is largely his terminology which seems to me irrelevant.

Incidentally, your Humanism has very little in common with the Humanism of the Americans, and is much more formidable.

I have just read your preface, your prefatory essay, to Mauriac's *Dieu et Mammon*, and admire the subtlety of your treatment of catholicism.[2]

I hope that you will have time to reply to this letter, busy as you are; meanwhile accept the New Year's wishes of myself and my wife.

Yours ever sincerely,

[T. S. Eliot]

1 – Fernandez, 'A Humanist Theory of Value', trans. TSE, C. 9 (Jan. 1930), 228–45.
2 – François Mauriac, *Dieu et Mammon* (Paris: Editions du Capitole, 1929). See further Charles du Bos, *François Mauriac et le problème du romancier catholique* (1933).

BIOGRAPHICAL REGISTER

Conrad Aiken (1889–1973): American poet and critic. Though he and Eliot were a year apart at Harvard, they became close friends, and fellow editors of *The Harvard Advocate*. Aiken wrote a witty memoir of their times together, 'King Bolo and Others', in *T. S. Eliot: A Symposium*, ed. Richard Marsh and Tambimuttu (1948), describing how they revelled in the comic strips of 'Krazy Kat, and Mutt and Jeff' and in American slang. In the 1920s he settled for some years in Rye, Sussex. His writings include volumes of poetry including *Earth Triumphant* (1914); the Eliot-influenced *House of Dust* (1921); *Selected Poems* (1929), which won the Pulitzer Prize; editions of *Modern American Poets* (1922) and *Selected Poems of Emily Dickinson* (1924); and *Collected Criticism* (1968). His eccentric autobiographical novel *Ushant: An Essay* (1952) satirises TSE as 'Tsetse'. On 7 Nov. 1952 TSE thanked Aiken for sending him an inscribed copy: 'It is certainly a very remarkable book. After the first few pages, I said to myself, this is all very well for a short distance, but can he keep it up through 365 pages without the style becoming oppressive? Anyway, you have done it, and I have read the book through with unflagging interest and I hope that it will have a great success.' Asked in Feb. 1953, by the editor of *The Carolina Quarterly*, if he would contribute to a symposium on *Ushant*, TSE replied on 17 Feb. that he had no time to prepare a critical piece but that '*Ushant* fully deserves such extended and varied critical treatment.' However, TSE was to write to Cyril Connolly on 17 Apr. 1963: 'Aiken is an old & loyal friend – I don't think he is a booby, though *Ushant* is a curiously callow work.' Stephen Spender noted in 1966 that Eliot 'once told me that he always felt disturbed and unhappy that . . . Aiken had had so little success as a poet. "I've always thought that he and I were equally gifted, but I've received a large amount of appreciation, and he has been rather neglected. I can't understand it. It seems unjust. It always worries me"' ('Remembering Eliot', *The Thirties and After* [1978], 251). See too *Selected Letters of Conrad Aiken*, ed. Joseph Killorin (1978); Edward Butscher, *Conrad Aiken: Poet of White Horse Vale* (1988).

Richard Aldington (1892–1962): poet, critic, translator, biographer, novelist. A friend of Ezra Pound, he was one of the founders of the Imagist movement; a contributor to *Des Imagistes* (1914); assistant editor of *The Egoist*. In 1913 he married the American poet H.D., though they were estranged and in due course separated (albeit they did not divorce until 1938). In 1914 he volunteered for WWI, but his enlistment was deferred for medical reasons: he went on active service in June 1916 and was sent to France in December. (TSE replaced him as Literary Editor of *The Egoist*.) During the war, he rose from the ranks to be an acting captain in the Royal Sussex Regiment. He drew on his experiences in the poems of *Images of War* (1919) and the novel *Death of a Hero* (1929). After WWI, he became friends with TSE, working as his assistant on *The Criterion* and introducing him to Bruce Richmond, editor of the *TLS* (for which TSE wrote some of his finest essays). From 1919 Aldington himself was a regular reviewer of French literature for the *TLS*. In 1928 he went to live in France, where, except for a period in the USA (1935–47), he spent the rest of his life. He is best known for his early Imagist poetry and translations (see for example his edition of *Selections from Rémy de Gourmont*, 1928), for his WWI novel *Death of a Hero* (1929), and for the controversial *Lawrence of Arabia: A Biographical Inquiry* (1955), which is widely held to have damaged his own reputation. In 1931, he published *Stepping Heavenward*, a lampoon of TSE – who is portrayed as 'Blessed Jeremy Cibber': 'Father Cibber, O.S.B.' – and Vivien ('Adele Palaeologue'). This ended their friendship. His estrangement from Eliot was further publicised in an essay written in the 1930s but published only in 1954, *Ezra Pound and T. S Eliot: A Lecture*, which takes both poets to task for their putatively plagiaristic poetry. He published further biographies, including a controversial study of his friend D. H. Lawrence, *Portrait of a Genius, But* ... (1950); *Complete Poems* (1948); and *Life for Life's Sake* (memoirs, 1941). See also *Richard Aldington: An Intimate Portrait*, ed. by Alister Kershaw and Frédéric-Jacques Temple (1965), which includes a brief tribute by Eliot (with a comment on the 'cruel' *Stepping Heavenward*); 'Richard Aldington's Letters to Herbert Read', ed. by David S. Thatcher, *The Malahat Review* 15 (July 1970), 5–44; Charles Doyle, *Richard Aldington: A Biography* (1989); *Richard Aldington: An Autobiography in Letters*, ed. Norman T. Gates (1992); and *Richard Aldington & H. D.: Their lives in letters 1918–61*, ed. Caroline Zilboorg (2003).

W. H. Auden (1907–73), prolific poet, playwright, librettist, translator, essayist and editor. He was educated at Gresham's School, Holt, Norfolk, and at Christ Church, Oxford, where he co-edited *Oxford Poetry* (1926, 1927), and where his friend Stephen Spender hand-set about 30 copies of his first book, a pamphlet entitled *Poems* (1928). After going down from Oxford with a third-class degree in English in 1928, he visited Belgium and then lived for a year in Berlin. He worked as a tutor in London, 1929–30; then as a schoolmaster at Larchfield Academy, Helensburgh, Dunbartonshire, 1930–2; followed by the Downs School, Colwall, Herefordshire, 1932–5. Although Eliot turned down his initial submission of a book of poems in 1927, he would presently accept 'Paid on Both Sides: A Charade' for *The Criterion*; and Eliot went on for the rest of his life to publish all of Auden's books at Faber & Faber: *Poems* (featuring 'Paid on Both Sides' and thirty short poems, 1930); *The Orators* (1932); *Look, Stranger!* (1937); *Spain* (1936); *Another Time* (1940); *New Year Letter* (1941; published in the USA as *The Double Man*); *The Age of Anxiety* (1947); *For the Time Being* (1945); *The Age of Anxiety: A Baroque Eclogue* (1948); *Nones* (1952); *The Shield of Achilles* (1955); *Homage to Clio* (1960); and *About the House* (1966). Eliot was happy too to publish Auden's play *The Dance of Death* (1933), which was to be performed by the Group Theatre in London in 1934 and 1935; and three further plays written with Christopher Isherwood: *The Dog Beneath the Skin* (1935), which would be performed by the Group Theatre in 1936; *The Ascent of F6* (1936); and *On the Frontier* (1937). In 1935–6 Auden went to work for the General Post Office film unit, writing commentaries for two celebrated documentary films, *Coal Face* and *Night Mail*. He collaborated with Louis MacNeice on *Letters from Iceland* (1937); and with Isherwood again on *Journey to a War* (1939). His first libretto was *Paul Bunyan* (performed with music by Benjamin Britten, 1941); and in 1947 he began collaborating with Igor Stravinsky on *The Rake's Progress* (performed in Venice, 1951); and he later co-wrote two librettos for Hans Werner Henze. Other works include *The Oxford Book of Light Verse* (1938); *The Enchafèd Flood: The Romantic Iconography of the Sea* (1951); *The Dyer's Hand* (1963); and *Secondary Worlds* (1968). See further Humphrey Carpenter, *W. H. Auden: A Biography* (1981); Richard Davenport-Hines, *Auden* (1995); and Edward Mendelson, *Early Auden* (1981) and *Later Auden* (1999).

Montgomery ('Monty') Belgion (1892–1973), author, was born in Paris of British parents and grew up with a deep feeling for the language and culture of France. In 1915–16 he was editor-in-charge of the European edition of the *New York Herald*; and for the remainder of WW1 he joined up as a private in the Honourable Artillery Company, 1916–18, and was commissioned in the Dorsetshire Regiment. Between the wars he worked briefly for the Paris review *This Quarter* and then for newspapers including the *Daily Mail, Westminster Gazette* and *Daily Mirror*, and for a while he was an editor for Harcourt, Brace & Co., New York. In WW2 he became a captain in the Royal Engineers, and he spent two years in prison camps in Germany. In 1929 Faber & Faber brought out (on TSE's recommendation) his first book, *Our Present Philosophy of Life*. Later writings include *Reading for Profit* (1945) and booklets on H. G. Wells and David Hume.

Julian Benda (1867–1956): journalist, political-social philosopher, and critic. Born into a Jewish family in Paris, he studied history at the Sorbonne, and was recognised as a noted essayist and '*intellectuel*', writing for a variety of periodicals including *Revue Blanche, Nouvelle Revue Française, Mercure de France, Divan* and *Le Figaro*. A passionate upholder of the Graeco-Roman ideal of rational order and disinterestedness – Eliot said Benda's 'brand of classicism is just as romantic as anyone else's' – his works include *Dialogues à Byzance* (1900), complete with pro-Dreyfus pieces; *Le Bergsonisme: ou, Une Philosophie de la mobilité* (1912); *Belphégor: Essai sur l'esthétique de la présente société française* (1918); and *Le Trahison des clercs* (*The Treason of the Intellectuals*, 1927) – trans. by Richard Aldington in 1928. See further Ray Nichols, *Treason, Tradition, and the Intellectual: Julian Benda and Political Discourse* (1978).

Arnold Bennett (1867–1931), author and journalist (and son of a weaver and tailor who eventually qualified and practised as a solicitor), grew up among 'the five towns' of the Potteries and began work at the age of 16 in a solicitor's office; but he swiftly made a name for himself as journalist and prolific author. His best-selling novels include *A Man from the North* (1898), *Anna of the Five Towns* (1902), *Whom God hath Joined* (1906), and *The Old Wives' Tale* (1908) – the first book in the Clayhanger trilogy. His plays, including *The Great Adventure* (1913), were just as successful, with naturalistic and effective dialogue; and it was in his capacity as a capable dramatist that TSE consulted him in the early 1920s – ironically when Eliot was attempting to write a determinedly (and ultimately uncompleted) experimental play, *Sweeney Agonistes*. It says much for Bennett that he took TSE seriously and gave him advice that was valued – though Bennett was not keen on *The Criterion*. See *The Journals of Arnold Bennett*, ed. by N. Flowers (3 vols, 1932–5); and Margaret Drabble, *Arnold Bennett: A Biography* (1974).

Marguerite Caetani, née Chapin (1880–1963) – born in New London, Connecticut, she was half-sister to Mrs Katherine Biddle, and a cousin of TSE – was married in 1911 to the composer Roffredo Caetani, 17th Duke of Sermoneta and Prince di Bassiano (a godson of Liszt), whose ancestors included two Popes (one of whom had the distinction of being put in Hell by Dante). A patron of the arts, she founded in Paris the review *Commerce* – the title being taken from a line in St-John Perse's *Anabase* ('*ce pur commerce de mon âme*') – which ran from 1924 to 1932 (see Sophie Levie, *La rivista Commerce e il ruolo di Marguerite Caetani nella letteratura europea 1924–1932* [Rome: Fondazione Camillo Caetani, 1985]); and then, in Rome, *Botteghe oscure*, 1949–60, a biannual review featuring poetry and fiction from many nations – England, Germany, Italy, France, Spain, USA – with contributions published in their original languages. Contributors included André Malraux, Albert Camus, Paul Valéry, Ignazio Silone, Robert Graves, Archibald MacLeish, E. E. Cummings, Marianne Moore.

Richard Cobden-Sanderson (1884–1964), printer and publisher, was the son of the bookbinder and printer, T. J. Cobden Sanderson (1840–1922), who was Bertrand Russell's godfather; grandson of the politician and economist Richard Cobden (1804–65). He launched his publishing business in 1919 and was publisher of *The Criterion* from its first number in Oct. 1922 until it was taken over by Faber & Gwyer in 1925. He also published three books with introductions by TSE: *Le Serpent* by Paul Valéry (1924), Charlotte Eliot's *Savanarola* (1926), and Harold Monro's *Collected Poems* (1933). In addition, his firm produced books by Edmund Blunden and David Gascoyne, editions of Shelley, and volumes illustrated by Rex Whistler. He became a dependable friend as well as a colleague of TSE's. His wife was Gwladys (Sally) Cobden-Sanderson.

R. G. Collingwood (1889–1943), philosopher and historian; Fellow of Pembroke College, Oxford; later Waynflete Professor of Metaphysical Philosophy, Magdalen College. On 8 Mar. 1938 Collingwood would send TSE a copy of *The Principles of Art* (1938) – which declared: 'In literature, those who chiefly matter have made the choice, and made it rightly. The credit for this belongs in the main to one great poet, who has set the example by taking as his theme in a long series of poems a subject that interests every one, the decay of our civilisation' – with the personal comment: 'in a sense the book is dedicated to you; the concluding pages are all about *The Waste Land*, regarded . . . as a demonstration of what poetry has got to be if my aesthetic theory is to be true! I hope you will be able to forgive me for treating you as a *corpus vile*, and will understand that it is the highest compliment a poor devil of a philosopher has it in his power to pay you.' (TSE wrote to Thomas Stauffer, 17 Aug. 1944: 'Aesthetics was never my strong suit. In fact, it is one department of philosophy which I always shied away from, even in the days when I thought I was going to be a philosopher, and that is a long time ago. I think that instinct told me that the less I thought about general aesthetic theory the better for me. (Incidentally, do you know Collingwood's book *In Praise of Art*? [*The Principles of Art*] To a plain literary practitioner like myself, who, as F. H. Bradley said of himself, has no capacity for the abstruse, Collingwood seems very good).') Collingwood's other works include *Speculum Mentis, or, The Map of Knowledge* (1924), *Outlines of a Philosophy of Art* (1925), and *The Idea of History* (1945). See Fred Inglis, *History Man: The Life of R. G. Collingwood* (2009).

John Cournos (1881–1966) – Johann Gregorievich Korshune – naturalised American writer of Russian birth (his Jewish parents fled Russia when he was 10), worked as a journalist on the *Philadelphia Record* and was first noted in England as an Imagist poet; he became better known as novelist, essayist and translator. After living in England in the 1910s and 1920s, he emigrated to the USA. An unhappy love affair in 1922–3 with Dorothy L. Sayers was fictionalised by her in *Strong Poison* (1930), and by him in *The Devil is an English Gentleman* (1932). His other publications include *London Under the Bolsheviks* (1919), *In Exile* (1923), *Miranda Masters* (a *roman à clef* about the imbroglio between himself, the poet H.D., and Richard Aldington, 1926), and *Autobiography* (1935).

Ernst Robert Curtius (1886–1956), German scholar of philology and Romance literature. Scion of a family of scholars, he studied philology and philosophy at Strasbourg, Berlin, and Heidelberg, and taught in turn at Marburg, Heidelberg, and Bonn. Author of *Die Französische Kultur* (1931; *The Civilization of France*, trans. Olive Wyon, 1932); his most substantial work was *Europäische Literatur und Lateinisches Mittelalter* (1948; trans. by Willard R. Trask as *European Literature and the Latin Middle Ages*, 1953), a study of Medieval Latin literature and its fructifying influence upon the literatures of modern Europe. In a letter to Max Rychner (24 Oct. 1955) Eliot saluted Curtius on his seventieth birthday by saying that even though he had met him perhaps no more than twice in 35 years, he yet counted him 'among my old friends', and owed him 'a great debt': 'I have . . . my own personal debt of gratitude to acknowledge to Curtius, for translating, and introducing, *The Waste Land*. Curtius was also, I think, the first critic in Germany to recognise the importance of James Joyce. And when it is a question of other writers than myself, and especially when we consider his essays on French contemporaries, and his *Balzac*, and his *Proust*, I am at liberty to praise Curtius as a critic . . . [O]nly a critic of scholarship, discrimination and intellect could perform the services that Curtius has performed. For his critical studies are contributions to the study of the authors criticised, which must be reckoned with by those authors' compatriots. *We cannot determine the true status and significance of the significant writers in our own language, without the aid of foreign critics with a European point of view.* For it is only such critics who can tell us, whether an author is of European importance. And of such critics in our own time, Curtius is one of the most illustrious.' Eliot praised too 'that masterly work, *Europäische Litteratur und Lateinisches Mittelalter*, on which he had been at work during the years when freedom of speech and freedom of travel were suspended. It bears testimony to his integrity and indomitable spirit . . . Curtius deserves, in his life and in his work, the gratitude and admiration of his fellow writers of every European nation' (Eliot's letter is printed in full in 'Brief über Ernst Robert Curtius', in *Freundesgabe für Ernst Robert Curtis zum 14. April 1956* [Bern, 1956], 25–7.) See too Peter Godman, 'T. S. Eliot and E. R. Curtius: A European dialogue', *Liber: A European Review of Books*, 1: 1 (Oct. 1989), 5, 7; and J. H. Copley, '"The Politics of Friendship": T. S. Eliot in Germany Through E. R. Curtius's Looking Glass', in *The International Reception of T. S. Eliot*, ed. Elisabeth Däumer and Shyamal Bagchee (2007), 243–67.

Martin D'Arcy (1888–1976), Jesuit priest and theologian, entered the Novitiate in 1906, took a first in Literae humaniores at Pope's Hall – the Jesuit private hall of Oxford University – and was ordained a Catholic priest in 1921. After teaching at Stonyhurst College, in 1925 he undertook doctoral research, first at the Gregorian University in Rome, then at the Jesuit House at Farm Street, London. In 1927 he returned to Campion Hall (successor to Pope's Hall), where he lectured and tutored in philosophy at the university. He was Rector and Master of Campion Hall, 1933–45;

and Provincial of the British Province of the Jesuits in London, 1945–50. Charismatic and highly influential as a lecturer, and as an apologist for Roman Catholicism (his prominent converts included Evelyn Waugh), he also wrote studies including *The Nature of Belief* (1931) and *The Mind and Heart of Love* (1945). Louis MacNeice, in *The Strings Are False: An Unfinished Autobiography* (1965), wrote of Fr D'Arcy: 'he alone among Oxford dons seemed to me to have the glamour that medieval students looked for in their masters. Intellect incarnate in a beautiful head, wavy grey hair and delicate features; a hawk's eyes.' Lesley Higgins notes: 'Five of his books were reviewed in *The Criterion*, some by Eliot himself; his twenty-two reviews and articles in the latter certainly qualify him as part of what Eliot termed the journal's "definite . . . [and] comprehensive constellation of contributors".' See further H. J. A. Sire, *Father Martin D'Arcy: Philosopher of Christian Love* (1997); Richard Harp, 'A conjuror at the Xmas party', *TLS*, 11 Dec. 2009, 13–15.

Bonamy Dobrée (1891–1974), scholar, editor and critic, was to be Professor of English Literature at Leeds University, 1936–55. After service in the army during WW1 (he was twice mentioned in despatches and attained the rank of major), he read English at Christ's College, Cambridge, and taught in London and as a professor of English at the Egyptian University, Cairo, 1925–9. His works include *Restoration Comedy* (1924), *Essays in Biography* (1925), *Restoration Tragedy, 1660–1720* (1929), *Alexander Pope* (1951), and critical editions and anthologies. From 1921 to 1925 Dobrée and his wife Valentine resided at Larrau, a village in the Pyrenees, where he worked as an independent scholar. He was one of TSE's most constant correspondents. On 8 Sept. 1938, TSE would write to George Every SSM on the subject of the projected 'Moot': 'I think [Dobrée] would be worth having . . . He has his nose to the grindstone of the provincial university machine . . . but he is not without perception of the futilities of contemporary education. His mental formation is Liberal, but he has the rare advantage of being a man of breeding, so that his instincts with regard, for instance, to society, the community and the land, are likely to be right. He is also a person of strong, and I imagine hereditary, public spirit.' On 23 Feb. 1963, TSE urged his merits as future editor of Kipling's stories: 'He is far and away the best authority on Kipling . . . I have often discussed Kipling with him, and know that we see eye to eye about the stories. As for Dobrée's general literary achievements, they are very high indeed: his published work is not only very scholarly, but of the highest critical standing, and he writes well . . . If this job is ever done – and I

should like to see it done during my lifetime – Dobrée is the man to do it.'
See also Jason Harding, *The 'Criterion': Cultural Politics and Periodical
Networks in Inter-War Britain* (2002).

Charlotte Champe Stearns Eliot (1843–1929), the poet's mother, was
born on 22 October in Baltimore, Maryland, the second child and second
daughter of Thomas Stearns (1811–96) and Charlotte Blood Stearns
(1818–93). She went first to private schools in Boston and Sandwich,
followed by three years at the State Normal School, Framingham, Mass.,
from which she graduated in 1862. After teaching for a while at private
schools in West Chester, Pennsylvania, and Milwaukee, Wisconsin, she
spent two years with a Quaker family in Coatesville, Pa. She then taught
at Antioch College, Ohio, 1865–7; at her Framingham School; and at St
Louis Normal School. It was while she was at the last post that she met
Henry Ware Eliot, entrepreneur, whom she married on 27 October 1868.
She was Secretary of the Mission Free School of the Church of the Messiah
for many years. As her youngest son was growing up, she became more
thoroughly involved in social work through the Humanity Club of St
Louis, whose members were disturbed by knowing that young offenders
awaiting trial were being held for long periods with adults. In 1899, a
committee of two was appointed, with Mrs Eliot as chairman, to bring
about reform. It was in large part due to her campaigning and persistence
over several years that the Probation Law 1901 was approved; and in 1903,
by mandate of the Juvenile Court Law, a juvenile court was established
with its own probation officer and a separate place of detention. As a
girl, Charlotte had nursed literary ambitions, and throughout her life
wrote poems, some of which (such as 'Easter Songs' and 'Poems on the
Apostles') were printed in the *Christian Register*. In 1904 she published
William Greenleaf Eliot: Minister, Educator, Philanthropist, a memoir
of her beloved father-in-law (TSE's grandfather); and it came as a great
joy to her when TSE arranged for the publication of her *Savanarola: A
Dramatic Poem*, with an introduction by himself (London, 1926). When
she was shown the issue of *Smith Academy Record* containing TSE's 'A
Lyric' (1905), she said (as TSE would remember) 'that she thought it
better than anything in verse she had ever written'. TSE reflected further
on that fine declaration: 'I knew what her verse meant to her. We did
not discuss the matter further.' Inspired by a keen ethic of public service,
she was a member of both the Wednesday Club of St Louis and the
Missouri Society of the Colonial Dames of America, serving successively
as Secretary, Vice-President, and President. She chaired a committee to

award a Washington University scholarship that required the beneficiary to do a certain amount of patriotic work; and in 1917–18 she did further service as chair of the War Work committee of the Colonial Dames. After the death of her husband in January 1919, she moved home to Cambridge, Massachusetts.

Henry Ware Eliot, Jr (1879–1947), TSE's elder brother, went to school at Smith Academy, and then passed two years at Washington University, St Louis, before progressing to Harvard. At Harvard, he displayed a gift for light verse in *Harvard Celebrities* (Cambridge, Mass., 1901), illustrated with 'Caricatures and Decorative Drawings' by two fellow undergraduates. After graduating, he spent a year at Law School, but subsequently followed a career in printing, publishing and advertising. He attained a partnership in Husband & Thomas (later the Buchen Company), a Chicago advertising agency, from 1917 to 1929, during which time he gave financial assistance to TSE and regularly advised him on investments. He accompanied their mother on her visit to London in the summer of 1921, his first trip away from the USA. In February 1926, he married Theresa Anne Garrett (1884–1981), and later the same year the couple went on holiday to Italy along with TSE and Vivien. He was one of TSE's most regular and trusted correspondents. It was not until late in life that he found his true calling, as a Research Fellow in Anthropology at the Peabody Museum, Harvard: see his posthumous publication *Excavations in Mesopotamia and Western Iran, Sites of 4000 to 500 B.C.* (Harvard University: Peabody Museum of American Archaeology and Ethnology, 1950). In 1932 he published a detective novel, *The Rumble Murders*, under the pseudonym Mason Deal. He was instrumental in building up the T. S. Eliot collection at Eliot House (Houghton Library). Of slighter build than his brother – who remarked upon his 'Fred Astaire figure' – Henry suffered from deafness owing to scarlet fever as a child, and this may have contributed to his diffidence. Unselfishly devoted to TSE, whose growing up he movingly recorded with his camera, Henry took him to his first Broadway musical, *The Merry Widow*, which remained a favourite. It was with his brother in mind that TSE wrote: 'The notion of some infinitely gentle / Infinitely suffering thing' ('Preludes' IV).

Vivien Eliot, née Haigh-Wood (1888–1947). Born in Bury, Lancashire, on 28 May 1888, 'Vivy' was brought up in Hampstead from the age of 3. After meeting TSE in company with Scofield Thayer in Oxford early in 1915, she and TSE hastened to be married just a few weeks later, on

26 June 1915. (TSE, who was lodging at 35 Greek Street, Soho, London, was recorded in the marriage certificate as 'of no occupation'.) The marriage was not a happy one for either of them. She developed close friendships with Mary Hutchinson, Ottoline Morrell, and others in TSE's circle. Despite chronic personal and medical difficulties, they remained together until 1933, when TSE resolved to separate from her during his visit to America. She was never to be reconciled to the separation, became increasingly ill, and in 1938 was confined to a psychiatric hospital, where she died (of 'syncope' and 'cardiovascular degeneration') on 22 January 1947. She is the dedicatee of *Ash-Wednesday* (1930). She published sketches in *The Criterion* (under various pseudonyms with the initials 'F. M.'), and collaborated on *The Criterion* and other works. See Carole Seymour-Jones, *Painted Shadow: The Life of Vivienne Eliot* (2001).

Geoffrey Faber (1889–1961), publisher and poet, was educated at Malvern College and Christ Church, Oxford, where he took a first in Literae humaniores (1912). He was called to the bar by the Inner Temple (1921), though he was never to practise law. In 1919 he was elected a prize fellow of All Souls College, Oxford, which he went on to serve in the capacity of estates bursar, 1923–51. Before WW1 – in which he served with the London Regiment (Post Office Rifles), seeing action in France and Belgium – he spent 18 months as assistant to Humphrey Milford, publisher of Oxford University Press. After the war he spent three years working for Strong & Co. Ltd., brewers (there was a family connection), before going in for publishing on a full-time basis by joining forces with his All Souls colleague Maurice Gwyer and his wife, Lady Alsina Gwyer, who were trying to run a specialised imprint called the Scientific Press that Lady Gwyer had inherited from her father, Sir Henry Burdett: its weekly journal, the *Nursing Mirror*, was their most successful output. Following protractedly difficult negotiations, in 1925 Faber became chair of their restructured general publishing house which was provisionally styled Faber & Gwyer. After being introduced by Charles Whibley to T. S. Eliot, Faber was so impressed by the personality and aptitude of the 37-year-old American that he chose both to take on the running of *The Criterion* and to appoint Eliot to the board of his company (Eliot's *Poems 1909–1925* was one of the first books to be put out by the new imprint, and its first best-seller), which was relocated from Southampton Row to 24 Russell Square. By 1929 both the Gwyers and the *Nursing Mirror* were disposed of to advantage, and the firm took final shape as Faber & Faber, with Richard de la Mare and two additional Americans,

Frank Morley and Morley Kennerley, joining the board. Faber chaired the Publishers' Association, 1939–41 – campaigning successfully for the repeal of a wartime tax on books – and helping to set up the National Book League. He was knighted in 1954, and gave up the chairmanship of Faber & Faber in 1960. His publications as poet included *The Buried Stream* (1941) and *Twelve Years* (posthumously published, 1962),, and his works of non-fiction were *Oxford Apostles* (1933) and *Jowett* (1957), as well as an edition of the works of John Gay (1926). In 1920 he married Enid Richards, with whom he had two sons and a daughter. He died at his home in 1961.

John Gould Fletcher (1886–1950), American poet and critic, scion of a wealthy Southern family, dropped out of Harvard in 1907 (his father's death having secured him temporarily independent means) and lived for many years in Europe, principally in London; a friend of Ezra Pound, he became one of the mainstays of Imagism and published much original poetry. In later years he returned to his native Arkansas and espoused Agrarian values. His *Selected Poems* won the Pulitzer Prize in 1939. Fletcher wrote of TSE in *Life Is My Song: The Autobiography of John Gould Fletcher* (1937): 'As an editor, I found him to be practically ideal, willing for opinions to be mooted that ran contrary to his own avowed toryism, so long as those opinions were not merely emotional prejudices, but were backed up by something resembling intellectual judgment' (308). See also Fletcher, *Life for Life's Sake* (1941); *Selected Letters of John Gould Fletcher*, ed. Leighton Rudolph, Lucas Carpenter, Ethel C. Simpson (1996) – 'One of my difficulties with Eliot, whom I knew fairly well for nearly 15 years, was his intellectual snobbery' – Lucas Carpenter, *John Gould Fletcher and Southern Modernism* (1990); and Ben F. Johnson III, *Fierce Solitude: A Life of John Gould Fletcher* (1994).

Frank Stuart ('F. S.') Flint (1885–1960), English poet and translator, and civil servant, grew up in terrible poverty – 'gutter-born and gutter-bred', he would say – and left school at 13. But he set about to educate himself in European languages and literature (he had a deep appreciation of the French Symbolists and of Rimbaud), as well as in history and philosophy. In 1908 he started writing articles and reviews for the *New Age*, then for the *Egoist* and for *Poetry* (ed. Harriet Monroe). Quickly gaining in reputation and authority (especially on French literature – his influential piece on 'Contemporary French Poetry' appeared in Harold Monro's *Poetry Review* in 1912) – he soon became associated with T. E. Hulme,

Ezra Pound, Richard Aldington, and Hilda Doolittle; and he contributed poems to the *English Review* (ed. Ford Madox Hueffer) and to Pound's anthology *Des Imagistes* (1914). In 1920 he published *Otherworld Cadences* (The Poetry Bookshop); and with TSE and Aldous Huxley he was one of the contributors to *Three Critical Essays on Modern English Poetry*, in *Chapbook* II: 9 (March 1920). Between 1909 and 1920 he published three volumes of poetry, though his work as essayist, reviewer, and translator was the more appreciated: he became a regular translator and reviewer for *The Criterion* from the 1920s – and a member of the inner circle gathered round TSE – even while continuing to work in the statistics division of the Ministry of Labour (where he was Chief of the Overseas Section) until retiring in 1951. See also *The Fourth Imagist: Selected Poems of F. S. Flint*, ed. Michael Copp (2007).

E. M. Forster (1879–1970), novelist and essayist, was educated at King's College, Cambridge, where he gained a second in the classics tripos (and where he was elected to the exclusive Conversazione Society, the inner circle of the Apostles). Though intimately associated with the Bloomsbury group in London, where his circle of friends and acquaintances came to include Edward Marsh, Edward Garnett, Duncan Grant, Roger Fry, Lytton Strachey, and Leonard and Virginia Woolf, he derived much from visits to Italy, Greece, Egypt, and India – where he worked for a while as private secretary to the Maharaja of Dewas: that experience brought about one of his most acclaimed novels, *A Passage to India* (1924), which sold around one million copies during his lifetime. His other celebrated novels include *Where Angels Fear to Tread* (1905), *A Room with a View* (1908), *Howards End* (1910), and the posthumous *Maurice* (1971, written 1910–13), a work that addressed his homosexuality. He gave the Clark Lectures at Cambridge in 1927 – in succession to TSE – which were published as *Aspects of the Novel* (1927). He turned down a knighthood, but in 1953 he was appointed a Companion of Honour; and he received the OM in 1969. See also Forster, 'Mr Eliot and His Difficulties', *Life and Letters*, 2: 13 (June 1929), 417–25; P. N. Furbank, *E. M. Forster* (2 vols, 1977, 1978); *Selected Letters of E. M. Forster*, ed. by Mary Lago and P. N. Furbank (2 vols, 1983–5); and Nicola Beauman, *Morgan: A Biography of E. M. Forster* (1993).

H. J. C. Grierson (1866–1960): Regius Professor of Rhetoric and English Literature, University of Edinburgh, 1915–35; knighted in 1936; celebrated for his edition of *The Poems of John Donne* (2 vols, 1912) and *Metaphysical Lyrics and Poems of the Seventeenth Century* (1921) – which TSE reviewed in the *TLS*, 21 Oct. 1921. Cairns Craig, in 'The Last Romantics: How the Scholarship of Herbert Grierson Influenced Modernist Poetry' (*TLS*, 15 Jan. 2010, 14–15), argues that '*The Waste Land* is saturated with echoes of Grierson's *Metaphysical Lyrics and Poems*. When Eliot sent a copy of his *Collected Poems* to Grierson, it was inscribed "to whom all English men of letters are indebted".' (Letty Grierson remembers a slightly different wording, 'to whom all poets of today are indebted': noted in the Grierson catalogue issued by James Fergusson Books & Manuscripts 2010.) TSE contributed to *Seventeenth Century Studies Presented to Sir Herbert Grierson* (1938).

Maurice Haigh-Wood (1896–1980): TSE's brother-in-law. He was six years younger than his sister Vivien, and after attending Ovingdean prep school and Malvern School, trained at Sandhurst Military Academy, before receiving his commission on 11 May 1915 as a second lieutenant in the 2nd Battalion, the Manchester Regiment. He served in the infantry for the war, and on regular visits home gave TSE his closest contact with the nightmare of life and death in the trenches. After the war, he found it difficult to get himself established, but became a stockbroker, and he remained friendly with, and respectful towards, TSE even after his separation from Vivien in 1933. In 1930 he married a 25-year-old American dancer, Ahmé Hoagland, and they had two children.

John Hayward (1905–65), editor, critic, and anthologist, read modern languages at King's College, Cambridge. Despite the early onset of muscular dystrophy, he became a prolific and eminent critic and editor, bringing out in quick succession editions of the works of Rochester, Saint-Évremond, Jonathan Swift, Robert Herrick and Samuel Johnson. Other publications included *Complete Poems and Selected Prose of John Donne* (1929), *Donne* (1950), *T. S. Eliot: Selected Prose* (1953), *The Penguin Book of English Verse* (1958), and *The Oxford Book of Nineteenth Century English Verse* (1964). Celebrated as the learned and acerbic editor of *The Book Collector*, he was made a chevalier of the Légion d'honneur in 1952, a CBE in 1953. Writers including Graham Greene and Stevie Smith valued his editorial counsel; and Paul Valéry invited him to translate his comedy *Mon Faust*. Hayward advised TSE on various essays, poems, and plays including *The Cocktail Party* and *The Confidential Clerk*, and most helpfully of all on *Four Quartets*. See also Helen Gardner, *The Composition of "Four Quartets"* (1978).

When it was proposed during WW2 by Robert Nichols that Hayward might be nominated for the Oxford Chair of Poetry, TSE wrote on 27 July 1944: 'I would certainly back up any testimony for John to the best of my command of the resources of the language; but I am wondering whether, at this stage, it would not be best for you to have a talk to John and sound him. I believe that such a suggestion would come as a surprise to him; he might need winning over to it; or he might have positive objections and difficulties beyond any of which you or I are aware . . . I suppose John's best official credentials are his "Nonesuch" editions of Donne and Swift, and the work he has been engaged upon, off and on, for some years, on Dryden, for the Oxford Press. I don't think he has done much formal lecturing; but I believe he has sometimes addressed undergraduate societies, as well as talked regularly to Mrs Whatshername's young ladies, during these last years in Cambridge. I think he stands well as an editor of texts, and therefore as an English scholar . . . [M]y own preference had fallen upon Dobrée, among the possibles, as John had not occurred to my mind . . .'

Mary Hutchinson, née Barnes (1889–1977), a half-cousin of Lytton Strachey, married St John ('Jack') Hutchinson in 1910. A prominent Bloomsbury hostess, she was for several years the acknowledged mistress of the art critic, Clive Bell, and became a close, supportive friend of TSE and VHE. TSE published one of her stories ('War') in *The Egoist*, and she later brought out a book of sketches, *Fugitive Pieces* (1927), under the imprint of the Hogarth Press. She wrote a short unpublished memoir of TSE (Harry Ransom Humanities Research Center, Austin). See David Bradshaw, '"Those Extraordinary Parakeets": Clive Bell and Mary Hutchinson', *The Charleston Magazine*, in two parts: 16 (Autumn/Winter 1997), 5–12; 17 (Spring/Summer 1998), 5–11.

Aldous Huxley (1894–1963): novelist, poet and essayist, whose early novels *Crome Yellow* (1921) and *Antic Hay* (1923) were successful satires of post-war English culture. While teaching at Eton, Aldous told his brother Julian in December 1916 that he 'ought to read' Eliot's 'things', which are 'all the more remarkable when one knows the man, ordinarily just an Europeanized American, overwhelmingly cultured, talking about French literature in the most uninspired fashion imaginable'. For his part, Eliot thought Huxley's early poems fell too much under the spell of Laforgue (and of his own poetry), but Huxley went on to become, not only a popular novelist, but, as the author of *Brave New World* and

The Doors of Perception, an influential intellectual figure. See Nicholas Murray, *Aldous Huxley: An English Intellectual* (2002); Aldous Huxley, *Selected Letters*, ed. James Sexton (2007).

Wyndham Lewis (1882–1957), painter, novelist, philosopher, critic, was one of the major modernist writers. A friend of Ezra Pound, Lewis was the leading artist associated with Vorticism, and editor of *BLAST*, the movement's journal (1914–15), in which TSE's 'Preludes' and 'Rhapsody on a Windy night' appeared (July 1915). Lewis served as a bombardier and war-artist on the Western Front, 1916–18, and wrote memorable accounts of the period in his memoir *Blasting and Bombardiering* (1937), including brilliant portraits of TSE, Pound, and Joyce, and war-time and modernist London. TSE reviewed Lewis's first novel *Tarr* (1918) in *The Egoist* 5: 8 (Sept. 1918), describing him as 'the most fascinating personality of our time', in whose work 'we recognize the thought of the modern and the energy of the cave-man' (106). In turn, Lewis considered Eliot 'the most interesting man in London society' (7 Nov. 1918). TSE, who thought Lewis's work 'so imaginative and visually concrete' (letter to Philip Lane, 4 Dec. 1934), published pieces by him in the *Criterion* and, even though Lewis was notoriously cantankerous, kept up a lifetime's friendship with him. Lewis did a number of drawings of TSE, one of which hung in his flat – reproduced in vol. 2 of *Letters* – and his best-known portrait of him (rejected by the Royal Academy) is now in Durban. On Lewis's death, TSE wrote 'The Importance of Wyndham Lewis' in *The Sunday Times* (10 Mar. 1957), and a memoir in *Hudson Review* X: 2 (Summer 1957): 'He was . . . a highly strung, nervous man, who was conscious of his own abilities, and sensitive to slight or neglect . . . He was independent, outspoken, and difficult. Temperament and circumstances combined to make him a great satirist . . . I remember Lewis, at the time when I first knew him, and for some years thereafter, as incomparably witty and amusing in company . . .' TSE wrote too, for the magazine *Spectrum*: 'Wyndham Lewis was in my opinion one of the few men of letters of my generation whom I should call, without qualification, men of genius. It is for other painters and draughtsmen to praise his genius as a painter and draughtsman. I would only like to repeat what I have said several times before, that Lewis was the most prominent and versatile prose-writer of my time. I would also like to pay a special tribute to the work he did after he became blind. In *Self-Condemned* he seems to have written a novel greater than *Tarr* or *The Revenge for Love*; in *Monstre Gai* a sequel to *The Childermass* more remarkable than *The Childermass* itself. It is a great artist and one of the most intelligent men of my age who is dead' (letter to Hugh Kenner, 27 Mar 1957). See *The Letters of Wyndham Lewis*, ed. W. K. Rose (1963); Paul O'Keeffe, *Some Sort of Genius: A Life of Wyndham Lewis* (2000).

Thomas McGreevy (1893–1967) – the family name was 'McGreevy', but by the 1930s he would assume the more Irish spelling 'MacGreevy' – Kerry-born poet, literary and art critic, and arts administrator, worked for the Irish Land Commission before serving in WW1 as a second lieutenant in the British Royal Field Artillery: he fought at Ypres and the Somme, and was twice wounded. After reading History and Political Science at Trinity College, Dublin, he moved in 1925 to London, where he met TSE and started to write for the *Criterion*, *TLS* (with an introduction from TSE), and *Nation & Athenaeum*. His poem 'Dysert' appeared in *NC* 4 (Jan. 1926) under the pseudonym 'L. St. Senan' (the title was later changed to 'Homage to Jack Yeats'). In 1927 he took up teaching English at the École Normale Supérieur in Paris, where he became friends with Beckett and Joyce (to whom he had been introduced in 1924) and with Richard Aldington. (His promotional essay on Joyce's incipient *Finnegans Wake* – 'The Catholic Element in Work in Progress' – appeared in *Our Exagmination round his Factification for Incamination of Work in Progress* in 1929.) In addition, he journeyed through Italy with W. B. Yeats. Back in London in 1933, he lectured at the National Gallery and wrote for *The Studio*. Ultimately he was appointed Director of the National Gallery of Ireland, 1950–63. He was made Chevalier de la Légion d'Honneur, 1948; Cavaliere Ufficiale al merito della Repubblica Italiana, 1955; and Officier de la Légion d'Honneur, 1962. In 1929 he published a translation of Paul Valéry's *Introduction à la méthode de Léonard de Vinci* (*Introduction to the Method of Leonardo da Vinci*); and in 1931, two short monographs, *T. S. Eliot: A Study* and *Richard Aldington: An Englishman*; and his *Poems* would appear in 1934. His publications on art include *Jack B. Yeats: An Appreciation and an Interpretation* (1945) and *Nicolas Poussin* (1960). See also *The Collected Poems of Thomas MacGreevy: An Annotated Edition*, ed. Susan Schreibman (Dublin, 1991).

Frederic Manning (1882–1935): Australian writer who settled in 1903 in England, where he came to know artists and writers including Max Beerbohm, William Rothenstein, Richard Aldington, and Ezra Pound (the latter would compliment him as 'the first licherary ComPanionship in Eng/ of Ez'); author of *Scenes and Portraits* (1909; 2nd edn, revised and enlarged, 1930). Despite being an asthmatic, he served in the ranks

(Shropshire Light Infantry) in WW1, being involved for four months in heavy fighting on the Somme: this experience brought about his greatest achievement, a novel about the Western Front, *The Middle Parts of Fortune* (privately printed, 1929; standard text, 1977; expurgated as *Her Privates We*, credited pseudonymously to 'Private 19022', 1930; republished in full, with intro. by William Boyd, 1999) – 'the best book to come out of the First World War', Eliot is said to have said of it. In a letter to Aldington (6 July 1921), Eliot described Manning as 'undoubtedly one of the very best prose writers we have'; and he wrote of him in a later year: 'I did not know him well myself, though I have met him – I think directly after the first World War – and I have a precious copy which he gave me of *Her Privates We* and later I went to his funeral in Kensal Green . . . I remember him as a very careful and meticulous letter writer – one of few people I knew who put the first word of the next page at the bottom of every page of their letter' (letter to L. T. Hergenhan, 26 Oct. 1962). See Verna Coleman, *The Last Exquisite: A Portrait of Frederic Manning* (1990).

Henri Massis (1886–1970), right-wing Roman Catholic critic: contributor to *L'Action Française*; co-founder and editor of *La Revue Universelle*. Closely associated with Charles Maurras, his writings include *Jugements* (2 vols, 1924), *Jacques Rivière* (1925), and *La Défense de l'Occident* (1928). A defender of Mussolini and Salazar, his later works include *Chefs: Les Dictateurs et nous* (1939) and *Maurras et notre temps* (2 vols, 1951).

On 1 Nov. 1945 TSE wrote the following testimony: 'I, Thomas Stearns Eliot, British subject, of 24 Russell Square, London, w.c.1., England, doctor honoris causa of the Universities of Cambridge, Edinburgh, Leeds, Bristol, Columbia, Honorary Fellow of Magdalene College, Cambridge, a member of the board of directors of the publishing house of Faber & Faber, Ltd., London, testify that I have known Monsieur Henri Massis for over twenty years. The firm of publishers of which I am a director published an English translation of his *Défense de l'Occident*; and M. Massis was a contributor to a quarterly review, *The Criterion*, of which I was the editor. I saw M. Massis whenever I visited Paris, and when he visited London. I also received regularly *La Revue Universelle* of which on the death of Jacques Bainville he became the editor.

'The intellectual bond between myself and M. Massis was the common concern for the civilisation of Western Europe, the apprehension of the Germanic danger, and a similar diagnosis of its nature. Germany owed her highest achievement of culture to her allegiance to western civilisation; the future of Europe depended on whether Germany affirmed this allegiance, or whether she abandoned herself to her primitive instincts, seeking barbaric dominion in cultural isolation. After the rise of Hitler it was evident that Germany had taken the wrong course; that Germany was no longer one of the western peoples and that she had become a menace against which Europe should prepare herself. Such were my views, and such, I am sure, were the views of M. Massis, as his writings show. We were also in accord in attaching great importance to the development of the closest possible relations in every way, between France and England.

'My conversations with M. Massis, as well as his writings, left me with the strongest impression that he was not only a man of clear vision in these matters, but also a patriot of integrity and probity, who would never hesitate to sacrifice his own interests to those of his country. I should always have said that the love of France was one of his most conspicuous characteristics. And I cannot believe that so passionate a nationalist can be suspected seriously of having used his editorship of *La Revue Universelle* in order to ensure anything but the consolidation of an intellectual resistance to the plans of Germany for the subordination of his country.'

Charles Maurras (1868–1952): French poet, critic, political philosopher and polemical journalist; founding editor and moving spirit of the monarchist paper, *L'Action Française* (1908–44) – which was ultimately to support Pétain and Vichy during WW2. TSE was to write of Maurras, in a letter to Vernon Watkins dated 10 Apr. 1946: 'He was condemned as a collaborator and is in prison for the rest of his life unless he is later released on compassionate grounds. Maurras was one of those whose collaboration, if it can be called that, was the result of mistaken judgement and certainly not unpatriotic or self-interested motives.' Building on 'three traditions' – classicism, Catholicism, monarchism – Maurras's ideology was to become increasingly, intransigently, right-wing, authoritarian and anti-democratic. In 1925 TSE had planned to write a book about Maurras; and he later wrote 'The *Action Française*, M. Maurras and Mr. Ward', *MC.* 7 (March 1928). TSE said he had been 'a reader of the work of M. Maurras for eighteen years', and, far from 'drawing him away from' Christianity – during 1926 Maurras was even condemned by the Pope, with five of his books being placed on the *Index* – it had had the opposite effect. (Paul Elmer More wrote to Austin Warren on 11 Aug. 1929, of Eliot: 'some time between *The Waste Land* and *For Lancelot Andrewes* he underwent a kind of conversion, due largely I believe to the influence of Maurras and the Action Française' – quoted in Arthur Hazard Dakin, *Paul Elmer More* [Princeton, 1960], 269. However, Eliot would write this comment in the margin of his copy of Dakin's book on More: 'Hardly possible. But Maurras convinced me, as he convinced my friend Massis, of the social importance of the *Church*. But there is a gap here which Maurras could not bridge.') In a later essay, TSE cited Léon Daudet, Whibley, and Maurras as the 'three best writers of invective of their time' (*SE*, 499). Eliot would ultimately write of Maurras to William Force Stead, on 19 Mar. 1954: 'I am a disciple of Charles Maurras only in certain respects and with critical selection. I do owe Maurras a good deal, and retain my admiration for him, but I think he had serious errors of political judgment – in fact, he should have confined himself, I think, to the philosophy of politics, and never have engaged in political agitation at all. In that, however, I may be wrong – one never knows what things would have been like, had they been different.' See further James Torrens, SJ, 'Charles Maurras and Eliot's "New Life"', *PMLA* 89: 2 (Mar. 1974), 312–22.

Jean de Menasce (1902–73), theologian and orientalist (his writings include studies in Judaism, Zionism, and Hasidism), was born in Alexandria into an aristocratic Jewish Egyptian family and educated in Alexandria, at Balliol College, Oxford (where he was contemporary with Graham Greene and took his BA in 1924), and at the Sorbonne (*Licence es-Lettres*). In Paris, he was associated with the magazines *Commerce* and *L'Esprit*, and he translated several of TSE's poems for French publication: his translation of *The Waste Land* was marked '*revue et approuvée par l'auteur*'. He became a Catholic convert in 1926, was ordained in 1935 a Dominican priest – Father Pierre de Menasce – and went on to be Professor of the History of Religion at the University of Fribourg, 1938–48; Professor and Director of Studies, specialising in Ancient Iranian Religions, at the École Pratique des Hautes Études, Paris. Eliot came to consider him 'the only really first-rate French translator I have ever had' (letter to Kathleen Raine, 17 May 1944).

Harold Monro (1879–1932): poet, editor, publisher, and bookseller. In 1913 he founded the Poetry Bookshop at 35 Devonshire Street, London, where poets would meet and give readings and lectures. In 1912 he briefly edited *The Poetry Review* for the Poetry Society; then his own periodicals, *Poetry and Drama*, 1913–15, and *The Chapbook* (originally *The Monthly Chapbook*), 1919–25. From the Poetry Bookshop, Monro would put out a remarkable mix of publications including the five volumes of *Georgian Poetry*, ed. by Edward Marsh (1872–1953), between 1912 and 1922 (popular anthologies which sold in the region of 15,000 copies), the English edition of *Des Imagistes*, and the first volumes by writers including Richard Aldington, F. S. Flint, and Robert Graves, along with some of his own collections including *Children of Love* (1915) and *Strange Meetings* (1917). TSE was to accept *The Winter Solstice* for publication by Faber & Gwyer as no. 13 of the Ariel Poems. Though a homosexual, Monro was to marry the sister of a friend, 1903–16; and in 1920 he wed Alida Klemantaski (daughter of a Polish-Jewish trader), with whom he never cohabited but who was ever loving and supportive to him: both of them endeared themselves to Eliot, who would occasionally use the premises of the Poetry Bookshop for meetings of contributors to *The Criterion*. After Monro's death, TSE wrote a critical note for *The Collected Poems of Harold Monro*, ed. Alida Monro (1933), xiii–xvi. See further Joy Grant, *Harold Monro and the Poetry Bookshop* (1967); and Dominic Hibberd, *Harold Monro: Poet of the New Age* (2001).

Marianne Moore (1887–1972), American poet and critic, contributed to *The Egoist* from 1915. Her first book, *Poems*, was published in London in 1921. She went on to become in 1925 acting editor of *The Dial*, editor, 1927–9, and an important and influential modern poet. Eliot found her 'an extremely intelligent person, very shy . . . One of the most observant people I have ever met'. Writing to her on 3 April 1921, he said her verse interested him 'more than that of anyone now writing in America'. And in Eliot's introduction to her *Selected Poems* (1935), which he brought out from Faber & Faber, he stated that her 'poems form part of the small body of durable poetry written in our time'.

Thomas Sturge Moore (1870–1944), English poet, playwright, critic, and artist – and brother of the philosopher G. E. Moore – was christened Thomas but adopted his mother's maiden name 'Sturge' to avoid confusion with the Irish poet Thomas Moore. A prolific poet, author of 31 plays, and a loyal contributor to the *Criterion*, he was also a close friend of W. B. Yeats, for whom he designed bookplates and bookbindings. He published his first collection of poems, *The Vinedresser and Other Poems*, in 1899. See also *W. B. Yeats and T. Sturge Moore: Their Correspondence, 1901–1937*, ed. Ursula Bridge (1953); Frederick L. Gwynn, *Sturge Moore and the Life of Art* (1951).

Paul Elmer More (1864–1937), critic, scholar, and prolific writer, had grown up in St Louis, Missouri, and attended Washington University before going on to Harvard; at one time he had taught French to TSE's brother Henry. Initially a humanist, by the 1930s he assumed an Anglo-Catholic position not unlike that of TSE (who appreciated the parallels between their spiritual development). See also 'An Anglican Platonist: the Conversion of Paul Elmer More', *TLS*, 30 Oct. 1937, 792. At the outset of his career, More taught classics at Harvard and Bryn Mawr; thereafter he became a journalist, serving as literary editor of *The Independent* (1901–3) and the New York *Evening Post* (1903–9), and as editor of *The Nation* (1909–14), before finally turning to freelance writing and teaching. TSE keenly admired More's many works, in particular *Shelburne Essays* (11 vols, 1904–21), *The Greek Tradition* (5 vols, 1924–31), and *The Demon of the Absolute* (1928); and he went to great trouble in the 1930s in his efforts to secure a publisher for *Pages from an Oxford Diary* (1937), which More stipulated he would only ever publish in anonymity.

In 1937, TSE wrote in tribute: 'The place of Paul More's writings in my own life has been of such a kind that I find [it] easiest, and perhaps most effective, to treat it in a kind of autobiographical way. What is significant to me . . . is not simply the conclusions at which he has arrived, but the fact that he *arrived* there from somewhere else; and not simply that he came from somewhere else, but that he took a particular route . . . If I find an analogy with my own journey, that is perhaps of interest to no one but myself, except in so far as it explains my retrospective appreciation of the *Shelburne Essays*; but my appreciation of the whole work cannot be disengaged from the way in which I arrived at it.

'When I was an undergraduate at Harvard, More was editor of the *Nation*, and to occupy that position in those days was to be a public figure. I sometimes read the *Nation* and I sometimes read a Shelburne Essay, but I cannot remember that I liked or disliked More's writing . . . I certainly did not have the background for appreciating the kind of critical intelligence at work in the *Shelburne Essays* – to say nothing of Ste. Beuve. It was not until my senior year, as a pupil of [Irving] Babbitt's, that More's work was forced on my attention: for one of the obligations of any pupil of Babbitt was to learn a proper respect for "my friend More". But while one was directly exposed to so powerful an influence as Babbitt's, everything that one read was merely a supplement to Babbitt.

'It was not until one or two of the volumes of *The Greek Tradition* had appeared, that More began to have any importance for me. It was possibly Irving Babbitt himself, <in 1927 or 1928>, in a conversation in London, in 1927 or '28, during which I had occasion to indicate the steps I had recently taken, who first made me clearly cognizant of the situation.

In the later volumes of *The Greek Tradition*, and in the acquaintance and friendship subsequently formed, I came to find an auxiliary to my own progress of thought, which no English theologian <at the time> could have given me. The English theologians, born and brought up in surroundings of private belief and public form, and often themselves descended from ecclesiastics, at any rate living mostly in an environment of religious practice, did not seem to me to know enough of the new world of barbarism and infidelity that was forming all about them. The English Church was familiar with the backslider, but it knew nothing of the convert – certainly not of the convert who ~~came~~ had come such a long journey. I might almost say that I never met any Christians until after I had made up my mind to become one. It was of the greatest importance, then, to ~~meet~~ have at hand the work of a man who had come by somewhat the same route, to <almost> the same conclusions, at almost the same time: with a maturity, a weight of scholarship, a discipline of thinking, which I did not, and never shall, possess.

'I had met More only once in earlier years – at a reception given by the Babbitts to which some of Babbitt's pupils had the honor of invitation and that remained only a visual memory. My first meeting with him in London, however, seemed more like the renewal of an old acquaintance than the formation of a new one: More was a St. Louisan, and had known my family; and if he had remained a few years longer, ~~I also~~ he would have ~~learned my~~ <taught me> Greek ~~from him,~~ as ~~did~~ he had taught my brother' (*Princeton Alumni Magazine* 37 [5 Feb. 1937], 373–74); TS at Princeton C0896, Box 1, folder 3).

Frank Vigor Morley (1899–1980), son of a distinguished mathematician – his brothers were the writer Christopher, and Felix (who was to become editor of *The Washington Post*) – was brought up in the USA before travelling as a Rhodes Scholar to New College, Oxford, where he earned a doctorate in mathematics. After working for a while at the *Times Literary Supplement*, he became London Manager of The Century Company (Publishers) of New York. In 1929 he became a founding director of Faber & Faber, where he would be a close friend of TSE: for some time they shared a top-floor office at Russell Square. On 4 January 1932 Morley wrote of himself to F. Gilchrist Thompson of Jonathan Cape Ltd, which was to publish his book *Lamb before Elia* (1932): 'As to career it is, alas, not so much chequered as check-mated. I was born at Haverford, Penn., the seat of a Quaker College in which in due course I was entered, but the war intervened and caused a kind of tussle with

Quakerism in which I am sorry to say Quakerism was worsted. After a completely undistinguished period with the American Army I returned, supposedly to study mathematics, to a good place called Johns Hopkins University. Actually I played at mathematics but worked at a subject called lacrosse, which seems to be played by women in this country [UK] but which is still a serious blood-letting, Red Indian pursuit in my native black blocks. I was successively a seaman on the Pacific, a member of the United State [words missing,] temporary manufacturer of air-cooled motor cars, and then a Rhodes Scholar at New College, which paved the way for becoming a stoker in SS. Antwerp on the Harwich-Antwerp run across the North Sea. The only item in this which has any bearing on literary criticism is my brief yet glorious career in the [words missing.] After coming to England I always intended to go home but never quite got round to doing so – so here I still am inventing Brothers' Clubs to take the place of legitimate adventures'.

In 1933 when TSE separated from Vivien, Morley arranged convivial temporary accommodation for him near his farmhouse at Pike's Farm, Lingfield, Surrey. In 1939 Morley moved to the USA, where he became Vice-President of Harcourt Brace and Company (and during the war he served on the National War Labor Board in Washington, DC). In 1947 he returned with his family to England to take up the post of Director at Eyre & Spottiswoode. A large, learned, ebullient figure, he earned the sobriquet 'Whale' – though not merely on account of his corpulence: in his youth he had spent time aboard a whaling ship (he was revolted by the slaughter), and subsequently wrote (with J. S. Hodgson) *Whaling North and South* (1927) – which was reviewed in the *Monthly Criterion* by his friend Herbert Read. His other publications include *Travels in East Anglia* (1923), *River Thames* (1926), *Inversive Geometry* (1933), *My One Contribution to Chess* (1947), *The Great North Road* (1961), *The Long Road West: A Journey in History* (1971), and *Literary Britain* (1980); and contributions in verse (along with verses by Eliot, Geoffrey Faber and John Hayward) to *Noctes Binanianae* (1939).

Morley Kennerley told *The Times* (25 Oct. 1980) that 'one of his hobbies was to work out complicated problems for his friends, and for those baffled there were amazing practical jokes. Convivial lunches with interesting people were a joy to him ... He found jobs for many and squeezed me into Fabers where he generously put up with my sharing a corner of his room for some years. I was present all day during his interviews, dictation, visitors and often lunch. How he put up with all this I do not know. His correspondence with Ezra Pound was quite something, and I think he out-Pounded Pound. As his family say, he was a compulsive letter writer and was rarely without a pencil in his hand or pocket.'

In 1939, when Morley was on the point of returning to the USA, Geoffrey Faber wrote of him to the editor of *The Times*: 'Morley is a quite outstanding person . . . [His] first obvious quality is that he is a born "mixer", with an extraordinary range of friends in different walks of life. He is a very good talker, though rather fond – like many Americans – of spinning the yarn out. But he never spins without a purpose. As a negotiator he is in a class by himself. His judgment of men and situations is first rate. He knows the personnel of both the English and American publishing and journalistic worlds. As for his mental equipment, he took a doctorate at Oxford with a mathematical thesis. The story is that nobody in Oxford could understand it, and help had to be got from Cambridge. But he is at least as good a man of letters as he is a mathematician' (Faber Archive).

Lady Ottoline Morrell (1873–1938): daughter of Lieutenant-General Arthur Bentinck and half-sister to the Duke of Portland. In 1902 she married Philip Morrell (1870–1941), Liberal MP for South Oxfordshire 1902–18. A patron of the arts, she entertained a notable literary and artistic circle, first at 44 Bedford Square, then at Garsington Manor, nr. Oxford, where she moved in 1915. She was a lover of Bertrand Russell, who introduced her to TSE, and her many friends included Lytton Strachey, D. H. Lawrence, Aldous Huxley, Siegfried Sassoon, the Woolfs, and the Eliots. Her memoirs (ed. by Robert Gathorne-Hardy) appeared as *Ottoline* (1963) and *Ottoline at Garsington* (1974). See Miranda Seymour, *Life on the Grand Scale: Lady Ottoline Morrell* (1992, 1998).

Edwin Muir (1887–1959): Scottish poet, novelist, critic; translator (with his wife Willa) of Franz Kafka. TSE was to write to LW on 22 Aug. 1946: 'I am anxious to do anything I can for Muir because I think highly of his best poetry and I think he has not had enough recognition.' To his cousin Eleanor Hinkley, 25 Dec. 1955: 'I have always found Willa rather oppressive. Edwin is a sweet creature, who never says anything when his wife is present, and only an occasional word when she isn't. An evening alone with him is very fatiguing. But he is a good poet, and I believe, what is even rarer, a literary man of complete integrity. He is not really Scottish, but Orcadian – in other words, pure Scandinavian.' And in an obituary tribute: 'Muir's literary criticism had always seemed to me of the best of our time: after I came to know him, I realised that it owed its excellence not only to his power of intellect and acuteness of sensibility, but to those moral qualities which make us remember him, as you say justly, as "in some ways almost a saintly man". It was more recently that I came to regard his poetry as ranking with the best poetry of our time. As a poet he began late; as a poet he was recognised late; but some of his finest work – perhaps his very finest work – was written when he was already over sixty . . . For this late development we are reminded of the later poetry of Yeats; and Muir had to struggle with bad health also: but in the one case as in the other (and Muir is by no means unworthy to be mentioned together with Yeats) we recognise a triumph of the human spirit' (*The Times*, 7 Jan. 1959). Willa Muir privately commented on TSE's plaudits: 'Eliot, in his desire to present Edwin as an orthodox Christian, overdid, I think, the desolations and the saintliness. Edwin's wine could never be contained in any orthodox creed' (letter to Kathleen Raine, 7 Apr. 1960). TSE would later say of Muir: 'He was a reserved, reticent man . . . Yet his personality made a deep impression upon me, and especially the impression of one very rare and precious quality . . . unmistakable integrity'; and of his poems: 'under the pressure of emotional intensity, and possessed by his vision, he found almost unconsciously the right, the inevitable, way of saying what he wanted to say' ('Edwin Muir: 1887–1959: An Appreciation', *The Listener*, 28 May 1964, 872). Muir's publications include *First Poems* (Hogarth Press, 1925); *Transition: Essays on Contemporary Literature* (1926), *An Autobiography* (1954); *Selected Poems of Edwin Muir*, preface by TSE (1966); *Selected Letters of Edwin Muir*, ed. P. H. Butter (1974).

John Middleton Murry (1889–1957): English writer, critic, and editor, founded the magazine *Rhythm*, 1911–13, and worked as a reviewer for the *Westminster Gazette*, 1912–14, and the *Times Literary Supplement*, 1914–18, before becoming editor from 1919 to 1921 of the *Athenaeum*, which he turned into a lively cultural forum – in a letter of 2 July 1919, TSE called it 'the best literary weekly in the Anglo-Saxon world'. Richard Church thought him 'a dark, slippery character, who looked over my shoulder (probably into an invisible mirror) when talking to me, and referred to himself always in the third person . . . In spite of these characteristics . . . he was possessed by a strong literary sensibility.' In a 'London Letter' in *Dial* 72 (May 1921), Eliot considered Murry 'genuinely studious to maintain a serious criticism', but he disagreed with his 'particular tastes, as well as his general statements'. After the demise of the *Athenaeum*, Murry went on to edit *The Adelphi*. 1923–48. In 1918, he married Katherine Mansfield. He was friend and biographer of D. H. Lawrence; and as an editor he provided a platform for writers as various as George Santayana, Paul Valéry, D. H. Lawrence, Aldous Huxley, Virginia Woolf, and Eliot. His first notable critical work was *Dostoevsky* (1916); his most influential study, *The Problem of Style* (1922). Though as a Romanticist he was an intellectual opponent of the avowedly 'Classicist' Eliot, Murry offered Eliot in 1919 the post of assistant editor on the *Athenaeum* (which Eliot had to decline); in addition, he recommended him to be Clark lecturer at Cambridge in 1926, and was a steadfast friend to both TSE and his wife Vivien. Eliot wrote in a reference on 9 Sept. 1945 that Murry was 'one of the most distinguished men of letters of this time, and testimony from a contemporary seems superfluous. Several volumes of literary essays of the highest quality are evidence of his eminence as a critic; and even if one took no account of his original contribution, his conduct of *The Athenaeum*, which he edited from 1919 until its absorption into *The Nation*, should be enough to entitle him to the gratitude of his contemporaries and juniors. His direction of *The Adelphi* should also be recognised. Since he has devoted his attention chiefly to social and religious problems, he has written a number of books which no one who is concerned with the same problems, whether in agreement with him or not, can afford to neglect. I am quite sure that no future student of these matters who wishes to understand this age will be able to ignore them, and that no future student of the literary spirit of this age will be able to ignore Mr Murry's criticism.' He wrote to Murry's widow on 29 May 1957: 'The friendship between John and myself was of a singular quality, such that it was rather different from any other of my friendships. We did not often meet. We disagreed throughout many years on one point after another. But on the other hand, a very warm affection existed between us in spite of differences of view and infrequency of meetings. This affection was not merely, on my part, a feeling of gratitude for the opportunities he had given me early in my career during his editorship of *The Athenaeum*, but was something solid and permanent. He was one of the strangest and most remarkable men I have known, and no less strange and remarkable was the tie of affection between us.' See F. A. Lea, *The Life of John Middleton Murry* (1959); and David Goldie, *A Critical Difference: T. S. Eliot and John Middleton Murry in English Literary Criticism, 1919–1928* (1998).

F. S. Oliver (1864–1934), businessman and polemicist, was educated at Edinburgh and Trinity College, Cambridge, before joining forces in 1892 with Ernest Debenham in the firm of Debenham and Freebody (drapers, wholesalers, manufacturers), which they caused to flourish and expand (buying up Marshall and Snelgrove and Harvey Nichols); Oliver, who had become a wealthy man, retired as managing director in 1920. A radical Tory, he engaged himself in many public issues. His publications included *Alexander Hamilton* (1906), *Ordeal by Battle* (1915), and *The Endless Adventure* (3 vols, 1930–5).

Kenneth Pickthorn (1892–1975): historian and politician; Fellow of Corpus Christi College, Cambridge, from 1914; Dean, 1919–29; Tutor, 1927–35; President, 1937–44. From 1950 to 1966 he was to be the Conservative MP for a Midlands constituency; an independent-minded and outspoken parliamentarian, critical of cant, he was made a baronet in 1959, Privy Councillor in 1964. His publications included *Some Historical Principles of the Constitution* (1925) and *Early Tudor Government* (2 vols, 1934).

Ezra Pound (1885–1972), American poet and critic, was one of the prime impresarios of the modernist movement in London and Paris, and played a major part in launching Eliot as poet and critic – as well as Joyce, Lewis, and many other modernists. Eliot called on him at 5 Holland Place Chambers, Kensington, on 22 Sept. 1914, with an introduction from Conrad Aiken. On 30 Sept. 1914, Pound hailed 'Prufrock' as 'the best poem I have yet had or seen from an American'; and on 3 October called Eliot 'the last intelligent man I've found – a young American T. S. Eliot . . . worth watching – mind "not primitive"' (*Selected Letters of Ezra Pound*, 40–1). Pound was instrumental in arranging for 'Prufrock' to be published in *Poetry* in 1915, and helped to shape *The Waste Land* (1922), which Eliot dedicated to him as 'il miglior fabbro'. After their first meeting, the poets became friends, and remained in loyal correspondence for the rest of their lives. Having initially dismissed Pound's poetry (to Conrad Aiken, 30 Sept. 1914) as 'well-meaning but touchingly incompetent', Eliot went on to champion his work, writing to Gilbert Seldes (27 Dec. 1922): 'I sincerely consider Ezra Pound the most important living poet in the English language.' He wrote an early critical study, *Ezra Pound: His Metric and Poetry* (1917), and went on, as editor of *The Criterion* and publisher at Faber & Faber, to publish most of Pound's work in the UK, including *Selected Shorter Poems*, *The Cantos* and *Selected Literary Essays*. After his move to Italy in the 1920s, Pound became increasingly sceptical about the direction of TSE's convictions and poetry, but they continued to correspond. TSE wrote to James Laughlin, on the occasion of Pound's seventieth birthday: 'I believe that I have in the past made clear enough my personal debt to Ezra Pound during the years 1915–22.

I have also expressed in several ways my opinion of his rank as a poet, as a critic, as impresario of other writers, and as pioneer of metric and poetic language. His 70th birthday is not a moment for qualifying one's praise, but merely for recognition of those services to literature for which he will deserve the gratitude of posterity, and for appreciation of those achievements which even his severest critics must acknowledge' (3 Nov. 1955). After Eliot's death, Pound said of him: 'His was the true Dantescan voice – not honoured enough, and deserving more than I ever gave him.' See A. David Moody, *Ezra Pound: Poet: A Portrait of the Man and his Work* I: *The Young Genius 1885–1920* (2007), Humphrey Carpenter, *A Serious Character* (1988), *The Selected Letters of Ezra Pound 1907–1941*, ed. D. D. Paige (1950), and *Ezra Pound to His Parents: Letters 1895–1929*, ed. Mary de Rachewiltz, A. David Moody, Joanna Moody (Oxford, 2011).

Mario Praz (1896–1982): scholar and critic of English life and literature; author of *La Carne, la Morte e Il Diavolo nella Letteratura Romantica* (1930; *The Romantic Agony* (1933). Educated in Bologna, Rome and Florence, he came to England in 1923 to study for the title of *libero docente*. He was Senior Lecturer in Italian, Liverpool University, 1924–32; Professor of Italian Studies, Victoria University of Manchester, 1932–4; and Professor of English Language and Literature at the University of Rome, 1934–66. His many other publications include *Il giardino dei sensi* (1975). In 1952 he was conferred by Queen Elizabeth II with the title of Knight Commander of the British Empire (KBE). In 'An Italian Critic on Donne and Crashaw' (*TLS*, 17 Dec. 1925, 878), TSE hailed Praz's study *Secentismo e Marinismo in Inghilterra: John Donne – Richard Crashaw* (1925) as 'indispensable for any student of this period and these authors'. Later, in 'A Tribute to Mario Praz', he noted: 'His knowledge of the poetry of that period in four languages – English, Italian, Spanish and Latin – was encyclopaedic, and, fortified by his own judgment and good taste, makes that book essential reading for any student of the English "metaphysical poets" ' (*Friendship's Garland: Essays presented to Mario Praz on His Seventieth Birthday*, ed. Vittorio Gabrieli [1966].)

Alec (later Sir Alec) Randall (1892–1977), diplomat and writer, entered the Foreign Office in 1920. In the early 1920s he was Second Secretary to the Holy See. He ended his career as Ambassador to Denmark (where he was awarded the Grand Cross, Order of Dannebrog), 1947–52. He wrote on German literature for the *Criterion* and *TLS*. Later works include *Vatican Assignment* (1956) and *The Pope, the Jews and the Nazis* (1963).

Herbert Read (1893–1968): English poet and literary critic, and one of the most influential art critics of the century. Son of a tenant farmer, Read spent his first years in rural Yorkshire; at sixteen, he went to work as a bank clerk, then studied law and economics at Leeds University; later still, he joined the Civil Service, working first in the Ministry of Labour and then at the Treasury. During his years of service in WW1, he rose to be a captain in the Yorkshire regiment the Green Howards (his war poems were published in *Naked Warriors*, 1919); and when on leave to receive the Military Cross in 1917, he arranged to dine with TSE at the Monico Restaurant in Piccadilly Circus. This launched a lifelong friendship which he was to recall in 'T.S.E. – A Memoir', in *T. S. Eliot: The Man and his Work*, ed. Allen Tate (1966). Within the year, he had also become acquainted with the Sitwells, Ezra Pound, Wyndham Lewis, Richard Aldington, and Ford Madox Ford. He co-founded the journal *Art & Letters*, 1917–20, and wrote essays too for A. R. Orage, editor of the *New Age*. In 1922 he was appointed a curator in the department of ceramics and glass at the Victoria and Albert Museum; and in later years he was to work for the publishers Routledge & Kegan Paul, and as editor of the *Burlington Magazine*, 1933–9. By 1923 he was writing for *The Criterion*: he was to be one of Eliot's regular leading contributors and a reliable ally and adviser. In 1924 he edited T. E. Hulme's posthumous *Speculations*. His later works include *Art Now* (1933); the introduction to the catalogue of the International Surrealist Exhibition held at the New Burlington Galleries, London, 1936; *Art and Society* (1937); *Education through Art* (1943); and *A Concise History of Modern Painting* (1959). In 1947 he founded (with Roland Penrose) the Institute of Contemporary Art; and in 1953 he was knighted for services to literature. Eliot, he was to recall (perhaps only half in jest), was 'rather like a gloomy priest presiding over my affections and spontaneity'. According to Stephen Spender in 1966, Eliot said 'of the anarchism of his friend Herbert Read, whom he loved and esteemed very highly: "Sometimes when I read Herbert's inflammatory pamphlets I have the impression that I am reading the pronouncements of an old-fashioned nineteenth-century liberal"' ('Remembering Eliot', *The Thirties and After* [1978], 251). Joseph Chiari recalled TSE saying of Read: 'Ah, there is old Herbie, again; he can't resist anything new!' See Herbert Read, *Annals of Innocence and Experience* (1940); James King, *The Last Modern: A Life of Herbert Read* (1990);

and *Herbert Read reassessed*, ed. D. Goodway (1998). Jason Harding (*The 'Criterion'*: see citation under Dobrée) calculates that Read wrote 68 book reviews, 4 articles, and 5 poems for the *Criterion*.

I. A. Richards (1893–1979): theorist of literature, education, and communication studies. At Cambridge University he studied History but switched to moral sciences, graduating from Magdalene College, where in 1922 he was appointed College Lecturer in English and Moral Sciences. A vigorous, spell-binding lecturer, he was to the fore in the advancement of the English Tripos. His early writings – *The Foundations of Aesthetics* (with C. K. Ogden and James Wood, 1922), *The Meaning of Meaning* (also with Ogden, 1923), *Principles of Literary Criticism* (1924), *Science and Poetry* (1926), *Practical Criticism: A Study of Literary Judgment* (1929) – are foundational texts in modern English literary studies. After teaching at National Tsing Hua University in Peking, 1929–30, he repaired for the remainder of his career to Harvard University, where he was made a university professor in 1944. His other works include *Basic Rules of Reason* (1933), *Basic in Teaching: East and West* (1935), *Mencius on the Mind* (1932), *Coleridge on Imagination* (1934), *The Philosophy of Rhetoric* (1936), *Interpretation in Teaching* (1938), *Speculative Instruments* (1955), and translations from Plato and Homer. He was appointed Companion of Honour in 1963, and awarded the Emerson-Thoreau medal of the American Academy of Arts and Sciences, 1970. Out of the teaching term, he enjoyed with his wife Dorothy (1894–1986) an adventurous life of travel and mountain-climbing. See *Selected Letters of I. A. Richards, CH*, ed. John Constable (Oxford: Clarendon Press, 1990); John Constable, 'I. A. Richards, T. S. Eliot, and the Poetry of Belief', *Essays in Criticism* (July 1990), 222–43; *I. A. Richards and his Critics*, ed. John Constable (vol. 10 of *I. A. Richards: Selected Works 1919–1938* (2001); John Paul Russo, *I. A. Richards: His Life and Work* (1989).

Bruce Richmond (1871–1964), literary editor, was educated at Winchester and New College, Oxford, and called to the Bar in 1897. However, he never practised as a barrister; instead, George Buckle, editor of *The Times*, appointed him an assistant editor in 1899, and in 1902 he assumed the editorship of the fledgling *Times Literary Supplement*, which he commanded for 35 years. During this period, the *TLS* established itself as the premier academic and critical periodical in Britain. He was knighted in 1935. TSE, who was introduced to Richmond by Richard Aldington in 1919, enthused to his mother that year that writing the leading article for the *TLS* was the highest honour 'in the critical world of literature'. In a tribute, he recalled Richmond as possessing 'a bird-like alertness of eye, body and mind . . . It was from Bruce Richmond that I learnt editorial standards . . . I learnt from him that it is the business of an editor to know his contributors personally, to keep in touch with them and to make suggestions to them. I tried [at *The Criterion*] to form a nucleus of writers (some of them, indeed, recruited from *The Times Literary Supplement*, and introduced to me by Richmond) on whom I could depend, differing from each other in many things, but not in love of literature and seriousness of purpose. And I learnt from Richmond that I must read every word of what was to appear in print . . . It is a final tribute to Richmond's genius as an editor that some of his troupe of regular contributors (I am thinking of myself as well as of others) produced some of their most distinguished critical essays as leaders for the *Literary Supplement* . . . Good literary criticism requires good editors as well as good critics. And Bruce Richmond was a great editor' ('Bruce Lyttelton Richmond', *TLS*, 13 Jan. 1961, 17).

J. M. Robertson (1856–1933), author, journalist, politician, began his career as a clerk; then worked on newspapers including the *Edinburgh Evening News* and *National Reformer*. He was Liberal MP for Tyneside, 1908–18. Though self-taught, he was a prolific writer, publishing over 100 books and pamphlets including *The Problem of Hamlet* (1919), *Hamlet Once More* (1923), *Mr Shaw and the Maid* (1926) – a study of *St Joan* which TSE reviewed in *The Criterion* (Apr. 1926) – *and The Problems of Shakespeare's Sonnets* (1927), which TSE reviewed in *The Nation* (12 Feb. 1927). A fervent disintegrationist, Robertson sought to isolate the pure Shakespeare. TSE wrote to Duff Cooper on 30 Nov. 1949, in response to his book *Sergeant Shakespeare*: 'I must let you know that I am no longer under the influence of Robertson, and no longer quite agree with what I said about *Hamlet*.' See also Leo Storm, 'J. M. Robertson and T. S. Eliot: A Note on the Genesis of Modern Critical Theory', *Journal of Modern Literature* 5: 2 (Apr. 1976), 315–21; Martin Page, *Britain's Unknown Genius: The Life-Work of J. M. Robertson* (1984); *J. M. Robertson, 1856–1933: Liberal, Rationalist and Scholar*, ed. G. A. Wells (1985); Odin Dekkers, *J. M. Robertson: Rationalist and Literary Critic* (1998).

Edouard Roditi (1910–92): American-Jewish poet, critic, biographer, translator, and essayist. With a background that was partly Spanish-

Portuguese and partly Greek, he attended schools in England, and went up (for a single year, 1927–8) to Balliol College, Oxford. Precocious as both poet and translator, by the age of 12 he had translated into Latin and Greek a good deal of the poetry of Byron; and at 14 he put Gerard Manley Hopkins into French. His adult works included *Prison Within Prison: Three Elegies on Jewish Themes* (1941); the prose poems of *New and Old Testaments* (1983); collections of essays including *The Disorderly Poet* (1975) and a treatise, *De L'Homosexualité* (1962); as well as translations into English, German and French. The *Times* obituary remarked (18 May 1992): 'In 1926 he was sent to a Swiss clinic, where he set himself the task of translating the French poet Saint-John Perse's *Anabase* into English. A little later he discovered that T. S. Eliot was engaged in the same project, and so sent him his version, from which, he claimed, Eliot took up more than a few interpretations. But Eliot also made encouraging comments about some of the boy's original verse.'

On 11 Nov. 1936 TSE wrote on Roditi's behalf to the Undersecretary of State: 'I am glad to offer myself as a sponsor for Mr Edward Roditi in his application to be allowed to reside in this country. I have known Mr Roditi for some years as a poet and man of letters, and neither in my personal acquaintance nor in his literary work – he has been a contributor to *The Criterion* – have I regarded him as a foreigner in any way. He writes English as his native tongue, and his poetry has distinction and beauty. I believe his abilities, experience and education to be such that I should consider it for the good of English letters that he should be allowed to reside here. And so far as I know him personally, my opinion of him supports my opinion of his literary work' (UCLA).

Roditi later wrote to *The Jewish Quarterly*, no. 142 (38: 2, Summer 1991), 72: 'I was barely eighteen when I first met Eliot in 1928 because I too had undertaken a translation of Saint-John Perse's *Anabase* without knowing that its French author had already granted Eliot the right to translate and publish it in English.

'Eliot then proved to be very cordial and almost paternal in his typically reserved manner. After discussing our different interpretations of some of the more cryptic passages in *Anabase*, Eliot invited me to submit to him some of my own poems. From some of these he was soon able to conclude that I was of Jewish origin and attempting somehow to discover my Jewish identity in a few of my poems. Very kindly, he suggested corrections to these somewhat immature poems and encouraged me to continue submitting my poetry to him for guidance. After a while, he even suggested publishing in *The Criterion* one of my most overtly

Jewish poems – in fact one of the sections of my long elegy entitled "The Complaint of Jehuda Abravanel"; but this particular section of my poem had already been accepted for publication either in *The Spectator* or *The Jewish Review*. I then submitted a group of shorter poems and Eliot published three of these in *The Criterion*.

'I continued to see Eliot fairly regularly in London between 1928 and 1937 and can testify to the fact that he expressed to me on several occasions after 1933 his horror of the anti-Semitic outrages which were already occurring in Nazi Germany. My personal impression is that, after writing *The Waste Land*, Eliot had become a much more devout Christian, before writing the so-called "Ariel Poems" and *Ash Wednesday*. As a Christian he no longer felt or expressed the kind of somewhat immature and snobbish anti-Semitism that can be detected in the earlier poems and letters . . .'

See also Roditi, 'T. S. Eliot: Persoenlichkeit und Werk', *Der Monat* 3 (1948), 86–9; 'Corresponding with Eliot', *London Magazine* 28: 5/6 (Aug./Sept. 1988), 33–44. Roditi wrote two articles about St-John Perse, in *Contemporary Poetry*, 6: 3 (1944) and *La République libre*, 26 Jan. 1951.

William Rothenstein (1872–1945), Bradford-born son of Jewish immigrants, painter and administrator, was Principal of the Royal College of Art from 1919; knighted in 1931. See *Twelve Portraits* (F&F, 1928), *Men and Memories: Recollections of William Rothenstein* (2 vols, 1931–2); *Since Fifty: Men and Memories, 1922–1938* (1939); and Robert Speaight, *William Rothenstein: The Portrait of an Artist in His Time* (1962).

A. L. Rowse (1903–97), Cornish historian, was educated at Christ Church, Oxford, and elected a Prize Fellow of All Souls in 1925. He was a lecturer at Merton College, 1927–30, and taught also at the London School of Economics. His numerous books include *Sir Richard Grenville of the Revenge* (1937), *The England of Elizabeth* (1950), *William Shakespeare: A Biography* (1963), *Shakespeare the Man* (1973), *Simon Forman: Sex and Society in Shakespeare's Age* (1974), *All Souls in My Time* (1993), and volumes of poetry gathered up in *A Life* (1981). Though he failed in 1952 to be elected Warden of All Souls, he was elected a Fellow of the British Academy in 1958 and made a Companion of Honour in 1997. See Richard Ollard, *A Man of Contradictions: A Life of A. L. Rowse* (1999), and *The Diaries of A. L. Rowse* (ed. Ollard, 2003). TSE was to write to Geoffrey Curtis on 1 May 1944: 'Rowse is an old friend of mine, and a very touching person: the suppressed Catholic and the rather less suppressed Tory (with a real respect for Good Families), the miner's son and the All Souls Fellow, the minor poet and the would-be politician, the proletarian myth and the will-to-power, are always at odds in a scholarly retiring mind and a frail body. He is also very patronising, and one likes it.'

Bertrand Russell (1872–1970): one of the most influential twentieth-century British philosophers; co-author (with Alfred North Whitehead) of *Principia Mathematica* (1910–13), and author of innumerable other books including the popular *Problems of Philosophy* (1912), *Mysticism and Logic* (1918) – which was reviewed by TSE in 'Style and Thought' (*Nation* 22, 23 March 1918) – and *History of Western Philosophy* (1945). In 1914, Russell gave the Lowell lectures on 'Our Knowledge of the External World' at Harvard, where he encountered Eliot. On 27 March 1914, Russell described Eliot as 'very well dressed and polished, with manners of the finest Etonian type'. He later characterised him as 'proficient in Plato, intimate with French literature from Villon to Vildrach, and capable of exquisiteness of appreciation, but lacking in the crude insistent passion that one must have in order to achieve anything'. After their accidental meeting in 1914, Russell played an important role in introducing TSE to English intellectual life, as well as getting him launched as a reviewer for *International Journal of Ethics* and *The Monist*. However, it has been alleged that, not long after TSE's marriage, Russell may have had a brief affair with his wife Vivien – though in later years Russell would deny any such thing; on 28 May 1968 he wrote to Robert Sencourt: 'I never had any intimate sexual relations with Vivienne. The difficulty between Eliot and Vivienne sprang chiefly from her taking of drugs and the consequent hallucinations.' The three friends had shared lodgings for a period in 1916 at Russell's flat in London. Russell was a Conscientious Objector and vocal opponent of WW1, which led to a brief prison sentence in Wandsworth. In later years, TSE saw little of his one-time professor and friend, and he attacked Russell's philosophical and ethical views, in his 'Commentary' in the *Criterion* (April 1924), and elsewhere. Russell provides a partial account of his relationship with the Eliots in *The Autobiography of Bertrand Russell* II: *1914–1944* (1968). See also Ray Monk, *Bertrand Russell: The Spirit of Solitude* (1996).

Alexis St Leger Leger (1887–1975) – pen name **St-John Perse** – poet and diplomat. Scion of a Bourgignon family, he passed his early years on an island near Guadeloupe in the West Indies, but the family returned to France in 1899. After studying law at the University of Bordeaux, he joined the Foreign Office as an attaché and worked for six years as Secretary at the French Legation in Peking: his poem *Anabase* is inspired in part by aspects of his life and observations in China, which included a journey to Outer Mongolia. In 1921, at a conference in Washington, DC, he was recruited by Aristide Briand, Prime Minister of France, as his *chef de cabinet*; and after Briand's death in 1932 he retained high office, serving as Sécretaire Générale of the Foreign Office, 1933–40. Dishonoured by the Vichy regime (he was a Grand Officier of the Legion of Honour), he spent the years of WW2 in the USA (serving for a time as a 'consultant' to the Library of Congress); and he went back to France only in 1957 (he had formally closed his diplomatic career in 1950, with the title of Ambassadeur de France). His publications include *Éloges* (published with help from André Gide, 1911), *Anabase* (1924; trans. TSE as *Anabasis*, 1930), *Exil* (1942), *Pluies* (1943), *Vents* (1946), *Amers* (1957), and *Oiseaux* (1962). In 1924 he had published in *Commerce* a translation of the opening section of 'The Hollow Men'. He was made Nobel Laureate in Literature in 1960.

In a copy of *Anabase* (Paris: Librairie Gallimard/Éditions de La Nouvelle Revue Française, 1925: limited edition copy no. 160), St-John Perse wrote: 'A T. S. Eliot / dont j'aime et j'admire l'oeuvre / fraternellement / St. J. Perse.' (TSE Library)

In 1960 TSE was to recommend St-John Perse for the Nobel Prize. When requested on 10 Mar. 1960 by Uno Willers, secretary of the Svenska Akadamiens Nobelkommitté, to 'write down a more detailed motivation for your suggestion', TSE responded on 23 Mar. 1960: 'My interest in the work of St-John Perse began many years ago when I translated his *Anabase* into English. This task gave me an intimacy with his style and idiom which I could not have acquired in any other way. It seemed to me then, and it seems to me still, that he had done something highly original – and in a language, the French language, in which such originality is not easily attained. He had invented a form which was different from "free verse" as practised in France to-day, and different from the "prose-poem" in which some French writers, anxious to escape the limitations of the conventional metrics of their language, take refuge.

'He is the only French poet among my contemporaries, with the solitary exception of Supervielle, whose work has continued to interest me. With some of my contemporaries writing in other languages I feel a certain affinity – with Montale, for example, and with Seferis so far as I can judge from translations – with Perse, I have felt rather an influence which is visible in some of my poems written after I had translated *Anabase*.' He added: 'My remarks are, of course, to be taken as confidential, as I am always careful never to express in public my opinions of the relative value of the works of poets who are my contemporaries or my juniors.'

See also Richard Abel, 'The Influence of St.-John Perse on T. S. Eliot', *Contemporary Literature*, XIV: 2 (Spring 1973), 213–39.

Gilbert Seldes (1893–1970), journalist, critic, and editor, was a war correspondent before becoming editor of *The Dial*, 1920–3. His works include *The Seven Lively Arts* (1924) – an influential study of popular arts embracing the comic strip and popular songs as well as cinema and vaudeville – and *The Stammering Century* (1928). He wrote a number of 'New York Chronicles' for the *Criterion*. In later years he was a prolific essayist; he also wrote for the Broadway theatre, and became the first director of TV programmes for CBS News, and founding Dean of the Annenburg School for Communication, University of Pennsylvania. See Michael Kammen, *The Lively Arts: Gilbert Seldes and the Transformation of Cultural Criticism in the United States* (1996).

Robert Esmonde Gordon George – Robert Sencourt (1890–1969) – critic, historian and biographer. Born in New Zealand, he was educated in Tamaki and at St John's College, Oxford. By 1929 – perhaps to avoid confusion with Professor George Gordon (President of Magdalen College, Oxford) – he was to take the name of Robert Sencourt. He taught in India and Portugal before serving as Vice-Dean of the Faculty of Arts and Professor of English Literature, University of Egypt, 1933–6. *The Times* obituarist noted that he was 'born an Anglican [but] was converted to Roman Catholicism which alone could inspire him with the spiritual dimension of the life of grace . . . [He] was the most fervent and devout of religious men, with the same personal mysticism which makes his life of St John of the Cross a joy to read. Never fearing to speak his mind in religious matters, even when (as often) his view ran counter to the church's, he was intolerant of any form of ecclesiastical cant or humbug.' His books include *The Genius of the Vatican* (1935), *Carmelite and Poet: St John of the Cross* (1943), *St Paul: Envoy of Grace* (1948), biographies of George Meredith, the Empress Eugénie, Napoleon III, King Alfonso, and Edward VIII, and *T. S. Eliot: A Memoir*, ed. Donald Adamson (1971). On 17 July 1936 TSE was to write to the Master of Corpus Christi College, Cambridge, in support of Sencourt's application for the Chair of English at Bucharest: 'I should think Sencourt would do admirably for it. He is a New Zealander, and has lived abroad a great deal, largely in Italy and France, and has what would be called a cosmopolitan mind. He gets on well with foreigners – he had three years as Professor of English in Cairo, and is very tolerant of inferior races, and gets on well with them. He is an R.C. convert. He knows everybody or nearly everybody. George Gordon will probably speak for his work as an undergraduate at Oxford (some years ago). He is very much more than competent in English literature (you will learn his official qualifications from other sources), is I believe a firstrate horseman, and of physical courage to the point of recklessness. He is regarded as an odd creature, and a snob: but I know that his kindness and generosity are boundless. I will also say what one could not very well say in a formal testimonial, that I think he is absolutely good enough, and *not too good*, for such a position. It wouldn't be a question of blocks being chopped (rather badly) with a razor; he is just the right sharpness and weight; he wouldn't despise the job and he would do it thoroughly; and he would do his best to like and to understand his pupils. I think the Roumanians would be lucky to get him.' Similarly, two years later, when Sencourt applied to be Professor of English at Raffles College, Singapore, TSE urged the Universities Bureau on 11 Feb. 1938: 'I am eager to add my recommendation, as I am sure that no more suitable incumbent could be found: Mr. Sencourt is qualified for such a position to an unusual degree, both by his academic and literary attainments, by his experience of teaching, and in particular by his experience in teaching Orientals. He has furthermore all the social and personal qualifications – such as patience, tactfulness, and a cosmopolitan experience which gives him a sympathy with foreign minds.'

Sencourt wrote to TSE in Oct. 1930, after staying for a few days with him and VHE: 'I could hardly imagine a spirit more congenial and refreshing than yours . . . I know I can count on you both to give me more of what means so much to me.'

Edith Sitwell (1887–1964): poet, biographer, anthologist and novelist; editor of *Wheels* 1916–21. Her collection, *The Mother and Other Poems* (1915), was followed by *Clown's Houses* (1918) and *The Wooden Pegasus* (1920). In 1923, her performance at the Aeolian Hall in London of her cycle of poems, *Façade* (1922), with music by William Walton, placed her briefly at the centre of modernistic experimentation. Other writings include *Gold Coast Customs* (1929), *Collected Poems* (1930), *Fanfare for Elizabeth* (1946), *The Queens and the Hive* (1962), and *Taken Care Of* (memoirs, 1965). She was appointed a DBE in 1954. See John Lehmann,

A Nest of Tigers: Edith, Osbert and Sacheverell Sitwell in their Times (1968); and John Pearson, *Façades: Edith, Osbert and Sacheverell Sitwell* (1978). TSE published one of her poems in *The Criterion*.

James Smith (1904–72), critic and educator, won a double first in English and Modern Languages (French and German) from Trinity College, Cambridge. According to a profile in *Granta* (which he edited, 1925–6), he revived the Cam Literary Club, 'and even presided over it for a year, in order to introduce Cambridge to T. S. Eliot' (cited in John Haffenden, *William Empson: Among the Mandarins* [2005], 603). He was Vice-President of the Club (the President being Professor Sir Arthur Quiller Couch). Empson was to recall having his weekly supervisions with I. A. Richards and then treacherously 'listening to the James Smith group, who favoured T. S. Eliot and Original Sin' (195). Smith was to become an occasional contributor to *The Criterion* and to *Scrutiny*: he wrote on Empson's *Seven Types of Ambiguity* and on metaphysical poetry; and his other essays included studies of Croce, Wordsworth, Marlowe, Chapman, Webster, and Shakespeare (collected in the posthumous *Shakespearean and Other Essays*, 1974). In the 1930s he taught at King Edward VII School in Sheffield before becoming an HMI. During WW2 he was Director of the British Institute at Caracas; and after the war he became Professor of English at Fribourg. F. R. Leavis petitioned TSE on 19 Nov 1946 to support Smith's application: 'He is, in my opinion, an incomparably well-equipped man, but, by a series of accidents, he didn't start a university career when he ought to have done, & so has never held a university post before. He is not long back from Venezuela, where he spent five years establishing a British Institute – which (I have reason to know) he did magnificently . . . He is a man for whom I would do anything that lay in my power. It has always seemed to me a scandal that such pre-eminent qualifications shouldn't be used in a university. And I'm worried about him generally: it's absurd that he should have to go on living by hackwork. I've found his assistance in Downing-teaching very valuable, both before the war, & since he has been back, but there's no post for him. I can't imagine a better representative of English culture abroad. He's a classic & a philosopher, & can talk with authority about almost any aspect of England in French & German that to my ear are perfect. And he's a charming man, of complete integrity. (He's a Catholic, so would fit in at Freiburg, which is Dominican, I'm told.)' TSE replied to Leavis on 21 Nov. 1946, 'I have hardly been in touch with [Smith] for a number of years but I have enough confidence in him from my knowledge in the past to be very glad to give him this support', and he enclosed a testimonial: 'I have known Mr. Smith ever since he was an undergraduate at Cambridge where I formed a high opinion of his abilities. A little later I was a referee in connection with a dissertation which he submitted and was to report very favourably thereon. I regard Mr. Smith as a man of quite first rate abilities, and of exceptionally wide knowledge and interests.'

William Force Stead (1884–1967), poet, critic, diplomat, clergyman, was educated at the University of Virginia and served in WW1 as Vice Consul at the American Foreign Service in Liverpool. After working for a while in Florence, he was appointed in 1927 Chaplain of Worcester College, Oxford, where he became a Fellow. While in England, he befriended literary figures including W. B. Yeats, John Masefield, and Robert Bridges, as well as TSE – whom he was to baptise into the Anglican Church in 1927. In later years, after living through WW2 in Baltimore, he taught at Trinity College, Washington, DC. His published poetry included *Moonflowers* (1909), *The Holy Innocents* (1917), *Uriel: A Hymn in Praise of Divine Immanence* (1933), and an edition of Christopher Smart's *Rejoice in the Lamb: A Song from Bedlam* (1939) – a work which he discovered.

TSE wrote a testimonial on 4 Dec. 1938 (sent to the Dept. of English, University of Cairo, on 9 Dec.): 'I have known Mr. William Force Stead for over eleven years and count him as a valued friend. He is, first, a poet of established position and an individual inspiration. What is not so well known, except to a small number of the more fastidious readers, is that he is also a prose writer of great distinction: his book [*The Shadow of*] *Mt. Carmel* is recognised as a classic of prose style in its kind. And while the bulk of his published writing on English literature is small, those who know his conversation can testify that he is a man of wide reading and a fine critical sense.

'Mr. Stead is, moreover, a man of the world in the best sense, who has lived in several countries and is saturated in European culture. By both natural social gifts and cultivation, accordingly, he has a remarkable ability of sympathy with all sorts and conditions and races of men.

'I would say finally that I know from several sources, that Mr. Stead was most successful as a teacher of young men at Oxford; that he gained both the affection and the respect of his students; and that he exercised upon them a most beneficial influence. He has the scholarship necessary to teach English literature accurately, and the personal qualities necessary to make the subject interesting to his pupils; and I could not recommend anyone for the purpose with more confidence.' (Beinecke)

See 'Mr Stead Presents An Old Friend', *Trinity College Alumni Journal* 38: 2 (Winter 1965), 59–66; George Mills Harper, 'William Force Stead's Friendship with Yeats and Eliot', *The Massachusetts Review* 21: 1 (Spring 1980), 9–38.

Allen Tate (1899–1979), poet, critic, and editor, grew up in Kentucky and attended Vanderbilt University (where he was taught by John Crowe Ransom and became associated with the group of writers known as the Fugitives). He taught at various universities before becoming Poet-in-Residence at Princeton, 1939–42; Poetry Consultant to the Library of Congress, 1944–5; and editor of *The Sewanee Review*, 1944–6; and he was Professor of Humanities at the University of Minnesota (where colleagues included Saul Bellow and John Berryman), 1951–68. Eliot wrote of him in 1959: 'Allen Tate is a good poet and a good literary critic who is distinguished for the sagacity of his social judgment and the consistency with which he has maintained the least popular of political attitudes – that of the sage. He believes in reason rather than enthusiasm, in wisdom rather than system; and he knows that many problems are insoluble and that in politics no solution is final. By avoiding the lethargy of the conservative, the flaccidity of the liberal, and the violence of the zealot, he succeeds in being a representative of the smallest of minorities, that of the intelligent who refuse to be described as "intellectuals". And what he has written, as a critic of society, is of much greater significance because of being said by a man who is also a good poet and a good critic of literature' (*The Sewanee Review*, 67: 4 [Oct.–Dec. 1959], 576). Tate's publications include *Ode to the Confederate Dead* (1930), *Poems: 1928–1931* (1932), *The Mediterranean and Other Poems* (1936), *Reactionary Essays on Poetry and Ideas* (1936), and *The Fathers* (novel, 1938).

Harriet Shaw Weaver (1876–1961), English editor and publisher, whom Virginia Woolf described as 'modest judicious & decorous' (*Diary*, 13 April 1918). In 1912, Weaver began by giving financial support to *The Freewoman*, a radical periodical founded and edited by Dora Marsden, which was renamed in 1913 (at the suggestion of Ezra Pound) *The Egoist*. Weaver became editor in 1914, turning it into a 'little magazine' with a big influence in the history of literary Modernism. TSE followed in the footsteps of Richard Aldington and H.D. to became assistant editor in 1917 (having been nominated by Pound), and remained so until it closed in 1919. When Joyce could not secure a publisher for *A Portrait of the Artist as a Young Man*, Weaver in 1917 converted *The Egoist* into a press in order to publish it. She went on to publish TSE's first book, *Prufrock and Other Observations* (1917), Pound's *Dialogues of Fontenelle* and *Quia Pauper Amavi*, Wyndham Lewis's novel *Tarr*, and Marianne Moore's *Poems*, and other notable books. (She played a major role as Joyce's patron and confidante, and went on to be his literary executor and to help to put together *The Letters of James Joyce*.) TSE wrote in tribute in 1962: 'Miss Harriet Shaw Weaver . . . was so modest and self-effacing a woman that her generous patronage of men of letters was hardly known beyond the circle of those who benefited by it . . . Miss Weaver's support, once given, remained steadfast. Her great disappointment was her failure to persuade any printer in this country to take the risk of printing *Ulysses*; her subsequent generosity to James Joyce, and her solicitude for his welfare and that of his family, knew no bounds . . . [Working for her at *The Egoist*] was all great fun, my first experience of editorship. In 1932 I dedicated my *Selected Essays* to this good, kind, unassuming, courageous and lovable woman, to whom I owe so much. What other publisher in 1917 (the Hogarth Press was not yet in existence) would, I wonder, have taken *Prufrock*?' See also Jane Lidderdale and Mary Nicholson, *Dear Miss Weaver: Harriet Shaw Weaver, 1876–1961* (1970).

Charles Whibley (1859–1930) took a first in Classics in 1883 from Jesus College, Cambridge, and embarked on a career as journalist, author, and editor, and as a well-connected social figure (his intimates were to include Lord Northcliffe and Lady Cynthia Asquith). After working briefly for the publishers Cassell & Co., he wrote for the *Scots Observer* and the *Pall Mall Gazette* (for a while in the 1890s he was Paris correspondent, a posting which enabled him to become acquainted with Stéphane Mallarmé and Paul Valéry), for the *Daily Mail*, and above all for *Blackwood's Magazine* – where he produced for over 25 years a commentary, 'Musings without Method', comprised of sharp High-Tory substance and style. TSE hailed his column as 'the best sustained piece of literary journalism that I know of in recent times'. Richard Aldington jealously thought Whibley 'a pernicious influence' on Eliot: 'Eliot was already too much influenced by Irving Babbitt's pedantic and carping analysis of Rousseau – indeed to some extent he founded his prose style on Babbitt – and in Whibley he found a British counterpart to his old Harvard professor. Whibley was . . . a good scholar, but a hopeless crank about politics. He was the very embodiment of the English Tory don, completely out of touch with the realities of his time. "Whig" and "Whiggism" were his terms of contempt and insult to everybody he disliked, and anybody can see how Eliot picked them up. But Whibley took Eliot to Cambridge, where his conversation enchanted the dons and procured him friends and allies, vastly more important and valuable than the Grub Street hacks who had rejected him.' His friend F. S. Oliver wrote (17 April 1930), in some personal reminiscences put down at TSE's request, of 'the apparently impulsive and prejudiced character of C. W. that when he came to deal with the craft of writing he had no favour, or fear, or anger for friends or enemies. I never knew him once to praise goodnaturedly a book because it was written by a very close friend; nor have I ever known him to disprize a book with real merits, but which happened to be written by someone whose character and opinions he held in detestation. Contrary to the general idea of him he was one of the most *tolerant* people (as regards literature) that I have ever known . . . [I]t is this quality of truthful, courageous, penetrating, sympathetic literary criticism which I should put first among all his brilliant capacities . . . [H]e was I think the best critic who lived in my time.' Whibley's books included *William Pitt* (1906), *Political Portraits* (1917, 1923), and *Lord John Manners and his Friends* (1925). See TSE, *Charles Whibley: A Memoir* (The English Association Pamphlet no. 80, Dec. 1931).

Orlando (Orlo) Williams (1883–1967): Clerk to the House of Commons, scholar, and critic; contributor to *TLS*. Chevalier, Légion d'honneur. His publications include *The Clerical Organisation of the House of Commons 1661–1850* (1954); *Vie de Bohème: A Patch of Romantic Paris* (1913); *Some Great English Novels: The Art of Fiction* (1926).

Edmund Wilson (1895–1972): highly influential literary critic, social commentator and cultural historian; worked in the 1920s as managing editor of *Vanity Fair*; later as associate editor of *The New Republic* and as a prolific book reviewer. Major publications include *Axel's Castle: A Study in the Imaginative Literature of 1870–1930* (1931) – which includes a chapter on TSE's work, sources and influence – *The Triple Thinkers: Ten Essays on Literature* (1938), and *The Wound and the Bow: Seven Studies in Literature* (1941). TSE was to write to Geoffrey Curtis on 20 Oct. 1943: 'Edmund Wilson is a very good critic except that, like most of his generation in America, he has mixed his literary criticism with too much political ideology of a Trotskyite variety and perhaps he is also too psychological, but I have a great respect for him as a writer and like him as a man.'

Humbert Wolfe (1885–1940) – originally Umberto Wolff (the family became British citizens in 1891, and he changed his name in 1918) – poet, satirist, critic, civil servant. The son of Jewish parents (his father was German, his mother Italian), he was born in Bradford (where his father was a partner in a wool business), and went to the Grammar School there. After graduating from Wadham College, Oxford, he worked at the Board of Trade and the Ministry of Labour, and spent time as UK representative at the International Labour Organisation in Geneva. He found fame with *Requiem* (1927), and in 1930 was mooted as a successor to Robert Bridges as Poet Laureate. He edited over 40 books of verse and prose, and wrote many reviews. See Philip Bagguley, *Harlequin in Whitehall: A Life of Humbert Wolfe, Poet and Civil Servant, 1885–1940* (1997).

Leonard Woolf (1880–1969): writer and publisher; husband of Virginia Woolf, whom he married in 1912. A friend of Lytton Strachey and J. M. Keynes at Cambridge, he played a central part in the Bloomsbury Group. He wrote a number of novels, including *The Village and the Jungle* (1913), as well as political studies including *Socialism and Co-operation* (1919) and *Imperialism and Civilization* (1928). As founder-editor, with Virginia Woolf, of the Hogarth Press, he was responsible for publishing TSE's *Poems* (1919) and *The Waste Land* (1922). In 1923 he became literary editor of *The Nation & Athenaeum* (after TSE had turned it down), commissioning many reviews from him, and he remained a firm friend. See *An Autobiography* (2 vols, 1980); *Letters of Leonard Woolf*, ed. Frederic Spotts (1990); Victoria Glendinning, *Leonard Woolf: A Life* (2006).

Virginia Woolf (1882–1941), novelist, essayist, and critic, was author of *Jacob's Room* (1922), *Mrs Dalloway* (1925), and *To the Lighthouse* (1927), *A Room of One's Own* (1928), a classic of modern feminist criticism, and *The Common Reader* (1925). Daughter of the biographer and editor Leslie Stephen (1832–1904), she married Leonard Woolf in 1912, published her first novel *The Voyage Out* in 1915, and founded the Hogarth Press with her husband in 1917. The Hogarth Press published TSE's *Poems* (1919), *The Waste Land* (1923), and *Homage to John Dryden* (1923). TSE published in the *Criterion* Woolf's essays and talks including 'Kew Gardens', 'Character in Fiction', and 'On Being Ill'. Woolf became a friend and correspondent; her diaries and letters give firsthand accounts of him. Woolf wrote to her sister Vanessa Bell on 22 July 1936: 'I had a visit, long ago, from Tom Eliot, whom I love, or could have loved, had we both been in the prime and not in the sere; how necessary do you think copulation is to friendship? At what point does "love" become sexual?' (*Letters*, vol. 6). Eliot wrote in 1941 that Woolf 'was the centre, not merely of an esoteric group, but of the literary life of London. Her position was due to a concurrence of qualities and circumstances which never happened before, and which I do not think will ever happen again. It maintained the dignified and admirable tradition of Victorian upper middle-class culture – a situation in which the artist was neither the servant of the exalted patron, the parasite of the plutocrat, nor the entertainer of the mob – a situation in which the producer and the consumer of art were on an equal footing, and that neither the highest nor the lowest.' To Enid Faber on 27 Apr. 1941: 'she was a personal friend who seemed to me (mutatis considerably mutandis) like a member of my own family; and I miss her dreadfully, but I don't see her exactly as her relatives see her, and my admiration for the ideas of her milieu – now rather old-fashioned – is decidedly qualified.' See further Hermione Lee, *Virginia Woolf* (1996).

INDEX OF CORRESPONDENTS
AND RECIPIENTS

GENERAL INDEX

Conan Doyle, Arthur, 475n, 540–1

Connes, George: *The Shakespeare Mystery*, 142n

Connington, J. J. (Alfred Walter Stewart), 511

Connolly, Cyril: 'Chang!', 203

Conrad, Joseph, 378n; *Heart of Darkness*, 573

Constable & Co., 515n, 640

'Contemporanea' (TSE), 438n

'Contemporary Literature' (TSE), 319–21

'Conversation Galante' (TSE), 182

Cooke, A. H., 619–20

'A Cooking Egg' (TSE), 737n

Copley, John, **668n**

Coppard, A. E., 195n

Corbière, Tristan, 129, 130n, 234, 444, 646n

Cornhill Magazine, 106

Corry, Andrew, **470n**

Coty, François, 24n; *Contre le communisme*, 23

Coulanges, Fustel de, 218, 233

Coulton, G. G.: *Art and the Reformation*, 189

Cournos, Helen, 736

Cournos, John, **752**; Russian Chronicle, 51, 146, 687, 736; naturalisation, 145–6; in H.D.'s *Bid Me to Live*, 478n; *A Modern Plutarch*, 214n; *Tales of Soviet Russia*, 376

Coward, Noël, 622–3

Cowley, Abraham, 450–1

Craig, Edward Gordon, **734n**

Crane, Hart, 565; 'The Bridge', 182, 279n

Crankshaw, Edward, **276n**

Crashaw, Richard, 266n, 268, 322, 449, 450, 488n, 625, 704n, 708

Crawford, Charles: *Collecteana*, 347, 353

The Criterion: and payment to F&G, 1, 2; Lady Rothermere withdraws support, 2, 5, 7n, 11, 22, 57–8, 71n, 93, 115, 141, 209–10, 343; financing, 8, 10, 24, 26n, 32–3, 37, 38–40, 44, 58, 74–5, 76, 93–4, 118, 141–2, 185, 569; film reviews, 8; quarterly not monthly, 10, 27, 32, 38, 51, 54, 58, 59, 74, 76, 87, 99, 125, 135; uncertain future, 18, 29; FVM as interim fund manager, 32, 71, 78–9; TSE rebuffs 'Parisian' moniker, 34–5, 48; pricing, 36, 90, 581; TSE on metaphysics in, 36; Russian Chronicle, 51,

146, 687, 736; May Sinclair's cheque, 71; annual expenses as quarterly, 83; F&G subsidies, 83, 94; shareholdings, 84, 201; *Hound and Horn* modelled on, 85n; list of guarantors, 94n, 189, 208, 209–10, 539; surfeit of material, 106, 116, 355, 400, 638; poor payment to contributors, 128, 202, 350, 395; American sheets for Doubleday meeting, 132; 'school of criticism', 133–4; circular issued, 142; *Commerce* 'arrangement', 185, 191–2, 204; subscription forms, 192, 257, 298; informal dinners, 202, 213, 714; German periodicals review, 222, 341; Harrison's critique of, 230; German Chronicle, 236, 276, 589, 594, 606–7, 623, 631, 727; Italian Notes, 247, 257, 498; French periodicals review, 252, 545; Music Chronicle, 257, 274, 381, 645; lunch gathering, 331n; bad English in, 355; *Die Europäische Revue* arrangement, 356; Mauron deal, 358; avoiding mention of TSE, 363, 612, 644; New Year's Dinner, 364–5, 366, 380, 740–2; humanism in, 367, 430, 546, 578, 585, 612–13, 664, 726; rule on reviewers, 383; scattered audience for, 391; serial rights, 395; *Life and Letters* arrangement, 397, 404n; lack of time pressure, 402; BD on, 408n; American Chronicle, 422–3; avoids reviewing single novels, 440; untimeliness of, 455; Dutch Chronicle, 473; avoids repetition of authors, 479; and F&G liquidation, 487–8; 'The Five Reviews' Award', 501–2, 628, 632, 717–18; policy on natural history, 553; publishing on commission, 567; position of secretary, 576; American periodicals review, 577–8, 610; and F&F series, 584; discussion on value, 644; TSE's salary, 652; exchange circularising, 665; as distinct from F&F, 685

TSE CONTRIBUTIONS: 'The *Action Française*, M. Maurras and Mr Ward', 79n; article on Ward, 25, 30; *Ash-Wednesday*, 264; Chesterton memorial note, 197n; 'A Commentary', 33, 34n, 38n, 41, 220n, 249n, 254, 321n, 335, 342, 371n, 373n, 501n, 520n, 570n, 717n; correspondence with Ward, 205n; 'The Literature of Fascism', 177n, 323, 340, 378; 'Mr. Barnes and Mr. Rowse',

and husband's electorate, 481n; sends flowers to Eliots, 524; Fishbourne house, 613; VHE on CWE's death, 615; TSE and VHE on her friendship, 616, 643; sends bowl to TSE, 729; sends necklace to VHE, 731; VHE postpones meeting, 739

Hutchinson, St John ('Jack'), **207n**, 212–13, 361, 481n, 615, 616, 730

Hutton, William, Dean of Winchester, **101n**, 117

Huxley, Aldous, **761–2**; Colefax poetry reading, 111n; fond of OM, 176; TSE's introduction to Caetani, 184, 204, 259, 299, 569, 623; Curtius reads, 248n; fights Newman's battle, 320; as *Calendar* contributor, 384n; possible review of in C., 481; in *This Quarter*, 517n; and Curtius proposal, 727; *Antic Hay*, 319n; *Crome Yellow*, 679n; *Do What You Will*, 648

Huxley, Maria, 176, 184, 204, 259, 299, 569n, 623

Huxley, T. H., 320

Ibsen, Henrik, 361n, 362

'The Idealism of Julien Benda' (TSE), 19, 53, 146n, 162, 170–1, 176

Ignatius Loyola, St: *The Spiritual Exercises*, 451

The Illustrated Who's Who, 63n

Ingram, Kenneth: Massis's Prayer Book controversy request, 119–20, 123–4; Catholic Literature Association invitation, 364; and More's *Pages*, 507, 526–7; 'L'affaire du Prayer-Book et l'Église Anglicane', 152

Institute of Intellectual Relations, 241

International Centre of Fascist Studies, 526, 641n

'Introduction to Goethe' (TSE), 374

The Irish Statesman, 338

Isaacs, Jacob ('Jack'), 27n, 98

Isherwood, Christopher, 682n, 695

'Isolated Superiority' (TSE), 13n

Iwasaki, Yozan T.: *Three Women Poets of Modern Japan* (with Hughes), 271n

Jack, Peter Monro, **294n**

Jacob, E. F., 597n

Jacob, Max, 61n

Jacobs, A. A., 736–7

James, Alfred E. (Messrs James & James),

181–2, 188, 242–3, 429, 442–3, 456, 470

James, Henry, 137–8, 318, 430n, 573

James, Norah J.: *Sleeveless Errand*, 466–8

James, William, 162n

James VI and I, King, 85, 263n

Jameson, Storm, 141

Janes, W. L., 463, 547

Janni, Ettore: *Machiavelli*, 334

J. B. Pinker & Sons, 619n

Jeans, J. H., 618, 668; *Astronomy and Cosmogony*, 179, 251, 312

Jeffers, Robinson: *Roan Stallion, Tamar, and Other Poems*, 286, 290

Joachim, Harold H., **411n**

John of the Cross, St, 325, 451

John Murray, 640

John Quinn collection, New York, 715

John Simon Guggenheim Memorial Foundation, 306, 337–8, 698, 699–700, 719–20, 733

Johnson, Dr Samuel, 172, 449; Clarendon Press edition, 486; *Lives of the Poets*, 450, 451; *London* (intro. by TSE), 486n, 531; *Vanity of Human Wishes*, 531n

Jolas, Eugène, 186n

Jonathan Cape Ltd, 115n, 116, 170n, 253n, 255

Jones, David, 4n

Jones, P. Mansell, **607n**, 608–9, 659–60; *Tradition and Barbarism*, 607n

Jones, Seymour, 615n

Jonson, Ben, 345

Joseph, H. W. B., 180n, 191

Joseph II, Emperor, 290n

Joubert, Joseph: *Pensées and Letters*, 440

The Journey of the Magi; French translation, 61–2, 84–5; and Heseltine, 97; Joseph on, 191n; sales, 412; Monro's anthology, 516–17; *Untermeyer's* anthology, 527; St-John Perse admires, 601n; French translation, 631

Jowett Society, 284–5

Joyce, James, **151n**; *Ulysses* serialised in *Little Review*, 55; McGreevy compares with TSE, 107n; Uppsala job, 151; TSE on *Ulysses*, 151n; advises McGreevy, 216n; studies by Curtius, 248n; Crosby publishes, 279n; censorship of, 320, 335n; TSE on F&F plans, 555; TSE on need for C. critique, 577; TSE lunch with JDH, 615; Pinker payments, 619; Curtius essay, 637, 638n; TSE on *Ulysses* publication,

690; *Anna Livia Plurabelle*, 555, 577, 592–3, 596, 616, 619, 620, 634, 691; *Pomes Penyeach*, 528n; *A Portrait of the Artist as a Young Man*, 634; *Shem and Shaun*, 577; *see also* Gilbert, Stuart
Joynson-Hicks, Sir William, 253n, 348
Junius: *The Letters of Junius* (ed. Everett), 235
Justin Martyr, St, 263

Kafka, Franz, 732
Kalamazoo Ltd, 496n, 497, 499
Kant, Immanuel, 407
Kassner, Rudolf, 150, 623
Kauffer, E. McKnight, **68n**, 245n, 266, 340, 714
Kauffer, Marion and Ted, 730
Kaye-Smith, Sheila, 287n
Keats, John, 266n, 322; 'Hyperion', 323
Kent, Muriel, 578, 692–3
Kessel, Joseph, 218
Keynes, John Maynard, 262n; *The Economic Consequences of the Peace*, 262n
Keyserling, Hermann Alexander Graf, 631
King, Henry, Bishop of Chichester, 450
King's College Literary Society, London, 574
Kingsley, Revd Charles, 510n
Kipling, Rudyard: BD's essay on, 18, 571; Methuen seeks to defend, 102–3; TSE on, 162n
Kirchwey, Freda, **421n**
Kirstein, Lincoln, **85n**, 318–19, 395, 536, 547–8
Knickerbocker, William S., **130n**
Knowledge and Experience in the Philosophy of F. H. Bradley (TSE), 305n, 412n
Knox, Evoe, 364n
Knox, Ronald, **675n**; *The Belief of Catholics*, 675
Kuhlemann, Johannes Th.: *Tristan da Cunha*, 160n
Kyd, Thomas, 344

The Ladies Home Journal, 647, 660, 713
Laforgue, Jules, 129, 130n, 646n
Lafourcade, Georges, 657, 708; *La Jeunnesse de Swinburne*, 234
Lambert, R. S., 516n
'Lancelot Andrewes' (TSE), 85n

Landor, Walter Savage, 238n
Lanux, Pierre de, 124n
Larbaud, Valery, 238n, 240, 350
Larsson, R. Ellsworth, **140n**, 573–4; 'O City, Cities', 141n; 'Listen! Listen', 141n, 171
Laski, Harold, 231–2, 234, 241–2, 334
Latimer, Hugh, Bishop of Worcester, 183
Latini, Brunetto, 261n
Laud, William, Archbishop of Canterbury, 102n, 173n, 183, 450, 451
Law, William, 102n
Lawrence, D. H.: Crosby publishes, 279n; TSE on censorship of, 320; as *Calendar* contributor, 384n; recommends Dahlberg, 405n, 406, 440; TSE's 'contempt' for, 428n; Dahlberg on, 441n; *NS* on censorship of, 467n; in *This Quarter*, 517n; BD's essay on, 571; 'Mother and Daughter', 356, 377; *Pornography and Obscenity*, 642, 676, 702, 704n
Lawrence, T. E., 269n
Lawrence, W. J.: 'The Elizabethan Private Playhouse', 519–20; 'The Mystery of the *Hamlet* First Quarto', 404; 'The Pirates of *Hamlet*', 404
Lawrence & Wishart, 384n
Layton-Bennett, K. A., 476, 480
Leach, Henry Goddard, 19n, 52–3, 154, 660n
Leavis, F. R., 170n, 407n, 495n
Lee, Vernon, 681n, 682
Lenin, V. I., 376n
Leslie, Sir Shane, **502n**
Leval, Roger de, 61n
Leverson, Ada (née Beddington), **366n**; *Before the Fall of the Curtain*, 366; *Reading from Left to Right*, 366
Lévi, Madame, 668n, 669n
Lewis, Wyndham, **762–3**; TSE on working with, 10; contributes to *Little Review*, 55; Praz reviews, 67n; value of *Tarr*, 109; McGreevy reviews, 161; Connolly reviews, 203n; receives Campbell poem, 221n; on Garman, 385; as possible Strachey reviewer, 407; at Oxford Poetry Society, 530n; TSE's query to Praz, 632; and Curtius proposal, 727; TSE recommends to Heretics, 738; and JMM's study group, 743; *Tarr*, 438; *Time and Western Man*, 277n; *The Wild Body*, 216n
Liddon, Dr Henry, **455n**

Mann, Thomas, 501n, 628

Manning, Frederic, **763–4**; reports on Randall's typhoid, 2; on Rothenstein drawing of TSE, 494n

Mansfield, Katherine, 257

Marichalar, Antonio, **6n**; proposed Goya article for *C.*, 7; Valéry article enquiry, 125; as *C.* contributor, 256

Maritain, Jacques: TSE proposes *Forum* essay on, 53; contributes to *1928*, 61n; Smith on, 211n; as *C.* contributor, 240; TSE reviews *Three Reformers*, 275, 359, 478n; Barnes's essay, 339, 369; possible *Symposium* contribution, 590; TSE's introduction to Jones, 607, 608–9, 659n; *Prayer and Intelligence* (with R. Maritain), 359

Maritain, Raissa, 359n

Marlowe, Christopher: Spenser influence, 336–7, 344–7, 353; *Dido, Queen of Carthage*, 336n, 337, 343, 344, 346, 347, 353; *Doctor Faustus*, 345; *Hero and Leander*, 345; *The Jew of Malta*, 113n, 336n, 337, 346; *Lucan's First Book*, 344; *Richard III*, 344; *Tamburlaine*, 336n, 337, 344, 346, 347, 353

Marsden, Dora: *The Definition of the Godhead*, 310, 466, 512–13

Marshall, Arthur Calder, **529n**, 723

Martindale, C. C., 702–3

Marvell, Andrew, 450, 451, 458n

Massingham, Harold John, 518–19

Massis, Henri, **764–5**; TSE seeks ALR's opinion, 5; contributes to *1928*, 61n; seeks Prayer Book controversy information, 91–2, 119–20, 123–4, 152; TSE seeks *C.* articles, 218, 317; Fletcher's review, 222–3; Gaxotte introduction for TSE, 232; Proust manuscript, 233; TSE enquires about *La Gazette des Nations*, 316; TSE seeks position for his daughter, 497, 499, 508–9, 511, 543; *Defence of the West*, 26; *Jugements*, 160

Mathiez, Albert: *The French Revolution*, 415

Mauriac, François: *Dieu et Mammon*, 746

Maurois, André, 315n, 387n, 627; 'The Past and Future of Love', 333

Mauron, Charles, 358, **612n**

Maurras, Charles, **765–6**; *C.* Prologue delayed, 22–3, 24; and *L'Action Française*, 25n; and Comte, 26; TSE proposes *Forum*

essay on, 53; TSE defends against *Church Times*, 64–5, 77; Heseltine's defence, 96n; English lack interest in, 98; TSE defends against Ward, 148–9; Randall's criticism, 223; ignorance of foreign affairs, 378n; TSE's *Dante* dedication, 582–3; TSE's introduction to Jones, 607, 609, 659; *L'Action Française et le Vatican* (with Daudet), 73; *L'Anglais qui a connu la France*, 226, 502–3; *Chemin de Paradis*, 25; *Le conseil de Dante*, 582n, 583; 'Prologue to an Essay on Criticism. II', 79

May, Derwent, 424n

Mayne, E. C.: *Life of Lady Byron*, 552n, 627n

Maxton, James, **676n**

Mazower, André, 246, 543–4, 550–1, 559

Meinong, Alexis: *Über Annahmen*, 305n

Menai, Huw (Hugh Owen Williams), 273, 414–15, 737; *The Passing of Guto and Other Poems*, 410, 485, 491, 695–6

Menasce, Jean de, **766**; as 'nicest type of Jew', 30; translation of *TWL* title, 63; translates TSE poems, 133, 168–9, 575, 623, 630–1; TSE reports on to Caetani, 185; TSE seeks meeting with, 194; TSE invites to *C.* dinner, 202

Mercier, Louis: *Le movement humaniste aux Etats-Unis*, 466

The Mercury, 201, 202

Merton College, Oxford, 470–1

Messages, 91

Methuen, Paul Methuen, 3rd Baron, 37

Methuen & Co.: new edition of *SW*, 20, 22, 41, 46, 80, 294; TSE on del Re anthology, 51–2; seeks to protect Kipling, 102–3; Petronius correction, 112, 119; Bennett's Marlowe edition, 336n; TSE's advice to Barnes, 640

Mew, Charlotte, 693n; *The Farmer's Bride*, 504

Middleton, Thomas, 266n, 419; *The Changeling*, 418n; *A Game at Chess*, 689

Miles, Hamish, 481, 648, 721

Miles, Susan, *see* Roberts, Ursula

Millett, Ursula, 658–9

Milton, John: Grierson's article, 114–15, 238; TSE's BBC synopsis, 450; Williams on, 472n; *Samson Agonistes*, 322

Mind, 393

Minto, William, 348, 351

Mirrlees, Robin, 111n, 114n

(preface by TSE), 137n, 138n, 342
Mozart, Wolfgang Amadeus, 290n
Mudie's, 516n
Muggeridge, Malcolm, 183n, 272n, 403
Muir, Edwin (Edward Moore), 771–2; and
  'C. school of criticism', 133–4, 147; and
  Macleod, 147; essay on Kafka, 732; 'T. S.
  Eliot', 246n
Munson, Gorham B., **210n**
Murder in the Cathedral (TSE), 425n
Murray, D. L., 117, 183n
Murray, Gilbert, 626n
Murray, John Tucker, 743
Murry, John Middleton, 772–3; TSE on
  Babbitt essay, 16; TSE seeks Shakespeare
  books review, 142, 143n; C. controversy
  with TSE, 169; on rejection of New Prayer
  Book, 173–5; Harrison praises, 230n;
  reviews Brémond in *TLS*, 302n, 309,
  325; wants TSE's Babbitt sequel, 453;
  TSE postpones meeting, 462, 479; and
  Morrow essay, 613; TSE offers humanism
  essays, 638–9; reviews Fausset, 649, 665,
  742; on Babbitt, 665n; dislikes Wilson
  Knight's work, 684; TSE shows Shafer
  essay, 726; religion study group, 743; on
  Fernandez, 745, 746; 'The Detachment of
  Naturalism', 568n, 742n; *God*, 585, 622,
  680n, 690n; *The Life of Jesus*, 622, 671
Murry, Violet, 143n
Mussolini, Benito, 65n, 339n, 641, 693,
  740n
Myers, L. H., **39n**

Namier, L. B., *Structure of Politics at the
  Accession of George III*, 495
Nance, John W., 711, 722–3
Nash, John, 4n
Nash, Paul, 4n
Nashe, Thomas, 337n, 344, 346, 419
The Nation & The Athenaeum: RA's de
  Gourmont offer, 98; Sturge Moore as
  reviewer, 120; TSE on Muir's article,
  133–4, 147; TSE–Chesterton tiff, 202;
  Bates as reviewer, 250n; and Hall protest,
  253; McGreevy as reviewer, 286n; BD and
  Belphégor review, 611; comparison with
  Listener, 735
Nesbitt, Thomas H., 47
Neue Rundschau, 633n
Neue Schweizer Rundschau, 79, 215, 396,
  420, 441, 589n

The New Adelphi: JMM on, 16n; Prayer
  Book debate, 173–5; Bates as reviewer,
  250n; Orrick as contributor, 301; and
  JMM's transformation, 325; 'pays
  nothing' to contributors, 453; TSE
  recommends Morrow, 613; *Shafer* article
  rejected, 726; TSE recommends Belgion
  for review, 743
The New Criterion, see *Criterion, The*
The New Criterion Ltd: allocating stock to
  guarantors, 58, 201; owns C.'s paper, 84
New Prayer Book, 142, 173–5
New Republic, 136, 138, 162n, 225
The New Statesman: C. as 'Parisian', 34–5,
  48; TSE reviews *A Defence of Idealism*
  (Sinclair), 57n; TSE on *Sleeveless Letter*
  case, 466–8; and Campbell poems, 600;
  Scott Moncrieff letter, 705; Belgion review,
  721
Newman, Cardinal John Henry, 320, 729;
  Apologia Pro Vita Sua, 510
Newton, Thomas, *Seneca his Tenne
  Tragedies* (ed.), 29n
Nichols, Robert, **144n**, 151
Nickerson, Hoffman: *The American Rich*,
  656
Nicolson, Harold, 390n, 400
Nicolson, Vita, see Sackville-West, Vita
Nietzsche, Friedrich, 65, 87, 431, 498n
Nievo, Ippolito: *Le confessioni di un
  ottuagenario*, 708
1928, 61–2
The Nineteenth Century and After, 80, 81n,
  596–7, 669
Nonesuch Press, 196n, 281, 389, 403n
Norman, Charles, **276n**, 306; 'Dead Men
  Under Buildings', 277n
North, Sir Thomas, 260
Norton, W. W., 18n
'*Not in Gallup*' (TSE), 388n
'Note sur Mallarmé et Poe' (TSE), 6
'A Note on Poetry and Belief' (TSE), 228
Nouvelle Revue Française, 107, 230n, 313,
  367, 396, 501n, 557n, 608
Nuova Antologia, 501n
Nursing Mirror, 154n, 155n, 156, 435,
  477n

O'Brien, Edward, 694n
O'Brien, Howard Vincent, **93n**
O'Connor, Thomas Power, **372n**
Ó'Faoláin, Seán, **251n**; Irish famine story,

192, 599n, 600; *Anabasis* (trans. TSE), 124, 126, 179–80, 298–9, 569, 599–600, 601–2, 623, 673–4, 691, 698, 705; 'Les Éloges', 214n, 599n; 'La Gloire des Rois', 124n, 214n

Saint-Simon, Louis de Rouvroy, duc de, 425n

Sainte-Beuve, Charles Augustin, 267n

Saintsbury, George: *Minor Poets of the Caroline Period*, 450, 451

'Salutation' (TSE), 59, 101, 182

Sampson, Ashley: 'The School Master', 694

Sands, Ethel, 94n, 200n, **226n**, 312, 539n

Santayana, George, 728

Sassoon, Siegfried, 4n, 377n; *Memoirs of a Fox Hunting Man*, 488n

Saturday Evening Post, 647, 660

The Saturday Review, 137, 274, 491n, 591n

Scharlieb, Dame Mary, 287n

Scheler, Märit, 357–8, 631, 696

Scheler, Max, **578**; C. publishes new work, 229, 240; death, 249, 357; and humanism, 284; popularising in England, 631; English rights, 631; and *Hound and Horn*, 718; TSE requests essays, 735; *Philosophische Anthropologie*, 358, 677, 696

Schiller, Friedrich, 367n

Schloezer, Boris de: *Igor Stravinsky* (trans. EP), 217, 338–9, 563

Schlumberger, Jean: 'L'enfant qui s'accuse', 378, 382, 400, 409

Schneider, H. W.: *The Making of the Fascist State*, 498n

Scholartis Press, 625

Schwartz, Delmore, 104n

Scientific Press, 154n, 159n, 435, 462n

Scott, E. T., 675–6

Scott, S. Herbert, *The Eastern Churches and the Papacy*, 289

Scott, Sir Walter, 167, 515n

Scott Moncrieff, C. K., 75n; 'The Death of Albertine' (trans.), 703–4

The Scottish Association for the Speaking of Verse, 473–4

Secker, Martin, 135

'Second Thoughts on Humanism' (TSE), 395, 452, 453, 459, 464, 483, 493, 533–4, 568n

Seizin Press, 570n

Seldes, Gilbert, **783**; American Chronicle for C., 422–3; *The Stammering Century*, 423

Selected Essays: 1917–1932 (TSE), 113n,

582n

Selwyn, Revd E. G., **670n**, 720–1

Sencourt, Robert, *see* George, Robert Esmonde Gordon

Seneca his Tenne Tragedies (intro. by TSE), 29, 55

Sewanee Review, 104n

Seymour, Miranda, 428n

Seymour-Jones, Carole, 428n

Shafer, Robert: 'Retort upon Tate', 726

Shah, Sirdar Ikbal Ali (Ikbal Ali Khan), 205n

Shakespeare, William: amended *SW* passage, 103n; TSE seeks JMM review, 142, 143n; as prose or poetry, 260; More on, 266; Wilson Knight on, 293n; and Spenser, 345; as no thinker, 393, 394, 397; Richter's book, 503–4; TSE's comparison with Dante, 605n; Wilson Knight's essays, 666n, 672, 684; Gundolf's volumes, 680, 692, 696, 708–9; *King Lear*, 394, 397; *The Tempest*, 394, 397; *The Winter's Tale*, 394

Shakespeare Association, 154, 697

Shakespeare and the Stoicism of Seneca (TSE), 138–9, 153–4, 394

Shaw, George Bernard, **709n**; Turner on Strachey on, 34n; supports Hall, 291n; on Irish censorship, 321–2; and TSE on 'intelligent censorship', 373n; and Strachey, 407n; Freeman on, 549n; 'supports' Copley's Umano proposal, 668n; TSE's Umano enquiry, 709; *The Intelligent Woman's Guide to Socialism*, 231, 232n, 234, 235, 236n, 239, 241–2, 247, 263

Sheed, F. J., **477n**, 667

Sheed & Ward, 272n, 477n, 667

Sheffield, Ada (née Eliot), 244, 398n, 650

Sheffield, Alfred Dwight, 398

Sheffield, Revd D. Z., 398

Shelley, Percy Bysshe: vandalised statue, 165; TSE's Crashaw comparison, 266n, 488n; Garman's essay, 384; planned Sitwell essay, 626, 635, 654, 689; Maurois on, 627; 'To a Skylark', 704; *The Triumph of Life*, 322, 323

Shenstone, William, 496

Sherlock, Chesla C., 713n

Shoolbred's Removals and Warehousing, 645

Shorthouse, J. H.: *John Inglesant*, 311n, 449